Animal Law

Animal Law

Cases and Materials

SIXTH EDITION

Bruce A. Wagman

RILEY SAFER HOLMES & CANCILA
ADJUNCT PROFESSOR OF LAW
UNIVERSITY OF CALIFORNIA, HASTINGS COLLEGE OF THE LAW
UNIVERSITY OF CALIFORNIA, BERKELEY LAW
LECTURER
STANFORD LAW SCHOOL

Sonia S. Waisman

PARTNER, McCLOSKEY, WARING, WAISMAN & DRURY LLP

Pamela D. Frasch

ASSOCIATE DEAN, ANIMAL LAW PROGRAM
EXECUTIVE DIRECTOR, CENTER FOR ANIMAL LAW STUDIES
LEWIS & CLARK LAW SCHOOL

CAROLINA ACADEMIC PRESS
Durham, North Carolina

ISBN   978-1-5310-1099-7
e-ISBN   978-1-5310-1100-0
LCCN   2018967081

Carolina Academic Press
700 Kent Street
Durham, North Carolina 27701
Telephone (919) 489-7486
Fax (919) 493-5668
www.cap-press.com

Printed in the United States of America

Contents

Table of Cases

Principal cases are listed in italics, while cases cited in the editors' notes and footnotes are not. Where a principal case is also referenced in the notes or footnotes, the principal pages are also italicized.

Preface to the First Edition, 2000

For over five years, we have been asked the same question when we inform colleagues and friends that we teach or practice animal law: "What is 'Animal Law'?" That repeated inquiry made clear the need for this casebook; you are reading our answer. Since it is the first on the subject, we acknowledge and accept the responsibility of introducing this new and developing area to many of our readers. We also recognize the crucial role this book can play in increasing awareness, practice and education of animal law.

Our introductory chapter deals in part with the definition of "animal"— something we thought was obvious before we began studying the area. Even prefatory to that, we must define "animal law"—for our readers as well as for those who will ask them the same question we have been asked. Quickly-phrased definitions are inherently unsatisfactory, but we will provide one as a starting point: Animal law is, in its simplest (and broadest) sense, statutory and decisional law in which the nature—legal, social or biological—of nonhuman animals is an important factor. After reading this book and/or taking a course in animal law, students and practitioners will better understand and be able to articulate their own definition.

Animals appear in cases of all sorts, and we notably do not define animal law to mean "any case with an animal." A few illustrations may be helpful here. A personal injury lawsuit for damages related to plaintiff's ingestion of contaminated meat is not animal law, even though the meat involved was part of an animal. Compare the *Provimi Veal* case in which plaintiffs claimed damages because the veal they bought was not properly labeled, allegedly subjecting them to unknown dangers. That case *is* animal law—not because meat was involved but because plaintiffs' thinly-veiled agenda was to increase protection of veal calves, or perhaps to stop veal production. As another paired example, consider a breach of contract action involving the sale of horses. If the horses are simply the chattel in a dispute over delivery or financial terms, the case is probably not animal law—although their current status as legal property is a fundamental assumption in the case. If, however, the case focuses on the horses' inability to perform (*e.g.*, to race or breed), or to get along with other horses, it might be an animal law case.

These scenarios are not meant to clarify or confuse (although they may do some of each). Rather, they demonstrate that, while there is no defining hallmark, with time one knows an animal law case when one sees it. What should become apparent from a glimpse at the Table of Contents is that the unique status and qualities of nonhuman animals affect every area of the law. What is not immediately obvious—but should become so—is that each affected area of the law must be adapted to deal with those qualities.

Animal law as a matter of statute is easier to identify and define. Statutes affecting the use and abuse, sale and management, protection and killing of animals are all part of animal law—and we could have produced a four-volume casebook solely on statutory animal law. Instead we have hand-picked a limited sampling of cases and statutes by way of introduction. As with any general survey course, there are many statutes, cases and issues not even considered here that may merit considerable study.

As we publish this book, animal law remains a frontier subject in both courts and law schools. Its underpinnings, however, are ancient. Indeed, the opening chapter includes descriptions of a period when nonhuman animals were defendants punished for their "crimes" against humans. They were even represented by counsel. In one case, the defendants, a group of rats, entered pleas in abatement arguing (through counsel) they could not be prosecuted or compelled to appear because they could not travel to the courthouse safely.

A collective sigh of relief should be breathed here. Our view of animal law includes *only* as a historical footnote the time when nonhuman animals were criminal defendants. This is a course and a legal specialty heading on four legs into the millennium. Much like the nascent environmental law of the late 1950s and 1960s, and the growth in courses under that name in the 1970s and 1980s, animal law is a monolithic, ascending field with a very large wingspan.

One other important note. This is affirmatively *not* a book about animal rights law. Since we take the prerogative of definition, our version of animal law is not synonymous with "animal rights" activism or with any particular political, moral or ethical agenda. Rather, it is an objective and logical specialization of a challenging area—one with a growing number of cases and statutes, increasing public and practical interest, and significantly different historical, legal and philosophical foundations than most other law school courses. We acknowledge some of the cases discussed here were brought by animal protection groups aiming to establish "rights" for nonhuman animals in our society. (*Provimi Veal* might be one example.) Certainly the question of what rights animals should or do have will be raised as a natural consequence of reading the casebook. Our collective personal goal, though, is to survey the field overall and raise awareness and consciousness of challenging and uncommon legal issues. It is our hope the casebook and any corresponding course would be as stimulating and pertinent to the meat-eating hunter as to the ethical vegan or vegetarian.

Each of us has taught one or more Animal Law courses over the past five years; in that short time the number of animal law classes and court cases, as well as public interest in the field, has grown considerably. It appears the trend will continue and animal law as a legal discipline is here to stay.

We believe there has been a reticence in many legal quarters to teach, learn or practice in the area specifically because of the absence of meaningful assistance and coverage. Thus the other great motivator for our "answer" to the question about the nature of animal law: We hope this casebook will serve as a valuable guide to students and professors stepping onto this new frontier and provide more law schools with a template for animal law courses of their own. Our greatest wish is that our readers be stimulated to work in the field and become able advisors to and practitioners in a burgeoning herd of animal law attorneys.

Preface to the Sixth Edition

It is hard to believe that the First Edition of *Animal Law* was published almost 20 years ago in 2000. Now, five editions later, literally thousands of lawyers and others have embraced the academic and real-world applications of animal law, and we take some pride in knowing that this book is part of a well-established, multidisciplinary, highly effective legal field of new principles and doctrines that have changed the way the world views animals. Animal law's effect is not just in the law schools, legislatures and courts, but in a shifting societal understanding of the mechanisms of social change for animals.

As we stated in the Preface to the Fifth Edition, the field is now active and attractive to commentators, practitioners and academics who see the challenging issues we face, and to more and more individuals who are part of the changing landscape of the area. Animal law sections of local and state bar associations continue to grow in number and importance, with the American Association of Law Schools and the American Bar Association doing their part to encourage and promote consideration of new ideas to further advance the discussion.

With this rapid growth comes the need for an update of this casebook. Our efforts this time have mirrored those of past revisions, seeking and incorporating input from all types of users of the book. The idea was to continue to improve the text to provide more informative, current, and useful guides to the areas addressed here.

As in the past, much of the prior editions' text still remains, but throughout the book we have added recent cases and removed those that now may be less relevant given the new cases that abound. This edition includes discussion of new legislation and addresses ideas that have become more significant or are more commonly raised. We have also added a new section on the "Ag-Gag" laws that have been the subject of attention over the past few years.

With our eyes on course structure and the shifting approaches taken by practitioners, many tough decisions had to be made about which cases, issues and areas would be included and which would be omitted. We adhered in large part to the original definition of animal law stated in the Preface to the First Edition and believe that the current version presents the opportunity to discuss virtually every issue pertinent to the field as it now exists.

Of course, because animal law has grown so rapidly and expansively, our coverage of each given topic must necessarily become more condensed and summary in fashion. At this point, *Animal Law* is like most casebooks in that it cannot possibly include all aspects of each issue raised. But we have endeavored to include cases and extensive Notes that will stimulate discussion and thought among our readers and raise questions about topics not specifically addressed in the text.

As we have said before, we remain extremely grateful, honored and privileged to have contributed to the field through this casebook, especially considering the fact that this text may be used by many as an introduction to the major concepts animal lawyers face, or as a starting point for future exploration by burgeoning practitioners.

Acknowledgments

Bruce Wagman thanks Deborah for everything, and all the animals, in and out of the house, for everything else.

Sonia Waisman dedicates this edition to Pablo and Lola, and in loving memory of Wilma, Freddie and Mooki.

Pamela Frasch thanks Victor and Elizabeth Kisch for their constant support, and dedicates this book in loving memory to Beverly Frasch, Donna Mae Hanson, Jenny, Ruby, and Abby.

This book is dedicated to all animals.

Editors' Note

Most of the cases and other materials appearing in these pages have been edited. The deletion of sentences is indicated by ellipses; the deletion of full paragraphs is indicated by asterisks; the deletion of citations is not indicated. Most footnotes have been excised. The remaining footnotes retain their original numbering. Editors' footnotes are lettered.

The editors confirmed that all website links referenced in the narratives and Notes in this edition were functioning properly as of publication. However, these links are not within our control and we recognize that URLs can change without notice and that links sometimes malfunction. We apologize if that occurs with any of the links referenced in this book.

The editors gratefully acknowledge permission to reprint the following secondary sources:

Derek W. St. Pierre, *The Transition from Property to People: The Road to the Recognition of Rights for Non-human Animals*, 9 Hastings Women's L. J. 255 (Summer 1998). © 1998 by University of California, Hastings College of the Law. Reprinted from Hastings Women's Law Journal, Vol. 9, No. 2 (pages 260–1, 269–70), by permission.

Steven M. Wise, *The Legal Thinghood of Animals*, 23 B.C. Envtl. Aff. L. Rev. 471. (Spring 1996). Boston College Environmental Affairs Law Review. Pages 543–45. Reprinted with permission.

David Favre, *Equitable Self Ownership of Animals*, 50 Duke L.J. 473 (2001). Duke Law Journal. Pages 479–80, 497–98, 501–02. Reprinted with permission.

Barbara Bennett Woodhouse, *Who Owns the Child? Meyer and Pierce and the Child as Property*, 33 Wm. & Mary L. Rev. 995 (1992). Pages 1044–45, 1056. Reprinted with permission.

William Alsup, *A Passion for the Wild, The Recorder* (Dec. 16, 1998), p. 5. This article is reprinted with permission from *The Recorder* Newspaper in San Francisco, © The Recorder 1999.

David Favre and Vivien Tsang, *The Development of Anti-Cruelty Laws During the 1800s*, 1993 Det. C.L. Rev. 1 (Spring 1993). Detroit College of Law Review. Pages 2–4, 13–15, 17, 20–22.

Animal Law

Chapter 1

What Is an Animal?

Section 1. Defining "Animal"

As with many areas of law, the first logical and necessary step is to define the subject of study. What is a corporation, legally speaking? What is real property? What is a contract? In this instance, what is an "animal"?

When you think of animals, you may first think of companion animals, animals found in zoos, farm animals or wildlife. Merriam-Webster's Third New International Dictionary Unabridged (2002) contains various definitions of the noun "animal." The first definition is very broad: "an organism of the kingdom Animalia being characterized by a requirement for complex organic nutrients . . . by cells that lack cellulose walls, and usually by greater mobility. . . ." *Id.* at 85. The subsequent definitions define "animal" as "a brute or beast as distinguished from man," "any creature except a human being," and "a mammal as distinguished from a bird, reptile, or other nonmammal." *Id.*

In the animal law field, the word has many meanings. As the cases and statutes in this chapter indicate, the definition in each situation depends on a variety of factors. This inquiry is often crucial to the outcome of litigation involving issues related to which "animals" are (or are not) covered by the legal doctrines addressed in the cases.

As you read through this section, consider how you would rule in these cases and how you would define "animal."

Knox v. Massachusetts Soc'y for the Prevention of Cruelty to Animals

Appeals Court of Massachusetts, Plymouth, 1981
425 N.E.2d 393

DREBEN, Justice. The plaintiff, a concessionaire, intended to award goldfish as a prize in a game of chance at the Brockton Fair in July, 1980. When informed by the defendant Massachusetts Society for the Prevention of Cruelty to Animals (MSPCA) that such conduct would violate G.L. c. 272, §80F, the plaintiff sought and obtained from a Probate Court judge a temporary restraining order against the enforcement of the statute. The defendant MSPCA filed a counterclaim seeking a declaration that the statute prohibited the conduct contemplated by the plaintiff. After a hearing, the judge granted a preliminary injunction against enforcement.

The plaintiff and the defendant submitted a statement of agreed facts and, upon request of the parties, the judge reported the case to this court.

The undisputed facts are as follows. For twenty-two years the plaintiff has been running a concession business in various states throughout the country. The defendant MSPCA became aware that the plaintiff intended to run a concession booth at the Brockton Fair where he would award a live goldfish (in a clear plastic bag containing water) as a prize to any person who succeeded in tossing a ping pong ball into one of a number of goldfish bowls aligned in the plaintiff's booth. Some of the bowls were to contain live goldfish. Officers of the MSPCA (*see* G.L. c. 147, § 10) notified the plaintiff that his offering of goldfish as prizes in connection with a game of skill or chance would violate G.L. c. 272, § 80F. That statute, as inserted by St. 1977, c. 112, provides in relevant part: "No person shall offer or give away any live animal as a prize or an award in a game, contest or tournament involving skill or chance. . . ."

*   *   *

The question raised by the report is whether the word "animal" includes goldfish. Unlike statutes of some other States, or other Massachusetts legislation relating to animals, *see, e.g.*, G.L. c. 132B, § 2 (pesticide control act), G.L. c. 272, § 80F, does not define the word "animal." The section is one of a series of provisions designed to prevent cruelty and neglect to animals; some of the provisions protect animals generally, *e.g.*, G.L. c. 272, §§ 77 and 81, and some are concerned with the treatment of certain animals and classes of animals, *e.g.*, G.L. c. 272, §§ 78A, 85A. These statutes are "directed against acts which may be thought to have a tendency to dull humanitarian feelings and to corrupt the morals of those who observe or have knowledge of those acts." *Commonwealth v. Higgins*, 277 Mass. 191, 194, 178 N.E. 536 (1931).

In *Commonwealth v. Turner*, 145 Mass. 296, 300, 14 N.E. 130 (1887), after construing "[t]he offense" to be "against the public morals, which the commission of cruel and barbarous acts tends to corrupt", the court applied the statute to a defendant who let loose a fox to be hunted by dogs even though a fox was a "noxious animal" which could lawfully be killed by hunting with dogs. In the course of its opinion, the court noted, "The word 'animal', in its common acceptation, includes all irrational beings." This broad definition, which accords with most dictionary meanings, leaves us little to contribute by deliberating on where the line should be drawn on any taxonomic scale. *See* Model Penal Code § 250.11, Comment 2 (Official Draft 1980) (cruelty to animals). We merely conclude, in interpreting this humane statute designed to protect animals subject to possible neglect by prize winners, that G.L. c. 272, § 80F, applies to goldfish.

*   *   *

The matter is remanded to the Probate Court to vacate the injunction and to enter a judgment declaring that the word "animal" as used in G.L. c. 272, § 80F, includes goldfish.

So ordered.

Notes

1. *Knox* held that a statute prohibiting "any live animal" as a prize applied to goldfish. In a somewhat different context, in February 2000 the Trapholt Art Museum in Western Denmark opened an exhibit featuring ten goldfish, each swimming in a separate blender. As part of the exhibit, each spectator had the option of turning on a blender. Several fish were "blended" by museum visitors. The police ordered the plugs pulled after receiving complaints from a local group, the Union for the Protection of Animals. The museum director, Peter Meyer, claimed he had not expected the blenders to be turned on. He nonetheless defended the work, concluding that it did not encourage people to blend the fish, but instead addressed ethical questions in society. "We have abortions and we have respirators where we choose whether to keep people alive or not. We have become rulers of the decision on life and death in a new way. . . . This work of art exemplifies this decision in a precise image." Christian Wienberg, *Goldfish in Blenders Cause Outrage*, Associated Press, Feb. 14, 2000. Meyer was later quoted as stating, "[W]e fail to understand why the museum should be ordered to intervene in a work of art. If an art work is to be altered, it must be the artist who is ordered to do so." *Museum Fined for Goldfish-in-a-Blender Exhibit*, Deutsche Presse-Agentur, Nov. 24, 2000. The manufacturer of the blenders used in the exhibit, however, characterized the exhibit as "sadistic." *Goldfish Exhibit "Sadistic,"* Sunday Telegraph (Sydney, Australia), Feb. 20, 2000, at 48. The exhibit subsequently toured South and Central America "amid huge controversy," but apparently ran into legal problems only in Denmark.

Did the Danish museum, the artist or the curators in South and Central America consider goldfish to be "animals" subject to legal protection? Does culture define whether a given animal is granted a certain legal status? (The same type of issue is addressed in Chapter 3, Section 8, in connection with three exhibits at the Guggenheim Museum.)

According to a 2003 BBC News story:

> Recent research had shown that fish recognised individual "shoal mates," social prestige and even tracked relationships. Scientists had also observed them using tools, building complex nests and exhibiting long-term memories. The scientists added: "Although it may seem extraordinary to those comfortably used to pre-judging animal intelligence on the basis of brain volume, in some cognitive domains, fishes can even be favourably compared to non-human primates."

Scientists Highlight Fish "Intelligence," BBC News, Aug. 31, 2003.

Scientists regularly confirm these notions, with one of the latest discoveries being that fish feel pain. *See, e.g.,* Tim Carman, *Scientists say fish feel pain. It could lead to major changes in the fishing industry.* Wash. Post, May 24, 2018 ("The accumulated research on fish pain has recently hit the public with the impact of a blunt object. In January, Hakai magazine published a comprehensive feature . . . , which Smithsonian magazine republished under the more provocative title, 'It's Official: Fish Feel

Pain.'"). The science is not lost on business and industry either. *See, e.g.,* Katrina Fox, *Vegan Seafood Is About to Become Big Business — And Not a Moment Too Soon,* FORBES, Aug. 6, 2018 ("Scientific evidence has found that fish are sentient and feel both physical and emotional pain, as do crabs, lobsters and other crustaceans.").

Should sentience or intelligence matter in determining whether fish should be protected as "legal animals" for purposes of exhibitions such as that at the Trapholt Art Museum? What about in contexts other than museum exhibitions?

2. Now that you have considered whether and in what contexts fish may be "animals," think about birds, addressed in the following case and Notes.

Lock v. Falkenstine
Court of Criminal Appeals of Oklahoma, 1963
380 P.2d 278

NIX, Judge. This is an original proceeding wherein the Petitioners seek a Writ of Prohibition directed to Allen Falkenstine, the County Judge of Blaine County, to prevent him from proceeding to trial in a case where defendants are accused of fighting gamecock. Wherein it is charged that to so do is a violation of Title 21 O.S.A. § 1682, which provides:

"Every person who maliciously, or for any bet, stake, or reward, instigates or encourages any fight between animals, or instigates or encourages any animal to attack, bite, wound or worry another, is guilty of a misdemeanor."

THE COURT OF CRIMINAL APPEALS, IN DETERMINING THIS ISSUE, IS NOT CHARGED WITH THE DUTY OR RESPONSIBILITY OF EXPRESSING ITS OPINION AS TO THE MORALITY OF THE EVENT OR THE PEOPLE PARTICIPATING IN FIGHTING COCKS.

There are those who would refer to it as an age old sport, dating back 400 years before Christ, and dignified by such participants as George Washington, Andrew Jackson, Henry Clay, and Benjamin Franklin, all of whom were purported to relish cock fighting. On the other hand, there are those who consider it a bestial, barbaric and inhuman act, saying that those who engage in such amusement are destitute of human feelings.

This highly controversial subject has been discussed pro and con for centuries. It is reported that Abraham Lincoln said to a group of citizens, who wished to wipe out gamecock fighting by Federal Law: "As long as the Almighty permitted intelligent men, created in his image and likeness, to fight in public and kill each other while the world looks on approvingly, it's not for me to deprive the chickens of the same privilege."

THE DIVERSITY OF OPINIONS RELATIVE TO GAMECOCK FIGHTING IS OF LITTLE CONCERN TO THIS COURT, WE ARE CONCERNED ONLY WITH THE QUESTION OF WHETHER OR NOT OUR STATUTE IS SO DESIGNED AS TO PROHIBIT IT UNDER PENALTY OF LAW.

The petition herein questions the constitutionality of the Statute heretofore cited, alleging that it is not sufficiently definite and certain in its description of the conduct prohibited and penalized to enable one of ordinary experience and understanding to know the law and to avoid violating the same.

The Attorney General does not herein question their right to obtain relief by Prohibition, but is content to assert that "gamecocks" are *animals* and therefore are covered by the Statute.

This Statute has been given earnest consideration by the Court in an attempt to place upon it the proper interpretation and determine just what the Legislature intended to include by employment of the word "Animals". The Court is thoroughly cognizant of the fact, that, biologically speaking, every living creature is presumed to be of the animal species and several courts have construed numerous types of fowl to come within the term. Before the science of Biology was in existence, a distinction was made between living creatures in the Holy Scriptures, and often referred to as "beasts of the fields, fish of the sea, and fowls of the air". In the beginning, it was said in Genesis 1.26:

"And God said, Let us make man in our image, after our likeness: and let them have dominion over the fish of the sea, and over the fowl of the air, and over the cattle, and over all the earth, and over every creeping thing that creepeth upon the earth."

And, in Genesis 2.19:

"And out of the ground the Lord God formed every beast of the field and every fowl of the air. . . ."

The Statute in question was enacted by Dakota in 1887, adopted by the Oklahoma Territory in 1890, yet it is presented to this Court as one of first impression. Rarely have people been prosecuted under this Statute, and the Court has not been called upon by way of appeal for an interpretation of the Law or a Declaration as to its validity.

* * *

The language adopted in the case of *United States v. Reese*, 92 U.S. 214 (1875), is highly pleasing to this Court:

"Penal statutes ought not to be expressed in language so uncertain. If the legislature undertakes to define, by statute, a new offense and provides for its punishment, it should express its will in language that need not deceive the common mind. Every man should be able to know with certainty when he is committing a crime. It would certainly be dangerous if the Legislature could set a net large enough to catch all possible offenders and leave it to the courts to step inside and say who could be rightfully detained and who should be set at large. This would, to some extent, substitute the Judicial for the Legislative Department of the Government."

Guided by the "judicial yardstick" created by the rules adopted in the foregoing cases, we approach the Statute's validity.

Is the Statute clear and explicit? Is it certain? Can a man of ordinary intelligence understand it? Does it deceive the common mind? Does a person of ordinary intelligence know when the Statute is being violated? Can the Court judicially determine the Legislative intent?

The Statute appears on its face to prohibit instigating fights between animals, whereby one may attack, bite, wound, or worry another. Then the question inevitably arises: Is a "gamecock" an animal? Though we respect those courts that have held that various kinds of fowl fall within that category, and likewise agree that the science of Biology holds them to be such; . . . we are charged with the duty of concluding whether the man of "ordinary intelligence" would consider a rooster an animal. Surely, we would not expect a man of ordinary intelligence to fathom the law on the same footing as a learned Judge, or be as well versed in genetics as a student of biology. We feel that the Statute is *not* explicit, nor is it certain. And that persons of ordinary intelligence would have difficulty understanding what it attempts to prohibit.

In the State of Arizona, a person was charged with cockfighting under the "Cruelty to Animals" statute. The Supreme Court of Arizona in *State v. Stockton, et al.,* 333 P.2d 735, 736, 737, had this to say:

> The solution of the questions presented must be found in the interpretation of the statute above quoted. Biologically speaking, there can be no doubt that birds or fowls are animals and where the intent is manifest in the language of a statute the same may be and has been held to be true in the field of law. In arriving at the intention of a statute resort will be had to the words, context, subject matter, effects and consequence, spirit and reason (or purpose) of the law, etc. *Isley v. School District No. 2 of Maricopa County,* 81 Ariz. 280, 305 P.2d 432. When the legislative intent is ascertained by the application of the cardinal rules of interpretation that intent must be followed. *Ernst v. Collins,* 81 Ariz. 178, 302 P.2d 941.
>
> After a careful study of the above statute we confess we are unable to find from the words, context, subject matter, spirit or purpose of the act a clear indication of an intent on the part of the legislature to include a gamecock in the *category of animals,* or to make it a crime for a person or persons to conduct a cockfight wherein such gamecocks are subjected to needless suffering. To so interpret the above statute in accordance with the contentions of the State would render it vague, indefinite and uncertain and therefore in violation of the due process clause of Art. 2, § 4 of the State Constitution, A.R.S.

If the Statute is to be construed literally, it would be virtually impossible to exaggerate its limitations. These are some of the things that a literal interpretation would prohibit, and make unlawful:

A boy urging his beagle hound to catch a rabbit;

The rancher hunting coyotes with stag hounds;

Those who hunt fox or wolves with hounds;

The mountain man who traps and catches wild hogs with dogs for food for his family;

The farmer who dogs a breachy sow from his corn patch;

Even the rural widow, who erects a martin box to encourage those birds to occupy the same and make war on hawks coming within their territory.

One can readily see the confusion that would exist if the Court attempted to interpret the Statute as to what it covers and what it does not cover. The legislature in its wisdom, surely could find the language to say in certain terms what the Statute is intended to prohibit. The Oklahoma Statute makes no attempt to define animals, yet the legislature has described the species that come under certain provisions; and the Court is at a loss to ascertain why that was not done in the Statute before us.

In Title 21 O.S.A. §§ 1716–1719, which pertain to Larceny, the legislature makes a distinction between "domestic animals" and "domestic fowls". Section 1716 relates to the Larceny of any "horse, jackass, jennet, mule, cow or hog." It is provided in the section that the word "horse" as used in this act, shall include all animals of the "equine species", and the word "cow" shall include all animals of the "bovine species". It was later amended to include sheep or goats and they are not included in the definition of "bovine species". Dogs are not included in the act, but separate sections, Title 21 O.S.A. §§ 1717–18 deal with dogs. Dogs and cats are dealt with as "domestic animals" in Title 21 O.S.A. § 1691; and Title 21 O.S.A. § 1684 deals with trapping "birds" in a cemetery.

So it is apparent the Legislature in the past has portrayed the ability to identify the species of animals it has reference to when enacting a Statute.

The Statute in question was first adopted 76 years ago when men were labeled pioneers engaged in building a country during a time when "cock fighting" was not the vogue, and it is highly doubtful if an intent to prohibit the fighting of gamecocks entered the author's mind. It would be more practical to assume that most men of that period kept a dog and was proud of its fighting ability, and the law was designed to prohibit instigating fights between dogs. However, the Court should not be made to speculate and a literal construction of "instigating a fight between animals whereby one may attack, bite wound, or worry another" includes so many offenses as to render the Statute an absurdity. . . .

It is most difficult to arrive at the Legislative intent of the Statute in question, either from the words, context, subject matter, effects or consequences; or spirit or reasoning of the law without undue speculation. Research on the question reveals forty-one states, Hawaii, District of Columbia, and Alaska have specific statutes against fighting gamecocks. We feel that our Legislature is capable of enacting a specific law if it so desires, free of uncertainty, understandable by people of ordinary intelligence; and sufficiently clear and explicit as to remove all doubt.

We are compelled to arrive at the conclusion that the Statute is invalid.

It is not clear or explicit. It is uncertain. It does not apprise a man of ordinary intelligence of what crime subjects him to penalty, and is not subject to judicial interpretation without undue speculation.

The Legislature is now in session and if it so desires, it can make a direct approach to the act complained of by making cock-fighting an offense against the State. It will then be understood to be a criminal offense by the ordinary layman and he will then know what is and what is not forbidden by law.

The Writ of Prohibition is hereby granted, and the petitioners ordered discharged.

Notes

1. In 1982, the Oklahoma legislature added the words "with the exception of dogs" after "between animals" in the statute at issue in *Lock*. This appears to be an attempt to solve the "void for vagueness" challenge to the statute, and demonstrate that the lawmakers really meant *all* animals, except dogs, and that they were not concerned with the laundry list of hypothetical acts of cruelty the court used to support its decision. In 2002, by voter initiative, Oklahoma expressly banned cockfighting. OKLA. STAT. title 21, §§ 1692.1–1692.9 (2003). The statute was upheld after being challenged on state and federal constitutional grounds. *Edmondson v. Pierce*, 91 P.3d 605 (Okla. 2004).

At some level, an overlay of logic and common sense should inform judicial and prosecutorial decisions. Consider the list of acts that the *Lock* court is concerned could fall under the coverage of the anti-cruelty statute, and then consider interpretations of the statute that would exclude them.

2. In *People v. Baniqued*, 85 Cal. App. 4th 13 (2000), a California appellate court considered a statute that defined "animal" to include "every dumb creature." In the context of a cockfighting case, the court concluded that roosters and other birds are encompassed by this broad definition of "animal."

In *State ex rel. Miller v. Claiborne*, 505 P.2d 732 (Kan. 1973), however, the Kansas Supreme Court considered an anti-cruelty statute with no definition of "animal," and concluded that gamecocks were not animals within the meaning of the statute. The court supported its holding as follows:

> We incline towards the views expressed in the foregoing cases [including *Lock*], even though we must recognize that biologically speaking a fowl is an animal; a sentient, animate creature as distinguished from a plant or an inanimate object. In [reaching this conclusion], we are influenced by a number of considerations.
>
> First of all, we harbor the opinion that in the common everyday experience of mankind, chickens are seldom thought of as animals; rather, they

are birds, with avian characteristics, in contrast to beast of the field. We tend to agree with the two professors who testified, one from Kansas State University, the other from Oklahoma State, that persons of common intelligence would consider a chicken a bird, not a hair-bearing animal.

* * *

We hold no brief for what some persons term the "noble sport of cock-fighting." Neither are we called upon to rhapsodize over the spectacle of two game and plucky birds fighting to the death for the edification of human spectators. Ours is but the function of interpreting the law as we find it, and in our opinion, the legislature has not clearly evinced an intention to include fowls within the prohibitions of [the anti-cruelty statute].

Id. at 735.

3. The Tennessee legislature attempted to avoid this debate, at least with respect to gamecocks, by enacting a statute prohibiting the fighting and baiting of "any bull, bear, dog, cock, or other animal." "Swine" was added to the list in 2007, although the reference to "other animal" remains open to interpretation for any being other than those enumerated. Tenn. Code Ann. § 39-14-203 (2013). *See also* N.Y. Agric. & Mkts. § 351 (Consol. 2013) (defining "animal fighting" to mean "any fight between cocks or other birds, or between dogs, bulls, bears or any other animals. . . ."); *State v. Tabor*, 678 S.W.2d 45 (Tenn. 1984) (applying prior statute with similar language). *But see Oregon Game Fowl Breeders Ass'n v. Smith*, 516 P.2d 499, 504 (Or. Ct. App. 1973) ("to require that the legislature specifically outlaw cockfighting despite the fact that cockfighting can be construed as prohibited by the cruelty to animals statutes would be to invite proliferation of statutes, which, in turn, often leads to absurd results"). In *Smith*, however, the anti-cruelty statute defined "animal" to include birds, and the legislative history indicated that the inclusion of birds was specifically for the purpose of including cockfighting within the scope of the Act. *Id.*

4. In *State v. Buford*, 331 P.2d 1110 (N.M. 1958), the New Mexico Supreme Court held that gamecocks were animals under New Mexico's anti-cruelty statute but that cockfighting did not constitute illegal animal cruelty, based largely on the court's *post hoc* interpretation of legislative intent. Forty years later, a notation to New Mexico Statutes, section 30-18-1, New Mexico's general anti-cruelty statute, cited *Buford* for the proposition that the anti-cruelty statute "was not passed with the intention of prohibiting such sports as cockfighting." That notation finally was deleted by amendment in 2007. Although New Mexico had expressly prohibited dogfighting since the 1981 enactment of section 30-18-9 of the New Mexico Statutes, the law remained silent with respect to cockfighting until 2007, when an express prohibition against cockfighting was added. Cockfighting is discussed further in Chapter 3.

5. In other contexts, various courts have implicitly or explicitly concluded that chickens are "animals." *See, e.g., Morning Fresh Farms, Inc. v. Weld County Board of Equalization*, 794 P.2d 1073, 1074 (Colo. Ct. App. 1990) (eggs were an "animal product" such that a business met the statutory definition of "farm" and was exempt

from personal and property tax); *Molbert Bros. Poultry & Egg Co. v. Montgomery*, 261 So. 2d 311, 314 (La. Ct. App. 1972) (in a breach of contract case arising from the purchase and sale of diseased chickens, the plaintiff argued that "the word animals as used in LSA-C.C. Art. 2535 does not include chickens and bases the argument on the definitions found in Webster's dictionary"; the court was "more impressed" with another statute, LSA-C.C. Art. 3419, which referred to "chickens, turkeys, geese, ducks and other domestic animals"); *Kimple v. Schafer*, 143 N.W. 505, 507 (Iowa 1913) (based on customary practices the court concluded that the legislature did not intend to prohibit chickens from running at large, but the court's discussion referred to chickens as "animals").

6. Just as courts have reached different conclusions as to whether gamecocks are "animals," in the next case an appellate court and the state's highest court reached diametrically opposed conclusions when interpreting *Buford* (see Note 4), in determining whether wild animals fall within the scope of an anti-cruelty statute protecting "any animal."

State v. Cleve

Supreme Court of New Mexico, 1999
980 P.2d 23

[*Defendant Cleve snared a wild deer in a wire trap, causing the deer to suffer. He was charged and convicted of cruelty to animals under New Mexico's anti-cruelty statute.*]

* * *

III. Interpretation of section 30-18-1

Section 30-18-1 provides:

Cruelty to animals consists of:

A. torturing, tormenting, depriving of necessary sustenance, cruelly beating, mutilating, cruelly killing or overdriving any animal;

B. unnecessarily failing to provide any animal with proper food or drink; or

C. cruelly driving or working any animal when such animal is unfit for labor.

The Court of Appeals concluded that the phrase "any animal" plainly means all animals, including game animals. The Court of Appeals relied on the lack of definition for "animal" in section 30-18-1, unlike the cruelty statutes of some other states, and the lack of alternative protection for many animals if they were excluded from section 30-18-1. Additionally, the Court of Appeals reviewed other criminal statutes relating to animals containing specific references to domesticated animals and concluded that the lack of specificity in section 30-18-1 was a deliberate choice of the Legislature. We disagree with the Court of Appeals' construction of section 30-18-1.

In *State v. Buford*, 65 N.M. 51, 331 P.2d 1110 (1958), this Court reviewed a statute nearly identical to section 30-18-1 in defining cruelty to animals. The prosecution in *Buford* charged the defendant with cruelty to animals in relation to a cockfighting incident. In determining whether New Mexico's cruelty-to-animals statute prohibited cockfighting, we discussed the cruelty-to-animals statutes of a number of other states. In addition, we reviewed England's Cruelty to Animals Act, which also prohibited the overdriving, abusing, or torturing of any animal and which defined any animal as meaning horses, dogs, cats, and other domestic animals. We assumed in *Buford* that gamecocks fell within the phrase "any animal" in New Mexico's cruelty-to-animals statute. In addition, we acknowledged that the terms torture and torment "would seem to embrace fighting cocks equipped with artificial spurs or gaffs capable of cutting deep wounds and sharp gashes in the cocks." However, we "look[ed] at the statute as a whole," and we noted that "[t]he language of the statute . . . seems to apply only to brute creatures and work animals and the history shows that it was passed in relation to other laws governing livestock. As a result, because, unlike most statutes, no New Mexico statute specifically prohibited cockfighting, we applied the rule of lenity and determined that "the type of cruelty to animal statute we are construing was not passed with the intention of prohibiting such sports as cockfighting."

The Court of Appeals concluded that our discussion of the cruelty-to-animals statute applying only to brute creatures and work animals constituted *dicta*. We disagree. *Obiter dictum* is defined as "[w]ords of an opinion entirely unnecessary for the decision of the case." Black's Law Dictionary 1072 (6th ed. 1990). The language quoted above from *Buford* clearly demonstrates that our discussion of the history and scope of the cruelty statute, far from being idle observation, was essential to our analysis of the Legislature's intent and directly influenced our holding that the statute did not apply to cockfighting. While it is true that we assumed without deciding that the cruelty statute protected gamecocks, we did not assume that the phrase "any animal" had the broad meaning attributed to it by the Court of Appeals in this case. Instead, as noted in *Buford*, some courts had apparently held gamecocks to be domestic animals within the provisions of cruelty-to-animals statutes expressly limited to the protection of domesticated animals. Thus, we understand *Buford* as assuming that, even though the history of New Mexico's cruelty statute suggested that it applied only to work animals, the Legislature also intended to protect domesticated animals such as gamecocks from cruelty, though not from such sports as cockfighting. To the extent *Buford* stands for the proposition that the Legislature, in enacting the cruelty to animals statute, primarily intended to protect work animals and that the Legislature did not intend to prohibit such sports as cockfighting, it is binding precedent in New Mexico, and the State fails to argue that it should be overruled.

In any event, we are persuaded that *Buford* accurately captures the history and scope of cruelty to animals statutes in New Mexico, including the present version contained in section 30-18-1. First, although under the plain language rule the phrase "any animal" would seem to imply a broad meaning, the language of the statute as a whole negates such an implication. Section 30-18-1 contains three subsections. Section 30-18-1(B) and section 30-18-1(C) prohibit behavior that could only apply to domesticated animals or wild animals previously reduced to captivity, unnecessarily failing to provide proper food or drink and cruelly working an animal that is unfit for labor. Despite such a necessarily limited scope, both of these subsections include the phrase "any animal." Clearly, the Legislature did not intend to create a duty on the part of the public to provide sustenance to wild animals. Similarly, while section 30-18-1(A) prohibits some conduct that could apply to both domesticated and wild animals, such as torturing, tormenting, cruelly beating, mutilating, or cruelly killing any animal, it also proscribes conduct, such as depriving of necessary sustenance and overdriving, that necessarily excludes wild animals. We do not believe the Legislature intended a different meaning for the phrase "any animal" between different subsections of the same statute and within a single subsection. To the contrary, we believe the Legislature intended that the phrase "any animal" denote domesticated animals and wild animals in captivity throughout section 30-18-1. In fact, the statute at issue in *Buford*, which did not contain discrete subsections like section 30-18-1, provided:

> If any person torture, torment, deprive of necessary sustenance, cruelly beat, mutilate, cruelly kill or overdrive *any animal*, or unnecessarily fail to provide *the same* with proper food or drink, or cruelly drive or work *the same* when unfit for labor, he shall be punished by a fine. . . .

1887 N.M. Laws, ch. 1, § 1 (emphasis added). We believe the use of "the same" to describe "any animal," like the repeated use of "any animal" in section 30-18-1, supports a conclusion that the Legislature intended the same meaning for the phrase throughout the statute. As with section 30-18-1(B)–(C), it is clear that the Legislature did not intend the latter prohibitions in the prior statute to apply to wild animals. Therefore, from the contextual language of section 30-18-1, we conclude that the Legislature intended the phrase "any animal" to mean domesticated animals and wild animals previously reduced to captivity.

In addition to the language of the statute, we believe the history of section 30-18-1 and other statutes *in pari materia* also support the conclusion that the Legislature did not intend to include wild animals in section 30-18-1. As previously mentioned, section 30-18-1, enacted by 1963 N.M. Laws, ch. 303, § 18-1, replaced a cruelty statute enacted by the Legislature in 1887. The Legislature placed the statute under a general article entitled "Animals." This article contains seven separate sections relating to criminal offenses involving animals. *See* 1963 N.M. Laws, ch. 303, §§ 18-1 to -7 (codified at N.M.S.A. 1978, §§ 30-18-1 to -2, -3 to -7 (1963)). In addition to the cruelty-to-animals prohibition in section 18-1, the other statutes in the article are as follows: section 18-2 prohibits the injury of "any animal or domesticated fowl which is the property of another;" section 18-3 prohibits the unlawful branding of "any animal which is the property of another;" section 18-4 prohibits the "unlawful disposition of animal," including "abandoning any livestock," taking livestock for use without the owner's consent, and "driving or leading any animal being the property of another from its usual range, without the consent of the owner;" section 18-5 prohibits the illegal confinement of animals and refers to "any cow," "any bull," "offspring of livestock," and "any freshly branded animal;" section 18-6 prohibits the transporting of stolen livestock; and section 18-7 prohibits the misrepresentation of pedigree "of any animal." We believe that these statutes, enacted in conjunction with section 30-18-1, under the same article, and regarding a similar subject matter, are *in pari materia* with section 30-18-1. Each of these other statutes exclusively concern livestock and other animals possessed by humans, yet these statutes variously use the phrase "any animal" to describe the domesticated animals covered by the statute. Similar to the history of the statute at issue in *Buford*, *see Buford*, 331 P.2d at 1115 (stating that "the history [of the cruelty to animals statute] shows that it was passed in relation to other laws governing livestock"), we believe these statutes clarify that the phrase "any animal" in section 30-18-1 extends only to domestic animals and wild animals previously reduced to captivity. Thus, we conclude that the Legislature enacted the entire article, 1963 N.M. Laws, ch. 303, §§ 18-1 to -7, with the exclusive purposes of controlling certain human behavior in relation to domesticated animals and protecting the property rights of the owners of domesticated or previously captured wild animals.

Finally, we presume that the Legislature was aware of *Buford* and our interpretation of the former cruelty-to-animals statute, 1887 N.M. Laws, ch. 1 § 1, when it repealed that statute and enacted section 30-18-1 in 1963. The Legislature could have easily inserted a definition of "animal" in section 30-18-1 if it had disapproved of our interpretation of the scope of the statute in *Buford*. Instead, the Legislature reenacted the statute with largely stylistic changes in the definition of the crime.

From the context surrounding the enactment of section 30-18-1, we conclude that the Legislature intended the phrase "any animal" to include domesticated animals and wild animals in captivity and did not intend to include other wild animals. We disagree with the Court of Appeals' assessment that such an intent would be absurd or unjust. While many may regard it presently desirable for New Mexico to protect all animals, including wild animals, from human cruelty, "[a] statute is to be interpreted as the Legislature understood it at the time it was passed." Our role in statutory interpretation is not to sculpt the most just law possible out of the words used by the Legislature or to attribute the meaning to a statute that contemporary ideals would deem preferable. Our role is to determine the intent of the Legislature. It has not been uncommon, both at the time the Legislature enacted section 30-18-1 and at present, for state legislators to limit cruelty to animals statutes to domesticated animals and wild animals in captivity. *See, e.g.*, Iowa Code § 717B.1(1)(b) (1995) (excluding from the crimes of animal abuse and neglect, among other things, "[a]ny game, fur-bearing animals, fish, reptile, or amphibian" unless owned, confined, or controlled by a person); N.H. Rev. Stat. Ann. § 644:8 (1996 & Supp. 1998) (proscribing cruelty to "any animal" and defining "animal" to mean "a domestic animal, a household pet or a wild animal in captivity"); Okla. Stat. title 21, § 1685 (Supp.

1999) (proscribing cruelty to "any animal in subjugation or captivity, whether wild or tame, and whether belonging to [the accused] or to another"); Tex. Penal Code Ann. §42.09(c)(1) (West Supp. 1999) (defining "animal" in a cruelty to animals statute as "a domesticated living creature and wild living creature previously captured"). A policy decision of this nature should not be second-guessed by the judiciary. The decision to extend the scope of an existing statute to reflect changing values is a matter for the Legislature, and absent an amendment to section 30-18-1, we presume that the Legislature continues to intend that the statute apply according to its original meaning. In light of the history of cruelty to animals statutes in New Mexico, we believe that the Legislature intended to exclude wild animals from the protections of section 30-18-1. Because we do not believe that such a result can be characterized as either absurd or unjust under the circumstances surrounding the statute's enactment, we are not persuaded that the Legislature must have had a different intent. Thus, we conclude that wild game animals, including the deer snared by Cleve in this case, are not covered by section 30-18-1.

* * *

Notes

1. In light of this ruling, if you were a New Mexico legislator seeking to protect wild game animals, in what manner would you propose to revise section 30-18-1?

2. In *Animal Legal Defense Fund, Inc. v. Espy*, 23 F.3d 496 (D.C. Cir. 1994), the court considered the definition of "animal" in the Animal Welfare Act (AWA) (discussed at length in Chapter 6, Section 2), the principal law protecting animals used in commercial endeavors such as research, exhibitions, and sales. At the time of that case, the controlling definition (7 U.S.C. §2132(g)) read:

> The term "animal" means any live or dead dog, cat, monkey (nonhuman primate mammal), guinea pig, hamster, rabbit, or such other warm-blooded animal, as the Secretary may determine is being used, or is intended for use, for research, testing, experimentation, or exhibition purposes, or as a pet. . . .

As the court explained:

> The new legislation qualified this expansion with various exclusions, *e.g.*, for horses not used for research, farm animals used for food, and livestock used to improve nutrition, breeding or production efficiency.
>
> After the 1970 amendments and an extensive rulemaking, the Department issued the regulation that is now contested. The Secretary defined "animal" essentially as it was defined in the statute except that the regulation expressly excluded "birds, aquatic animals, rats and mice." . . .
>
> In 1989 two of the plaintiff-appellees, the Animal Legal Defense Fund and the Humane Society of the United States, requested that the Secretary again conduct a rulemaking to re-examine the exclusion. The Department

refused, relying, it said, on the Act, its legislative history, and considerations of "the manpower, funds, and other resources available to administer effectively our animal welfare program."

Id. at 498.

The *Espy* case is discussed more fully in Chapter 5, with respect to the issue of plaintiffs' standing. Standing requires a showing of "injury in fact" that is fairly traceable to the defendant's actions and is redressable by the requested relief. Because the court ultimately concluded the plaintiffs in *Espy* did not meet that standard, it did not reach the merits of the case. If the court had gone beyond the standing issue, how do you think it would have ruled?

After groups filed a rulemaking petition to amend the AWA definition of "animals" to include birds, rats and mice bred for use in research, and after further litigation (discussed in Chapters 5 and 6), Congress passed the "Farm Security and Rural Investment Act of 2002," which amended the definitional provision of the AWA to exclude "(1) birds, rats of the genus Rattus, and mice of the genus Mus, bred for use in research, [and] (2) horses not used for research purposes" from protection under the AWA. This effectively ended the effort to have birds, rats and mice specifically bred for research use—who comprise more than ninety percent of the animals used in biomedical and toxicity research—protected by the AWA.

3. As is evident from the statutes and cases discussed in this section, courts and legislatures seem to be searching for a balance to protect living creatures other than humans, without extending that protection to a point that may seem unreasonable and possibly unenforceable as well. A prime example of the possible backlash effect of taking anti-cruelty to the extreme can be seen in the following situation.

In 1997, California state laws and guidelines regarding the use of animals in science classrooms prohibited cruelty to animals subjected to research projects. A high school student was disqualified from participating in a science fair because his project, which tested the effects of radiation on fruit fly reproduction, violated the contest's rules prohibiting any project that caused cruelty to animals; the "animals" at issue were the fruit flies that died during his research. The director of the fair received an onslaught of complaints asserting that it was absurd to exclude such research from the contest. Ultimately, the school board apologized to the student's father and asked him to act as a judge at the fair, in which the student participated. The student did so well at the local fair that he continued on to the state contest.

Do you agree with the school board's initial decision to disqualify the student? Consider where you would have drawn the line, and why.

4. Many found it unreasonable for the high school to construe "animals" to include fruit flies. Compare that with the definition of "animal" in the following statute, which was designed to protect human property interests (in animals who were subject to research), as opposed to protecting animals as beings in their own right:

> "Animal" means any warm or cold-blooded animal or insect which is being used in food or fiber production, agriculture, research, testing, or education, however, shall not include any animal held primarily as a pet.

N.Y. Agric. & Mkts. Law § 378(1)(b) (2017) ("Unlawful tampering with animal research").

5. In addition to California, some other states also have enacted express antivivisection statutes applicable to schools, as further noted in Chapter 6.

6. Having studied the definitions (or lack thereof) of "animal" in the preceding Notes and cases, consider the excerpts from selected state anti-cruelty statutes in Appendix A. Consider which beings would be included within the various definitions and which would be omitted, assuming there is no legislative history to assist in the analysis. If you were a legislator, would you include a definition of "animal" in your state's anti-cruelty statute? If so, which one?

Some state anti-cruelty statutes do not define the animals they are intended to protect, leaving law enforcement agencies and courts with less certainty and potentially with broader discretion in addressing cruelty. The uncertainty can also be problematic and ultimately leaves the courts to interpret the statutes and to determine which animals are or are not covered by the statute. Where criminal statutes are at issue, ambiguity can lead to reversals of convictions after successful constitutional challenges for lack of notice and vagueness. Sometimes, though, even the inclusion of a definition has not provided sufficient guidance to the courts. Anti-cruelty statutes are addressed more fully in Chapter 3.

Section 2. Classifications of Animals

United States v. Park

United States Court of Appeals, Ninth Circuit, 2008
536 F.3d 1058

McKEOWN, Circuit Judge. Ron and Mary Park own and operate a dog kennel, Wild River Kennels, on property along the Clearwater River in Idaho. Their property is subject to a scenic easement that was granted to the United States, which prohibits commercial activity but permits livestock farming. In this appeal, we are asked to determine the unusual question whether dogs are "livestock." Despite a gut inclination that the answer might be "no," resolution of the issue is not so clear, thus precluding summary judgment at this stage of the proceeding. As it turns out, the term "livestock" is ambiguous at best and much broader than the traditional categories of horses, cattle, sheep, and pigs.

I. BACKGROUND

In 1973, Earl and Iona Monroe, the owners of a plot of land along the Middle Fork of the Clearwater River in Idaho, including a two-acre tract known as Tract

160A, granted the United States a scenic easement in accordance with the Wild and Scenic Rivers Act. . . .

Ron and Mary Park purchased Tract 160A in 1989. . . . In 1997, they began advertising that they were offering a dog training and kennel business, Wild River Kennels, on the property.

In early 1998, the Forest Service notified the Parks that their dog training and kennel business violated the terms of the easement. According to the Forest Service, the kennel was an unauthorized commercial activity and there were new structures associated with it that had been built without prior approval. The Parks met with the Forest Service to discuss the dog kennel, but did not resolve the issue. Several years later, the dispute remained unsettled. In 2003, the parties exchanged letters on the matter, but, again, did not come to a resolution.

The United States filed suit in 2005. On cross-motions for summary judgment, the Parks argued that their dog kennel constituted "livestock farming," which is specifically permitted by the terms of the easement. The government contended that, under Idaho law, dogs are not livestock.

The district court held that the easement terms were "unambiguous," stating that "[r]egardless of how broadly one defines livestock farming, the Parks' activities do not fall within its terms." The court did not look to any particular source to define "livestock farming," but commented that the government's citations to Idaho law "further yield support for its interpretation." The district court granted summary judgment in favor of the government and ordered the Parks to cease their commercial operation and remove any associated structures or convert them to noncommercial use. The court's order that the Parks remove or convert the structures was stayed pending this appeal.

* * *

II. ANALYSIS

A. LIVESTOCK FARMING

* * *

The scenic easement permits the Parks to engage in "livestock farming," but does not define this term. Still, we have no difficulty concluding that the district court erred in holding that "livestock," even broadly defined, could not include dogs.

The term "livestock" stems from the Middle Ages, when it was used as a measure of wealth or to refer to property that could be moved, particularly to a market for trade. Online Etymology Dictionary, *http://www.etymonline.com* (last visited July 25, 2008). Later, the term began to be used in a more limited sense to describe cattle. *Id.* Today, the dictionary definition of "livestock" is sweeping, capturing every type of domesticated animal. For example, Merriam-Webster's Collegiate Dictionary defines "livestock" as "animals kept or raised for use or pleasure; *esp:* farm animals kept for use and profit." *MERRIAM-WEBSTER COLLEGIATE*

DICTIONARY 728 (11th ed. 2003). The Oxford English Dictionary is in accord and defines "livestock" as "animals, esp. on a farm, regarded as an asset." *THE CONCISE OXFORD DICTIONARY OF CURRENT ENGLISH* 797 (9th ed. 1995). Even Black's Law Dictionary defines "livestock" broadly as "domestic animals and fowls that (1) are kept for profit or pleasure, (2) can normally be confined within boundaries without seriously impairing their utility, and (3) do not normally intrude on others' land in such a way as to harm the land or growing crops." *BLACK'S LAW DICTIONARY* 953 (8th ed. 2004); *see also Levine v. Conner*, 540 F. Supp. 2d 1113, 1116 (N.D. Cal. 2008) (analyzing the dictionary definitions of the word "livestock" and observing that "the scope of domestic animals used or raised on a farm can potentially extend to guinea pigs, cats, dogs, fish, ants, and bees.").

Despite the broad definitions in the dictionaries, we recognize that "livestock" has been used to describe a more limited set of animals such as cattle, horses, and pigs. The government calls our attention to § 25-1101 of the Idaho Code, which limits "livestock" to a narrow set of animals, namely, "cattle, horses, mules, or asses." Idaho Code § 25-1101. That section, however, pertains to brands and identifications affixed to the hide of an animal. Not surprisingly, this provision is not the only one in the Idaho Code that defines "livestock:" § 25-3601 states that cassowary, ostrich, emu, and rhea are "livestock" and § 25-3701 adds fallow deer, elk, and reindeer to the list. Idaho Code §§ 25-3601, 25-3701.

Idaho is not alone in having a statutory definition of "livestock" that identifies certain specific animals as "livestock." A cursory survey of case law and federal and state statutes uncovers multiple definitions of "livestock" that include particular subsets of domestic animals. For example, federal regulations under the Fair Labor Standards Act define "livestock" to include "cattle, sheep, horses, goats, and other domestic animals ordinarily raised or used on the farm," but notes that "[t]urkeys and domesticated fowl are considered poultry and not livestock." 29 C.F.R. § 780.328. Turning to state law, the Court of Appeals of Michigan has observed that Michigan law defines "livestock" as "horses, stallions, colts, geldings, mares, sheep, rams, lambs, bulls, bullocks, steers, heifers, cows, calves, mules, jacks, jennets, burros, goats, kids and swine, and fur-bearing animals being raised in captivity." *People v. Bugaiski*, 224 Mich. App. 241, 568 N.W.2d 391, 392 (Mich. Ct. App. 1997) (citing Mich. Comp. Laws § 287.261(2)) (emphasis omitted). In Iowa, "livestock" is defined as "cattle, horses, sheep, goats, swine (other than feeder swine), or any other animals of the bovine, equine, ovine, caprine or porcine species." Iowa Admin. Code r. 21-66.1(1). The Iowa Code also includes "all species of deer, elk, and moose raised under confinement or agricultural conditions for the production of meat, the production of other agricultural products, sport, or exhibition" as "livestock." *Id.*

The language in the easement does not provide us with any more clarity on the meaning of the term. The statement of purpose neither compels nor eliminates a definition. The word "farming," which follows "livestock," is unhelpful because "to farm" is simply defined as "to engage in raising crops or animals."

MERRIAM-WEBSTER'S COLLEGIATE DICTIONARY supra at 454. The government urges us to apply the definition of "livestock" that is found in §25-1101, but there is nothing in the easement that unambiguously points us in this direction.

* * *

Given the lack of a uniform definition of "livestock" and the absence of any guidance within the four corners of the easement, we conclude that the term is ambiguous and summary judgment was premature.

* * *

REVERSED AND REMANDED.

Notes

1. On remand, a bench trial was held. The federal district court found Idaho state statutes unhelpful in defining "livestock" in the context of the case and looked instead to the plain meaning and dictionary definitions of the term. *United States v. Park*, 658 F. Supp. 2d 1236, 1244 (D. Idaho 2009). In doing so, the court found that "dogs can be considered livestock in the generic sense of the word," and went on to find that dogs were "livestock" under the facts of that case. *Id.* at 1245.

> It is clear from the evidence, that neither party to the scenic easement expressed an intent as to whether dogs should be considered "livestock." The Court concludes that dogs are livestock or pets depending on their purpose and/or usage. Like the example of the bison being considered at times livestock and at times zoo animals, the Court finds dogs are at times livestock when they are used for work on a farm such as herding animals, or used for profit when dogs are bred for sale or used for hunting. A dog could be considered livestock when it is being kenneled for profit just like pasturing horses for profit. While it is true that dog kenneling can be also commercial activity, it is a type of commercial activity allowed under the broad reservation for "general crop and livestock farming."

> Of course a dog can also be on real property without being livestock. A family dog that does not work on the farm, is not bred, or is not used to help produce food when a person hunts, is just a family pet and is not livestock. Under the facts of this case, the Court finds that the dogs being used on the easement property for breeding, hunting and boarding are dogs being used for work and/or profit and can be considered "livestock" under the plain meaning of the term livestock. Moreover, this conclusion is consistent with the rules of contract construction when the term is ambiguous and the Court cannot determine the parties' intent.

Id. at 1246–47.

2. Despite the holding in *Park*, "livestock" usually refers to traditional farm animals. Nevertheless, as in that case, some statutory definitions could be construed to include dogs and cats. *See, e.g., St. Petersburg Kennel Club, Inc. v. Smith*, 662 So. 2d

1270 (Fla. Dist. Ct. App. 1995) (greyhound racing dogs are not "livestock"); *People v. Bugaiski*, 568 N.W.2d 391, 392–93 (Mich. Ct. App. 1997) (under a definition of "livestock" listing specific types of animals and including "fur-bearing animals being raised in captivity," the court considered the doctrine of *ejusdem generis* (grouping things of the same nature) and concluded domestic dogs were not "livestock" under the statute). *But see* KAN. STAT. ANN. § 79-1301 (2018) ("a dog shall be considered as personal property and have all the rights and privileges and be subject to like lawful restraints *as other livestock*" (emphasis added)). Some state statutes expressly exclude dogs, cats and other "companion animals" from the definition of livestock. *See, e.g.*, CAL. BUS. & PROF. CODE § 4825.1(d) (2018) (definition applicable to veterinary medicine: "'Livestock' includes all animals, poultry, aquatic and amphibian species that are raised, kept, or used for profit. It does not include those species that are usually kept as pets such as dogs, cats, and pet birds, or companion animals, including equines.").

3. In *State v. Nelson*, 499 N.W.2d 512, 514 (Minn. Ct. App. 1993), the court reversed a conviction under a zoning ordinance criminalizing the raising or handling of livestock, concluding that "a pet rooster does not plainly fall within the definition of livestock as used in the ordinance." The ordinance at issue encompassed "all livestock" and "any animal causing a nuisance." The question of whether the rooster was an "animal causing a nuisance" was waived, and the case was prosecuted solely on a theory that, under the ordinance, a rooster was livestock as a matter of law:

> Since "livestock" is not defined in the ordinance, Maplewood relies on a dictionary definition of the term as "domestic animals kept for use on a farm or raised for sale and profit." *Webster's New Twentieth Century Dictionary* 1059 (2d ed. 1979). Other authorities have also defined livestock broadly enough to encompass roosters. *See, e.g., Meader v. Unemployment Compensation Div.*, 64 Idaho 716, 136 P.2d 984, 987 (1943) ("Livestock" in its generic sense includes all domestic animals.).
>
> At least as commonly, however, the term livestock is defined as separate from chickens. Minnesota's own statutes consistently define "livestock" as "cattle, sheep, swine, horses, mules and goats." *See, e.g.*, Minn. Stat. § 17A.03, subd. 5 (1990). When the legislature intends to reach chickens, it uses the term poultry, often in conjunction with livestock. *See* Minn. Stat. § 169.81, subd. 8 (1990) (regulating "livestock or poultry loading chute trailers"); Minn. Stat. § 343.21, subd. 8 (1990) (cruelty to animals provision referring to "livestock or poultry exhibitions"). Clearly the lawmakers of this state understand livestock to be a category of animal distinct from poultry.
>
> Other state statutes also define livestock to include four-legged animals, but not chickens or other poultry. *See, e.g.*, Colo. Rev. Stat. § 35-46-101(2) (1984) ("livestock" defined as "horses, cattle, mules, asses, goats, sheep, swine, buffalo, and cattalo"); Neb. Rev. Stat. § 54-101(15) (1988) ("livestock" means "any domestic cattle, horses, mules, donkeys, sheep, or swine").

Because the meaning of livestock is not entirely certain, we turn to rules of construction to resolve the ambiguity. Minnesota courts have often recognized that because zoning ordinances restrict common law rights, they should be strictly construed against the governmental unit and in favor of property owners. In light of this principle, we give "livestock" a less inclusive meaning than does the city and conclude that the term as used in the Maplewood Zoning Ordinance does not reach chickens or other poultry.

499 N.W.2d. at 514.

In the following case, a court considered whether hens were "recognized household pets" under a residential development's restrictive covenants.

Eldorado Improvement Association, Inc. v. Billings

Court of Appeals of New Mexico, 2016
374 P.3d 737

SUTIN, Judge. This case pits a subdivision association against several subdivision residents who keep hens as pets. The dispute is over a subdivision covenant that disallows "animals, birds, or poultry" on residents' lots unless kept as "recognized household pets." The subdivision association sued the defendant hen owners to rid their properties of hens. The defendants (the owners) claimed that their hens met the recognized household pet exception. On motions for summary judgment, the district court agreed with the subdivision association and required the owners to remove their hens from their lots. In this Opinion, we at times refer to "chickens" and to "hens" but we also use "poultry," because "poultry" appears in Section 11 of the subdivision covenants and because the parties concentrate on using "poultry" in their briefs. We hold that the restrictive covenant does not disallow the owners from keeping hens that are recognized as household pets and that the district court erred in requiring the owners to remove the hens.

BACKGROUND

Eldorado at Santa Fe Subdivision is a residential development located in Santa Fe County, New Mexico, and was established in 1972 with protective covenants. . . . The [amended] covenants state that their purpose, among other purposes, is to provide "an attractive rural setting for residential neighborhoods and home sites" and to encourage "individual expression consistent with the historical traditions of the region." The plaintiff here, Eldorado Community Improvement Association, Inc. (the association), has many subdivision-related administrative tasks, not the least of which is to enforce violations of the covenants.

At issue in this case is Section 11 of the covenants, which reads:

Household pets. No animals, birds[,] or poultry shall be kept or maintained on any lot, except recognized household pets which may be kept thereon in reasonable numbers as pets for the pleasure and use of the occupants but not for any commercial use or purpose. . . .

No other section in the covenants has any direct bearing on keeping animals, birds, or poultry on residential lots.

Section 11 forbids residential lot owners from keeping poultry on residential lots in the subdivision. At the same time, Section 11 provides an exception that permits poultry as well as animals or birds to be kept on residential lots under certain conditions, namely, as long as the poultry are "recognized household pets . . . for the pleasure and use of the occupants[,]" kept on the lot in reasonable numbers, and "not [kept] for any commercial use or purpose." There exists no issue here as to number of hens or as to commercial use or purpose. Nothing in Section 11 gives free reign to expansive poultry operations and no issue exists as to any such use here.

Both sides filed motions for summary judgment. . . . As to interpreting the critical, ambiguous words, the district court determined that chickens were not recognized household pets and could not be kept or maintained on any lot in the subdivision. The court granted the association's motion and ordered the owners to remove their chickens from their properties. The owners appeal. . . .

DISCUSSION

* * *

Definitions

Because the issues in this case focus on the meaning of certain covenant terms, we begin with definitions. A "bird" is "any of a class . . . of warm-blooded vertebrates distinguished by having the body more or less completely covered with feathers and the forelimbs modified as wings." *Merriam-Webster's Collegiate Dictionary* 125 (11th ed. 2005). A "chicken" is a "common domestic fowl[.]" *Id.* at 213. A "hen" is "a female chicken[.]" [*Id.* at] 580. A "fowl" is a "bird of any kind[.]" Chickens are poultry. [*Id.* at] 972. "Poultry" are "domesticated birds kept for eggs or meat[.]" *Id.* Finally, "a domesticated animal kept for pleasure rather than utility" and "kept for companionship or pleasure" is a pet. [*Id.* at] 926. The parties do not spar much over what a "pet" is. The definitions do not state that pets cannot also have utility. For purposes here, hens kept as a source of eggs are poultry, and hens also kept as a source of companionship or pleasure can be a pet. It is manifestly unclear, however, what "recognized" means.

The District Court's Decision

* * *

The district court ultimately agreed with the owners that the phrase "recognized household pets" was not defined in the covenants and was unclear on its face. However, upon determining that the covenant was ambiguous, the district court looked to [*Agua Fria Save the Open Space Ass'n v. Rowe* (N.M. Ct. App. 2011)] and in doing so went beyond our Supreme Court's interpretative rules for determining restrictive covenant meaning. . . .

* * *

... In granting summary judgment, the district court concluded that the owners' interpretation of Section 11 was "inconsistent with the uniformity contemplated by the covenants" and would "create an illogical result[.]" The district court determined that the owners' interpretation would "render the covenant meaningless" and was "inconsistent with the intent and purposes of the covenants when analyzed under the modern rule of construction and results in foreseeable illogical results when analyzed under the general rule of construction." In addition, the district court expressed concern that "[c]onstruing the covenant to allow individual owners complete freedom to designate any creature they want as a household pet would frustrate the purposes of the covenants and create a dangerous precedent leaving other property owners without [any] recourse (unless it was a nuisance under the covenants)." Furthermore, the court determined that the owners' interpretation "would open the door to an unlimited multitude of different kinds of creatures being kept inside and outside of homes . . . without regulation or control under the covenants (except nuisances) leaving the other homeowners without recourse." These determinations were significantly driven by the association's extrinsic evidence offered to uncover the covenants' original meaning.

The Evidence

The district court considered the developer's 1972 covenants and even considered the reputation of the subdivision in the 1970s and 1980s. It considered evidence that the association historically viewed the covenant not to permit chickens—a history, as explained by the court, that indicated that chickens had not been considered by the association as recognized household pets and that the association had historically taken enforcement action against individual owners who had chickens on their property. Also, according to the court, no historical evidence existed that chickens or other livestock had been contemplated by the developer or accepted by the association as allowable.

The association's evidence in major part consisted of affidavits. William Donohue, who was general manager of the association beginning in 2006, provided an affidavit and documents relating to what the association's "policy and practice" was and had been. He also reported on the association's planning and enforcement activities, on its grants of variances, and on holding an election on proposed alternative covenant amendments. . . .

In the owners' view, even were the foregoing extrinsic evidence allowable, any opinion of the current association board or past boards, any surmised intent of the original developer in 1972, any surmised intent of voters in 1995 apart from the language in the covenant, and any hearsay evidence presented by a subdivision home builder, constituted elusively speculative and fleeting evidence. . . .

The association also presented an affidavit of Dr. Kristy Pabilonia, an associate professor and diagnostic veterinarian at Colorado State University, and an expert in commercial poultry populations and backyard poultry flocks, both rural and urban. . . . She stated that "[p]oultry has not historically been considered 'household pets,' . . . She further stated that her scientific surveys of owners of backyard poultry flocks showed that 86% maintained chickens as a source of food, meat, or eggs, and that 42% maintained chickens as pets, companions, or hobby animals. . . . The district court concluded that "[t]his significantly indicates that in broader society[,] chickens are not recognized as household pets by most."

* * *

The Covenant Must Be Construed to Favor the Owners

The notions expressed in the covenants of maintaining the "pastoral" and "rural" nature of the area and the historical traditions of the region would appear to lend themselves to allowing animals, birds, and poultry as recognized pets. If the Eldorado community did not want poultry because poultry were not recognized as household pets, it is reasonable to assume that the residents would have removed the language that anticipates and permits poultry as household pets. We do not think that it is reasonable to read the language of Section 11 to reflect an intent that the only way poultry could be "recognized" as household pets was if the association or a large number but less than a majority of lot owners recognized poultry as such.

We agree with the district court that the covenant language was unclear and ambiguous. Ambiguity is created when provisions are reasonably and fairly susceptible to different constructions. . . . And restrictive use covenants involve valuable property rights and extrinsic evidence should not provide the basis for interpretation of those covenants.

* * *

Further, it is important to keep in mind that restrictive "covenants constitute valuable property rights of the owners of all lots in the tract." Reliance on restrictive covenants is a valuable property right. Thus, the rules set out by our Supreme Court in *Hill* are controlling in the case before us.

What the developer may have had in mind, how individual association members over time may have viewed the language, whether the association over time successfully enforced Section 11 without court assistance, and any "community" or "broader society" sense of Section 11's meaning, constitute fleeting and speculative proof of meaning in this case, as did that of Dr. Pabilonia regarding when the advent of chickens as pets may have emerged in contemporary society. Dr. Pabilonia actually confirmed that a substantial percentage of chicken owners keep chickens as pets.

We therefore disagree that Section 11 disallows hens that can be and are treated as pets. And we disagree that to allow hens as household pets creates or opens up any likely circumstances of ruination as expressed by the association and the district court that warrants an interpretation that allowing the hens as pets could never have been intended at any time and under any circumstance. We are not persuaded that in permitting pet chickens "the sky will fall." Such a Chicken Little-esque view of possible results and calamity is not convincing. . . .

CONCLUSION

Section 11 of the covenants cannot be enforced under the circumstances in this case to preclude the owners from keeping their hens as recognized household pets. We reverse the judgment of the district court.

IT IS SO ORDERED.

Notes

1. While courts like the New Mexico court above and the Minnesota court in *State v. Nelson* (Note 3 preceding *Eldorado Community Improvement Ass'n v. Billings*) recognize that chickens can be pets, those chickens (and other birds used for food) who are not pets do not have even the minimal protection of laws governing the slaughter of other "non-pet" animals for food. Roughly nine billion chickens and other birds are raised or slaughtered for food each year in the United States. In *Levine v. Vilsack*, 587 F.3d 986 (9th Cir. 2009), poultry eaters concerned about food-borne illnesses and organizations representing poultry slaughterhouse workers concerned about working conditions sued the United States Department of Agriculture (USDA), challenging the USDA's interpretive rule excluding chickens, turkeys and other avian species from coverage under the Humane Methods of Slaughter Act (HMSA) of 1958, 7 U.S.C. §§ 1901 *et seq.* (discussed in Chapter 6), which addresses the slaughter and handling for slaughter of "livestock." The federal district court ruled in favor of the USDA, finding that Congress intended to exclude birds from the term "livestock" in the HMSA, leaving them without protection under the HMSA. On appeal, the Ninth Circuit concluded that plaintiffs had no standing to sue; it therefore vacated the judgment and remanded the case for dismissal. Thus, those birds who are not "pets" are also not "livestock" for purposes of the HMSA (which applies in virtually every American slaughterhouse), and are unprotected by federal law.

2. It should now be apparent that defining "animal" under various laws or deciding whether to characterize animals as "livestock" or "pets" may not necessarily be a straightforward determination — and that the actual legal definition may have broader implications.

The same holds true for the term "domestic animal." Before reading the following cases, consider how you would define that term. Consider the same question after reading the cases and Notes that follow.

Holcomb v. Van Zylen

Supreme Court of Michigan, 1913
140 N.W. 521

BIRD, Justice. The defendant's dog "raised havoc" with plaintiff's turkeys, and the damage which resulted is sought to be recovered in this action. The declaration is based on the statute. C.L. 1897, § 5593. The demurrer which was interposed by the defendant raises the sole question whether a turkey is an animal within the meaning of this statute.

The statute upon which the action is planted provides in part that: "If any dog shall have killed or assisted in killing, wounding or worrying any sheep, lamb, swine, cattle or other domestic animal," etc. As turkeys are not specifically named, it is clear that, if they are embraced within the statute, the authority for so doing must be found in the words "or other domestic animal." An animal is defined by Bouvier as "any animate being which is not human, endowed with the power of voluntary motion." This comprehensive definition seems to have been accepted in legal matters as the proper one.

The courts have dealt with the question from many different angles, and in nearly every instance they have adopted this definition, and have construed the term "animal" so as to include fowls. In *Huber v. Mohn*, 37 N.J. Eq. 432, the question arose in the construction of a will, where the testator had given "his horses and all other animals on the premises," and it was held that the words "all other animals" carried with them the fowls on the premises. A statute which prohibited domestic animals from running at large in the highway was construed so as to include turkeys. *McPherson v. James*, 69 Ill. App. 337. In construing a statute prohibiting cruelty to animals, a goose was held to be an animal. *State v. Bruner*, 12 N.E. 103. A like result was reached in the criminal cases of *People v. Klock*, 48 Hun (N.Y.) 275 and *Reg. v. Brown*, 24 Queen's Bench Division, 357. The question is a new one in this court, and when it was first suggested by one of the briefs in the case that there were animals which grew feathers, it was a severe strain on the writer's credulity to accept it without reserve; but an examination of the question has brought with it the conviction that turkeys are animals under the generally accepted definition of that term as used in the law.

The question, therefore, is whether the Legislature, in passing the act, had in mind this comprehensive definition of the word "animal," or whether it had in mind the popular and well-understood subdivisions of that term, namely, fowls, birds, reptiles, insects, *etc.* Either view could be accepted without doing violence to the language of the act. But the fact that the statutes involving this question have been generally construed by other courts in accordance with the general definition induces us to follow them, and hold that the words "or other domestic animal" should be construed as including domestic turkeys.

As the same conclusion was reached by the trial court, its order overruling the demurrer will be affirmed, and the writ of *certiorari* dismissed, with costs to the plaintiff.

Notes

1. The *Holcomb* court had little trouble concluding that turkeys and other birds are included within the definitions of both "animal" and "domestic animal." In the absence of legislative history related to a particular statute, is there a legal

justification for applying a different interpretation to roosters in the cockfighting cases?

2. For most Americans, dogs and cats might epitomize the term "domestic animal," but as the following cases demonstrate, that has not always been true.

Commonwealth v. Massini

Superior Court of Pennsylvania, 1963
188 A.2d 816

WOODSIDE, Judge. This is an appeal from a sentence imposed upon the defendant for the violation of §941 of The Penal Code of June 24, 1939, P.L. 872, 18 P.S. §4941.

This section provides that "Whoever wilfully and maliciously kills, maims or disfigures any domestic animal of another person, or wilfully and maliciously, administers poison to any such animal, or exposes any poisonous substance, with the intent that the same shall be taken or swallowed by animals, fowl or birds, is guilty of a misdemeanor, . . ."

The Statutory Construction Act of May 28, 1937, P.L. 1019, § 101, 46 P.S. § 601 provides: "The following words and phrases, when used in any law hereafter enacted, unless the context clearly indicates otherwise, shall have the meaning ascribed to them in this section: . . . (37) 'Domestic Animal,' any equine animal, bovine animal, sheep, goat and pig."

The defendant shot and killed his neighbor's cat. A cat is not one of the animals defined in the Statutory Construction Act, *supra*, as a "domestic animal." The legislature has directed us to accept the definitions of the Statutory Construction Act when used in any law thereafter enacted, unless the context clearly indicates otherwise. The relevant part of the section, which the defendant stands convicted of having violated, must therefore be read as follows: "Whoever wilfully and maliciously kills any equine animal, bovine animal, sheep, goat or pig of another person is guilty of a misdemeanor." It is evident, of course, that the defendant by shooting a cat did not violate such provision.

The court below submitted to the jury whether the dead cat had been a domestic animal, ignoring the statutory definition of such animal. In its opinion, the court attempted to demonstrate that some cats, including the one that was shot, can fall within the dictionary definitions of domestic animal. That is not the issue. When the legislature defines the words it uses in a statute, neither the jury nor the court may define them otherwise.

* * *

The omission of cats from the definition of domestic animals was not a mere oversight by the legislature, but was based upon long recognized law. At common law a cat could not be the subject of larceny, having no intrinsic value in the eyes of the law. But this is not important, for, as we have seen, the legislature may, for reasons of its own, define a word differently than it is generally used or defined. "'The legislature must be intended to mean what it has plainly expressed. . . . It matters not, in such a case, what the consequences may be.'"

* * *

If the legislators wish to make it a violation of § 941 of The Penal Code, *supra*, to kill a cat, they can easily do so, but the decision must be theirs and not ours. The judges of this Commonwealth cannot decide what acts should be crimes regardless of how immoral or wicked we might think them to be. If the act which a person commits is not a crime at common law and the legislature has not clearly declared that act to be a crime, we have no power to make it a crime.

As killing a cat is not a violation of the section of The Penal Code which the defendant was convicted of violating, he must be discharged. Having reached this conclusion, we need not refer to the other objections raised by the appellant to his conviction and sentence.

Judgment of sentence is arrested and the defendant discharged.

Commonwealth v. Comella

Commonwealth Court of Pennsylvania, 1999
735 A.2d 738

MCGINLEY, Judge. Sandra Comella (Comella) appeals from an order of the [trial court] which dismissed her appeal from the order of a district justice finding Comella guilty of harboring a dangerous dog under section 502-A(a)(1)(ii) of the Dog Law (Law), sentenced her to pay a fine of $300.00 plus costs and found her guilty as charged.

> [*Section 502-A(a)(1)(ii) provided:*
>
> *(a) Summary offense of harboring a dangerous dog. Any person who has been attacked by one or more dogs, or anyone on behalf of such person, a person whose domestic animal has been killed or injured without provocation, the State dog warden or the local police officer may file a complaint before a district justice, charging the owner or keeper of such a dog with harboring a dangerous dog. The owner or keeper of the dog shall be guilty of the summary offense of harboring a dangerous dog if the district justice finds beyond a reasonable doubt that the following elements of the offense have been proven:*
>
> *(1) The dog has done one or more of the following: . . . (ii) Killed or inflicted severe injury on a domestic animal without provocation while off the owner's property.*]

On January 4, 1998, Comella was walking her two dogs when she stopped on the side of her house to put some refuse in a container. As she did this, Comella dropped the leash of one of her dogs. At this time Mary Jo Salmen (Salmen), Comella's neighbor, was walking her dog. Comella's dog ran toward Salmen and her dog. Salmen ran screaming from the scene. Comella's dog attacked Salmen's dog.

Salmen's dog was seriously injured and underwent surgery for puncture wounds it received for cuts in the chest, back, hindquarters, nose and tail. The dog received at least ten stitches and was placed on pain medication and antibiotics. . . .

On January 9, 1998, animal control officer, John Decker (Decker), cited Comella pursuant to section 502-A of the Law that stated that Comella "did unlawfully keep or harbor a dangerous dog."

* * *

[On appeal,] Comella contends that the phrase "domestic animal" as used in section 502-A(a)(1)(ii) of the Law, P.S. §459-502-A(a)(1)(ii), does not apply to dogs for purposes of determining whether a dog who attacks another dog should be registered as dangerous under the Law. The term, "domestic animal" is defined in section 102 of the Law, 3 P.S. §459-102, as "any equine animal or bovine animal, sheep, goat, pig, poultry, bird, fowl, confined hares, rabbits and mink, or any wild or semiwild animal maintained in captivity." This definition is contained in the 1996 amendments to the Law. Prior to this amendment, section 102, the general definition section of the Law did not contain a definition for the term, "domestic animal." However, prior to amendment, section 501-A of the Law, 3 P.S. §459-501-A, the definitional section for the portion of the Law dealing with dangerous dogs, defined a domestic animal as "Any dog, cat, equine animal, bovine animal, sheep, goat or porcine animal." When the Law was amended in 1996, this section was deleted. Comella asserts that because the new definition does not include dogs and because the deleted definition section did include dogs, section 502-A(a)(1)(ii) of the Law does not apply when one dog attacks another dog.[3]

* * *

This Court's aim in statutory construction is to ascertain and effectuate the intent of the legislature. When the language of a statute is clear and unambiguous, any further deliberation as to its meaning is unwarranted. If the words of a statute are not explicit, we may consider, among other matters, the occasion and necessity for the statute, the circumstances under which it was enacted, the mischief to be remedied, the object to be attained, the former law, if any, including other statutes upon the same or similar subjects, the consequences of a particular interpretation, the contemporaneous legislative history and the legislative and administrative interpretations of the statute. Ordinarily, a change in the language of a statute indicates a change in the legislative intent. However, when interpreting a statute, the practical results of a particular interpretation must be considered. Further, the legislature cannot be presumed to have intended a result that is absurd or unreasonable.

---

3. For further support, Comella notes that Section 501 of the Law, 3 P.S. §459-501(a), which makes it legal to kill certain dogs distinguishes between dogs and domestic animals because the section states "Any person may kill any dog which he sees in the act of pursuing or wounding or killing any domestic animal, wounding or killing other dogs, cats or household pets."

We must reject Comella's interpretation. The Law contains some ambiguity as dogs are not specifically identified in the definition of a domestic animal but a dog is commonly characterized as a domestic animal. The term, "dog" is defined in section 102 of the Law, 3 P.S. § 459-102, as "the genus and species known as *Canis familiaris.*" Webster's Third International Dictionary (1986) defines "*canis*" as "the chief and type genus of the dog family including the domestic dogs, the wolves and jackals, and sometimes in older classifications of foxes." The same dictionary defines "dog" as "a carnivorous mammal (*Canis familiaris*) of the family *Canidae* that has been kept in a domesticated state by man since prehistoric times."

It is clear that dogs are commonly considered domestic animals. While cognizant of the importance of a statute's exact wording, we must also examine whether the application of that wording leads to an absurd result. Under the Law, a dog's owner could be convicted of harboring a dangerous dog if the dog attacked an animal that is classified as domestic under the Law such as a horse, cow, sheep, or goat or even an ostrich which is being kept in captivity. Under Comella's interpretation of the Law, a dog could repeatedly attack dogs and cats when not on its own property, and the owner would not be a violator of the Law. We do not believe that the Legislature intended such an absurd result. Although Comella contends that the clear intent of the 1996 amendment is to protect agricultural animals, we simply do not believe that the legislature intended to exclude dogs and, for that matter, cats from the definition of a domestic animal. Section 102 of the Law states that "the following words and phrases when used in this act [the Law] shall have, unless the context clearly indicates otherwise, the meanings given them in this section." Here, the context indicates that the accepted meaning of the term "domestic animal" controls.

Accordingly, we affirm.

Notes

1. Can you reconcile the approach to statutory interpretation taken by the Pennsylvania courts in *Massini* in 1963 and in *Comella* thirty-six years later?

2. In *McKinney v. Robbins*, 892 S.W.2d 502 (Ark. 1995), defendant shot and killed plaintiff's dog when the dog roamed onto defendant's property. Defendant asserted that the dog was vicious and had previously killed his cats and threatened his child and guests. Defendant relied on a state statute (ARK. STAT. ANN. § 20-19-102(b)(2)), which permitted the owner of a domesticated animal to kill a dog that kills his domesticated animal. Plaintiff contended that pet kittens were not "domesticated animals" under the statute and that the killing of his dog was, therefore, not justified. According to the definition in the controlling statute, "'domesticated animals' includes, but is not limited to, sheep, goats, cattle, swine, and poultry." The court looked to the legislative history, which dated back to 1887, and concluded that the "pattern of legislative acts appears to limit reprisals only to dogs which kill livestock." *Id.* at 504. The court also applied the doctrines of *ejusdem generis* (members of the enumeration suggest a class) and *noscitur a sociis* (a term may be defined by the accompanying words). The *McKinney* court ultimately held that "domesticated

animals," as used in the statute, was limited to livestock and did not cover domestic pets. The court justified its holding as follows:

> There is a practical aspect to our holding today. The genesis of the 1887 Act was manifestly a need to protect livestock in the form of sheep against marauding dogs. Sheep represented livelihood and a means of sustenance. The same is true of the other kinds of livestock added to the statute over more than a hundred years. To extend the definition of "domesticated animals" which is limited by its terms to examples of livestock to include pets would expand the effect of the Act far beyond what, we believe, was intended by the General Assembly.

Id. The court distinguished a 1914 Maine Supreme Court case where a plaintiff's foxhound had been killed by the defendant for taunting his cat, and the defendant was found to be free of liability. *Thurston v. Carter*, 92 A. 295 (Me. 1914). The statute in that case provided that dogs could be killed for worrying or killing "any domestic animal," but it did not contain a list of livestock as the Arkansas statute did. The *Thurston* court concluded that cats were domestic animals under the Maine statute at issue in 1914.

In *Thurston*, the court first looked to dictionary definitions, then considered the historical relationship between cats and humans, as well as English law and the then-present view:

> The time of its first domestication is lost in the mists of the dawn of history, but it is apparent that the cat was a domestic animal among the early Egyptians, by whom it came to be regarded as sacred, . . . which could scarcely have been feasible if the animal was then wild. From that date to this, it has been a dweller in the homes of men. In no other animal has affection for home been more strongly developed, and in none, when absent from home, can the *animus revertendi* be more surely assumed to exist.
>
> * * *
>
> It is clear, therefore, from the popular meaning of the word "domestic" and from our knowledge of its habits gained from fact and experience that the cat is a domestic animal. In the Laws of England it is laid down that the common law follows the civil law in classifying animals in two divisions as follows: "(1) domestic or tame (*domitae* or *mansuetae naturae*). This class includes cattle, horses, sheep, goats, pigs, poultry, cats, dogs, and all other animals which by habit or training live in association with man. 1 Halsbury, 365."
>
> * * *
>
> But it is urged that the cat is not the subject of larceny, and therefore its owner can have but a qualified property therein. Among the ancient Britons, it was held to have intrinsic value, and the theft of a cat was punishable by fine. When, however, larceny became punishable capitally, the courts,

to mitigate the severity of the law, held that certain animals were not the subject of larceny as not fit for food, or as base, or as kept only for pleasure, curiosity, or whim. And Hawkins, speaking of the subjects of larceny, says: "Thirdly, they ought not to be things of a base nature, as dogs, cats, foxes, monkeys, ferrets, and the like, which, however they may be valued by their owner, shall never be so regarded by the laws, that for their sakes a man shall die."

* * *

A cat which is kept as a household pet may be properly considered a thing of value. It ministers to the pleasures of its owner, and serves, as was said by Coke of falcons, *ob vitae solaitum* [as a comfort for life].

* * *

The change of sentiment respecting animals and the light in which they are regarded at the present day [which was then 1914] is admirably shown in the provisions of law punishing cruelties inflicted upon them, and their sweeping character is indicated in the provision that the word "animal" as employed in our statutes upon this subject "includes every living brute creature." On the other hand, while enactments are numerous giving damages for injuries caused by various animals and providing for their license and regulation, our statutes are silent as to the "harmless necessary cat."

Id. at 295–96.

In *United States v. Gideon*, 1 Minn. 292 (Minn. 1856), the defendant was indicted for shooting a dog in violation of a statute that provided that "every person who shall willfully and maliciously kill, maim or disfigure any horses, cattle, or other beasts of another person . . . shall be punished. . . ." The court reasoned:

It may be difficult to determine in all respects what animals the term "beasts," as used in the statute, includes; but it may be fairly assumed, as it seems to me, that all such as have, in law, no value, were not intended to be included in that general term. Horses and cattle have an intrinsic value which their names import, and it is but reasonable to suppose that the intention of the law was, in using the term "beasts," to include such other animals as may properly come under the name of beasts, and as have an intrinsic value in the same sense that there is value in horses, oxen and cows . . . , but it would be going quite too far to hold that dogs were intended. A criminal offense should not be created by an uncertain and doubtful construction of a statute. If there be any doubt in the case, penal statutes are to be so construed as not to multiply felonies, unless the construction be supported by express words, or by a reasonable implication. My opinion, therefore, is that the shooting [of] a dog is not an indictable offense under the statute referred to.

But if I am wrong in this opinion, there is still the fatal objection left, that no value was alleged or proved. Blackstone, in his 4 Com. 236, says: "As to these animals which do not serve for food, and which the law therefore, holds to have no intrinsic value, as dogs of all sorts, and other creatures kept for whim and pleasure, though a man may have a bare property therein, and maintain a civil action for the loss of them, yet they are not of such estimation as that the crime of stealing them amounts to a larceny." It is equally necessary to sustain this indictment, even admitting that it should be sustained in any event, that the dog killed should have been charged and proved to be of value. . . . The simple word or name of dog, then, not importing value, and no value being alleged or proved, the verdict cannot be sustained.

Id. at 296–97.

More than a century later, the Vermont Supreme Court based its holding on similar reasoning in *Morgan v. Kroupa*, 702 A.2d 630 (Vt. 1997). Plaintiff had lost his companion dog, and defendant found him, and plaintiff claimed a right to the dog under a lost property statute. The court found the statute's reference to a "stray beast" applied to "a farm animal of considerable value" but not to a lost pet. Defendant, who had cared for the dog for a year, was entitled to keep him and claim an interest greater than plaintiff. The dissenting justice in *Morgan v. Kroupa* disagreed, concluding that "[t]o separate some species of domesticated animals from others on an attempted livestock-pet dichotomy is a purely arbitrary interpretation of the statute."

3. According to the *Gideon* court, in 1856 penal statutes had been enacted in England against persons found guilty of stealing dogs, but there were no similar American laws. Presently, however, numerous states have enacted specific statutes against dog theft, and a growing number of states are classifying the crime as a felony, rather than a misdemeanor. *See, e.g.*, OR. REV. STAT. § 164.055 (2017).

4. Historical artifacts document that dogs and cats have been highly-regarded companion animals throughout the world for thousands of years. *See, e.g.*, Mary Elizabeth Thurston, THE LOST HISTORY OF THE CANINE RACE: OUR FIFTEEN THOUSAND-YEAR LOVE AFFAIR WITH DOGS (1996); *Nahrstedt v. Lakeside Village Condo. Ass'n*, 78 P.2d 1275, 1292 (Cal. 1994) ("Beyond dispute, human beings have long enjoyed an abiding and cherished association with their household animals.") (Arabian, J., dissenting) (excerpted in Chapter 7).

5. A veterinary ethics text has defined the term "companion animal" as "referring to any nonhuman animal involved with one or more human beings in a relationship which is 'at the very least a continuous, bidirectional relationship . . . that brings a significant benefit to a central aspect of the lives of each, which is in some sense voluntary, and in which each party treats the other not just as something entitled to respect and benefit in its own right, but also as an object of admiration, trust, devotion, or love.'" *Krasnecky v. Meffen*, 777 N.E.2d 1286, 1287 n.6 (Mass. App. Ct. 2002), citing to the plaintiffs' reference to Tannenbaum, Veterinary Ethics 125 (1989). In that case, defendants' two dogs entered plaintiffs' property and killed seven of plaintiffs' sheep. Plaintiffs alleged that the sheep were their companion

animals and sought damages for emotional distress and loss of companionship. The plaintiffs asserted that the term "companion animal" is not limited to cats and dogs and that the evidence established that the slain sheep were pets and "companion animals" to them. The evidence indicated that "the plaintiffs regarded the sheep as their 'babies' and spent six or seven hours a day with them, giving them names and celebrating their birthdays with special food and balloons." It further indicated that they "patted, hugged, and brushed the sheep and baked snacks for them" and that "[w]hen the sheep were young, the plaintiffs welcomed them into their home for up to four weeks at a time, bottle fed them, and allowed them to run through their home." The court acknowledged that, under the circumstances, "it was reasonably foreseeable that the plaintiffs would suffer emotional distress upon learning of the slaughter of the sheep and seeing their bodies." Nevertheless, the court held that the damages sought for emotional distress and loss of companionship were not available for harm to companion animals. (Emotional distress and loss of companionship damages are discussed in Chapter 4.)

6. Interpreting a statutory meaning of "wild animals," two Wisconsin state courts reached opposite conclusions as to whether a buck (adult male) deer kept in a fenced-in "deer display" at a park is a "wild" animal. In *Hudson v. Janesville Conservation Club*, 472 N.W.2d 247 (Wis. Ct. App. 1991) (*depublished*), plaintiff was injured when a buck deer charged him while he was standing inside the deer pen feeding other deer. The statute at issue immunized property owners from liability for any injury resulting from a wild animal attack; such statutes encourage landowners to open their lands for recreational use by the public. Neither the statute nor any controlling case law defined "wild animal." Considering the numerous authorities cited by both sides to support their respective positions, the appellate court concluded reasonable persons could differ as to whether the term "wild animal" includes captive buck deer. The court then looked to legislative intent: "[a]n obvious concern of owners of large tracts of land was potential attacks on recreational users by animals not in captivity." The court concluded legislative intent would not be advanced by interpreting "wild animal" to include animals held in captivity. According to the court, if captive animals were "wild animals," victims of animal attacks at zoos could not state a negligence cause of action against the property owner, which would not further the intended purpose of opening private lands to recreation. Accordingly, the court held a captive buck deer was not a "wild animal" as used in the statute and plaintiff's claim was valid.

The Wisconsin Supreme Court disagreed. *Hudson v. Janesville Conservation Club*, 484 N.W.2d 132 (Wis. 1992). The majority did not find an animal's captivity dispositive of whether the animal is "wild" within the meaning of the statute at issue. The majority first looked to dictionary definitions of the term, commenting that "wild animal" is "not a technical term." Looking to legislative intent, the court took the following approach:

> A wild animal is a wild animal, regardless of its captivity. If the legislature had meant to restrict the meaning of the term "wild animal" so that

it did not include those wild animals held in captivity, it could easily have done so. However, it did not.

* * *

If a type of animal normally survives without human assistance in a state of nature, or is nondomesticated and usually is of outdoor habitation, or is of an untamable disposition, then we are of the opinion that the animal is probably wild, as that term is used in sec. 895.52(2)(b).

Id. at 135 n.5, 136. The court discussed an 1879 case (*Spring Co. v. Edgar*, 99 U.S. 645, 658 (1879)) in which the United States Supreme Court had concluded that it was then "a matter of common knowledge" that a male deer is a wild animal. The buck in that case was also captive. The court commented that "[a]lthough many things have changed since 1879, we do not think that the nature of deer has evolved to the point where a male deer is now considered a domestic animal, whether captive or not." The court quoted from a text stating that young deer and older does are generally gentle and affectionate, but that older bucks often develop an "ugly disposition" and, during certain times of the year, "may fight anything." *Id*. Later in the opinion, the court quoted from an earlier case discussing wild deer and stating that it does not matter "that an animal of this kind may be to some extent tame and domesticated; the natural wildness and ferocity of his nature but sleeps, and is liable to be awakened at any moment, suddenly and unexpectedly, under some provocation, as was the case in this instance." The majority therefore reversed the appellate decision and held that a captive buck deer was a wild animal within the meaning of the statute.

The *Hudson* court and those courts it cited all made a distinction between female and male deer, suggesting female deer remain gentle and affectionate while male deer become unruly and unmanageable. If the plaintiff in *Hudson* had been injured by a young female deer, rather than by a charging buck, do you think the result would have been different?

7. In Oregon, the case of Snowball, a pet deer, brought much media attention. The Oregon Department of Fish and Wildlife determined that Snowball should be sent to an elk farm, and not maintained as a family pet. A county judge then ordered that Snowball be returned to her adoptive human family. The Department of Fish and Wildlife expressed concern that the judge's ruling would set a dangerous precedent: "We are concerned that this ruling opens the door to people removing wildlife from the wild. . . . If a District Attorney chooses not to prosecute, an individual will simply get the animal back. That's not good for Oregon's wildlife." Steve Mayes, *State Will Appeal Order to Return Deer*, Oregonian, Oct. 27, 2007, at D2. On appeal, the court reversed the trial court ruling and held that individuals cannot lawfully possess wildlife without a valid permit. *Filipetti v. Dept. of Fish & Wildlife*, 197 P.3d 535 (Or. Ct. App. 2008). Snowball was returned to the Department of Fish and Wildlife and was sent to a wildlife safari petting zoo.

8. In *Zinter ex rel. Lyons v. Oswskey*, 633 N.W.2d 278 (Wis. Ct. App. 2001) (unpublished), the court considered whether a pet rabbit was a "wild animal." The court

recognized that there are different types of rabbits and that rabbits may be of a domesticated or wild species. Relying upon Wisconsin statutes and the reasoning in *Hudson*, the court noted that this determination does not depend on whether the rabbit is treated as a pet — *i.e.,* if the defendants merely caged a wild rabbit, the rabbit would remain "wild" under the statute. *Compare People v. Hepburn*, 688 N.Y.S.2d 428 (N.Y. City Ct. 1999) (wolf hybrid kept as a pet, born in captivity and domesticated from birth, was not "wildlife" under statute defining "wildlife" as "'wild game' and all other animal life 'existing in a wild state'").

9. The cases establish that the circumstances under which an animal is raised can transform (from a legal standpoint) a wild animal into a companion, domestic or domesticated animal. Consider, for example, the problems that arise when chimpanzees are kept in private homes as pets. Because they are naturally wild, all of their needs are impossible to meet in captivity, especially outside of professionally-run sanctuaries, and chimpanzees in private homes often live in cruel (and sometimes illegal) conditions of neglect and deprivation. In part because of this dangerous combination (and also because of their natural tendencies), there have been a series of publicized instances where captive chimpanzees have attacked and injured their caregivers and other bystanders. For example, the Davises were a couple who kept a chimpanzee named Moe in their home (and yard) in West Covina, California for almost thirty years. In 1998, he escaped from his enclosure and bit a police officer. Hector Becerra, *Chimp's Removal Raises a Cry Worthy of Tarzan*, L.A. TIMES, Oct. 3, 1999. The next year he bit off the tip of a woman's finger. *Id.* Moe was removed from the Davises' care and, after a lengthy legal battle between the municipality and the Davises, he was eventually caged at Animal Haven Ranch, a private wildlife facility in Southern California. Rich Schapiro, *The Worst Story I Ever Heard*, ESQUIRE MAGAZINE, Feb. 17, 2009. On March 3, 2005, while the Davises were visiting Moe at the ranch, two other chimpanzees escaped from their enclosure and attacked the Davises. *Id.* Both chimpanzees had to be shot and killed to end the attack. Mr. Davis lost his genitals, all of his fingers, most of his face, and part of his foot in the attack. *Id.*

Two chimpanzees kept in a private home in Montana escaped in January 2009 and bit a woman; the chimps had bitten at least thirty people over the previous several years. Linda Halstead-Acharya, *Health Board Orders Chimps Quarantined*, BILLINGS GAZETTE, Mar. 13, 2009. Their owner was charged with misdemeanor public nuisance. *Rizzotto Makes Initial Appearance on Public Nuisance Charge*, BILLINGS GAZETTE, Mar. 26, 2009. (Chimpanzees are prohibited as pets in Montana, but these two were imported just prior to the ban.)

One month later, in Connecticut, Charla Nash was attacked and critically wounded by Travis, a 14-year-old pet chimpanzee owned by her friend. Chase Wright, *Chimp Victim Blind for Life*, STAMFORD NEWS, Apr. 7, 2009. She experienced brain damage and also lost both of her hands, her eyes and parts of her face as a result of the attack. *Id.* Travis's owner stabbed Travis with a kitchen knife and struck him repeatedly with a shovel in her failed attempts to stop the attack before Travis was shot and killed by police. Stephanie Gallman, *Chimp Attack 911 Call: 'He's Ripping Her Apart!'*, CNN.com, Feb. 18, 2009, *available at http://www.cnn.com/2009/US/02/17/chimpanzee.attack/*. The victim's conservator filed a civil suit against the chimp's owner. *Nash v. Herold*, 2010 Conn Super. LEXIS 1237 (Conn. Super. Ct., Stamford-Norwalk Jud. Dist., May 18, 2010) (denying motion to dismiss strict liability claim). According to news reports, a $4 million settlement was reached in 2012 with the deceased owner's estate. Nash's efforts to sue the state for her injuries were unsuccessful. Sasha Goldstein, *Charla Nash, mauled by Travis the chimp, denied the right to sue Connecticut for $150M*, New York Daily News, Apr. 2, 2014; Tina Susman, *Woman maimed in chimp attack loses bid to sue Connecticut*, L.A. Times, Apr. 3, 2014.

A few months after the attack by Travis, in June 2009, Connecticut enacted a law banning the possession and importation of chimpanzees, orangutans and gorillas, although existing law at the time of the attack already restricted ownership of chimpanzees like Travis. *See* Conn. Gen. Stat.§ 26-55 (2008) ("No person shall import or introduce into the state, or possess or liberate therein, any live fish, wild bird, wild mammal, reptile, amphibian or invertebrate unless such person has obtained a permit. . . ."). The law in place in 2017 banned the possession of a "potentially dangerous animal," defined to include the aforementioned primates. Conn. Gen. Stat. § 26-40a (2017). The law excluded from the definition a "primate that weighs less than thirty-five pounds at maturity and that was imported or possessed by a person in this state prior to October 1, 2010." Conn. Gen. Stat. § 26-40a (b) (2017).

10. Other legal issues may arise when private individuals keep exotic animals in their homes. Two decades before the 2009 chimpanzee attacks, the court in the following case determined that the monkey (significantly different in size, genetics and behavior than a chimpanzee) maintained in the defendants' home was a domesticated animal under the facts presented in that case.

City of Rolling Meadows v. Kyle
Appellate Court of Illinois, First District, Third Division, 1986
494 N.E.2d 766

RIZZI, Justice. Plaintiff, City of Rolling Meadows, brought an action against defendant, Audrey Kyle, for keeping an undomesticated animal, a monkey, in her home in violation of a city ordinance. Following an evidentiary hearing, the court entered judgment in favor of plaintiff. Defendant subsequently filed a motion to vacate the judgment and a motion for a new trial. The trial court denied both motions. Defendant appeals. We reverse.

The monkey in question here, Yondi, has resided with defendant and her husband since she was 2 days old. At the time this suit was commenced, Yondi and the Kyles had been living in Rolling Meadows for the preceding 7 years. The citation issued by the city of Rolling Meadows charged defendant with violating a municipal ordinance which provides:

Keeping animals other than domesticated pets.

> No person, firm or corporation shall own or keep within the city any bees, goats, sheep, hogs, cattle, fowl, reptile or serpent, spider, or other animal normally wild, dangerous to human life or carnivorous in nature, other than domesticated house pets, and each day such animal is kept in violation of this section shall constitute a separate and distinct offense. The word "fowl" shall include chickens, turkeys, geese, and ducks. It is no defense to a violation of this section that the owner or keeper of any animal or reptile which is prohibited in this section has attempted to domesticate such animal or reptile.

City of Rolling Meadows, Ordinance, section 4-28 (1981).

Defendant and her husband testified extensively regarding the domesticity of Yondi and the commonly understood meaning of the words "domesticated house pets." The city presented no evidence indicating its definition of "domesticated house pets." . . .

The court essentially determined that (1) a monkey is an animal normally wild and incapable of being domesticated or defined as a domesticated house pet, (2) the phrase "other than domesticated house pets" refers to cats and dogs, and (3) taken as a whole, ordinance 4-28 bars the keeping of monkeys within the city limits.

At issue here is the construction and application to be given the phrase "other than domesticated house pets" as set forth in ordinance 4-28. Defendant contends that contrary to the trial court's ruling, proper statutory construction of ordinance 4-28 requires that (1) the phrase "other than domesticated house pets" be construed to modify the preceding phrase "or other animal normally wild, dangerous to human life or carnivorous in nature" in order to allow even cats or dogs to be kept as pets within the city, and (2) the phrase "domesticated house pets" be defined according to its commonly understood meaning. Defendant further contends that it is a question of fact in each case whether or not an animal normally wild, dangerous to human life or carnivorous in nature has been domesticated within the meaning of the ordinance.

* * *

We believe that the drafters of ordinance 4-28 intended the phrase "other than domesticated house pets" to modify the entire preceding phrase "or other animal normally wild, dangerous to human life or carnivorous in nature." Were we to follow the city's argument that "domestic house pets" modifies nothing and refers only to dogs and cats, ordinance 4-28 would prohibit residents from keeping all other animals normally wild, dangerous to human life or carnivorous in nature, including such commonly kept house pets as birds, gerbils, hamsters, mice, rabbits, guinea pigs, tropical fish and turtles.

Furthermore, adoption of the city's interpretation of ordinance 4-28 would ban any pet store located within the city of Rolling Meadows from selling any animals other than cats and dogs. We do not believe that the drafters of ordinance 4-28 intended the ordinance to be construed in such a restrictive manner, since such a construction would be neither logical, useful nor reasonable.

Having determined that the phrase "other than domesticated house pets" modifies the phrase "or other animal normally wild, dangerous to human life or carnivorous in nature," we must next consider defendant's argument that the phrase "domesticated house pets" should be defined according to its commonly understood meaning.

Here, the word domesticated, as referring to house pet, has not been defined by the drafters. When a term of a statute is not defined by the legislature, courts are to presume that the term was intended to have its ordinary and popularly understood meaning absent legislative intent to the contrary. The legislature is presumed not to intend unjust, absurd or unreasonable consequences. Ordinance 4-28 lacks a legislative history to aid us in our interpretation of the meaning of the term domesticated, and the record shows that the city presented no evidence regarding the drafter's intended definition of the term. Consequently, we are required to adopt the common and approved usage of the term domesticated.

In view of our determination that the phrase "other than domesticated house pets" modifies the phrase "or other animal normally wild, dangerous to human life or carnivorous in nature," we must reject the trial court's definition of domesticated house pets as being limited to cats and dogs. Moreover, in ordinary usage, and as defined by both legal and standard dictionaries, the word domestic means made domestic or converted to domestic use. Where the word domestic or domesticated is descriptive of the word animals, these terms connote an animal wild by nature which has been so reclaimed as to become tame, under the dominion and control of its owner, associated with family life or accustomed to living in or near the habitations of men. . . . Absent evidence to the contrary, we believe that the drafters of ordinance 4-28 intended to adopt these common meanings of the term domesticated house pets. Any other interpretation would be inconsistent with case law, the rules regarding statutory construction, and common understanding and usage of the English language.

In her remaining argument, defendant contends that it is a question of fact in each case whether or not an animal normally wild, dangerous to human life, or carnivorous in nature has been domesticated within the meaning of ordinance 4-28. Defendant therefore argues that the trial court erred in deciding that as a matter of law, a normally wild animal, such as a monkey, cannot be domesticated. We agree with defendant.

Our interpretation of the language of ordinance 4-28 requires a trial court to first determine whether an animal in question is normally wild, dangerous to human life, or carnivorous in nature, and then to determine whether the animal is domesticated. Application of the commonly understood definition of the term domesticated house pet to an individual animal necessarily involves a factual determination. While we recognize that a monkey is an animal normally wild, we do not believe that such a classification is dispositive of the question of domesticity in all cases. Rather, it is clear that Illinois recognizes that animals wild by nature may be domesticated. *See* Ill. Rev. Stat. 1983, ch. 8, par. 24; *Ulery v. Jones* (1876) 81 Ill. 403.

Here, the evidence shows that Yondi is a lesser spotted white nose quenon [sic] monkey, registered as an endangered species pursuant to the Endangered Species Act (16 U.S.C. § 1531 *et seq.* (1982)), born in captivity in Kenya, Africa and raised by defendant since the age of two days. Yondi is now approximately 15 years old and weighs six pounds. The uncontroverted evidence is that Yondi makes intelligent communications through a variety of vocalizations and gestures, and that she is toilet trained. She receives the same inoculations and vaccinations as a child, including tuberculosis, polio, diphtheria and booster shots. Yondi has accompanied defendant and her husband on trips to Europe, Asia, Africa and Latin America. The record also shows that Yondi is a highly sociable animal and interacts equally well with people and animals. Moreover, the record is devoid of any evidence that Yondi poses a danger to the community.

Under the circumstances, we conclude that the evidence presented to the trial court concerning the proper interpretation of the term "domesticated house pet" and its application to Yondi establishes as a matter of law that Yondi is a domesticated animal. The trial court erred in finding defendant in violation of ordinance 4-28.

Accordingly, the judgment of the circuit court is reversed.

WHITE, Justice, dissenting. I would hold that the City of Rolling Meadows ordinance forbids keeping within the city an "animal normally wild," and that Yondi, a monkey, is such an animal. Keeping Yondi within the city is therefore a violation of the ordinance. The majority states that the record "shows that Yondi is a highly sociable animal," but Yondi is still a monkey, and in the words of the ordinance, "It is no defense to a violation of this section that the owner . . . has attempted to domesticate such animal. . . ."

I would affirm the judgment of the trial court.

Notes

1. In *Lakeshore Hills, Inc. v. Adcox*, 413 N.E.2d 548 (Ill. App. Ct. 1980), the defendant kept a twelve-year-old, 575-pound Canadian black bear named Yogi on his lot in a subdivision which permitted the keeping of "household pets," which term was undefined. Yogi was kept in a cage within a cage. The defendant testified that Yogi was a fifth-generation captive and was quite gentle and held no animosity towards humans, including young children. The trial court granted a preliminary injunction compelling the defendant to remove Yogi from the property, concluding that it is "contrary to the nature of people to live with or in the immediate vicinity of bears" and "contrary to the nature of bears to live in a cage in a yard busy with the incidents of suburban life." *Id.* at 550. The appellate court affirmed the injunction, concluding that although Yogi was a fifth-generation captive and lacked claws and fangs, "Yogi is a bear and not a domestic household animal." *Id. See also Cavaliere*

v. Skelton, 40 S.W.2d 844 (Ark. Ct. App. 2001) (where defendants kept Bengal tigers at their residence, they did not contest plaintiffs' assertion that the tigers were not "household pets" within the meaning of the community's restrictive covenant); *Warren County Combined Health District v. Rittenhouse*, 689 N.E.2d 1036, 1039 (Ohio Ct. App. 1997) ("The mere fact that the cougars have become accustomed to interaction with man from living in captivity simply does not alter their wild and untame nature so as to render them domesticated animals."). *But see Turudic v. Stephens*, 31 P.3d 465, 471 (Or. Ct. App. 2001) (where one of the plaintiffs testified that two cougars they kept on their property were an "integral part" of their family life and that they had a "very strong bond" with the animals, the court concluded that "although the cougars may be more exotic than goldfish or hamsters, they are, nevertheless, indisputably family pets").

2. In *Gallick v. Barto*, 828 F. Supp. 1168 (M.D. Pa. 1993), the central issue was whether ferrets are "wild animals." In a lengthy opinion, the court first considered general facts about ferrets, referring to a dictionary definition of a ferret as "a kind of weasel, easily tamed and used for hunting or killing of rabbits, rats, etc. . . ." The court then discussed Pennsylvania law on wild animals, concluding that because Pennsylvania's Game and Wildlife Code provides that a wild animal is any animal that is not a domestic animal under the general definitions provision, and because that provision does not list ferrets as domestic animals, ferrets therefore must be wild animals. The court next looked to the historical reasons for keeping ferrets ("ferrets have been kept by humans for some time basically because of their propensity to attack small animals"; "they were first brought to this country from Europe in 1875 to hunt for rabbits"; "while people have kept ferrets, they have done so for the limited purpose of hunting, and ferrets serve that purpose only because of their ferocity") and then noted that "several states do not allow residents to possess ferrets, while others put limits on ferret ownership." Unlike the court in *City of Rolling Meadows*, the court concluded that "whether *these particular* ferrets were tame is not the issue, since a wild animal may be tame without changing its essential nature." The court ultimately held:

> In sum, we are of the view that ferrets are an inverse of the types of dogs we have noted above. A pit bull may be considered a domestic animal because dogs generally are considered domestic animals. Therefore, a pit bull is a domestic animal with dangerous propensities.
>
> A ferret, on the other hand, is a wild animal which people may, to a point, be successful in keeping in their home. Therefore, a ferret is a wild animal with domestic propensities. However, those propensities do not change its essential character as a wild animal. We hold that a ferret is a wild animal.

Id. at 1174.

In *New York City Friends of Ferrets v. City of New York*, 876 F. Supp. 529 (S.D.N.Y. 1995), the court upheld the constitutionality of the City's interpretation of the local rule as prohibiting the keeping of ferrets, but left open the determination of whether ferrets are in fact "a species which is wild, ferocious, fierce, dangerous or naturally inclined to do harm." *See 1700 York Assocs. v. Kaskel*, 701 N.Y.S.2d 233, 242 (N.Y. Civ. Ct. 1999).

3. What reasons support different treatment under the law for different species of "companion" animals? What criteria should be examined to determine if an individual member of a species can be a companion animal? Should the courts examine the animals as individuals or as a species?

4. California's Business & Professions Code section 4825.1 expressly includes horses and other equine species as "companion animals." Although not all of California's statutory definitions do the same (*see, e.g.,* CAL. FOOD & AGRIC. CODE §§ 14205, 18663), section 4825.1 does reflect some legislative recognition that horses may maintain some special status. *See also* 510 ILL. COMP. STAT. ANN. 70/2.01a (2017) (defining "companion animals" to include equines). On the other hand, the Virginia Code defines "companion animal" to mean:

> any domestic or feral dog, domestic or feral cat, nonhuman primate, guinea pig, hamster, rabbit not raised for human food or fiber, exotic or native animal, reptile, exotic or native bird, or any feral animal or any animal under the care, custody, or ownership of a person or any animal which is bought, sold, traded, or bartered by any person. . . .

VA. CODE ANN. § 3.2–6500 (2017). The statute specifically excludes "agricultural animals," which are defined as "all livestock and poultry." "Livestock," in turn, is defined to include "all domestic or domesticated: . . . equine animals. . . ." Thus, horses are not considered companion animals under the Virginia statutory definitions applicable to Title 3.2 ("Agriculture, Animal Care and Food"), Subtitle V ("Domestic Animals"), Ch. 65 ("Comprehensive Animal Care") of the Virginia Code.

In *State v. Robertson*, 2016 Tenn. Crim. App. LEXIS 401 (May 27, 2016), the defendant was charged with aggravated cruelty under an indictment alleging that he, "with no justifiable purpose, cause[d] serious physical injury to a companion animal, to wit: a horse" belonging to another person, in violation of a Tennessee statute. However, the court ruled that the indictment failed to state an offense because the statute did not apply to equine animals. The statute at issue (TENN. CODE ANN. § 39-14-212) applied only to "companion animals," which were defined as "any non-livestock animal as defined in 39-14-201." Section 39-14-201(3) defined "non-livestock animal" as:

> [A] pet normally maintained in or near the household or households of its owner or owners, other domesticated animal, previously captured wildlife, an exotic animal, or any other pet, including but not limited to, pet rabbits, a pet chick, duck, or pot bellied pig that is not classified as "livestock" pursuant to this part . . . .

While the statute (Section 39-14-201(2)) defined "livestock" to include equines, the court also noted that the aggravated cruelty to animals statute expressly stated that "the provisions of this section do not apply to equine animals or to animals defined as livestock by the provisions of 39-14-201." TENN. CODE ANN. § 39-13-212(n).

Similarly, the Texas Penal Code has separate sections for the offenses of "Cruelty to Nonlivestock Animals" (Section 42.092) as opposed to "Cruelty to Livestock Animals" (Section 42.09). The former applies to cruelty to "animals," defined to mean "a domesticated living creature, including any stray or feral cat or dog, and a wild living creature previously captured," but expressly excluding "an uncaptured wild living creature or a livestock animal." TEX. PENAL CODE § 42.092(a)(2) (2017). "Livestock animal" is defined to include horses. TEX. PENAL CODE § 42.09(b)(5) (2017).

Chapter 2

Property and Beyond: The Evolution of Rights

Section 1. Slaves

Africans brought to America as slaves were the property of their owners. Slave owners could sell their slaves and buy others and, with very limited exceptions (that were virtually never enforced), do whatever they wanted with their human possessions. This represents the paradigmatic "humans-as-property" situation. The propriety of abolishing slavery and freeing former slaves is beyond dispute. Yet analyzing the reasons for doing it—and the way in which it occurred—may shed further light on the reasons why we might (or might not) decide to abolish the property status of animals.

An oft-cited case addressing the status of slaves as property is *Dred Scott v. Sandford*, 60 U.S. 393 (1856), a 240-page decision, with nine separate opinions (six concurring with the Court's opinion, and two dissenting). Dred Scott was the descendant of Africans brought to America as slaves. In 1834, Scott was a slave belonging to Dr. Emerson. That year Emerson took Scott from Missouri (a slave state) to Illinois (a "free state" where slavery was forbidden). They stayed in Illinois until 1836, when Emerson brought Scott to Fort Snelling in the Louisiana Territory. They stayed there until 1838. Emerson subsequently sold Scott to Sandford, who returned with Scott and his family to Missouri. Scott sued Sandford in Missouri, where they both lived, after Sandford assaulted and confined Scott, his wife, and his children. The Court acknowledged the alleged assault and imprisonment were "no more than what [Sandford] might lawfully do if [the Scotts] were of right his slaves at such times." The Court framed the issue before it:

> Can a negro, whose ancestors were imported into this country, and sold as slaves, become a member of the political community formed and brought into existence by the Constitution of the United States, and as such become entitled to all the rights, and privileges, and immunities, guarantied [*sic*] by that instrument to the citizen? One of which rights is the privilege of suing in a court of the United States in the cases specified in the Constitution.

Id. at 403. The answer was a resounding "no." The Court found that descendants of slaves were neither "people of the United States" nor "citizens" according to the "sense in which the word citizen is used in the Constitution of the United States." The Court therefore held slaves could "claim none of the rights and privileges which

47

that instrument provides for and secures to citizens of the United States. "On the contrary, they were at that time considered as a 'subordinate and inferior' class of beings, who had been subjugated by the dominant race, and, whether emancipated or not, remained subject to their authority, and had no rights or privileges but such as those who held the power and the Government might choose to grant them." *Id.* at 404–05.

> . . . [T]he right of property in a slave is distinctly and expressly affirmed in the Constitution. The right to traffic in it, like an ordinary article of merchandise and property, was guaranteed to the citizens of the United States, in every State that might desire it, for twenty years. And the Government in express terms is pledged to protect it in all future time, if the slave escapes from his owner. This is done in plain words—too plain to be misunderstood. And no word can be found in the Constitution which gives Congress a greater power over slave property, or which entitles property of that kind to less protection than property of any other description. The only power conferred is the power coupled with the duty of guarding and protecting the owner in his rights.

Id. at 451. Justice Catron concurred, concluding, "Scott was Dr. Emerson's lawful property in Missouri." *Id.* at 527.

Justice McLean could not accept the Court's holding. He dissented, stating "[a] slave is not a mere chattel. He bears the impress of his Maker, and is amendable to the laws of God and man; and he is destined to an endless existence." *Id.* at 550. Justice Curtis also disagreed with the majority, writing that "persons held to service under the laws of a State are property only to the extent and under the conditions fixed by those laws; . . . they must cease to be available as property, when their owners voluntarily place them permanently within another jurisdiction, where no municipal laws on the subject of slavery exist. . . ." *Id.* at 625.

Numerous cases from the nineteenth and early twentieth centuries explored whether a slave, as property, could be the beneficiary of other property, such as land, money, or even himself (known as "manumission"). Because many state statutes specifically prohibited emancipation, slave owners tried other vehicles such as wills and trusts that would allow for the removal of slaves to Northern states or foreign countries where they would be recognized as free persons.

In several instances, the courts had to determine the status of slaves whom an executor or trustee had been directed to free, but had not yet freed. Parties opposing the transfers argued that, as chattel, slaves could not take any legally cognizable interest in themselves. For example, in *Pleasants v. Pleasants*, 2 Call 319 (Va. 1800), it was argued that the gift of a slave essentially to himself could not really be a trust because it was unthinkable "that the legatees have the legal estate, and that the beneficial interest, that is the labour of the slaves, is in the slaves themselves." *Id.* at 324.

In *Shaw v. Ward*, 175 N.C. 192 (1918), however, the court supported a slave's right to be a beneficiary by relying on parallel trusts for animals as authority:

[I]t is not true that a trust is void because its beneficiaries are *non sui juris*. There are too many instances upheld by the courts of devises which have been made by eccentric testators of property to trustees to be held for the support and maintenance of dumb animals, . . . idiots or other incompetents, and even for the support of aliens in those States where they can not own realty, to require a citation of authorities that the fee simple is in the trustee for the purpose of the trust. . . . This trust was valid. . . .

Id. at 193.

Parties opposing transfers to slaves also argued that the transfer instruments were void because the beneficiaries were not capable of suing to enforce their rights. Courts generally rejected such arguments and held that the executors' oaths, the testators' confidence in their executors, and, ultimately, the courts themselves (where a suit was brought by one who *could* sue, *e.g.*, where an executor sought a court's guidance) provided sufficient guarantees of the instruments' execution. *See, e.g., Dunn v. Amey*, 1 Leigh 465 (Va. 1829); *Leach v. Cooley*, 6 S. & M. 93 (Miss. 1846); *Cleland v. Waters*, 19 Ga. 35 (1855).

In *M'Cutchen v. Marshall*, the United States Supreme Court upheld an instrument directing an executor to emancipate, observing that:

As a general proposition, it would seem a little extraordinary to contend, that the owner of property is not at liberty to renounce his right to it, either absolutely, or in any modified manner he may think proper. As between the owner and his slave, it would require the most explicit prohibition by law, to restrain this right. Considerations of policy, with respect to this species of property, may justify legislative regulation, as to the guards and checks under which such manumission shall take place; especially, so as to provide against the public's becoming chargeable for the maintenance of slaves so manumitted.

33 U.S. (8 Pet.) 220, 238 (1834). The court in *Cleland* similarly stated:

If any point may be considered as settled by the *consistent decisions* of the slave States, the cases establish the proposition, that unless restrained by positive enactment, a testator may, by his will, effect the manumission of his slaves, by vesting the title to them in trustees, for the purpose of their removal to a free State, there to enjoy their freedom.

19 Ga. at 51 (emphasis in original).

This reasoning did not extend to freed slaves suing on their own behalf in a slave state. In *Mitchell v. Wells*, 37 Miss. 235 (1859), the court rejected the right of a freed slave living in Ohio to sue in Mississippi, by finding that the logical conclusion of conferring such a right would be the extension of the same right to great apes:

Suppose that Ohio, still further afflicted with her peculiar philanthropy, should determine to descend another grade in the scale of her peculiar humanity, and claim to confer citizenship on the chimpanzee or the ourang-outang (the most respectable of the monkey tribe), are we to be told that "comity" will require of the States not thus demented, to forget their own policy and self-respect, and lower their own citizens and institutions in the scale of being, to meet the necessities of the mongrel race thus attempted to be introduced into the family of sisters in this confederacy?

Id. at 264.

Early cases also recognized and discussed the unique position slaves held as both property and non-property (persons) depending on the circumstances. In *Fable v. Brown*, 10 S.C. Eq. (1 Hill. Eq.) 378, 382 (1835), the chancellor stated:

There is certainly considerable difficulty in this, and other questions which arise out of the condition of slaves. Our statute considers them as chattels, yet, in many cases, they are treated by our laws as persons, and reasonable persons accountable for their actions. They are punished for crimes, which chattels could not be. It is their equivocal condition, which creates the difficulty.

Notwithstanding these difficulties, early courts were very aware of the economic interest of slave owners and slave states in maintaining the status quo slave system. For example, the *Mitchell* court stated:

... [Mississippi's] climate, soil, and productions, and the pursuits of her people, their habits, manners, and opinions, all combine not only to sanction the wisdom, humanity, and policy of the system thus established by her organic law and fostered by her early legislation, but they require slave labor. It was declared in the convention that framed the Federal Constitution, by some of their delegates, that Georgia and South Carolina would become barren wastes without slave labor. . . .

37 Miss. at 252–53.

Consider the following commentary on similar arguments for maintaining the property status of animals:

The economic interests implicated in the status of nonhuman animals as property are enormous. In this country alone, billions of animals are slaughtered each year for human consumption. Yet, the true economic pressures for social evolution are being artificially staved off. For example, government subsidization of animal agriculture defrays its true cost. Further, the environmental impact of pollution from factory farms is not regulated. If animal agriculture were faced with economic reality, forced to bear its own costs without government subsidization and responsibility for its environmental impact, its days would surely be numbered.

Derek St. Pierre, *The Transition from Property to People: The Road to the Recognition of Rights for Non-Human Animals*, 9 HASTINGS WOMEN'S L.J. 255, 269–70 (1998).

In addition to the perception that slavery was an economic necessity, other courts proclaimed that slavery was consistent with the natural order of life.

To inculcate care and industry upon the descendants of Ham, is to preach to the idle winds. To be the "servant of servants" is the judicial curse pronounced upon their race. And this Divine decree is unreversible. It will run on a parallel with time itself. And heaven and earth shall sooner pass away, than one jot or tittle of it shall abate. Under the superior race and nowhere else, do they attain to the highest degree of civilization; and any experiment, whether made in the British West India Islands, the coast of Africa, or elsewhere, will demonstrate that it is a vain thing for fanaticism, a false philanthropy, or anything else, to fight against the Almighty. His ways are higher than ours; and humble submission is our best wisdom, as well as our first duty! Let our women and old men, and persons of weak and infirm minds, be disabused of the false and unfounded notion that slavery is sinful, and that they will peril their souls if they do not disinherit their offspring by emancipating their slaves!

American Colonization Society v. Gartrell, 23 Ga. 448, 464–65 (1857).

The *Transition* article discusses the erosion of the belief that African-Americans were properly classified as property in colonial America:

> ... As illustrated below, some of the Northerners of the new nation agreed and understood "all men" to include slaves.
>
> The Massachusetts Constitution of 1780 echoed the above sentiments of liberty and equality. In fact, the Supreme Court of Massachusetts held that these words, in light of the Revolution, ended slavery. The Court could find no justification for denying slaves the "natural rights of man-kind" and held that we all share "that innate desire for liberty which heaven, without regard to complexion or shape, has planted in the human breast."
>
> The Pennsylvania legislature reflected a similar perspective of Revolutionary ideology and rhetoric. The passage of the Pennsylvania Gradual Abolition Act of 1780 spelled out the Pennsylvania legislature's recognition of the rights common to all individuals. "Negro and Mulatto slaves ... [could no longer be denied] the common blessings that they were by nature entitled to." The perspectives of both Massachusetts and Pennsylvania show the recognition of the similarity between slaves and the rest of their society. The Virginia Supreme Court also expressed its concerns by the freeing of a family of mixed racial ancestry because they "lacked any visible features of Negroes." This breakdown in the concept of "other" eroded the foundation upon which differential treatment was based.

Id. at 264–65.

Notes

1. As you read through the rest of this chapter, consider how the arguments of economic necessity and "divine decree" reconcile with more recent decisions relating to the property status and treatment of animals. Also consider whether

analyzing the legal similarities and distinctions between humans and nonhuman animals, particularly in the context of slavery, is a legitimate exercise. What benefit, if any, do you think can be gained in such discourse? Conversely, do you think such an exercise minimizes or de-legitimizes the legal, political, economic, and social struggles of African-Americans?

2. Applying the language used by the Supreme Court in *Dred Scott*, are nonhumans "considered as a subordinate and inferior class of beings, who ha[ve] been subjugated by the dominant race, and, whether emancipated or not, yet remain[] subject to their authority[?]" Consider the distinctions and similarities between humans and nonhuman animals, which might support (or oppose) the exercise of human authority over nonhumans.

3. To fully appreciate the reasons for deeming sentient beings legal property, make a list of the rationales for and against granting rights to slaves. Perform the same exercise for nonhumans. Compare the two lists and analyze which characteristics of humans probably led to the ultimate rejection of the property status of slaves. Which of those do nonhumans share?

4. In *Dred Scott*, the Court found a slave did not become free by entering a free state. With respect to wild animals, the rule may be the opposite. "[N]o individual property rights exist as long as the animal remains wild, unconfined, and undomesticated. Unqualified property rights in wild animals can arise when they are legally removed from their natural liberty and made the subject of man's dominion. This qualified right is lost, however, if the animal regains its liberty." *Nicholson v. Smith*, 986 S.W.2d 54, 60 (Tex. 1999). *See also Pierson v. Post*, 3 Cai. 175 (N.Y. Sup. Ct. 1805) (addressing the question of "whether Lodowick Post, by the pursuit with his hounds in the manner alleged in his declaration, acquired such a right to, or property in, the fox, as will sustain an action against Pierson for killing and taking him away," the court held there was no basis for legal action).

5. Animals are bought and sold as property, but can they legally own property? In Chapter 8 you will read about "animal trusts" in which animals can be bequeathed money or property. Under those circumstances do they, in essence, "own" that money or property? In one reported instance, a British investment analyst advised an Old English sheepdog named William "to such good effect that the dog's worldly wealth — in the shape of stocks and shares — has risen in eleven years from nothing to almost £100,000." J. Leigh Mellor, *Hath a Dog Money? Is It Possible a Cur Can Lend Three Thousand Ducats?*, 16 TAXATION 357 (Feb. 1985). The author attacks the notion that an animal can own property, asserting:

> The view that a dog is not a "legal entity" with respect, has meaning only in a particular context. It is a "legal entity," *i.e.*, is recognised as existing by the law, when the question of its license arises, for instance. However, the writer is prepared to swallow hard and assume for the moment that William can own property. On this assumption the writer accepts that William could not *himself* be assessed to tax. Nor could anyone else be on

William's behalf under Part VII, Taxes Management Act 1970, because he is not a "person," still less a "body of persons." No question of receivership arises, *Ibid.*, section 77 provides that part VII (except section 76) "shall apply in relation to capital gains tax as it applies in relation to income tax, and subject to any necessary modifications." The writer is of the view that those concluding words are insufficient to metamorphose William to a "person."

Id.

6. Consider whether great apes, or any other animals, may be defined as "persons" for some purposes, and "property" for others?

7. For further discussion of the issues raised in this section, *see* Marjorie Spiegel, THE DREADED COMPARISON: HUMAN AND ANIMAL SLAVERY (1997).

Section 2. Women

This section examines the development of legal protections for, and rights of, women in America. With some parallels and doctrinal overlap with the preceding section, it demonstrates the development of increasing rights accorded American women, both in terms of political and financial power. The history of the suffrage and women's liberation movements may serve as examples and road maps for the potential for change in the way society and the law treat animals.

Until the late nineteenth century, married women occupied a status of "legal nonexistence," and their "degraded position" rendered them "a combination vessel, chattel, and household drudge." *Montgomery v. Stephan*, 101 N.W.2d 227, 230 (Mich. 1960). *See also Wait v. Pierce*, 209 N.W. 475, 477 (Wis. 1926) (under the common law, "the wife was little more than a chattel of the husband"); *Theama ex rel. Bichler v. City of Kenosha*, 344 N.W.2d 513, 515 (Wis. 1984) (noting "archaic common law doctrine that upon marriage, the woman assumed the status of a chattel and was legally nonexistent"). *See generally* Margaret Thornton, *Loss of Consortium: Inequality Before the Law*, 10 SYDNEY L. REV. 259 (1984).

A husband's legal right to his wife's services was first recognized in 1618. *Guy v. Livesey*, 79 Eng. Rep. 428 (K.B. 1618). Although a husband could sue a third party over injury to his wife, at common law the right of a wife "was apparently no more than the capacity to sustain the injury, because she could not recover damages on account of it, and when the damages were recovered in an action in which her husband joined, the damages belonged to the husband and not to the wife." *Wait v. Pierce*, 209 N.W. 475, 480 (Wis. 1926). At common law,

> [t]he wife, by her coverture [marriage], ceased to have control of her actions or her property, which became subject to the control of her husband, who alone was entitled, during the marriage, to enjoy the possession of her lands, and who became owner of her goods and might sue for her

demands. The wife could neither possess nor manage property in her own right, could make no contract of a personal nature which would bind her, and could bring no suit in her own name. In short, she lost entirely all the legal incidents attaching to a person acting in her own right. The husband alone remained *sui juris*, as fully as before marriage.

Burdeno v. Amperse, 14 Mich. 91, 92 (1866). In contrast, unmarried women have always had the freedom to contract and the right to hold and convey property. *Wait v. Pierce, supra*, 209 N.W. at 478.

Toward the end of the nineteenth century, state legislatures began enacting so-called "Married Women's Property Acts" to "relieve married women of the disabilities of coverture," at least with respect to the ability to enter into certain specified property contracts. *Cohen v. Wollner, Hirschberg & Co.*, 72 Ala. 233, 236 (1882); *City Finance Co. v. Kloostra*, 209 N.W.2d 498, 499 (Mich. Ct. App. 1973) (quoting portion of Michigan's version of the Act enacted in 1917). "The impact of the Married Woman's Property Acts was greater than women being able to retain their property and enter into contracts. The Acts meant that the perception of women was slowly changing during the later half of the nineteenth century." Deborah H. King, *Clara Shortridge Foltz: Angel and Revolutionary*, 11 HASTINGS WOMEN'S L.J. 179, 197 (Summer 2000).

The contemporary view of women as full rights-bearing citizens was affirmed in a different context in *Planned Parenthood v. Casey*, 505 U.S. 833 (1992). In that case, the Supreme Court considered the constitutionality of a Pennsylvania statute requiring, among other things, that a married woman notify her husband before obtaining an abortion. In rejecting this requirement the Court looked to the status of women as viewed by the Court a century earlier in *Bradwell v. State*, 83 U.S. 130 (1873) ("a woman had no legal existence separate from her husband, who was regarded as her head and representative in the social state") and reasoned that this notification aspect of the Pennsylvania statute "embodies a view of marriage consonant with the common-law status of married women but repugnant to this Court's present understanding of marriage and of the nature of the rights secured by the Constitution." *Planned Parenthood*, 505 U.S. at 898.

Obviously, since the 1850s there has been a revolutionary change in the notion that women might be classified as lacking the rights of citizenship or being considered as some type of property. This shift is due in large part to the political movements that have alerted and educated the populace to discrimination and injustice based on gender, and the need for change. What other forces may have contributed to the shift in protections and rights recognition for women? Can parallels be seen in the current efforts to obtain increased rights for nonhumans?

It took more than a century for the status of women to evolve from chattel to equal protection under the U.S. law, with repeated staunch opposition from the courts. For example, in the 1800s, courts routinely denied women admission to state bars to practice law. *See, e.g., In re Goodell*, 39 Wis. 232 (1875) (describing it as a "departure[] from nature" and "treason against [nature]" for a woman to practice law; four years later the state legislature enacted a statute explicitly prohibiting denial of admission based on gender and the state court majority granted Ms. Goodell's re-application for admission); *Bradwell v. State*, 83 U.S. 130 (1872) ("The paramount destiny and mission of woman are to fulfil the noble and benign offices of wife and mother. This is the law of the Creator. And the rules of civil society must be adapted to the general constitution of things, and cannot be based upon exceptional cases."); *In re Ricker*, 29 A. 559, 559 (N.H. 1890) (concluding that women were not "citizens" for purposes of a statute allowing admission to the bar for "any citizen" of certain age, moral character and qualifications). *See also In re Robinson*, 131 Mass. 376 (1881) (accord). This was gradually rectified by legislative action on a state-by-state basis, to expressly allow women to be admitted to practice law.

More than a century later, the United States Supreme Court held that Virginia's categorical exclusion of women from the Virginia Military Institute (VMI) denied equal protection to women. *United States v. Virginia*, 518 U.S. 515 (1996). The opinion reflected the evolved view that "'[i]nherent differences' between men and women, we have come to appreciate, remain cause for celebration, but not for denigration of the members of either sex or for artificial constraints on an individual's opportunity." *Id*. at 532. The Court further emphasized that sex classifications "may not be used, as they once were, to create or perpetuate the legal, social, and economic inferiority of women." *Id*. at 534. The Court recognized that, as with any societal change, the "inclusion of women in settings where, traditionally, they were not wanted inevitably entails a period of adjustment." *Id*. at 545 n.15.

VMI argued against admission of women, asserting that alterations required to accommodate the change would necessarily be so "radical" and "drastic" as to transform and "destroy" VMI's program. *Id*. at 540. As the Court noted, such a prediction is "hardly different from other 'self-fulfilling prophecies' once routinely used to deny rights and opportunities." *Id*. at 542–43. The Court cited instances where these fears were voiced in connection with advances for women, but the same has been and continues to be true for advancing protections for other groups. *See, e.g., Mitchell v. Wells*, 37 Miss. 235, 252–53 (1859) (concluding that Mississippi "require[d] slave labor" and noting that certain delegates to the Constitutional Convention that framed the U.S. Constitution claimed "Georgia and South Carolina would become barren wastes without slave labor"); *People v. Hall*, 4 Cal. 399 (1854) (holding that the testimony of a Chinese witness was inadmissible, based on what the court deemed to be "public policy" to keep the races separate in legal matters). The *People v. Hall* opinion included the following racist justification for excluding Chinese-Americans from testifying:

> The same rule which would admit them to testify, would admit them to all the equal rights of citizenship, and we might soon see them at the polls, in the jury box, upon the bench, and in our legislative halls.

> This is not a speculation which exists in the excited and over-heated imagination of the patriot and statesman, but it is an actual and present danger.

The anomalous spectacle of a distinct people, living in our community, recognizing no laws of this State, except through necessity, bringing with them their prejudices and national feuds, in which they indulge in open violation of law; whose mendacity is proverbial; a race of people whom nature has marked as inferior, and who are incapable of progress or intellectual development beyond a certain point, as their history has shown; differing in language, opinions, color, and physical conformation; between whom and ourselves nature has placed an impassable difference, is now presented, and for them is claimed, not only the right to swear away the life of a citizen, but the further privilege of participating with us in administering the affairs of our Government.

Id. at 404–05.

The continuing progression towards equality and away from property status is demonstrated by the appointment of Hillary Rodham Clinton, a married woman, as the Secretary of State, and then her selection as the Democratic candidate for the office of President of the United States. While animal advocates are not seeking the same scope of "equal rights" for nonhumans that women and other groups of humans have fought for (and in some instances continue to fight for), the long and arduous process for the status of women to evolve from chattel to equal protection under the law provides a good template for the efforts required to change the status quo for nonhumans, and at some level increase the protections they obtain from the law.

Section 3. Children

During the first part of their lives, young humans have an undisputed (except by the young humans themselves, on occasion) need for care and protection by their parents (usually) and society at large. The reasons are obvious: vulnerability (physical, emotional and intellectual) and their innocence about the dangers of the outside world, both the natural and manmade aspects. In this sense, parallels can be drawn between nonhuman animals and human children. The development of protections for children and the issues raised in this section, therefore, may serve as a valuable analog in considering legal protections for nonhumans who are similarly vulnerable.

Historically and until relatively recently, children were considered the property of their parents. This concept is well-established in early Judeo-Christian writings. Joyce Ann Mercer, *Legal and Theological Justice for Abused Adolescent Girls*, 9 J.L. & Religion 451 (1992). The belief in a "God-ordained hierarchy" (using Mercer's terminology), in which fathers have unquestioned control over their wives and children, served not only to preserve the male monopoly on religious authority, but also to support the attitude that the family is a private domain and as such should be free from state interference. Legal doctrine tracked this religious construct. Under English common law, children were treated as chattel and their fathers had complete rights over them—including the power to terminate the child's life. *See, e.g., King v. Greenhill*, 111 Eng. Rep. 922 (K.B. 1836). Early American law adopted the eighteenth century English common law view that children were to be regarded as chattels of the family and wards of the State. James Kent, COMMENTARIES ON AMERICAN LAW (14th ed., Oliver Wendell Holmes ed., Little Brown 1873).

Indeed, just as the common law protected a man's right to use his property as he wished, so the common law also protected his right to govern his family as he wished. Some examples include the "rule of thumb," which permitted a man to beat his spouse or children with a stick as long as it was not thicker than his thumb, or the rule permitting children to be put to death merely for cursing or striking their father. Steven Mintz & Susan Kellogg, DOMESTIC REVOLUTIONS: A SOCIAL HISTORY OF AMERICAN FAMILY LIFE 54 (1988). One commentator argues that

> [c]ommon law rights, although firmly rooted in tradition and necessary to maintenance of the traditional order, often reinforced inequalities of power and justified the oppression of the weaker by the stronger. . . . Knowing the potential of the common law to make abuse and exploitation seem ordinary and natural, we ought to treat "rights" rooted in the common law with heightened suspicion rather than with heightened respect.

Barbara Bennett Woodhouse, *Child Abuse, the Constitution, and the Legacy of Pierce v. Society of Sisters*, 78 U. DET. MERCY L. REV. 479, 483–84 (2001).

Control and custody of one's children historically have been guaranteed by the Due Process clause of the Fourteenth Amendment. *Meyer v. Nebraska*, 262 U.S. 390, 400 (1923). *Meyer* was followed by *Pierce v. Society of Sisters*, 268 U.S. 510 (1925), which ostensibly addressed parents' "rights" to send their children to private schools. However, the *Pierce* decision has had a much more far-reaching impact. It is routinely cited as the basis for (1) privacy rights in child-bearing decisions free from state interference; (2) liberty interests of fathers to raise their biological children; and (3) parents' rights to raise their children according to the parents' moral values. Woodhouse, *supra*, at 481. *Meyer* and *Pierce* also addressed the literal "ownership" of children, with traditionalists arguing that the state's attempts to put any limits on parental authority were an infringement on parents' "God-given rights." Those opposed to the traditional point of view argued that children are future citizens of the larger community and, thus, the community generally should have a voice in determining what is best for the child. *Id.* at 482.

The Supreme Court's longstanding reliance on the Fourteenth Amendment's guarantee of liberty interests to protect parents' ownership rights in their children may have delayed some legal protections for children. And it was not until the early 1980s that lawyers were assigned to represent children themselves; this was so even in cases where their very liberty was at issue, such as in criminal and juvenile delinquency proceedings. *Id.* at 479.

Much earlier though, in the 1850s, a movement began to remove children from unhealthy living conditions and to provide them with suitable housing and education. Out of this movement grew a larger effort to protect all abused children. Because the children in question had not been abandoned, but nonetheless needed to be removed from their parents' homes, a legal basis for seizing them was created: a community interest in "children's rights." Linda Gordon, HEROES OF THEIR OWN LIVES 55–57 (U. Ill. Press 2002) (1988). This societal/judicial intervention was an obvious attack on traditional power structures and "property rights" in children, particularly when parental treatment was brutal. The welfarists justified the attack by invoking the competing child's "right" to decent treatment and by arguing that community control over such matters provided a long-term benefit to the community. *Id.* In 1892, children's rights were described by Reverend M.J. Savage as "moral, not legal rights, and included the right to be born in health, to have a happy childhood, and to have proper education." Minot J. Savage, *The Rights of Children*, 6 ARENA MAG. 8, 13 (1892). Much of the debate and writings at the time discussed children as assets of the community rather than as parents' exclusive property. The children's rights movement, however, established minimum standards of care that parents were required to provide. The failure to do so constituted a violation of the children's rights, justifying community intervention. Barbara Bennett Woodhouse, *Who Owns the Child? Meyer and Pierce and the Child as Property*, 33 WM. & MARY L. REV. 995, 1052 (1992).

Momentum began to build in favor of state and federal legislation protecting basic children's rights. The courts, however, were reluctant to follow suit. Child custody cases generally referred to children's "interests," not rights, and explored a child's "best interests" as a paramount concern only when it was an even contest between two parents, not as between one or both parents and a third-party caretaker or the state. *Harper v. Tipple*, 184 P. 1005, 1006 (Ariz. 1919).

Over time, courts have refined the view of children as mere chattels to mean that parents have a natural and legal right to the custody, control and care of their minor children. *See, e.g., Niewiadomski v. United States*, 159 F.2d 683 (6th Cir. 1947). This parental right in rearing one's family has been characterized as the "highest of natural rights," *Shappy v. Knight*, 475 S.W.2d 704 (Ark. 1972), "sacred," *Moore v. Burdman*, 526 P.2d 893 (Wash. 1974), and "paramount." *White v. Appleton*, 304 So. 2d 206 (Ala. Civ. App. 1974).

But what if a child decides, and deserves, otherwise? The legal doctrine of "emancipation" was invented to deal with those situations.

"Emancipation" as it relates to children refers to the freeing of a minor child from the control of his or her parents. As defined in an early case, "[e]mancipation is an entire surrender of all right to the care, custody, and earnings of the child, as well as renunciation of parental duties. It leaves the child, so far as the parent is concerned, free to act on its own responsibility, in accordance with its own will and pleasure, with the same independence as though it were 21 years of age." *Inhabitants of Lowell v. Inhabitants of Newport*, 66 Me. 78 (1876).

Emancipation may be express or implied. When parents agree with a child who is old enough to care for and provide for himself, that he may do so outside of the family, there is express emancipation. *See, e.g., Swenson v. Swenson*, 227 S.W.2d 103 (Mo. Ct. App. 1950) (expressly emancipated minor occupies same legal relation to parents as if he had attained full age; legal duty of parents to maintain and support him and defray his necessary expenses is extinguished).

Implied emancipation requires no agreement. *Rounds Bros. v. McDaniel*, 118 S.W. 956 (Ky. 1909); *Brosius v. Barker*, 136 S.W. 18 (Mo. Ct. App. 1911). *See also Alice C. v. Bernard G.C.*, 602 N.Y.S.2d 623 (App. Div. 1993) (under "withdrawal from parental control doctrine," a child is deemed emancipated so as to relieve parent of support obligation if she abandons parental home without sufficient cause and refuses to comply with reasonable parental demands).

Child emancipation cases tend to fall into two general groups: those that focus on the impact of emancipation on (1) the parents (*see, e.g., Swenson v. Swenson*, 227 S.W.2d 103 (Mo. Ct. App. 1950) ("emancipation" of a child is the relinquishment by parent of control and authority over child, conferring on him right to his earnings and terminating parents' legal duty to support child); and *Ream v. Watkins*, 27 Mo. 516 (1858) (where father emancipates son and relinquishes claim to his services, son will be entitled to the fruits of his own labor until the father sees fit to resume his authority)), and (2) the child. *See, e.g., Kingsley v. Kingsley*, 623 So. 2d 780 (Fla. 1993) (establishing right to emancipation and representation by guardian *ad litem*). *See also* Alison Brumley, *Comment: Parental Control of a Minor's Right to Sue in Federal Court*, 58 U. CHI. L. REV. 333 (Winter 1991) (discussing tension between parents' and children's rights and states' interests in protecting children).

In the Interest of Kingsley, No. JU90-5245, 1992 WL 551484 (Fla. Cir. Ct. Oct. 21, 1992) (the trial court opinion preceding *Kingsley, supra*), appears to be the first case in which a child sued his parents for "divorce" (termination of parental rights). This case is significant for two reasons: First, a child was able to terminate his parents' rights and interests in him when the state failed to do so; and second, the appellate court emphasized the need for children to use a guardian *ad litem* or "next friend" to obtain access to the courts.

Notes

1. Some litigants and advocates argue that a "best interests of the animal" standard should be adopted by legislatures and applied by courts in cases addressing custody of companion animals, whether involving marital dissolution or disputes over ownership between unmarried individuals. In 2017, Alaska became the first state to legislate that the court has discretion to take into consideration an animal's "well-being" when determining custody of a companion animal in marital dissolution cases. ALASKA STAT. § 25.24.160(a)(5) (enacted 2016; effective Jan. 17, 2017). Illinois followed, with a statute that expressly *requires* courts to consider the animals' interests. 750 ILL. COMP. STAT. 5/503(n) (enacted 2017; effective Jan. 1, 2018). Anecdotally, there is some evidence to suggest that individual judges may opt to apply a standard akin to "best interests of the animals" when adjudicating this type of case, even without legislation. For more on this issue, see Chapter 7, Section 3.

2. The concept of emancipation for minors is rooted in the assumption that the minor is able to care for him or herself without parental assistance. Can the same assumption ever be made for domesticated animals? If not, are there other bases upon which we can draw legal comparisons between children and nonhuman animals and which would result in enhanced "rights" for both groups?

3. The creative use of animal anti-cruelty laws in an early New York case involving the abuse of a foster child is often credited with sparking the beginnings of the modern children's rights movement. A discussion of the link between animal abuse and human violence and the story of Henry Bergh of the ASPCA and his efforts to protect foster child "Mary Ellen" from further abuse can be found in Chapter 3.

4. Do you think it is appropriate to compare nonhuman animals to human children within the context of working to extend or roll back protections of nonhuman animals? If not, why not? If so, what are the most compelling arguments to be made both in favor and in opposition to enhanced animal protections?

Section 4. Humans with Severe and Permanent Cerebral Impairments

On March 31, 2005, Terri Schiavo died after being in a persistent vegetative state for close to fifteen years. Her death was preceded by a lengthy and widely publicized (and politicized) legal battle between her husband, who wanted to discontinue life support (which would likely have hastened her death), and her parents, who wanted to continue that support and custodial care indefinitely. For years, the pros and cons of both approaches were argued in the media as a series of lawsuits and legislative efforts proceeded. Despite the fact that the debate between the parties was ultimately over who had the authority to decide if Ms. Schiavo lived or died, one question that was never credibly debated was whether Ms. Schiavo, in her vegetative state, was legally a "person" entitled to full protections under the law. Because of her genetic membership in the human species, and despite the loss of those abilities that some might claim define us as human, Ms. Schiavo's advocates never had to argue her entitlement to rights as a legal "person."

The legal definition of "person" (like the legal definition of "animal") varies depending on the context. Since we know that historically certain humans have not been considered "persons" under the law, what makes a human a legal "person"—is it biology or some other factor? One argument might be that it is our ability to think and feel that makes us human. In her persistent vegetative state, Ms. Schiavo did not demonstrate these crucial attributes of "humanness." So, what is it that determines one's entry into the circle of legally protected "persons"? Is it simply DNA? If so, should a chimpanzee—whose DNA is more than 98% identical to ours—be considered a legal "person"? In this section, we briefly explore the history of the disability rights movement for the purpose of analyzing whether the concepts underlying this movement overlap with, or are relevant to, the efforts of some to expand the legal status of nonhuman animals to legal "persons."

Prior to the disability rights movement, which came of age in the 1960s and 1970s, society made certain assumptions regarding the disabled. For example, people with cognitive disabilities were to be sheltered and kept separate from the rest of the population. John V. Jacobi, *Federal Power, Segregation, and Mental Disability*, 39 Houston L. Rev. 1231 (Spring 2003). Until recently, the well-being of the cognitively disabled was in the hands of their families or, for those without families, in the hands of society, which often relegated them to institutions or abandoned them to homelessness. Barbara L. Antonello, *Problems of Enforcing the Rights of the Mentally Retarded*, 48 Notre Dame L. Rev. 1314 (1972–1973).

Courts generally defer to the treatment decisions of mental health professionals in psychiatric institutions, applying a hands-off policy with respect to treatment decisions. According to some commentators, this type of policy affords the disabled no citizenship rights, thrusting them into a "lower legal caste." Alexander D. Brooks, Bruce J. Winick, Foreword, *Mental Disability Law Comes of Age*, 39 Rutgers L. Rev. 235, 236 (1987). Consider the following speech delivered at an American Association on Mental Deficiency conference in 1971:

> Human rights in our society are not guaranteed or protected by good will alone. The fabric of our society, even many of its customs, is dictated, controlled or modified by law. The mentally retarded, in spite of pious protestations of good will, are still too often regarded as a sub-specie of Homo sapiens. It is inherent in our ethic, and latterly, of our jurisprudence, that the weaker need and must receive society's protection. Their "rights," their human rights, if you will, depend, therefore, not on their own strength, but how society translates government, the agencies of government, and the people who are entrusted with the task of implementing, or making effective this protection, express this protection through legislation, administration and custom.

Address by Joseph T. Weingold, American Association on Mental Deficiency regional meeting, in Grossinger, New York (Oct. 1971), *cited in* Antonello, *supra*, at 1314 n.2.

One reason offered for the treatment of the cognitively disabled as, essentially, "second-class citizens" is our ostensible need to distance the unimpaired majority from those dealing with disability. "We are ... desperate to erect an impenetrable borderline between 'us' and 'them'" in order to protect ourselves and our self image, and in doing so we either "infantilize" or "demonize" the cognitively disabled. Michael L. Perlin, *"Where the Winds Hit Heavy on the Borderline": Mental Disability Law, Theory and Practice, "Us" and "Them"*, 31 Loy. L.A. L. Rev. 775, 787–89 (1998).

Despite its slow beginning, the cognitive disability rights movement made significant progress in the latter half of the twentieth century. For example, in 1952, the National Institute of Mental Health published the Draft Act Governing

Hospitalization of the Mentally Ill (P.H.S. Pub. No. 51), which was an attempt to standardize the dramatically varying state laws on the subject. Cases began to establish the constitutional rights of the mentally ill as the civil rights movement expanded into the mental health arena, and federal cases began to address the conditions of public mental institutions, which many considered "abysmal." Brooks & Winick, *supra*, at 237. One of the first rights to emerge for confined mentally ill patients was the right to receive treatment for their diseases. Such rights were grounded in constitutional theories of equal protection and the Eighth Amendment, which arguably compensated for the lack of procedural due process in the involuntary commitment of patients. For example, *Rouse v. Cameron*, 373 F.2d 451 (D.C. Cir. 1966), addressed the constitutional rights of a defendant who had been involuntarily and summarily committed after being found not guilty by reason of insanity for a dangerous crime. These rights were more fully fleshed out in subsequent cases such as *Wyatt v. Aderholt*, 503 F.2d 1305 (5th Cir. 1974), which held that involuntarily committed mentally disabled individuals have a right to treatment and rehabilitation.

A 1966 case, *Lake v. Cameron*, 364 F.2d 657, 660 (D.C. Cir. 1966), held that "deprivations of liberty solely because of dangers to ill persons themselves should not go beyond what is necessary for their protection." Thus, *Lake* introduced the notion that if we must contain or confine someone who cannot take care of himself, we can only do it to the extent the *confined individual* needs it. In the mid-1970s, Congress enacted the Developmentally Disabled Assistance and Bill of Rights Act,[a] which established protections for persons with developmental disabilities, including the right to appropriate treatment, services and rehabilitation for such disabilities. In 1982, the Supreme Court decided *Youngberg v. Romeo*, 457 U.S. 307 (1982), holding that state institution residents had rights to personal security, reasonably safe conditions of confinement, freedom from unreasonable bodily restraint, and to such minimally adequate rehabilitation or training as may be reasonably required to ensure safety and freedom from undue restraint. The Americans with Disabilities Act of 1990, 42 U.S.C. §§ 12101–12213, provides additional protection to those suffering from cognitive disabilities, protecting them from discrimination related to their particular disability. The Supreme Court later held that the unjustified placement or retention of persons in institutions constitutes a form of discrimination based on disability prohibited by Title II of the Americans with Disabilities Act. *Olmstead v. L.C.*, 527 U.S. 581 (1999).

American courts "generally hold that incompetent human beings are entitled to the same dignity rights as are competent human beings." Steven M. Wise, *Hardly a Revolution: The Eligibility of Nonhuman Animals for Dignity-Rights in a Liberal Democracy*, 22 Vt. L. Rev. 793, 873 (1998). This was the case in *Care & Protection of Beth*, 587 N.E. 2d 1377 (Mass. 1992), where the judgment of a ten-month-old child in a persistent vegetative state was substituted for that of her guardian. The

---

a. This law was subsequently replaced by the Developmental Disabilities Assistance and Bill of Rights Act of 2000, 42 U.S.C. §§ 15001–15115.

guardian requested an order that the child be resuscitated in the event of cardiac or respiratory arrest, but the court concluded that the child would refuse resuscitative measures. The court held that regardless of the child's condition, the child had dignity that could not be offended by resuscitation attempts. *See also Schmidt v. Schmidt*, 459 A.2d 421, 422–23 (Pa. 1983) (twenty-six-year-old woman with the cognitive ability of a child between four-and-a-half and eight years, can decide whether to visit a parent); *Youngberg v. Romeo*, 457 U.S. 307, 309–16 (1982) (holding that a person with the cognitive capacity of an eighteen-month-old child has an inextinguishable liberty right to personal security).

Wise argues that if humans in persistent vegetative states (and fetuses and infants) are afforded rights, then courts must do so for animals as well:

> [T]o avoid the arbitrariness, lack of integrity, and invidious discrimination antithetical to the overarching principles and values of traditional Western law, courts would have to recognize that nonhuman animals who possess capacities for autonomy and self-determination of similar degree, or their equivalents, also possess a dignity sufficient to trigger a realistic and nonarbitrary degree of dignity-rights as well. . . . If humans who lack the capacity for choice possess the power rights necessary to prevent violations of their fundamental immunity-rights or to vindicate violations of their fundamental claim-rights, the capacities for autonomy and self-determination cannot be necessary for dignity and legal personhood, even if they are sufficient for it.

Wise, *supra*, at 874–75. If it is not the fully rational cognitive ability of humans that is necessary to obtain certain legal rights, Wise queries why humanness is a prerequisite to obtaining such rights. "If merely being human was sufficient for legal personhood, why would [judges] bother to employ the equality-busting legal fiction that anencephalic infants and humans in persistent vegetative states possess dignity? . . . What is sufficient for legal personhood turns not upon species membership, but upon the possession of important qualities." *Id.* at 885–87. While what constitutes an "important quality" may be debated, it is clear that many animals possess attributes similar to those of humans. For example, some animals have an intellect very close to that of humans and, in some instances, greater than that of certain humans (including those in vegetative states). Consider the non-human members of the great ape family (the scientific family to which humans belong). These animals "are all rational beings with complex emotional lives and strong social bonds that last a lifetime. All can be harmed, and they are aware that they are being harmed. The fact that the framers of the Constitution did not know these facts does not render our modern understanding unfaithful to their essential objectives. . . . [T]he Constitution is able to adapt to the knowledge and social realities of its time." Lee Hall & Anthony Jon Waters, *From Property to Person: The Case of Evelyn Hart*, 11 Seton Hall Const. L.J. 1, 16 (2000).

For further discussion on advocates' efforts to expand personhood status for nonhuman animals, *see* Section 6 of this chapter.

Notes

1. Great apes are rational, self-aware, possess self-control and have a sense of the past and future. They have the capacity to relate to and have concern for others, are curious, and communicate among themselves. Hall & Waters, *supra,* at 18-27. Should these traits qualify them for status as legal persons—or at least for consideration of some of the protections given to other beings similarly situated (like humans)? Consider John Locke's concept of a person (which applies equally to many species) as a "thinking intelligent being that has reason and reflection and can consider itself as itself, the same thinking thing, in different times and places." John Locke, *Essay on Human Understanding*, Bk. II, ch. 9, p. 29 (1690), quoted by Hall & Waters, *supra,* at 18.

2. It is clear from this discussion that the condition of "humanness" may not be essential to becoming a "person" under the law and obtaining all the rights associated with such classification. While genetics usually plays a role, the definition of "person" is a legal chameleon. Corporations and ships may be legal persons in some situations, and the bundle of rights granted to humans may vary depending on their status (illegal alien, immigrant, cognitively incompetent, child), and not their biological makeup.

Is it too great a cognitive leap to allow animals—given their undisputed commonalities with humans in terms of feeling and consciousness—to become legal persons in the eyes of the law, in situations where their dignity and autonomy is at stake? If not, one must address the practical dilemma that arises when rights and autonomy are given to beings not fully able to fend for themselves. Some animal law scholars have argued that legal concepts of guardianship should apply and that trustees and beneficiaries can be used in these situations. (*See* Chapter 8 for a thorough discussion of the use of trusts and will provisions for the benefit of nonhuman animals.)

Section 5. Potential Humans—Fetuses, Embryos and Prezygotes: Property, Persons or Something in Between?

The status of animals under the law and the longstanding debate over abortion share some theoretical ground, considering that from conception to adulthood, human genetic material occupies various positions along a spectrum from pure property to personhood. The comparison of this treatment—legal, ethical, societal—to that of nonhumans thus supplements the discussion of animals as property, and provides food for thought when considering greater protections for nonhumans.

For purposes of this section, "potential humans" include genetic material, such as human sperm and eggs, as well as unborn humans *in utero* or otherwise developing towards that goal. Like nonhuman animals, what we will call in this section "potential humans" are not "persons" in the eyes of the law, at least not completely. *See* Richard Stith, *Location and Life: How Stenberg v. Carhart Undercut Roe v. Wade*, 9 WM. & MARY J. OF WOMEN & L. 255 (2003) (arguing that personhood does not occur until long after birth). "Arguing that embryos and fetuses are persons in a strict sense is about as convincing as saying animals are." Kayhan Parsi, *Metaphorical Imagination: The Moral and Legal Status of Fetuses and Embryos*, 4 DePAUL J. HEALTH CARE L. 703, 708 (1999). If these biological entities are not persons, are they property? Both? Neither? Or some other middle-ground status?

As discussed in this section, potential humans occupy a legal status on the continuum between property and personhood—one that provides an interesting counterpoint to concepts regarding the potential (and actual) status of animals. One question might be, what legal difference does it make what they are called—as opposed to how they are treated? Ultimately, the degree of legal protection is all that matters to all interested parties.

To determine the legal status of a potential human, we must first revisit the traditional characteristics that make something property. "Ownership is not a single concrete entity but a bundle of rights and privileges as well as of obligations." *Union Oil Co. v. State Bd. of Equal.*, 60 Cal. 2d 441, 447 (1963). Property owners have the right to: (i) possess and exclude all others from the property; (ii) use and dispose of the property; (iii) the fruits and profits of the property; and (iv) destroy it. Judged by those standards, as discussed in this section, the creators (parents) of these entities—with the notable exception of a fetus viable out of the womb—may have something like a property right in their potential humans (although that right may vary in degree between the male and female parent).

During the first trimester of pregnancy, abortion is a right granted to all American females. *Roe v. Wade*, 410 U.S. 113 (1973). Since *Roe v. Wade*, the cases involving a woman's right to terminate her pregnancy, and the ownership rights and duties relating to fetuses and embryos, as well as unfertilized frozen eggs and sperm, have been the subject of much debate and political discourse.

Whether a potential human is legally a "person" or property, or something in between, has never been answered decisively. In fact, based on judicial and legislative treatment, the degree to which they have been treated like persons or property has shifted over time. Currently, the answer seems to depend as much on the law and science as it does on philosophy, and shifts both with changing morals and the location of the potential human. As one example, consider the unborn child of a slave. Slaves were the property of their owners. Therefore, at whatever stage of growth the potential human was, she presumably was also the property of her mother's owners.[b] Even that, of course, could change. If her mother escaped to a free

---

b. The analogy between human slaves as property and potential humans as property has not been lost on the pro-life movement, which has attempted to make the connection between freeing the slaves and ending abortion. *See, e.g.*, Paul A. Gerike, *Comment, Human Biological Material: A Proprietary Interest or Part of the Monistic Being?*, 17 OHIO N.U. L. REV. 805 (1991) (discussing a

state, and bore the potential human there, the former slave's child probably would be a legal person—while her mother would still be her owner's property under the *Dred Scott* decision discussed earlier in this chapter.

Before a fetus is viable outside the womb (previability), American women currently have the right to the "use and disposition" of their potential human property, with the concomitant right to profit from that use. It has been widely reported that at one point financial consideration was being offered and paid for fetal tissues. Nancy E. Field, Note, *Evolving Conceptualizations of Property: A Proposal to De-Commercialize the Value of Fetal Tissue*, 99 YALE L.J. 169, 169–70, 170 n.7 (1989) ("*Fetal Tissue*") (discussing solicitations for fetal tissue and reports that one medical practitioner sold thousands of fetal kidneys to an American medical supply corporation). This practice ended with the federal moratorium on research on fetal tissue from aborted fetuses. *Id.* at 183.

The concept of a fetus as property—subject to the rules of contract—has come up in the "gestational carrier" arena as well. A gestational carrier, also known as a "surrogate mother," is a woman who agrees to be inseminated and carry a child from fetus through to live birth, and then turn the child over to the party with whom she contracts. Most gestational carriers enter into agreements with the intended parents, which require the gestational carrier to act in the best interests of the intended parents and the fetus; this includes an agreement to carry the fetus to term. Because "there is no precise legal theory analogous to the terms" of such a contract, one commentator has suggested the contract creates a trust relationship with the potential human being *both* the trust property and an intended beneficiary of the trust. K. Yamamoto & S. Moore, *A Trust Analysis of a Gestational Carrier's Right to Abortion*, 70 FORDHAM L. REV. 93 (Oct. 2001). (Compare this to David Favre's theory of equitable self-ownership, discussed in the next section of this chapter, in which Professor Favre suggests the ownership of animals may be logically split between the human owner and the animals themselves.)

The indeterminate nature of fetal legal status is also evident in other areas of the law. At common law and in most jurisdictions, a fetus "in existence at the time of a testator's death that is subsequently born alive," and who would have been entitled to a share of an inheritance if she had already been born, is entitled to share an inheritance equal to her living siblings. James Drago, Note, *One for My Baby, One More for the Road: Legislation and Counseling to Prevent Prenatal Exposure to Alcohol*, 7 CARDOZO WOMEN'S L.J. 163, 164 (2001). While the common law simply recognized this right to receive property, modern inheritance law actually recognizes fetuses as legal persons. *Id.*

---

speech by U.S. Supreme Court Justice Clarence Thomas in which he cited an article comparing the right to abortion with the right to own slaves; and an article by Nat Hentoff, stating "pro-lifers should be compared to the abolitionists since 'like the slave, the fetus is property and its owner can dispose of it'").

Legislators also have provided fetuses with a panoply of protections not available to most forms of property. Many states have "fetal protection acts," which criminalize harm to a fetus, regardless of its status as person or property. Much like the animal anti-cruelty laws, these statutes arguably are granting special protections to a unique form of property.

Over the years, courts in some states have allowed tort actions to be brought on behalf of fetuses alleging injury. *See, e.g., Bonbrest v. Kotz*, 65 F. Supp. 138 (D.D.C. 1946) (allowing cause of action for prenatal injuries as long as fetus is born alive); *Smith v. Brennan*, 157 A.2d 497 (N.J. 1960) (fetus born alive can sue for a prenatal, pre-viability injury). The potential for claims by the unborn varies by jurisdiction. *Compare Danos v. St. Pierre*, 383 So. 2d 1019 (La. Ct. App. 1980) (tort action by stillborn fetus permitted); *Connor v. Mokem Co.*, 898 S.W.2d 89 (Mo. 1995) (nonviable unborn child is a person capable of asserting a claim for wrongful death) and *Amadio v. Levin*, 501 A.2d 1085 (Pa. 1985) (allowing estate to recover for individual medical and funeral costs, economic losses, and pain and suffering) and *Farley v. Sartin*, 466 S.E.2d 522 (W. Va. 1995) (viability not determinative factor in whether fetus is "person" for purposes of recovery under wrongful death statute) *with Justus v. Atchison*, 565 P.2d 122, 125 (Cal. 1977) (no wrongful death action available to stillborn) and *Dietrich v. Inhabitants of Northampton*, 138 Mass. 14 (1884) (fetus was part of mother and had no independent legal identity). In some instances, guardians *ad litem* have been appointed on behalf of fetuses in cases involving potential injury to the fetus or marital dissolution of the parents.

Thus, the same entity that is treated like property with respect to its mother, may have a cause of action as if it were a legal "person" in connection with its relationships with others. This will depend on state-specific law and on whether the fetus emerges into the world alive. Is this distinction reconcilable on legal grounds? On ethical grounds?

Similarly, in the criminal arena, in nearly forty states, homicide charges may be brought where the state can demonstrate a fetus was killed. *See, e.g.,* CAL. PENAL CODE § 187(a). In most of those states, the criminal prohibition applies to an unborn child at *any* stage of development, from fertilization onwards. *See, e.g.,* TEX. PENAL CODE § 1.07. So in this particular legal context, it is a crime to "murder" what is otherwise treated as property, at least with respect to its mother.

A fertilized egg in the laboratory (*in vitro*), rather than in the woman's body (*in vivo*), is treated as, and may even be considered, a form of property for multiple purposes. For example, in *York v. Jones*, 717 F. Supp. 421 (E.D. Va. 1989), a couple (the Yorks) sued for possession and transfer of their frozen fertilized egg ("pre-zygote," as the court referred to it) from one reproductive services company to another. The court found the parties had entered into a bailment relationship when the Yorks entrusted the reproductive services company with the pre-zygote. All parties acknowledged the couple's *property rights* in the pre-zygote, and the contract between the parties explicitly provided that, in the event of divorce, legal ownership of the pre-zygote must be determined by a court "in a property settlement."

Id. at 426. *See also* Steven Maynard-Moody, THE DILEMMA OF THE FETUS: FETAL RESEARCH, MEDICAL PROGRESS, AND MORAL POLITICS 83–86 (1995) (noting nonviable fetal remains are simply discarded as byproducts of surgery or treated as human tissue with correlative rights of the tissue owner; and the potential "quasi-property rights" held by a family if a dead fetus is considered a dead person).

In *York*, the court "assumed without deciding that the subject matter of the dispute was 'property.'" *Davis v. Davis*, 842 S.W.2d 588, 596 (Tenn. 1992). The *Davis* court addressed the issue head on. In the context of a divorce case, the court considered a "custody" dispute, which would determine the fate of the "cryogenically-preserved product of *in vitro* fertilization (IVF), commonly referred to in the popular press and the legal journals as 'frozen embryos.'" *Id.* at 589. The court noted that "semantic distinctions are significant in this context, because language defines legal status and can limit legal rights." *Id.* at 592. In fact, there had been much dispute at trial about whether the "four-to eight-cell entities" in that case properly should be referred to as "embryos" or "pre-embryos," with resulting differences in legal analysis. *Id.* at 593.

> [The distinction between embryo and pre-embryo] deserves emphasis only because inaccuracy can lead to misanalysis such as occurred at the trial level in this case. The trial court reasoned that if there is no distinction between embryos and preembryos, as [one expert] theorized, then [that expert] must also have been correct when he asserted that "human life begins at the moment of conception." From this proposition, the trial judge concluded that the eight-cell entities at issue were not preembryos but were "children in vitro." He then invoked the doctrine of *parens patriae* and held that it was "in the best interest of the children" to be born rather than destroyed.

Id. at 594. *See also* LA. REV. STAT. ANN. § 9:121-9:133 (2009) (Louisiana statute entitled "Human Embryos" forbids intentional destruction of a "viable *in vitro* fertilized ovum" (§ 9:129) and declares that disputes between any parties regarding an "*in vitro* fertilized ovum" are to be resolved in the "best interest" of such ovum (§ 9:131)). Section 9:123 provides: "An *in vitro* fertilized ovum exists as a juridical person until such time as the *in vitro* fertilized ovum is implanted in the womb; or at any time when rights attach to an unborn child in accordance with law."

The *Davis* court noted that one of the "fundamental issues" in the case was whether the pre-embryos involved should be considered persons or property under the law. 842 S.W.2d at 594. Based on Tennessee statutory law, the court concluded they could not be considered persons under Tennessee law. *Id.* In the absence of guidance from the courts on this issue, the Tennessee Supreme Court looked to ethical standards set by the American Fertility Society:

> Three major ethical positions have been articulated in the debate over preembryo status. At one extreme is the view of the preembryo as a human subject after fertilization, which requires that it be accorded the rights of a person. This position entails an obligation to provide an opportunity

for implantation to occur and tends to ban any action before transfer that might harm the preembryo or that is not immediately therapeutic, such as freezing and some preembryo research.

At the opposite extreme is the view that the preembryo has a status no different from any other human tissue. With the consent of those who have decision-making authority over the preembryo, no limits should be imposed on actions taken with preembryos.

A third view—one that is most widely held—takes an intermediate position between the other two. It holds that the preembryo deserves respect greater than that accorded to human tissue but not the respect accorded to actual persons. The preembryo is due greater respect than other human tissue because of its potential to become a person and because of its symbolic meaning for many people. Yet, it should not be treated as a person, because it has not yet developed the features of personhood, is not yet established as developmentally individual, and may never realize its biologic potential.

Id. at 596, quoting from Journal of the American Fertility Society (vol. 53, no. 6), at 34S–35S (June 1990 report of the Ethics Committee of The American Fertility Society: Ethical Considerations of the New Reproductive Technologies). The referenced report concluded that "special respect is necessary to protect the welfare of potential offspring . . . [and] creates obligations not to hurt or injure the offspring who might be born after transfer [by research or intervention with a preembryo]." *Id*. (Bracketed text added by the *Davis* court.) After thorough analysis, the *Davis* court concluded that

preembryos are not, strictly speaking, either "persons" or "property," but occupy an interim category that entitles them to special respect because of their potential for human life. It follows that any interest that [the divorcing wife and husband] have in the preembryos in this case is not a true property interest. However, they do have an interest in the nature of ownership, to the extent that they have decision-making authority concerning disposition of the preembryos, within the scope of policy set by law.

Id. at 597. Based on the foregoing and additional factors, including constitutional rights to privacy and balancing of the parties' interests, the court awarded custody to the husband, who "would prefer to see the 'frozen embryos' discarded" than to have his former wife (who no longer wished to be impregnated with them herself) donate them to a childless couple. *Id*. at 590, 604–05. For practical purposes, this meant the clinic was "free to follow its normal procedure in dealing with unused preembryos," as long as that procedure did not conflict with the court's opinion. *Id*. at 605.

Most courts, when faced with couples arguing over frozen embryos have ruled in favor of the individual arguing against procreation. In a novel case, a San Francisco Superior Court judge ruled that embryos a couple had frozen before their divorce would be destroyed, pursuant to a contract to that effect signed by both parties. In the 83-page opinion, the court acknowledged that "the fate of nascent life, which the embryos in this case represent, must be determined in a court by reference to cold legal principles." The court found that the parties were fully informed, and so the ruling was based on strict application of property/contract law, despite the defendant's claim that she had a First Amendment right to procreate. *Stephen Findley v. Mimi Lee*, Case No. FDI-13-780539 (Cal. Super. Ct., San Fran. Cty. Nov. 18, 2015).

A related topic concerns an individual's property rights in his or her DNA (the basic building blocks of genetic material). In *Moore v. Regents of the University of California*, 793 P.2d 479 (Cal. 1990), the California Supreme Court held that property rights do not exist in excised body tissue or in proteins contained therein. The court reasoned that, because one person's proteins are indistinguishable from those of another, there is no property right. In another case, however, an intermediate appellate California court took a slightly different approach and held that there *is* a property right in the frozen sperm of a deceased donor. *Hecht v. Superior Court*, 16 Cal. App. 4th 836 (1993).

Thus, potential humans—when nonviable and potentially after that time—fit the legal definition of property.[c] Nevertheless, courts, legislatures and commentators are reticent to give them solely property status. *Fetal Tissue, supra*, at 822 ("I disagree that there's just a sliding scale or continuum with property at one point along the spectrum and human beings at another. I think there's a sharp distinction between something that is property and something that is not property.") And, despite the fact that, at some level, they are at the whim of their "parents," potential humans have a panoply of legal protections (as well as the moral force based on their potential existence outside the womb)—at least with respect to the acts of third parties—which demonstrate they are something much more than property. Like animals, and to a greater or lesser degree depending on the stage of their existence, potential humans dwell in a hybrid place between property and person.

Section 6. Nonhumans

In making the argument that nonhuman animals deserve certain legally-protected rights, one must assume that status as a "human" or a "person" (however that is defined) is not essential to possessing legal rights—or at least the kind of protections that prevent abuse. Some refuse to make that leap. Indeed, even within the animal protection community there is a continuing debate as to whether animals should be granted rights as nonhuman "persons" or should simply be granted an elevated property status.

In other contexts, as noted earlier in this chapter, it is well established that being human is not essential to obtaining legal status that is akin to personhood. For

---

c. After the first trimester of pregnancy, and subject to some federal limits, states may legislate the right to abortion, potentially modifying those property rights.

example, corporations have long been considered "persons" under the Fourteenth Amendment, *Smythe v. Ames*, 169 U.S. 466, 522 (1898), but are not covered by the Fifth Amendment right against self-incrimination. *Bellis v. United States*, 417 U.S. 85 (1974). And ships historically have been provided legal status that might be the envy of modern animals and their advocates. *See, e.g., Tucker v. Alexanderoff*, 183 U.S. 424, 438 (1902) ("A ship is born when she is launched, and lives so long as her identity is preserved."). These are obvious important legal fictions that do not recognize any inherent qualities of sentiency or humanness in the corporation or ship, but simply acknowledge the need—and establish the affirmative legal right—to allow lawyers to bring issues involving them before the courts.

On the other hand, being human does not always guarantee status as a legal person. For example, it is unclear whether illegal aliens are rights-holders under the Fourth Amendment. *See United* States *v. Guitterez*, 983 F. Supp. 905 (N.D. Cal. 1998), *rev'd*, 203 F.3d 833 (9th Cir. 1999) (table case) (reversing district court ruling that illegal aliens have no Fourth Amendment protection); *but see United States v. Verdugo-Urquidez*, 494 U.S. 259 (1990) (holding that a Mexican citizen taken from his residence in Mexico by American authorities without a warrant, and tried in the United States, had no Fourth Amendment rights); *United States v. Esparza-Mendoza*, 265 F. Supp. 2d 1254, 1259 (N.D. Utah 2003), *aff'd*, 386 F.3d 953 (10th Cir. 2004) (holding that illegal aliens gain Fourth Amendment protection only when they become part of the national community or have otherwise developed sufficient connections with the United States to be considered part of that community).

As of the publication of this edition, nonhuman animals are still property under the law of all fifty states, and that status seems to be entrenched. Nevertheless, the courts have struggled with and continued to bend and modify this concept, both implicitly and expressly. *See, e.g., Morgan v. Kroupa*, 702 A.2d 630, 633 (Vt. 1997) ("[M]odern courts have recognized that pets generally do not fit neatly within traditional property principles. . . . Instead, courts must fashion and apply rules that recognize their unique status. . . ."). Many of the cases in this book reflect that tension. Even though the courts and the law may not always be able to adequately reconcile how the conundrum of a sentient being as property confounds traditional legal applications, many courts have simultaneously recognized greater protections or considerations for animals while clinging to the property label and status.

One latter-day example of this continuing development is demonstrated by *State v. Newcomb*, 359 Or. 756 (2016), discussed further in Chapter 3. In *Newcomb*, the legal issue was whether an animal owner had a Fourth Amendment right to privacy in what was "inside" her property/dog—specifically, blood samples taken to diagnose the dog's condition. The Oregon Supreme Court held that while animals retain their property status at law, the law does not and should not treat them the same as inanimate property. The Court acknowledged the biological fact that they are sentient beings with lives of their own, and recognized that this changed how they should be treated. The Court held that the search (taking the blood samples) was permissible.

Previously, in *State v. Fessenden/Dicke*, 355 Or. 759, 769-70 (2014), the Oregon Supreme Court recognized:

> As we continue to learn more about the interrelated nature of all life, the day may come when humans perceive less separation between themselves and other living beings than the law now reflects. However, we do not need a mirror to the past or a telescope to the future to recognize that the legal status of animals has changed and is changing still[.]

For an analysis of the socio-legal constructions of "the animal" in *State v. Newcomb* and in a 2016 Canadian case, see Richard Jochelson & James Gacek, *"Ruff" Justice: Canine Cases and Judicial Law Making As an Instrument of Change*, 24 ANIMAL L. 171 (2018).

The historical and practical explanation for the property position animals hold in our society often has been attributed to their commercial value and the need to be able to control this symbol (literal and figurative) of wealth. Others believe non-humans' status has a more cultural basis.

> The legal thinghood of nonhuman animals has existed continuously since the dawn of law in Near Eastern and Western legal systems. It has encumbered nonhuman animals for so long because even the most funda-mental legal rights of beings will go unrecognized by a society that accepts a hierarchical cosmology in which those beings are seen as inherently infe-rior or that fails to connect law to the values of liberty and equality. . . .

> It was only in the eighteenth century that Western legal philosophy com-menced its long separation from a theology that was seen as the ultimate source of law and posited the inherent and immutable superiority of human over nonhuman animals. The vertical cosmologies that created the legal thinghood of nonhuman animals in Hebrew, Greek, Roman and finally Western law were only scientifically discredited in the nineteenth century. Their ruin spurred demands for human equality and opened the possibility for judges at last to consider that nonhuman animals might transcend legal thinghood under the proper circumstances as a matter of logic.

* * *

> The twentieth century also has witnessed the birth of scientific disci-plines and discoveries that have powerfully supported Darwin's notion of evolution by natural selection and have steadily and more truly revealed the natures of both human and nonhuman animals. Yet scientific facts that contradict beliefs so old and cherished that they appear self-evident may take a long time to illuminate judicial decisions. The ancient idea of the legal thinghood of nonhuman animals will continue to grip the com-mon law to the degree that judges are either affected by the disproven cos-mologies upon which it rests or value precedent over justice. While many Americans still reject Darwinism and embrace primitive hierarchical cos-mologies, few modern judges consciously rest their decisions upon them.

Numerous twentieth-century judicial decisions have characterized nonhuman animals as property, and continue to do so. The reason that an exceedingly small number of decisions actually have sought to justify the status of nonhuman animals as human property is that judges normally fail to perceive that it requires justification.

Steven Wise, *The Legal Thinghood of Animals*, 23 B.C. Envtl. Aff. L. Rev. 471, 543–45 (1996).

Several other commentators have critically examined the longstanding practice of classifying animals as property. *See, e.g.*, Taimie L. Bryant, *Sacrificing the Sacrifice of Animals: Legal Personhood for Animals, the Status of Animals as Property, and the Presumed Primacy of Humans*, 39 Rutgers L.J. 247 (Winter 2008); Gary L. Francione, *Animals, Property, and Legal Welfarism: "Unnecessary" Suffering and the "Humane" Treatment of Animals*, 46 Rutgers L. Rev. 721 (1994); Thomas G. Kelch, *Toward a Non-Property Status for Animals*, 6 N.Y.U. Envtl. L.J. 531 (1998); and Derek W. St. Pierre, *The Transition from Property to People: The Road to the Recognition of Rights for Non-human Animals*, 9 Hastings Womens L.J. 255 (Summer 1998) (*"Transition"*) (cited earlier in this chapter).

In *Transition*, St. Pierre posits one theory for the foundational concepts that gave rise to all subsequent assumptions about the "lesser" status of animals:

> Historically, Western culture has understood the universe as a linear hierarchical ascendancy. This concept, known as the Great Chain of Being, is one of the most powerful presuppositions in Western thought. The Great Chain of Being is the idea that there is a natural hierarchy, in essence a ladder, which designates a place for everything. Location on the ladder is ordained by a designed and ordered universe. Plants occupy the lower rungs, nonhuman animals are further up the ladder, humans are even higher up and the upper rungs are occupied by angelic forms with God atop the whole.
>
> The Great Chain of Being has been central to the development of thought in Western systems; specifically, two reasons are given as the justification for the legal status of animals as property. The first has a theological basis, established in the Bible. In Genesis, man is given "dominion over the fish of the sea, and over the birds of the air, and over the cattle, and over all the earth, and over every creeping thing that creeps upon the air." A second justification rests in the "inferior" status of nonhuman animals. Historically, nonhuman animals were viewed as lacking a "soul," a "mind," a "will," or whatever attribute it was thought makes humans uniquely human. The Great Chain of Being fed into and supported this idea because only those beings on the upper rungs, humans and angelic beings, were found capable of rational thought. This second reason is a classic creation of the concept of "other." By focusing on differences, accentuating what separates human animals from nonhuman animals, our society has created yet another of its many dualisms by which animal exploitation is justified.

> This creation of a dualism and "other" through the confluence of scientific and social rationale spawns some interesting anomalies. For example, the use of nonhuman animals in vivisection places those animals somewhere in a state of limbo. Modern science presumes that nonhuman animals are genetically similar enough to humans that experiments on them will help to predict human reaction. Yet it is also simultaneously posited that nonhuman animals are so different that they do not merit ethical consideration or legal protection.

Id. at 260–61. For further analysis of the moral, ethical and legal issues raised in the effort to obtain rights for nonhuman primates, *see* Adam Kolber, *Standing Upright: The Moral and Legal Standing of Humans and Other Apes*, 54 Stanford L. Rev. 163 (2001). For an early philosophical viewpoint and overview of the issues, *see* Peter Singer, Animal Liberation 18 (Harper Perennial Modern Classics 2009) (1990) (discussing the concept of "speciesism"). In its simplest form, speciesism is a bias based on genetic makeup, just as racism is a bias based on race. Singer believes speciesism to be an invidious form of prejudice which, like other prejudices founded on immutable conditions, is grounded in false notions of the differences between beings. The term is now often used to refer to any difference in treatment between humans and nonhumans (or between one group of nonhumans and another), even if sound justifications exist for that differential treatment. (For example, there is a general consensus that companion animals need protection from dangers in the outside world such as cars. But the decision to confine one's dog to a safe home, and not to confine one's adult children, is based in rational thought, not some level of unjustified discrimination.) In Singer's original definition, though, speciesism

> is exactly the kind of arbitrary difference that the most crude and overt kind of racist uses in attempting to justify racial discrimination. This does not mean that to avoid speciesism we must hold that it is as wrong to kill a dog as it is to kill a human being in full possession of his or her faculties. The only position that is irredeemably speciesist is the one that tries to make the boundary of the right to life run exactly parallel to the boundary of our own species.

Id. at 18.

Are animal "rights" and the Great Chain of Being mutually exclusive? Christopher Stone, an early commentator on environmental issues, felt that "until [a] rightless thing receives its rights, we cannot see it as anything but a thing for the use of 'us'—those who are holding rights at the time." Christopher D. Stone, Should Trees Have Standing? Toward Legal Rights for Natural Objects 8 (Tioga Pub. Co. 1988) (1974). Stone wrote a law review article of the same title in 1972. He subsequently revisited the issue in *Should Trees Have Standing? Revisited: How Far Will Law and Morals Reach? A Pluralistic Perspective*, 59 S. Cal. L. Rev. 1 (1985). *See also* Christopher D. Stone, Should Trees Have Standing?: And Other Essays on Law, Morals and the Environment (1996).

Another scholar, while acknowledging the common law's derogation of animals to property status, also believes the common law may be used to change that status:

> [T]he common law is not an impotent steed fenced by history; it has the liberty and, in fact, the duty to migrate to higher ground when facts and moral awareness dictate. Although some have argued that the common law is not a ripe mechanism for change as it relates to the protection of the interests of animals, a fresh judicial view of the status of animals is, perhaps, the best means presently available to change the legal view of animals as property, given that legislative efforts to protect interests of animals have been largely ineffective.

Thomas G. Kelch, *Toward a Non-Property Status for Animals*, 6 N.Y.U. ENVTL. L.J. 531, 532 (1998).

Revisiting the question of personhood discussed in the previous sections of this chapter, consider the dilemmas posed by giving personhood status and rights to animals unable to protect themselves from humans. Instead of granting them actual rights, is there a way to give some heightened protection to those who both have their own interests and, by virtue of modern societal structures, need our protection? Anti-cruelty laws are an obvious example of this. Animal law commentators have devised other theories of guardianship and substituted judgment to suggest solutions to this dilemma. For example, Professor David Favre has proposed a theory based in traditional concepts: "It is possible to imagine and articulate a legal paradigm in which a nonhuman animal has equitable self-ownership and, thus, status within the legal system, while a human retains legal title to the animal in question." David Favre, *Equitable Self Ownership for Animals*, 50 DUKE L.J. 473, 476 (2000). He explains that this separation is possible since title, like property, is a "cluster of legally enforceable rights relative to a given object." *Id.* at 477. He proposes "an intermediate ground between being only property and being freed of property status, where the interests of animals are recognized by the legal system but the framework of property law is still used for limited purposes." *Id.* at 476.

> As property laws are a human construct and not an inherent characteristic of physical objects, there is always conceptual space for innovation. One of the premises for our new property paradigm is that living objects have "self-ownership." That is, unless a human has affirmatively asserted lawful dominion and control so as to obtain title to a living object, then a living entity will be considered to have self-ownership. . . .

> * * *

> After the creation of this new property status, nothing changes about the nature or interests of the self-owned animal, as they have no knowledge of what property status we might impose upon them. The changes will arise in how we humans consider and relate to the animals in question. The premier relationship being created is between the self-owned animal and the guardian. The nature of the duty toward the self-owned animal will arise

out of two primary legal sources, anti-cruelty laws and the concepts developed for defining the parent-child relationship.

* * *

What interests of the self-owned animal will the guardian need to take into account? The focus should be on life-supporting and species-defining activities. Consider the example of a human infant who has an interest in receiving food so he or she can live and grow. It is an interest recognized by adult humans and easily asserted, such that if it is shown that a human with responsibility is ignoring this fundamental interest of an infant for which they have responsibility, then the courts may intervene and do whatever is required to fulfill that interest. This can occur whether or not the infant has self-awareness of the interference with his or her self-interest. The human may or may not have breached the duty to the state as set out in criminal law, but the court will certainly have the authority to make sure that the needs of the child are met.

* * *

The second category of relationships is between the self-owned animal and others besides the guardian. As entities with legally recognized interests, self-owned animals have sufficient status as juristic persons so as to be able to hold equitable interests in other property. Thus, a chimpanzee with self-owned animal status could have an equitable interest in a building or a bank account. Property could come to him or her by gift, will, or perhaps through purchase by the guardian on the chimpanzee's behalf. The guardian of the self-owned chimpanzee will be a trustee for such assets with an obligation to use the assets for the interests of the equitable owner, the chimpanzee.

* * *

Animals are not humans and are not inanimate objects. Presently, the law has only two clearly separated categories: property or juristic persons. But, by using existing concepts of property law, it is possible to construct a new paradigm that gives animals the status of juristic persons without entirely severing the concept of property ownership. It is a blending of the two previously separated categories. The new status can initially be created by the actions of individual humans, but in time the legislature may want to speak on the topic and regularize some of the rules and relationships. Creating this new status will impose duties upon the guardians. The potential legal duties can be ascertained by reference to our long-existing anti-cruelty laws and the obligations existing within the parent-child relationship. When these sources do not provide a sufficient answer, the powers of the court of equity can be tapped to resolve disputes. With these steps, the issue of justice for nonhuman animals can begin to be addressed.

Id. at 479–80, 497–98, 501–02.

The law currently recognizes two types of title—legal and equitable—that an owner holds in property. Professor Favre's creative solution envisions a separation of titles by accepted legal procedure. This split can be accomplished by one of two methods: either (1) a private lawsuit brought by the existing owner, where the owner transfers only the equitable title to the animal, or (2) judicial or legislative action granting animals equitable title in themselves. *Id.* at 493–94. Favre's theory has historical analogy in the methods used during slavery abolition, where slave owners could hand title over to the slaves themselves, effectively freeing them, or where slavery was abolished by governments. *Id.* at 491–92.

Favre's theory focuses on the relationship between animal and owner/guardian and suggests that connection should be viewed by the law more like the custodial relationship between parent and child and less like ownership of an inanimate object that has no "self." *Id.* at 484. "Just as the parents of the child must sort out what is in the best interests of the children, so the animal guardians must . . . decide what is in the best interests of the self-owned animal." *Id.* at 501. Favre's intent, of course, is to establish greater protection for the animal at issue: "Once the separation of legal and equitable title occurs for any one animal, then the nature of having legal title will change, as the legal title holder must recognize and take into account the interests of the equitable title holder." *Id.* at 494–95.

Compare the practical application of Favre's theory to guardianship in general. Guardians and conservators exist to safeguard the rights and interests of their wards, who generally are minors or incompetent persons, and courts enforce those obligations. *State ex rel. Michelson v. Superior Court for King County*, 251 P.2d 603 (Wash. 1952); *Richelson v. Mariette*, 149 N.W. 553 (S.D. 1914); *State v. District Court of the Ninth Judicial Dist. in and for Gallatin County*, 99 P. 291 (Mont. 1909). Depending on the capabilities of the ward, guardians/conservators may be appointed by a court to carry out certain duties and powers that the ward is incapable of exercising. *Matter of Guardianship of Hedin*, 528 N.W. 2d 567 (Iowa 1995). The guardians have no authority, rights or duties except those that a court or statute imposes upon them and, therefore, their role may be adapted to the particular ward they oversee. *State of Cal. v. Frito-Lay, Inc.*, 474 F.2d 774 (9th Cir. 1973); *Parker v. Ohio Oil Co.*, 186 So. 604 (La. 1930); *State ex rel. Emmons v. Hollenbeck*, 394 S.W. 2d 82 (Mo. Ct. App. 1964). Consider the California statutory explanation of a limited conservatorship for developmentally disabled adults:

> A limited conservatorship may be utilized only as necessary to promote and protect the well-being of the individual, shall be designed to encourage the development of maximum self-reliance and independence of the individual, and shall be ordered only to the extent necessitated by the individual's proven mental and adaptive limitations.

Cal. Prob. Code § 1801(d) (2008). This is the essence of Favre's construct: the caretaker, or legal title holder, of an animal must assume a role designed for the intellectual/sentient level at which the animal functions, while the animal holds equitable title to himself.

How does one reconcile the self-ownership suggested for animals with the fact that their guardians would need to make many of their decisions for them? Courts often use the concept of "substituted judgment" to describe the role of one who must make decisions for those who are unable to do so. "In making a substituted judgment determination, the court dons the mental mantle of the incompetent and substitutes itself as nearly as possible for the individual in the decision-making process." *Care & Protection of Beth*, 587 N.E.2d 1377, 1382 (Mass. 1992). Some believe we can apply this concept to those who care for animals. *See, e.g.*, Carolyn B. Matlack, WE'VE GOT FEELINGS TOO!: PRESENTING THE SENTIENT PROPERTY SOLUTION (Log Cabin Press 2006) (proposing a "sentient property" classification to describe certain animals as somewhere in between property and legal "persons"; this concept has been controversial among animal advocates because it does not ordain animals with full personhood status, and also because this definition of sentient property does not necessarily include farmed animals or those regulated by the federal Animal Welfare Act). *See also* Connecticut's Public Act 16-30 (providing for court-appointed advocates for dogs and cats in cruelty cases); David Favre, *Living Property: A New Status for Animals Within the Legal System*, 93 MARQ. L. REV. 1021 (2010) (proposing animals should obtain legal rights as a special type of property).

In a dogfighting case that received national attention, a law professor was appointed as a "guardian" and special master to oversee evaluations and recommendations for the seized dogs. The case is discussed in more detail in Chapter 3. *See also* Alexis Curry Fox, *Using Special Masters to Advance the Goals of Animal Protection Law*, 15 ANIMAL L. 87 (2009).

Commentators, advocates and activists continue to take a variety of approaches to suggest changes to the dominant paradigm of animals as property. For example, In Defense of Animals (IDA), a California non-profit group, launched a campaign called "They Are Not Our Property, We Are Not Their Owners." The campaign sought to have local and state governments amend ordinances, regulations and laws to replace the word "owner," when used in reference to nonhumans (usually companion animals), with "guardian." The change in language did not alter the effect of any laws with respect to animals in any way, and it does not affect the property status of nonhumans. One state (Rhode Island, in 2001) and many cities made the change, but the campaign did not succeed in making any substantive changes.

In a related vein, over the past several years, various animal advocacy groups have used litigation in their efforts to elevate animals to a higher legal status, with the goal that the animals themselves would obtain certain legal rights. In each of these cases, the filings were extensive and included numerous expert affidavits in support of the facts and theories set forth. Each effort has tried to make the leap from property to some form of "personhood" with significant philosophical and ethical support, while trying to change the legal status quo. And every one of the efforts has been rebuffed by the courts hearing the cases. For example, in *Cetacean Community v. Bush*, 386 F.3d 1169, 1171 (9th Cir. 2004), the plaintiffs were "all of the world's whales, porpoises, and dolphins," seeking to challenge the federal government's use of sonar which was harmful to the cetacean plaintiffs. The district court dismissed the case for lack of standing, and the Ninth Circuit Court of Appeals affirmed. Then, in *Tilikum v. Sea World Parks & Entertainment, Inc.*, 842 F. Supp. 2d 1259 (S.D. Cal. 2012), People for the Ethical Treatment of Animals brought suit on behalf of five orca whales, claiming they had been imprisoned as slaves in violation of the Thirteenth Amendment to the federal Constitution's proscription of involuntary servitude. The federal court in California held the cetaceans had no standing because they were not humans. Adopting or copying the *Tilikum* model of thinking with another imprisonment-related claim, two years later three separate lawsuits were filed in three separate courts in New York State within a few days, seeking to have four captive chimpanzees moved to sanctuary. These cases all relied on the *habeas corpus* doctrine most typically used to free prisoners who are illegally incarcerated. *See, e.g., People ex rel. Nonhuman Rights Project, Inc. v. Lavery,* 998 N.Y.S.2d 248 (App. Div. 2014). The *habeas corpus* suits were all rejected, with two different bases for the dismissals: that the plaintiffs had no standing because chimpanzees are not persons entitled to the protections of *habeas corpus,* and that *habeas corpus* does not apply when a petitioner seeks to change the place and means of confinement rather than the confinement itself. (The plaintiffs were arguing the chimpanzees should go from one form of confinement to another.) Moving from chimpanzees to elephants, the same group filed a case in late 2017, on the same *habeas corpus* grounds, with the same result. The court dismissed the case, finding that the plaintiff had no relationship with the subject elephants, and that the complaint was "wholly frivolous on its face." *See Nonhuman Rights Project, Inc. v. R.W. Commerford & Sons, Inc.,* 2017 Conn. Super. LEXIS 5181 (Conn. Super. Ct., Litchfield Jud. Dist. Dec. 26, 2017) (unreported op.).

Despite the losses in American courts, international courts and legislatures have taken steps towards significantly greater protections for animals, which might even be called animal rights. For example, while the courts were denying *habeas corpus* to chimpanzees in America, advocates for two chimpanzees and an orangutan in South America were actually successful in their efforts. Suica, the chimp involved in the first case—in Brazil—died in his cage at the zoo where he had been living during the litigation, one day after the judgment.[d] The second ruling was in Argentina in 2014, when a court ruled that Sandra the orangutan was a non-human person unlawfully deprived of her freedom, and should be moved to a sanctuary.[e] And in 2016, an Argentina court ruled in a one-page opinion that a chimpanzee named Cecilia possessed the requisite rights to be awarded the *habeas* writ.[f]

---

d. *See* https://www.animallaw.info/case/sui%C3%A1.

e. *See, e.g.,* Richard Lough, *Court Rules Orangutan Held in Argentina Zoo Is 'Non-Human Person' And Can Be Freed,* HUFFINGTON POST, Dec. 21, 2014.

f. *See, e.g.,* Gabriel Samuels, *Chimpanzees have rights says Argentinian judge as she orders Cecilia be released from zoo,* INDEPENDENT (U.K.), Nov. 7, 2016.

In 2015, the Delhi High Court in India ruled that birds "have fundamental rights including the right to live with dignity and they cannot be subjected to cruelty by anyone . . ." The opinion effectively banned keeping birds in cages, holding that "all the birds have fundamental rights to fly in the sky and all human beings have no right to keep them in small cages for the purposes of their business or otherwise."[g]

And also in 2015, New Zealand amended its Animal Welfare laws, declaring that animals are "sentient beings," expanding the protections given to them, and banning the use of animals in cosmetics-related research and testing.[h]

In December 2017, Spain announced its intention to have its legislative body change the designation of animals from "objects" to "beings," which would instantly increase protections for animals, and prevent their passage through estates as property or their use in debt collection as property to be sold.[i] Earlier that year, Portugal enacted a comparable legislative change; and two years earlier, France made a similar change in its Civil Code, with a new section (515-14) stating that animals are sentient living beings.[j]

Notes

1. The notion of animals as more than mere property—and rather, as beings warranting "dignity"—may be gaining some momentum. *See, e.g.,* Erica R. Tatoian, *Animals in the Law: Occupying a Space Between Legal Personhood and Personal Property*, 31 J. Envtl. L. & Litig. 147 (2015); Frank Bruni, *According Animals Dignity*, N.Y. Times, Jan. 14, 2014, at A27 ("An era of what might be called animal dignity is upon us. You see signs everywhere. . . . 'Those creatures big and small that have fed, frightened, entertained, comforted and awed us are no longer just them' []. 'Increasingly, they are us.'"). *See also* Muhamed Sacirbey, *Is Animal Rights the Next Human Rights?*, Huffington Post, Jan. 9, 2014 (former U.N. Ambassador considers the question of whether "the passion of the animal rights movement [will] soon become part of an international debate at the United Nations and related institutions").

2. A modified "personhood" theory was developed in an article discussing Poland's treatment of religious/ritual slaughter exemptions to humane slaughter

---

g. *See Birds have fundamental rights, can't be kept in cages: Delhi High Court,* The Economic Times, May 17, 2015.

h. *See* http://www.legislation.govt.nz/bill/government/2013/0107/latest/DLM5174807.html?path=bill%2fgovernment%2f2013%2f0107%2flatest&col=bill&fid=DLM5174807&search=sw 096be8ed81047b83 sentient 25 se&p=1 *(text of law);* http://www.hngn.com/articles/95818/20150527/animal-rights-new-zealand-government-rules-that-animals-have-feelings-in-new-animal-welfare-amendment-bill.htm.

i. *See* https://global.fm/news/spain-announces-landmark-animal-rights-ruling/; Claire Toureille, *Spain decides whether dogs are living beings or objects,* Int'l Business Times (UK Ed.), Dec. 12, 2017.

j. *See, e.g., New legal status that defines animals as 'living, feeling beings' into force this week,* The Portugal News, Apr. 5, 2017; Henry Samuel, *France finally upgrades animals from 'furniture status,* Telegraph (UK), Oct. 31, 2014; C. civ § 515-14.

laws (discussed in Chapter 6). The universally accepted method of humanely slaughtering food animals involves initially rendering them unconscious and insensitive to pain or any stimuli (by "stunning"), before the actual slaughter process begins. However, because certain ritual slaughter methods (most notably Kosher slaughter under Jewish law and Halal slaughter under Islamic law) require that animals be conscious when they are slaughtered, an exception has been written into nearly every slaughter law that eliminates the stunning requirement for animals slaughtered in a ritual manner. (Thus, animals are shackled and hung upside down, while conscious, before they are killed.) Poland's legislature and courts included the exemption, then removed it, then added it back. In an article discussing these decisions, the authors rejected the "radical proposal" that animals be granted personhood, and posited the idea of identifying animals as "non-personal subjects of the law":

> The recognition of animals as non-personal subjects of the law entails making their vital interests legally relevant considerations that must be taken into account in all decisions that could materially impact their well-being. The obvious differences between human beings and non-human animals suggest that the latter should enjoy only one legal right—to have one's individual, subjective interests taken into account whenever they may be seriously affected by decisions or actions of third persons. The concept of a non-personal subjecthood avoids the obvious difficulties in attributing animals with the whole bundle of rights (most of which are bluntly inconsistent with the nature of even the most developed non-human animals) implicated by the ordinary concept of personhood in law.
>
> Conferring to animals the right to have their interests taken into account does not determine *per se* the outcome of necessary balancing of their subjective interests with other competing considerations. It only requires that they cannot be completely or disproportionately ignored. Thus, the idea of non-personal subjecthood clearly is not intended as a panacea to all of the current legal problems of animal suffering. The deliberate vagueness of [its] practical implications may be its advantage rather than weakness. It allows for flexibility without which any elevation of the legal status of animals is doomed to fail. This way of thinking aims to reconcile most of the socially accepted forms of exploiting animals while paving the way towards gradual balancing of their interests with human benefits.

Aleksandra Lis and Tomasz Pietrzykowski, *Animals as Objects of Ritual Slaughter: Polish Law after the Battle over Exceptionless Mandatory Stunning*, GLOBAL J. OF ANIMAL LAW 1, 13 (Vol. 2, 2015).

3. In a 2018 article undertaking a comparative analysis of several legal systems, including Switzerland and Germany, while focusing primarily on Israeli law, the authors argue that "constitutional law cannot provide adequate protections for animals and, contrary to conventional wisdom, might even impair their protection."

Ariel L. Bendor & Hadar Dancig-Rosenberg, *Animal Rights in the Shadow of the Constitution*, 24 Animal L. 99 (2018).

4. If indeed the property status of animals were to be abolished, what would be the legal and practical effects on the commercial use of animals? What would happen to the animals themselves—should they be put in sanctuaries, sterilized, or is there some other means of dealing with animals who otherwise would have become food? Are any of those scenarios in the animals' best interests? Can you conceive of any other arrangement that might be more appropriate?

5. Having considered the property concepts raised in this chapter, go back to the introductory portion of this chapter and review the questions posed there. Has your opinion of the potential for change been altered, disproven, or confirmed?

Chapter 3

Criminal Law

No other area of animal law has received as much attention as that involving crimes of animal abuse and neglect. Every state has its own set of anti-cruelty laws, and some counties and even smaller governmental entities have supplemental laws. Given the number of different approaches and philosophies concerning animal protection, there are significant variations among the laws, but there are many similarities as well. This chapter introduces the principal concepts underlying those laws and discusses the issues and challenges inherent in applying and enforcing them. This chapter does not cover the more basic information necessary to understand the foundational concepts of general criminal law or procedure, but focuses instead on theories, language, legal procedures, and challenges specific to different types of anti-cruelty laws and abuse and neglect prosecutions.

Generally speaking, the criminal laws that protect animals from abuse and neglect can be reviewed, analyzed, and interpreted in the same way as any other criminal statute. Law enforcement and criminal defense attorneys should approach the investigation and gathering of evidence as they would any other case; prosecutors must prove every statutory element, including any *mens rea* requirement, beyond a reasonable doubt; and the defense has available all of the relevant arguments, defenses, and procedural options it would in any type of criminal case. However, there are some specific issues commonly found in animal abuse and neglect cases that may not arise in standard criminal prosecutions. In this chapter we focus on those issues as well as common language seen in many anti-cruelty laws and common themes in the cases involving those laws.

We begin with an interesting historical look at how, outside of the secular courts, criminal laws once included acts done by animals themselves.

Section 1. Historical Perspective

The Criminal Prosecution and Capital Punishment of Animals

E. P. EVANS (Faber & Faber Ltd., 1987) (1906)

It is said that Bartholomew Chassenée, a distinguished French jurist of the sixteenth century, made his reputation at the bar as counsel for some rats, which had been put on trial before the ecclesiastical court of Autun on the charge of having feloniously eaten up and wantonly destroyed the barley-crop of that province. On complaint formally presented by the magistracy, the official or bishop's vicar, who exercised jurisdiction in such cases, cited the culprits to appear on a certain day and appointed Chassenée to defend them.

In view of the bad repute and notorious guilt of his clients, Chassenée was forced to employ all sorts of legal shifts and chicane, dilatory pleas and other technical objections, hoping thereby to find some loophole in the meshes of the law through which the accused might escape, or at least to defer and mitigate the sentence of the judge. He urged, in the first place, that inasmuch as the defendants were dispersed over a large tract of country and dwelt in numerous villages, a single summons was insufficient to notify them all; he succeeded, therefore, in obtaining a second citation, to be published from the pulpits of all the parishes inhabited by the said rats. At the expiration of the considerable time which elapsed before this order could be carried into effect and the proclamation be duly made, he excused the default or non-appearance of his clients on the ground of the length and difficulty of the journey and the serious perils which attended it, owing to the unwearied vigilance of their mortal enemies, the cats, who watched all their movements, and with fell intent, lay in wait for them at every corner and passage. On this point Chassenée addressed the court at some length, in order to show that if a person be cited to appear at a place, to which he cannot come with safety, he may exercise the right of appeal and refuse to obey the writ, even though such appeal be expressly precluded in the summons.

* * *

One of the strong points made by the counsel for the defence in prosecutions of this kind was that these insects were sent to punish man for his sins, and should therefore be regarded as agents and emissaries of the Almighty, and that to attempt to destroy them or to drive them away would be to fight against God (*s'en prendre à Dieu*). Under such circumstances, the proper thing to do would be, not to seek legal redress and to treat the noxious creatures as criminals, but to repent and humbly to entreat an angry Deity to remove the scourge.

* * *

In 1519, the community of Stelvio, in Western Tyrol, instituted criminal proceedings against the moles or field-mice,[1] which damaged the crops "by burrowing and throwing up the earth, so that neither grass nor green thing could grow." But "in order that the said mice may be able to show cause for their conduct by pleading their exigencies and distress," a procurator, Hans Grinebner by name, was charged with their defence, "to the end that they may have nothing to complain of in these proceedings." Schwarz Mining was the prosecuting attorney, and a long

---

1. . . . Field-mice are exceedingly prolific rodents, and in modern as well as in mediaeval times have often done grievous harm to husbandry and arboriculture by consuming roots and fruits and gnawing the bark of young trees. The recklessness of hunters in exterminating foxes, hedgehogs, polecats, weasels, buzzards, crows, kits, owls and similar beasts and birds, which are destructive of field-mice, has frequently caused the latter to multiply so as to become a terrible plague. This was the case in England in 1813–14 and in Germany in 1822, and again in 1856.

list of witnesses is given, who testified that the serious injury done by these creatures rendered it quite impossible for tenants to pay their rents. The counsel for the defendants urged in favour of his clients the many benefits which they conferred upon the community, and especially upon the agricultural class by destroying noxious insects and larvae and by stirring up and enriching the soil, and concluded by expressing the hope that, if they should be sentenced to depart, some other suitable place of abode might be assigned to them. He demanded, furthermore, that they should be provided with a safe conduct securing them against harm or annoyance from dog, cat or other foe. The judge recognized the reasonableness of the latter request, in its application to the weaker and more defenceless of the culprits, and mitigated the sentence of perpetual banishment by ordering that "a free safe-conduct and an additional respite of fourteen days be granted to all those which are with young and to such as are yet in their infancy; but on the expiration of this reprieve each and every must be gone, irrespective of age or previous condition of pregnancy."

Not only were insects, reptiles and small mammals, such as rats and mice, legally prosecuted and formally excommunicated, but judicial penalties, including capital punishment, were also inflicted upon larger quadrupeds.

* * *

The culprits are a miscellaneous crew, consisting chiefly of caterpillars, flies, locusts, leeches, snails, slugs, worms, weevils, rats, mice, moles, turtle-doves, pigs, bulls, cows, cocks, dogs, asses, mules, mares and goats. . . . Also as late as 1864 at Pleternica in Slavonia, a pig was tried and executed for having maliciously bitten off the ears of a female infant aged one year. The flesh of the condemned animal was cut in pieces and thrown to the dogs, and the head of the family, in which the pig lived, as is the custom of pigs among the peasants of that country, was put under bonds to provide a dowry for the mutilated child, so that the loss of her ears might not prove to be an insuperable obstacle to her marriage. It would be incorrect to infer from the tables just referred to that no judicial punishment of animals occurred in the tenth century or that the fifteenth, sixteenth, and seventeenth centuries were peculiarly addicted to such practices. It is well known that during some of the darkest periods of the Middle Ages and even in later times the registers of the courts were very imperfectly kept, and in many instances the archives have been entirely destroyed. It is highly probable, therefore, that the cases of capital prosecution and conviction of animals, which have been collected and printed by Berriat-Saint-Prix and others, however thorough their investigations may have been, constitute only a very small percentage of those which actually took place.

Beasts were often condemned to be burned alive; and strangely enough, it was in the latter half of the seventeenth century, an age of comparative enlightenment, that this cruel penalty seems to have been most frequently inflicted. Occasionally a merciful judge adhered to the letter of the law and curbed its barbarous spirit by sentencing the culprit to be slightly singed and then to be strangled before being committed to the flames. Sometimes brutes were doomed to be buried alive.

Animals are said to have even been put to the rack in order to extort confession. It is not to be supposed that, in such cases, the judge had the slightest expectation that any confession would be made; he wished merely to observe all forms prescribed by the law, and to set in motion the whole machinery of justice before pronouncing judgment. The statement of a French writer, Arthur Mangin (*L'Homme et la Bête.* Paris, 1872, p. 344), that "the cries which they uttered under torture were received as confessions of guilt," is absurd. No such notion was ever entertained by their tormentor. "The question," which under the circumstances would seem to be only a wanton and superfluous act of cruelty, was nevertheless an important element in determining the final decision, since the sentence of death could be commuted into banishment, whipping, incarceration or some milder form of punishment, provided the criminal had not confessed his guilt under torture. The use of the rack might be, therefore, a merciful means of escaping the gallows. Appeals were sometimes made to higher tribunals and the judgments of the lower courts annulled or modified. In one instance a sow and a she-ass were condemned to be hanged; on appeal, and after a new trial, they were sentenced to be simply knocked on the head. Occasionally an appeal led to the acquittal of the accused.

In 1266, at Fontenay-aux-Roses, near Paris, a pig convicted of having eaten a child was publicly burned by order of the monks of Sainte Genevièbr. In 1386, the tribunal of Falaise sentenced a sow to be mangled and maimed in the head and forelegs, and then to be hanged, for having torn the face and arms of a child and thus caused its death. Here we have a strict application of *lex talionis*, the primitive retributive principle of taking an eye for an eye and a tooth for a tooth. As if to make the travesty of justice complete, the sow was dressed in man's clothes and executed on the public square near the city-hall at an expense to the state of ten sous and ten deniers, besides a pair of gloves to the hangman.

It is rather odd that Christian law-givers should have adopted a Jewish code against sexual intercourse with beasts and then enlarged it so as to include the Jews themselves. The question was gravely discussed by jurists, whether cohabitation of a Christian with a Jewess or *vice versa* constitutes sodomy. Damhouder is of the opinion that it does, and Nicolaus Boër cites the case of a certain Johannes Alardus or Jean Alard, who kept a Jewess in his house in Paris and had several children by her; he was convicted of sodomy on account of this relation and burned, together with his paramour, "since coition with a Jewess is precisely the same as if a man should copulate with a dog." Damhouder, in the work just cited, includes Turks and Saracens in the same category, "inasmuch as such persons in the eye of the law and our holy faith differ in no wise from beasts."

But to resume the subject of the perpetration of felonious homicide by animals, on the 10th of January, 1457, a sow was convicted of "murder flagrantly committed on the person of Jehan Martin, aged five years, the son of Jehan Martin of Savigny," and sentenced to be "hanged by the hind feet to a gallows-tree (*a ung arbre esproné*)." Her six sucklings, being found stained with blood, were included in the indictment as accomplices; but "in lack of any positive proof that they had assisted in mangling the deceased, they were restored to their owner, on condition that he should give bail for their appearance, should further evidence be forthcoming to prove their complicity in their mother's crime."

Notes

1. The cases in which animals were prosecuted and punished were brought in ecclesiastical (also known as spiritual) courts. The ecclesiastical court system, based in England but present across Europe, was intended to have authority mainly over religious matters, although the descriptions above make clear that they also reviewed matters of the flesh. The ecclesiastical courts had much more authority before the development of current court systems. "Canon law," which began with these courts, underlies many of our modern judicial doctrines. A current version of the ecclesiastical courts still exists in some European jurisdictions, but its authority is limited to church matters.

2. Under current American law, nonhuman animals are no longer accused, arrested, tried or convicted in courts of law for crimes against humans or against other nonhuman animals, presumably (at least in part) because they are viewed as incapable of possessing the appropriate *mens rea* that would support culpability, and because they are categorized as property. Comparing the cases in the excerpt above with the current status of animals, were animals accorded more or less rights or protections in sixteenth century ecclesiastical courts than they are in modern courts today? Did they, in a sense, receive more respect by being recognized as capable of intentional thought and motive, and by being entitled to legal representation? Or, were these cases simply a way for people to seek some sort of vengeance for acts done by animals, to find a scapegoat, regardless of the species? What would be the salutary effects (if any) of a resurrection of the laws and procedures described above? Does the treatment of animals in these cases mean that earlier societal evaluation of nonhumans included an appreciation of animals' own cultures, personalities, or sentience?

3. For a thorough review of the practice of animal trials and the lessons modern practitioners can learn from them, *see* K. Sykes, *Human Drama, Animal Trials: What the Medieval Animal Trials Can Teach Us About Justice for Animals*, 17 ANIMAL L. 273 (2011). The author argues that old animal trials "have something to teach us about both the promise and the limitations of using legal tools like personhood, standing, and legal rights — the machinery of the human justice system — to further the emancipation of animals."

4. When considering that historically animals could be charged, convicted, and sentenced for alleged wrongdoing, it is notable that this practice continues in one specific area of animal law. So-called "dangerous dog laws," in the form of local ordinances or state laws, describe procedures and sanctions for dogs who bite, attack, kill, or sometimes even just "harass" both humans and other animals. *See, e.g., www.animallaw.info/topic/state-dangerous-dog-laws*. If a dog has engaged in behavior that triggers the applicable dangerous dog law, then the arbiter (often an administrative hearing officer) has the authority to issue orders that impact both

the dog and the owner. These orders can include a requirement that the offending dog wear a muzzle in public or that the dog be killed. While a limited number of ordinances require a hearing to determine if the dog will be classified as "dangerous," "vicious," or some other designation, in the majority of cases the local animal control authority makes the determination and then gives the dog's owner the right to rebut its conclusion at a specifically requested hearing. Adam Karp, *Defending Against Dangerous Dog Classifications*, 128 Am. Jur. *Proof of Facts* 3d § 291 (2012). Some commentators are concerned that some dangerous dog laws violate due process principles. A more thorough discussion of these ordinances is set forth later in this chapter.

5. Contemporary American anti-cruelty laws have their roots in early English laws that recognized the need to provide some protection to nonhuman animals:

> Notwithstanding the political independence that the United States obtained from Great Britain during the late 1700s and early 1800s, there was still a considerable transfer of ideas from the intellectually mature mother country to the newly formed and basically frontier United States. The first articulations of concern for the moral and legal status of animals appeared in British writing. . . .

> Jeremy Bentham, an English barrister, was one of the few legal writers who addressed the issue of animals and the legal system. His *Introduction to the Principles of Morals and Legislation* (1789) was closely studied at the time by a large number of individuals, some of whom went on to propose legislation for the protection of animals. Bentham argued that there was no reason why animals should not be accorded protection under the law. He pointed out that animals, "on account of their interests having been neglected by the insensibility of the ancient jurists, stand degraded into the class of *things*." Within a footnote entitled "Interests of the inferior animals improperly neglected in legislation," Bentham argued that the capacity for suffering is the vital characteristic that gives a being the right to legal consideration. The final sentence of the footnote is often used today as a rallying cry for those seeking to promote the cause of animal rights. "The question is not, Can they *reason?* nor, Can they *talk?* but *Can they suffer.*"

> Having made the intellectual arguments for concern about animals, the British followed up with changes to the legal system. On May 15, 1809, Lord Erskine addressed Parliament in support of the bill he had introduced for the protection of animals. This date may represent the first time animal protection was seriously debated by a full legislative body. . . .

> The bill passed the House of Lords, but was defeated in the House of Commons. Some thirteen years later the battle was taken up again, this time by Richard Martin. On June 10, 1822, he succeeded in obtaining passage of a law known as "Dick Martin's Act . . . An Act to Prevent the Cruel and Improper Treatment of Cattle."

* * *

The life of Henry Bergh is set out elsewhere and will not be repeated here. His impact on the legal world began in 1866. After his return from a trip to Europe, where he observed both the cruelty inflicted upon animals and the efforts of the Royal Society for the Protection of Animals on behalf of animals, he became focused on the animal cruelty issue. Because of his social and political connections, it was not difficult for him to approach the New York legislature in Albany.

Although not a lawyer, Henry Bergh was able to direct the drafting of substantially different legislation [than previous laws, which focused more on property issues and less on humane considerations]. He also understood that the mere passage of legislation was insufficient—without dedicated enforcement the laws will never actually reach out and touch the lives of the animals about which he was concerned. Therefore, beside the drafting and passage of new criminal laws, he sought the charter of an organization which, like the Royal Society of London, would be dedicated to the implementation of the law. He asked the New York Legislature for a statewide charter for the American Society for the Prevention of Cruelty to Animals ("A.S.P.C.A."), whose purpose, as set forth in its constitution, was "[t]o provide effective means for the prevention of cruelty to animals throughout the United States, to enforce all laws which are now or may hereafter be enacted for the protection of animals and to secure, by lawful means, the arrest and conviction of all persons violating such laws." This was granted on April 10, 1866. Henry Bergh was unanimously elected as the A.S.P.C.A.'s first president, a position he continued to hold until his death in 1888.

Henry Bergh realized the shortcomings of the existing New York law and, therefore, sought strengthening amendments. His first attempt was in 1866 when the prior language of 1829 was amended to read: "Every person who shall, by his act or neglect, maliciously kill, maim, wound, injure, torture, or cruelly beat any horse, mule, ox, cattle, sheep, or other animal, belonging to himself or another, shall, upon conviction, be adjudged guilty of a misdemeanor."

This law represented several significant steps forward for animals. First, the provisions applied regardless of the ownership of an animal. Second, the negligent act, as well as the intentional act, of an individual could lead to criminal liability. Third, the list of illegal actions was expanded. Note that the word "cruelly" modified only the word "beat."

* * *

As a follow up to the second section of the 1866 Act, section 7 of the 1867 Act made illegal the abandonment of any "maimed, sick, infirm or disabled creature." Under the previous law it was not at all clear what could be done with an abandoned animal. Under this law, a magistrate or the captain of the police could authorize the destruction of such a creature.

* * *

While the New York law would not have happened but for the energy and drive of Henry Bergh, his actions clearly struck a responsive cord [*sic*] in a number of individuals around the country. Evidence of society's readiness for animal protection legislation is found in the rapid adoption of the legislation and the creation of animal protection societies around the country. Bergh was the catalyst, but the actions in many other states required the work and support of others outside the political power and influence of Bergh. Besides the drafting of the laws, Bergh's other major contribution was the generation of publicity about the issues. Because of the force of his personality and the visible way in which he ran his campaigns against animal cruelty, he was able to generate a large volume of newspaper coverage, first in New York and then around the country.

Within a few years Massachusetts, Pennsylvania, Illinois, New Hampshire, and New Jersey had adopted the same pattern of legislation as that in New York, including new criminal laws and the chartering of state Societies for the Prevention of Cruelty of Animals ("S.P.C.A."). One exception to the pattern is Maryland, which did not adopt any statute until 1890 and then adopted a very short provision clearly not based on New York's statute. . . .

Apparently, the legislation was lost on the wagon trains heading for California. It did not adopt any legislation until 1872 when the California Legislature adopted a law similar to the 1829 New York legislation. It was not until 1900 that California passed the more comprehensive legislation adopted thirty years earlier in New York.

David Favre & Vivien Tsang, *The Development of Anti-Cruelty Laws During the 1800s*, 1993 DET. C.L. REV. 1, 2–4, 13–15, 17, 20–22 (Spring 1993) (footnotes and citations omitted).

6. Anti-cruelty statutes historically have addressed multiple concerns that should be considered when reading this chapter and evaluating social and judicial reactions to animal cruelty. First, and perhaps somewhat counterintuitively, the legislative intent behind the early anti-cruelty laws was in part to protect personal (human) property rights in animals. This is clearly demonstrated in early versions of many statutes, which only criminalized conduct if it was directed at animals owned by others—in other words, it was not illegal to commit the same acts upon one's own animals or wild animals. (And in most American jurisdictions, wild animals are not protected by the anti-cruelty laws.) Second, anti-cruelty laws represent a type of moral legislation and the establishment of a code of behavior that includes the notion that unjustified cruelty to some living beings is immoral or unacceptable. Third, many anti-cruelty laws (particularly laws passed in recent years) implicitly recognize the sentience of animals, incorporating the human view of their ability

to suffer. Fourth, current rationale for the importance and passage of stronger anti-cruelty laws is that such laws are necessary because restricting cruelty to animals will also reduce violence against humans by helping identify individuals likely to engage in such conduct.

As a basis for the second (moral) aspect of anti-cruelty laws, courts have cited Mahatma Gandhi, who is credited with saying that "the greatness of a nation and its moral progress can be measured by the way its animals are treated." One challenge in this area is that morality, except at the extremes, is a subjective concept. Therefore, the creation and application of the anti-cruelty laws requires legislatures and courts to balance the goal of enforcing moral codes against other (and perhaps incompatible) individual rights. In *Paris Adult Theatre I v. Slaton*, 413 U.S. 49 (1973), for example, the Supreme Court upheld a Georgia law prohibiting pornographic films shown in a private setting to consenting adults, because of the "legitimate state interest" in "the quality of life and the total community environment, the tone of commerce in the great city centers, and, possibly, the public safety itself." *Id.* at 57–58. The Court emphasized that regulation of morality through criminal statutes is common and appropriate: "Bearbaiting and cockfighting are prohibited only in part out of compassion for the suffering animals; the main reason they were abolished was because it was felt that they debased and brutalized the citizenry who flocked to witness such spectacles." *Id.* at 68 n.15 (quoting Irving Kristol, ON THE DEMOCRATIC IDEA IN AMERICA 33 (1972)).

7. Over the past few decades, there has been mounting scientific and popular evidence of the direct link between animal abuse and human violence. It is now well established that individuals who mistreat animals are much more likely to do the same to people, particularly those who are more vulnerable by virtue of relative physical strength or inter-family dynamics (*e.g.*, children, the elderly, spouses). The evidence also shows that the violence continuum goes both ways; that is, those who abuse people are more likely to abuse animals. This is now commonly referred to as "The Link."

The Link refers to the interconnected nature of animal cruelty and human violence, including child abuse, elder abuse, and domestic violence. In domestic violence situations, threatened and actual violence toward nonhuman animals can act as a tool to manipulate or terrorize the intended human target, such as a spouse or children. *See, e.g., People v. Garcia*, 812 N.Y.S.2d 66 (App. Div. 2006) (domestic abuse situation where a goldfish was killed in front of children after physical and psychological abuse of their mother) (excerpted later in this chapter). Animal cruelty exhibited by a child often signals that the child has been abused and/or the child may behave violently toward humans in the future. For more information on The Link, see Section 7 of this chapter.

As this information has made its way to social services, law enforcement, educators and the courts, there has been a renewed focus on anti-cruelty laws. The idea that criminalizing animal cruelty can also prevent abuse of humans has been proven to be valid. Anti-cruelty laws are now often seen as a way of potentially preventing domestic abuse by identifying those who might commit those crimes before they occur. The following section, as well as Section 7 of this chapter, explores this concept and its impact on the development of anti-cruelty laws in more depth.

Section 2. State Anti-Cruelty Statutes

A. Introduction

Every state has a set of anti-cruelty statutes. Although some advocates agree that these laws do not afford animals legal rights,[a] the laws do provide the principal (and, in some cases, the only) legal protection available to animals in America. Animal cruelty may be considered an infraction, a misdemeanor, or a felony, depending on the severity of the crime and other factors. Most conduct encompassed by anti-cruelty laws is classified as a misdemeanor offense; however, as of March, 2014, all fifty states and the District of Columbia had at least one felony anti-cruelty law.[b] But this is a relatively recent development—a majority of felony anti-cruelty laws were enacted after 1993. Considering that the first state anti-cruelty law[c] was passed in the early 1800s, the heightened legislative activity since 1994 suggests a pronounced change in the level of interest and willingness of the public to address animal abuse and neglect through the legislative process, and to emphasize the importance of those laws to society.

Each state (and each of hundreds of local jurisdictions) has developed its own anti-cruelty laws with variations in language and application. In addition to basic prohibitions against abuse, cruelty, neglect, animal fighting, and sexual assault of animals, there are a number of provisions and exemptions found in most statutes, the most common of which are set out here.

B. Common Provisions

1. *Community Service.* Courts (in most cases, not just animal cruelty) may order a certain number of hours of some task as part of sentencing or as a condition of probation. A controversial order from some courts has been to require animal abusers to perform their service in animal shelters.

---

a. *But see* Cass R. Sunstein, *Standing for Animals (With Notes on Animal Rights)*, 47 UCLA L. Rev. 1333 (2000) and Cass R. Sunstein, *Centennial Tribute Essay: The Rights of Animals*, 70 U. Chi. L. Rev. 387 (2003) (suggesting that a wide range of animal rights, particularly *vis-à-vis* anti-cruelty laws, already are protected).

b. On March 14, 2014, South Dakota became the fiftieth state to enact a felony-level anti-cruelty law.

c. The first anti-cruelty law passed within what is now the continental United States was in 1641 by the Massachusetts Bay Colony. Article 92, entitled "Body of Liberties" stated "No man shall exercise any Tyranny or Cruelty towards any creature which is usually kept for man's use."

2. *Counseling.* In an effort to change offenders' conduct, some anti-cruelty laws specifically authorize or mandate evaluations and psychological or psychiatric treatment of convicted offenders.

3. *Cross-Reporting.* Humane officers may be required or allowed to report suspected or known child abuse that is identified when they investigate animal cruelty. One such bill was passed in Illinois in June 2009. The bill amends the Humane Care for Animals Act (510 ILL. COMP. STAT. 70/18) and the Abused and Neglected Child Reporting Act (325 ILL. COMP. STAT. 5/4) to provide for cross-reporting of child and animal abuse. Under the new provisions, animal control officers, Department of Agriculture investigators and humane society investigators must report suspected child abuse, and specialists with the Department of Children and Family Services must report suspected animal abuse.

4. *Definition of "Animal."* As established in Chapter 1, the statutory definitions and judicial interpretation of the term "animal" vary widely from state to state, and even in different statutes within the same state. This has obvious significant impact on whether particular species receive any protection under relevant anti-cruelty laws.

5. *Penalties.* Every anti-cruelty law violation carries with it some form of penalty, usually prescribed by that state's general misdemeanor and felony penalty provisions.

6. *Preconviction Costs of Care and Forfeiture.* Some states have laws that allow or require courts (upon petition by seizing agencies) to order defendants who own the animals they abused to pay the costs of caring for seized animals. Those laws often include a procedure that provides for a quick, pretrial, post-seizure hearing to assess the costs of care for seized animals. Where those preconviction costs are not paid in the time prescribed by statutes, defendants may automatically forfeit their rights in the animal victims to the seizing agencies. Experience shows that in most cases defendants refuse to pay the costs of care, so that these pivotal laws reduce the costs placed on shelters by large-scale animal abuse cases and provide great value to animals who can be more quickly adopted to permanent homes, rather than be sequestered in a shelter for the time it takes for a case to proceed to final judgment (which could be years).

7. *Post-Conviction Reimbursement for Costs of Care.* Most states have laws that place a lien on animals for the total costs of care of seized animals, assuming there is a conviction. Because most cases settle, and many animal abuse defendants are judgment-proof, these laws may not provide a significant benefit to seizing agencies.

8. *Restitution.* Where the defendant does not own the animal victims, a restitution order typically means that the person convicted must pay the owner of the affected animal for economic loss, including, for example,

veterinary bills. Many states employ similar provisions within their general criminal codes.

9. *Veterinarian Reporting.* As of early 2018, fifteen states required veterinarians to report suspected or known animal cruelty; and another twenty states addressed animal cruelty reporting by veterinarians by statute or regulation but did not mandate it. Veterinarians often receive some form of immunity for this reporting. *See* American Veterinary Medical Association Website, *https://www.avma.org/KB/Resources/Reference/AnimalWelfare/Pages/Abuse-Reporting-requirements-by-State.aspx* (last visited February 2018).

C. Common Exemptions

Most anti-cruelty laws include one or more exemptions, which can significantly weaken an otherwise strong animal protection law by excluding from coverage (1) whole classes of animals, such as wildlife or farm animals; or (2) specific activities, such as hunting or mutilations performed for cosmetic reasons (*e.g.*, tail docking or ear cropping of dogs, and declawing of domestic cats). Some common exemptions are outlined below.

1. *Traditional Veterinary Practices*

The practice of veterinary medicine is regulated by each state's veterinary practices statutes. What the state laws define as "traditional veterinary practices" varies state to state, but there are some general similarities. These include diagnosis and treatment of an animal's disease and injury, administration of prescription medication to animals, and diagnosis of pregnancy or fertility. Most states define "animal" for the purposes of their veterinary practices statute as any animal other than a human, including mammals, birds, reptiles, amphibians, and fish. Broad definitions of "veterinary practices" and "animals" create broad exemptions to anti-cruelty statutes.

For instance, in Pennsylvania, cosmetic surgery for animals is included as a traditional veterinary practice. 63 PA. STAT. ANN. § 485.3(10). Cosmetic surgery for animals usually includes declawing (amputating the "toes" of domestic cats), ear cropping, and tail docking, among others. The coverage of these practices by the state's traditional veterinary practice statute exempts them from the state's anti-cruelty statute.

2. *Animals Used for Medical, Educational or Scientific Research*

Most states exempt actions undertaken during the course of medical, educational or scientific research from their anti-cruelty statutes.

Minimal standards with respect to the treatment of laboratory animals in federally-funded research are set by the Animal Welfare Act (AWA) (7 U.S.C. §§ 2131–2159), discussed in detail in Chapter 6, Section 2. (The AWA does not govern the actual research protocols, but only treatment and housing of animals.) As such, states generally defer to federal law regarding the treatment of laboratory animals.

A small number of states have made special considerations for laboratory animals. New Mexico's statute, for example, exempts federally-funded research facilities covered by the AWA from coverage under the anti-cruelty laws, except when research activities include conduct that is "knowingly" outside of the standards set by internally approved protocols. N.M. STAT. ANN. § 30-18-1(I)(6).

3. *Hunting, Fishing and Trapping*

Hunting, fishing and trapping are considered a cultural heritage by many Americans and are protected, approved and regulated activities in every state. In line with this reality, these practices also are included within exemptions to anti-cruelty statutes in most states. Such exemptions generally provide that nothing in the anti-cruelty statutes should be construed to interfere with state or federal game laws covering these activities, or certain other hunting, fishing and trapping activities that are legal but otherwise unregulated. Additionally, some species of wildlife obtain protection from harm, harassment, hunting or killing from a variety of federal and state laws such as the federal Endangered Species Act (16 U.S.C. §§ 1531–1544) and parallel state statutes, Marine Mammal Protection Act (16 U.S.C. §§ 1361–1407), Migratory Bird Conservation Act (16 U.S.C. §§ 715–715s), and many others. However, the vast majority of animals that are hunted, fished and trapped do not qualify for these protections. As a consequence, many acts that would be considered criminal cruelty if done to a companion animal, such as a dog or cat, are legal if done to any wildlife that is either unprotected by state law, or subject to hunting and fishing regulations governing their taking.

4. *Farmed Animals and Routine Practices*

Common "standard animal husbandry practices" and treatment of animals used in food production are usually exempt from state anti-cruelty statutes. As a consequence, "standard animal husbandry practices," such as unanesthetized castration, debeaking, tail docking, ear cropping, and dehorning are all permissible. For a thorough discussion of the many legal challenges faced by advocates working on behalf of farmed animals, see Chapter 6, Section 1.

5. *Pest Control*

State anti-cruelty statutes often exempt what are commonly referred to as "commercially acceptable" means of pest control. The protected conduct may include, but is not limited to the use of fumigation, pesticides, poisoned bait, traps and sterilization. The use of these methods applies to a broad range of "pests," from cockroaches to deer.

The category "pest" itself is broad and amorphous and often undefined by statute. Different species of animals can be considered "pests" depending on the statutory definitions (or absence thereof), as well as the damage they inflict and the geographical location in which the damage takes place. Moreover, the same species may be both a "pest" to some and a pet to others. New Jersey, for example, exempts "[t]he killing or disposing, by a reasonable or commercially acceptable method or means, of" a rat or mouse, "provided that the animal is not a pet." N.J. STAT. ANN. §4:22-16(f). Control of some pests may be covered by the anti-cruelty statutes, although pest control is often seen as a facet of modern life, and an accepted practice. Because of that fact, even where there is no express exemption provision, courts may find that there is an unwritten but implied exemption for common practices.

6. *Entertainment*

Most forms of entertainment involving animals are exempt from state anti-cruelty statutes. Zoos, aquaria, circuses, horse racing and rodeos are just a few examples of operations and practices that commonly are exempt—though they may be subject to state and federal regulation with respect to their operations. Entertainment involving animals is quite lucrative, and in some states, it is as integral to the cultural tradition of the state as hunting, fishing, and trapping. There is a limitation placed on exempted animal entertainment, however. Unacceptable forms of entertainment involving animals—dogfighting and cockfighting for example— have been prohibited by state laws. *See also* the *People v. Thomason* case discussed later in this chapter.

Horse racing is a profitable and popular form of animal entertainment. Perhaps the most famous example is the Kentucky Derby. A very specific exemption in Kentucky's anti-cruelty statute states that the killing of an animal is legal if performed "[f]or purposes relating to sporting activities, including but not limited to horse racing at organized races and training for organized races." KY. REV. STAT. ANN. §525.130(2)(e).

Similarly, western states tend to show the same deference to common rodeo events. Nevertheless, some states include a separate exemption specifically for rodeos, though some state and local ordinances mitigate the potential harm rodeos may cause to an animal, such as Wisconsin's state-wide ban on electric prods in rodeos. WIS. STAT. §951.07.

Treatment of captive wildlife, such as those in zoos, aquaria, and circuses, is regulated by state laws as well as the federal Animal Welfare Act (AWA). The AWA does not preempt state laws with respect to animals in entertainment, but serves as a regulatory floor to treatment of these animals. Some animals also qualify for additional standards of care established by other state and federal laws. In recent years, various jurisdictions have passed state laws and/or local ordinances to help protect captive wildlife from abuses in these industries. Several jurisdictions have banned the use of bullhooks—long sticks with razor-sharp hooks on the end used to control elephants. Other localities have taken a more restrictive stance and completely prohibited the use of wild (also known as "exotic") animals in circuses or other public exhibition.

Each year, there is significant legislative activity relating to state anti-cruelty laws, making it difficult to have a completely up-to-date recitation of all the provisions in one place. A very useful tool for those interested in reviewing any of the fifty states' anti-cruelty laws is a compendium entitled *Animal Protection Laws of the United*

States of America and Canada. When this edition of the casebook went to press, the most recent edition had been published in early 2018 and covered every state's law for 2017. It is available at no cost from the Animal Legal Defense Fund at *http://aldf .org/resources/advocating-for-animals/animal-protection-laws-of-the-united-states-of -america-and-canada/*. The compendium provides the actual language of the laws as well as information about the different laws in table form (and hyper-linked) for easy comparison.

D. Issues and Challenges Facing Prosecutors and Law Enforcement

The high degree of legislative activity in the anti-cruelty area is not universally matched by a similar level of attention and resources by the law enforcement agencies and prosecutors charged with upholding these laws. While specialty divisions focused on animal cruelty do exist in some police departments and district attorneys' offices, as a general matter these agencies face a number of challenges, both internally and externally, that may restrict their ability to handle animal abuse cases promptly and thoroughly. In 2004, dozens of interviews were conducted with members of law enforcement in six geographically diverse states: California, New York, Colorado, Illinois, Texas and Florida. These interviews brought to light a number of impediments authorities face when investigating and prosecuting animal cruelty cases, including the following:[d]

Training. Police officers and prosecutors rarely receive adequate training on proper techniques to investigate and litigate animal abuse cases. This problem is compounded by the fact that often the newest and least-experienced prosecutors are assigned to handle these cases.

Personal Bias. Police officers, prosecutors and judges have their own life experience and history with biases about what type of case is worthy of attention and resources. If police officers or prosecutors generally think of animals (or animal abuse) as less worthy of attention than their other cases and victims, it is unlikely they will be inclined to pursue these cases vigorously, unless pressed to do so. Judges, likewise, may consider animal abuse cases less important and therefore give them short shrift in their courtrooms.

Financial Burdens. Police departments and prosecutors' offices are funded with public tax dollars and often need additional funds to cover the demand of their caseloads. When forced to prioritize cases, it is the rare official who will consider putting animal abuse cases above those involving human

---

d. Pamela D. Frasch first presented findings from this research project on November 6, 2004, at Yale Law School. A written report on the findings can be found in the INTERNATIONAL HANDBOOK OF ANIMAL ABUSE AND CRUELTY: THEORY, RESEARCH, AND APPLICATION (Frank R. Ascione ed., 2008).

victims. Even prosecutors who take animal abuse seriously may find it difficult to convince their supervisors that doing so is an appropriate use of precious time and resources.

Community Pressure. Putting resources into an animal abuse case can divide a community. For example, if the perpetrators are perceived as being sympathetic or otherwise upstanding citizens (such as may occur in certain neglect cases or in exceptional circumstances in other cases), authorities may come under considerable community pressure to drop the charges or to pursue limited sanctions against the wrongdoers, while those who side with the animals may demand the opposite.

Animals as Victims. Until recently, animals had never been considered victims under the statutes intended to protect them, which created difficulties when charging a defendant accused of harming multiple animals in a single event. As the cases in Section 3 of this chapter reflect, under recent Oregon case law, animals now are considered victims, at least for certain purposes.

E. Special Procedural Issues in Animal Cruelty Cases

1. *Evidence.* Animals are property under the law and, as such, have the unique distinction of being both "evidence" and victims entitled to some degree of protection under the anti-cruelty statutes. This dual classification can be a complicating factor when a motion to suppress evidence is filed in a cruelty case. Defense counsel may seek to suppress evidence (any animals) obtained through an allegedly improper search. As a result, animal control agents or police officers may be reluctant to seize animals without a warrant (even if there is immediate danger to the animals) because they are concerned that the seizure will be invalidated later. This hesitation can result in further suffering or death, or in the animals being removed by the defendant before a warrant is obtained; likewise, a successful motion to suppress can result in the return of the animals to their alleged abuser. Like any other criminal matter, however, it is important to remember that law enforcement officers may seize evidence of a crime, even if the evidence is an animal—and that in cruelty cases any animal subjected to cruelty is indeed evidence and the means by which the criminal act is achieved. In addition, the "plain view" and "exigent circumstances" exceptions to the Fourth Amendment's warrant requirements may support taking an animal into custody without prior judicial approval. Suffering animals thus can be treated in the same way as an officer would treat contraband or instrumentalities of a crime.

2. *Pretrial Forfeiture.* Prosecutors may seek pretrial forfeiture of any seized animals so they can be placed in permanent homes before trial. (Some state statutes specifically provide for this process under "costs-of-care" laws, discussed previously in Section 2.B of this chapter.) Defendants may argue that the forfeiture would be an unconstitutional taking of property without compensation. Courts examining the issue will likely consider whether due process requirements of notice and a hearing have been satisfied, and prosecutors must convince a court that no

constitutional violations occurred in connection with the seizure and/or forfeiture. This may resolve the entire case for the animals and the defendants—increasingly, where seizures are upheld, prosecutors are seeking early forfeiture (or surrender) of ownership rights in exchange for dismissal of the action.

3. *Proving Ownership.* Animal ownership is vital to establish when a defendant is accused of neglecting any animals the authorities believe s/he owns and for whom that defendant has a duty to provide minimum care. In such cases, proof of ownership is an element of the crime and defendants may try to avoid liability by contesting ownership. In most cases, however, circumstantial evidence can be used to prove this fact even where direct evidence (*e.g.,* license applications or a breeder's bill of sale) is not available.

4. *Examination of Remains.* Where animals have died as a result of suspected cruelty, it is important to preserve the evidence through a documented post-mortem examination as soon as possible. Chain-of-custody procedures must be followed to ensure the evidence will be admissible. Prosecutors who have seized the evidence may also have a duty to preserve it for the defendants, who may want access to an animal's body to do their own independent testing and analysis of cause of death or injuries.

5. *Conditions of Release.* Courts have considerable discretion to set the terms of probation for a convicted defendant. In recent years, more prosecutors are asking for "no contact with animals" provisions as a condition of release. (Note that "no contact" is distinguishable from "no possession." The former prohibits physical contact with any animal regardless of whether the defendant has actual possession. This is important in those cases where the likelihood of further abuse is high and the defendant's friends, relatives, or acquaintances possess animals.) A related condition prohibits any contact by the defendant with any providers of care for the seized animals in a given case. As discussed previously, the link between animal abuse and human violence is well established and more and more prosecutors are making a special effort to ensure the safety of the human caregivers in addition to that of the animals.

6. *Desmond's Law.* Connecticut General Statutes § 54-86n, commonly known as Desmond's Law, went into effect in October of 2016. The law is named after a dog who was beaten, starved, and strangled by his owner in 2012. Desmond's owner avoided jail time by taking part in a pre-trial diversionary program intended to help defendants with mental illnesses who are charged with crimes that are not of a serious nature. Public outcry against what some deemed a soft punishment for Desmond's owner led to the development and passage of Desmond's Law. The statute allows judges to appoint lawyers and supervised law students as volunteer advocates in animal cruelty, welfare and custody cases involving dogs or cats, to promote "the interests of justice." Additional efforts are underway in other states to adopt similar provisions. For a more detailed analysis of Desmond's Law, see Jessica Rubin, *Desmond's Law: A Novel Approach to Animal Advocacy,* 24 ANIMAL L. 243 (2018).

Section 3. Animals as "Victims" of Crimes

As noted in Section 2.D of this chapter, until relatively recently animals had not been considered victims under statutes intended to protect them. As the cases below reflect, however, this has changed in at least one jurisdiction.

In *State of Oregon v. Hess*, 273 Or. App. 26 (2015), the defendant appealed a judgment of conviction for seven counts of first-degree animal neglect and thirty-eight counts of second-degree animal neglect that were based on defendant's failure to provide minimum care for her cats. She contended, among other claims, that the trial court erred by excluding expert testimony that she suffered from Obsessive Compulsive Personality Disorder, which compelled her to acquire cats for which she was unable to provide minimum care, and, thus, she did not act voluntarily as required to impose criminal liability under the Oregon statute at issue. With respect to the issue of abused animals as victims:

> Defendant contended at sentencing that all of the guilty verdicts should merge into a single conviction because the cats were her property and, thus, not victims, leaving only one victim of her crimes—the public. The trial court disagreed, reasoning that the animal-neglect statutes were enacted to protect animals, thus making each cat a victim for purposes of subsection (2) of the anti-merger statute, ORS 161.067. The court entered a judgment of conviction on all 45 counts.
>
> * * *
>
> Defendant . . . assigns error to the trial court's failure to merge the guilty verdicts on the 45 animal-neglect counts into a single conviction for first-degree animal neglect. Defendant argues that the trial court erred in concluding that each animal was a separate victim for purposes of Oregon's anti-merger statute, ORS 161.067(2), which provides that, "when the same conduct or criminal episode, though violating only one statutory provision involves two or more victims, there are as many separately punishable offenses as there are victims." The state responds that the trial court did not err in refusing to merge defendant's guilty verdicts, relying on *Nix*, 355 Or. at 798.
>
> In *Nix*, the Supreme Court addressed and rejected the same argument that defendant makes on appeal. However, the court ultimately vacated its decision in *Nix* because it concluded that it did not have jurisdiction of the appeal. Although the court vacated its decision in *Nix*, we nonetheless are persuaded by the *Nix* court's reasoning on the merger question, and we adopt it. Hence, we conclude that the trial court did not err in entering convictions on all 45 of the animal neglect counts.

273 Or. App. at 33, 35.

Despite the fact that *Nix* was vacated on jurisdictional grounds, the *Hess* court adopted its reasoning and, so as to provide a fuller picture, the *Nix* case is excerpted here:

State v. Nix

Supreme Court of Oregon, 2014
355 Or. 777, 334 P.3d 437
(*Vacated*, 356 Or. 768 (2015))

In this criminal case, defendant was found guilty of 20 counts of second-degree animal neglect. ORS 167.325 (2009). Oregon's "anti-merger" statute, ORS 161.067, provides that, when the same conduct or criminal episode violates only one statute, but involves more than one "victim," there are "as many separately punishable offenses as there are victims." The issue in this case is whether defendant is guilty of 20 separately punishable offenses, which turns on the question whether animals are "victims" for the purposes of the anti-merger statute.

* * *

On review before this court, defendant renews his argument that "the ordinary meaning of the word 'victim' means a 'person,'" not an animal. According to defendant, "[a]nimals are defined as property under Oregon law," and "[t]here is no statute that allows property to be seen as a victim" of a criminal offense. In defendant's view, the victim of an animal neglect case is either the public at large or the owner of the animal.

The state responds that the ordinary meaning of the word "victim" is not as narrow as defendant contends and that, to the contrary, it commonly is used to refer both to animals and to human beings. Moreover, because individual animals directly suffer the harm that is central to the crime of animal neglect, as set out in ORS 167.325, they are the "victims" of that crime. According to the state, the text and history of the statute make clear that the legislature was concerned with the capacity of animals to suffer abuse and neglect. Indeed, the state argues, the legislature expressly structured the animal neglect statutes "such that the degree of the crime corresponds to the extent of the animal's suffering." Thus, in the state's view, the statutes evince a concern to protect more than a general public interest in animal welfare; rather, those statutes reflect the legislature's intention to protect individual animals from suffering.

The issue before us is one of statutory construction . . . . Our goal is to ascertain the meaning of the statute that the legislature most likely intended.

. . . At issue in this case is the meaning of the word "victims" as it is used in [ORS 161.067].

In the absence of evidence to the contrary, we assume that the legislature intended that the wording of an enactment to be given its ordinary meaning. The ordinary meaning of the word "victim" reflected in a dictionary of common usage is:

> "**1** : a living being sacrificed to some deity or in the performance of a religious rite **2** : someone put to death, tortured, or mulcted by another : a person subjected to oppression, deprivation, or suffering <a ~ of war> <a ~ of intolerance> <fell a ~ to prohibition era gangsters> **3** : someone who suffers

death, loss, or injury in an undertaking of his own <became a ~ of his own ambition> **4** : someone tricked, duped, or subjected to hardship : someone badly used or taken advantage of <felt himself the ~ of his brother's shrewdness—W.F. Davis> < little boys, as well as adolescent girls, became the willing ~s of sailors and marines—R.M. Lovett>

"**syn** PREY, QUARRY: VICTIM applies to anyone who suffers either as a result of ruthless design or incidentally or accidentally <the victim sacrificed on these occasions is a hen, or several hens—J.G. Frazer> < was the girl born to be a victim; to be always disliked and crushed as if she were too fine for this world—Joseph Conrad> <lest such a policy precipitate a hot war of which western Europe would be the victim—Quincy Wright> ***."

Webster's Third New Int'l Dictionary 2550 (unabridged ed 1983).

In that light, it can be seen that defendant's contention that the "plain meaning" of the word "victim" refers only to persons, and not to animals, is predicated on a selective reading of the dictionary definitions. The first sense listed in the definition, for example, refers broadly to "a living being," not solely to human beings. And the synonymy gives as an example of the word "victim" the sacrifice of animals. The ordinary meaning of the word "victim," then, is capable of referring either to human beings, animals, or both.[3]

Illustrative examples of the plain meaning of "victim" to refer to animals are not difficult to locate. Especially in the context of animal cruelty, it is common to refer to animals as "victims." As far back as the mid-nineteenth century, John Stuart Mill referred to the "unfortunate slaves and victims of the most brutal part of mankind; the lower animals." John Stuart Mill, 2 *Principles of Political Economy: With Some of Their Applications to Social Philosophy* 579 (1864). Rachel Carson complained of cruelty to all, "whether its victim is human or animal." . . . Closer to home, an article in the Oregon State Bar Bulletin reported that, "[t]he Oregon Legislature has repeatedly and consistently articulated a strong public policy favoring the aggressive prosecution of animal cruelty cases by enacting statutes requiring police officers to make arrests in cases of animal abuse and to pay for and provide care to victim animals." *Full-Time Prosecutor to Litigate Animal Cruelty Cases Statewide*, Or State Bar Bulletin, May 2013.

Having established the common, ordinary meaning of the term "victim," the question is whether anything in the statute at issue suggests that the legislature meant something different. Certainly nothing in the wording of ORS 161.067(2)

---

3. The idea of animals being regarded as "victims" is not a new one. *Animals as Offenders and Victims*, 21 Alb LJ 265, 266 (1880) (recounting the history of animal welfare laws in Europe and noting that eventually legislation prohibited cruelty to animals "not out of regard to the owner, but in mercy to the creature itself"). In a related vein, there are records of legal proceedings being brought against animals as named parties to legal proceedings as early as the Middle Ages in Europe and as recently as the twentieth century in this country. . . .

suggests that the word "victim" cannot refer to animals. If anything, the phrasing of the statute — which refers to the violation of another statutory provision — suggests that the meaning of the word "victim" will depend on the underlying substantive statute that the defendant violated.

The legislative history sheds no light on the matter. . . . .

* * *

To summarize our analysis so far: The ordinary meaning of the word "victim" as it is used in ORS 161.067(2) can include both human and non-human animals, and nothing in the text, context, or legislative history of the statute necessarily precludes an animal from being regarded as such. This court's cases construing the term "victim" as it is used in that statute hold that, in fact, the meaning of the term is not to be found in an analysis of ORS 161.067(2) itself, but rather, it derives from the underlying substantive criminal statute that defendant has been found to have violated.

Whether each of the animals that defendant neglected was a "victim" for the purposes of the anti-merger statute, then, depends on whether the legislature regarded them as such for the purposes of the substantive offense of second-degree animal neglect. More particularly, it depends on "who suffers harm that is an element of the offense." *Glaspey*, 337 Ore. at 565. We turn to that issue.

ORS 167.325 (2009) provides:

> "A person commits the crime of animal neglect in the second degree if, except as otherwise authorized by law, the person intentionally, knowingly, recklessly or with criminal negligence fails to provide minimum care for an animal in such person's custody or control."

An "animal" means "any nonhuman mammal, bird, reptile, amphibian or fish." ORS 167.310(1) (2009). "Minimum care" refers to "care sufficient to preserve the health and well-being of an animal and, except for emergencies or circumstances beyond the reasonable control of the owner, includes, but is not limited to," such requirements as food, water, shelter, and reasonably necessary veterinary care. ORS 167.310(7) (2009). For domesticated animals, "minimum care" also includes access to adequate shelter, continuous access to an area that is adequate for "exercise necessary for the health of the animal," being kept at a "temperature suitable for the animal," and being "[k]ept reasonably clean and free from excess waste or other contaminants that could affect the animal's health." *Id.*

The phrasing of the offense reveals that the legislature's focus was the treatment of individual animals, not harm to the public generally or harm to the owners of the animals. The offense is committed by failing to provide required care to "an animal," regardless of who owns it. The required care includes the minimum necessary "to preserve the health and well-being" of that animal. It is the individual animal that "suffers harm that is an element of the offense. *Glaspey*, 337 Ore. at 565.

The larger context of the statutory offense confirms that the legislature's focus is on the treatment of individual animals. Second-degree animal neglect is a component of a more comprehensive set of offenses concerning the care of animals, offenses that are structured to correspond to the extent of an animal's suffering. The statutes begin with animal neglect in the second degree, which, as we have noted, is committed when a person fails to provide minimum care. When the person's failure to provide minimum care "results in serious physical injury or death to the animal," that person commits animal neglect in the first degree. ORS 167.330. When a person "intentionally, knowingly, or recklessly causes physical injury to an animal," that person commits the offense of animal abuse in the second degree. ORS 167.315. And when a person intentionally, knowingly, or recklessly causes "serious physical injury" or "[c]ruelly causes the death of an animal," that person commits animal abuse in the first degree. ORS 167.320. Finally, when a person "[m]aliciously kills an animal" or "[i]ntentionally or knowingly tortures an animal," that person commits the offense of aggravated animal abuse in the first degree, a Class C felony. ORS 167.322.

In each instance, the offense is committed against "an animal," and the relative seriousness of the offense is gauged in accordance with the relative degree of harm to or suffering of that animal. If the animal suffers a lack of minimum care, the offense is second-degree animal neglect. But if the animal is subjected to torture, the offense is felony aggravated animal abuse. In any reasonable sense of the word, the "victim" of those offenses is the individual animal that suffers the neglect, injury, cruelty, torture, or death.

Other aspects of the larger statutory scheme similarly confirm the legislature's focus on the suffering of individual animals. ORS 167.350, for example, provides that, in addition to other penalties that a court may impose for violations of the animal cruelty laws, the court may order the forfeiture of a defendant's rights in the animal. ORS 167.350(1). The same statute provides that, if a court orders such a forfeiture, it may further order "that the rights be given over to an appropriate person or agency demonstrating a willingness to accept and care for the animal." ORS 167.350(2). The statute also provides that a court may also require the owner to repay the reasonable costs incurred by any person or agency caring for the animal during the pendency of the charges. In each instance, again, the focus is on the care of the animal who has suffered the harm of neglect or abuse. ORS 167.350(3).

* * *

The legislative history of ORS 167.325, particularly in the larger context of the history of animal cruelty legislation, confirms what our textual analysis so strongly suggests. At common law, cruelty to animals did not constitute an offense.

The first animal cruelty legislation on this continent can be traced to the Puritan "Body of Liberties" from the Massachusetts Bay Colony, which prohibited cruelty to "any bruite [sic] Creature which are usuallie [sic] kept for man's use." Massachusetts Body of Liberties § 92 (Ward 1641); Thomas G. Kelch, *A Short History of (Mostly) Western Animal Law: Part II*, 19 Animal L 347, 350 (2013) (quoting Body of Liberties). By its terms, the law protected the animals only as property of their owners, and even then, only as to commercially valuable animals that were "usuallie kept for man's use."

* * *

In the nineteenth through the twentieth centuries, some states began to pass anti-cruelty laws that were intended to deter immoral conduct; the emphasis still was not on protecting the animals themselves. . . .

Other states, however, enacted legislation targeting cruelty to animals for the sake of preventing the animals themselves from suffering, not merely as property to be protected or as a way of improving public morality. . . . .

* * *

The preceding history confirms that the principal purpose of adopting the legislation that became ORS 167.325 was to prevent the suffering of animals. Although early animal cruelty legislation may have been directed at protecting animals as property of their owners or as a means of promoting public morality, Oregon's animal cruelty laws have been rooted—for nearly a century—in a different legislative tradition of protecting individual animals themselves from suffering. . . .

We therefore conclude that defendant is incorrect that the real "victim" of the crime of second-degree animal neglect is either the public or the animal owner. . . . Moreover, *Glaspey* makes clear that the "victim," for the purposes of ORS 161.067(2), is the one that "suffers harm that is an element of the offense." *Glaspey*, 337 Ore. at 565. Public harm is not an element of the offense of second-degree animal neglect. Harm to the individual animal is.

Nor is there in any indication that the legislature regarded the "victim" of animal neglect to be the owner of the animal. To be sure, Oregon law regards animals as the property of their owners. But it does not necessarily follow from that fact that owners of abused or neglected animals are the victims of the offense. Indeed, it would be anomalous to conclude that the "victim" of animal neglect is the owner of the animal when it is the owner who is charged with having committed the offense.[5] What is more, ORS 167.325 provides that, in the event of a conviction for animal neglect or animal cruelty, a court may order that the defendant forfeit any rights he or she had in the animal that has been neglected or abused—an odd consequence if the real victim of the offense is the animal's owner.

In concluding that animals are "victims" for the purposes of ORS 161.067(2), we emphasize that our decision is not one of policy about whether animals are deserving of such treatment under the law. That is a matter for the legislature. Our decision is based on precedent and on a careful evaluation of the legislature's intentions as expressed in statutory enactments. Our prior decisions hold that the meaning of the word "victim" for the purposes of ORS 161.067(2) necessarily depends on what the legislature intended in adopting the underlying substantive criminal statute that the defendant violated. In this case, the underlying substantive criminal statute,

---

5. Of course, animal cruelty offenses may be committed by persons other than the owner of the animal. We do not need to address whether, in those circumstances, the owner—in addition to the animal—may be regarded as a victim of the offense, and we express no opinion on that issue.

ORS 167.325, protects individual animals from suffering from neglect. In adopting that statute, the legislature regarded those animals as the "victims" of the offense. It necessarily follows that the trial court in this case erred in merging the 20 counts of second-degree animal neglect into a single conviction.

The decision of the Court of Appeals is affirmed. The judgment of the circuit court is reversed, and the case is remanded for entry of separate convictions on each guilty verdict for a violation of ORS 167.325 and for resentencing.

Notes

1. Connecticut's Desmond's Law (CONN. GEN. STAT. § 54-86n) (noted immediately before the discussion of *Hess* in Section 2.E of this chapter) allows judges to appoint lawyers and supervised law students as volunteer advocates in cases of cruelty to dogs or cats. These volunteer advocates represent "the interests of justice." Following in line with the holdings in *Hess* and *Nix*, Desmond's Law recognizes the various factors to be considered in these cases. What advantages and drawbacks can you see to the approach of treating animals as crime victims?

2. In *People v. Brunette*, 194 Cal. App. 4th 268 (2011), the court considered a different question regarding the meaning of "victim" in an animal cruelty case. One issue there was whether the county animal services agency, which had incurred costs in treating and caring for dozens of emaciated and severely ill dogs from the defendant's property, was entitled to restitution under California Penal Code section 1202.4 (California's "Victims' Bill of Rights"), which allows restitution for an entity "when that entity is a direct victim of a crime." The court held that the animal services agency was not the direct victim of defendant's animal cruelty. Nevertheless, the court relied on the anti-cruelty statute as the basis for a restitution award for the costs of care for the animals seized from defendant.

3. In *People v. Garcia*, 812 N.Y.S.2d 66 (App. Div. 2006), excerpted later in this chapter, both the pet goldfish and the children who were forced to watch the fish be sadistically killed were arguably victims of the crime, though not in any formal legal sense. There, the question was whether the fish was a "companion animal" under the statute, which transformed the crime from a misdemeanor into a felony. The court answered that question in the affirmative.

4. For further analysis, *see* L. Chiesa, *Why is it a Crime to Stomp on a Goldfish?—Harm, Victimhood and the Structure of Anti-Cruelty Offenses*, 78 MISS. L.J. 1 (2008); Douglas E. Beloof, *Crime Victims' Rights: Critical Concepts for Animal Rights*, 7 ANIMAL L. 19 (2001).

5. The following case addresses a related issue of whether an enhanced penalty for use of a deadly weapon under a Texas statute applies only to crimes against human victims.

Prichard v. State

Court of Criminal Appeals of Texas, 2017
533 S.W.3d 315

ALCALA, J. This case addresses whether a deadly weapon finding is permissible for the use or exhibition of a deadly weapon against a nonhuman. In his petition for discretionary review, Robert Monte Prichard, appellant, argues that a deadly weapon finding is improper when the only thing injured or killed as a result of a defendant's criminal conduct is an animal rather than a human being. Rejecting that argument, the court of appeals upheld a deadly weapon finding in this case in which appellant was convicted of animal cruelty and the deadly force was directed only against a dog. We conclude that the language of the deadly weapon statute is ambiguous with respect to whether a deadly weapon finding may be made for weapons used or exhibited against nonhumans, and thus, we must consider extra-textual factors to discern the Legislature's intent as to this matter. We determine that an analysis of those factors supports our determination that a deadly weapon finding may be made for human victims only. We, therefore, we reverse the judgment of the court of appeals.

I. Background

While purportedly disciplining his pet dog, appellant killed her by repeatedly hitting her head with a shovel and then drowning her in a swimming pool. He was indicted for the state-jail felony of cruelty to a non-livestock animal. *See* Tex. Penal Code §42.092(b)(1), (c). In a separate paragraph, the indictment also alleged that the shovel and pool water, singly or in combination, constituted the use of a deadly weapon in the commission of the offense. A jury convicted appellant of the offense as charged in the indictment and, in a special issue in the verdict form, made a finding that appellant had used a deadly weapon. This finding made the state-jail felony offense punishable within the punishment range for a third-degree felony. *See id.* § 12.35(c). The jury sentenced appellant to six and one-half years' imprisonment. The trial court's judgment reflected that appellant had been convicted of a third-degree felony and the judgment showed an affirmative finding of a deadly weapon.

On appeal, appellant argued that the evidence was insufficient to support the jury's deadly weapon finding because that finding should be limited only to human victims and no evidence showed that a human had been harmed or placed at risk of harm as a result of appellant's conduct. Appellant challenged the deadly weapon finding primarily based on three theories.

＊ ＊ ＊

II. Analysis

＊ ＊ ＊

B. The Deadly Weapon Statute is Ambiguous

After examining the statutory language, we determine that the statute is ambiguous because a reasonable person could read its terms as applying either to only humans or to all organisms that are capable of cessation of life.

1. The Statute's Language

The deadly weapon statute at issue here is set forth in Article 42.12, § 3g(a)(2), which provides for a stricter penalty for an offender who has "used or exhibited [a deadly weapon] during the commission of a felony offense or during immediate flight therefrom." Tex. Code Crim. Proc. art. 42.12, § 3g(a)(2) (West 2013). A "deadly weapon" includes "anything that in the manner of its use or intended use is capable of causing death or serious bodily injury." Tex. Penal Code § 1.07(a)(17)(B). The term "serious bodily injury" is defined as "bodily injury that creates a substantial risk of death or that causes death, serious permanent disfigurement, or protracted loss or impairment of the function of any bodily member or organ." *Id.* § 1.07(a)(46). "Bodily injury" means "physical pain, illness, or impairment of physical condition." *Id.* § 1.07(a)(8) . . . .

Although our review in this case examines the deadly weapon statute, the question before us is exceedingly narrow. The issue is whether the intended target of the exhibition or use of a deadly weapon may be a nonhuman. . . .

2. The Deadly Weapon Statute's Language is Ambiguous

A review of the statute's language, as it generally applies to offenses in the penal code and as it specifically applies in the context of the animal-cruelty statute, reveals that it is ambiguous with respect to whether it was intended to apply to only humans or to all living organisms. Reasonable people could reach opposite conclusions about the meaning of the statutory language as it pertains to this question. Furthermore, this Court's precedent supports our conclusion that the deadly weapon statute is ambiguous.

* * *

b. The Deadly Weapon Statute in the Context of Animal-Cruelty Statute

Despite the ambiguity in the deadly weapon statute as it generally applies to offenses in the penal code, the State argues that the particular statutory language in the animal-cruelty statute under which appellant was convicted in this case plainly permits a deadly weapon finding. Section 42.092 of the Penal Code, entitled "Cruelty to Nonlivestock Animals," states, "A person commits an offense if the person intentionally, knowingly or recklessly: (1) tortures an animal or in a cruel manner kills or causes serious bodily injury to an animal." Tex. Penal Code § 42.092(b)(1).

The State contends that the animal-cruelty statute's use of the phrase "kills or causes serious bodily injury to an animal" necessarily includes the use of a deadly weapon because (1) the phrase "serious bodily injury" appears in both the deadly weapon statute and animal-cruelty statute and (2) it is impossible to inflict serious bodily injury or death without the use of a deadly weapon. A close comparison of the deadly weapon statute and animal-cruelty statute reveals that, although they each incorporate the same phrase "serious bodily injury," they use different terms for the loss of life, they criminalize the loss of life under different circumstances, and the term has varied meanings in the two statutes. Thus, we are unpersuaded that the plain language of the animal-cruelty statute reveals the Legislature's intent to permit a deadly weapon finding.

It is true that the animal-cruelty statute and the deadly weapon statute each use the same phrase "serious bodily injury," but it is also true that the two statutes use entirely different terms for the cessation of life. The animal-cruelty statute uses the term "kill" and the deadly weapon statute uses the word "death." This choice of vocabulary suggests that the interests at stake are quite different in that the penal code, within which the animal cruelty statute appears, expressly permits the lawful killing of nonlivestock animals under certain circumstances. The animal-cruelty statute states, "It is an exception to the application of this section that the conduct engaged in by the actor is a generally accepted and otherwise lawful: (1) form of conduct occurring solely for the purpose of or in support of: (A) fishing, hunting, or trapping; or (B) wildlife management, wildlife or depredation control, or shooting preserve practices . . . ; or (2) animal husbandry or agriculture practice involving livestock animals." Tex. Penal Code § 42.092(f). Recognizing that cessation of the life of certain animals is lawful under certain circumstances, the animal cruelty statute used the word "kill." In contrast, the deadly weapon statute incorporates the definition of deadly weapon that uses the broader word "death." A killing involves a death, but a death does not necessarily involve a killing. Unlike the authorized killing of an animal, the penal code provides no exceptions to offenses that cause death or serious bodily injury to a person. *See id.* § 9.02 ("It is a defense to prosecution that the conduct in question is justified under this chapter."); *see also id.* § 2.02.

Although both relevant statutes use the identical phrase "serious bodily injury," the statutes are materially different in their descriptions about the cessation of life, with the animal-cruelty statute permitting certain killings, and the deadly weapon statute more broadly using the word "death." Given these differences in the two statutes, we do not consider the fact that the Legislature used part of the phrase in the deadly weapon statute, "serious bodily injury," but not the entire phrase "serious bodily injury or death," to render the statutory language plain so as to reveal the Legislature's intent to permit a deadly weapon finding for violations of the animal-cruelty statute.

* * *

The State also suggests that the language in the animal-cruelty statute that includes the phrase "to an animal" in the context of "kills or causes serious bodily injury to an animal" necessarily means that the Legislature intended to permit a deadly weapon finding. The State argues that it is impossible to kill or cause serious bodily injury without the use of a deadly weapon. Although the State's reading of the statute may be a reasonable interpretation of the language, we conclude that it is equally reasonable that the Legislature did not intend for this language to permit a deadly weapon finding, and thus that the meaning of the statute is ambiguous. The phrase "to an animal" could connote the meaning that the State suggests, but it could equally have been inserted there by the Legislature to limit the applicability of the statute to animals that are specifically identified in the definition. The statute defines "animal" as "a domesticated living creature, including any stray or feral cat or dog, and a wild living creature previously captured. The term does not include an uncaptured wild living creature or a livestock animal." *Id.* §42.092(a)(2). The word "animal" in that statute is distinguished from "livestock animal" that is covered in a different section. Section 42.09, entitled "Cruelty to Livestock Animals," defines "livestock animal" as "(A) cattle, sheep, swine, goats, ratites, or poultry commonly raised for human consumption; (B) a horse, pony, mule, donkey, or hinny; (C) native or nonnative hoofstock raised under agriculture practices; or (D) native or nonnative fowl commonly raised under agricultural practices." *Id.* §42.09(b)(5). Thus, the reference to killing or causing serious bodily injury "to an animal" could reasonably suggest that the Legislature intended to permit a deadly weapon finding for the death of an animal, but, alternatively, it could also mean that the statute was merely defining the types of creatures to which the statute was intended to apply. For this reason, the language in the animal-cruelty statute is ambiguous rather than plain with respect to whether it would specifically permit a deadly weapon finding.

* * *

Given that reasonable people could disagree about the meaning of the statutory language, the deadly weapon statute is ambiguous as to whether it applies only to humans. Nothing in the plain language of the statute limits the victim of the use or exhibition of the deadly weapon to humans only, and for all of the reasons explained above, reasonable minds may disagree about whether the Legislature intended for this statute to be limited to only humans.

* * *

C. Extra-Textual Analysis

Having determined that the plain language is ambiguous, we may consider extra-textual factors, including (1) the legislative history, (2) the objective of the statute, and (3) the consequences of a particular construction, to determine the Legislature's intent in enacting the statute.

1. Legislative History

In *Plummer*, this Court described the legislative record discussing the specific terms in the deadly weapon statute as "skimpy." *Plummer* [*v. State*, 410 S.W.3d 855, 861 (Tex. Crim. App. 2013)]. The general purpose of the statute, however, is well documented in that the Legislature apparently intended to provide more severe punishment against actors who risk serious bodily injury or death for crimes against people. One witness testifying before the 1977 Senate subcommittee on the deadly weapon provision stated that it was "intended to send a message to criminals to leave their firearms at home." *Id.* All of the discussion during the hearing centered on the commission of dangerous, violent felonies towards people, and the use of obvious weaponry, such as guns, grenades, and knives. . . .

Although the legislative history is silent with respect to whether the Legislature specifically intended to more severely punish defendants who victimize animals or plants as well as humans, the substance of the arguments presented in favor of the legislation suggest that the focus of the statute was to protect people from criminals who bring firearms and other weapons to commit their offenses. There is nothing in the legislative history to suggest that the statute was enacted to enhance the penalties for deadly weapons used or exhibited against nonhumans. Moreover, as explained above, because a primary purpose of the deadly weapon statute is to deter using or exhibiting deadly weapons in a criminal act because their presence increases the likelihood of violence and the severity of injuries by escalating the dangers involved, that rationale fails when the crimes are directed against nonhumans. For example, a mugger who produces a knife or a firearm to compel his victim's wallet creates a far more dangerous situation than if unarmed because the victim can perceive the weapon and understand the increased threat. With respect to an animal, it is extraordinarily unlikely that an animal would comprehend the significance of a deadly weapon in its interaction with a person. The legislative history, therefore, weighs in favor of permitting a deadly weapon finding for humans only.

2. The Objective of the Statute

Considering the objective of the statute, we determine that it is unlikely that the Legislature intended to broadly include nonhumans as the entity against whom the deadly weapon was used or exhibited. A deadly weapon finding significantly affects the gravity of the punishment, carrying with it serious legal consequences that may affect probation eligibility, parole, and the punishment range. . . .

* * *

3. Consequences of Construction

In considering the consequences of the construction of the statute, we conclude that it is more likely that the Legislature intended to limit the deadly weapon statute to humans. Although we are unpersuaded by many of appellant's arguments, we agree with his ultimate contention that it would be absurd to read the broadly written statute as permitting a deadly weapon finding for nonhuman victims.

* * *

In further considering the consequences of the construction suggested by the State, we are persuaded that the application of the deadly weapon statute to animal-victims in the animal-cruelty statute would lead to absurd results not intended by the Legislature through its broad phrasing in the statute. Appellant argues that allowing serious bodily injury to include nonhumans creates a slippery slope whereby causing death or serious bodily injury to any living creature could result in a deadly weapon finding. We agree. Permitting a deadly weapon finding in this case would necessarily mean that killing all animals could result in a deadly weapon finding. If this Court interpreted the broad phrasing in the deadly weapon statute to permit a deadly weapon finding for killing an animal covered in the animal-cruelty statute, that finding would significantly enhance the punishment that could be imposed against a defendant for causing serious bodily injury to or the death of, for example, frogs, lizards, turtles, and rats. The finding would not be limited to, for example, cats, dogs, or horses, or other animals that many people may view as pets or loved ones. . . .

Of course, we do not hold that it would be irrational or absurd for the Legislature to write a statute that expressly permits deadly weapon findings to elevate the punishment for exhibiting or using a deadly weapon that may threaten or cause serious bodily injury or death to certain animals or plants or even to all animals or plants. Rather, we hold that, given the broadness of the particular statutory language in the deadly weapon statute, and given our consideration of the extra-textual factors, here the Legislature's apparent intent as to this statute was to permit a deadly weapon finding for those weapons that are used or exhibited against humans only.

In sum, the extra-textual factors weigh in favor of a conclusion that the Legislature's intent was to limit deadly weapon findings for human victims only. Taking the legislative history, the objective of the statute, and the consequences of the interpretations of the statute into consideration, we conclude that the Legislature intended to permit a deadly weapon finding only if the recipient of the use or exhibition of the deadly weapon was a human. The parties agree that the recipient of the use or exhibition of the deadly weapon in this case was a nonhuman. We, therefore, hold that the evidence was insufficient to sustain the deadly weapon finding in this case, and we order that the trial court's judgment delete the deadly weapon finding [¶] . . . and remand the case to the trial court for a new punishment hearing.

* * *

Notes

1. Consider a similar analysis in *Commonwealth v. J.A.*, 478 Mass. 385 (2017). In that case, when the defendant was fourteen years old "he tortured a friend's dog by shoving a soap dispenser into the dog's vagina, resulting in serious internal injuries to the dog." (The dog underwent surgery and survived.) He was indicted as a "youthful offender" rather than as a "delinquent child," subjecting him to penalties that could include an adult sentence in state prison, as opposed to "rehabilitative penalties and remedies" if he had been convicted as a delinquent child. The youthful offender statute applied to offenses involving "serious bodily harm." Defendant moved to dismiss his conviction, arguing that "serious bodily harm" under that statute did not encompass harm to animals, only to human victims. The juvenile court judge granted the motion and the Massachusetts high court affirmed. In seeking to determine legislative intent, the court noted that, by its terms, the statute "neither expressly includes nor excludes bodily harm to animals." The court then considered language used in animal protection statutes, concluding that "[w]hen the Legislature intends a statute to protect animals, it does so directly and unambiguously." It went on to note that "[b]y and large, the statutes that prohibit the infliction of serious bodily injury apply only to human beings."

> Notably, the only place where the term "bodily injury" is used specifically to refer to both humans and animals is in the statute that provides for restraining orders to protect a person or a member of his or her family or household, including "domesticated animal[s]." This lone example demonstrates again that when the Legislature intends to include animals as victims in a statute, it does so expressly.

Id. at 388. Finally, the legislative history did not convince the court otherwise. The court pointed out that although the juvenile would not be treated as an adult, the Commonwealth could proceed by way of a complaint for delinquency, "where the flexibility to order mental health treatment exists."

As a matter of public policy, what are the pros and cons of treating the juvenile in this case as a delinquent rather than as a youthful offender? Consider the views in the *Commonwealth v. J.A.* concurring opinion below.

The concurring judge agreed with the statutory interpretation of the majority but went on to address broader public policy issues regarding the treatment and protection of animals in our society.

> A dog was horrifically tortured, and because her torturer was a teenager, the Commonwealth had limited recourse. I agree with the court that bodily harm to animals does not fall within the purview of the youthful offender statute as drafted. I write separately to highlight the Legislature's ability to amend the youthful offender statute or promulgate other legislation to better protect animals and the public.

> Preventing animal cruelty is a tenet of our collective humanity and a crucial public policy goal in Massachusetts. *See Commonwealth v. Duncan,* 467 Mass. 746, 751 (2014) ("Our statutes evince a focus on the prevention of both intentional and neglectful animal cruelty"). The Commonwealth also has a strong interest in identifying young people with violent tendencies and in preventing additional violence.

> Not only is preventing animal cruelty and abuse an important public policy goal for the sake of the animals, but the link between juvenile animal cruelty and abuse and later adulthood violence is well established as well. [Citing studies regarding the clear link between abuse of animals and abuse of other humans. See discussion of the link later in this chapter.]

> A juvenile who intentionally harms an animal displays a concerning propensity for viciousness. If the Commonwealth can respond to juvenile animal abuse effectively, it may help spare future victims, animal and human alike.

> The youthful offender statute, if amended, can provide the Commonwealth more flexibility when dealing with such disquieting cases of animal cruelty. Prosecutors then may be able to enlist the comprehensive assistance

of the criminal justice system in addressing allegations of animal cruelty that may be harbingers of violence to come.

Although there may be other avenues available to the Commonwealth, the youthful offender statute could have been the most appropriate response. If the Legislature wishes to empower prosecutors to respond to similar acts of animal brutality, it may expand the reach of the youthful offender statute and other statutes proscribing violence to better address animal abuse and cruelty in the Commonwealth.

Id. at 390–92 (*concurring op.*).

2. It is almost certain that when enacting the statutes at issue in *Prichard* and *J.A.* the legislatures were focused on human crime victims and did not consider whether they would have wanted the statutes to apply to the same crimes against animal victims. As the concurring judge in *J.A.* noted, legislatures act prospectively and cannot reasonably consider and specifically address every possible circumstance where the statute may be at issue, so that some flexibility in interpretation is appropriate for courts looking at challenges such as these. If it were to become common practice for legislatures to expressly refer to human and animal victims when enacting criminal statutes, could they avoid the problem of an expansive construction that may prompt a court to deem a statute overly broad, vague or ambiguous?

3. If an anti-cruelty statute is vague or does not provide proper notice to potential defendants, due process protections may prevent convictions. In *Commonwealth v. Kneller*, 971 A.2d 495 (Pa. Super. Ct. 2009), Wendy Kneller handed her boyfriend a pistol and told him to kill her dog, because the dog had bitten her child. The jury found Kneller guilty of criminal conspiracy to commit cruelty to animals. The appellate court reversed, finding the relevant state statute was not only confusing, but seemed to actually permit the shooting of one's own dog or cat. The statute provided: (1) "The killing of a dog or cat by the owner of that animal is not malicious if it is accomplished in accordance with" authorized methods of destruction, including an overdose of barbiturates; and (2) "Nothing in this act shall prevent a person or humane society organization from destroying a pet animal by means of firearms." *Id.* at 496. When read together, the court interpreted these provisions to mean that "in general one cannot kill an animal, *but* the owner of a dog or cat can destroy that dog or cat by means of an overdose of barbiturates or 'by means of firearms.'" *Id.* at 496–97 (emphasis in original). The court acknowledged that the legislature may have intended this provision to apply only to the humane killing of sick, injured, or unwanted animals, or animals with violent tendencies, but such intent was not clearly stated. Since other alternative (and equally reasonable) interpretations existed, the court concluded the legislature did not provide reasonable notice that shooting one's dog was a criminal act and, under such circumstances, the defendant's criminal conviction could not be upheld. *Id.* at 498 ("[A]s with all criminal statutes, if the legislature wishes to

make it criminal to shoot one's own dog or cat, it must do so in a clear, unambiguous manner.").

4. In *State v. Newcomb*, 359 Or. 756 (2016), excerpted later in this chapter, the Oregon Supreme Court addressed whether the defendant's constitutional privacy interests in her animal property were violated by the testing of her severely neglected dog's blood after a lawful seizure of the dog. In line with the foregoing cases, the court found that "the trial court . . . at least implicitly found that Dr. Hedge performed the tests for medical reasons by analogizing this case in its ruling to one in which an abused child taken into custody is medically examined for purposes of diagnosis and treatment." *Id.* at 769 n.12.

Section 4. Affirmative Acts of Cruelty

The next two sections divide animal cruelty cases based on one parameter (affirmative versus passive conduct of the defendants) that provides an important way of distinguishing the variations in conduct and motive. This distinction affects societal views of the crime and proof requirements at trial and sentencing. Ultimately, all animal cruelty cases rely on evidence of the effect of the defendant's conduct upon the animals in question, but the manner of presenting and proving these cases is dictated in part by the differences highlighted in these sections.

This section discusses circumstances involving some degree of active conduct by the defendant, as distinguished from acts of omission resulting in harm, such as starving, failing to provide appropriate veterinary care, or other neglect. Cockfighting, dogfighting, and other types of animal fighting are crimes in all fifty states and would qualify as affirmative acts of cruelty. Affirmative acts, however, should not be confused with intentionality. One can intentionally fail to feed a cat just as easily as one can intentionally kick a dog. Both affirmative acts and acts of omission usually require a specific *mens rea* standard to be met. However, acts of omission can be prosecuted as animal cruelty without proving an intentional act has been committed. The specific language of the applicable statute will determine the *mens rea* (if any is required) that must be proven to successfully prosecute a case.

As the following cases demonstrate, vagueness issues also arise in the use of qualifying words such as "cruelly," "unjustifiably," "maliciously," and "willfully." On one hand such terms provide some discretion and flexibility to the interpretation of anti-cruelty laws; on the other hand, the qualifying language can also reduce prosecutors' ability to prove cruelty. This could be by legislative design or a problem with the drafting. As you read the following cases, consider what value, if any, such qualifiers add to an anti-cruelty statute. And consider in this context, as you did with the preceding cases, whether the absence of such language could make prosecution more difficult or subject the statute to charges of overbreadth and/or vagueness.

Oliver v. City of Anaheim

United States Court of Appeals, Ninth Circuit, 2012
490 Fed. App'x. 890 (Unpublished)

KOZINSKI, CHIEF JUDGE, and REINHARDT, CIRCUIT JUDGE. [*C.B. Oliver and his father were arrested by police officers who believed they had violated California's anti-cruelty law when they "bash[ed] a mother opossum on the head three times with a metal shovel." The Olivers, after avoiding criminal convictions, sued the officers and the City of Anaheim under 42 U.S.C. section 1983 for violating their constitutional rights, based on the Olivers' argument that it was indisputable that their acts did not violate the statute. The City defended, claiming qualified immunity because the law was not established that the Olivers' act was not criminal. In reversing that holding, the Ninth Circuit ruled:*] The officers had no probable cause to arrest C.B. and Oliver because the act the officers believed C.B. committed—trying to kill the opossum by hitting it with a shovel—isn't a crime. While section 597(a) of the California Penal Code prohibits the intentional and malicious killing of animals, section 599c provides, "No part of this title shall be construed . . . as interfering with the right to destroy . . . any animal known as dangerous to life, limb, or property." Regulations confirm that opossums are dangerous by explicitly permitting their killing. Cal.Code Regs. tit. 14, § 472(a). The regulations do prohibit certain ways of killing animals, but hitting them with a shovel is not among them. Cal .Code Regs. tit. 14, § 475. Indeed, if section 597(a) were construed as prohibiting the killing of wild opossums, it would impermissibly nullify California's laws that permit killing them.

People v. Thomason, 84 Cal.App.4th 1064 (2000), held that mice bought at a feed store were not "dangerous to life, limb, or property," as required by section 599c. By contrast, wild opossums are dangerous to property. *See* T.P. Salmon et al., Univ. of Cal., Pub. No. 74123, Pest Notes: Opossum 2 (2005). Indeed, the opossum C.B. allegedly struck had injured the family's bulldogs. *Thomason* is also inapposite because the defendant there tortured the mice. The police here had no evidence that plaintiffs did anything more than try to kill the opossum, which they were entitled to do.

Because C.B.'s act wasn't criminal, there was no cause to arrest him. And, without an underlying criminal act, Oliver couldn't have been an accessory or an aider and abettor. The arrests violated the plaintiffs' constitutional rights. Therefore, the officers are not entitled to qualified immunity. Nor are they entitled to immunity under state law because a reasonable officer could not have believed that the arrests of C.B. and Oliver were lawful.

Reversed and Remanded.

WATFORD, Circuit Judge, dissenting:

The question facing the officers in this case was whether bashing a mother opossum on the head three times with a metal shovel constitutes "maliciously and intentionally . . . wound[ing] a living animal" in violation of California Penal Code section 597(a). I am not sure such conduct in fact violates the statute; even today, California law remains unclear on that score. At the same time, nothing in California law has clearly established that such conduct does *not* violate the statute. The best guidance available on the scope of section 597(a) is *People v. Thomason*, which held that, even though animals covered by Penal Code section 599c and associated game regulations may be killed at will, they are still protected by section 597(a)'s prohibition on malicious and intentional wounding. Whether bashing a mother opossum on the head three times with a metal shovel is sufficiently egregious to constitute a malicious and intentional wounding is certainly debatable. But the very fact that reasonable minds could disagree is what entitles the officers to qualified immunity here.

Notes

1. The doctrine of qualified immunity at issue in the *Oliver* case serves to protect law enforcement from civil liability for conduct that could reasonably be interpreted as having been done in good faith. The Ninth Circuit majority, faced with the facts in *Oliver*, found no possibility that a reasonable officer might believe that bashing a mother opossum over the head constituted criminal animal cruelty, despite the prohibition against "intentional and malicious cruelty." Under the rule in this case, is there any level of cruelty or killing not enumerated in the regulations cited in the case that would trigger criminal liability in killing the opossum or would at least provide qualified immunity to an officer arresting the defendants? What if the defendants had caught the opossum in a cage and then drowned her? Set her on fire? Hung her by her tail and stoned her until she was dead?

2. In this case, the majority distinguished between animals that are "dangerous to life, limb, or property" and those that are not, concluding that wild opossums pose such a danger based on its interpretation of California regulations allowing the killing of "nongame mammals." The court went on to state that torturing mice (not dangerous, according to the court) is wholly different than trying to kill an opossum (supposedly dangerous) with a shovel. Yet the dissenting judge believed that because such a distinction under law is "certainly debatable" the officers should have been entitled to qualified immunity for their role in arresting the perpetrators.

3. A constant source of frustration for animal protection advocates are the lines drawn between different species of animals, based solely on their utility to humans, for purposes of determining levels of protection. For example, companion animals such as dogs and cats typically enjoy heightened protections when compared to wildlife and farmed animals. This creates dissonance in the types of activities humans can engage in with one species as compared to another. Under the law in most jurisdictions, a homeowner can use virtually any method to rid the premises of unwanted pests (such as mice, rats, snakes, birds), no matter how painful or prolonged the process may be. If an animal such as a snake or a mouse is identified as a "companion animal," however, would those same actions be deemed criminal under the anti-cruelty statutes? If so, do you consider this disparate treatment for the same animal under different circumstances to be appropriate and defensible?

People v. Voelker

Criminal Court of the City of New York, Kings County, 1997
172 Misc. 2d 564, 658 N.Y.S.2d 180

MORGENSTERN, Judge. Can a defendant insulate himself from prosecution on First Amendment grounds by televising the criminal acts of decapitating three live, conscious iguanas in violation of the State's anti-cruelty statute?

Defendant was arrested on October 2, 1996 and charged with three counts of Overdriving, Torturing and Injuring animals pursuant to section 353 of the Agriculture and Markets Law ("AML"). These charges stem from a videotaped incident wherein defendant is alleged to have cut off the heads of three live, conscious iguanas without justification. Defendant was arraigned in criminal court on November 19, 1996. A superseding complaint was filed on November 22, 1996.

Defendant moves to dismiss the accusatory instrument . . . upon the ground that it is facially insufficient in that it fails to adequately allege every element of the offense charged. . . . Defendant also maintains that dismissal is required because the statute is being unconstitutionally applied.

The complaint in this case alleges, in pertinent part, that on or about and between February 6, 1996 and August 2, 1996 at 85 Havemeyer Street, apartment 1L, in Brooklyn, the defendant allegedly cut off the heads of three live, conscious iguanas without justification. The complaint alleges further that Assistant District Attorney Todd Davis (hereinafter deponent) is in possession of and has viewed a videotape showing the defendant committing the acts alleged. Additionally, the complaint alleges that deponent was informed:

> by Michael Pescatore that informant is the owner of the building at the above location, that he has viewed the videotape mentioned above, that the room pictured in said videotape is inside the above location, and that informant leased the apartment that includes said room at the above location to Eric Voelker from February 6, 1996 to the present; [and]

> by Frank Fitzgerald that informant recorded said videotape on August 9, 1996, from a television broadcast by Manhattan Neighborhood Network of the show entitled "Sick and Wrong," and that informant saw the same incident broadcast on an earlier edition of the show, "Sick and Wrong," aired on August 2, 1996.

Defendant maintains that an essential element of AML § 353 is an "unjustifiable act" toward an animal, and that the allegation that defendant cut off the heads of three live iguanas, "without justification," is conclusory and insufficient. Defendant contends that killing the animals in this case was justified and necessary and that any pain or suffering was temporary, unavoidable and without criminal intent.

The People maintain that the term "without justification" means just what it says, that defendant cut off the heads of three animals without apparent justification.

Thus, the allegations in the accusatory instrument provide reasonable cause to believe that the defendant committed the offense charged and establish, if true, every element of the offense charged.

The People maintain further that defendant's alleged "justification defense" does not support the motion to dismiss and that the issue of justification is a question of fact to be determined at trial. Additionally, the People argue that defendant's acts were unjustified in that defendant violated the State's anti-cruelty statute by cutting off the heads of three conscious iguanas and that the mere fact that defendant thereafter allegedly cooked and consumed these animals does not justify defendant's actions.

* * *

AML § 353 provides that:

> A person who overdrives, overloads, tortures or cruelly beats or unjustifi-ably injures, maims, mutilates or kills any animal, whether wild or tame, and whether belonging to himself or to another, . . . or causes, procures or permits any animal to be overdriven, overloaded, tortured, cruelly beaten, or unjustifiably injured, maimed, mutilated or killed, . . . or in any way fur-thers any act of cruelty to any animal, or any act tending to produce such cruelty, is guilty of a misdemeanor. . . .

An "Animal" is defined as "every living creature except a human being" (AML § 350[1]), and "torture" is defined as "every act, omission, or neglect, whereby unjus-tifiable physical pain, suffering or death is caused or permitted" (AML § 350[2]).

In *People ex rel. Freel v. Downs*, 136 N.Y.S. 440 (1911), defendant, captain of a ship, was convicted of causing, procuring and permitting turtles to be transported in a manner that caused unnecessary and unjustifiable pain and suffering. The turtles had their fins pierced and were tied together through the holes with a string. The court explained that "[t]he question as to whether the pain caused to such crea-tures, often classed as dull nervous organisms, is 'justifiable' or not, cannot be easily answered." *Id.* at 445. Moreover, the court held that the question of what constitutes cruelty is an issue of fact to be decided upon all the evidence in a prosecution for cruelty to animals. *Id.* at 446.

Defendant cites the *Downs* decision (*supra*) for the proposition that where the acts against the animal are "temporary, unavoidable, and without criminal intent . . . than [sic] it is not torture as that term is here employed." Defendant's reliance on *Downs* is misplaced in that he misquotes the *Downs* decision. In *Downs*, *supra*, at 444, the court held that:

> [t]he torture that would justify a criminal prosecution must be some mode of inflicting bodily pain that is unjustifiable and unnecessary; but if the pain and suffering is temporary, unavoidable and without criminal intent, *and necessary to preserve the safety of the property involved and to overcome any danger or injury to such property, then it is not torture as that term is employed in legal parlance.* (Emphasis added.)

Thus, it is clear that the justification for killing or torturing the animals must be of the type necessary to preserve the safety of property or to overcome danger or injury, or the type of legal justification specifically authorized by law. Moreover, whether an act of cruelty and infliction of pain was justified or unjustified is a question to be determined by the trier of facts based upon the moral standards of the community.

In this case, to establish a *prima facie* case of overdriving, torturing and injuring animals, the information must contain nonhearsay factual allegations which establish that defendant did torture or unjustifiably injure, maim, mutilate or kill three live iguanas.

This court holds that the acts of cutting off the heads of three conscious iguanas are acts which certainly injure, maim, mutilate and kill. This court holds further that the term "without justification" is not a legal conclusion but a factual allegation that means what it says, *i.e.*, with no apparent justification; to demand that the People address an infinite number of justification defenses would place an undue burden on the People requiring them to supply trial quality evidence in the body of an accusatory instrument. Whether or not the People can prove that defendant "unjustifiably" committed these acts is a matter best left to the trier of facts. . . .

The fact that defendant has set forth what he calls a "justification defense" in his motion does not compel a different result since defendant does not claim that his acts were necessary to preserve the safety of property or to overcome danger or injury. Moreover, in considering a motion to dismiss for facial insufficiency, the court is bound by the four corners of the accusatory instrument and may not consider extraneous allegations contained in a motion to dismiss or an answer to a motion to dismiss.

Accordingly, defendant's motion to dismiss for facial insufficiency is denied.

Defendant also moves for dismissal upon the ground that AML § 353 is being unconstitutionally applied in that the motivation for the prosecution of defendant is that he chose to televise an act that is normally relegated to the back room of a restaurant, and that such content-based restrictions on speech are unconstitutional.

There is no question that government action that stifles speech on account of its message, or that requires the utterance of a particular message favored by the government, contravenes an individual's rights under the First Amendment. *Turner Broadcasting v. F.C.C.*, 512 U.S. 622 (1994). However, it is well established that a content-neutral restriction on speech will be upheld if "it furthers an important or substantial governmental interest; if the governmental interest is unrelated to the suppression of free expression; and if the incidental restriction on alleged First Amendment freedoms is no greater than is essential to the furtherance of that interest." *Id.* at 662, *quoting United States v. O'Brien*, 391 U.S. 367, 377 (1968).

Contrary to defendant's contention, this court holds that the animal cruelty statute at issue is not a content-based restriction on speech. Rather, it is a restriction against torturing, injuring, maiming, mutilating or killing animals. The statute is not directed at any form of communication. Furthermore, the People correctly point out that although the statute might prohibit the torturing of an animal as a form of expression, such a statute would not be unconstitutional where it serves a legitimate governmental interest, and that the United States Supreme Court has indicated that a neutral anti-cruelty statute which is limited to the Government's legitimate interest in the prevention of cruelty to animals may be upheld despite its effect on religious observance. *Church of Lukumi Babalu Aye v. City of Hialeah*, 508 U.S. 520, 538 (1993).

Moreover, defendant is not being prosecuted because he televised the decapitation of the iguanas. The televising of the decapitations merely provided law enforcement officials with a way to observe defendant engage in criminal activity. A defendant cannot shelter himself from prosecution by the mere televising of a criminal act. Taking defendant's argument to its logical conclusion, a defendant could televise any criminal act and seek to shield himself from prosecution on First Amendment grounds. Such an argument defies common sense and cannot be sustained.

The court holds that AML § 353 is not being unconstitutionally applied in this case. Accordingly, defendant's motion to dismiss is denied on this ground.

Notes

1. The court in *Voelker* notes that after the iguanas were killed, they were eaten. Is there, or should there be, an ethical or legal difference between killing cows behind slaughterhouse walls and killing iguanas on cable television, if the principal purpose behind both activities is to consume the killed animals as food? What about killing iguanas behind closed doors? How would you articulate the difference?

2. New York's anti-cruelty statute AML § 353 uses the adverb "unjustifiably" to modify "injures, maims, mutilates or kills any animal." As you read in Section 2, the language in state anti-cruelty statutes varies, but many have some variation of this phrasing when referring to injury or death of an animal ("unjustifiable" or "unnecessary").

3. Though the number of wild green iguanas around the world is dropping due to habitat loss, and they are a treasured companion animal on the mainland United States, they are considered a pest in Puerto Rico. Iguanas are herbivores and their appetite for fruit often conflicts with the interests of Puerto Rican farmers. With no natural predators on the island, their numbers have soared over the last few decades. While local lawmakers are still debating the sale of iguana meat, hunting tourism for the animals has stepped in as a form of population control. For a fee, spotters take hunters, armed with air rifles and pellet guns, to areas where iguana populations swell. The harvested meat can be eaten while on the island or sent back home with the hunter. Arian Campo-Flores, *To Battle Iguanas, Puerto Rico Has New Plan: Put Them on Menu*, Wall St. J., Aug. 19, 2012. Do you think this is what the drafters of statutes such as AML § 353 mean by "justifiable"?

4. In the last few decades, websites have been created showing animal cruelty in grotesque detail. These so-called "crush videos" and related websites have been targeted by society and animal protection groups. According to a House Committee Report,

> such videos feature the intentional torture and killing of helpless animals, including cats, dogs, monkeys, mice, and hamsters. H.R. Rep. No. 106-397, p. 2 (1999). Crush videos often depict women slowly crushing animals to death "with their bare feet or while wearing high heeled shoes," sometimes while "talking to the animals in a kind of dominatrix patter" over "[t]he cries and squeals of the animals, obviously in great pain." *Ibid.* Apparently these depictions "appeal to persons with a very specific sexual fetish who find them sexually arousing or otherwise exciting." *Id.,* at 2–3.

U.S. v. Stevens, 559 U.S. 460, 465–66 (2010).

In 1999, President Bill Clinton signed 18 U.S.C. § 48 into law. The law prohibited interstate commerce in, and commercial gain from, the distribution of depictions of animal cruelty, including crush videotapes. In 2010, the United States Supreme Court struck it down as unconstitutional on overbreadth/First Amendment (free speech) grounds, in a case involving the sale of videotapes of dogfighting. *U.S. v. Stevens,* 559 U.S. 460 (2010). (*Stevens* is excerpted in Chapter 5.) Later that year, Congress modified 18 U.S.C. § 48 with a narrower law specifically geared to crush videos, entitled the "Animal Crush Video Prohibition Act of 2010." A federal district court ruled that the new law also violated the First Amendment, but on appeal the Fifth Circuit reversed the lower court decision, thereby reinstating the revised law. *State v. Richards,* 755 F.3d 269 (5th Cir. 2014). Crush videotapes were also at issue in the *People v. Thomason* case referenced by the Ninth Circuit in *Oliver,* above, and excerpted in Section 8 of this chapter.

People v. Dunn

Court of Appeal of California, First Appellate District, 1974
39 Cal. App. 3d 418, 114 Cal. Rptr. 164

DRAPER, P.J. Charged with maliciously maiming, wounding and killing animals which were the property of another (Pen. Code § 597, subd. (a)), appellant was found guilty by a jury and was admitted to probation on condition he serve six months in county jail and make restitution. He appeals.

Appellant lived on 23 acres of land in a large tract over which animals, belonging to one Cabezut, had ranged freely for some years. Appellant had planted some fruit trees. Some of Cabezut's livestock began to feed on the newly planted trees. Appellant never complained to Cabezut but drove off the animals by throwing rocks. On March 15, 1973, however, he fired at them, using a .22 rifle on one occasion, and a shotgun on another. Two colts were killed, a mare was so seriously wounded in the neck and stomach that she had to be put out of her misery, and a jackass, also shot in the stomach, survived.

The trial court instructed the jury that malice was an element of the crime, and defined malice as "an intent to do a wrongful act" (Pen. Code § 7, subd. 4, 2d cl.) but refused to instruct that such malice must be directed to "another person," *i.e.*, the owner. Subdivision (a) of section 597 makes it an offense to "maliciously" maim, wound, or kill the animal of another. Subdivision (b) proscribes acts of cruelty to "any animal," whether owned by the defendant or another. Subdivision (b) does not use the word "maliciously." Hence appellant argues that the malice required by subdivision (a) necessarily must be against the owner himself. We cannot agree.

As initially enacted in 1872, section 597 provided that "[e]very person who maliciously kills, maims, or wounds an animal, the property of another, or who maliciously and cruelly beats, tortures, or injures any animal, whether belonging to himself or another, is guilty of a misdemeanor." The 1905 amendment omitted the word "maliciously" from the definition of the offense against an animal not owned by another. It is apparent, however, that the intent was not to alter the direction or object of the malice. Rather, the amendment added numerous specific acts of cruelty to an animal owned by a defendant. Each of these was of a nature—*e.g.*, "tortures," "torments," "cruelly beats"—necessarily implying the necessity of malice in the second sense of the code definition (Pen. Code § 7, subd. 4, 2d cl.), "an intent to do a wrongful act." The code commissioner's note to the 1905 amendment states that its purpose is to consolidate two existing sections "for the more effectual prevention of cruelty to animals." This emphasizes that the Legislature by no means intended to switch emphasis from the cruelty to animals element to a factor of malice toward the animal's owner.

Thus we find no error in the court's failure to instruct that the word "maliciously" imports a wish to "vex, annoy, or injure another person." That instruction would be proper under a statute designed to proscribe malicious mischief, but has no place in a statute intended to prohibit cruelty to animals, which section 597 clearly is intended to do.

The court instructed the jury that appellant's remedy against the strays was to drive them off or to confine them, and to sue their owner for damage to the land or crops and for the expense of keeping the animals if captured. This instruction was correct. It further instructed that appellant could use reasonable force to drive off the animals but that use of force beyond that limit is regarded by the law as excessive and unjustified, and subjects the user of such force to the legal consequences thereof. The court correctly refused to instruct that Cabezut had a duty to confine his animals to prevent them from trespassing, and that the jury should weigh this duty against appellant's duty to refrain from use of excessive force. We find no error.

Judgment affirmed.

Notes

1. In *People v. Tessmer*, 137 N.W. 214 (Mich. 1912), the defendant was convicted of animal cruelty after putting a strap around the tongue of a bay mare owned by someone else and pulling it with all his strength. The injuries were so severe that the

animal had to be euthanized. The defendant claimed he was angry at the animal for her refusal to work, rather than at the animal's owner. He argued that this absence of malice toward the owner precluded a conviction. The court held that the jury need not find the malice directed toward the animal's owner to find the defendant guilty. Rather, the court affirmed the trial court's jury instruction that stated in part: "If you find from the evidence in this case that [defendant] had the intent to do the act charged against him in the information unlawfully, it makes no difference whether it be from spite or revenge or hope of gain and profit; malice may be presumed from that conduct." *Id.* at 216.

2. Much like the court in *Tessmer*, the *Dunn* court dismissed the argument that the jury should have been instructed that the term "maliciously" means a wish to vex, annoy, or injure another *person*. The court held it was sufficient to prove there was merely "intent to do wrong." Does this finding suggest that animals should be afforded legal protection based on their own independent interest in not being harmed?

3. Very often, animals suffer the consequences of their owners' acts or omissions. For example, some states give livestock owners or even non-owner third parties broad discretion to kill a dog they believe to have chased, harassed or killed livestock. *See, e.g., Katsaris v. Cook*, 180 Cal. App. 3d 256 (1986) (statute allowed trespassing dog to be killed where livestock are on the property, regardless of the dog's conduct), excerpted in Chapter 4.

4. Many of the anti-cruelty laws date back more than 100 years, when societal views of dogs (and most animals, especially companion animals) were markedly different than today. As these views have developed, laws relating to livestock-chasing dogs have come under increasing public scrutiny. The self-help doctrine, which authorizes the killing of animals without due process, may at some point be reconsidered. Since we have left the period in which ecclesiastical courts were prosecuting animals for their crimes, does it make sense to shift responsibility to the owners of animals who do harm? Consider the benefits and disadvantages of this approach.

5. Consider the following case: "A pro-tem judge and candidate for Multnomah County [Oregon] circuit judge is drawing criticism for ordering a homeless man's three dogs confiscated and destroyed if he doesn't pay fines for not licensing them. Mary A. Overgaard ordered Spanky, Tuffy and Baby Girl euthanized if Jimmy Dean Workman does not pay $60 in fines within 45 days of the dogs being seized." David R. Anderson, *Judge's Order Against Dogs Bites Back*, Oregonian, May 7, 1998, at D2. The court's order caused immediate public response due to the perception that the dogs would be required to pay with their lives for the owner's infraction. As a result of public pressure, Judge Overgaard amended her order to provide that the dogs be confiscated and placed for adoption if the fines were not timely paid. Do you think the judge was taking the animals' interests into consideration when amending the order, or might she have had another rationale? Should exceptions to licensing rules be introduced for people of limited means?

6. The practice of blaming and punishing animals for human actions has a long, interesting history in Europe (as you know from Section 1 of this chapter) and in this country as well. For example, in 1692 (during the same period as the famous Salem witch trials) John Bradstreet was accused of bewitching a dog into committing a crime in Massachusetts. Bradstreet wisely fled to New Hampshire to avoid prosecution. However, the dog was not so lucky—she was tried, found guilty and subsequently hanged. *See* Daniel Pickering, DICTIONARY OF WITCHCRAFT 232 (London, Cassell 1996).

7. As noted in Section 2 of this chapter and as discussed in Chapter 6, many states have express exemptions from the anti-cruelty statutes for most customary farming practices, although more egregious acts of cruelty arguably could be prosecuted under the general anti-cruelty statutes. Prosecutors surely distinguish between farmed animals and companion animals when considering a case for prosecution, even in those states or situations where there is no specific exemption for practices with respect to farmed animals. Should a different standard apply to farmed animals when determining whether a particular act rises to the level of criminal cruelty or neglect? For further analysis of anti-cruelty laws as they apply to farmed animals, *see generally*, David J. Wolfson, *McLibel*, 5 ANIMAL L. 21 (1999); Steven J. Havercamp, *Are Moderate Animal Welfare Laws and a Sustainable Agricultural Economy Mutually Exclusive? Laws, Moral Implications, and Recommendations*, 46 DRAKE L. REV. 645 (1998); David J. Wolfson, *Beyond the Law: Agribusiness and the Systematic Abuse of Animals Raised for Food or Food Production*, 2 ANIMAL L. 123 (1996).

8. In all cases of animal abuse, the importance of an adequate and immediate veterinary exam and report cannot be overstated. Some veterinarians do not have the requisite training to complete a forensic examination or recognize signs of abuse. In these cases, lawyers should get involved early and actively to identify qualified veterinary personnel to assist in the analysis of injuries and causation. Prosecutors or those helping them should immediately evaluate the evidence that will be most convincing at trial—both in terms of establishing the elements of the crime and presenting the most compelling facts. Pictures, videotapes, and detailed medical records are the types of documentation most likely to become (or at least preserve) evidence and ultimately to prove a cruelty case. In *Celinski v. State*, 911 S.W.2d 177, 180–181 (Tex. Ct. App. 1995), for example, the court upheld a jury verdict convicting the defendant based largely on circumstantial evidence, including cat hair and fluid recovered from the inside of a microwave, and supporting testimony from a veterinarian. As stated by the court, "any theory that a large amount of cat fur was left in the microwave oven by some other cat, or by some process other than torture, is neither reasonable nor consistent with the evidence." *Id.* at 181.

9. Evidence of cruelty is sometimes lost (either through the death of an animal or healed wounds) in the time between the commission of the crime and the initial investigation. Therefore, it is imperative that shelter workers, veterinarians, and

others who are likely to be among the first in contact with abused animals have the tools necessary to recognize, report, and create a record of animal cruelty. Currently, few resources exist for these individuals to learn how to recognize and report cruelty—although educational and training materials and sessions are increasing. *See, e.g.,* Recognizing & Reporting Animal Abuse: A Veterinarian's Guide (Patricia Olsen ed., 1998); *http://www.aspca.org/fight-animal-cruelty/how -to-recognize-cruelty.html* (last visited Feb. 2018); and the Tufts Animal Care and Condition (TACC) scales for assessing body condition, weather and environmental safety, and physical care in dogs, created by Dr. Gary Patronek, *http://vet.tufts.edu /wp-content/uploads/tacc.pdf* (last visited Feb. 2018).

10. Courts considering cruelty cases often determine penalties based on animals' demonstrable physical injuries. Generally, however, prosecutors do not consider animals' psychological pain and suffering because most courts (and juries) are not receptive to the notion that such an injury is significant enough to be considered; nor has psychological injury ever been considered a meaningful part of any evaluation of the severity of the crime. Yet it is a scientifically and medically accepted fact that at least some animals do experience this kind of injury. *See, e.g.,* Marc Bekoff, "Animal Emotions: Exploring Passionate Natures: Current interdisciplinary research provides compelling evidence that many animals experience such emotions as joy, fear, love, despair, and grief—we are not alone," 50 BioScience 861-70 (Oct. 1, 2000). Should courts considering anti-cruelty cases take animals' psychological pain and suffering into account in determining the penalties? How would you prove this at trial given the fact that, generally speaking, animals cannot communicate using human language?[e]

People v. Garcia

Supreme Court of New York, Appellate Division, First Department, 2006
812 N.Y.S.2d 66, 29 A.D.3d 255

CATTERSON, Justice. The earliest known domestic animal appears to be the dog, a companion to mankind as early as 15000 B.C. Goats, sheep, pigs and cows followed in domestication in the next 10,000 years. Horses, however, did not succumb to the lure of mankind's presence until 4000 B.C. . . . The goldfish's leap from domesticated fish to family pet and companion may have happened as early as 1368 during the Ming Dynasty. The goldfish's popularity in the West began as the first public aquarium opened in London in 1853. Keeping goldfish as companions and pets in the United States has been popular since that time.

---

e. A few notable exceptions exist, though they have never been used in court. There have been a number of chimpanzees and one gorilla who have been able to communicate directly with humans using American Sign Language. For more information, *see* Roger Fouts & Stephan Turkel Mills, Next Of Kin—What Chimpanzees Have Taught Me About Who We Are (1997); The Great Ape Project: Equality Beyond Humanity (Paola Cavalieri & Peter Singer eds. 1993).

Agriculture and Markets Law § 353-a(1), "Aggravated cruelty to animals," represents the Legislature's recognition that man's inhumanity to man often begins with inhumanity to those creatures that have formed particularly close relationships with mankind. The scope of section 353-a(1) is a question of first impression for the Appellate Division, and the instant case compels the conclusion that its reach is broad.

On August 2, 2003, Emelie Martinez was living in an apartment with the defendant, her three children, Juan Torres, Crystal and Emaleeann, and Jesus Rabassa, an 18-year-old high school student. Juan was nine years old, Crystal eight and Emaleeann five. Also living in the apartment were two dogs, a cat, and three goldfish named after the children, Junior, Crystal and Emma.

At about 3:00 a.m., Martinez awoke on the sofa to find the defendant standing over her, holding the fish tank. She asked him what he was doing. The defendant threw the fish tank into the television set, saying, "That could have been you." The fish tank shattered, as did the television screen and a portion of a glass wall unit. The defendant also destroyed Juan's VCR by ripping it out and throwing it against the wall unit.

Eventually, the defendant and Martinez began cleaning up the mess. Juan came out of his room, with the girls behind him, crying. The defendant turned to Juan and said, "You want to see something awesome?" and stomped on Juan's fish, killing the fish. Martinez had to calm the children before she could continue cleaning up the mess.

* * *

The trial court also convicted the defendant of aggravated cruelty to animals, a felony. The court determined that the pet goldfish of Martinez and her children was a companion animal within the meaning of Agriculture and Markets Law § 353-a(1) and § 350(5), and that the statute is not unconstitutionally vague.

* * *

The defendant argues that his "stomping of young Juan's pet goldfish" is a misdemeanor pursuant to Agriculture and Markets Law § 353 (unjustifiable killing of any animal, whether wild or tame), and not a felony because a fish is not a "companion animal" and his "stomping" did not constitute "aggravated cruelty" within the meaning of the statute.

Agriculture and Markets Law § 353-a(1) provides: "A person is guilty of aggravated cruelty to animals when, with no justifiable purpose, he or she intentionally kills or intentionally causes serious physical injury to a companion animal with aggravated cruelty. For purposes of this section, 'aggravated cruelty' shall mean conduct which: (i) is intended to cause extreme physical pain; or (ii) is done or carried out in an especially depraved or sadistic manner."

The term "companion animal" is defined in section 350(5):

"Companion animal" or "pet" means any dog or cat, and shall also mean any other domesticated animal normally maintained in or near the household of the owner or person who cares for such other domesticated animal. "Pet" or "companion animal" shall not include a "farm animal" as defined in this section.

The defendant contends that a fish is not a companion animal because it is not domesticated and because there is no reciprocity or mutuality of feeling between a fish and its owner, such as there is between a dog or a cat and its owner.

In the absence of a definition in the statute, the defendant, citing 4 Am Jur 2d, Animals § 2 (at 346 [Lawyers Coop Publ 1995]), defines "domesticated animals" as those that "no longer possess the disposition or inclination to escape," and claims that "if dropped in a pond and offered the opportunity to swim away, a goldfish will do so without any hesitation and not look back." He maintains that the statute's reference to "any other" domesticated animal limits "companion animal[s]" to those that are similar to dogs or cats, that is, those with a degree of sentience sufficiently elevated to enable them to enter into a relationship of mutual affection with a human being. Furthermore, "[b]eloved household pets (fish) may be, but 'companion animals' in the same vein as dogs or cats they are not."

The defendant's contention that all household pets are equal but some are more equal than others is manifestly not derived from the statute. The Legislature simply did not require a reciprocity of affection in the definition of "companion animal." To the contrary, the statutory language is consistent with the People's contention that, "domesticated" is commonly understood to mean "to adapt (an animal or plant) to life in intimate association with and to the advantage of humans." Thus, a goldfish such as the one herein is a domesticated rather than a wild animal within the common meaning of the term. Moreover, the goldfish was, as the statute requires, "normally maintained in or near the household of the owner or person who cares for [it]." Indeed, acknowledging that the goldfish is one of the most common household pets, defense counsel stipulated at trial that there are "millions of fish owners throughout the country."

The defendant's argument that goldfish are not domesticated animals because given the opportunity they would leave home is without merit. While this trait arguably distinguishes fish from dogs and, probably to a lesser extent cats, it fails to take into account that many other animals commonly considered pets, such as hermit crabs, gerbils, hamsters, guinea pigs and rabbits, would depart for less confining venues and greener pastures if given the opportunity. Loyalty, if that is what it is, is merely another characteristic urged by defendant—but not included by the Legislature—as a defining feature of a companion animal.

Moreover, Agriculture and Markets Law § 353-a(2) provides that "[n]othing contained in this section shall be construed to prohibit or interfere in any way with anyone lawfully engaged in hunting, trapping, or fishing. . . ." (Emphasis added.) This provision would be superfluous if a fish could not be considered a companion animal.

While the defendant maintains that the statute's definition of "companion animal" is unconstitutionally vague, we find, as did the trial court, the statute sufficiently clear to apprise a person of ordinary intelligence that the sort of conduct in which the defendant engaged comes within the statute's prohibition.

The defendant further asserts that because the fish's death was instantaneous, it was not accompanied by "extreme physical pain" or accomplished with "especial[]" depravity or sadism, and that therefore the killing was not accomplished with any heightened level of cruelty. The trial court correctly observed that the legislative history of the statute indicates that the crime was established in recognition of the correlation between violence against animals and subsequent violence against human beings. Thus, it must be inferred that the Legislature's concern was with the state of mind of the perpetrator rather than that of the victim.

* * *

Notes

1. Refer back to Chapter 1 regarding classifications of "animal," "wild animal," and "domestic animal." "Companion animal" is the most recent entry into the multiple ways animals are categorized in the law. Recall the cases in Chapter 1 that discussed people keeping cougars, bears, monkeys, and deer. Would they be companion animals under the New York statute? Note that the definitions apply in different contexts so that, for example, a monkey might be a companion animal for purposes of evaluating criminal cruelty, but a prohibited wild animal under a law limiting the types of animals that can be kept in a jurisdiction.

2. The court clearly believed that Junior (the goldfish) was the victim of the crime. But Juan was also a victim, as he was forced to watch Junior be sadistically killed. The trial court opinion suggests that the impact of Garcia's conduct on Juan may have been a factor in determining whether Garcia was guilty of a crime: "[W] hile humans can and do kill and eat fish on a regular basis, they do not do so if the fish at issue is a pet goldfish belonging to a young child . . . [D]efendant's killing of Junior, the fish, under these circumstances could only have been undertaken for the purpose of destroying a creature the boy held dear, namely his pet." *People v. Garcia*, 777 N.Y.S.2d 846, 852 (Sup. Ct. 2004). Do you think the impact of Garcia's conduct on Juan should have been a factor for purposes of conviction or sentencing?

Waters v. People

Supreme Court of Colorado, 1896
23 Colo. 33, 46 P. 112

CAMPBELL, J. This prosecution, instituted by the humane society . . . where the plaintiff in error (defendant below) was found guilty and sentenced to pay a fine, resulted in a conviction and a fine. . . . To this latter judgment the defendant prosecutes his writ of error in this court.

In the county court, by an agreement of parties, the cause was submitted to the decision of the court, without a jury, upon this agreed statement of facts:

The defendant was at the time of the matter complained of in this case a member of what is known as the "County Club," the same being an organization of gentlemen, for the purpose of amusement, and its operations were carried on in El Paso county, Colorado.

That on or about the 12th day of January, 1895, the defendant, together with other members of said club, owned forty (40) live doves, which they had obtained and kept in confinement for the purpose of using them as targets to shoot at for their amusement; that at said time the doves were placed in traps singly and released therefrom, and then and there shot by the defendant as targets, for sport and amusement of himself and other members of the club; that some of the doves were shot and killed outright by defendant, while some were wounded and then captured and immediately killed by persons employed for that purpose; others shot by defendant escaped apparently unhurt; it was impossible to know whether all were unhurt or not, or whether they were seriously injured or not; that the wounding of said doves was not for the purpose of inflicting pain or to torture the same thereby, but resulted from want of skill, the purpose of the defendant being then and there to kill the birds outright; that the doves which were killed outright or wounded, and then captured and killed, were subsequently used as food by defendant and others.

The validity of the judgment below depends upon the construction of the following provisions of our statute:

Every person who ... tortures, torments, ... or needlessly mutilates or kills ... any animal, or causes or procures it to be done, ... shall, upon conviction, be punished. ...

Mills' Ann. Stats. § 104.

In this act the word 'animal' shall be held to include every living dumb creature; the words 'torture,' 'torment' and 'cruelty' shall be held to include every act, omission or neglect whereby unnecessary or unjustifiable pain or suffering is caused, permitted, or allowed to continue when there is a reasonable remedy or relief. ...

Mills' Ann. Stats. § 117.

While this controversy is real, and the prosecution was instituted by the humane society in good faith, counsel for the people and the defendant, both in the court below and here, with the sole desire to obtain a decision upon the legal proposition involved, have, with commendable accord, eliminated all matters the consideration of which might tend to embarrass or obscure the one vital question in the case. It is proper further to remark that the plaintiff in error is not chargeable with moral delinquency, or with malicious intent wantonly to violate a law of the land; but, rather, as a law abiding citizen, he has purposely done the act complained of in order to furnish a test case wherein may be determined his controverted right, and that of his associates, to shoot live birds from a trap for sport and amusement.

At the common law the act done would not be a crime or a misdemeanor. If it is such now, it is because of our statute. As an abstract question, men of equal refinement and intelligence, either because of a difference in taste or training, or in their surroundings and occupations, might well differ as to the moral obliquity of the act of shooting live doves as they were released from a trap. The scholarly ascetic, whose chief pleasures are found in the library, or the man whose life is devoted to the welfare of the lower animals, might suffer excruciating pain if such an act was committed in his presence; while the sportsman, whose recreations are gunning and fishing, might look with pleasure upon what, to him, was "an ancient and honorable pastime."

What is a popular diversion, or a harmless amusement, cannot always be accurately determined. That which was so considered in the decade past may not be so regarded to-day, and that which is so to-day may be tabooed, as such, in the near future; and so men equally conscientious, intelligent and law-abiding, may, not only at different times, but during the same period of time, differ as to these questions.

It is of common knowledge that within the past few years, as incident to the progress of civilization, and as the direct outgrowth of that tender solicitude for the brute creation which keeps pace with man's increased knowledge of their life and habits, laws, such as the one under consideration, have been enacted by the various states having the common object of protecting these dumb creatures from ill treatment by man. Their aim is not only to protect these animals, but to conserve public morals, both of which are undoubtedly proper subjects of legislation. With these general objects all rightminded people sympathize. There may be, however, and are, radical differences of opinion as to the extent to which such legislation ought to go.

With the policy or wisdom of such enactments we have nothing to do. Our duty, and our only concern, is to give proper effect to such legislation, and to interpret or construe its provisions in the light of the object which the general assembly had in view when the law was passed in response to the demand of an enlightened public sentiment. . . .

The Pennsylvania statute is: "Any person who shall . . . wantonly or cruelly illtreat . . . any animal," shall be punished. The Missouri statute is: "If any person shall . . . torture, torment, . . . needlessly mutilate or kill . . . any living creature, he shall be punished,. . . ." The Massachusetts statute is: "Every owner . . . or person having charge or custody of an animal who . . . knowingly and willfully authorizes or permits it to be subjected to unnecessary torture, suffering or cruelty of any kind, shall be punished, . . ." The North Carolina Code is: "If any person shall willfully . . . torture, torment, . . . or needlessly mutilate or kill . . . any . . . animal, ..."

In the case before the Pennsylvania court the special verdict of the jury was that the defendant was a member of a gun club which held pigeon shooting matches for a test of skill of marksmanship. At one of these matches, for said purpose, the defendant with a gun fired upon pigeons liberated from a trap, and killed one and wounded another. The wounded bird alighted upon a tree, when it was soon killed by a member of the club, according to the prevailing custom, and the two pigeons thus killed were then sold for food, as the rule of the club provided. Upon these facts the court held that the case was not within the statute. The object of the defendant being to acquire skill and perfect himself in shooting on the wing, the fact that in such exercise he wounded, but did not kill, one of the birds, was held not to constitute the act an unlawful, wanton or cruel shooting or wounding. The learned chief justice who wrote the opinion concludes by saying: "We do not say there might not be a violation of the act at a shooting match, but, in our view, the facts found by the jury do not bring this case within it."

So far as we are advised, the Missouri statute has not been before the supreme court of that state, but . . . the St. Louis court of appeals has passed upon it. The facts were that as a man threw up pigeons, two at a time, the defendant shot and killed them in the air with a gun, to show his skill, and the pigeons so killed were eaten as food. The court . . . held that the pigeons were not "needlessly or unnecessarily" killed, but that the killing, done in the indulgence of a healthful recreation and during "an exercise tending to promote strength, bodily agility and courage," cannot be considered as a violation of the statute. The court refers to and emphasizes the fact that there was "no mutilation or anything approaching to it." What would have been the decision of the court had there been in that case, as there was here, a wounding and mutilating of a number of the birds, we can only conjecture. Upon a rehearing, [the court] said that the test of judicial interpretation of the statute was what application of the descriptive words employed was intended by the legislature. While the learned judge found no moral justification for the acts charged in the general truth that the policy of a good government was not to suppress innocent manly exercise, nevertheless he could not believe that it was within the legislative contemplation by an indefinite prohibition to interfere with pigeon shooting from traps, which, for so long a time, had been identified with a mere popular diversion that was not considered needless.

These are the only cases cited by plaintiff in error which support his construction of our statute. It will be observed that the Pennsylvania statute is not so broad as ours, and contains no prohibition against needlessly mutilating or torturing, as does our statute, and is aimed only at wanton and cruel ill treatment. Had it, in these particulars, contained provisions like or similar to ours, and had the facts been the same as in the case at bar, the court might have considered the statute violated.

The Missouri statute in its specific inhibitions is very much like ours,—substantially the same,—and were the facts of the Bogardus Case, and the one under consideration the same, the former would be on all fours with this, and a precedent precisely in point; but as there was no mutilation of the pigeons, as in the case at bar, we are justified in the inference that the decision might have been different, as the court called special attention to the fact that there was nothing approaching to a mutilation of the birds.

In *Commonwealth v. Turner*, 145 Mass. 296, the defendant had charge of a fox, and permitted it to be turned loose to be hunted by dogs which pursued, caught and mangled the fox. This was held to be a violation of the statute, and against public morals, which the statute sought to protect. The reasoning of the court is instructive, and, as it seems to us, conclusive. At the common law, fox hunting and shooting pigeons from a trap were equally lawful, and if fox hunting, in the circumstances stated, is prohibited, so, too, is shooting at captive pigeons liberated from a trap.

In *State v. Porter*, 112 N.C. 887, the facts were identical with the facts in this. Indeed, the agreed statement of facts in this record seems to have been copied literally from the special verdict in that case, with such changes only as were necessary as to the name of the club and the county, and using the word "doves" in this statement instead of "pigeons" in the special verdict. The North Carolina statute, unlike the others quoted, contains the same definition of "torture," "torment" and "cruelty" as does our statute, and the decision there was that the statute was violated.

The holding of the Massachusetts and North Carolina courts is, in our judgment, not only warranted under their respective statutes, but is in harmony with the advance in enlightened public opinion at this day as to the protection of dumb animals, which, we think, was unquestionably within the contemplation of the legislative mind at the time of the enactment of our statute. Indeed, it would seem that the language of our statute is too plain for construction.

In the North Carolina statute, like ours, the words "torment," "torture" and "cruelty" include every act whereby unnecessary or unjustifiable pain or suffering is caused. The shooting of wild animals in the forest and fishing in the streams do not come within the statute. We have other laws covering these things, and they are permitted at certain seasons of the year. Every act that causes pain and suffering to animals is not prohibited. Where the end or object in view is reasonable and adequate, the act resulting in pain is, in the sense of the statute, necessary or justifiable, as where a surgical operation is performed to save life, or where the act is done to protect life or property, or to minister to some of the necessities of man. But the killing of captive doves, as they are released from a trap, merely to improve one's skill of marksmanship, or for sport and amusement, though there is no specific intention to inflict pain or torture, is, within the meaning of this act, unnecessary and unjustifiable. The same degree of skill may otherwise be readily acquired, and so there was no necessity for the shooting of these doves. Other rational sport and amusement are within easy access of the gentlemen of the Country Club, and so the avowed object of this shooting is neither adequate nor reasonable; hence, under this act, unjustifiable.

Where, as here, the acts charged are admittedly done, not to furnish food, but merely for the sport and amusement of the defendant and his associates, the facts clearly bring the case within the ban of the statute. In contemplation of this law, the pain and suffering caused by such acts are disproportionate to the end sought to be attained, and furnish no adequate or reasonable excuse for the acts which, to be necessary or justifiable, must be prompted by a worthy motive and a reasonable object.

The judgment, for the reasons given, is affirmed.

Notes

1. Should the analysis of what constitutes animal cruelty differ based on whether an animal is killed for food or for other—less "socially acceptable"—reasons? Recall *Voelker*, where three iguanas were decapitated on television and subsequently eaten. Does the motivation or the purpose of the act change the nature of the act? How do you think the courts would (or should) treat this issue?

2. How do courts draw the line between recreation like hunting and the pigeon shoot here, and animal cruelty?

Section 5. Failure to Act

In virtually every state, failing to provide minimum care for some animals generally constitutes animal cruelty or neglect. Although such laws apply to cases involving even a single animal, many neglect cases involve substantially greater numbers of animals, as you saw in the *Hess* and *Nix* cases earlier in this chapter. "Animal hoarding" or "collecting" is addressed in the next section of this chapter. Neglect cases (whether with single animals or multiple animals) can be the worst for the animal victims because the suffering—which often involves chronic pain and disease—can continue for months or even years before being discovered.

State v. Hershey
Oregon Court of Appeals, 2017
286 Or. App. 824, 401 P.3d 256

DUNCAN, J. In this criminal case, defendant appeals the judgment convicting him of first-degree animal neglect, ORS 167.330. Defendant moved to suppress evidence gathered as a result of law enforcement officers' warrantless entry onto his property, arguing that the entry violated his rights under Article I, section 9, of the Oregon Constitution. The trial court denied that motion, concluding that the search was justified under the emergency aid exception to the warrant requirement as we had recently interpreted that exception. *See State v. Fessenden*, 258 Or. App. 639, 649 (2013), *aff'd on other grounds sub. nom. State v. Fessenden/Dicke*, 355 Or. 759 (2014). Defendant assigns error to that ruling. Addressing the narrow question properly before us, we conclude that, under the totality of the circumstances, there were specific and articulable facts from which the officers could, and did, reasonably conclude that the entry was necessary in order to provide emergency aid to defendant's cattle. We therefore affirm.

We review a trial court's denial of a defendant's motion to suppress for errors of law. We are bound by the trial court's explicit and implicit findings of fact if there is constitutionally sufficient evidence in the record to support them. We state the facts consistently with that standard.

At the time of the hearing on defendant's motion to suppress, Sheriff Glerup was the Sheriff of Harney County . . . [,] had more than 31 years' experience in law enforcement and had investigated "several" animal abuse and neglect cases in the county. Sergeant Needham was a deputy sheriff in Harney County, who, at the time of the motion hearing, had conducted approximately 10 major animal abuse and neglect investigations.

On July 8, 2013, Needham went to defendant's property in Burns, Oregon, in response to a call from Noelle Hauck, who lived on a nearby ranch and had reported "that [defendant's] cows were starving, and/or had no water or food." Needham drove to the property, but was unable to see the cattle. There is a hill with a lip, which can conceal the cattle from view from the highway.

Needham called defendant, who was at the coast, and explained that the sheriff's office had received a report about the condition of defendant's cattle. Defendant told Needham that the cattle "were okay," and that he had fired the workers who had been taking care of them approximately a week earlier but had arranged for a man named Brandon Baron to take care of the cattle.

* * *

The next day, Noelle Hauck's husband, Scott Hauck, "a long-term rancher * * * who's run cattle for most of his life," whose ranch is "not far from" defendant's property, and who was "very familiar with" cattle, called the sheriff's office and spoke to Glerup. Scott Hauck told Glerup that, "in his opinion[,] the animals were near death."

As Needham later summarized at the motion hearing, the Haucks had reported that "the cows were thin, that they appeared to be starving, no food, and that they were trying to get out of the property to obtain food and/or water." The animals appeared "to be dying" and "near death." According to Needham, the Haucks' reports were based on their personal observations of the cattle from the highway.

In addition, Needham spoke with the persons who lived directly to the west of the gate to defendant's property. They said that they had thrown "a small amount of hay over the fence because the cows looked like they were starving," and that "the cows had been coming down the road, to the gate area, trying to get out."

According to Glerup, after Scott Hauck's call, "[t]hat's when * * * Sergeant Needham contacted Brandon Baron by phone, and we learned that what we had been told by [defendant] was not true, that [Baron] was not hired to take care of" the cattle. Baron told Needham that defendant had contacted him a few days earlier because he had gotten a call that the cattle were out on the highway. Baron said that defendant asked him to check, and to put them back onto his property if they were out. Baron told Needham that he agreed to check for the cattle on the highway—he did not find them there—but that he had never been hired to take care of the cattle.

After Needham spoke with Baron, he briefed Glerup, and Glerup decided that they would to go out to the property. At the motion hearing, Needham testified that he and Glerup "were concerned about the health and safety of the cattle, that they were possibly dying on the property, and we knew that [defendant] was out of town, and that there was no apparent person taking care of the cattle." When asked if he believed that the entry onto defendant's property "was necessary to render immediate aid or assistance to the cows," and whether it was his "belief that they needed immediate aid or assistance, and without that immediate aid or assistance they would suffer serious physical injury or death," Needham answered, "Absolutely."

Also at the motion hearing, Glerup described the information he had when he decided that they had to enter defendant's property immediately: "We had two local people that were very familiar with cows and cattle, and they were telling us that they were in very poor health, and they—they feared for their safety and their lives." When asked if he felt that it was necessary to enter the property to render immediate aid or assistance to the cows, he said, "Yes," and that in his view it was their "duty" to ensure the safety of the cattle.

Glerup and Needham entered defendant's property, where they made observations and gathered evidence of animal neglect. Defendant was ultimately charged with five counts of first-degree animal neglect, ORS 167.330, and one count of second-degree animal neglect, ORS 167.325.

Defendant moved to suppress the evidence gathered as a result of the officers' entry onto his property. In response, the only justification that the state advanced for the warrantless entry was the emergency aid doctrine. The parties both filed memoranda recognizing that a Court of Appeals' decision, *Fessenden*, had recently held that that doctrine could apply to nonhuman animals. The parties also agreed on the legal analysis for determining whether the requirements of the emergency aid doctrine had been satisfied. The dispute before the trial court at the suppression hearing was whether the state had met its burden of proving that those requirements had been satisfied. At the conclusion of the hearing, the trial court made findings, concluded that the emergency aid doctrine applied, and denied the motion to suppress.

Pursuant to negotiations, defendant agreed to a stipulated facts trial on one count of first-degree animal neglect, with the understanding that he would be able to appeal the denial of his motion to suppress, and the state agreed to dismiss the remaining counts.

On appeal, defendant argues that the trial court erroneously denied his motion to suppress because the state failed to establish that the warrantless entry onto his property was justified under an exception to the warrant requirement. He argues that the state failed to meet its burden of establishing the requirements for emergency aid . . . .

* * *

Article I, section 9, prohibits unreasonable searches and seizures. Under Article I, section 9, warrantless searches and seizures are per se unreasonable, unless they fall within an established exception to the warrant requirement. *State v. Baker*, 350 Or. 641, 647 (2011).

Generally, an officer must have a warrant to enter or search a person's premises. However, an officer may enter or search a person's premises without a warrant if the requirements of the emergency aid exception to the warrant requirement are satisfied. . The Supreme Court set out those requirements in *Baker*:

> "[A]n emergency aid exception to the Article I, section 9 warrant requirement is justified when police officers have an objectively reasonable belief, based on articulable facts, that a warrantless entry is necessary to either render immediate aid to persons, or to assist persons who have suffered, or who are imminently threatened with suffering, serious physical injury or harm."

350 Or. at 649 (footnotes omitted). To establish that the requirements of the emergency aid exception are satisfied, the state must prove that, at the time of the warrantless entry, the officers had the subjective belief "that there was an immediate need to aid or assist a person who has suffered (or is imminently threatened with suffering) serious physical injury or harm" and that that "belief [was] objectively reasonable." The emergency aid exception does not require probable cause to believe that a crime has been or is being committed. *Fessenden/Dicke*, 355 Or. at 765. "It permits warrantless entry, search, or seizure, regardless of whether the officer has probable cause to believe that a crime has been or is being committed, as long as the officer reasonably believes it necessary to "'render immediate aid to persons * * * who have suffered, or who are imminently threatened with suffering, serious physical injury or harm.'" *Id.* (quoting *Baker*, 350 Or. at 649 (omission in *Fessenden/Dicke*)).

In *Fessenden*, this court held that the emergency aid exception can justify warrantless searches and seizures to protect animals "when law enforcement officers have an objectively reasonable belief, based on articulable facts, that the search or seizure is necessary to render immediate aid or assistance to animals that have suffered, or which are imminently threatened with suffering, serious physical injury or cruel death, unless that injury or death is being inflicted lawfully." 258 Or. App. at 646. We further held that the emergency aid exception justified the warrantless search and seizure at issue in *Fessenden*, which was of a horse that, as observed by an animal control officer, was "near death from starvation, * * * in imminent danger of suffering organ damage (either directly from starvation or as the result of falling), and * * * [in need of] emergency medical care." *Id.* at 649-50. We explained:

> "Given the possibility of imminent death, as well as the unnecessary suffering associated with starvation and organ failure * * *, [the animal control officer] * * * could reasonably conclude that he should take immediate steps to save the horse, or at least alleviate its suffering[.]"

Id. at 650.

As in *Fessenden*, we conclude that the emergency aid exception justifies the warrantless entry at issue here. At the time of the warrantless entry, the officers knew that, in July, in Burns, Oregon, defendant was away from his property and his cattle had not been cared for in at least a week. They also knew that neighbors had observed that the cattle lacked food and water and were starving and trying to escape the property. According to the neighbors, the cattle appeared to be "dying" and "near death."

Based on those facts, Glerup and Needham subjectively believed that it was necessary to enter defendant's property to render immediate aid or assistance. . . . That belief was objectively reasonable; the circumstances known to the officers at the time of their entry onto the property were sufficient to support an objectively reasonable belief that the cattle were presently dying from starvation and dehydration and were near death. As in *Fessenden*, we conclude that, "[g]iven the possibility of imminent death, as well as the unnecessary suffering associated with starvation," the officers could reasonably conclude that they "should take immediate steps to save" the cattle, or to alleviate their suffering. 258 Or. App. at 650.

Defendant argues that the articulated facts do not show that there was a true emergency. He argues that the fact that the officers waited a day before entering the property shows that they did not believe that a true emergency existed. But the officers explained how the information that they had changed over time, and how their concerns escalated. . . . Under the totality of the circumstances, it was also reasonable to conclude that it was necessary to render immediate aid or assistance to the cattle, and that, without that immediate aid or assistance they would suffer serious physical injury or death.

Defendant also argues that the officers could have taken the time to call defendant back, or should have sought a search warrant. But, as we have concluded, it was reasonable to believe that the cattle needed immediate aid at the time the officers entered defendant's property, and the officers did act immediately after learning that the cattle had not had anyone taking care of them for a week.

In sum, the officers' belief that immediate action was necessary to provide aid to the cattle, which appeared to be "dying" and "near death," was reasonable under the circumstances. Accordingly, the trial court did not err when it denied defendant's motion to suppress.

Affirmed.

* * *

Notes

1. In the combined cases of *State v. Fessenden* and *State v. Dicke*, 355 Or. 759 (2014), referenced heavily in *Hershey*, the court held that the emergency aid exception to the warrant requirement applies not just to humans but also includes animals. The court relied on the basic rule of "reasonableness" that is at the core of the Fourth Amendment and Article 1, section 9 of the Oregon Constitution. In the

Fessenden/Dicke case, an officer responded to a neighbor's complaint of a suffering horse and found a profoundly emaciated animal. Based on his training and experience, the officer reasonably believed that emergency action was required to save this horse, so he seized her and took her to a veterinarian. The horse survived. At trial and on appeal, the defendants argued that the officer needed a search warrant, claiming that "a danger to an animal's life is not the kind of emergency that is necessary to diminish constitutional provisions." The court disagreed. Citing the *Nix* case, the court held that the legislative protections afforded to animals under Oregon's criminal law support the conclusion that it is constitutionally reasonable to render emergency aid to a suffering animal.

2. Oregon is not the first state to confront this issue and rule that the life of an animal justifies application of the emergency aid (or exigent circumstances) exception to the warrant requirement. Other states that have so ruled include California, Florida, Georgia, Illinois, Indiana, Massachusetts, Missouri, Montana, New York, Ohio, Texas, Vermont, and Wisconsin. *See, e.g., Recchia v. City of Los Angeles Dept. of Animal Svcs.,* 889 F.3d 553 (9th Cir. 2018) (exigent circumstances exception to Fourth Amendment applies to seizure of animals in need of urgent care); *Broden v. Marin Humane Soc'y,* 70 Cal. App. 4th 1212 (1999) (Fourth Amendment exigency exception applies to emergencies involving animals where animals are suffering).

3. In the following case, the defendant did not dispute that her severely neglected dog was lawfully seized, but she asserted that the removal of his blood for testing after he was seized violated her protected privacy interest in her property—her dog's blood.

State v. Newcomb

Supreme Court of Oregon, 2015
359 Or. 756, 375 P.3d 434

LINDER, S. J.

Defendant was convicted of second-degree animal neglect (ORS 167.325) after she failed to adequately feed her dog, Juno, resulting in his malnourishment. Before trial, defendant moved to suppress blood test results showing that Juno had no medical condition that would have caused him to be malnourished, which in turn indicated that Juno was malnourished because he was starving. Defendant argued that the state had violated both Article I, section 9, of the Oregon Constitution, and the Fourth Amendment to the United States Constitution by failing to obtain a warrant before testing the dog's blood. The trial court denied the motion and allowed the state to introduce the test results during trial. Defendant appealed to the Court of Appeals, which agreed with defendant that she had a protected privacy interest in her dog's blood that required the state to obtain a search warrant, unless the circumstances fit within an exception to the warrant requirement. Because the state had failed to obtain a warrant, and because no exception to the warrant requirement applied, the Court of Appeals reversed. We allowed the state's petition for review to resolve whether defendant had a protected privacy interest in her dog's blood under Article I, section 9, of the Oregon Constitution or the Fourth Amendment to the United States Constitution. As explained below, on these facts, we conclude that she did not. We accordingly reverse the decision of the Court of Appeals and affirm the decision of the trial court.

* * *

On review, the only issue before us is the lawfulness of testing Juno's blood; defendant no longer disputes that Juno was lawfully seized. The chief point of contention between the parties is whether defendant had a protected privacy interest in Juno's blood once Juno was in the state's lawful custody and care. That, in turn, is essentially a disagreement over whether drawing and testing Juno's blood was a "search" for purposes of either Article I, section 9, or the Fourth Amendment. The parties further dispute whether, if the blood testing was a search for constitutional purposes, that search was reasonable in these circumstances despite the state's failure to get a warrant. Consistently with our approach to analyzing constitutional claims, we examine first whether the state's conduct constituted a search under Article I, section 9, and then consider defendant's *Fourth Amendment* claim only if we conclude that no state constitutional violation occurred.

II. ANALYSIS

A. *Article I, Section 9*

Article I, section 9, of the Oregon Constitution provides in part: "No law shall violate the right of the people to be secure in their persons, houses, papers, and effects, against unreasonable search, or seizure." Implicit in that guarantee against unreasonable searches and seizures is a significant limitation: The provision applies only when government officials engage in conduct that amounts to a search or a seizure. *State v. Owens*, 302 Ore. 196, 205–06 (1986). For purposes of Article I, section 9, a search occurs only if governmental action invades "a protected privacy interest." A seizure occurs only if, through governmental action, "there is a significant interference with a person's possessory or ownership interests in property." Although the two interests—privacy and ownership/possession—are not necessarily coextensive, property law concepts of ownership and possessory rights can bear significantly on the existence or nonexistence of a protected privacy interest in the property. Ultimately, "the privacy protected by Article I, section 9, is not the privacy that one reasonably *expects* but the privacy to which one has a *right*." *State v. Campbell*, 306 Ore. 157, 164 (1988) (emphasis in original; citation omitted). And the right to privacy that Article I, section 9, protects is the freedom from scrutiny as "determined by social and legal norms of behavior, such as trespass laws and conventions against eavesdropping." *Id.* at 170 (citations omitted).

The general issue that this case presents is one that has come before the court with some frequency before: the extent to which the state may examine property without a warrant after it has lawfully seized that property in the course of a criminal investigation. On the other hand, this case presents—as most cases raising search and seizure issues do — its own set of distinctive facts and circumstances within that context. Here, the seized property was a living animal — Juno, the dog — not an inanimate object or other insentient physical item of some kind. Central to the issue that we must resolve is whether that distinctive fact makes a legal difference.

In defendant's view, it does not. Defendant relies on ORS 609.020, which states: "Dogs are hereby declared to be personal property." Defendant maintains that, for purposes of Article I, section 9, a dog is the same as any other item of property that can be lawfully owned or possessed, such as a stereo or a folder. As a general proposition, under that construct, when the state lawfully seizes inanimate property, it may "observe, feel, smell, shake and weigh" lawfully seized property or otherwise "thoroughly examine" its exterior without obtaining a warrant. *Owens*, 302 Ore. at 206. But examining the "interior" of the property to reveal other property that it may contain is another matter. Whether such an examination is an unlawful search depends on whether the contents are open to view or the property "by [its] very nature announce[s] [its] contents (such as by touch or smell) * * *." *Id.* (no warrant required to withdraw and test white powder visible in lawfully seized clear vial to confirm probable cause that powder was cocaine). Defendant's position is that Juno was the legal equivalent of a closed opaque container, one that did not announce its contents, so that a warrant was required before the state could examine its contents.

In *Owens*, however, this court recognized that "not all containers * * * merit the same protection under Article I, section 9." The same is true of personal property more generally: Not all things that can be owned and possessed as personal property merit the same constitutional protection in the same circumstances. With regard to living animals, and domestic pets in particular, we have recognized that "some animals, such as pets, occupy a unique position in people's hearts and in the law," one that is not well-reflected in the "cold characterization of a dog * * * as mere property." *State v. Fessenden/Dicke*, 355 Ore. 759, 769 (2014) (latter quotation from *Rabideau v. City of Racine*, 243 Wis.2d 486, 491 (2001)). Whether defendant had a protected privacy interest that was invaded by the withdrawal and testing of Juno's blood requires us to examine the nature of the property involved and the circumstances of the governmental intrusion into that property.

As to the nature of the property involved — here, a living animal — we are aided by our analysis in *Fessenden/Dicke*. The issue there was whether the state could, without a warrant, lawfully seize an animal (a horse) believed to have been criminally neglected. In concluding that traditional exigent circumstances doctrine extended to animals in such a circumstance, this court explored the nature of the relationship of humans to the animals that they own and possess, as well as the social and legal norms that attend to that relationship. The observations that we made in that regard are helpful in the context of the legal issue that this case presents.

Under Oregon's statutes, animals generally, as well as dogs in particular, are deemed "property." 355 Ore. at 767-68 (citing statutes); ORS 609.020 (declaring dogs to be property). Animals generally therefore can be lawfully owned and possessed much as other property can be.[9] But the welfare of animals is subject to a series of explicit statutory protections that are distinct to animals and do not apply to inanimate property. Indeed, "Oregon's animal welfare statutes impose one of the nation's most protective statutory schemes[.]" *Id.* The crimes of animal abuse and neglect are themselves reflections of the distinctive nature of animals as property. *Id.* at 767-69 (discussing animal neglect and other animal welfare statutes as illustrating unique legal and social status of animals). A person commits first-degree animal abuse if the person, with any of several culpable mental states, causes serious physical injury to or cruelly causes the death of an animal. ORS 167.330(1). A person commits second-degree animal neglect if the person, with any of several culpable mental states, "fails to provide minimum care for an animal in [that] person's custody or control." ORS 167.325(1). Significantly, the obligation to provide minimum care arises for anyone who has custody or control of an animal; it is not limited to those who have lawful possession or custody of the animal. "Minimum care," in turn, means "care sufficient to preserve the health and well-being of an animal" and includes, in addition to adequate nutrition, "[v]eterinary care deemed necessary by a reasonably prudent person to relieve distress from injury, neglect or disease." ORS 167.310(7). If the failure to provide minimum care results in death or serious physical injury, the crime is elevated to first-degree animal neglect. ORS 167.330(1).

Reflected in those and other laws that govern ownership and treatment of animals is the recognition that animals "are sentient beings capable of experiencing pain, stress and fear[.]" *Fessenden/Dicke*, 355 Ore. at 768 (quoting ORS 167.305(1)). To be sure, the protection given to animals under Oregon law does not place them on a par with humans. Among other things, there are legally sanctioned ways for humans to kill animals, and many animals may be "treated or mistreated" by those who own or lawfully possess them as long as their treatment is within the boundaries of "good animal husbandry" or "animal research." *Id.* at 768-69 (citing statutes; noting special legal protections for domestic animals, "colloquially known as pets"). The important point for this case, however, is not that Oregon law permits "humans to treat animals in ways that humans may not treat other humans." *Id.* at 768. What matters here is that Oregon law prohibits humans from treating animals in ways that humans are free to treat other forms of property.[11] Oregon law also places affirmative obligations on those who have custody of an animal to ensure that animal's basic welfare; those obligations have no analogue for inanimate property.

---

9. Under Oregon law, there are many exceptions to a person's ability to lawfully own and possess certain animals. See, e.g., ORS 167.365(1) (person commits crime of "dogfighting" if person knowingly "[o]wns, possesses, keeps, breeds, trains, buys, sells or offers to sell a fighting dog"); ORS 609.341 (special state permits required to keep "exotic" animals). There are also many limits on animal owners' rights of dominion and control over some animals. *See, e.g.,* ORS 609.098(1)(c) (unlawful to use dog as a weapon in the commission of a crime); ORS 811.200(1) (unlawful to carry dog on certain parts of a vehicle operated on highway without specified protective measures).

11. A person can be as cruel or abusive as she wants to her own stereo or folder, and can neglect the maintenance of a car to the point where it will not operate, without legal consequence. The same is not true of an animal that a person owns or has custody of or control over.

Those observations alone are not enough to resolve the issue before us. As an abstract proposition, we accept that a person who owns or lawfully possesses an animal, and who thus has full rights of dominion and control over it, has a protected privacy interest that precludes others from interfering with the animal in ways and under circumstances that exceed legal and social norms. Thus, for example, if a dog owner walks his dog off-leash down the street, and the friendly dog runs over to greet a passerby who pets it, that act of petting the dog would invade no possessory or privacy interest; a contact of that kind would fall well within social norms and conventions, even if by petting the dog the passerby discovers something concealed from plain view (*e.g.*, that under the dog's thick fur coat, the dog is skin and bones to the point of serious malnourishment). On the other hand, if the passerby produces a syringe and expertly withdraws a sample of the dog's blood in the time that it would take to greet and pet the dog, that contact would violate the owner's possessory and privacy interests, even if the passerby did so for a valuable scientific study (*e.g.*, whether local animals were infected with an easily-transmitted virus); such a contact would fall well outside social norms and conventions. As those examples suggest, determining the existence of a constitutionally protected privacy right in property depends not only on the nature of the property itself, but also on the nature of the governmental intrusion and the circumstances in which it occurred. We must consider those, too, in resolving the issue before us.

Here, when Dr. Hedge tested Juno's blood, defendant had lost her rights of dominion and control over Juno, at least on a temporary basis. Juno at that point had been lawfully seized and taken into custody based on probable cause to believe that he had been criminally neglected. The specific neglect that the officer believed Juno to have suffered was that Juno was starving. Juno's physical appearance and behavior provided the officer with significant support for his belief—Juno was near-emaciated, was dry-heaving, and was "eating at random things" in the yard. The officer had, as well, a citizen report of neglect and defendant's own admission that she had no food for the dog. The officer, who believed Juno needed medical treatment, asked defendant for her consent to take Juno into custody for medical evaluation, but defendant refused. When the officer then seized Juno over defendant's protest, both to preserve evidence and to render aid to the dog, Juno was lawfully taken into the state's protective custody. *Fessenden/Dicke*, 355 Ore. at 773 (animal entitled to "statutory protection" through seizure without warrant if officer has probable cause to believe animal has been criminally neglected, neglect is ongoing, and seizure is necessary to prevent further serious imminent harm to animal).

Juno was not beyond danger simply because he had been removed for the time from defendant's dominion and control, however. Juno's condition appeared serious and required medical attention. To ensure appropriate medical care for Juno, Dr. Hedge drew and tested Juno's blood to determine whether he was suffering from some other medical condition that might cause his malnourishment. When the blood tests failed to reveal any other medical condition that would have caused Juno to be seriously emaciated, Dr. Hedge put Juno on a special feeding protocol.

Given the specific context involved here—the lawful seizure of a dog based on probable cause to believe the dog was suffering from malnourishment, followed by drawing and testing the dog's blood to medically diagnose and treat the dog—we conclude that defendant had no protected privacy interest in Juno's blood that was invaded by the medical procedures performed. In these circumstances, we agree with the state that Juno is not analogous to, and should not be analyzed as though he were, an opaque inanimate container in which inanimate property or effects were being stored or concealed. Juno's "contents"—in terms of what was of interest to Dr. Hedge—were the stuff that dogs and other living mammals are made of: organs, bones, nerves, other tissues, and blood. As the prosecutor argued at trial, inside Juno was just "more dog."[13] The fact that Juno had blood inside was a given; he could not be a living and breathing dog otherwise. And the chemical composition of Juno's blood was a product of physiological processes that go on inside of Juno, not "information" that defendant placed in Juno for safekeeping or to conceal from view.[14]

That fact has significance in the context of the legal and social norms for the care and welfare of animals that we have already discussed. A dog is personal property under Oregon law, a status that gives a dog owner rights of dominion and control over the dog. But Oregon law simultaneously limits ownership and possessory rights in ways that it does not for inanimate property. Those limitations, too, are reflections of legal and social norms. Live animals under Oregon law are subject to statutory welfare protections that ensure their basic minimum care, including veterinary treatment. The obligation to provide that minimum care falls on any person

---

13. At least, that was true in this case. It might not be true under different facts. Dogs and other animals at least *can* be used as repositories of information and inanimate effects, and can have more inside them than just "more dog." Many animals—and dogs in particular—for example *are* repositories for information through the use of "microchip" technology that permits a scanner, from outside the dog, to retrieve information encoded on the microchip. *See generally Microchip implant (animal)* at *https://en.wikipedia.org/wiki/Microchip_implant_(animal)* (accessed May 30, 2016) (describing use of microchips placed under skin of farm and ranch animals, as well as domestic pets, as common means of identification).

It is at least doubtful that a dog's owner would have a cognizable *privacy* interest in the information planted in a dog for the specific purpose of being able to externally identify the dog. On the other hand, hypothetically, if what was planted "inside" the dog was a microchip containing stolen secret government data, the owner's or possessor's protected privacy interest, even if the dog had been lawfully seized on probable cause to believe it contained the stolen data, might be the same as in an opaque inanimate container. In short, whatever the answer to the question whether the owner has a protected privacy interest in an object planted inside a dog, the dog is at least more analogous to an inanimate container in such a circumstance.

14. To be sure, Dr. Hedge had to extract Juno's blood to test it; she could not determine the chemical state of Juno's blood through some non-invasive procedure. As Groucho Marx famously quipped:

"Outside of a dog, a book is man's best friend. Inside of a dog, it's too dark to read."

But what Dr. Hedge withdrew here was "more dog," not a separate item of property that defendant had placed inside Juno to either safeguard or conceal from public view in the same way that property nested within other property involves. That fact, although not necessarily dispositive, properly bears on the analysis.

who has custody and control of a dog or other animal. A dog owner simply has no cognizable *right*, in the name of her privacy, to countermand that obligation. That conclusion follows with equal or greater force when, as here, the dog is in the state's lawful protective custody on probable cause that the dog is suffering injury as a result of neglect, at which point the owner has lost her property rights of dominion and control over the dog. An examinations of the dog's physical health and condition in that circumstance, pursuant to a medical judgment of what is appropriate for diagnosis and treatment, is not a form of governmental scrutiny that, under legal and social norms and conventions, invades a dog owner's protected privacy rights under Article I, section 9.

That conclusion resolves this case for purposes of Article I, section 9. We emphasize, however, that our decision is limited to the circumstances that this case presents. As we said in *Fessenden/Dicke*, 355 Ore. at 769–70:

> "As we continue to learn more about the interrelated nature of all life, the day may come when humans perceive less separation between themselves and other living beings than the law now reflects. However, we do not need a mirror to the past or a telescope to the future to recognize that the legal status of animals has changed and is changing still[.]"

Assessing an animal owner's constitutionally protected interests of possession and privacy in his or her animal in that evolving landscape of social and behavioral norms presents, at best, "difficult questions," and we are well-advised in that context "to observe the wise limitations on our function and to confine ourselves to deciding only what is necessary to the disposition of the immediate case." *Id.* at 770–71.

Consequently, our holding is confined to circumstances in which the state has *lawfully* seized a dog or other animal on probable cause to believe the animal has been neglected or otherwise abused. It is also confined to the general kind of intrusion that occurred in this case—a medically appropriate procedure for diagnosis and treatment of an animal in ill-health. In those particular circumstances, we conclude that the warrantless withdrawal and testing of Juno's blood did not violate Article I, section 9.

B. *The Fourth Amendment*

The remaining question before us is whether the analysis under the Fourth Amendment requires a different result. Although worded somewhat differently, the guarantee of the Fourth Amendment parallels that of Article I, section 9. The Fourth Amendment protects "[t]he right of the people to be secure in their persons, houses, papers, and effects, against unreasonable searches and seizures[.]" As is true of Article I, section 9, a "seizure" under the Fourth Amendment occurs when there is "some meaningful interference with an individual's possessory interest" in property. And a "search" for purposes of the Fourth Amendment occurs when an individual's protected privacy interest is infringed.

The test under the Fourth Amendment to determine if a particular governmental action invades a protected privacy interest differs, at least in how it is articulated, from the test under Article I, section 9. Rather than turn on an individual's "right" of privacy, the Fourth Amendment test has both a subjective and an objective component, and thus involves "two discrete questions." The first is whether an individual has manifested an expectation to preserve something as private; the second is whether that subjective expectation of privacy is one "that society is prepared to recognize as reasonable." In application, however, the Fourth Amendment privacy test takes into account the same and similar considerations as the test under Article I, section 9, and the two tests often lead to the same result in like circumstances.

Understandably, then, the parties' Fourth Amendment arguments closely track the arguments they make under Article I, section 9. Ultimately, the issue under the Fourth Amendment reduces to the same question as under Article I, section 9: Whether defendant had a protected privacy interest in the withdrawal and testing of her dog's blood for purposes of medical treatment after the dog had been lawfully taken into custody on probable cause to believe that he had been criminally neglected. To date, the Supreme Court has not had a case requiring it to examine an individual's privacy interests in a dog or other animal, either generally or in circumstances in which the animal is in the government's lawful custody. But the Court's cases suggest that the analysis under the Fourth Amendment would not differ in a significant way from the analysis we have made under Article I, section 9.

In particular, the different nature of that property that this case involves — a living animal, one that is not ordinarily and was not here used as a repository into which other property was placed — would have bearing on the Fourth Amendment analysis. The same is true of the nature and circumstances of the government intrusion that we have discussed — those, too, would be factors in the Fourth Amendment analysis. And the laws and social norms of behavior that we have discussed as they pertain to animal welfare generally, and minimum care in particular, are significant under the Fourth Amendment analysis in determining what expectations of privacy society will recognize as legitimate.

In short, the guidance available to us from current Fourth Amendment jurisprudence leads us to the same factors that we have considered in analyzing the issue under Article I, section 9. No purpose would be served by repeating ourselves. For the reasons we have discussed in our analysis under Article I, section 9, we conclude under the Fourth Amendment that defendant had no protected privacy that was violated by the withdrawal and testing of Juno's blood without a warrant.

The decision of the Court of Appeals is reversed. The judgment of the circuit court is affirmed.

Note

The following case raises questions about prosecutorial discretion in relation to a neglect case involving a single animal. When reading, consider whether the number of animals at issue could or should have had an impact on the decision to prosecute. What about financial resources? Should a defendant's ability to afford basic food, shelter, and veterinary care be part of the prosecutorial equation?

Martinez v. State of Texas

Court of Appeals of Texas, Fourth District, San Antonio, 2001
48 S.W.3d 273

RICKHOFF, Justice. This appeal requires us to review a sad case. We reach this legal result with some discomfort. As appellate judges we cannot apply our own philosophy of justice, but may only apply the law to the facts of a particular case. After doing so here, we must affirm.

Appellant Andrea Martinez, an eighty-three year old widow, is known in her neighborhood for taking in homeless animals. She was charged with cruelty to animals, and convicted by a jury. *See* Tex. Pen Code Ann. § 42.09(a)(2). . . . The trial court assessed punishment at one year confinement and fined Martinez one thousand dollars. The trial court probated the sentence and the fine for two years on the condition that Martinez perform one hundred hours of community service at a local animal shelter. Martinez raises five appellate issues.

SUFFICIENCY OF THE EVIDENCE

In two issues, Martinez challenges the sufficiency of the evidence supporting her conviction. Specifically, Martinez argues that the evidence is legally and factually insufficient to prove she "intentionally or knowingly" withheld care for the animal she called "Lobo." . . . [W]e find that the evidence is legally and factually sufficient to support the verdict.

Martinez was charged with intentionally and knowingly "failing unreasonably to provide necessary food, care, or shelter for an animal in [her] custody." *See* Tex. Pen. Code Ann. § 42.09(a)(2). . . . To prove this allegation, the State presented the testimony of Rudy Davila, an animal cruelty investigator for the City of San Antonio. Davila explained that he was asked to investigate a complaint of animal cruelty involving a dog being kept at Martinez's home. Davila testified that upon arriving at Martinez's home, he observed several dogs in the back yard, one of which was separated from the others. Davila stated that most of the dogs appeared healthy, but the separated dog was lethargic, non-responsive, and suffering from a severe skin condition. Davila described the dog as having very little hair and open wounds. Davila explained that he could not determine the dog's skin color because its skin was completely crusted-over. Davila further testified that the dog appeared malnourished, explaining that the dog's back vertebrae were distinctly visible and the dog's abdominal wall had a severe tuck. Davila identified the infected dog in several photographs that were admitted into evidence.

Davila explained that he questioned Martinez about the dog's condition. According to Davila, Martinez told him a friend gave her the dog two years before after trying to cure the dog's skin condition with flea powder. When questioned about Martinez's demeanor, Davila indicated that Martinez did not appear upset or worried about the dog. Davila opined that the dog had not received reasonable care, noting the dog did not appear to have been treated for parasitic sarcoptic mange.

Davila explained that he did not smell sulfur on the dog, a scent that would indicate the dog was being treated. Davila stated he decided to seize the dog due to the severity of the dog's condition. He explained how Martinez signed a consent form, marking it to indicate the dog was "not wanted." Davila stated that after he took the dog to the animal control facility, a veterinarian decided to euthanize the dog.

The State also presented the testimony of Dr. Robert Granberry, a veterinarian. After examining the photos of the infected dog, Granberry opined that the animal probably had scabies or sarcoptic mange in an advanced stage. . . . Granberry testified that the dog in the photographs had been neglected in its care.

After viewing this evidence in the light most favorable to the verdict, we conclude that a rational jury could have found all elements of the State's allegation. The evidence demonstrates that an animal in Martinez's custody did not receive the medical treatment it needed to survive. The decision to euthanize the animal upon its arrival at the shelter shows the unreasonableness of failing to treat the animal. Although Martinez maintains that no evidence of intent or knowledge exists, a jury may infer a culpable mental state from the circumstances surrounding the offense of cruelty to animals. *See Pine v. State*, 889 S.W.2d 625, 629 (Tex. App. 1994). Here, the evidence indicates obvious and severe illness, and a long-neglected need for treatment. Presented with such an obvious need for treatment, a jury could easily infer intent or knowledge. As a result, the evidence is legally sufficient to support the verdict. However, even viewed without the light of the prism of "in the light most favorable to the prosecution," the evidence is still sufficient.

* * *

CONCLUSION

The jury, faced with the evidence discussed above, had no choice but to find Martinez guilty. She should not have accepted the dog or kept it without treatment for so long. The facts, however, offer compelling mitigation.[1]

---

1. In my view, anyone visiting this home should have realized Martinez, poor, isolated, and elderly, needed assistance. One would think the first question these authorities would ask after, "Where is the dog?" would be, "Do you have any children, grandchildren, friends, or relatives who can help you so this does not happen again?" After Davila investigated she surrendered the dog and was compliant. Perhaps she could have been educated without the rigors of a full courtroom experience—nothing more than a helpful follow-up visit for the benefit of the other, healthy dogs.

Failure to provide necessary care is cruelty to animals and a criminal offense, even though the record in this case reveals neglect arising out of a lack of resources rather than outright cruelty. Whether a case like this one rises to the level of outrageousness suggested by intentional behavior is properly for others to decide. *Cf. Tilbury v. State*, 890 S.W.2d 219, 220 (Tex. App.-Fort Worth 1994) (upholding conviction of cruelty to animals committed by shooting and killing two dogs). Whether there is a need to deter others similarly situated from committing this violation is also beyond our judgment. Martinez lives on four-hundred dollars monthly Social Security benefits, has no transportation, her husband passed away two months prior to trial, and the record failed to reveal any helpful family members. She did what she could short of calling for the dog's removal. Performing community service at an animal shelter may be difficult in light of Martinez's prior hardship in traveling to the veterinarian. Perhaps another Good Samaritan will appear to assist

The judgment of the trial court is affirmed.

LOPEZ, J., concurred.

If there was ever a case that screamed for prosecutorial discretion, it is this case. Ms. Martinez, an 83 year old widow, is known in her neighborhood for taking in, and caring for, stray dogs—acts most of us would never consider. Yet for whatever reason, Martinez takes in homeless animals like the one at issue here, and somehow manages to stretch her meager income to care for animals that would otherwise roam our city's streets. While the jury faced with the evidence discussed in the majority opinion had no choice but to find Martinez guilty, I question why this case was ever prosecuted at all.

Martinez lives on $400.00 per month in Social Security benefits. She has no transportation. While the evidence demonstrates that Martinez did not do everything that was needed to properly care for the infected dog, the evidence indicates that she did what she felt she could do. Nonetheless, nothing indicates that Martinez is a cruel person. When the animal cruelty investigator went to Martinez's home to investigate the complaint of animal cruelty, Martinez surrendered the infected dog at the investigator's request. Notably, however, the investigator also found healthy dogs at Martinez's home. Those dogs were separated from the infected dog to prevent them from becoming ill.

All the testimony from Martinez's trial indicates that the infected dog required professional treatment—care that costs money that Martinez did not have. With the dog in the hands of the animal control authorities, what purpose was served by prosecuting this little old woman? Surely, nothing was gained except to alienate a senior member of our community from the justice system that should protect her.

Although this case should never have been prosecuted, the damage done could have been minimized by the trial court. Cruelty to animals is a Class A misdemeanor, punishable by up to one year in jail. The trial court sentenced Martinez to the maximum punishment. A one-year sentence, even though probated, seems unnecessarily severe in circumstances such as these. Perhaps the trial court intended to exercise leniency by probating Martinez's sentence and ordering her to perform 100 hours of community service at the local animal shelter. Nonetheless, performing this service will require numerous trips to and from the shelter, each trip requiring money for transportation. On a $400.00 a month income, even this effort will be a challenge.

Hopefully, Martinez's love for animals will facilitate her efforts to perform her community service and to put this experience behind her. As for my part in this case, I concur in the judgment only.

---

her. We can only hope Martinez's love for animals will find an appropriate outlet in her community service, allowing this sad experience to become meaningful.

Notes

1. Many statutes prohibiting animal neglect as a form of cruelty require that the defendant "intentionally" or "knowingly" fail to provide minimum care to an animal. Even though the defendant in *Martinez* maintained that no evidence of knowledge or intent was presented at trial, the appellate court concluded a jury could infer a culpable mental state from the circumstances, specifically, the poor condition of the animal. *See also Pelloni v. Commonwealth of Virginia*, 781 S.E.2d 368 (Va. Ct. App. 2016), a case involving the neglect of defendant's dog:

> [A]ppellant acted consciously and intentionally over the course of several weeks in declining to provide food or water or basic veterinary services to Hannibal with an awareness of the likelihood that such failures would result in "inhumane injury or pain" leading to death. While he may not have committed these omissions for the purpose of inflicting Hannibal with "pain or inhumane injury," appellant admitted he knew Hannibal had been sick for at least a week and watched the puppy shaking as he died the morning of July 31, 2014. In light of his admission, appellant's refusal to provide basic veterinary care for Hannibal, demonstrates his intentionality and his awareness of the likely result of his inaction. . . . Appellant's decision to allow these conditions to continue for several weeks could lead a reasonable factfinder to conclude that appellant "willfully inflict[ed] inhuman injury or pain" on Hannibal in violation of Code § 3.2-6570(F).

781 S.E.2d at 373.

2. The defendant in *Martinez* was an elderly individual with limited funds. The concurring justice agreed that the anti-cruelty law was violated, but thought prosecution was inappropriate because the defendant was a "little old woman." The defendant in *Pelloni* also claimed he had limited funds to care for the dogs. Does the "little old woman" elicit greater sympathy than the adult male in *Pelloni*? Should a defendant's age or economic status be taken into account before a decision to prosecute animal abuse is made or before a conviction is rendered? Some prosecutors may be reluctant to take neglect cases where an overt act of violence is not involved, and where the defendant is more sympathetic due to age or circumstances. However, it is important to remember that neglect cases may actually involve more suffering over a longer period of time than certain cases of affirmative cruelty.

People v. Brian

Appellate Department, Superior Court of California, Los Angeles, 1980
110 Cal. App. 3d Supp. 1, 168 Cal. Rptr. 105

SAETA, J. A jury found defendant guilty of violating Penal Code section 597, subdivision (b). The charge involved neglect of animals she owned. On appeal defendant claims that the evidence was insufficient to show that she had the intent to harm or neglect her animals.

The facts are presented to us in a settled statement which presents a sometimes disjointed summary of the many witnesses' testimony. Defendant owned three horses, several dogs, cats, goats and some fowl. In July 1978 she left her home for an eastern trip. She told her stepfather (Duff) and a feedstore employee (Madrid) she would return about September 1. Defendant made vague arrangements with Duff and Madrid for feeding of her animals before she left her home. Madrid commenced caring for the animals; Duff paid for the food.

About August 15, Duff left the area, the animals being in good condition at that time. Madrid fed the animals for about one month more — to about September 14. Defendant found out, by a phone call to Duff on September 8, that Duff would no longer pay for feed. (Defendant had been delayed in her return to her home by two car breakdowns.) On September 14, defendant called Duff, the Antelope Valley Sheriff, Madrid and Chindale (a friend) seeking care for the animals until her return. Apparently, Madrid refused both defendant's and Chindale's requests to work further as he had already paid out $60 of his own money for feed. Chindale testified that she volunteered to pay for the feed in her conversation with Madrid.

The animal control officer posted the premises on September 19. Defendant returned the same day. She was charged with neglect of her animals on or about September 19, 1978. There is substantial evidence that some of the animals were in a thin and dehydrated condition due to a shortage of food, water, shelter and protection from the weather. Thus the only issue is whether or not defendant had the requisite intent to be guilty of violating the statute charged.

People v. Farley (1973) 33 Cal.App.3d Supp. 1 held that the offense in question "requires proof of negligence, but not more." We disagree. In our view, a conviction of Penal Code section 597, subdivision (b) requires proof of *criminal* negligence, a higher standard of culpability than that required in *Farley*. The *Farley* court felt bound by two prior Court of Appeal decisions, *People v. Harris* (1966) 239 Cal. App.2d 393 and *People v. Beaugez* (1965) 232 Cal.App.2d 650. These cases interpreted Penal Code section 273a, an analogous statute involving permitting children to be endangered. *Harris* in turn, relied on *Beaugez* in deciding that ordinary negligence was the only element of intent in child endangering. We think the analogy to child endangering decisions is apt, but that *Beaugez* and *Harris* have been weakened in their persuasiveness, since *Farley* was decided, in *People v. Peabody* (1975) 46 Cal.App.3d 43. *Peabody* . . . held that "Penal Code section 273a, subdivision (1) requires proof of criminal negligence which means that the defendant's conduct must amount to a reckless, gross or culpable departure from the ordinary standard of due care; it must be such a departure from what would be the conduct of an ordinarily prudent person under the same circumstances as to be incompatible with a proper regard of human life." This standard is higher than the ordinary negligence standard specified in *Farley*. . . .

Peabody distinguishes *Beaugez* by stating that *Beaugez* was concerned, not with the quantum of negligence, but, rather with whether the statute was constitutionally vague. We agree with this interpretation and are more persuaded by *Peabody* than by *Harris* or *Beaugez* given the trend in the law . . . toward limiting the number of crimes where no intent or limited criminal intent will be allowed. . . .

In our case defense counsel, relying on *People v. Farley*, suggested the instruction that was given. We do not find this invited error as we do not discern any tactical purpose deliberately decided up by the defendant's trial counsel. Absent such a purpose or tactic, the duty still rests upon the trial court to render a full and correct instruction on the important element of the requisite criminal intent.

On retrial the court should instruct the jury . . . with a paraphrase of the definition of criminal negligence from *People v. Peabody, supra*, so that it applies to animals, not children. In addition, the trial court should be aware of the rule of law that a principal is not criminally liable for the criminal act of his agent unless he authorized, consented to, advised, aided or encouraged the specific act. *People v. Travers* (1975) 52 Cal.App.3d 111, 114. *Travers* held that this principle does not apply to strict liability criminal offenses, but, as we have seen Penal Code section 597, subdivision (b) is not a strict liability offense. The court, on request, should instruct on this principle if the evidence shows, as it did at the first trial, that defendant was relying on friends and employees (Madrid) to care for her animals in her absence.

The judgment of conviction is reversed.

Notes

1. The *Brian* case establishes "criminal negligence" as the appropriate *mens rea* in animal neglect cases, just as it is in child neglect cases. Is there justification for changing the *mens rea* requirement depending on the species or category of victim involved? If so, how would you articulate the different standards in the following abuse cases: animal, spousal, child, elder.

2. The *Brian* court interpreted California Penal Code section 597(b) relating to animal neglect. In *People v. Alvarado*, 125 Cal. App. 4th 1179 (2005), the court considered whether California Penal Code section 597(a), relating to affirmative animal cruelty, constitutes a general or specific intent crime. The statute provides that "[e]very person who maliciously and intentionally maims, mutilates, tortures, or wounds a living animal or maliciously and intentionally kills an animal" is guilty of a violation of section 597(a). Manual Alvarado was charged with two counts of animal cruelty after killing two dogs that he and his girlfriend owned. After conviction on both counts, Alvarado appealed, contending the court erred by failing to instruct the jury that he acted with *specific intent* to "maim, mutilate, torture, wound or kill a living animal." The court rejected this argument, concluding that under section 597(a) no specific intent is required for conviction. Rather, a general intent to do the prohibited acts, without reference to any intent to do a further act or achieve a future consequence, is all that is required. In Alvarado's case, his actions against the dogs were sufficient to convict him even if he did not specifically intend to "maim, mutilate, torture, wound or kill a living animal."

3. In the period from 2005 through 2018, there were a number of arrests and convictions of slaughterhouse employees for shocking acts of cruelty to the animals they were handling. Where it could be proved that the company management was aware of the cruelty committed by its employees, the managers were in some situations also criminally prosecuted. In some circumstances, companies could be held liable for the actions of their employees if the employees acted in accordance with company policies but contrary to the provisions of federal or state laws related to animal cruelty or humane slaughter.

4. Where prosecutors seek criminal charges against employers of individuals involved in acts of animal cruelty, it may be necessary to show that the agent's acts were authorized, requested, commanded, performed or recklessly tolerated by the board of directors or by a high managerial agent acting on behalf of the corporation within the scope of their office or employment. *State v. Adjustment Dept. Credit Bureau Inc.*, 483 P.2d 687 (Idaho 1971). *See also People v. Travers*, 52 Cal. App. 3d 111, 114 (1975) (principal is not criminally liable for the criminal act of his agent unless he authorized, consented to, advised, aided or encouraged the specific act).

5. In 2007, an undercover investigation of the Hallmark Meat Packing Plant in Chino, California, produced extensive documentation of animal cruelty. The investigation led to the filing of criminal and civil charges against two plant employees and reportedly the largest beef recall (143 million pounds of meat) in U.S. history. A plant manager pled no contest to two felony counts of animal cruelty and two misdemeanor counts of cruelty to downed (non-ambulatory) animals and was sentenced to nine months in jail and three years of felony probation. Another worker was sentenced to six months in jail for illegally moving a downed animal. Associated Press, *California Beef Plant Worker Sentenced in Abuse Case*, USA TODAY (Sept. 24, 2008). (A related civil case — *United States of America, ex rel The Humane Society of the United States v. Hallmark Meat Packing Co., et al.*, 2013 U.S. Dist. LEXIS 126945 (C.D. Cal. Apr. 30, 2013) — is discussed in Chapter 6.)

When equally egregious incidents were caught on tape at the Pilgrims Pride chicken processing plant in Moorefield, West Virginia, the special prosecutor presented the case to a grand jury, but the grand jury refused to indict the chicken plant workers or their managers. Vicki Smith, *Jury Won't Indict Chicken Plant Workers*, Associated Press (Jun. 8, 2005). *See also Workers at Chicken Plant Escape Criminal Charges*, GLOBE AND MAIL (Canada), Jan. 12, 2005, at A10.

6. For more information on corporate liability for criminal acts, *see generally*, 18B Am. Jur. 2d Corporations §§ 2134–2149 (1985); H. Lowell Brown, *Vicarious Criminal Liability of Corporations for the Acts of Their Employees and Agents*, 41 Loy. L. Rev. 279 (1995).

Section 6. Hoarding

Animal "hoarding" or "collecting" has long been a problem across the nation—current estimates are that it affects more than 250,000 animals in the United States each year. Recognition of the magnitude of the problem in recent years has caused animal advocacy groups and law enforcement to focus more of their resources on the special challenges in hoarding cases. It also has emerged as an important topic for study among legal scholars as well as mental health and veterinary health experts. For example, the Cummings School of Veterinary Medicine at Tufts University supports a project known as the Hoarding of Animals Research Consortium ("HARC"). According to the project website (_http://www.tufts.edu/vet/cfa/hoarding/_) (last visited Feb. 2018), HARC was established by "a group of researchers who collaborated from 1997–2006 to define and better understand the problem of animal hoarding." That group created a community intervention manual in 2006, and since then the work of HARC continues under the leadership of Dr. Gary Patronek and Jane Nathanson.

The terms "hoarder" and "collector" are used interchangeably and refer to people who keep multiple animals who are concurrently neglected in a manner that causes suffering of varying degrees. Animal hoarders are usually charged (if at all) under a state's general animal anti-cruelty statute, although both Hawaii and Illinois have passed law explicitly prohibiting "animal hoarding." Under the Illinois law, animal hoarders, like all others, are subject to punishment for animal neglect. 510 Ill. Comp. Stat. 70/3. Under the statute, however, if a defendant meets the definition of a "companion animal hoarder," the court must order the person to undergo mental evaluation and appropriate treatment. _Id._ Illinois defines a "companion animal hoarder" as:

> a person who (i) possesses a large number of companion animals; (ii) fails to or is unable to provide what he or she is required to provide under section 3 of this Act [510 ILCS 70/3]; (iii) keeps the companion animals in a severely overcrowded environment; and (iv) displays an inability to recognize or understand the nature of or has a reckless disregard for the conditions under which the companion animals are living and the deleterious impact they have on the companion animals' and owner's health and well-being.

510 Ill. Comp. Stat. 70/2.10 (2009).

From a prosecution standpoint, hoarding cases can be among the most difficult to handle because of the number of animals involved, the amount of resources needed to rescue, treat, and foster the animals, and the case management issues that may arise when there are tens or even hundreds of potential criminal counts based on a single discovery of hoarding.

People v. Riazati

Court of Appeal, Fourth District, Division 1, California, 2011
195 Cal. App. 4th 514

NARES, J. Manuchehr Riazati accumulated at his residence more than 90 animals, which the County of San Diego Department of Animal Services (Department) ultimately seized pursuant to a search warrant after animal control officers made multiple unsuccessful attempts to persuade Riazati to rectify code violations concerning the living conditions of the animals. A jury convicted Riazati of two counts of felony animal neglect (rabbits & dogs) and four counts of misdemeanor animal neglect (chickens, birds, guinea pigs & a duck) in violation of Penal Code section 597, subdivision (b) (hereafter section 597(b)). The court suspended imposition of sentence for five years, granted formal probation to Riazati, and ordered him to pay $42,263 in restitution and fines.

Riazati appeals, contending (1) the evidence is insufficient to support any of his six animal neglect convictions because there is no evidence he "failed to properly provide food, water, or shelter to the six species of animals under his care in a manner that created a high risk of death" to the animals, and thus there is no evidence he acted with the gross negligence required for a conviction under section 597(b); and (2) the court prejudicially erred and violated his rights to due process and a fair trial by instructing the jury (at Riazati's request) that he could be found guilty of animal neglect under section 597(b) if his acts or omissions created a high risk of great bodily injury to an animal under his care, thereby reducing the prosecution's burden of proof.

We conclude (1) Riazati is barred under the doctrine of invited error from challenging the jury instructions on the elements of the offense of animal neglect (§597(b)) and the definition of gross negligence given by the court, because his repeated and successful requests for those instructions were the result of a deliberate tactical choice at trial; (2) Riazati's instructional error claim is unavailing on the merits because the challenged instructions are correct statements of applicable law; and (3) the evidence is sufficient to support all six of his section 597(b) animal neglect convictions. Accordingly, we affirm the judgment.

FACTUAL BACKGROUND

A. *The People's Case*

It is undisputed that the Department received complaints about the condition of animals at Riazati's residence and that during multiple visits there on and between February 28 and April 16, 2008, Department officers observed more than 90 animals.

February 28

On February 28, Shalimar Oliver, an animal control officer employed by the Department, responded to a complaint from one of Riazati's neighbors regarding an aggressive dog on Riazati's roof that was trying to jump down and possibly attack people walking by. When Officer Oliver arrived at Riazati's home, she observed in the front yard various items of junk and holes in the ground that were filled with water with insects flying around. She detected a strong, foul odor emanating from both the front yard and the home. While knocking on the front door, Officer Oliver heard dogs barking and the sound of a lot of birds inside the home.

When Riazati answered the door, Officer Oliver, who was assisted by other officers, identified herself and explained she was there to investigate the complaint the Department had received. Riazati said one of his dogs might have been able to get on the roof from bales of straw located on the side of the house. Officer Oliver and Riazati entered the side yard on the left side of the home and observed a tethered juvenile German Shepherd-type dog, which was not sheltered from the elements and was lying in a muddy area with insects flying around it. The dog had no access to food or water.

In the back yard, Officer Oliver saw a large number of "random junk items," such as an old toilet, and smelled a very noticeable odor of feces and urine. She testified that the feces "smelled as though it had been there for a while." During the visit, Officer Oliver observed five dogs on the property. They did not have dog tags, and only one was licensed. As Riazati, who was becoming argumentative and uncooperative, did not want to purchase licenses through Officer Oliver, she issued a correctable citation.

When Riazati went inside to get his identification, Officer Oliver noticed an enclosed patio with a sliding glass door. A chicken that had come through the vertical blinds was leaning its head against the glass door in an unresponsive and atypical manner. Through the blinds Officer Oliver saw rabbits and guinea pigs, and she could hear birds, some of which were flying through the vertical blinds.

After explaining to Riazati her concern about the animals, Officer Oliver entered the enclosed back patio to check on their welfare. With free-roaming rabbits and guinea pigs at her feet, she noticed she was standing on what appeared to be soiled hay and feces. She saw at least 20 rabbits running around and numerous noisy birds flying around. She saw about 30 birds, most of which were caged. Officer Oliver counted nine chickens, including the free-roaming chicken she saw leaning against the glass door; eight were in a cage that did not give them enough room to move around. The room had a very strong odor of a combination of feces and urine, and the sharp scent of ammonia associated with urine caused Officer Oliver's eyes to water. The ventilation was inadequate because the windows in the room were barely open. The free-roaming chicken appeared weak. Feces appeared to be on the birdseed inside the bird cages, and the color of the water in the cages was brownish green. Some of the water had feces in it. The coats of some of the rabbits and guinea pigs appeared to be stained with feces.

From the enclosed back patio, Officer Oliver was able to see more animals in the living room-kitchen area. When she entered those areas, Officer Oliver saw on the kitchen floor stains of significant size that appeared to be smeared feces. She smelled in both the kitchen and the living room the same strong odor of feces and urine. She found a glass aquarium full of finches and saw one that was missing a large amount of feathers, which caused her concern that other birds were picking on it. She was also concerned about the poor sanitation inside that aquarium. She found an adult Boxer dog inside a crate covered by a blanket. The dog appeared to be thin, and it had no access to water. Officer Oliver advised Riazati about how to properly feed the dog.

Riazati did not allow Officer Oliver and the other officers to further inspect the house. Officer Oliver explained to Riazati the violations she observed, advised him how to improve the conditions of the animals, and issued him a notice of complaint. The violations she noted were inadequate food, inadequate water, inadequate ventilation, and inadequate sanitation. Riazati relinquished a rat, and Officer Oliver took no other animals because the Department's aim was to educate people and give them a chance to correct the violations.

March 8

Officer Oliver, accompanied by police officers, returned to Riazati's home on March 8. The front yard appeared to be in about the same condition. In the back yard, the items of junk appeared to have been rearranged in different piles, but were still cluttering the yard. The rabbits and guinea pigs had been moved into a penned area in the back yard. Officer Oliver did not see rabbit pellet food, leafy greens, or other food in that area, and she testified she could not recall seeing any water there. Insects were buzzing around. She was concerned about the poor sanitation in the pen as the animals were living in their own filth.

Officer Oliver saw four of the five dogs, and their condition was the same as it had been on February 28. She continued to be concerned with shelter and sanitation. The penned area for the dogs did not have a roof, and the odor was strong and foul.

Many of the birds had been moved into the back yard. The cages were on top of each other, allowing the birds in the upper cages to urinate and defecate on the birds in the lower cages. The bird food was still contaminated with feces and urine, and the water appeared to have feces in it. The shelter for the birds was inadequate as there was no roof over most of the cages.

The condition of the finches in the glass aquarium inside the house was the same. Officer Oliver was concerned about the urine and feces in the food and water.

Riazati had removed some of the soiled hay and feces in the enclosed patio. However, a significant amount remained.

Officer Oliver advised Riazati he needed to fix the issues concerning food, water, and shelter for the animals. She orally advised Riazati what he needed to do as to each type of animal.

* * *

March 21

On March 21, Officer Oliver, accompanied by another Department officer, again returned to Riazati's home. She took photographs of the front and back yards and most of the inside of the house. Riazati told her he had not had time to make many corrections. He told Officer Oliver he was trying to sell one of the dogs.

The condition of the front yard was improved, but not significantly. The yard was still cluttered and the odor of feces was still there. The Boxer dog still appeared to be thin.

The condition of the back yard was similar to the condition Officer Oliver had previously observed. She was concerned about the shelter of the caged birds, cockatiels and parakeets, as the tray top was insufficient. She was still concerned about sanitation as the water in the cages was brownish green and had feces in it. The food containers did not contain edible food. Officer Oliver saw feces in the bird seed. The birds did not have adequate shelter from extreme temperatures. She also testified that sanitation was poor because of the amount of feces in the cages.

Officer Oliver was also concerned about the condition of the estimated 20 rabbits in the back yard. Bales of hay were part of the fencing for the enclosure, but the animals did not have adequate shelter from the sun. Sanitation was poor as there were feces everywhere. Officer Oliver did not see any rabbit food. Guinea pigs were with the rabbits. The conditions had not changed much since Officer Oliver's last visit. She observed an empty bowl with feces in it. Another container that was too high for the animals to reach was full of brownish water that was not suitable for drinking. The officers smelled the odor of a dead animal and found a dead young rabbit locked inside a cage.

A lot of the clutter had been cleared out of the back area of the enclosed patio, but some cages were still in the room. Hay and feces were still on the floor.

In the living room-kitchen area, several bird cages were still piled on top of each other so that the birds on top would urinate and defecate on the birds in the lower cage. The bird food and water were still contaminated with feces. The finches were still in a fish tank. The food and water in the tank were contaminated with feces and urine. The water was brownish green. Riazati had not fixed anything that Officer Oliver had asked him to fix.

Officer Oliver observed an adult German Shepherd dog that was confined in the back kennel area of the back yard and heard another dog that appeared to be confined in a crate in one of the bedrooms. She observed a chicken in the back yard that had inadequate shelter and contaminated food and water.

Riazati was no longer at home when the officers finished their inspection. Officer Oliver posted preimpoundment notices on the front door instructing Riazati what he needed to do to correct the violations.

* * *

Execution of the search warrant on April 16

The Department obtained a search warrant to retrieve the animals from Riazati's home. Several other Department officers as well as several police officers assisted Officer Oliver in executing the search warrant on April 16. The execution of the warrant was photographed and videotaped. The videotape was admitted into evidence and played for the jury.

Officer Oliver testified that during the execution of the search warrant, she observed no significant change in the condition of the animals in the back yard. Feces covered the bottom of cages. The water in the water bowls for the rabbits and guinea pigs was brownish green and contained feces.

The officers found two rabbits inside Riazati's garage. Officer Oliver testified the rabbits were standing on wire flooring, the tray beneath the wiring was saturated with urine and feces, and the water was contaminated.

The officers found another rabbit in a cage in the kitchen area. Officer Oliver testified the rabbit had some serious wounds on its back end that the medical operations manager needed to inspect.

A water container in the dog kennel area of the back yard appeared to have bacteria growing inside it, and the water was green. Larvae were growing in a water bowl. The officers also found a dog food bowl that contained old food and another food bowl with food that smelled rotten. The officers found three dogs inside the house. A dog in a crate had dirty water and the amount of the water was insufficient.

Officer Oliver again found birds inside Riazati's home. The only change in the condition of the birds was that they had been moved back inside the house. The food bowls in the cages contained a heavy amount of feces. Water bowls contained water that was discolored and contaminated with feces.

In the back yard, the officers found a free-roaming duck, which they caged. They also found a chicken in the back yard where the birds were previously located. The shelter for the chicken consisted of a piece of plastic over the wire cage, which was insufficient, and feces were all over the cage.

During the execution of the search warrant, the officer seized and inventoried 90 animals.

Medical examination of the seized animals

All of the seized animals were taken to the Central Animal Shelter, where they were examined by Dr. Julie Maher, a Department veterinarian. The German Shepherd had hair loss around the tail, indicating malnutrition and exposure to dirty conditions. It also had scars on both ears, indicating fly bites resulting from poor sanitation. Another dog, a Chow Chow puppy, had green nasal discharge and abnormally quiet lungs, indicating bacteria, fluid, and pus in the lungs. Maher put the dog, which was suffering from pneumonia, on antibiotics. The puppy was very underweight, had lost the muscle mass along his spine, and had no palpable fat.

Tapeworms were seen in the stools of the Chow Chow and a couple of the other seized dogs, including another German Shepherd.

Maher testified she watched the video and saw the photographs of the living conditions of the animals at Riazati's home and opined there were too many rabbits there, they did not have enough uncluttered and safe living space, and they had inadequate food and water. The guinea pigs should have had a solid cage floor because they are prone to get sores on their feet from wire bedding. They also should have had a sipper bottle with water and a place to hide because they are a very nervous prey species. Maher testified that the main medical problems she observed regarding the majority of the rabbits and guinea pigs were dehydration and low body weight, which she opined was caused by underfeeding. The young, dehydrated, brownish-red rabbit with abscesses over his pelvis and on his back probably suffered those wounds as a result of other rabbits biting him. The rabbit, whose fur was dirty with feces, also had tattered ears. Maher opined the ears were tattered as a result of fighting with other rabbits, overcrowding, and/or lack of sanitation and food.

Maher examined the duck, which was emaciated and covered with feces. No shelter or bathing water was provided for the duck in Riazati's backyard.

Maher also examined the chicken, which was emaciated. Maher opined the chicken was starving from inappropriate or not enough food at the time it was seized.

Maher opined the birds were not provided adequate shelter. The cages were full of feces, and they were overcrowded. Birds should not eat their own feces, which contain bacteria and parasites that can cause disease. She also opined the birds had inadequate food, which appeared to be covered with bird droppings. The water for the birds was contaminated with bird droppings, algae, or bacteria. Contaminated water transmits parasitic, bacterial, and fungal diseases.

B. *The Defense Case*

Moghadase Tavakoli, Riazati's mother, indicated she found her brown rabbit had injured its back in a cage at her home. She called Riazati, who applied medication to the injury and took the rabbit.

David Adam Baruch, Riazati's neighbor, went to Riazati's house twice between February 28 and April 16. On the first visit he saw water and food in the bird cages. He did not smell feces in the house. Baruch did not recall seeing a brown rabbit in a cage. He returned to Riazati's home on April 14. He saw birds in cages inside the house and rabbits and guinea pigs in the penned area outside the house, but no dogs. He did not see any dead rabbits, and the rabbits acted normally. Riazati's rabbits had adequate food and water and appeared hydrated and of proper weight.

Ehsan Bagheri–Anderson, Riazati's nephew, went to Riazati's house in early March after he learned about the Department officer's visit on February 28. He looked inside the bird cages, which were clean, and saw clean water and food.

Bagheri–Anderson returned to Riazati's house in early April. Riazati was cleaning the brown rabbit's injury, applying hydrogen peroxide and an ointment. The water in the rabbit's cage was clear.

Bagheri–Anderson again returned to Riazati's house on April 13 and took video footage inside the house. He videotaped the bird cages to show the water and food. He also videotaped the rabbits. He opined that Riazati provided clear, good water, appropriate food, and shelter for the animals.

Defense expert Gayle Roberts, a veterinarian who had no formal training in animal neglect cases and did not personally examine the animals or see their living conditions before the April 16 video, relied on the records to form her opinions. A rabbit may develop a skin condition as a result of a bite wound, and it is appropriate to treat such a skin condition at home with hydrogen peroxide and Neosporin. She opined that among the rabbits at Riazati's home were no common rabbit problems one would expect when the food, water, and shelter are inadequate. In the April 16 video, the rabbits looked playful, bright, and alert. While one bowl of water looked contaminated with feces, rabbits could drink it. The injured rabbit was alone in a cage, which was appropriate to prevent the other rabbits from hurting it further.

Although the German Shepherd had fly strike scars, fly strikes are normally not fatal and are common with outside dogs. None of the dogs had distemper, diarrhea, kennel cough, heat stroke, hookworm, roundworm, or coccidiosis. Roberts testified the video showed the dogs were friendly, greeting the officers and jumping on them. She would have expected to see signs of vomiting or diarrhea if the dogs had been eating rotten food. Although the Chow was diagnosed with pneumonia, it was not coughing at intake and its alleged nasal discharge was not apparent in the video. Roberts indicated there was no evidence the three dogs, the German Shepherd and the two German Shepherd mixes, were improperly fed or watered, and it was appropriate to house the sick Chow separately. She indicated that tapeworms are not a major risk to an animal's life.

Birds sometimes defecate in their water and food bowls and sometimes put food in their water, which can discolor it. Roberts indicated that birds eat around feces in their food. The bird with feather loss was overplucking its own feathers.

On cross-examination, Roberts testified she had never before encountered a client who had so many animals. She would not give her dog the food and water shown in certain photographs of Riazati's yard. She acknowledged the food could be a cause of disease if a dog ate it, and it was possible the water could also lead to disease if a dog drank it.

DISCUSSION

I. CLAIM OF INSTRUCTIONAL ERROR

Riazati contends the court prejudicially erred and violated his rights to due process and a fair trial by instructing the jury (at Riazati's request) that he could be found guilty of animal neglect under section 597(b) if his acts or omissions created a high risk of "great bodily injury" to an animal under his care, thereby reducing the prosecution's burden of proof. He asserts that "the problem lies in the inclusion of 'great bodily injury' as an element in the present offense." For reasons we shall discuss, we conclude Riazati's contention is unavailing because (1) he is barred under the doctrine of invited error from challenging on appeal this portion of the jury instructions on animal neglect (§597(b)) and the definition of gross negligence given by the court, and (2) the instructions are correct statements of the applicable law.

A. *Background*

In the People's trial brief, the prosecutor noted there is no standard jury instruction on the elements of a violation of section 597(b) and requested that the court give the jury the instruction on animal cruelty that the Court of Appeal approved in *People v. Speegle* (1997) 53 Cal.App.4th 1405, 1412–1413 (*Speegle*), which informed the jury in that case that the prosecution was required to prove the defendant committed a "grossly negligent act or omission" that "caused danger to an animal's life."[3]

The prosecutor also requested an instruction on the definition of "gross negligence" based on *People v. Brian* (1980) 110 Cal.App.3d Supp. 1, 4–5 (*Brian*), in which the appellate department of the superior court held that a conviction under section 597(b) for animal neglect requires proof of criminal negligence, not ordinary negligence, which the court defined as conduct amounting to a reckless, gross, or culpable departure from the ordinary standard of due care; in other words, conduct that is such a departure from what would be the conduct of an ordinarily prudent person under the same circumstances as to be incompatible with a proper regard for animal life.

During a discussion regarding jury instructions after the parties rested, defense counsel objected to the instructions proposed by the prosecutor. Specifically, Riazati's counsel objected to the portion of the proposed instruction stating that in order to prove animal neglect, the People must prove that Riazati committed an act or omission that "caused danger to an animal's life." Defense counsel stated: "I do not believe that is the standard under gross negligence. Gross negligence requires something much more . . . [S]*omething more is required than just mere danger to an animal's life* if we are talking about gross negligence." (Italics added.) Relying on *People v. Rodriguez* (1960) 186 Cal.App.2d 433 (*Rodriguez*), which involved an appeal from an involuntary manslaughter conviction and addressed the meaning of criminal negligence, Riazati's counsel argued that a finding of gross negligence requires proof the defendant's alleged act or omission caused a "high degree of risk" of "death or great bodily injury." . . .

. . . [E]ssentially agreeing with defense counsel, the prosecutor then asked the court to give the definition of gross negligence set forth in CALCRIM No. 970, which addresses the crime of shooting a firearm in a grossly negligent manner and

---

3. Footnote text missing.

provides in part: "A person acts with gross negligence when: [¶] 1. He or she acts in a reckless way that *creates a high risk of death or great bodily injury* [; AND] [¶] 2. A reasonable person would have known that acting in that way would create such a risk." (Italics added.)

* * *

C. *Analysis*

At issue in this appeal is the italicized language in the two instructions that informed the jury it could find Riazati guilty of animal neglect in violation of section 597(b) if it found beyond a reasonable doubt that he committed a reckless act or omission that created a high risk of "great bodily injury" to an animal.

* * *

2. *Riazati's instructional error claim is unavailing on the merits*

In *Speegle, supra,* 53 Cal.App.4th at page 1415, the Court of Appeal observed that, "[i]n our society, those who mistreat animals are the deserved object of obloquy, and their conduct is wrongful of itself and not just as a matter of legislative declaration." An example of such "legislative declaration" regarding the mistreatment of animals may be found in the enactment of section 597(b), which proscribes specified acts and omissions that are the product of grossly negligent conduct and are deemed to be acts of animal cruelty or neglect.

As pertinent here, and with exceptions not applicable in this case, section 597(b) provides: "[E]very person who ... deprives of necessary sustenance, drink, or shelter ... any animal, or causes ... any animal to be so ... deprived of necessary sustenance, drink, shelter; ... and whoever, having the charge or custody of any animal, either as owner or otherwise, subjects any animal to needless suffering, or ... fails to provide the animal with proper food, drink, or shelter or protection from the weather, ... is, for every such offense, guilty of a crime punishable as a misdemeanor or as a felony or alternatively punishable as a misdemeanor or a felony and by a fine of not more than twenty thousand dollars ($20,000)."

Riazati acknowledges that criminal liability under section 597(b) may be imposed on a person who has custody of, or is responsible for providing care to, an animal and commits an act or omission proscribed by that subdivision that recklessly exposes the animal to a high risk of *death,* as the court properly instructed the jury in this case. In *Speegle, supra,* 53 Cal.App.4th at pages 1412–1413, the Court of Appeal upheld an instruction (which was also given in the instant case) that "[s]ubjecting an animal to needless suffering and failure to provide an animal with proper food, drink or shelter are both unlawful [under section 597(b)] when a person ... commits an act or omission which would inherently produce danger to an animal's *life.*" (Italics added.)

Speegle, however, did not address the issue of first impression presented here of whether criminal liability under section 597(b) may be imposed on a person who has custody of, or is responsible for providing care to, an animal and commits an act or omission proscribed by that subdivision that recklessly exposes the animal to a high risk of *great bodily injury*. We conclude that criminal liability may be imposed on such a person under section 597(b). Nothing in the language set forth in section 597(b) indicates a legislative intent to proscribe grossly negligent conduct that exposes an animal under a person's care to a high risk of death, but to shield that same person from criminal liability for engaging in grossly negligent conduct that exposes the animal to a high risk of great bodily injury. On the contrary, as pertinent here, the statute is broadly written to encompass grossly negligent conduct that "deprives [any cared-for animal] of necessary sustenance, drink, or shelter"; or "causes ... any animal to be so ... deprived of necessary sustenance, drink, [or] shelter"; or "subjects any animal to needless suffering." (§597(b).) As a practical matter, and as a matter of common sense and experience, great bodily injury to an animal is often the precursor to the animal's death. Thus, an interpretation of section 597(b) permitting the imposition of criminal liability for grossly negligent conduct that exposes a cared-for animal to a high risk of great bodily injury is consistent with the Legislature's judicially recognized intent to protect such animals from grossly negligent conduct that exposes them to a risk of death. (See *Speegle, supra*, 53 Cal.App.4th at pp. 1412–1413; *People v. Youngblood* (2001) 91 Cal. App.4th 66, 70.) In this regard, we emphasize that the risk of great bodily injury to an animal created by the allegedly culpable conduct of the defendant must be a high risk. Stated differently, the risk of great bodily injury to the cared-for animal created by the defendant's alleged gross negligence, in order to support a conviction for animal cruelty or animal neglect under section 597(b), must be a high risk.

In sum, we conclude the court did not commit instructional error or violate Riazati's rights to due process and a fair trial.

* * *

Notes

1. Compare the court's determination in *Riazati* to *State v. Thompson*, 33 N.W.2d 13 (Iowa 1948). In *Thompson*, the defendant was convicted of cruelty to animals. He had been picking up stray and unwanted dogs and shipping them to a serum company for a year. On the date of his arrest and for the preceding three months, the defendant had rented a vacant lot, where he kept the dogs in pens until they were sold. Thirty-eight dogs were impounded from the site. The dogs were very thin, quite hungry, in "very bad condition" and suffering from mange (a dangerous inflammatory disease caused by mites) and distemper (a viral infection that is potentially fatal, especially in puppies). At the time of their rescue, in the heat of the day, few if any of the pens had water in them. On appeal, the court followed the standard rule that a guilty verdict will not be set aside on the grounds of insufficient evidence unless the evidence is so utterly wanting that the verdict cannot be sustained. The court nevertheless reversed the conviction, holding that there was no evidence the dogs suffered unjustifiable pain or distress because the evidence only showed they were panting and their tongues were hanging out; that while the dogs

were thin and appeared to be hungry, they were strays and accustomed to eating from garbage cans for their sustenance; and that mange and distemper can develop even in well-cared-for animals. The court concluded the evidence was insufficient to sustain a conviction of cruelty to animals by unnecessarily failing to provide proper food, drink and shelter.

2. Another case that demonstrates the problems of addressing hoarding is *Animal Legal Defense Fund (ALDF) v. Woodley*, 640 S.E.2d 777 (N.C. Ct. App. 2007). In that case, undisputed trial testimony established that in October 2004 the Woodleys, who were breeder/hoarders, had close to 450 dogs, many suffering severely and all living in filth with basic health needs neglected. Local law enforcement and animal control had received reports of overcrowding and neglect for years, and multiple dogs bought from the Woodleys were sick or had died. Prior efforts to address the problems had failed. For example, in 2000, an investigation of the premises resulted in no cruelty charges and no animal rescue but simply a requirement that the Woodleys divert the discharge of canine waste products from an adjoining stream to city sewers. In August 2004, an individual who bought three dogs from the Woodleys and personally observed the conditions filed cruelty charges. When the case came before the court, however, it was dismissed for lack of evidence. Finally, in November of 2004, ALDF became involved, performed its own investigation, and filed a civil action pursuant to North Carolina General Statutes Chapter 19A, which allows private citizens and groups to sue for animal cruelty and force the surrender of abused animals. The Woodleys appealed from an injunction forfeiting all of their rights in the animals and the removal of the animals from their control, arguing in part that Chapter 19A was unconstitutional in that it purported to grant standing to persons that had suffered no injury. The court rejected this argument and affirmed the trial court's ruling in the civil action. (Constitutional standing is addressed at length in Chapter 5.) In connection with both the civil action and the companion criminal case against the Woodleys, ALDF worked with local authorities. The Woodleys ultimately were convicted on multiple counts of animal cruelty.

The *Woodley* case took place in a small town south of Raleigh, North Carolina, which had a limited animal control budget and staff and a shelter with only a very small number of kennels available for housing stray or abandoned dogs. The story behind the case reveals the complex and multidisciplinary organization that needs to be established to manage large hoarding situations. ALDF relied on local citizens at every stage of the case. By way of example:

a) Concerned citizens first contacted ALDF to alert it of the neglect and suffering of the Woodleys' dogs;

b) ALDF began a thorough investigation, interviewing everyone its lawyers could find who had information about the site, tracking down friends of the Woodleys, and even getting testimony from individuals who were helping the Woodleys remove dogs from their property;

c) ALDF relied on veterinarians around the state to handle special medical care needed by the majority of the dogs;

d) ALDF relied on full-time volunteer veterinarians to conduct daily visits to the Woodleys' property while the litigation was pending and to provide daily consultation and care for the dogs for almost a year after the case was first filed;

e) A local volunteer designed an interactive database that allowed quick access to all pertinent information about each dog, volunteer, foster location and other data;

f) Full-time volunteer shelter managers brought their expertise and oversaw the entire shelter operation; and

g) Hundreds of volunteers assisted in the rescue and the daily care of the dogs prior to fostering.

The case illustrates the overwhelming strain hoarding places on local communities, which is one reason many consider hoarding the number one problem affecting companion animals in America today. The other main reason, of course, is the level of neglect and suffering seen in a majority of hoarding cases, the chronic nature of the medical problems and the long-term pain and psychological effects involved with many of those conditions.

3. "Typical" hoarding cases involve large numbers of animals, ranging from forty to over one thousand, and the animals involved are usually dogs or cats. Exotic animal and farm animal hoarders have been identified as well. Most distressing to animal protection groups are the consequences of hoarding, of which the following conditions are the most common:

a) Moderate to severe tooth and mouth decay, with animals losing many if not all of their teeth, and jawbones rotting from poor hygiene;

b) Eye disease resulting in extremely painful conditions as well as blindness;

c) Chronically matted fur caked with feces and urine;

d) Filthy housing with months of urine and feces forming the "floor" of boxes and caging;

e) "Urine scalding" where animals' sensitive skin is burned from the acidic nature of the urine they are forced to lie in for extended periods;

f) Psychological trauma that may last a lifetime and make rescued hoarding victims especially difficult to care for and adopt out to permanent homes; and

g) Extreme malnutrition and starvation.

See also Josh Marquis, The Kittles Case and its Aftermath, 2 ANIMAL L. 197 (1996); Colin Berry, Long-Term Outcomes in Hoarding Cases, 11 ANIMAL L. 167 (2005).

4. Hoarding poses problems for communities generally, and new legislation may provide relief. For example, Oregon's nuisance abatement scheme (OR. REV. STAT. § 105.550, *et seq.*) allows for an action to restrain or enjoin a nuisance to be brought by "the Attorney General, district attorney, county attorney, city attorney or a person residing or doing business in the county where the property is located" and to seek damages "for mental suffering, emotional distress, inconvenience and interference with the use of property suffered by the plaintiff by reason of the activities constituting a nuisance." OR. REV. STAT. § 105.560(1)-(2). In 2015, the Oregon legislature amended this scheme to specifically address the issues faced by communities plagued with animal abuse, irresponsible breeding, hoarding, and animal fighting. Section 105.597(1)-(4) describes circumstances in which a property may be subject to the nuisance abatement scheme:

(1) Any place being used on a continuous, regular or sporadic basis for carrying out any of the following activities, except with regard to activities and animals described under ORS 167.335 [which provides a list of exemptions to animal cruelty], whether or not carried out with a particular mental state:

(a) Causing physical injury or serious physical injury, both as defined in ORS 167.310 or cruelly causing death.

(b) Killing maliciously as defined in ORS 167.322 or committing torture as defined in ORS 167.322.

(c) Failing to provide minimum care as defined in ORS 167.310.

(d) Possession of a domestic animal as defined in ORS 167.310 by a person described under ORS 167.332.

(2) Any place appearing to be vacant at which a domestic animal or equine, both as defined in ORS 167.310, are present and have been left without provision for minimum care as defined in ORS 167.310.

(3) Any place being used on a continuous, regular or sporadic basis for carrying out any of the following activities, whether or not carried out with a particular mental state:

(a) Training or keeping an animal for use in an exhibition of fighting as defined in ORS 167.355.

(b) Preparing for, occupation for, promoting, conducting or participating in an exhibition of fighting as defined in ORS 167.355.

(c) Possessing, keeping, breeding, training, buying, selling or offering for sale a fighting dog as defined in ORS 167.360.

(d) Promoting, conducting, participating in or performing services in furtherance of a dogfight as defined in ORS 167.360.

(e) Occupation, keeping or use of the place for a dogfight as defined in ORS 167.360.

(f) Exchanging for commerce raw fur of a domestic cat or dog as defined in ORS 167.390, or products that include the fur of a domestic cat or dog, if the fur is obtained through a process that kills or maims the domestic cat or dog.

(g) Possessing, keeping, rearing, training, buying, selling or offering for sale a fighting bird as defined in ORS 167.426.

(h) Promoting, conducting, participating in or performing services in furtherance of a cockfight as defined in ORS 167.426.

(i) Occupation, keeping or use of the place for a cockfight as defined in ORS 167.426.

(4) Any place being used on a continuous, regular or sporadic basis for carrying out any of the following activities:

(a) Sexual assault of an animal as described in ORS 167.333.

(b) Possession of dogfighting paraphernalia as described under ORS 167.372.

(c) Selling or offering for sale equipment other than paraphernalia described in paragraph (b) of this subsection with the intent that the equipment be used to train a fighting dog as defined in ORS 167.360.

(d) Possessing, controlling or otherwise having charge at the same time of more than 50 sexually intact dogs that are two or more years of age for the primary purpose of reproduction.

(e) Manufacturing, buying, selling, bartering, exchanging, possessing or offering for sale a gaff or slasher as those terms are defined in ORS 167.426, or other sharp implement designed for attachment to the leg of a fighting bird as defined in ORS 167.426, with the intent that the gaff, slasher or other sharp implement be used in a cockfight as defined in ORS 167.426.

(f) Manufacturing, buying, selling, bartering, exchanging, possessing or offering for sale equipment other than equipment described in paragraph (e) of this subsection with the intent that the equipment be used to train or handle a fighting bird as defined in ORS 167.426 or to enhance the fighting ability of a fighting bird.

5. Do you think the Oregon approach is reasonable? Are there privacy rights that need to be considered? Property rights? Discuss possible affirmative defenses a defendant could bring to combat a nuisance charge.

People v. Youngblood

Court of Appeal of California, Third Appellate District, 2001
91 Cal. App. 4th 66, 109 Cal. Rptr. 2d 776

NICHOLSON, J. The defendant accumulated 92 cats and kept them in a 7-foot-by-11-foot trailer, providing less than one square foot for each cat. Convicted by jury of felony animal cruelty and placed on probation, she appeals. She asserts the trial was tainted by instructional error, due process violations, and evidence that should have been suppressed. We affirm.

PROCEDURE

The defendant was charged by information with seven counts of animal cruelty in violation of Penal Code section 597, subdivision (b). Count 1 alleged cruelty to all 92 of the cats, while counts 2 through 7 alleged cruelty to one specified cat each. The jury found the defendant guilty of count 1 but not guilty of counts 2 through 7. The court placed the defendant on five years of formal probation with a condition that she serve 92 days in county jail. The court also ordered her not to possess or care for any cat or dog, except for a cat named Holly Angel.

FACTS

On December 31, 1998, Officer Robert Carter of Placer County Animal Control responded to a complaint that an excessive number of cats were being kept under poor health and living conditions in a small trailer. Officer Carter went to the property and saw a residence with a small trailer near the garage. He smelled a strong odor of ammonia, which he associated with animal urine, when he left his truck and started toward the residence. Terrance Deveany, the owner of the property, responded when Officer Carter knocked on the door. Deveany told Officer Carter the trailer belonged to the defendant.

Officer Carter approached the trailer and looked inside through the windows. He saw at least 35 cats in the trailer. At various places in the trailer, he saw fecal matter and urine. Many of the cats were sneezing and had eye discharge. Officer Carter telephoned the on-call magistrate and obtained a search warrant for the trailer. The officer then called for a tow truck. As they were hooking up the trailer to the tow truck, the defendant arrived at the property. She stated she was taking care of the cats and believed there were between 80 and 90 in the trailer. She tried to give Officer Carter a vial with medicine for the cats, but he would not accept it because it was not adequately marked. The trailer was towed to the DeWitt Center so it could be placed in a building before being opened to prevent loss of control of the cats.

When the trailer was first opened at the DeWitt Center, Officer Carter entered with a video camera and recorded the conditions inside the trailer. The videotape was played for the jury.

The cats, 92 in all, were removed from the trailer and assigned numbers for identification. Most of the cats appeared unhealthy. They were examined and treated by a veterinarian. Her initial summary of the condition of the cats is as follows:

> Most of the cats were covered in urine and feces. There [were] many that were malnourished, emaciated. Cats were sick with upper respiratory, herpes virus. They had ear mites, fleas. There [were] cats with neurologic[al] problems. There [were] cats that were missing portions of their limbs or had deformed limbs. There [were] cats with urine scald, and there [were] cats that were either blind or partially blind in one or both eyes and cats that were missing eyes, too.

The veterinarian also described other ailments suffered by the cats. Many of the problems described by the veterinarian, such as dehydration, chronic malnourishment, anorexia, urine scald, and severe infection, occur as a result of inadequate care over a long period.

The defendant testified. She lived in Sacramento County. In October 1998, she put the cats, about 35 to 40 at the time, in the trailer and moved them to the Deveany property in Placer County because Sacramento Animal Control officials told her she could not have more than four cats. She lived with the cats at first, either in the trailer or in a tent next to the trailer, feeding the cats and cleaning up after them. She brought additional stray cats from the Sacramento County neighborhood to the trailer. Eventually, she moved back to Sacramento County and visited the trailer to care for the cats. During the last two weeks before animal control seized the trailer, the defendant was sick and did not visit the cats as often. She contended that the messy conditions inside the trailer were a result of the removal of the trailer to the DeWitt Center. She knew she had too many cats, but she asserted she was trying to save their lives.

DISCUSSION

* * *

IV. Instruction Concerning Defense of Necessity

The defendant requested an instruction on the defense of necessity. She claimed that she was keeping the cats to save them from euthanasia at animal control. The trial court rejected the instruction and denied the defendant's request that she be permitted to present argument to the jury on the defense. On appeal, the defendant asserts the trial court erred. We conclude that, under the facts of this case, the defense of necessity was not available.

"The defense of necessity is 'founded upon public policy and provides a justification distinct from the elements required to prove the crime.' The situation presented to the defendant must be of an emergency nature, threatening physical harm, and lacking an alternative, legal course of action. The defense involves a determination that the harm or evil sought to be avoided by such conduct is greater than that sought to be prevented by the law defining the offense charged. Necessity does not negate any element of the crime, but represents a public policy decision not to punish such an individual despite proof of the crime. An important factor of the necessity defense involves the balancing of the harm to be avoided as opposed to the costs of the criminal conduct." (*In re Eichorn* (1998) 69 Cal.App.4th 382, 389.) "Necessity is an affirmative public policy defense, in effect a plea in avoidance and justification, which comes into focus only after all elements of the offense have been established." (*People v. Waters* (1985) 163 Cal.App.3d 935, 938.) When public policy considerations do not support a defense of necessity, the trial court need not instruct on that defense.

Since the defense of necessity is based on public policy, we must look to public policy to determine whether the defense was available to the defendant on the facts presented here. "[A]side from constitutional policy, the Legislature, and not the courts, is vested with the responsibility to declare the public policy of the state." (*Green v. Ralee Engineering Co.* (1998) 19 Cal.4th 66, 71.)

The duties of a facility that acts as a depositary of living animals are spelled out in the Civil Code. (*See* Civ. Code § 1834 *et seq.*) "A depositary of living animals shall provide the animals with necessary and prompt veterinary care, nutrition, and shelter, and treat them kindly." The Legislature has expressly stated the public policy of this state concerning euthanasia of animals. If an animal is adoptable or, with reasonable efforts, could become adoptable, it should not be euthanized. However, if an animal is abandoned and a new owner cannot be found, the facility "shall thereafter humanely destroy the animal so abandoned." Particularly relevant to this case and the defendant's assertions is a finding made by the Legislature in 1998: "The Legislature finds and declares that it is better to have public and private shelters pick up or take in animals than private citizens." (Stats. 1998 ch. 752, § 1.)

The Food and Agricultural Code provides specifically for what a shelter must do when a stray cat is impounded. (*See* Food & Agr. Code, § 31752.) The facility must hold the stray cat for owner redemption for a designated time, usually between four and six days. Prior to the euthanasia of the cat, the facility, at the request of a nonprofit, animal rescue or adoption organization, must release the cat to the requesting organization. During the holding period, the facility must scan the cat for a microchip that identifies the owner. Concerning an animal seized by authorities, the Penal Code provides:

> "A veterinarian may humanely destroy an impounded animal without regard to the prescribed holding period when it has been determined that the animal has incurred severe injuries or is incurably crippled. A veterinarian also may immediately humanely destroy an impounded animal afflicted with a serious contagious disease unless the owner or his or her agent immediately authorizes treatment of the animal by a veterinarian at the expense of the owner or agent." (Pen. Code, § 597.1, subd. (i).)

To utilize a term from preemption analysis, these statutes occupy the field of what to do with stray cats. The defendant is not at liberty to impose her own will over the public will. Her assertion that it was necessary for her to keep the cats instead of passing them on to animal control flies in the face of legitimately adopted public policy. Accordingly, since her proffered necessity defense is against public policy, the trial court properly denied her request for the necessity instruction and prohibited her from arguing the defense to the jury.

DISPOSITION

The judgment is affirmed.

Notes

1. Hoarding and neglect cases are sometimes the most difficult to prosecute, not only because they involve high numbers of animals, but because the legal requirement for appropriate minimum care is not well established. Many state statutes define the standard of care in very general terms such as "food in sufficient quantity." Is it appropriate or desirable for legislatures to craft more specific minimum care standards? Is it feasible?

2. Neglect crimes are often misdemeanors (unless defendants are repeat offenders), even though the harm suffered can be severe and ongoing for years and may cause more pain and suffering than an affirmative act of cruelty. If animal injuries were taken into consideration, cruelty would be judged not by the actor's intent but by the animal victims' experience. Should these statutes be amended to provide for increased penalties depending on the victim's experience?

3. Whether animals can and should be forfeited before or after a criminal conviction is hotly contested. Should the state have the power to require that all rights in abused animals be forfeited before a conviction? If so, what are the ownership implications if the defendant ultimately is acquitted? How do the facts in a hoarding case—with tens or even hundreds of animals threatening to overwhelm local facilities—play into these considerations?

Any court can ban those convicted of animal cruelty from possessing animals for a period of time as part of a probation or a condition of supervised release. Several states have codified this general rule, statutorily authorizing courts to include such a ban as part of the post-conviction sentence. *See, e.g.,* Alaska Stat. § 11.61.140(f). Other states, such as Oregon and Delaware, require a ban on ownership, usually for five to fifteen years following conviction. Or. Rev. Stat. § 167.332; Del. Code Ann. tit. 11, § 1325(c)-(d). As a matter of public policy, once an individual has been convicted of neglect or an affirmative act of cruelty, should s/he be banned from possessing any animal for a set period of time? If you think a ban is appropriate, should it be in perpetuity, or with an opportunity for review after a set period, or for a designated period from the outset?

Section 7. Restitution and Costs of Care

As discussed earlier in this chapter, many states have "costs of care statutes," which provide for applications for the costs incurred by agencies or nonprofit groups involved in the seizure and maintenance of animals in cruelty cases. These laws require hearings soon after seizure to immediately assess costs against the criminal defendant. The applicable costs under the statutes typically include the costs of seizure, veterinary care, and daily impoundment and care costs. If the court approves the application for costs, the defendant must pay those costs either for the initial period after seizure, or possibly the entire time that the case is pending. Under such statutes, if payment is not made, defendants forfeit their rights in the animals to the seizing agency. As noted previously, these laws are extremely valuable for seizing agencies and the animals, and greatly reduce the costs placed on shelters by large-scale animal abuse or neglect cases, because if defendants forfeit the animals, they can be adopted out to permanent homes, rather than be sequestered in a shelter for the time it takes for a case to proceed to final judgment (which could be years). *See, e.g.,* N.C. Gen. Stat. § 19A-70; 18 Pa. Cons. Stat. § 30.1 *et seq.*; Cal. Penal C. § 597.1(h).

At the other end of a criminal case, convicted defendants may be liable for all the costs of care for the animals since seizure. For example, California Penal Code section 597(f) provides in part: "A person convicted of a violation of this section by causing or permitting an act of cruelty, as defined in section 599b, shall be liable to the impounding officer for all costs of impoundment from the time of seizure to the time of proper disposition." In *People v. Speegle*, 53 Cal. App. 4th 1405 (1997), discussed in *Prichard v. State*, the defendant was charged and convicted on eight counts of felony cruelty under California Penal Code section 597, after animal control officers seized two hundred poodles, one cat and three horses from her property.

The conditions at Speegle's property were extremely egregious, with rotting corpses being eaten by the animals who were still alive, dead dogs in freezers and virtually all of the animals severely suffering. The defendant argued the statute was ambiguous about which "costs of impoundment" may be recovered. She asserted that the court should apply the interpretation most favorable to her, namely, limiting the obligation for reimbursement to the eight animals on which her convictions for felony cruelty specifically relied. The court responded to this argument as follows:

> The phrase "costs of impoundment" in the second part of the statute refers necessarily to "*all animals* lawfully seized and impounded *with respect to the violation*" (§ 597, subd. (f), emphasis supplied) in the first part of the statute. "With respect to" is a general phrase requiring only a logical or causal connection in a general transactional sense with the violation, as opposed to a limited phrase such as "for," "from," or "as a result of" the violation (which would require a direct connection). The general connection is further reflected in the use of the plural "all animals" (rather

than "the animal"), while also using the singular "the violation" (which itself rests on cruelty to the singular "any animal"). Thus, on its face, an impoundment officer may recover costs for animals other than the direct victims of a defendant's violation of the statute.

Even if "with respect to" could be considered ambiguous, we do not find the language *reasonably* susceptible of the interpretation which the defendant gives it. In the panoply of statutes from section 596 through 599f, the Legislature has manifested an unmistakable intent to prevent cruelty to animals and to provide for the removal of animals from the custody of those not fit to keep them. We thus interpret the present statute as allowing the removal of *all* animals in the keeping of a defendant found to be capable of cruelty, regardless of whether the other animals have been victims of a violation of the statute, as a rational means of ensuring the safety of the other animals. To limit the impoundment power under the statute (as the defendant would interpret it) would have the result of requiring an unwieldy prosecution of a separate count for every animal (much like the initial 70-odd page information in this matter) in order to remove them from abusive conditions. We reject the proffered interpretation.

Id. at 1417 (emphasis in original).

In *People v. Brunette,* 194 Cal. App. 4th 268 (2011), discussed in Section 3 of this chapter, the defendant operated a dog breeding facility. After inspections revealed more than 80 severely emaciated, sick, dead and dying dogs, the dogs were removed and those who could be saved were treated and cared for by the county animal services agency. Defendant was charged and convicted of multiple counts of felony and misdemeanor animal cruelty and ordered to pay more than $127,000 in restitution to the agency for the cost of treating and caring for dozens of dogs, as expressly allowed under California's anti-cruelty statutes. The appellate court affirmed the restitution order, except for the trial court's imposition of an interest charge.

Note

There is an important distinction between the costs-of-care statutes that provide for preconviction forfeiture for nonpayment (discussed in the first paragraph of this section), and the more common allowance for a lien to be placed on the animals after a conviction and final judgment (such as that at issue in the *Speegle* case). The latter laws provide little motivation for criminal defendants, since they are often judgment-proof and not concerned about this aspect of the law. And it is unlikely that most criminal defendants, convicted or not, ever pay any money for the animals they have abused.

The costs of mounting a criminal prosecution are always at issue, and prosecutors often face the dilemma of whether to bring individual charges based on every abused animal confiscated, thereby embarking on a lengthy and costly trial, or to limit the charges to the most egregious acts of cruelty, thereby risking the return of multiple animals (on whose behalf charges are not brought) to the alleged abuser. How would you balance these competing interests?

Section 8. Animals in Sport and Entertainment

A wide range of activities in which animals are the central participants fit into this heading. An illustrative, but not exclusive, list includes: (1) rodeos; (2) animal fighting; (3) swim-with-the-dolphins programs; (4) dog (usually Greyhound) racing, horse racing and other horse competitions; (5) hunting (including "standard," canned and Internet hunting) and fishing; (6) crush videos; (7) zoos and aquaria; (8) circuses and other animal exhibitions; (9) television and film use; and (10) dog, cat, and horse shows. In each case, animals are used for the enjoyment of humans. This subsection touches upon some, but not all, of this conduct.

Some of these activities have been outlawed in all states (dogfighting and cockfighting); some are regulated by specific laws and by industry standards (horse racing, dog racing, hunting, and fishing); and some are governed only by internal rules of trade groups (dog and cat shows). The laws prohibiting cruelty to animals also arguably apply to most of these activities in some states (while others may have applicable exemptions, as discussed throughout the book), although prosecutions are rare for the more popular of these activities.

A significant distinction can be made between dogfighting, cockfighting and crush videos, on the one hand—where death or injury is the desired effect, at least from the human participants' points of view—and dog and cat shows, on the other, where the "best in show" awards suggest that a well-behaved and pampered animal is involved. The distinctions may be less clear when comparing other types of activities.

An emerging issue is that of animals used in art. In September of 2017, the Guggenheim Museum in New York City pulled three exhibits from its "Art and China After 1989: Theater of the World" show, after experiencing enormous backlash from the public and animal advocacy groups who claimed the exhibits depicted animal cruelty. One exhibit, "Dogs That Cannot Touch Each Other," consists of a video in which eight trained fighting dogs face each other on treadmills just far enough from each other so that they cannot touch. The dogs exhaust themselves over the course of seven minutes trying to get to the others, without success. Another video, titled "A Case Study of Transference," portrays a heavily tattooed boar and a heavily tattooed sow copulating. "Dogs That Cannot Touch Each Other" and "A Case Study in Transference" were filmed in 2003 and 1994 respectively. The third exhibit that was pulled is titled "Theatre of the World" and consists of a wood and metal dome with heat lamps under which various creatures, such as lizards, cockroaches, beetles, and scorpions, exist for three months at a time. The supposed artistic "purpose" of this exhibit is to allow the creatures to kill one another or die of fatigue or starvation. At least two of the three exhibits undeniably cause pain and suffering to the animals involved. (It is unclear if the tattoos in "A Case Study of Transference" are real, or how the boar and sow were treated or manipulated in the making of the exhibit.)

Proponents of these exhibits claim that the outcry is inappropriate because it seeks to have the Guggenheim Museum censor the depiction of art. (The same issues arose in connection with the opposition to the "goldfish in a blender" exhibit discussed in Chapter 1, Section 1.) After the Guggenheim agreed to pull all three exhibits, Ai Weiwei, a social activist and contemporary Chinese artist featured in the show, stated: "When an art institution cannot exercise its right for freedom of speech, that is tragic for modern society. Pressuring museums to pull down artwork shows a narrow understanding about not only animal rights but also human rights." Robin Pogrebin, *Guggenheim Museum Is Criticized for Pulling Animal Artworks*, N.Y. TIMES, Sept. 26, 2017. Of course, the Guggenheim was actually exercising its "right for freedom of speech" when it decided not to display the challenged exhibits.

In contrast, some artists use animal cruelty in their artwork as an advocacy tool. Photographer Jo-Anne McArthur photographs conduct inside factory farms, slaughterhouses, and zoos around the world, exposing a world rarely seen by the general public. "Our photographs portray issues and images that no one wants to look at. The greatest challenge in animal advocacy is getting people not only to look, but to not turn away. We are presenting scenes of horror, and it's natural for them to want to turn away." Leah Edgarton, *ACE Interviews: Jo-Anne McArthur*, Animal Charity Evaluators, July 25, 2016, *https://animalcharityevaluators.org/blog/ace -interviews-jo-anne-mcarthur* (last visited Feb. 25, 2018).

What is the difference between the scenes of suffering Ai Weiwei defends as "art" and those Jo-Anne McArthur captures? Does the characterization of a depiction of animal cruelty as art provide it with special legal protection and immunity from challenge? Or are there certain expressions or uses that should never be considered (and protected) as art under any circumstances? In considering this, review the *Voelker* and *Thomason* cases discussed earlier, where acts of "entertainment" were not protected simply because they were being filmed for viewers.

A. Hunting

State v. Kuenzi

Court of Appeals of Wisconsin, 2011
332 Wis. 2d 297, 796 N.W. 2d 222

LUNDSTEN, J. It is alleged here that Rory and Robby Kuenzi were operating their snowmobiles on a trail in Waupaca County when they came across a large number of deer in a field. They charged the deer with their snowmobiles, ramming and running over at least five. At one point, Robby Kuenzi rode on top of a downed deer and did a "burn out," causing the deer's abdomen to rip open. The Kuenzis tied a strap around the neck of another downed live deer, dragged it to a tree, and secured it there. The Kuenzis apparently planned to retrieve that deer later, but never returned.

The Kuenzis were criminally charged under the animal cruelty statute, WIS. STAT. § 951.02. Both men moved to dismiss the charges, and the circuit courts granted the motions.

The Kuenzis' primary argument is that the animal cruelty statute cannot be applied to their actions, no matter how cruel or senseless, because they were engaged in taking "wild animals" and the taking of non-captive wild animals is a hunting activity regulated by WIS. STAT. ch. 29. In the Kuenzis' view, chapter 29, and only that chapter, regulates hunting and, therefore, they may take a wild animal by any means without fear of prosecution so long as their means are not specifically prohibited by chapter 29. We disagree and, accordingly, reverse and direct the courts to reinstate the charges.

Background

The criminal complaints in these cases allege the following facts. In January 2009, a sheriff's deputy, acting on a tip, found five deer with significant injuries near a snowmobile trail in Waupaca County. Four of the deer were dead, and the fifth had to be euthanized. Several of the deer had broken legs, and one of these had apparently crawled some distance before dying. Another deer, found tied to a tree, had apparently suffocated trying to free itself. Tracks at the scene suggested that snowmobiles were used to injure and kill the deer.

* * *

The State charged Rory Kuenzi with six counts and Robby Kuenzi with five counts of party to the crime of mistreatment of animals under WIS. STAT. § 951.02. The charges were Class I felonies because the alleged mistreatment was intentional and resulted in death. *See* WIS. STAT. § 951.18(1) ("Any person who intentionally violatess. 951.02, resulting in the mutilation, disfigurement or death of an animal, is guilty of a Class I felony.").

Prior to trial, both of the Kuenzis moved to dismiss the charges, arguing that prosecution under WIS. STAT. § 951.02 controverted hunting regulations under chapter 29, something prohibited by WIS. STAT. § 951.015(1). The circuit courts granted the motions and the State appeals. Because both cases present the same legal issue and are based on the same underlying facts, they have been consolidated for purposes of this appeal.

Discussion

* * *

A. The General Statutory Scheme

Chapter 951, titled "Crimes Against Animals," prohibits several acts directed toward animals. . . . The prohibition at issue here is cruel mistreatment under WIS. STAT. § 951.02. It provides:

> No person may treat any animal, whether belonging to the person or another, in a cruel manner. This section does not prohibit bona fide experiments carried on for scientific research or normal and accepted veterinary practices.

Our attention is on the first sentence, which prohibits "cruel" treatment of "any animal."

Chapter 951 defines "cruel" as "causing unnecessary and excessive pain or suffering or unjustifiable injury or death." WIS. STAT.§ 951.01(2). The term "animal" is also defined in chapter 951. It broadly includes "every living . . . [w]arm-blooded creature, except a human being." WIS. STAT. § 951.01(1). Thus, on its face, §951.02's cruel mistreatment prohibition applies to all animals, including wild animals such as the deer in this case.

The Kuenzis do not argue that, when their behavior is viewed in the context of taking wild deer, their alleged behavior did not cause "unnecessary and excessive pain or suffering or unjustifiable injury or death." That is, the Kuenzis do not argue that their conduct was not "cruel," as that term is used in §951.02. The Kuenzis do argue that, despite the broad definition of "animal," we should interpret "any animal" as excluding wild animals. We address this argument later in the opinion.

In addition to its several prohibitions, chapter 951 contains language intended to resolve conflicts that may arise between enforcement actions under that chapter and other laws. WISCONSIN STAT. § 951.015(1) provides:

> [Chapter 951] may not be interpreted as controverting any law regulating wild animals that are subject to regulation under ch. 169, the taking of wild animals, as defined in s. 29.001(90), or the slaughter of animals by persons acting under state or federal law.

Generally speaking, chapter 169 regulates captive wild animals and chapter 29 regulates non-captive wild animals. Thus, chapter 951 may not be applied in ways that controvert three categories of animal regulation laws: (1) laws regulating captive wild animals in chapter 169, (2) laws regulating the taking of non-captive "wild animals, as defined in s. 29.001(90)," and (3) federal and state laws regulating the slaughter of animals. Our focus here is on the second category of laws, those concerning the taking of non-captive wild animals.

Both the State and the Kuenzis assume that §951.015(1)'s use of the phrase "the taking of wild animals" and the reference to the definition of "wild animals" in WIS. STAT. § 29.001(90) are meant as a general reference to chapter 29. That is, the parties assume that the legislature meant to impose a general prohibition on enforcement actions under chapter 951 that "controvert" chapter 29 regulations and, more generally, chapter 29's regulatory scheme. We agree.

Our review of chapter 29, titled "Wild Animals and Plants," reveals that most of its provisions directly or indirectly regulate the taking of non-captive "wild animals." Under that chapter, persons obtain approvals and then may take wild animals subject to restrictions found in the chapter and related DNR regulations. The purpose of the regulations is to "conserve the fish and game supply and ensure the citizens of this state continued opportunities for good fishing, hunting and trapping." WIS. STAT. § 29.014(1).

To sum up, §951.02 prohibits "cruel" treatment of "any animal." The term "any animal" is broadly defined so that, on its face, the term encompasses the wild deer at issue in this case. The Kuenzis do not argue that their alleged behavior was not "cruel" within the meaning of chapter 951. And, a prosecution under §951.02 may not "controvert" laws regulating the taking of non-captive wild animals under chapter 29. With this overview in mind, we turn to the Kuenzis' specific arguments.

B. The Kuenzis' Arguments

1. Whether non-captive wild animals are "animals" under WIS. STAT. § 951.02

The Kuenzis argue that the term "animal" in §951.02 should not be read as including non-captive wild animals, such as the deer in this case. They assert that, except for the cruel mistreatment prohibition, all of the prohibitions in chapter 951, by their terms, do not apply to non-captive wild animals. They reason that, because the other prohibitions do not apply to non-captive wild animals, it follows that the cruel mistreatment provision shares this limitation. We disagree.

First, the legislature defines "animal" in chapter 951 — and, thus, in §951.02 — in a way that unambiguously includes non-captive wild animals. . . . Here, the legislature has provided a clear definition that includes all warm-blooded animals.

Second, the limited reading advocated by the Kuenzis is inconsistent with the wording the legislature chose to use to avoid conflicts with chapter 29. Rather than exclude all non-captive wild animals from coverage, the legislature instead prohibits enforcement that controverts chapter 29 laws and regulations governing "the taking of wild animals." By prohibiting a subset of takings—those that controvert chapter 29—the legislature necessarily conveys its belief that there are takings that do not controvert chapter 29.

Third, assuming for purposes of this discussion only that the cruel mistreatment provision is the sole prohibition in chapter 951 that is capable of application to non-captive wild animals, that fact does not support the Kuenzis' interpretation. It does not help the Kuenzis because there is no inconsistency in having several specific prohibitions directed at domesticated and captive wild animals and also a general prohibition on inflicting "unnecessary and excessive pain or suffering or unjustifiable injury or death" on all animals.

* * *

Accordingly, we reject the Kuenzis' argument that the term "animal" in §951.02 does not include the wild deer in this case.

2. Whether a cruel mistreatment prosecution under chapter 951 controverts chapter 29

The Kuenzis argue that an enforcement action against them under chapter 951 "controverts" chapter 29. They reason as follows:

- The Kuenzis' conduct constituted "taking" deer because the term "taking" is commonly understood as taking *by any means.*

- The term "hunting" is defined in chapter 29 to include "taking."

- The Kuenzis were, therefore, engaged in "hunting" as that term is used in chapter 29.

- Because laws regulating the hunting of non-captive wild animals are found in chapter 29, it "controverts" chapter 29 to prosecute the Kuenzis under chapter 951.

The first three steps in this reasoning are clear, and we briefly comment on those steps immediately below. What is less clear is how, in the Kuenzis' view, the enforcement action here "controverts" chapter 29.

As to whether the Kuenzis' actions fall under the term "hunting," we first note our agreement with amicus Wisconsin Wildlife Federation's view that the Kuenzis' conduct is not generally considered "hunting." The Federation states:

> Based on discussions with many of its members and other hunters, the Federation has found that virtually all hunters found the alleged acts of the Defendants in this matter appalling and their characterization as "acts of hunting" to be demeaning and inaccurate. It is safe to say that Wisconsin sportsmen and women do not consider such conduct to be forms of hunting.

Although we agree with the Federation's take on the common use of the term hunting, it is a different matter whether the Kuenzis' conduct is subject to regulation under chapter 29 because that conduct fits the broad definition of hunting in that chapter. On this topic, the State and the Kuenzis agree, as they should, that the term "hunting" in chapter 29 is so broadly defined that it includes taking wild animals by any means. The legislature chose to define "hunting" as including "shooting, shooting at, pursuing, taking, capturing or killing or attempting to capture or kill any wild animal." WIS. STAT. § 29.001(42).

Although hunters in their conversations would not likely talk about the allegations against the Kuenzis as hunting, the alleged conduct is "hunting" for regulatory purposes under chapter 29. Thus, we turn our attention to the last step of the Kuenzis' reasoning, their assertion that, because laws regulating the hunting of non-captive wild animals are found in chapter 29, it "controverts" chapter 29 to prosecute the Kuenzis under chapter 951.

We begin by observing that the Kuenzis frame their argument in terms of multiplicity. That is, they contend that constitutional double jeopardy rights are implicated and multiple prosecutions for the same conduct under both chapter 29 and chapter 951 are prohibited. It is apparent, however, that this case ultimately turns on the meaning of the "controverting" provision, As the Kuenzis admit, if §951.015(1) does not prohibit applying the cruel mistreatment statute to the taking of wild animals, then there is no multiplicity problem.

The first "controverting" argument we address involves the Kuenzis' assumption that, on its face, WIS. STAT. § 951.015(1) simply directs that, if the more *general* cruel mistreatment provision in chapter 951 "controverts" the more *specific* provisions in chapter 29, then the more specific chapter 29 provisions govern. The Kuenzis reason that, because there is already a well-established canon of statutory construction providing that the specific governs the general, the may-not-be-interpreted-as-controverting language in §951.015(1) must mean something more. And, the Kuenzis go on, that something more is the legislature's desire to override the general rule that, if an act forms the basis for a prosecution under more than one statutory provision, prosecutions may proceed under all such provisions. *See* WIS. STAT. § 939.65. The flaw in this reasoning is that we are not presented with a general/specific overlap.

Chapter 29 contains many prohibitions, but none against cruel mistreatment. For example, the record reveals that the Kuenzis were charged with "closed season" violations under WIS. STAT. §§ 29.055 and 29.971(11). The cruel mistreatment charge, however, is not a more general version of chapter 29's prohibitions on closed season hunting. And, even if there might be a general/specific relationship between the cruel mistreatment statute and some other particular prohibition in chapter 29, or a regulation promulgated thereunder, it is inaccurate to characterize the cruel mistreatment statute as more general with respect to chapter 29 as a whole. Accordingly, this general/specific argument is a non-starter—its premise is wrong.

In a distinct argument, the Kuenzis begin with what they assert is the State's position—that every hunter who violates a law under chapter 29 is also guilty of cruel mistreatment under chapter 951. The Kuenzis then assert that such an interpretation is absurd because, among other reasons, it would render moot the penalty provisions of chapter 29. Again, the Kuenzis' argument is a non-starter, and again the reason is a flawed premise.

The Kuenzis' assumption that every violation of chapter 29 is a violation of the cruel mistreatment statute is based on their assertion that the State expressly or implicitly takes that position. This is not accurate. We acknowledge that some statements made by the State, viewed in isolation, might be read that way. But it is clear that it is the State's position that cruel mistreatment violations may occur regardless whether the conduct does or does not involve a violation of chapter 29.

In the State's view, one we share, the cruel mistreatment of wild animals must be assessed based on the backdrop of common hunting practices and, in that context, the question is whether the alleged acts caused "unnecessary and excessive pain or suffering or unjustifiable injury or death." Quite obviously, the normal course of hunting frequently involves the infliction of pain and suffering and, just as obviously, the infliction of such pain and suffering does not subject hunters to prosecution under the cruel mistreatment statute. What is absurd is the Kuenzis' assertion that it is the State's view that "all hunting intentionally causes unnecessary pain or suffering or unjustifiable injury or death" and, therefore, that all hunting violates the cruel mistreatment statute.

Because their premise is wrong, so too is the Kuenzis' solution, namely, an interpretation of the "controverting" limitation in §951.015(1) as forbidding application of the cruel mistreatment statute to any taking of a wild animal, no matter how cruel and senseless.

What remains is the Kuenzis' bald assertion that, if conduct is "hunting" as that term is broadly defined in chapter 29, such conduct necessarily is regulated *only* under chapter 29 and, therefore, the application of chapter 951 to any acts directed against wild animals is prohibited. This argument withers under even cursory scrutiny.

If the legislature intended a blanket prohibition on applying the cruel mistreatment statute to the taking of wild animals, it could have done so with simple direct wording, such as this: "This chapter may not be applied to the taking of wild animals." The legislature did not. To the contrary, as we explain . . . above, the "controverting" limitation plainly contemplates that chapter 951 may be applied to the taking of wild animals. This is plain because the limitation in §951.015(1) only prohibits interpretations—i.e., applications of chapter 951—to "the taking of wild animals" when such interpretations/applications controvert chapter 29.

. . . In sum, the Kuenzis have failed to explain how their prosecution controverts in any manner regulations contained in, or promulgated under, chapter 29.

Conclusion

For the reasons discussed, we reverse the orders of the circuit courts dismissing the charges against the Kuenzis. We remand with directions to reinstate the charges in both cases.

Orders reversed and causes remanded with directions.

Notes

1. The *Kuenzi* court aptly summarized the unique relationship between hunting and anti-cruelty laws, which establish parallel and complementary sets of prohibitions. While shooting a deer outside of the official hunting season could lead to a conviction for unlawful hunting, a hunter who tortures an animal during hunting season can be charged and convicted for violation of the anti-cruelty laws.

Is there any contradiction between the anti-cruelty and hunting and fishing laws? Consider the broader range of laws impacting animals and how distinctions are made when comparing specific practices or species. For example, it would be a crime to castrate a dog or cat without anesthesia, and yet the law allows, without consequence, the unanesthetized castration of male calves, pigs and sheep.

2. As you read the next case, consider whether the activities engaged in by the defendant could be viewed as "hunting" or whether this was a straightforward non-hunting cruelty case. Should the species involved, or the instrumentality used, be relevant to the analysis? Should different standards apply with regard to the same activity if the characterization of that activity shifts?

Boushehry v. State

Court of Appeals of Indiana, Second District, 1995
648 N.E.2d 1174

KIRSCH, Judge. Fereydoon "Fred" Boushehry was charged with eleven criminal offenses arising out of the killing of two Canadian geese. He was ultimately convicted of seven of those charges. . . . He was acquitted of the remaining four offenses.

We restate the issues Boushehry raises on appeal as:

I. Whether there was sufficient evidence to support his convictions for criminal recklessness and cruelty to an animal.

II. Whether he was properly convicted of violating IC 14-2-4-1(1) and (2).

III. Whether his convictions and sentences violate double jeopardy principles.

We affirm in part and reverse in part.

FACTS

The facts most favorable to the judgment of conviction establish that on September 26, 1991, Jim Waugh was working in a subdivision Boushehry was developing. Boushehry approached Waugh and asked him if he wanted to shoot some geese. Waugh agreed, and the two men went to a nearby vacant lot next to Boushehry's home. Then, Waugh took a .22-caliber rifle out of the trunk of his car, and fired two or three shots, killing one goose and wounding another. When Waugh fired his rifle, he was approximately twenty-five yards away from the geese. The shots were fired in the direction of Shelbyville Road in Marion County, Indiana, which bordered the vacant lot. Waugh put the rifle back into the trunk of his car and resumed his work. Boushehry later told Waugh that he cut the heads off the geese and put the geese in the sink in Boushehry's garage.

On the same day, Chestena Rodgers was watching television in her home in the same subdivision when she heard gunshots outside. She looked out the window and saw Waugh put a rifle in a gun case which he then put in the trunk of a car. Ms. Rodgers looked toward the vacant lot and saw Boushehry chasing a goose that had a broken wing. Boushehry caught the goose, grabbed it by the neck, and started walking toward his house. Ms. Rodgers' son, Craig, saw Boushehry carry the goose into Boushehry's garage and return carrying the goose and a shiny object. Craig saw Boushehry make a "slitting" motion across the goose and then throw the goose to the ground. The goose flopped around on the ground before becoming still. Boushehry then picked up that goose and another goose that was already dead, and carried them both into his garage.

Also on September 26, 1991, Conservation Officer Paul Bykowski responded to a report that someone was illegally taking Canadian geese in Boushehry's subdivision. Officer Bykowski went to the Boushehry residence where Mrs. Boushehry consented to let him look in the garage. As Mrs. Boushehry led Officer Bykowski to the open garage door, he noticed a trail of blood and feathers leading from the vacant lot into the garage, ending at a utility sink toward the back of the garage. Officer Bykowski saw two freshly killed Canadian geese in the utility sink.

The time set by the Federal Fish and Wildlife Service for taking Canadian geese in 1991 was October 26 to November 3, and again from November 21 to January 20. The court took judicial notice that September 26 does not fall within either of these two time periods.

DISCUSSION AND DECISION

* * *

B. Cruelty To An Animal

Boushehry next contends there was insufficient evidence to support his cruelty to an animal convictions. Cruelty to an animal is proscribed by IC 35-46-3-12 (1988 Ed.) which provides:

"(a) A person who knowingly or intentionally:

(1) tortures, beats or mutilates a vertebrate animal resulting in serious injury or death to the animal; or

(2) kills a vertebrate animal without the authority of the owner of the animal; commits cruelty to an animal, a Class A misdemeanor."

Boushehry was charged with two counts of "knowingly tortur[ing] or mutilat[ing] a vertebrate animal, to-wit: 1 Canada [sic] Goose, resulting in death to the animal."

Boushehry claims there was insufficient evidence to establish that either he or Waugh tortured or mutilated the geese. The State counters that the shooting of the geese constituted mutilation. Because IC 35-46-3-12 does not define "mutilate," we must take the term in its plain, or ordinary and usual, sense.

The evidence supports Boushehry's guilt of only one count of cruelty to an animal. Waugh shot two geese. One goose died instantly; there was no evidence presented at trial that either Boushehry or Waugh tortured or mutilated this goose in achieving its death. The act of shooting the goose is not enough alone to establish cruelty to an animal by either torture or mutilation. Because Boushehry was charged with only the torturing or mutilation death of the geese, his conviction for cruelty to an animal based on the death of the goose who died from the gunshot, absent evidence that the goose was tortured or mutilated, cannot stand.

With respect to the wounded goose, the record supports Boushehry's conviction for cruelty to an animal. This goose continued to live after it was shot. The record reflects that the gunshot resulted in injury to the goose's wing. Boushehry then slit the throat of the injured goose. This act constituted mutilation in its plain, or ordinary and usual, sense.

Boushehry testified at trial that he killed the injured goose to put it out of its misery, a defense recognized under the statute. IC 35-46-3-12(b)(3). It was for the trier of fact to determine the weight and credibility to be afforded Boushehry's claim that he killed the goose to prevent it from suffering. We will not disturb that determination.

The dissent concludes that this conviction should also be reversed because the uncontroverted testimony of Chestena Rogers, Craig Rogers and Boushehry establish that the goose was suffering when Boushehry killed it. The evidence is also uncontroverted that Boushehry was responsible for causing the injuries that induced the goose's suffering. When the defendant's unlawful act causes the animal's suffering, he should not escape penal consequences by claiming that killing the animal was necessary to prevent continued suffering.

CONCLUSION

We dispose of Boushehry's convictions and sentences as follows:

* * *

2. One of Boushehry's convictions and sentence for cruelty to an animal is reversed and ordered vacated. The other conviction and sentence for cruelty to an animal is affirmed.

* * *

Notes

1. While many hunters hunt on federal or state lands, many others prefer to hunt on privately owned hunting ranches. Some hunting ranches stock only native game species on multi-thousand-acre ranches, where hunters conduct themselves in typical fashion similar to that done on government-owned lands. Other hunters pay for the opportunity to visit "canned hunting" ranches, where they kill exotic animals that have been purchased by the ranches or raised in captivity. The animals on canned hunting ranches are kept in corrals and let out of the corrals or trailers just as the participants arrive. Many of the animals on these "canned hunting" ranches are bred and raised in captivity, regularly fed and habituated to the presence of humans, and have lost their natural instincts to avoid people, as compared with their wild counterparts.

Some hunters question this brand of hunting. Writing about canned hunting, one hunting enthusiast concluded that "ignoring [this] cancer within our ranks is indefensible and makes us hypocrites in the eyes of nonhunters." Ted Kerasote, *The Future of Hunting*, Sports Afield, Sept. 1992, at 106. *See also,* Manny Fernandez, *Blood and Beauty on a Texas Exotic-Game Ranch*, N.Y. Times, Oct. 19, 2017.

2. Often, "canned hunt" animals have come from zoos that sell them as surplus. Between 1992 and mid-1998, more than 19,000 mammals left the nation's accredited zoos. Linda Goldston, *The Animal Business: Many Zoos Give Away or Sell Off Surplus Mammals, Which Often End Up Exploited or Even Hunted Despite Safeguards*, San Jose Mercury News, Feb. 7, 1999, at 1A. Almost 40% of these former zoo animals went to dealers, auctions, hunting ranches, unidentified individuals,

unaccredited zoos or game farms. *Id. See also* Rick Orlov, *Animal Transfer Policies Tightened*, Daily News L.A., Sept. 3, 1999, at N4.

3. In 2004, "Internet hunting" began to garner some attention. A Texas rancher offered to provide users the opportunity to shoot deer, antelope or wild pigs using a remote-controlled rifle with a "webcam" mounted on it—thus allowing computer users to shoot captive wildlife from anywhere in the world without ever leaving their houses. "Live-shot.com" and other sites met with serious resistance from animal protection and some hunting groups, as well as state wildlife agencies. Opponents contacted legislators and several states began curtailing the practice.

On March 20, 2005, Virginia became the first state to ban Internet hunting. Va. Code § 29.1-530.3. By February 2018, thirty-eight states had similar prohibitions.

4. Many states provide specific statutory protection against harassment of hunters. These laws make interference with a person's legal taking of an animal unlawful and punishable by fines and/or imprisonment. Hunter harassment laws are addressed more extensively in Chapter 5.

5. Poaching, or illegal hunting, is a serious problem worldwide. Often driven by the black market trade in animal parts for trinkets and traditional medicines, poaching is a significant factor threatening the world's endangered species. For example, the high demand for ivory (mainly from elephants) on the black market has led to the loss of millions of elephants, tens of thousands per year as of 2018. Though elephants are a protected species under the Convention on International Trade in Endangered Species of Wild Fauna and Flora (CITES), not all countries who have signed on to the treaty have effective local enforcement statutes—and even where they do, corruption and the difficulty of enforcement make the laws somewhat ineffective. However, the dire situation facing elephants appears to be leading to change.

Hong Kong reportedly has the largest ivory market in the world. Hong Kong's law known as "Cap 586" gives effect to CITES and the ban on international sales of ivory. Though Cap 586 banned the trade of ivory after the global trade ban took effect in 1989, the ordinance allowed for the trade of pre-1989 ivory. This loophole allowed for illegally acquired ivory to be traded virtually unnoticed, simply by labeling it as pre-1989 product.

Cap 586 was amended in 2018 in an effort to increase protections. The changes increased the penalties for wildlife parts trafficking generally and placed a complete ban on the ivory trade in Hong Kong. Lawmakers hope that this will slow the depopulation of elephants while deterring wildlife traffickers from using Hong Kong as a shield for illegal activity. The ban will take full effect in 2021. It is being implemented in phases to prevent the complete disruption of the business of law-abiding merchants. On mainland China, similar efforts were equally successful, and as of December 2017, lawful, government-sanctioned trade in ivory came to a close.

In the United States, the U.S. Fish and Wildlife Service completed a rulemaking process under the Endangered Species Act (ESA), prohibiting the import and export of African elephant ivory (with limited exceptions) effective July 6, 2016. 50 C.F.R. Part 17 (81 Fed. Reg. 36388 (June 6, 2016)). The final rule also "prohibits take of live African elephants in the United States," with the intended goal of "helping to ensure that elephants held in captivity receive an appropriate standard of care." *Id.* The prohibition on "takes" in the U.S. is "the same as the prohibition on take of Asian elephants, which has been in place since 1976 when the Asian elephant was listed under the ESA." *Id.*

As of 2018, several states now make it "unlawful to purchase, sell, offer for sale, possess with intent to sell, or import with intent to sell ivory [from any species] or rhinoceros horn," subject to certain limited exceptions. Cal. Fish & Game Code § 2022.

B. Rodeos and Bull Runs

Rodeos attract viewers and competitors in many states. These public events typically include a number of demonstrations and exhibitions that involve brutal and sometimes fatal interactions between human participants and horses, bulls and calves. While animal protection groups have criticized rodeos and racing for years, a number of states have specific exemptions to their anti-cruelty laws for standard rodeo and practices.

In an action filed against various Northern California school districts by two animal protection organizations and an individual on behalf of her child, plaintiffs sought to prevent defendants from having students attend the Grand National Rodeo as part of a school-sponsored activity. As alleged in the plaintiffs' second amended complaint:

> 21. On October 24, 2002, the Cow Palace hosted a Free Arena Performance for school children (hereinafter referred to as School Day) for the Grand National Rodeo (Rodeo). Approximately 7,000 students and teachers, including Defendant teachers, attended as part of a school-sponsored activity. This activity has occurred annually for at least the past twenty years.

> * * *

> 25. The Rodeo is a competition sponsored by the Professional Rodeo Cowboys Association (PRCA) consisting of six events in which animals are frightened, injured and even killed. These events include calf roping, bareback bronc riding, saddle bronc riding, bull riding, steer wrestling and team roping. The Rodeo also includes barrel racing, a non-PRCA sponsored event.

> 26. Calf roping involves a frightened calf sent running into the arena. Different methods are used in order to prompt the calf to run. These include twisting the calf's tail, raking the tail painfully over the slats of the chute, and slapping the calf. A man on horseback then pursues the calf and attempts to throw a rope around the calf's neck. If done properly, he then

throws the calf to the ground and ties three legs, holding this position for at least six seconds. Often during this event, the calf suffers a 'jerk-down.' In a jerk-down the calf is abruptly jerked over backwards, landing on his back, causing pain and occasionally severe injury and death.

27. In bull riding, saddle bronc riding and bareback bronc riding, a 'flank' or 'bucking' strap is wrapped around a horse (bronc) or bull's flank tight enough to cause such discomfort that the horse or bull bucks in an attempt to remove the irritant. During the bucking, a man rides the frantic animal, getting points for staying on the animal and for the number of times his spurs are raked into the sides of the animal.

* * *

30. School Day at the Rodeo consists of bareback bronc riding, saddle bronc riding, bull riding, barrel racing, team penning and drill team.

31. Apart from the pain inflicted in the course of the above events, many animals have been injured during the Rodeo. In 1982 a calf and a horse suffered broken legs. In 1984 a calf was severely injured. In 1985 a calf and a horse suffered broken backs, a horse suffered a swollen knee, two horses suffered cuts, and one horse suffered a facial injury. In 1986, a horse suffered a fractured rear hock. In 1987, four animals suffered leg injuries and five animals suffered lacerations. In 1990 a horse suffered a shattered disk and a horse suffered a cut eye. In 2000 a bull broke its neck.

* * *

33. During the 2000 Rodeo a bull was killed in the presence of many children, causing severe emotional distress to the children and adults witnessing the event. This distress included nightmares about the incident.

34. Teachers, including Defendant teachers, are given educational material for the School Day Rodeo to distribute to their students. This material describes the history of the rodeo and the events at the rodeo, and it portrays the rodeo in a positive manner. This material is also used to encourage students to attend the rodeo. The material fails to mention the pain and suffering inflicted on the animals and fails to warn children of the cruel treatment and suffering of the animals that they are about to witness.

In Defense of Animals v. San Francisco Unified School Dist., Case No. 413659 (Cal. Super. Ct., San Francisco County) (second amended complaint, filed April 2003). The complaint alleged violations of the following sections of the California Education Code: (i) section 233.5, which requires the promotion of "humane treatment of living creatures"; (ii) section 51540, which states that "[i]n the public elementary and high schools or in public elementary and high school school-sponsored activities and classes held elsewhere than on school premises, live vertebrate animals shall not, as part of a scientific experiment or [for] *any purpose whatsoever*: . . . (b) Be injured through other treatments, including, but not limited to anesthetization or electric shock. . . ." (emphasis added); and (iii) section 60042, which requires that educational materials should "encourage . . . the humane treatment of animals. . . ."

The court granted summary judgment in favor of the defendants on procedural grounds and dismissed the case.

Setting aside any procedural basis the court may have had for its ruling, consider the statutes along with the allegations in the complaint and any general knowledge you may have about rodeos. Do you think it can properly be concluded as a matter of law that school-sponsored trips to rodeos comply with the language and intent of the California statutes? If you were the trier of fact, what factors would you consider to make your determination at trial?

More recently, activists have targeted the particular rodeo practice of "horse tripping." Horse tripping is an event that originated in Mexican rodeos called charreadas. Horses are lassoed around the front legs, causing the horses to trip forward and crash into the ground, potentially causing significant pain or injury. A number of states have now specifically outlawed horse tripping. *See, e.g.,* ARIZ. REV. STAT. § 13-2910.09; CAL. PENAL CODE § 597g; FLA. STAT. ANN. § 828.12; 510 ILL. COMP. STAT. 70/5.01; ME. REV. STAT. ANN. title 7, § 3972; NEB. REV. STAT. § 54-911; N.M. STAT. ANN. § 30-18-11; OKLA. STAT. title 21, § 1700; R.I. GEN. LAWS § 4-20-4; and TEX. PENAL CODE § 42.09.

In *Animal Legal Defense Fund (ALDF) v. Great Bull Run, LLC,* 2014 U.S. Dist. LEXIS 78367 (N.D. Cal. June 6, 2014), ALDF and People for the Ethical Treatment of Animals brought a civil action under California's unfair competition law based on the claim that defendants' "great bull run" (GBR) events violated various California criminal anti-cruelty statutes. In denying defendants' motion to dismiss, the court explained:

> Plaintiffs describe GBR's events as:
>
>> people on horses us[e] ropes as whips to scare as many as three dozen bulls—each of which weighs approximately 1,500 pounds—to charge towards as many as 1,000 people arrayed along a quarter-mile track. As the bulls approach at speeds faster than humans can run, the participants try to keep up while avoiding the stampede at their heels. Many runners intentionally run as close to the bulls as possible to provoke them. An eyewitness at the most recent bullrun event in Florida reported that several runners taunted and punched the bulls as they ran by.
>
> Each GBR event draws approximately 3,000 paying participants. . . .
>
> * * *
>
> Plaintiffs allege that the Great Bull Run events subject bulls to needless suffering, distress, and unnecessary cruelty. They state that, according to veterinary experts, bull runs are dangerous for the animals because bulls may become entangled with other bulls or runners, causing them to slip and break their legs or get gored. Bull runs are also inherently stressful to

the bulls, who find themselves in an unfamiliar location surrounded by loud noises, often after having travelled for days in cramped transport trailers. Plaintiffs allege that GBR and Lone Star take advantage of this fear and confusion to motivate the animals to stampede.

Id. at *3-*4. The court found plaintiffs had standing to bring their unfair competition action based on allegations that plaintiffs "diverted significant resources to investigate and counteract [d]efendants' events." "Organizational plaintiffs have standing under the [unfair competition law] where they divert resources as a result of a defendant's alleged unlawful business practices." *Id.* at *18. In 2015, the parties entered into a consent decree, settling the case and ending the GBR in California. 2015 WL 5168588.

C. Animal Racing

Horse racing is big business and a common activity in many states. Greyhound racing also occurs, but in very few states, with Florida (where the most Greyhound racing occurs) voting in 2018 to end the practice by 2021. There is virtually no reported case law involving animal racing in which animal cruelty is at issue. Rather, controversy about the industry tends to revolve around gambling and performance-related cheating through the inappropriate use of steroids and other drugs to enhance individual performance, and many courts have dealt with business disputes between and among racehorse and Greyhound owners, breeders, trainers and racing facilities. These lawsuits typically involve contract, insurance and other ownership or business-related matters, where treatment of the animals is not at issue. The following short excerpt from *Di Mario v. Coppola*, 10 F. Supp. 2d 213 (E.D.N.Y. 1998) offers a brief history of the industry:

> The horse racing industry has a long and rich tradition from which modern trade usage and custom is derived. Contests of speed between horses are among the oldest diversions of humanity. *See* 11 Encyclopedia Britannica 714 (1967). Horse racing owes much of its development to the Greeks, who by 1200 B.C. had developed and refined the sport of chariot contests. *See* Melvin Bradley, Horses: A Practical and Scientific Approach 36 (1981). Racing without chariots is said to have later developed independently, though it was "an important part of the first Olympic games" of 776 B.C. *Id.* As early as 1500 B.C. "Kikkuli of the land of Matinni" composed a lengthy treatise on the breeding and training of horses. 11 Encyclopedia Britannica 714 (1967).
>
> Modern day racing, "the sport of kings," owes its origin to the nobility of England who developed racing as a popular amusement. *Id.* at 714–15. It is the traditions of Western Europe's aristocracy that have defined modern equine standards and practices, including the industry's reliance on oral "gentlemen's" agreements. *But cf.* John J. Kropp, *et al.*, *Horse Sense and the UCC: The Purchase of Racehorses*, 1 Marq. Sports L.J. 171, 173 (1991) ("The days of handshake deals in the horse business are rapidly coming to an end.").

The *American Stud Book* was established in 1873. It traces the history and origin of Thoroughbreds in America. *See* Bradley, *supra*, at 40, 42–43. Both the *General Stud Book* and *American Stud Book*, referred to as horse registries, are maintained and controlled by breed associations. 11 Encyclopedia Britannica 715–16, 719. These organizations ensure that no horses bred through artificial insemination or embryo transfer are registered. *See* Stephen Budiansky, The Nature of Horses 238 (1994). Unlike the dairy-cattle business, the horse industry restricts breeding methods to maintain tradition and control. *See id.* at 236–39. This adherence to strict regulation has engendered specialized termination and customs.

After successful male Thoroughbred racehorses have finished their career, they are often retired to a breeding farm. This is referred to as being retired "to stud." The owner of the stallion either retains the breeding rights or "syndicates" the animal. *See id.* In syndication the ownership interest in the thoroughbred is divided into shares, designed to provide access to breeders "when sole ownership is cost-prohibitive." Timothy Nicholas Sweeney, *Keflas v. Bonnie Brae Farms: A Practical Approach to Thoroughbred Breeding Syndications and Securities Laws*, 75 Ky. L.J. 419, 422 (1987).

10 F. Supp. 2d at 216–17.

One illegal practice that is unrelated to racing, but rather to a specialized form of equine display, is "soring." Soring involves the intentional infliction of pain to a horse's legs or hooves, usually through cutting the horse with a sharp blade and/or applying caustic and burning chemicals, to force the horse to perform an artificial, exaggerated gait known as "high stepping." Soring is exceptionally painful to the horse, particularly when weight is put on the hoof. It is a common practice in the Tennessee Walking Horse industry, which values the high hoof lift that horses demonstrate in response to the pain they feel from walking. The exaggerated gait/hoof lift is considered to be a sign of top performance in certain competitions.

This widespread practice has been prohibited since 1970 under the Horse Protection Act (HPA), PL 91-540, 15 U.S.C. §§ 1821–1831. The HPA prohibits the showing, sale, auction, exhibition or transport of sored horses. The law was amended in 1976 to allow horse industry organizations to train and license their own inspectors, known as Designated Qualified Persons, to examine horses at shows for signs of soring. This practice has been criticized for creating a clear conflict of interest, as the inspector is beholden to the organization for his or her job. Activists, long frustrated by this approach and the resulting lack of official intervention against those who engage in soring, started gathering evidence themselves. In mid-2013, Jackie McConnell, a Collierville, Tennessee horse trainer pled guilty to twenty-two counts of animal cruelty related to the use of soring on his horses, and was sentenced to house arrest for a year, fined $25,000 and prohibited from owning and training horses for twenty years. McConnell's guilty plea came after the Humane Society of the United States in 2011 filmed an undercover video inside a training stable, showing caustic chemical substances being applied to Tennessee Walking Horses' legs and hooves, and the horses then being beaten to make them stand and walk.

Notes

1. Despite some well-publicized issues like that of soring, horse exhibition and racing are big businesses and widely accepted nationwide. Dog racing, on the other hand, is not. As of February 2018, dog racing was illegal in forty states. In four states (Connecticut, Kansas, Oregon and Wisconsin), all dog racing has ceased despite there being no legal prohibition against the practice. As of December 2018, commercial dog racing remained active in just six states — Alabama, Arkansas, Iowa, Florida, Texas and West Virginia. However, as previously mentioned, in November 2019, Florida (by far the biggest dog racing state) enacted a law that would shut down all eleven tracks in that state down by 2021. For the latest developments on dog racing issues, see *https://www.grey2kusa.org/about/states.php* (last visited Dec. 2018). Even in states where dog racing itself is not prohibited, betting on the results of dog races may be illegal. *See, e.g., Reed v. Fulton*, 384 S.W.2d 173, 176 (Tex. Ct. App. 1964).

2. What distinction between dogs and horses justifies the dichotomy in the reaction by many to the racing industries related to the two species? Why do you think this chasm has developed? For a broad historical and contemporary perspective of the practice and the controversy, *see* Addie Patricia Assay, Comment, *Greyhounds: Racing to their Deaths*, 32 Stetson L. Rev. 433 (2003). As a further concern for animal advocates, the Comment points out that "[a]s many as 100,000 small animals, mostly domestic rabbits and wild jackrabbits, [used as 'bait'] are maimed and killed in a variety of ways every year by persons involved in the greyhound-racing industry." *Id.* at 438.

3. In 1990, the Humane Society of the United States estimated that 50,000 Greyhounds were destroyed each year in connection with the racing industry. Sharon H. Smith, *Dog Lovers Helping Greyhounds Mistreated at Spanish Tracks*, Buffalo News, May 7, 1999, at 2C. By 2007, the efforts of various animal protection and Greyhound rescue organizations significantly increased the adoption of "retired" Greyhounds and inspections of conditions of Greyhounds at racetracks had been increased. As of 2018, the number of racing Greyhounds being destroyed each year reportedly had dropped to between 2,000 and 3,000. *https://www.grey2kusa.org/pdf /GREY2KUSANationalFactSheet.pdf* (last visited Dec. 2018). These figures do not take into account dogs who are killed before they reach the racetrack or the extensive number of other species of animals killed as part of the dog racing industry that are mentioned in Note 2.

4. In 2001, a Massachusetts state trial court dismissed a defamation suit against a ballot measure committee and its individual members, where the purpose of the ballot measure was to end Greyhound racing in the state. The suit arose from television ads stating that Greyhound racing kills thousands of Greyhounds nationwide

and showing images suggesting that racing Greyhounds are abused, neglected and killed. Defendants had also made public statements to the media during the campaign that Greyhounds at the Massachusetts Greyhound racing track were killed, regardless of health or age, when they were slow. In dismissing the suit, the court found reasonable factual support that "greyhounds are needlessly killed and abused in Massachusetts by the racing industry." *Sarkis v. Grey2K*, No. 00-4891-E (Mass. Super. Ct. Apr. 13, 2001).

5. As described by the Fifth Circuit, the contractual arrangements between Greyhound owners and race tracks are generally as follows:

> Contracts between dog owners and the tracks are made on a season-to-season basis. Under these contracts, the owner of the track agrees to let the dog owner race at his track, and in return the dog owner promises to race a certain number of dogs at the track. The dog owner receives a share of the track's profits and competes with other dog owners for prize money awarded for dogs who win, place, or show.

Fulton v. Hecht, 580 F.2d 1243, 1245 (5th Cir. 1978). *See also Wilson v. Sandstrom*, 317 So. 2d 732 (Fla. 1975) (contractual dispute between race track operator and kennel/dog owners).

6. Greyhound racing is not the only type of dog racing that has garnered media attention. Each year in the Iditarod Trail Sled Dog Race, dozens of dog "musher" teams race roughly 1,150 miles from Anchorage to Nome, Alaska, in approximately nine to fourteen days. The first Iditarod race was held in 1973. In 1997, the Anchorage Daily News, which has been a sponsor of the race, reported that according to newspaper accounts, "at least" 107 dogs had died in the Iditarod races up to that time. Doug O'Harra and Natalie Phillips, *Wanted: Healthy, Happy Dogs,* ANCHORAGE DAILY NEWS, Feb. 23, 1997. This number does not take into account the number of puppies killed in the process known as "culling," where dogs are killed before they ever race because they are not deemed to possess the optimum characteristics for the race. According to an earlier article in the Anchorage Daily News, many mushers consider "killing unwanted sled-dog puppies [to be] part of doing business." *Id. See also Mushers Say Most "Culling" Not Cruel,* ANCHORAGE DAILY NEWS, Oct. 6, 1991, at B1. According to the 1991 article, Mat-Su Borough Animal Control unit received 3,060 musher dogs in 1990 and 65% of those were killed. According to the article, dog mushers often prefer to kill their "culled" puppies themselves rather than bring them to the animal control unit because it may be "inconvenient or overly bureaucratic" to utilize the official route. The reported death statistics also do not take into account dogs who die in between the annual races from injuries suffered during the race or in training, or caused by the conditions in which Iditarod dogs may be kept, such as staying tethered in the outdoors for much of the time they are in training or racing. According to the 1997 article, race officials stated that they lacked complete records of dog deaths. A 2016 documentary, *Sled Dogs*, by Canadian filmmaker Fern Levitt, provides a critical examination of commercial mushing businesses and the Iditarod.

D. Breeding, Veterinary and Shelter Issues

Breeding practices often are at issue in the animal racing industry as well as among dog and cat breed enthusiasts, pet store owners and others who are seeking financial gain, bragging rights or prestige through the ownership, use and sale of certain animals. The following case explores one common requirement for breed groups involved in dog shows, and an interesting legal twist in connection with those practices.

Hammer v. American Kennel Club

Court of Appeals of New York, 2003
1 N.Y.3d 294, 803 N.E.2d 766

GRAFFEO, J. Plaintiff Jon H. Hammer is the owner of a purebred Brittany Spaniel dog with a 10-inch-long natural tail. Defendant American Kennel Club (AKC) sponsors competitions that utilize a breed standard promulgated by defendant American Brittany Club (ABC). The standard penalizes Brittany Spaniels with tails longer than four inches. The issue in this appeal is whether Agriculture and Markets Law § 353 grants plaintiff, who wishes to enter his dog and compete without penalty in breed contests, a private right of action to preclude defendants from using a standard that encourages him to "dock" his Brittany Spaniel's tail. Because we conclude that it would be inconsistent with the applicable legislative scheme to imply a private right of action in plaintiff's favor, we affirm the Appellate Division order dismissing the complaint.

Defendant ABC is the national parent club for Brittany Spaniels and is one of 148 different breed clubs affiliated with defendant AKC. As explained in AKC's official publication, "The Complete Dog Book," members of breed clubs vote to adopt particular standards, which are then submitted to the AKC for approval and use in AKC-sanctioned competitions, such as the Westminster Kennel Club show. According to defendants, these standards represent the "ideal" for each breed and establish guidelines for dog show judges, breeders and purchasers of purebred dogs.

Defendants' standard for Brittany Spaniels provides that dogs should be "[t]ailless to approximately four inches, natural or docked. The tail not to be so long as to affect the overall balance of the dog. . . . Any tail substantially more than four inches shall be severely penalized." Notably, unlike other deviations from the standards, such as height and coloration, a longer tail does not disqualify a dog from competition.

In 2001, plaintiff commenced this action against defendants for declaratory and injunctive relief. The gravamen of plaintiff's complaint is that the Brittany Spaniel breed standard encourages owners to violate Agriculture and Markets Law § 353, a penal statute prohibiting animal cruelty, because it is cruel to dock a dog's tail. Plaintiff claims that defendants discriminate against him by excluding him from meaningful participation in AKC competitions because he is unwilling to dock his dog's tail. He therefore seeks a declaration that the breed standard violates New York law and an injunction precluding defendants from using the allegedly illegal standard in judging breed competitions.

AKC and ABC moved separately to dismiss the action, arguing that plaintiff lacked standing to secure civil relief for the alleged violation of section 353. . . .

Where a penal statute does not expressly confer a private right of action on individuals pursuing civil relief, recovery under such a statute "may be had only if a private right of action may fairly be implied" (*Sheehy v. Big Flats Community Day*, 73 N.Y.2d 629, 633 [1989]; *see also Carrier v. Salvation Army*, 88 N.Y.2d 298, 302 [1996]). This inquiry entails consideration of three factors: "(1) whether the plaintiff is one of the class for whose particular benefit the statute was enacted; (2) whether recognition of a private right of action would promote the legislative purpose; and (3) whether creation of such a right would be consistent with the legislative scheme" (*Carrier*, 88 N.Y.2d at 302). In assessing whether a private right of action can be implied, we have acknowledged that

> the Legislature has both the right and the authority to select the methods to be used in effectuating its goals, as well as to choose the goals themselves. Thus, regardless of its consistency with the basic legislative goal, a private right of action should not be judicially sanctioned if it is incompatible with the enforcement mechanism chosen by the Legislature or with some other aspect of the over-all statutory scheme.

Sheehy, 73 N.Y.2d at 634–635.

Article 26 of the Agriculture and Markets Law regulates the treatment of animals and contains provisions previously codified in the former Penal Code, Penal Law and Code of Criminal Procedure. Plaintiff relies on section 353 of that article, which states that a person who "cruelly beats or unjustifiably injures, maims, mutilates or kills any animal" or permits such treatment of any animal is guilty of a misdemeanor, contending that this criminal statute also creates a civil private right of action.

The Legislature explicitly addressed the enforcement of animal protection statutes in two provisions. Section 371 of the Agriculture and Markets Law requires police officers and constables to enforce violations of article 26 and further authorizes "any agent or officer of any duly incorporated society for the prevention of cruelty to animals" to initiate a criminal proceeding. In addition, section 372 enables magistrates to issue search and arrest warrants "[u]pon complaint under oath . . . that the complainant has just and reasonable cause to suspect that any of the provisions of law relating to or in any wise affecting animals are being or about to be violated." Through the adoption of these two sections, the Legislature established that enforcement authority lies with police and societies for the prevention of cruelty to animals and violations would be handled in criminal proceedings.

This is not a criminal action and plaintiff is not asking law enforcement officials to charge defendants with violations of the law subject to criminal penalties. Indeed, plaintiff has not alleged that these organizations are cruelly or unjustifiably injuring or maiming any dogs and admittedly does not intend to conform his dog's tail length to the breed standard. Therefore, neither plaintiff nor defendants have engaged in any conduct that violates the law as plaintiff interprets it.[2]

The statute does not, either expressly or impliedly, incorporate a method for private citizens to obtain civil relief. In light of the comprehensive statutory enforcement scheme, recognition of a private civil right of action is incompatible with the mechanisms chosen by the Legislature.

* * *

Notes

1. There are private organizations, like the AKC and the ABC discussed in the case, that provide formal registration for purebred animals, organize dog and cat shows, and are involved in lobbying efforts. These breed groups have regularly opposed the introduction of laws requiring that all shelter and homeless animals be sterilized—even where there are specific exemptions for breeders and others. These "spay-neuter laws" effectively decrease the number of cats and dogs euthanized in local animal shelters each year (by reducing the number of animals overall), estimated at four to five million. Almost all of these animals are killed solely because of overpopulation and overcrowding, which are direct consequences of a failure to sterilize companion animals and the decision by some members of the public to buy their companion animals from commercial breeders as opposed to adopting them from shelters.

2. In *Hammer*, the court concluded that no express or implied civil private right of action existed under the criminal anti-cruelty laws for a dog owner to sue the AKC for effectively excluding his dog from competition because he refused to cut off (dock) the dog's tail. By dismissing the case on that basis, the court did not reach the issue of whether docking a dog's tail is a cruel act in violation of New York's anti-cruelty laws. The docking of tails and cropping of ears necessarily is painful; yet these procedures are widely accepted and required practices for people involved in entering certain breeds in dog shows and competitions. Should anti-cruelty laws prohibit cosmetic surgery on companion animals?

3. The City of West Hollywood has been at the forefront of animal protection and welfare issues, enacting ordinances to protect animals, including an ordinance banning the nontherapeutic declawing of cats, which resulted in the following lawsuit brought by the California Veterinary Medical Association.

California Veterinary Medical Ass'n v. City of West Hollywood

Court of Appeal of California, Second District, 2007
152 Cal. App. 4th 536, 61 Cal. Rptr. 3d 318

PERLUSS, P.J. Echoing Gandhi's teaching that a society's moral progress is best judged by its treatment of animals, the City of West Hollywood has banned as cruel

---

2. It is therefore unnecessary for us to determine here whether dog tail docking violates section 353 of the Agriculture and Markets Law.

and inhumane the practice of animal declawing unless necessary for a therapeutic purpose. Believing West Hollywood's prohibition of recognized veterinary medical procedures within its city limits was both inappropriate and ill-advised, the California Veterinary Medical Association (CVMA) filed an action for declaratory and injunctive relief, asserting the ordinance was preempted by the California Veterinary Medical Practice Act (VMPA or Act) (Bus. & Prof. Code §4800 *et seq.*) and by Business and Professions Code section 460, which precludes cities and counties from prohibiting certain individuals licensed by the State from engaging in their business or profession "or any portion thereof."

On cross-motions for summary judgment the trial court concluded West Hollywood's anti-declawing ordinance was preempted by section 460 and entered judgment in favor of the CVMA, declaring the ordinance invalid and enjoining further enforcement. We reverse. Although section 460 prohibits local legislation imposing separate and additional licensing requirements or other qualifications on individuals holding state licenses issued by agencies of the Department of Consumer Affairs (DCA), it does not preclude otherwise valid local regulation of the manner in which a business or profession is performed. Similarly, although West Hollywood's adoption of an anti-cruelty measure prohibiting nontherapeutic declawing of animals has an incidental impact on veterinarians practicing within its city limits, the ordinance is not preempted by virtue of the state's regulation of veterinary medicine through the VMPA or its implementing regulations.

FACTUAL AND PROCEDURAL BACKGROUND

1. West Hollywood's Prohibition of Declawing Animals for Nontherapeutic Purposes

On April 21, 2003 the City of West Hollywood, finding that onychectomy (declawing) and flexor tendonectomy procedures cause "unnecessary pain, anguish and permanent disability" to animals. . . . The ordinance prohibits any person, "licensed medical professional or otherwise," from performing or causing either procedure to be performed "by any means on any animal within the city, except when necessary for a therapeutic purpose." (West Hollywood Mun. Code §9.49.020.)[3]

In detailed findings supporting adoption of the ordinance, West Hollywood recited the bases for its conclusion the practice of animal declawing is cruel and inhumane unless necessary for a therapeutic purpose: "Contrary to most people's understanding, declawing consists of amputating not just the claws but the whole phalanx (up to the joint), including bones, ligaments, and tendons. [¶] . . . Declawing is not a simple cosmetic procedure akin to a manicure or a pedicure. On the

---

3. "Therapeutic purpose" is defined as "the necessity to address the medical condition of the animal, such as an existing or recurring illness, infection, disease, injury or abnormal condition in the claw that compromises the animal's health. 'Therapeutic purpose' does not include cosmetic or aesthetic reasons or reasons of convenience in keeping or handling the animal." (West Hollywood Mun. Code, §9.49.020.)

contrary, to remove a claw, the bone, nerve, joint capsule, collateral ligaments, and the extensor and flexor tendons must all be amputated. Thus, declawing is not a 'simple,' single surgery but ten separate, painful amputations of the third phalanx up to the last joint of each toe. In human terms, this is akin to cutting off the last joint of each finger. [¶] ... [¶] ... Complications can include excruciating pain, damage to radial nerve, hemorrhage, bone chips that prevent healing, painful re-growth of deformed claw inside the paw which is not visible to the eye, necrosis, lameness, and chronic back and joint pain as shoulder, leg and back muscles weaken. ..." (West Hollywood Mun. Code, § 9.49.010(a), (b) & (d).)

2. The Opinion from the DCA Legal Office

Following adoption of West Hollywood's ban on declawing, ... the DCA legal office [determined that] "a city cannot prohibit a licensed veterinarian from practicing any aspect of the veterinary medical work that falls within the perimeter of the state license. ... Such local regulation of veterinary practice in different jurisdictions would ultimately create a chaotic and confusing situation where it would be difficult for licensed veterinarians to know which veterinary procedures are legal or not depending on the jurisdiction. ... Such a balkanization of professional practice ultimately would lead to different standards of practice throughout the state ... [and] will inevitably make it very difficult for the Board to enforce the Veterinary Medical Practice Act."

* * *

4. Cross-motions for Summary Judgment and the Trial Court's Order

After conducting initial discovery the CVMA and West Hollywood filed cross-motions for summary judgment. The CVMA [argued that] "whether moral or immoral, ethical or unethical," these procedures are part of the practice of veterinary medicine as defined by the VMPA and, therefore, West Hollywood's effort to ban those procedures is preempted by the state's licensing laws.

* * *

DISCUSSION

* * *

2. State Regulation of the Practice of Veterinary Medicine

The VMPA creates a Veterinary Medical Board within the DCA to exercise licensing, regulatory and disciplinary functions and to protect the public with respect to the practice of veterinary medicine in California. The Board is authorized to adopt rules and regulations as necessary to implement the Act.

* * *

The VMPA and the regulations adopted by the Board contain comprehensive provisions setting minimum standards for sanitation and hygiene at sites where veterinary medicine is practiced; and the Legislature has expressly preempted the field of enforcing the cleanliness and sanitary requirements of the Act. The VMPA and regulations also provide extensive rules governing the education, licensing and function of "registered veterinary technicians," including a detailed specification of animal health care tasks that may and may not be performed by technicians and unregistered assistants.

* * *

3. General Principles of Preemption

The California Constitution reserves to a county or city the right to "make and enforce within its limits all local police, sanitary, and other ordinances and regulations not in conflict with general laws." "'If otherwise valid local legislation conflicts with state law, it is preempted by such law and is void.'"

* * *

"'[I]t is well settled that local regulation is invalid if it attempts to impose additional requirements in a field which is fully occupied by statute.'"

* * *

Local ordinances within the scope of a city's traditional police powers are presumed valid: The party challenging the ordinance has the burden of demonstrating preemption.

* * *

4. Section 460 Does Not Preempt the West Hollywood Anti-declawing Ordinance

As discussed, the trial court found that onychectomy and flexor tendonectomy are surgical operations upon an animal and that performing such procedures are part of the practice of veterinary medicine. Accordingly, the court concluded West Hollywood's prohibition of those procedures by any person, including licensed veterinarians, was precluded by section 460, which provides, "No city or county shall prohibit a person, authorized by one of the agencies in the Department of Consumer Affairs by a license, certificate, or other such means to engage in a particular business, from engaging in that business, occupation, or profession or any portion thereof."

The DCA's legal office had reached a similar conclusion. . . .

* * *

West Hollywood advances three arguments in support of its contention the trial court erred in concluding section 460 bars adoption of its anti-declawing ordinance. First, because nontherapeutic declawing procedures are inhumane and, by definition, serve no legitimate medical purpose, performing such procedures is not a "portion" of the practice of veterinary medicine. Second, because the ordinance is an anti-cruelty measure and is not directed solely to veterinarians, but to any person who authorizes or performs such procedures, including the owner of the animal, it is outside the scope of section 460, even as that statute was interpreted by the DCA's legal office and by the trial court. Finally, by its terms section 460 prohibits local governments from imposing additional licensing conditions or qualification as a requirement for working within their jurisdiction but does not preclude local regulation of the manner in which state licensees actually perform their business or profession. Although the first two contentions lack merit, we agree the trial court (and the DCA's legal office) misconstrued the scope of section 460 and thus erred in concluding that statute expressly preempts West Hollywood's anti-declawing ordinance.

a. Onychectomy and flexor tendonectomy are currently part of the practice of veterinary medicine

* * *

We need not enter, let alone attempt to resolve, the debate whether nontherapeutic declawing is "cruel" or can ever be justified as a moral or ethical matter; for it is clear that at present it is part of the conventional practice of veterinary medicine, at least in the United States.[9] Were it not, there would be little need for the West Hollywood ordinance in the first place. Nonetheless, the question remains whether section 460 prohibits a local government from making such political judgments when they restrict in some manner the traditional method by which a state licensee conducts his or her business or profession.

* * *

c. Section 460 prohibits local licensing requirements and qualifications but does not preclude otherwise valid local regulation of the manner in which a business is operated or profession is practiced

Section 460 forbids a city or county from prohibiting, in whole or in part, any person licensed or certified by one of the agencies within the DCA from engaging in his or her business or profession. The trial court ... interpreted this prohibition to include not only local legislation imposing separate and additional licensing requirements or other qualifications on individual licensees ... but also regulations affecting the manner in which the licensed profession itself is practiced. . . . This expansive interpretation of section 460 misconstrues the literal language of the statute itself and misperceives the policy it was intended to implement.

* * *

d. The DCA legal opinion is not entitled to heightened deference

. . . Although courts are bound by an agency's rulemaking as long as it is authorized by the enabling legislation, "the binding power of an agency's interpretation of a statute or regulation is contextual: Its power to persuade is both circumstantial and dependent on the presence or absence of factors that support the merit of the interpretation."

---

9. Similarly, although we may decry unnecessarily combative and overly aggressive litigation tactics as "unprofessional" and approve the imposition of sanctions to deter such behavior, the lawyers who engage in this conduct are surely practicing law.

* * *

[Here, n]either the context nor the circumstances of the DCA's legal opinion weigh in favor of according its broad interpretation of section 460 any heightened deference in this case.

* * *

5. The Veterinary Medicine Practice Act Does Not Preempt the West Hollywood Anti-declawing Ordinance

As discussed above, performing onychectomies and flexor tendonectomies, whether or not necessary for therapeutic purposes, is currently part of the practice of veterinary medicine. Nonetheless, neither the VMPA nor the regulations adopted by the Board mandate or expressly approve those procedures. Accordingly, West Hollywood's Ordinance No. 03-656 does not directly conflict with or contradict the VMPA. . . . Similarly, because the VMPA and related regulations do not prohibit nontherapeutic declawing procedures, West Hollywood's ordinance is not coextensive with, and plainly does not duplicate, state law. . . . Finally, although the VMPA specifically preempts enforcement of sanitation and hygiene requirements developed for the premises where veterinarians practice, the Legislature has not expressly declared its intention to fully occupy the field of regulating the practice of veterinary medicine.

Although local regulation of veterinarians is not expressly preempted by the VMPA, the CVMA contends the practice of veterinary medicine is highly regulated by the state and thus the West Hollywood ordinance is preempted by "legislative implication" because it impermissibly enters an area fully and completely occupied by general law. . . . In advancing this argument the CVMA misconstrues the nature of West Hollywood's anti-declawing ordinance and, as a result, misapprehends the scope of the implied preemption doctrine.

. . . [I]t is by no means clear the VMPA fully occupies the field of regulating that practice. Of course, the fact the state has legislated on the same subject does not necessarily preclude the exercise of local authority: A city or county may make additional regulations, different from those established by the state, if not inconsistent with the purpose of the general law. . . . Those commendable objectives hardly constitute the type of extensive regulation of the practice of veterinarian medicine that would support an inference the subject has become either exclusively a matter of state concern or one in which the state interest is so paramount it will not tolerate additional local action.

* * *

As for the third test for implied preemption—"the adverse effect of a local ordinance on the transient citizens of the state outweighs the possible benefit to the locality" (*Sherwin-Williams, supra,* 4 Cal. 4th at p. 898)—because onychectomies and flexor tendonectomies performed for nontherapeutic reasons are, by their very definition, nonemergency procedures, any negative impact on transient citizens is difficult to imagine. As noted in the opinion from the DCA's legal office, owners may freely go to a neighboring city and have the operation performed there and bring the cat back to West Hollywood. Although the CVMA asserts local regulation of veterinary practice could ultimately result in a chaotic situation in which licensed veterinarians struggle to know what procedures are legal in which jurisdictions, this speculative fear of "fragmented localization" is, in our view, wholly insufficient to overcome West Hollywood's significant interest in exercising its police power to set minimum standards for the humane treatment of animals within its borders.

. . . The Legislature has no doubt preempted discrete areas impacting the practice of veterinary medicine (most clearly licensing and enforcement of sanitary standards), but not the entire field.

Even if we were to find the VMPA fully occupies the field of regulating veterinary medicine, that conclusion would not be determinative of the validity of Ordinance No. 03-656. By its terms, the ordinance is a general measure to prevent animal cruelty — an area concededly not preempted by the state [16] — not a regulation of the practice of veterinary medicine. To be sure, one effect of the ordinance is to prevent veterinarians in West Hollywood from performing declawing procedures unless medically necessary; but the ordinance also prohibits animal owners and their employees (breeders, for example) from performing the procedures, which they otherwise might do even though not licensed as a veterinarian (§ 4827, subd. (a)), and makes it a criminal offense for the owner ("the animal guardian") to order the procedure.

* * *

West Hollywood's ordinance prohibiting onychectomy and flexor tendonectomy procedures has a valid principal purpose plainly within the city's police power — the prevention of animal cruelty — and only a secondary or incidental effect on a field arguably preempted by the state. Because this incidental restriction of a particular form of surgical procedure to therapeutic purposes does not materially interfere with any legislative purpose expressed in the VMPA, West Hollywood's ordinance is not preempted by state law.

* * *

The judgment is reversed. . . .

Notes

1. As demonstrated by the *West Hollywood* case and the veterinary malpractice cases in Chapter 4, as well as those in the farmed animal area, animal law may place animal guardian/owners and animal welfare advocates on opposite sides of

---

16. Responding to an argument in West Hollywood's opening brief, the CVMA acknowledges a provision of the San Francisco Municipal Code that sets minimum standards for the humane treatment of companion dogs is valid even if applied to a veterinarian who fails to adequately provide for a dog in his or her care.

various legal issues. Just as the threat of heightened damages in animal injury cases and under statutes allowing for noneconomic damages has received strong opposition from some veterinary groups as well as from insurance companies that provide veterinary malpractice insurance, so too may any incursion into veterinary practice create a conflict. Some veterinarians disapprove of a number of controversial practices—including declawing, debarking, tail docking and ear cropping. Traditionally, however, the veterinary lobby and the organizations that represent them react against any suggestion that the ultimate decision as to whether these practices are undertaken should be made by anyone but veterinarians.

2. Governmental and official veterinary policy also may clash with the interests of animal protection and advocacy groups within the confines of municipal shelters. These facilities are typically run by local city or county governments. While in more urban areas there may be a number of private shelters that carry out similar functions, in most localities there is only one shelter, run by the county. The problems of limited budgets and employees who may not be well-trained in animal control skills and philosophies leads, in some places, to problems for the animals and severe tensions between animal advocates and shelter managers.

3. Each state has specific laws governing the treatment of animals who end up in municipal possession and control. The most typical state-controlled parameters are (1) the amount of time between when animals arrive at a shelter and when they can be legally euthanized (known as the "holding period"), and (2) the methods of euthanasia that may be employed. Shelters may be overseen by state agencies (such as departments of agriculture or health and safety), with local governments or private nonprofits responsible for day-to-day activities. As discussed in the following Note, some states, like California, have adopted extensive laws and regulations, while others, like Kentucky, delegate most of the responsibility for animal control to local governments.

4. In 1999, California adopted the "Hayden Act," which amended and supplemented several state laws, all relating to the treatment of animals in California shelters. The motivation was to shift shelter policies from management and euthanasia to increased encouragement of adoptions from shelters. California Penal Code section 599d embodies that sentiment:

> (a) It is the policy of the state that no adoptable animal should be euthanized if it can be adopted into a suitable home. Adoptable animals . . . [manifest] no sign of a behavioral or temperamental defect that could pose a health or safety risk or otherwise make the animal unsuitable for placement as a pet, and have manifested no sign of disease, injury, or congenital or hereditary condition that adversely affects the health of the animal or that is likely to adversely affect the animal's health in the future.

> (b) It is the policy of the state that no treatable animal should be euthanized. A treatable animal shall include any animal that is not adoptable but that could become adoptable with reasonable efforts. . . .

The Hayden Act has generated a number of lawsuits in which plaintiffs—usually rescue groups—sue the California counties responsible for compliance with the Hayden Act. The following issues have been raised:

a) *Failure to comply with the statutory holding period.* Euthanization of animals is only allowed after a defined period, with limited exceptions. Shelters have been accused of euthanizing animals earlier than allowed or for unsupportable reasons.

b) *Use of drop boxes.* Some shelters provide bins that allow individuals to place animals in a box when a shelter is closed. Plaintiffs have challenged the legality of the boxes under the Hayden Act.

c) *Differential treatment for owner-relinquished and abandoned animals.* Animals come into shelters in two general ways—when they are picked up by animal control officers or when their owners bring them in and turn them over to the shelter because they no longer want the animals. At one point, Los Angeles County shelters allegedly were euthanizing owner-relinquished animals without waiting for the statutory holding period to expire and denying them veterinary care. These practices were challenged and the county changed its policies as the result of a settlement between the parties.

d) *Exclusion of rescue groups.* Tensions often run high between shelter administrators and authorized rescue groups who are sometimes their most vocal critics. The Hayden Act entitles rescue groups to a pre-euthanasia right to adopt shelter animals and the question of the breadth of that right is a point of ongoing debate.

e) *Failure to provide veterinary care.* The Hayden Act requires that veterinary care be delivered to animals in need. Counties have been sued for failing to comply with that requirement.

5. States like Kentucky have gone in the opposite direction of California and the Hayden Act, abdicating almost all responsibility for shelter management and animal care and control to local authorities. The Kentucky statutes regarding shelters lay out a set of minimum standards, but place all obligation on the counties, so that state agencies and officials have no duties whatsoever with respect to shelter problems. *See, e.g.,* KY. REV. STAT. ANN. §§ 258.119, 258.195.

6. "Pet leasing" is a recent practice in which consumers who are unable to afford the price of a new pet (almost always a dog) enter into contracts with pet stores who then turn the contract management over to leasing/finance companies. The retailers assign the contracts to the leasing companies, and the consumer pays a monthly fee, usually for a few years, which ultimately greatly exceeds the actual cost of the dog. At the end of the lease, consumers can pay one more lump sum and own the dog. During the period of payment, any default on payment technically results in a loss of rights to the dog. As of the end of 2018, three states—California, New York

and Nevada—had banned pet leasing. *See, e.g.,* Cal. Civ. Code § 1670.10; Nev. Rev. Stat. Ann. § 597-997.

7. Growing attention has been paid to the sale in pet stores of dogs, cats and rabbits from "puppy mills" and breeders.[f] In response, scores of state and local governments across the U.S. have enacted legislation to limit sales of puppies, kittens and rabbits in their jurisdictions.[g] The means by which sales are curtailed is usually through bans on the retail (pet store) sales of any puppies, kittens or rabbits, or a requirement that those animals only be sourced from rescues and local humane societies. For more information about specific ordinances, see *https://bestfriends .org/resources/puppy-mills/jurisdictions-retail-pet-sale-bans*. Many of the ordinances also faced legal challenges from pet stores, breeders and puppy mills, but the bans have been upheld in virtually every case. *See, e.g., Park Pet Shop v. City of Chicago*, 872 F.3d 495 (7th Cir. 2017); *Perfect Puppy, Inc. v. City of E. Providence, R.I.*, 807 F.3d 415 (1st Cir. 2015); *Missouri Pet Breeders Ass'n v. County of Cook*, 119 F. Supp. 3d 865 (N.D. Ill. 2015); *Puppies 'N Love v. City of Phoenix*, 116 F. Supp. 3d 971 (D. Ariz. 2015), *vacated due to subsequent legislation*, 283 F. Supp. 3d 815 (D. Ariz. 2017); *Maryeli's Lovely Pets, Inc. v. City of Sunrise*, 2015 U.S. Dist. LEXIS 98451 (S.D. Fla. 2015). For further discussion, see Chapter 6, Section 2.

E. Television, Film, Zoos, Circuses and Aquaria

Although many people may enjoy seeing animals in zoos and circuses and as animal "actors" in films and television, extensive reports of abuse in these settings have raised significant concern about the treatment of animals in these industries, most of which occurs far from the public eye. Because of the secretive nature of the conduct, the abuses are hard to uncover and enforce. Correspondingly, there is a dearth of case law addressing the treatment of animals in these contexts.

Since 1980, a clause in the Screen Actors Guild (SAG) contract with television and film producers has granted sole authority for monitoring the treatment of animals in movies, television shows, commercials, and music videos to the Film and Television Unit of the American Humane Association (AHA). Ralph Frammolino and James Bates, *Questions Raised About Group That Watches Out for Animals in Movies*, L.A. Times, Feb. 9, 2001, at A1. Although the contract covers "most significant productions in the U.S.," according to the article, "interviews and internal documents" revealed that (at least in 2001) the Unit "lacks any meaningful enforcement power

---

f. The term "puppy mill" is defined as a business involved in high volume breeding operations that provide little or extremely poor basic care for their animals (which may include puppies, kittens, or rabbits), sell animals with a myriad of health and behavioral issues to an unsuspecting public, and place expensive burdens on local consumers and taxpayer-funded animal shelters.

g. Over 254 cities have enacted legislation to address the tragic consequences of puppy mill production. *See, e.g., https://bestfriends.org/resources/states-local-pet-sale-bans*. California was the first state to have passed such a ban. *See, e.g.,* Cal. Health & Safety Code § 122354.5 (effective Jan. 1, 2018; operative Jan. 1, 2019), and as amendments to other Code sections.

under the SAG contract, depends on major studios to pay for its operations and is rife with conflicts of interest." *Id.*

Beginning in the 1980s, the methods of training wild animals came under some level of public scrutiny. Former trainers like the late Pat Derby (who founded Performing Animal Welfare Society (PAWS) in California, a sanctuary for retired entertainment animals) decried the treatment and abuse of great apes, large cats, elephants and many other species. Groups like PAWS provide sanctuary for former animal actors and may lobby for legislation banning ownership of exotic animals and the use of these animals in some forms of entertainment.

Trainers and professional animal caretakers are rarely charged with criminal animal cruelty except when the most egregious conduct comes to light. One such instance was the case of Rose-Tu, an elephant at the Oregon Zoo in Portland. The evidence presented in that case showed that a zookeeper had used a sharpened ankus (commonly known as a "bull hook") to inflict 176 documented puncture wounds on Rose-Tu. Her rectum also allegedly was sodomized with the ankus. Roger Anthony, *Keeper Won't Face Charges*, Oregonian, Aug. 16, 2000, at B01; R. Gregory Nokes, *Animal Abuse Bill Would Aid Prosecution*, Oregonian, Jan. 25, 2001, at D06; Peter Farrell, *Elephant Keeper Pleads No Contest*, Oregonian, Mar. 6, 2001, at B01. At the time, Oregon's anti-cruelty laws required a minimum showing of "physical injury," which was defined—based on a definition initially created for crimes against humans—to mean "impairment of physical condition or substantial pain." Because the injuries primarily were limited to surface wounds, the issue of whether Rose-Tu's physical condition was impaired came into question. In addition, experts were required to testify as to whether Rose-Tu suffered pain and whether the pain was substantial. In the end, the zookeeper was convicted. In addition, the case served to highlight the problems in the definition and was used to galvanize support for the passage of a law that made numerous changes to Oregon's animal protection laws. One change was a new definition of physical injury that obviated the need to present evidence of pain in an abuse case. The new standard instead simply requires evidence of "physical trauma," which is defined as "fractures, cuts, punctures, bruises, burns or other wounds." Or. Rev. Stat. § 167.310(9).

In 1988, zoo keepers at the San Diego Zoo took an 18-year-old African elephant named Dunda, "chained her legs, pulled her to the ground, and beat her on the head with ax handles during several sessions over two days." Jane Fritsch, *Beatings, Abuse: Elephants in Captivity: A Dark Side*, L.A. Times, Oct. 5, 1988, at 1. One of the five participants was quoted as describing the blows as "home run swings." *Id.* This incident and the investigations that followed "provided a rare opportunity for the public to get a behind-the-scenes look at measures sometimes taken to control elephants." *Id.* Officials of the Zoological Society of San Diego, which operates the San Diego Zoo, stated they considered the beatings to be, as paraphrased in the article, "an appropriate method of disciplining a dangerous animal." *Id.* There was a mix of opinion in this regard among various zoo keepers across the country who commented publicly about the incident. *Id.* The city attorney's criminal investigation concluded the treatment was a cruel but accepted practice and that there was insufficient evidence to prosecute the zoo keepers for cruelty. The USDA fined the park, but as a result of the incident and public outcry, a new state anti-cruelty law was enacted that criminalized any discipline of elephants that scarred their hide (CAL. PENAL CODE § 596.5), notwithstanding that this was deemed by many in the industry to be a necessary and customary practice for training and handling elephants at zoos and circuses.

Notes

1. On October 23, 2013, the Los Angeles City Council unanimously voted to ban the use of bullhooks (as well as baseball bats, axe handles and pitchforks) on circus elephants. According to news reports at the time, the ban passed because council members believed that bullhooks are dangerous to the elephants and that there are more humane ways to control elephant behavior. The ordinance has the practical effect of making it difficult for many traveling zoos and circuses to perform in Los Angeles, as bullhooks are commonly used by those entities and are the only means by which circus employees can control the elephants. The ban was phased in over a three-year period. Since that time, Rhode Island and California have enacted statewide bans on the use of bullhooks and more than fifty localities across the country have enacted similar laws. *See* R.I. GEN. LAWS § 4-1-43; CAL. FISH & GAME CODE § 2128.

2. Taking the elephant issue one step further, New York has banned the use of elephants in "any type of entertainment act," defined to mean "any exhibition, act, circus, trade show, carnival, ride, parade, race, performance or similar undertaking which is primarily undertaken for the entertainment or amusement of a live audience." However, the law does not apply to institutions accredited by the Association of Zoos and Aquariums. N.Y. AGRIC. & MKTS. (Consol. 2018). The law goes into effect October 19, 2019.

3. Expanding beyond just elephants, many jurisdictions have banned the use of all exotic (wild) animals in displays and shows, impacting the bottom line of once profitable companies such as Feld Entertainment, which ran the Ringling Brothers circus. Facing intense criticism on the heels of the popularity of these bans nationwide, Ringling Brothers announced in March of 2015 that it would retire its elephants over the course of three years. The elephants were in fact retired by May of 2016. One year later, following years of declining attendance at its performances, Ringling Brothers permanently shut down.

4. Taxpayer claims have been the basis for civil lawsuits arising out of alleged violations of criminal anti-cruelty statutes in the treatment of elephants in zoos. For example, in *Leider v. Lewis,* 2 Cal. 5th 1121 (2017), plaintiffs sued the L.A. zoo and its director for alleged elephant abuse in violation of several California anti-cruelty statutes. They sought injunctive and declaratory relief as taxpayers under California Code of Civil Procedure section 526a, which authorizes individuals to bring a private right of action to restrain the illegal or wasteful expenditure of public funds.

In *Leider*, the plaintiffs alleged that the city's criminal mistreatment of elephants at the L.A. zoo amounted to such an illegal and wasteful expenditure of public funds. The California Supreme Court held that the statutory bar against equitable relief to enforce the criminal law precluded the taxpayer action.

In *Animal Legal Defense Fund v. Cal. Expositions & State Fairs,* 239 Cal. App. 4th 1286 (2015), another Section 526a taxpayer lawsuit, plaintiffs alleged that defendants wasted taxpayer money and staff time by obtaining, transporting and exhibiting pregnant pigs housed in farrowing crates at a state fair every summer, in violation of two of California's anti-cruelty statutes, Penal Code sections 597 and 597t. Consistent with the later decision by the high court in *Leider*, the court held that California's anti-cruelty laws are not enforceable through taxpayer lawsuits.

In *Sebek v. City of Seattle,* 172 Wash. App. 273 (2012), plaintiffs filed suit as taxpayers against the city, alleging that Woodland Park Zoological Society (Zoo) was a *de facto* agency of the city that violated state and local animal cruelty laws by the manner in which they housed elephants. Even though the city had provided payment to the Zoo to operate and manage a "state of the art zoo," the operating agreement made it clear that the Zoo had exclusive control over operation of the elephant exhibit. For that reason, the court held the Zoo was not a *de facto* agency of the city and, thus, taxpayer standing could not be conferred on plaintiffs for purposes of suing the city for animal cruelty.

5. In late 2011, a lawsuit was filed, naming five orca whales as plaintiffs. The case was brought on their behalf by their "next friends" (guardians/representatives) People for the Ethical Treatment of Animals and several other individuals. *Tilikum v. Sea World Parks & Entertainment*, 842 F. Supp. 2d 1259 (N.D. Cal. 2012) (also discussed in Chapter 2). The complaint alleged that the orcas were being held by Sea World in violation of the Thirteenth Amendment to the U.S. Constitution, which prohibits slavery and involuntary servitude. This novel approach sought to capitalize on the precise language of the Thirteenth Amendment, which simply describes what activities are prohibited without specifying to whom the benefit of the prohibition should flow; "Neither slavery nor involuntary servitude . . . shall exist within the United States or any place subject to their jurisdiction." (U.S. Const. amend. XIII, § 1.) Not surprisingly, the court granted defendants' motion to dismiss, finding that plaintiffs had no standing.

6. In *Animal Legal Defense Fund (ALDF), et al. v. Sidney Jay Yost*, Civil Case No. ED CV 05-01066 RGK (E.D. Cal., filed Nov. 23, 2005), ALDF and the Chimpanzee Collaboratory (a great ape advocacy group), along with two individuals, sued an individual known in the entertainment industry as an animal trainer, alleging that he routinely beat, punched and continuously abused chimpanzees (and other exotic animals) under his control. The individual plaintiffs alleged that they had witnessed the defendant's actions, and plaintiffs sued him for alleged violations of the Endangered Species Act and the California anti-cruelty law, California Penal Code section 597. The complaint also alleged violations of California's false advertising/deceptive trade practices laws, based on the defendant's alleged claims that he

"affection train[ed]" chimpanzees "with love, respect, and positive reinforcement." Complaint, ¶ 86 (quoting the defendant's representations). The complaint included a description of chimpanzees generally and the effects of abuse:

> Chimpanzees suffer emotional and physical pain "just as we do and often for the same reasons." Roger Fouts, *On the Psychological Well-Being of Chimpanzees*, 1 Journal of Applied Animal Welfare Science 65 ("Psychological Well-Being of Chimpanzees"), 69 (1998). Indeed, chimpanzees engage in higher-level cognitive behavior, including rational and conceptual thought, problem solving, creative thinking and strategizing. *See, e.g.,* S. Savage-Rumbaugh, D. Rumbaugh and Boysen, *Symbolic communication between two chimpanzees (pan troglydytes)*, Science 201, 641–44 (1978); B.T. Gardner & R.A. Gardner, *Two-Way Communication with an Infant Chimpanzee*, Behavior of Nonhuman Primates, Vol. 4 (1971). When faced with abuse, they respond like humans subjected to abuse. They cry and scream, and utter sounds with distinct meanings. Jane Goodall, *The Chimpanzees of Gombe: Patterns of Behavior* 125 (1986). They are aware of themselves and others as distinct individuals. R. Fouts and S.T. Mills, *Next of Kin* ("*Next of Kin*") 155 (1997) (chimpanzees express understanding of humans' distress, physical pain and anger); J. van Hooff, *Understanding Chimpanzees* 276–84 (1994). Their social relations with one another and with humans are wide-ranging and complex. William Karesh, *Appointment at the Ends of the World: Memoirs of a Wildlife Veterinarian* 299 (1999); Psychological Well-Being of Chimpanzees, 69. It is virtually undisputed that "chimpanzees have emotions similar to those which in ourselves we label pleasure, joy, sorrow, boredom and so on." *See* Goodall, p. 118; *see also Next of Kin* 155 (chimpanzees expressing sadness, pleasure). Thus, when they are beaten or abused, they suffer pain and psychological harm.

Complaint, ¶ 2. The defendant counterclaimed against each of the plaintiffs, for publication of the allegations on a website and stating that defendant was involved in beatings of the animals under his care and additional animal cruelty. By order dated March 27, 2006, the court granted the plaintiffs' motion to strike the counterclaim, based on California's "anti-SLAPP statute" (CAL. CIV. PROC. CODE § 425.16(b)(1)). In December of that year, the parties entered into a settlement agreement in which Yost (who denied all claims) agreed to give up the chimpanzees in his care to two sanctuaries designated by plaintiffs and to cease all future contact of any kind with all primates.

7. Over the last twenty-five years, special attention has been paid to the treatment of great apes, especially chimpanzees, in the entertainment industry. Investigations and exposés of this treatment have established that the great apes often are beaten with fists, sticks and other objects, and kicked and mentally and psychologically abused, to get them to "act" as necessary for performing and filming, as plaintiffs reported in *Yost* and in *People for the Ethical Treatment of Animals v. Bobby Berosini*, 111 Nev. 615 (1995).

For a thorough discussion and analysis of the use of chimpanzees in entertainment, with considerations of the potential for legal change, *see* Lorraine Fischer, *"No Animals Were Harmed . . .": Protecting Chimpanzees from Cruelty Behind the Curtain*, 27 Hastings Comm. & Ent. L.J. 405 (2005).

8. Some believe computer-generated imaging and digital animation, along with repeated protests by activists, have resulted in the decreased used of live "wild" animals (particularly chimpanzees) in the entertainment industry. *See* Amanda Covarrubias, *When the Show's Over for Hollywood Chimps*, L.A. Times, Mar. 22, 2005. This trend did not progress fast enough, however, to save two horses from dying during the 2005 filming of a remake of the 1940s film "My Friend Flicka." *See, e.g.*, Associated Press, *Second Horse Killed During "Flicka" Filming in So. Cal.*, Contra Costa Times, Apr. 27, 2005; Dana Bartholomew, *Horse Dies on Set of "Flicka" Remake*, L.A. Daily News, Apr. 25, 2005.

Similar problems plagued the HBO horse-racing drama "Luck" — in 2012 three horses died during the show's production. The bad press, low ratings and criticism HBO received for the harm done to horses resulted in cancellation of the show after only a few episodes. *http://www.huffingtonpost.com/2012/03/14/luck-canceled -hbo-dustin-hoffman_n_1346185.html*. Prior to cancellation, Barbara Casey, who had worked for the American Humane Association (AHA) on site for the show, monitoring the treatment of the actor animals, sued both HBO and the AHA. Her suit claimed that HBO and its producers facilitated and covered up animal cruelty and that she was wrongfully terminated from her employment at AHA in retaliation for exposing abuses that had occurred on film and television shoots for which the AHA had given its "no animals were harmed in the making" stamp of approval.

There is some evidence that advanced technology could be the future of zoos and aquaria, as well. A virtual reality aquarium opened in New York City's Times Square in 2017. Through surround sound, high-resolution images, and state-of-the-art immersive experiences featuring photo-real animation, the exhibit, called Encounter: Ocean Odyssey, takes visitors from the ocean floor through various underwater habitats, allowing virtual interaction with coral, various species of fish, and dolphins. This type of technology is allowing people to experience animal-based entertainment in a way that removes the possibility of harming animals.

9. Efforts to create or increase the legal protections that should be afforded to "performing" animals in mainstream film and television face significant hurdles, in part because of the public's assumption that those animals they see on the big screen necessarily must be well cared for, and the dichotomy between the perception of how animals are feeling and the reality of their experience. The factual setting for the case below alerted the world to a dark underside of the film and animal exploitation industry and is the first reported criminal prosecution of a producer of "crush videotapes" brought under California's general anti-cruelty law.

People v. Thomason

Court of Appeal of California, Second District, 2000
4 Cal. App. 4th 1064, 101 Cal. Rptr. 2d 247

LILLIE, P. J. The issue of defendant's guilt was submitted to the trial court on the testimony taken at the preliminary hearing and a videotape received in evidence. It found defendant guilty of three felony counts of cruelty to animals (mice, rats, newborn mice) in violation of Penal Code section 597, subdivision (a). He appeals from the judgment. We affirm.

FACTS

On information from a Ventura County District Attorney investigator who had learned, through a chat room and subsequent conversation with defendant, that he had produced a "crush video" depicting rats, mice and baby mice ("pinkies") being crushed and killed by a female under heel of her shoe, Officer William Le Baron and other officers conducted a search of defendant's apartment for any evidence of his production and distribution of videos. Officer Le Baron found 30 or 40 videos in defendant's closet, then asked defendant for the crush video he had filmed with codefendant Diane Aileen Chaffin. Defendant told the officer the videotape was with the others and labeled "Diane." Officer Le Baron found two "Diane" videotapes which, defendant stated, had been filmed at the home of Chaffin's parents. Other items seized were defendant's computer containing chat room conversations relating to crush videos, clips taken from crush videos and still images.

The videotape in evidence is 60 minutes long and shows Chaffin crushing numerous mice, baby mice and rats under the heel of her shoe and under her bare feet. Part of the videotape depicts a mouse being held down and Chaffin crushing the animal to death; the mice and rats were "stepped on to the point where intestines and innards are torn apart and taken out of them. It is then smashed into the ground until the mouse or rat or pinkie appears to be dead and it stops moving." Involved were 12 animals consisting of four mice, six baby mice and two rats. They were all taunted, maimed, tortured, mutilated, disemboweled and ultimately slowly killed under the heel of a shoe. The videotape depicts Chaffin stepping on the shoulder of a mouse with the heel of her shoe, causing the mouse to spin in circles, then Chaffin crushing its head. In one instance a mouse is taped down by its tail to prevent escape before being crushed to death. These videotapes were produced by codefendant Chaffin and defendant to sell for profit. Defendant obtained the animals from The Feed Barn, a store that sells feeder mice used to feed other animals.

I. Penal Code section 597, Subdivision (a) Applies to Defendant

Appellant contends that Penal Code section 597, subdivision (a), does not apply to rodents, which are different from animals within the meaning of the statute in that they may be killed at any time by any means because they represent a health and property hazard and are "known as dangerous to life or property" (Pen. Code, § 599c), thus, are exempt under Penal Code section 597, subdivision (a).

Penal Code section 597, subdivision (a) in pertinent part provides: "Except as provided in subdivision (c) of this section or section 599c, every person who maliciously and intentionally maims, mutilates, tortures, or wounds a living animal, or maliciously and intentionally kills an animal, is guilty of an offense punishable by imprisonment in the state prison. . . ."

Penal Code section 599c provides:

"No part of this title shall be construed as interfering with any of the laws of the state known as the 'game laws,' or any laws for or against the destruction of certain birds, nor must this title be construed as interfering with the right to destroy any venomous reptile, or any animal known as dangerous to life, limb, or property, or to interfere with the right to kill all animals used for food, or with properly conducted scientific experiments or investigations performed under the authority of the faculty of a regularly incorporated medical college or university of this state."

Penal Code section 599b provides in part: "In this title the word 'animal' includes every dumb creature; the words 'torment,' 'torture,' and 'cruelty' include every act, omission, or neglect whereby unnecessary or unjustifiable physical pain or suffering is caused or permitted. . . ."

Penal Code section 597, subdivision (a), makes it unlawful to mistreat any "living animal," which applies to rodents, and the term "animal" includes every "dumb creature" (Pen. Code, § 599b) which also applies to rodents, and appellant does not contend otherwise. And no reasonable person can argue that the malicious and intentional "'torment,' 'torture,' and 'cruelty,'" defined in Penal Code section 599b and as applied here, did not cause "unnecessary or unjustifiable physical pain or suffering" to the mice, rats and baby mice. However, appellant contends that rodents are "animal[s] known as dangerous to life, limb, or property" under section 599c, and have been "historically treated" as such "because of the disease they carry [*i.e.,* bubonic plague, hantavirus])," and "may be eradicated anytime using any means," referring to traps and poison commonly used by homeowners and restaurants to kill mice and rats. As to this defendant, we reject the contention.

First, "any living animal" (Pen. Code, § 597, subd. (a)) used in various state cruelty to animals statutes applies to domesticated animals and wild animals in captivity (*State v. Cleve* (1999) 127 N.M. 240), raccoons and any dumb living creature (*Wilkerson v. State* (Fla. 1981) 401 So. 2d 1110, 1111), and any dumb creature (*State v. Kaneakua* (1979) 61 Hawaii 136). Both parties agree, as do we, there is no California case in point, and this is a case of first impression.

Second, the rats, mice and baby mice used by defendant in his crush video were not wild animals, but bred for a domestic purpose—food for other animals. However, they were not used by defendant for this purpose, but to intentionally and maliciously maim, mutilate, torture and wound before ultimately slowly killing them, all for sexual gratification of others and for commercial gain. They differ from the rodents that run wild—rats and mice, denizens of alleys, garbage cans, and sewers—that carry disease to restaurants and households and destroy property. The rats and mice used by defendant were not wild nor were they destroyed by him as hazardous to health or property. He obtained the animals from The Feed Barn, a store which sells feeder mice used to feed other animals. These bred rats and mice do not run wild but are kept in cages, and are not "dangerous to life, limb or property." They clearly do not fall within the exception described in Penal Code section 599c.

Nor does Penal Code section 599c permit the destruction of all mice and rats, wild or bred, by "using any means," as contended by him. Penal Code section 599c applies only to specific animals known to pose a danger to life, limb or property. Among them are not the animals used by defendant bred and raised in captivity. We belabor this point because this, too, is the reason Food and Agricultural Code section 5401, relied on by appellant, does not support his argument that all rats and mice "may be eradicated anytime." This section provides that "[a]ny *premises* . . . which are infected or *infested* with any *pest*, or premises where any pest is found, are a *public nuisance*. . . ." (Italics added.) This statute cannot apply to defendant under the evidence in this case. Here the rats and mice cannot be classified as "pests" because they were bred and kept in cages; there was no "infestation" of any "premises," for defendant purchased them and voluntarily brought them to Chaffin's home where the video was made, not to eradicate as a public nuisance, but for the private purpose to intentionally and maliciously torture, maim, mutilate wound and ultimately kill.

Nor does Health and Safety Code section 116125 aid appellant. This section, too, requires one possessing "any place that is *infested* with rodents" to destroy them "by poisoning, trapping, and other *appropriate* means." (Italics added.) Appellant argues that "crushing rodents is not proscribed" therefore, what he did "was clearly lawful." "Appropriate means" to eradicate the "pests" surely does not include "any means available" as urged by appellant, nor does it embrace maliciously and intentionally maiming, taunting, torturing, wounding and disemboweling before crushing the mutilated animal to a slow death. But the fallacy in appellant's argument as to the applicability of both of the above sections is that the evidence does not support the necessary premise that the rats and mice were killed for health and safety purposes. The facts are, that they were voluntarily brought to the "premises" or "place" to make crush videos, and were ultimately killed after maiming, torturing and mutilating the animals, all for profit and for the sexual gratification of others.

Third, even if the bred mice and rats used by defendant could be classified as animals "known as dangerous to life, or property," it is one thing to kill by traps or poison, rats and mice that run wild and create a health hazard, but quite another to intentionally and maliciously maim, mutilate, and torture the animals until they die, for the purpose of making and selling videotapes for commercial gain. Known as crush videos, they are fetish videos in which small animals are taunted, maimed, tortured and ultimately crushed to death under the heel of a shoe or bare feet of a provocatively dressed woman. The live animals are stepped on until their intestines and innards are torn apart, then disemboweled after which the animal is smashed on the ground until it dies or stops moving. The videotape exhibit depicts the codefendant talking to four mice, six baby mice and two rats, taunting them, stepping on the shoulder of a mouse with the heel of her shoe, causing the animal to spin around in circles before crushing its head. It also shows a mouse taped to the floor by its tail to prevent its escape before being mutilated and crushed to death.

Assuming Penal Code section 599c could be construed to permit the destruction of all mice and rats, wild or bred and domesticated, as deadly or dangerous or destructive, it does not permit defendant to intentionally and maliciously torture or maim or taunt or mutilate or wound or disembowel and kill any living animal in the process. As the trial judge stated, "it is my view beyond a reasonable doubt that what I saw on that tape was malicious torture . . . no animal, whether the animal is a deer or rat or a rodent, a mouse—no animal under the Fish and Game Code, or any other code, is subject to that kind of malicious torture that I saw."

Our construction of Penal Code sections 597, subdivision (a), 599b and 599c is supported by the plain language used in those sections, "giving the words their ordinary meaning", a reasonable meaning and admitting a "'construction that comports most closely with the apparent intent of the Legislature, with a view to promoting rather than defeating the general purpose of the statute. . . .'"

Even if the killing of mice and rats should fall within the exception to Penal Code section 597, subdivision (a), as set up in Penal Code section 599c, intentionally and maliciously torturing, mutilating, wounding, tormenting and maiming the animals causing unnecessary physical pain or suffering before slowly killing them do not.

II. Challenge to Vagueness of Penal Code section 597, Subdivision (a)

Appellant contends that "the statute [(Pen. Code, §597, subd. (a))], as applied to rodents [is] constitutionally infirm as void for vagueness," violating his due process rights "for failing to notify the public that one who exterminates rodents for the 'wrong purpose' is criminally liable while one who exterminates rodents for another purpose [protection of health and property] is not subject to prosecution." Appellant ignores two cogent points—it is not only the extermination of the animals that is at issue, but how it is carried out—the intent and the purpose; and it is not all rodents that are at issue, but only those bred in captivity for use of food for other domesticated animals, that are not pests that infest premises, are caged and cannot run wild, and pose no danger spreading disease or destroying property.

Respondent contends that appellant lacks standing to challenge Penal Code section 597 as vague because "his conduct clearly falls under the statute's purview," and "a person to whom a statute may constitutionally be applied will not be heard to challenge that statute on the ground that it may conceivably be applied unconstitutionally to others, in other situations not before the Court." If a statute "clearly applies to a criminal defendant's conduct, the defendant may not challenge it on grounds of vagueness."

Appellant challenges his conviction on the ground that those in other situations not before the court, such as those who use traps or poison to exterminate rats and mice may also be committing unlawful acts because whether the killing of rodents is lawful as pests harmful to health and property or unlawful under Penal Code section 597, subdivision (a), they suffer the same effects and the exterminator may feel "joy in trapping a rat in his attic and listening as it slowly dies," or gain pleasure from baiting or poisoning "a rodent causing a slow and painful death" because of damage it did to the wiring of his house, and asks, is the exterminator "subject to prosecution?" However, defendant did not use traps or poison and the rodents were intentionally and maliciously tormented, tortured, maimed, mutilated, disemboweled and ultimately slowly killed, not to exterminate them for health reasons nor to save property from being destroyed, but for videotaping for sexual gratification and commercial profit. Section 597, subdivision (a) "clearly applies to defendant's conduct." Thus, for lack of standing of appellant to challenge section 597, subdivision (a), we reject his contention that it is "constitutionally vague [in] that it fails to distinguish between lawful killing of rodents and unlawful."

DISPOSITION

The judgment is affirmed.

Notes

1. Consider how different individuals can have dramatically different reactions to essentially the same activity. For example, in the case you just read, the defendant was convicted of animal cruelty for his role in producing videotapes depicting rodents being crushed to death. However, millions of rodents are crushed and killed every year in spring-loaded mousetraps and other devices which often result in slow, painful deaths—a dictionary definition of "torture." The first activity (crush video conduct) is roundly condemned by society, but enjoyed by a small minority, while the second is completely acceptable and legal, though likely never enjoyed. In both instances, the rodent experiences pain and suffering; arguably, if left in a trap for days to die slowly, the "acceptable" practice is crueler than that depicted in the crush video, because it prolongs the suffering. Consider this dichotomy (between animal suffering and human reactions) in connection with the recurrent question of whether the effect on the victim should matter in defining animal cruelty. If an animal's pain or suffering is offensive, why should one activity be legal and the other illegal? Describe the legal, social and ethical bases that may support such a distinction.

2. The criminal conduct at issue in *Thomason*—the production of crush videos—generated strong opposition from much of the public. 18 U.S.C. § 48, discussed earlier in this chapter and in the *U.S. v. Stevens* case excerpted in Chapter 5, was directed at shutting down that video market, but was initially drafted more broadly to prohibit depictions of all illegal animal cruelty, well beyond the production of crush videos. In *Stevens*, the U.S. Supreme Court found that the statute's breadth rendered it unconstitutional. 559 U.S. 460 (2010).

F. Animal Fighting

Many types of animal fighting have been part of American and other cultures for years. Dogfighting, cockfighting, bullfighting and "hog-dog fighting" (between dogs and pigs) are among the most well known. Bullfighting is illegal in the United States, and every state has now outlawed dogfighting and cockfighting.

1. Cockfighting

Fifty years ago, the treatment of cockfighting varied widely from state to state. Since the late 1970s, however, an almost unanimous societal rejection of cockfighting occurred—although not without resistance. In 2005, after Oklahomans passed a 2002 initiative banning cockfighting (Okla. Stat. Ann. title 21, § 1692(1)-(9)), one Oklahoma legislator—a long-time defender of the practice—hoped to revive cockfighting by proposing that fighting roosters wear boxing gloves attached to their spurs and lightweight vests configured with electronic sensors to record hits and help keep score: "It's like fencing that you see on the Olympics, you know, where they have little balls on the ends of the swords and the fencers wear vests." *Oklahoma Senator Wants Cockfights, With Gloves*, Reuters News, Jan. 26, 2005.

In 2007, New Mexico and Louisiana became the last states to outlaw cockfighting. Nearly fifty years earlier, the New Mexico Supreme Court upheld a lower court's ruling that cockfighting did not come within the terms of the statute prohibiting cruelty to animals. *State v. Buford*, 331 P.2d 1110 (N.M. 1958) (discussed in Chapter 1). The court noted that from early times cockfighting had been considered a "lawful and honorable" sport in New Mexico. It compared cockfighting to calf roping, steer riding and other similar activities. The court also pointed out that in 1887, five days after passage of the original statute that prohibited cruelty to animals, a statute was passed that, in effect, amended the law prohibiting Sunday cockfighting. The court concluded that by that amendment the legislature recognized again that cockfighting was legal on weekdays and thus had never intended to criminalize it.

The federal "Animal Fighting Venture Prohibition" within the Animal Welfare Act makes it "unlawful for any person to knowingly sponsor or exhibit an animal in an animal fighting venture." 7 U.S.C. § 2156 (2008). This crime is a felony punishable by up to five years in prison for each violation. The law also makes it unlawful for a person to "(e) ... knowingly sell, buy, transport, or deliver in interstate or foreign commerce a knife, a gaff, or any other sharp instrument attached, or designed or intended to be attached, to the leg of a bird for use in an animal fighting venture." 7 U.S.C. § 2156(e). Each violation of this provision is punishable by fines and up to three years in prison.

Nevertheless, these laws do not mean that cockfighting events do not continue to be held clandestinely. *See, e.g., Martin v. King*, 2018 U.S. App. LEXIS 100 (10th Cir. Unpub. Jan. 3, 2018) (law enforcement officials seized 435 hens and roosters, 285 baby chickens and 200 eggs from a cockfighting and breeding operation, all of which were destroyed by the animal control agency due to the illegal use of anabolic steroids and prescribed medications).

Cockfighting is also addressed in Chapter 1, in the context of defining "animal," and in the discussions of *State v. Buford*, 331 P.2d 1110 (N.M. 1958), *Lock v. Falkenstine*, 380 P.2d 278 (Okla. 1963) and *State ex rel. Miller v. Claiborne*, 505 P.2d 732 (Kan. 1973).

2. Dogfighting

Ash v. State

Supreme Court of Arkansas, 1986
290 Ark. 278, 718 S.W.2d 930

SMITH, Justice. Act 862 of 1981 prohibits persons from promoting dog fighting, engaging in dog fighting, being present at a dog fight, or committing various acts connected with dog fighting. Ark. Stat. Ann. §§ 41-2918.1 and -2918.2 (Supp. 1985). At about 10:00 p.m. on May 10, 1985, after a search warrant had been obtained, ten law enforcement officers entered a building behind the residence of Darryl and Winifred Hook in Fort Smith. A dog fight between two American pit bull terriers was in progress. Fifteen persons were present. The police arrested all of them except the Hooks' 12-year-old son, who was videotaping the dog fight. The police took possession of the videotape and of a copy of the rules for dog fighting, which was found in a filing cabinet in the building.

All of the persons arrested, except Mrs. Hook, were charged with witnessing a dog fight presented as a public spectacle or with being present at a dog fight. Mrs. Hook was charged with promoting or engaging in dog fighting or possessing a dog for that purpose. Darryl Hook was among those arrested, but he was charged separately and is not a party to this case. The defense offered no evidence. The jury found all these appellants guilty and assessed a $3,000 fine against each of them except Mrs. Hook, who was fined $5,000. The Court of Appeals transferred the case to us as presenting an issue of construing the word "promotes" in the statute.

The raided "garage" area, as described in the testimony and as shown by the videotape, had been converted into an arena for dog fighting. The rules comprise five single-spaced typewritten pages. The rules provide that the pit is to be an enclosure not less than 14 feet each way, with sides 30 inches high and a carpeted floor. The pit in the Hooks' garage appears to have been in general conformity with the rules. The rules contemplate that each of the two dogs will be in the pit with its handler. The referee, if one is present, is also in the pit. At a signal from the referee the dogs begin to fight. The term "scratch" is not defined. One dog must scratch first; after that they scratch alternately until one fails to scratch and thereby loses the contest. No dog is required or allowed to "scratch to a dead dog"; in that event the live dog is the winner. There is a detailed rule for determining the winner or declaring a draw if the dogs quit fighting, though the handlers may allow the fight to continue. A dog that jumps out of the pit is automatically the loser.

The proof leaves no doubt that when the garage area was raided there was a dog fight in progress, and all the appellants except Mrs. Hook were present. Consequently counsel do not even attempt to argue that the evidence, if admissible, was not sufficient as to all the appellants except Mrs. Hook. . . . We have no hesitancy in affirming the convictions of those present during the dog fight.

Mrs. Hook's case is not equally as open-and-shut, but the proof as a whole leaves us with no doubt about its sufficiency to support the verdict. The State introduced the sworn testimony she had given in connection with her husband's trial; the jury was of course not informed of that setting for the testimony. She said she and her husband had formerly lived in California, where dog fighting was then legal. They fought the passage of a law to make it illegal, but the law was passed. They left California for that reason. "We moved here because there [were] no laws against dog fighting." She denied knowing that dog fighting had been made illegal in Arkansas. The Hooks had lived at the residence in Fort Smith for seven years when she testified. She said she and her husband had raised pit bulls for over ten years and owned six of the dogs at the time she testified. (The testimony and the photographs in the record show that the kennel building is of concrete block construction, with a concrete floor. It has a roof over it. There are 12 separate enclosures for dogs, in two stories having six pens each. The front of each enclosure consists of chain-link fencing attached to steel posts set in concrete. The entire structure is enclosed by a chain-link fence.)

Mrs. Hook testified that the pit, which takes up most of the garage space in the other outbuilding, was made for dog "rolling," by which two dogs are placed together to see if they will fight. "If they do, then you just don't let them." She conceded that a pit is not needed for dog rolling; the dogs could just be put on the ground. (The pit is apparently also a permanent installation, not put together for the one evening. In addition to the garage space, that outbuilding also contains a storage room and an apartment with two bedrooms and two baths. One bath is readily accessible to the pit area via the storage room. That accessibility would be of importance if the owners of the dogs agreed to abide strictly by the rules, which have detailed instructions for washing and drying each dog immediately before the dogs are put in the pit to fight.)

Mrs. Hook testified that on the morning of the day of the raid, May 10, she arose as usual at about seven o'clock. At some time later she left to report for work at her job at 3:30 p.m. Before she left five or six people had arrived from "different places," some of them bringing dogs with them. When asked if the people were there to fight dogs, she replied, "I don't know," which was her usual response to questions about her awareness of dog fighting on the premises. She saw nothing wrong about dog fighting or about her 12-year-old son's having operated the video camera during the fight. She said she and her husband owned the dogs they had and that all four members of the family helped take care of the animals. The dogs like to exercise and would run for hours on a treadmill. At one point she did say about her husband, "He has fought dogs."

On that day Mrs. Hook returned home shortly before 11:00 p.m., after the raid and arrests had taken place. When she got home, the people who had brought their dogs before she left were still there and were among those arrested. She herself was arrested when she got home. It was not unusual, she testified, for numbers of people to show up at her house, but as far as she knew they were not there to fight dogs. She said that was the first time she even knew of dogs having been fought there.

The argument on appeal is that since Mrs. Hook was away during the dog fight, the State's proof was not sufficient to support her conviction. That, however, depends upon whether the State produced substantial evidence to show her to be guilty of having "promoted" dog fighting, even though she did not engage in it that night. The word promote means to "further; encourage; advance." Webster's New International Dictionary (2d ed. 1934). The court included in its instructions to the jury two that are now pertinent: [One] explained that the jurors were not required to set aside their common knowledge, but had the right to consider the evidence in the light of their own observations and experiences in the affairs of life. [The other] told the jurors that they were the sole judges of the witnesses' credibility and specified some of the matters to be considered in determining the truth or falsity of the witness's testimony.

The Hooks had admittedly come to Arkansas partly because dog fighting was then legal here. Mrs. Hook, no matter how inactively she may have participated in the dog fighting, knew that a structure had been built in the back yard for the specific purpose of housing pit bull dogs, with accommodations to contain dogs other than their own. She was familiar with the pit and knew it could be used for dog fighting. Both the kennels and the arena were of a permanent nature, solidly built. Mrs. Hook knew that her husband had fought dogs; she herself saw nothing wrong with dog fighting. She realized that numbers of people came to the house from time to time and brought pit bull terriers with them. She must have known that something was going on to attract those visitors. She and her children had helped to take care of the dogs, washing them and feeding them. In short, from the evidence presented the jury could reasonably have concluded that Mrs. Hook was aware that on property owned by her and her husband an arena had been built for the specific purpose of clandestine dog fighting and that she was aware that it was being so used. The jury could find that she "promoted" dog fighting. The direct and circumstantial evidence to support the jury's verdict is more than sufficient to meet the test of substantiality.

Affirmed.

Notes

1. Is the court suggesting that mere knowledge that dogfighting is occurring is tantamount to "promoting" dogfighting? Alternatively, do you think Mrs. Hook's

conviction may have hinged on the fact that she co-owned the property where the dogfighting occurred and that she may have profited from her husband's illegal activities?

2. Why was the defendant's fine two-thirds higher than the fines of those persons who actually participated in the dogfighting? By assessing a substantial fine against Mrs. Hook, was the court trying to send a message to the public about dogfighting?

3. Does this ruling create an affirmative duty for anyone aware of dogfighting to report it to authorities or risk the possibility of being charged under the statute?

4. As of 2013, dogfighting was a felony in all fifty states. The practice nevertheless continues, and one estimate has put the number of people involved in dogfighting in the United States at 40,000. *Dogfighting a Booming Business, Experts Say*, CNN (July 19, 2007) (*http://www.cnn.com/2007/US/07/18/dog.fighting/*). A variety of reasons may account for the continued occurrence of dogfighting, including limited penalties, the overwhelming costs of running extended and extensive investigations into dogfighting rings (and therefore the absence of enforcement and prosecution), and the reality that it is often difficult to catch dogfighters because most dogfights occur at hidden locations and on very short notice. Besides the obvious cruelty issues, dogfighting attracts other crime, including gambling, drug use and weapons violations.

5. The most famous case of dogfighting occurred in 2007 and involved a professional football player, Michael Vick. At the time of his arrest, Vick was the quarterback for the Atlanta Falcons and a famous sports figure. Vick and several others pled guilty to federal crimes connected with their operation of a dogfighting establishment on Vick's property. Because of his fame as a sports figure, Vick's conduct became front-page news for weeks. He was sentenced to twenty-three months in federal prison and was suspended from the National Football League for his conduct, which included financing the dogfighting operation and killing dogs who were not aggressive enough to be used as fighting dogs. After being released from prison, Vick returned to football and participated in public education about the cruelty inherent in dogfighting.

Controversy surrounded much of the case, but especially the disposition of the dogs. Forty-eight dogs were rescued from Vick's home. Many individuals and animal protection groups believed the dogs should be humanely euthanized. Others believed they should be saved. In almost all other dogfighting cases, the animals seized are euthanized as soon as they are no longer needed as evidence of the crime (and the owner surrenders them). Dogs in dogfighting operations are routinely euthanized because of uncertainty about their demeanors and aggressiveness, coupled with the significant resource investment it may take to rehabilitate fighting dogs. Many argue that the resources used to save one fighting animal could instead fund the rescue of many homeless dogs who do not come from similar situations.

In the Vick case, almost all of the dogs ultimately were saved. A panel of experts was sent to evaluate the dogs and the dogs were then taken in by a number of groups and adoptive families. Before the dogs were placed, the federal court entered an order, appointing Rebecca Huss, a law professor, as the Guardian/Special Master of the dogs. Special Masters are often used in settling discovery disputes. This order was significant both because it recognized Professor Huss as a "guardian" and because the court used the Special Master designation in this context. *See also* Alexis Curry Fox, *Using Special Masters to Advance the Goals of Animal Protection Law,* 15 Animal L. 87 (2009).

6. After the Vick case, Illinois enacted a first-of-its-kind law that prohibits individuals convicted of certain felonies from owning unsterilized dogs or dogs who have been adjudicated "vicious." 720 Ill. Comp. Stat. 5/12-36. The enumerated felonies include dogfighting, animal cruelty and many drug crimes. The legislative intent behind the law was to minimize the chances of a return to prior illegal conduct by individuals who have demonstrated their predilection for such activity. Drug crimes were likely included because of the undisputed connection between drug use and animal fighting.

7. In *Hargrove v. State*, 253 Ga. 450 (1984), defendants challenged the constitutionality of Georgia's dogfighting statute. The crux of their argument was that the harsher penalty for dogfighting offenses, as compared to the lesser penalty for cockfighting offenses, constituted a violation of the Equal Protection Clause of the U.S. Constitution, as well as the Constitution's prohibition against cruel and unusual punishment. The court disagreed, citing the legislature's broad discretion in classifying crimes and punishments.

8. In *Moody v. State*, 320 S.E.2d 545 (Ga. 1984), fifty-nine people who were spectators at a dogfight were indicted for violating Georgia's dogfighting statute. Defendants appealed the lower court's denial of their motion to quash the indictment, arguing "that since different versions of dogfighting bills included 'spectators' and that the present law is silent on this matter, the legislature never intended those who were 'merely present' to be prosecuted." The Georgia Supreme Court rejected this argument, holding:

> It is clear that the legislature intended to outlaw dogfighting and set a mandatory punishment. Because of the nature of the activity, conduct other than actually placing a dog in a pit is prohibited. The statute is aimed at those who intentionally participate on any level because without such participation the purpose of dogfighting, *i.e.*, profit or gambling sport would not exist. . . .

Id. at 545.

The court suggests that one of the legislature's rationales for making penalties for dogfighting harsher than those for violating the standard animal anti-cruelty statute is that dogfighting also involves gambling. If this is so, the state would logically also create a harsher penalty for cockfighting—an activity which also involves gambling and animal cruelty. Are there other reasons to distinguish the two?

Section 9. Cross-Protecting: The Link between Animal Abuse and Human Violence

A. Introduction

The connection between human violence and animal abuse has long made intuitive sense to most people. In 1751, the artist William Hogarth printed a series of four engravings, entitled "The Four Stages of Cruelty." The engravings follow the criminal path of "Tom Nero" starting with his torture of a dog in the first engraving, theft and murder in the next two engravings, and ending with the final engraving (entitled "The Reward of Cruelty") which depicts Tom as a corpse being publicly dissected, having been convicted and hung for his crimes. The engravings illustrate what has now become a well-known phenomenon—that those who abuse animals are also likely to commit acts of violence against other humans (and vice versa). As the table below indicates, some of the more infamous criminals of our time also had a history of violence against animals.

Name	Crime Against Humans	Crime Against Animals
David Berkowitz ("Son of Sam")	Thirteen murders/attempted murders	Shot neighbor's dog
Ted Bundy	Mass murderer	Spoke of a grandfather who regularly tortured animals in his childhood
Jeffrey Dahmer	Mass murderer	Killed neighborhood pets, impaled dogs' heads on sticks
Richard Aleen Davis	Kidnapped and murdered Polly Klaas	Doused cats with gasoline and set them on fire
Albert DeSalvo ("Boston Strangler")	Mass murderer	Shot arrows into boxes of trapped cats and dogs
James Huberty	Killed twenty-one people at a fast food restaurant	Shot neighbor's dog
Edmund Emil Kemper III	Murdered mother and seven other women	Abused dogs and cats
Brenda Spencer	Fired forty shots into a crowd of children, killing two and wounding nine	Set tails of cats and dogs on fire
Luke Woodham	Killed mother and two classmates	Tortured and killed his dog
Lee Boyd Malvo	Killed ten people with a rifle	Killed numerous cats with a slingshot when he was a teenager
Eric Harris and Dylan Klebold	Shot and killed twelve classmates at Columbine High School	Bragged to classmates about mutilating animals

More recently, Nikolas Cruz murdered seventeen people at Marjory Stoneman Douglas High School in Parkland, Florida on Valentine's Day in 2018. His social media accounts displayed photos of slaughtered toads. Responding to a comment on one of the photos, Cruz stated: "I killed a lot of them. I went on a massacre of these things once." Julie Turkewitz, *Florida Shooting: Nikolas Cruz Confessed to Police That He Began Shooting Students in the Hallways*, N.Y. Times, Feb 15, 2018.

In recent years, sociologists, criminologists, psychologists and other scholars and practitioners have gone beyond anecdotal or intuitive bases for believing "the link" (as the connection between animal cruelty and human violence is now known) exists. They now investigate, document and produce peer-reviewed studies exploring this pathology. Many reliable studies have been published,[h] several of which are discussed here.

The first well-documented evidence of the link came from a study of eighty-four prison inmates that found that 75% of those charged with violent crimes had early records of cruelty to animals. Daniel Hellman & Nathan Blackman, *Enuresis, Firesetting and Cruelty to Animals: A Triad Predictive of Adult Crime*, 122 Am. J. Psychiatry 1431 (1966).

A 1985 study found that 25% of 152 aggressive inmates had committed five or more acts of animal cruelty as children, as compared to 6% of a study group of nonaggressive inmates. Alan R. Felthous & Stephen R. Kellert, *Childhood Cruelty Toward Animals Among Criminals and Noncriminals*, 38 Hum. Relations § 12 (1985). In a second study by the same researchers, criminals were interviewed one-on-one to obtain historical descriptions of violent acts against animals. The results provided further support of "an association between childhood cruelty to animals and later aggressive behaviors against people." Alan R. Felthous & Stephen R. Kellert, *Violence Against Animals and People: Is Aggression Against Living Creatures Generalized?*, 14 Bull. Am. Acad. Psychiatry Law 55 (1986).

The largest study of serial sex killers as of the publication of this edition of the casebook found that 36% admitted to committing animal cruelty as children; 46% admitted to committing animal cruelty as adolescents; and 36% admitted to committing animal cruelty as adults. Ressler et al., Sexual Homicides: Patterns and Motives (1988).

There is also a high correlation between family violence and animal cruelty. A 1983 study of New Jersey families referred to youth and family services for reasons of child abuse reported that 60% of the cases had at least one member of the household

---

h. A number of these studies can be found in: Cruelty to Animals and Interpersonal Violence: Readings in Research and Application (Randall Lockwood & Frank R. Ascione eds., 1998); International Handbook of Animal Abuse and Cruelty: Theory, Research, and Application (Frank R. Ascione ed., 2008); and also at the following websites: Humane Society of the United States, *http://www.hsus.org*; Humane Research Council, *http://www.humanespot.org*; American Humane Association, *http://www.americanhumane.org*; The Latham Foundation, *http://www.latham.org*.

who physically abused nonhumans. Notably, it was sometimes the children acting out on the abuse that they had suffered. DeViney et al., *The Care of Pets Within Child Abusing Families*, 4 INT'L J. STUD. ANIMAL PROBS. 321 (1983). A study in England resulted in similar findings: 83% of families reported for animal abuse had also been identified as at-risk families for child abuse and other violations by social service agencies. James S. Hutton, *Animal Abuse as a Diagnostic Approach in Social Work: A Pilot Study*, in CRUELTY TO ANIMALS AND INTERPERSONAL VIOLENCE: READINGS IN RESEARCH AND APPLICATION 417 (Randall Lockwood and Frank R. Ascione eds., 1998). The professional journal Social Work printed a manual for therapists designed to predict potential violent behavior from patients which, not surprisingly, includes animal cruelty as a "factor highly associated with violent, antisocial behavior." Barbara Star, *Patient Violence/Therapist Safety*, 29 SOC. WORK 25 (1984).

A 1997 study by the Massachusetts Society for the Prevention of Cruelty to Animals (MSPCA) and Northeastern University found that 70% of people who committed violent crimes against animals also had criminal records for violent, property, drug or disorderly conduct crimes. In demonstrating the syndrome of abuse, the study also found that 56% of animal abusers who committed other crimes, committed those crimes prior to the animal offense. Carter Luke et al., CRUELTY TO ANIMALS AND OTHER CRIMES: A STUDY BY THE MSPCA AND NORTHEASTERN UNIVERSITY (1997). This finding conflicted with the previously generally-accepted premise that violent individuals start by abusing animals and then graduate to human victims. Current thinking is in line with the principle that animal abuse is not so much a harbinger of future violence as it is part of an overall pattern of antisocial, community-based violence.

The Chicago Police Department studied 322 animal cruelty arrests from 2001–2004 and discovered that 70% of those arrested had other felony charges, including homicides; 86% had multiple arrests; 70% had narcotics charges; 65% had been charged with violent offenses; 27% had previous firearms charges; 13% had been arrested on sex crime charges; and 59% were alleged gang members. CHICAGO POLICE DEPARTMENT STATISTICAL SUMMARY OF OFFENDERS CHARGED WITH CRIMES AGAINST COMPANION ANIMALS, JULY 2001–JULY 2004, Chicago Police Department (Illinois 2008).

Scholars have begun to evaluate the link from a legal perspective as well. The following law review articles provide a good start to those students wishing to explore this issue further. *See* Susan Crowell, Comment, *Animal Cruelty as it Relates to Child Abuse: Shedding Light on a "Hidden" Problem*, 20 J. JUV. L. 38 (1999) (discussing the relationship between animal cruelty and child abuse and arguing for more legal intervention in instances of animal abuse); Dianna J. Gentry, *Including Companion Animals in Protective Orders: Curtailing the Reach of Domestic Violence*, 13 YALE J. L. & FEMINISM 97 (2001) (examining animal abuse within the context of domestic violence and suggesting a "best interest of the animal" test for resolving animal custody disputes); Charlotte A. Lacroix, *Another Weapon for Combating Family Violence: Prevention of Animal Abuse*, 4 ANIMAL L. 1 (1998) (arguing that acts of cruelty against family pets are a form of family violence and should be treated as such); Beth Ann Madeline, Comment, *Cruelty to Animals: Recognizing Violence Against Nonhuman Victims*, 23 U. Haw. L. Rev. 307 (2000) (arguing that cruelty to nonhuman animals constitutes "violent crime" and should be punished accordingly); Jared Squires, *The Link Between Animal Cruelty and Human Violence: Children Caught in the Middle*, 8 Ky. Children's Rts. J. 2 (Winter 2000) (reviewing the link between animal cruelty and violence against humans, the importance of this link to child advocates, and innovative therapies now used to address this issue); Seymour Moskowitz, *Saving Granny From the Wolf: Elder Abuse and Neglect—The Legal Framework*, 31 Conn. L. Rev. 77 (1998) (exploring the link between animal abuse and elder abuse); Frank Ascione and Kenneth Shapiro, *People and Animals, Kindness and Cruelty: Research Directions and Policy Implications*, 65 Journal of Soc. Issues 56 (2009) (addressing the challenges of defining and assessing the relation between animal abuse and childhood mental health).

Finally, there are practical and public policy considerations that take on renewed prominence as a result of learning about the link. Research has spotlighted the problem that abused women face when trying to decide if, when and how to leave their abusers. Often these women have companion animals who are not welcome at domestic violence shelters, but who face possible abuse if left behind. Some studies show that a significant percentage of women in that situation either delay leaving their abusive situation or simply refuse shelters out of concern for their pets, thus leaving themselves and the pets in an environment where further abuse is likely to occur. *See, e.g.*, Frank R. Ascione et al., *Battered Pets and Domestic Violence: Animal Abuse Reported by Women Experiencing Intimate Violence and by Nonabused Women*, 13 Violence Against Women 354 (2007) (vast majority of studied women residing at domestic violence shelters were distraught about abuse experienced by family pets and substantial minority said they delayed seeking shelter because of concerns for their pets' welfare); Catherine A. Faver & Elizabeth B. Strand, *To Leave or To Stay?: Battered Women's Concern for Vulnerable Pets*, 18 J. Interpers. Violence 1367 (2003) (almost half of pet-owning battered women reported real or threatened animal abuse by their partner and more than one-quarter reported that concern for their pets affected their decision to leave or stay with the batterer).

In response to this problem, many communities have established programs that provide a safe, confidential haven for the pet while the woman is in residence at a domestic violence shelter. For examples of both on-site and off-site shelter programs, *see* American Humane Website, Pets and Women's Shelters (PAWS) Program, *http://www.americanhumane.org/human-animal-bond/programs/pets-and-womens-shelters/*.

B. Case Law

The following cases explore the connection between animal abuse and human violence, the overlap of animal and child protection laws, and the way in which inter-agency cooperation can result in better protection for both animals and humans. When reading these cases, keep in mind the following questions:

1. Did the animal cruelty impact the perceived seriousness of the child abuse?

2. Were the child protection laws used to advance the prosecutor's argument with respect to the animal abuse charges?

3. How do the penalties for animal abuse, child abuse and domestic violence compare?

4. What preventive measures could be taken to provide for early and effective intervention in each of the cases?

Schambon v. Commonwealth

Supreme Court of Kentucky, 1991
821 S.W.2d 804

LAMBERT, Justice. Appellants were convicted of eight counts of first degree sodomy, three counts of first degree criminal abuse, twenty-one counts of second degree sodomy, and twenty-eight counts of second degree cruelty to animals. Appellant Barbara Schambon was also convicted of one count of incest. Both were sentenced to a total of eighty-five years in prison and appeal as a matter of right.

In June of 1989, the Warren County Animal Shelter was informed of the presence of animals in a garage. The animals were without food or water and the garage was without any ventilation. The shelter's employees contacted the county dog warden who, accompanied by a deputy sheriff, investigated the complaint. Upon arriving at the location, they noticed a strong dog feces odor coming from the house. The warden then walked to the detached garage. Upon opening the door, he noticed chain link pens containing some seventeen to twenty-three poodles, Yorkshire terriers, and Pomeranians. The garage was not ventilated and the temperature was in excess of ninety degrees. The floor was covered with three to five inches of dog feces, no dog food was noticeable and the water dish was empty. In one of the pens, a poodle was eating the remains of a Pomeranian. The warden reported that the stench was "overpowering." The two officials removed the dogs from the garage. After loading the dogs into a truck, the warden returned to the animal shelter while the deputy remained to investigate the situation.

After loading the dogs into the warden's truck, the deputy talked to several neighbors who had gathered to observe the situation. The deputy attempted to locate the owners of the house. One of the neighbors told him that the children who lived in the house were across the street at their babysitter's home. The deputy went to the house and spoke to the sitter, but the sitter would not let him talk to the children.

However, one of the children overheard the deputy's inquiries and volunteered that her mother was in the house across the street. The girl left the babysitter and went across the street and crawled in a window. A few minutes later, appellant Barbara Schambon appeared at the front door.

The deputy informed appellant that he and the warden had removed the dogs from the garage. Appellant told the deputy that if he walked around to the back, she would talk to him inside the house. When the deputy entered the house, he noticed that two walls were lined with cages containing cats. He observed that the litter boxes were overflowing with feces. He also could hear additional animals barking and crying. While in the kitchen, he saw a badly decomposed Pomeranian lying on the floor in its bodily fluids. Dirty dishes and pots and pans were scattered around the kitchen and the stove was "alive" and "growing" with fungus and moss. A Guinea pig was sitting in a cage on the kitchen counter.

Upon being questioned, appellant maintained that the dogs had been fed and watered. She stated that the animals belonged to her husband and that she had told him to take care of them. She admitted that they had not been groomed. The deputy went outside the house in an effort to avoid becoming nauseated, and upon his refusal to re-enter the house, appellant slammed the door. The deputy left the premises.

After the dog warden returned the dogs to the animal shelter, he obtained a search warrant for the house. Later that afternoon, the warden, the animal shelter manager, and the deputy returned to the house. When they arrived, appellant Floyd Schambon was standing in the driveway. He was arrested for cruelty to animals. Upon searching the house, the officials noted that dog feces was everywhere, including the walls and the beds.

While the authorities were searching the house, the four children returned from the babysitter's. The children were C.S., a son age thirteen; E.S., a daughter age ten; A.S., a daughter age eight, and R.S., a son age five. While the deputy talked to the children, appellant Barbara yelled and ordered them not to talk to anyone. She informed the deputy that he had no right to talk to her children and that she would contact her attorney and sue him.

After the animals were taken to the shelter, the staff cleaned and treated them. Most of the dogs had to be sheared because their hair was completely matted with feces. One poodle was so badly matted that it had to be sedated before it could be sheared. Most of the dogs were underweight and infested with lice and fleas. Many of the dogs had ear, eye and penis infections. Several of the dogs had parvo and distemper. One Pomeranian puppy died from parvo within an hour of arrival at the shelter and a poodle died from distemper the following week. Other dogs had mange and ringworm. A Yorkshire terrier had toenails an inch and a half long and one gave birth to puppies at the shelter. Both puppies died immediately after birth.

Due to the unsanitary conditions of appellants' house, the children were removed pursuant to an emergency custody order and placed in foster homes. The two boys were placed in the foster care of Mr. and Mrs. Bobby Bright while the two girls were placed in another foster home.

* * *

[Editors' note: The foster families learned that severe sexual and physical abuse occurred, which the court described but which is not included here.]

After receiving directed verdicts on numerous counts, both appellants were convicted and sentenced to eighty-five years in prison. They now appeal.

* * *

II. SEVERANCE

(a) Appellants contend that the trial court erred when it declined to sever the animal cruelty charges from the sexual abuse charges.

RCr 6.18 permits the joinder of two or more offenses in the same indictment if the offenses are of the same or similar character or based on the same acts or transactions connected together or constitute parts of a common scheme or plan. Additionally, RCr 9.12 permits two or more indictments to be consolidated for trial if those offenses could have been joined in a single indictment.

Joinder is inappropriate, however, when it appears that a party or the Commonwealth will be prejudiced by the joinder of offenses or of parties in a single indictment. RCr 9.16. If a party will be prejudiced, the trial court must order separate trials of counts or defendants or provide whatever other relief justice requires. The decision to join or sever is within the sound discretion of the trial court and an exercise of that discretion will not be disturbed unless clear abuse and prejudice are shown.

In the case at bar, appellants filed a pre-trial motion to sever the animal offenses from the sex offenses. After conducting a hearing on the motion, the trial court found that the offenses were intertwined and that the evidence of animal cruelty was essential to establish the physical abuse offenses and, as such, joinder was appropriate. In reaching this decision, the trial court noted that the circumstances of animal cruelty actually led to the criminal abuse and sex charges and that appellants' mistreatment of the animals reflected upon their state of mind when they committed the physical and sexual abuse.

To convict appellants of criminal abuse, it was necessary to prove that the environment in which the children lived subjected them to a risk of physical injury. This proof included testimony as to the deplorable conditions in the house and garage, specifically, the presence of diseased cats, dogs and other animals in the house and garage. Additionally, proof of the presence of animal feces and the carcasses of dead animals in the house was presented. This same proof was used to prove the animal cruelty charges. The record revealed that the trial court thoroughly contemplated the possibility of prejudice before ruling on the motion. There was no abuse of discretion.

(b) Appellants also contend that it was error for the trial court to refuse to try them separately. We reiterate that RCr 9.16 provides for separate trials only upon a showing of prejudice to the complaining party. In applying this rule, the trial court has broad discretion and an exercise of that discretion will not be overturned absent a clear showing of abuse.

Appellants base their claim here on the theory that, excluding the animal cruelty charges, none of the evidence admitted against one of them would have been admissible against the other. As a result, it is contended that both were prejudiced by the admission of the evidence relating to the other.

Although appellants' contention as to the admissibility of evidence in separate trials may be correct, there was no showing that the jury could not distinguish the evidence relevant to each appellant, resulting in unfair prejudice. Appellants have not shown that the jury could not "individualize each defendant in relation to the mass [of evidence]." *Kotteakos v. United States*, 328 U.S. 750 (1946).

(c) Appellants also claim that the Commonwealth's bill of particulars misled them as to what crimes they were defending against and, as such, violated their right to due process. From a plain reading of the document, it appears that some of the charges were misnamed, but appellants were put on unmistakable notice that they would be required to defend against charges arising out of "deviate sexual intercourse." Their conduct was particularly described. Appellants' defenses to the charges were complete denials. As such, their defenses would not have been any different if the bill of particulars had been flawless. Appellants could not have been misled or prejudiced in their defenses.

* * *

CONCLUSION

Upon review of appellants' convictions, this Court has addressed every contention with any possible merit. We have omitted appellants' absurd contentions that they were entitled to a directed verdict of acquittal and omitted unpreserved contentions of prosecutorial misconduct during summation on the firm conviction that it did not amount to palpable error. The judgments of the trial court are affirmed.

All concur.

Notes

1. The case is an example of the value of "cross-reporting" and the potential value of cross-training for animal abuse, domestic violence, elder abuse and child abuse investigators.

2. *Schambon* presents a good argument for psychological evaluation and treatment of animal abusers. In most jurisdictions, courts are not required, but do have the discretion, to order convicted defendants to undergo diagnostic testing and any potentially helpful treatment. There is little data on the success of such programs. Should psychological evaluation and treatment be required after any animal abuse conviction or only for certain types of animal abuse?

3. Animal advocates have made tremendous gains over the last fifteen years by strengthening anti-cruelty laws and educating legislators about the recognized link between animal abuse and human violence. For example, in 2003 Oregon became the first state to legislatively recognize the link when it passed section 167.320 of the Oregon Revised Statutes. The law increases any misdemeanor first-degree animal abuse to a felony if the defendant previously has been convicted of animal abuse, domestic violence or child abuse, or commits the animal abuse in front of a minor.

4. It is interesting to note that the child protection movement was, in large part, an offshoot of early animal protection legislation. The case of Mary Ellen Wilson has become legendary in this regard. In 1874, Mary Ellen was a 9-year-old girl who had been horribly abused by her parents. Neighbors became concerned and reported the mistreatment to the public health department. Despite a public health nurse's best efforts to engage the police or the district attorney on Mary Ellen's behalf, she discovered that no law existed to protect the child from her parents' treatment. The nurse then turned to the Society for the Prevention of Cruelty to Animals (SPCA) for assistance, arguing that the girl's abuse would be illegal if she was an animal. The SPCA petitioned to have Mary Ellen removed from her home under laws governing the welfare of animals. One year later, in 1875, the first Society for the Prevention of Cruelty to Children was organized in New York. For more information on this story and the beginnings of the children's rights movement, *see* Eric Shelman & Stephen Lazoritz, OUT OF THE DARKNESS: THE STORY OF MARY ELLEN WILSON (1998).

State v. Thompson

Court of Appeals of North Carolina, 2000
139 N.C. App. 299, 533 S.E.2d 834

LEWIS, Judge. Defendant was tried at the 23 February 1998 session of Durham County Superior Court on two counts of first-degree statutory rape, one count of statutory rape of a person fourteen years of age, one count of first-degree statutory sex offense, and three counts of taking indecent liberties with a minor. The alleged offenses occurred in December 1993, January 1994, and February 1996. The jury returned a verdict of guilty as to all charges, and defendant now appeals.

* * *

Several witnesses at trial, including N and one of her brothers, testified that defendant also physically abused N's siblings and the family cat. Specifically, the evidence showed that defendant hit the siblings with boxing gloves, forced them to fight each other with boxing gloves, beat one brother with a cane, burned the leg of another brother by igniting lighter fluid on it, and strangled and drowned the family cat. This abuse occurred in N's presence.

. . . Defendant . . . contests the evidentiary basis for admitting his alleged physical abuse of N's siblings and his alleged abuse of the family cat.

Our Supreme Court has clarified that Rule 404(b) is "a clear general rule of *inclusion* of relevant evidence of other crimes, wrongs or acts by a defendant, subject to but *one exception* requiring its exclusion if its *only* probative value is to show that the defendant has the propensity or disposition to commit an offense of the nature of the crime charged." *State v. Coffey*, 326 N.C. 268, 278–79 (1990). We conclude the contested evidence here was admissible for purposes other than merely to show defendant's propensity to commit sex crimes of the type charged.

* * *

We next consider whether the trial court improperly admitted the evidence of defendant's prior physical abuse of N's siblings and his physical violence against the cat. We again emphasize that "evidence of other offenses is admissible so long as it is relevant to any fact or issue other than the character of the accused." *State v. Weaver*, 318 N.C. 400, 403 (1986). Significantly, although this alleged abuse was committed on N's siblings and pet (as opposed to N herself), it occurred *in N's presence*. N testified that she saw defendant beat her siblings several times with a cane and with boxing gloves. She also testified that defendant strangled and drowned their cat in her presence.

In sex abuse cases, the victim's state of mind can be relevant. When it is relevant, any evidence tending to show the victim is afraid of her abuser, or evidence explaining why the victim never reported the sexual incidents to anyone, is admissible. At trial, defendant relied heavily on N's failure to report the sexual abuse in suggesting that such abuse never in fact occurred. By bringing forth this defense, defendant thereby specifically made N's state of mind relevant. The State could therefore introduce any evidence tending to explain N's state of mind. The evidence of physical abuse and animal abuse here did just that: it tended to explain N's fear of defendant and why she never reported all the incidents of sexual abuse. N even specifically testified that she never reported the sexual abuse because, in light of all the other abuse that she witnessed, she knew he would beat her if she did report it.

We do express caution with a trial court's admitting evidence of animal abuse and/or physical abuse in cases only involving sex abuse. Such evidence must be relevant, and being lewd and despicable does not necessarily make it relevant. Furthermore, such evidence has the potential of being highly prejudicial to a defendant and thus should be scrutinized carefully by the trial judge. We emphasize that the *only* reason the evidence is admissible here is because the physical and animal abuse was done in N's presence and because defendant specifically made N's state of mind relevant. To the extent evidence of physical and/or animal abuse not done in N's presence was admitted, such admission was error, but would not have changed the outcome so as to require a new trial. We therefore reject defendant's first argument.

* * *

Note

Judges have discretion to decide whether to include animals in protective orders in these types of cases. Some states also have codified this judicial authority. For example, in 2006 Maine amended its protective order statute to expressly allow a court to enter "an order concerning the care, custody or control of any companion animal or companion livestock owned, possessed, leased, kept or held by either party or a minor child residing in the household," in addition to any other relief allowed under Maine's protective order statute. Me. Rev. Stat. Ann. title 19-A, § 4997 (2006). This statute was the first of its kind in the United States and was inspired by a model statute proposed in a law review article published in 2001. *See* Dianna J. Gentry, *Including Companion Animals in Protective Orders: Curtailing the Reach of Domestic Violence*, 13 Yale J.L. & Feminism 97 (2001). *See also* Joan MacLeod Heminway and Patricia Graves Lenaghan, *Safe Haven Conundrum: The Use of Special Bailments to Keep Pets Out of Violent Households*, 12 Tenn. J.L. & Pol'y 79 (2017).

Chapter 4

Torts

Since the 1990s, there has been an increased focus on the ways in which courts and legislatures deal with tort issues of liability and damages in connection with injuries to, and by, animals. A rapidly growing number of cases, published opinions, statutes, law review articles and items in the popular media have addressed the issues covered in this chapter. Litigators, legislators and commentators have proposed new legal theories and variations on existing theories, and discussed the current state of the law and reasons that changes may be warranted. This chapter provides an overview and sampling of these recent developments, as well as the historical fundamentals of "animal tort law" that form the basis for these and future changes.

Courts sometimes have blurred the lines between theories of liability and damages in their discussion of the legal issues involving animals, making a linear organization of the topics difficult. This chapter attempts to clarify those lines of demarcation and, to the extent possible, sets out a roadmap for this area of the law.

Section 1. Theories of Liability

In animal law tort cases, plaintiffs' counsel's determination of which causes of action to assert in a complaint has significance, not only on the measure of damages that may be available, but also on the public policy issues that may be raised and that may be unique to animal law cases. For example, will the court be asked to view the animals at issue, if they are companion animals, with some special legal status as family members who are also considered property under the law? Can plaintiff include an intentional tort, which opens the door to emotional distress and punitive damages (as discussed in Section 3)? Is intentional infliction of emotional distress (with its particular standards of proof) available in the case? What are the advantages and disadvantages (both strategic and with respect to potential recovery) of asserting claims that depend upon the property status of animals, such as trespass to chattels or, in cases involving government entities or agents, Fourth Amendment violations? Are property-based claims and those alleging a valuable relationship between humans and animals mutually exclusive, or can both serve the ultimate goals of these cases? These issues are addressed in the cases and Notes that follow.

A. Intentional Torts

While not all fact patterns support an intentional tort claim, in those instances where such a claim can be asserted, plaintiffs in cases involving animal injuries may be in a better position to obtain a higher damages award. Thus, intentional tort claims can be the key to a plaintiff's success. The intentional torts most commonly applicable to these cases are intentional infliction of emotional distress, outrage, trespass to chattel and conversion. In determining the likelihood of success on such claims, advocates must of course evaluate the law of the particular jurisdiction, as the law varies significantly among the states.

Plotnik v. Meihaus

Court of Appeal of California, Fourth District, Division 3, 2012
208 Cal. App. 4th 1590, 146 Cal. Rptr. 3d 585

RYLAARSDAM, Acting P.J.—Plaintiffs David and Joyce Plotnik sued their neighbor, defendant John Meihaus, Jr. (Meihaus), and two of his sons, defendants Greg Meihaus and John Meihaus III, alleging both contract and tort claims. In part, plaintiffs sought recovery for the emotional distress they suffered when Meihaus injured their dog. The superior court entered a judgment on jury verdicts that awarded David Plotnik over $175,000 against all defendants and Joyce Plotnik over $255,000 against Meihaus. The awards included emotional distress damages resulting from the dog's injury. In response to defendants' motion for new trial, the superior court entered an amended judgment after plaintiffs accepted a remittitur reducing the damage awards to $146,600 for David Plotnik and $205,209.53 for Joyce Plotnik. . . .

Defendants appeal from both the original and amended judgments. While some of their claims have merit, requiring a further reduction of the amended judgment's damage awards, we hold California law allows a pet owner to recover for mental suffering caused by another's intentional act that injures or kills his or her animal.

FACTS AND PROCEDURAL BACKGROUND

Plaintiffs and their two children moved into a home in Laguna Niguel in 2003. The rear portion of the property slopes upward, abutting the Meihauses' lot. At the time, a three-foot-high fence on the property line separated the two parcels. [¶] Plaintiffs claimed that, shortly after moving into their home, they began to have problems with the Meihaus family. [*The court then summarized various disputes between the parties unrelated to plaintiffs' dog that ensued over the following years.*]

* * *

Things came to a head on April 9, 2009. David Plotnik testified that, around noon, he went to the backyard and began photographing yard clippings. Romeo, the family's 12- to 15-pound, 12-inch-tall miniature pinscher was with him. He denied Romeo was barking or growling. Plotnik heard loud banging against the opposite side of the rear fence. When he opened the gate, Romeo ran into the Meihauses' backyard. Losing sight of Romeo, Plotnik assumed the dog ran to the front of their residence. He returned to his lot and began walking along the adjacent public street. At that point, he heard Romeo barking and then squeal. He hurried home, arriving in time to see Romeo roll down the slope through the open gate and hit a tree.

Plotnik went through the gate and saw Meihaus holding a bat, returning to his house. He confronted Meihaus, yelling "Why did you hit our dog?" Plotnik testified Meihaus raised the bat to waist level, came within two feet of him, yelling, "'You need to be more courteous and get your dogs to stop barking.'" Plotnik then accused Meihaus of damaging the side yard fence and throwing debris over the rear fence, all of which Meihaus denied. Claiming Romeo was agitated and kept barking and growling at him, Meihaus testified he obtained a bat from the garage and used it to "guide" Romeo back to the Plotniks' yard. He denied striking the dog.

After this exchange, Plotnik returned to his residence to check on Romeo. The dog had difficulty walking. The family took him to a veterinarian. Eventually, Romeo needed surgery to repair his right rear leg. The surgery cost $2,600 and Joyce Plotnik paid another $209.53 for a stroller to help Romeo get around after the surgery. At trial, the veterinarian opined Romeo's leg injury resulted from a traumatic event.

* * *

Plaintiffs filed this lawsuit. Meihaus responded with a cross-complaint for breach of contract against plaintiffs. [¶] The parties submitted a 33-page verdict form to the jury that sought rulings on 32 issues. . . . *** [¶] Four issues concerned Meihaus's injuring plaintiffs' dog. On special verdicts 6 and 7, for trespass to personal property, the jury found Meihaus intentionally harmed Romeo. It awarded David Plotnik damages of $2,600 for economic loss and $20,000 for emotional distress. In addition, the jury awarded Joyce Plotnik economic damages of $209.53 and emotional distress damages of $30,000. . . .

* * *

DISCUSSION

* * *

4. *The Attack on Romeo*

Plaintiffs sought damages from Meihaus on causes of action for trespass to personal property and negligence arising from his injuring Romeo by striking the dog with a bat. On the trespass count, the jury awarded plaintiffs both economic damages for Romeo's surgery and postoperative care, plus damages for the emotional distress each plaintiff suffered as a result of the incident. . . .

The primary issue here is whether plaintiffs can recover under the trespass to personal property cause of action for the emotional distress they suffered resulting from Meihaus's injuring Romeo by striking him with a bat. Generally, "[f]or the breach of an obligation not arising from contract, the measure of damages, except where otherwise expressly provided by this Code, is the amount which will compensate for all the detriment proximately caused thereby, whether it could have been anticipated or not." (Civ. Code, § 3333.)

Citing *Zaslow v. Kroenert* (1946) 29 Cal.2d 541, *Intel Corp. v. Hamidi* (2003) 30 Cal.4th 1342, and *McMahon v. Craig* [(2009)] 176 Cal.App.4th 1502, Meihaus argues "California [has] rejected the concept that an animal owner may recover emotional distress damages due to injuries his animal received at the hands of a[nother]. . . ." We disagree.

"Under California law, trespass to chattels 'lies where an intentional interference with the possession of personal property *has proximately caused injury.*' [Citation.]" (*Intel Corp. v. Hamidi, supra,* 30 Cal.4th at pp. 1350–1351.) "Where the conduct complained of does not amount to a substantial interference with possession or the right thereto, but consists of intermeddling with or use of or damages to the personal property, the owner has a cause of action for trespass. . . ." (*Zaslow v. Kroenert, supra,* 29 Cal.2d at p. 551; *see Jamgotchian v. Slender* (2009) 170 Cal.App.4th 1384, 1400–1402 [owner of horse injured in race could sue track steward for trespass when steward rejected request to scratch horse from race and prevented animal's removal from track grounds].)

Dogs are considered personal property. (*Johnson v. McConnell* (1889) 80 Cal. 545, 548–549 [22 P. 219]; Pen. Code, § 491; Civ. Code, § 3340.) Generally, trespass to personal property allows one to "recover only the actual damages suffered by reason of the impairment of the property or the loss of its use. [Citations.]" (*Zaslow v. Kroenert, supra,* 29 Cal.2d at p. 551.) In *Kimes v. Grosser* (2011) 195 Cal.App.4th 1556, the court held a pet owner could recover "the [reasonable and necessary] costs of care of the pet attributable to the injury" caused by another. (*Id.* at p. 1558.)

But no case cited by Meihaus prohibits the recovery of damages for emotional distress. McMahon[2] did not involve an action for trespass to personal property. In *Zaslow,* the plaintiff unsuccessfully sought the entire value of personal property a cotenant wrongfully removed from the premises and placed in storage even though the plaintiff was afforded an opportunity to recover possession of his effects. *Intel Corp. v. Hamidi, supra,* 30 Cal.4th 1342, involved a defendant using the plaintiff's internal e-mail system to send messages to its employees. The court merely held "the tort does not encompass, and should not be extended to encompass, an electronic communication that neither damages the recipient computer system nor impairs its functioning." (*Id.* at p. 1347.) And in *Kimes,* the court expressly noted the "[p]laintiff is not seeking damages for emotional distress." (*Kimes v. Grosser, supra,* 195 Cal.App.4th at p. 1558, fn. 1.) Since "the language used in any opinion is to be understood in the light of the facts and the issue then before the court[,] . . . cases

---

2. In *McMahon v. Craig,* 176 Cal. App. 4th 1502, 97 Cal. Rptr. 3d 555 (2009), the court declined to allow recovery of damages for emotional distress or loss of companionship caused by a veterinarian's negligent treatment of a dog that resulted in the dog's death. The *Plotnik* court agreed with the *McMahon* court and reversed the award of emotional distress damages for negligence in connection with the harm to the Plotniks' dog.

are not authority for propositions not considered. [Citation.]" (*McDowell and Craig v. City of Santa Fe Springs* (1960) 54 Cal.2d 33, 38 [4 Cal. Rptr. 176, 351 P.2d 344], citation omitted.)

We believe good cause exists to allow the recovery of damages for emotional distress under the circumstances of this case. In the early case of *Johnson v. McConnell, supra,* 80 Cal. 545, the court noted "while it has been said that [dogs] have nearly always been held 'to be entitled to less regard and protection than more harmless domestic animals,' it is equally true that there are no other domestic animals to which the owner or his family can become more strongly attached, or the loss of which will be more keenly felt." (*Id.* at p. 549.) Additionally, one can be held liable for punitive damages if he or she willfully or through gross negligence wrongfully injures an animal. (Civ. Code, § 3340.) Intentionally maiming, mutilating, torturing, or wounding an animal also constitutes a crime. (Pen. Code, § 597, subd. (a).)

Trespass to personal property often arises in circumstances where a defendant's interference with another's property falls short of that required for a conversion cause of action. Thus, cases have described this tort as "the 'little brother of conversion.'" (*Intel Corp. v. Hamidi, supra,* 30 Cal.4th at p. 1350) In *Gonzales v. Personal Storage, Inc.* (1997) 56 Cal.App.4th 464, the court recognized "the limits imposed with respect to recovery for emotional distress caused by a defendant's negligence do not apply when distress is the result of a defendant's commission of the distinct torts of trespass, nuisance or conversion" (*id.* at p. 475), and held "damages for emotional distress growing out of a defendant's conversion of personal property are recoverable" (*id.* at p. 477). Cases involving actions for trespass to real property and nuisance have also recognized a party may recover emotional distress damages.

Furthermore, cases in other states have recognized a pet owner may recover for mental suffering caused by another's wrongful acts resulting in the pet's injury or death. (*Womack v. Von Rardon* (2006) 133 Wn.App. 254, 263 [cat set on fire; "malicious injury to a pet can support a claim for, and be considered a factor in, measuring a person's emotional distress damages"]; *La Porte v. Associated Independents, Inc.* (Fla. 1964) 163 So.2d 267, 269 [garbage collector hurled can at tethered dog, killing it; "the affection of a master for his dog is a very real thing and ... the malicious destruction of the pet provides an element of damage for which the owner should recover, irrespective of the value of the animal ..."]; *Brown v. Crocker* (La. Ct.App. 1962) 139 So.2d 779, 781–782 [affirming recovery of damages "for shock and mental anguish experienced" for "death of ... mare" and "loss of [stillborn] colt" "as a result of ... shooting"]; see Annot., Recovery of Damages for Emotional Distress Due to Treatment of Pets and Animals (2001) 91 A.L.R.5th 545.)

Consequently, while we reverse the damages awarded plaintiffs on their negligence claim, we uphold both the economic and emotional distress damages plaintiffs recovered for trespass to personal property arising from Meihaus's act of intentionally striking Romeo with a bat.

Notes

1. In *Banasczek v. Kowalski*, 10 Pa. D. & C. 3d 94 (Luzerne Cty. 1979), the defendant intentionally shot two of plaintiff's dogs. In an action for trespass, defendant demurred (moved to dismiss) on the grounds that "there [was] no basis in Pennsylvania law for compensation for emotional distress and mental anguish to plaintiff as a result of the loss of a pet dog." The court overruled the demurrer, holding that "the more enlightened view is to allow recovery for emotional distress in the instance of malicious destruction of a pet." *Id.* at 97. The Third Circuit Court of Appeals has relied on *Banasczek* in allowing a claim of emotional distress under similar facts. *Brown v. Muhlenberg Township*, 269 F.3d 205 (3d Cir. 2001) (police officer shot and killed plaintiffs' dog):

> Officer Eberly argues in essence that the killing of a pet under any circumstances would not be recognized by the Pennsylvania courts as extreme or outrageous [*a prong of the prima facie case for intentional infliction of emotional distress*]. We believe the *Banasczek* court was correct in rejecting a similar contention. Given the strength of community sentiment against at least extreme forms of animal abuse and the substantial emotional investment that pet owners frequently make in their pets, we would not expect the Supreme Court of Pennsylvania to rule out all liability [*for emotional distress*] predicated on the killing of a pet.

Id. at 218.

2. In determining which intentional tort theories to assert in a complaint, plaintiffs must consider whether to include claims based on the property status of the harmed animal—such as conversion and trespass to chattels—in conjunction with, or instead of, intentional infliction of emotional distress or similar torts.

> Conversion is the unjustified and willful interference with a chattel that deprives a person entitled to the property of possession. Wrongful intent is not an element of conversion and good faith is not a defense to conversion. Trespass to chattels is something less than a conversion. It is the intentional interference with a party's personal property without justification that deprives the owner of possession or use. While a plaintiff must show that the interference was intentional, no intent to deprive the owner must be shown.

Sexton v. Brown, 2008 Wash. App. LEXIS 2504 (Unpub. Oct. 20, 2008) (in a veterinary malpractice case, the court found questions of fact precluding dismissal of conversion and trespass to chattels claims as a matter of law). *See also Copenhaver v. Borough of Bernville*, 2003 U.S. Dist. LEXIS 1315 (E.D. Pa. Jan. 9, 2003) (where police shot and killed plaintiff's dog, the court considered the trespass to chattels claim, noting that "[a]lthough it is an intentional tort, the court should not focus on alleged specific intent to commit a wrong, but rather on the alleged wrongdoer's intent to exercise control over the chattel"; because the complaint alleged that only one of the defendants intended to exercise control over plaintiff's dog, the claim was dismissed as to the other defendants).

As the above cases demonstrate, depending on the jurisdiction and the facts of the case, property-based intentional tort claims may be a means of obtaining or at least being permitted to seek recovery of emotional distress damages and punitive damages. (The valuation aspect of this type of case is discussed in Section 3 of this chapter.) Note that *Gonzales v. Personal Storage, Inc.*, 56 Cal. App. 4th 464 (1997), cited by the *Plotnik* court, in which the court affirmed a jury award of emotional distress damages arising from a conversion claim, involved irreplaceable family heirlooms. For cases involving animals, *see, e.g., Bluestone v. Bergstrom*, Case No. 00CC00796 (Cal. Super. Ct., Orange Cty. Mar. 28, 2001) (in a veterinary malpractice case, the trial court relied on *Gonzales v. Personal Storage* and overruled a motion to strike a claim for emotional distress damages where the complaint included claims for conversion, deceit and trespass to chattels); *Lincecum v. Smith*, 287 So. 2d 625 (La. Ct. App. 1973) (conversion action where defendant found plaintiffs' puppy and authorized the veterinarian to euthanize him because of the puppy's failing eyesight and the poor prognosis for restoring his sight; damages awarded for mental anguish).

In another veterinary malpractice case, however, a California court distinguished the *Jamgotchian* case cited in *Plotnik* and rejected the plaintiff's trespass to chattels claim, which it viewed as an inappropriate attempt to circumvent the one-year statute of limitations applicable to veterinary malpractice claims.

> In a recent California reported decision involving trespass to an animal as chattel, a race horse owner sued a racing steward, alleging that the steward was liable for trespass to chattels because he had prevented the owner from retrieving his horse from the grounds of a race track and required that the horse be raced against the owner's wishes. (*Jamgotchian v. Slender* (2009) 170 Cal.App.4th 1384, 1387 (*Jamgotchian*).) During the race, the horse was injured. (*Id*. at p. 1392.) On appeal from an order granting the defendant's motion for summary judgment, the appellate court found that a triable issue of fact existed as to whether the defendant had intentionally interfered with the plaintiff's right to possession of the horse. (*Id*. at pp. 1401–1402.)

> In the present case, the trial court concluded this cause of action was barred by the one-year statute of limitations for veterinary malpractice. The court also observed that plaintiff cited to no cases in which a veterinarian had been held liable for trespass to chattels based on acts of veterinary malpractice. We agree with the court's reasoning. Unlike the issue in *Jamgotchian*, the allegations of this claim arise solely out of defendant's treatment of Elvira [plaintiff's dog]. The allegations state an action for veterinary malpractice and, as such, the claim is barred by the statute of limitations. (Code Civ. Proc., § 340, subd. (c).)

Mink v. Encina Veterinary Clinic, Inc., 2011 Cal. App. Unpub. LEXIS 4441 (June 13, 2011), at *23–*24.

In the *Mink* case, defendants recommended surgery and Elvira was operated on to remove an intestinal lump; a week later a second surgery was performed to repair a leak at the site of the first surgery. Elvira received various treatments, including chemotherapy, over the following several weeks, but her condition worsened and she was euthanized less than two months after plaintiff initially brought her to the defendants. As described by the court, the "gist of the complaint is that defendants wrongfully coerced plaintiff into agreeing to excessive treatments for Elvira." In addition to rejecting plaintiff's trespass to chattels claim, the court also rejected plaintiff's conversion claim.

3. In *Womack v. Von Rardon*, 135 P.3d 542 (Wash. Ct. App. 2006), cited by the *Plotnik* court, the court adopted a new cause of action in Washington for "malicious injury to a pet," which supported emotional distress damages. *Id.* at 543. In that case, two boys took plaintiff's cat, Max, from her front porch to a nearby school and, after dousing Max with gasoline, set him on fire. Max suffered extensive burns and had to be euthanized. The youths were ordered to pay restitution to a local animal care organization. In the civil lawsuit brought against the boys and their parents, plaintiff asserted a claim for the tort of outrage, which was dismissed. On appeal, the court identified the three elements of the outrage tort: (1) extreme and outrageous conduct, (2) intentional or reckless infliction of emotional distress, and (3) plaintiff's resulting actual severe emotional distress. The court concluded that "[w]hat happened to Max was deplorable, but the record does not sufficiently establish the required severity." *Id.* at 545. *See also Criscuolo v. Grant County*, 2014 U.S. Dist. LEXIS 17493 (E.D. Wash. Feb. 10, 2014) (reconfirming that "a cause of action for malicious injury to a pet is recognized in Washington, so long as the harm was malicious").

4. As *Womack* illustrates, courts are not precluded from expanding the potential claims for injuries to animals. Given this fact, one commentator has proposed the adoption of another new tort—"intentional interference with the primary interests of an animal." David S. Favre, *Judicial Recognition of the Interests of Animals— A New Tort*, 2005 MICH. ST. L. REV. 333 (2005). Under this cause of action, which envisions an animal as plaintiff, the plaintiff must establish: (1) the existence of an interest which is of fundamental importance to the plaintiff animal; (2) defendant's interference with or harm to that interest (by act or omission); and (3) the weight and nature of the animal's interests substantially outweigh defendant's. Professor Favre's article provides sound reasoning, as well as substantial legal precedent, supporting this theory.

5. In *Scheele v. Dustin*, 998 A.2d 697 (Vt. 2010), the parties stipulated that, as a direct and proximate result of the defendant's intentional act of shooting at and causing the death of plaintiffs' dog, plaintiffs suffered severe emotional distress. The parties also stipulated that plaintiffs incurred economic and noneconomic damages. In appealing the trial court's denial of their claim for noneconomic damages, plaintiffs asked the Vermont high court to either "extend the common law to permit such damages to the degree that they are not otherwise recognized" in Vermont or, alternatively, to recognize "a new common law cause of action for malicious injury to a dog," as the Washington court had done in *Womack*. The Vermont

court declined to do either, deferring to the legislature to expand the law in this manner. Without deciding whether the defendant's conduct in that case rose to the level of malice and moral culpability necessary to support an award of punitive damages, the court emphasized that punitive damages are the proper remedy where a defendant's conduct rises to the level of malice or is done with evil intent, and that plaintiffs had made the strategic decision to omit them from the stipulation and had not appealed the presumed waiver.

Burgess v. Taylor
Court of Appeals of Kentucky, 2001
44 S.W.3d 806

SCHRODER, Judge. This appeal questions whether the tort of intentional infliction of emotional distress can apply to the conversion and slaughter of pet horses. We opine that the conduct of the offender rather than the subject of the conduct determines whether the conduct was outrageous. Hence, we affirm.

Judy Taylor ("Taylor") was the owner of two registered Appaloosa horses, nicknamed Poco and P.J. Taylor had owned Poco for 14 years (since he was a foal) and P.J. for 13 years (since her birth). Taylor loved Poco and P.J. as if they were her "children." Taylor and others testified that the horses were gentle and affectionate, and, having spent their entire lives together, were inseparable. After Taylor and her husband separated in 1994, Taylor remained at the marital residence where the horses lived, and she assumed sole responsibility for their care.

Due to a variety of medical problems, including myasthenia gravis, it was difficult for Taylor to perform some of the physical tasks necessary to properly care for her horses by herself. Taylor did not want to sell or separate Poco and P.J. Therefore, she decided to try to find someone with a farm who would like to care for both of them in exchange for the enjoyment of having them—a common arrangement in the horse world sometimes referred to as a "free-lease agreement." Taylor's brother suggested that his friends, Lisa and Jeff Burgess, who had a small farm with horses of their own, might be interested in such an arrangement. Taylor subsequently spoke to the Burgesses, explained her situation and the arrangement she was looking for. Taylor testified that she explained to Lisa that she never wanted to lose contact with or control of Poco and P.J., that she wanted to be able to visit them, and if the Burgesses ever didn't want to keep them anymore, Taylor would take them back or find another place for them to live. Lisa agreed, assuring Taylor that she loved and was knowledgeable about horses, that she had a nice pasture for them to live in together, that she liked helping people, and that Taylor could come and visit the horses any time she wanted. Believing that she had found a good place for her horses, Taylor agreed to let Poco and P.J. go live with the Burgesses. Taylor did not transfer ownership of the horses, nor ever indicate to the Burgesses that she no longer wanted them. On August 31, 1994, the Burgesses came to Taylor's residence to pick up Poco and P.J. Later that evening, Lisa called Taylor to tell her that they had led them around their new pasture and that the horses were doing fine.

Within the next few days, Lisa Burgess called Eugene Jackson, a known slaughter-buyer, to say she had two horses for sale. On September 6, 1994, Jackson purchased Poco and P.J. from the Burgesses for a total of $1,000.00.

Taylor waited a week before planning her first visit in order to give Poco and P.J. time to adjust to their new surroundings. She bought some film and treats for the horses and called Lisa to say that she would like to come and see Poco and P.J. and take some pictures. Lisa told Taylor "they're gone," that she had given them to a man she had met on a trail ride, but she did not know his name. Upset and frightened, Taylor said she needed to know who he was and where her horses were so she would know they were okay and could bring them back to her home. Lisa said she would find out and let Taylor know. The Burgesses then asked their friend, Kenny Randolph, to cover for them by lying and telling Taylor that he had the horses. Randolph never had possession of Poco and P.J. at any time and admitted his role in the events when questioned by a Harrison County, Indiana police detective.

Not hearing from Lisa, and after learning about the dangers of the slaughter market at a humane event over the weekend, Taylor called back and begged Lisa to tell her where Poco and P.J. were. At first, Lisa refused to tell her. Eventually, she lied and said that they were with a Kenny Randolph in the Corydon area of Indiana. Taylor called Randolph and told him she wanted to see her horses. Randolph, lying, told Taylor that he had them, but was not going to let her see them or tell her where they were. Taylor pleaded with him to tell her, and he eventually gave her vague directions to a fictitious location in the Frenchtown, Indiana area where he said they were in a pasture. He refused to give her specific directions or the name of the "gravel road" the pasture was supposedly on. Frantic, Taylor drove to the area and tried to find the gravel road Randolph spoke of. Taylor tried every road she found, stopping and asking people along the way if they had seen the horses, but was, of course, unsuccessful. Finally, it became dark, and a distraught Taylor had to return home.

With the aid of Victoria Coomber, a humane investigator, and Sharon Mayes, president of a local humane organization, in early October 1994, Taylor learned that Poco and P.J. had been purchased from the Burgesses by Eugene Jackson, a known slaughter-buyer, and then sold to Jason Ryan of the Ryan Horse Company, a business which supplies horses to slaughterhouses. Ryan Horse Company sold them to the Beltex Corporation in Texas where they were slaughtered in late September.

. . . Taylor filed an action in Jefferson Circuit Court. . . . The jury returned a verdict against the Burgesses, finding that they had breached their agreement with Taylor and that they had intentionally inflicted emotional distress on Judy Taylor.

The jury awarded Taylor $1,000.00, representing the fair market value of the horses for the breach of the free-lease agreement; $50,000.00 in compensatory damages for outrageous conduct; and $75,000.00 in punitive damages, for a total of $126,000.00.

* * *

[*In discussing the "tort of outrage" (analogous to intentional infliction of emotional distress), the court noted:*] Compelling evidence was presented at trial establishing Taylor's love for her horses and concern that they were in a good place. Recognizing that love, Lisa Burgess called Judy Taylor the evening she picked up the horses to tell her that she led them around their new pasture and the horses were doing fine. The jury heard evidence of subsequent phone calls by a distraught and frightened Taylor to Lisa Burgess and Kenny Randolph, begging to know where her horses were. The Burgesses knew that Poco and P.J. were heading to slaughter, and that Taylor was, in reality, pleading for their lives. Yet, in the face of Taylor's pleas for the horses she loved like children, the Burgesses continued to lie and refuse to tell her where they were. This Court cannot characterize this emotional torment inflicted by the Burgesses upon Taylor as anything other than "heartless, flagrant, and outrageous." [Restatement (Second) of Torts § 46, cmt. f (1965).]

* * *

Finally, the evidence indicates that Taylor suffered severe emotional distress. Taylor testified that when she learned what had happened to Poco and P.J., she broke down, knowing that "my babies were dead." Since then she has suffered from many panic attacks, and has had major problems with high blood pressure for which she must receive medical care. She suffers from anxiety and depression, for which she takes medication, and has had many thoughts of suicide. She described overwhelming feelings of loss and failure. She testified she has trouble sleeping and has recurring nightmares in which she hears Poco's scream in her head. Taylor testified that she has sought help from her doctor and social workers but cannot get over what happened.

Having reviewed the record, we opine that Taylor offered sufficient evidence to establish the elements of the tort of outrage, and the trial court properly submitted the claim to the jury. On appeal, we give deference to the jury's determination of conflicting facts and the reasonable inferences drawn from the facts. Having reviewed the evidence in the light most favorable to Taylor, we believe that the jury verdict was supported by sufficient evidence.

Next, the Burgesses contend that, under Kentucky law, "the proper award of damages for the loss or damage to an animal is the value of that animal, not emotional damages for that loss." We disagree. *Faulkner Drilling Co., Inc. v. Gross*, Ky. App., 943 S.W.2d 634 (1997) established that an action for tort may be combined with a breach of contract and that punitive damages may also be asserted. *Cincinnati, N.O. & T.P. Ry. Co. v. Rankin*, 153 Ky. 730, 156 S.W. 400 (1913), cited by the Burgesses to support their argument for fair market value, did not involve a claim for emotional damages and did not hold that there cannot be a claim for intentional infliction of emotional distress. *Cincinnati, N.O. & T.P. Ry. Co.* involved the liability of a common carrier transporting livestock under a tariff contract and is not relevant to this case. There was no allegation that pets were involved and the case was before *Craft* [*v. Rice*, 671 S.W.2d 247 (1984)]. There are no cases in Kentucky holding that a finding of intentional infliction of emotional distress or punitive damages is precluded simply because the facts giving rise to the claim involve an animal. Indeed, we conclude that the second element in application of the tort of the intentional infliction of emotional distress depends on the facts of the case as to the offender's conduct and not to the subject of said conduct.

[*The Burgesses' final argument was that the jury's award of $50,000.00 of compensatory and $75,000.00 of punitive damages for emotional distress was excessive. The trial court had concluded that "the jury's award was not excessive and based only on sympathy, passion and prejudice." The appellate court held that "the trial court did not abuse its discretion in so finding."*]

Notes

1. In *Rabideau v. City of Racine*, 627 N.W.2d 795 (Wis. 2001), where the defendant off-duty police officer (who happened to be plaintiff's neighbor) shot plaintiff's dog (who allegedly was threatening defendant's family), the court rejected the plaintiff's negligent infliction of emotional distress theory and then reviewed the Wisconsin standards for intentional infliction of emotional distress and applied them to the facts of that case.

Next, we consider Rabideau's claim of intentional infliction of emotional distress. Four elements must be established for a plaintiff to maintain such a claim. A plaintiff must demonstrate (1) that the defendant's conduct was intentioned to cause emotional distress; (2) that the defendant's conduct was extreme and outrageous; (3) that the defendant's conduct was a cause-in-fact of the plaintiff's emotional distress; and (4) that the plaintiff suffered an extreme disabling emotional response to the defendant's conduct. *Alsteen*, 21 Wis. 2d at 359–60; Wis. JI — Civil 2725. We agree with the court of appeals' conclusion that summary judgment is warranted here.

The first *Alsteen* element requires the plaintiff to demonstrate that the defendant acted with the intent to cause emotional harm. "One who by extreme and outrageous conduct intentionally causes severe emotional distress to another is subject to liability for such emotional distress and for bodily harm resulting from it." *Id.* at 358 (emphasis omitted). In this case, there is no material issue of fact in the record that suggests that Officer Jacobi acted for the purpose of causing Rabideau emotional harm.

Rabideau argues that she need only show that Officer Jacobi acted intentionally when he shot Dakota. She contends that by shooting Dakota while she was present, Officer Jacobi would have known that his act would cause her severe emotional distress. Rabideau argues that such knowledge is tantamount to intentionally causing severe emotional distress because "a person is presumed to intend 'the natural and probable consequences of his acts voluntarily and knowingly performed.'"

The presumption cited by Rabideau . . . is generally applied in criminal cases. Rabideau's application in this case of the general rule that an accused is presumed to intend the natural and probable consequences of his act obfuscates what is required by the first element of this cause of action. The plaintiff must establish that the purpose of the conduct was to cause emotional distress. There is no question that Officer Jacobi intended to fire his weapon at Dakota. However, there is no evidence to indicate he did so to cause emotional distress to Rabideau. Certainly that was a by-product, but that is insufficient standing alone. This is a limitation upon the cause of action for the intentional infliction of emotional distress. There must be something more than a showing that the defendant intentionally engaged in the conduct that gave rise to emotional distress in the plaintiff; the plaintiff must show that the conduct was engaged in for the purpose of causing emotional distress. While intent may be evidenced by inferences from words, conduct or the circumstances in which events occurred, in the present case there is no asserted fact as to this element. Accordingly, we are not persuaded by Rabideau's argument, and we affirm the court of appeals' grant of summary judgment.

Id. at 802–03.

While the court concluded that the particular facts in that case did not establish a *prima facie* case for intentional infliction of emotional distress, it was in accord with *Burgess'* holding that such a claim would lie, even if the defendant carried out his plan to inflict emotional distress on plaintiff by perpetrating violence on a nonhuman.

2. Similarly, under different facts, in *Langford v. Emergency Pet Clinic*, 644 N.E.2d 1035 (Ohio Ct. App. 1994), where plaintiff sued a clinic and pet cemetery that had buried her dog in a mass grave, the court granted summary judgment for defendants because plaintiff failed to prove that their conduct was intentional or reckless, or that she had suffered mental anguish beyond her endurance. Notably, the court implied that under appropriate circumstances such a claim might be presented, but the court went on to point out that the mental anguish in such situations must be "'so serious and of a nature that no reasonable man could be expected to endure it.'" (This standard is higher than most states' interpretation of the tort, where the emotional distress need only be extreme, though not unbearable.) *See also Oberschlake v. Veterinary Associates Animal Hospital*, 785 N.E.2d 811 (Ohio Ct. App. 2003) (recognizing that *Langford* "impliedly indicated that dog owners may present claims for intentional infliction of emotional distress," but nonetheless concluding that "[e]ven conceding the bond between many humans and their pets, the burden is one that would be very difficult to meet," and rejecting the claim in that veterinary malpractice case).

3. In Nevada, a court allowed a claim for intentional infliction of emotional distress to survive a motion to dismiss where plaintiff's dog became ill while plaintiff was away and the dog was brought to a veterinary hospital, which subsequently informed the plaintiff that he had thirteen days to pick up the dog, but when he returned to get his dog within that time period, the hospital had euthanized

the dog. *Thompson v. Lied Animal Shelter*, 2009 U.S. Dist. LEXIS 86137 (D. Nev. Aug. 10, 2009).

B. Negligence

The elements of a standard negligence claim are the same whether the claim is for damage to inanimate property, injury to a person or harm to an owned (whether commercially used or companion) animal. A negligence cause of action may be equally available to the plaintiff in any of these circumstances. In cases involving alleged tortious harm to an animal, plaintiffs may assert a negligence cause of action and seek emotional distress damages or they may assert the separate but related cause of action for negligent infliction of emotional distress (NIED). The latter is the focus of our discussion here.

As you have learned already, animals are viewed as property under the law. With rare exceptions, negligent harm to property will not support an emotional distress claim; and virtually every state has carved out a narrow set of circumstances under which an NIED claim can be asserted even for harm to another human.

A growing number of courts have acknowledged that animals are more than mere inanimate objects of property, and that they may be considered as valued members of the family. Thus far, though, courts generally have stopped short of recognizing a viable cause of action for NIED for harm to a companion animal, unless the law of the particular jurisdiction permits such a claim in cases of harm to personal property. Despite the daunting odds, claims for NIED continue to be asserted in animal law cases with the hope of ultimately convincing a court to allow the claim to reach the jury.

McDougall v. Lamm

Supreme Court of New Jersey, 2012
211 N.J. 203, 48 A.3d 312

HOENS, Justice. In this appeal, we are asked to consider whether a pet owner should be permitted to recover for emotional distress caused by observing the traumatic death of that pet. Asserting that pets have achieved an elevated status that makes them companions in the lives of human beings, plaintiff Joyce McDougall asks this Court to hold that pets should no longer be considered to be mere personal property. With that fundamental shift in the way that pets are seen in the eyes of the law as her backdrop, plaintiff asks us to permit her to recover for the emotional distress she endured after she watched her dog as it was shaken to death by a larger dog.

The basis in our law for recovering emotional distress damages arising out of observing the traumatic death of another was first expressed by this Court in *Portee v. Jaffee*, 84 N.J. 88, 417 A.2d 521 (1980). Since that time, the doctrine has been narrowly applied and we have carefully limited the circumstances in which such relief is available. In considering potential expansions of the relief permitted under

Portee, we have never concluded that it can be applied to the observation of a death, however traumatic, by one who did not share a close familial relationship or intimate, marital-like bond with the victim.

The question that we confront today is whether a bond with a pet meets that carefully circumscribed criteria. Although we recognize that many people form close bonds with their pets, we conclude that those bonds do not rise to the level of a close familial relationship or intimate, marital-like bond. We therefore decline to expand the traditionally and intentionally narrow grounds established in *Portee* to include claims arising from the death of a pet.

We reach this conclusion for three essential reasons. First, we do so because expanding the cause of action recognized in *Portee* to include pets would be inconsistent with the essential foundation of the *Portee* claim itself. Second, creating a cause of action based on observing the death of a pet would result in an ill-defined and amorphous cause of action that would elevate the loss of pets to a status that exceeds the loss of all but a few human beings. Third, creating a new common law cause of action of this type would conflict with expressions of our Legislature found in both the statutory cause of action designed to address wrongful death of humans and in the statutes that govern rights and responsibilities of dog owners.

The bond shared between humans and animals is often an emotional and enduring one. Permitting it to support a recovery for emotional distress, however, would require either that we vastly expand the classes of human relationships that would qualify for *Portee* damages or that we elevate relationships with animals above those we share with other human beings. We conclude that neither response to the question presented would be sound.

I.

* * *

On June 7, 2007, plaintiff was walking along a street in Morris Plains with her dog Angel, a nine-year old "maltipoo" [*half maltese and half poodle*]. According to plaintiff, a large dog, belonging to defendant Charlot Lamm, ran out from defendant's house. That dog, which was growling and snarling, stopped and sniffed plaintiff's dog, then looked at her and paused. After a moment, the larger dog grabbed plaintiff's dog by the neck, picked it up and shook it several times before dropping it and returning to defendant's yard. According to plaintiff, she screamed and tried to figure out if she could help the dog before attempting to telephone for help. She later learned that her dog had died.

* * *

Plaintiff's complaint alleged in its first count that defendant was negligent in maintaining her dog and demanded compensatory damages. In the second count of the complaint, plaintiff alleged that, as a result of witnessing the events up to and including the dog's death, she suffered significant and continuing emotional distress and discomfort and demanded damages for that emotional distress.

Defendant moved for partial summary judgment, seeking dismissal of plaintiff's emotional distress claim. In ruling on that motion, the court noted that the law categorizes dogs as a form of personal property. Although expressing sympathy to plaintiff for the loss she felt, the court observed that there is no cause of action in New Jersey that permits an emotional distress claim based on the loss of property. For those reasons, the court dismissed plaintiff's emotional distress claim and limited plaintiff's claim for damages to the dog's intrinsic value.

* * *

Plaintiff appealed the dismissal of her emotional distress claim, arguing that although New Jersey does not permit a pet owner such as plaintiff to recover for emotional distress, the better rule would be to recognize the cause of action for the loss of a companion dog. In opposition, defendant argued that the law is clear that only economic damages can be recovered for the loss of a pet. Defendant urged the appellate panel not to permit plaintiff's claim to proceed, warning that it would set a dangerous precedent to expand the scope of bystander recovery to non-humans. The Appellate Division affirmed the judgment of the trial court . . . .

* * *

III.

We begin our consideration of the issue raised on appeal with an explanation of the historical developments relating to the *Portee* doctrine, following which we consider the role that pets play in the lives of their owners and whether recognizing the cause of action plaintiff requests would be consistent with *Portee*.

A.

Historically, plaintiffs could only recover for emotional anguish arising from a defendant's negligence if the plaintiff suffered some form of physical injury in addition to the emotional injury. The requirement that emotional injury be accompanied by a physical injury arose in part from a policy concern that emotional injuries could be more "'easily feigned without detection.'" *Jablonowska v. Suther,* 195 N.J. 91, 102, 948 A.2d 610 (2008) (quoting *Ward v. W. Jersey & Seashore R.R. Co.,* 65 N.J.L. 383, 386, 47 A. 561 (Sup.Ct.1900)).

The historical physical injury requirement was eventually replaced by a requirement that the plaintiff be within the "zone of risk," but this was only a permissible substitute if accompanied by the risk of substantial bodily injury or sickness.

The evolution in the requirements for an emotional distress claim culminated in this Court's decision in *Portee, supra.* [*In that case, plaintiff witnessed her son's death when he was trapped in an elevator door.*]

Among other claims, the plaintiff in *Portee* filed suit seeking to recover damages for her mental and emotional distress. Although both the trial and appellate courts dismissed plaintiff's claims, this Court reversed, holding that she had stated a claim for negligent infliction of emotional distress. Relying on a decision of the California Supreme Court, (citing and discussing *Dillon v. Legg,* 68 Cal. 2d 728, 69

Cal. Rptr. 72, 441 P.2d 912, 920 (1968)), this Court identified four elements that a plaintiff must prove to recover for emotional distress as a bystander: "(1) the death or serious physical injury of another caused by defendant's negligence; (2) a marital or intimate, familial relationship between plaintiff and the injured person; (3) observation of the death or injury at the scene of the accident; and (4) resulting severe emotional distress." *Portee,* at 101, 417 A.2d 521. In the three decades since *Portee* was decided, the four-element test has remained in place as the framework for a bystander's emotional distress claim in New Jersey.

The four elements were intentionally designed to create a narrow class of claimants who could be readily identified, to fix criteria that could not be easily feigned, and to identify those who were foreseeable plaintiffs. Therefore, "recovery for negligent infliction of emotional harm requires that it must be reasonably foreseeable that the tortious conduct will cause genuine and substantial emotional distress or mental harm to average persons." *Decker v. Princeton Packet, Inc.,* 116 N.J. 418, 430, 561 A.2d 1122 (1989).

Because this appeal only requires consideration of whether a pet can fulfill *Portee's* requirement that the relationship qualify as "a marital or intimate[ ] familial" one, we focus only on that element. In *Portee,* this Court described the existence of an intimate familial relationship as the "most crucial" of the four inquiries. We explained that "the presence of deep, intimate, familial ties between the plaintiff and the physically injured person . . . makes the harm to emotional tranquility so serious and compelling." We held that an intimate familial relationship is "an essential element of a cause of action for negligent infliction of emotional distress."

* * *

B.

We begin with an analysis of the essential underpinnings on which plaintiff bases her request that we recognize this cause of action. Those points, for our analytical purposes, include her contentions about the role that pets play in the lives of their owners and the principles identified in the decisions reached by other jurisdictions that have confronted the question now before this Court.

Plaintiff's arguments concerning the expansion of the *Portee* cause of action rest on the assertion that pets play a role in the lives of their owners that cannot be equated with property and that the loss of a pet therefore cannot be fairly compensated by resort to property loss principles. Fundamental to this aspect of her argument is the implicit assumption that there is a class of animals, referred to as companion animals, *see* Debra Squires-Lee, Note, *In Defense of Floyd: Appropriately Valuing Companion Animals in Tort,* 70 N.Y.U. L. Rev. 1059, 1059 & n.2 (1995) (explaining genesis and implications of companion animal designation), with which an owner, referred to as an animal guardian, interacts in a manner akin to a relationship with other humans.

Those underlying presumptions, in turn, give rise to the argument that courts must abandon the historical legal categorization of pets as a form of property and permit compensation commensurate with the special status to which their role in the lives of humans is entitled. In attempting to define the features by which courts can identify companion animals, and thereby distinguish between them and any other kind of animals with which people interact, the commentators on this subject have suggested that we look to

> the relationship that they share with their guardians. Humans and companion animals share their lives; daily emotional and social interactions establish a bond and a connection. "With companion animals it is the relationship itself which is important to the owner." Each relationship depends on the personalities and nature of the individuals involved.

Id. at 1065 (citation omitted).

Although plaintiff does not expressly ask this Court to embrace this theory or the definitions it proposes, her arguments on appeal require us to recognize this underlying premise as part of our analysis of whether plaintiff's proposed cause of action comports with our existing *Portee* jurisprudence and how adopting it would work in practice.

Plaintiff does expressly invite this Court to find persuasive the reasoning of those jurisdictions that have permitted recovery in circumstances similar to her own, while rejecting the reasoning of the majority of other jurisdictions that have declined to do so. Numerous other jurisdictions have considered whether to permit recovery for emotional distress for pet owners witnessing the death or injury of their pet. *See* Jay M. Zitter, *Recovery of Damages for Emotional Distress Due to Treatment of Pets and Animals*, 91 A.L.R. 5th 545, [3] (2012) (collecting cases).

The majority of jurisdictions that have considered whether pet owners should be permitted to recover for emotional distress arising from the death of the pet have declined to authorize the cause of action.

* * *

[IV.a]

* * *

B.

Our framework for determining whether to recognize a new common law cause of action, as we have explained, "derive[s] from considerations of public policy and fairness." *Hopkins v. Fox & Lazo Realtors*, 132 N.J. 426, 439, 625 A.2d 1110 (1993). More specifically, deciding whether one party owes another a duty of care "involves identifying, weighing, and balancing several factors—the relationship of the parties, the nature of the attendant risk, the opportunity and ability to exercise care, and the public interest in the proposed solution." *Ibid.* Underlying all of those

---

a. The opinion has two sections designated as "III." The section designated as "[IV]" in this text refers to the second section III in the opinion.

considerations, however, is an analysis of whether the harm suffered was foreseeable, for in the absence of foreseeability of harm, the other factors will not be advanced by the imposition of a duty and the outcome will inevitably be unfair.

* * *

In the end, we decline plaintiff's request that we expand the class of individuals authorized to bring a *Portee* claim by extending it to individuals who have witnessed the traumatic death of a pet for several reasons.

First, we do not doubt that plaintiff was attached to her dog and that she had strong emotional ties to it. Nevertheless, we have strictly limited the kinds of relationships that can support a *Portee* claim precisely because of our intention to preserve the essential principle of foreseeability so as to serve the ends of fairness to all parties. It would make little sense, we think, to permit plaintiff to recover for her emotional distress over the loss of her dog when she would be precluded from any such recovery if she instead had the misfortune of watching the neighbor's child, whom she regarded as her own, torn apart by a wild animal. [*Eyrich ex rel. Eyrich v. Dam*, 193 N.J. Super. 244, 259–61, 473 A.2d 539 (App. Div. 1984).] Our carefully limited authorization for *Portee* damages, which would not permit recovery for observing the death of most humans, simply cannot permit recovery for watching the death of a non-human.

Second, expanding the *Portee* cause of action to permit recovery of emotional distress damages based upon the death of a pet would be inconsistent with existing statutes. It would be a clear conflict with the expression of our Legislature in the Wrongful Death Act, N.J.S.A. 2A:31-1 to -6. That statutory cause of action limits recovery for wrongful death by survivors to pecuniary damages, regardless of the closeness of consanguinity. N.J.S.A. 2A:31-5. Permitting plaintiff to recover emotional distress damages based on the loss of her pet would effectively create a class of pet owners with rights in excess of those the Legislature has granted to family members suffering the loss of another human. Moreover, recognizing the cause of action would conflict with the Legislature's statutory scheme for regulating dog owners and for addressing dangerous dogs, see, e.g., N.J.S.A. 4:19-38 (criminalizing the silencing of a dog); N.J.S.A. 4:22-20 (defining abandonment of a domestic animal as a disorderly persons offense); N.J.S.A. 4:19-16 (setting forth liability of dog owners for injuries inflicted by their dog's bite). To the extent that the imposition of a duty of care through recognizing a tort remedy serves to alter or deter conduct, *see Kelly* [*v. Gwinnell*, 96 N.J. 538, 548, 476 A.2d 1219 (1984)] (discussing deterrent effect of new cause of action against social hosts who directly serve alcohol to guests whom they know will be driving), our Legislature has not been silent.[3]

---

3. Although it would not preclude this Court from recognizing a common law remedy, we note that our Legislature has not enacted bills that have been introduced to create a statutory cause of action for non-economic damages of this type. Assembly Bill No. 2411, 211 Leg., Reg. Sess. (2004); Assembly Bill No. 2012, 211 Leg., Reg. Sess. (2004) (introduction of bills that would have permitted recovery of non-economic damages for the loss of a pet, capped at $20,000).

Third, we do not question plaintiff's argument that, for many people, their pets are not merely property. That alone, however, cannot support a cause of action for emotional distress damages. Instead, that value is recognized through the precedents that permit the measure of recovery for the loss of the pet to exceed its replacement value and to include the intrinsic value of the pet. Plaintiff's damage award in this matter, as an illustration, appropriately exceeded even the highest cost that she estimated would be needed to replace the dog with another one.

Fourth, there is no clear line of demarcation that we can draw in order to distinguish which pet owners would qualify for a *Portee* recovery and which would not. Unlike the plain and obvious emotional bond one has to the easily-identified universe of people that to date we have limited to parent, child, spouse or an individual with whom one shares a marital-like or intimate familial relationship, there is no manner in which to identify the class of pet owners or pets that would be included in such a cause of action.

Nor is it sufficient to describe some pets as companion animals, because the descriptive definition of the role played by companion animals would equally apply to innumerable human relationships. Surely utilizing that articulation as our basis would suggest that a school teacher, coach, regular babysitter, housekeeper or live-in au pair could claim an equally close bond with a child that would potentially support a *Portee* claim. Moreover, as the same commentator recognizes, our attachment to our pets is uniquely individualized, *see* Squires-Lee, *supra*, 70 N.Y.U. L. Rev. at 1065 (conceding that "[e]ach relationship depends on the personalities and nature of the individuals involved"), as a result of which there could be no agreement as to which ones would certainly provoke the requisite level of emotional upheaval, were we to witness their traumatic death, that would be foreseeable and thus entitled to the extraordinary remedy recognized in *Portee* and its progeny.

Fifth, as we have recognized, we consider pets to be unlike property in the traditional sense. However, by not expanding the scope of a *Portee* claim to include their loss, we forestall the argument, raised by some of the commentators, that an expansion of the cause of action would inevitably open the door to claims that attachments to inanimate forms of property should likewise be honored. Thus, we need not be concerned with future applications by children of long-deceased parents claiming to have strong emotional ties to family heirlooms, photographs or meaningful gifts who would argue that witnessing the destruction of those things entitles them to be compensated for their alleged distress.

In the end, we leave the *Portee* cause of action where we found it. We leave it to serve the limited and specific purposes for which it was designed, permitting it to compensate certain individuals for the traumatic loss of carefully defined classes of other individuals. We perceive no basis in law or in public policy to depart from that meaning of the doctrine or to expand it in the manner that plaintiff requests.

Notes

1. Much of the same reasoning was relied on by the Wisconsin Supreme Court a decade earlier in *Rabideau v. City of Racine*, 627 N.W.2d 795 (Wis. 2001), a case where the plaintiff witnessed her neighbor (an off-duty police officer) shooting her dog, who later died from the injuries.

> At the outset, we note that we are uncomfortable with the law's cold characterization of a dog, such as Dakota, as mere "property." Labeling a dog "property" fails to describe the value human beings place upon the companionship that they enjoy with a dog. A companion dog is not a fungible item, equivalent to other items of personal property. A companion dog is not a living room sofa or dining room furniture. This term inadequately and inaccurately describes the relationship between a human and a dog.

Id. at 798. The court went on to note the longstanding association between dogs and humans "since 6,300 B.C.," that dogs are "so much a part of the human experience" and that "of course, dogs continue to provide humans with devoted friendship." Nevertheless, like the New Jersey court in *McDougall*, the court fell back on historical common law precedent characterizing animals as property, precluding NIED claims (or emotional distress damages for negligence claims) in cases of damage to "property," and limiting the circumstances under which an NIED claim can be asserted (noting that "this rule of nonrecovery applies with equal force to a plaintiff who witnesses as a bystander the negligent injury of a best friend who is human as it does to a plaintiff whose best friend is a dog"), as well as on the fear of a "slippery slope."

> Our decision is based upon well-established public policy criteria. We are particularly concerned that were such a claim to go forward, the law would proceed upon a course that had no just stopping point. Humans have an enormous capacity to form bonds with dogs, cats, birds and an infinite number of other beings that are non-human. Were we to recognize a claim for damages for the negligent loss of a dog, we can find little basis for rationally distinguishing other categories of animal companion.

Id. Accordingly, the *Rabideau* court affirmed the grant of summary judgment, dismissing the claim for damages for negligence. However, the court did reverse the trial court's finding that the claim was frivolous, concluding that the plaintiff "set forth a substantial argument in good faith for an extension, modification or reversal of existing law."

2. As noted, the courts in *McDougall* and *Rabideau* clearly acknowledged the bond between humans and their companion animals, yet fell back on public policy concerns in refusing to allow claims of negligent infliction of emotional distress in cases where the victim is a nonhuman. Is the "slippery slope" rationale persuasive in your view? Be prepared to discuss arguments for and against this majority rule.

3. As is not atypical, the *McDougall* court intertwined its discussion of the emotional distress cause of action with the question of the appropriate measure of damages for negligent harm to a companion animal. The latter issue is addressed in Section 3 of this chapter.

4. *McDougall* and *Rabideau* are in accord with almost every court that has examined a negligent infliction of emotional distress claim for harm to a companion animal. The *McDougall* opinion provides a lengthy list of cases supporting the majority view (at 48 A.3d at 321–22), and which address the cause of action and/or the proper measure of damages. The court summarized its view of the basis for those decisions and it went on to distinguish the few cases that have allowed emotional distress damages for injuries to companion animals.

5. In *Oberschlake v. Veterinary Associates Animal Hospital*, 785 N.E.2d 811 (Ohio Ct. App. 2003), which is one of the cases cited by the *McDougall* court, the court explained its view of the limitations on this claim, including the "bystander" requirement, which was met in *McDougall* and *Rabideau*, but which generally is not met in veterinary malpractice cases such as *Oberschlake*.

> Whether or not one agrees with the view that pets are more than personal property, it is clear that Ohio does not recognize non-economic damages for injury to companion animals. Moreover, even if non-economic damages were allowed, Ohio limits recovery for negligent infliction of emotional distress to situations where a plaintiff-bystander observes an accident and suffers "emotional injury that is both severe and debilitating." The Ohio Supreme Court has described this type of injury as "beyond trifling mental disturbance, mere upset or hurt feelings. * * * Serious emotional distress describes emotional injury which is both severe and debilitating. Thus, serious emotional distress may be found where a reasonable person, normally constituted, would be unable to cope adequately with the mental distress engendered by the circumstances of the case."
>
> In the present case, the allegations in the complaint indicate that neither of the Oberschlakes were bystanders. In fact, the dog was left at the veterinary hospital and was picked up some time after the surgery was performed. As the Ohio Supreme Court has stressed on various occasions, "the only logical definition of 'bystander' is 'one who is at the scene.' 'Bystander' does not include a person who was nowhere near the accident scene and had no sensory perception of the events surrounding the accident."
>
> As a further point, being "shocked" over improper surgery to a dog does not present the type of severe and debilitating emotional injury required for negligent infliction of emotional distress. Accordingly, even if Ohio law permitted the award of non-economic damages, negligent infliction of emotional distress would not have been an appropriate cause of action.

Id. at 814.

6. Louisiana is an exception to the general rule, and allows for emotional distress damages for injuries to animals witnessed by their owners. Under Louisiana law, "a domestic animal is considered corporeal movable property." *Barrios v. Safeway Ins. Co.*, 97 So. 3d 1019, 1022 (La. Ct. App. 2012). An award for mental anguish resulting from negligent harm to property is permissible "when the owner is present or nearby and suffers psychic trauma as a result," requiring the plaintiff to prove "psychic trauma in the nature of or similar to a physical injury as a direct result of the property damage." *Id.* at 1022, 1023. In *Barrios*, plaintiffs' seventeen-year-old son was walking with the family's twelve-year-old Labrador retriever, Yellow, when they were struck by a vehicle driven by defendant Darrell Cuti. Plaintiff Matthew Barrios was injured and Yellow died on the scene. Matthew's parents (but not Matthew) sued as owners of Yellow for "mental anguish and property damage" resulting from the death of their dog. The trial judge awarded them a total of $10,000 for mental anguish and loss of Yellow's value that they suffered because of Yellow's death. Mr. Cuti's insurer (a co-defendant in the case, as permitted under Louisiana's direct action statute) appealed the award. In affirming the trial court's judgment, finding no abuse of discretion, the appellate court explained:

> In deciding the damages award, the trial judge found that Yellow was killed as a result of Mr. Cuti's negligence. The trial judge noted that the plaintiffs were nearby and they immediately arrived at the accident scene to find their beloved dog deceased. The trial judge cited testimony from Mr. and Mrs. Barrios that established that Yellow was loved by the Barrioses and was extremely valuable to them. Mr. Barrios retrieved Yellow's remains the day after the accident from Animal Control and buried Yellow on his property. The trial judge reasoned that the plaintiffs suffered a severe loss and severe emotional distress as a result of the loss of their pet.

> In her reasons for judgment, the trial judge stated the following:

>> The plaintiffs testified that they both have suffered severe emotional distress as a result of the loss of their beloved pet. Ellen Barrios stated that Yellow was part of the family and that they are still grieving. Austin Barrios stated that he spent a lot of time with the dog as a member of the family and that he was still grieving over the loss of Yellow. The car accident that resulted in Yellow's death was on Yellow's birthday, a day that the family celebrated with a cook-out and a cake. Yellow was viewed by its owners as more than property, but as a member of the family. Austin Barrios testified that if he was not working then he was with Yellow.

> Although a pet is considered corporeal movable property in Louisiana, clearly, pets are not inanimate objects. This Court takes judicial notice of the emotional bond that exists between some pets and their owners and the "family" status awarded some pets by their owners. In the present matter, the trial judge based her award of $5,000.00 each to the Barrioses on her

finding that they had a close family-like relationship with Yellow; that the dog was a part of their lives for approximately twelve years and that his loss caused them psychic trauma.

Id. at 1023–24.

7. For a number of years, Hawaii took the same rare approach taken in Louisiana, permitting recovery for emotional distress resulting from the negligent destruction of property. In *Campbell v. Animal Quarantine Station*, 632 P.2d 1066 (Haw. 1981), the plaintiffs' dog Princess died of heat prostration when employees of the state quarantine station left her in an unventilated hot van for over an hour. The court built on established Hawaiian precedent allowing for the award of damages for serious mental distress resulting from harm to property, even where that harm was caused by the defendant's negligent (rather than intentional) act. The seminal case was *Rodrigues v. State*, 472 P.2d 509 (Haw. 1970), which allowed recovery for emotional distress arising from damage to a house. In 1986, however, the Hawaii legislature passed a law abolishing emotional distress claims arising "solely out of damage to property or material objects." HAW. REV. STAT. § 663-8.9. The statute was part of a sweeping tort reform effort, triggered by numerous claims filed after Hurricane Iniki, where claimants sought emotional distress damages arising from damage to their homes and belongings. There is no indication that the *Campbell* case or the effect on cases of harm to companion animals were considered at all in the legislative process.

C. Fourth Amendment Claims for Tortious Harm to Companion Animals by Public Officials

Unfortunately, since the 1990s there has been an increasing number of shooting of dogs by police officers. According to one source, "[t]he most widely cited estimate from the U.S. Department of justice is that every day, police officers kill 25 to 30 dogs — or some 10,000 per year." Arin Greenwood, *Courts are awarding significant damages to families whose dogs are killed by police*, ABA JOURNAL (Apr. 2018).

We have already seen this issue arise in several of the Note cases earlier in this chapter. Often the animal victim's human guardians do not pursue legal action in response. Where they do file suit, they are required to follow specialized procedures for suing officials in tort. The cases typically allege violations of the dog owners' Fourth Amendment federal constitutional rights in claims brought under 42 U.S.C. § 1983.

"Every circuit that has considered the issue has held that the killing of a companion dog constitutes a 'seizure' within the meaning of the Fourth Amendment." *Viilo v. Eyre*, 547 F.3d 707, 710 (7th Cir. 2008) ("*Viilo*"), *See also Robinson v. Pezzat*, 818 F.3d 1, 7 (D.C. Cir. 2016) (quoting *Viilo*); *Brown v. Battle Creek Police Dep't*, 844 F.3d 556, 566 (6th Cir. 2016); *Mayfield v. Bethards*, 826 F.3d 1252, 1259 (10th Cir. 2016). Reasonableness is the touchstone of any Fourth Amendment seizure analysis.

In these "constitutional tort" cases, the officers' actions will be deemed constitutional only if they were "reasonable" under the circumstances. *Viilo,* 547 F.3d at 710. The court must look to the "totality of the circumstances to determine whether the destruction of property was reasonably necessary to effectuate the performance of the law enforcement officer's duties." *San Jose Charter of the Hells Angels Motorcycle Club v. City of San Jose,* 402 F.3d 962, 975 (9th Cir. 2005). Courts consider multiple factors in analyzing whether a seizure of a dog is reasonable under the totality of the circumstances, including, but not limited to: "Whether the dog was 'at-large' or whether the owner was available and willing to assert control over the dog"; the breed of the dog; whether there was "time to find an alternative solution to gain control of the dog"; whether non-lethal means were available to control the dog; and whether the dog posed a danger to the officer or the public. *Branson v. Price,* 2015 U.S. Dist. LEXIS 126652, *14 (D. Colo. Sept. 21, 2015).

The seizure becomes unlawful when it is more intrusive than necessary. *Id.* "To determine whether the shooting of plaintiff's dog was reasonable, the court must balance the nature and quality of the intrusion on plaintiff's Fourth Amendment interests against the countervailing governmental interests at stake." *Perez v. City of Placerville,* 2008 U.S. Dist. LEXIS 83172, *25 (E.D. Cal. Sept. 9, 2008). "[U]se of deadly force against a household pet is reasonable only if the pet poses an immediate danger and the use of force is unavoidable." *Viilo,* 547 F.3d at 710; *Robinson v. Pezzat,* 818 F.3d at 7 (quoting *Viilo* and citing *San Jose Charter*); *Brown v. Battle Creek Police Dep't,* 844 F.3d at 566 (noting that a "large number" of federal circuit courts apply this standard and citing numerous cases from other circuits).

This reasonableness analysis relates to the "qualified immunity" defense available under Section 1983:

> "The doctrine of qualified immunity protects government officials 'from liability for civil damages insofar as their conduct does not violate clearly established statutory or constitutional rights of which a reasonable person would have known.'" Qualified immunity provides government officials "breathing room to make reasonable but mistaken judgments, and protects all but the plainly incompetent or those who knowingly violate the law." "[W]hether an official protected by qualified immunity may be held personally liable for an allegedly unlawful official action generally turns on the 'objective legal reasonableness' of the action . . . assessed in light of the legal rules that were 'clearly established' at the time it was taken."

> To determine whether a police officer is entitled to qualified immunity, this Court applies a two-prong test: "(1) whether the facts, when taken in the light most favorable to the party asserting the injury, show the officer's conduct violated a constitutional right; and (2) whether the right violated was clearly established such 'that a reasonable official would understand that what he is doing violates that right.'"

Brown v. Battle Creek Police Dep't, 844 F.3d at 565.

Not surprisingly, in determining whether officers have a viable qualified immunity defense, courts look to the facts and evidence presented. In some cases, courts have denied summary judgment to police officers on the issue of qualified immunity and allowed the plaintiffs to present their case to the jury at trial. For example, in *Viilo*, the court summarized the testimony and concluded as follows:

> Despite the police testimony, at least seven witnesses testified that Bubba wasn't interfering with the officers when he was shot for the third and fourth time. Rather, according to the witnesses, he was attempting to limp back to his owner. It should go without saying that this testimony, if it is credited by the jury, does not support the conclusion that the decision to shoot Bubba a third and fourth time was reasonable.

Viilo, 547 F.3d at 710. *See also Cabisca v. City of Rochester*, 2017 U.S. Dist. LEXIS 154295 (W.D.N.Y. Sept. 21, 2017) (where facts concerning the circumstances of the officer's shooting of plaintiff's dog were in dispute, the court denied the defendants' motion for summary judgment on the Fourth Amendment claim); *Branson v. Price*, 2015 U.S. Dist. LEXIS 126652 (D. Colo. Sept. 21, 2015).

In *Fuller v. Vines*, 36 F.3d 65 (9th Cir. 1994), plaintiffs (a father and his son) alleged they were in their yard with their dog, Champ (a twelve-year-old Labrador/ Great Dane mix), when two police officers passed by. Plaintiffs alleged that, as the officers approached, Champ merely stood up from where he had been lying. The officers contended Champ charged them, barking and growling. Plaintiffs allegedly pleaded with the officers not to shoot their dog and told them that Champ could be controlled. The officers shot Champ twice, and he died shortly thereafter. The officers claimed the son charged at them with a weapon after the shooting. Plaintiffs, on the other hand, alleged that when the son objected to the shooting, one officer pointed a gun at him and threatened to send him "to the morgue." *Fuller v. Vines*, 1996 U.S. Dist. LEXIS 3622, *4 (N.D. Cal. Mar. 25, 1996). The Ninth Circuit held that Champ was "property" that can be seized and that killing him constituted a seizure under the Fourth Amendment. On remand, the jury rendered the following special verdict: In shooting the dog, one of the officers violated plaintiffs' constitutional rights causing damages totaling $143,000, plus $10,000 in punitive damages; in assaulting the son, the other defendant was liable for damages of $77,000, plus $25,000 in punitive damages.

The Ninth Circuit considered this issue again in *San Jose Charter of Hells Angels Motorcycle Club v. City of San Jose*, 402 F.3d 962 (9th Cir. 2005), where police officers shot and killed three dogs, refusing to allow family or bystanders to assist one of the dogs who lay bleeding to death. The Ninth Circuit concluded:

> Here, the intrusion was severe. The officers shot and killed one of Souza's dogs, and two of the Vieiras' dogs. We have recognized that dogs are more than just a personal effect. *See Miller v. Clark County*, 340 F.3d 959, 968 n.13 (9th Cir. 2003). The emotional attachment to a family's dog is not comparable to a possessory interest in furniture. As noted in Lori Vieira's journal,

the effect of her being handcuffed just yards from where her dog Sam lay
dead and bleeding was extremely traumatic.

Id. at 975. In analyzing the issue, the court considered the fact that the police entry
teams had a week to plan the execution of the entry and they had advance knowledge of the presence of two guard dogs at one of the properties, giving the officers
"substantial time to develop strategies for immobilizing the dogs." *Id.* at 977. The
Ninth Circuit held that the shootings constituted an unreasonable seizure and an
unreasonable execution of search warrants in violation of the Fourth Amendment,
and affirmed the trial court's denial of the officers' summary judgment motion
claiming qualified immunity.

In *Criscuolo v. Grant County*, 540 Fed. Appx. 562 (9th Cir. Aug. 8, 2013), the officer claimed he was justified in shooting the plaintiff's dog, Slyder, in order to protect the officer's police dog, Maddox. The district court found that the shooting was
reasonable and, alternatively, that the officer was subject to qualified immunity. The
Ninth Circuit reversed the grant of summary judgment on the Fourth Amendment
claims and remanded for further proceedings, explaining:

> A reasonable trier of fact could find that Lamens [the officer] unreason-
> ably shot Slyder after the dogs separated, because Slyder posed no immi-
> nent threat to Maddox even though the events occurred rapidly. Criscuolo
> and other witnesses claim that right before Lamens fired, Slyder was not
> springing toward Maddox, Slyder was stationary or retreating at a distance
> of 10-20 feet from Lamens and Maddox, and Criscuolo was one to two feet
> away and about to leash Slyder.

Id. at 563. *See also Silva v. City of San Leandro*, 744 F. Supp. 2d 1036 (N.D. Cal. 2010)
(where police officers shot plaintiffs' dog, having known the dog was in the house
before they entered, the court denied defendants' summary judgment motion based
on questions of fact as to whether defendants violated plaintiffs' Fourth Amendment rights and whether qualified immunity applied).

In *Brown v. Muhlenberg Township.* 269 F.3d 205 (3d Cir. 2001), as plaintiffs were
in the process of moving from their home, unbeknownst to them their Rottweiler, Immi, wearing her bright pink collar with tags, wandered onto the neighboring parking lot. Defendant police officer saw her and approached her. Immi started
barking as the officer approached. Plaintiff Kim Brown looked out from an open
window and saw Immi and the officer facing each other as the officer reached for his
gun. She screamed, "That's my dog, don't shoot!" *Id.* at 209. The officer hesitated a
few seconds then fired five shots at Immi. He continued firing as she tried to crawl
away. *Id.* The Third Circuit held:

> The Browns had a possessory interest in their pet. In Pennsylvania, by
> statute, "All dogs are . . . declared to be personal property and subjects of
> theft." [Citations omitted.] It necessarily follows that Immi was property
> protected by the Fourth Amendment and that Officer Eberly's destruc-
> tion of her constituted a Fourth Amendment seizure. Accordingly, we join

two of our sister courts of appeals in holding that the killing of a person's dog by a law enforcement officer constitutes a seizure under the Fourth Amendment. *Fuller*, 36 F.3d at 68; *Lesher v. Reed*, 12 F.3d 148, 150–51 (8th Cir. 1994).

Id. at 210.

Considering the "reasonableness" of the officer's conduct in *Brown*, the court concluded that "the state may not, consistent with the Fourth Amendment, destroy a pet when [she] poses no immediate danger and the owner is looking on, obviously desirous of retaining custody." *Id.* at 211. Like the Ninth Circuit in *Fuller* and *San Jose Charter*, the Third Circuit held that the officer was not entitled to qualified immunity in defense of the Fourth Amendment claim. *Id.* at 212. The court, therefore, reversed the district court's grant of summary judgment in favor of the police officer. *See also Robinson v. Pezzat*, 818 F.3d 1 (D.C. Cir. 2016) (reversing the district court's grant of summary judgment in favor of the officer who shot plaintiff's dog); *Jones v. Lopez*, 689 Fed. Appx. 337 (5th Cir. Unpub. 2017) (questions of fact "as to what danger the dog posed to the police officers," and therefore on the applicability of qualified immunity defense, where police shot and killed plaintiff's eight-year-old Boxer who allegedly had no history of aggressive behavior and was recovering from a recent surgery).

On the other hand, some courts have granted summary judgment for officers, finding their conduct reasonable as a matter of law. In *Warboys v. Proulx*, 303 F. Supp. 2d 111 (D. Conn. 2004), for example, the canine victim was a "pit bull" approaching the officer (and his dog) at a rate of six feet per second. Because the court concluded it would have been too late to act if the officer had waited, the court held the officer acted reasonably, as a matter of law, in shooting the dog in the head — despite evidence that the owner/guardian was nearby and shouted to the officers that the dog was friendly and would not hurt them. *Id.* at 114. *See also Brown v. Battle Creek Police Dep't*, 844 F.3d 556 (6th Cir. 2016) (affirming the grant of summary judgment for the officers; finding that, as a matter of law, the officer's shooting of plaintiffs' two dogs while executing a warrant to search a gang member's home for controlled substances was reasonable and therefore protected by the qualified immunity defense); *Altman v. City of High Point, N.C.*, 330 F.3d 194 (4th Cir. 2003) (reversing trial court's denial of summary judgment, the majority held the officers' conduct in shooting plaintiffs' dogs was reasonable as a matter of law, factoring in the dogs' breed; the dissenting judge concluded the majority had misinterpreted the law and the factual evidence); *Dziekan v. Gaynor*, 376 F. Supp. 2d 267 (D. Conn. 2005) (granting defendant's summary judgment motion on qualified immunity; even though the court took plaintiff's version of the facts as true, including the statement that the dog would not bite and that plaintiff could have put him on a leash, the court concluded that the officer "could have reasonably assumed that the dog posed an imminent threat to his safety" and that he was "objectively reasonable in his belief that his conduct would not violate clearly established law").

Courts have recognized that there can be a Fourth Amendment seizure where an officer injures but does not kill an individual's dog. *See, e.g., Pettit v. State of New Jersey*, 2011 U.S. Dist. LEXIS 35452, *16 (D.N.J. Mar. 30, 2011) ("Although the dog, Trooper, in the present matter did not die as a result of the shooting, the Court assumes, without deciding, that the shooting and wounding of a dog by a law enforcement officer is a sufficiently meaningful interference with an owner's possessory interests in his property as to constitute a seizure."); *Esterson v. Broward County Sheriff's Dept.*, 2010 U.S. Dist. LEXIS 117490, *10 (S.D. Fla. Nov. 4, 2010) ("Despite the fact that Fred [the Dalmatian dog] was not killed by the shooting does not mean there was no seizure."). In both of these cases, however, the courts granted summary judgment for the defendants, finding the shootings reasonable as a matter of law. In *Esterson*, for example, the court found the shooting to be reasonable where plaintiff's Dalmatian allegedly charged at the officer when she was investigating a complaint regarding a barking dog on the premises. In *Pettit*, the evidence indicated the officer shot the dog "as the dog was about to spring," after the officer tried to avoid using force and after the dog "leaped aggressively" at him and landed approximately five feet in front of him. 2011 U.S. Dist. LEXIS 35452 at *20.

In addition, as the following case demonstrates, where the jury finds in favor of the officers based on the testimony and evidence presented at trial, a court of appeal, constrained by the applicable standard of review, may not be willing to overturn that finding.

Carroll v. County of Monroe

United States Court of Appeals, Second Circuit, 2013
712 F.3d 649

PER CURIAM:

Plaintiff-Appellant Sherry Carroll ("the plaintiff") appeals from a March 9, 2012, decision and order of the United States District Court for the Western District of New York, which denied the plaintiff's motion to set aside a jury verdict or, in the alternative, for a new trial. After a two-day trial, the jury found that the plaintiff failed to prove her claim—brought under 42 U.S.C. § 1983—that the shooting of her family's dog by Deputy James Carroll ("Deputy Carroll") during the execution of a search warrant of her home was an unconstitutional seizure in violation of the Fourth Amendment. On appeal, the plaintiff contends that the Defendants-Appellees' failure to train its officers regarding non-lethal means to secure dogs and to formulate a plan to restrain the plaintiff's dog using non-lethal means rendered Deputy Carroll's shooting of her dog unconstitutional as a matter of law.

BACKGROUND

The facts of this case are undoubtedly tragic. On October 11, 2006, Deputy Carroll and other officers from the Greater Rochester Area Narcotics Enforcement Team executed a "no-knock" warrant for the plaintiff's home. A no-knock warrant permits officers to enter a residence without knocking and announcing their presence and is issued when there is reason to believe that the occupants of the residence will, if the officers announce themselves prior to entry, pose a significant threat to officer safety or attempt to destroy evidence. The officers in this case used a battering ram to break through the front door, and Deputy Carroll, who was in charge of securing the entryway, was the first to enter the house. Deputy Carroll immediately saw a dog growling, barking, and quickly and aggressively approaching him. Once the dog had advanced to within a foot of him, Deputy Carroll fired one shot from his shotgun at the animal's head and killed him. According to Deputy Carroll, the plaintiff was not close enough to the dog to help restrain him from charging at the officers.

Prior to executing the warrant, Sergeant Michael DeSain briefed the team and mentioned that a dog would be present at the plaintiff's home. The team did not discuss a plan for controlling the dog or formulate a strategy to neutralize any threat the dog might pose by non-lethal means. Additionally, although the County had a written policy prohibiting the use of lethal force against an animal unless the animal posed a danger to officers or other persons, the County did not formally train its officers about how to handle encounters with dogs during searches. The officers testified that they would call animal control to help secure a dog when executing a normal warrant but never planned for non-lethal means to secure a dog during execution of a no-knock warrant.

The officers explained that executing a no-knock warrant requires them to move through the entryway (also called the "fatal funnel") as quickly as possible to avoid becoming easy targets for armed occupants. In DeSain's words, the officers "don't have the time" to use nonlethal means during execution of a no-knock warrant when confronted by a dog in the fatal funnel "because our lives are at risk entering that door." Moreover, the officers explained that any delay in securing the entryway and moving through the house could facilitate the destruction of evidence. They emphasized, however, that shooting a dog was often unnecessary during execution of a no-knock warrant when, for example, an owner is able to restrain the dog or where the dog runs away, lies down, or poses no threat to officer safety.

DISCUSSION

Federal Rule of Civil Procedure 50 provides that a motion for judgment as a matter of law will be granted only if there was no "legally sufficient evidentiary basis" for the jury to find for the nonmoving party. This is a "particularly heavy burden where, as here, the jury has deliberated in the case and actually returned its verdict in favor of the non-movant." *Cash v. Cnty. of Erie*, 654 F.3d 324, 333 (2d Cir. 2011) (internal quotation marks omitted). Therefore, we may set aside a verdict "only if there exists such a complete absence of evidence supporting the verdict that the jury's findings could only have been the result of sheer surmise and conjecture, or the evidence in favor of the movant is so overwhelming that reasonable and fair minded persons could not arrive at a verdict against it." *Id.* (internal quotation marks omitted). We must "consider the evidence in the light most favorable to the [nonmoving party] and . . . give that party the benefit of all reasonable inferences that the jury might have drawn in [its] favor." *Tolbert v. Queens Coll.*, 242 F.3d 58, 70 (2d Cir. 2001) (internal quotation marks omitted). Although the death of her dog was regrettable, we cannot conclude that the plaintiff has met this heavy burden.

As a number of our sister circuits have already concluded, the unreasonable killing of a companion animal constitutes an unconstitutional "seizure" of personal property under the Fourth Amendment. *See, e.g., Altman v. City of High Point*, 330 F.3d 194, 204–05 (4th Cir. 2003); *Brown v. Muhlenberg Twp.*, 269 F.3d 205, 211 (3d Cir. 2001); *Fuller v. Vines*, 36 F.3d 65, 68 (9th Cir. 1994), *overruled on other grounds by Robinson v. Solano Cnty.*, 278 F.3d 1007 (9th Cir. 2002); *Lesher v. Reed*, 12 F.3d 148, 151 (8th Cir. 1994). To determine whether a seizure is unreasonable, a court must "balance the nature and quality of the intrusion on the individual's Fourth Amendment interests against the importance of the governmental interest alleged to justify the intrusion" and determine whether "the totality of the circumstances justified [the] particular sort of . . . seizure." *Tennessee v. Garner*, 471 U.S. 1, 8–9 (1985) (internal quotation marks omitted). We have long held that the plaintiff has the burden to prove that a seizure was unreasonable. *See Ruggiero v. Krzeminski*, 928 F.2d 558, 562–63 (2d Cir. 1991).

There is no dispute that Deputy Carroll's shooting of the plaintiff's dog was a severe intrusion given the emotional attachment between a dog and an owner. *See San Jose Charter of Hells Angels Motorcycle Club v. City of San Jose*, 402 F.3d 962, 975 (9th Cir. 2005) ("*Hells Angels*"). On the other hand, ensuring officer safety and preventing the destruction of evidence are particularly significant governmental interests. Additionally, courts have held that, at least in some circumstances, it is reasonable for an officer to shoot a dog that he believes poses a threat to his safety or the safety of the community. *See, e.g., Altman*, 330 F.3d at 205–06; *Brown*, 269 F.3d at 210–11. The key question, then, is whether a jury could reasonably conclude that the plaintiff had failed to prove that Deputy Carroll's actions were unreasonable under the totality of the circumstances.

A reasonable jury certainly could have found—based on the evidence presented—that no amount of planning or training would have changed the unfortunate outcome in this case. The plaintiff offered no evidence that any non-lethal means of controlling her dog would have allowed the officers to quickly escape the "fatal funnel" and effectively execute the no-knock warrant. In other words, the jury could have reasonably found that Deputy Carroll would still have needed to shoot the plaintiff's dog even if the officers had developed a non-lethal plan to restrain the dog.

Although the plaintiff's counsel mentioned the possibility of using pepper spray, a taser, or a catch pole, the plaintiff offered no evidence that these non-lethal means would have been effective or that it would have been unreasonable for the officers to decide not to use them. Deputy Carroll testified that he had never heard of pepper spray effectively controlling an aggressive dog, and he also explained that the department did not own tasers at the time. A jury could reasonably conclude that using a catch pole in the middle of the entryway would compromise officer safety and unreasonably delay the search, allowing the occupants to destroy evidence, or worse, arm themselves. The jury could further have reasonably found that an officer in Deputy Carroll's position should not be required to enter a house holding pepper spray or a taser and thereby compromise his ability to defend himself from possible gunfire. Also, unlike scenarios in which a dog might not pose a genuine threat to officer safety, *see, e.g., Erwin v. Cnty. of Manitowoc,* 872 F.2d 1292, 1299–1300 (7th Cir. 1989), there was sufficient evidence here for the jury to find that Deputy Carroll reasonably feared for his safety when the plaintiff's dog aggressively approached him in the entryway. In sum, the jury was entitled to believe the officers' testimony that non-lethal methods would not have been effective in this particular case, and we cannot say that its verdict was wholly without a "sufficient evidentiary basis." Fed. R. Civ. P. 50(a).

We do not believe that the Ninth Circuit's decision in *Hells Angels*—on which the plaintiff bases nearly her entire argument—compels a different result. Although we agree with the Ninth Circuit that the failure to plan adequately for the presence of dogs during a search could contribute to a Fourth Amendment violation under certain circumstances, *see Hells Angels,* 402 F.3d at 976–78, the officers' conduct there was far more unreasonable than the police conduct here. The officers in *Hells Angels* executed normal (*i.e.,* knock and announce) warrants to search two residences where they knew dogs would be present. At one residence, the officers did not encounter the dog until they had already cleared the residence and—for unknown reasons—ventured into the backyard; the dog then charged at an officer, and the officer killed the dog. *Id.* at 968. The other residence was encircled by a tall fence, and three guard dogs were on the opposite side. *Id.* at 969. After an officer poked one dog with his shotgun and the dog did not retreat, the officer shot at the dogs (killing two) so that the police could cut through the fence and safely move toward the residence. *Id.*

In both instances, the officers had ample time to utilize non-lethal means without compromising their safety or the search, especially given that they were not executing no-knock warrants and were not in a "fatal funnel." The officer at the first residence could simply have left the dog outside and conducted the search in complete safety, and the officers at the second residence were separated from the dogs by a fence. If the officers had formulated a better plan for the search, they would probably not have needed to shoot the dogs. In fact, as the Ninth Circuit pointed out, the execution of the warrant at the second residence might have been *better* served by non-lethal means because the gunfire alerted the occupants of police presence and could have allowed them time to destroy evidence.[1] *Id.* at 976. Under these cir-

---

1. To the extent the Ninth Circuit implied that use of a battering ram might similarly undermine an officer's justification that shooting a dog was necessary to prevent the destruction of evidence by ruining the element of surprise, *see id.* at 976, we do not agree. When, as in this case,

cumstances, there is little doubt that better planning would have obviated any need to shoot the dogs, but, as explained above, a reasonable jury would not necessarily have been required to reach the same conclusion in this case. At any rate, even on the much stronger facts in *Hells Angels*, the Ninth Circuit simply held that summary judgment on qualified immunity grounds for the defendants was not warranted, and that the case could proceed to trial. It did not hold, as the plaintiff would have us do, that the plaintiffs there were entitled to judgment as a matter of law.

As a cautionary note, however, we do not mean to endorse the defendants' apparent position that the failure to plan for the known presence of a dog is always acceptable when the police are executing a no-knock warrant. We merely decide that under the particular facts of this case, especially given the high burden that a party must meet to successfully challenge a jury verdict, the jury was not unreasonable to conclude that the plaintiff did not meet her burden of proof. There may very well be circumstances under which a plaintiff could prove that lack of an adequate plan rendered the shooting of his or her dog unreasonable even during execution of a no-knock warrant, and we urge the defendants to consider whether more comprehensive training and planning would better serve the public, as well as its officers, in the future.[2]

* * *

For the foregoing reasons, the judgment of the district court is affirmed.

Notes

1. Fourth Amendment claims most frequently arise in cases where government officials shoot and injure or kill companion animals, generally dogs, while searching premises for other reasons. However, these claims may arise in other contexts, such as where the seizure of the animals was the government's intended goal. For example, in *Maldonado v. Fontanes*, 568 F.3d 263 (1st Cir. 2009), animals belonging to residents of public housing complexes were taken in two successive raids, within days of the Municipality of Barceloneta assuming control of the public housing complexes from the Puerto Rico Public Housing Administration. Residents of three such complexes brought a civil rights suit under 42 U.S.C. § 1983 against the Mayor of Barceloneta, "protesting the precipitous seizures and cruel killings of their pet cats and dogs" and asserting "violations of their Fourth Amendment rights to be free from unreasonable seizures of their 'effects'" and their Fourteenth Amendment procedural and substantive due process rights. Plaintiffs alleged that before that

---

entry is achieved upon one thrust of the battering ram, it only provides the occupants with a few seconds of advanced warning and is hardly enough time to allow for the destruction of evidence. The occupants would only have had the chance to destroy evidence in this case if the officers had been delayed by trying to control the dog using non-lethal means.

2. Deputy Carroll, in particular, has apparently killed two other dogs in the course of executing no-knock search warrants, which indicates that officers in the County encounter these situations more frequently than they would probably prefer and that planning and training—while not always constitutionally required—may be advisable to avoid future tragedies and future litigation.

transfer they had been permitted to have pets, and that only a few days before the raids residents were told to "surrender their pets" or face eviction from their homes. They alleged that "after many of the pets were seized, the pets were killed by slamming them into the sides of vans and by hurling the survivors off a 50-foot-high bridge" and that some plaintiffs "eventually found their family pets dead under the bridge." *Id.* at 266. Ten days after the Municipality assumed the position of administrator of public housing complexes, it resigned that position.

The mayor, in his personal capacity, moved to dismiss all damages claims against him on grounds of qualified immunity. That motion was denied and, on an interlocutory appeal, the First Circuit affirmed the denial.

Having failed to obtain an early dismissal based on the pleadings, in subsequent proceedings the mayor and the other defendants moved for summary judgment. *Maldonado v. Municipio de Barceloneta*, 682 F. Supp. 2d 109 (D.P.R. 2010). For purposes of summary judgment, taking all inferences in favor of the plaintiffs, the court concluded that the animals taken from outside their homes could not reasonably have been thought to be strays, the defendants had not established that any of the animals taken posed an immediate threat to life and liberty, and the plaintiffs who allegedly voluntarily gave up their pets were coerced into doing so and, therefore, did not "consent" to the seizure. Accordingly, the court denied defendants' summary judgment motion on Fourth Amendment grounds for those plaintiffs whose dogs or cats were taken, and allowed the case to go forward to trial.

The case later settled, with the municipal defendants paying a total of $300,000 to the plaintiffs whose pets had been seized. *Maldonado v. Municipio de Barceloneta*, 2011 U.S. Dist. LEXIS 93130 (D.P.R. Aug. 19, 2011).

2. Another example is *Mayfield v. Bethards,* 826 F.3d 1252 (10th Cir. 2016), where two deputies saw plaintiffs' two dogs lying in plaintiffs' unfenced front yard, the deputies entered the yard without a warrant and both deputies began shooting at the dogs. One of the deputies missed the first dog, who fled back into the house, while the other deputy shot at the second dog, Majka, three times, killing her on the front porch. The deputy who killed Majka argued, based on the explanation in his police report, that even if the Fourth Amendment applied, the killing was reasonable because "he thought she had attacked livestock and he believed Kansas law allows anyone to kill a dog reported to have done so." *Id.* at 1256. (Such statutes and fact patterns are discussed in Section 4 of this chapter.) The case reached the Tenth Circuit on appeal from a motion to dismiss, early in the case, where the court's review was limited to the complaint and any documents it incorporated, which did not include the police report but did attach a letter in which plaintiffs had written to the sheriff disputing "as a case of 'mistaken identity' an accusation that Majka had mauled a neighbor's livestock a year before [the deputy] shot her." *Id.* at 1256-57. Applying the standards applicable to a motion to dismiss—accepting the allegations in the complaint as true and viewing all reasonable inferences from those facts in favor of the plaintiffs—the court denied the motion to dismiss, inferring that the

killing was not a reasonable seizure and therefore that the complaint asserted facts sufficient to show a violation of plaintiffs' "clearly established" Fourth Amendment rights. *Id.* at 1258, 1259.

3. At least one court has relied on state dog licensing statutes (under which it was a misdemeanor to possess unlicensed dogs) to deem unlicensed dogs "contraband"—*i.e.*, "property that is illegal to produce or possess"—and not protected by the Fourth Amendment but that ruling was reversed on appeal. *Smith v. City of Detroit*, 2017 U.S. Dist. LEXIS 121387, *15-*20 (E.D. Mich., So. Div., Aug. 2, 2017) *reversed*, 2018 U.S. App. LEXIS 28890 (6th Cir. Oct. 15, 2018).

4. On the other hand, in 2016 a dog owner reportedly received a settlement of $262,000 after a police officer shot his dog. Lucy Schouten, *What's a dog worth? Colorado court says $262,000*, CHRISTIAN SCIENCE MONITOR, Jan. 26, 2016. According to the article, a neighbor filmed the encounter and the video showed the dog "cowering before three officers." The article reported that there were websites tracking police shootings, citing to *https://www.facebook.com/DogsShotbyPolice/* and noted that at least one writer for The Washington Post has suggested that police try tactics that have helped post office employees, citing to *https://www.washingtonpost.com/posteverything/wp/2015/11/13/police-can-shoot-your-dog-for-no-reason-it-doesnt-have-to-be-that-way/*. According to the article, to provide a similar resource to the police as one that is provided to the post office, the National Canine Research Council (described as a New York-based think tank) has provided a series of instructional videos for police who may be involved in encounters with dogs. *See http://nationalcanineresearchcouncil.com/police-resources/*.

5. In 2014, a Maryland police officer investigating a robbery shot and killed a family's dog. In 2017, after trial in the family's lawsuit, a jury reportedly awarded $1.26 million, described as "the largest civil judgment in U.S. history for a pet's death at the hands of police." Arin Greenwood, *Courts are awarding significant damages to families whose dogs are killed by police*, ABA JOURNAL (Apr. 2018). The court later reduced the judgment to $207,500 under a Maryland statute limiting government liability. According to the same ABA Journal article, in 2017, the city of Hartford, Connecticut settled for $885,000 with a family whose dog was shot and killed during what the Second Circuit deemed to be an unlawful search.

6. For more on police killings of companion dogs, see Genette Gaffney, *6,083 Dogs Shot and Killed: The Unknown Puppycide Epidemic in America*, 24 ANIMAL L. 197 (2018).

Section 2. Veterinary Malpractice

The majority of actions contemplated and brought with respect to injuries to or deaths of companion animals in America involve the conduct of veterinarians. This is no comment on the quality of veterinary medicine or veterinarians, but a function of the fact that guardians bring their companion animals to veterinarians on a regular and increasing basis, and that the results do not always turn out the way the guardians expected. As in the human medical arena, in some instances this is because of negligence (or, in the very rare case, intentional acts) of the veterinarian.

Section 1 of this chapter considered theories of liability that could apply in veterinary malpractice cases as well as in other contexts. Section 3 will address damages and valuation issues that apply to veterinary malpractice cases as well as to other cases of alleged tortious harm to companion animals. This section addresses solely the standard of care and theories of liability specific to veterinary malpractice, which is a significant enough area of the law to warrant a separate discussion.

In medical malpractice cases, physicians have long been held to the standard of care ordinarily possessed by other similarly situated physicians. As discussed in the Notes after *Price v. Brown* below, the same standard generally has been applied to veterinarians. In cases of veterinary malpractice, as opposed to medical malpractice, however, the practical effect of this standard on the parties to the litigation and the circumstances under which it may be applied are not always clear.

Price v. Brown

Supreme Court of Pennsylvania, 1996
545 Pa. 216, 680 A.2d 1149

ZAPPALA, Justice. The issue presented in this appeal is whether a complaint based upon an alleged breach of a bailment agreement states a cause of action for injury or death suffered by an animal that has been entrusted to a veterinarian for surgical and professional treatment. We hold that allegations of breach of a bailment agreement are insufficient to state a cause of action against a veterinarian who has performed surgery on an animal when the animal suffers an injury as a result or does not survive the surgery.

On May 4, 1993, Tracy Price filed a complaint against Nancy O. Brown, a veterinarian, alleging that she had delivered her English Bulldog to Dr. Brown for surgical treatment to correct a prolapsed urethra. Dr. Brown performed the surgery on August 30, 1991. The next evening, Price visited the dog at the veterinary hospital. She inquired into the dog's condition after observing that the dog was panting strenuously and appeared groggy. She requested that the dog be monitored on a 24-hour basis and was assured that would be done by an unidentified agent of Dr. Brown's. Price alleged that the dog was left unattended after midnight that evening. During the morning of September 1, 1991, the dog died.

In her complaint, Price asserted liability based only upon a theory of bailment. Price alleged that the dog had been entrusted to Dr. Brown in reliance upon the promise and representation that she would perform the necessary surgery and return the dog to her in the same general good health as before. Price alleged that Dr. Brown had breached the agreement by failing to monitor the dog's condition and by failing to return the dog in good health. Price alleged that the fair market value of the dog was $1,200.00 and demanded judgment in that amount.

Preliminary objections in the nature of a demurrer were filed to the complaint. By order dated October 12, 1993, the trial court sustained the preliminary objections and dismissed the complaint without prejudice. The trial court concluded that allegations of a breach of a bailment agreement, without more, are insufficient to state a cause of action against a veterinarian for death or injury to an animal entrusted to his or her care for professional treatment.

The Superior Court reversed, finding that the complaint was sufficient to state a cause of action for breach of a bailment agreement and that the issue of whether a bailment agreement existed under the specific facts alleged was a matter for the fact finder. The court did not consider the allegation that Dr. Brown failed to monitor the dog overnight and its implications of negligent care, reasoning that where the owner of an animal chooses to bring a cause of action in bailment rather than negligence the only relevant question is whether sufficient facts are presented to support an implied agreement between the parties. The matter was remanded for further proceedings.

We granted allocatur and now reverse and reinstate the trial court's order dismissing the complaint.

* * *

As to a cause of action based on the negligence of a veterinarian in the performance of his/her professional duties or services, we note at the outset that malpractice claims have traditionally arisen in the context of services provided by the legal and medical professions. Similar to the practice of law or medicine, the vocation of veterinary medicine involves specialized education, knowledge, and skills. We conclude, therefore, that professional negligence concepts also extend to veterinary medicine.

The practice of veterinary medicine is extensively regulated in Pennsylvania under the Veterinary Medicine Practice Act, 63 P.S. §485.1 *et seq*. "Veterinary medicine" is defined as the "branch of medicine which deals with the diagnosis, prognosis, treatment, administration, prescription, operation or manipulation or application of any apparatus or appliance for any disease, pain, deformity, defect, injury, wound or physical condition of any animal or for the prevention of or the testing for the presence of any disease." 63 P.S. §485.3(9).

The Act established a State Board of Veterinary Medicine within the Department of State whose duties include, *inter alia*, the adoption of rules and regulations governing the practice of veterinary medicine, approval of qualifications of applicants for a license to practice, and regulation of licensed veterinarians. 63 P.S. §§485.4, 485.5. A person who intends to practice veterinary medicine in Pennsylvania must obtain a license and maintain registration. The board may license to practice veterinary medicine any applicant who pays the requisite fee and submits satisfactory evidence that he or she: (1) is at least eighteen years old; (2) has graduated from an approved school or college of veterinary medicine; (3) has passed a license examination required by the board; and (4) has not been convicted of a felonious act prohibited by The Controlled Substance, Drug, Device and Cosmetic Act. 63 P.S. § 485.9.

To state a cause of action based upon the negligent acts or omissions of a veterinarian in the performance of professional duties or services, the plaintiff must plead (1) the employment of the veterinarian or other basis for the duty; (2) the veterinarian's failure to exercise the appropriate standard of care; and (3) that the veterinarian's departure from that standard was the proximate cause of the animal's injury or death. A plaintiff must specifically allege that the veterinarian was negligent in the performance of his professional services. . . .

* * *

[*Editors' Note: Since plaintiff had not asserted a claim alleging professional negligence, the court reinstated the trial court order dismissing the case.*]

CASTILLE, JUSTICE (dissenting). The majority here holds that a complaint based upon a breach of bailment agreement is insufficient to state a cause of action against a veterinarian who performs surgical procedures on an animal where the animal suffers an injury or expires as a result of these procedures. Instead, the majority creates a new cause of action, veterinary medical malpractice, and holds that in such situations as here this new cause of action extends to veterinarians who perform surgical or medical procedures on an animal in a negligent manner. Because I believe that bailment theories are adequate to address such situations and that professional medical malpractice concepts should not be extended by this Court to the field of veterinary medicine, I must respectfully dissent.

As noted by the majority, a "bailment" is a delivery of personalty for the accomplishment of some purpose upon a contract, express or implied, that after the purpose has been fulfilled, the personalty shall be redelivered to the person who delivered it in the same or an agreed to altered form. Typical bailment agreements involve items of personal property such as automobiles. The present case concerns delivery of a pet dog to a veterinarian for surgical procedures. Under Pennsylvania law, dogs are recognized as personal property. *See* 3 P.S. § 459.601(a), The Dog Law. Case law within this jurisdiction demonstrates that animals may be the subject of bailments. Thus, since dogs by statute are personal property in the eyes of the law, they are capable of being the subject of a bailment agreement.

Since dogs are capable of being the subject of a bailment agreement, the bailor (dog owner) bears the ultimate burden of proof in a bailment cause of action. As stated in *Schell v. Miller N. Broad Storage Co.*, 16 A.2d 680 (Pa. Super. Ct. 1940):

> When the bailor has proved a bailment, a demand and failure to deliver, it then becomes incumbent upon the bailee to go forward with proofs not necessarily showing that he used proper care in handling the bailment but merely showing by clear and satisfactory proof that the goods were lost, and

the manner that they were lost. When the bailee has furnished such proof satisfactory to the court and jury and if such proofs do not disclose lack of due care on his part, then the bailor, if he should recover, must prove negligence on the part of the bailee and the bailee's negligence becomes a vital issue.

Id. at 683–84. I believe that this standard of proof imposes a reasonable burden on veterinarians in situations involving medical or surgical procedures on animals since a veterinarian will still have to explain the course of treatment for the animal in question and adequately explain why the animal was not returned as per the bailment agreement. Therefore, since an animal is subject to bailment agreements and no undue burden is placed on veterinarians by the bailment cause of action, I believe that bailment theories are adequate to address situations where veterinarians perform medical or surgical procedures on an animal and the animal is not returned in the same condition as when it was delivered.

Like the majority, I recognize that veterinarians are somewhat similar to physicians and surgeons in that they are medically educated individuals who provide a great service to society and that their practice is extensively regulated by the Commonwealth. I, however, do not believe that it follows from these similarities that medical malpractice principles normally applied only to physicians and surgeons who operate on human beings should be extended to veterinarians. Such an expansion is unwarranted because the subject matter of the treatment (humans, as opposed to animals) is vastly different. . . .

I also believe that medical malpractice principles should not be extended to veterinarians because, unlike medical malpractice actions in physician and surgeon cases, the victim of veterinary malpractice is incapable of bringing a cause of action against the veterinarian. . . . As personal property, a dog or any other animal, unlike a human being, cannot bring a cause of action against the veterinarian who treated it. Rather, the animal's owner must institute the suit and the owner of the animal is not legally the direct victim of the malpractice.

Moreover, I find it improper for the majority here to create a veterinary medical malpractice cause of action because if such causes of action are to be extended to the owners of animals, be they pets or otherwise, I believe such a mandate should come from the General Assembly and not this Court.

Thus, I believe existing bailment theories provide an adequate and fair remedy to owners who unfortunately lose the faithful companionship of their pet animals or the use and benefit of their working animals from injuries or death suffered as a result of medical or surgical procedures performed by veterinarians. . . .

* * *

Notes

1. In *Price v. Brown*, the complaint was dismissed because the plaintiff failed to assert a claim for professional negligence, but instead alleged only breach of

the bailment agreement. The medical purpose for which plaintiff's bulldog was entrusted to the veterinarian's care was a material fact in the court's determination. Under *Price*, would a bailment claim lie if an animal is simply kenneled at a veterinarian's office, as opposed to being there for medical treatment?

2. Should the standards regarding bailment differ depending on whether the bailed property is an inanimate object or a living sentient being? Should it matter whether the living being is kept for profit or whether that being is considered by the owner/guardian as a family member?

3. For a discussion of the interplay between bailment and veterinary malpractice causes of action, *see* Katie Scott, Note: *Bailment and Veterinary Malpractice: Doctrinal Exclusivity, or Not?*, 55 HASTINGS L.J. 1009 (2004).

4. *Standard of Care: Historical Background*

In human medical malpractice cases, physicians have long been held to the standard of "learning, skill and ability which others similarly situated ordinarily possess." *Williams v. Reynolds*, 263 S.E.2d 853, 855 (N.C. Ct. App. 1980). "Similarly situated" has been described as "envision[ing] a standard of professional competence and care customary in the field of practice among practitioners in similar communities." *Id*. The same standard generally has been applied in veterinary malpractice cases. *See, e.g., id*. (considering "accepted medical practices respecting the treatment of a horse" in similar communities).

In *Conkey v. Carpenter*, 106 Mich. 1 (1895), a veterinarian sued to collect his fees for services rendered treating a horse. The court required the plaintiff to establish his qualifications as a veterinarian as a predicate to collection. Although *Conkey* was not a malpractice case, the court noted that "[p]hysicians who are graduates of medical colleges, or are admitted to practice under the laws of the State, will be presumed competent, and malpractice will then be the only question to determine in the individual case." *Id*. at 5. The court set forth the standard of care for physicians and surgeons, noting it applied equally to veterinary surgeons since "[i]t requires education to be able to treat diseases of dumb animals as well as diseases of men." *Id*. at 4–5.

In *Bekkemo v. Erickson*, 242 N.W. 617 (Minn. 1932), plaintiff sued a veterinarian for failing to correctly diagnose and treat plaintiff's hogs. Although the cause of action sounded in negligence, the court essentially applied a medical malpractice standard, holding the defendant to the standard of "ordinary care as established by the standards of veterinary medicine in his community." *Id*. at 619. *See also Cook v. Dayton*, 8 Haw. 8 (1889) (expressly recognizing malpractice cause of action against veterinarian).

The analysis flows in both directions. In *Gillette v. Tucker*, 65 N.E. 865 (Ohio 1902), the court expressly adopted a similar malpractice analysis for all doctors, regardless of the species they treated. In *Gillette*, the defendant was a surgeon. The court followed prior case law, stating:

[W]e found a pointed authority in the case of *Williams v. Gilman*, 71 Me. 21. While that case involved the conduct or misconduct of a veterinary surgeon, we have no doubt its doctrine may be applied to the conduct of surgeons practicing their profession upon a human being.

Id. at 869. The court went on to discuss the standard of care for physicians, again comparing veterinary and medical practice:

This [standard of care], we believe, is a sound and salutary rule to govern the relation existing between the patient and the surgeon, who practices his profession and undertakes the serious operation described in this record. If such care is due to a dumb animal, it is surely due to a human being.

Id.

5. *Standard of Care: More Recent Cases*

Some courts in more recent cases have taken a similar approach:

As often happens, the pet (in this case, a Great Dane puppy) took ill on the weekend and the owner was unable to reach a veterinarian. To those who are not indoctrinated in this field of unusual medicine, a veterinarian in relatively suburban Nassau County may, with no disrespect meant to either medical specialty, be referred to with love and affection as a "pet's family pediatrician."

Animal Hospital of Elmont, Inc. v. Gianfrancisco, 418 N.Y.S. 2d 992, 993 (Dist. Ct., 2d Dist., Nassau Cty. 1979). *See also Fackler v. Genetzky*, 595 N.W.2d 884, 889 (Neb. 1999) (relying on an 1890 Nebraska case to apply "standards of professional negligence to a malpractice action involving a veterinarian"); *Ladnier v. Norwood*, 781 F.2d 490, 492 (5th Cir. 1986) ("Louisiana courts have turned to medical malpractice cases in analyzing veterinary malpractice cases"; applying the same standards); *Mutual Service Cas. Co. v. Ambrecht*, 142 F. Supp. 2d 1101, 1111 (N.D. Iowa 2001) (court noted in *dicta* that facts alleged against veterinarian "seem to fit squarely within a claim for professional malpractice").

In *Williamson v. Prida*, 75 Cal. App. 4th 1417, 1425 (1999), the court held that the medical malpractice standard applies to veterinary malpractice cases. To reach this conclusion, the court looked to out-of-state cases and California statutes, such as California Code of Civil Procedure sections 340.5 and 597.5 (treating both types of cases the same for purposes of the statute of limitations) and California Business & Professions Code section 4800 *et seq.* (categorizing both medical doctors and veterinarians as licensed health care providers). *See also Quigley v. McClellan*, 214 Cal. App. 4th 1276 (2013) (citing to *Williamson v. Prida* to require expert testimony to establish the community standard of care and causation, as required in medical malpractice cases).

In several states there is conflicting authority on this issue. *See Storozuk v. W.A. Butler Co.*, 203 N.E.2d 511 (Ohio Ct. of Common Pleas 1964) (the court looked to other Ohio statutes to conclude that "malpractice" within the meaning of Ohio Revised Code section 2305.11, which sets forth the statute of limitations for certain "malpractice" claims, includes the practice of veterinary medicine); *Turner v. Sinha*, 582 N.E.2d 1018 (Ohio Ct. App. 1989) (applying standard of care "as applied to professionals"); *Williams v. Midland Acres, Inc.*, 77 N.E.3d 583 (Ohio Ct. App. 2017) (applying the standard of care set forth in *Turner*, and reversing grant of summary judgment in favor of the defendant on plaintiff's veterinary malpractice claims based on conflicting expert affidavits); *Cerimele v. Van Buren*, 2013 Ohio App. LEXIS 1159 (Ct. App. Mar. 29, 2013) (quoting the standard set forth in *Turner*, noting the requirement for expert testimony in veterinary malpractices cases as in medical malpractice cases). *But see Hitchcock v. Conklin*, 669 N.E.2d 563 (Ohio Ct. App. 1995) (refusing to expand the meaning of "malpractice" beyond those professions specified in the statute, the court concluded that section 2305.11 does not include veterinarians).

In *Southall v. Gabel*, 28 Ohio App. 2d 295, 277 N.E.2d 230 (1971), the plaintiff alleged that the defendant veterinary clinic so mishandled her three-year-old horse (Pribal), that Pribal sustained physical injuries and emotional trauma, and that Pribal's emotional stability deteriorated thereafter, until he finally had to be euthanized. In *dicta* supporting its holding that the case involved negligence, rather than malpractice, the court stated:

> The very essence of "malpractice" is the patient-physician relationship upon which the trial court relied in this case. The conclusion of the court is a bit strained in this case when it is noted that it was the left front knee of the colt "Pribal" that required surgery and not that of his owner, the plaintiff, Mrs. Southall. The patient-physician relationship was that between the colt and Dr. Gabel, the defendant. That, in the slang vernacular, is "a horse of a different color." . . . Until the Supreme Court speaks, veterinarians are not included in the definition of malpractice.

Id. at 298, 299. For a full recitation of the facts of this case, *see Southall v. Gabel*, 293 N.E.2d 891 (Ohio Muni. Ct., Franklin Cty. 1972) (trial after remand of appellate decision above).

A similar split of authority exists in Texas. *See Downing v. Gully*, 915 S.W.2d 181, 183 (Tex. Ct. App. 1996) ("Because there is currently no case law in Texas establishing how veterinary negligence cases are to be analyzed, we will, as other jurisdictions have done, adopt the standard applied to physicians and surgeons in medical malpractice cases."); *McGee v. Smith*, 107 S.W.3d 725, 727 (Tex. Ct. App. 2003) (relying on the standard in *Downing*, the court required the plaintiff to present expert testimony to support his claim, as a medical malpractice plaintiff would have to do); *Gonzalez v. S. Tex. Veterinary Assocs.*, 2013 Tex. App. LEXIS 15215 (Ct. App. Dec. 19, 2013) (following the standard set forth in *Downing*, the court reversed summary judgment in favor of the veterinary clinic based on plaintiff's expert report regarding standard of care and the clinic's failure to comply with it). *But see Pruitt v. Box*, 984 S.W.2d 709, 711 (Tex. Ct. App. 1998) (expressly disagreeing with *Downing*, the court was "not convinced that the standard applicable to medical malpractice on human beings should be applied to veterinary malpractice cases in light of Texas law relegating animals to personal property status").

In another case, a Texas court cited to *Downing* as part of its rationale for not allowing a claim for damages for pain and suffering and for mental anguish in a veterinary negligence case. *Zeid v. Pearce*, 953 S.W.2d 368, 370 (Tex. Ct. App. 1997). The court concluded that since the Texas Supreme Court has precluded bystander recovery for mental anguish in medical malpractice cases, the court saw "no reason why the same rule would not apply in cases involving death due to veterinary malpractice." *Id.*

The law establishing the standard of care based on that in "similar communities" has undergone significant changes in many jurisdictions with respect to medical malpractice cases. *See* Joseph H. King, Jr., *The Standard of Care for Veterinarians in Medical Malpractice Claims*, 58 TENN. L. REV. 1, 21 n.85 (1990). According to King, since there appears to be no reason to treat the two professions differently in this regard, it is likely that courts in veterinary cases will follow the lead of the more recent medical malpractice cases on this issue. *Id. See, e.g., Ladnier, supra,* 781 F.2d at 493 (veterinarians "should be held, like physicians, to the standard of care expected of practitioners in their specialty, namely, equine medicine").

In one case, where a racetrack veterinarian was sued for malpractice, the court rejected the "locality rule" in favor of a higher standard:

> [A]ssuming *arguendo* the locality rule applies to veterinarians, it was designed to protect small town physicians from charges that they failed to exercise big city expertise which they reasonably would not have. However, where a defendant is part of a professional community, he or she is bound by the possibly higher standards notwithstanding such association extends beyond the defendant's geographic locality or even State lines. We take judicial notice that numerous major racetracks are being operated through the State of New York. In the absence of any evidence that the level of expertise being practiced by veterinarians at these facilities is less than that existing at racetracks in Pennsylvania, Delaware and New Jersey, we decline to apply a lesser standard.

Restrepo v. State of New York, 550 N.Y.S.2d 536, 541 (Ct. Cl. 1989). *See also Carter v. Louisiana State University*, 520 So. 2d 383, 387 (La. 1988) ("locality standard is inapplicable to a veterinary specialist").

5.a. As in medical malpractice cases, if the conduct was not within the realm of professional negligence, and needed no expert testimony, plaintiffs may not be required to prove a breach of the standard of care or meet other malpractice requirements.

> As a general rule, expert testimony is necessary to establish the applicable standard of care, as well as deviation from such standard, which resulted in injury, unless the case is one within the experience and observation of

the average layperson. [¶] It has been held that expert testimony may be dispensed with in a veterinary malpractice action "where the very nature of the acts complained of bespeaks improper treatment and malpractice."

Astarita v. Croton Animal Hospital, 2016 N.Y. Misc. LEXIS 3311, *8 (N.Y. City Ct., Westchester Cty. Sept. 19, 2016).

In *Moses v. Richardson*, 2001 Cal. App. Unpub. LEXIS 1154 (Ct. App. Nov. 29, 2001), defendant performed an endoscopic exam on plaintiffs' horse, Rossa, while Rossa was exercising on a treadmill. After the exam, as the technician was slowing the treadmill to turn it off, Rossa caught her back hooves between the moving belt and a metal plate at the end of the treadmill. Her legs were seriously injured and she had to be euthanized. Plaintiffs sued the veterinarian, his technician and the veterinary facility, alleging negligence. After the close of plaintiffs' case, the veterinarian moved for nonsuit on the ground that plaintiffs did not present expert veterinary testimony on the standard of care applicable to him or the technician. The trial court denied the motion, finding that the negligence claims were not based on professional malpractice but on the handling of a horse and operation of a treadmill, issues on which plaintiffs had presented expert testimony. After completion of the trial, the jury found in favor of the plaintiffs; defendants appealed.

On appeal, defendants relied on *Williamson v. Prida, supra,* to support their position that expert medical testimony on the standard of care was required. The appellate court rejected this argument, noting that treadmills are used both inside and outside the veterinary context and that a horse should be handled the same on a treadmill regardless of the setting. The court noted that if a horse was injured on a treadmill at a training facility, expert medical testimony would not be required to prove negligence. The court affirmed the judgment.

5.b. *Ladnier, supra,* raised (but did not resolve) another issue—statutory consent to medical treatment and battery claims. Plaintiff asserted a claim under the Louisiana "Consent to Medical Treatment" statute (LA. REV. STAT. ANN. § 40:1299.40). Plaintiff argued that it would be "logical and fair" to apply the statute in the context of a veterinary malpractice case. The court noted that the basis of the statute is traced to the tort of battery. The court commented, in *dicta*, that "[t]herefore, it seems equally 'logical' that the statute should be applied only to human patients." 781 F.2d at 494. The Fifth Circuit, however, did not rule on this issue.

Consider in this context the case of *In the Matter of Lillian Kline*, No. A-1788-95T5 (N.J. Super. Ct. App. Div. July 12, 1996), where a service dog was attacked by teenagers throwing stones. In permitting the service dog's owner/guardian recovery under New Jersey's crime victims' compensation law, the court concluded "in view of the function of the dog as a veritable extension of appellant's own body, an injury to the dog is tantamount to an injury to appellant's person." Do you think Lillian Kline would also have had a viable claim for battery against the teenagers? What if the dog had been harmed by veterinary malpractice? (This case is discussed further in Chapter 7.)

5.c. Do veterinarians serve "patients" or "clients" (or both)? Does the answer dictate which standard of care (*i.e.*, medical malpractice versus simple negligence) should apply in veterinary cases? Consider the argument by some judges in the above cases that because the physician-patient relationship in veterinary negligence exists between the animal and the veterinarian, the "community standard" approach should not be used. The interests of animals aside, are there valid public policy reasons for applying the medical malpractice standard to veterinarians, or does a simple negligence standard make more sense?

How might the application of a professional malpractice standard as opposed to a negligence standard, or *vice versa*, impact the parties or affect the outcome of the case?

6. *Statutes Applicable to "Health Care Providers"*

As noted above, in some jurisdictions statutory law includes veterinarians in the definition of "health care providers," at least in certain contexts. This may raise questions beyond "standard of care" issues. Lawyers filing veterinary malpractice actions should carefully consider any similar statutory provisions in their own jurisdiction to determine whether and to what extent it may impact procedure and possibly the outcome of the lawsuit as well.

One might expect that applying medical malpractice statutes to veterinarians would be helpful to plaintiffs, by holding veterinarians to a high standard and possibly recognizing the animals as their patients with appropriate duties owed to those patients. However, given that medical malpractice legislation generally is enacted to protect health care providers rather than plaintiffs, it may be more advantageous for plaintiffs if such statutes do not apply to veterinarians and veterinary facilities.

For example, in *Sherman v. Kissinger*, 195 P.3d 539 (Wash. Ct. App. 2008), the defendants (a veterinarian and veterinary clinic) asserted that Washington's medical malpractice statute applied to veterinarians and served to bar the plaintiff's claims for breach of fiduciary duty, negligent misrepresentation, conversion, trespass to chattels and breach of bailment contract. Looking to the entire legislative scheme and the purpose behind it, the court concluded that it did not apply to veterinarians or veterinary clinics, and ruled in favor of the plaintiff on this issue. *See also Sexton v. Brown*, 2008 Wash. App. LEXIS 2504 (Unpub. Oct. 20, 2008) (same, relying on *Sherman*).

Under the Washington statutory scheme, "health care provider" did not explicitly include veterinarians, and was construed to be limited to providers of human health care. *Sherman*, 195 P.3d at 546. In contrast, "health care providers" under California's Medical Injury Compensation Reform Act ("MICRA"), includes veterinarians. Cal. Civ. Code § 3332(c). *See also Williamson v. Prida*, 75 Cal. App. 4th 1417, 1425 (1999) ("Veterinarians, like medical doctors, are licensed health care providers (Bus. & Prof. Code § 4800 *et seq.*).").

In *Scharer v. San Luis Rey Equine Hospital, Inc.*, 204 Cal. App. 4th 421 (2012), the plaintiff did not file her lawsuit within the one-year statute of limitations applicable to claims against veterinarians. CAL. CIV. PROC. CODE § 340(c). Plaintiff asserted that Code of Civil Procedure section 364, which was enacted as part of MICRA, applied to toll the statute of limitations during the period of advance notice to the health care provider required under the statute. The court acknowledged that veterinarians are "health care providers" under MICRA, but affirmed summary judgment in favor of the defendants, concluding:

> Veterinarians ... do fall within the definition of "health care provider" contained in Code of Civil Procedure section 364, subdivision (f)(1). However, actions seeking damages from veterinarians for alleged injury or death to an animal are not actions for "professional negligence" as the Legislature has defined that term, in section 364, subdivision (f)(2), because that definition applies only to a health care provider's negligence that results in "a personal injury or wrongful death." Actions for veterinary malpractice, however, seek damages for *property damage* because animals are a form of personal property under California law.

Id. at 427.

In two Connecticut cases, the defendant veterinary hospitals and veterinarians, rather than the plaintiffs, relied upon similar statutes to support their position. They argued that the veterinary malpractice claims were governed by statutes expressly written for medical malpractice cases. The court rejected that argument, because the statute (Connecticut General Statutes § 52-190a) was a tort reform statute drafted "in derogation of the common law" and therefore should receive a strict construction and not be extended to veterinary malpractice. The statute applied to actions seeking "damages resulting from personal injury or wrongful death." Because dogs are personal property, the plaintiff had no such claim. *Broderick v. Pond,* 2010 Conn Super. LEXIS 3206, *5–*8 (New Haven Jud. Dist., Dec. 10, 2010) (denying defendants' motion to dismiss). *See also Philip v. Norwich Veterinary Hospital,* 2012 Conn. Super. LEXIS 1905 (New London Jud. Dist., July 25, 2012) (quoting from and agreeing with *Broderick,* the court denied defendants' motion to dismiss on the same ground).

Section 3. Damages and Valuation

[We] note the obvious dissonance between the emotional investment at the heart of the human-pet relationship and the current legal system, which identifies this eleven-year-old cocker spaniel with chronic health problems as "property," subject to suit for conversion and identified in terms of her economic worth. Given the parties' considerable expenditure in this case, it goes without saying that Jazz's significance as a cherished member of Aguillard's family—as well as her importance to her caretakers of almost three years, Tiffany Madura and Richard Toro—far exceeds her market value. Thus, while resolving this appeal in accordance with the applicable law governing ownership of chattel, we recognize that there are important non-economic interests at stake in this case. As one commentator has remarked,

> People do not plan memorial services, or invest in serious medical treatment for their books or lawnmowers. They don't plan to pay more in insurance premiums than the purchase price or replacement cost of the property they seek to protect. Individuals do not leave money for their bicycles in their wills, or seek visitation arrangements for their televisions upon the termination of their marriages.

Aguillard v. Madura, 257 S.W.3d 494, 503 n.15 (Tex. Ct. App. 2008) (quoting Kathy Hessler, *Mediating Animal Law Matters*, 2 J. ANIMAL L. & ETHICS 21, 28 (2007)) (owner of a dog lost in Hurricane Katrina brought a conversion action against a person who allegedly had adopted the dog from a rescue group).

As in other tort cases, compensatory, emotional distress and punitive damages may be available in cases involving injury to or death of animals. Emotional distress damages are available where an intentional tort has been committed and sometimes in cases where defendant's conduct was reckless or amounted to gross negligence, but generally not in cases of simple negligence. Punitive damages are also available for intentional torts, but such damages focus on the conduct and financial means of the tortfeasors, as opposed to the harm suffered by the plaintiffs and their animals.

The primary focus in this section is on compensatory damages, including potential claims for damages for loss of companionship. In cases arising from harm to companion animals, valuation of the harmed animal is especially significant. Different courts have developed different criteria and labels for the damages awardable in such cases. Market value, "intrinsic value," "peculiar value," and "actual value to the owner" are some of the terms used by the courts. As you will see in this section, the case law and doctrines in this area have been constantly developing through the courts and legislative enactments.

This section provides a sampling of cases throughout the country addressing these issues, starting with several decades of Florida and New York cases. It also notes legislative enactments where applicable. There is some overlap with the issues in Section 1, as considerations of damages and available claims are logically intertwined. Although public policy issues are implicated throughout this chapter, this section ends with a focused discussion of public policy issues related to the valuation of companion animals particularly, though not exclusively, in veterinary malpractice cases.

La Porte v. Associated Independents, Inc.

Supreme Court of Florida, 1964
163 So. 2d 267

THOMAS, Justice. An action for damages was brought by the petitioner, then plaintiff, against the defendant, now respondent, based on facts we will presently, briefly relate. The plaintiff, was awarded a verdict of $2,000 compensatory damages and $1,000 punitive damages. The subsequent judgment was appealed to the District Court of Appeal, Second District, and there reversed for reconsideration not of "the issue of liability, but for determination only of compensatory and punitive damages."

The appellate court observed that appellant was contending error had been committed by the trial judge when he charged the jury that the plaintiff could recover for alleged mental suffering. The question here is simplified by the apparent concession on the part of the respondent that under the evidence the jury could believe the petitioner was entitled to recover both compensatory and punitive damages, which have been allowed, however, the respondent complains that the element of mental suffering was injected improperly by the judge's instruction.

The respondent is a corporation engaged in the business of collecting garbage. Among its customers was the petitioner. Early one morning, while the petitioner was occupied in the preparation of breakfast, a garbage collector came for the refuse. The petitioner had tethered her pet, a miniature dachshund, Heidi, outside the house and beyond reach of the garbage can. Heidi was pedigreed and had been purchased two years before. She saw the garbage man empty the can and hurl it in the direction of the dog. Upon hearing her pet yelp, the petitioner went outside to find Heidi injured. The collector laughed and left. Heidi expired from the blow.

In the afternoon petitioner consulted a physician who later testified that she was upset to the point of marked hysteria and in such a plight that she could not recount the experience coherently. The doctor testified also that he had been treating her for nervousness for the past two years. But there is no need to pursue the matter of the effect of Heidi's demise upon her nervous system.

The narrow point for decision is whether or not the element of mental suffering was properly submitted to the jury for their consideration in assessing damages. It is humanly impossible, of course, to extract from the record whether or not the jury was influenced by that feature or, if so, to what extent. In these circumstances if no such factor should have been considered the opinion of the District Court of Appeal should not be disturbed so that upon re-trial the instruction on the point might be eliminated. If such damages are recoverable then the judgment of the trial court should prevail.

The petition for review here was based on an alleged conflict between the decision of the District Court of Appeal in the instant case and decisions of the Supreme Court in *Kirksey v. Jernigan*, 45 So. 2d 188; *Crane v. Loftin*, 70 So. 2d 574, and *Slocum v. Food Fair Stores of Florida*, 100 So. 2d 396.

In the first of these cases it was shown that an undertaker had possessed and embalmed the body of a child without authority of the parent and had refused to surrender the body until a fee for the embalming was paid. The action of the parent for compensatory and punitive damages was dismissed in the trial court. The Supreme Court reversed the judgment and undertook to distinguish cases involving mental suffering from intentional or malicious torts and those in which mental suffering may have resulted from negligent acts. This court acknowledged its commitment to the rule that there could be no recovery for mental pain unconnected with physical hurt in an action arising from "negligent breach of a contract [when] simple negligence [was] involved."

The court then remarked that the rule would not, however, be extended to cases purely in tort "where the wrongful act is such as * * * reasonably [to] imply malice," or when from "great indifference to the persons, property, or rights of others, such malice will be imputed as would justify the assessment of exemplary or punitive damages."

It is to us obvious from the facts we have related that the act performed by the representative of the respondent was malicious and demonstrated an extreme indifference to the rights of the petitioner. Having this view we think there was no prohibition of punitive damages under the rule just cited relative to awarding compensation for mental pain, as would be the case if there had been physical injury resulting only from simple negligence. There must have been no dispute before the District Court of Appeal about the propriety of punitive damages for that court observed in the opinion: "Appellant [respondent] acknowledges that, under the version of the evidence which the jury must have accepted, appellee [petitioner] was entitled to recover both compensatory and punitive damages," leaving, as we have already written, the sole question whether or not in setting the amount of damages mental suffering could be considered as the trial court had charged.

The District Court of Appeal held that *generally* in the case of injury to, or destruction of, a dog only the market value of the animal or some special or pecuniary value could establish the amount of the loss. Then the court concluded with the flat statement: "It is improper to include an allowance for sentimental value of the dog to its owner." The restriction of the loss of a pet to its intrinsic value in circumstances such as the ones before us is a principle we cannot accept. Without indulging in a discussion of the affinity between "sentimental value" and "mental suffering", we feel that the affection of a master for his dog is a very real thing and that the malicious destruction of the pet provides an element of damage for which the owner should recover, irrespective of the value of the animal because of its special training such as a Seeing Eye dog or sheep dog.

The respondent tries to distinguish between the *Kirksey* case, *supra*, and the instant one on two bases, namely, that in the former the body of a child was involved and in the latter a dog; that in the former there was a personal transaction between the undertaker and complainant while in the latter there was none since the garbage gatherer "did not even know the plaintiff was anywhere within sight, nor had he ever met her or seen the dog previously." As to the first of these we hasten to say that the anguish resulting from the mishandling of the body of a child cannot be equated to the grief from the loss of a dog but that does not imply that mental suffering from the loss of a pet dog, even one less an aristocrat than Heidi, is nothing at all. As for the matter of contact between the miscreant and the injured person, the attempted distinction is just too fine for us to accept.

We think upon serious consideration that the opinion of the District Court of Appeal sufficiently collides with our opinion in the cited case to justify our assuming jurisdiction and in such event, as we have often held, we extend our power to determination of the merits.

* * *

For the reasons given, the writ of *certiorari* is granted and the judgment of the District Court of Appeal is quashed with directions to order the judgment of the trial court reinstated.

Notes

1. What do you think the cause(s) of action was/were in *La Porte*?

2. Why might the court have "hasten[ed] to say that the anguish resulting from the mishandling of the body of a child cannot be equated to the grief from the loss of a dog"? Keep that comment in mind when reading the *Corso* case following these Notes.

3. As reflected in *La Porte*, even without legislative guidance courts may permit the recovery of exemplary (punitive) damages for intentional harm to animals. Some states, however, have enacted statutes expressly allowing punitive damages in cases of intentional (or even grossly negligent) harm to animals. For example, California Civil Code section 3340 (enacted in 1872) provides as follows:

> Injuries to animals. For wrongful injuries to animals being the subject of property, committed willfully or by gross negligence, in disregard of humanity, exemplary damages may be given.

Id. See also Mont. Code Ann. § 27-1-222 (enacted in 1895; same language, but entitled "Exemplary Damages for Inhumane Injury to Animals"); Okla. Stat. title 23, § 68 (same, entitled "Exemplary Damages for Injuries to Animals"). Under North Dakota Century Code, title 36, "Livestock" ("Exemplary Damages for Wrongful Injuries to Domestic Animals"), punitive damages are available for injury to "any animal." N.D. Cent. Code § 36-21-13. In addition, North Dakota expressly allows exemplary damages in cases of harassment of domestic animals by a motorized vehicle. N.D. Cent. Code § 39-08-19.

4. While the punitive damages award in *La Porte* was just $1,000, according to a news article, sixty years later an Oregon jury awarded $100,000 "in emotional harm" and $139,500 in punitive damages after two hunters killed the plaintiff's three Great Pyrenees sheepdogs, asserting that they thought the dogs were wild dogs. Kailey Fisicaro, *Civil verdict reached on livestock dogs killed in 2012*, The Bulletin (Bend, Or.), Mar. 11, 2016.

5. *La Porte* addressed the measure of damages in a case where the court found it "obvious" that defendant's acts were "malicious and demonstrated an extreme indifference" to the plaintiff's rights. Subsequent Florida cases in the context of negligence claims have both relied upon and distinguished *La Porte*.

For example, in *Knowles Animal Hospital, Inc. v. Wills*, 360 So. 2d 37 (Fla. Ct. App., 3d Dist. 1978), plaintiffs' dog was severely burned and disfigured after being left by veterinary staff on a heating pad after surgery. Plaintiffs alleged gross negligence and sought compensatory and punitive damages. The jury found against the defendant veterinary hospital, and the hospital appealed. The appellate court relied in part on *La Porte* to hold that the trial court did not err when it allowed the jury to consider the element of the plaintiffs' mental pain and suffering. The court affirmed the judgment, concluding that the jury viewed the "neglectful conduct which resulted in the burn injury suffered by the dog to have been of a character amounting to great indifference to the property of the plaintiffs, such as to justify the jury award." *Id.* at 38–39 (citing to *Levine v. Knowles*, 197 So. 2d 329 (Fla. Ct. App., 3d Dist. 1967)).

Under substantially similar facts, the court reached the same result fourteen years later, relying on *Knowles v. Wills* to hold that the trial court had improperly granted partial summary judgment dismissing claims for punitive damages and emotional distress. *Johnson v. Wander*, 592 So. 2d 1225 (Fla. Ct. App., 3d Dist. 1992).

Twelve years later, however, Florida's First Appellate District took a different approach and reached a different result. In *Kennedy v. Byas*, 867 So. 2d 1195 (Fla. Ct. App., 1st Dist. 2004), as explained to the editors by plaintiff's counsel, plaintiff's dog Fred suffered from bouts of gastric torsion (twisting of the stomach), a condition that can be fatal if the patient is not properly monitored after initial treatment, to ensure that the stomach untwists itself and that the torsion does not recur within the next few hours. Plaintiff told the defendant veterinarian (an emergency room doctor who had not treated Fred before) about Fred's history of torsion. The veterinarian indicated he knew how to treat Fred's problem. According to plaintiff's counsel, however, it appeared that instead of monitoring Fred through the night defendant simply left Fred unattended. The hospital did not contact plaintiff during the night to apprise him of Fred's condition. When plaintiff arrived the following morning to bring Fred home as planned, the attendant handed him a box containing Fred's body.

In the veterinary malpractice suit that followed, the trial court granted the defendant's motion for partial summary judgment, dismissing plaintiff's claim for emotional distress damages. In affirming that ruling, the Court of Appeals considered and rejected *Knowles* and *Johnson* based on Florida's "impact rule," and distinguished *LaPorte*.

> The "impact rule" requires some physical impact prior to the recovery of damages for emotional distress. *Id.* at 1050. Petitioner requests that we abandon the "impact rule" in this case and allow the recovery for emotional distress in cases involving veterinary malpractice. In *Welker v. S. Baptist Hosp. of Fla., Inc.*, 864 So. 2d 1178 (Fla. 1st DCA Jan. 8, 2004), this court recognized that the impact rule is not an unyielding inflexible rule of law and in some cases damages for emotional distress may be recovered

absent physical impact. We identified those types of cases where an exception to the impact rule was likely to be applied:

> There exist common threads in all of the foregoing cases in which the court established exceptions to the impact rule. In all, the likelihood of emotional injury was clearly foreseeable; the emotional injury was likely to be significant; the issue of causation was relatively straightforward; and it was unlikely that creating an exception to the rule would result in a flood of fictitious or speculative claims.

Id.

One area that was identified as having the gravity of emotional injury and lack of countervailing policy concerns to justify exceptions to the impact rule involves familial relationships, such as injury to a child as a result of malpractice. We decline to extend this exception to malpractice cases involving animals. As we stated in *Bennett v. Bennett*, 655 So. 2d 109, 110 (Fla. 1st DCA 1995) [*excerpted in Chapter 8 of the text*], "While a dog may be considered by many to be a member of the family, under Florida law animals are considered to be personal property."

In making this point we have not overlooked the decision of the Florida Supreme Court in *La Porte v. Associated Indeps., Inc.*, 163 So. 2d 267, 269 (Fla. 1964), where the supreme court stated, "Without discussing the affinity between 'sentimental value and mental suffering' we feel that the affection of a master for his dog is a very real thing and that the *malicious* destruction of the pet provides an element of damage for which the owner should recover." (Emphasis supplied). *La Porte*, however, may be distinguished from the instant case. In *La Porte*, the defendant's behavior was malicious—the defendant threw a garbage can at the plaintiff's pet; in the instant case we are dealing with an allegation of simple negligent behavior by a veterinarian who was trying to provide treatment. *See Nichols v. Sukaro Kennels*, 555 N.W.2d 689, 691 (Iowa 1996) (distinguishing *La Porte* on the basis that their case involved negligence rather than malicious behavior).

We acknowledge there is a split of authority on whether damages for emotional distress may be collected for the negligent provision of veterinary services. See Jay M. Zitter, Annotation, *Recovery of Damages for Emotional Distress Due to Treatment of Pets*, 91 A.L.R.5th 545, §§ 3 and 4. We find ourselves in agreement, however, with the New York courts which recognize that while pet owners may consider pets as part of the family, allowing recovery for these types of cases would place an unnecessary burden on the ever burgeoning caseload of courts in resolving serious tort claims for individuals. [*Citing to* Johnson v. Douglas, *a trial court decision noted later in the text*.] We decline to carve out an exception to the impact rule for cases involving veterinary malpractice.

Kennedy, 867 So. 2d at 1197–98.

The published decision in *Kennedy v. Byas* refers only to "simple negligence." According to plaintiff's counsel, however, Kennedy actually alleged gross negligence. According to counsel, the court chose to ignore that fact, even though plaintiff explicitly and repeatedly brought it to the court's attention. Given this fact, do you think another court applying Florida law could have reached a different result here? How do you think the *La Porte* court would have ruled under the facts in *Kennedy*? If gross negligence rather than simple negligence were alleged, should it change the result?

One year after the *Kennedy* decision, yet another district of Florida's appellate courts had an opportunity to address this issue. In *Arendes ex rel. Arendes v. Lee County*, 899 So. 2d 493 (Fla. Ct. App., 2d Dist. 2005), the complaint alleged that plaintiffs' dog, Winston, was picked up by animal control officers and impounded after having left plaintiffs' yard. Winston died from overheating while at the county shelter waiting to be picked up by his family. The complaint alleged that the staff veterinarian denied employees' requests to move the visibly overheating dog to a cooler place (the shelter had no air conditioning on the mid-summer day he was impounded) or take other measures to relieve his distress. The third amended complaint asserted causes of action for negligence, gross negligence and intentional infliction of emotional distress, among others (including breach of bailment). The Court of Appeals, without discussion of any of the issues, affirmed the trial court's ruling, which granted a motion to dismiss plaintiffs' claims for mental pain and suffering, loss of capacity for enjoyment of life and loss of society.

What public policy issues are implicated by the Florida cases?

Corso v. Crawford Dog and Cat Hospital, Inc.

Civil Court of the City of New York, Queens County, 1979
97 Misc. 2d 530, 415 N.Y.S.2d 182

SEYMOUR FRIEDMAN, Judge. The facts in this case are not in dispute. On or about January 28, 1978, the plaintiff brought her 15 year old poodle into the defendant's premises for treatment. After examining the dog, the defendant recommended euthanasia and shortly thereafter the dog was put to death. The plaintiff and the defendant agreed that the dog's body would be turned over to Bide-A-Wee, an organization that would arrange a funeral for the dog. The plaintiff alleged that the defendant wrongfully disposed of her dog, failed to turn over the remains of the dog to the plaintiff for the funeral. The plaintiff had arranged for an elaborate funeral for the dog including a head stone, an epitaph, and attendance by plaintiff's two sisters and a friend. A casket was delivered to the funeral which, upon opening the casket, instead of the dog's body, the plaintiff found the body of a dead cat. The plaintiff described during the non-jury trial, her mental distress and anguish, in detail, and indicated that she still feels distress and anguish. The plaintiff sustained no special damages.

The question before the court now is two-fold. 1) Is it an actionable tort that was committed? 2) If there is an actionable tort is the plaintiff entitled to damages beyond the market value of the dog?

Before answering these questions the court must first decide whether a pet such as a dog is only an item of personal property as prior cases have held, *Smith v. Palace Transportation Co., Inc.*, 142 Misc. 93, 253 N.Y.S. 87. This court now overrules prior precedent and holds that a pet is not just a thing but occupies a special place somewhere in between a person and a piece of personal property.

As in the case where a human body is withheld, *Zaslowsky v. Nassau County Public General Hospital*, 27 Misc. 2d 379, 209 N.Y.S. 2d 921, *Diebler v. American Radiator and Standard Sanitary Corp.*, 196 Misc. 618, 92 N.Y.S. 2d 356, the wrongfully withholding or, as here, the destruction of the dog's body gives rise to an actionable tort.

In ruling that a pet such as a dog is not just a thing I believe the plaintiff is entitled to damages beyond the market value of the dog. A pet is not an inanimate thing that just receives affection it also returns it. I find that plaintiff Ms. Corso did suffer shock, mental anguish and despondency due to the wrongful destruction and loss of the dog's body.

She had an elaborate funeral scheduled and planned to visit the grave in the years to come. She was deprived of this right.

This decision is not to be construed to include an award for the loss of a family heirloom which would also cause great mental anguish. An heirloom while it might be the source of good feelings is merely an inanimate object and is not capable of returning love and affection. It does not respond to human stimulation; it has no brain capable of displaying emotion which in turn causes a human response. Losing the right to memorialize a pet rock, or a pet tree or losing a family picture album is not actionable. But a dog that is something else. To say it is a piece of personal property and no more is a repudiation of our humaneness. This I cannot accept.

Accordingly, the court finds the sum of $700 to be reasonable compensation for the loss suffered by the plaintiff.

Notes

1. The court in which the *Corso* case was heard, and that issued this opinion, is the lowest level court in New York. Thus, despite the stated intentions of the opinion, the court did not have the authority to, and could not, "overrule[] prior precedent." Regardless of whether it had the power to ignore controlling rulings, the court declined to follow New York case law, stating it was granting companion animals special status "somewhere in between a person and a piece of personal property."

2. *Corso* and the *Brousseau* case that follows these Notes reflect the courts' recognition of the need for a change in approach in cases involving animals. Both have been relied upon for years as well-reasoned decisions whose rationale should be adopted by other courts, in New York and elsewhere.

3. Notably, the *Corso* case did not involve harm to a companion animal. Rather, it is akin to the mishandled human corpse cases, where the plaintiff suffers emotional distress when the corpse of a loved one is misplaced or lost. Thus, it is not a case that determines the value of the animal, but only the value of the *connection* between the plaintiff and her deceased companion, and the resulting emotional distress of the plaintiff after the mishandling. Recall the Florida *La Porte* court's comment that "the anguish resulting from the mishandling of the body of a child cannot be equated to the grief from the loss of a dog." Can that be reconciled with the reasoning in *Corso*?

4. In *Guth v. Freeland*, 28 P.3d 982 (Haw. 2001), the Hawaii Supreme Court held that the state statute precluding recovery of emotional distress damages for negligent damage to property (discussed in Section 1 of this chapter in conjunction with *Campbell v. Animal Quarantine Station*, 632 P.2d 1066 (Haw. 1981)) does not apply to claims of negligent infliction of emotional distress arising from the negligent mishandling of a human corpse, based on the conclusion that a corpse is not "property" or a "material object" under the statute. The majority looked to the "special circumstances" in such a case, and distinguished it from a case that would encourage the "attachment to material possessions," which the court agreed should be discouraged by society. 28 P.3d. at 987. In a separate opinion, concurring in the result, one justice concluded that a human corpse is not "property" under the statute because it "is not the object of sale or transfer or of some use stemming from its intrinsic nature and, thus, is not property in the commonly understood sense." *Id.* at 992 (Acoba, J., concurring in part and dissenting in part) (internal citation omitted).

Could a "special circumstances exception" apply in cases of tortious harm to companion animals? Should society and the legal system place a different value on the emotional bond between a person and his living companion animal who is killed by the tortious act of another than the value it places on the emotional distress caused by the mishandling of the body of a deceased human family member? If so, on what basis?

5. At common law there were no property rights in human corpses. *Colavito v. New York Organ Donor Network, Inc.*, 438 F.3d 214, 223 (2d Cir. 2006). Duties with respect to corpses were excluded from common law "because burials were matters of ecclesiastical cognizance." *Newman v. Sathyavaglswaran*, 287 F.3d 786, 791 (9th Cir. 2002). In one form or another, most states have now recognized claims for "tortious interference with a corpse," although some jurisdictions simply consider it as a part of a negligent or intentional infliction of emotional distress claim. *See, e.g., Amaker v. Kings County*, 540 F.3d 1012 (9th Cir. 2008). In many jurisdictions such claims are subject to the general rule that emotional distress damages will be awarded only if the tortious conduct was intentional or malicious, as opposed to negligent. *See, e.g., Ely v. Hitchcock*, 58 P.3d 116, 122 (Kan. Ct. App. 2002). The legal claim for interference with a corpse is generally recognized to derive from a "quasi-property" right. *Amaker*, 540 F.3d at 1015. "Later, however,

some courts began to recognize that the recovery for mishandling of a corpse was in reality solely for mental anguish and was not due to the injury of any separate 'quasi-property' right." *Midtown Hospital v. Miller*, 36 F. Supp. 2d 1360, 1367 (N.D. Ga. 1997).

Might there be any application for a "quasi-property" status for companion animals? If so, would this more likely be advantageous or potentially detrimental to the broader goals of animal advocates? Consider the plaintiffs' argument in *Lockett v. Hill*, 51 P.3d 5 (Or. Ct. App. 2002), seeking a "constitutive property" status for companion animals. In *Lockett*, defendant's dogs chased and killed plaintiffs' cat. The trial court found that defendant was negligent and awarded plaintiffs $1,000 in compensatory damages but denied plaintiffs' claims for negligent infliction of emotional distress and loss of companionship. Plaintiffs appealed, arguing that they should be compensated for emotional distress resulting from witnessing the death of their pet. In their appeal, they urged the court to consider their cat, and companion animals generally, as constitutive property.

> Generally, a person cannot recover for negligent infliction of emotional distress if the person is not also physically injured, threatened with physical injury, or physically impacted by the tortious conduct. The rule, however, is not absolute. Under one exception, such recovery may occur if "the defendant's conduct infringed on some legally protected interest apart from causing the claimed distress ***." "The term 'legally protected interest' refers to an independent basis of liability separate from the general duty to avoid foreseeable risk of harm," and "the identification of such a distinct source of duty is the *sine qua non* of liability for emotional distress damages unaccompanied by physical injury." Further, emotional distress damages cannot arise from infringement of every kind of legally protected interest, but from only those that are "of sufficient importance as a matter of public policy to merit protection from emotional impact."

> Thus, because defendant's pit bulls did not physically injure or even tortiously touch plaintiffs, they must prove that: (1) defendant not only negligently allowed his dogs to run free, thereby foreseeably injuring plaintiffs' cat; (2) in so doing, defendant breached a legal duty to them over and above the general duty to avoid foreseeable harm; and (3) the breach of duty resulted in the invasion of an interest that is sufficiently important to merit, if it is harmed, an award of damages for emotional distress.

> ... [P]laintiffs rely on a theory of "constitutive property." That theory is based on the proposition that ownership or possession of certain personal property, like a pet, can become a central aspect of the owner's/guardian's sense of identity. In support of this proposition, plaintiffs cite Steven M. Wise, *Wrongful Death of a Companion Animal*, 4 Animal L. 33 (1998). Wise refers to pets, for which he uses the term "companion animals," as "quasi-children" who "may also be metaphorical extensions of their owners" to the

extent that "the wrongful killing of one's companion animal may threaten the way in which an owner constitutes herself: in losing her companion animal, she loses a vital part of herself." *Id.* at 67–68. According to plaintiffs, Oregon courts have already identified a person's interest in constitutive property as a legally protected interest. They rely on *Mooney v. Johnson Cattle,* 291 Ore. 709, 717 (1981), in which the Supreme Court commented in *dictum* that "such noneconomic values as personal association, love of a place, and pride in one's work * * * add up to one's sense of identity." The companionship of a pet, plaintiffs argue, is similar in kind to the "values" named in *Mooney.*

Plaintiffs then argue that we have the authority to declare that wrongful destruction of such "constitutive" property is a breach of duty or invasion of an interest on which emotional damages can be based. . . . Plaintiffs, in other words, ask us to acknowledge that people have a legally protectible interest in the integrity of constitutive property and that a companion animal is such property and then to declare that that interest is one the interference with which should support an award of damages for emotional distress.

The fatal flaw in plaintiffs' logic occurs at the first step. Our authority to make policy choices in this context is limited to deciding which independent legally protectible interests are sufficiently important to serve as the foundation for emotional distress damages; it does not extend to creating independent legally protectible interests. . . . [P]laintiffs have directed us to no authority for the proposition that defendant's negligent conduct breached a duty over and above the duty to avoid foreseeable risk, that is, that defendant's negligent conduct interfered with an interest that is protected by something beyond negligence law. The trial court did not err in denying plaintiffs' claim for damages based on emotional distress.

Id. at 6–8. While adoption of such a theory may have expanded the plaintiffs' recovery in this case, would it offer any potential benefit to the animals themselves?

Brousseau v. Rosenthal

Civil Court of the City of New York, New York County, 1980
110 Misc. 2d 1054, 443 N.Y.S.2d 285

MARGARET TAYLOR, J. This small claims action presents the question of how to make plaintiff whole in dollars for the defendant's negligence in causing the death of plaintiff's dog.

The evidence adduced at trial shows that on July 28, 1979 Ms. Brousseau delivered her healthy, eight-year-old dog for boarding at Dr. Rosenthal's kennel. When she returned to the kennel on August 10, she was told that her dog had died on August 6. In this bailment for mutual benefit, defendant will be held only to a standard of ordinary care. . . . Nevertheless, defendant's failure to return the bailed dog presumptively establishes his negligence, shifting the burden of proving due care to the defendant bailee.

That the usual rules apply to bailees of animals is not disputed. The policy that affords to the bailor the benefit of the presumption of negligence recognizes that the facts and proof surrounding the property's loss are peculiarly within the knowledge and control of the bailee. In this case, where plaintiff consented to an autopsy of the dog, but where no report was forthcoming, and where contradictory explanations of the loss were proffered by defendant, but no competent proof was adduced as to the cause of the dog's death, the fairness of this rebuttable presumption of negligence is manifest.

Having found that plaintiff is entitled to recover, we must devise a formula for computing the fair measure of her damages.

Although the general rules and principles measure damages by assessing the property's market value, the fact that Ms. Brousseau's dog was a gift and a mixed breed and thus had no ascertainable market value need not limit plaintiff's recovery to a merely nominal award. 1 ALR3d 999. An element of uncertainty in the assessment of damages or the fact that they cannot be calculated with absolute mathematical accuracy is not a bar to plaintiff's recovery.

Although the courts have been reluctant to award damages for the emotional value of an injured animal, *Stettner v. Graubard*, 82 Misc. 2d 132 (Town Court of Harrison, Westchester County 1975); *Smith v. Palace Transportation Co.*, 142 Misc. 93 (Municipal Ct., Manhattan 1931), the court must assess the dog's actual value to the owner in order to make the owner whole. *Blauvelt v. Cleveland*, 198 App. Div. 229 (1921); *Smith v. Palace Transp. Co., supra*; 94 ALR 731–735. The court finds that plaintiff has suffered a grievous loss. The dog was given to her when it was a puppy in August, 1970 shortly after plaintiff lost her husband. To this retired woman who lived alone, this pet was her sole and constant companion. Plaintiff testified that she experienced precisely the kind of psychological trauma associated with the loss of a pet that has received increased recent public attention. *See, e.g.,* A. Fischer, *When a Pet's Death Hurts Its Master*, New York Times, May 8, 1980, p. 3, col. 5. As loss of companionship is a long-recognized element of damages in this State, *see Millington v. Southeastern Elevator Co.*, 22 N.Y.2d 498 (1968), [1] the court must consider this as an element of the dog's actual value to this owner. *Blauvelt v. Cleveland, supra*.

Plaintiff must also be made whole for the protective value to her of this part-German Shepherd. The testimony indicates that plaintiff relied heavily on this

---

1. Although loss of companionship has been excluded both as an element of damages in wrongful death cases and as an independent common law action, *Liff v. Schildkrout*, 49 N.Y.2d 622, 427 N.Y.S.2d 746, 404 N.E.2d 1288 (1980) that holding was based upon the statutory preemption and upon the statutory language of EPTL 5-4.3. Because there is no analogous wrongful death statute that governs damages for the loss of an animal, the policies behind the loss of consortium cases impact upon the court's consideration in the instant case.

well-trained watchdog and never went out into the street alone at night without the dog's protection. Since the dog's death, plaintiff does not go out of her apartment after dark. In addition, her home was burglarized and a watch given to her on retirement was stolen while she was watching television in her own back bedroom. Had the dog been alive, no one would have entered her apartment undetected, for the dog would have barked vigorously at the mere sound of a presence in the hallway outside her apartment.

Resisting the temptation to romanticize the virtues of a "human's best friend," it would be wrong not to acknowledge the companionship and protection that Ms. Brousseau lost with the death of her canine companion of eight years. The difficulty of pecuniarily measuring this loss does not absolve defendant of his obligation to compensate plaintiff for that loss, at least to the meager extent that money can make her whole. The dog's age is not a depreciation factor in the court's calculations, for "manifestly, a good dog's value increases rather than falls with age and training." *Stettner v. Graubard, supra*, 368 N.Y.S.2d at 685. The court therefore awards judgment to plaintiff in the sum of $550 plus costs and disbursements.

Notes

1. In *Animal Hospital of Elmont, Inc. v. Gianfrancisco*, 418 N.Y.S. 2d 992 (Dist. Ct. 2d Dist. Nassau Cty. 1979), a veterinary hospital sued the defendant for failure to pay for medical care for his Great Dane puppy. The hospital notified the defendant in writing that he owed $199 and that if he failed to pay the bill and pick up the puppy within ten days, the puppy would be disposed of in accordance with state law. This notice, however, did not comply with New York statutory requirements. The hospital ultimately sent the puppy to the local shelter, where he was killed. The court ruled that the defendant owed the $199, but also ruled the hospital's failure to abide by state law entitled defendant to damages for the value of the dog. In formulating those damages, the court noted

> there are many factors which in the appropriate case may be taken into consideration in an effort to establish the extent of that value, not the least of these would be the age of the animal, the purchase price, pedigree, training, show quality, and last, but not least, the length of time the puppy had been living with the defendant.

Id. at 994–95. The damages were limited, but the court's thoughtful opinion (excerpted below) evinces a clear recognition of the bond between humans and their companion animals:

> The magic of Lassie is not just a movie script made in magic land USA, but for many a young boy and girl it may well be the theme song for their feelings about a little dog that just happens to live at home with them, and for most of these persons who have dogs at home, the greatest problem, pooper-scooper notwithstanding, is that these dogs believe quite honestly that they are human beings and members of the family.

In a sense this decision might be dedicated to just such a four-legged member of the family. The facts are, at least at the beginning, not uncommon to many a home, where a pet permits his owners to live with him.

Id. at 992–93.

Twenty-two years later, a different judge in the same Nassau County court acknowledged the bond but refused to permit causes of action for emotional distress based on the bond to stand. *Johnson v. Douglas,* 723 N.Y.S.2d 627 (N.Y. Supr. Ct., Nassau Cty. 2001).

2. A number of courts applying New York law have declined to consider animals as a special type of property. For example, in *Young v. Delta Air Lines, Inc.,* 432 N.Y.S.2d 390 (App. Div. 1980), plaintiff sought emotional distress damages in connection with the death of her dog during transport. The court found that "New York law does not permit recovery for mental suffering and emotional disturbance as an element of damages for loss of a passenger's property." *Id.* at 391.

In *Gluckman v. American Airlines, Inc.,* 844 F. Supp. 151 (S.D.N.Y. 1994), Floyd (a dog found by the teenaged plaintiff on a camping trip) died from heat exposure while flying on the defendant airline. When the airline's agents brought Floyd to plaintiff, Floyd had collapsed from the heat, his face and paws were bloody, there was blood all over his crate and the condition of the crate evidenced a panicked effort to escape. The court relied on *Young* to dismiss summarily the claim for negligent infliction of emotional distress. Dismissing the intentional infliction of emotional distress claim, the court noted that such a claim is not viable under New York law unless the conduct is "intentionally directed at the plaintiff." The court concluded that "[a]s deplorable as it may be for American to have caused the death of an innocent animal," there was no allegation that the airline's conduct was directed intentionally at Gluckman. *Id.* at 158.

Gluckman's complaint also included a cause of action for loss of companionship. Plaintiff relied on *Corso* and *Brousseau* to support this claim. The court first distinguished *Brousseau* on the ground that the *Brousseau* court "did not find that the loss of a pet's companionship alone sustained a separate cause of action, but rather, that it was one factor available to assess the dog's actual value to the owner." *Id.* at 158. The court then discussed *Corso:*

Although *Corso v. Crawford Dog and Cat Hosp., Inc.,* which holds that "a pet occupies a special place somewhere in between a person and a piece of property," is more on point, the *Corso* court recognized that it was overruling prior precedent.

In viewing a pet as more than property, however, the *Corso* opinion, and the few cases that follow it, are aberrations flying in the face of overwhelming authority to the contrary. *See, e.g., Snyder v. Bio-Lab, Inc.,* 405 N.Y.S.2d 596 (1978) ("[a]s with personal property generally, the measure of damages for injury to, or destruction of, an animal is the amount which will compensate the owner for the loss and thus return him, monetarily, to the status he was in before the loss"); *Stettner v. Graubard*, 368 N.Y.S.2d 683 (1975) (sentiment will not be considered in assessing market value for purposes of determining measure of damages for destruction of dog). In addition, the *Corso* court provides no legal reasoning why prior precedent should be overruled in categorizing pets as more than property. Moreover, and most importantly, none of the decisions cited by plaintiff, including *Corso*, recognize an independent cause of action for loss of companionship. Rather, these cases provide a means for assessing the "intrinsic" value of the lost pet when the market value cannot be determined. *See, e.g., Hersh v. Heiffler*, N.Y.L.J., Oct. 18, 1975, at 16 (noting that where market value cannot be determined, factors such as the animal's age, health and character may be considered in assessing damages); *Zager v. DiMilia*, N.Y.L.J., Aug. 5, 1987, at 13 (same). Accordingly, the Court finds that there is no independent cause of action for loss of the companionship of a pet.

Id. As discussed in the Notes that follow, courts in other jurisdictions have rejected a cause of action for loss of companionship, distinguishing *Brousseau* on the same basis.

Finally, Gluckman's complaint included a cause of action for Floyd's pain and suffering. The court rejected this claim, noting that the plaintiff had agreed no such cause of action had been recognized. *See also Oberschlake v. Veterinary Associates Animal Hospital*, 785 N.E.2d 811, 814 (Ohio Ct. App. 2003) ("We note that the Oberschlakes have also included a claim for Poopi's own emotional distress. Although Poopi was obviously directly involved in the incident, a dog cannot recover for emotional distress — or indeed for any other direct claims of which we are aware. We recognize that animals can and do suffer pain or distress, but the evidentiary problems with such issues are obvious. As a result, the claims on Poopi's behalf were also not viable.").

Do you agree with the *Oberschlake* court's conclusion that the "evidentiary problems with [proving an animal's pain and suffering] are obvious"? Are there instances where a human victim's emotional distress would present analogous evidentiary difficulties? Juries are logically better positioned to place a dollar value on a human victim's pain and suffering than on a nonhuman victim's, but if appropriate evidence is presented, would it be any different than a jury deciding other issues that are the subject of expert testimony or circumstantial evidence? What if the nonhuman victim was a chimpanzee who was injured but not killed by the defendants' tortious act and who could communicate through sign language?

Do you think the plaintiff in *Gluckman* lost credibility with the court in seeking damages for the animal's own pain, suffering and emotional distress? Do you think any state legislature in the foreseeable future may be willing to consider a statute allowing such claims to proceed to the jury? If the case involves an intentional tort as opposed to merely negligence, should that make a difference?

3. As can be seen throughout this text, where courts are apprehensive to act, legislatures may step in. In an effort to promote such legislative action, the Animal

Legal Defense Fund, a national non-profit legal animal advocacy organization, has proposed the following language to be enacted by state legislatures:

Civil Right of Action

> Any guardian of an animal subjected to a violation of the [animal protection statutes] may bring a civil action to recover the damages sustained by the animal and guardian. Damages may include, but are not limited to, the pecuniary value of the animal, veterinary expenses incurred on behalf of the animal, any other expenses incurred by the guardian in attempting to mollify the effects of the violation, pain and suffering of the animal, emotional distress and any loss of companionship suffered by the guardian. In addition to such actual damages as may be proven, the guardian shall also be awarded a sum of not less than $1000.00 for each violation to which the animal was subjected. In addition, the court shall award reasonable attorney's fees and costs incurred by the guardian in the prosecution of the action. The remedies provided in this section are in addition to, and do not replace or supplant, any other remedies allowed by law. The court may enter injunctive orders as are reasonably necessary to abate further violations of the [animal protection statutes] by the defendant.

> Commencement of a cause of action under this section shall occur within three years from the date on which injuries were first identified by the guardian.

This or similar language could be added as a component to supplement statutes like Tennessee's General Patton Act, TENN. CODE ANN. § 44-17-403 (discussed in Note 10, *infra*, and set out in full in Appendix B). Under this proposed statute, the guardian of an animal may seek recovery for the animal's pain and suffering from acts of cruelty. How would you prove such damages? To what extent would the evidence be similar to that required to prove a person's emotional distress? What type of expert testimony might be helpful? Would the analysis be the same for a statute providing such relief for veterinary malpractice? Should the damages be the same?

4. In 2002, a New York State intermediate appellate court addressed some of these issues and, like the *Gluckman* court, refused to apply the reasoning of *Corso* and *Brousseau*. In *Lewis v. DiDonna*, 743 N.Y.S.2d 186 (App. Div. 3d Dept. 2002), the plaintiff sued Eckerd Drug Store, its parent companies, and the pharmacist whose mislabeling of a prescription bottle resulted in her dog's death. The trial court dismissed plaintiff's cause of action for loss of companionship, but allowed her to introduce proof of loss of companionship at trial, on the issue of damages for her other claims. This approach—allowing the companionship to be a factor in damages, but not a claim of its own—is consistent with holdings in other cases, but the New York appellate court disagreed: "[S]ince loss of companionship is not a cognizable cause of action in this State, it should not be recognized as a factor of damages, and [the trial court] erred in allowing plaintiff the opportunity to present such proof, whatever that may be, at the time of trial." The case was not appealed to New York's high

court. In accord are *DeJoy v. Niagara Mohawk Power Corp.*, 786 N.Y.S.2d 873 (App. Div., 4th Dept. 2004) and *Whitmore v. Niagara Mohawk Power Corp.*, 786 N.Y.S.2d 762 (App. Div., 4th Dept. 2004) (companion cases in which the court relied on *Johnson* and *Lewis*, with no analysis of the issue). In both cases, plaintiffs' horses were electrocuted when defendant's wires fell: "An animal owner may not recover damages for loss of companionship, which we view here as legally equivalent to emotional distress, resulting from the death of the animal."

Is there a way to harmonize all of these cases? As a plaintiff's counsel, what might be an ideal situation for trying to bring a case before New York's highest court— both in terms of having the court agree to hear the case and in terms of achieving the desired result?

5. The approach of these more recent New York courts to loss of companionship claims is the majority rule. *See, e.g., McMahon v. Craig*, 176 Cal. App. 4th 1502 (2009) ("given California law does not allow parents to recover for the loss of companionship of their children, we are constrained not to allow a pet owner to recover for loss of the companionship of a pet"); *Kaufman v. Langhofer*, 222 P.3d 272, 279 (Ariz. Ct. App. 2009) (in a veterinary malpractice case arising out of the death of plaintiff's scarlet macaw, the court cited to *McMahon* and other cases and was "unwilling to expand Arizona common law to allow a plaintiff to recover emotional distress or loss of companionship damages for a pet negligently injured or killed"); *Jankoski v. Preiser Animal Hospital Ltd.*, 510 N.E.2d 1084 (Ill. App. Ct. 1987) (no claim for loss of companionship for the death of plaintiff's dog; distinguishing cases involving the death of a human child); *Harabes v. Barkery, Inc.*, 791 A.2d 1142, 1146 (N.J. Super. Ct. Law Div. 2001) (dog died from extremely hot conditions over an extended period of time in a grooming room; "there is no reason to believe that emotional distress and loss of companionship damages, which are unavailable for the loss of a child or spouse, should be recoverable for the loss of a pet dog"); *Oberschlake v. Veterinary Associates Animal Hospital*, 785 N.E.2d 811, 815 (Ohio Ct. App. 2003) ("no authority in Ohio that would allow recovery for loss of companionship of animals"); *Krasnecky v. Meffen*, 777 N.E.2d 1286, 1289–90 (Mass. App. Ct. 2002) (refusing to allow recovery for loss of companionship of slain sheep regarded by the plaintiffs as their "babies" because Massachusetts wrongful death statutes limit recovery to persons); *Daughen v. Fox*, 539 A.2d 858 (Pa. Super. Ct. 1988) (summarily rejecting "loss of companionship" claim for death of companion animal); *Pickford v. Masion*, 98 P.3d 1232 (Wash. Ct. App. 2004) (declining to extend loss of companionship to death of, or injury to, a pet).

The *Daughen* court described "companionship" as "included in the concept of consortium, which is a right growing out of a marriage relationship giving to each spouse the right to the companionship, society and affection of each other in their life together." 539 A.2d at 865 n.5. Considering this definition, if loss of consortium/ companionship is extended to parents and their children, what would be the rationale for not extending it to a plaintiff and his or her companion animal where they share "the companionship, society and affection of each other in their life together"?

On the other hand, where such claims are limited by wrongful death statutes to certain close human family members (spouses, often parents and/or children and occasionally siblings, but rarely more remote family than that), is it reasonable to expect a court to allow such a claim when the deceased is a nonhuman that the law deems to be "property," even if that nonhuman is considered by the plaintiff to be a family member? Should a plaintiff be permitted to present evidence as to his relationship with the deceased animal, allowing the jury to decide whether in a given case the animal was "like a child" to the plaintiff and whether, therefore, an award of damages for loss of companionship is warranted?

6. While the New Jersey *Harabes* court seemed to blur the distinction, the Illinois *Jankoski* case distinguished between allowing a cause of action for loss of companionship (sought by the plaintiff in that case) and allowing this loss to be considered in measuring the amount of damages. *See also Animal Hospital of Elmont, Inc. v. Gianfrancisco*, 418 N.Y.S.2d 992 (Dist. Ct. 2d Dist. Nassau Cty. 1979). As in *Gluckman*, discussed in Note 2, the *Jankoski* court also distinguished *Brousseau v. Rosenthal*:

> The *Brousseau* court did not, as plaintiffs ask us to do, recognize loss of companionship as an independent cause of action, but rather considered it as an element to be used in measuring the actual value of the dog for purposes of calculating damages in a property damage case. In doing so, it followed the previously discussed rules regarding the assessment of damages in cases where the object destroyed has no market value. In line with these cases, we believe that the law in Illinois is that where the object destroyed has no market value, the measure of damages to be applied is the actual value of the object to the owner. The concept of actual value to the owner may include some element of sentimental value in order to avoid limiting the plaintiff to merely nominal damages. It appears clear that damages in such cases, while not merely nominal, are severely circumscribed.

> The plaintiffs in the case at bar, however, expressly disavow any sort of limited recovery for property damage. Rather, they are asking us to extend the independent cause of action for loss of companionship ... to permit recovery by a dog owner for the loss of companionship of a dog. We do not believe that this is consistent with Illinois law.

Jankoski, supra, 510 N.E.2d at 1087.

What is the effect, if any, when courts ignore the distinction between a cause of action for loss of companionship and a claim for damages for loss of an animal, which allows consideration of loss of companionship as a factor in determining the amount of damages?

7. Even where courts recognize the bond between humans and their companion animals, which is happening more and more, they may still reach the same result. In *Ammon v. Welty*, 113 S.W.3d 185 (Ky. Ct. App. 2002), for example, the county dog warden shot plaintiffs' dog ("Hair Bear") in the head (the warden's customary method of euthanasia), after Hair Bear had been found roaming freely beyond his

property without identification. State law mandated that all stray animals must be kept for seven days before being euthanized, but the county warden did not wait the full statutory period. Hair Bear's family sued the warden (among others) seeking damages for loss of companionship and punitive damages. The court rejected plaintiffs' loss of companionship claim, finding such a claim was severely circumscribed.

> It is undisputed that Hair Bear, an unregistered mixed breed with no particular training or skill other than as a companion, had no market value. Yet, the Ammons urge this court to permit them to prove Hair Bear's value as a beloved and devoted pet.
>
> The affection an owner has for, and receives from, a beloved dog is undeniable. It remains, however, that a dog is property, not a family member. The Ammons request damages for loss of consortium, a common law remedy limited, until recently, to the marital relationship. In *Giuliani v. Guiler*, the court reasoned that it was time for the common law to recognize that the loss suffered by a child as a result of the wrongful death of a parent should be no different from the claim of parents for the loss of a child's consortium recognized in KRS 411.135. The action remains one, however, dependent on the familial relationship. The loss of love and affection resulting from the loss or destruction of personal property is not compensable.

Ammon v. Welty, 113 S.W.3d at 187–88.

On the other hand, some courts in other jurisdictions, such as Oregon for example, have recognized loss of companionship claims. *See, e.g., Smith v. Cook*, Civil Case No. CCV0303790 (Or. Cir. Ct. Clackamas Cty. July 21, 2003) (rejecting defendants' argument that the tort did not exist in Oregon); *Quick v. Inavale Veterinary Clinic*, Civil Case No. 0310168 (Or. Cir. Ct. Benton Cty. Oct. 4, 2004) (denying motion to dismiss loss of companionship claim). Both of these cases ultimately settled for undisclosed amounts.

8. What arguments could you make for and against applying loss of companionship as a measure of damages in this context? To whom would you make that argument — the courts or state legislatures?

9. In *Rabideau v. City of Racine*, 627 N.W. 2d 795 (Wisc. 2001), Chief Justice Abrahamson wrote separately to emphasize the bond between humans and companion animals and to urge the legislature to follow the lead of lawmakers in other states.

> I wish to emphasize that this case is about the rights of a pet owner to recover in tort for the death of her dog. Scholars would not classify this case as one about animal rights. Professor Martha Nussbaum has pointed out that one's love of a pet should not be mistaken for concern about the ethical rights of animals. [13] Professor Nussbaum explains this error as follows:

---

13. *See* Martha C. Nussbaum, Book Review: Animal Rights: The Need for a Theoretical Basis,

Commonly, we conflate two sorts of people: animal lovers and people who are sensitive to the ethical rights of animals. This conflation is a great error. In human life, we can easily take its measure: men may be genuine lovers of women while treating them extremely badly. . . . Even people who treat well the particular women they love may not care at all about women's rights generally.

Professor Nussbaum further explains the difference between animal lovers and proponents of animal rights by noting that while many of us have affectionate relationships with animals such as dogs and cats and horses, we also eat meat and eggs and wear leather, and we do not concern ourselves with the conditions under which these goods are produced. For purposes of recovery for negligent infliction of emotional distress, this court treats the death of a dog the same as it treats injury to or death of a best friend, a roommate, or a nonmarital partner: It allows no recovery.

Having concluded that the plaintiff's only remedy is for loss of property, the majority opinion declines to give guidance to the circuit court and litigants about damages for the death of the dog. This issue was not briefed. At least one state has enacted a law that allows up to $4,000 recovery of non-economic damages such as loss of the reasonably expected companionship, love, and affection of a pet resulting from the intentional or negligent killing of the pet. [Tenn. Code Ann. § 44-17-403 (2001).] Such a statute allows the legislature to make a considered policy judgment regarding the societal value of pets as companions and to specify the nature of the damages to be awarded in a lawsuit.

627 N.W. 2d at 806–07. *See also Oberschlake v. Veterinary Assocs. Animal Hospital*, 785 N.E.2d 811, 815 (Ohio Ct. App. 2003) (Young, J., concurring) (in a veterinary malpractice case, the judge "reluctantly agree[d]" that under the then-current state of Ohio law "the owners of a pet animal have no claim for non-economic injuries to their pets," and he urged the Ohio General Assembly to "at least consider recognizing pets as companion animals and allow owners to recover reasonable damages for their loss of or injury to a much-loved pet"); *Kondaurov v. Kerdasha*, 629 S.E. 2d 181, 186–87 (Va. 2006) ("It is beyond debate that animals, particularly dogs and cats, when kept as pets and companions, occupy a position in human affections far removed from livestock. Especially in the case of owners who are disabled, aged or lonely, an emotional bond may exist with a pet resembling that between parent and child, and the loss of such an animal may give rise to grief approaching that attending the loss of a family member. The fact remains, however, that the law in Virginia, as in most states that have decided the question, regards animals, however beloved, as personal property . . . Our decisions have never approved an award of damages

---

reviewing Steven M. Wise, Rattling the Cage: Toward Legal Rights for Animals, 114 Harv. L. Rev. 1506 (2001).

for emotional distress resulting from negligently inflicted injury to personal property . . . We conclude that permitting such an award would amount to a sweeping change in the law of damages, a subject properly left to legislative consideration.").

What do you think Chief Justice Abrahamson was trying to achieve by distinguishing between animal lovers and "people who are sensitive to the ethical rights of animals"? She concluded that *Rabideau* was not about animal "rights." Do you agree? For a discussion of what "rights" might be in this context, *see* Cass Sunstein, *A Tribute to Kenneth L. Karst: Standing for Animals (With Notes on Animal Rights)*, 47 U.C.L.A. L. Rev. 1333 (June 2000).

10. The Tennessee statute (Tenn. Code Ann. § 44-17-403) referenced by Chief Justice Abrahamson was enacted in June 2001, making Tennessee the first state to codify the right to recover damages for emotional distress and loss of companionship for tortious harm to a companion animal. The statute originally was referred to as the "T-Bo Act," named after the dog of Tennessee Senator Steven Cohen (D-Memphis). T-Bo had been attacked and killed by another dog. Upon learning that in Tennessee damages were limited to the fair market value of the animal who had been his close companion, Senator Cohen sponsored the T-Bo Act. The statute was subsequently amended and renamed the "General Patton Act of 2003." The text of the law is set forth in full in Appendix B.

Illinois followed suit and enacted the "Humane Care for Animals Act," effective January 1, 2002. (510 Ill. Comp. Stat. Ann. 70/16.3). The text of this statute also is set forth in full in Appendix B. Since that time, similar or broader legislation has been proposed and debated in a number of other jurisdictions, but when this edition went to press no other state had yet enacted any such statute.

Carefully review, compare and contrast the text of the Illinois and Tennessee statutes. Be ready to discuss possible advantages and disadvantages of each as it is written, its limitations, possible alternative language, and arguments on both sides of the issue regarding potential ramifications of broadening the scope of the statutes. Also consider the possible advantages if the state legislature in a particular jurisdiction has not spoken on the issue. Could that give the courts more flexibility to address the issues in a progressive way under the common law?

11. For one commentator's legislative proposal for Florida, primarily modeled after legislation proposed in Colorado in 2003, see Marcella S. Roukas, *Determining the Value of Companion Animals in Wrongful Harm or Death Claims: A Survey of U.S. Decisions and Legislative Proposal in Florida to Authorize Recovery for Loss of Companionship*, 3 J. Animal Law 45 (2007). For a broader argument in favor of expanding the tort of loss of consortium to include companion animals, see David Favre & Thomas Dickinson, *Animal Consortium*, 84 Tenn. L. Rev. 893 (Summer 2017).

12. The concurring opinion in a 1994 Texas case also argued the law should afford for damages when defendants' conduct affects the bond between plaintiffs and their companion animals. In *Bueckner v. Hamel*, 886 S.W.2d 368 (Tex. Ct. App. 1994), plaintiff sued a hunter for killing his dogs. The court awarded plaintiff actual

and punitive damages. Justice Andell concurred, but would have expanded plaintiff's recovery:

> I write separately . . . to address what I consider to be a more substantial basis for affirming this award, namely, the intrinsic or specific value of domestic animals as companions and beloved pets. The issue is whether bereaved pet owners must accept the market value of their pets as the measure of actual damages for their pets' wrongful killing, or if they have the option of accepting either the market value or the special value. I consider the general rule of market value to be inadequate for assessing damages for the loss of domestic pets.

Id. at 373 (Andell, J., concurring). Justice Andell addressed the issue of market versus special value, distinguishing *Porras v. Craig*, 675 S.W.2d 503 (Tex. 1984) (involving a claim for special value based on the personal value of real property) and noting the special characteristics of animals:

> As I have observed above, *Porras* did not involve domestic pets, but real property. Real property, although highly prized, does not have characteristics that can make it a widely recognized member of the family. It is common knowledge among pet owners that the death of a beloved dog or cat (or other domestic animal) can be a great loss. This is true even if that loss is the result of a prolonged illness or of an automobile accident rather than an intentional shooting as in the present case.

* * *

> Because of the characteristics of animals in general and of domestic pets in particular, I consider them to belong to a unique category of "property" that neither statutory law nor case law has yet recognized.

> Many people who love and admire dogs as family members do so because of the traits that dogs often embody. These represent some of the best of human traits, including loyalty, trust, courage, playfulness, and love. This cannot be said of inanimate property. At the same time, dogs typically lack the worst of human traits, including avarice, apathy, pettiness, and hatred.

> Scientific research has provided a wealth of understanding to us that we cannot rightly ignore. We now know that mammals share with us a great many emotive and cognitive characteristics, and that the higher primates are very similar to humans neurologically and genetically. It is not simplistic, ill-informed sentiment that has led our society to observe with compassion the occasionally televised plight of stranded whales and dolphins. It is, on the contrary, a recognition of a kinship that reaches across species boundaries.

> The law must be informed by evolving knowledge and attitudes. Otherwise, it risks becoming irrelevant as a means of resolving conflicts. Society

has long since moved beyond the untenable Cartesian view that animals are unfeeling automatons and, hence, mere property. The law should reflect society's recognition that animals are sentient and emotive beings that are capable of providing companionship to the humans with whom they live. In doing so, courts should not hesitate to acknowledge that a great number of people in this country today treat their pets as family members. Indeed, for many people, pets are the only family members they have.

Losing a beloved pet is not the same as losing an inanimate object, however cherished it may be. Even an heirloom of great sentimental value, if lost, does not constitute a loss comparable to that of a living being. This distinction applies even though the deceased living being is nonhuman.

* * *

Bueckner, 886 S.W.2d at 376–78 (Andell, J., concurring).

In comparison, in *City of Canadian v. Guthrie*, 87 S.W.2d 316 (Tex. Ct. App. 1932), plaintiff sued for the value of his mare, who was shot and killed by a city employee after the plaintiff failed to pay the bill for her boarding. In addition to the mare's market value, the plaintiff sought to recover $100 for her "sentimental value" and $500 in punitive damages. The court held market value was the proper measure of damages, because "in the cold, unsympathetic eye of the law, sentimental value is not recognized as a basis for damages."

In *Zeid v. Pearce*, 953 S.W.2d 368 (Tex. Ct. App. 1997), the plaintiffs sought damages for pain and suffering and for mental anguish in a veterinary malpractice case, when their dog had died from an allergic reaction after receiving vaccinations. The court first cited to an 1891 Texas case for the "longstanding Texas rule" that "the recovery for death of a dog is the dog's market value, if any, or some special or pecuniary value to the owner that may be ascertained by reference to the dog's usefulness or service." The court found this rule to be inconsistent with the plaintiffs' claim. The plaintiffs relied on Justice Andell's concurring opinion in *Bueckner v. Hamel* to support their claim. The court noted that "if Justice Andell's conclusion is correct," damages for the special or intrinsic value of plaintiffs' dog may have been allowable. The plaintiffs, however, had not sought such damages. The court did not agree that Justice Andell's opinion entitled the plaintiffs to damages for pain and suffering and for mental anguish under Texas law.

Subsequently, in *Petco Animal Supplies, Inc. v. Schuster*, 144 S.W.3d 554 (Tex. Ct. App. 2004), the court considered the damages available to individuals whose dog had been harmed by defendants' negligence (not veterinary malpractice/professional negligence, but pure negligence by a groomer whose actions led to the death of plaintiffs' dog), and concluded that, as a matter of law, damages were not recoverable for mental anguish and related counseling costs, "'intrinsic value' loss of companionship," or related lost wages. Nine years later, the Texas Supreme Court addressed these issues in the following case.

Strickland v. Medlen[b]

Texas Supreme Court, 2013

397 S.W.3d 184

OPINION BY: Don R. Willett

Beauty without Vanity, Strength without Insolence, Courage without Ferocity, And all the Virtues of Man without his Vices

Texans love their dogs. Throughout the Lone Star State, canine companions are treated — and treasured — not as mere personal property but as beloved friends and confidants, even family members. Given the richness that companion animals add to our everyday lives, losing "man's best friend" is undoubtedly sorrowful. Even the gruffest among us tears up (every time) at the end of *Old Yeller*.

This case concerns the types of damages available for the loss of a family pet. If a cherished dog is negligently killed, can a dollar value be placed on a heartsick owner's heartfelt affection? More pointedly, may a bereaved dog owner recover emotion-based damages for the loss? In 1891, we effectively said no, announcing a "true rule" that categorized dogs as personal property, thus disallowing non-economic damages. In 2011, however, a court of appeals said yes, effectively creating a novel — and expansive — tort claim: loss of companionship for the wrongful death of a pet.

In today's case, involving a family dog that was accidentally euthanized, we must decide whether to adhere to our restrictive, 122-year-old precedent classifying pets as property for tort-law purposes, or to instead recognize a new common-law loss-of-companionship claim that allows non-economic damages rooted solely in emotional attachment, a remedy the common law has denied those who suffer the wrongful death of a spouse, parent, or child, and is available in Texas only by statute.

We acknowledge the grief of those whose companions are negligently killed. Relational attachment is unquestionable. But it is also uncompensable. We reaffirm our long-settled rule, which tracks the overwhelming weight of authority nationally, plus the bulk of amicus curiae briefs from several pet-welfare organizations (who understand the deep emotional bonds between people and their animals): Pets are property in the eyes of the law, and we decline to permit non-economic damages rooted solely in an owner's subjective feelings. True, a beloved companion dog is not a fungible, inanimate object like, say, a toaster. The term "property" is not a pejorative but a legal descriptor, and its use should not be misconstrued as discounting the emotional attachment that pet owners undeniably feel. Nevertheless, under established legal doctrine, recovery in pet-death cases is, barring legislative reclassification, limited to loss of value, not loss of relationship.

We reverse the court of appeals' judgment and render judgment in favor of the Petitioner.

---

b. The extensive footnotes throughout this lengthy opinion are not noted or included here.

I. Factual and Procedural Background

In June 2009, Avery, a mixed-breed dog owned by Kathryn and Jeremy Medlen, escaped the family's backyard and was promptly picked up by Fort Worth animal control. Jeremy went to retrieve Avery but lacked enough money to pay the required fees. The shelter hung a "hold for owner" tag on Avery's cage to alert employees that the Medlens were coming for Avery and ensure he was not euthanized. Despite the tag, shelter worker Carla Strickland mistakenly placed Avery on the euthanasia list, and he was put to sleep.

Jeremy and his two children learned of Avery's fate a few days later when they returned to retrieve him. Devastated, the Medlens sued Strickland for causing Avery's death and sought "sentimental or intrinsic value" damages since Avery had little or no market value but was irreplaceable. Strickland specially excepted, contending such damages are unrecoverable in pet-death cases. The trial court directed the Medlens to amend their pleadings to "state a claim for damages recognized at law." The Medlens amended their petition to drop the words "sentimental value" but realleged damages for Avery's "intrinsic value." Strickland specially excepted on the same basis, and the trial court, sure that Texas law barred such damages, dismissed the suit with prejudice.

The court of appeals reversed, becoming the first Texas court to hold that a dog owner may recover intangible loss-of-companionship damages in the form of intrinsic or sentimental-value property damages. Addressing our 1891 decision in *Heiligmann v. Rose* [81 Tex. 222 (1981)], which pegged dog-loss damages to market value or a value ascertained from the dog's "usefulness and services," the court of appeals stated, "Texas law has changed greatly since 1891" and "sentimental damages may now be recovered for . . . all types of personal property." Specifically, the court said our more recent, non-dog property cases "explicitly held that where personal property has little or no market value, and its main value is in sentiment, damages may be awarded based on this intrinsic or sentimental value." The court of appeals pivoted, too, on our expression in *Heiligmann* that the dogs "were of a special value to the owner," and took from this phrase that special value "may be derived from the attachment that an owner feels for his pet." Emphasizing these iron truths — that "[d]ogs are unconditionally devoted to their owners" and owners, reciprocally, have a deep attachment "to their beloved family pets" — the court of appeals declared "the special value of 'man's best friend' should be protected." Thus, given "the special position pets hold in their family, we see no reason why existing law should not be interpreted to allow recovery in the loss of a pet at least to the same extent as any other personal property." Reinstating the Medlens' claim, the court of appeals concluded: "Because an owner may be awarded damages based on the sentimental value of lost personal property, and because dogs are personal property, the trial court erred in dismissing the Medlens' action against Strickland."

This appeal followed, posing a single, yet significant, issue: whether emotional-injury damages are recoverable for the negligent destruction of a dog.

II. Discussion

America is home to 308 million humans and 377 million pets. In fact, "American pets now outnumber American children by more than four to one." In a nation with about 78 million pet dogs and 86 million pet cats (and 160 million pet fish), where roughly 62% of households own a pet, it is unsurprising that many animal owners view their pets not as mere personal property but as full-fledged family members, and treat them as such:

- A study found that 70% of pet owners thought of their pets as family members.
- 45% of dog owners take their pets on vacation.
- Over 50% of pet owners say they would rather be stranded on a deserted island with a dog or cat than with a human.
- 50% of pet owners report being "very likely" to put their own lives in danger to save their pets, and 33% are "somewhat likely" to risk their lives.
- In 2012, Americans spent roughly $53 billion on their pets.

The human-animal bond is indeed powerful. As the Medlens' second amended petition states: "The entire Medlen family was devastated by the loss of Avery, who was like a family member to them." Countless Texas families share this pets-as-family view, but Texas law, for a century-plus, has labeled them as "property" for purposes of tort-law recovery.

A. Our Precedent Limits Damages in Dog-Death Tort Cases to "Market Value, If the Dog Has Any," or "Special or Pecuniary Value" Linked to the Dog's "Usefulness and Services"

1. Our 1891 Heiligmann Decision Ties "Special Value" to a Dog's Economic Attributes, Not Subjective or Emotional Considerations

Our analysis begins with *Heiligmann v. Rose*, our 1891 case upholding $75 in damages for the poisoning of three "well trained" Newfoundland dogs. *Heiligmann* articulated some key valuation principles for animal cases. First, we classified dogs as personal property for damages purposes, not as something giving rise to personal-injury damages. Second, we declared a "true rule" for damages that flags two elements: (1) "market value, if the dog has any," or (2) "some special or pecuniary value to the owner, that may be ascertained by reference to the usefulness and services of the dog."

In *Heiligmann*, the dogs "were of fine breed, and well trained," with one using different barks to signal whether an approaching person was a man, woman, or child. While the owner could sell each dog for $5, they had no market value beyond that, but the Court upheld damages of $25 each:

> There is no evidence in this case that the dogs had a market value, but the evidence is ample showing the usefulness and services of the dogs, and that they were of special value to the owner. If the jury from the evidence should be satisfied that the dogs were serviceable and useful to the owner, they

could infer their value when the owner, by evidence, fixes some amount upon which they could form a basis.

The Medlens insist that *Heiligmann* does not limit recovery to an amount based *solely* on the dog's economic usefulness and services. Rather, when the Court mentioned certain dogs lacking market value but having "a special value to the owner," we meant something far broader and distinct from the dogs' commercial attributes. Similarly, argue the Medlens, when the Court in *Heiligmann* noted a dog's "special or pecuniary value to the owner," the word "or" indicates two distinct categories of non-market value dogs—those with a special value to the owner, and those with a pecuniary value to the owner. We disagree.

Given its ordinary, contextual meaning, *Heiligmann* tied the recovery of "special or pecuniary value" to the dogs' "usefulness and services"—their economic value, not their sentimental value. While we referenced evidence "showing the usefulness and services of the dogs, and that they were of a special value to the owner," the next conditional sentence pegs the jury. Thus, a dog's "special or pecuniary value" refers not to the dog-human bond but to the dollars-and-cents value traceable to the dog's usefulness and services. Such value is economic value, not emotional value based on affection, attachment, or companionship. In short, *Heiligmann's* use of the word "special" does not authorize "special damages" and does not refer generically to a dog's ability to combat loneliness, ease depression, or provide security. The valuation criteria is not emotional and subjective; rather it is commercial and objective.

2. Our Post-Heiligmann Cases Do Not Relax the No Emotional-Injury Damages Rule for Animal-Death Cases

Alternatively, the Medlens assert that three *post-Heiligmann* decisions—*City of Tyler v. Likes* [962 S.W.2d 489 (Tex. 1997)], *Porras v. Craig* [675 S.W.2d 503 (Tex. 1984], and *Brown v. Frontier Theatres, Inc.* [369 S.W.2d 299 (Tex. 1963)]—viewed collectively, entitle property owners to seek intrinsic or sentimental-value damages for certain destroyed property that lacks market value or "special or pecuniary" value. Because dogs are considered property under Texas law, they should be treated no differently, argue the Medlens. Accordingly, Avery's intrinsic value to them, including companionship, is recoverable. We decline to stretch our *post-Heiligmann* decisions this far.

Our decision a half-century ago in *Brown* involved irreplaceable family heirlooms such as a wedding veil, pistol, jewelry, hand-made bedspreads and other items going back several generations—in other words, family keepsakes that "have their primary value in sentiment." Such one-of-a-kind heirlooms have a "special value . . . to their owner," and damages may factor in "the feelings of the owner for such property." Notably, on the same day we decided *Brown* fifty years ago, we reaffirmed in another case the default damages rule for destroyed non-heirloom property lacking market or replacement value: "the actual worth or value of the articles to the owner . . . excluding any fanciful or sentimental considerations."

While they rely chiefly on *Brown*, the Medlens also cite our decisions in *Porras* and *Likes*, but neither offers much pertinent guidance here. In *Porras*, a landowner sued someone for clearing several large trees from his land. The landowner testified about what the land meant to him and his wife, not in market terms but in personal terms. We recognized that the landowner had been injured by the destruction of trees, even though the property's overall market value may have actually *increased*. We remanded for a new trial to determine the "intrinsic value" of the felled trees— that is, its ornamental (aesthetic) value and its utility (shade) value. That assessment concerning real property is not rooted in an owner's subjective emotions, as here. While Porras permitted recovery of the "intrinsic value" of the trees, the plaintiff did not seek, nor did the Court discuss, the trees' sentimental value. Here, the Medlens have suffered lost companionship and are seeking, as a form of "intrinsic value" property damages, recovery for Avery's role as a cherished family member. The court of appeals read too much into *Porras*, which did not import sentimental considerations into measuring "intrinsic value." And we decline to expand *Porras's* notion of "intrinsic value" to animal cases, specifically to include the subjective value a dog owner places on his pet's companionship, particularly when *Porras* itself excluded such subjective notions.

Likes is likewise uninstructive. In *Likes*, the plaintiff alleged that a municipality negligently flooded her house and destroyed "many personal irreplaceable items." The principal issue was whether mental-anguish damages are recoverable for the negligent destruction of personal property. We answered no, though we acknowledged *Brown's* sentimental-value rule for property of which the "greater value is in sentiment and not in the market place." Again, mental anguish is a form of personal-injury damage, unrecoverable in an ordinary property-damage case. The Medlens' emotion-based claim is, like the mental-anguish claim in *Likes*, based wholly on negligent damage to personal property. But *Likes* bars personal-injury-type damages in a case alleging negligent property damage. In short, neither *Porras* nor *Likes* provides the Medlens much support. Distilled down, the pivotal question today is straightforward: whether to extend *Brown's* special rules for family heirlooms to negligently destroyed pets.

Heiligmann remains our lone case directly on point, and after a century-plus we are loathe to disturb it. An owner's attachment to a one-of-a-kind family keepsake as in *Brown* is sentimental, but an owner's attachment to a beloved pet is more: It is emotional. Pets afford here-and-now benefits—company, recreation, protection, etc.—unlike a passed-down heirloom kept around chiefly to commemorate past events or passed family members. We agree with the amicus brief submitted by the American Kennel Club (joined by several other pet-welfare groups): "While no two pets are alike, the emotional attachments a person establishes with each pet cannot be shoe-horned into keepsake-like sentimentality for litigation purposes." Finally, as explained below, permitting sentiment-based damages for destroyed heirloom property portends nothing resembling the vast public-policy impact of allowing such damages in animal-tort cases.

Loss of companionship, the gravamen of the Medlens' claim, is fundamentally a form of *personal-injury* damage, not property damage. It is a component of loss of consortium, including the loss of "love, affection, protection, emotional support, services, companionship, care, and society." Loss-of-consortium damages are available only for a few especially close family relationships, and to allow them in lost pet cases would be inconsistent with these limitations. Therefore, like courts in the overwhelming majority of other states, the Restatement of the Law of Torts, and the other Texas courts of appeals that have considered this question, we reject emotion-based liability and prohibit recovery for loss of the human-animal bond.

We do not dispute that dogs are a special form of personal property. That is precisely why Texas law forbids animal cruelty generally (both civilly and criminally), and bans dog fighting and unlawful restraints of dogs specifically—because animals, though property, are unique. Most dogs have a simple job description: provide devoted companionship. We have no need to overrule *Brown's* narrow heirloom exception today; neither do we broaden it to pet-death cases and enshrine an expansive new rule that allows recovery for what a canine companion meant to its owner. The Medlens find it odd that Texas law would permit sentimental damages for loss of an heirloom but not an Airedale. Strickland would find it odd if Texas law permitted damages for loss of a Saint Bernard but not for a brother Bernard. The law is no stranger to incongruity, and we need not jettison *Brown* in order to refuse to extend it to categories of property beyond heirlooms.

The "true rule" in Texas remains this: Where a dog's market value is unascertainable, the correct damages measure is the dog's "special or pecuniary value" (that is, its actual value)—the economic value derived from its "usefulness and services," not value drawn from companionship or other non-commercial considerations.

We recognize that the benefit of most family dogs like Avery is not financial but relational, and springs entirely from the pet's closeness with its human companions. Measuring the worth of a beloved pet is unquestionably an emotional determination—what the animal means to you and your family—but measuring a pet's value is a legal determination. We are focused on the latter, and as a matter of law an owner's affection for a dog (or ferret, or parakeet, or tarantula) is not compensable.

B. Compelling Pet Welfare and Social Policy Reasons Counsel Against Permitting Emotion-Based Damages in Dog-Death Cases

This is a significant case not only for pet owners but also, as several animal-welfare groups underscore, for pets themselves. Appreciating this case's significant implications, numerous animal-advocacy organizations have submitted amicus curiae briefs. And while there is no unanimous "pro-pet" position—organizations committed to animal well-being are arrayed on both sides—the vast majority of pet-friendly groups oppose the Medlens' request for emotion-based damages, lest greater liability raise the cost of pet ownership and ultimately cause companion animals more harm than good.

Several animal-welfare groups—organizations that understand the intense grief and despair occasioned by a pet's death—insist that relational-injury damages would adversely impact pet welfare. For example, the American Kennel Club, joined by the Cat Fanciers' Association and other pro-animal nonprofits, worry that "pet litigation will become a cottage industry," exposing veterinarians, shelter and kennel workers, animal-rescue workers, even dog sitters, to increased liability: "Litigation would arise when pets are injured in car accidents, police actions, veterinary visits, shelter incidents, protection of livestock and pet-on-pet aggression, to name a few." As risks and costs rise, there would be fewer free clinics for spaying and neutering, fewer shelters taking in animals, fewer services like walking and boarding, and fewer people adopting pets, leaving more animals abandoned and ultimately put down. The Texas Veterinary Medical Association sounds alarms of "vast unintended consequences," asserting its members would have no choice but to practice defensive medicine "to safeguard against potential claims of malpractice." The unfortunate outcome, they contend, would be higher prices for veterinary care, thus fewer owners bringing in their pets for needed treatment. Families, particularly lower-income families, will avoid preventive care for their pets, not seek needed care for ill or injured pets, and be more apt to euthanize a pet. The Texas Municipal League and other government associations worry about police officers and animal-service employees being second-guessed for split-second decisions they must make in the field when they encounter loose and potentially dangerous animals. Not all dogs are good-natured, they warn, and government workers must be free to take swift action to protect citizens rather than worrying about lawsuits that, even if successfully defended, drain finite taxpayer resources.

The opposing amici, including the Texas Dog Commission and eleven Texas law professors, emphasize that the court of appeals' judgment is consistent with our property-valuation precedent, which allows for sentimental-value damages for the loss of a dog. On this heirloom point, the Medlens pose a unique hypothetical, asserting they could seek sentimental damages if a taxidermied Avery had been negligently destroyed. If property is property, and if they could seek sentimental value for a stuffed Avery destroyed long after death, why can't they recover for a euthanized Avery destroyed while alive? For the reasons stated above and below, we are unpersuaded.

A decade ago we explained: "When recognizing a new cause of action and the accompanying expansion of duty, we must perform something akin to a cost-benefit analysis to assure that this expansion of liability is justified." On this score, the pet-welfare amici make a forceful case. While recognizing that dogs are treasured companions whose deaths generate tremendous sorrow, they persuade us that loss-of-companionship suits are apt to impact pets adversely. We decline to recognize a new cause of action, so we need not calibrate the public-policy impact of such claims (something legislators are better equipped to do). But, were we to consider that analysis, we could not overlook two legal-policy impacts: (1) the anomaly of elevating "man's best friend" over multiple valuable human relationships; and (2) the open-ended nature of such liability.

The court of appeals' decision works a peculiar result, effectively allowing "wrongful death" damages for pets. Loss of companionship is a component of loss of consortium—a form of personal-injury damage, not property damage—and something we have "narrowly cabined" to two building-block human relationships: husband-wife and parent-child. The Medlens request something remarkable: that pet owners have the same legal footing as those who lose a spouse, parent, or child.

Moreover, they seek damages they plainly could not seek if other close relatives (or friends) were negligently killed: siblings, step-children, grandparents, dear friends, and others. Our cases reject loss-of-consortium recovery for such losses. Losing one's pet, even one considered family, should not invite damages unavailable if an actual human family member were lost. Put differently, the Medlens seek emotion-based damages for the death of "man's best friend" when the law denies such damages for the death of a human best friend. For all their noble and praiseworthy qualities, dogs are not human beings, and the Texas common-law tort system should not prioritize human-animal relationships over intimate human-human relationships, particularly familial ones. Analogous would be anomalous.

It would also invite seemingly arbitrary judicial line-drawing. Certainly, if we anointed a common-law claim for loss of pet companionship, we could prescribe limits, but the issue is not whether the Court can draw lines, but whether it should. After all, people form genuine bonds with a menagerie of animals, so which "beloved family pets" (the court of appeals' description) would merit such preferred treatment? Domesticated dogs and cats only (as in a Tennessee statute)? Furry, but not finned or feathered? What about goldfish? Pythons? Cockatiels? There seems to be no cogent stopping point, at least none that does not resemble judicial legislation.

Similarly, while statutory damage caps exist in various types of cases involving people, the court of appeals' decision leaves matters wholly unconfined. Such broad, unstructured liability would invite peculiar results. Under *Heiligmann*, for example, if a Westminster best-of-breed champion with a $20,000 market value is negligently destroyed, that would be its owner's top-end recovery. But if a 15-year-old frail dog with no market value dies, the owner could sue for unlimited emotional-injury damages. We could impose damages limits, but such fine-tuning is more a legislative function than a judicial one. The Medlens and amici urge a damages model based on a pet's primary value, but that, too, in-vites gamesmanship. The owner of a well-trained dog with legitimate market or pecuniary value, like a service animal, would be better off saying his beloved pet was a "worthless mutt" (to avoid a less-rewarding recovery under *Heiligmann*), yet a lovable, part-of-the-family mutt that the owner adored with all his heart (to maximize sentimental damages under *Brown*). Our tort system cannot countenance liability so imprecise, unbounded, and manipulable.

C. The Legislature Is Best Equipped to Weigh and Initiate Broad Changes to Social and Civil-Justice Policy, Including Whether to Liberalize Damages Recovery in Pet-Death Cases

The Medlens seek a sweeping alteration of Texas tort-law principles, upending a century-plus of settled rights, duties, and responsibilities. The judiciary, however, while well suited to adjudicate individual disputes, is an imperfect forum to examine the myriad policy trade-offs at stake here. Questions abound: who can sue, who can be sued, for what missteps, for what types of damages, for how much money? And what of the societal ripple effects on veterinarians, animal-medicine manufacturers, insureds and insurers, pet owners, pet caretakers, and ultimately pets themselves? Pet-death suits portend fundamental changes to our civil-justice system, not incremental adjustments on a case-by-case basis. They require detailed findings and eligibility criteria, which in turn require the careful balancing of a range of views from a range of perspectives, something best left to our 181-member Legislature. If lawmakers wish, they can hold hearings and then, after hearing testimony and weighing arguments, craft meticulous, product-of-compromise legislation that allows non-economic damages to a controllable and predictable degree.

We also draw counsel from the history of Texas common law, which, though it has allowed sentimental damages for the loss of an heirloom, has not done so for the loss of a person, instead deferring to the Legislature. One explanation is that with heirlooms, the value is sentimental; with people, the value is emotional. The reason the common law historically declined to create a wrongful-death action is not because the common law is incapable of setting reasonable parameters, or because such parameters are impossible or necessarily capricious. Rather it is because such parameters are most optimally informed by policy- and value-laden judgments the Legislature is better equipped to make. The difficulties of measuring damages for the loss of human life and identifying the beneficiaries entitled to recover were deemed by the common law too great. Because the judiciary was an imperfect decider, courts decided legislatures should decide. And our legislature did so, authorizing a statutory wrongful-death action for reasons it was better suited to calibrate. Having historically declined to recognize a common-law action for the loss of a human, the common law should not, for mostly the same reasons, recognize one for the loss of a pet.

Our precedent on the legal valuation of companion animals has endured for 122 years, and while we decline today to expand the damages available to bereaved pet owners, we understand the strength of the human-animal bond. Few Texans consider their pets throw-away commodities. Perhaps the Legislature will enact a more generous valuation formula for family pets. Valuation derives fundamentally from values, and elected legislators may favor scrapping the "property" label and reclassifying companion pets as something more elevated. The Legislature has passed a Wrongful Death Statute for humans; it has not (yet) for animals. Given the competing public-policy considerations, we believe if there is to be expanded recovery in pet-death cases, it, too, should be confronted legislatively, not judicially.

* * *

As a matter of Texas common law, emotion-based damages are unrecoverable, but whether to permit such liability statutorily is a quintessential legislative judgment. Societal attitudes inexorably change, and shifting public views may persuade the Legislature to extend wrongful-death actions to pets. Amid competing policy interests, including the inherent subjectivity (and inflatability) of emotion-based damages, lawmakers are best positioned to decide if such a potentially costly expansion of tort law is in the State's best interest, and if so, to structure an appropriate remedy.

III. Conclusion

To his dog, every man is Napoleon; hence the constant popularity of dogs.

It is an inconvenient, yet inescapable, truth: "Tort law . . . cannot remedy every wrong." Lines, seemingly arbitrary, are required. No one disputes that a family dog—"in life the firmest friend"—is a treasured companion. But it is also personal property, and the law draws sensible, policy-based distinctions between types of property. The majority rule throughout most of America—including Texas since 1891—leavens warm-heartedness with sober-mindedness, applying a rational rule rather than an emotional one. For the reasons discussed above, we decline to (1) jettison our 122-year-old precedent classifying dogs as ordinary property, and (2) permit non-economic damages rooted in relational attachment.

Under Texas common law, the human-animal bond, while undeniable, is uncompensable, no matter how it is conceived in litigation—as a measure of property damages (including "intrinsic value" or "special value . . . derived from the attachment that an owner feels for his pet"), as a personal-injury claim for loss of companionship or emotional distress, or any other theory. The packaging or labeling matters not: Recovery rooted in a pet owner's feelings is prohibited. We understand that limiting recovery to market (or actual) value seems incommensurate with the emotional harm suffered, but pet-death actions compensating for such harm, while they can certainly be legislated, are not something Texas common law should enshrine.

We reverse the court of appeals' judgment and render judgment in favor of Strickland.

Notes

1. Unless and until the Texas state legislature addresses this issue or the Texas Supreme Court revisits it in a future case, the law is settled in Texas. As discussed below, because tort doctrine is a state law concern, that is not the case elsewhere. For example, the "intrinsic value" measure of damages has been adopted in other jurisdictions and in other contexts. The concept is particularly significant in cases arising from harm to companion animals. Although "intrinsic value" certainly is not a new concept, its application seems to hinge on variable factors on a case-by-case basis. In the veterinary malpractice case excerpted below (*Sherman v. Kissinger,*

195 P.3d 539, 546–49 (Wash. Ct. App. 2008)), the court summarized Washington precedent on the issues.

It is well established, and Sherman does not dispute, that as a matter of law pets are characterized as personal property. . . . .

In *McCurdy v. Union Pac. R. Co.,* 68 Wash. 2d 457 (1966), the Washington Supreme Court sets forth a three part analysis for the measure of damages for the loss of personal property.

> If the property is a total loss the measure of damages is the value of the property destroyed or damaged. This is its market value, if it has a market value. If the property is damaged but not destroyed, the measure of damages is the difference between the market value of the property before the injury and its market value after the injury. (Again, if it has a market value.) If the property does not have a market value, then if a total loss, the measure of damages is the cost to replace or reproduce the article. If it cannot be reproduced or replaced, then its value to the owner may be considered in fixing damages.

Id. at 467.

In *McCurdy,* because there was evidence of the property's market value, the court reversed the trial court's refusal to give a jury instruction on market value. The court defined "market value" to mean the "reasonable sum of money which the property would bring on a fair sale, by a man willing to sell, but not obligated to sell, to a man willing to buy, but not obligated to buy." *Id.* at 467. Because the measure of damages was disputed, the court held that on remand the trial court should instruct the jury to first consider whether there was a market value for the property before considering intrinsic value damages. "If the jury, having been instructed on market value, nevertheless finds that there was no market value, then [the property's] actual or intrinsic value, including consideration of its value to the owner, may be used by the jury in fixing damages." *Id.* at 469.

In *Mieske v. Bartell Drug Co.,* 92 Wash. 2d 40 (1979), the jury awarded the plaintiffs damages for family movie films that were destroyed. On appeal, the court adopted the measure of damages set forth in *McCurdy* and rejected the argument that as a matter of law the plaintiffs were entitled only to damages for the cost of replacing the film because blank film "is not what the plaintiffs' lost." Because the plaintiffs in *Mieske* proved that there was no market value and the destroyed film could not be replaced, the court held that the plaintiffs were entitled to the value to the owner, also referred to as the intrinsic value of the property. However, recognizing that there was a subjective element to intrinsic value damages, the court clarified that while not explicitly stated in *McCurdy,* if the jury decides that the proper measure of damages is the value to the owner, the jury cannot consider sentimental value. "[W]hile not stated in *McCurdy,* we have held that in the third *McCurdy* situation, [value to the owner] damages are not recoverable for the sentimental value which the owner places on the property. . . ." The court in *Mieske* defined sentimental value as "indulging in feeling to an unwarranted extent" or being "affectedly or mawkishly emotional." Webster's Third International Dictionary (1963). *Mieske,* 92 Wash. 2d at 45. In describing the measure of damages for the intrinsic value of the property, the court also acknowledged it is somewhat imprecise, but concluded that the difficulty of assessing intrinsic value should not preclude damages where the plaintiff establishes there is no market or replacement value.

> Necessarily the measure of damages in these circumstances is the most imprecise of the three categories. Yet difficulty of assessment is not cause to deny damages to a plaintiff whose property has no market value and cannot be replaced or reproduced.

Id. at 44.

In proving intrinsic value, while the owner can testify about the value of the property, that testimony is not binding. Rather in determining damages, the fact finder must consider the evidence objectively from the perspective of a reasonable owner in the plaintiff's position. *James v. Robeck,* 79 Wash. 2d 864, 869 (1971). In *Stephens v. Target Corp.,* 482 F. Supp. 2d 1234 (9th Cir.2007), the court suggested that one way the jury could determine intrinsic damages was to "consider the dog's utility (for lack of a better term) in assessing its intrinsic value; such an assessment is confined by the limitation on sentimental or fanciful value set forth in *Mieske,* 593 P.2d at 1311."

However, it is well established that a pet owner has no right to emotional distress damages or damages for loss of human-animal bond based on the negligent death or injury to a pet. In *Pickford v. Masion,* 124 Wash. App. 257, 260 (2004), we held that the plaintiff was not entitled to recover damages for negligent infliction of emotional distress or damages for loss of companionship and the human-animal relationship for the negligent death or injury of a pet. However, in *Womack v. Rardon,* 133 Wash. App. 254, 263 (2006), the court held that malicious injury to an animal can support a claim for emotional distress damages.

Kissinger's and BVH's reliance on *Dillon v. O'Connor,* 68 Wash. 2d 184 (1966) to argue that as a matter of law Sherman's damages are limited to market value, is misplaced. In *Dillon,* the defendant negligently killed the plaintiff's dog while driving his car. The plaintiff sued for the market value of his trained four-year-old hunting dog. While the supreme court stated that the dog's training and pedigree were factors the jury could consider in determining the fair market value, the court held the jury instruction that authorized the jury to award damages for factors "over and above" market value was an erroneous statement of the law and ambiguous.

While the measure of damages for personal property is a question of law, the plaintiff bears the burden of producing evidence to show which measure of damages applies. *McCurdy,* 68 Wash.2d at 467; *Womack,* 133 Wash. App. at 261 (the party claiming damages bears the burden of proof). The amount of damages is a question of fact and the fact finder has the ultimate authority to weigh the evidence and determine the amount of damages in a particular case.

Consequently, where, as here, the plaintiff seeks to establish that the third measure of damages applies, the plaintiff must produce evidence showing that the property does not have a fair market value and cannot be replaced. If the plaintiff claiming damages meets this burden, the burden then shifts to the other party to present evidence on the measure of damages.

Sherman v. Kissinger, 195 P.3d 539, 547–49 (Wash. Ct. App. 2008) (finding questions of fact as to whether plaintiff's toy poodle with a clotting disorder had a market value).

2. The interplay between market value and intrinsic value varies by jurisdiction. After *Sherman,* in Washington plaintiffs must prove their animals had no market value in order to be entitled to seek intrinsic value damages. The same holds true in Oregon. *Green v. Leckington,* 236 P.2d 335 (Or. 1951). In contrast, in California, plaintiffs cannot recover "peculiar value" damages unless they *can* prove some market value (see Note 7).

3. In the Washington cases, the courts were quite clear that intrinsic value is not equivalent to and (at least theoretically) does not include sentimental value. As a practical matter, however, what value of any nature was there in a family's home movies in the Washington *Mieske* case, for example, if not sentimental value? What about in family photographs? Or "heirlooms" that do not have a market value?

It has been said that the courts allow recovery for the emotional component through the use of legal fiction that the owner is not being directly compensated for the emotional harm but, rather, for the "value to the owner," which includes an element of the owner's feelings for the pet. 1 D. Dobbs, Remedies § 5.15(3), at 899–900 (1993). In employing that fiction, the courts are "denying in one breath that * * * emotional harm damage can be recovered, but awarding * * * damages for the personal value to the owner, specifically including the owner's feelings as a part of this value." 1 D. Dobbs, Remedies § 5.15(3), at 899–900.

Anzalone v. Kragness, 826 N.E.2d 472, 477–78 (Ill. App. Ct. 2005). In *Anzalone,* the plaintiff's cat was attacked by a dog while being boarded at an animal hospital. The court cited extensively from, and followed, *Jankoski v. Preiser Animal Hospital, Ltd.,* 510 N.E.2d 1084 (Ill. App. Ct. 1987), applying an "actual value to the owner" standard for damages. Unlike the cases discussed and excerpted above which, at least theoretically, reject the notion of "sentimental" value, the *Jankoski* court held that the value to the owner may "include some element of sentimental value." *Id.* at 1087.

4. In *Leith v. Frost*, 899 N.E.2d 635 (Ill. App. Ct. 2008), plaintiffs' dog, Molly, was killed by defendants' dog. Addressing the issue of damages, the court held:

> The trial court reasoned that under Illinois law, a dog is considered to be personal property. The cost of repairs to personal property is usually the measure of damages, but when the cost of repairs exceeds the fair market value of the personal property, the value of the personal property becomes the ceiling on the amount of damages which can be recovered. The court awarded plaintiff damages in the amount of $200, the amount of Molly's fair market value, according to [] testimony.
>
> Even if it were true that anyone would pay $200 for a 7 1/2-year-old dachshund that is not a show dog, the reality is that Molly had merely nominal value at the time of the injury. A reasonable person in defendant's position should have reasonably foreseen that if his dogs escaped from their enclosure and injured plaintiffs' family pet, plaintiffs would feel compelled to pay considerably more than a nominal amount for veterinary care. It is common knowledge that people are prepared to make great sacrifices for the well-being and continued existence of their household pets, to which they have become deeply attached. They feel a moral obligation toward these animals. Emotionally, they have no choice but to lay out great expenditures when these animals suffer a serious physical injury. Illinois courts recognize that certain items of personal property, such as heirlooms, photographs, trophies, and pets have no market value. *Jankoski*, 157 Ill. App. 3d at 820. Damages for harm to such items of property are not restricted to nominal damages. "[R]ather, damages must be ascertained in some rational way from such elements as are attainable. *** [T]he proper basis for assessing compensatory damages in such a case is to determine the item's 'actual value to [the] plaintiff'[;] *** the plaintiff is 'entitled to demonstrate its value to him by such proof as the circumstances admit.'" *Jankoski*, 157 Ill. App. 3d at 820, quoting *Long v. Arthur Rubloff & Co.*, 27 Ill. App. 3d 1013, 1026 (1975). We specifically adopt the rationale of *Burgess v. Shampooch Pet Industries, Inc.*, 35 Kan. App. 2d 458, 463 (2006), in which the Court of Appeals of Kansas held: "[W]hen an injured pet dog with no discernable market value is restored to its previous health, the measure of damages may include, but is not limited to, the reasonable and customary cost of necessary veterinary care and treatment."
>
> In the present case, plaintiffs have demonstrated how much Molly is worth to them by paying $4,784 for the dog's veterinary care. Plaintiffs are not claiming a windfall; this is the amount they actually have paid or have contractually obligated themselves to pay. To prevent the award of damages from being nominal, we modify the trial court's judgment so as to award plaintiffs $4,784 in compensatory damages instead of $200.

Leith, 899 N.E.2d at 640–41.

The *Leith* court fashioned a remedy that supposedly approximated the "actual value to the owner," but relied solely on the veterinary costs paid by plaintiffs. While the veterinary costs represent one aspect of the damages caused by defendants' wrongdoing, those costs may have little connection to the plaintiffs' evaluation of their damages upon loss of their companion animal. The obvious analogue to those costs are medical costs incurred in a personal injury case, which are always awarded, *in addition to* any calculation of other compensatory damages.

As in *Leith*, and as the following case and the Notes after it demonstrate, courts are becoming more inclined to recognize companion animals as a unique form of property and allow plaintiffs to at least seek damages accordingly where plaintiffs seek actual out-of-pocket costs, even if those costs exceed the market value of their companion animals, although as noted in the following case, this approach is not new.

Barking Hound Village LLC v. Monyak

Georgia Supreme Court, 2016
299 Ga. 144, 787 S.E.2d 191

THOMPSON, CHIEF JUSTICE.

The subject matter of this case is near and dear to the heart of many a Georgian in that it involves the untimely death of a beloved family pet and concerns the proper measure of damages available to the owners of an animal injured or killed through the negligence of others. Observing that pet dogs are considered personal property under Georgia law, but finding that not all dogs have an actual commercial or market value, the Court of Appeals held that where the actual market value of the animal is nonexistent or nominal, the appropriate measure of damages would be the actual value of the dog to its owners. The Court of Appeals concluded that the actual value of the animal could be demonstrated by reasonable veterinary and other expenses incurred by its owners in treating its injuries, as well as by other economic factors, but held that evidence of noneconomic factors demonstrating the dog's intrinsic value to its owners would not be admissible.

This Court granted certiorari to consider whether the Court of Appeals erred in holding that the proper measure of damages for the loss of a pet dog is the actual value of the dog to its owners rather than the dog's fair market value. Because we find that longstanding Georgia precedent provides that the damages recoverable by the owners of an animal negligently killed by another include both the animal's fair market value at the time of the loss plus interest, and, in addition, any medical and other expenses reasonably incurred in treating the animal, we affirm in part and reverse in part the Court of Appeals' decision.

The damages at issue in this case arise from the death of a mixed-breed dachshund owned by Robert and Elizabeth Monyak. In 2012, the Monyaks boarded Lola, their 8½-year-old dachshund mix, for ten days at a kennel owned by Barking Hound Village, LLC ("BHV") and managed by William Furman. Along with Lola, the Monyaks boarded their 13-year-old mixed-breed Labrador retriever, Callie, who had been prescribed an anti-inflammatory drug for arthritis pain—medication which the Monyaks gave to kennel personnel with directions that it be administered to Callie. Three days after picking up their dogs from BHV, Lola was diagnosed with acute renal failure. Despite receiving extensive veterinary care over a nine-month period, including kidney dialysis treatment, Lola died in March 2013.

The Monyaks sued BHV and Furman for damages alleging that while boarded at the kennel Lola was administered toxic doses of the medication prescribed for Callie, a much larger dog. The Monyaks asserted various claims of negligence against BHV and Furman, and sought compensatory damages, including over $67,000 in veterinary and other expenses incurred in treating Lola. In addition, alleging fraud and deceit on the part of the defendants, the Monyaks sought litigation expenses and punitive damages.

BHV and Furman moved for summary judgment on all the Monyaks' claims asserting that the measure of damages for the death of a dog was capped at the dog's fair market value and that, in this case, the Monyaks failed to prove Lola had any market value; thus their claims were barred as a matter of law. Alternatively, the defendants sought partial summary judgment on the Monyaks' claims for punitive damages and fraud.

In its order denying summary judgment to the defendants . . . , the trial court held the Monyaks would be permitted to present evidence of the actual value of the dog to them, as demonstrated by reasonable veterinary and other expenses incurred in her treatment, as well as evidence of noneconomic factors demonstrating the dog's intrinsic value.

On appeal, the Court of Appeals affirmed the trial court's ruling rejecting a market value cap on damages. Finding the evidence showed Lola had little or no market value,[2] the Court of Appeals observed that "[w]here the absence of a market value is shown, 'the measure of damages . . . is the actual value to the owner[,]'" quoting *Cherry v. McCutchen*, 65 Ga. App. 301, 304 (1941). Noting, however, that, in Cherry, no recovery was allowed for the sentimental value of the object to the owner, the Court of Appeals concluded that damages for the intrinsic value of the dog to the Monyaks were not recoverable.

* * *

1. The parties agree, and Georgia law clearly provides, that a pet dog has value and is considered the personal property of its owner. As a result, the owner of a dog may maintain an action against anyone who wantonly, maliciously, intentionally, or negligently injures or kills it.

---

2. Evidence in the record showed that the Monyaks adopted Lola from a rescue center when she was about two years old, there was no purchase price for the dog, she was not a pure breed or a show dog, she had never generated any revenue, and that at the time she was boarded at the kennel, her market value to the public at large was nonexistent or nominal.

2. Having established that dogs are personal property for which a suit for damages will lie, we look to Georgia precedent in order to determine the appropriate measure of damages recoverable by a dog's owners in such actions. In so doing, we find the Court of Appeals erred in deciding that application of an actual value to owner standard was the appropriate measure of recoverable damages, but additionally find that a cap on all damages based on application of the fair market value standard as urged by defendants is likewise incorrect.

Generally, in a suit to recover damages to personal property it is a well-established principle that "a plaintiff cannot recover an amount of damages against a tortfeasor greater than the fair market value of the property prior to impairment." However, over 120 years ago this Court decided that such a limitation was not appropriate in negligence cases involving the injury or death of an animal. See *Telfair County v. Webb*, 119 Ga. 916, 918 (1904); *Atlanta Cotton-Seed Oil Mills v. Coffey*, 80 Ga. 145, 150 (1887). Instead, this Court determined that where an animal is negligently injured and subsequently dies as a result of those injuries, the proper measure of damages recoverable by the animal's owner includes not only the full market value of the animal at the time of the loss plus interest, but also expenses incurred by the owner in an effort to cure the animal. See *Webb*, 119 Ga. at 918; *Coffey*, 80 Ga. at 150.

* * *

. . . [W]hile a cap on the recovery of loss of use damages exists for an injured animal, there is no such cap on the amount of damages recoverable with respect to actual expenditures associated with the animal's treatment and recovery. Thus, where the injured animal survives, its owner is entitled to receive loss of hire and diminution in market value *up to* the full market value of the animal in addition to the animal's reasonable medical costs and treatment; whereas, when the animal fails to recover, damages are limited to the market value of the animal plus interest, as well as the reasonable costs expended on its care and treatment.

In adopting a different measure of damages for use in tort cases involving injury to animals, this Court relied on a prominent 19th century legal treatise on negligence, and notes, in which the authors promoted such a distinction and articulated the rationale behind it, stating:

> [I]n cases of injury to animals . . . the plaintiff ought to recover for expenses reasonably incurred in efforts to cure them, in addition to the depreciation in their value, or to their whole value where they are finally lost. The law would be inhumane in its tendency if it should prescribe a different rule, even where the animal eventually dies, since it would then offer an inducement to the owner to neglect its suffering.

Shearman & Redfield, Negligence § 603, at 680–681 (2nd ed. 1870).

By ensuring that property owners whose animals are negligently injured by another are able to recoup reasonable expenses incurred in attempting to save the animal, this Court's decisions in *Webb* and *Coffey* are consistent with the position taken by courts in a majority of states, including those which have adopted an actual value to the owner measure of damages to determine a pet dog's worth.

At the time this lawsuit was filed, the Monyaks' injured dog was still alive and the veterinary fees incurred were in the neighborhood of $10,000. The fact that the dog's treatment ultimately proved unsuccessful and the animal died nine months later should not prevent the Monyaks from seeking compensatory damages for the reasonable veterinary fees incurred in their attempt to save their pet. Rather, we conclude, pursuant to long-established Georgia precedent, that the proper measure of damages recoverable by the Monyaks for the negligent injury and death of their dog includes both the dog's fair market value plus interest *and* any reasonable medical costs and other expenses they incurred in treating the animal for its injuries.

3. While we are sympathetic to the concerns expressed by the parties and others regarding the difficulties in establishing the fair market value of a family pet,[5] this Court long ago stated that "[t]he value of a dog may be proved as that of any other property, by evidence that he was of a particular breed, and had certain qualities, and by witnesses who knew the market value of such animal, if any market value be shown." *Woolfolk*, 128 Ga. at 635 [1907]. . . .

Georgia law provides that direct testimony regarding market value is opinion evidence and a witness need not be an expert to testify as to an object's value so long as the witness has had an opportunity to form a reasoned opinion. . . .

4. Although we find the Court of Appeals erred in applying an actual value to owner measure of damages in this case, we find no error in that court's determination that Georgia precedent does not allow for the recovery of damages based on the sentimental value of personal property to its owner. Instead, we agree with those courts which have held that the unique human-animal bond, while cherished, is beyond legal measure.

This does not mean, however, that all qualitative evidence regarding the plaintiffs' dog is inadmissible. As in *Chalker* [*v. Raley*, 73 Ga. App. 415 (1946)], we see no reason why opinion evidence, both qualitative and quantitative, of an animal's particular attributes — e.g., breed, age, training, temperament, and use — should be any less admissible than similar evidence offered in describing the value of other types of personal property. The key is ensuring that such evidence relates to the value of the dog in a fair market, not the value of the dog solely to its owner.

---

5. We note that amicus briefs have been filed in this case by numerous entities concerned with the care and treatment of animals both in this State and nationwide. These groups include the Georgia Veterinary Medical Association, American Veterinary Medical Association, American Kennel Club, Cat Fanciers' Association, Animal Health Institute, National Animal Interest Alliance, American Pet Products Association, American Animal Hospital Association, Pet Industry Joint Advisory Council and the Animal Legal Defense Fund. The primary issue addressed by amici, however, is whether the law in Georgia should allow for the recovery of damages based on a pet's sentimental value to its owner, a position properly rejected by the Court of Appeals in this case and not disputed by either party on appeal.

5. As previously stated in Division 2 of this opinion, in addition to recovering the fair market value of their deceased dog plus interest, the Monyaks would be entitled to recover the reasonable veterinary and other expenses they reasonably incurred in trying to save her. Whether the veterinary costs and other expenses incurred by a pet owner in obtaining treatment for an animal negligently injured by another are reasonable will depend on the facts of each case. As observed by the Massachusetts Appeals Court in a case involving tortious injury to a dog,

> [a]mong the factors to be considered are the type of animal involved, the severity of its injuries, the purchase and/or replacement price of the animal, its age and special traits or skills, its income-earning potential, whether it was maintained as part of the owner's household, the likelihood of success of the medical procedures employed, and whether the medical procedures involved are typical and customary to treat the injuries at issue.

Irwin v. Degtiarov, 8 N.E.3d 296, 301 (Mass. App. Ct. 2014).

* * *

6. For the foregoing reasons, we reverse the Court of Appeals' decision in this case to the extent it holds that the proper measure of damages recoverable in tort cases involving the negligent injury to or death of an animal is one based on the actual value of the animal to its owner. We affirm, however, that portion of the Court of Appeals' decision holding that damages representing an animal's sentimental value to its owner are not recoverable, although we find that descriptive evidence, both qualitative and quantitative, is admissible to establish an animal's attributes for determining its fair market value, as well as for determining the reasonableness of an owner's expenditures for veterinary expenses. Accordingly, we remand this case to the Court of Appeals for further proceedings consistent with this opinion.

Notes

1. Courts in other jurisdictions have taken the same approach as the courts in *Leith* (in the Notes before this case) and *Barking Hound Village* in allowing recovery of veterinary costs *in addition* to fair market value. For example, in *Rego v. Madaliski*, 63 N.E.3d 190 (Ohio Ct. App. 2016), the court cited to *Leith* and *Barking Hound Village*, among others, in concluding:

> [W]e cannot ignore the growing number of courts outside of Ohio which have awarded veterinary expenses for injuries caused by attacks from other dogs [citing *Leith*] and grooming or kennel injuries [citing *Barking Hound Village* and *Burgess v. Shampooch*]. . . . In addition, various courts and law review articles have discussed the plausibility of reclassifying companion animals under a "semi-property" classification suggesting such terms as companion property, or sentient property. *See, generally*, William C. Root, Note, 47 Vill. L. Rev. 423 (2002); Lauren M. Sirois, Comment, 163 U. Pa. L. Rev. 1199 (2015).

We agree with and acknowledge that pets do not have the same characteristics as other forms of personal property, such as a table or sofa which is disposable and replaceable at our convenience. Accordingly, additional factors should be considered in fashioning an appropriate economic damages award due to loss or injury. Such factors include fair market value, age of the pet, pedigree, training, breeding income, recommendation of the treating veterinarian, circumstances of the injury, and anticipated recovery. The overriding consideration is the reasonableness of the expenses and is fact specific. *Irwin v. Degtiarov*, 8 N.E.3d at 301 (Mass. App. 2014). Importantly we note that

> [a]lthough the owner's affection for the animal may be considered in assessing the reasonableness of the decision to treat the animal, the owner cannot recover for his or her own hurt feelings, emotions, or pain. Nor is the owner entitled to recover for the loss of the animal's companionship or society. *Id.* at 302.

Rego, 63 N.E.3d at 192. Based on the foregoing, the *Rego* court remanded to the trial court for a damages hearing to determine the amount of damages beyond fair market value that the plaintiff was entitled to recover after her dog was "seriously injured" from an attack by the defendant's dog. When the complaint was filed, the veterinary bills were more than $10,000.

In *Kimes v. Grosser*, 195 Cal. App. 4th 1556 (2011), the defendant allegedly shot the plaintiff's pet cat, Pumkin, with a pellet gun while Pumkin was sitting on a fence between the parties' neighboring properties. Emergency surgery costing $6,000 saved Pumkin's life, but left him partially paralyzed, and the plaintiff incurred an additional $30,000 in expenses caring for the cat because of his injuries. In that case the plaintiff was "not seeking loss of companionship, unique noneconomic value, or the emotional value of the cat, but rather the costs incurred as a result of the shooting." *Id.* at 1560 n.3. The defendants filed motions in limine to exclude evidence of such expenses on the theory that liability was limited to the cat's fair market value, and the defendants described Pumkin as "an adopted stray of very low economic value." *Id.* at 1558. The trial court granted the motion, the plaintiff then declined to proceed (effectively conceding that the cat had no market value), and the case was dismissed. The appellate court reversed the judgment dismissing the case, remanding to the trial court to allow the plaintiff to present evidence of the bills incurred. The court held that plaintiff was entitled to recover reasonable and necessary costs; and defendants were entitled to present evidence as to why the costs were unreasonable under the circumstances. Looking to cases involving damage to unique property other than companion animals, the court focused on the tangible nature of the costs actually incurred by the plaintiff.

> In this case, plaintiff is not plucking a number out of the air for the sentimental value of damaged property; he seeks to present evidence of costs incurred for Pumkin's care and treatment by virtue of the shooting — a

"rational way" of demonstrating a measure of damages apart from the cat's market value. That evidence is admissible as proof of plaintiff's compensable damages, and the trial court erred in granting the motions to exclude it. (*See also* Evid. Code, § 823 ["the value of property for which there is no relevant, comparable market may be determined by any method of valuation that is just and equitable"].) Plaintiff is entitled to have a jury determine whether the amounts he expended for Pumkin's care because of the shooting were reasonable.

Kimes, 195 Cal. App. 4th at 1561–62.

The same approach was taken in *Martinez v. Robledo*, 210 Cal. App. 4th 384 (2012) (discussing *Kimes* extensively, finding it persuasive and reaching the same result). *Martinez* was actually a consolidated appeal of two cases—one in which the plaintiff's neighbor shot plaintiff's German Shepherd when he entered the neighbor's property, requiring his leg to be amputated and resulting in close to $21,000 in veterinary costs; and another in which the defendant veterinarian left a piece of gauze in plaintiff's nine-year-old Golden Retriever during surgery and the veterinarian offered to refund the $4,866.16 cost of the original surgery but not the $37,766.06 for the emergency surgery and veterinary care required to save the dog's life by removing gauze remnants and treating the damage caused by the gauze. The defendants argued that to "permit animal owners—or at least the owners of otherwise 'valueless' animals—to effectively dictate a value by their unilateral choice concerning the amount they are willing to spend for veterinary care is to treat animals as *sui generis*, as fundamentally different from any other sort of personal property." But, as the court pointed out, "the law already treats animals differently from other forms of property." The court noted felony animal cruelty laws across the country, federal pet evacuation legislation in the wake of Hurricane Katrina and cases in other jurisdictions reflecting "the widespread socially-accepted significance of animals and their connection with people." The court also looked to California statutes, concluding that "[i]n California, the Legislature has recognized since 1872 that animals are special, sentient beings, because unlike other forms of property, animals feel pain, suffer and die." The court therefore found "the usual standard of recovery for damaged personal property—market value—is inadequate when applied to injured pets." *Accord Hyland v. Borras*, 719 A.2d 662, 664 (N.J. Super. Ct., App. Div. 1998) (where defendant's dog injured plaintiff's dog, "[i]t is purely a matter of 'good sense' that defendants be required to 'make good the injury done' as the result of their negligence by reimbursing plaintiff for the necessary and reasonable expenses she incurred to restore the dog to its condition before the attack). *But see Smith v. Wisconsin Mutual Ins. Co.*, 2016 Wisc. App. LEXIS 209, *6 (Unpub. Apr. 7, 2016), in which the court rejected a claim for more than $12,000 in veterinary and related expenses to save a badly injured 11-year-old dog who had been attacked by another dog, instead limiting damages to the lesser of the cost of repair or a "replacement dog of the same breed." In so ruling and "declin[ing] to extend Wisconsin's 'keepsake' rule to pets," the *Smith* court rejected the plaintiffs' contention that because elderly dogs such as theirs typically have no market value, the rule applicable to family heirlooms and keepsakes (special value to the owner) should apply.

The *Hyland* court noted, without reaching, the "more difficult question of whether and when a plaintiff should, if ever, be awarded non-economic damages for such a loss." In raising this issue, which was not before the court, the court cited to Debra Squires-Lee, Note, *In Defense of Floyd: Appropriately Valuing Companion Animals*, 70 N.Y.U. L. Rev. 1059 (1995), which was written about the *Gluckman v. American Airlines* case discussed earlier in this chapter.

Does the fact that the actual financial expenditures recovered exceed the market value of the "property" increase the potential import of these cases? Or does the close tie to out-of-pocket expenses actually reduce the value attributed to the animals at issue?

2. In various contexts outside the realm of animal law, courts have taken the practical approach of explicitly recognizing that sentimental value may be recoverable in certain circumstances, even where there is also a nominal market value to the damaged or destroyed property. The *Brown v. Frontier Theatres* case relied upon by the *Strickland* plaintiffs is a prime example. Although the *Strickland* court declined to apply *Brown*'s "special value" analysis to companion animal cases, courts in other jurisdictions may find the analogy more compelling.

> The law recognizes that articles of small market value of which their owner is despoiled may have a special value to him as heirlooms . . .

> As a general rule recovery for sentimental value for personal property cannot be had in a suit for the loss of property for personal use such as wearing apparel and household goods. This rule has been applied in Texas so as to deny the recovery for sentimental value in a suit for the loss of heirlooms. However, in our opinion such is not the rule to be applied in a suit to recover for the loss or destruction of items which have their primary value in sentiment.

> It is a matter of common knowledge that items such as these generally have no market value which would adequately compensate their owner for their loss or destruction. Such property is not susceptible of supply and reproduction in kind, and their greater value is in sentiment and not in the market place. In such cases the most fundamental rule of damages that every wrongful injury or loss to persons or property should be adequately and reasonably compensated requires the allowance of damages in compensation for the reasonable special value of such articles to their owner taking into consideration the feelings of the owner for such property. Where such special value is greater than the market value, it becomes the only criterion for the assessment of damages.

Brown v. Frontier Theaters, Inc., 369 S.W.2d 299 (Tex. 1963) (fire damage to the tenant's property from negligent failure to repair electrical wiring defects). *See also*

Bond v. A.H. Belo Corp., 602 S.W.2d 105 (Tex. Civ. App. 1980) (relying on *Brown*, the court awarded the appellant the sentimental value of pictures, birth records and newspaper clippings lost by a newspaper reporter, which pertained to her efforts to find her natural parents). *But see Edmonds v. U.S.*, 563 F. Supp. 2d 196, 203 (D.D.C. 2008) (noting the views in *Campins*, excerpted below, and in *Bond*, but concluding that it would "follow the Restatement and the majority of courts, and apply the rule that in the case of missing family photos, special value to the owner can be recovered, but sentimental value cannot").

3. In *Stifft's Jewelers v. Oliver*, 678 S.W.2d 372 (Ark. 1984), the plaintiff had brought four rings to the defendant jeweler for repair. Three of the rings—her engagement ring, her mother's diamond ring, and her grandmother's garnet ring—were lost. The jury awarded $3,800 for the market value of the rings and $4,000 for the rings' sentimental value. On appeal, the Arkansas Supreme Court recognized that sentimental value may be a measure of damages in some cases, though not under the facts of that case.

> In order to determine correctly the measure of damages, the nature of the action must first be determined. While appellants have provided us with a tort theory, they are bound to proceed on a contract theory. . . . [¶] The question here is the amount of damages that can be established with reasonable certainty under the facts of this case. Since there was a market value established for the rings, we must now determine whether a special or sentimental value is greater than the market value, and what the parties understood their obligations to be. We look to our holding in *Morrow, et al. v. First National Bank of Hot Springs*, 261 Ark. 568, 550 S.W.2d 429 (1977) for guidance. There we reaffirmed the adoption of the "tacit agreement test" for the recovery of special damages for a breach of contract. We stated: "By that test the plaintiff must prove more than the defendant's mere knowledge that a breach of contract will entail special damages to the plaintiff. It must also appear that the defendant at least tacitly agreed to assume responsibility."
>
> Here the appellees have not pointed out where the appellant company was made aware of the sentimental value of the rings. Neither do they show any tacit agreement by appellant to assume responsibility.
>
> There could be circumstances where the value of the property is primarily sentimental and the jury could determine that value, provided there was a tacit agreement by the parties. However, the circumstances do not exist here because no tacit agreement was made and the alleged sentimental value of the lost rings is so highly speculative in this case that it was not a proper element of damages for consideration by the jury. We strike that part of the judgment for sentimental value.

Id. at 373.

The *Stifft's* holding relied in large part on the fact that plaintiff's case was being evaluated under a bailment theory. Under this standard, then, where a plaintiff brings his companion animal to a veterinarian or a groomer such that a bailment contract is created, and the plaintiff makes clear his emotional bond with and sentimental attachment to his companion animal, if that animal is harmed while in the care of that veterinarian or groomer, the plaintiff should have a viable claim for damages for sentimental value. Is that bond a given, when companion animals are brought to veterinarians for services which all parties know will usually exceed the market value of the animals?

4. California has codified the reasoning in the *Stifft's Jewelers* case in Civil Code § 3355, which allows an award of "peculiar value" damages: "Where certain property has a peculiar value to a person recovering damages for deprivation thereof, or injury thereto, that may be deemed to be its value against one who had notice thereof before incurring a liability to damages in respect thereof, or against a willful wrongdoer." As interpreted in the standard California Civil Jury Instruction 3093L in order to recover damages for the unique value of personal property, the plaintiff must prove that (1) the property "had some market value," (2) the property "had unique value" to the plaintiff, and (3) either that the defendant "had notice of this unique value before the harm" or that the defendant's "conduct was intentional and wrongful."

5. In *Campins v. Capels*, 461 N.E.2d 712 (Ind. Ct. App. 1984), various items of jewelry were stolen. The thief was convicted and the plaintiffs brought a civil action against the jeweler who had purchased and melted down the stolen jewelry. The items destroyed included three national racing championship rings awarded by United States Auto Club, that had significant sentimental value to their owner.

> The emphasis in the cases where the actual value of the goods exceeded the market value or where there was no market value at all is upon looking at all the circumstances and the available elements of loss in a rational, reasonable fashion. For example, the South Carolina Supreme Court stated, "any method adopted, which is obviously fair, and which duly conserves the rights and interest of the party to be made liable, will satisfy legal requirements." *McCready v. Atlantic Coast Line Railroad Co.*, 48 S.E.2d 193, 196–97 (S.C. 1948). We believe the best method to ensure fairness to both parties is to receive a wide range of elements for consideration in the actual value. This range of evidence gives the trier of fact sufficient latitude to intelligently determine the amount of damages. Such elements that have been introduced and relied upon are often such typical factors as cost of replacement, original cost, and cost to reproduce. But our courts and juries have also examined elements of a less prosaic nature, such as the proposed use of woodland for a forestry course, uniqueness (*Lack v. Anderson*, (La. Ct. App. 1946) 27 So. 2d 653), the feelings of the owner (*Harvey v. Wheeler Transfer & Storage Co.*, (1938) 227 Wis. 36), and the cost to build and decorate a

room to match a single painting. We believe that sentimental value, in limited circumstances, is also such a consideration.

When we refer to sentimental value, we do not mean mawkishly emotional or unreasonable attachments to personal property. *See Mieske v. Bartell Drug Co.*, (1979) 92 Wash.2d 40. Rather, we are referring to the feelings generated by items of almost purely sentimental value, such as heirlooms (*Brown v. Frontier Theatres, Inc.*, (Tex. 1963) 369 S.W.2d 299), family papers and photographs (*Bond v. A.H. Belo Corp.*, (Tex. Civ. App. 1980) 602 S.W.2d 105), handicrafts, (*Monahan v. Scott Cleaning Co.*, (Mo. Ct. App. 1922) 241 S.W. 956), and trophies (*Shaffer v. Honeywell, Inc.*, (S.D. 1976) 249 N.W.2d 251). What we are referring to basically are those items *generally* capable of generating sentimental feelings, not just emotions peculiar to the owner. In other words, any owner of these USAC rings would have similar feelings.

* * *

By our decision here, we simply conclude that certain property, by its very nature, has an element of sentiment essential to its existence. In this case, we refer to symbols for achievements of national stature and recognition and the calculation of their actual value. But we must also add the proviso that even for significant awards or mementos we do not intend to permit fanciful speculation as to their worth. We must fashion our remedy within the realm of sensibility, as here, where $750 is only slightly above the established range of replacement values. Such would naturally also be our standard in valuing similar significant awards, such as an Oscar, the Heisman Trophy, or an Olympic medal, where the recipient retains the honor despite the loss of the trophy, such trophy being merely the symbol of the achievement and perhaps replaceable by a surrogate. A certain amount of sentiment is inherent in the value of these objects to the owner, and each case must be based on its own facts. But we must refrain from considering all but reasonable estimates of that element of sentiment. We believe in this case, Capels's $750 figure was just such a reasonable value of each ring with the sentiment included therein.

Id. at 720–23.

6. Companion animals would seem to epitomize the type of property for which sentimental value could be taken into account when assessing the loss to the plaintiff. Certainly "man's best friend" should be considered as "*generally* capable of generating sentimental feelings, not just emotions peculiar to" his guardian, such that any guardian of the victim dog (or other companion animal) in any given case "would have similar feelings." On the other hand, if an animal advocate's strategic goal is to advance the worth of companion animals as individual beings whose interests should be factored more heavily into a court's analysis, does "sentimental value" advance or hinder this goal?

The *Campins* court was cautious to "fashion our remedy within the realm of sensibility." Similarly, the Illinois *Jankoski* court, while allowing "some element of sentimental value in order to avoid limiting the [plaintiff] to merely nominal damages," acknowledged that the "damages in such cases, while not merely nominal, are severely circumscribed." 510 N.E.2d at 1087. If you consider the damages permitted to be sought or the sums awarded in most of the cases in this chapter, you will note that they generally were nominal in amount.

Because the "value to the owner" is a substitute for the fair market value, it produces only small recovery in the loss of a nonpedigreed pet. M. Livingston, [*The Calculus of Animal Valuation: Crafting a Viable Remedy,*] 82 Neb. L. Rev. [783,] 789–90 [2004]. For instance, the *Brousseau* court awarded the plaintiff $550 plus costs, despite having found that the plaintiff, a retired widow who lived alone, relied heavily on her well-trained watch dog, which was her sole and constant companion, never went out alone at night without his protection, and, after the dog's death, was burglarized, which would not have happened had the dog been alive. *Brousseau*, 443 N.Y.S.2d at 286–87.

None of the foregoing cases questioned the right to maintain a cause of action under the theory of destruction of personal property. It is well established that "[i]t is not necessary for the maintenance of an action for killing a [pet], that it should be shown to be of any pecuniary value. It is for the jury to [be the] judge of the value." *State v. M'Duffie,* 34 N.H. 523, 526 (1857). As discussed, there is no formula for computing the value of the pet to her owner. *See also Brousseau*, 443 N.Y.S.2d at 287; 1 D. Dobbs, Remedies §5.16(3), at 907 ("'Value to the owner' cannot yield any dollar figure by computation, by analysis or by empirical investigation"). Professor Dobbs commented that "[s]ince value to the owner is stated as a measure [of damages] but cannot function as one, all this is very unsatisfactory in theory." Despite that fact, the "value to the owner" as a measure of damages is widely used in small cases. . . .

Anzalone v. Kragness, 826 N.E.2d 472, 478 (Ill. App. Ct. 2005) (reversing dismissal of complaint based on lack of specificity in the damages alleged, commenting that "[g]ranted, the amount of $100,000 claimed by plaintiff as damages [for her cat's death] is excessive under existing precedent; nevertheless, that is not a proper basis for dismissing the complaint").

7. There is no mathematical formula for computing the value of a companion animal, but many factors may be evaluated in proving damages in these cases. Age, duration of relationship, special skills, and pedigree are obvious factors, but, in addition, science and society have confirmed that companion animals provide calculable, identifiable psychological and medical health benefits that can be used in assessing the damages from their loss. Other approaches are discussed below.

8. As addressed further in the following Notes, opponents to the concept of allowing recovery for sentimental value (or for emotional distress or loss of companionship) often argue that allowing recovery for the sentimental value of a companion animal would result in excessive awards and have far-reaching ramifications beyond the "realm of sensibility" (to use the *Campins* court's phrasing). Do you think this is a plausible concern? Might the mere fact of the awards in the cases discussed in this section effectuate change in how our society views and values animals and ultimately how it may afford legal recognition of their interests, or are the awards insignificant for this purpose if their dollar value remains nominal? Consider all of these questions as you read Notes 9 and 10.

9. Undoubtedly, class discussion to this point has addressed some of the public policy issues that flow from this area of the law. This Note and the Notes that follow further delve into the core issues in the public policy debate that have come to the forefront as the debate over non-economic damages and the valuation of companion animals, particularly though certainly not solely in veterinary malpractice cases, has heated up.

The primary arguments against allowing awards of non-economic damages in veterinary malpractice cases have been based in the usual fears of opening the "floodgates of litigation" and veterinary industry concerns about increased costs:

> The essence of the veterinary response, however, is that any legal acknowledgment of companion animal value beyond mere purchase price will cause drastic increases in veterinary insurance and treatment costs— increases it is claimed will be economically cataclysmic for the profession *and* for pet owners. In recent years this resonating argument has become the baby that prevents any state from throwing out the dirty bath water of the previous century's animal jurisprudence.

> Surprisingly, though, the assertion that veterinary costs and prices will dramatically rise as a result of increased compensation is commonly made and accepted without any mathematical verification. Even academic advocates of higher civil damages for animal loss often feel obliged to concede that the potential for ancillary increases in veterinarians' liability exposure is the Achilles heel of their argument. In actuality, the exact opposite may be true: *The near total absence of veterinary negligence deterrents under current law may turn out to be the strongest economic reason for draining the baby's bath water as soon as politically possible.*

Christopher Green, *The Future of Veterinary Malpractice Liability in the Care of Companion Animals*, 10 Animal L. 163, 167–68 (2004) (emphasis in original; footnotes and citations omitted).[c]

---

c. This article provides a thorough and detailed analysis of practical and public policy concerns, concluding that "allowing civil recovery for loss of companionship to the owner is both 'good law and solid economics.'" *Id.* at 250. The author updates it annually to assure that it remains current

We will consider both issues—insurance and treatment costs as well as the deterrent factor—in turn. With respect to the former, statistics indicate that, unlike medical and legal malpractice insurance rates, veterinary malpractice insurance premiums have not risen significantly in many years, unaffected even by the rate of inflation. According to Green, this reflects a market failure—a "disruption in optimal functioning in the market," where "some interference is shielding or protecting the price unnaturally from the fluctuating equilibrium of the marketplace." *Id*. at 177. By refusing to allow recovery of more than nominal damages, he argues, "courts remove the opportunity for pet-owning consumers [who Green sees as the 'true consumers' of veterinary malpractice insurance] to take advantage of their cost spreading numbers and insure themselves at the increased level of compensation that adequately matches their increased valuation of pets." *Id*.

With artificially low insurance rates for so many years and concerns about increasing numbers of malpractice claims and higher settlement values than in the past, some may conclude veterinarians have reasons to be concerned about a risk of skyrocketing insurance costs. There is, however, evidence to the contrary. According to Green, "the actuarial experts at the second largest veterinary malpractice insurer calculate that allowing up to $25,000 in compensation for the negligent killing of a companion animal would only increase the average pet owner's veterinary expenses by less than 13¢ per year." *Id*. at 220. As of 2018, this remained the only published actuarial study on this issue. Green, 2018 Update.

Even if this assessment is wholly inaccurate and a significantly higher rate increase results, veterinarians can spread that risk to those who pay for veterinary services. Spreading the risk should result in nothing more than a *de minimis* impact on each individual owner/guardian. Yet some veterinarians, particularly in rural or lower income areas, argue that many persons already refuse costly treatment and that higher prices simply will result in more animals being abandoned or euthanized when their guardians are unwilling or unable to pay for life-saving treatment.

On the other hand, studies indicate that an ever-growing percentage of animal guardians are ready to do whatever it takes for their animals and that veterinary practices have been expanding as a result. For example,

> [a]ccording to an American Veterinary Medical Association [AVMA] study reported in 1998, $11.1 billion was spent on health care for companion dogs, cats, and birds in 1996, an increase of 61% from expenditures in 1991. As of 1998, there were twenty board-certified veterinary specialties, ranging from anesthesiology to toxicology. . . . In a 1996 survey by the American

---

and relevant. *See, e.g.,* Christopher Green, *2018 Update to: The Future of Veterinary Malpractice Liability in the Care of Companion Animals*, 10 ANIMAL L. 163, 167–68 (2004) (obtained from the author May 8, 2018) ("Green, 2018 Update").

Animal Hospital Association, 38% of respondents stated they would spend
any amount of money to save the life of their animal companion.

Sonia S. Waisman and Barbara R. Newell, *Recovery of "Non-Economic" Damages
For Wrongful Killing Or Injury Of Companion Animals: A Judicial And Legislative
Trend*, 7 ANIMAL L. 45, 61–62 (2001) (footnotes and citations omitted). According to the AVMA, in 2001 U.S. consumers spent $19.08 billion on veterinary care
(Green, *supra*, at 170 n.21) and by 2011, they spent $28 billion on veterinary care
alone. (Green, 2018 Update.) In 2012, Americans spent roughly $53 billion on their
pets. *Strickland v. Medlen*, 397 S.W.3d 184, 188 (Tex. 2013). And in 2017, that number reportedly increased to $69.51 billion. (Green, 2018 Update.)

10. As one commentator has noted, the dichotomy between veterinarians caring for animal patients, and then denying their guardians recovery when those
animals are injured, raises a "question of fairness." Veterinarians understand that
they are health care providers who, for many of their human clients, function similarly to the way a pediatrician functions for parents of human children. "Veterinarians emphasize the importance of the human-animal bond and should not be
able to then argue that the bond is irrelevant when it is time to determine damages
in malpractice actions." Rebecca J. Huss, *Valuation in Veterinary Malpractice*, 35
LOY. U. CHI. L.J. 479, 531 (2004). Should concepts of equity and fairness enter into
this debate?

In weighing the issues, "traditional objections to recognizing expanded awards
for the loss of pet animals that include an emotional distress component" (policy
concerns such as "fraudulent claims, disproportionate liability, the impact on cost
of veterinary care and other goods and services, and the difficulties of assessing
damages in an accurate, consistent and fair way") must be counterbalanced by "the
traditional tort law policy objectives of compensation, deterrence and reflection of
societal values." Margit Livingston, *The Calculus of Animal Valuation: Crafting a
Viable Remedy*, 82 NEB. L. REV. 783, 811–14, 824 (2004) (cited repeatedly in *Anzalone v. Kragness*, 826 N.E.2d 472 (Ill. App. Ct. 2005)).

11. Regarding the so-called "traditional tort law policy objectives" of compensation and reflection of societal values, Livingston argues that awarding emotional
distress damages in these cases is supported by "social science evidence . . . [that]
establishes the depth of the human-animal bond and the profound grief experienced by humans when their companion animals die; [t]he circumstances of a
tortious death . . . typically intensify that grief." *Id.* at 826. *See also* Waisman and
Newell, *supra*, at 57–64.

12. What duty should veterinarians have with respect to the emotional well-
being of their human clients who pay for services? What about with respect to the
nonhuman patients they treat?

13. With respect to deterrence, it has been argued that existing mechanisms to
regulate veterinarians fail to "adequately police veterinary malfeasance" or deter

veterinary harm. Green, *supra*, at 179. Green cites examples of courts failing to sanction problem veterinarians and veterinary malpractice insurance companies continuing to insure them. *Id.* at 179–80. Moreover, standard veterinary practices often are exempt from state anti-cruelty statutes and other criminal laws. Further, "the penalties assessed by state licensing boards also are often too lenient to meaningfully reprimand veterinarians who cause negligent or intentional animal harm." *Id.* at 183. According to Green, "years of disciplinary statistics clearly demonstrate that these regulatory bodies rarely take serious action in instances of negligence or professional incompetence—essentially eliminating the likelihood of any meaningful enforcement of the veterinary standard of care." *Id.*

If Green is correct, the answer to these problems may be administrative, legislative, litigation-related, or a combination of all three. The obvious problem of state veterinary boards is that the industry is monitoring itself, which leads to potential conflicts of interest and leniency. Criminal liability for negligent acts is unlikely, leaving only new legislative solutions or civil litigation, which currently provides no deterrence because of the lack of adequate damages.

14. Another problem with animal injury cases is the courts' and society's difficulties in adequately assessing the appropriate damages. Some believe "[c]ourts are unsure of how to value the intrinsic worth of companion animals or their companionship; therefore they have hesitated to permit such damages and instead have deferred to state legislatures" which, in the few states that have enacted statutes addressing this issue, have proposed arbitrary damages caps that may exempt veterinary malpractice and other situations, and that are viewed as being "unsatisfactory in either compensating for loss or deterring future harm to companion animals." Elaine T. Byszewski, *Valuing Companion Animals in Wrongful Death Cases: A Survey of Current Court and Legislative Action and a Suggestion for Valuing Pecuniary Loss of Companionship*, 9 ANIMAL L. 215, 231–32 (2003). *See also* Huss, *Valuation in Veterinary Malpractice* (cited in Note 11 above), at 501 (noting a growing uncertainty about available remedies, and that "[p]roviding more consistency in the damages available in these cases allows both parties to understand fully the ramifications of their actions if malpractice occurs and, if necessary, to adjust their behavior accordingly"). As discussed in the preceding Notes, even where courts have allowed recovery for "intrinsic value" or "actual value to the owner," they have been cautious to limit the amount of such recovery.

To provide some predictability, Byszewski proposed that animals be valued in these cases by using the so-called "investment approach" that is often applied in cases of a child's wrongful death. Byszewski, at 236–40. This approach, refined by forensic economists Thomas Ireland and John Ward, sets "a child's pecuniary value, . . . equal to 'at least the flow of expenditures the parents have already made plus the value of the flow of expenditures on the child the parents would have been willing to make in the future.' [Citation]. . . . Ireland and Ward pointed out that 'many of the issues involved with investments in pets are similar to those with children.'" *Id.* at 237 (internal citation omitted). Byszewski explains:

Because the investment approach focuses on the average investment guardians are willing to make, it provides a straightforward way to value the entire pecuniary loss that guardians face upon the deaths of their companion animals. That is, when a person decides to become a guardian to a companion animal, the value she places on her companion is at least equal to the financial expenditures she expects to make over the lifetime of the animal. With this economic postulate in mind, courts and legislatures can use the investment approach to accurately value loss of companion animals, which will promote efficient levels of compensation and deterrence.

Id. at 240.

Do you think valuation of companion animals in a similar way to human children would offend accepted social values?

15. For a discussion of one method of valuation of companion animals, see Geordie Duckler, *The Economic Value of Companion Animals: A Legal and Anthropological Argument for Special Valuation*, 8 Animal L. 199, 221 (2002) ("Companion animals, to the extent that they have a social 'purpose' created by humans, are most emphatically non-commercial objects valued entirely for the comfort and well-being that they impart to their owners as a benefit of ownership."). For a discussion of moral theories of animal rights and how they affect legal standards of care for companion animals, *see* Rebecca Huss, *Valuing Man's and Woman's Best Friend: The Moral and Legal Status of Companion Animals*, 86 Marq. L. Rev. 47 (2002).

16. One issue that is the subject of debate among animal advocates, as noted in Chapter 2 and in Section 1.C of this chapter, is whether classifying a companion animal as property is beneficial or detrimental to the plaintiffs in these cases. For arguments on both sides of the issue, see Lynn Epstein, *Resolving Confusion in Pet Owner Tort Cases: Recognizing Pets' Anthropomorphic Qualities Under a Property Classification*, 26 S. Ill. U.L.J. 31, 46 (2001) ("[C]lose attention ought to be given to the adoption of a more uniform approach wherein courts would consider standardized claims that . . . serve to compensate owners for the special bond they have established with their pet. To assure uniformity in this approach, courts should continue to classify the pet as property. . . . Even though relegating pets to property status, pet owners must still be permitted recovery for the intrinsic value of their injured pet. This policy must permit the fact finder to fairly analyze the loss of the pet's companionship to the owner. . . ."). *But see* William C. Root, *"Note: Man's Best Friend": Property or Family Member? An Examination of the Legal Classification of Companion Animals and Its Impact on Damages Recoverable for Their Wrongful Death or Injury*, 47 Vill. L. Rev. 423, 446 (2002) ("Courts must realize that the law's categorization of companion animals as property is archaic and does not reflect society's values or expectations. Removing the 'property' label will give the courts more flexibility to expand the damages recoverable for the injury to or death of a companion animal.").

Section 4. Competing Interests: Companion Dogs and Farm Animals

There is a longstanding tension between owners/guardians whose dogs roam about freely in rural communities and may be inclined to chase or attack various types of farm animals, and those who raise and keep animals for profit. Historically, the laws in the Western states have favored the interests of livestock owners, often giving them the right to kill dogs who interfere with or even threaten farmed animals. The following case reflects that tension and the balancing efforts courts may take in considering the interests on both sides.

Katsaris v. Cook

California Court of Appeal, First District, Division 4, 1986
180 Cal. App. 3d 256, 225 Cal. Rptr. 531

POCHÉ, Acting P.J. Plaintiff and appellant, Steven Katsaris, brought an action for damages, negligence and intentional infliction of emotional distress resulting from the shooting of his two dogs by defendant and respondent, Melvin Kenneth Cook. Also named as defendants are Cook's employers, Robert C. and Betty Harvey. Defendants' motion for a judgment was granted at the close of plaintiff's case and judgment entered. Plaintiff appeals. We affirm the judgment as to plaintiff's claims for damages and negligence, but remand the emotional distress claim to the trial court for its further consideration.

I.

Steven Katsaris lived alone on a 120-acre plot of land adjacent to an 80-acre ranch occupied by Mr. and Mrs. Harvey. Katsaris kept two Belgian sheep dogs—a female who was his pet and a male who had been specially trained to provide personal protection for Katsaris. As was his custom when he left town, in May 1982, when Katsaris was away on business he left the dogs in the care of two neighbor boys, Patrick and Jeff Schuette, 15 and 14 years old respectively. About 8 a.m. on May 17, 1982, while the boys were cleaning the dogs' kennels, the sheep dogs wandered away and would not come when called. Despite the boys' efforts and those of their father, the dogs remained loose.

About 1 in the afternoon the dogs were shot on the Harveys' property by their employee, 19-year-old Melvin Cook. Cook's accounts of the shooting were highly inconsistent. In a declaration he claimed the dogs lacked identification, were biting and mauling the Harveys' own dog who was chained up, and were worrying cattle penned nearby. At trial Cook testified that the sheep dogs were not biting or mauling the Harveys' dog, but were merely growling which upset the cattle, and that after he shot the sheep dogs he had not looked for identification tags on them.

Furthermore, he testified that it was his decision to dispose of the two corpses by dumping them into a ditch on the Harveys' property. According to Cook's declaration and his statement to the sheriff, he dumped the corpses at the direction of the Harveys or of Mr. Harvey. Cook told Mrs. Harvey about the shooting when she arrived home late in the afternoon of the 17th.

When Katsaris returned from his business trip on the evening of May 17 he found a note from the Schuette brothers telling him the dogs were loose. He searched without success that evening. The next day he widened his search by visiting various neighbors, including the Harveys, to inquire about his dogs and ask that they call him if the dogs were spotted. Mrs. Harvey denied seeing the dogs. On the following day, May 19, Katsaris again visited the Harvey home and showed Mrs. Harvey photographs of the dogs. She once more denied having seen the sheep dogs.

Ten days after the dogs disappeared Katsaris was taken to identify their decomposed remains by the Schuette family, one of whose sons had been told about the shooting by Cook. When the remains were discovered only the female still wore her collar and neither dog had ID tags.

II.

Katsaris contends the trial court erred when it granted defendants' motion for a judgment . . . as to all three of his claims. The trial court found that Food and Agricultural Code section 31103 precluded all three claims. That section provides in pertinent part that "any dog entering any enclosed or unenclosed property upon which livestock or poultry are confined may be seized or killed by the owner or tenant of the property or by any employee of the owner or tenant. No action, civil or criminal, shall be maintained against the owner, tenant, or employee for the seizure or killing of such dog."

The judicial construction of this statute is apparently a matter of first impression. Katsaris advances an interpretation of section 31103 which requires the dog to enter either a walled and roofed ("enclosed") or an unroofed and partly open pen, coop or corral ("unenclosed") area containing animals before it can be seized or killed.

* * *

By enacting section 31103 the Legislature found the public's interest in protecting farm animals outweighed the dog owners' right to permit their animals to roam freely on land occupied by livestock.[2] To promote the Legislature's goal,

---

2. Statutes such as section 31103 apparently reflect the dog's disadvantaged status at common law where it was not considered property. (Comment, *Animal Law in California* (1985) 12 Pepperdine L. Rev. 567, 590.) However, we cannot say that in modern day California, where ranches are often located next door to suburbia, that there is no longer any need to protect livestock from packs of or *from* individual roaming dogs. Reports of farm animals being killed or mutilated periodically appear in the news media such as a recent article entitled *When Pets Become Killers*. (S.F. Chronicle (Mar. 7, 1986) at p. 6, cols. 1–4).

In discussing dogs and the common law the dissent makes much of the language "lawful inclosure" in the case of *Sabin v. Smith* (1915) 26 Cal. App. 676, 680. (Dis. opn., *post*, p. 272.) Both the *Sabin* case and the earlier case of *Johnson v. McConnell* (1889) 80 Cal. 545, 548, were cases construing Civil Code section 3341 which permitted killing a dog caught in the act of worrying, wounding,

it gave livestock owners, in section 31103, a privilege to kill or seize trespassing dogs.[3]

* * *

If the policy choice made by the Legislature in enacting section 31103 is to protect livestock owners from economic loss stemming from the death or injury of their animals, then arguably conduct by livestock owners which goes beyond what is necessary to protect their livestock from trespassing dogs is not covered by the privilege.

Any conduct necessary to the killing of a trespassing dog will be within the privilege. Decisions by the owner of livestock about when, where or how to kill a trespassing dog and dispose of its body, as well as the owner's delegation of those decisions to his employees, is conduct which comes within the privilege.

In applying this test to the case before us we conclude that the trial court correctly granted defendants' motion for judgment as to the first cause of action—the claim for damages arising from the killing of the dog. The question before us is whether the motion for judgment was also properly granted as to Katsaris' other two claims, the causes of action for negligence and for intentional infliction of emotional distress. Are both these claims likewise within the privilege created by section 31103?

---

or killing farm animals. In *Sabin* the worrying dog had actually entered the enclosure in which the worried poultry was kept. Thus, the *Sabin* case quite understandably emphasized that the fowl were enclosed, and hence helpless, as justification for the poultry owner's need to take immediate action to protect his property rights in the chickens. The *Sabin* court found protection for animals not enumerated in the statute, hence the rule stated in the case is really a fact-specific worse case, *e.g.*, dog within the enclosure, which permitted the court to rely upon a general common law right to act even where statute provided no privilege for the actor. (Dis. opn., *post*, p. 271).

In *Johnson* the court makes no reference to any common law rule because the case is construing the specific provisions of Civil Code section 3341. To that end the court distinguishes a case reaching the opposite result under a differently worded statute. (*Johnson v. McConnell, supra*, 80 Cal. at p. 551.)

3. * * *

The 1921 law added a number of new features to California dog law. It made it unlawful for "any person to permit any dog . . . to run at large on any farm on which livestock or domestic fowl are kept, . . ." (Current § 30955, added by Stats. 1921, ch. 757, § 3, p. 1306.) Likewise the 1921 law permitted impound of a dog "straying on any farm whereon livestock or domestic fowl are kept." (1921 Stats., ch. 757, § 4, p. 1306.) We read the new provision in the 1929 amendment permitting the killing of a dog "entering any enclosed or unenclosed property upon which livestock or poultry are confined" to be a change in the prior law. Whether the change was a good or a bad legislative decision is irrelevant to our inquiry. It has long been the rule that the police power of the state permits it to regulate, even to the point of death, the lives of dogs. "[F]rom time immemorial, [dogs have] been considered as holding their lives at the will of the [L]egislature, . . ." (*Sentell v. New Orleans &c. Railroad Co.* (1897) 166 U.S. 698, 702.)

* * *

The dissent is much distressed by the harshness of the reading we adopt for section 31103. Yet the dissent does not mention that any county may avoid the harsh result of sections 31102 and 31103 by adopting the stricter provisions for control of trespassing dogs embodied in sections 31152 and 31153.

Katsaris alleged that the Harveys negligently permitted guns to be kept and to be shot on the ranch near habitable structures, that they negligently supervised, and that they negligently withheld facts of the dogs' deaths. In all of these claims except the last, if the duty of care was breached by the shooting of the dogs, the claim is barred by section 31103. In the last claim—which alleges that the Harveys negligently failed to tell Katsaris what had happened—the alleged breach was not an act necessary to the killing itself, and thus would not be barred by the statute. The trial court could have granted the motion for judgment on the ground that the Harveys had no duty to tell Katsaris what had happened to his dogs, and therefore Katsaris had not established a prima facie case of negligence. Instead, the court found the negligence claim barred by section 31103. Because there is no duty to speak, Katsaris has no claim for negligent infliction of emotional distress against the defendants. Therefore, we affirm the granting of the motion for judgment on the second cause of action.

Katsaris' third cause of action was for intentional infliction of emotional distress. If the factual basis of this claim lies in the manner in which the defendants killed the dogs or disposed of their bodies, then the privilege of section 31103 bars the claim. Both the manner of killing and of disposing of the carcasses are matters so intimately linked to the deaths that they are within the scope of the privilege. However, to the extent that the basis of the claim lies in Mrs. Harvey's post shooting assertions that she knew nothing about the dogs or their whereabouts, her conduct does not come within the scope of the privilege created by section 31103.

To prevail on his intentional distress claim Katsaris would have to prove that Mrs. Harvey's conduct was extreme and outrageous, that she acted with intent to cause him emotional distress or with reckless disregard of the probability of causing him emotional distress, that he suffered severe distress, and that her conduct was the actual and proximate cause of his injury. . . .

Normally the test of extreme and outrageous conduct is an objective one—would the conduct involved outrage the "average member of the community?" The outrageousness of the conduct may arise instead, however, from the actor's knowledge of the plaintiff's particular susceptibility. In the case at hand Mrs. Harvey arguably knew by the time of Katsaris' second visit to her house that he was extremely concerned by the disappearance of the dogs and anxious to locate them.

The specific intent required for intentional infliction of emotional distress is that the defendant either acted intending to inflict the injury or with the realization that the injury was substantially certain to result from his conduct. Alternatively, the defendant may fulfill the specific intent requirement if he acts recklessly in disregard of the likelihood that he will cause emotional distress to the plaintiff.

Reckless disregard can, like any other specific intent, be proven circumstantially by inference from the conduct of the actor. In the context of section 31103, however, it is not, as a matter of law, sufficient to prove reckless disregard by showing merely that the livestock owner failed to notify the dog's owner of its death, or failed upon inquiry by the dog's owner to tell him what happened to the dog or lied in response to inquiry by the owner.

Unless these limitations circumscribe an emotional distress claim made where the killing itself is privileged under section 31103, the purpose of the section's privilege will be hopelessly undercut. The irate dog owner whose pet has been killed will not be able to bring an action for damages for the loss of the dog, but he will be able to get a jury on the claim that the livestock owner intentionally caused the dog owner emotional anguish by failing to notify him of his pet's death, or by not being truthful or forthcoming when asked about its fate. A more lenient rule would disturb the balance of economic interests apparently intended by the Legislature.[4] Livestock owners, insulated by section 31103 from often negligible liability for the value of the destroyed dog, would instead be exposed to potentially substantial liability for the dog owner's emotional suffering.

Because Mrs. Harvey's post shooting conduct was not within the scope of the privilege created by section 31103, the trial court erred when it granted the motion for judgment as to the claim for intentional infliction of emotional distress. On a motion for judgment the trial court is authorized to, and required to act as a trier of fact. Here the trial court viewed the emotional distress claim as barred by section 31103, and thus it did not reach the merits of that claim. We remand to the trial court for the limited purpose of determining, in light of the foregoing discussion, whether Katsaris proved his claim for intentional infliction of emotional distress.

The judgment is reversed insofar as it dismisses plaintiff's cause of action for intentional infliction of emotional distress; in all other respects the judgment is affirmed. Each party to bear its own costs on appeal.

CHANNELL, J., concurred.

SABRAW, J.—I concur and dissent.

Today we speak of but the killing of two dogs—perhaps not a thing of great moment to some—but to others the loss of a dog leaves memories of loyalty and devotion seldom equaled in any other relationship. In the words of Lord Byron: "Near the spot are deposited the remains of one who possessed beauty without vanity, strength without insolence, courage without ferocity, and all the virtues of Man, without the vices. This praise, which would be unmeaning flattery if inscribed over human ashes, is but a just tribute to the memory of Boatswain, a dog." (Lord Byron, Inscription to the monument of a Newfoundland dog (1808).)

When Mr. Katsaris returned home in the evening of May 17, 1982, to find his two Belgian Tervuren sheep dogs missing he immediately undertook what eventually turned into a 10-day vigil and nightmare in search of his 2 "constant companions"

---

4. Section 31103 is one of a group of statutes which have been criticized because they protect the economic interests of some members of the public (here livestock owners) at the expense of a property loss suffered by other members of the public (here dog owners whose pets are destroyed).

and "protector[s]." He went to all of his neighbors with pictures of the dogs seeking information from anyone who might have seen them. He got up early in the morning and called and walked the woods. He went into town. He checked with the dog pound daily. The local radio station cooperated with announcements. A notice was placed in the local newspaper. He hired an airplane so he could search from the air. Each day he continued his search on foot for his friends. He searched at night after dark with a flashlight. On occasion sympathetic friends would join in the search. He visited two psychics in search of clues. He hired a helicopter to join in the search. In his contacts with his immediate neighbors, the Harveys, even photographs of the dogs did not produce any knowledge of their whereabouts or fate — nor did the passing of the 7th, the 8th or the 9th day. On the 10th day at a point of grief, disappointment and despair and at a time when he "was finding it harder to lose those dogs almost than when my daughter was killed," a phone call interrupted the unknowing. The dogs had been found by a friend in a ditch on the Harvey Ranch "maybe a quarter of a mile from my fence line, maybe an eighth of a mile." When he saw the dogs in the ditch "they had been there 10 days in the heat. There were maggots crawling from the cavities. We loaded the remains of the dogs, took them up to my place and buried them." The long vigil was over.

We are called upon to interpret statutes which authorize one man to kill another man's dog. We know that in any civilized society the authority to kill any living being must be viewed with the greatest of caution. I submit under today's rules we condone the killing of a dog only as a last resort. We have come a long way from the old common law concept of a dog not even being considered property. Not only is he more than property today, he is the subject of sonnets, the object of song, the symbol of loyalty. Indeed, he is man's best friend.

My colleagues in the majority would have us conclude that mere trespassing by a dog anywhere on a neighbor's land where livestock or poultry are kept is legal justification for killing the dog. There is neither legislative history, rules of construction, nor the thread of today's civilized attitudes in support of the statutory interpretation given by the majority. We have come too far from the law of the Pecos for that brand of "taking the law into one's own hands" remedy to survive today. We have in this age of surfacing humanitarianism recognized the need for pet doctors, pet hospitals, pet cemeteries and even a society for the prevention of cruelty to pets. All of this stands in stark contrast to the majority's interpretation of the code sections in question as giving livestock owners the unbridled authority to decide "when, where or how to kill a trespassing dog and dispose of its body. . . ."

If we had only Food and Agricultural Code section 31103 to guide us in our task, the majority opinion could find some support as a logical reading of the statute. Closer scrutiny, however, leads to a contrary conclusion. In this instance we have over 100 years of statutory history and case law as well as closely related statutes such as section 31102 to assist us. Virtually all of this material is ignored by the majority. My analysis of these materials convinces me that the Legislature intended the term "enclosed" in section 31103 ("entering any *enclosed* or unenclosed property upon which livestock or poultry are *confined*" (italics added)) to refer to a barn or like structure, and the term "unenclosed" to refer to a corral, coop, pen or like structure where animals are confined. The animals would not be otherwise "confined" if such types of structures were not intended by the statutory language used.

* * *

ANALYSIS

* * *

Contrary to the impression created by the majority, I agree that the Legislature was concerned as it obviously should be with livestock owners being able to protect their animals from aggressive, marauding dogs. However, the majority's interpretation ignores the clear intent of the Legislature over the last 57 years to protect domestic animals from *aggressive* canine behavior, not mere failure to observe man-made boundaries.

For lack of any better authority to support their position, the majority relies on a recent press account of dog attacks on livestock. I, for one, find the threat of dogs (including packs of wild poodles) with split personalities a slim reed on which to base interpretation of the statute before us. In any event, the "evidence" cited by the majority is more appropriately suited to legislative hearings than it is to our task of interpreting the existing statute.

I believe that the interpretation that I have given provides the true legislative intent which resulted from the delicate balancing on the one hand of the clear and absolute right of owners of livestock and fowl to have an immediate self-help remedy to protect their flock from threatening dogs, and, on the other hand, the need to exercise care in not authorizing the senseless and unwarranted killing of a dog who happens to wander over the wrong boundary line.

Notes

1. Many states have codified the liability of the guardians of dogs who injure or kill "livestock." *See, e.g.,* Ala. Code § 3-1-1 (permitting recovery of double the value of all livestock injured or killed if the dog "has been known to kill or worry sheep or other stock"); Minn. Stat. Ann. § 347.01 (civil liability "without proving notice to or knowledge by" the dog owner/guardian that the dog "was mischievous or disposed to kill or worry any domestic animal"; "owner of any dog that kills or pursues domestic livestock is guilty of a petty misdemeanor"); S.D. Codified Laws § 40-34-2 (civil and criminal (misdemeanor) liability for "owning, keeping or harboring a dog that chases, worries, injures or kills any poultry or domestic animal"); Idaho Code § 25-2806 (permitting livestock owners/guardians or others to kill "any dog, not on the premises of its owner or possessor, worrying, wounding, or killing any livestock or poultry which are raised and kept in captivity for domestic or commercial purposes"); Ohio Rev. Code Ann. § 955.28 (subject to certain qualifications, "a dog that is chasing or approaching in a menacing fashion or apparent attitude of attack, that attempts to bite or otherwise endanger, or that kills or injures a person or a dog that

chases, injures, or kills livestock, poultry, or other domestic animal, or other animal, that is the property of another person, except a cat or another dog, can be killed at the time of that chasing, approaching, attempt, killing, or injury").

At least one court has declined to extend such a statute to apply where defendants' dog caused the plaintiff's horse to rear up and fall on top of the plaintiff, causing her severe injuries. *Fishman v. Kotts*, 179 P.3d 232, 237 (Colo. Ct. App. 2007).

2. Most statutes of this type were first enacted in the mid to late 1800s. The Iowa statute, as originally enacted in 1862, provided that it was "lawful for any person to kill a dog . . . when the dog is caught in the act of worrying, chasing, maiming, or killing any domestic animal." IOWA CODE § 351.27. In 2007, however, the legislature amended the statute to delete the term "worrying." The case of *State v. West*, 741 N.W. 2d 823, 2007 WL 2963990, *5 n.3 (Iowa Ct. App. 2007) (unpublished table op.) was brought under the pre-2007 statute. The defendant had shot and killed his neighbor's two dogs who were running back and forth along a fenced-in enclosure for deer he raised and sold to petting zoos, game farms and for breeding. The defendant was convicted, but the appellate court reversed his conviction, declining to imply a reasonableness requirement in the pre-2007 statute to justify shooting. The 2007 amendment increased the level of requisite danger that a dog has to be creating in order to provide statutory immunity for killing the dog. Under the facts in *West*, the conviction might have been affirmed under the amended statute, since the dogs were outside of the fenced-in area in which the deer were kept.

3. The amendment to the Iowa statute demonstrates the shifting sentiments of courts and legislatures with respect to the continuing conflict between farmed animal protection and the penalties for failure to control owned dogs. The statutory changes discussed in the preceding Note demonstrate that public policy may be moving toward a view that dogs can be killed only when "guilty" of actual injury to farmed animals. *See also Propes v. Griffith*, 25 S.W.3d 544 (Mo. Ct. App. 2000) (where plaintiff's dogs were in defendants' sheep pasture but were not barking at, chasing or attempting to bite the sheep and defendant was able to grab the dogs by the collar to remove them from the pasture, and then drove to have plaintiff's dogs euthanized, the court affirmed the judgment and award of punitive damages against the defendants).

How should courts and legislatures resolve the competing property interests of farmed animal owners and dog owners/guardians? Where the competing interests are those of a pecuniary nature (and possible threat to the life of a sentient being) versus the life of a companion animal, often the economic interest has prevailed. What public policy arguments could be made for and against this result?

The issue could also be framed as the farmed animal owner/guardian's right to protect those beings under his control who cannot protect themselves versus the responsibility of dog owners/guardians to supervise their dogs. Does this present a legally significant difference from a situation where one neighbor's dog is chasing another neighbor's cat?

4. Based on the readings in this section, draft a proposed statute that satisfies, or at least considers, both sides of the issue.

5. In *Parker v. Parker*, 195 P.3d 428 (Or. Ct. App. 2008), plaintiff brought his horse with him when he visited his son, the defendant. Defendant's dog ran toward the horse and barked, causing the horse to run into a steel fence and sustain fatal injuries. The issue on appeal was whether an Oregon statute that imposes strict liability and entitles a "livestock" owner to damages from the owner of a dog that "injured, chased, wounded or killed" the livestock (ORS 609.140(1)) applied to the facts of that case. The court concluded that it did. "Livestock" was defined, for purposes of that statute, to include horses, so the definition of "livestock" was not an issue. The court reaffirmed its earlier decision interpreting a related statutory provision, where the court had determined that (1) "chasing" requires no predatory intent, and (2) "injuring" requires no contact between the dog and the livestock. *Roach v. Jackson County*, 151 Or. App. 33, 37, 37 n.3 (1997) (interpreting ORS 609.155, which provides for impoundment of dogs found "killing, wounding, injuring or chasing livestock"). The court had concluded in *Roach* that "injuring" could include injuring livestock by causing the animal to "run[] into a fence or similar barrier." *Id*. The court in *Parker* rejected defendant's argument that the plaintiff was not within the class of persons intended to be protected by the statute because the horse was injured on property that was not owned or controlled by the plaintiff.

6. In *Mayfield v. Bethards*, 826 F.3d 1252 (10th Cir. 2016), discussed in Section 1.C of this chapter, a deputy saw plaintiffs' two dogs lying in plaintiffs' unfenced front yard, entered the yard without a warrant and shot one of the dogs, explaining in his police report, that even if the Fourth Amendment applied, the killing was reasonable because "he thought she had attacked livestock and he believed Kansas law allows anyone to kill a dog reported to have done so." The plaintiffs had attached to the complaint their letter to the sheriff saying the accusation that the dog had mauled a neighbor's livestock *a year earlier* was a case of mistaken identity. In affirming the district court's denial of the deputy's motion to dismiss, the Tenth Circuit looked to the Kansas statute and earlier case law interpreting it.

> Section 47-646 of the Kansas Statutes allows "any person at any time to kill any dog which may be found injuring or attempting to injure any livestock." Kan. Stat. Ann. §47-646. According to Deputy Bethards, the Kansas Supreme Court in *McDonald v. Bauman*, 199 Kan. 628, 433 P.2d 437 (Kan. 1967), interpreted this statute to permit a person not only to kill an offending dog caught in the act of injuring or attempting to injure livestock, but also to pursue and kill the dog after it has returned to its owner's land. But that case cannot be read as broadly as Deputy Bethards suggests.
>
> In *McDonald*, the defendant shot a dog he caught attacking his hogs, chased the dog to its home, and then shot the dog several more times.

The dog survived and its owner sued to recover the veterinarian expenses incurred in treating the gunshot wounds. After the jury returned a verdict in favor of the defendant, the dog owner appealed. The Kansas Supreme Court affirmed, holding that section 47-646 allows a person to shoot a trespassing dog "which he finds on his premises injuring or attempting to injure" livestock "either at the time the dog is found in the act . . . or within a reasonable time thereafter," which includes "the right within such reasonable time, if necessary, to pursue such dog after it has left his premises, and to shoot . . . such dog off his premises."[5] *Id.* at 442. In reaching that conclusion, the Kansas Supreme Court identified two prerequisites that make application of the statute a fact-intensive inquiry. First, *McDonald* places the burden of proof on a defendant seeking to rely on the statute "to show by a preponderance of the evidence that he was justified in shooting the dog." *Id.* at 443. Second, where the aggrieved livestock owner pursues the dog onto its owner's property and shoots it, the defendant must establish that he entered the dog owner's land "with authority, or under such circumstances that authority to enter such other's land may be implied." *Id.* And the Kansas Supreme Court further explained that whether a livestock owner in hot pursuit has entered the dog owner's property with consent or implied consent is a question for the jury. Thus, *McDonald* supports rather than refutes the district court's denial of Deputy Bethards's motion to dismiss.

Mayfield, 826 F.3d at 1257.

Section 5. Injuries Caused by Animals

The doctrine of strict liability for harm caused by animals has its roots in English common law. The rules for recovery for such harm have varied, however, depending on the category of animal who caused the harm. Historically, the doctrine was applied when livestock wandered freely and caused harm when trespassing onto another's property. The rationale was that owners/guardians, being aware of the animals' natural tendencies to roam, should keep them under control. Similarly, knowledge of "wild" animals' natural tendencies prompted application of strict liability when such animals, used in circuses and public exhibits, or in private ownership, attacked attendees or visitors. However, even where courts purport to apply the doctrine of strict liability in these cases, defendants often are not found to be liable if they did not act negligently in failing to properly restrain or control the animal. Moreover, if the plaintiff's own knowing and voluntary conduct caused the

---

5. Significantly, neither section 47-646 nor *McDonald* addresses the killing of a dog on its owner's property by either a private third party or a police officer acting in his official capacity in response to an accusation by a livestock owner about an attack the third party or police officer did not witness.

injury, the doctrines of contributory or comparative negligence may bar recovery even in a strict liability case.

With respect to harm caused by domesticated/companion animals, the common law rule is that the owner/guardian will not be liable unless she or he knew or should have known of the animal's "vicious or violent propensities." *See, e.g., Doyle v. Monroe County Deputy Sheriff's Ass'n*, 195 Misc. 2d 358, 360 (N.Y. Supr. Ct., Monroe Cty. 2003). As discussed in this section, however, this rule has been abrogated in most jurisdictions by strict liability statutes, particularly with respect to dog bites.

The opinions that follow provide examples of courts applying the foregoing theories, first in cases involving wild animals, then in those involving domesticated animals. For further background on the history and development of tort law in connection with harm caused by animals, *see, e.g.,* RESTATEMENT (SECOND) OF TORTS §§ 504–518 ("Liability of Possessors and Harborers of Animals"); W. Page Keeton et al., PROSSER AND KEETON ON THE LAW OF TORTS § 76 at 538–43 (5th ed. 1984); David S. Favre & Murray Loring, ANIMAL LAW 189–217 (1983); Glanville Williams, LIABILITY FOR ANIMALS (1939).

Baugh v. Beatty

California Court of Appeal, Second District, Division 2, 1949
91 Cal. App. 2d 786, 205 P.2d 671

WILSON, J. From a judgment in favor of defendants in an action to recover damages for personal injuries, plaintiff appeals. He has also purportedly appealed from the order denying a new trial.

Plaintiff, a minor 4 years of age, was taken by his parents to the circus operated by defendants. Following the performance in the main tent they went to see the animals in the "animal tent" and it was there that plaintiff was bitten by a chimpanzee, sustaining the injury which is the basis of this action.

The chimpanzee was in a circus wagon cage in the front of which there were perpendicular iron bars set about 3 inches apart. There was no meshed wire inside or around the bars of the cage to prevent the ape from reaching his arms through the bars. The wagon, together with other wagons containing animals, was set back approximately 5 feet from a rope or chain, which was about 3 feet above the ground, and which passed through holes in the poles holding up the tent. There was no fence under the rope to keep small children back and no guard in the vicinity of the cage. At the time of the incident there were from 100 to 200 people along the rope in front of four or five animal cages and some of the ladies in the crowd were reaching over the rope and feeding peanuts to the chimpanzee. At plaintiff's request his father put him down. The child worked his way through the crowd, under the rope and up to the cage containing the ape. The boy was next seen holding a peanut up to the animal which reached through the bars, grabbed the child's hand and bit him.

* * *

Plaintiff asserts that the court erred in refusing to give two instructions requested by him: (1) covering the duty of an operator of a business toward an invitee in keeping the premises in a condition reasonably safe, and (2) an instruction on the attractive nuisance doctrine.

It is plaintiff's contention that the jury should have been instructed on the theory of negligence in failing to take reasonable precautions against injury to plaintiff as a business invitee, as well as that on the liability for injury by a wild animal. A cause of action against the owner of an animal for injuries inflicted by it may be based upon negligence as well as upon the ground of the keeping of an animal known to be vicious. The complaint raises both issues and although they are contained in the one count, no demurrer having been interposed, an objection may not be raised for the first time on appeal. However, if the animal which inflicted the injury is vicious and dangerous, known to defendant to be such, an allegation of negligence on the part of defendant is unnecessary and the averment, if made, may be treated as surplusage.

A litigant requesting it is entitled to instructions presenting his theory of the case and if inconsistent causes of action or defenses are alleged, the instructions covering them must necessarily be based upon conflicting and contradictory hypotheses. However, a wild animal is presumed to be vicious and since the owner of such an animal, or the owner of an animal which is known by him to be vicious and dangerous, is an insurer against the acts of the animal to anyone who is injured, and unless such person voluntarily or consciously does something which brings the injury on himself, the question of the owner's negligence is not in the case. There was, therefore, no prejudicial error in the court's refusal to give the requested instruction on negligence.

Plaintiff's contention that the court erred in refusing to give his requested instruction on the attractive nuisance doctrine is not tenable. The instruction refers to the keeping of an "artificial and dangerous contrivance." An animal in a cage is not artificial and it does not fall within the definition of the word "contrivance" which is defined in Webster's New International Dictionary (2d ed.) (1947), page 580 as "a mechanical device; an appliance." Whether the attractive nuisance doctrine could be extended so far as to include a caged animal it is not necessary for us to determine, since the doctrine is not applicable to the facts in the present case. It is conceded that plaintiff was a business invitee and not being a trespasser there is no need to invoke the doctrine, which is but an exception to the rule that the owner of premises is under no obligation to keep it in a safe condition for trespassers.

The court instructed the jury with respect to the liability of the keeper of a vicious or dangerous animal, known to be such by its owner.[1] Although plaintiff has

---

1. "Where injury is done by a vicious or otherwise dangerous animal, known to be such by its owner, the owner is liable to the injured person in a sum that will compensate him reasonably for

not raised any objection to this instruction, it was not proper in the instant case since the animal was of the class of animals *ferae naturae*, of known savage and vicious nature, and hence an instruction on the owner's knowledge of its ferocity was unnecessary.

* * *

[With respect to plaintiff's contributory negligence, whether] a minor of tender years has conducted himself with the care and prudence due from one of his years and experience is strictly a question of fact for the jury.... What the jury should have been told to determine was whether under the circumstances of the case plaintiff knowingly or consciously placed himself in danger.

Judgment reversed....

Notes

1. In *Baugh*, the court noted that a jury instruction regarding defendant's knowledge of the chimpanzee's "ferocity" was unnecessary. More recent cases and commentators are in accord. For example, in a case where a circus leopard fatally attacked a five-year-old boy who was passing by the center ring as the leopard waited to perform, the court explained:

> We have already spoken twice in this opinion regarding the nature of the potential harm associated with the display of wild beasts and we begin from this springboard. The proposition should require no expert testimony. We are not speaking of domesticated animals gone amuck. We are concerned with naturally wild and ferocious animals whose basic instincts are predatory from the day they are born. This observation cannot reasonably be a matter of dispute. In the absence of proper safeguards, even a caged wild animal presents a "manifest danger" to persons attracted to such an exhibit. This is the composition of that with which we here deal.

> A dangerous propensity is presumed in wild animals and the keepers of such, at least, have been held strictly liable. Prosser and Keeton, *Torts*, § 76 at 542 (5th ed. 1984). "No member of such a species, however domesticated, can ever be regarded as safe, and liability does not rest upon any experience with the particular animal." *Ibid*. Taking all relevant circumstances of

---

all detriment suffered by him and resulting from the injury, unless the injured person knowingly and voluntarily invited the injury and brought it upon himself. To have done that, he voluntarily must have done something with respect to the animal that induced the injury and which he either knew, or should have known was dangerous. The principle of law does not require a finding that the owner was negligent. The liability attaches to his ownership of such an animal, with knowledge of its dangerous character, and makes him an insurer against injury done by it. Thus, in applying this rule of law, you are required first to ask and answer the question. Was the plaintiff injured by a vicious or dangerous animal? If so, two other questions must be answered: 1. Was that animal then owned by the defendants in this action? 2. Did the owners then have knowledge of the dangerous character of the animal?"

the matter before us into consideration, we are satisfied that whether wild animals are said to be a nuisance per se, ultra hazardous or abnormally dangerous, the fact remains that exposure of the public to them creates a "serious risk of harm to . . . others which cannot be eliminated by the exercise of the utmost care" and the liability of all those producing that exposure should be absolute.

Our path is lighted by analogy from the products liability cases. The principal and perhaps only difference between those and our situation is there it is an inanimate thing which is unleashed upon the public whereas we are dealing with animals. . . . We think it not unreasonable to believe that the benefits bestowed by a few hours (or perhaps minutes) of entertainment or recreation for those who like this sort of thing hardly justify the possibility, if not the probability, of disasters such as the one which occurred here. The magnitude of the risk certainly outweighs the social utility. In such a case those who provide the extraordinary risk must share the responsibility.

* * *

As a matter of public policy, it is unthinkable that we should refuse to insulate those who contribute to putting a defective car on the road from claims by the ultimate purchaser for injuries resulting from the defect, then tell one injured by a wild beast that he has no claim against those who put that beast on the road. . . .

Certainly considerations such as these motivated those who decided *Stamp v. Eighty-Sixth Street Amusement Co.*, 159 N.Y.S. 683 (App. Term 1916), cited by [the trial court] here. That case charged not only the owner with responsibility, but also "any third person . . . if he takes part in the owner's keeping of" a vicious animal (there lions). [*Id.*] at 684. We are satisfied that the *Stamp* court would do what we do here today. To the extent that *Theobald v. Grey Public Relations, Inc.*, 39 A.D.2d 902, 334 N.Y.S.2d 281 (1972) might be thought to disagree with *Stamp*, we point out only that *Theobald* obviously was much more concerned with the quantum of damages than anything else. To the extent it excused from liability one defendant, it did that in six printed lines, without reference to *Stamp*, without citation of one authority and without an explication, beyond a meager factual statement, of its theory on the dismissal. . . .

Eyrich v. Robert Earl, d/b/a Robert Bros. Circus, 495 A.2d 1375, 1377–78 (N.J. Super. Ct., App. Div. 1985).

2. In the *Stamp* case, cited approvingly by the *Eyrich* court, three of the lions used in a vaudeville act escaped from their cages and entered the orchestra while another act was in progress. The *Stamp* plaintiff was injured by the panicked crowds and not by the lions. The court nonetheless applied the general rule of strict liability against the harborer of wild animals, concluding the crowd's panic was "directly caused by

the natural fear of an unsecured vicious animal and was a result which might well have been foreseen by the defendant."

3. In the *Theobald* case, distinguished and essentially discounted by the *Eyrich* court, plaintiff was attacked by a lion at a car show. The jury returned a verdict of strict liability in the amount of $250,000 against all defendants—the auto dealer that used the lion, the public relations company that arranged for the lion to be present at the show, the animal agency that provided the lion, and the sponsor of the show. On appeal, the majority reduced the award to $150,000 and overturned the verdict against the sponsor. The dissenting judge disagreed with the majority on both grounds and opined that there was sufficient proof to sustain the verdict on a negligence theory.

4. The doctrine of strict liability for harm arising from the keeping of wild animals derives from English law. In the leading English case, *May v. Burdett*, 9 Q.B. 101, 115 E.R. 1213 (1846), the court explained the rule as follows:

> The precedents, both ancient and modern, with scarcely an exception, merely state the ferocity of an animal and the knowledge of the defendant without any allegation of negligence or want of care. *** The conclusion to be drawn from an examination of all the authorities appears to us to be this: That a person keeping a mischievous animal with knowledge of its propensities is bound to keep it secure at his peril, and that, if it does mischief, negligence is presumed, without express averment.

As reflected in *Baugh v. Beatty*, though, historically some courts refused to apply the doctrine where the injured party's own negligence contributed to the injury. *See also Opelt v. Al. G. Barnes & Co.*, 41 Cal. App. 776 (1919) (affirming judgment in favor of defendant where a circus leopard scratched a ten-year-old boy who had crossed a rope to approach the leopard's cage).

5. Circuses and other traveling shows that use animals present not only a danger to humans, as reflected in *Eyrich* but, according to veterinarians, animal behaviorists, animal advocates and a growing public consensus, they also cause unnecessary suffering to the animals. As a result of efforts by national and grassroots organizations to increase public awareness, a growing number of localities are banning circuses and other exhibitions, such as roadside zoos, that use animals. For more on this issue, see Chapter 3, Section 5 and Chapter 6, Section 2.

6. The general rule of law is that "a landowner cannot be held liable for the acts of animals *ferae naturae*, that is, indigenous wild animals, occurring on his or her property unless the landowner has actually reduced the wild animals to possession or control, or introduced a non-indigenous animal into the area." *Belhumeur v. Zilm*, 949 A.2d 162, 164–65 (N.H. 2008) (no liability for injuries from attack by wild bees nesting in a tree on defendants' property), quoting *Nicholson v. Smith*, 986 S.W.2d 54, 60 (Tex. Ct. App. 1999). This rule arises from "a common law doctrine tracing its origins back to the Roman empire whereby wild animals are presumed to be owned by no one specifically but by the people generally." *Id.* (footnote omitted).

7. Cases involving harm caused by domesticated animals are much more common than those involving harm caused by wild animals. Administrative and legal actions related to dog bites occur frequently. The following case—which does not involve a dog bite—demonstrates a court's analysis in the absence of strict liability (illustrated by the statutes discussed in the Notes following) for injuries caused by animals.

Drake v. Dean

California Court of Appeal, Third District, 1993
15 Cal. App. 4th 915, 19 Cal. Rptr. 2d 325

PUGLIA, P.J. Plaintiff filed this action to recover for personal injuries sustained when she was injured by defendants' dog. The complaint alleges two counts sounding respectively in strict liability and negligence. A jury returned a verdict in favor of defendants. On appeal, plaintiff contends the trial court erred in admitting certain evidence and in refusing to give certain instructions, including the standard instructions on negligence. Relying on *dicta* in this court's decision in *Hagen v. Laursen* (1953) 121 Cal. App. 2d 379, the trial court indicated that instructions on negligence, if given, would be modified to limit defendants' duty to the taking of ordinary care to avoid harm by a domestic animal with dangerous propensities of which defendants knew or should have known. We hold that the *dicta* in this court's opinion in *Hagen v. Laursen, supra,* upon which the trial court relied, is incorrect to the extent it would engraft onto negligence legal criteria applicable to strict liability. Thus, the *Hagen* court erred in stating that in an action for negligent harm done by defendants' dog, plaintiff must plead and prove that the injury was the result of "the vicious character or evil propensity of the dog" which character or propensity is both "abnormal with regard to the usual actions of these animals" and known to the owner or keeper of the animal. (*Hagen, supra*, 121 Cal. App. 2d at p. 382). Since plaintiff presented sufficient evidence of negligence to entitle her to instructions on that theory, unalloyed with legal principles applicable to strict liability, we shall reverse.

Plaintiff and Judy Hightower, both members of the Jehovah's Witnesses Congregation, were engaged in their ministry, going house to house to discuss the Bible with those who might be interested. As they walked along the driveway toward defendants' house, Hightower noticed defendants' dog, Bandit, sitting near the corner of the house. She said, "Look out, . . . it's a pit bull." Before plaintiff could react, Bandit arrived on the run, jumped on plaintiff and knocked her to the ground. Plaintiff suffered a broken hip and lacerations to her head where it struck some rocks.

Plaintiff testified that before entering onto defendants' property, she received no indication of Bandit's presence. There was no fence surrounding the property, nor were there any signs advising a dog was present or warning against solicitation.

At the time of these events, Bandit was leashed to a chain attached to a 100-foot guy wire which allowed him to run across the front yard of defendants' property and gave him access to the driveway.

After Bandit knocked plaintiff to the ground, Hightower shouted for help, whereupon defendant Robert Dean emerged from his house. According to Hightower, Dean told her Bandit "had a habit of jumping on people."

Dean denied making any such statement. He testified Bandit was well trained, well behaved and liked people. He denied Bandit had a propensity for jumping on people. There was evidence no complaint concerning Bandit had ever been received by the Shasta County Animal Control Office. Several witnesses testified that in their experience Bandit was a well-behaved, gentle animal.

Bandit was an American Staffordshire Terrier, known commonly as a pit bull, and weighed approximately 65 pounds. Plaintiff produced evidence that historically pit bulls were bred for their aggressiveness. Defendant offered evidence that pit bulls are not inherently dangerous to people. Dean did admit Bandit once barked at a stranger and would not let him come up the driveway toward the house.

Near the conclusion of the evidence counsel and the court discussed jury instructions. All agreed plaintiff was entitled to instructions on strict liability for harm done by a domestic animal with known vicious or dangerous propensities abnormal to its class. As to plaintiff's theory of negligence, plaintiff requested the jury be instructed with BAJI Nos. 3.00 and 3.10 on the general principles of negligence. Defendants objected, arguing there could be no finding of negligence absent evidence defendants knew of a dangerous propensity on the part of Bandit.

Relying on *Hagen v. Laursen, supra*, 121 Cal. App. 2d 379, the trial court ruled it would not give BAJI No. 3.00 or 3.10 unless those instructions were modified. In a discussion with counsel the court suggested the jury should be instructed it could find negligence only if it found Bandit had a dangerous propensity of which defendants knew or should have known. Given the choice of negligence instructions so modified or no instructions on negligence, plaintiff chose the latter alternative. The matter was submitted to the jury solely on the theory of strict liability. By special verdict, the jury found Bandit did not have "a particular vicious or dangerous propensity" and judgment was entered for defendants.

I

California has long followed the common law rule of strict liability for harm done by a domestic animal with known vicious or dangerous propensities abnormal to its class. (*E.g., Hillman v. Garcia-Ruby* (1955) 44 Cal. 2d 625, 626 and authorities cited therein; *Hicks v. Sullivan* (1932) 122 Cal. App. 635, 638 and authorities cited therein.) This rule is set forth in section 509 of the Restatement Second of Torts (Restatement Second): "(1) A possessor of a domestic animal that he knows or has reason to know has dangerous propensities abnormal to its class, is subject to liability for harm done by the animal to another, although he has exercised the utmost care to prevent it from doing the harm. [¶] This liability is limited to harm that results from the abnormally dangerous propensity of which the possessor knows or has reason to know."

"[Because] [t]he great majority of dogs are harmless . . . the possession of characteristics dangerous to mankind . . . is properly regarded as abnormal to them." (Rest. 2d, § 509, com. f.). . . .

It is because dangerous propensities are abnormal to dogs as a class that the rule of strict liability comes into play. . . . "When an owner has reason to believe his dog is savage, ill-tempered, mischievous or dangerous to persons and property, he may be kept only at the owner's risk, who will become liable for damages resulting from such conduct of the dog which exhibits such known traits or character." (*Hicks v. Sullivan*, *supra*, 122 Cal. App. at p. 638.)

"Thus, one who keeps a large dog that he knows to be accustomed to fawn violently upon children and adults is liable under [section 509] for harm done by its dangerous playfulness or over-demonstrative affection. . . . [¶] . . . [Likewise] [i]f the possessor knows that his dog has the playful habit of jumping up on visitors, he will be liable without negligence when the dog jumps on a visitor, knocks him down and breaks his hip. . . ." (Rest. 2d, § 509, coms. c, i.)

* * *

In this case plaintiff adduced evidence pit bulls historically were bred for their aggressiveness and that Bandit, who weighed 60 to 70 pounds, had a tendency, known to defendants, to jump on people and in fact jumped on plaintiff, knocking her down and breaking her hip.

The jury was instructed on strict liability in terms of BAJI No. 6.66, as follows: "If you find that the plaintiff was injured by the dog owned or kept by the defendant and that before the plaintiff was injured by said animal the defendant knew or had reason to know of the particular vicious or dangerous trait or propensity in the animal which caused plaintiff's injuries, you will find in favor of the plaintiff and against the defendant and award the plaintiff such damages as you find that the plaintiff suffered from injuries which legally resulted from such vicious or dangerous trait or propensity. [¶] An owner or keeper of an animal has reason to know of the trait or propensities of the animal when the owner or keeper has notice of facts that a reasonable person would have."

Plaintiff complains, however, that the trial court erred in refusing her special instruction on strict liability, which stated: "The (a) vicious propensities and dangerous character of a dog and (b) knowledge thereof by his owner may be inferred from evidence that the dog was kept (1) tied (2) as a watchdog and also (3) from his size and breed."

* * *

II

We address plaintiff's contention it was error to refuse her proffered negligence instructions. The common law recognizes negligence as a distinct legal theory of recovery for harm caused by domestic animals that are not abnormally dangerous. Restatement Second section 518 provides: "Except for animal trespass, one who possesses or harbors a domestic animal that he does not know or have reason to know to be abnormally dangerous, is subject to liability for harm done by the animal if, but only if . . . (b) he is negligent in failing to prevent the harm."

* * *

On the other hand, "[t]here are certain domestic animals so unlikely to do harm if left to themselves and so incapable of constant control if the purpose for which it is proper to keep them is to be satisfied, that they have traditionally been permitted to run at large. This class includes dogs. . . ." (Rest. 2d, § 518, com. j.)

* * *

In determining the keeper's liability for negligence for injuries inflicted by a domestic animal, the criterion usually adopted is one of reasonable anticipation of the occurrence, *i.e.*, foreseeability. (*Hagen v. Laursen, supra*, 121 Cal. App. 2d 379, 383; *see* 4 Am. Jur. 2d, *Animals*, § 89, p. 337.)

Endresen v. Allen (Wyo. 1978) 574 P.2d 1219 involved a dog with a proclivity to escape from the yard and chase motor vehicles. The dog escaped and chased plaintiff, who was riding a motorcycle, causing plaintiff to crash and sustain injury. Plaintiff sued the dog's owner on theories of negligence and violation of a local ordinance requiring dogs to be kept off the public streets. Since plaintiff's theories did not include strict liability, dangerous propensity of the dog abnormal to its class was not an issue. Concerning negligence, the reviewing court commented: "We think that there was sufficient evidence of negligence to justify submission to the finder of the facts the question whether defendants should reasonably have anticipated that injury would result from their failure properly to secure the dog and whether they negligently failed properly to secure the dog." (*Endresen v. Allen, supra*, 574 P.2d at p. 1222.)

In *DeRobertis v. Randazzo* (1983) 94 N.J. 144 the jury returned a verdict in favor of plaintiff, a five-year-old child bitten by defendant's dog. Although the judgment was reversed on other grounds, the court explained both strict liability and negligence were viable theories of recovery: "If a plaintiff proves scienter, a dog-owner is absolutely liable for injuries caused by the dangerous characteristic of the dog. . . ." (*DeRobertis v. Randazzo, supra*, 462 A.2d at p. 1267.) Citing Restatement Second section 518, the court commented: "If, on the other hand, the plaintiff is unable to prove that the owner knew or should have known of the dog's dangerous characteristics, then the owner is liable only if the plaintiff is able to prove that the owner acted negligently in keeping the dog." (*Id.* at pp. 1266–1267.)

In *Hagen v. Laursen, supra*, 121 Cal. App. 2d 379, plaintiff was injured when defendants' two dogs ran against plaintiff, a neighbor who was visiting on defendants' property, and caused her to fall and injure herself. Plaintiff sued on theories of general negligence and negligence per se arising from defendants' alleged violation of a dog control ordinance. Plaintiff secured a judgment and defendants appealed. Defendants' sole contention on appeal was that the evidence was insufficient as a matter of law to support the judgment. On the negligence *per se* theory this court held plaintiff failed to prove she was within the class for whose protection the ordinance was enacted. (*Id.* at p. 386.)

This court also held plaintiff failed to prove general negligence predicated on any act or omission of defendants. Defendants' two dogs were Irish setters, approximately five years old and weighing respectively thirty-five and forty-five pounds, more or less. "On the occasion when plaintiff was injured the dogs were frolicking, occasionally going into the road and back to their home grounds. They romped and played with each other; would jump at each other, wrestle, run, roll over, pretend to bite each other, and generally indulge in the antics usual with dogs at play. Their actions were described as the average play of a dog. No one had seen them run into anyone while playing, before [plaintiff] received her injuries. They were not shown to have been more boisterous than dogs usually are. There was no evidence that these dogs were vicious." (121 Cal. App. 2d at p. 380.)

"[Plaintiff] was well acquainted with the dogs and had often observed them at play. At the time of the accident [plaintiff] had seen the dogs playing and while this was going on had gone across the road and onto the premises of [defendants] where she stood conversing with a group of people, which included [defendant] and some relatives of [plaintiff]. The dogs were frolicking about, the women were talking; [plaintiff] stood with her back toward the area in which the dogs were for the moment at play and did not, therefore, see them approaching her. Others, however, including [defendant] saw the dogs coming, but no one said or did anything. One or perhaps both of the dogs while so playing and frolicking ran against the back of [plaintiff's] legs at about the knees, causing her to fall sharply to the ground and to suffer a broken hip and various less serious bruises and lacerations. There was nothing in the nature of an attack by either animal." (121 Cal. App. 2d at p. 381.)

After an excursive discussion in which legal principles governing strict liability and negligence were conflated (121 Cal. App. 2d at pp. 382–383), this court analyzed defendants' contention that the evidence, as a matter of law, was insufficient to prove a charge of general negligence: "Giving full play to the rule that negligence is usually a question of fact, still negligence cannot be here predicated upon any act or omission of [defendant]. The ground of liability here is reasonable anticipation of the occurrence and reasonable opportunity to act. Dogs at play rarely run against stationary objects whether tree, post or person. They generally look where they are going and this is self-preservation. We are unable to see where in the situation confronting her [defendant] could reasonably be held to anticipate that the playing dogs would blindly run into a group of people and knock one of them down. . . . Here was misadventure pure and simple without liability. . . ." (*Id.* at p. 383.)

As the Restatement Second section 518 and the cases indicate, negligence may be predicated on the characteristics of the animal which, although not abnormal to its class, create a foreseeable risk of harm. As to those characteristics, the owner has a duty to anticipate the harm and to exercise ordinary care to prevent the harm. (See *Hagen v. Laursen, supra,* 121 Cal. App. 2d at pp. 382–383.). . . .

* * *

Although the jury found Bandit had no vicious or dangerous propensity, that finding did not resolve the question of negligence tendered by plaintiff's complaint. Plaintiff alleged defendants "negligently . . . failed to . . . control" Bandit. Thus, there were issues whether Bandit posed a risk of harm to others; whether that risk was reasonably foreseeable; and if so, whether defendants failed to exercise ordinary care to avert that risk by controlling Bandit.

Unlike *Hagen v. Laursen, supra,* where the dogs' conduct prompted the court to observe that "dogs at play rarely run into stationary objects whether tree, post or person" (121 Cal. App. 2d at p. 383), the facts here prompt us to observe that it is not unknown for dogs to jump on people. (*E.g., see* Rest. 2d § 509, com. i.) Thus, it may reasonably be anticipated that a dog which has jumped on people before will do it again, whereas it is not reasonable to suppose that a dog that has, for whatever reason, run into an immovable object will not have been discouraged from repeating that conduct. Thus, we cannot say as a matter of law that no reasonable jury could find defendants could not have anticipated either the event or the harm that resulted. Plaintiff presented evidence that defendant Dean knew Bandit "had a habit of jumping on people," from which an inference could be drawn that such conduct was reasonably foreseeable. And, as we have indicated, the special verdict does not necessarily exclude the possibility the jury credited that evidence.

Moreover, even though the jury found jumping on people not to be a dangerous propensity, we cannot say that a jury which exonerated Bandit of a vicious or dangerous propensity, if instructed on negligence, would necessarily have found that Bandit's conduct was not potentially harmful even though the jury did not regard it as vicious or dangerous. Instead, the jury may have regarded Bandit's conduct as playful or perhaps as manifesting an unrestrained friendliness and thus have been disinclined to characterize it as vicious or dangerous.

The evidence also presented a question for the jury on the issue of breach, *i.e.,* whether defendants, knowing of Bandit's potential to do harm, exercised ordinary care to avert that harm by adequately controlling him. Although Bandit was on a leash, the radius of the tether gave him access to defendants' driveway on which visitors to defendants' house approached.

We conclude the trial court erred prejudicially in refusing to instruct the jury on negligence unalloyed with strict liability.[6]

---

6. The dissent mistakenly ascribes to the majority the position, obviously unsupportable in law, that it is "foreseeable that dogs, *regardless of their prior characteristics*, will react to strangers coming on their owners' property in a dangerous and harmful way." (Italics added, dis. opn., *post*, at p. 943.) The dissenting justice then mistakenly taxes the majority with the "misapprehension that the owners of a *peaceful dog* are liable in negligence if the animal causes some injury to a person

We acknowledge that in refusing standard negligence instructions, the trial court was led into error by this court's decision in *Hagen v. Laursen, supra.* We do not disagree with the holding of *Hagen v. Laursen*, nor do we fault the *Hagen* court's analysis to the extent it applied the law of negligence to the facts of the case. (121 Cal. App. 2d at pp. 383–386.) However, the *Hagen* court also discussed strict liability (*id.* at pp. 382–383) and cited cases in which strict liability was in issue whereas in the case before it there was no issue of strict liability presented. Although the discussion was unnecessary to the court's holding and therefore *dicta*, its presence in a case involving only negligence very strongly implies that the principles of strict liability there discussed are applicable in an action for negligence. To the extent *Hagen* so implies, it is overruled.

The judgment is reversed. Plaintiff is to recover costs.

Notes

1. In *Drake*, the court admitted expert testimony regarding the characteristics and propensities of specific breeds of dogs. *See also Hill v. Williams*, 144 N.C. App. 45 (2001) (defendants' negligence was not based on their knowledge of any "vicious propensities" of their own dog, but they were "chargeable in a negligence action with knowledge of the general propensities of a Rottweiler dog as reflected in plaintiff's evidence"). Dogs of the so-called "pit bull breed" (which does not actually exist, but refers to a collection of breeds all characterized by similar physical traits), in particular, have been the focus of controversy amid claims of their vicious tendencies. Not all courts, however, are ready to accept this condemnation of the breed:

> On the subject of the propensities of pit bull terriers as a breed there are alternative opinions that preclude judicial notice such as was taken by the [lower] court. While many sources, including the authorities relied upon by the [lower] court, assert the viciousness of pit bulls in general, numerous other experts suggest that, at most, pit bulls possess the potential to be trained to behave viciously.

> Furthermore, scientific evidence more definitive than articles discussing the dogs' breeding history is necessary before it is established that pit bulls, merely by virtue of their genetic inheritance, are inherently vicious or unsuited for domestic living, such as, for instance, wolves and leopards

---

and the owners could have prevented the harm had they confined or controlled the dog." (Italics added, dis. opn., *post*, at p. 943.)

We acknowledge that the dog is man's best friend and have no desire to spurn or betray that friendship nor design to hold his master liable for conduct of the dog in acting as dogs characteristically and commonly act, *i.e.*, peacefully and harmlessly. Moreover, we acknowledge that the owner is not liable in negligence for any harmful conduct of his dog that was not reasonably foreseeable. Here, however, there was evidence from which a jury instructed on negligence could have found Bandit's conduct was harmful and reasonably foreseeable and that defendants did not exercise ordinary care in so controlling Bandit as to avert his known potential to cause harm.

would be. No statistical analysis is offered to demonstrate that a high percentage of the total number of pit bulls has engaged in violent incidents.

Carter v. Metro North Assocs., 680 N.Y.S.2d 239, 240–41 (App. Div. 1998) (citations omitted). The court held the plaintiff (a tenant who had been bitten by another tenant's pit bull) failed to establish the dog had vicious propensities or, even assuming *arguendo* it had such propensities, that the defendant landlord was aware of them. As such, plaintiff could not support a strict liability claim, and the complaint was dismissed. The dissenting judge agreed it was improper to take judicial notice of the vicious propensities of pit bulls, but cited to authorities "to support the proposition that a degree of viciousness may be implied solely by virtue of the specific breed involved." *Id.* at 242 (Mazzarelli, J., dissenting). The dissent commented that pit bulls can bite with a force of nearly 2000 pounds per square inch — twice the force of an average Doberman Pinscher or German Shepherd. *Id.*

Should an animal's strength or power alone be sufficient to classify the animal, be it a species or a particular breed of a species, as "vicious" for purposes of imposing a strict liability standard? This *per se* designation is equivalent to identifying the breed as a wild animal for purposes of owner liability for injuries caused by any dog within the breed.

2. In some states, as under the common law, "all dogs, regardless of breed or size, are presumed to be harmless, domestic animals. . . . The presumption is overcome by evidence of a known or dangerous propensity as evidenced by specific acts of the particular animal." *Poznanski v. Horvath*, 749 N.E.2d 1283, 1286 (Ind. Ct. App. 2001).

In *Mieloch v. Country Mutual Insurance Company*, 628 N.W.2d 439 (Wis. Ct. App. 2001) (unpublished table op.) (text of opinion at 2001 Wisc. App. LEXIS 398), the court found "no precedent or support for the proposition that the propensities of other dogs, whether related by blood *or breed*, create an obligation from one dog keeper to provide such information to another when effecting the transfer of control of a particular dog." (Emphasis added.) The court further noted that a dog's propensities towards other dogs would not provide the owner/guardian with prior knowledge, actual or constructive, that the dog might bite a person. (Dog behaviorists regularly state that there is no cross-species transfer of aggressive activity. For example, the fact that a dog has acted on her innate prey drive in chasing small animals (including cats) does not provide any relevant information with respect to the potential for that dog to bite a person.) In that case, plaintiffs (professional dog trainers) alleged that defendants negligently failed to warn them of their dog's propensity to bite. Plaintiffs relied in particular on the fact that, previously, the dog's father and grandmother both allegedly had bitten people and on the fact that, previously, the dog himself allegedly had bitten another dog. The court rejected these facts as a basis for the claim, and affirmed summary judgment in favor of the defendants.

Similarly, in *Pfeffer v. Simon*, 2003 Tex. App. LEXIS 2495 (Unpub. Mar. 26, 2003), where defendant's Scottish Terrier bit plaintiff on the lip when she tried to pet him, knowledge that the dog previously had eaten defendant's pet cockatiel did not constitute evidence that he was "dangerous" or had "vicious propensities abnormal to his class," where there was no information regarding the circumstances surrounding that incident. The court affirmed summary judgment in favor of the defendant.

3. The common law rules that find dog owner/guardians liable only where they have been negligent or knew of their dogs' dangerous propensities have been abrogated by statute in most states. These jurisdictions thus have done away with the "first bite is free" rule and instead codified a strict liability standard for dogs who bite. A good example is the Oklahoma statute at issue in *Nickell v. Sumner*, 943 P.2d 625 (Okla. 1997), which provides: "The owner or owners of any dog shall be liable for damages to the full amount of any damages sustained when his dog, without provocation, bites or injures any person while such person is in or on a place where he has a lawful right to be." OKLA. STAT. title 4, §42.1. In *Nickell*, a dog allegedly chased and tried to bite the horse plaintiff was riding, causing the horse to buck and throw the plaintiff. The court held statutory liability would not be imposed because the dog attacked the horse rather than the plaintiff. *Id*. at 629. "What is missing from this case is an act of aggression by a dog toward or upon a person." *Id*. The court therefore did not reach the issue of whether there must be physical contact between a person and a dog for the statute to apply.

Contrast *Boitz v. Preblich*, 405 N.W.2d 907 (Minn. Ct. App. 1987), in which a running Springer Spaniel accidentally bumped into the plaintiff, causing him to fall and injure himself. In considering the applicability of Minnesota Statutes section 347.22 (which applies when a dog "attacks or injures any person"), the court held the statute could apply, and remanded the case for trial. The court noted the statute was not limited only to a biting attack, but to any act that "injures": "For instance, some dogs, particularly the larger ones, may without malice rear up and place their front paws on small children or elderly or disabled persons, causing them to fall and suffer injuries." *Id*. at 910. In discussing what it termed "common law scienter," however, the court noted that a mere tendency to run does not constitute a dangerous propensity. *Id*. *See also* Illinois Animal Control Act (ILL. COMP. STAT. ANN. §510/5-16) (strict liability for "full amount of the injury proximately caused" if an owned animal "attacks, attempts to attack or injures any person" without provocation). Although many dogs may be defensive when approached and/or touched by strangers, greeting or petting an animal generally is not deemed to constitute provocation. *See, e.g., Severson v. Ring*, 615 N.E.2d 1 (Ill. App. Ct. 1993); *Smith v. Pitchford*, 579 N.E.2d 24 (Ill. App. Ct. 1991) (plaintiff's mere presence on private property does not constitute provocation, regardless of how his movements may be interpreted by the animal).

In *Anderson v. Christopherson*, 816 N.W.2d 626 (Minn. 2012), the Minnesota Supreme Court addressed the same statute discussed in *Boitz*. Relying on previous Minnesota precedent, the court noted that the statute applied if the dog was a "direct and immediate cause" of a person's injury. The majority found a question of fact as to whether the statute applied where a large dog ran out of a house and attacked plaintiff's 20-pound Schnauzer while he was walking the dog on a leash; the plaintiff fell and broke his hip while attempting to separate the two dogs. The majority remanded the case for trial. The dissent would have held that the defendant was entitled to judgment as a matter of law, concluding that "[c]reating liability for a dog owner not only when his dog directly and immediately injures the plaintiff, but also when the plaintiff is injured because the plaintiff decided to respond to the dog's actions, is not contemplated by the statute and is inconsistent with our case law." *Id.* at 636 (Gildea, C.J., dissenting).

4. Where a veterinarian is bitten while treating a dog, these statutes may not apply, and many courts invoke a "veterinarian's rule" similar to the "firefighter's rule" that precludes liability for injury to firefighters acting in the scope of their occupation. *See, e.g., Nelson v. Hall*, 165 Cal. App. 3d 709, 715 (Cal. Ct. App. 1985) ("A veterinarian or a veterinary assistant who accepts employment for the medical treatment of a dog, aware of the risk that any dog, regardless of its previous nature, might bite while being treated, has assumed this risk as part of his or her occupation."); *Brady v. White*, 2006 Del. Super. LEXIS 390 (Sept. 27, 2006) (same, construing Delaware statute).

California Civil Code section 3342 provides: "The owner of any dog is liable for the damages suffered by any person who is bitten by the dog while in a public place or lawfully in a private place, including the property of the owner of the dog, regardless of the former viciousness of the dog or the owner's knowledge of such viciousness." In *Priebe v. Nelson*, 39 Cal. 4th 1112 (2006), the California Supreme Court considered whether the "veterinarian's rule" exception to section 3342 — "a recognized application of the doctrine of primary assumption of risk, [under which] a dog owner who contracts with a veterinarian to treat his or her dog is generally exempt from liability should the dog bite or injure the veterinarian or veterinarian's assistant during such medical treatment" — should likewise apply to bar a kennel worker's strict liability claim against a dog owner for injuries sustained from a dog bite while the worker was caring for the owner's dog boarded at the kennel. The court answered the question in the affirmative, holding that the doctrine applies in this situation, and affirming a defense verdict.

5. A large number of cases involving dog bites move through administrative and judicial proceedings across the country. State statutes and local ordinances generally govern the designation of dogs as "potentially dangerous," "dangerous," "potentially vicious" and "vicious." Each county, usually through its health, police or animal control departments, is the first line of authority that deals with dogs who bite or injure humans or other animals. The owner of a dog who has been involved in such an incident will be informed if the local agency intends to proceed with a hearing on whether the dog and owner should be subject to sanctions. The designation (dangerous/vicious) may carry with it a variety of potential consequences, which range from a warning with no restrictions, to muzzle and leash restrictions, all the way to euthanization. The initial hearing is usually somewhat informal, although it must comply with basic due process protections, and the ramifications

for the dog and owner can be severe. The results of the hearing are usually appeal-
able to a court of general jurisdiction, where an administrative challenge or a trial
de novo may be available.

Civil litigation also often results from dog bites. Plaintiffs who have been bitten
sue dog owners in cases that are similar in most respects to standard personal injury
cases. An appreciation of animal law issues is very helpful in these cases, especially
for the defense, where counsel may be defending both the dog and dog's owner/
guardian. These cases can involve significant injuries and thus large demands for
compensatory damages, as well as demands for judicial orders directly impacting
the dog, such as those noted above relative to dangerous dog designations, and thus
may present complex issues.

For a discussion of "dangerous dog" cases and related dog behavior issues, see
Schaffner, J., *A Lawyer's Guide to Dangerous Dog Issues* (2009); Cynthia A. McNeely
& Sarah A. Lindquist, *Dangerous Dog Laws: Failing to Give Man's Best Friend a Fair
Shake at Justice*, 3 J. Animal Law 99 (2007).

6. Outside the context of tort liability, various states and local municipalities
have enacted breed-specific bans, often targeting so-called pit bull breeds. Numerous courts have addressed the constitutionality of such statutes and ordinances,
with varying results. This issue is addressed in Chapter 5, Section 2.

7. Strict liability statutes generally apply only to owners/guardians or possessors
of an animal. With respect to those who do not own or possess the dog who bit,
but who own the real property on which the dog resided, courts generally find no
liability absent the property owner's knowledge of the dog's presence and his purported "dangerous propensity." *See, e.g., Uccello v. Laudenslayer*, 44 Cal. App. 3d 741,
746–47 (1975) (duty of care exists only if premises owner had (i) knowledge of presence of dangerous animal; (ii) knowledge of dangerous propensity; and (iii) right to
remove animal by retaking possession of premises); *Batra v. Clark*, 110 S.W.3d 126
(Tex. Ct. App. 2003) (absentee landlord not liable because he had no actual knowledge, and imputed knowledge was not enough). *See also Braun v. York Properties,
Inc.*, 583 N.W.2d 503, 508 (Mich. Ct. App. 1998) (pet size restrictions in lease did not
impose a duty upon the landlord to protect others from harm caused by a companion animal exceeding the size restrictions); *Parrish v. Wright*, 828 A.2d 778, 783 (Me.
2003) ("Maine law has not established a duty of a property owner not on the premises to require invitees or licensees to control their dogs . . . or a duty of a property
owner to train the animals of those the owner permits onto the property.").

Strict liability statutes in some state address landlord liability by defining "owner"
to include anyone who "permits [the dog] to remain on or about the premises owned
or occupied by him." *Benningfield v. Zinmeister*, 367 S.W.3d 561 (Ky. 2012) (construing Kentucky Revised Statutes section 258.095(5) to include landlords if permission
to keep the dog on the premises could be shown; but holding the landlord in that
case was not liable because an attack across the street from his property was not "on
or about" the premises).

In Ohio, the strict liability statute applies to persons who "harbor" a dog, and a landlord is deemed to "harbor" a dog if the landlord permits the dog in common areas of the property. *Weisman v. Wasserman*, 2018 Ohio App. LEXIS 335 (Jan. 25, 2018) (reversing summary judgment for the landlord, finding questions of fact as to whether the dog attacked the child within the tenant's apartment unit or in the hallway, which is a common area). Under Ohio common law, the plaintiff must show that the landlord harbored the dog with knowledge of the dog's vicious tendencies. *Id.* at *7.

In South Carolina, landlords are completely immune from liability for the acts of a tenant's dog—even if the landlord had knowledge of potential danger to third parties. In *Gilbert v. Miller*, 586 S.E.2d 861 (S.C. Ct. App. 2003), the court followed precedent holding that "a landlord could not be vicariously liable under the common law for the actions of a tenant's dog even where the landlord knew of the animal's vicious propensities and could have foreseen the injury, had adequate time to terminate a month-to-month tenancy, and failed to terminate the lease." *Id.* at 863, citing *Mitchell v. Bazzle*, 404 S.E.2d 910, 911–12 (S.C. Ct. App. 1991). The Wisconsin rule is in accord. *See Smaxwell v. Bayard*, 682 N.W. 2d 923 (Wis. 2004) (holding only the "owner or keeper" of a dog is responsible for injuries from a dog bite on premises owned by the defendant). *But see Holcomb v. Colonial Assocs., LLC*, 597 S.E.2d 710 (N.C. 2004) (landlord who is not a dog's "owner or keeper" may be liable under a negligence (premises liability) standard for the actions of a tenant's dog who attacks a third party).

Under what circumstances, if any, should a landlord be held vicariously liable if a tenant's dog bites?

8. In a breed-specific twist on landlord liability in dog bite cases, Maryland's high court expressly modified the common law in that state as it related to attacks by pit bull and cross-bred pit bull dogs against humans, establishing a standard that "when an owner or a landlord is proven to have knowledge of the presence of a pit bull or cross-bred pit bull . . . or should have had such knowledge, a *prima facie* case is established." The court went on to hold: "It is not necessary that the landlord (or the pit bull's owner) have actual knowledge that the specific pit bull involved is dangerous. Because of its aggressive and vicious nature and its capability to inflict serious and sometimes fatal injuries, pit bulls and cross-bred pit bulls are inherently dangerous." *Tracey v. Solesky*, 427 Md. 627, 636 (Md. 2012), *abrogated by statute*, MD. CODE ANN., CTS. & JUD. PROC. §3-1901. On reconsideration, the court amended its original opinion to delete any reference to "cross-breds, pit bull mix, or cross-bred pit bull mix." *Id.* at 667.

In response, the Maryland state legislature abrogated those rulings, expressly stating its intent to do so, enacting the following statute:

> **Common law of liability for other than owner.** In an action against a person other than an owner of a dog for damages for personal injury or death caused by the dog, the common law of liability relating to attacks by dogs

against humans that existed [before *Tracey v. Solesky*], is retained as to the person without regard to the breed or heritage of the dog.

Md. Code Ann. § 3-1901(b).

9. What are the competing public policies between retaining the common law rule and adopting a strict liability rule for dog bites? Should the laws include *any* injuries by dogs, or just bites? Should the laws include injuries caused by other domestic animals?

10. Where strict liability is applied by statute in dog bite cases, the courts seem inclined to maintain the species limitation. In *Jackson v. Mateus*, 70 P.3d 78 (Utah 2003), the Utah Supreme Court rejected the plaintiff's argument that the statute, which expressly applied to dogs but not cats, should be construed to apply to cats as well. Plaintiff argued that the same public policy issues apply equally to harm caused by cat bites. Finding the merits of the contention "debatable," the court construed the statute as drafted and deferred to the legislature. The court also refused to construe local ordinances regarding "vicious" animals to require cat owners/ guardians to muzzle or restrain their cats. *See also Pullan v. Steinmetz*, 16 P.3d 1245 (Utah 2000) (same court declined to extend the strict liability rule to bites by horses, applying instead the "dangerous propensity abnormal to its class" standard, when a horse bit the hand of a twelve-year-old girl); *Bauman v. Auch*, 539 N.W.2d 320, 325 (S. Dak. 1995) (noting the word "vicious" may be more applicable to a dog than to a horse, the court focused instead on whether the horse had a "dangerous propensity abnormal to its class").

Some courts have focused on the negligence requirement of knowledge of a vicious or dangerous propensity. *See, e.g., Ennen v. White*, 598 N.E.2d 416, 419 (Ill. App. Ct. 1992) ("To recover under the common law negligence theory, plaintiff had to allege the horse was predisposed to commit such an injury and defendants knew of its predisposition."); *Wardrop v. Koerner*, 617 N.Y.S.2d 946, 947 (App. Div. 1994) ("It is fundamental that a horse is a domestic animal and that the owner or person charged with its care is not liable for injury caused by the animal unless he or she knew or should have known of its vicious or violent propensities.").

In *Rhodes v. MacHugh*, 361 P.3d 260 (Wash. Ct. App. 2015), the court declined to extend the strict liability theory to injuries caused by rams (male sheep). The court acknowledged that rams (as well as bulls and stallions) have not historically been regarded as being abnormally dangerous animals to keep so as to impose a strict liability standard upon their owners, but noted that the reason is "because its dangerous propensities are 'normal' for its species." The court discussed public policy reasons for not applying strict liability to owners of such animals "because it is often the very characteristics that cause males to be dangerous that make them useful to society." *Id.* at 111, quoting comments in the Restatement (Second) of Torts ("the virility which makes [bulls, stallions and rams] dangerous is necessary for their usefulness in performing their function in the socially essential breeding of livestock;" "the slightly added risk due to their dangerous character is counterbalanced by the desirability of raising livestock"). Might that same analysis apply to a pit bull dog if he or she was, for example, a police or military dog, i.e., would that "socially essential" function, justify overriding "dangerous propensity" arguments in a tort case?

11. To "encourage equine activities," many states have enacted statutes limiting the liability of horse owners/guardians and equestrian facilities for injuries arising from the inherent risks of equine activities. Ala. Code § 6-5-337. *See also* Ariz. Rev. Stat. § 12-553; Del. Code Ann. title 10, § 8140; Fla. Stat. § 773.02; Idaho Code § 6-1802 ("Equine Activities Immunity Act"); Ill. Comp. Stat. Ann. § 745/47-10 ("Equine Activity Liability Act"); Mich Comp. Laws § 691.1661 *et seq.* (same); Or. Rev. Stat. § 30.687 *et seq.*; Wis. Stat. § 895.481. Such statutes expressly or implicitly codify a rebuttable presumption of assumption of the risk (*see, e.g.,* Me. Rev. Stat. title 7, § 4103-A), but allow recovery for intentional or negligent acts. They generally contain language similar to the following: "[Subject to specified exceptions] an equine activity sponsor, an equine professional or another person, is not liable for an injury to or the death of a participant or property damage resulting from an inherent risk of an equine activity." Mich. Comp. Laws § 691.1663. "Equine activity" is generally defined as follows:

> Equine shows, fairs, competitions, performance, or parades that involve any or all breeds of equines and any of the equine disciplines, including, but not limited to, dressage, hunter and jumper horse shows, grand prix jumping, three-day events, combined training, rodeos, driving, pulling, cutting, polo, steeplechasing, English and western performance riding, endurance trail riding and western games, and hunting.

Colo. Rev. Stat. § 13-21-119(2)(c)(I) (2004). Horse racing (regulated by other statutes) is expressly exempted from many of these statutes. *See, e.g.,* Mo. Rev. Stat. § 537.325(3); Tenn. Code Ann. § 44-20-104.

The following are just a few examples of cases interpreting these statutes: *Bothell v. Two Point Acres, Inc.*, 965 P.2d 47 (Ariz. Ct. App. 1998) (statute did not apply where injury did not arise from activity directly relating to horseback riding — rope being used to lead horse to grassy area tightened around plaintiff's hand when horse was startled while being led by plaintiff); *Muller v. English*, 472 S.E.2d 448, 453 (Ga. Ct. App. 1996) (risk of being kicked by horse on fox hunt is inherent risk within scope of statute; noting that fox hunting is a "very dangerous sport" and that "[t]he unusual hazards of fox hunting have been recognized for over 150 years"); *Carl v. Resnick*, 714 N.E.2d 1 (Ill. App. Ct. 1999) (plaintiff was not engaged in "equine activity" because she was riding her own horse when defendant's horse kicked at her horse, striking and injuring plaintiff's leg); *Amburgey v. Sauder*, 605 N.W.2d 84 (Mich. Ct. App. 1999) (statute applied where horse allegedly lunged at and bit plaintiff as she walked past the stall); *Friedli v. Kerr*, No. M1999-02810-COA-R9-CV, 2001 Tenn. App. LEXIS 108 (Unpub. Feb. 23, 2001) (riding in a horse-drawn carriage was not an "equine activity" under the statute). *See also Burke v. McKay*, 679 N.W.2d 418 (Neb. 2004) (eighteen-year-old injured while participating in rodeo had "assumed the risk"; summary judgment affirmed in favor of defendant).

In *Swigart v. Bruno*, 13 Cal. App. 5th 529 (2017), in an endurance horseback riding event the defendant's horse bumped the rear of another horse, causing that horse to kick the defendant's horse, who then bolted, striking the plaintiff, who was standing nearby. Affirming summary judgment in favor of the defendant, the court concluded that because the defendant's horse "merely acted or behaved as a horse," the plaintiff had not raised an issue of material fact as to whether the horse had vicious or dangerous propensities.

Several states have expanded their equine liability statutes to provide the same protections for those engaged in "llama activities" (defined in a similar manner as "equine activities," but adapted as appropriate for current uses of llamas). *See, e.g.,* Colo. Rev. Stat.§ 13-21-119; Ga. Code Ann.§ 4-12-3. Louisiana expanded its equine liability statute in 1999 to apply to any "farm animal activity." La. Rev. Stat. § 9:2795.1. However, it expressly provides that it is not intended to prohibit or limit liability under Louisiana's products liability statute. La. Rev. Stat. § 9:2795.1.D. In 2003, Louisiana created a separate statute applicable only to "equine activities." La. Rev. Stat. § 9:2795.3.

12. For an analysis of equine liability statutes, *see* Terence J. Centner, *The New Equine Liability Statutes*, 62 Tenn. L. Rev. 997 (1995). *See also* Sharlene A. McEvoy, *The Rise of Equine Activity Liability Statutes*, 3 Animal L. 201 (1997).

13. Similar but broader "Recreational Activity Liability" statutes have been construed to apply to equine activities. *See, e.g., King v. CJM Country Stables*, 315 F. Supp. 2d 1061 (D. Haw. 2004) (concluding that Hawaii Revised Statute section 663-1.54 covers equine activities, but finding a question of fact as to whether being bitten by a horse was an inherent risk of horseback riding); *Walters v. Grand Teton Crest Outfitters, Inc.*, 804 F. Supp. 1442 (D. Wyo. 1992) (where a hunter was thrown by a mule who acted "spooked and jumpy" before he rode her, Wyoming's Recreation Safety Act applied, but the court found a question of fact as to whether, under the facts of that case, being thrown was an "inherent risk"—defined by statute to be one "which cannot reasonably be eliminated, altered or controlled").

Chapter 5

Constitutional Law

Section 1. Legal Standing, Justiciability and Other Limiting Doctrines

The justiciability doctrines are the procedural gatekeepers of the federal courts, setting up limitations on access to the courts, because they are courts of limited jurisdiction. A justiciable question or case is one that is properly before a court for a decision on the dispute, *i.e.*, that meets the requirements for justiciability. Legal standing is the most controversial and the most heavily-litigated of the justiciability doctrines. Standing is a prerequisite for a party to have a dispute decided by a court; without standing, a case cannot and will not proceed. Standing in federal court is governed by constitutional limitations, created by the Supreme Court from the "case and controversy" requirement of Article III, section 2 of the federal Constitution. "[T]he question of standing is whether the litigant is entitled to have the court decide the merits of the dispute or of particular issues." *Warth v. Seldin*, 422 U.S. 490, 498 (1975).

Federal court standing is thus a constitutional minimum and a necessity if a dispute is to be heard. Courts and commentators agree the case law on standing presents one of the most confused areas of federal jurisprudence. The cases have been erratic at best in describing and defining the contours of the doctrine. The Supreme Court has openly acknowledged the problem. *See, e.g., Valley Forge Christian College v. Americans United for Separation of Church and State*, 454 U.S. 464, 475 (1982) (standing "not defined with complete consistency in all of the various cases decided by this Court"). Standing is also a threshold question, and a court's determination of the issue should not include any consideration of the merits of a lawsuit. Nevertheless, commentators generally agree the Supreme Court's standing precedent has taken its direction based on the Court's perception of the merits and value of bringing particular actions or types of actions. Since the early 1970s, environmental law and animal law have been at the forefront of the debate over the proper use of standing doctrine by the judiciary.

It is important to understand and appreciate this procedural barrier that frames and informs the role of the federal courts and the ability of litigants to pursue political, moral and ethical agendas before judges (as opposed to legislators). As it develops, standing doctrine delineates and redefines the barriers to and the opportunities for access to the federal courts. Standing is a limiting doctrine, and the courts have used it effectively as such, but litigants seeking to present their arguments have carved out a space for potential claims within the doctrine.

As will be discussed in the cases in this section, there are both textual (constitutional) and judicially-created ("prudential") standing requirements. The former are mandatory, the latter discretionary (although invoked automatically in all cases where an exception does not apply). The constitutional requirements, as defined by the Supreme Court, are that (1) the plaintiff has suffered, or is in imminent danger of suffering, an "injury in fact"; (2) the plaintiff's injury must be fairly traceable to defendant's conduct; and (3) a favorable ruling on plaintiff's claim(s) will remedy the problem of which plaintiff complains. The requirements, especially the latter two, dovetail to varying degrees in the opinions. The prudential standing limitations (which foster judicial management of cases, according to the Supreme Court) are: (1) the plaintiffs and the relief sought must fall within the "zone of interests" protected by the statute under which the claims are made; (2) plaintiffs cannot raise "generalized grievances" shared by all members of society; (3) "citizen" or "taxpayer" suits — brought only on the basis that the plaintiff is experiencing the alleged harm based on her status in one of these two categories — are rarely permitted; and (4) plaintiffs usually may not raise the complaints of third parties without showing some independent, individualized injury.

There are literally hundreds of law review articles and dozens of treatises analyzing the Supreme Court's standing doctrine and cases. For several articles focusing directly on animal law standing issues, *see* Marguerite Hogan, *Standing for Nonhuman Animals: Developing a Guardianship Model From the Dissents in* Sierra Club v. Morton, 95 Cal. L. Rev. 513 (April 2007); Katherine A. Burke, *Can We Stand For It? Amending The Endangered Species Act With An Animal-Suit Provision*, 75 U. Colo. L. Rev. 633 (Spring 2004); Cass Sunstein, *Standing for Animals (With Notes on Animal Rights)*, 47 UCLA L. Rev. 1333 (2000) and Joseph Mendelson, *Should Animals Have Standing? A Review of Standing Under the Animal Welfare Act*, 24 B.C. Envtl. Aff. L. Rev. 795 (Summer 1997).

The main focus of this section is standing in federal court because, for a number of reasons, the most significant animal protection cases generally are brought in federal court and plaintiffs therefore must satisfy Article III standing or their lawsuit will be dismissed. Before considering the federal standing cases, and as a matter of further introduction, however, the first case is a state court case that demonstrates a more relaxed state law standing doctrine and summarizes other justiciability/limiting doctrines.

Jones v. Beame

Court of Appeals of New York, 1978
45 N.Y.2d 402, 380 N.E.2d 277

BREITEL, C.J. These two appeals share a common quality: in each the plaintiffs would embroil the courts in the administration of programs the primary responsibility for which lies in the executive branch of government. In each the courts are obliged to decline the invitation. Accepting the responsibility would violate the constitutional scheme for the distribution of powers among the three branches of government and involve the judicial branch in responsibilities it is ill-equipped to assume.

In the *Jones* appeal plaintiffs are private persons and organizations concerned with the inadequate, and therefore cruel, treatment of animals, as a result of fiscal crisis, in municipal zoos in the City of New York in violation of applicable statutes. They seek declaratory and injunctive relief against the municipal officials charged with ultimate responsibility for operation of the zoos. As the appeal reaches this court, all of the causes of action in the amended complaint have been dismissed on motion either for legal insufficiency or lack of standing.

In the *Bowen* appeal plaintiffs, the City of Long Beach and its city manager, are concerned with the premature placement in private homes and hotels of mental patients discharged into the community in violation of applicable law. They seek declaratory and injunctive relief against the State departments charged with responsibility for the care and treatment of the mentally ill on the assertions that the patients, while still mentally ill, were discharged into the community in excessive numbers and without adequate supervision. As the appeal reaches this court, the complaint has been sustained on motion as legally sufficient.

[Dismissal of *Jones* is upheld, and *Bowen* is also dismissed.] In both cases the allegations of fact are accepted as true. . . . [P]laintiffs, however sincerely motivated, may not interpose themselves and the courts into "the management and operation of public enterprises". Involved are, as in the [*Matter of Abrams v. New York City Tr. Auth.*, 39 N.Y.2d 990, 992 (1976)] case, "questions of judgment, discretion, allocation of resources and priorities inappropriate for resolution in the judicial arena", the responsibility for which is "lodged in a network of executive officials, administrative agencies and local legislative bodies."

In the *Jones* case, involving the zoos, the City of New York, in prolonged fiscal crisis, threatened with bankruptcy, dependent on State and Federal fiscal assistance, and constrained by close regulation, has curtailed services and personnel in efforts to achieve a balanced budget. Its choices have been hard and the measures taken often Draconian, not only at the expense of its animal charges but also of its children in the schools, its poor, its highways and transportation, its courts, jails, hospitals, museums, libraries, police and fire services, and indeed of its whole range of municipal services. Obviously, it is untenable that the judicial process, at the instance of particular persons and groups affected by or concerned with the inevitable consequences of the city's fiscal condition, should intervene and reorder priorities, allocate the limited resources available, and in effect direct how the vast municipal enterprise should conduct its affairs.

In the *Bowen* case, involving the "dumping" on communities of mentally ill patients, the complexities relate not to fiscal measures alone, but to theories and programs for deinstitutionalizing, for the sake of the patients, the inmates of the crowded and evermore crowding mental hospitals. In the State too there are fiscal problems, although not as grave as those affecting the City of New York. The State's fiscal problem is not necessarily solvable by increased taxation because of the fear that it would accelerate the removal of taxpayers and enterprise from the State. Thus, there may be no easy answer in allocating the State's tax-created resources to assist the fiscally troubled City of Long Beach in handling the problems created by the influx of mental patients. Even more intractable are the conflicting views as to the better therapy for mental patients, that is, whether to treat them in institutions or in private settings in the community.

Hence, inescapably, in both cases there are questions of broad legislative and administrative policy beyond the scope of judicial correction. Not only is the situs of responsibility elsewhere, but the judicial process is not designed or intended to assume the management and operation of the executive enterprise.

* * *

The problem of judicially manageable questions is usually described as one of justiciability, not just one of standing. Although much has been written on justiciability, its meaning and application remain uncertain. For example, considered as nonjusticiable, that is, inappropriate or sometimes even improper for judicial inquiry or adjudication, have been political questions, issues that have become moot, and challenges in which only an advisory opinion is sought. Even within a particular category of justiciability, as with political questions, the line separating the justiciable from the nonjusticiable has been subtle, and with the passage of time, it might be said, has even moved.

There is one recurrent theme: the court as a policy matter, even apart from principles of subject matter jurisdiction, will abstain from venturing into areas if it is ill-equipped to undertake the responsibility and other branches of government are far more suited to the task. As put by the then Chief Judge Wyzanski, speaking with respect to a political question, abstention was "a recognition that the tools with which a court can work, the data which it can fairly appraise, [and] the conclusions which it can reach as a basis for entering judgments, have limits." *United States v. Sisson*, 294 F. Supp. 511, 515.

In the instant cases much effort was expended in detailing the concern of the plaintiffs with the issues presented, avowedly to demonstrate that if anyone has standing to litigate these issues, plaintiffs do. In this, plaintiffs are probably correct. The difficulty is not, however, whether plaintiffs are the wrong ones to present and litigate the issues; the point is that the courts are the wrong forum for resolution of the disputes. The proper forums are the Legislature and the elected officials of State and local government. It is there that the accommodations can be made in determining priorities and allocating resources.

In short, resolution of the ultimate issues rests on policy, and reference to violations of applicable statutes is irrelevant except in recognized separately litigable matters brought to enforce them.

* * *

Notes

1. What are the factual similarities between the inadequately cared-for zoo animals and displaced mental patients involved in the two cases? What are the legally significant similarities? Why do you think the court consolidated the two cases?

2. Courts do not enjoy plenary discretion in reviewing matters brought before them; the judiciary's power to review a matter is subject to a number of textually-mandated and self-imposed limitations. These justiciability doctrines determine *who* may go to court ("standing to sue"), *when* in the course of a dispute a judicial response is allowed ("ripeness" and "mootness"), and *what* issues are or are not appropriate for judicial resolution (political questions, collusive actions, advisory opinions).

Courts traditionally refrain from addressing cases that involve a "political question" because such an action supposedly does not present a justiciable controversy; and the political question doctrine is used when the judiciary wants such questions to be handled by one or both of the other branches of the government. The standards for assessing which issues are political questions are not very clear, but the courts retain a significant degree of freedom in defining the concept. The leading case of *Baker v. Carr*, 369 U.S. 186 (1962), held that courts should defer ruling when there exists

> a textually demonstrable constitutional commitment of the issue to a coordinate political department; or a lack of judicially discoverable and manageable standards for resolving it; or the impossibility of deciding without an initial policy determination of a kind clearly for nonjudicial discretion; or the impossibility of a court's undertaking independent resolution without expressing lack of the respect due coordinate branches of government; or an unusual need for unquestioning adherence to a political decision already made; or the potentiality of embarrassment from multifarious pronouncements by various departments on one question.

Id. at 217. These criteria have an obvious level of subjectivity allowing judicial deferral of sensitive issues.

What other options were available to the *Jones v. Beame* court?

3. Article III of the federal Constitution does not bind state courts. Although standing is often an insurmountable barrier in federal court, and is more relaxed in some states, there are several reasons why animal advocates do not bring cases in state courts. First, many federal statutes provide for exclusive jurisdiction in the federal courts. Second, even where jurisdiction is not exclusive, where the federal government or its agencies are sued, defendants can remove the case from state to federal court. Third, some advocates believe that federal judges, who are insulated from the popular pressure of being selected by voters, may be more willing to issue opinions criticizing governmental entities or effecting change for animals that may be contrary to the status quo.

Sierra Club v. Morton

Supreme Court of the United States, 1972
405 U.S. 727, 92 S. Ct. 1361

STEWART, JUSTICE.

I.

The Mineral King Valley is an area of great natural beauty nestled in the Sierra Nevada Mountains in Tulare County, California, adjacent to Sequoia National Park. It has been part of the Sequoia National Forest since 1926, and is designated as a national game refuge by special Act of Congress. Though once the site of extensive mining activity, Mineral King is now used almost exclusively for recreational purposes. Its relative inaccessibility and lack of development have limited the number of visitors each year, and at the same time have preserved the valley's quality as a quasi-wilderness area largely uncluttered by the products of civilization.

The United States Forest Service, which is entrusted with the maintenance and administration of national forests, began in the late 1940s to give consideration to Mineral King as a potential site for recreational development. Prodded by a rapidly increasing demand for skiing facilities, the Forest Service published a prospectus in 1965, inviting bids from private developers for the construction and operation of a ski resort that would also serve as a summer recreation area. The proposal of Walt Disney Enterprises, Inc., was chosen from those of six bidders, and Disney received a three-year permit to conduct surveys and explorations in the valley in connection with its preparation of a complete master plan for the resort.

The final Disney plan, approved by the Forest Service in January 1969, outlines a $35 million complex of motels, restaurants, swimming pools, parking lots, and other structures designed to accommodate 14,000 visitors daily. This complex is to be constructed on 80 acres of the valley floor under a 30-year use permit from the Forest Service. Other facilities, including ski lifts, ski trails, a cog-assisted railway, and utility installations, are to be constructed on the mountain slopes and in other parts of the valley under a revocable special-use permit. To provide access to the resort, the State of California proposes to construct a highway 20 miles in length. A section of this road would traverse Sequoia National Park, as would a proposed high-voltage power line needed to provide electricity for the resort. Both the highway and the power line require the approval of the Department of the Interior, which is entrusted with the preservation and maintenance of the national parks.

Representatives of the Sierra Club, who favor maintaining Mineral King largely in its present state, followed the progress of recreational planning for the valley with close attention and increasing dismay. . . . In June 1969 the Club filed the present suit in the United States District Court for the Northern District of California, seeking a declaratory judgment that various aspects of the proposed development contravene federal laws and regulations governing the preservation of national parks, forests, and game refuges, and also seeking preliminary and permanent injunctions restraining the federal officials involved from granting their approval or issuing permits in connection with the Mineral King project. The petitioner Sierra Club sued as a membership corporation with "a special interest in the conservation and the sound maintenance of the national parks, game refuges and forests of the country," and invoked the judicial-review provisions of the Administrative Procedure Act, 5 U. S. C. § 701, *et seq.*

After two days of hearings, the District Court granted the requested preliminary injunction. It rejected the respondents' challenge to the Sierra Club's standing to sue, and determined that the hearing had raised questions "concerning possible excess of statutory authority, sufficiently substantial and serious to justify a preliminary injunction...." The respondents appealed, and the Court of Appeals for the Ninth Circuit reversed. 433 F.2d 24. With respect to the petitioner's standing, the court noted that there was "no allegation in the complaint that members of the Sierra Club would be affected by the actions of [the respondents] other than the fact that the actions are personally displeasing or distasteful to them," *id.* at 33. ...

The Sierra Club filed a petition for a writ of *certiorari* which we granted, 401 U.S. 907, to review the questions of federal law presented.

II.

The first question presented is whether the Sierra Club has alleged facts that entitle it to obtain judicial review of the challenged action. Whether a party has a sufficient stake in an otherwise justiciable controversy to obtain judicial resolution of that controversy is what has traditionally been referred to as the question of standing to sue. Where the party does not rely on any specific statute authorizing invocation of the judicial process, the question of standing depends upon whether the party has alleged such a "personal stake in the outcome of the controversy," *Baker v. Carr*, 369 U.S. 186, 204, as to ensure that "the dispute sought to be adjudicated will be presented in an adversary context and in a form historically viewed as capable of judicial resolution." *Flast v. Cohen*, 392 U.S. 83, 101. Where, however, Congress has authorized public officials to perform certain functions according to law, and has provided by statute for judicial review of those actions under certain circumstances, the inquiry as to standing must begin with a determination of whether the statute in question authorizes review at the behest of the plaintiff.[3]

The Sierra Club relies upon § 10 of the Administrative Procedure Act (APA), 5 U. S. C. § 702, which provides:

---

3. Congress may not confer jurisdiction on Art. III federal courts to render advisory opinions, or to entertain "friendly" suits, *United States v. Johnson*, 319 U.S. 302, or to resolve "political questions," *Luther v. Borden*, 7 How. 1, because suits of this character are inconsistent with the judicial function under Art. III. But where a dispute is otherwise justiciable, the question whether the litigant is a "proper party to request an adjudication of a particular issue," *Flast v. Cohen*, 392 U.S. 83, 100, is one within the power of Congress to determine.

A person suffering legal wrong because of agency action, or adversely affected or aggrieved by agency action within the meaning of a relevant statute, is entitled to judicial review thereof.

Early decisions under this statute interpreted the language as adopting the various formulations of "legal interest" and "legal wrong" then prevailing as constitutional requirements of standing. But, in *Data Processing Service v. Camp*, 397 U.S. 150, and *Barlow v. Collins*, 397 U.S. 159, decided the same day, we held more broadly that persons had standing to obtain judicial review of federal agency action under § 10 of the APA where they had alleged that the challenged action had caused them "injury in fact," and where the alleged injury was to an interest "arguably within the zone of interests to be protected or regulated" by the statutes that the agencies were claimed to have violated.

* * *

[*The question presented in this case is:*] what must be alleged by persons who claim injury of a noneconomic nature to interests that are widely shared[?]

III.

The injury alleged by the Sierra Club will be incurred entirely by reason of the change in the uses to which Mineral King will be put, and the attendant change in the aesthetics and ecology of the area. Thus, in referring to the road to be built through Sequoia National Park, the complaint alleged that the development "would destroy or otherwise adversely affect the scenery, natural and historic objects and wildlife of the park and would impair the enjoyment of the park for future generations." We do not question that this type of harm may amount to an "injury in fact" sufficient to lay the basis for standing under § 10 of the APA. Aesthetic and environmental well-being, like economic well-being, are important ingredients of the quality of life in our society, and the fact that particular environmental interests are shared by the many rather than the few does not make them less deserving of legal protection through the judicial process. But the "injury in fact" test requires more than an injury to a cognizable interest. It requires that the party seeking review be himself among the injured. The impact of the proposed changes in the environment of Mineral King will not fall indiscriminately upon every citizen. The alleged injury will be felt directly only by those who use Mineral King and Sequoia National Park, and for whom the aesthetic and recreational values of the area will be lessened by the highway and ski resort. The Sierra Club failed to allege that it or its members would be affected in any of their activities or pastimes by the Disney development. Nowhere in the pleadings or affidavits did the Club state that its members use Mineral King for any purpose, much less that they use it in any way that would be significantly affected by the proposed actions of the respondents.

The Club apparently regarded any allegations of individualized injury as superfluous, on the theory that this was a "public" action involving questions as to the use of natural resources, and that the Club's longstanding concern with and expertise in such matters were sufficient to give it standing as a "representative of the public." This theory reflects a misunderstanding of our cases involving so-called "public actions" in the area of administrative law.

* * *

The trend of cases arising under the APA and other statutes authorizing judicial review of federal agency action has been toward recognizing that injuries other than economic harm are sufficient to bring a person within the meaning of the statutory language, and toward discarding the notion that an injury that is widely shared is *ipso facto* not an injury sufficient to provide the basis for judicial review. We noted this development with approval in *Data Processing, supra*, at 154, in saying that the interest alleged to have been injured "may reflect 'aesthetic, conservational, and recreational' as well as economic values." But broadening the categories of injury that may be alleged in support of standing is a different matter from abandoning the requirement that the party seeking review must himself have suffered an injury.

Some courts have indicated a willingness to take this latter step by conferring standing upon organizations that have demonstrated "an organizational interest in the problem" of environmental or consumer protection. *Environmental Defense Fund v. Hardin*, 138 U.S. App. D.C. 391, 395, 428 F.2d 1093, 1097. It is clear that an organization whose members are injured may represent those members in a proceeding for judicial review. *See, e.g., NAACP v. Button*, 371 U.S. 415, 428. But a mere "interest in a problem," no matter how longstanding the interest and no matter how qualified the organization is in evaluating the problem, is not sufficient by itself to render the organization "adversely affected" or "aggrieved" within the meaning of the APA. The Sierra Club is a large and long-established organization, with a historic commitment to the cause of protecting our Nation's natural heritage from man's depredations. But if a "special interest" in this subject were enough to entitle the Sierra Club to commence this litigation, there would appear to be no objective basis upon which to disallow a suit by any other bona fide "special interest" organization, however small or short-lived. And if any group with a bona fide "special interest" could initiate such litigation, it is difficult to perceive why any individual citizen with the same bona fide special interest would not also be entitled to do so.

The requirement that a party seeking review must allege facts showing that he is himself adversely affected does not insulate executive action from judicial review, nor does it prevent any public interests from being protected through the judicial process. It does serve as at least a rough attempt to put the decision as to whether review will be sought in the hands of those who have a direct stake in the outcome. That goal would be undermined were we to construe the APA to authorize judicial review at the behest of organizations or individuals who seek to do no more than vindicate their own value preferences through the judicial process. The principle that the Sierra Club would have us establish in this case would do just that.

As we conclude that the Court of Appeals was correct in its holding that the Sierra Club lacked standing to maintain this action, we do not reach any other questions presented in the petition, and we intimate no view on the merits of the complaint. The judgment is Affirmed.

MR. JUSTICE POWELL and MR. JUSTICE REHNQUIST took no part in the decision of this case.

MR. JUSTICE DOUGLAS, dissenting. I share the views of my Brother BLACK-MUN and would reverse the judgment below.

The critical question of "standing" would be simplified and also put neatly in focus if we fashioned a federal rule that allowed environmental issues to be litigated before federal agencies or federal courts in the name of the inanimate object about to be despoiled, defaced, or invaded by roads and bulldozers and where injury is the subject of public outrage. Contemporary public concern for protecting nature's ecological equilibrium should lead to the conferral of standing upon environmental objects to sue for their own preservation. *See* Stone, *Should Trees Have Standing? — Toward Legal Rights for Natural Objects*, 45 S. Cal. L. Rev. 450 (1972). This suit would therefore be more properly labeled as *Mineral King v. Morton*.

Inanimate objects are sometimes parties in litigation. A ship has a legal personality, a fiction found useful for maritime purposes. The corporation sole — a creature of ecclesiastical law — is an acceptable adversary and large fortunes ride on its cases. The ordinary corporation is a "person" for purposes of the adjudicatory processes, whether it represents proprietary, spiritual, aesthetic, or charitable causes.

So it should be as respects valleys, alpine meadows, rivers, lakes, estuaries, beaches, ridges, groves of trees, swampland, or even air that feels the destructive pressures of modern technology and modern life. The river, for example, is the living symbol of all the life it sustains or nourishes — fish, aquatic insects, water ouzels, otter, fisher, deer, elk, bear, and all other animals, including man, who are dependent on it or who enjoy it for its sight, its sound, or its life. The river as plaintiff speaks for the ecological unit of life that is part of it. Those people who have a meaningful relation to that body of water — whether it be a fisherman, a canoeist, a zoologist, or a logger — must be able to speak for the values which the river represents and which are threatened with destruction.

I do not know Mineral King. I have never seen it nor traveled it, though I have seen articles describing its proposed "development."[5] The Sierra Club in its com-

---

5. Although in the past Mineral King Valley has annually supplied about 70,000 visitor-days of simpler and more rustic forms of recreation — hiking, camping, and skiing (without lifts) — the Forest Service in 1949 and again in 1965 invited developers to submit proposals to "improve" the Valley for resort use. Walt Disney Productions won the competition and transformed the Service's idea into a mammoth project 10 times its originally proposed dimensions. For example, while the Forest Service prospectus called for an investment of at least $3 million and a sleeping capacity of at least 100, Disney will spend $35.3 million and will bed down 3,300 persons by 1978. Disney also plans a nine-level parking structure with two supplemental lots for automobiles, 10 restaurants and 20 ski lifts. The Service's annual license revenue is hitched to Disney's profits. Under Disney's projections, the Valley will be forced to accommodate a tourist population twice as dense as that

plaint alleges that "one of the principal purposes of the Sierra Club is to protect and conserve the national resources of the Sierra Nevada Mountains." The District Court held that this uncontested allegation made the Sierra Club "sufficiently aggrieved" to have "standing" to sue on behalf of Mineral King.

Mineral King is doubtless like other wonders of the Sierra Nevada such as Tuolumne Meadows and the John Muir Trail. Those who hike it, fish it, hunt it, camp in it, frequent it, or visit it merely to sit in solitude and wonderment are legitimate spokesmen for it, whether they may be few or many. Those who have that intimate relation with the inanimate object about to be injured, polluted, or otherwise despoiled are its legitimate spokesmen.

The Solicitor General, whose views on this subject are in the Appendix to this opinion, takes a wholly different approach. He considers the problem in terms of "government by the Judiciary." With all respect, the problem is to make certain that the inanimate objects, which are the very core of America's beauty, have spokesmen before they are destroyed. It is, of course, true that most of them are under the control of a federal or state agency. The standards given those agencies are usually expressed in terms of the "public interest." Yet "public interest" has so many differing shades of meaning as to be quite meaningless on the environmental front. . . .

[T]he pressures on agencies for favorable action one way or the other are enormous. The suggestion that Congress can stop action which is undesirable is true in theory; yet even Congress is too remote to give meaningful direction and its machinery is too ponderous to use very often. The federal agencies of which I speak are not venal or corrupt. But they are notoriously under the control of powerful interests who manipulate them through advisory committees, or friendly working relations, or who have that natural affinity with the agency which in time develops between the regulator and the regulated.

The Forest Service—one of the federal agencies behind the scheme to despoil Mineral King—has been notorious for its alignment with lumber companies, although its mandate from Congress directs it to consider the various aspects of multiple use in its supervision of the national forests.[7]

---

in Yosemite Valley on a busy day. And, although Disney has bought up much of the private land near the project, another commercial firm plans to transform an adjoining 160-acre parcel into a "piggyback" resort complex, further adding to the volume of human activity the Valley must endure. Michael Frome cautions that the national forests are "fragile" and "deteriorate rapidly with excessive recreation use" because "the trampling effect alone eliminates vegetative growth, creating erosion and water runoff problems. The concentration of people, particularly in horse parties, on excessively steep slopes that follow old Indian or cattle routes, has torn up the landscape of the High Sierras in California and sent tons of wilderness soil washing downstream each year." M. Frome, The Forest Service 69 (1971).

7. . . . "Clearcutting," somewhat analogous to strip mining, is the indiscriminate and complete shaving from the earth of all trees—regardless of size or age—often across hundreds of contiguous acres. . . .

The voice of the inanimate object, therefore, should not be stilled. That does not mean that the judiciary takes over the managerial functions from the federal agency. It merely means that before these priceless bits of Americana (such as a valley, an alpine meadow, a river, or a lake) are forever lost or are so transformed as to be reduced to the eventual rubble of our urban environment, the voice of the existing beneficiaries of these environmental wonders should be heard.[8]

Perhaps they will not win. Perhaps the bulldozers of "progress" will plow under all the aesthetic wonders of this beautiful land. That is not the present question. The sole question is, who has standing to be heard?

Those who hike the Appalachian Trail into Sunfish Pond, New Jersey, and camp or sleep there, or run the Allagash in Maine, or climb the Guadalupes in West Texas, or who canoe and portage the Quetico Superior in Minnesota, certainly should have standing to defend those natural wonders before courts or agencies, though they live 3,000 miles away. Those who merely are caught up in environmental news

---

8. Permitting a court to appoint a representative of an inanimate object would not be significantly different from customary judicial appointments of guardians ad litem, executors, conservators, receivers, or counsel for indigents.

The values that ride on decisions such as the present one are often not appreciated even by the so-called experts.

"A teaspoon of living earth contains 5 million bacteria, 20 million fungi, one million protozoa, and 200,000 algae. No living human can predict what vital miracles may be locked in this dab of life, this stupendous reservoir of genetic materials that have evolved continuously since the dawn of the earth. For example, molds have existed on earth for about 2 billion years. But only in this century did we unlock the secret of the penicillins, tetracyclines, and other antibiotics from the lowly molds, and thus fashion the most powerful and effective medicines ever discovered by man. Medical scientists still wince at the thought that we might have inadvertently wiped out the rhesus monkey, medically, the most important research animal on earth. And who knows what revelations might lie in the cells of the blackback gorilla nesting in his eyrie this moment in the Virunga Mountains of Rwanda? And what might we have learned from the European lion, the first species formally noted (in 80 A. D.) as extinct by the Romans?

"When a species is gone, it is gone forever. Nature's genetic chain, billions of years in the making, is broken for all time." Conserve—Water, Land and Life, Nov. 1971, p. 4.

Aldo Leopold wrote in Round River 147 (1953):

"In Germany there is a mountain called the Spessart. Its south slope bears the most magnificent oaks in the world. American cabinetmakers, when they want the last word in quality, use Spessart oak. The north slope, which should be the better, bears an indifferent stand of Scotch pine. Why? Both slopes are part of the same state forest; both have been managed with equally scrupulous care for two centuries. Why the difference?

Kick up the litter under the oaks and you will see that the leaves rot almost as fast as they fall. Under the pines, though, the needles pile up as a thick duff; decay is much slower. Why? Because in the Middle Ages the south slope was preserved as a deer forest by a hunting bishop; the north slope was pastured, plowed, and cut by settlers, just as we do with our woodlots in Wisconsin and Iowa today. Only after this period of abuse was the north slope replanted to pines. During this period of abuse something happened to the microscopic flora and fauna of the soil. The number of species was greatly reduced, i.e., the digestive apparatus of the soil lost some of its parts. Two centuries of conservation have not sufficed to restore these losses. It required the modern microscope, and a century of research in soil science, to discover the existence of these 'small cogs and wheels' which determine harmony or disharmony between men and land in the Spessart."

or propaganda and flock to defend these waters or areas may be treated differently. That is why these environmental issues should be tendered by the inanimate object itself. Then there will be assurances that all of the forms of life which it represents will stand before the court—the pileated woodpecker as well as the coyote and bear, the lemmings as well as the trout in the streams. Those inarticulate members of the ecological group cannot speak. But those people who have so frequented the place as to know its values and wonders will be able to speak for the entire ecological community.

Ecology reflects the land ethic; and Aldo Leopold wrote in A Sand County Almanac 204 (1949), "The land ethic simply enlarges the boundaries of the community to include soils, waters, plants, and animals, or collectively: the land." That, as I see it, is the issue of "standing" in the present case and controversy.

Notes

1. The Administrative Procedure Act (APA), 5 U.S.C. section 701 *et seq.*, provides that "a person suffering legal wrong because of agency action, or adversely affected or aggrieved by agency action within the meaning of a relevant statute, is entitled to judicial review thereof." 5 U.S.C. § 702. After the APA was passed in 1946, its judicial review provisions became the basis for most suits by citizens seeking review of federal agency actions. Beginning in the 1960s, lower courts expanded plaintiffs' access to federal court to the limits of section 702, in response to pressure from environmental and citizens' organizations that were displeased by agency actions. Cass Sunstein, *Standing and the Privatization of Public Law*, 88 COLUM. L. REV. 1432 (1988); Richard B. Stewart, *The Reformation of American Administrative Law*, 88 HARV. L. REV. 1669 (1975).

As environmental law began to flourish and environmental legislation became more prevalent (particularly in the 1970s), courts were increasingly accessible to the public, primarily due to the citizen suit provisions of most of the key federal environmental statutes. *See, e.g.*, Clean Air Act § 307(b), 42 U.S.C. § 7607(b), Clean Water Act § 509(b), 33 U.S.C. § 1369(b); the Comprehensive Environmental Response, Compensation, and Liability Act § 310, 42 U.S.C. § 9654; the Resource Conservation and Recovery Act § 7006(a), 42 U.S.C. § 6976; the Safe Drinking Water Act § 1449, 42 U.S.C. § 300j-8; the Toxic Substances Control Act § 19, 15 U.S.C. § 2618. Such provisions often include an express private right of action that facilitates judicial review of agency actions under the relevant statutes. These statutes typically specify the kinds of agency actions that are eligible for review as well as when, where and how review can be obtained. *See, e.g.*, Clean Air Act § 304(a) & (b); 42 U.S.C. § 7604(a) & (b). As a result, today the APA serves a back-up function where a private right of action is not afforded under the relevant statute. That is, those who want to sue a federal agency usually look to the APA, especially if the underlying statutes contain no citizen suit provision.

2. Describe a proper plaintiff under the Supreme Court's holding in *Sierra Club v. Morton*, which remains the seminal case (along with *Defenders of Wildlife v. Lujan*,

which follows these Notes) for standing issues in environmental as well as animal protection contexts. *See, e.g.,* Christopher Stone, Should Trees Have Standing? Law, Morality and the Environment (3d Ed. Oxford U. Press 2010); Joseph Mendelson, *Should Animals Have Standing? A Review of Standing Under the Animal Welfare Act,* 24 B.C. Envtl. Aff. L. Rev. 795 (Summer 1997).

3. On remand, *Sierra Club v. Morton,* 348 F. Supp. 219 (N.D. Cal. 1972), the district court denied defendants' motion to dismiss the second amended complaint, holding Sierra Club could proceed on the merits.

4. As a factual postscript, Mineral King remains an incorporated section of the Sequoia National Forest. The Sierra Club, among other nature lovers, organizes regular day and overnight trips into the still-untouched wilderness there. Disney subsequently located to a less remote site in Kissimee, Florida, and built Disneyworld.

5. Consider the following excerpt from an article written by William Alsup, Justice Douglas's clerk in the October 1971 term (and later a federal judge in the Northern District of California):

> Douglas was a lifelong mountaineer and conservationist. Stricken with polio as a child, he force-marched himself up and down the Cascades near Yakima, Wash. His spindly legs grew strong. So did his affection for the wilderness. That affection stayed with him throughout his meteoric career until his death in 1979. He read Aldo Leopold and Gifford Pinchot and was committed to a responsibility to the earth. He saved the C&O Canal — which runs from Georgetown to Cumberland, Md. — from destruction in 1954. To do so, he led a group of 37 on a 180-mile, eight-day protest against paving it over to make a highway. Today, it is a national monument. He opposed dam after dam on wild rivers. The Corps of Engineers, the TVA, the Bureau of Reclamation, and the Forest Service, among others, were all on his public enemies list. They had abandoned their charters to protect the public interest, he felt, and had combined with corporate moguls to flatten, grind up, pollute and destroy the earth.
>
> His reverence for the wild and his legal career crossed paths in *Sierra Club.* . . . Although the lawsuit arose after a cluster of landmark environmental statutes had been enacted. . . . , the courts were still refusing, by and large, to confer standing on individuals or organizations to sue under the Administrative Procedure Act to challenge agency action in violation of federal laws and regulations governing national parks and forests. The industry of environmental litigation we now know was non-existent.

FIGHTING A SWISS SKI VILLAGE

> Mineral King Valley lies at the southern end of the Sierra. It has been home to bald eagles, peregrine falcons, pine martens, wolverines and even spotted owls. Located just outside Sequoia National Park, it was under the

control of the Forest Service. Throughout the 1960s, the Forest Service and Walt Disney were planning to transform Mineral King into a replica of a ski village in the Swiss Alps, with as many as 27 chairlifts and two mega-hotels. It would be six times the size of Squaw Valley.

. . . [O]ral argument was on Nov. 17, 1971.

When the argument was over that morning, Justice Douglas returned to his chambers, where he remained alone. He finished his draft just before he had to return to the bench that afternoon. The result was his famous separate opinion in *Sierra Club.* . . .

Justice Douglas' draft opinion framed the issue much differently from the way it had been presented below and by the parties during argument. Instead of focusing on whether the plaintiff would be sufficiently aggrieved he wrote that "environmental suits should be litigated in the name of the inanimate object about to be despoiled, defaced or invaded by roads and bulldozers."

* * *

The draft was vintage Douglas, written in his own hand, from the heart. No one on the court had drawn so much strength from the land as had Douglas. To him, the land and its way of life developed over the eons, had a right to endure, or at least to be heard out before being sacrificed. A court, he felt, could select a guardian *ad litem* to represent Mineral King or any other ecosystem, just as a court could select a proper person to argue for the protection of a ward of the court.

His original manuscript was exceedingly close to the final text of his separate opinion. Douglas further insisted on a series of footnotes critiquing the Forest Service and its clear-cutting of timberlands. He called me in, showed me a stack of reference material on point, and told me to draft the notes for his review. Read consecutively, the footnotes tell a story. They were, however, secondary to his main idea.

William Alsup, *A Passion for the Wild*, THE RECORDER, Oct. 16, 1998, at 5.

In light of Alsup's disclosure, reconsider Justice Douglas' dissent. Was it based on sound judicial reasoning, or was it self-interested judicial activism? Even if every member of the Court agreed, would Douglas' position be a constitutionally defensible ruling for the Supreme Court in light of Article III?

6. While Justice Douglas' ideas were not accepted by the Supreme Court, the idea of a guardian *ad litem* for animals has obtained some recognition in a variety of contexts. *See, e.g.*, Rebecca Huss, *Lessons Learned: Acting As Guardian/Special Master In The Bad Newz Kennels Case,* 15 ANIMAL L. 69 (2008); CONN. GEN. STAT. 54-86n (2017) ("Desmond's Law," allowing the appointment of advocates to represent the "interests of justice" in animal welfare and custody cases) (discussed in Chapter 3).

7. Protection of Mineral King would save both habitat and those beings who live there—that is, the environment *and* the animals. Are the interests of the environmental and animal protection movements always the same? Can they clash without reconciliation? Compare the agendas of the two movements and consider how their positions might differ in the following situation: Roaming herds of wild boars inhabit an island and are single-handedly destroying a native plant population whose species is found nowhere but on the island. In an attempt to protect the plants, the U.S. Department of Fish and Game sends sharpshooters out to gun down the boars from a helicopter and leave them to die. Compare the interests of environmental organizations, whose goal is to preserve endangered animal and plant populations, as contrasted with animal protectionists, who object to the killing. Consider the likelihood of a compromise or a clash between the groups.

8. A similar scenario to that proposed in Note 7 presented itself in *Animal Lovers Volunteer Ass'n v. Weinberger*, 765 F.2d 937 (9th Cir. 1985). On San Clemente Island off the coast of southern California, Navy personnel were planning on shooting feral (wild) goats from helicopters, because "removal of goats running wild on San Clemente was necessary to protect endangered or threatened animals and plants in a critical habitat covering approximately one third of the island." Plaintiff (ALVA) sued to enjoin the shooting, claiming "that the environmental impact statement prepared by the Navy for the removal program was so inadequate as to violate the National Environmental Policy Act (NEPA), 42 U.S.C. §§ 4321, 4332." (NEPA is summarized in Chapter 9. In short, NEPA requires environmental review where federal agencies are involved in actions that may impact the environment and it has been an effective tool to prevent or delay federal agencies that have not adequately evaluated their actions.)

The Ninth Circuit affirmed ALVA's dismissal on standing grounds, holding it had not demonstrated injury in fact:

> If goats were an endangered species, or if ALVA sought to protect the plants endangered by the goats, ALVA's position would be different. If ALVA showed that the Navy's program would affect its members' aesthetic or ecological surroundings, its position also might be different. But ALVA has alleged no such cognizable injury to its members. A mere assertion of organizational interest in a problem, unaccompanied by allegations of actual injury to members of the organization, is not enough to establish standing.

ALVA and its members could not view the goats because they were excluded from San Clemente Island because of the military work being done there. Its members could not step on the island to see the capricide, and therefore the Ninth Circuit ruled there was no standing because there was no "direct sensory impact" on its members.

9. Given that most humans have five senses, consider other "sensory impacts" and how those might be grounds for injury in fact under Article III.

10. In *ALVA*, the court cited additional grounds for rejecting ALVA's standing:

> ALVA has not differentiated its concern from the generalized abhorrence other members of the public may feel at the prospect of cruelty to animals. To have standing, a party must demonstrate an interest that is distinct from the interest held by the public at large. ALVA lacks the longevity and indicia of commitment to preventing inhumane behavior which gave standing to Fund for Animals [an older organization that had been making the same animal welfare claims before ALVA], and which might provide standing to other better known organizations. While an organization's standing is not simply a function of its age or fame, those factors become highly relevant when the organization, like ALVA, has no history which antedates the legal action it seeks to bring, and can point to no activities which demonstrate its interest, other than pursuing a legal action.

Should a "demonstrated organizational stake"—or the longevity of the organization's history—be part of the constitutional analysis as to whether there is a sufficiently adverse case or controversy? Consider this example: You and your classmates learn that a local hunting club is about to start shooting dogs on campus for sport, and that the federal government has approved the hunt. You form a group, Law Students for Campus Dogs, and file an action to stop the killing. Without considering the merits, should your organization's "age" matter in determining whether there is an injury in fact?

11. Regardless of the Ninth Circuit's concern about its viability or authenticity, ALVA proved it was not a one-case group in *Animal Lovers Volunteer Ass'n v. Carlucci*, 849 F.2d 1475 (9th Cir. 1988) (unreported table op.). In that case, ALVA challenged another government eradication program, this one involving the slaughter of red foxes in the Seal Beach National Wildlife Refuge, which lies within the Seal Beach Naval Weapons Station. The alleged purpose of the project was to protect two endangered bird species believed to be threatened by the foxes. ALVA stated two injuries—the anticipated aesthetic injury from the lost opportunity to observe the foxes, and the fact that "the eradication project [might] increase the rodent population and thereby adversely affect [plaintiffs'] health . . . ." Finding plaintiffs' proximity to the area of planned eradication provided a "geographical nexus," the court denied defendants' motion to dismiss for lack of standing. Is that result consistent with *ALVA* and *Sierra Club*?

12. The cognizable interest in *viewing* wildlife was recognized by the court in *Humane Society of the U.S. v. Hodel*, 840 F.2d 45, 52 (D.C. Cir. 1988) (*Hodel*): "The gist of [the Humane Society's] grievance is that the existence of hunting on wildlife refuges forces Society members to witness animal corpses and environmental degradation, in addition to depleting the supply of animals and birds that refuge visitors seek to view. These are classic aesthetic interests, which have always enjoyed protection under standing analysis." *See also National Wildlife Federation v. Hodel*, 839 F.2d 694 (1988) (wildlife organization had standing to challenge Interior

Department surface-mining regulations that allegedly threatened to degrade the landscape); *Alaska Fish & Wildlife Federation v. Dunkle*, 829 F.2d 933, 937 (9th Cir. 1987) (decrease in number of migratory birds "has injured those who wish to hunt, photograph, observe, or carry out scientific studies").

13. A very common form of standing where animal protection groups are involved is called "representational" or "associational" standing—where organizations bring actions on behalf of their members. The elements of associational standing are set out in *Hunt v. Washington State Apple Advertising Commission*, 432 U.S. 333, 343 (1977):

> An association has standing to bring suit on behalf of its members when:
> (a) its members would otherwise have standing to sue in their own right;
> (b) the interests it seeks to protect are germane to the organization's purpose; and (c) neither the claim asserted nor the relief requested requires the participation of individual members in the lawsuit.

This is a very important tripartite test seen in many environmental and animal law cases. The second germaneness requirement "mandate[es] mere pertinence between litigation subject and organizational purpose," and so is usually easily met where groups are suing over animal interests. *Hodel*, 840 F.2d at 58. It is an "undemanding," "modest but sensible standard." *Id.* at 59. While there may be outlier cases in which a plaintiff-group's purpose is completely out of line with the claims stated, in almost every case an animal welfare group satisfies that prong when it brings cases in alignment with its mission.

14. *Sierra Club* illustrates a recurring procedural quandary in environmental and animal-protection litigation. Plaintiffs who seek to enjoin particular actions commonly move for a preliminary injunction as a short-term remedy based either on the scientifically provable ultimate injury to a species or habitat, or more routinely the potential harm to the plaintiffs. The goal of a preliminary injunction is both to avert irreparable injury while litigation of the matter is conducted and, more importantly, to ensure that any subsequent decision rendered by the court about the (im)propriety of the defendant's actions is not mooted by, in the case of the environment or animals, elimination of the "resource" plaintiffs seek to protect. 11A Wright, Miller & Kane, Federal Practice and Procedure: Civil 2d §2947. Injunctive relief is crucial in animal and environmental cases since any damage to the resource could be irreversible and non-compensable.

Although the requirements vary somewhat between courts, parties moving for a preliminary injunction generally must establish that (1) they are likely to win on the merits; (2) they will suffer irreparable injury if the preliminary injunction is denied; (3) the risk of harm posed by not granting the preliminary injunction outweighs the risk of imposing a burden on the defendant if the plaintiff subsequently loses on the merits; and (4) the public interest will be served by the injunction. A leading case on the standard in federal court is *Winter v. Natural Resources Defense Council, Inc.*, 555 U.S. 7 (2008), which is excerpted in Chapter 9.

The first of the four precepts of the traditional test—the "likelihood of success on the merits"—may force a modified approach to standing. By requiring courts to look ahead to the substance of a matter, the test implicates a "standing on the merits" analysis. Remember the first requirement for standing is injury-in-fact. As *Hodel* and *Sierra Club* illustrate, satisfaction of the injury-in-fact requirement in animal protection cases involves not just a showing that a species or group is being or will be adversely affected by the challenged activity, but also an indication that such adverse effects be characterized as detrimental to some cognizable interest of the plaintiff—a leap that courts may be reluctant to make.

15. *Hodel* held the second injury asserted by the Humane Society's members—the harm that hunting causes to both the members' interests in not having to view dead animals or the degradation of the environment when visiting wildlife refuges and their interest in preventing or limiting the reduction of the animal populations that the members seek to view—was "clearly cognizable." The court's justification for this holding was based in large part on *Sierra Club*'s holding that "the fact that particular environmental interests are shared by the many rather than the few does not make them less deserving of legal protection through the judicial process." *Sierra Club*, 405 U.S. at 734. This holding stands in important contrast with the prudential rule that plaintiffs do not have standing to bring "generalized grievances"—*i.e.*, that standing does not lie where the resolution of a dispute would affect all (or a substantial majority of the) members of society.

Lujan v. Defenders of Wildlife

Supreme Court of the United States, 1992
504 U.S. 555, 112 S. Ct. 2130

JUSTICE SCALIA delivered the opinion of the Court with respect to Parts I, II, III-A, and IV, and an opinion with respect to Part III-B, in which THE CHIEF JUSTICE, JUSTICE WHITE, AND JUSTICE THOMAS join.

This case involves a challenge to a rule promulgated by the Secretary of the Interior interpreting §7 of the Endangered Species Act of 1973 (ESA), 87 Stat. 892, as amended, 16 U.S.C. §1536, in such fashion as to render it applicable only to actions within the United States or on the high seas. The preliminary issue, and the only one we reach, is whether respondents here, plaintiffs below, have standing to seek judicial review of the rule.

I

The ESA, 87 Stat. 884, as amended, 16 U.S.C. § 1531, *et seq.*, seeks to protect species of animals against threats to their continuing existence caused by man. *See generally TVA v. Hill*, 437 U.S. 153, 98 S. Ct. 2279, 57 L. Ed. 2d 117 (1978). The ESA instructs the Secretary of the Interior to promulgate by regulation a list of those species which are either endangered or threatened under enumerated criteria, and to define the critical habitat of these species. 16 U.S.C. §§ 1533, 1536. Section 7(a)(2) of the Act then provides, in pertinent part:

> Each Federal agency shall, in consultation with and with the assistance of
> the Secretary [of the Interior], insure that any action authorized, funded,
> or carried out by such agency . . . is not likely to jeopardize the continued
> existence of any endangered species or threatened species or result in the
> destruction or adverse modification of habitat of such species which is
> determined by the Secretary, after consultation as appropriate with affected
> States, to be critical.

6 U.S.C. § 1536(a)(2).

In 1978, the Fish and Wildlife Service (FWS) and the National Marine Fisheries Service (NMFS) . . . promulgated a joint regulation stating that the obligations
imposed by § 7(a)(2) extend to actions taken in foreign nations. 43 Fed. Reg. 874
(1978). [In 1986, the Interior Department revised the regulations, requiring] consultation only for actions taken in the United States or on the high seas. . . .

Shortly thereafter, respondents, organizations dedicated to wildlife conservation
and other environmental causes, filed this action against the Secretary of the Interior, seeking a declaratory judgment that the new regulation is in error as to the geographic scope of § 7(a)(2) and an injunction requiring the Secretary to promulgate a
new regulation restoring the initial interpretation. . . .

II

* * *

The party invoking federal jurisdiction bears the burden of establishing its
standing. Since they are not mere pleading requirements but rather an indispensable part of the plaintiff's case, each element must be supported in the same way
as any other matter on which the plaintiff bears the burden of proof, *i.e.*, with the
manner and degree of evidence required at the successive stages of the litigation. At
the pleading stage, general factual allegations of injury resulting from the defendant's conduct may suffice, for on a motion to dismiss we "presume that general
allegations embrace those specific facts that are necessary to support the claim." In
response to a summary judgment motion, however, the plaintiff can no longer rest
on such "mere allegations," but must "set forth" by affidavit or other evidence "specific facts," Fed. Rule Civ. Proc. 56(e), which for purposes of the summary judgment
motion will be taken to be true. And at the final stage, those facts (if controverted)
must be "supported adequately by the evidence adduced at trial." When the suit
is one challenging the legality of government action or inaction, the nature and
extent of facts [required] depends considerably upon whether the plaintiff is himself an object of the action (or forgone action) at issue. If he is, there is ordinarily
little question that the action or inaction has caused him injury, and that a judgment preventing or requiring the action will redress it. When, however, as in this
case, a plaintiff's asserted injury arises from the government's allegedly unlawful
regulation (or lack of regulation) of someone else, much more is needed. In that
circumstance, causation and redressability ordinarily hinge on the response of the
regulated (or regulable) third party to the government action or inaction — and

perhaps on the response of others as well. . . . Thus, when the plaintiff is not himself the object of the government action or inaction he challenges, standing is not precluded, but it is ordinarily "substantially more difficult" to establish.

III

* * *

A

Respondents' claim to injury is that the lack of consultation with respect to certain funded activities abroad "increas[es] the rate of extinction of endangered and threatened species." . . . To survive the Secretary's summary judgment motion, respondents had to submit affidavits or other evidence showing, through specific facts, not only that listed species were in fact being threatened by funded activities abroad, but also that one or more of respondents' members would thereby be "directly" affected apart from their "'special interest' in the subject." [T]he Court of Appeals focused on the affidavits of two Defenders' members—Joyce Kelly and Amy Skilbred. Ms. Kelly stated that she traveled to Egypt in 1986 and "observed the traditional habitat of the endangered Nile crocodile there and intend[s] to do so again, and hope[s] to observe the crocodile directly," and that she "will suffer harm in fact as the result of [the] American . . . role . . . in overseeing the rehabilitation of the Aswan High Dam on the Nile . . . and [in] developing . . . Egypt's . . . Master Water Plan." Ms. Skilbred averred that she traveled to Sri Lanka in 1981 and "observed the habitat" of "endangered species such as the Asian elephant and the leopard" at what is now the site of the Mahaweli project funded by the Agency for International Development (AID), although she "was unable to see any of the endangered species"; "this development project," she continued, "will seriously reduce endangered, threatened, and endemic species habitat including areas that I visited . . . [, which] may severely shorten the future of these species"; that threat, she concluded, harmed her because she "intend[s] to return to Sri Lanka in the future and hope[s] to be more fortunate in spotting at least the endangered elephant and leopard." When Ms. Skilbred was asked at a subsequent deposition if and when she had any plans to return to Sri Lanka, she reiterated that "I intend to go back to Sri Lanka," but confessed that she had no current plans: "I don't know [when]. There is a civil war going on right now. I don't know. Not next year, I will say. In the future." We shall assume for the sake of argument that these affidavits contain facts showing that certain agency-funded projects threaten listed species—though that is questionable. They plainly contain no facts, however, showing how damage to the species will produce "imminent" injury to Mses. Kelly and Skilbred. That the women "had visited" the areas of the projects before the projects commenced proves nothing. As we have said in a related context, "'Past exposure to illegal conduct does not in itself show a present case or controversy regarding injunctive relief . . . if unaccompanied by any continuing, present adverse effects.'" And the affiants' profession of an "intent" to return to the places they had visited before—where they will presumably, this time, be deprived of the opportunity to observe animals of the endangered species—is simply not enough. Such "some day" intentions—without any description of concrete plans, or indeed even any specification of when the some day will be — do not support a finding of the "actual or imminent" injury that our cases require.[2]

Besides relying upon the Kelly and Skilbred affidavits, respondents propose a series of novel standing theories. The first, inelegantly styled "ecosystem nexus," proposes that any person who uses any part of a "contiguous ecosystem" adversely affected by a funded activity has standing even if the activity is located a great distance away. This approach, as the Court of Appeals correctly observed, is inconsistent with our opinion in *National Wildlife Federation*, which held that a plaintiff claiming injury from environmental damage must use the area affected by the challenged activity and not an area roughly "in the vicinity" of it. It makes no difference that the general-purpose section of the ESA states that the Act was intended in part "to provide a means whereby the ecosystems upon which endangered species and threatened species depend may be conserved," 16 U.S.C. § 1531(b). To say that the Act protects ecosystems is not to say that the Act creates (if it were possible) rights of action in persons who have not been injured in fact, that is, persons who use portions of an ecosystem not perceptibly affected by the unlawful action in question. Respondents' other theories are called, alas, the "animal nexus" approach, whereby anyone who has an interest in studying or seeing the endangered animals anywhere on the globe has standing; and the "vocational nexus" approach, under which anyone with a professional interest in such animals can sue. Under these theories, anyone who goes to see Asian elephants in the Bronx Zoo, and anyone who is a keeper of Asian elephants in the Bronx Zoo, has standing to sue because the Director of the Agency for International Development (AID) did not consult with the Secretary regarding the AID-funded project in Sri Lanka. This is beyond all reason. Standing is not "an ingenious academic exercise in the conceivable,"

---

2. The dissent acknowledges the settled requirement that the injury complained of be, if not actual, then at least imminent, but it contends that respondents could get past summary judgment because "a reasonable finder of fact could conclude . . . that . . . Kelly or Skilbred will soon return to the project sites." This analysis suffers either from a factual or from a legal defect, depending on what the "soon" is supposed to mean. If "soon" refers to the standard mandated by our precedents — that the injury be "imminent," — we are at a loss to see how, as a factual matter, the standard can be met by respondents' mere profession of an intent, some day, to return. But if, as we suspect, "soon" means nothing more than "in this lifetime," then the dissent has undertaken quite a departure from our precedents. Although "imminence" is concededly a somewhat elastic concept, it cannot be stretched beyond its purpose, which is to ensure that the alleged injury is not too speculative for Article III purposes — that the injury is "certainly impending." It has been stretched beyond the breaking point when, as here, the plaintiff alleges only an injury at some indefinite future time, and the acts necessary to make the injury happen are at least partly within the plaintiff's own control. In such circumstances we have insisted that the injury proceed with a high degree of immediacy, so as to reduce the possibility of deciding a case in which no injury would have occurred at all. There is no substance to the dissent's suggestion that imminence is demanded only when the alleged harm depends upon "the affirmative actions of third parties beyond a plaintiff's control." Our cases mention third-party-caused contingency, naturally enough; but they also mention the plaintiff's failure to show that he will soon expose himself to the injury. . . .

but as we have said requires, at the summary judgment stage, a factual showing of perceptible harm. It is clear that the person who observes or works with a particular animal threatened by a federal decision is facing perceptible harm, since the very subject of his interest will no longer exist. It is even plausible—though it goes to the outermost limit of plausibility—to think that a person who observes or works with animals of a particular species in the very area of the world where that species is threatened by a federal decision is facing such harm, since some animals that might have been the subject of his interest will no longer exist. It goes beyond the limit, however, and into pure speculation and fantasy, to say that anyone who observes or works with an endangered species, anywhere in the world, is appreciably harmed by a single project affecting some portion of that species with which he has no more specific connection.[3]

Notes

1. *Lujan* remains the leading Supreme Court opinion on standing in environmental and animal cases. This may seem odd, given that the plaintiffs' sole failing with respect to standing was their failure to buy plane tickets. In a concurring opinion, Justices Kennedy and Souter wrote:

> While it may seem trivial to require that Mses. Kelly and Skilbred acquire airline tickets to the project sites or announce a date certain upon which they will return, this is not a case where it is reasonable to assume that the affiants will be using the sites on a regular basis, nor do the affiants claim to have visited the sites since the projects commenced. With respect to the Court's discussion of respondents' "ecosystem nexus," "animal nexus,"

---

3. The dissent embraces each of respondents' "nexus" theories, rejecting this portion of our analysis because it is "unable to see how the distant location of the destruction *necessarily* (for purposes of ruling at summary judgment) mitigates the harm" to the plaintiff.... The dissent may be correct that the geographic remoteness of those members (here in the United States) from Sri Lanka and Aswan does not "*necessarily*" prevent such a finding—but it assuredly does so when no further facts have been brought forward (and respondents have produced none) showing that the impact upon animals in those distant places will in some fashion be reflected here. The dissent's position to the contrary reduces to the notion that distance *never* prevents harm, a proposition we categorically reject. It cannot be that a person with an interest in an animal automatically has standing to enjoin federal threats to that species of animal, anywhere in the world. Were that the case, the plaintiff in *Sierra Club*, for example, could have avoided the necessity of establishing anyone's use of Mineral King by merely identifying one of its members interested in an endangered species of flora or fauna at that location. JUSTICE BLACKMUN's accusation that a special rule is being crafted for "environmental claims," is correct, but *he* is the craftsman. JUSTICE STEVENS, by contrast, would allow standing on an apparent "animal nexus" theory to all plaintiffs whose interest in the animals is "genuine." Such plaintiffs, we are told, do not have to visit the animals because the animals are analogous to family members. We decline to join JUSTICE STEVENS in this Linnaean leap. It is unclear to us what constitutes a "genuine" interest; how it differs from a "nongenuine" interest (which nonetheless prompted a plaintiff to file suit); and why such an interest in animals should be different from such an interest in anything else that is the subject of a lawsuit.

and "vocational nexus" theories, *ante,* I agree that on this record respondents' showing is insufficient to establish standing on any of these bases. I am not willing to foreclose the possibility, however, that in different circumstances a nexus theory similar to those proffered here might support a claim to standing.

2. Cases addressing substantive provisions of the Endangered Species Act are included in Chapter 9.

3. Is Justice Scalia raising the constitutional minimum injury required to establish standing? Who is the proper plaintiff now, and what does s/he need to show? How "imminent" does the injury need to be for a plaintiff to establish standing?

4. The Court rejects the "contiguous ecosystem" standing argument out of hand. Could scientific evidence change the Court's mind, *e.g.,* what if plaintiffs could prove that as a matter of scientific fact, the results of environmental destruction and transformation have a ripple effect throughout the world that would result in an effect at their home? Should the current scientific state of the art regarding the environmental effects of distant conduct be considered in developing the standing doctrine? If so, does constitutional doctrine consequently change with increases in scientific knowledge?

Note also that Justice Scalia suggests plaintiffs want to have standing to challenge any action throughout the world. He sets up a "relative distance" standard (similar to a proximate cause tort analysis) that could lead to a series of inconsistent opinions from lower courts trying to determine how close to an environmentally-injurious event one needs to be in order to have standing to challenge that event.

5. Does the Court's holding contradict Congressional intent in enacting the Endangered Species Act? Could, or did, Congress intend such a high standard of involvement before a plaintiff could successfully seek to enforce the ESA? For a discussion of standing under the ESA and a proposal for an "animal-suit" provision to enable advocates to sue under the ESA on behalf of endangered animals, see Katherine A. Burke, *Can We Stand For It? Amending The Endangered Species Act With An Animal-Suit Provision,* 75 U. Colo. L. Rev. 633 (Spring 2004).

6. In *Citizens to End Animal Suffering and Exploitation, Inc. ("CEASE") v. New England Aquarium,* 836 F. Supp. 45 (D. Mass. 1993), plaintiffs were Kama, a dolphin, and three animal protection groups; the Aquarium, the Navy and two agencies were defendants. The gravamen of the complaint was that (a) Kama had been illegally transferred from the Aquarium to participate in a Navy sonar study, and (b) the Navy was not following federal law with respect to the capture of dolphins for its programs, which resulted in fewer dolphins in the wild for plaintiffs to see.

The court found plaintiffs had no standing with respect to Kama because, among other reasons, plaintiffs could not actually identify Kama or state when he had left the Aquarium. On the issue of plaintiffs' concern about the number of animals available for viewing in the wild, the court found this overstepped Justice Scalia's "outermost limits" defined in *Lujan*: "Even if plaintiffs could demonstrate that [the defendants'] actions have resulted in the depletion of wild dolphins somewhere, plaintiffs have not offered any evidence that the depletion occurs in any particular place, or that their members have or will be harmed by the depletion in that place." *Id.* at 53.

7. The *CEASE* plaintiffs also alleged procedural and informational injuries as a basis for standing. Again citing *Lujan*, the court rejected the procedural harm claim, which related to the organizations' claims that they were injured by the government's failure to engage in required notice and comment rulemaking procedures, thereby precluding plaintiffs from obtaining the information necessary to both advise their members of developments and to prepare legal challenges. The court recognized the overlap in such cases between informational and procedural harms:

> [T]he strongest argument which can be made concerning informational harm is that the improper failure of the government to disseminate information injures the ability of organizations and their members to participate in the political process to promote public policies they prefer. Adequate information about government activity is important to the exercise of fundamental political rights, including the rights to vote, to speak and write in an effort to influence the votes of others, and to lobby Congress and the President. In this sense, informational rights are instrumental to the exercise of procedural rights; the two rights are integrally related.

836 F. Supp. at 56.

Given that connection, the court held, based on *Lujan* and other cases, that neither procedural nor informational injury claims alone conferred standing. Where such an injury is claimed, a plaintiff generally must establish some other Article III injury in fact, some "concrete and particularized" injury affecting plaintiff and not the public at large.

A different standing analysis applies where an organization is suing on its own behalf for injuries to the organization *qua* organization. In that situation, the organization must satisfy the tripartite test under Article III and prove some injury to its actual corporate missions or goals, or specific programs. The following case presents one example.

The Humane Society of the United States v. United States Postal Service

United States District Court, District of Columbia, 2009
609 F. Supp. 2d 85

James Robertson, District Judge.

The Animal Welfare Act, 7 U.S.C. § 2156, makes it unlawful to use the United States mail to advertise an animal or certain sharp instruments for use in "animal fighting ventures." The Postal Reorganization Act renders mail that is punishable under the Animal Welfare Act "nonmailable." 39 U.S.C. § 3001. Invoking those statutes, the Humane Society of the United States petitioned the United States Postal Service ("USPS") to declare nonmailable a monthly periodical entitled *The Feathered Warrior*. The Humane Society sought judicial review of USPS's denial of that petition, asserting that the denial was arbitrary, capricious, an abuse of discretion, or otherwise not in accordance with the law. See 5 U.S.C. § 706(2)(A).

* * *

Facts

USPS delivers *The Feathered Warrior* to a few thousand subscribers every month, charging a discounted periodical rate for postage. About two-thirds of the magazine's content is advertisements. The Humane Society alleges that more than ninety percent of the ads are criminal solicitations for the sale of fighting animals and weapons whose purchase is illegal under federal law and the laws of many states. There are also ads for the sale of cockfighting supplies, illegal steroids, and animal fighting venues (*i.e.*, cockfighting clubs) in states where cockfighting is illegal; ads for illegal animal fights; and listings of champions in recent cockfights. Publications like *The Feathered Warrior* are recovered in seventy-five percent or more of law enforcement raids of illegal animal fights and are offered in evidence to prove criminal culpability.

The Humane Society is often called upon by law enforcement to provide care and shelter for fighting animals seized in raids of animal fighting ventures, and it expects that the calls for such service will continue. The costs to the Humane Society, for the equipment, transportation, veterinary supplies, and personnel needed to respond to such calls, usually on an emergency basis and without prior notice, run to hundreds of thousands of dollars.

The Humane Society alleges that USPS's continuing willingness to deliver *The Feathered Warrior* violates the Postal Reorganization Act's requirement that material in violation of the Animal Welfare Act be declared nonmailable. The Humane Society also asserts that the circulation of *The Feathered Warrior* violates USPS's own Domestic Mail Manual ("DMM").

The Animal Welfare Act states in relevant part that:

(c) ... It shall be unlawful for any person to knowingly use the mail service of the United States Postal Service or any instrumentality of interstate commerce for commercial speech for purposes of advertising an animal, or an instrument described in subsection (e), for use in an animal fighting venture, promoting or in any other manner furthering an animal fighting venture except as performed outside the limits of the States of the United States.

* * *

(e) ... It shall be unlawful for any person to knowingly sell, buy, transport, or deliver in interstate or foreign commerce a knife, a gaff, or any other sharp instrument attached, or designed or intended to be attached, to the leg of a bird for use in an animal fighting venture.

7 U.S.C. § 2156.

The Postal Reorganization Act makes "[m]atter the deposit of which in the mails is punishable under . . . section 26 of the Animal Welfare Act *nonmailable.*" 39 U.S.C. § 3001(a) (emphasis added).

* * *

On June 18, 2008, after this suit was filed, §2156 was amended again, inserting an express ban on mailing "advertising" materials for fighting animals and cockfighting weapons. 7 U.S.C. § 2156.

Analysis

1. *Standing*

* * *

Here, alleging financial injury and a need to shift programming and organizational resources, the Humane Society asserts organizational standing. USPS disputes the claim of organizational standing, asserting that the Humane Society has not been injured, that its expenditures cannot be traced to the actions of USPS, and that an order forcing USPS to declare *The Feathered Warrior* nonmailable would not decrease illegal animal fights or the number of law enforcement raids on such fights. In evaluating this dispute, I must "assume the merits in favor of the party invoking . . . jurisdiction."

A. *Injury*

Injury-in-fact is "an invasion of a legally protected interest that is (i) concrete and particularized rather than abstract or generalized, and (ii) actual or imminent rather than remote, speculative, conjectural or hypothetical."

USPS does not dispute the Humane Society's claim that answering law enforcement requests for assistance to animals seized from illegal fights costs hundreds of thousands of dollars. It argues instead that those expenses invade no legally protected interest of the Humane Society because the Humane Society is a volunteer — that the fact that the Humane Society *chooses* to try and eliminate illegal animal fights makes the related expenditures a self-inflicted wound insufficient to establish injury-in-fact. Additionally, USPS argues that there is no actual or imminent harm because the Humane Society cannot identify any future raids in which the Humane Society will be called in to assist.

The Humane Society has spent decades trying to reduce illegal animal fighting in the United States. Its decision to dedicate time and resources to achieving this goal may be a voluntary budgetary decision, but if the need to care for animals on an emergency basis is increased by USPS's circulation of *The Feathered Warrior,* then the financial injury to the Humane Society is neither voluntary nor self-inflicted. *See Havens Realty Corp. v. Coleman,* 455 U.S. 363, 378–79 (1982) (if discriminatory actions taken by the defendants have "perceptibly impaired" the plaintiff's programs, "there can be no question that the organization has suffered injury in fact"); *see also Abigail Alliance for Better Access to Developmental Drugs v. Eschen-bach,* 469 F.3d 129, 133 (D.C. Cir. 2006) (citing cases that have found organizational standing under *Havens*).

The fact that the Humane Society cannot name the exact date and location of the next raid of an illegal animal fight does not affect its standing. *See Emergency Coal. to Defend Educ. Travel,* 545 F.3d 4, 9–10 [(D.C. Cir. 2008)] (noting that "some day" intentions do not create an actual or imminent injury, but events that occur consistently are more concrete and specific and can serve as the basis for injury-in-fact).

B. *Causation and redressability*

To establish the causation element of standing, a plaintiff must demonstrate that its injury is "fairly traceable" to the defendant's actions, "as opposed to the independent action of a third party not before the court." To establish redressability, a plaintiff must establish that it is "likely, as opposed to merely speculative, that a favorable decision by this court will redress the injury suffered." *Id.*

USPS argues that its distribution of *The Feathered Warrior* is not a substantial factor in the decision of animal fighting enthusiasts to engage in illegal animal fights, and that the Humane Society's injury is therefore not fairly traceable to USPS's decision on the mailability of *The Feathered Warrior.* The Humane Society argues, on the other hand, that causation and redressability exist because the circulation of *The Feathered Warrior* promotes animal fights and therefore likely increases the number of animals injured in illegal animal fights.

Standing to challenge government conduct that allegedly causes a third party to injure the plaintiff can exist *either* "where the challenged government action authorized conduct that would otherwise have been illegal," *or* "where the record presented substantial evidence of a causal relationship between the government policy and the third-party conduct, leaving little doubt as to causation and the likelihood of redress." *Renal Physicians Ass'n,* 489 F.3d [1267, 1275 (D.C. Cir. 2007)] (internal quotations omitted). The Humane Society arguably meets both tests. Under the first one, the Humane Society challenges government action that authorizes what it alleges is the illegal acceptance of mail matter. Under the second, the record does present "substantial evidence of a causal relationship" between the continued mailing of *The Feathered Warrior* and illegal animal fighting, including a declaration by Ann Chynoweth, the Senior Director of the Animal Cruelty and Fighting campaign for the Humane Society. Chynoweth states that the distribution of *The Feathered Warrior* promotes and furthers illegal animal fighting ventures in at least five ways: (1) it advertises animal fights, (2) specific animal fighting ventures would not exist without the publication because it would be more difficult to procure animals and supplies for the fights, (3) it advertises birds that won at past fights and therefore encourages attendance at particular fights, (4) it advertises fighting animals, and (5) it publishes fight results from particular venues. The Humane Society also points to an academic study examining the market forces of cockfighting. *See* Donna K. Darden & Steven K. Worden, *Marketing Deviance: The*

Selling of Cockfighting, 4 Journal of Human-Animal Studies 211, 228 (1996). In that study, the authors state that "[t]he major third party intermediary or facilitator in the marketing of fighting chickens is the magazine." *Id.* Although the article also states that "[w]ord-of-mouth is still the most effective means of advertising and promoting in all forms of marketing," the article notes that in the world of cockfighting, magazines such as *The Feathered Warrior* are the only intermediary or facilitator of product sales. *Id.*

C. *Prudential standing*

In addition to the constitutional standing requirements, a plaintiff must also satisfy prudential standing requirements. The Humane Society can establish prudential standing if its injury is within the zone-of-interests protected or regulated by the Animal Welfare Act. . . .

Congress enacted § 2156 of the Animal Welfare Act, and has repeatedly amended it over the years, to assure the humane treatment of animals and to protect animals from being abused in illegal animal fights. *See* 7 U.S.C. § 2131. The Humane Society's reason for existence is to protect animals, and, as indicated in its declarations to this court and at oral argument, it has dedicated time and resources for over fifty years to eliminate or reduce the number of illegal animal fights. Its grievance is well within the zone-of-interests protected or regulated by the Animal Welfare Act. *See Animal Welfare Inst. v. Kreps,* 561 F.2d 1002, 1007 (D.C. Cir. 1977) ("Where an act is expressly motivated by considerations of humaneness toward animals, who are uniquely incapable of defending their own interests in court, it strikes us as eminently logical to allow groups specifically concerned with animal welfare to invoke the aid of the courts in enforcing the statute.").

* * *

Note

In addition to the associational standing discussed in some of the preceding cases, an organization can also sue on its own behalf if it can prove a cognizable injury to the organization itself. One form of this type of standing—known as *"Havens* standing"—is found where an organization alleges financial injury to itself, unrelated to any injury to its members, caused by defendants' allegedly illegal conduct, which forced the organization to divert funds it would have used elsewhere to investigate or effect change with respect to those illegal acts. If the challenged acts "have perceptibly impaired" the plaintiff organization's ability to serve its members and carry out its mission, "there can be no question that the organization has suffered injury in fact. Such concrete and demonstrable injury to the organization's activities—with the consequent drain on the organization's resources—constitutes far more than simply a setback to the organization's abstract social interests . . ." *Havens Realty Corp. v. Coleman,* 455 U.S. 363, 379 (1982) (citing *Sierra Club v. Morton,* 405 U.S. at 739). This can be a very valuable alternative argument for standing, as *HSUS v. USPS* makes clear. *See also Organic Consumers Ass'n v. Sanderson Farms, Inc.,* 284 F. Supp. 3d 1005, 1010-12 (N.D. Cal. 2018) ("direct organizational standing" established where plaintiff organizations were forced to divert resources from other programs in order to educate consumers and research misrepresentation claims by chicken producer and distributor); *Animal Legal Defense Fund v. Great Bull Run, LLC*, 2014 WL 2568685, *5 (N.D. Cal. June 6, 2014) (animal welfare organization established standing where it "allege[d] the diversion of organizational resources to identify and counteract Defendants' events, which frustrate Plaintiffs' missions").

Animal Legal Defense Fund v. Espy

United States Court of Appeals, District of Columbia Circuit, 1994
23 F.3d 496

SENTELLE, CIRCUIT JUDGE.

* * *

I.

In 1966 Congress enacted the Animal Welfare Act to improve the treatment of certain animals. In its original form the Act protected "live dogs, cats, monkeys (nonhuman primate mammals), guinea pigs, hamsters, and rabbits." 7 U.S.C. § 2132(h) (Supp. II 1965–66). Four years later, Congress expanded the reach of the Act, adding dead animals and a catch-all phrase — the subject of dispute here. The controlling definition now reads:

> The term "animal" means any live or dead dog, cat, monkey (nonhuman primate mammal), guinea pig, hamster, rabbit, or such other warm-blooded animal, as the Secretary may determine is being used, or is intended for use, for research, testing, experimentation, or exhibition purposes, or as a pet. . . .

* * *

After the 1970 amendments and an extensive rulemaking, the Department issued the regulation that is now contested. The Secretary defined "animal" essentially as it was defined in the statute except that the regulation expressly excluded "birds, aquatic animals, rats and mice." 36 Fed. Reg. 24,917, 24,919 (1971).

* * *

In 1989 two of the plaintiff-appellees, the Animal Legal Defense Fund and the Humane Society of the United States, requested that the Secretary again conduct a rulemaking to re-examine the exclusion. The Department refused, relying, it said, on the Act, its legislative history, and considerations of "the manpower, funds, and other resources available to administer effectively our animal welfare program." Letter from James W. Glosser (June 8, 1990), Joint Appendix ("J.A.") at 46. These associations, joined by two individual members, sued to enjoin the Secretary from excluding birds, mice and rats and to set aside the denial of their rulemaking petition.

II.

* * *

On appeal, the Secretary has elected not to challenge the District Court's rulings on justiciability. [The District Court found that plaintiff-appellees had standing.] That waiver cannot satisfy the constitutional standing requirements, for Article III limits federal jurisdiction and "every federal appellate court has a special obligation to satisfy itself not only of its own jurisdiction, but also that of the lower courts in a cause under review, even though the parties are prepared to concede it."

* * *

Appellees comprise two individual plaintiffs and two organizations. The individuals are Dr. Patricia Knowles and William Strauss. . . .

A.

Knowles is a psychobiologist who worked from 1972 to 1988 in laboratories covered by the Animal Welfare Act but is not presently so employed.[3] Knowles has used rats and mice as a researcher at various institutions registered under the Act. She alleges that the agency's failure to define rats and mice as animals rendered her "unable to effectively control the care and treatment these institutions afforded the rats and mice she used"; that "the inhumane treatment of these animals will directly impair her ability to perform her professional duties as a psychobiologist"; and that "she will be required to spend time and effort in an attempt to convince the facility of the need for humane treatment." Plaintiff's Amended Complaint ("Complaint").

We need not decide whether such aesthetic and professional injuries are sufficiently concrete to create a justiciable claim, for Knowles has failed to demonstrate an additional element of constitutional standing: the requirement that the plaintiff's injury be presently suffered or imminently threatened.

In *Lujan* [*v. Defenders of Wildlife,* 504 U.S. 555 (1992)] the Court described the imminence requirement in these terms:

> Although "imminence" is concededly a somewhat elastic concept, it cannot be stretched beyond its purpose, which is to ensure that the alleged injury is not too speculative for Article III purposes—that the injury is "certainly impending". It has been stretched beyond the breaking point when, as here, the plaintiff alleges only an injury at some indefinite future time, and the acts necessary to make the injury happen are at least partly within the plaintiff's own control.

Lujan, 112 S. Ct. at 2138 n.2.

Knowles' allegations fail for just those reasons. Her claim of standing rests on the following assertion of future injury:

---

3. It is unclear whether Knowles currently performs animal research at all. Even if she does, it must by her own account be at an institution outside the coverage of the statute, and whatever professional or aesthetic injury she presently suffers is not fairly traceable to the Secretary's illegal failure to regulate.

> In order to further my career and gain professional advancement, I will be required to engage in further research. That research will necessitate using rats and mice in some follow-up research to my doctoral dissertation and in other psychobiological research I have planned. Since I have seen abuses (intentional or not) throughout my education and career, I have every reason to expect and fear that similar abuses will happen again when I conduct research on rats and mice.

Admittedly her claim is marginally more impressive than that advanced by the affiants in *Lujan*; not because Knowles' statement of intent to subject herself to the future harm is plausible in light of her profession . . . , but because *Lujan* contrasts vague intentions with "[a] description of concrete plans." But the central question is the immediacy rather than the specificity of the plan, for the underlying purpose of the imminence requirement is to ensure that the court in which suit is brought does not render an advisory opinion in "a case in which no injury would have occurred at all." 112 S. Ct. at 2139 n.2.

For all the record shows that is precisely what happened here. Knowles merely states that at some undefined future time she "will be required to engage in further research," and even that is in part not literally true. She will not be required to do so. Whether she will do so is wholly within her control. Six years ago Dr. Knowles decided that her energies could most profitably be spent on activities other than research. That choice has determined the present state of affairs, in which she suffers no injury and will not do so unless she makes a further choice to subject herself to it. We cannot say that the injury she seeks to litigate is "certainly impending." Knowles has failed to carry her burden to demonstrate constitutional standing, and we lack power to consider her claim.

B.

Plaintiff Strauss is an attorney and a member of one of the oversight committees that registered facilities are required to establish under the Act. *See* 7 U.S.C. § 2143(b) (1988). Strauss alleges that he was chosen as the member intended to "provide representation for general community interests in the proper care and treatment of animals." § 2143(b)(1)(B)(iii). As a committee member he is charged with various duties: inspecting his facility to ensure compliance with the Act, reporting on violations of standards promulgated by the Secretary, and ensuring that the animals' living conditions will be appropriate for their species in accordance with the Secretary's regulations.

Strauss alleges that the agency's failure to promulgate standards governing the humane treatment of birds, rats and mice has left him "without relevant guidance" in evaluating the treatment and conditions of those animals and in providing representation for general community interests in animal care. He cannot adequately perform his statutory duties as a member of the committee because he is "without guidance in the form of specific, detailed regulations that instruct him how to ensure that . . . the institution he serves will comply with the Act to minimize pain and distress to the animals it uses." *Id.* at 193. Finally, the lack of regulations for birds, rats and mice hampers his ability to ensure that those animals' living conditions are appropriate for their species, as the Act allegedly requires.

Strauss has failed to present a cognizable claim of injury in fact. He has not even alleged any extra-legal aesthetic or personal injury of the sort that underlies Knowles' claim. He simply maintains that the Secretary has impeded his attempts to enforce the provisions of the statute, in his role as representative of "general community interests." His suit amounts to nothing more than an attempt to compel executive enforcement of the law, detached from any factual claim of injury. That type of suit has no place in the federal courts, for "vindicating the public interest (including the public interest in government observance of the Constitution and laws) is the function of Congress and the Chief Executive." *Lujan*, 112 S. Ct. at 2145 (emphasis omitted).

C.

The Fund and the Society complain that the exclusion of birds, rats and mice from the definition of "animal" hampers their attempts to gather and disseminate information on laboratory conditions for those animals. If the definition were broadened, regulated laboratories would be legally obliged to provide information about their treatment of the animals to the Secretary, who in turn would include it in his annual report to Congress; the organizations could in turn acquire it and use it in public education and rulemaking proceedings. Similarly, the constricted definition of "animal" makes it difficult for the organizations to "work with" the laboratories and to educate them about the humane treatment of birds, rats and mice, for there is no legal requirement that the laboratories consider the welfare of those animals.

The district court held that these allegations conferred "informational standing" on the organizations. Although informational injury satisfies the minimum requirements of Article III standing, it does not fall within the "zone of interests" protected or regulated by the Animal Welfare Act.

... The [zone of interests] test precludes review of administrative action if the particular interest asserted is "so marginally related to or inconsistent with the purposes implicit in the statute that it cannot reasonably be assumed that Congress intended to permit the suit." Put conversely, the prospective litigant must show either a congressional intent to protect or regulate the interest asserted, or some other indication that the litigant is a suitable party to pursue that interest in court.

A continuous line of circuit precedent holds that claims of informational injury can surmount the zone of interests threshold only in very special statutory contexts. . . .

* * *

Competitive Enterprise Institute v. NHTSA, 901 F.2d 107, 122 (D.C. Cir. 1990), announced that informational injury is justiciable where the information sought is "essential to the injured organization's activities . . . [and] lack of the information will render those activities infeasible." . . . .

* * *

Action Alliance [*of Sr. Citizens v. Heckler*, 789 F.2d 931 (D.C. Cir. 1986)] is consistent with the principle that informational injury, without more, does not fall within the zone of interests of the statute under which suit is brought. There the organizations' purpose was to advise their members of the members' own rights under the statute, rather than simply to educate all those who desire to promote the statute's substantive purposes. . . .

. . . [T]o come within the zone of interests of the statute under which suit is brought, an organization must show more than a general corporate purpose to promote the interests to which the statute is addressed. Rather it must show a congressional intent to benefit the organization or some indication that the organization is "a peculiarly suitable challenger of administrative neglect."

The Animal Welfare Act precludes any such showing, for the general informational and educative interests in animal welfare upon which the organizations base their suit are, by the terms of the Act, the province of a different institution altogether. The very section that orders the Secretary to promulgate standards for the humane treatment of animals, 7 U.S.C. § 2143, also establishes oversight committees of private citizens, whose members "represent society's concerns regarding the welfare of animal subjects used at such facility." § 2143(b)(1). The committees inspect their laboratories semiannually to "ensure compliance with the provisions of this Chapter to minimize pain and distress to animals," § 2143(b)(3), and file a public report on the conditions and welfare of the animals, § 2143(b)(4)-(5). The evident congressional intent to entrust to the committees the functions of oversight and the dissemination of information precludes any inference that other private advocacy organizations are "peculiarly suitable challengers of administrative neglect."

It is simply not enough that the organizations exist to promote interests congruent with the humanitarian purposes of the statute, broadly conceived. We owe fidelity as well to the means by which the statute pursues its purposes, and on the face of the Act the organizations are not the intended representatives of the public interest in animal welfare. The organizations have not asserted any claim within the zone of interests protected by the Act, and their suit may not be heard.

III.

As the record discloses no claim of justiciability that survives application of the constitutional and statutory restrictions on our power to hear the case, the decision of the district court is vacated and the case remanded with directions to dismiss.

Notes

1. Because they are judicially created, and not constitutionally mandated, prudential requirements like the zone-of-interests test can be altered or overridden by Congress. *See United Food & Commercial Workers Union Local 751 v. Brown Group,*

Inc., 517 U.S. 544, 552 (1996). "Citizen suit provisions," which grant private rights of action, exist in many environmental statutes. These provisions can override the zone-of-interests requirement, but not the constitutional requirements under Article III.

2. The breadth of the actual interest "zone" varies depending on the statutory provision(s) at issue. Therefore, what falls within the scope of a statute's zone-of-interests for one purpose (*e.g.*, judicial review of an administrative action under the review provisions of the Administrative Procedure Act) may not do so for another purpose (*e.g.*, asserting a private right of action under a statute in circumstances which render the APA inapplicable). *See Clarke v. Securities Indus. Ass'n*, 479 U.S. 388, 400 n.16 (1987) (holding that the crucial inquiry in determining prudential standing is whether Congress intended a particular class of plaintiffs be provided the right to challenge an agency's violation of a law or regulation; respondent satisfied zone-of-interests test because interest which he asserted had plausible relationship to policies underlying statute in question); *see also Association of Data Processing Serv. Orgs., Inc. v. Camp*, 397 U.S. 150, 156 (1970).

3. This case demonstrates the continued hurdles animal advocates face to achieve constitutional standing. Outline the requirements for a successful plaintiff after this case.

4. This court undertook a *sua sponte* review of its jurisdiction to hear the case, based on longstanding rules that (1) a court has jurisdiction to determine its jurisdiction, and (2) a court has no jurisdiction over an action where the plaintiff has not met the constitutional minimum for standing. This rule is clear with respect to *constitutional* Article III standing issues—but is the court equally empowered to investigate prudential standing doctrine on its own?

With respect to the constitutional requirements, the court cites *FW/PBS, Inc. v. Dallas*, 493 U.S. 215 (1990). That decision held that Article III requires federal appellate courts to determine not only their own jurisdiction, "but also that of the lower courts in a cause under review [in the appellate court], even though the parties are prepared to concede it." *Id.* at 231.

With respect to the zone-of-interests requirement, however, the court's independent review may not be as well-founded. As justification for its review of ALDF's prudential standing, the court relied on the fact that the zone-of-interests test "serves the institutional obligations of the federal courts, rather than being a privilege of the parties that they may conclusively waive" and on "the prudential concern that federal courts should not adjudicate generalized grievances." 23 F.3d at 499. The court "examined legislative materials bearing on the zone of interests test even though the parties and the court below assumed the test was satisfied, . . . and ha[d] found it dispositive," *id.*, yet the court did not elaborate on which legislative materials it had examined or what exactly it had gleaned from them.

The Supreme Court has not explicitly ruled on the propriety of *sua sponte* review of prudential standing. Of the circuit courts that have made a determination on the issue, one besides the *Espy* court has ruled the prudential requirements cannot be waived and can thus be reviewed *sua sponte*, *Community First Bank v. National Credit Union Admin.*, 41 F.3d 1050 (6th Cir. 1994), while one "has not decisively settled the matter," *UPS Worldwide Forwarding, Inc. v. U.S. Postal Service*, 66 F.3d 621, 626–27 n.6 (3d Cir. 1995), and another seems to have suggested that the prudential requirements can be waived and thus precluded from review (presumably even *sua sponte* review). *See Lindley v. Sullivan*, 889 F.2d 124 (7th Cir. 1989).

5. *Bennett v. Spear*, 520 U.S. 154 (1997), established that where a citizen suit provision is available, environmental and animal protection statutes can be used by anyone affected by a decision made under those laws. In *Bennett*, plaintiffs were parties with economic interests that would be negatively impacted by a decision to restrict water access in order to protect endangered species. Plaintiffs sued under the Endangered Species Act ("ESA") and challenged the correctness of a biological opinion by the Fish and Wildlife Service that the restriction was necessary to maintain the habitat of two varieties of endangered fish. While two lower courts held plaintiffs' injuries did not fall within the ESA's zone of interests because plaintiffs had no interest in the endangered species, the Supreme Court disagreed. Crucial to this finding was the Court's holding that the citizen suit provision "negates the zone of interests." Thus, advocacy groups on both sides of the issue can use the citizen suit provisions to seek to overturn government action they believe is wrong.

6. The question of whether animals, as opposed to people, can obtain standing to sue, has been raised on various occasions. The next case provides a summary of the issues courts consider in these cases.

Cetacean Community v. Bush

United States Court of Appeals, Ninth Circuit, 2004
386 F.3d 1169

Before: HUG, ALARCÓN, and W. FLETCHER, Circuit Judges.

WILLIAM A. FLETCHER, Circuit Judge:

We are asked to decide whether the world's cetaceans have standing to bring suit in their own name under the Endangered Species Act, the Marine Mammal Protection Act, the National Environmental Protection Act, and the Administrative Procedure Act. We hold that cetaceans do not have standing under these statutes.

I. Background

The sole plaintiff in this case is the Cetacean Community ("Cetaceans"). The Cetacean Community is the name chosen by the Cetaceans' self-appointed attorney for all of the world's whales, porpoises, and dolphins. The Cetaceans challenge the United States Navy's use of Surveillance Towed Array Sensor System Low Frequency Active Sonar ("SURTASS LFAS") during wartime or heightened threat conditions. The Cetaceans allege that the Navy has violated, or will violate, the Endangered Species Act ("ESA"), 16 U.S.C. §§ 1531–1544, the Marine Mammal Protection Act

("MMPA"), 16 U.S.C. §§ 1371–1421h, and the National Environmental Policy Act ("NEPA"), 16 U.S.C. §§ 4321–4347.

The Navy has developed SURTASS LFAS to assist in detecting quiet submarines at long range. This sonar has both active and passive components. The active component consists of low frequency underwater transmitters. These transmitters emit loud sonar pulses, or "pings," that can travel hundreds of miles through the water. . . . Through their attorney, the Cetaceans contend that SURTASS LFAS harms them by causing tissue damage and other serious injuries, and by disrupting biologically important behaviors including feeding and mating.

The negative effects of underwater noise on marine life are well recognized. An analysis accompanying the current regulations for the Navy's use of SURTASS LFAS summarizes the harmful effects as follows:

> Any human-made noise that is strong enough to be heard has the potential to reduce (mask) the ability of marine mammals to hear natural sounds at similar frequencies. . . . Very strong sounds have the potential to cause temporary or permanent reduction in hearing sensitivity. In addition, intense acoustic or explosive events may cause trauma to tissues associated with organs vital for hearing, sound production, respiration, and other functions. This trauma may include minor to severe hemorrhage.

67 Fed. Reg. 46,778; *see also* Nat'l Parks & Conservation Ass'n v. Babbitt, 241 F.3d 722, 737 n.4 (9th Cir. 2001) (noting that the "acoustic environment appears to be very important to humpback whales"). The current regulations, governing routine peacetime training and testing, have been challenged in a separate action. Natural Res. Def. Council, Inc. v. Evans, 279 F. Supp. 2d 1129, 1191 (N.D. Cal. 2003) ("NRDC") (issuing permanent injunction restricting the Navy's routine peacetime use of LFA sonar "in areas that are particularly rich in marine life").

The Cetaceans do not challenge the current regulations. Instead, they seek to compel President Bush and Secretary of Defense Rumsfeld to undertake regulatory review of use of SURTASS LFAS during threat and wartime conditions. . . .

Defendants moved to dismiss the Cetaceans' suit [and the District Court held] that the Cetaceans lacked standing under the ESA, the MMPA, NEPA and the Administrative Procedure Act ("APA").

The Cetaceans timely appeal. We review the district court's standing decision de novo. We agree with the district court that the Cetaceans have not been granted standing to sue by the ESA, the MMPA, NEPA, or the APA. We therefore conclude that dismissal under Rule 12(b)(6) for failure to state a claim was correct, and we affirm the district court.

II. Our Decision in *Palila IV*

The Cetaceans contend that an earlier decision of this court requires us to hold that they have standing under the ESA. We first address that decision. In *Palila v.*

Hawaii Department of Land and Natural Resources, 852 F.2d 1106, 1107 (9th Cir. 1988) (*"Palila IV"*), a suit to enforce the ESA, we wrote that an endangered member of the honeycreeper family, the Hawaiian Palila bird, "has legal status and wings its way into federal court as a plaintiff in its own right." *Id.* We wrote, further, that the Palila had "earned the right to be capitalized since it is a party to these proceedings." *Id.*

* * *

After due consideration, we agree with the district court that *Palila IV's* statements are nonbinding dicta. A statement is dictum when it is "'made during the course of delivering a judicial opinion, but . . . is unnecessary to the decision in the case and [is] therefore not precedential.'" *Best Life Assur. Co. v. Comm'r,* 281 F.3d 828, 834 (9th Cir. 2002) (quoting *Black's Law Dictionary* 1100 (7th ed.1999)). The line is not always easy to draw, however, for "where a panel confronts an issue germane to the eventual resolution of the case, and resolves it after reasoned consideration in a published opinion, that ruling becomes the law of the circuit, regardless of whether doing so is necessary in some strict logical sense." *United States v. Johnson,* 256 F.3d 895, 914 (9th Cir. 2001).

. . . [I]n *Palila IV,* immediately after we stated that the Palila "wings it way into the federal court as a plaintiff in its own right," we noted that "the Sierra Club and others brought an action under the [ESA] on behalf of the Palila." *Palila IV,* 852 F.3d at 1107.

We have jurisdiction if at least one named plaintiff has standing to sue, even if another named plaintiff in the suit does not. Because the standing of most of the other parties was undisputed in *Palila I–IV,* no jurisdictional concerns obliged us to consider whether the Palila had standing. *Cf. Hawksbill Sea Turtle v. FEMA,* 126 F.3d 461, 466 n.2 (3d Cir. 1997) (allowing turtle to remain named in case caption, but not deciding whether it had standing because named human parties did). Moreover, we were never asked to decide whether the Palila had standing.

In context, our statements in *Palila IV* were little more than rhetorical flourishes. They were certainly not intended to be a statement of law, binding on future panels, that animals have standing to bring suit in their own name under the ESA. Because we did not hold in *Palila IV* that animals have standing to sue in their own names under the ESA, we address that question as a matter of first impression here.

III. Standing

Standing involves two distinct inquiries. First, an Article III federal court must ask whether a plaintiff has suffered sufficient injury to satisfy the "case or controversy" requirement of Article III. To satisfy Article III, a plaintiff "must show that (1) it has suffered an 'injury in fact' that is (a) concrete and particularized and (b) actual or imminent, not conjectural or hypothetical; (2) the injury is fairly traceable to the challenged action of the defendant; and (3) it is likely, as opposed to merely speculative, that the injury will be redressed by a favorable decision." *Friends of the Earth, Inc. v. Laidlaw Envtl. Sys. (TOC), Inc.,* 528 U.S. 167, 180–81 (2000).

If a plaintiff lacks Article III standing, Congress may not confer standing on that plaintiff by statute. A suit brought by a plaintiff without Article III standing is not a "case or controversy," and an Article III federal court therefore lacks subject matter jurisdiction over the suit. In that event, the suit should be dismissed under Rule 12(b)(6).

Second, if a plaintiff has suffered sufficient injury to satisfy Article III, a federal court must ask whether a statute has conferred "standing" on that plaintiff. Non-constitutional standing exists when "a particular plaintiff has been granted a right to sue by the specific statute under which he or she brings suit." [*City of Sausalito v. O'Neill*, 386 F.3d 1186, 1199 (9th Cir. 2004).] To ensure enforcement of statutorily created duties, Congress may confer standing as it sees fit on any plaintiff who satisfies Article III. Where it is arguable whether a plaintiff has suffered sufficient injury to satisfy Article III, the Supreme Court has sometimes insisted as a matter of "prudence" that Congress make its intention clear before it will construe a statute to confer standing on a particular plaintiff. In that event, the suit should be dismissed under Rule 12(b)(6).

A. Article III Standing

Article III does not compel the conclusion that a statutorily authorized suit in the name of an animal is not a "case or controversy." As commentators have observed, nothing in the text of Article III explicitly limits the ability to bring a claim in federal court to humans. *See* U.S. Const. art. III; *see also* Cass R. Sunstein, *Standing for Animals (With Notes on Animal Rights*), 47 UCLA L. Rev. 1333 (2000) (arguing that Congress could grant standing to animals, but has not); Katherine A. Burke, *Can We Stand For It? Amending the Endangered Species Act with an Animal–Suit Provision,* 75 U. Colo. L. Rev. 633 (2004) (same).

Animals have many legal rights, protected under both federal and state laws. In some instances, criminal statutes punish those who violate statutory duties that protect animals. . . . In other instances, humans whose interests are affected by the existence or welfare of animals are granted standing to bring civil suits to enforce statutory duties that protect these animals. The ESA and the MMPA are good examples of such statutes.

It is obvious that an animal cannot function as a plaintiff in the same manner as a juridically competent human being. But we see no reason why Article III prevents Congress from authorizing a suit in the name of an animal, any more than it prevents suits brought in the name of artificial persons such as corporations, partnerships or trusts, and even ships, or of juridically incompetent persons such as infants, juveniles, and mental incompetents. . . .

If Article III does not prevent Congress from granting standing to an animal by statutorily authorizing a suit in its name, the question becomes whether Congress has passed a statute actually doing so. We therefore turn to whether Congress has granted standing to the Cetaceans under the ESA, the MMPA, NEPA, read either on their own, or through the gloss of Section 10(a) of the APA.

B. Statutory Standing

* * *

2. The ESA

The ESA contains an explicit provision granting standing to enforce the duties created by the statute. The ESA's citizen-suit provision states that "any person" may "commence a civil suit on his own behalf . . . to enjoin any person, including the United States and any other governmental instrumentality or agency . . . who is alleged to be in violation of any provision of this chapter or regulation. . . ." 16 U.S.C. § 1540(g)(1)(A). The ESA contains an explicit definition of the "person" who is authorized to enforce the statute:

> The term "person" means an individual, corporation, partnership, trust, association, or another private entity; or any officer, employee, agent, department, or instrumentality of the Federal Government, or any State, municipality, or political subdivision of a State, or of any foreign government; any State, municipality, or political subdivision of a State; or any other entity subject to the jurisdiction of the United States.

Id. § 1532(13).

The ESA also contains separate definitions of "species," "endangered species," "threatened species," and "fish and wildlife." [Discussion of each of these definitions excerpted. See Chapter 9 for further discussion of the ESA.]

* * *

It is obvious both from the scheme of the statute, as well as from the statute's explicit definitions of its terms, that animals are the protected rather than the protectors. The scheme of the ESA is that a "person," as defined in §1532(13), may sue in federal district court to enforce the duties the statute prescribes. Those duties protect animals who are "endangered" or "threatened" under §1532(6) and (20). The statute is set up to authorize "persons" to sue to protect animals whenever those animals are "endangered" or "threatened." Animals are not authorized to sue in their own names to protect themselves. There is no hint in the definition of "person" in §1532(13) that the "person" authorized to bring suit to protect an endangered or threatened species can be an animal that is itself endangered or threatened.

We get the same answer if we read the ESA through Section 10(a) of the APA. . . . [L]ike the ESA, Section 10(a) of the APA grants standing to a "person." "Person" is explicitly defined to include "an individual, partnership, corporation, association, or public or private organization other than an agency." Notably absent from that definition is "animal." *Data Processing*, 397 U.S. at 156, and *Clarke*, 479 U.S. at 400 n.16, instruct us that Section 10(a) means that we should read the underlying statute to grant standing generously, such that "persons" who are "adversely affected or aggrieved" are all persons "arguably within the zone of interests" protected by the underlying statute. See *Bennett*, 520 U.S. at 163. But, as with the ESA, these cases do not instruct us to expand the basic definition of "person" beyond the definition provided in the APA.

3. The MMPA

Unlike the ESA, the MMPA contains no explicit provision granting standing to enforce its duties. The MMPA imposes a moratorium on "taking" a marine mammal without a permit, and prohibits "incidental, but not intentional" takes without a letter of authorization. 16 U.S.C. § 1371(a)(51)(1). . . . But the statute says nothing about the standing of a would-be party, such as the Cetaceans, who seek to compel someone to apply for a letter of authorization, or for a permit.

Relying on Section 10(a) of the APA, as well as *Data Processing* and *Clarke,* we have held that affected "persons" with conservationist, aesthetic, recreational, or economic interests in the protection of marine mammals have standing to seek to compel someone to apply for a permit under the MMPA. But, as discussed above, Section 10(a) of the APA does not define "person" to include animals. No court has ever held that an animal—even a marine mammal whose protection is at stake— has standing to sue in its own name to require that a party seek a permit or letter of authorization under the MMPA. *See Citizens to End Animal Suffering & Exploitation, Inc.,* 836 F. Supp. at 49 (rejecting such a suit). Absent a clear direction from Congress in either the MMPA or the APA, we hold that animals do not have standing to enforce the permit requirement of the MMPA.

4. NEPA

NEPA requires that an environmental impact statement ("EIS") be prepared for "major Federal actions significantly affecting the quality of the human environment. . . ." 42 U.S.C. § 4332(2)(C). As is true of the MMPA, no provision of NEPA explicitly grants any person or entity standing to enforce the statute, but judicial enforcement of NEPA rights is available through the APA. Interpreting NEPA broadly, we have recognized standing for individuals and groups of individuals who sue to require preparation of an EIS, when they contend that a challenged federal action will adversely affect the environment. However, we see nothing in either NEPA or the APA that would permit us to hold that animals who are part of the environment have standing to bring suit on their own behalf.

[IV.] Conclusion

We agree with the district court in *Citizens to End Animal Suffering & Exploitation, Inc.,* that "[i]f Congress and the President intended to take the extraordinary step of authorizing animals as well as people and legal entities to sue, they could, and should, have said so plainly." In the absence of any such statement in the ESA, the MMPA, or NEPA, or the APA, we conclude that the Cetaceans do not have statutory standing to sue.

AFFIRMED.

Notes

1. In *Citizens to End Animal Suffering and Exploitation, Inc. (CEASE) v. New England Aquarium*, 836 F. Supp. 45 (D. Mass. 1993), the court rejected standing for Kama, a dolphin, for various reasons, including his species and, as noted in Note 5

before *HSUS v. USPS*, plaintiffs' inability to be able to identify him. Like the court in *Cetacean Community*, the *CEASE* court also refused to "impute to Congress or the President the intention to provide standing to a marine mammal without a clear statement in the statute." As the *Cetacean Community* court quoted from *CEASE* in the conclusion of its opinion, "[i]f Congress and the President intended to take the extraordinary step of authorizing animals as well as people and legal entities to sue, they could, and should, have said so plainly." Some commentators accord some significance to the fact that the court believed that Congress could, if it so desired, grant standing to animals.

2. Another case in which the court rejected an animal's standing was *Naruto v. Slater*, 888 F.3d 418 (9th Cir. 2018). Naruto was a crested macaque monkey who had allegedly manipulated a camera owned by Mr. Slater to take "selfie" photos of himself. Naruto's self-appointed lawyers sued Mr. Slater, arguing that Naruto, and not Mr. Slater, owned the copyright on the photographs. Although the decision was based on an evaluation of the elements of a claim under the federal Copyright Act of 1976, and not under Article III, the ultimate outcome was the same: Naruto did not satisfy the standing requirements of the Copyright Act because he was not human. Confusing the requirements of standing with the standards for stating a claim under the Copyright Act, the court held that the monkey's *claim* satisfied Article III, but still found the monkey himself had no "statutory standing"—even though standing is a constitutional doctrine.

The Ninth Circuit's opinion came as a surprise, because the parties had actually settled the case and moved to dismiss the appeal and vacate the district court's ruling rejecting standing. In an unusual response, the Ninth Circuit declined to vacate the ruling and instead notified the parties that it intended to rule on the appeal in spite of the settlement, stating, in an unsigned order: "As one of our colleagues once warned in a similar context, 'courts are wary of abetting "strategic behavior" on the part of institutional litigants whose continuing interest in the development of the law may transcend their immediate interest in the outcome of a particular case.'"

3. Although a lack of standing traditionally has been the basis for rejecting virtually every challenge where an animal is a plaintiff, other potential problems arise where lawyers claim to represent animals. If the animal is represented by counsel, how was that relationship formed? Is it legally sound? If not, it is certainly the case that simply announcing that you are an animal's lawyer (whether it be a single monkey or chimpanzee, or the entire population of cetaceans) does not create the requisite legal engagement or satisfy state law requirements.

Lawyers who claim to represent individual animals almost certainly have not engaged in the practices—required by state bar associations and state law—to properly establish the attorney-client relationship. In his famous dissent in *Sierra Club v. Morton* (excerpted earlier in this chapter), Justice Douglas suggested that environmental groups should be able to "speak for the trees." But in the environmental area, and even more so in the animal welfare area, there may be a broad range of opinions as to what is the best outcome for an animal or group of animals. What if two animal legal advocates both announce that they represent a single animal, and have different views on the best result for the animal? There is no known mechanism or procedure for a court or administrative body to decide who the animal's lawyer really is. And in the *Naruto* case, the Ninth Circuit took the organization claiming to represent Naruto to task, finding that despite its claim to be the monkey's "next friend," it had operated on its own and had "failed to live up to the title of 'friend,'" making decisions unrelated to Naruto's interests. *Naruto v. Slater*, 888 F.3d 418, 421 n.3 (9th Cir. 2018); *see also id.* at 437 n.11 (Smith, J., concurring).

Animal Legal Defense Fund v. Glickman

United States Court of Appeals, District of Columbia Circuit, 1998
154 F.3d 426

WALD, CIRCUIT JUDGE. The 1985 amendments to the Animal Welfare Act ("AWA") direct the Secretary of Agriculture to "promulgate standards to govern the humane handling, care, treatment, and transportation of animals by dealers, research facilities, and exhibitors." They further provide that such standards "shall include minimum requirements" for, *inter alia*, "a physical environment adequate to promote the psychological well-being of primates." *Id*. Pursuant to this authority, the United States Department of Agriculture ("USDA") issued regulations for primate dealers, exhibitors, and research facilities that included a small number of mandatory requirements and also required the regulated parties to "develop, document, and follow an appropriate plan for environment enhancement adequate to promote the psychological well-being of nonhuman primates. The plan must be in accordance with the currently accepted professional standards as cited in appropriate professional journals or reference guides, and as directed by the attending veterinarian." 9 C.F.R. § 3.81 (1997). Although these plans must be made available to the USDA, the regulated parties are not obligated to make them available to members of the public.

The individual plaintiffs, Roseann Circelli, Mary Eagan, and Marc Jurnove, challenge these regulations on the ground that they violate the USDA's statutory mandate under the AWA and permit dealers, exhibitors, and research facilities to keep primates under inhumane conditions. The individual plaintiffs allege that they suffered aesthetic injury during their regular visits to animal exhibitions when they observed primates living under such conditions.

* * *

We hold that Mr. Jurnove, one of the individual plaintiffs, has standing to sue. Accordingly, we need not pass on the standing of the other individual plaintiffs. . . .

I. BACKGROUND

A. *Marc Jurnove's Affidavit*

Mr. Jurnove's affidavit is an uncontested statement of the injuries that he has suffered to his aesthetic interest in observing animals living under inhumane conditions. . . .

For his entire adult life, Mr. Jurnove has "been employed and/or worked as a volunteer for various human and animal relief and rescue organizations." "By virtue of [his] training in wildlife rehabilitation and [his] experience in investigating complaints about the treatment of wildlife, [he is] very familiar with the needs of and proper treatment of wildlife." "Because of [his] familiarity with and love of exotic animals, as well as for recreational and educational purposes and because [he] appreciates these animals' beauty, [he] enjoys seeing them in various zoos and other parks near [his] home."

Between May 1995 and June 1996, when he filed his affidavit, Mr. Jurnove visited the Long Island Game Farm Park and Zoo ("Game Farm") at least nine times. Throughout this period, and since as far back as 1992, the USDA has not questioned the adequacy of this facility's plan for the psychological well-being of primates.

Mr. Jurnove's first visit to the Game Farm, in May 1995, lasted approximately six hours. *See id.* While there, Mr. Jurnove saw many animals living under inhumane conditions. For instance, the Game Farm housed one primate, a Japanese Snow Macaque, in a cage "that was a distance from and not in view of the other primate cages." "The only cage enrichment device this animal had was an unused swing." Similarly, Mr. Jurnove "saw a large male chimpanzee named Barney in a holding area by himself. He could not see or hear any other primate." Mr. Jurnove "knew that chimpanzees are very social animals and it upset [him] very much to see [Barney] in isolation from other primates." The Game Farm also placed adult bears next to squirrel monkeys, although Jurnove saw evidence that the arrangement made the monkeys frightened and extremely agitated.

The day after this visit, Mr. Jurnove began to contact government agencies, including the USDA, in order to secure help for these animals. Based on Mr. Jurnove's complaint, the USDA inspected the Game Farm on May 3, 1995. According to Mr. Jurnove's uncontested affidavit, however, the agency's resulting inspection report "states that [the USDA inspectors] found the facility in compliance with all the standards." Mr. Jurnove returned to the Game Farm on eight more occasions to observe these officially legal conditions.

On July 17, 18, and 19, 1995, he found "virtually the same conditions" that allegedly caused him aesthetic injury during his first visit to the Game Farm in May. For instance, Barney, the chimpanzee, and Samantha, the Japanese Snow Macaque, were still alone in their cages. This time, Mr. Jurnove documented these conditions with photographs and sent them to the USDA. Nevertheless, the responding USDA inspectors found only a few violations at the Game Farm; they reported "nothing" about many of the conditions that concerned Mr. Jurnove and that he had told the agency about, such as "the fact that numerous primates were being housed alone" and the lack of adequate stimulation in their cages.

Mr. Jurnove devoted two trips in August and one in September to "videotaping the conditions that the inspection missed," and on each trip he found that the inhumane conditions persisted. At the end of September, the USDA sent three inspectors to the Game Farm in response to Mr. Jurnove's continued complaints and reportage; they found violations, however, only with regard to the facility's fencing.

Mr. Jurnove returned to the Game Farm once more on October 1, 1995. Indeed, he only stopped his frequent visits when he became ill and required major surgery. After his health returned, Mr. Jurnove visited the Game Farm in April 1996, hoping to see improvements in the conditions that he had repeatedly brought to the USDA's attention. He was disappointed again; "the animals [were] in literally the same conditions as [he] had seen them over the summer of 1995." Mr. Jurnove's resulting complaints prompted the USDA to inspect the Game Farm in late May 1996. For the fourth time, the agency found the facility largely in compliance, with a few exceptions not relevant to the plaintiffs' main challenge in this case. In June 1996, Mr. Jurnove filed the affidavit that is the basis of his claim here. He concluded this affidavit by stating his intent to "return to the Farm in the next several weeks" and to "continue visiting the Farm to see the animals there."

B. *The Plaintiffs' Complaint*

The plaintiffs' complaint elaborates a two-part legal theory based on the factual allegations in the individual plaintiffs' affidavits. First, the plaintiffs allege that the AWA requires the USDA to adopt specific, minimum standards to protect primates' psychological well-being, and the agency has failed to do so.

* * *

Second, the plaintiffs contend that the conditions that caused Mr. Jurnove aesthetic injury complied with current USDA regulations, but that lawful regulations would have prohibited those conditions and protected Mr. Jurnove from the injuries that he describes in his affidavit.

* * *3

C. *Procedural History*

The United States District Court, Judge Charles R. Richey, held that the individual plaintiffs had standing to sue, finding in their favor on a motion for summary judgment. *See* 943 F. Supp. at 54–57.[4] On the merits, the district court held that 9 C.F.R. § 3.81 violates the Administrative Procedure Act ("APA") because it fails to set standards, including minimum requirements, as mandated by the AWA; that the USDA's failure to promulgate standards for a physical environment adequate to

---

3. Although the crux of the plaintiffs' complaint alleges that the USDA failed to promulgate minimum standards as required by the AWA, the complaint also states that the USDA has inadequately enforced even its existing regulations, by allegedly failing to inspect facilities and by allegedly instructing its inspectors to avoid documenting violations. As the district court found, *see* 943 F. Supp. at 62–64, the USDA's decisions about whether to undertake enforcement actions are generally unsuitable for judicial review. The plaintiffs have not appealed that judgment to this court.

4. The district court also held that ALDF had standing to sue in its own capacity on its notice and comment claim, *see* 943 F. Supp. at 53–54, and found for ALDF on the merits, *see id.* at 61–62.

promote the psychological well-being of primates constitutes agency action unlawfully withheld and unreasonably delayed in violation of the APA; and that the USDA's failure to issue a regulation promoting the social grouping of nonhuman primates is arbitrary, capricious, and an abuse of discretion in violation of the APA.

A split panel of this court held that none of the plaintiffs had standing to sue and accordingly did not reach the merits of their complaint. *See* 130 F.3d at 466. This court granted rehearing in banc, limited to the question of Marc Jurnove's standing.

II. ANALYSIS

* * *

We find that Mr. Jurnove's allegations fall well within the [constitutional standing] requirements.

A. *Injury in Fact*

Mr. Jurnove's allegations solidly establish injury in fact. As his affidavit indicates, Mr. Jurnove "enjoys seeing [animals] in various zoos and other parks near [his] home" "because of [his] familiarity with and love of exotic animals, as well as for recreational and educational purposes and because [he] appreciates these animals' beauty." He decided to tour the primate cages at the Game Farm "in furtherance of [his] appreciation for exotic animals and [his] desire to observe and enjoy them." During this tour and the ones that followed, Mr. Jurnove suffered direct, concrete, and particularized injury to this aesthetic interest in observing animals living under humane conditions. At this particular zoo, which he has regularly visited and plans to keep visiting, he saw particular animals enduring inhumane treatment. He developed an interest, moreover, in seeing these particular animals living under humane treatment. As he explained, "what I observed [at the Game Farm] was an assault on my senses and greatly impaired my ability to observe and enjoy *these captive animals*." (emphasis added). "I want to observe, study, and enjoy these animals in humane conditions."

Simply put, Mr. Jurnove has alleged far more than an abstract, and uncognizable, interest in seeing the law enforced. To the contrary, Mr. Jurnove has made clear that he has an aesthetic interest in seeing exotic animals living in a nurturing habitat, and that he has attempted to exercise this interest by repeatedly visiting a particular animal exhibition to observe particular animals there. This interest was allegedly injured, however, when Mr. Jurnove witnessed the actual living conditions of the primates described and named in his affidavit. It is, of course, quite possible that many other people might visit the same zoo, observe the same animals there, and suffer similar injuries upon seeing these animals living under inhumane conditions. But the fact that many may share an aesthetic interest does not make it less cognizable, less "distinct and palpable."

The Supreme Court has repeatedly made clear that injury to an aesthetic interest in the observation of animals is sufficient to satisfy the demands of Article III standing. . . .

The key requirement, one that Mr. Jurnove clearly satisfies, is that the plaintiff have suffered his injury in a personal and individual way—for instance, by seeing with his own eyes the particular animals whose condition caused him aesthetic injury. . . .

This court's precedent, moreover, specifically recognizes that people have a cognizable interest in "viewing animals free from . . . 'inhumane treatment.'" In *Animal Welfare Institute v. Kreps*, 561 F.2d 1002 (D.C. Cir. 1977), the plaintiff organizations alleged, *inter alia*, an interest in "enjoying Cape fur seals alive in their natural habitat under conditions in which the animals are not subject to . . . inhumane treatment," 561 F.2d at 1007. This court held that these plaintiffs' aesthetic interests satisfied the requirements of standing. *See id.* at 1007–10.[5] Similarly, *Humane Society v. Hodel* found standing based on a complaint "that the existence of hunting on wildlife refuges forces Society members to witness animal corpses and environmental degradation, in addition to depleting the supply of animals and birds that refuge visitors seek to view," 840 F.2d at 52. As this Court noted, "these are classic aesthetic interests, which have always enjoyed protection under standing analysis." *Id.*[6]

The Ninth Circuit has similarly recognized an aesthetic interest in observing animals living under humane conditions. In *Fund for Animals, Inc. v. Lujan*, 962 F.2d 1391 (9th Cir. 1992), the plaintiffs alleged aesthetic injuries stemming from

5. The dissent attempts to limit *Animal Welfare Institute* to support standing only where the challenged governmental action is "diminishing the opportunity to observe [the animal], not affecting the quality of the observation." Dissent at 6. This statement does not accurately reflect either the injury alleged in *Animal Welfare Institute* or this court's holding in that case. In articulating the nature of their aesthetic injury, the *Animal Welfare Institute* plaintiffs alleged an interest in observing Cape fur seals who lived under "not . . . inhumane" conditions, 561 F.2d at 1007—in other words, an interest in the *quality* of animal life, rather than the *quantity* of animals alive. To be sure, the "inhumane treatment" that concerned these particular plaintiffs revolved, as the dissent notes, around the manner in which the seals were being killed. *See id.* at 1012–13. But this fact does not reduce the plaintiffs' claim to one challenging the government only for causing the diminishment of an animal population. To the contrary, the plaintiffs in *Animal Welfare Institute* were alleging aesthetic injury based on how the Cape fur seals were living and *how* they were dying; the plaintiffs did not simply focus on the fact that the seals were, in fact, dying. Moreover, in holding that the plaintiffs' aesthetic interests would satisfy the requirements of standing if the plaintiffs could establish that they were among the injured, this court never distinguished between the plaintiffs' claims based on the quality of animal life and those based on the number of animals in existence.

6. Not surprisingly, the dissent also reads *Humane Society v. Hodel* to support standing only where the challenged governmental action has or will deplete the supply of an animal population. In fact, the case explicitly rejects that reading. The complaint in *Humane Society v. Hodel* stated *both* "that the existence of hunting on wildlife refuges forces Society members to witness animal corpses and environmental degradation" (a claim based on the quality of the aesthetic experience of observing animals) and that the challenged hunting regulations also "depleted the supply of animals and birds that refuge visitors seek to view" (a claim based on the *number* of animals in existence). 840 F.2d 45 at 52. This court, moreover, clearly recognized both of these claims, stating: "*These* are classic aesthetic *interests*, which have always enjoyed protection under standing analysis." *Id.* (emphasis added).

the mistreatment of bison, who were subject to a population management plan that operated by shooting animals who strayed outside the boundaries of Yellowstone. In finding standing, the court observed "that the Fund's members had standing to sue because of the psychological injury they suffered from viewing the killing of the bison in Montana. Mr. Pacelle testified that several Fund members had been emotionally harmed when they saw bison 'who were just standing outside the boundary of the park shot and crumbled [sic] to their feet.'" *Id.* at 1396 (quoting testimony and citing *Humane Society v. Hodel*, 840 F.2d 45 (D.C. Cir. 1988)).[7]

The dissent attempts further to build on the suggestion put forth at oral argument that no one should be able to establish constitutional standing based on an aesthetic interest in observing animals living under humane conditions because definitions of what is "humane" may differ so widely. But the dissent, again, forgets that not every aesthetic interest can form the basis for a lawsuit; our injury-in-fact test protects only those aesthetic interests that have been "legally protected." 504 U.S. at 560. At its heart, the dissent's complaint may reflect a fear that the AWA does not do enough to define what it means by "humane," although the statute does indicate, in its sections focusing on animal research, a particular concern with minimizing "animal pain and distress." *See, e.g.,* 7 U.S.C. § 2143(a)(3)(A). Yet "humane" does convey a basic meaning of compassion, sympathy, and consideration for animals' health, safety, and well-being, and it is not that unusual for this court to apply relatively broad statutory language to particular claims by looking to the normal usage of words, even when different people may disagree as to their application to a variety of factual situations.

Analogously, the Supreme Court and this circuit have frequently recognized the injury in fact of plaintiffs who suffered aesthetic injury stemming from the condition and quality, or despoliation, of an environmental area that they used. In *Mountain States Legal Foundation*, for instance, the plaintiffs asserted injury flowing from government action that would allegedly make the Kootenai National Forest more vulnerable to forest fire. This court found an "aesthetic and environmental interest[ ] in having such areas free of devastating forest fire . . . clearly sufficient for Article

---

7. It was suggested, not altogether facetiously, at oral argument that recognition of an aesthetic interest in observing animals might be problematic because it could encapsulate the aesthetic interest of a sadist in seeing animals living under *in*humane conditions and the injury he suffered upon seeing particular animals living in a humane environment. There is a major difficulty with this argument. The meaning of "injury in fact" under our constitutional standing test does not incorporate every conceivable aesthetic interest. To the contrary, our standing jurisprudence defines injury in fact as "an invasion of a *legally protected interest.*" *Defenders of Wildlife*, 504 U.S. at 560 (emphasis added). Thus, if the hypothetical sadist challenged the regulations at issue here (presumably, for being too protective of animal welfare), he would not be able to establish injury in fact because the AWA, the relevant statute, recognizes no interest in sadism. To the contrary, it requires dealers, exhibitors, and research facilities to treat animals *humanely. See* 7 U.S.C. § 2143. This sadist would also find his claim immediately excluded under the APA, which only grants standing to people "adversely affected or aggrieved by agency action *within the meaning of a relevant statute.*" 5 U.S.C. § 702 (1994) (emphasis added). . . .

III standing." 92 F.3d at 1234. Similarly, in *Montgomery Environmental Coalition v. Costle*, 646 F.2d 568 (D.C. Cir. 1980), the plaintiffs challenged the Environmental Protection Agency's ("EPA's") regulation of "two sewage treatment plants that discharge pollutants into the Potomac River and its tributaries," 646 F.2d at 573. They "professed an interest in the preservation and enhancement of the natural environment situated along the Potomac estuary," *id.* at 576, and alleged that the EPA had issued "permits too lax to protect the water quality of the Potomac," *id.* at 573. This court found standing.

* * *

Indeed, *Humane Society v. Hodel*, which recognized an aesthetic interest in seeing animals living under humane conditions, explicitly acknowledged the usefulness of analogizing such an aesthetic interest to a plaintiff's interest in the condition of an environmental area that he uses. That case drew on our opinion in *National Wildlife Federation v. Hodel*, 839 F.2d 694 (D.C. Cir. 1988), which held that a wildlife organization had standing to challenge regulations that allegedly threatened to degrade the environment, *see* 839 F.2d at 703–16. The *Humane Society* court noted that the two cases involved "strikingly analogous" injuries, explaining: "There the National Wildlife Federation's standing rested in part on the aesthetic injuries to those members who complained of viewing degraded landscapes, and here the Humane Society's standing similarly rests on the aesthetic injuries to members who complain of viewing the despoliation of animals." 840 F.2d at 52.

In the environmental context, too, however, plaintiffs must establish that they have actually used or plan to use the allegedly degraded environmental area in question. It is this failure to show such direct use that has resulted in the denial of standing in several high-profile environmental cases. [*Discussing Sierra Club and other cases.*]

* * *

Other circuits have also recognized injury in fact based on injury to a plaintiff's interest in the quality and condition of an environmental area that he used.

* * *

These myriad cases recognizing individual plaintiffs' injury in fact based on affronts to their aesthetic interests in observing animals living in humane habitats, or in using pristine environmental areas that have not been despoiled, articulate a second principle of standing. It has never been the law, and is not so today, that injury in fact requires the elimination (or threatened elimination) of either the animal species or environmental feature in question. . . .

To be sure, a number of cases that have recognized standing based on an aesthetic interest in the observation of animals have involved government action that allegedly threatened to diminish the overall supply of an animal species. *See Defenders of Wildlife*, 504 U.S. at 562; *Japan Whaling Ass'n*, 478 U.S. at 231 n.4. But there is no case that we know of establishing that the elimination of a species or even the deaths of particular animals is an indispensable element of the plaintiffs' aesthetic injury, and we see no reason to import such a requirement into our standing doctrine so late in the day. Indeed, the standing cases that do stress the threat of diminished animal populations were those brought under conservation statutes whose mission is to preserve the number of animals in existence. . . . It is not surprising, then, that the plaintiffs who brought suit to allege violations of these statutes would emphasize that the challenged agency action threatened to diminish the supply of an animal species, in contravention of the express purpose of those conservation statutes. In contrast, the Animal Welfare Act, with which we deal here, is explicitly concerned with the quality of animal life, rather than the number of animals in existence. It seeks "to promote the psychological well-being of primates." Pub. L. No. 99-198, § 1752, 99 Stat. 1354, 1645 (1985) (codified at 7 U.S.C. § 2143(a) (1994)) (emphasis added). Quite naturally, suits alleging violations of this statute will focus on the conditions under which animals live. *Cf. ALDF II*, 29 F.3d at 722 ("The primary purpose of the [Federal Laboratory Animal Welfare] Act is to ensure the humane care and treatment of various animals used in research or for exhibition or kept as pets. 7 U.S.C. § 2131. To this end, the Act requires, *inter alia*, that the Secretary of Agriculture 'promulgate standards to govern the humane handling, care, treatment, and transportation of animals by dealers, research facilities, and exhibitors. *Id.* § 2143(a)(1)'"). Along these lines, this court has already noted in *Animal Welfare Institute*, which recognized injury in fact based on an aesthetic interest in seeing animals living under humane conditions, that "where an act is expressly motivated by considerations of humaneness toward animals, who are uniquely incapable of defending their own interests in court, it strikes us as eminently logical to allow groups specifically concerned with animal welfare to invoke the aid of the courts in enforcing the statute." 561 F.2d at 1007. Moreover, and perhaps more importantly, it does not make sense, as a matter of logic, to suppose that people suffer aesthetic injury from government action that threatens to wipe out an animal species altogether, and not from government action that leaves some animals in a persistent state of suffering. To the contrary, the latter seems capable of causing more serious aesthetic injury than the former.

Mr. Jurnove has adequately alleged injury to an aesthetic interest in observing animals living under humane conditions. His affidavit describes both the animal exhibition that he regularly visits, and the specific animals there whose condition caused Mr. Jurnove injury. It requires no expansion of existing standing doctrine to find that he has established a cognizable injury in fact.

B. *Causation*

Plaintiffs allege that the AWA, 7 U.S.C. § 2143, requires the USDA to adopt explicit minimum standards to govern the humane treatment of primates, and that the agency did not do so. They further contend that the conditions that caused Mr. Jurnove injury complied with current USDA regulations, but that lawful regulations would have prohibited those conditions and protected Mr. Jurnove from the injuries that his affidavit describes. We find that these allegations satisfy the causation prong of Article III standing.

As Mr. Jurnove's affidavit elaborates, he allegedly suffered aesthetic injury upon observing conditions that the present USDA regulations permit. Mr. Jurnove, for instance, "saw a large male chimpanzee named Barney in a holding area by himself. He could not see or hear any other primate." Mr. Jurnove also "viewed a monkey cage [containing one Japanese Snow Macaque] that was a distance from and not in view of the other primate cages." As the plaintiffs observe, *see* First Amended Complaint ¶¶ 84, 95, 114–17, the housing of these two primates appears to be compatible with current regulations, which state only that "the environment enhancement plan must include specific provisions to *address* the social needs of nonhuman primates of species known to exist in social groups in nature. Such specific provisions must be in accordance with currently accepted professional standards, as cited in appropriate professional journals or reference guides, and as directed by the attending veterinarian." 9 C.F.R. § 3.81(a) (emphasis added). Thus, an exhibition may apparently comply with the procedural requirement that this standard creates—by establishing a plan that "addresses" the social needs of primates—and still leave a primate caged singly. Similarly, 9 C.F.R. § 3.81(a)(3) provides that "individually housed nonhuman primates must be able to see and hear nonhuman primates of their own or compatible species unless the attending veterinarian determines that it would endanger their health, safety, or well-being." Here again, the regulation is structured so that an exhibitor that secured the approval of the veterinarian in its employ could comply with the regulation without actually housing nonhuman primates within the sight or sound of other primates. Contrary to the dissent, *see* Dissent at 13–14, plaintiffs do not suggest that the regulation is flawed simply because it leaves room for bribery in securing a veterinarian's consent to an exception; rather, they contend that the regulation gives exhibitors too much leeway to shop around for a compliant veterinarian and that placing such broad and unguarded discretion in the hands of the veterinarian in an exhibitor's own employ is an insufficient safeguard to protect primate well-being. Whatever the ultimate merits of the plaintiffs' case, they most definitely assert that the AWA requires minimum standards to prohibit or more rigidly restrict the occasions on which such allegedly inhumane treatment can occur.

Mr. Jurnove's affidavit also states that "the pen next to the adult bears housed the squirrel monkeys ... I observed the monkeys repeatedly walking over to the door and sniffing and acting very upset when the bears came near." Plaintiffs allege that the current regulations permit the housing of incompatible species next to each other. Specifically, these regulations state that "nonhuman primates may not be housed *with* other species of primates or animals unless they are compatible." 9 C.F.R. § 3.81(a)(3) (emphasis added). This provision does not expressly regulate animals housed *next* to each other, but in separate cages. But even if section 3.81(a)(3) does apply to the situation that Mr. Jurnove observed, it includes the caveat that "compatibility of nonhuman primates must be determined in accordance with generally accepted professional practices and actual observations, as directed by the attending veterinarian," thus again permitting wide discretion on the part of the local veterinarian.

Similarly, Mr. Jurnove's affidavit observes that "the only cage enrichment device [a Japanese Snow Macaque] had was an unused swing." The plaintiffs allege that such a situation is perfectly legal under the present regulations, *see* First Amended Complaint ¶ 84, which provide only that "the physical environment in the primary enclosures must be enriched by providing means of expressing noninjurious species-typical activities." 9 C.F.R. § 3.81(b). The regulations do not include any specific requirements governing the particular kind or number of enrichment devices. According to the plaintiffs, providing only a single swing, and one that the primate appears to shun, offends the AWA's mandate for minimum standards, although it is perfectly compatible with 9 C.F.R. § 3.81(b).[9]

The USDA's own actions in this case further support the plaintiffs' allegation that the agency's current regulations allow the conditions that allegedly caused Mr. Jurnove injury. As Mr. Jurnove's affidavit makes clear, the Game Farm has repeatedly submitted to inspection by the USDA. The allegedly inhumane conditions at the Game Farm have persisted precisely because the USDA inspectors have concluded on the basis of these visits that in every important aspect the conditions at the Game Farm comply with the USDA regulations. If the USDA had found the Game Farm out of compliance with current regulations, or if the governing regulations had themselves been more stringent, the Game Farm's owners would have been forced (in order to remain in accord with the law) to either alter their practices or go out of business and transfer their animals to exhibitors willing to operate legally; either scenario would protect Mr. Jurnove's aesthetic interest in observing animals living under humane conditions. Instead, however, the USDA has not questioned the legality of the Game Farm's plan since 1992. Since May 1995, when Mr. Jurnove began visiting the Game Farm and complaining to the agency, the USDA inspectors have examined, and largely approved, the actual conditions at the facility at least four times. The USDA's first inspection report "states that [the USDA inspectors] found the facility in compliance with all the standards." Jurnove Affidavit ¶ 18. Although subsequent inspection reports identify a few conditions that Mr. Jurnove agrees violate the USDA regulations, the USDA continued—in at least three more inspection reports—to conclude that the Game Farm was in compliance with existing USDA regulations in all other respects, including presumably the existence of a plan that met the regulations' standards.[10]

---

9. The United States argues that Mr. Jurnove has not demonstrated causation, on the ground that the above-described injuries are self-inflicted. The assertion appears to turn on the fact that Mr. Jurnove first traveled to the Game Farm "in [his] capacity as an equine investigator, [after being] apprised that several ponies needed to be checked on at that location." This argument may—or may not—have merit with regard to equine mistreatment at the Game Farm. However, there is no need in this case to offer any opinion about whether so-called "self-inflicted" wounds can give rise to standing. According to Mr. Jurnove's uncontested affidavit, he visited the primates at the Game Farm, the subject of the present suit, out of an aesthetic interest in observing animals living under humane conditions.

10. The dissent makes much of the fact that Mr. Jurnove occasionally expresses doubt in his affidavit about the soundness of the USDA's multiple determinations that the Game Farm was in

* * *

This circuit's case law confirms the proposition that a plaintiff satisfies the causation prong of constitutional standing by establishing that the challenged agency rule permitted the activity that allegedly injured her, when that activity would allegedly have been illegal otherwise. . . . *Telephone and Data Systems, Inc. v. FCC*, 19 F.3d 42 (D.C. Cir. 1994), recently explained that "one narrow proposition at least is clear: injurious private conduct is fairly traceable to the administrative action contested in the suit if that action authorized the conduct or established its legality," *id.* at 47.

* * *

. . . The proper comparison for determining causation . . . is between what the agency did and what the plaintiffs allege the agency should have done under the statute. The plaintiffs' legal theory of this case, which we accept for purposes of determining Mr. Jurnove's standing, is grounded on their view that animal exhibitors are in fact governed by a mandatory legal regime. Specifically, the plaintiffs allege that the AWA requires the USDA to establish specific, mandatory requirements that establish humane living conditions for animals. According to this view, the AWA itself prohibits the conditions that allegedly injured Mr. Jurnove, and the USDA regulations misinterpret the statute by permitting these conditions. Both the Supreme Court and this circuit have repeatedly found causation where a challenged government action *permitted* the third party conduct that allegedly caused a plaintiff injury, when that conduct would have otherwise been illegal. Neither court has ever stated that the challenged law must *compel* the third party to act in the allegedly injurious way. . . .

* * *

Mr. Jurnove's affidavit accordingly falls well within our established causation requirement for constitutional standing. He alleges that the USDA failed to adopt the specific, minimum standards that the AWA requires. He further describes how the conditions that caused him injury complied with current USDA regulations,

---

compliance with essentially all of the relevant regulations, contending that "the thrust of the affidavit" is that "the USDA went through the motions and wrote up incorrect reports." Dissent at 12. This argument is flawed on two counts. First, Mr. Jurnove's affidavit is the wrong place to look for a statement of the plaintiffs' legal theory of this case. Mr. Jurnove is not a lawyer and his affidavit purports to articulate only his alleged injuries. The plaintiffs' legal arguments are put forth in their complaint, where they explicitly allege that the conditions at the Game Farm that caused Mr. Jurnove injury complied with the present USDA regulations. Second, even if we were to look to Mr. Jurnove's affidavit to determine the plaintiffs' legal theory, the "thrust of the affidavit" is certainly not that the conditions at the Game Farm violated the USDA's regulations. Indeed, so far as the record before us reflects, no decisionmaking authority has ever made the determination that there are widespread regulatory violations at the Game Farm. And the USDA, the agency with regulatory control over the Game Farm, repeatedly came to the opposite conclusion, finding that the Game Farm was in legal compliance with the USDA regulations that the plaintiffs challenge here.

and alleges that regulations complying with the AWA would have prohibited those conditions and protected him from the injuries that his affidavit recounts.

C. *Redressibility*

We also find that Mr. Jurnove has satisfied the redressibility element of constitutional standing. Mr. Jurnove's affidavit alleges that he has a current routine of regularly visiting the Game Farm and provides a finite time period within which he will make his next visit, stating that he plans to "return to the Farm in the next several weeks" and to "continue visiting the Farm to see the animals there." Jurnove Affidavit ¶ 43. As the plaintiffs' complaint argues, more stringent regulations, which prohibit the inhumane conditions that have consistently caused Mr. Jurnove aesthetic injury in the past, would necessarily alleviate Mr. Jurnove's aesthetic injury during his planned, future trips to the Game Farm. Tougher regulations would either allow Mr. Jurnove to visit a more humane Game Farm or, if the Game Farm's owners decide to close rather than comply with higher legal standards, to possibly visit the animals he has come to know in their new homes within exhibitions that comply with the more exacting regulations.

* * *

Circuit Judge SENTELLE, with whom Judge SILBERMAN, Judge GINSBURG, and Judge KAREN LeCRAFT HENDERSON join, dissenting:

* * *

... Because I believe the majority significantly weakens existing requirements of constitutional standing, I dissent.

I.

* * *

It is ... imperative to exercise prudence when deciding a case-like the case before us today-that would lower existing Article III barriers to standing. We should not lightly tinker with the constitutional source of federal judicial power, even when we may sympathize with the ideological goals of plaintiffs in a particular case.

* * *

II.

A. *Injury-in-Fact*

... The majority concludes that Jurnove has articulated a "concrete and particularized" injury to his "legally protected interest" in "observing animals living under humane conditions."....

Despite the majority's assertion to the contrary, today's ruling is indeed a departure from existing aesthetic injury jurisprudence. Granted, "the desire to use or observe an animal species, even for purely esthetic purposes, is undeniably a cognizable interest for purpose of standing." However, as we have observed before, the Supreme Court cases addressing aesthetic injury resulting from the observation of animals are limited to cases in which governmental action threatened to reduce the number of animals available for observation and study.

Nor has this circuit previously crossed this diminution-of-the-species line and found the existence of a constitutional interest in the conditions under which one views animals. The majority misleadingly suggests that we did so in *Animal Welfare Institute v. Kreps,* 561 F.2d 1002, 1007 (D.C.Cir.1977). In fact, that decision does not make it at all clear what the nature of the injury is which the court found sufficient. . . . Insofar as the majority claims that our decision adopted the view that the conditions of observation constitute a cognizable interest such that interference therewith constitutes injury-in-fact for Article III standing purposes, the opinion simply will not bear that weight.

In that case, environmental groups had filed a lawsuit that challenged a decision by the Secretary of Commerce to waive a statutory moratorium on the taking or importation of marine mammals or marine mammal products. . . . The plaintiffs alleged in their lawsuit that the government's action would "contribute to the death and injury of marine mammals and injury to the ecosystem of the South Atlantic Ocean." The plaintiffs articulated their aesthetic injury as follows:

> Through sanctioning the seal harvesting method of the South African Government, the [Secretary's] decision impairs the ability of members of the Plaintiff organizations to see, photograph, and enjoy Cape fur seals alive in their natural habitat under conditions in which the animals are not subject to excessive harvesting, *inhumane treatment* and slaughter of pups that are very young and still nursing.

* * *

. . . *Animal Welfare Institute,* then, involved allegations that governmental action will "contribute to the death" of seals. Accordingly, this case falls squarely within the line of Supreme Court precedents recognizing claims of aesthetic injury to governmental action diminishing the opportunity to observe, not affecting the quality of the observation.

The majority also cites *Humane Society v. Hodel,* 840 F.2d 45 (D.C. Cir. 1988), seemingly for the proposition that viewing animals free from inhumane treatment is a constitutionally cognizable injury. But this case too comes within the Supreme Court's diminution-of-the-species parameters, specifically recognizing as cognizable the "deplet[ion] [of] the supply of animals and birds that refuge visitors seek to view."

Although the Supreme Court and this circuit have not recognized a cognizable injury-in-fact to an aesthetic interest based on the circumstances of observation, that does not mean that interference with such an interest could not amount to a constitutional injury-in-fact. Rather, as I set forth above, I believe it is necessary to proceed with caution when venturing into constitutionally uncharted waters.

Having removed the diminution-of-the-species touchstone of existing case law, the majority opens an expanse of standing bounded only by what a given plaintiff finds to be aesthetically pleasing. Aesthetic injury is, by its nature, a matter of individual taste. For example, although Jurnove might find it aesthetically pleasing to view primates kept in groups, another person might prefer to watch them kept alone. Still another person might prefer to see primates in brightly colored cages, or in cages in which recordings of Mozart piano concertos are played around the clock, or not in cages at all. Under the majority's theory, it appears that Article III encompasses the injury of a person who states that he has an aesthetic interest in seeing primates kept under such conditions, and that he believes primates that are not kept under these conditions are treated inhumanely.

Jurnove's injury, recognized by the majority as constitutionally cognizable, is in seeing particular animals treated humanely. "Humane" is defined as "marked by compassion, sympathy, or consideration for other human beings or animals." WEBSTER'S NEW COLLEGIATE DICTIONARY 556 (1973). Humaneness, like beauty, is in the eye of the beholder: one's individual judgment about what is or is not humane depends entirely on one's personal notions of compassion and sympathy. I find it difficult to imagine a more subjective concept than this.

* * *

In recognizing Jurnove's purely subjective injury, the majority radically departs from our precedent . . .

* * *

. . . Jurnove's notion of what is "humane" depend[s] solely on his own value preferences. And no objective standard could possibly measure degrees of a concept — humaneness — that is based entirely on one's subjective emotions. Under existing law, a plaintiff may establish a "concrete and particularized" injury when his interest in observing or studying animals is directly affected by the reduction in the number of animals to be viewed or studied. Today's decision goes much further, recognizing an aesthetic injury based solely on a plaintiff's subjective emotional response to something he sees. Under today's decision, one's individual preference in viewing animals in a particular way is thought to be constitutionally injured when government regulations do not require the animals to be kept in a way that comports with one's taste. I would . . . hold that such a purely subjective injury is outside the boundaries of Article III. The majority's contrary conclusion amounts to constitutional recognition of the "psychological consequence presumably produced by observation of conduct with which one disagrees." . . . [T]his is "not an injury sufficient to confer standing under Art. III. . . ."

* * *

. . . Accordingly, I would find that [Jurnove] has not met his burden of demonstrating a cognizable injury-in-fact. This conclusion alone would bar Jurnove from seeking relief in federal court.

B. *Causation*

Even if I shared my colleagues' belief that an interference with a plaintiff's aesthetic sensibilities absent a diminution in the opportunity to exercise those sensibilities is sufficient to make out the injury-in-fact element of constitutional standing, I still could not conclude that the plaintiffs had established that Jurnove has constitutional standing on the present complaint. Even if such an injury were cognizable, and even if the complaint has set forth that cognizable injury, their attempt at standing stumbles at the second stile: they have not established causation.

In analyzing the "causation" element of constitutional standing, we ask whether it is "substantially probable" that the challenged acts of the defendant—as opposed, for example, to the acts of an absent third party—caused a plaintiff's particularized injury. Causation, therefore, is related to but distinct from "redressability," which requires that the relief sought by the plaintiffs is likely to alleviate the plaintiff's injury.

. . . A plaintiff who claims to have been injured by the government's regulation of a third party must "adduce facts showing that the unfettered choices made by independent actors have been or will be made in such manner as to produce causation and permit redressability of injury."

. . . Since Jurnove is asserting injuries attributed to the government's regulation of a third party, his claims of causation must be considered with "exacting scrutiny."

The cornerstone of Jurnove's claims of causation is that existing regulations permit the conditions that troubled him. . . . However, the gravamen of the affidavit is not that the events Jurnove witnessed were legal, but that USDA is shirking its obligation to enforce the law, and is only halfheartedly inspecting the Game Farm in order to mollify Jurnove. . . . In light of the thrust of the affidavit (that USDA went through the motions and wrote up incorrect reports), Jurnove's legal claims of causation (that the regulations *permitted* the conditions he witnessed) seem disingenuous.

* * *

According to the majority, causation is established if a plaintiff demonstrates that challenged governmental action "authorizes" the plaintiff's injuries. But the majority uses the term "authorize" in a very loose way. For example, 9 C.F.R. § 3.81(a)(3) provides that "individually housed nonhuman primates must be able to see and hear nonhuman primates of their own or compatible species unless the attending veterinarian determines that it would endanger their health, safety, or well-being." According to the majority, this regulation authorized the Game Farm to house nonhuman primates out of the sight or hearing of other primates.

The majority's view of "authorization" here is beyond expansive. The regulation says that individually housed primates *must* be able to see and hear other primates unless the attending veterinarian determines otherwise. Thus, one of two things must be true under existing law if a primate were housed out of the sight or hearing of other primates. Either the attending veterinarian determined that housing such a primate within the sight or hearing of another primate "would endanger their health, safety, or well-being," or the veterinarian did not, in which case the housing of the primate would violate the regulation. According to the majority, the regulation authorizes inhumane treatment of primates. How? An exhibitor that *secured the approval of the veterinarian in its employ* could comply with the regulation without actually housing nonhuman primates within the sight or sound of other primates." ([E]mphasis added). The obvious innuendo of this sentence is that an exhibitor could bribe its staff veterinarian to determine falsely that a given primate's "health, safety, or well-being" would be endangered, thus permitting the primate to be housed away from the sight or sound of other primates. But if this were so, any inhumane treatment would be the result of the exhibitor's failure to follow existing regulations, and would not be traceable to the regulations themselves.

The majority also addresses the causation of Jurnove's alleged aesthetic injury in seeing squirrel monkeys housed next to adult bears "repeatedly walking over to the door and sniffing and acting very upset when the bears came near." The majority acknowledges that under existing regulations, "[n]onhuman primates may not be housed with other species of primates or animals unless they are compatible." . . . The majority's causation analysis comes down to this: when a provision does not "expressly regulate" certain treatment, the regulations "authorize" such treatment. Surely this analysis proves too much. There are an infinite variety of things not "expressly regulated" by section 3.81, and according to the majority's reasoning any injury caused by those things is fairly traceable to the government's failure to "expressly regulate" them. I cannot subscribe to such a wide-ranging theory of causation.

I find frightening at a constitutional level the majority's assumption that the government causes everything that it does not prevent. The majority rejects as "a false premise" the proposition that "[t]he proper comparison for determining causation is . . . between what the agency did and the status quo before the agency acted." I submit that consistent with our constitutional tradition of limited government that is precisely the correct premise for causation.

* * *

It is no answer to say that USDA's regulations do not *prohibit* the allegedly inhumane conditions that [Jurnove] observed at the Game Farm. What matters, under our consistent case law, is whether the third party conduct follows directly on the heels of a government decision that affirmatively approved that conduct. Jurnove has made no such submission.

C. *Redressability*

I would further hold that Jurnove fails the test of redressability. . . . The [challenged] regulation provides that "[t]he physical environment in the primary enclosures must be enriched by providing means of expressing noninjurious species-typical activities." 9 C.F.R. § 3.81(b). According to Jurnove (and the majority), these regulations authorized the Game Farm to keep primates in an offensive single-swing cage.

To find redressability on Jurnove's claims would require that we ignore the well-established rule that Article III standing requires it to "be likely, as opposed to merely speculative, that the injury will be redressed by a favorable decision."

. . . Under Jurnove's theory, to comply with the "minimum standards" mandate of the AWA, the new regulation would require certain specific cage enrichment devices to be included. But due to the fuzzy nature of Jurnove's asserted injury, it would require sheer speculation to presume that any enrichment devices specified in a future regulation would satisfy Jurnove's aesthetic tastes. We only know that Jurnove does *not* like seeing primates kept in cages with only one enrichment device. We do not know what conditions would satisfy his individual taste. We do not know, for example, how many enrichment devices Jurnove would prefer to see, or of what type.

This problem—how could we possibly know whether a future regulation comports with Jurnove's aesthetic interests—is directly related to the nature of Jurnove's claimed injury itself. When an animal viewer asserts an aesthetic interest in not seeing a species diminished, it is easy to tell when that injury is redressed: a judicial order may prevent the government from diminishing the species. But when, as here, a plaintiff asserts that a regulation has injured an unquantifiable interest (the plaintiff's own taste), it seems to me nearly impossible to redress such an injury by a general court order directing the government to try again.

* * *

Notes

1. Finally a plaintiff survived a standing challenge—at least for the moment. Yet the strident dissent, written by Judge Sentelle and joined by three other judges, including then-future Supreme Court Justice Ruth Ginsburg, took issue with every aspect of the majority opinion. Perhaps the most telling—and bizarre—statement of the dissent was that "[a]ccording to the majority's theory, a sadist with an interest in seeing animals kept under inhumane conditions is constitutionally injured when he views animals kept under humane conditions."

Notably, Judge Sentelle wrote the original D.C. Circuit panel opinion rejecting standing, which is reversed by the full D.C. Circuit here. For an argument that animal protections should not be expanded and that animals should not have standing, *see* David R. Schmahmann and Lori J. Polacheck, *The Case Against Rights for Animals*, 22 B.C. Envtl. Aff. L. Rev. 747 (Spring 1995). For a further thorough analysis and historical background of the case, *see* Rob Roy Smith, *Standing on Their Own Four Legs: The Future of Animal Welfare Litigation After Animal Legal Defense Fund v. Glickman*, 29 Envtl. L. 989 (Dec. 1999).

2. *Killing versus torturing, destroying a species versus causing suffering to living members of a species, eliminating a habitat/reducing the number of animals of a given species versus maintaining inadequate conditions for animals.* The dissent draws clear

lines between each of these pairings. For the future, what level of injury do you think will be required for animal protection plaintiffs? Whose injury must it be? Has the degree of effect on animals or the environment been a factor considered by the Supreme Court? Is Judge Sentelle trying to add another barrier that might stop animal protection plaintiffs at the courthouse door? Who would be the proper plaintiff for the dissenting judges?

3. If the legislature is the proper forum, what could the legislature do for the plaintiffs in this case?

4. Compare the plaintiffs in prior cases—is there a constitutionally significant difference in terms of injury in fact, causation, redressability?

5. Judicial review of the actions of federal agencies became more prevalent in the 1970s and 1980s. At the same time, beginning with the Supreme Court's ruling in *Vermont Yankee Nuclear Power Corp. v. NRDC*, 435 U.S. 519 (1978), a rule of deference was applied to agency decisions. Agency actions must meet the minimum requirements of the Administrative Procedure Act. The leading case in the area is *Chevron U.S.A. v. NRDC*, 467 U.S. 837 (1984), which held courts should defer to agencies' interpretations of statutes unless such interpretations are "arbitrary and capricious" or contravene the unequivocal provisions of a statute.

Chevron bestowed upon agencies the authority to determine questions of law, arguably violating the separation-of-powers doctrine. *See Marbury v. Madison*, 5 U.S. (1 Cranch) 137, 177 (1803) ("It is emphatically the province and duty of the judicial department to say what the law is."); *see also* Cass R. Sunstein, *Law and Administration After Chevron*, 90 COLUM. L. REV. 2071, 2075 (1990) (stating that *Chevron* has become "a kind of Marbury, or counter-Marbury, for the administrative state"). Before *Chevron*, courts were selectively—and inconsistently—deferential toward agencies' interpretations of statutes; for instance, courts rarely deferred to agencies' interpretations of "pure questions of law." *See NLRB v. Hearst Publications*, 322 U.S. 111, 130 (1944); *see also* Sunstein, *supra*, at 2081–82 & nn. 47–48, 2094–96; Antonin Scalia, *Judicial Deference to Administrative Interpretations of Law*, 1989 DUKE L.J. 511, 512–13. The *Chevron* decision adopted a two-step review process for agencies' interpretations of a statute:

> When a court reviews an agency's construction of the statute which it administers, it is confronted with two questions. First, always, is the question whether Congress has directly spoken to the precise question at issue. If the intent of Congress is clear, that is the end of the matter; for the court, as well as the agency, must give effect to the unambiguously expressed intent of Congress. If, however, the court determines Congress has not directly addressed the precise question at issue, the court does not simply impose its own construction on the statute, as would be necessary in the absence of an administrative interpretation. Rather, if the statute is silent or ambiguous with respect to the specific issue, the question for the court is whether the agency's answer is based on a permissible construction of the statute.

467 U.S. at 842–43. The Court elaborated in a related footnote:

> The court need not conclude that the agency construction was the only one it permissibly could have adopted to uphold the construction, or even the reading the court would have reached if the question initially had arisen in a judicial proceeding.

Id. at 843 n.11. If a statutory provision is ambiguous, the court must defer to agencies' interpretation of the provision even if the court disagrees with that interpretation unless the agency's interpretation is arbitrary and capricious or otherwise violates federal law. *Id.* at 845.

6. Since *Glickman*, a regular viewer of animal exhibitions has standing to challenge USDA regulations that allegedly violate the AWA. The zone-of-interests analysis favors animal protection plaintiffs. The court may have added to the list of those with standing by including "'those who in practice can be expected to police the interests that the statute protects.'" (quoting *Mova Pharmaceutical Corp. v. Shalala*, 140 F.3d 1060, 1075 (D.C. Cir. 1998)). With *Glickman*, watchdogs as well as those individually injured have standing to sue, although they must still satisfy Article III, section 2. This parallels the court's conclusion that even aesthetic or "emotional" injuries like those claimed by Mr. Jurnove satisfy the zone-of-interests requirement under the AWA.

7. Subsequently, animal advocates made one final judicial challenge to the "birds, rats and mice" rule excluding those species from the animals covered by the Animal Welfare Act, as had been done by the plaintiffs in *Animal Legal Defense Fund v. Espy*, 23 F.3d 496 (D.C. Cir. 1994), excerpted earlier in this chapter. The case, *Alternative Research & Development Foundation v. Glickman*, 101 F. Supp. 2d 7 (D.D.C. 2000), began with another standing decision. Building on the decisions in both *Espy* and *ALDF v. Glickman*, the court held plaintiff Kristine Gausz had standing. The facts asserted were:

> Kristine Gausz is a psychology student at Beaver College. As part of her course requirements at the college, she participates in laboratory experiments involving rats. She alleges that as a result of the defendants' failure to include birds, mice and rats in the AWA's definition of "animal," Beaver College is permitted to use rats for laboratory experiments without providing them with humane care. The lack of humane care in the lab has caused the plaintiff regularly to observe laboratory rats that receive "inadequate housing, water, food, and veterinary care." Complaint, Para. 18. Gausz claims aesthetic and emotional injury resulting from her observation of these mistreated animals. She further alleges that she has spent her own time and money to "rectify the inhumane treatment" of the rats. Complaint, Para. 19.

* * *

> [*Ms. Gausz's affidavit further stated*] that she "want[s] to observe and study the laboratory rats, however, I am personally, aesthetically, emotionally,

and profoundly disturbed when observing rats treated and cared for inhumanely. Repeatedly, I have observed rats that were suffering and subject to deplorable living conditions, which has been an assault on my senses."

Id. at 11. The court rejected defendants' claim that Gausz's injuries were not cognizable because they arose during employment, as opposed to during recreational activities. Because the AWA was based on considerations of humane treatment, anyone focused on those issues (in whatever capacity) could assert an injury. The court found causation, or "traceability," as well, since the USDA's lack of regulations was the source of Gausz's injuries. The court expressly rejected the government's arguments that plaintiff's injuries were not traceable to the lack of AWA coverage because (a) the AWA did not *require* inhumane treatment or (2) Gausz could treat her experimental subjects humanely.

8. Another important standing decision came out of *American Society for the Prevention of Cruelty to Animals v. Ringling Bros. and Barnum & Bailey Circus*, 317 F.3d 334 (D.C. Cir. 2003), in which several animal protection groups and an elephant trainer challenged the mistreatment of elephants by circus employees. The court focused on Tom Rider, a former trainer for the circus, who said that he

> formed a "strong, personal attachment to these animals." Employees of Ringling Bros. beat the elephants with sharp bull hooks, kept the elephants in chains for long periods of time, and forcibly removed baby elephants from their mothers at an earlier age than they could normally be weaned in the wild. These actions have negative impacts on the elephants' behavior "wherever they perform or are exhibited." Rider has seen the elephants show stressful "stereotypic" behavior as a result. Department of Agriculture inspectors saw lesions and rope burns on the elephants. Rider left his job at Ringling Bros. because of the mistreatment of the elephants. He would like to work with the elephants again and would attempt to do so if the elephants were relocated. Rider would also like to visit the elephants, but is unwilling to do so because he would suffer "aesthetic and emotional injury" from seeing the animals unless they are placed in a different setting or are no longer mistreated.

Id. at 336. The court held that Rider had established injury in fact because it could "see no principled distinction between the injury that person suffers when discharges begin polluting the river and the injury Rider allegedly suffers from the mistreatment of the elephants to which he became emotionally attached during his tenure at Ringling Bros.—both are part of the aesthetic injury."

9. *ASPCA v. Ringling, ALDF v. Glickman,* and *ARDF v. Glickman* all demonstrate the value—for standing purposes—of a plaintiff with direct contact with animals affected by adverse action, whether that contact is formalized or more personal.

10. The history of the *ASPCA v. Ringling Brothers* case demonstrates the vigor with which both sides will advocate for their cause. The case spanned approximately nine years and included a six-week bench trial. In addition to the 2003 D.C. Circuit's

standing opinion, the case generated a constant stream of protracted discovery disputes and extensive motions that resulted in numerous, and often lengthy, court opinions over the years. *See, e.g., ASPCA v. Ringling Bros.*, 2007 WL 4261699 (D.D.C. Dec. 3, 2007); *ASPCA v. Ringling Bros.*, 2007 WL 625937 (D.D.C. Feb. 26, 2007) (plaintiffs' motion for attorneys' fees after successful motion to compel); *ASPCA v. Ringling Bros.*, 244 F.R.D. 49 (D.D.C. 2007) (denying defendants' request for leave to add Racketeer Influenced and Corrupt Organizations Act (RICO) counterclaim to answer and to add affirmative defense of unclean hands doctrine). Along the way, the defendants prevailed in part on a summary judgment motion that limited the scope of plaintiffs' claim because certain elephants who were allegedly abused were not covered by the Endangered Species Act (ESA). *ASPCA v. Ringling Bros.*, 502 F. Supp. 2d 103 (D.D.C. 2007). After trial, having had the opportunity to observe Tom Rider on the stand and subjected to cross-examination, the court concluded that Rider's testimony regarding his injury-in-fact was "not credible," depriving plaintiffs of standing, and entered judgment in favor of the defendant. *ASPCA v. Feld Entertainment*, 677 F. Supp. 2d 55, 83 (D.D.C. 2011). On appeal, the D.C. Circuit affirmed and additionally found that plaintiff Animal Protection Institute had not satisfied its alternative (informational and *Havens*) bases for standing. *ASPCA v. Feld Entertainment*, 659 F.3d 13 (D.C. Cir. 2011).

The case did not end there, however. Ringling Bros.' parent company, Feld Entertainment, Inc. (Feld), filed a motion to recoup its attorneys' fees, which the court granted. *Animal Welfare Institute v. Feld Entertainment, Inc.*, 944 F. Supp. 2d 1 (D.D.C. 2013) (the first named plaintiff changed after ASPCA settled with Feld in late 2012 (in connection with Feld's lawsuit discussed in Note 11 below) and the court granted ASPCA's motion to remove its name from the case caption to reflect its dismissal in this case).

11. In a strategic move of turning the defense into an offense, Feld sued the plaintiffs in the *ASPCA v. Ringling Bros.* case, their lawyers and a related group, claiming that Tom Rider was bribed to be a plaintiff in the underlying ESA lawsuit. Feld relied on the federal RICO Act (18 U.S.C. § 1961, *et seq.*) and the Virginia Conspiracy Act (Va. Code Ann. § 18.2-499-500) and alleged a conspiracy to "permanently ban Asian elephants in circuses and to defraud [Feld] of money and property, with the ultimate object of banning Asian elephants in all forms of entertainment and captivity." *Feld Entertainment, Inc. v. ASPCA*, 523 F. Supp. 2d 1, 2 (D.D.C. 2007) (quoting from Feld's complaint). Upon motion by the animal advocacy groups, the court stayed all proceedings in Feld's action, pending resolution of the underlying ESA lawsuit. *Id.* After judgment in the ESA lawsuit, the stay was lifted. The defendants filed motions to dismiss, which the district court granted in part and denied in part, in a lengthy opinion. *Feld Entertainment, Inc. v. ASPCA*, 873 F. Supp. 2d 288 (D.D.C. 2012).

12. All related litigation in the Ringling Brothers saga ended with settlements in 2014. *See, e.g.,* Thomas Heath, *Ringling Circus prevails in 14-year legal case; collects $16M from Humane Society, others*, Wash. Post, May 16, 2014.

13. Despite the settlements and partial success of Feld's litigation, in 2017 Ringling Brothers circus officially ended, with elephants having been removed in 2016, as discussed in Chapter 3.

14. Like in circuses, many exotic animals used in films, television, advertising and public exhibition are forced to act in unnatural ways on command. (See discussion in Chapter 3.) Eyewitnesses, primatologists and animal behaviorists have reported that such behavior can only be controlled by negative, usually painful, reinforcement. Great apes and other primates are often removed from their nursing mothers near birth to disrupt their natural instincts and begin the process of fear inducement and pain avoidance that produces a proper "show." Activists try to alert the public about the mistreatment of animals when they are offstage, hoping the knowledge will prompt the public to stop patronizing such shows. When Bobby Berosini, who had a Las Vegas show including a number of orangutans who he beat regularly, was caught on film, he sued the groups responsible. *People for the Ethical Treatment of Animals v. Bobby Berosini*, 111 Nev. 615, 895 P.2d 1269 (1995) took two trips to the Nevada Supreme Court before finally being resolved against Berosini.

Berosini sued for invasion of privacy and for defamation. One of the most notable aspects of the *Berosini* ruling was the court's logical conclusion that pictures or videotape of animal cruelty could never be considered false, and therefore can never be defamatory. Berosini challenged the videotapes of his beatings of the orangutans, but because they were "true," that claim was rejected. Additionally, Berosini claimed the beatings were necessary and justified for his act. Since Berosini did not deny the acts and claimed they were proper, the court found their depiction could not be defamatory. The court also recognized the subjective nature of cruelty, so that an opinion that he was acting cruelly could not be defamatory as a statement of fact about him.

Judicial opinions like *Berosini* provide an educational function as well, validating the claims of activists alleging cruel treatment of animals:

> All of the members of this court have viewed the tape; and what is shown on the tape is clear and unequivocal: Berosini is shown, immediately before going on stage, grabbing, slapping, punching and shaking the animals while several handlers hold the animals in position. The tape also shows Berosini striking the animals with a black rod approximately ten to twelve inches long. Perhaps Berosini has some explanation or justification for this conduct; but, the videotape accurately portrays what he was doing to these animals on at least nine different occasions. Berosini, himself, was forced to admit at trial that there was no visual inaccuracy in the images represented on the tape.

* * *

The animal rights activists all see Berosini's treatment of his animals as cruel and abusive, an opinion shared by the defendants in this case. Jane

Goodall, Ph.D., Director of the Gombe Stream Research Centre and expert in primate behavior viewed the tape in this manner:

> In this video, I saw the following sequence of events: A door opened and five men, each leading a young orang by one hand, walked along a bare passage towards the (presumably concealed) camera. With these ten primates was a sixth man, wearing a bow tie. At the end of the passage the whole group stopped. The orangs, still standing upright, appeared quiet and well behaved. I saw no signs of disobedience in any of them at any time. Yet as they stood there—apparently waiting to go onstage for a performance—the man in the bow tie began to abuse the orangs. Suddenly he would seize one of them by its hair and pull and push it towards and away from him with violent movements. He would slap one of them, or punch it with his fist. Most of the abuse was directed towards the larger orangs. Once he pulled one round to face him, then slapped it hard over the muzzle. Occasionally he hit one of them over the shoulders with a heavy implement, shaped like a conductor's baton.
>
> During these entirely unprovoked assaults the handlers restrained the orangs by both arms, holding them upright. They gave the impression that they were expecting the abuse and positioning their charges in readiness to receive it.

Dr. Goodall was of the opinion that what she saw on the videotape involved "severe psychological cruelty as well as physical abuse," and recommended that the five orangutans depicted in the videotape "be confiscated immediately and placed in the hands of caring and responsible people who could try to cure them of their psychological (and perhaps physical) wounds."

* * *

[*Because opinions differ as to what constitutes animal cruelty, the court found Dr. Goodall's statements were protected, "evaluative opinions."*] We are dealing here with two very strongly held, contrary opinions on how animals should be treated. We agree completely with *amicus*, Nevada State Press Association, Inc., that "without taking sides on the activities or the strongly-held beliefs of either party, it is nevertheless clear that open and robust debate on controversial and contested issues of this kind could not long survive a succession of such multi-million dollar judgments."

Id. at 620, 623–25. The court also rejected Berosini's claims for invasion of privacy.

15. The opinion represented the culmination of many years of attempts by PETA to shut down Berosini's act, or at least expose his practices. Many felt Berosini's conduct was more reprehensible because it involved orangutans, a highly intelligent ape closely related to humans. Although loners, orangutans exhibit a significant family structure and mother-child bond. H. Lyn White Miles, *Language and the Orang-Utan: The Old 'Person' of the Forest, in* THE GREAT APE PROJECT, EQUALITY BEYOND HUMANITY 42–57 (Paola Cavalieri & Peter Singer eds., 1993).

16. Rehearing of the first opinion in *Berosini* was granted because Judge Lehman, a member of the previous panel, was on the advisory board of a local humane society. *PETA v. Berosini*, 894 P.2d 337 (Nev. 1995). The humane society's board of trustees included a local news columnist and PETA member who was involved in bringing Berosini's actions to public attention. Although the court found Judge Lehman had only met the columnist two or three times at group meetings, and that the goals of the local humane society and PETA were substantially different, rehearing was granted based on a Nevada ethical rule prohibiting the appearance of impropriety.

17. PETA spent years pursuing Berosini in court to obtain the attorneys' fees and costs to which the court held PETA was entitled. In 2004, the federal district court in Las Vegas ordered Berosini to pay additional sums for the attorneys' fees incurred by PETA trying to locate assets to obtain payment of previously ordered fees and costs. *Roush v. Berosini*, No. CV-S-98-482-PMP-LRL (D. Nev. Nov. 18, 2004).

Section 2. Due Process — Challenges and Claims

"Breed-specific legislation" (BSL) like the ordinances discussed in the following cases is the subject of ongoing controversy nationwide. BSL refers to local and state laws that prohibit or limit ownership and possession of specific breeds of dogs. By one view, these laws are simply an extension of state and local laws that ban exotic, dangerous or wild animals. By another view, the laws are discriminatory targeting of an identifiable group of dogs solely because of their "race." The number of such laws increased significantly throughout the last thirty years, as the number of reports of attacks by certain breeds has also spiked.

American Dog Owners Association v. The City of Yakima

Supreme Court of Washington, En Banc, 1989
113 Wash. 2d 213, 777 P.2d 1046

DOLLIVER, JUSTICE. In January 1987, there were three attacks by pit bull dogs on unsuspecting citizens in Yakima. On July 28, 1987, the City of Yakima adopted ordinance 3034 which bans dogs known by the owners to be pit bulls, specifically the breeds Bull Terrier, American Pit Bull Terrier, Staffordshire Bull Terrier, and American Staffordshire Terrier, as well as dogs "identifiable" as having any pit bull variety as an element of their breeding. The ordinance allows owners of pit bulls licensed prior to the enactment to keep their pets subject to certain rules. The ordinance also allows a judge to release an apprehended dog on a showing that the dog will not return to the city or that the dog was misidentified.

Plaintiffs David Carvo and Mark and Bonnie Johnson own dogs that may come under the ordinance. Plaintiff American Dog Owners Association has members in

Yakima owning dogs that may come under the ordinance. In August 1987, Yakima notified the Johnsons that they may be subject to the ordinance. All plaintiffs sued Yakima, seeking injunctive and declaratory relief as well as damages. A temporary restraining order was issued.

Both parties moved for summary judgment prior to trial. In support of their motion, the plaintiffs offered affidavits stating that an ordinary person would mis-identify mixed breeds and that no scientific method can determine breed. Defendant City of Yakima offered affidavits showing the identifiability and vicious propensity of pit bulls and outlining the procedures required of the City to prove an animal comes under the ordinance. The trial judge granted defendant's motion for summary judgment. Plaintiffs assign error. The matter was certified to the Supreme Court. We accept certification and affirm.

I

Plaintiffs argue first that Yakima City Ordinance 3034, codified in Yakima City Code 6.18.010, *et seq.*, is unconstitutionally vague, claiming that a person of ordinary intelligence cannot reasonably tell what is prohibited. In *Seattle v. Huff*, 111 Wn. 923 (Wash. 1989), we reaffirmed that "[a]n ordinance is presumed constitutional and the party challenging the constitutionality of the law has the burden of proving it is unconstitutionally vague beyond a reasonable doubt." *Huff*, at 928. For the ordinance to be vague beyond a reasonable doubt, the plaintiff must show at least one of two procedural elements is missing: "adequate notice to citizens and adequate standards to prevent arbitrary enforcement." *Seattle v. Huff, supra* at 929. Adequate notice requires the law to be sufficiently definite so that a person of ordinary intelligence can reasonably tell what is prohibited. However, "[i]mpossible standards of specificity are not required." *Blondheim v. State*, 529 P.2d 1096 (Wash. 1975). Neither is absolute agreement. "'[I]f [persons] of ordinary intelligence can understand a penal statute, notwithstanding some possible areas of disagreement, it is not wanting in certainty.'" *Seattle v. Eze*, 759 P.2d 366 (Wash. 1988).

We find Yakima City Ordinance 3034 gives sufficient notice. The four breeds outlined in the ordinance are understood to refer to dogs satisfying detailed professional standards. Yakima animal control officers presently use these standards along with illustrations to identify dogs. This standard is stricter than a lay person would have to apply. Moreover, the ordinance has provisions to protect those who already own pit bulls and those who happen to travel through town with a pit bull. Other courts have held pit bull ordinances may give notice without painstaking definitions. *State v. Peters*, 534 So. 2d 760, 766 (Fla. Dist. Ct. App. 1988), where the ordinance was explicit, held that alternative definitions of pit bull did not violate notice requirements. *State v. Robinson*, 44 Ohio App. 3d 128 (1989), where the ordinance was not explicit, determined that "[a]lthough the statute lacks a specific definition of pit bull dog, mathematical certainty is not always essential." Likewise an unpublished Ohio Court of Appeals case upheld an ordinance without a definition of pit bull because the phrase "pit bull" has a discernible meaning.

Although *American Dog Owners Ass'n, Inc. v. Lynn*, 533 N.E.2d 642 (1989) found that statute "not sufficiently definite," *Lynn*, at 646, the definition there was "devoid of any reference to a particular breed." *Id.* The Yakima ordinance here names four particular breeds. We decline to follow *Lynn*.

A statute must have adequate standards to prevent arbitrary enforcement. This forbids "criminal statutes that contain no standards and allow police officers, judge, and jury to subjectively decide what conduct the statute proscribes . . . in any given case." But a statute is not necessarily unconstitutional because it requires subjective evaluations by an officer. The real question is whether it "invites an inordinate amount of police discretion."

We find adequate standards for identification in the professional standards and illustrations used by the City and in the burden of proof which rests on the City to show that a particular dog meets the professional standard and that no reason exists to impede the dog's destruction. Furthermore, as outlined by the assistant city attorney in her affidavit, the City is required to prove that the dog at the time of pickup was over 6 months old, known by the owner to be either a purebred or mixed breed of the four listed breeds and identifiable as one of those breeds. The Yakima ordinance is constitutional even though some inoffensive pit bulls might be banned. Over-breadth is only a problem when it "'. . . reaches a substantial amount of constitutionally protected conduct.'" *Huff*, at 925. Dogs are subject to police power and may be destroyed or regulated to protect citizens. Thus, "property in dogs is of an imperfect or qualified nature," *Sentell*, at 701, and "a harmless or inoffensive American Pit Bull Terrier may be banned in order to abate the threat . . . presented by other American Pit Bull Terriers." *Garcia v. Tijeras*, 767 P.2d 355, 363 (1988).

The Yakima ordinance is also constitutional although it will not stop all dog bites nor remove unidentifiable pit bull mixes. A municipality may "address threats in a piecemeal fashion," *Garcia*, 767 P.2d at 361, as long as there is a rational basis for the decision. The Yakima ordinance was enacted as a public safety measure after three unprovoked attacks by pit bulls.

Finally, the plaintiffs fail to show vagueness "beyond a reasonable doubt." *Huff*, at 928. In fact, the plaintiffs admit acquiring their pets believing them to be pit bulls, although they now aver they cannot identify the breed.

* * *

The trial court is affirmed.

Note

After being in effect for thirty-one years, the Yakima ordinance discussed in the preceding case was overturned in August 2018, according to local news reports. *See, e.g.,* http://www.yakimaherald.com/news/local/yakima-city-council-votes-to-end -pit-bull-ban/article_112a2a68-a5b6-11e8-aae2-1bd28ea79539.html.

Garcia v. The Village of Tijeras

Court of Appeals of New Mexico, 1988
108 N.M. 116, 767 P.2d 355

BIVINS, JUDGE. Plaintiffs appeal from a judgment upholding the constitutionality of an ordinance of the Village of Tijeras, New Mexico, banning the ownership or possession of a breed of dog "known as American Pit Bull Terrier." They challenge the ordinance on the grounds that it: (1) is void for vagueness; (2) violates substantive and procedural due process; and (3) provides for the taking of private property without just compensation. Plaintiffs do not question the authority of the Village to enact the ordinance. We affirm.

FACTS

The Village of Tijeras (Village) is a small, semi-rural community located within Bernalillo County with a population of approximately 312 residents. Eighteen of the eighty households within the Village possessed one or more pit bull dogs at the time the ordinance was enacted. For some time prior to enactment of the ordinance, Village residents had been repeatedly subjected to attacks on their persons and animals by pit bull dogs. Many of their animals were killed and several residents were injured in the attacks. Two months prior to enactment of the ordinance, a nine-year-old girl was severely mauled by pit bull dogs on her way home from school.

Following a series of town meetings for the purpose of discussing the problem presented by these dogs, the Village passed Ordinance No. 32 on May 14, 1984. Section Vl, Paragraph I of Ordinance No. 32 makes it unlawful:

> to own or possess in the Village any dog of the breed known as American Pit Bull Terrier. Any such dog may be impounded by the Mayor or Animal Control Officer to be destroyed as provided herein. It shall be held until a determination is made by a court of competent jurisdiction that the animal is an American Pit Bull Terrier and shall accordingly order that the dog be destroyed.

A month later, plaintiffs filed suit seeking declaratory judgment holding the Village ordinance unconstitutional. Plaintiffs Melvin L. Garcia, Raymond A. Sanchez, and David J. Wilson are residents of the Village and each is the owner of one or more American Pit Bull Terriers. Plaintiff Margaret H. Amacker is a resident of Bernalillo County and is the owner of four "domestic animals which may be classified as American Pit Bull Terriers." Amacker is also the president and registered agent for the Duke City Pit Bull Terrier Club, and travels frequently to the Village with her four animals.

After denying defendant's motion for summary judgment, the matter proceeded to trial. The trial court entered its findings of fact and conclusions of law upholding the ordinance. Judgment was entered in favor of the Village. This appeal follows.

DISCUSSION

. . . [A]ll legislative acts are presumed to be constitutional. . . . In reviewing the constitutionality of a statute or ordinance, we indulge in every presumption favoring validity of the enactment. This court is obliged to uphold the enactment unless it is satisfied beyond all reasonable doubt that it exceeds constitutional limitations. The party attacking a statute or ordinance has the burden of establishing its invalidity.

All of plaintiffs' arguments are based on asserted violations of their right to due process.

1. *Vagueness*

Plaintiffs first argue that the challenged ordinance fails to define the term "known as American Pit Bull Terrier" with sufficient specificity and is, therefore, void for vagueness. They contend the term is incapable of precise interpretation. Plaintiffs note that the term "American Pit Bull Terrier" is used only by the United Kennel Club, that the American Kennel Club uses the term "American Staffordshire Terrier" to register the same breed, that the American Kennel Club also registers the "Staffordshire Bull Terrier" and the "Bull Terrier," and that all of these breeds might be described as "pit bulls."

The trial court found that the American Pit Bull Terrier is a recognized breed of dog readily identifiable by laymen. We understand the trial court's finding to have been that the breed can be identified by persons who are not qualified to be dog show judges. Plaintiffs have challenged this finding as not supported by substantial evidence. They further argue that the breed varies so much in physical characteristics that it is difficult for the average person to ascertain, with certainty, whether a dog is in fact an American Pit Bull Terrier.

Plaintiffs also contend that owners of mixed-breed dogs, which might be to some percent pit bull, will have no idea whether the ordinance applies to them at all, because the ordinance lacks meaningful standards that could be used to identify those dogs subject to its prohibition. Plaintiffs note that a person might drive through the Village of Tijeras with a pit bull in his or her vehicle without any prior notice of the ordinance.

Under these circumstances, plaintiffs argue that the phrase "known as" is open to a number of interpretations. They contend that this phrase is independently vague. Plaintiffs have standing to challenge the ordinance, on vagueness grounds, only as it applies to them. One to whose conduct a statute clearly applies may not successfully challenge it for vagueness. *Parker v. Levy*, 417 U.S. 733 (1974).

There was testimony at trial that the term "pit bull" is the generic term for "American Staffordshire Terrier." There was also testimony at trial that there is no difference between the American Staffordshire Terrier and the American Pit Bull Terrier.

In addition, there was testimony that each breed of dog has a typical physical appearance termed as "phenotype," and that an unregistered dog can be identified as being of the breed "American Pit Bull Terrier" by its physical characteristics, or phenotype. Several witnesses testified that they could recognize an American Pit Bull Terrier by its physical characteristics.

We believe this evidence supports a determination that the breed American Pit Bull Terrier is a breed of dog recognized by its physical appearance. Given our obligation to indulge every presumption in favor of constitutionality, we interpret the term "known as" in light of the testimony at trial. Thus, we interpret the ordinance to include not only dogs that are registered, but also dogs that are recognizable, as American Pit Bull Terriers or American Staffordshire Terriers.

* * *

2. Rational Relation

Plaintiffs argue that the Village ordinance at issue violates substantive due process. In order to withstand scrutiny under the fifth and fourteenth amendments to the United States Constitution and similar provisions in our state Constitution, N.M. Const. art. II, §§ 4 & 18, a statute or ordinance must bear a rational relationship to a legitimate legislative goal or purpose.

That the Village had a legitimate purpose in enacting the ordinance—the protection of the health and safety of Village residents—is undisputed. However, plaintiffs contend that the ordinance is not rationally related to that purpose. We disagree. The trial court's findings were to the effect that American Pit Bull Terriers presented a special danger to the health and safety of Village residents. The evidence supports this determination.

As we have already stated, eighteen of the eighty households in the Village possessed pit bull dogs, a proportion approaching 25%. Village witnesses testified concerning a number of specific incidents involving pit bull attacks in the Village. The trial court found that there had been several serious attacks involving American Pit Bull Terriers.

* * *

As a complement to the testimony regarding specific incidents, the Village also presented evidence establishing that the American Pit Bull Terrier breed possesses inherent characteristics of aggression, strength, viciousness and unpredictability not found in any other breeds of dog. The testimony indicates that American Pit Bull Terriers are frequently selected by dogfighters specifically because of their extraordinary fighting temperament. In a fight or attack, they are very aggressive and the most tenacious dog of any breed. They continue their attack until they are separated or their victim is destroyed. Unlike other breeds of dog that "bite and slash" in an attack, pit bulls will "bite and hold," thereby inflicting significantly more damage upon their victim.

Testimony was also presented that pit bulls are especially dangerous due to their unpredictability. It is impossible to tell from looking at a pit bull whether it is aggressive or not. American Pit Bull Terriers have been known to be friendly and docile at one moment, willing to sit on your lap and lick your face, and at the next moment to attack in a frenzied rage. A pit bull in the grip of such a fighting frenzy will not respond to attempts to deter its attack. Such frenzies can occur at any time and for no apparent reason. There was testimony to the effect that such berserk frenzies do not occur in other breeds of dog. This behavior has been substantiated by a number of reports from owners of American Pit Bull Terriers. There was further evidence to show that, in proportion to their population, more dog-bite incidents are caused by American Pit Bull Terriers than by other breeds.

Other evidence tended to establish that the American Pit Bull Terrier is an exceptionally strong and athletic dog. Extraordinary measures are required for confining American Pit Bull Terriers, such as a six-foot chainlink fence with an overhanging ledge to keep the dogs from jumping out, and six-inch wide, one-foot deep concrete footings around the base to keep the dogs from digging under. They have exceptionally strong bites, possibly twice the strength of bites of other dogs. They can grip cyclone fencing and tear it from its mounting, and have been known to destroy sheet metal panels by ripping them apart with their teeth.

Testimony by a representative of the Animal Humane Association in Albuquerque established that the society takes in many stray dogs of every breed and mix-breed. Some have exhibited aggressive behavior towards other dogs, but none have ever caused the kinds of injuries or exhibited the aggressive behavior shown by American Pit Bull Terriers. The Albuquerque Animal Humane Association and other humane societies do not adopt out pit bull dogs because of their potential for attacks on other animals and people.

Plaintiffs produced contrary evidence to the effect that environment and training are more important than genetics in determining the behavior of a dog. Many breeders, including plaintiff Amacker, breed American Pit Bull Terriers for the show ring, where aggressiveness towards humans would disqualify them. Evidence was presented concerning the history of this breed of dog that indicated it was not bred for aggressiveness towards humans. Many owners of American Pit Bull Terriers report that they are loyal and gentle family pets. Evidence was presented to establish that other breeds of dog are responsible for more of the total number of bite incidents every year than are American Pit Bull Terriers.

Notwithstanding this evidence presented by plaintiffs, the evidence presented by the Village was extensive and was derived from credible sources. What is true of some American Pit Bull Terriers may well not be true of others. However, where evidence is conflicting, we defer to the fact finder and uphold the findings if supported by substantial evidence. Substantial evidence is relevant evidence that a reasonable mind might accept as adequate to support a conclusion. We believe the evidence amply supports the trial court's findings concerning the threat to the safety of the residents of the Village presented by American Pit Bull Terriers.

In light of the instances of personal injury and property damage in the Village attributable to American Pit Bull Terriers, of the unusual prevalence of dogs of this breed in the Village, and of the evidence presented concerning the inherent characteristics of aggression, strength, and unpredictability of this breed, we find the ordinance banning possession of American Pit Bull Terriers is reasonably related to protecting the health and safety of the residents of the Village. Thus, we hold that the Village ordinance does not violate substantive due process. . . .

The Village was entitled to combat the special threat it faced from pit bulls, and the Village's action was clearly rationally related to efforts to combat that threat. The trial court's carefully drafted decision was narrowly tailored to the unique situation presented; so is our holding affirming that decision.

Plaintiffs also contend that an ordinance banning only one breed of dog rather than all breeds, pure and mixed, bears no rational relationship to a legitimate governmental purpose. Although this argument was raised in the context of their due process claim, we view it as alleging a violation of equal protection. Even so, we find that the Village's classification, whereby owners of American Pit Bull Terriers are treated differently than owners of other breeds of dog, is not violative of either due process or equal protection. Where the challenged ordinance does not trammel fundamental rights or involve a suspect classification, the court presumes the constitutionality of the discriminatory classification.

* * *

3. Procedural Due Process

Plaintiffs argue that the ordinance violates due process in that it fails to provide owners of American Pit Bull Terriers notice and an opportunity to be heard prior to the destruction of their dogs. We disagree.

The ordinance on its face provides that a dog identified as an American Pit Bull Terrier "may be impounded . . . [and] held until a determination is made by a court of competent jurisdiction that the animal is an American Pit Bull Terrier. . . ." The plain language of the ordinance contemplates that a hearing will be held to determine whether a dog is an American Pit Bull Terrier prior to the destruction of the dog. That the ordinance does not expressly set out the procedures to be followed with respect to notice of the hearing and an owner's right to appear and be heard is not fatal.

It is well settled that if an act can be applied or interpreted so as to avoid constitutional conflict, such construction should be adopted by the court. Moreover, we indulge in every presumption favoring validity of the enactment. We therefore conclude that the express requirement of a judicial determination provided by the ordinance contemplates that such determination will comport with due process requirements, namely, that a hearing will be held before a court of competent jurisdiction and that the owner of the impounded animal will be provided notice of the hearing and an opportunity to appear before the court to present evidence and defenses to the action. Accordingly, the opportunity to be heard and present evidence would occur at a meaningful time, that is, prior to the destruction of the dog.[3]

---

3. Section III, paragraph B of the ordinance also provides that notice of impoundment and

We therefore reject plaintiffs' challenges under this point.

4. *Taking of Property Without Just Compensation*

Plaintiffs argue that the ordinance violates due process in that it allows the taking of private property without just compensation. This argument is likewise without merit. Plaintiffs correctly note that, in New Mexico, dogs are deemed personal property. *See* NMSA 1978, § 77-1-1. However, it is well established that property and property rights are held subject to the proper exercise of the police power. *Mitchell v. City of Roswell*, 111 P.2d 41 (N.M. 1941). "[A] reasonable regulation enacted for the benefit of the public health, convenience, safety or general welfare is not an unconstitutional taking of property in violation of . . . due process . . ." *Id.* at 44. The ordinance, being a proper exercise of the Village's police power, is not a deprivation of property without due process even though it allows for the destruction of private property.

Cases cited by plaintiffs for the proposition that the state may not order the destruction of private property absent extreme, imperative or overruling necessity do not support their claim. The United States Supreme Court in *Webb's Fabulous Pharmacies, Inc. v. Beckwith*, 449 U.S. 155 (1980), and *Sentell v. New Orleans & Carrollton R.R.*, 166 U.S. 698 (1897), recognized that there can be a deprivation of private property where justified as a legitimate exercise of the police power.

Even if it were assumed that dogs are property in the fullest sense of the word, they would still be subject to the police power of the State, and might be destroyed or otherwise dealt with, as in the judgment of the legislature is necessary for the protection of its citizens. A legislative enactment is justified as a legitimate exercise of the police power if it is reasonably necessary to preserve and protect the public health, safety, morals or welfare. We deem that test to be satisfied here. The extent of damages previously inflicted by American Pit Bull Terriers in the Village, coupled with the evidence of the animal's potential threat and unpredictability, furnish such necessity.

In the matter before us, the Village has legitimately exercised the police power to curtail a menace to the public health and safety. Plaintiffs cite to *Dennis* for the proposition that a legislative body may not, under the guise of the police power, impose restrictions that are unnecessary and unreasonable on the use or enjoyment of private property. In *Dennis*, an arson statute, which was drafted so broadly that it imposed criminal sanctions even on those who might burn structures for entirely legitimate and beneficial purposes, was determined to be an unreasonable exercise of the police power.

* * *

In the present case, evidence demonstrates that American Pit Bull Terriers present a special threat to Village residents, over and above any threat they might offer

---

procedures for redemption will be given to the owners in accordance with applicable Bernalillo County Ordinances, which the ordinance purports to incorporate by reference.

to the public in general. This evidence consisted of testimony establishing that there is a high percentage of pit bull dogs in relation to the population of the Village, and that Village residents had been repeatedly subjected to attacks on their persons and animals by American Pit Bull Terriers for some time prior to enactment of the ordinance. In light of this evidence, the Village could properly determine that an ordinance banning American Pit Bull Terriers was necessary for the protection of its citizens. That a harmless or inoffensive American Pit Bull Terrier may be banned in order to abate the threat to safety of the Village presented by other American Pit Bull Terriers does not render the ordinance invalid.

We also point out that the geographic scope of this ordinance is limited. Plaintiffs and other pit bull dog owners in the Village may remove their dogs from the Village. We also note that the Village notified everyone prior to enforcing the ordinance. Under these circumstances, a finding that a taking requiring compensation has occurred is much less compelling.

It is not entirely clear from the ordinance itself under what circumstances an impounded American Pit Bull Terrier would be destroyed. If the provisions for impounding vicious animals were to be incorporated by the reference to impounding as a procedure, the dog owner apparently would be permitted to redeem the animal. In this record, there is no claim that any dog has been destroyed or is threatened with destruction. We believe the question of whether the provision for destruction is a compensable taking is not ripe for judicial determination; therefore, we do not reach it.

Plaintiffs' last claim of error therefore is also rejected.

CONCLUSION

Under the facts of this case, we hold that Village of Tijeras Ordinance No. 32 is not violative of the United States or New Mexico Constitutions insofar as it prohibits the ownership or possession of American Pit Bull Terriers within the Village limits. The judgment of the district court is affirmed.

Notes

1. In most challenges to these types of BSL laws, the challengers have lost, with courts finding the ordinances complied with due process requirements, sufficiently described the type of dogs prohibited, and were immune from other constitutional challenges. In the rare situation where the ordinances were found invalid, there was an easy fix to correct the identified problems. Nevertheless, advocates continue to press the issues. *See, e.g., Frost v. City of Sioux City*, 2017 U.S. Dist. LEXIS 150955 (N.D. Iowa Sept. 18, 2017).

2. Vocal support for and against these laws is growing. Supporters view what are sometimes referred to as the "bully breeds" (e.g., American Staffordshire Terriers, American Pit Bull Terriers, and others) as inherently dangerous, given the repeated media reports of incidents involving these breeds, and the severity of the injuries.

They simply see BSL as an extension of laws that protect the public from unreasonably dangerous activities, or that outlaw other wild and potentially dangerous animals.

3. There is no question that local and state governments can regulate the animals allowed within a jurisdiction. BSL opponents state an ethical fairness argument, but legally they have very limited ability to challenge such an ordinance on constitutional grounds, assuming it is clearly written and well-constructed. The best defense to these laws may be education and lobbying to stop the sentiment that BSL is effective, to change the perception that the "bully breeds" are inherently dangerous, and to strike at the bigger issues causing the attacks.

For a compelling argument that BSL is a misplaced idea based on sensational media attention and does not solve the problems it seeks to correct, see Ann Schiavone, *Barking Up the Wrong Tree: Regulating Fear, Not Risk*, 22 ANIMAL L. 9 (2015).

Opponents of the laws point out that most incidents involving injuries by dogs are caused by irresponsible owners or intentional training of dogs to fight or attack, and that the most maligned breeds are not inherently dangerous or vicious. In fact, the real irony is that bully breeds were originally known for their kind and gentle nature, and their ability to get along well with children and families.

4. The targeting of pit bulls and their owner-guardians has at times gained significant legal ground. In *Tracey v. Solesky*, 427 Md. 627, 636 (2012), *abrogated by statute*, MD. CODE ANN., CTS. & JUD. PROC. § 3-1901, the Maryland Court of Appeals (the state's highest court) held that landlords were strictly liable for injuries inflicted by pit bulls who live on their properties: "Because of [their] aggressive and vicious nature and [their] capability to inflict serious and sometimes fatal injuries, pit bulls and cross-bred pit bulls are inherently dangerous." Animal advocates sought a legislative nullification of that ruling and obtained it with the above cited statute, which simply returned "the common law of liability relating to attacks by dogs against humans" to that in effect prior to the case, so that liability would be judged "without regard to the breed or heritage of the dog." MD. CODE ANN., CTS. & JUD. PROC. § 3-1901(b).

5. The City of Denver has had a long history with its ordinance banning "pit bulls." A challenge to section 8-55 of the Revised Municipal Code of the City and County of Denver ("Pit bulls Prohibited") was rejected in *Colorado Dog Fanciers v. City and County of Denver, Colorado*, 820 P.2d 644 (Colo. 1991), which addressed claims similar to those in the *American Dog Association* and *Garcia* cases—due process, equal protection and vagueness, and also a claim that that the ordinance constituted a violation of the Fifth Amendment to the U.S. Constitution as a government taking of private property. As to due process, the court found the ordinance did not violate procedural due process where the ordinance was not fundamentally unfair and the burden of proof upon the dog owner in the civil context was valid.

In 2004, the Colorado legislature enacted a law prohibiting local governments from adopting BSL. COLO. REV. STAT. ANN. § 18-9-204.5(5)(a) (Municipalities cannot enact any rule that "regulate[s] dangerous dogs in a manner that is specific to breed."). Since this directly conflicted with the Denver ordinance, Denver sued the state, seeking a ruling that its law was still valid. A Denver judge upheld the ordinance, concluding that the question of breed regulation of dogs was an issue of "home rule" reserved to Denver's authority. The State did not follow through on its appeal of this issue.

Since the State withdrew its appeal, it appeared that the State silently agreed with the lower court that home rule authority prevails on this issue. Alternatively, it simply may not have felt strongly enough about the state law to continue the litigation.

A further legal challenge to the Denver ban was brought in federal court in 2008. *Dias v. City and County of Denver*, 567 F.3d 1169 (10th Cir. 2009). Plaintiffs, who owned pit bulls, claimed the ordinance was vague and violated their substantive due process rights. The district court dismissed the case; on appeal, the Tenth Circuit held that plaintiffs had alleged sufficient facts to state a claim for substantive due process, and remanded the case for further proceedings. On June 27, 2012, plaintiff Sonya Dias announced that the case had settled without further judicial findings, leaving the Tenth Circuit's opinion in place, but effecting no change in the law.

6. BSL most often is based on the breed's supposed propensity for violence and injury. Over the past forty years similar ordinances have been adopted and then repealed for German Shepherds, Rottweilers and Doberman Pinschers. Litigation also has arisen regarding governmental bans on "wolfdogs," hybrid breeds between domestic dogs and wolves. *See, e.g., Michigan Wolfdog Ass'n, Inc. v. St. Clair County*, 122 F. Supp. 2d 794 (E.D. Mich. 2000).

7. Under what authority does a state or local government have the right to restrict the *number* of animals a person may have on their property? What kind of evidence is required for such a statute to pass constitutional muster?

8. Assuming the authority exists to restrict the type and number of animals on private property, does the authority apply to other property?

9. In *American Dog Owners Ass'n v. City of Lynn*, 533 N.E.2d 642 (Mass. 1989), plaintiffs challenged three ordinances restricting pit bull ownership. Like the two principal cases preceding these Notes, the appeal addressed the question of whether the ordinances violated due process because they were unconstitutionally vague. The City of Lynn admitted there was no objective standard to determine whether a dog was a "pit bull." Based largely on the absence of any readily-definable requirements, the regulation was found to be void because it was unconstitutionally vague and because of the lack of fairness it provided to dog owners. Are *City of Lynn* and *City of Yakima* distinguishable?

10. Because of their property status, governmental regulations regarding dogs are subject to legal property doctrines. For example, plaintiffs can sue government officials under 42 U.S.C. § 1983 for deprivation of property, where a government actor's conduct results in the loss, injury or killing of one or more dogs. For a detailed discussion of cases regarding the application of that statute, see Chapter 4, Section 1.C.

11. Particular dogs (as opposed to breeds) are also subject to the governmental regulation because of their property status if they act in socially unacceptable ways. Incidents involving dogs injuring people or other animals are often subject to state and/or local laws, colloquially referred to as "dangerous dog laws." The laws vary from jurisdiction to jurisdiction (often from town to town), but include certain basic constitutional protections for animal owners whose animals may be taken away or euthanized. In *Phillips v. San Luis Obispo County Dept. of Animal Regulation*, 183 Cal. App. 3d 372 (1986), the court reversed the trial court's ruling that a dog who had bitten humans on several occasions be put to death, so that, as stated by the appellate court, "Missy, a female black Labrador, [could] live, and 'go out in the midday sun.'" The City of San Luis Obispo had ordered her killed and the trial court had affirmed. Plaintiffs challenged the ruling based on a lack of due process. Because of the constitutional prohibition on the deprivation of property without notice and a pre- or post-seizure (as well as pre-destruction) hearing, and because Missy's owners had not been given the opportunity to be heard, the death sentence was vacated.

12. If notice and an opportunity to be heard are provided, can the government then kill a dog who has misbehaved? Are there alternatives to destruction that might be considered? Why is killing, as opposed to fines or other penalties, one of the punishments of choice? When a dog is killed under a constitutionally-sound ordinance, is the wrongdoer being punished?

13. In *Zuniga v. San Mateo Dept. of Health Services (Peninsula Humane Soc'y)*, 218 Cal. App. 3d 1521 (1990), plaintiff's dogs were seized based on allegations that plaintiff was involved in dogfighting activities. (Dogfighting is outlawed in all fifty states and at the federal level.) While the dogs were impounded, one of them had puppies. The animal control officers declared the puppies "inherently dangerous" based on the following:

(1) the parents of the puppies were fighting dogs; (2) county employees, including a veterinarian, testified that the puppies were observed to have "dangerous propensities including extremely aggressive behavior requiring the puppies to be housed separately so they would not injure each other"; and (3) appellant was a known dogfighter, with criminal dogfighting charges pending.

In addition, the hearing officer viewed video tapes of appellant at a dogfight and examined veterinary records indicating that the adult dogs seized from appellant's home had severe multiple lacerations.

Id. at 1531. The court found the hearing officers' determination invalid, in what could be seen as a response to BSL:

The evidence received by the hearing officer relates mainly to [*the alleged dogfighter's*] actions and his mistreatment of the parent animal. The only evidence relevant to the puppies' "inherent nature" was the observed aggressive behavior toward each other while caged together and certain possible assumptions about their nature from the condition and use of their mother. The latter assumptions can be given only minimal weight, as the subjects of heredity and genetics are generally matters calling for the consideration of expert opinion. There was no evidence to demonstrate whether female dogs who are trained to fight are likely to give birth to dangerous puppies. As a matter of common knowledge, we would agree that wild animals or poisonous reptiles may possess an inherent nature that makes them dangerous to the public safety if not properly confined. However, we find no evidence to support a finding that the essential character or inherent nature of these [then] six-month-old puppies confined in kennels constitutes a threat to the public safety.

Regarding the reported aggressive behavior, there is no indication that the puppies threatened human health and safety, as required under the ordinance definition. Nor was there evidence that the young puppies had ever harmed each other or engaged in unprovoked attacks on humans or other animals. The governing ordinance does not make aggressive behavior among caged puppies the criteria for a finding of dangerousness. Moreover, the unspecified aggressive behavior observed by the county staff fails to support a finding of an *inherently* dangerous nature, because in the absence of testimony regarding the cause of such behavior, it could be easily attributed to a number of factors including the fact of being caged.

Commentators have noted that a dog's propensity to bite results from a combination of many factors, including a genetic predisposition towards aggression, lack of early socialization with people, specific training to fight, the quality of care provided by the owner, and the behavior of the victim. (Lockwood, Vicious-Dog Legislation-Controlling the Pit Bull, 13 Univ. Dayton L. Rev. 267, 270, citing a 1987 study.) "Thus a dog whose genetic predisposition is to be aggressive may present little or no danger if the dog is well-trained and reasonably supervised, whereas an animal with little innate tendency to bite may become dangerous if improperly trained, socialized, supervised, treated, or provoked." (*Ibid.;* Note, The New Breed of Municipal Dog Control Laws: Are They Constitutional? (1984) 53 Cinn.L.Rev. 1067, 1077 [citing a survey showing that "pit bull" type dogs are not uniquely dangerous].)

There was no evidence presented at the hearing regarding the proposed future disposition of the puppies which would support a finding that any factors indicating a danger to the public would result. Absent expert evidence on the cause and nature of the puppies' perceived aggressive behavior which might fulfill the ordinance requirement of "inherent nature," or any indication of how the nature of the puppies adversely impacts public health or safety, the hearing officer's conclusion regarding an inherently dangerous nature is singularly speculative.

It is somewhat ironic that respondent, who controlled all but one of the above factors having some impact on the maturing puppies' nature, now seeks to declare them dangerous. A more realistic assumption is that in order to discount its own contribution to the lack of socialization and training of the caged puppies, respondent, of necessity, must advance the theoretical argument that these puppies were congenitally "dangerous animals," a proposition for which no competent evidence was offered or received. Thus, we are compelled to agree with appellant that the finding of dangerousness is not supported by the evidence in the record.

Id. at 1532–33. The dog owner had been barred, as part of his criminal probation, from regaining possession of the puppies. He was entitled, however, to assign his interest in the dogs (because they were personal property) to his attorney. He made the transfer and, therefore, the Humane Society was required to turn them over to her.

Section 3. First Amendment

A. Free Exercise of Religion

Church of the Lukumi Babalu Aye v. City of Hialeah

Supreme Court of the United States, 1993
508 U.S. 520, 113 S. Ct. 2217

JUSTICE KENNEDY delivered the opinion of the Court, except as to Part II-A-2.*

The principle that government may not enact laws that suppress religious belief or practice is so well understood that few violations are recorded in our opinions. . . .

Our review confirms that the laws in question were enacted by officials who did not understand, failed to perceive, or chose to ignore the fact that their official actions violated the Nation's essential commitment to religious freedom. The challenged laws had an impermissible object; and in all events the principle of general applicability was violated because the secular ends asserted in defense of the laws were pursued only with respect to conduct motivated by religious beliefs. We invalidate the challenged enactments and reverse the judgment of the Court of Appeals.

I. A.

This case involves practices of the Santeria religion, which originated in the 19th century. When hundreds of thousands of members of the Yoruba people were brought as slaves from western Africa to Cuba, their traditional African religion absorbed significant elements of Roman Catholicism. The resulting syncretion, or

---

* The Chief Justice, Justice Scalia, and Justice Thomas join all but Part II-A-2 of this opinion. Justice White joins all but Part II-A of this opinion. Justice Souter joins only Parts I, III, and IV of this opinion.

fusion, is Santeria, "the way of the saints." The Cuban Yoruba express their devotion to spirits, called orishas, through the iconography of Catholic saints, Catholic symbols are often present at Santeria rites, and Santeria devotees attend the Catholic sacraments.

The Santeria faith teaches that every individual has a destiny from God, a destiny fulfilled with the aid and energy of the orishas. The basis of the Santeria religion is the nurture of a personal relation with the orishas, and one of the principal forms of devotion is an animal sacrifice. The sacrifice of animals as part of religious rituals has ancient roots. Animal sacrifice is mentioned throughout the Old Testament, and it played an important role in the practice of Judaism before destruction of the second Temple in Jerusalem. In modern Islam, there is an annual sacrifice commemorating Abraham's sacrifice of a ram in the stead of his son.

According to Santeria teaching, the orishas are powerful but not immortal. They depend for survival on the sacrifice. Sacrifices are performed at birth, marriage, and death rites, for the cure of the sick, for the initiation of new members and priests, and during an annual celebration. Animals sacrificed in Santeria rituals include chickens, pigeons, doves, ducks, guinea pigs, goats, sheep, and turtles. The animals are killed by the cutting of the carotid arteries in the neck. The sacrificed animal is cooked and eaten, except after healing and death rituals.

Santeria adherents faced widespread persecution in Cuba, so the religion and its rituals were practiced in secret. The open practice of Santeria and its rites remains infrequent. The religion was brought to this Nation most often by exiles from the Cuban revolution. The District Court estimated that there are at least 50,000 practitioners in South Florida today. *See* 723 F. Supp. at 1470.

B.

Petitioner Church of the Lukumi Babalu Aye, Inc. (Church), is a not-for-profit corporation organized under Florida law in 1973. The Church and its congregants practice the Santeria religion. The president of the Church is petitioner Ernesto Pichardo, who is also the Church's priest and holds the religious title of Italero, the second highest in the Santeria faith. In April 1987, the Church leased land in the city of Hialeah, Florida, and announced plans to establish a house of worship as well as a school, cultural center, and museum. Pichardo indicated that the Church's goal was to bring the practice of the Santeria faith, including its ritual of animal sacrifice, into the open. The Church began the process of obtaining utility service and receiving the necessary licensing, inspection, and zoning approvals. Although the Church's efforts at obtaining the necessary licenses and permits were far from smooth, it appears that it received all needed approvals by early August 1987.

The prospect of a Santeria church in their midst was distressing to many members of the Hialeah community, and the announcement of the plans to open a Santeria church in Hialeah prompted the city council to hold an emergency public session on June 9, 1987. The resolutions and ordinances passed at that and later meetings are set forth in the Appendix following this opinion.

A summary suffices here, beginning with the enactments passed at the June 9 meeting. First, the city council adopted Resolution 87-66, which noted the "concern" expressed by residents of the city "that certain religions may propose to engage in practices which are inconsistent with public morals, peace or safety," and declared that "the City reiterates its commitment to a prohibition against any and all acts of any and all religious groups which are inconsistent with public morals, peace or safety." Next, the council approved an emergency ordinance, Ordinance 87-40, which incorporated in full, except as to penalty, Florida's animal cruelty laws. Fla. Stat. ch. 828 (1987). Among other things, the incorporated state law subjected to criminal punishment "whoever . . . unnecessarily or cruelly . . . kills any animal." § 828.12.

The city council desired to undertake further legislative action, but Florida law prohibited a municipality from enacting legislation relating to animal cruelty that conflicted with state law. § 828.27(4). To obtain clarification, Hialeah's city attorney requested an opinion from the attorney general of Florida as to whether § 828.12 prohibited "a religious group from sacrificing an animal in a religious ritual or practice" and whether the city could enact ordinances "making religious animal sacrifice unlawful." The attorney general responded in mid-July. He concluded that the "ritual sacrifice of animals for purposes other than food consumption" was not a "necessary" killing and so was prohibited by § 828.12. Fla. Op. Atty. Gen. 87-56, Annual Report of the Atty. Gen. 146, 147, 149 (1988). The attorney general appeared to define "unnecessary" as "done without any useful motive, in a spirit of wanton cruelty or for the mere pleasure of destruction without being in any sense beneficial or useful to the person killing the animal." *Id.* at 149, n.11. He advised that religious animal sacrifice was against state law, so that a city ordinance prohibiting it would not be in conflict.

The city council responded at first with a hortatory enactment, Resolution 87-90, that noted its residents' "great concern regarding the possibility of public ritualistic animal sacrifices" and the state-law prohibition. The resolution declared the city policy "to oppose the ritual sacrifices of animals" within Hialeah and announced that any person or organization practicing animal sacrifice "will be prosecuted."

In September 1987, the city council adopted three substantive ordinances addressing the issue of religious animal sacrifice. Ordinance 87-52 defined "sacrifice" as "to unnecessarily kill, torment, torture, or mutilate an animal in a public or private ritual or ceremony not for the primary purpose of food consumption," and prohibited owning or possessing an animal "intending to use such animal for food purposes." It restricted application of this prohibition, however, to any individual or group that "kills, slaughters or sacrifices animals for any type of ritual, regardless of whether or not the flesh or blood of the animal is to be consumed." The ordinance contained an exemption for slaughtering by "licensed establishment[s]" of animals specifically raised for food purposes." Declaring, moreover, that the city council "has determined that the sacrificing of animals within the city limits is contrary to the public health, safety, welfare and morals of the community," the city council adopted Ordinance 87-71. That ordinance defined "sacrifice" as had Ordinance 87-52, and then provided that "it shall be unlawful for any person, persons, corporations or associations to sacrifice any animal within the corporate limits of the City of Hialeah, Florida." The final Ordinance, 87-72, defined "slaughter" as "the killing of animals for food" and prohibited slaughter outside of areas zoned for slaughterhouse use. The ordinance provided an exemption, however, for the slaughter or processing for sale of "small numbers of hogs and/or cattle per week in accordance with an exemption provided by state law." All ordinances and resolutions passed the city council by unanimous vote. Violations of each of the four ordinances were punishable by fines not exceeding $500 or imprisonment not exceeding 60 days, or both.

Following enactment of these ordinances, the Church and Pichardo filed this action pursuant to 42 U.S.C. §1983 in the United States District Court for the Southern District of Florida. Named as defendants were the city of Hialeah and its mayor and members of its city council in their individual capacities. Alleging violations of petitioners' rights under, inter alia, the Free Exercise Clause, the complaint sought a declaratory judgment and injunctive and monetary relief. The District Court granted summary judgment to the individual defendants, finding that they had absolute immunity for their legislative acts and that the ordinances and resolutions adopted by the council did not constitute an official policy of harassment, as alleged by petitioners. 688 F. Supp. 1522 (S.D. Fla. 1988).

After a 9-day bench trial on the remaining claims, the District Court ruled for the city, finding no violation of petitioners' rights under the Free Exercise Clause. 723 F. Supp. 1467 (S.D. Fla. 1989).

The Court of Appeals for the Eleventh Circuit affirmed in a one-paragraph per curiam opinion. *Judgt. order reported* at 936 F.2d 586 (1991). Choosing not to rely on the District Court's recitation of a compelling interest in promoting the welfare of children, the Court of Appeals stated simply that it concluded the ordinances were consistent with the Constitution.... It declined to address the effect of *Employment Div., Dept. of Human Resources of Ore. v. Smith*, 494 U.S. 872 (1990), decided after the District Court's opinion, because the District Court "employed an arguably stricter standard" than that applied in *Smith*....

II.

The Free Exercise Clause of the First Amendment, which has been applied to the States through the Fourteenth Amendment, provides that "Congress shall make no law respecting an establishment of religion, or *prohibiting the free exercise thereof....*" (Emphasis added.) The city does not argue that Santeria is not a "religion" within the meaning of the First Amendment. Nor could it. Although the practice of animal sacrifice may seem abhorrent to some, "religious beliefs need not be acceptable, logical, consistent, or comprehensible to others in order to merit First Amendment protection." *Thomas v. Review Bd. of Indiana Employment Security Div.*, 450 U.S. 707, 714 (1981). Given the historical association between animal sacrifice and religious worship, petitioners' assertion that animal sacrifice is an integral part of their religion "cannot be deemed bizarre or incredible." *Frazee v. Illinois Dept. of Employment Security*, 489 U.S. 829, 834, n.2 (1989). Neither the city nor the courts below, moreover, have questioned the sincerity of petitioners' professed desire to conduct animal sacrifices for religious reasons. We must consider petitioners' First Amendment claim.

In addressing the constitutional protection for free exercise of religion, our cases establish the general proposition that a law that is neutral and of general applicability need not be justified by a compelling governmental interest even if the law has the incidental effect of burdening a particular religious practice. Neutrality and general applicability are interrelated, and, as becomes apparent in this case, failure to satisfy one requirement is a likely indication that the other has not been satisfied. A law failing to satisfy these requirements must be justified by a compelling governmental interest and must be narrowly tailored to advance that interest. These ordinances fail to satisfy the *Smith* requirements. We begin by discussing neutrality.

A.

In our Establishment Clause cases we have often stated the principle that the First Amendment forbids an official purpose to disapprove of a particular religion or of religion in general. These cases, however, for the most part have addressed governmental efforts to benefit religion or particular religions, and so have dealt with a question different, at least in its formulation and emphasis, from the issue here. Petitioners allege an attempt to disfavor their religion because of the religious ceremonies it commands, and the Free Exercise Clause is dispositive in our analysis.

At a minimum, the protections of the Free Exercise Clause pertain if the law at issue discriminates against some or all religious beliefs or regulates or prohibits conduct because it is undertaken for religious reasons. Indeed, it was "historical instances of religious persecution and intolerance that gave concern to those who drafted the Free Exercise Clause." *Bowen v. Roy*, 476 U.S. 693, 703 (1986) (opinion of Burger, C. J.). These principles, though not often at issue in our Free Exercise Clause cases, have played a role in some. In *McDaniel v. Paty*, 435 U.S. 618 (1978), for example, we invalidated a state law that disqualified members of the clergy from holding certain public offices, because it "impose[d] special disabilities on the basis of . . . religious status," *Employment Div., Dept. of Human Resources of Ore. v. Smith*, 494 U.S. at 877. On the same principle, in *Fowler v. Rhode Island*, 345 U.S. 67 (1953), we found that a municipal ordinance was applied in an unconstitutional manner when interpreted to prohibit preaching in a public park by a Jehovah's Witness but to permit preaching during the course of a Catholic mass or Protestant church service.

1.

Although a law targeting religious beliefs as such is never permissible, if the object of a law is to infringe upon or restrict practices because of their religious motivation, the law is not neutral; and it is invalid unless it is justified by a compelling interest and is narrowly tailored to advance that interest. There are, of course, many ways of demonstrating that the object or purpose of a law is the suppression of religion or religious conduct. To determine the object of a law, we must begin with its text, for the minimum requirement of neutrality is that a law not discriminate on its face. A law lacks facial neutrality if it refers to a religious practice without a secular meaning discernible from the language or context. Petitioners contend that three of the ordinances fail this test of facial neutrality because they use the words "sacrifice" and "ritual," words with strong religious connotations. We agree that these words are consistent with the claim of facial discrimination, but the argument is not conclusive. The words "sacrifice" and "ritual" have a religious origin, but current use admits also of secular meanings. *See* Webster's Third New International Dictionary 1961, 1996 (1971). *See also* 12 Encyclopedia of Religion 556 ("The word sacrifice ultimately became very much a secular term in common usage"). The ordinances, furthermore, define "sacrifice" in secular terms, without referring to religious practices. We reject the contention advanced by the city that our inquiry must end with the text of the laws at issue. Facial neutrality is not determinative. The Free Exercise Clause, like the Establishment Clause, extends beyond facial discrimination. The Clause "forbids subtle departures from neutrality," *Gillette v. United States*, 401 U.S. 437, 452 (1971), and "covert suppression of particular religious beliefs," *Bowen v. Roy, supra*, at 703 (opinion of Burger, C.J.). Official action that targets religious conduct for distinctive treatment cannot be shielded by mere compliance with the requirement of facial neutrality. The Free Exercise Clause protects against governmental hostility which is masked as well as overt. "The Court must survey meticulously the circumstances of governmental categories to eliminate, as it were, religious gerrymanders."

The record in this case compels the conclusion that suppression of the central element of the Santeria worship service was the object of the ordinances. First, though use of the words "sacrifice" and "ritual" does not compel a finding of improper targeting of the Santeria religion, the choice of these words is support for our conclusion. There are further respects in which the text of the city council's enactments discloses the improper attempt to target Santeria. Resolution 87-66, adopted June 9, 1987, recited that "residents and citizens of the City of Hialeah have expressed their concern that certain religions may propose to engage in practices which are inconsistent with public morals, peace or safety," and "reiterate[d]" the city's commitment to prohibit "any and all [such] acts of any and religious groups." No one suggests, and on this record it cannot be maintained, that city officials had in mind a religion other than Santeria. It becomes evident that these ordinances target Santeria sacrifice when the ordinances' operation is considered. Apart from the text, the effect of a law in its real operation is strong evidence of its object. To be sure, adverse impact will not always lead to a finding of impermissible targeting. For example, a social harm may have been a legitimate concern of government for reasons quite apart from discrimination. The subject at hand does implicate, of course, multiple concerns unrelated to religious animosity, for example, the suffering or mistreatment visited upon the sacrificed animals and health hazards from improper disposal. But the ordinances when considered together disclose an object remote from these legitimate concerns. The design of these laws accomplishes instead a "religious gerrymander," *Walz v. Tax Comm'n of New York City, supra*, at 696 (Harlan, J., concurring), an impermissible attempt to target petitioners and their religious practices.

It is a necessary conclusion that almost the only conduct subject to Ordinances 87-40, 87-52, and 87-71 is the religious exercise of Santeria church members. The texts show that they were drafted in tandem to achieve this result. We begin with Ordinance 87-71. It prohibits the sacrifice of animals, but defines sacrifice as "to unnecessarily kill . . . an animal in a public or private ritual or ceremony not for the primary purpose of food consumption." The definition excludes almost all killings of animals except for religious sacrifice, and the primary purpose requirement narrows the proscribed category even further, in particular by exempting kosher slaughter, *see* 723 F. Supp. at 1480. We need not discuss whether this differential treatment of two religions is itself an independent constitutional violation. It suffices to recite this feature of the law as support for our conclusion that Santeria alone was the exclusive legislative concern. The net result of the gerrymander is that few if any killings of animals are prohibited other than Santeria sacrifice, which is proscribed because it occurs during a ritual or ceremony and its primary purpose is to make an offering to the orishas, not food consumption. Indeed, careful drafting ensured that, although Santeria sacrifice is prohibited, killings that are no more necessary or humane in almost all other circumstances are unpunished. Operating in similar fashion is Ordinance 87-52, which prohibits the "possession, sacrifice, or slaughter" of an animal with the "intent to use such animal for food purposes." This prohibition, extending to the keeping of an animal as well as the killing itself, applies if the animal is killed in "any type of ritual" and there is an intent to use the animal for food, whether or not it is in fact consumed for food. The ordinance exempts, however, "any licensed [food] establishment" with regard to "any animals which are specifically raised for food purposes," if the activity is permitted by zoning and other laws. This exception, too, seems intended to cover kosher slaughter. Again, the burden of the ordinance, in practical terms, falls on Santeria adherents but almost no others: If the killing is—unlike most Santeria sacrifices— unaccompanied by the intent to use the animal for food, then it is not prohibited by Ordinance 87-52; if the killing is specifically for food but does not occur during the course of "any type of ritual," it again falls outside the prohibition; and if the killing is for food and occurs during the course of a ritual, it is still exempted if it occurs in a properly zoned and licensed establishment and involves animals "specifically raised for food purposes." A pattern of exemptions parallels the pattern of narrow prohibitions. Each contributes to the gerrymander.

Ordinance 87-40 incorporates the Florida animal cruelty statute, Fla. Stat. § 828.12 (1987). Its prohibition is broad on its face, punishing "whoever . . . unnecessarily . . . kills any animal." The city claims that this ordinance is the epitome of a neutral prohibition. The problem, however, is the interpretation given to the ordinance by respondent and the Florida attorney general. Killings for religious reasons are deemed unnecessary, whereas most other killings fall outside the prohibition. The city, on what seems to be a *per se* basis, deems hunting, slaughter of animals for food, eradication of insects and pests, and euthanasia as necessary. *See id.* at 22. There is no indication in the record that respondent has concluded that hunting or fishing for sport is unnecessary. Indeed, one of the few reported Florida cases decided under §828.12 concludes that the use of live rabbits to train greyhounds is not unnecessary. *See Kiper v. State*, 310 So. 2d 42 (Fla. App.), *cert. denied*, 328 So. 2d 845 (Fla. 1975). Further, because it requires an evaluation of the particular justification for the killing, this ordinance represents a system of "individualized governmental assessment of the reasons for the relevant conduct," *Employment Div., Dept. of Human Resources of Ore. v. Smith*, 494 U.S. at 884. As we noted in *Smith*, in circumstances in which individualized exemptions from a general requirement are available, the government "may not refuse to extend that system to cases of 'religious hardship' without compelling reason." *Id., quoting Bowen v. Roy*, 476 U.S. at 708 (opinion of Burger, C. J.). Respondent's application of the ordinance's test of necessity devalues religious reasons for killing by judging them to be of lesser import than nonreligious reasons. Thus, religious practice is being singled out for discriminatory treatment.

We also find significant evidence of the ordinances' improper targeting of Santeria sacrifice in the fact that they proscribe more religious conduct than is necessary to achieve their stated ends. It is not unreasonable to infer, at least when there are no persuasive indications to the contrary, that a law which visits "gratuitous restrictions" on religious conduct, *McGowan v. Maryland*, 366 U.S. at 520 (opinion of Frankfurter, J.), seeks not to effectuate the stated governmental interests, but to suppress the conduct because of its religious motivation.

The legitimate governmental interests in protecting the public health and preventing cruelty to animals could be addressed by restrictions stopping far short of a flat prohibition of all Santeria sacrificial practice.[10] If improper disposal, not the sacrifice itself, is the harm to be prevented, the city could have imposed a general regulation on the disposal of organic garbage. It did not do so. Indeed, counsel for the city conceded at oral argument that, under the ordinances, Santeria sacrifices would be illegal even if they occurred in licensed, inspected, and zoned slaughterhouses. Thus, these broad ordinances prohibit Santeria sacrifice even when it does not threaten the city's public health. The District Court accepted the argument that narrower regulation would be unenforceable because of the secrecy in the Santeria

---

10. Respondent advances the additional governmental interest in prohibiting the slaughter or sacrifice of animals in areas of the city not zoned for slaughterhouses and the District Court found this interest to be compelling, *see* 723 F. Supp. 1467, 1486 (S.D. Fla. 1989). This interest cannot justify Ordinances 87-40, 87-52, and 87-71, for they apply to conduct without regard to where it occurs. Ordinance 87-72 does impose a locational restriction, but this asserted governmental interest is a mere restatement of the prohibition itself, not a justification for it. In our discussion, therefore, we put aside this asserted interest.

rituals and the lack of any central religious authority to require compliance with secular disposal regulations. It is difficult to understand, however, how a prohibition of the sacrifices themselves, which occur in private, is enforceable if a ban on improper disposal, which occurs in public, is not. The neutrality of a law is suspect if First Amendment freedoms are curtailed to prevent isolated collateral harms not themselves prohibited by direct regulation.

Under similar analysis, narrower regulation would achieve the city's interest in preventing cruelty to animals. With regard to the city's interest in ensuring the adequate care of animals, regulation of conditions and treatment, regardless of why an animal is kept, is the logical response to the city's concern, not a prohibition on possession for the purpose of sacrifice. The same is true for the city's interest in prohibiting cruel methods of killing. Under federal and Florida law and Ordinance 87-40, which incorporates Florida law in this regard, killing an animal by the "simultaneous and instantaneous severance of the carotid arteries with a sharp instrument"—the method used in kosher slaughter—is approved as humane. *See* 7 U.S.C. § 1902(b); Fla. Stat. § 828.23(7)(b) (1991); Ordinance 87-40, § 1. The District Court found that, though Santeria sacrifice also results in severance of the carotid arteries, the method used during sacrifice is less reliable and therefore not humane. If the city has a real concern that other methods are less humane, however, the subject of the regulation should be the method of slaughter itself, not a religious classification that is said to bear some general relation to it.

Ordinance 87-72—unlike the three other ordinances—does appear to apply to substantial nonreligious conduct and not to be overbroad. For our purposes here, however, the four substantive ordinances may be treated as a group for neutrality purposes. Ordinance 87-72 was passed the same day as Ordinance 87-71 and was enacted, as were the three others, in direct response to the opening of the Church. It would be implausible to suggest that the three other ordinances, but not Ordinance 87-72, had as their object the suppression of religion. We need not decide whether Ordinance 87-72 could survive constitutional scrutiny if it existed separately; it must be invalidated because it functions, with the rest of the enactments in question, to suppress Santeria religious worship.

2.

In determining if the object of a law is a neutral one under the Free Exercise Clause, we can also find guidance in our equal protection cases. As Justice Harlan noted in the related context of the Establishment Clause, "neutrality in its application requires an equal protection mode of analysis." *Walz v. Tax Comm'n of New York City*, 397 U.S. at 696 (concurring opinion). Here, as in equal protection cases, we may determine the city council's object from both direct and circumstantial evidence. Relevant evidence includes, among other things, the historical background of the decision under challenge, the specific series of events leading to the enactment or official policy in question, and the legislative or administrative history, including contemporaneous statements made by members of the decisionmaking body. These objective factors bear on the question of discriminatory object. That the ordinances were enacted "'because of,' not merely 'in spite of,'" their suppression of Santeria religious practice is revealed by the events preceding their enactment. Although respondent claimed at oral argument that it had experienced significant problems resulting from the sacrifice of animals within the city before the announced opening of the Church, Tr. of Oral Arg. 27, 46, the city council made no attempt to address the supposed problem before its meeting in June 1987, just weeks after the Church announced plans to open. The minutes and taped excerpts of the June 9 session, both of which are in the record, evidence significant hostility exhibited by residents, members of the city council, and other city officials toward the Santeria religion and its practice of animal sacrifice. The public crowd that attended the June 9 meetings interrupted statements by council members critical of Santeria with cheers and the brief comments of Pichardo with taunts. When Councilman Martinez, a supporter of the ordinances, stated that in prerevolution Cuba "people were put in jail for practicing this religion," the audience applauded. Other statements by members of the city council were in a similar vein. For example, Councilman Martinez, after noting his belief that Santeria was outlawed in Cuba, questioned: "If we could not practice this [religion] in our home-land [Cuba], why bring it to this country?" Councilman Cardoso said that Santeria devotees at the Church "are in violation of everything this country stands for." Councilman Mejides indicated that he was "totally against the sacrificing of animals" and distinguished kosher slaughter because it had a "real purpose." The "Bible says we are allowed to sacrifice an animal for consumption," he continued, "but for any other purposes, I don't believe that the Bible allows that." The president of the city council, Councilman Echevarria, asked: "What can we do to prevent the Church from opening?"

Various Hialeah city officials made comparable comments. The chaplain of the Hialeah Police Department told the city council that Santeria was a sin, "foolishness," "an abomination to the Lord," and the worship of "demons." He advised the city council: "We need to be helping people and sharing with them the truth that is found in Jesus Christ." He concluded: "I would exhort you . . . not to permit this Church to exist." The city attorney commented that Resolution 87-66 indicated: "This community will not tolerate religious practices which are abhorrent to its citizens. . . ." *Id.* Similar comments were made by the deputy city attorney. This history discloses the object of the ordinances to target animal sacrifice by Santeria worshippers because of its religious motivation.

3.

In sum, the neutrality inquiry leads to one conclusion: The ordinances had as their object the suppression of religion. The pattern we have recited discloses animosity to Santeria adherents and their religious practices; the ordinances by their own terms target this religious exercise; the texts of the ordinances were gerrymandered with care to proscribe religious killings of animals but to exclude almost all secular killings; and the ordinances suppress much more religious conduct than is necessary in order to achieve the legitimate ends asserted in their defense. These ordinances are not neutral, and the court below committed clear error in failing to reach this conclusion.

B.

We turn next to a second requirement of the Free Exercise Clause, the rule that laws burdening religious practice must be of general applicability. All laws are selective to some extent, but categories of selection are of paramount concern when a law has the incidental effect of burdening religious practice. The Free Exercise Clause "protect[s] religious observers against unequal treatment, and inequality results when a legislature decides that the governmental interests it seeks to advance are worthy of being pursued only against conduct with a religious motivation."

The principle that government, in pursuit of legitimate interests, cannot in a selective manner impose burdens only on conduct motivated by religious belief is essential to the protection of the rights guaranteed by the Free Exercise Clause. The principle underlying the general applicability requirement has parallels in our First Amendment jurisprudence. In this case we need not define with precision the standard used to evaluate whether a prohibition is of general application, for these ordinances fall well below the minimum standard necessary to protect First Amendment rights.

Respondent claims that Ordinances 87-40, 87-52, and 87-71 advance two interests: protecting the public health and preventing cruelty to animals. The ordinances are underinclusive for those ends. They fail to prohibit nonreligious conduct that endangers these interests in a similar or greater degree than Santeria sacrifice does. The underinclusion is substantial, not inconsequential. Despite the city's proffered interest in preventing cruelty to animals, the ordinances are drafted with care to forbid few killings but those occasioned by religious sacrifice. Many types of animal deaths or kills for nonreligious reasons are either not prohibited or approved by express provision. For example, fishing—which occurs in Hialeah—is legal. Extermination of mice and rats within a home is also permitted. Florida law incorporated by Ordinance 87-40 sanctions euthanasia of "stray, neglected, abandoned, or unwanted animals," Fla. Stat. § 828.058 (1987); destruction of animals judicially removed from their owners "for humanitarian reasons" or when the animal "is of no commercial value," § 828.073(4)(c)(2); the infliction of pain or suffering "in the interest of medical science," § 828.02; the placing of poison in one's yard or enclosure, § 828.08; and the use of a live animal "to pursue or take wildlife or to participate in any hunting," § 828.122(6)(b), and "to hunt wild hogs," § 828.122(6)(e).

The city concedes that "neither the State of Florida nor the City has enacted a generally applicable ban on the killing of animals." Brief for Respondent 21. It asserts, however, that animal sacrifice is "different" from the animal killings that are permitted by law. *Id.* According to the city, it is "self-evident" that killing animals for food is "important"; the eradication of insects and pests is "obviously justified"; and the euthanasia of excess animals "makes sense." *Id.* at 22. These ipse dixits do not explain why religion alone must bear the burden of the ordinances, when many of these secular killings fall within the city's interest in preventing the cruel treatment of animals. The ordinances are also underinclusive with regard to the city's interest in public health, which is threatened by the disposal of animal carcasses in open public places and the consumption of uninspected meat. Neither interest is pursued by respondent with regard to conduct that is not motivated by religious conviction. The health risks posed by the improper disposal of animal carcasses are the same whether Santeria sacrifice or some nonreligious killing preceded it. The city does not, however, prohibit hunters from bringing their kill to their houses, nor does it regulate disposal after their activity. Despite substantial testimony at trial that the same public health hazards result from improper disposal of garbage by restaurants, restaurants are outside the scope of the ordinances. Improper disposal is a general problem that causes substantial health risks but which respondent addresses only when it results from religious exercise.

The ordinances are underinclusive as well with regard to the health risk posed by consumption of uninspected meat. Under the city's ordinances, hunters may eat their kill and fishermen may eat their catch without undergoing governmental inspection. Likewise, state law requires inspection of meat that is sold but exempts meat from animals raised for the use of the owner and "members of his household and nonpaying guests and employees." Fla. Stat. § 585.88(1)(a) (1991). The asserted interest in inspected meat is not pursued in contexts similar to that of religious animal sacrifice.

Ordinance 87-72, which prohibits the slaughter of animals outside of areas zoned for slaughterhouses, is underinclusive on its face. The ordinance includes an exemption for "any person, group, or organization" that "slaughters or processes for sale, small numbers of hogs and/or cattle per week in accordance with an exemption provided by state law." *See* Fla. Stat. § 828.24(3) (1991). Respondent has not explained why commercial operations that slaughter "small numbers" of hogs and cattle do not implicate its professed desire to prevent cruelty to animals and preserve the public health. Although the city has classified Santeria sacrifice as slaughter, subjecting it to this ordinance, it does not regulate other killings for food in like manner.

We conclude, in sum, that each of Hialeah's ordinances pursues the city's governmental interests only against conduct motivated by religious belief. The ordinances "have every appearance of a prohibition that society is prepared to impose upon [Santeria worshippers] but not upon itself." This precise evil is what the requirement of general applicability is designed to prevent.

III.

A law burdening religious practice that is not neutral or not of general application must undergo the most rigorous of scrutiny. To satisfy the commands of the First Amendment, a law restrictive of religious practice must advance "'interests of the highest order'" and must be narrowly tailored in pursuit of those interests. The compelling interest standard that we apply once a law fails to meet the *Smith* requirements is not "water[ed] . . . down" but "really means what it says." A law that targets religious conduct for distinctive treatment or advances legitimate governmental interests only against conduct with a religious motivation will survive strict scrutiny only in rare cases. It follows from what we have already said that these ordinances cannot withstand this scrutiny. First, even were the governmental interests compelling, the ordinances are not drawn in narrow terms to accomplish those interests. As we have discussed . . . all four ordinances are overbroad or underinclusive in substantial respects. The proffered objectives are not pursued with respect to analogous nonreligious conduct, and those interests could be achieved by narrower ordinances that burdened religion to a far lesser degree. The absence of narrow tailoring suffices to establish the invalidity of the ordinances.

Respondent has not demonstrated, moreover, that, in the context of these ordinances, its governmental interests are compelling. Where government restricts only conduct protected by the First Amendment and fails to enact feasible measures to restrict other conduct producing substantial harm or alleged harm of the same sort, the interest given in justification of the restriction is not compelling. It is established in our strict scrutiny jurisprudence that "a law cannot be regarded as protecting an interest 'of the highest order' . . . when it leaves appreciable damage to that supposedly vital interest unprohibited." . . . [T]he ordinances are underinclusive to a substantial extent with respect to each of the interests that respondent has asserted, and it is only conduct motivated by religious conviction that bears the weight of the governmental restrictions. There can be no serious claim that those interests justify the ordinances.

IV.

The Free Exercise Clause commits government itself to religious tolerance, and upon even slight suspicion that proposals for state intervention stem from animosity to religion or distrust of its practices, all officials must pause to remember their own high duty to the Constitution and to the rights it secures. Those in office must be resolute in resisting importunate demands and must ensure that the sole reasons for imposing the burdens of law and regulation are secular. Legislators may not devise mechanisms, overt or disguised, designed to persecute or oppress a religion or its practices. The laws here in question were enacted contrary to these constitutional principles, and they are void.

Reversed.

* * *

JUSTICE BLACKMUN, with whom JUSTICE O'CONNOR joins, concurring in the judgment.

* * *

When a law discriminates against religion as such, as do the ordinances in this case, it automatically will fail strict scrutiny under *Sherbert v. Verner*, 374 U.S. 398, 402–403, 407 (1963) (holding that governmental regulation that imposes a burden upon religious practice must be narrowly tailored to advance a compelling state interest). This is true because a law that targets religious practice for disfavored treatment both burdens the free exercise of religion and, by definition, is not precisely tailored to a compelling governmental interest.

Thus, unlike the majority, I do not believe that "[a] law burdening religious practice that is not neutral or not of general application must undergo the most rigorous of scrutiny." In my view, regulation that targets religion in this way, *ipso facto*, fails strict scrutiny. It is for this reason that a statute that explicitly restricts religious practices violates the First Amendment. Otherwise, however, "the First Amendment . . . does not distinguish between laws that are generally applicable and laws that target particular religious practices." *Smith*, 494 U.S. at 894 (opinion concurring in judgment).

It is only in the rare case that a state or local legislature will enact a law directly burdening religious practice as such. Because respondent here does single out religion in this way, the present case is an easy one to decide.

A harder case would be presented if petitioners were requesting an exemption from a generally applicable anticruelty law. The result in the case before the Court today, and the fact that every Member of the Court concurs in that result, does not necessarily reflect this Court's views of the strength of a State's interest in prohibiting cruelty to animals. This case does not present, and I therefore decline to reach, the question whether the Free Exercise Clause would require a religious exemption from a law that sincerely pursued the goal of protecting animals from cruel treatment. The number of organizations that have filed amicus briefs on behalf of this interest, however, demonstrates that it is not a concern to be treated lightly.

Notes

1. The Santerians dropped the remains of sacrificed animals in various public and private places, raising concerns of disease and a notable violation of the laws against the dumping of garbage. *See, e.g.,* A.J. Dickerson, *Secretive Religion Makes Waves in South Florida*, ASSOCIATED PRESS, June 7, 1987. In *Mormon Church v. United States*, 136 U.S. 1 (1890), the Court held that government can prohibit "open offenses against the enlightened sentiment of mankind, notwithstanding the pretense of religious conviction by which they may be advocated and practiced." *Id.* at 50. In *Mormon Church*, the "offense" was polygamy. In the Santeria case, one supposed offense was animal sacrifice, but the Court highlights the difficulty with isolating that killing of animals. If the sole reason for the Santerian practice was to litter the landscape with animal corpses in streets, parks and cemeteries, under the guise of a religious practice, that might support a prohibition. But the "enlightened sentiment of mankind" is clearly a fluid and a subjective one, determined as much by the makeup of the Supreme Court as the mores of society.

2. Assuming the ordinances were directed at the Santeria religion, the city was required to prove a compelling state interest to support upholding them. Are any compelling interests shown? Has the Court rejected cruelty to animals as a

compelling interest? Other compelling interests identified by the lower courts (and ignored by the Supreme Court) include the prevention of a deleterious influence on children witnessing the slaughter and remains of sacrificed animals, and the health hazards presented by the appearance in the community of a steady stream of dead animals, often discarded in inappropriate places and left for days.

3. Do you think the outcome would have been different if the Hialeah ordinances were forty years old? How about 200?

4. The result of this case may have been preordained, not by the First Amendment or the case law, but by what one commentator has termed the "central contradiction in society's attitude toward animals—*i.e.*, some killing of animals is acceptable, but other killing of animals is not . . ." Henry Mark Holzer, *Contradictions Will Out: Animal Rights vs. Animal Sacrifice In the Supreme Court*, 1 ANIMAL L. 79, 102 (1995).

5. Courts dealing with issues of animal sacrifice may accept it as an important religious sacrament. Consider *People v. Keichler*, 129 Cal. App. 4th 1039 (2005). In that case, the defendant was convicted of racially-motivated hate crimes against three "members of the Hmong community." The victims sought, as restitution, the costs of "spirit calling" ceremonies, traditional services for healing traumatized individuals. "These ceremonies require, among other things, the sacrifice of animals." *Id.* at 1043. The victims sought restitution for "a pig, two cows, and several chickens" who were killed as part of the ceremony. *Id.* The California Court of Appeal found these appropriate items of damages.

6. In 2014, the *Lukumi* case was cited approvingly by the Polish Constitutional Tribunal (similar to the U.S. Supreme Court, but limited to addressing constitutional questions and constitutional conflicts with statutory law), in a case which rejected statutorily-imposed exemptions to Poland's humane slaughter laws for ritual slaughter, as discussed further in Chapter 6, Section 1.B. *See* Aleksandra Lis and Tomasz Pietrzykowski, *Animals as Objects of Ritual Slaughter: Polish Law after the Battle over Exceptionless Mandatory Stunning*, GLOBAL J. OF ANIMAL LAW 1, 13 (Vol. 2, 2015).

7. In addition to federal constitutional provisions, some states have strengthened the protection of religious freedom, which may provide additional protections for religious sacrifice. The Texas Religious Freedom and Restoration Act (TRFRA), Texas Civ. Practice and Remedies Code §§ 110.001 *et seq.*, prevents state or local governments from substantially burdening religious practices unless the ban promotes a compelling government interest in the least restrictive manner. *Id.* at § 110.003. Jose Merced was a Santerian priest who engaged in animal sacrifice (such as that described in the *Lukumi Babalu Aye* case) within the city limits of Euless, Texas. Euless prohibited the keeping of more than four animals as well as the slaughter of any animals within city limits. In *Merced v. Kasson*, 577 F.3d 578 (5th Cir. 2009), the Fifth Circuit found the Euless ordinances were barred by the TRFRA. Notably, the court did not address Merced's federal constitutional claims. Thus, the *Merced* opinion is based solely on the Texas religious freedom law.

8. In *Lukumi Babalu Aye*, the First Amendment's protection of the free exercise of religion clashed in part with the public policy against animal cruelty. The "religious" passion many people have for animals may also create interesting doctrine. Many people with just such a passion are, or are converting to, a vegan diet and lifestyle. Vegans, who are strict vegetarians, will not eat, wear or otherwise use animal products or byproducts of any kind. Many vegans combine this practice with a firmly held ethical and moral belief that each animal life is sacred and that animals should not be used or exploited by humans. Because this belief is akin to a religious belief, veganism has been asserted as a basis for First Amendment legal challenges.

Federal courts have adopted a variety of tests to determine whether a belief constitutes a "religious belief" or a "religion." Some of the cases approach the issue in the context of the First Amendment Free Exercise Clause. *Cf. United States v. Seeger*, 380 U.S. 163, 176 (in determining whether conscientious objector to military service was exercising his First Amendment right, Supreme Court held that a religious belief is "[a] sincere and meaningful belief which occupies in the life of its possessor a place parallel to that filled by" God in members of traditional religions) (1970); *Welsh v. United States*, 398 U.S. 333, 339 (1970) (conscientious objector case; First Amendment protects "moral, ethical, or religious beliefs about what is right and wrong . . . held with the strength of traditional religious convictions"). Other courts have looked at the question under federal housing and employment laws, under the repealed federal Religious Freedom Restoration Act and in other contexts.

Consider *Friedman v. Southern California Permanente Medical Group*, 102 Cal. App. 4th 39 (2002), in which plaintiff claimed that his veganism was akin to a religious belief and that an adverse employment action violated a California fair employment statute. *Id.* at 44. Plaintiff had applied for employment with defendant and was informed that he could not be hired without a mumps vaccine. Plaintiff refused to take the vaccine, because it was grown in chicken embryos. "To be vaccinated, it was alleged, 'would violate [plaintiff's] system of beliefs and would be considered immoral by [him].'" When plaintiff refused to be vaccinated with the mumps vaccine, defendants withdrew the "employment offer." *Id.* (quoting complaint).

The key issue before the court was whether veganism was a "religious creed" under the regulations promulgated pursuant to the California statute. After a lengthy discussion, the California Court of Appeal settled on a tripartite analysis set out in *Africa v. Commonwealth of Pa.*, 662 F.2d 1025, 1032 (3d Cir. 1981):

> First, a religion addresses fundamental and ultimate questions having to do with deep and imponderable matters. Second, a religion is comprehensive in nature; it consists of a belief-system as opposed to an isolated teaching. Third, a religion often can be recognized by the presence of certain formal and external signs.

The *Friedman* court's analysis of whether plaintiff's veganism was a religious creed follows:

We do not question plaintiff's allegation that his beliefs are sincerely held; it is presumed as a matter of law that they are. However, we disregard conclusory allegations, for example, that plaintiff's beliefs "occupy a place in [his] life parallel to that filled by God in traditionally religious individuals adhering to the Christian, Jewish or Muslim Faiths." First, plaintiff believes "that all living beings must be valued equally and that it is immoral and unethical for humans to kill and exploit animals even for food, clothing and the testing of product safety for humans"; further, it is "a violation of natural law" to transgress this belief. There is no allegation or judicially noticeable evidence plaintiff's belief system addresses fundamental or ultimate questions. There is no claim that veganism speaks to: the meaning of human existence; the purpose of life; theories of humankind's nature or its place in the universe; matters of human life and death; or the exercise of faith. There is no apparent spiritual or otherworldly component to plaintiff's beliefs. Rather, plaintiff alleges a moral and ethical creed limited to the single subject of highly valuing animal life and ordering one's life based on that perspective. While veganism compels plaintiff to live in accord with strict dictates of behavior, it reflects a moral and secular, rather than religious, philosophy. Second, while plaintiff's belief system governs his behavior in wide-ranging respects, including the food he eats, the clothes he wears, and the products he uses, it is not sufficiently comprehensive in nature to fall within the provisions of [the California law]. Plaintiff does not assert that his belief system derives from a power or being or faith to which all else is subordinate or upon which all else depends. Third, though not determinative, no formal or external signs of a religion are present. There are no: teachers or leaders; services or ceremonies; structure or organization; orders of worship or articles of faith; or holidays.

Absent a broader, more comprehensive scope, extending to ultimate questions, it cannot be said that plaintiff's veganism [is a "religious creed."] Rather, plaintiff's veganism is a personal philosophy, albeit shared by many others, and a way of life. As Associate Justice Werdegar has aptly noted, religious belief is other than "a philosophy or way of life." Therefore, plaintiff's veganism is not a religious creed within the meaning of the FEHA. We quite obviously do not resolve the question of whether a vegan lifestyle that results from a religious belief otherwise meeting the standard in [the regulation]is subject to [statutory] coverage.

Id. at 70–71. The case does not foreclose another challenge. Based on the opinion, it is quite possible that a more detailed complaint would have satisfied this court that plaintiff actually was exercising a constitutionally-protected "religious creed" in his veganism, rather than simply a "personal philosophy."

For further analysis of this issue and argument in favor of veganism or "animal rights" as a protected religion, *see, e.g.*, Rebecca Schwartz, *Employers, Got Vegan?: How Ethical Veganism Qualifies for Religious Protection Under Title VII*, 24 ANIMAL

L. 221 (2018); Bruce Friedrich, *The Church of Animal Liberation: Animal Rights as 'Religion' Under the Free Exercise Clause*, 21 ANIMAL L. 65 (2014).

9. In *Jones v. Butz*, 374 F. Supp. 1284 (S.D.N.Y. 1974), excerpted in Chapter 6, plaintiffs challenged certain provisions of the Humane Methods of Slaughter Act, 7 U.S.C. §§ 1901–1907. The court acknowledged plaintiffs had a "commitment to the principles of humane treatment of animals and to the separation of church and state [that was] deeply held and sincere. . . ." Plaintiffs' First Amendment challenge was based on the Establishment Clause and the Free Exercise Clause. They claimed that the Act's declaration that kosher/ritual slaughter was humane had a religious purpose, constituting a violation of the Establishment Clause, citing the fact that rabbis and experts on kosher slaughter testified before Congress in support of the rule, even though it meant that fully conscious animals could be shackled and hung by their back legs before they were slaughtered. Basing its holding on a series of Establishment Clause cases, the court held that Congress permissibly determined that this practice was humane, and the fact that the act coincided with those religious practices did not amount to a constitutional violation.

Plaintiffs' Free Exercise claim was quickly rejected by the court because they did not establish any effect on any of their claimed religious practices—although they did state the origins of the type of assertions made by the plaintiff in *Friedman*. And in contrast to the *Friedman* court, the *Jones* court seemed to accept without argument that plaintiffs' commitment toward the humane treatment of the animals satisfied the Supreme Court test of sincerity and deeply-held belief that is required to state a First Amendment case in the first instance.

Do you think that in *Jones v. Butz*, a viable claim could have been brought under the Humane Methods of Slaughter Act based on a plaintiff's veganism? Could such a claim be brought by "compassionate carnivores" who eat animal products but believe that all animals should be treated and killed in a "humane" manner?

B. Freedom of Speech

United States v. Stevens

Supreme Court of the United States, 2009
559 U.S. 460, 129 S. Ct. 1984, 173 L.Ed.2d 1083

ROBERTS, C. J., delivered the opinion of the Court, in which STEVENS, SCALIA, KENNEDY, THOMAS, GINSBURG, BREYER, and SOTOMAYOR, JJ., joined. ALITO, J., filed a dissenting opinion.

Congress enacted 18 U.S.C. § 48 to criminalize the commercial creation, sale, or possession of certain depictions of animal cruelty. The statute does not address underlying acts harmful to animals, but only portrayals of such conduct. The question presented is whether the prohibition in the statute is consistent with the freedom of speech guaranteed by the First Amendment.

I

Section 48 establishes a criminal penalty of up to five years in prison for anyone who knowingly "creates, sells, or possesses a depiction of animal cruelty," if done "for commercial gain" in interstate or foreign commerce. § 48(a). A depiction of "animal cruelty" is defined as one "in which a living animal is intentionally maimed, mutilated, tortured, wounded, or killed," if that conduct violates federal or state law where "the creation, sale, or possession takes place." § 48(c)(1). In what is referred to as the "exceptions clause," the law exempts from prohibition any depiction "that has serious religious, political, scientific, educational, journalistic, historical, or artistic value." § 48(b).

The legislative background of § 48 focused primarily on the interstate market for "crush videos." According to the House Committee Report on the bill, such videos feature the intentional torture and killing of helpless animals, including cats, dogs, monkeys, mice, and hamsters. H.R.Rep. No. 106-397, p. 2 (1999). Crush videos often depict women slowly crushing animals to death "with their bare feet or while wearing high heeled shoes," sometimes while "talking to the animals in a kind of dominatrix patter" over "[t]he cries and squeals of the animals, obviously in great pain." *Ibid.* Apparently these depictions "appeal to persons with a very specific sexual fetish who find them sexually arousing or otherwise exciting." *Id.,* at 2–3. The acts depicted in crush videos are typically prohibited by the animal cruelty laws enacted by all 50 States and the District of Columbia. But crush videos rarely disclose the participants' identities, inhibiting prosecution of the underlying conduct.

This case, however, involves an application of § 48 to depictions of animal fighting. Dogfighting, for example, is unlawful in all 50 States and the District of Columbia, and has been restricted by federal law since 1976. Stevens ran a business, "Dogs of Velvet and Steel," and an associated Web site, through which he sold videos of pit bulls engaging in dogfights and attacking other animals. . . . On the basis of these videos, Stevens was indicted on three counts of violating § 48.

Stevens moved to dismiss the indictment, arguing that § 48 is facially invalid under the First Amendment. The District Court denied the motion. It held that the depictions subject to § 48, like obscenity or child pornography, are categorically unprotected by the First Amendment. It went on to hold that § 48 is not substantially overbroad, because the exceptions clause sufficiently narrows the statute to constitutional applications. The jury convicted Stevens on all counts, and the District Court sentenced him to three concurrent sentences of 37 months' imprisonment, followed by three years of supervised release.

The en banc Third Circuit, over a three-judge dissent, declared § 48 facially unconstitutional and vacated Stevens's conviction. 533 F.3d 218. The Court of Appeals first held that § 48 regulates speech that is protected by the First Amendment. The Court declined to recognize a new category of unprotected speech for depictions of animal cruelty, and rejected the Government's analogy between animal cruelty depictions and child pornography.

The Court of Appeals then held that §48 could not survive strict scrutiny as a content-based regulation of protected speech. It found that the statute lacked a compelling government interest and was neither narrowly tailored to preventing animal cruelty nor the least restrictive means of doing so. It therefore held §48 facially invalid.

In an extended footnote, the Third Circuit noted that §48 "might also be unconstitutionally overbroad," because it "potentially covers a great deal of constitutionally protected speech" and "sweeps [too] widely" to be limited only by prosecutorial discretion. But the Court of Appeals declined to rest its analysis on this ground.

We granted certiorari.

* * *

III

Because we decline to carve out from the First Amendment any novel exception for §48, we review Stevens's First Amendment challenge under our existing doctrine.

A

Stevens challenged §48 on its face, arguing that any conviction secured under the statute would be unconstitutional. . . .

To succeed in a typical facial attack, Stevens would have to establish "that no set of circumstances exists under which [§48] would be valid," or that the statute lacks any "plainly legitimate sweep." . . . Here the Government asserts that Stevens cannot prevail because §48 is plainly legitimate as applied to crush videos and animal fighting depictions. Deciding this case through a traditional facial analysis would require us to resolve whether these applications of §48 are in fact consistent with the Constitution.

In the First Amendment context, however, this Court recognizes "a second type of facial challenge," whereby a law may be invalidated as overbroad if "a substantial number of its applications are unconstitutional, judged in relation to the statute's plainly legitimate sweep." Stevens argues that §48 applies to common depictions of ordinary and lawful activities, and that these depictions constitute the vast majority of materials subject to the statute. The Government makes no effort to defend such a broad ban as constitutional. Instead, the Government's entire defense of §48 rests on interpreting the statute as narrowly limited to specific types of "extreme" material. As the parties have presented the issue, therefore, the constitutionality of §48 hinges on how broadly it is construed. It is to that question that we now turn.

B

As we explained two Terms ago, "[t]he first step in overbreadth analysis is to construe the challenged statute; it is impossible to determine whether a statute reaches too far without first knowing what the statute covers." . . .

We read § 48 to create a criminal prohibition of alarming breadth. To begin with, the text of the statute's ban on a "depiction of animal cruelty" nowhere requires that the depicted conduct be cruel. That text applies to "any . . . depiction" in which "a living animal is intentionally maimed, mutilated, tortured, wounded, or killed." § 48(c)(1). "[M]aimed, mutilated, [and] tortured" convey cruelty, but "wounded" or "killed" do not suggest any such limitation.

The Government contends that the terms in the definition should be read to require the additional element of "accompanying acts of cruelty." The Government bases this argument on the definiendum, "depiction of animal cruelty," and on "'the commonsense canon of noscitur a sociis.'" As that canon recognizes, an ambiguous term may be "given more precise content by the neighboring words with which it is associated." Likewise, an unclear definitional phrase may take meaning from the term to be defined.

But the phrase "wounded . . . or killed" at issue here contains little ambiguity. . . . Nothing about that meaning requires cruelty.

While not requiring cruelty, § 48 does require that the depicted conduct be "illegal." But this requirement does not limit § 48 along the lines the Government suggests. There are myriad federal and state laws concerning the proper treatment of animals, but many of them are not designed to guard against animal cruelty. Protections of endangered species, for example, restrict even the humane "wound[ing] or kill[ing]" of "living animal[s]." § 48(c)(1). Livestock regulations are often designed to protect the health of human beings, and hunting and fishing rules (seasons, licensure, bag limits, weight requirements) can be designed to raise revenue, preserve animal populations, or prevent accidents. The text of § 48(c) draws no distinction based on the reason the intentional killing of an animal is made illegal, and includes, for example, the humane slaughter of a stolen cow.

What is more, the application of § 48 to depictions of illegal conduct extends to conduct that is illegal in only a single jurisdiction. Under subsection (c)(1), the depicted conduct need only be illegal in "the State in which the creation, sale, or possession takes place, regardless of whether the . . . wounding . . . or killing took place in [that] State." A depiction of entirely lawful conduct runs afoul of the ban if that depiction later finds its way into another State where the same conduct is unlawful. This provision greatly expands the scope of § 48, because although there may be "a broad societal consensus" against cruelty to animals, Brief for United States 2, there is substantial disagreement on what types of conduct are properly regarded as cruel. Both views about cruelty to animals and regulations having no connection to cruelty vary widely from place to place.

In the District of Columbia, for example, all hunting is unlawful. Other jurisdictions permit or encourage hunting, and there is an enormous national market for hunting-related depictions in which a living animal is intentionally killed. Hunting periodicals have circulations in the hundreds of thousands or millions. . . . Nonetheless, because the statute allows each jurisdiction to export its laws to the rest of the country, § 48(a) extends to any magazine or video depicting lawful hunting, so long as that depiction is sold within the Nation's Capital.

Those seeking to comply with the law thus face a bewildering maze of regulations from at least 56 separate jurisdictions. Some States permit hunting with crossbows, while others forbid it or restrict it only to the disabled. Missouri allows the "canned" hunting of ungulates held in captivity, but Montana restricts such hunting to certain bird species. The sharp-tailed grouse may be hunted in Idaho, but not in Washington.

The disagreements among the States—and the "commonwealth[s], territor[ies], or possession[s] of the United States," 18 U.S.C. § 48(c)(2)—extend well beyond hunting. State agricultural regulations permit different methods of livestock slaughter in different places or as applied to different animals. . . .

C

The only thing standing between defendants who sell such depictions and five years in federal prison—other than the mercy of a prosecutor—is the statute's exceptions clause. Subsection (b) exempts from prohibition "any depiction that has serious religious, political, scientific, educational, journalistic, historical, or artistic value." The Government argues that this clause substantially narrows the statute's reach: News reports about animal cruelty have "journalistic" value; pictures of bullfights in Spain have "historical" value; and instructional hunting videos have "educational" value. Thus, the Government argues, § 48 reaches only crush videos, depictions of animal fighting (other than Spanish bullfighting, see Brief for United States 47-48), and perhaps other depictions of "extreme acts of animal cruelty."

The Government's attempt to narrow the statutory ban, however, requires an unrealistically broad reading of the exceptions clause. As the Government reads the clause, any material with "redeeming societal value," "'at least some minimal value,'" or anything more than "scant social value," is excluded under § 48(b). But the text says "serious" value, and "serious" should be taken seriously. We decline the Government's invitation—advanced for the first time in this Court—to regard as "serious" anything that is not "scant." . . .

Quite apart from the requirement of "serious" value in § 48(b), the excepted speech must also fall within one of the enumerated categories. Much speech does not. Most hunting videos, for example, are not obviously instructional in nature, except in the sense that all life is a lesson. . . . The Government offers no principled explanation why these depictions of hunting or depictions of Spanish bullfights would be *inherently* valuable while those of Japanese dogfights are not. . . . There is simply no adequate reading of the exceptions clause that results in the statute's banning only the depictions the Government would like to ban.

The Government explains that the language of § 48(b) was largely drawn from our opinion in *Miller v. California*, 413 U.S. 15 (1973), which excepted from its definition of obscenity any material with "serious literary, artistic, political, or scientific value". . . .

In *Miller* we held that "serious" value shields depictions of sex from regulation as obscenity. Limiting *Miller*'s exception to "serious" value ensured that "'[a] quotation from Voltaire in the flyleaf of a book [would] not constitutionally redeem an otherwise obscene publication.'" We did not, however, determine that serious value could be used as a general precondition to protecting *other* types of speech in the first place. *Most* of what we say to one another lacks "religious, political, scientific, educational, journalistic, historical, or artistic value" (let alone serious value), but it is still sheltered from government regulation. . . .

Thus, the protection of the First Amendment presumptively extends to many forms of speech that do not qualify for the serious-value exception of § 48(b), but nonetheless fall within the broad reach of § 48(c).

D

Not to worry, the Government says: The Executive Branch construes § 48 to reach only "extreme" cruelty, and it "neither has brought nor will bring a prosecution for anything less." The Government hits this theme hard, invoking its prosecutorial discretion several times. . . .

This prosecution is itself evidence of the danger in putting faith in government representations of prosecutorial restraint. When this legislation was enacted, the Executive Branch announced that it would interpret § 48 as covering only depictions "of wanton cruelty to animals designed to appeal to a prurient interest in sex." No one suggests that the videos in this case fit that description.

To read § 48 as the Government desires requires rewriting, not just reinterpretation.

Our construction of § 48 decides the constitutional question; the Government makes no effort to defend the constitutionality of § 48 as applied beyond crush videos and depictions of animal fighting. . . .

Nor does the Government seriously contest that the presumptively impermissible applications of § 48 (properly construed) far outnumber any permissible ones. However "growing" and "lucrative" the markets for crush videos and dogfighting depictions might be, they are dwarfed by the market for other depictions, such as hunting magazines and videos, that we have determined to be within the scope of § 48. We therefore need not and do not decide whether a statute limited to crush videos or other depictions of extreme animal cruelty would be constitutional. We hold only that § 48 is not so limited but is instead substantially overbroad, and therefore invalid under the First Amendment.

* * *

Justice ALITO, dissenting.

The Court strikes down in its entirety a valuable statute, 18 U.S.C. § 48, that was enacted not to suppress speech, but to prevent horrific acts of animal cruelty — in particular, the creation and commercial exploitation of "crush videos," a form of depraved entertainment that has no social value. The Court's approach, which has the practical effect of legalizing the sale of such videos and is thus likely to spur a resumption of their production, is unwarranted. Respondent was convicted under § 48 for selling videos depicting dogfights. On appeal, he argued, among other things, that § 48 is unconstitutional as applied to the facts of this case, and he highlighted features of those videos that might distinguish them from other dogfight videos brought to our attention. . . .

* * *

I

* * *

The "strong medicine" of overbreadth invalidation need not and generally should not be administered when the statute under attack is unconstitutional as applied to the challenger before the court. . . .

I see no reason to depart here from the generally preferred procedure of considering the question of overbreadth only as a last resort. Because the Court has addressed the overbreadth question, however, I will explain why I do not think that the record supports the conclusion that § 48, when properly interpreted, is overly broad.

II

The overbreadth doctrine "strike[s] a balance between competing social costs." Specifically, the doctrine seeks to balance the "harmful effects" of "invalidating a law that in some of its applications is perfectly constitutional" against the possibility that "the threat of enforcement of an overbroad law [will] dete[r] people from engaging in constitutionally protected speech." *Ibid.* "In order to maintain an appropriate balance, we have vigorously enforced the requirement that a statute's overbreadth be substantial, not only in an absolute sense, but also relative to the statute's plainly legitimate sweep."

In determining whether a statute's overbreadth is substantial, we consider a statute's application to real-world conduct, not fanciful hypotheticals. Accordingly, we have repeatedly emphasized that an overbreadth claimant bears the burden of demonstrating, "from the text of [the law] *and from actual fact*," that substantial overbreadth exists. Similarly, "there must be a *realistic danger* that the statute itself will significantly compromise recognized First Amendment protections of parties not before the Court for it to be facially challenged on overbreadth grounds."

III

In holding that § 48 violates the overbreadth rule, the Court declines to decide whether, as the Government maintains, § 48 is constitutional as applied to two broad categories of depictions that exist in the real world: crush videos and depictions of deadly animal fights. . . . [T]he Court concludes that § 48 reaches too much protected speech to survive. The Court relies primarily on depictions of hunters killing or wounding game and depictions of animals being slaughtered for food. I address the Court's examples below.

A

I turn first to depictions of hunting. As the Court notes, photographs and videos of hunters shooting game are common. But hunting is legal in all 50 States, and § 48 applies only to a depiction of conduct that is illegal in the jurisdiction in which the depiction is created, sold, or possessed. §§ 48(a), (c). Therefore, in all 50 States, the creation, sale, or possession for sale of the vast majority of hunting depictions indisputably falls outside § 48's reach.

* * *

The Court's interpretation is seriously flawed. "When a federal court is dealing with a federal statute challenged as overbroad, it should, of course, construe the statute to avoid constitutional problems, if the statute is subject to such a limiting construction."

Applying this canon, I would hold that § 48 does not apply to depictions of hunting. . . . Virtually all state laws prohibiting animal cruelty either expressly define the term "animal" to exclude wildlife or else specifically exempt lawful hunting activities,[3] so the statutory prohibition set forth in § 48(a) may reasonably be interpreted not to reach most if not all hunting depictions.

Second, even if the hunting of wild animals were otherwise covered by § 48(a), I would hold that hunting depictions fall within the exception in § 48(b) for depictions that have "serious" (*i.e.*, not "trifling") "scientific," "educational," or "historical" value. While there are certainly those who find hunting objectionable, the predominant view in this country has long been that hunting serves many important values, and it is clear that Congress shares that view. . . . Thus, it is widely thought that hunting has "scientific" value in that it promotes conservation, "historical" value in that it provides a link to past times when hunting played a critical role in daily life, and "educational" value in that it furthers the understanding and appreciation of nature and our country's past and instills valuable character traits. And if hunting itself is widely thought to serve these values, then it takes but a small additional step to conclude that depictions of hunting make a non-trivial contribution to the exchange of ideas. Accordingly, I would hold that hunting depictions fall comfortably within the exception set out in § 48(b).

I do not have the slightest doubt that Congress, in enacting § 48, had no intention of restricting the creation, sale, or possession of depictions of hunting. Proponents of the law made this point clearly. Indeed, even *opponents* acknowledged that § 48 was not intended to reach ordinary hunting depictions.

---

3. See Appendix, *infra* (citing statutes); B. Wagman, S. Waisman, & P. Frasch, Animal Law: Cases and Materials 92 (4th ed. 2010) ("Most anti-cruelty laws also include one or more exemptions," which often "exclud[e] from coverage (1) whole classes of animals, such as wildlife or farm animals, or (2) specific activities, such as hunting"); . . . .

For these reasons, I am convinced that § 48 has no application to depictions of hunting. But even if § 48 did impermissibly reach the sale or possession of depictions of hunting in a few unusual situations . . . , those isolated applications would hardly show that § 48 bans a substantial amount of protected speech.

B

* * *

In sum, we have a duty to interpret § 48 so as to avoid serious constitutional concerns, and § 48 may reasonably be construed not to reach almost all, if not all, of the depictions that the Court finds constitutionally protected. Thus, § 48 does not appear to have a large number of unconstitutional applications. Invalidation for overbreadth is appropriate only if the challenged statute suffers from substantial overbreadth—judged not just in absolute terms, but in relation to the statute's "plainly legitimate sweep." As I explain in the following Part, § 48 has a substantial core of constitutionally permissible applications.

* * *

IV.A.1

As the Court of Appeals recognized, "the primary conduct that Congress sought to address through its passage [of § 48] was the creation, sale, or possession of 'crush videos.'" 533 F.3d 218, 222 (CA3 2008) (en banc). A sample crush video, which has been lodged with the Clerk, records the following event:

> "[A] kitten, secured to the ground, watches and shrieks in pain as a woman thrusts her high-heeled shoe into its body, slams her heel into the kitten's eye socket and mouth loudly fracturing its skull, and stomps repeatedly on the animal's head. The kitten hemorrhages blood, screams blindly in pain, and is ultimately left dead in a moist pile of blood-soaked hair and bone." Brief for Humane Society of United States as *Amicus Curiae* 2 (hereinafter Humane Society Brief).

It is undisputed that the *conduct* depicted in crush videos may constitutionally be prohibited. All 50 States and the District of Columbia have enacted statutes prohibiting animal cruelty. See 533 F.3d, at 223, and n. 4 (citing statutes); H.R. Rep., at 3. But before the enactment of § 48, the underlying conduct depicted in crush videos was nearly impossible to prosecute. These videos, which "often appeal to persons with a very specific sexual fetish," *id.*, at 2, were made in secret, generally without a live audience, and "the faces of the women inflicting the torture in the material often were not shown, nor could the location of the place where the cruelty was being inflicted or the date of the activity be ascertained from the depiction." *Id.*, at 3. Thus, law enforcement authorities often were not able to identify the parties responsible for the torture. . . .

In light of the practical problems thwarting the prosecution of the creators of crush videos under state animal cruelty laws, Congress concluded that the only effective way of stopping the underlying criminal conduct was to prohibit the commercial exploitation of the videos of that conduct. And Congress' strategy appears to have been vindicated. We are told that "[b]y 2007, sponsors of § 48 declared the crush video industry dead. Even overseas websites shut down in the wake of § 48. Now, after the Third Circuit's decision [facially invalidating the statute], crush videos are already back online." Humane Society Brief 5 (citations omitted).

2

The First Amendment protects freedom of speech, but it most certainly does not protect violent criminal conduct, even if engaged in for expressive purposes. Crush videos present a highly unusual free speech issue because they are so closely linked with violent criminal conduct. The videos record the commission of violent criminal acts, and it appears that these crimes are committed for the sole purpose of creating the videos. In addition, as noted above, Congress was presented with compelling evidence that the only way of preventing these crimes was to target the sale of the videos. Under these circumstances, I cannot believe that the First Amendment commands Congress to step aside and allow the underlying crimes to continue.

The most relevant of our prior decisions is *Ferber*, which concerned child pornography. The Court there held that child pornography is not protected speech, and I believe that *Ferber*'s reasoning dictates a similar conclusion here.

* * *

It must be acknowledged that § 48 differs from a child pornography law in an important respect: preventing the abuse of children is certainly much more important than preventing the torture of the animals used in crush videos. It was largely for this reason that the Court of Appeals concluded that *Ferber* did not support the constitutionality of § 48. 533 F.3d, at 228 ("Preventing cruelty to animals, although an exceedingly worthy goal, simply does not implicate interests of the same magnitude as protecting children from physical and psychological harm"). But while protecting children is unquestionably *more* important than protecting animals, the Government also has a compelling interest in preventing the torture depicted in crush videos.

The animals used in crush videos are living creatures that experience excruciating pain. Our society has long banned such cruelty, which is illegal throughout the country. In *Ferber*, the Court noted that "virtually all of the States and the United States have passed legislation proscribing the production of or otherwise combating 'child pornography,'" and the Court declined to "second-guess [that] legislative judgment." 458 U.S., at 758. Here, likewise, the Court of Appeals erred in second-guessing the legislative judgment about the importance of preventing cruelty to animals.

* * *

In short, *Ferber* is the case that sheds the most light on the constitutionality of Congress' effort to halt the production of crush videos. Applying the principles set forth in *Ferber*, I would hold that crush videos are not protected by the First Amendment.

B

Application of the *Ferber* framework also supports the constitutionality of § 48 as applied to depictions of brutal animal fights. (For convenience, I will focus on videos of dogfights, which appear to be the most common type of animal fight videos.)

First, such depictions, like crush videos, record the actual commission of a crime involving deadly violence. Dogfights are illegal in every State and the District of Columbia, and under federal law constitute a felony punishable by imprisonment for up to five years, 7 U.S.C. § 2156 *et seq.* (2006 ed. and Supp. II), 18 U.S.C. § 49 (2006 ed., Supp. II).

Second, Congress had an ample basis for concluding that the crimes depicted in these videos cannot be effectively controlled without targeting the videos. Like crush videos and child pornography, dogfight videos are very often produced as part of a "low-profile, clandestine industry," and "the need to market the resulting products requires a visible apparatus of distribution." *Ferber*, 458 U.S., at 760. In such circumstances, Congress had reasonable grounds for concluding that it would be "difficult, if not impossible, to halt" the underlying exploitation of dogs by pursuing only those who stage the fights. *Id.* at 759–760; see 533 F.3d, at 246 (Cowen, J., dissenting) (citing evidence establishing "the existence of a lucrative market for depictions of animal cruelty," including videos of dogfights, "which in turn provides a powerful incentive to individuals to create [such] videos").

The commercial trade in videos of dogfights is "an integral part of the production of such materials," *Ferber, supra,* at 761. As the Humane Society explains, "[v]ideotapes memorializing dogfights are integral to the success of this criminal industry" for a variety of reasons. For one thing, some dogfighting videos are made "solely for the purpose of selling the video (and not for a live audience)." *Id.,* at 9. . . .

Third, depictions of dogfights that fall within § 48's reach have by definition no appreciable social value. As noted, § 48(b) exempts depictions having any appreciable social value, and thus the mere inclusion of a depiction of a live fight in a larger work that aims at communicating an idea or a message with a modicum of social value would not run afoul of the statute.

Finally, the harm caused by the underlying criminal acts greatly outweighs any trifling value that the depictions might be thought to possess. As the Humane Society explains:

> "The abused dogs used in fights endure physical torture and emotional manipulation throughout their lives to predispose them to violence; common tactics include feeding the animals hot peppers and gunpowder, prodding them with sticks, and electrocution. Dogs are conditioned never to give up a fight, even if they will be gravely hurt or killed. As a result,

dogfights inflict horrific injuries on the participating animals, including lacerations, ripped ears, puncture wounds and broken bones. Losing dogs are routinely refused treatment, beaten further as 'punishment' for the loss, and executed by drowning, hanging, or incineration."

For these dogs, unlike the animals killed in crush videos, the suffering lasts for years rather than minutes. As with crush videos, moreover, the statutory ban on commerce in dogfighting videos is also supported by compelling governmental interests in effectively enforcing the Nation's criminal laws and preventing criminals from profiting from their illegal activities. See *Ferber, supra,* at 757–758; *Simon & Schuster,* 502 U.S., at 119.

In sum, § 48 may validly be applied to at least two broad real-world categories of expression covered by the statute: crush videos and dogfighting videos. Thus, the statute has a substantial core of constitutionally permissible applications. Moreover, for the reasons set forth above, the record does not show that § 48, properly interpreted, bans a substantial amount of protected speech in absolute terms. *A fortiori,* respondent has not met his burden of demonstrating that any impermissible applications of the statute are "substantial" in relation to its "plainly legitimate sweep." Accordingly, I would reject respondent's claim that § 48 is facially unconstitutional under the overbreadth doctrine.

* * *

For these reasons, I respectfully dissent.

Notes

1. As discussed in Chapter 3, Congress revised 18 U.S.C. section 48 in late 2010 to address the overbreadth argument on which the Court based its decision to reverse Stevens' conviction for distributing dogfighting videos. Congress specifically added a requirement that conduct violating section 48 must be "obscene," thereby incorporating the Supreme Court precedent defining obscenity found in *Miller v. California,* 413 U.S. 15 (1973). The first challenge to the new law came in 2013, when two defendants were charged with making and distributing animal crush videos in violation of the amended statute. The District Court for the Southern District of Texas found that the new law was unconstitutional because it restricted free speech in violation of the First Amendment. Focusing on the statute's requirement that the conduct be obscene and the Court's determination that crush videos are not "sexual" in nature, and thus not "obscene" under Supreme Court precedent, the court concluded "[t]he acts depicted in animal crush videos are disturbing and horrid. But '[t]he history of the law of free expression is one of vindication in cases involving speech that many citizens find shabby, offensive, or even ugly.'" *U.S. v. Richards,* 940 F. Supp. 2d 548, 559 (S.D. Tex. 2013).

The Fifth Circuit reversed, in *U.S. v. Richards,* 755 F.3d 269 (5th Cir. 2014), *cert. denied,* 135 S. Ct. 1547 (2015). The court held that the statute was not facially unconstitutional, specifically focusing on the fact that it contained a requirement of obscenity, which is illegal. The court remanded for further findings consistent with its opinion. After further review was rejected by the U.S. Supreme Court, Denise Richards (one of the two defendants in *Richards*) pled guilty and was sentenced in federal court. Additionally, while the federal case against Richards and her co-defendant (the actual producer of the video) was on appeal, they were separately convicted under state animal cruelty statutes and sentenced to several years in prison. Craig Malisow, *Finally, a Federal Conviction for Man Behind Animal Torture Videos,* HOUSTON PRESS, May 24, 2016.

2. Another area in which the use of animals for entertainment creates First Amendment issues is the clash between hunters and those opposed to hunting, with respect to the advocates' rights to protest what they believe is an unethical practice. So-called "hunter harassment laws" are directed at restricting the pro-test activities, but must be tempered by the constitutional right to free speech and debate. It is indisputable that the laws are a response to "political speech," which is afforded the highest protection. The cases analyzing them, two of which are excerpted below, balance the right to hunt and the state's right to regulate that activity, on the one hand, with the right to assemble and speak one's mind, on the other.

Dorman v. Satti

United States District Court, District of Connecticut, 1988
678 F. Supp. 375

ALAN H. NEVAS, JUDGE. This case requires the court to consider the consti-tutionality of Connecticut's newly-enacted Hunter Harassment Act, Conn. Gen. Stat. section 53a-183a, which penalizes those who interfere with or harass persons engaged in the "lawful taking of wildlife." The plaintiff was arrested under the Act after she had approached several hunters taking waterfowl in state marshlands near her home and verbally attempted to dissuade them from their hunt. Although the charge against her was subsequently dismissed, she brought this action pursuant to 42 U.S.C. section 1983 in order to adjudicate the Act's constitutionality. On cross motions for summary judgment, for the reasons set forth below, the court finds that the Act as written is unconstitutionally vague and overbroad.

Background

A. *The Act*

An Act concerning Harassment of Hunters, Trappers or Fishermen ("Hunter Harassment Act" or "the Act"), which became part of Connecticut's penal code by legislative enactment in 1985, provides that:

> No person shall: (1) Interfere with the lawful taking of wildlife by another person, or acts in preparation for such taking, with intent to prevent such taking; or (2) harass another person who is engaged in the lawful taking of wildlife or acts in preparation for such taking.

Conn. Gen. Stat. section 53a-183a. It is a class C misdemeanor, subjecting an offender to a fine and/or imprisonment for up to three months. Conn. Gen. Stat. §§ 53a-28 and 53a-36(3).

The Hunter Harassment Act is Connecticut's version of legislation that has been enacted in nearly half the states for the purpose of protecting lawful hunters from intentional interference by those who would disturb their hunt.[1] In adopting the Act the legislature clearly intended to provide an effective deterrent against persons who actively oppose hunting.[2] . . . A spokesman for the bill explained to his colleagues that examples of hunter "harassment" would include "intentionally blaring a radio when someone intended to go out and pursue game," giving "verbal abuse to someone who was preparing to go out into some public property perhaps to take game," and "spreading human hair around the facility [so that] game would be deterred." *Id.* at 3327 (Sen. Benson).

* * *

B. *The Arrest*

The plaintiff, Francelle Dorman, lived near a state forest containing marshland inhabited by a variety of waterfowl. By her own admission, Ms. Dorman is "morally opposed to the hunting and senseless killing of harmless and defenseless animals, including all waterfowl." Affidavit of Francelle Dorman, filed December 30, 1986, at para. 2.

On January 30, 1986, during the goose-hunting season, Ms. Dorman approached several hunters in the marsh with the intention of convincing them to abandon their plans to hunt. Complaint, filed Aug. 21, 1986, at para. 10. To that end, as she describes it, she "walked with the hunters, . . . [and] spoke to them about the violence and cruelty of hunting, of the beauty of the waterfowl and of their right to live

---

1. Other states' corresponding statutes, most of which were enacted within the past five years, include: Ariz. Rev. Stat. Ann. § 17-316 (1984); Del. Code Ann. title 7, § 731 (Supp. 1986); Ga. Code Ann. §§ 27-3-150 to -152 (1986); Idaho Code §§ 36-1510 (Supp. 1987); Ill. Ann. Stat. ch. 61, paras. 301–304 (Smith-Hurd Supp. 1987); La. Rev. Stat. Ann. §§ 56:648.1 to.3 (West 1987); Me. Rev. Stat. Ann. title 12, §§ 7541–7542 (Supp. 1987); Md. Nat. Res. Code Ann. § 10-422 (Supp. 1987); Mont. Code Ann. §§ 87-3-141 to -144 (1987); Nev. Rev. Stat. § 503.015 (1985); N.Y. Envtl. Conserv. Law § 11-0110 (McKinney Supp. 1988); N.D. Cent. Code § 20.1-01-31 (Supp. 1987); R.I. Gen. Laws § 20-13-16 (Supp. 1987); S.D. Codified Laws Ann. §§ 41-1-8 to -10 (1985); Tex. Parks & Wild. Code Ann. § 62.0125 (Vernon Supp. 1988); Utah Code Ann. § 23-20-29 (Supp. 1987); Vt. Stat. Ann. title 10, § 4708 (1984); W.Va Code § 20-2-2a (Supp. 1987). Such legislation is vigorously supported by the National Rifle Association.

2. One of the bill's supporters stated during floor debate that "we need to have some sort of deterrent. . . . There have been some instances where hunters' lives have been threatened by individuals clearly because of the emotional type of objection that there is to . . . taking of animals' lives." 28 S. Proc., Pt. 10, 1985 Sess., pp. 3328–29 (Sen. Benson). Another argued that "hunters are picked on often. . . . [They] should have the right to hunt in lands that are made available to them." *Id.* at 3332 (Sen. Eaton). And a third noted that "the people who are involved in this business of harassment are very apparent in their harassment . . . and they do it [purposely and] habitually and repeatedly." *Id.* at 330–31 (Sen. Gunther).

peacefully and without harm." *Id.* at para. 11. The hunters, in contrast, regarded her behavior as "antics" that were in "rude and blatant disregard of [their] rights [to] precious recreational time" and "to pursue [their] enjoyment of hunting." They advised Ms. Dorman that her actions were unlawful and, when she refused to leave, they summoned a state law enforcement officer who arrested her for violating the Hunter Harassment Act.

In a pretrial appearance in state court, the prosecutor conceded that the arrest had been premature because Ms. Dorman had only been "talking about what she was going to do to interfere with hunting geese." Transcript at 2 (April 22, 1986), *State v. Dorman*, No. CR-10-151085. At the prosecutor's request, the court dismissed the charge against Ms. Dorman for lack of probable cause.

C. *The Lawsuit*

On August 21, 1986, Ms. Dorman filed this action in federal court against C. Robert Satti, chief prosecutor for the New London Judicial District, and Lester J. Forst, Commissioner of Public Safety for the State of Connecticut, who are responsible for enforcing the laws of Connecticut and prosecuting violations thereof. The plaintiff grounds her suit in 42 U.S.C. section 1983, alleging that her arrest violated her rights under the first, fourth and fourteenth amendments; she seeks a declaratory judgment that the Hunter Harassment Act is unconstitutional on its face and as applied, and further seeks to have the court enjoin the defendants from enforcing and prosecuting under the Act.

* * *

The plaintiff has now moved for summary judgment pursuant to Rule 56, Fed. R. Civ. P., arguing that there exists no genuine issue of material fact and that, because the Act is unconstitutionally vague and overbroad, she is entitled to a judgment as a matter of law. The defendants have filed cross-motions for summary judgment, asserting the constitutionality of the Act. The court heard oral argument on September 23, 1987.

* * *

Discussion

The plaintiff asserts that the Hunter Harassment Act is facially—that is, wholly—invalid because it is unconstitutionally overbroad and vague. She grounds her argument in the premise that the statute so implicates free expression as to trigger both first amendment overbreadth analysis and the concomitant stringent review for vagueness. The defendants' position is that the plaintiff's analysis is inapposite because the Act regulates conduct, not speech. They argue that the Act is valid under the vagueness and overbreadth standards applicable to content-neutral statutes; that is, that it is reasonable regulation necessary to further substantial state interests.[5] They contend that, in effect, it is "nothing more than a reasonable time, place and manner restriction on certain conduct and incidental speech."

---

5. The authority to regulate the hunt is one of the state's ancient police powers, and is

A. *Vagueness and Overbreadth Review*

"In a facial challenge to the overbreadth and vagueness of a law, a court's first task is to determine whether the enactment reaches a substantial amount of constitutionally protected conduct." As a threshold matter, then, the court must determine whether the Hunter Harassment Act implicates the communicative aspect of the conduct it proscribes. If it does not, the Act will be regarded as content-neutral and the overbreadth challenge must fail. Furthermore, where conduct and not merely speech is involved, the Act's overbreadth "must not only be real, but substantial as well, judged in relation to the statute's plainly legitimate sweep." *Broadrick v. Oklahoma*, 413 U.S. 601, 615 (1973).

A vagueness analysis is somewhat, though not wholly,[6] different. To survive a "void for vagueness" attack, the Act must "give the person of ordinary intelligence a reasonable opportunity to know what is prohibited so that he may act accordingly," and "must provide explicit standards" so as to ensure it is not arbitrarily and discriminatorily enforced. "The issue thus is whether a person of 'common intelligence' would 'necessarily' wonder if his contemplated conduct were illegal." An enactment may be unambiguous in the sense that its terms are plain, but may nevertheless be vague in that it fails to provide a "reasonably ascertainable standard of guilt." Furthermore, when a penal statute's "literal scope, unaided by a narrowing state court interpretation," could reach such a fundamental right as freedom of speech sheltered by the first amendment, the void-for-vagueness doctrine "demands a greater degree of specificity than in other contexts."

It is not the proper function of the federal courts independently to construe a state statute so as to eliminate its vagueness or overbreadth. The validity of the

---

uncontested here. The general rule is that every person has the right to take game wherever and whenever he has a right to do so, subject to statutory regulations and so long as he does not infringe on the rights of others. The common law provides a remedy on trespass against anyone "interfering with another's right of hunting or taking game . . . if he does anything for the express purpose of destroying that right." 38 C.J.S. Game section 6 (1943). It is equally well established, however, that such regulation and remedy must come within constitutional limitations. *Id.* at section 8. Connecticut's extensive regulations of fish and game—and their taking—are located at Title 26 of the Connecticut General Statutes.

6. In approaching a combined overbreadth-vagueness claim, it is helpful to remember that: in many cases, the doctrines of vagueness and overbreadth are distinguishable. The former, originally a due process doctrine, applies when the statutory language is unclear, and is concerned with notice to the potential wrongdoer and prevention of arbitrary or discriminatory enforcement. The doctrine of overbreadth, in contrast, is exclusively a First Amendment product, and usually applies when the statutory language is clear, but encompasses activities in which people have a right to engage without interference. However, in a suit challenging an ambiguously worded statute for infringing upon First Amendment rights, the doctrines blend. The same evils are addressed, *i.e.*, application of the statute's sanctions to protected activity and deterrence of others from engaging in similar conduct, and the same remedies are available, *i.e.*, a narrowing interpretation or facial invalidation. As a result, some courts have made no attempt to distinguish the two doctrines when measuring a statute against the requirements of the First Amendment.

Hunter Harassment Act has not been litigated in the Connecticut courts. However, this court may look for well established state judicial interpretation of other statutes that may clarify this Act and effectively remove uncertainties which the statutory language may have created.

The plaintiff argues that the Act could be read to prohibit "either speech or conduct which occurs in the presence of a hunter, trapper or fisherman if [he] subjectively believes that he has been annoyed or his purposes opposed." Her interpretation arises from the fact that the Act fails to specify what conduct constitutes interference or harassment. Furthermore, that fact must be considered in context of the clause by which the Act protects "acts in preparation for" the lawful taking of wildlife, without limiting the effect of that clause to any time, place or circumstance. As such, she concludes, the Act impermissibly penalizes merely offensive or annoying speech uttered in a public place not properly subject to government regulation.

B. *Interference and Harassment*

As the Supreme Court recently reaffirmed, acts such as interference and harassment plainly encompass verbal as well as physical conduct, unless otherwise defined. *City of Houston v. Hill*, 482 U.S. 451 (1987) (rejecting as overbroad an ordinance making it unlawful to "in any manner oppose, molest, abuse or interrupt any policeman in the execution of his duty, or any person summoned to aid in making an arrest").

"Interference" offenses generally describe the prohibited conduct in concrete terms that are statutorily defined, often altogether avoiding the word "interfere." . . .

* * *

. . . [B]ecause the Act fails to define the nature of the interference it proscribes, its language implicitly sweeps as broadly as that of the *Houston* ordinance, and it thus cannot be saved by a limiting construction as was section 53a-167a. Second, in failing—by virtue of its "acts in preparation" clause—to limit the proscribed interference as to time and place, the Act carries its effect far beyond the proper scope of government regulation.

* * *

In arguing that the Act is content-neutral, the defendants note that the Act is silent as to the method or opinion of those whose conduct it proscribes. However, to be proscribed under the Act, conduct must have the objective of preventing hunting. It is as easy to accomplish that objective indirectly by verbally dissuading the hunter as directly by physical means. As such, the Act clearly encompasses communicative content.

C. *"Acts In Preparation"*

Having determined that the conduct the Act proscribes includes communication, it is necessary to find whether that communication is entitled to a First Amendment shield. The Act prohibits interference and harassment directed to "lawful taking" and to "acts in preparation for" lawful taking. "Lawful taking" clearly limits the protection to acts in times, places and circumstances identified by state fish and game laws and regulations, but "acts in preparation" are not defined or delimited. Thus, the "acts in preparation" clause can be reasonably read to encompass buying supplies long before the actual hunt takes place, which could not only include the purchase of weapons and ammunition, but could also include the purchase of food and clothing to be used on a hunting trip; consulting a road map on a public road; making plans during a workplace coffee break; or even getting a good night's sleep before embarking on a hunting trip. Conduct that intentionally interferes with those acts, or harassment of anyone undertaking them, is clearly subject to the Act as it is now framed.

In this aspect, the Act is strikingly different from those hunter harassment statutes enacted in other states that extend the legislation's scope beyond actual "lawful taking"; in those cases the statutes' broadened effect is expressly limited to "travel, camping, and other acts preparatory to taking, which occur on lands or waters upon which the affected person has the right or privilege to take such wildlife." While the Connecticut legislature is certainly not bound to adopt such alternative formulations, they do demonstrate that there exists the option of circumscribing the preparatory acts that the state may legitimately protect.

The state has a legitimate and substantial interest in managing and regulating the public lands designated for the preservation, enjoyment or taking of wildlife; the wildlife itself; and the activities of persons on those lands, including hunters. So long as the legislature elects to permit hunters to pursue their activity on property, during times, and under circumstances set aside for that purpose, it also may regulate the conduct of nonhunters in those contexts. Considerations of safety, alone, would justify such regulation, even if it impinges incidentally upon protected speech. On the other hand, the propriety of hunting and taking wildlife is a fair subject for spirited public debate. Once the hunter is outside the scope of his "lawful hunt" he is no different from any other unreceptive listener who must, "in vindication of our liberties," be "exposed to the onslaught of repugnant ideas." Because the Act extends its proscription to protected speech in forums not properly subject to state regulation, it is "unconstitutionally vague in its overly broad scope."

In conclusion, the Act as written "criminalizes a substantial amount of constitutionally protected speech." To the extent that the "acts in preparation" clause sweeps beyond the legitimate scope of the state's regulatory power over hunting and taking of wildlife, the Act is unenforceably vague in its overly broad scope. And to the extent that the prohibited harassment and interference governed by that clause include protected speech, the Act is unconstitutionally overbroad. The state is well within its power in protecting the legitimate rights of lawful hunters from harassing conduct, and "such conduct might constitutionally be punished under a properly tailored statute." But this Hunter Harassment Act is not such a statute.

Note

The district court's opinion was affirmed by the Second Circuit in *Dorman v. Satti*, 862 F.2d 432, 437 (2d Cir. 1988):

Although the Act would appear by its terms to be content-neutral, it clearly is designed to protect hunters from conduct—whether verbal or otherwise—by those opposed to hunting. Of course, to the extent that the Hunter Harassment Act can be considered content-based, it cannot withstand strict scrutiny. There is no showing that protecting hunters from harassment constitutes a compelling state interest. Nor is the statute narrowly drawn to serve any putative compelling state interest.

Many states enacted similar laws in the 1980s and 1990s. And while there have not been a significant number of additional reported cases since those here, courts continue to rule in a similar fashion. *See, e.g., Haagenson v. Pennsylvania State Police*, 490 Fed. Appx. 447 (3d Cir. 2012) (Pennsylvania hunter harassment law not unconstitutionally overbroad or vague where it prohibited "intentionally or knowingly" interfering with hunting).

State v. Miner

Court of Appeals of Minnesota, 1996
556 N.W. 2d 578

PETERSON, JUDGE. Appellants Jesse Miner and Renee Gardner each were charged with one count of harassing a hunter in violation of Minn. Stat. § 97A.037, subd. 1 (1994); one count of disturbing wild animals in violation of Minn. Stat. § 97A.037, subd. 2 (1994); one count of trespassing on public lands in violation of Minn. Stat. § 97A.037, subd. 3 (1994); and one count of trespassing on closed park lands in violation of Hennepin County ordinances. Appellants filed a pretrial motion to dismiss the charges of violating Minn. Stat. § 97A.037 on grounds that the statute was unconstitutional. The district court denied the motion.

Following a jury trial, the trial court dismissed the trespass charges. The jury found appellants guilty of the remaining charges. The trial court stayed the imposition of sentence and placed appellants on probation for one year.

On appeal, appellants argue that their convictions should be reversed because Minn. Stat. § 97A.037 is unconstitutional. This court granted the Minnesota Civil Liberties Union, Minnesota Bowhunters, Inc., and Minnesota Outdoor Heritage Alliance leave to file amicus briefs.

FACTS

Murphy-Hanrehan Park consists of over 2,000 acres of wooded areas, lakes, potholes, and fields. The park is used for recreational purposes, including mountain biking, horseback riding, hiking, cross-country skiing, and hunting. Every year in November, a bow hunt to control the deer population is held in the park. During the bow hunt, the park is closed to the general public, and only hunters whose names were drawn in a lottery are allowed in the park.

Appellants were among a group of individuals who went to the park during the bow hunt to protest the bow hunt and to talk to hunters to try to get them to change their minds about killing deer. Mark Waletzko, a bow hunter, testified that after he had been in his deer stand about one-half hour, he saw a group of about 13 people dressed in orange congregating in the parking lot. Waletzko testified that as the group approached his deer stand, they scared six deer and caused them to run by Waletzko's deer stand, but Waletzko was unable to shoot at the deer because the group of people was in his way. Waletzko did not think the group saw the deer. Waletzko said that when the group noticed him, someone said, "There's a Bambi killer." Waletzko testified that people in the group said things like, "You don't need the meat," and "You should let the deer live and let nature take its course." After talking to the group for about 15 minutes, Waletzko decided to call the Department of Natural Resources (DNR) to remove the group from the park. Waletzko identified appellants as members of the group he encountered.

Another bow hunter, Alfred Rausch, testified that when he arrived at his deer stand at about 7:00 a.m., he saw a group of people dressed in blaze orange talking, laughing, and carrying on. When the group was near Rausch, the person in front said, "There's a hunter in the tree." The same person then turned on a video camera and asked Rausch why he wanted to kill deer. Rausch testified that he heard people say, "Leave them alone," "Can't you enjoy nature," and "Why do you want to kill the deer?" According to Rausch, when he asked the group about their objective, one individual said, "Our objective here is to have you take all of your things and get out of the woods." When Rausch said he would not be leaving until about 11:00 a.m., the group sat down on a tree beneath his deer stand and talked among themselves. Rausch could not hear what they were saying. Rausch said he counted 12 people in the group. A short time later, about half the group got up and left. Rausch testified that as they were leaving, they grabbed some scent bombs, which Rausch had placed to attract deer, and threw them. Rausch testified that the presence of people under his deer stand interfered with his ability to hunt deer. Gardner was among the individuals who remained near Rausch.

Hennepin County Park Ranger Michael St. John responded to a call about appellants' group being in the park. St. John found a group of eight people walking in an open field in the park. St. John talked to the group briefly and escorted them to the parking lot where Scott County Sheriff's Deputy Mark Hartman issued tab charges to them. Miner was in this group. Hartman and DNR Conservation Officer Scott Carlson then went into the woods to look for the rest of the group. They found six individuals sitting on a log under Rausch's deer stand. When Hartman explained that the group had to leave the park, four people, including Gardner, stepped off the log like they were going to leave. Two people, however, protested about leaving. According to Hartman, the other four did not want to leave without the officers. The officers handcuffed the two who were protesting and escorted the group out of the woods.

ISSUES

I. Is Minn. Stat. §97A.037 (1994) an invalid, content-based restriction on the right to freedom of speech and expression as guaranteed by the First Amendment to the United States Constitution?

II. Is Minn. Stat. § 97A.037 a valid time, place, and manner restriction on protected expression?

III. Is Minn. Stat. § 97A.037 unconstitutionally vague or overbroad?

IV. Is Minn. Stat. § 97A.037 unconstitutional as applied to appellants?

ANALYSIS

I.

Minn. Stat. § 97A.037 (1994) provides:

> Subdivision 1. Interference with taking wild animals prohibited. A person who has the intent to prevent, disrupt, or dissuade the taking of a wild animal or enjoyment of the out-of-doors may not disturb or interfere with another person who is lawfully taking a wild animal or preparing to take a wild animal. "Preparing to take a wild animal" includes travel, camping, and other acts that occur on land or water where the affected person has the right or privilege to take lawfully a wild animal.

> Subd. 2. Disturbing wild animals prohibited. A person who has the intent to prevent or disrupt a person from lawfully taking the animals may not disturb or engage in an activity that will tend to disturb wild animals.

> Subd. 3. Persons intending to harass hunters, trappers, and anglers may not remain on land. A person who has intent to violate subdivision 1 or 2 may not enter or remain on public lands, or on private lands without permission of the owner.

* * *

Appellants argue that Minn. Stat. § 97A.037 is an invalid, content-based restriction on the exercise of First Amendment rights because only speech or expressive conduct that seeks to dissuade the taking of a wild animal is proscribed by the statute. Speech that disturbs a hunter is not prohibited, appellants contend, if there is no intent to dissuade. To illustrate their argument, appellants cite as an example a trail side vigil that disturbs a hunter. If vigil participants do not intend to prevent or disrupt the taking of a wild animal, they violate the statute only if they intend to dissuade the taking of a wild animal. Generally, statutes "enjoy a presumption of constitutionality which remains in force until the contrary is established beyond a reasonable doubt." *State v. Casino Mktg. Group, Inc.*, 491 N.W.2d 882, 885 (Minn. 1992). However, "any provision of law restricting [first amendment] rights does not bear the usual presumption of constitutionality normally accorded to legislative enactments." *Id.* (alteration in original).

When "deciding whether particular conduct possesses sufficient communicative elements to bring the First Amendment into play," *Texas v. Johnson*, 491 U.S. 397, 404, 109 S. Ct. 2533 (1989), the United States Supreme Court has asked whether "an intent to convey a particularized message was present, and [whether] the likelihood was great that the message would be understood by those who viewed it." *Id.*, 109 S. Ct. at 2539.

Minn. Stat. § 97A.037 appears not to regulate speech in that it prohibits only conduct that disturbs or interferes with another person who is lawfully taking, or preparing to take, a wild animal. But an examination of the plain language of the statute—specifically the word "dissuade"—persuades us that the statute is a content-based regulation of speech and expressive conduct.

"Dissuade" means "to deter (a person) from a course of action or a purpose by persuasion or exhortation." American Heritage Dictionary 539 (3d ed. 1992). In turn, "persuade" means "to induce to undertake a course of action or embrace a point of view by means of argument, reasoning, or entreaty," id. at 1352, and "exhort" means "to urge by strong, often stirring argument, admonition, advice, or appeal." Id. at 642. Combining these meanings, we conclude that an intent to dissuade the taking of a wild animal means an intent to use argument, reasoning, entreaty, admonition, advice, or appeal to deter the taking of a wild animal. In short, an intent to dissuade the taking of a wild animal means an intent to convey a particular message.

* * *

To the extent that Minn. Stat. § 97A.037 applies to a person whose only intent is to dissuade the taking of a wild animal or enjoyment of the out-of-doors, its purpose is related to the content of expression. An intent to convey a particular message is an element of the criminal offense created by the statute. Minn. Stat. § 97A.037 does not have only an incidental effect on some speakers or messages but not others. The statute expressly applies to a person because the person intends to convey a particular message. We, therefore, conclude that to the extent that Minn. Stat. § 97A.037 applies to a person whose only intent is to dissuade the taking of a wild animal or enjoyment of the out-of-doors, the statute is impermissibly content-based.

This conclusion, however, does not mean that Minn. Stat. § 97A.037 is invalid in its entirety.

* * *

II.

Appellants next argue that Minn. Stat. § 97A.037 fails to meet the requirements of a valid time, place, and manner restriction of protected expression. We will address this argument in light of our partial invalidation of the statute. The remaining provisions of Minn. Stat. § 97A.037 make it a crime for any person to disturb or interfere with another person who is lawfully taking or preparing to take a wild animal if the person acts with intent to prevent or disrupt the taking of a wild animal or enjoyment of the out-of-doors. It is immaterial whether a person who disturbs or interferes with a hunter intends the disturbance or interference to express an idea. On its face, the modified statute deals with conduct having no connection with speech; it does not restrict protected expression. We therefore conclude that the modified statute is not a facially invalid time, place, and manner restriction of protected expression.

III.

* * *

Unlike the Connecticut statute, Minn. Stat. § 97A.037, subd. 1, provides: "'Preparing to take a wild animal' includes travel, camping, and other acts that occur on land or water where the affected person has the right or privilege to take lawfully a wild animal." Although this provision includes a potentially wide range of activity, it limits application of Minn. Stat. § 97A.037 to times when and places where taking a wild animal is legal. *See State v. Bagley*, 474 N.W.2d 761, 766 (Wis. Ct. App. 1991) (acts preparatory to lawful hunting defy precise definition, but lack of precise definition did not render statute unconstitutionally vague; whether hunter was engaged in act in preparation for lawful hunting was fact question).

* * *

IV.

Finally, appellants argue that even if Minn. Stat. § 97A.037 is not facially invalid, it is unconstitutional as applied to them because they were engaging in constitutionally protected speech when they were arrested. They state that they had a polite conversation with two hunters, did not raise their voices or use any fighting words, and left the park when asked to do so by law enforcement authorities.

Even if we assume that appellants intended to express an idea by their conduct, the United State Supreme Court has rejected the view that an apparently limitless variety of conduct can be labeled "speech" whenever the person engaging in the conduct intends thereby to express an idea. *United States v. O'Brien*, 391 U.S. 367, 376 (1968). When "speech" and "nonspeech" elements are combined in the same course of conduct, a sufficiently important governmental interest in regulating the nonspeech element can justify incidental limitations on First Amendment freedoms. . . . [A] governmental regulation is sufficiently justified if it is within the constitutional power of the Government; if it furthers an important or substantial governmental interest; if the governmental interest is unrelated to the suppression of free expression; and if the incidental restriction on alleged First Amendment freedoms is no greater than is essential to the furtherance of the interest. *Id.* at 376–77, 88 S. Ct. at 1678–79.

Minn. Stat. § 97A.037 meets all of these requirements. The legislature possesses unquestioned authority to declare which acts or what course of conduct shall be deemed inimical to the public welfare so as to constitute a crime and to establish the appropriate punishment therefor.

Minn. Stat. § 97A.037 furthers the important governmental interest in regulating the taking of wild animals and protecting the right of individuals to hunt, fish, or otherwise take wild animals. *See* Minn. Stat. §§ 97A.015, subd. 47 (1994) ("'taking' means pursuing, shooting, killing, capturing, trapping, snaring, angling, spearing, or netting wild animals . . ."); 97A.025 (1994) (state owns wild animals of the state in its sovereign capacity for benefit of all people of the state). The state's interest in regulating the taking of wild animals and protecting the right of individuals to take wild animals is not related to the suppression of free expression.

Notes

1. *Dorman* and the *Miner* case illustrate the issues state courts have grappled with in addressing the constitutional tensions here. Courts analyzing similar statutes typically focus on some or all of the following questions:

a) What are the specific acts of the individual or individuals accused of interfering with or harassing hunters? Is there some verbal or speech component? To what degree is the challenged act conduct, and to what degree is it speech?

b) What is the intention of the interferer(s)? Are they trying to educate? To promote a political agenda? To spread a particular message? To protect individual animals?

c) Where does the offending conduct take place?

d) What conduct was interrupted, if any?

e) What was the legislative intent in creating the statute at issue?

f) What motivated the legislature to enact the laws involved?

2. In the absence of hunter harassment statutes, are there other legal bases for deterring and/or punishing the interferers? Are there other civil causes of action available to the hunters?

3. Courts employ a standard rule that, when speech and conduct are used in conjunction with one another to express an idea, "incidental" restrictions on First Amendment freedoms are allowed where there is "a sufficiently important governmental interest" in regulating the conduct. To conclude that a regulation serves purposes unrelated to the limitation of the content of expression and accordingly deem it "neutral," a court must determine, among other things, that any effects which the regulation might have on speakers or messages are only incidental.

"Incidentality" is determined on a case-by-case basis. The Supreme Court has drawn a clear distinction between incidental burdens, on the one hand, and facial (or "direct") burdens, on the other hand. *See, e.g., Church of the Lukumi Babalu Aye*, 508 U.S. 520 (1993) (excerpted and discussed earlier in this chapter). Unfortunately, there is no consistently-employed methodology for drawing this distinction.

4. Hunting protests bear significant parallels to abortion protests—a clash of constitutional rights occurs in both cases between the First Amendment right to free speech and the right to hunt/make an informed decision about termination of a pregnancy. Abortion and hunting are regulated activities that polarize political adversaries and bring their constitutional battles to the forefront of judicial disputes. In both scenarios, if the protest activity impinges upon another person's protected rights, the speech or conduct is subject to reasonable regulations on the time, place, and manner in which it is made. Any restrictions that draw distinctions based on the ideas or opinions expressed are arguably content-based and

presumptively invalid. In both contexts, protest is allowed if it does not infringe on the actors' protected conduct. The Supreme Court has held reasonable restrictions (including a "buffer zone" around abortion clinics, like those suggested around designated hunting areas in the cases here) may be imposed to maintain safety and order and to reconcile the competing interests.

5. Some individuals engage in protest and public challenges and target those who work in or are somehow connected to industries that use animals for commercial endeavors. First Amendment issues are raised by those cases as well, because the activists are exercising their rights to free speech. The courts have balanced that right with the interests of the targeted individuals in order to determine the limits of legal behavior in this area. *See, e.g., Huntingdon Life Sciences, Inc. v. Stop Huntingdon Animal Cruelty USA, Inc.,* 129 Cal. App. 4th 1228 (2005) (biomedical research).

6. In recent years, First Amendment rights of animal activists have clashed with farming interests with respect to "Ag-Gag" laws, so named because the laws at issue seek to penalize undercover investigators who wish to expose the activities in industrial farming settings. These laws, which are discussed in detail in Chapter 6, Section 1.C, may squelch public comment about the use of animals for food and fiber, and have been reviewed by the courts in recent years.

7. Defamation claims may also be made when issues of food safety are discussed. When television show host Oprah Winfrey had a program discussing the potential for bovine spongiform encephalopathy (also known as "mad cow disease") and its implications for the safety of the meat supply, she was unsuccessfully sued by a group of Texas beef industry interests. *See Texas Beef Group v. Winfrey,* 201 F.3d 680 (5th Cir. 2000), discussed in Chapter 6.

8. In a related context, there are several reported decisions in which animal advocates and activists have been sued by those whose practices they challenge. The plaintiffs, who are usually connected with industries that use animals in ways with which advocates disagree, state claims for defamation or invasion of privacy torts. Often the new publicity stemming from the case, as well as the defendants' opportunity to discuss plaintiffs' practices, can be damaging to plaintiffs even if they are successful. Because the advocates and activists are allegedly exposing illegal animal cruelty, they may have defenses not normally present in other cases with the same legal theories. *See, e.g., People for the Ethical Treatment of Animals [PETA] v. Berosini,* 894 P.2d 337 (Nev. 1995) (discussed earlier in this chapter; animal protection groups sued by Las Vegas animal abuser who beat and terrorized orangutans before live show); *PETA v. Berosini,* 111 Nev. 615, 895 P.2d 1269 (1995) (later opinion, same case); *Ouderkirk v. PETA,* 2007 U.S. Dist. LEXIS 29451 (E.D. Mich. 2007) (defamation claims by chinchilla breeders against animal protection group after disclosure of videotapes taken at breeders' facility).

Chapter 6

Commercial Uses of Animals

Section 1. Animals Raised and Slaughtered for Food

Farmed animals receive extremely limited legal protection, compared to those animals who are more visible and present on a daily basis, such as companion animals. Billions of animals are raised in the U.S. for food and fiber each year. The vast majority of people regularly consume the flesh of these animals, and wear their skins and fur/hair. Given the sheer number of animals involved and their importance to individuals and industry alike, it is counterintuitive that they do not receive at least the same level of protection as other types of animals. But, in fact, they do not, although this is slowly starting to change. This section of Chapter 6 explores the practices involved in farming animals, some examples of the legal actions that have been brought to challenge those practices, welfare-directed legislation, and what challenges remain for advocates seeking change, as well as for industry representatives who are fighting to maintain the status quo.

> If a donkey is badly beaten, a dog stoned, or a cat killed with a riding-whip, the chances are that a prosecution will ensue or a question be asked in Parliament; for public opinion and the law lay it down that the infliction of unnecessary suffering on animals is cruelty, an offence punishable by fine or imprisonment. But if in the dark and sacred precincts of our slaughterhouses some 8,000,000 sheep are killed yearly, *without first being stunned*, by a method, which even in the hands of an expert produces some seconds of acute suffering . . . , if thousands of cattle, stunned by inexperienced young slaughtermen, require two or more blows of that primitive instrument, the pole-axe; if pigs are driven in gangs into a small space and there killed, one by one, while the others squeal in terror round their dead bodies; if all this preventable suffering is inflicted daily in our slaughterhouses, what does the public opinion know of it, and what does the law care?

John Galsworthy, The Slaughter of Animals for Food 3 (1913) (emphasis in original).

In the late 1980s, approximately five billion animals were slaughtered in America for food each year.[a] By 2005, that number had doubled, equating to seventeen

---

a. C. David Coates, Old MacDonald's Factory Farm 18 (1989) ("*Factory Farm*"); Peter Singer, Animal Liberation 95 (revised ed. 1990).

thousand animals slaughtered for food each *minute* in the United States alone; the number remained generally the same in 2016.[b]

The family farms that were prevalent seventy years ago have now been replaced in large part by what are known as "factory farms"—so named because of the mass production techniques and modern business efficiency programs they have adopted. As a result, the vast majority of animals raised and slaughtered for food today are found on factory farms.[c] The goal of a factory farm is to turn out high volumes of standardized product at the lowest possible cost per "unit." "To this end all is fair; animals cease to be treated as individual living creatures—and traditional animal husbandry ethics are ignored."[d]

A. Conditions Under Which Animals Are Raised

In recent years there has been some development of laws in a limited number of states relating to the welfare of animals while being bred or raised for commercial purposes. At the federal level there are no such protections, and only limited regulation of the conditions under which animals are transported for slaughter. The "Twenty-Eight Hour Law," 49 U.S.C. § 80502, provides *de minimis* regulation relating solely to the transport of animals across state lines and applies only to a very small percentage of animals raised for food. The law requires that if animals are going to be transported "in a vehicle or vessel" for more than twenty-eight hours they must be given at least five hours of rest, watering and feeding. 49 U.S.C. § 80502(a)-(b) (2013).

Until 2006, the United States Department of Agriculture (USDA) took the position that only trains, but not trucks, were "vehicles," so that truck transport (the main form of transport of agricultural animals for decades) was not covered by the law. That year, in response to a petition for rulemaking submitted by the Humane Society of the United States, USDA conceded that trucks were vehicles, and confirmed its position that the law does not apply to birds, who represent 90 percent of the animals transported and killed for food; the only court addressing that question

---

b. U.S.D.A. National Agricultural Statistics Service (2005)—Poultry Slaughter: 2004 Annual Summary; and Livestock Slaughter: 2004 Annual Summary; U.S.D.A. Livestock Slaughter 2016 Summary (Pub. Apr. 2017).

c. In 1945 there were nearly six million farms in the United States; by 1987 there were less than 2.2 million. *Factory Farm*, at 19. That number remained more or less the same for a quarter of a century. *http:// www. bloomberg.com/ news/ 2013-02-19/ number-of-u-s-farms-fell-to-six-year-low -in-2012-usda-says-1-.html* (2.17 million farms in 2012).

d. *Factory Farm*, at 20. *See also* Amy Mosel, *What about Wilbur? Proposing a Federal Statute to Provide Minimum Humane Living Conditions for Farm Animals Raised for Food Production*, 27 Dayton L. Rev. 133, 136 (Fall 2001) ("Animals raised on the factory farm are treated like mere economic units, or widgets, as if they have no life, breath, nerves or feelings."). *See generally* Nicole Fox, *The Inadequate Protection of Animals Against Cruel Animal Husbandry Practices Under United States Law*, 17 Whittier L. Rev. 145 (Fall 1995).

has agreed with that interpretation.[e] *Clay v. New York Cent. R.R. Co.*, 231 N.Y.S. 424, 424 (N.Y. App. Div. 1928) ("Its provisions are confined to the transportation of animals in these words: 'cattle, sheep, swine or other animals.' It does not apply to poultry; birds are not animals.").[f]

By its title, one might expect that the Animal Welfare Act (AWA) (7 U.S.C. §§ 2131–2159) would apply to farmed animals, who represent more than 95 percent of the animals used in commerce. The AWA offers some protection for certain animals used in research and exhibitions, as well as for some of those in the pet industry, but it expressly excludes farmed animals raised for food from its coverage. 7 U.S.C. § 2132(g).

At the state level, the vast majority of anti-cruelty statutes expressly or impliedly (or by practical effect) provide little or no protection to animals raised for consumption. The majority of states expressly exempt at least some customary farming practices from the impact of anti-cruelty statutes. As one commentator has noted:

> The effect of this trend of amendments cannot be overemphasized. The trend indicated a nationwide perception that it was necessary to amend anticruelty statutes to avoid their possible application to animals raised for food or food production. Amendments specifically exempting customary husbandry practices indicate that, but for the exemption, such practices would be determined to be cruel.

David J. Wolfson, Beyond the Law: Agribusiness and the Systemic Abuse of Animals Raised for Food or Food Production 31 (1999).

---

e. More recently, a federal district court in California addressed the issue under the federal Humane Methods of Slaughter Act (HMSA) (discussed later in this chapter), concluding that Congress did not intend to include "poultry" within the definition of "livestock" under the HMSA, thereby leaving them with no protection under that law, but the ruling was vacated by the Ninth Circuit based on lack of standing. *Levine v. Conner*, 540 F. Supp. 2d 1113 (N.D. Cal. 2008), *vacated by*, *Levine v. Vilsack*, 587 F.3d 986 (9th Cir. 2009).

f. More generally, common carriers are subject to federal regulations governing the care and handling of animals during transportation. *See* 9 C.F.R. §§ 3.13–3.19 (dogs and cats); §§ 3.35–3.41 (guinea pigs and hamsters); §§ 3.60–3.66 (rabbits); §§ 3.86–3.92 (nonhuman primates); §§ 3.112–3.118 (marine mammals); and §§ 3.136–3.142 (warm-blooded animals other than the foregoing). Airlines, in particular, have been the focus of publicity and controversy when animals (primarily companion animals rather than those used for food) have suffered harm during transport. *See, e.g., Dalton v. Delta Airlines*, 570 F. 2d 1244 (5th Cir. 1978) (five greyhounds died en route from Ireland to Florida). In some cases farmed animals have been involved. *See, e.g., Hughes-Gibb & Co. v. The Flying Tiger Line, Inc.*, 504 F. Supp. 1239 (N.D. Ill. 1981) (sixty of plaintiff's breeding pigs allegedly suffocated to death during flight from Chicago to Manila on defendant's plane; issue was whether pigs were "damaged goods" or "destroyed goods"—*i.e.*, whether there was an economic value to the dead pigs—for purposes of the Warsaw Convention "notice of loss" requirements).

Under federal law, airlines are required to submit monthly reports "on any incidents involving the loss, injury, or death of an animal ... during air transport provided by the air carrier." 49 U.S.C. § 41721(a). "Air transport ... includes the entire period during which an animal is in the custody of an air carrier, from check-in of the animal prior to departure until the animal is returned to the owner or guardian of the animal at the final destination of the animal." 49 U.S.C. § 41721(e).

Where state legislatures have left enforcement to the state agricultural departments—agencies whose interests often seem to lie with the agribusiness industry and not with animal welfare or protection interests—they have "endowed the agribusiness community with complete authority to define what is, and is not, cruelty to the animals in their care." *Id.* As discussed in this chapter, while some states have begun to enact statutes to provide some protections or improved standards for the raising and slaughter of farmed animals, other states have enacted so-called "Ag-Gag" laws to keep the doors of agribusiness operations shuttered from public view for the benefit of the industry and to the detriment of the animals and the public. Ag-Gag laws are addressed in Section 1.C of this chapter.

Notwithstanding efforts to enact at least some limited statutory protections in some states, given the general lack of such protections for animals raised for food and fiber, animal advocates interested in ensuring better treatment for agricultural animals are left with the daunting task of using creative legal means to achieve their goals. Advocates have used litigation to raise public awareness of the harsh realities of factory farming, even where a complete legal victory may seem unlikely, given the political and regulatory climate. This chapter includes cases in which the plaintiffs are attempting to move regulators and courts toward the goal of reducing the amount of suffering experienced by farmed animals, as well as cases against the companies conducting the agribusiness operations—by consumers and/or advocacy organizations seeking to obtain and enforce farmed animal protections. It also includes lawsuits filed by state governments or industry representatives to undermine the animal protection laws. You will see that these cases arise in many contexts and present a wide variety of legal theories—including challenges to agency action in adopting regulations (as in the first case below), false advertising claims and criminal cases. Many of these cases present constitutional law issues such as standing, preemption and, with respect to Ag-Gag laws, for example, First Amendment and Equal Protection Clause issues as well. As discussed later in this chapter, members of Congress have weighed in on these issues, and legislative action and voter initiatives at the state level also have proven effective to some degree. The driving force of much of this section of the chapter is the tension between those who rely on the animals as part of their business, and those who see them as deserving of greater protections.

New Jersey Society for the Prevention of Cruelty to Animals v. New Jersey Department of Agriculture

Supreme Court of New Jersey, 2008
196 N.J. 366, 955 A.2d 886

HOENS, J. In 1996, with little discernable fanfare, the Legislature enacted a new section of the existing statute regulating animal cruelty. Although that statute, since at least 1898, had essentially left animal welfare and the protection of animals to the New Jersey Society for the Prevention of Cruelty to Animals ("NJSPCA") and its related county organizations, the Legislature decreed that the Department of

Agriculture ("the Department") would be vested with certain authority relating to the care and welfare of domestic livestock, commonly referred to as farm animals.

In doing so, the Legislature directed the Department to create and promulgate regulations that would set standards governing the raising, keeping, and marketing of domestic livestock, but it specified that the guiding principle to be utilized in establishing those standards was to be whether the treatment of these animals was "humane." The statute required the Department to consult with the New Jersey Agricultural Experiment Station[1] in developing and promulgating the regulations and established a presumption that compliance with those regulations would satisfy the other statutory standards defining animal cruelty. Although vesting the Department with this rulemaking function, the Legislature left the preexisting enforcement mechanisms, which have long relied on the NJSPCA, largely undisturbed.

This matter presents us with a broad challenge to the regulations promulgated by the Department pursuant to this legislative directive. More particularly, we are called upon to consider whether the Department, in promulgating the regulations relating to the care of domestic livestock: (1) failed in general to comply with the mandate of the Legislature that it create standards that are "humane," either objectively or as tested against the definition that the Department itself adopted; (2) created an impermissibly broad and vague category of permitted practices by referring to "routine husbandry practices" as generally acceptable; (3) failed to create an adequate regulatory scheme by utilizing undefined or ill-defined terms that cannot serve as objectively enforceable standards; and (4) embraced a variety of specific practices that are either objectively inhumane or supported by inadequate scientific evidence as to their usefulness, or that fail to meet any accepted definition of the term humane.

In part, the issues before this Court require us to evaluate the very methodology utilized by the Department in its creation of the challenged regulations; in part, the issues before us raise questions and debates arising from deeply held notions concerning the welfare of animals generally. Nonetheless, the dispute before this Court has nothing to do with anyone's love for animals, or with the way in which any of us treats our pets; rather, it requires a balancing of the interests of people and organizations who would zealously safeguard the well-being of all animals, including those born and bred for eventual slaughter, with the equally significant interests of those who make their living in animal husbandry and who contribute, through their effort, to our food supply.

In the end, our focus is not upon, nor would it be appropriate for us to address, whether we deem any of the specifically challenged practices to be, objectively,

---

1. The New Jersey Agricultural Experiment Station is a component of Rutgers, The State University of New Jersey. Its mission is "[t]o enhance the vitality, health, sustainability and overall quality of life in New Jersey by developing and delivering practical, effective solutions to current and future challenges relating to agriculture;...." New Jersey Agricultural Experiment Station, Vision and Mission Statement, *http:// njaes. rutgers.edu/ about/* (last visited July 8, 2008).

humane. To engage in that debate would suggest that we have some better understanding of the complex scientific and technical issues than we possibly could have, or that we are in some sense better able to evaluate the extensive record compiled by the Department than is that body itself. To engage in that discussion would also suggest that in a realm in which the Legislature has expressed its intention that an administrative agency bring its expertise to bear upon the issues, this Court is better equipped to do so. More to the point, it would suggest that we, rather than the Legislature or the Department, know which farming and livestock practices are objectively humane and which are not.

To accept such a challenge would be to overstep our role in our constitutional system, for it would be little more than our effort to substitute our view for that of the bodies authorized to act. It is, simply put, an invitation that we decline to accept. Rather, we confine our analysis, as we must, to a consideration about whether the agency in question did or did not carry out the function assigned to it by the Legislature, as tested in accordance with our ordinary standard of review of final agency actions and with due deference to the considerable expertise of that agency.

Notwithstanding all of the foregoing, our review of the record compels us to conclude that in its wholesale embrace of the regulations adopted by the Department, the Appellate Division erred. Because we find in those regulations both unworkable standards and an unacceptable delegation of authority to an ill-defined category of presumed experts, we conclude that the Department failed, in part, to carry out its mandate. We therefore conclude that some, but not all, of the regulations are invalid and we reverse only those aspects of the Appellate Division's judgment that concluded otherwise.

I.

The statute that created the underpinnings for the challenged regulations was first introduced for consideration by the Legislature on March 3, 1994. Designated as Senate Bill 713, . . . [t]he bill was designed to construct the framework for the adoption of standards to govern the care of domestic livestock as a part of the existing laws prohibiting cruelty to animals. . . . [¶] [New Jersey Governor Whitman] "recognize[d] the merit of this bill and its goal of setting standards for humane treatment of domestic livestock. . . ."

As enacted, the bill had two sections, the first of which was codified as N.J.S.A. 4:22-16.1. That section provides, in relevant part, as follows:

> a. The State Board of Agriculture and the Department of Agriculture, in consultation with the New Jersey Agricultural Experiment Station and within six months of the date of enactment of this act, shall develop and adopt, pursuant to the "Administrative Procedure Act," P.L. 1968, c. 410 (*C. 52:14B-1* et seq.): (1) standards for the humane raising, keeping, care, treatment, marketing, and sale of domestic livestock; and (2) rules and regulations governing the enforcement of those standards.

b. Notwithstanding any provision in this title to the contrary:

(1) there shall exist a presumption that the raising, keeping, care, treatment, marketing, and sale of domestic livestock in accordance with the standards developed and adopted therefor pursuant to subsection a. of this section shall not constitute a violation of any provision of this title involving alleged cruelty to, or inhumane care or treatment of, domestic livestock. . . .

[N.J.S.A. 4:22-16.1.]

The bill also amended N.J.S.A. 4:22-16, which more generally defines the manner in which the animal cruelty statutes are to be construed. The bill added a new section that created an exception to the animal cruelty statutes for any activity or practice performed in accordance with the regulations that the Department was directed to promulgate. . . .

A.

* * *

[T]he Department stated that it intended to "establish the minimum level of care that can be considered to be humane." 36 N.J.R. 2637 (June 7, 2004). Moreover, the Department noted that the regulations were developed after extensive "consultations with the New Jersey Agricultural Experiment Station, as well as with other academicians, the New Jersey Society for the Prevention of Cruelty to Animals, veterinarians, Department staff, extension agents, producers, and allied industries." . . .

As the Department understood its legislative mandate, and as it expressed that understanding as part of its adoption of these regulations in 2004, "[t]he rule proposal was designed to meet the complementary objectives of developing standards to protect animals from inhumane treatment and . . . fostering industry sustainability and growth." . . .

* * *

[O]n April 3, 2006, the Department, responding to continued criticism of one part of the previously promulgated regulations, proposed a further amendment that would alter the definitions and the regulations relating to a specific practice used in the management of poultry. *See* 38 N.J.R. 1491(a) (Dec. 4, 2006). In particular, the newly proposed regulations were designed to limit induced molting procedures and to ban full feed-removal forced molting[4] techniques.

---

4. Any forced molting procedure is designed to increase egg production. These procedures do so by essentially forcing the hen to molt and to lay eggs on an unnatural schedule. As adopted, the regulations do not ban such procedures in general. However, full feed-removal forced molting, which involves starving fowl or poultry for fourteen days, has been deemed to be inhumane and it has now been banned.

B.

Petitioners are a variety of entities, including the NJSPCA, and individuals which describe themselves collectively as "a wide coalition of animal protection organizations, consumers, farmers, and concerned citizens."

* * *

C.

The Appellate Division, in an unpublished opinion, rejected each of petitioners' challenges and sustained all of the challenged regulations. Relying in large part on the presumption of reasonableness afforded to acts of administrative agencies and the deferential standard of review that courts employ when reviewing matters involving an agency's scientific or technical expertise, the Appellate Division found no basis on which to invalidate any part of these regulations.

* * *

II.

Petitioners argue before this Court that the Appellate Division erred in its analysis and failed to recognize that the regulations authorize the continuation, as humane, of practices that are not. Asserting that the statute itself is remedial legislation entitled to be broadly read, petitioners argue that the Appellate Division failed to recognize the particular legislative purpose in utilizing the "humane" standard. According to petitioners, that standard was used by the Legislature to avoid simply allowing the continuation of practices that are merely routine or common. They assert that the Legislature intended instead to require the Department to consider separately whether any particular practice, even if commonly or routinely utilized, is in fact humane. Petitioners urge us to conclude that although the Department recognized this mandate, as evidenced by the definition of humane that it adopted, its regulations fall short by ignoring that definition and by effectively doing precisely what the Legislature sought to avoid.

Reiterating the specific arguments they expressed before the appellate panel, petitioners urge this Court to invalidate the regulations in their entirety. They argue that the regulations, by relying on the "routine husbandry practices" definition, created a safe harbor that cannot be sustained. Petitioners point out that because the definition of this phrase permits any practice, and equates it with a humane practice, if it is "commonly taught" at a wide variety of educational institutions, it amounts to an impermissible delegation of the Department's authority and permits as humane those practices that are not. Before this Court, petitioners have expanded this argument to include an assertion that the Department, in including this wide assortment of educational and other institutions within its definition, failed to review or analyze their curricula or their programs to ensure that any of them actually teaches practices that are humane. They assert that because of this shortcoming, the Department acted without an essential basis in the record, resulting in the adoption of regulations not entitled to the Court's deference.

Petitioners also reiterate the other arguments that they pressed before the Appellate Division[.] They urge the Court to conclude that the regulations fail to set an enforceable standard by utilizing language, such as "minimize pain," without further definition, so as to provide insufficient guidance to those charged with enforcement and that the regulations therefore fail to establish any standard. Finally, they point to a large number of particular practices that are permitted to be performed by the regulations but that, they assert, are not humane in accordance with the Department's definition or which are of dubious benefit according to the scientific evidence. In short, because the regulations have both specific shortcomings and general ones, petitioners urge this Court to invalidate the regulations in their entirety.

The Department urges this Court to affirm the Appellate Division's carefully analyzed and lengthy opinion and to uphold the regulations both in general and in all of their particulars. More specifically, the Department argues that its regulations should be afforded great deference and that the Appellate Division correctly determined that petitioners did not meet their heavy burden to overcome the agency's expertise in setting up appropriate standards. It stresses that its regulations are supported by an extensive record and represent its considered judgment in carrying out its role of both promoting viable agriculture and ensuring animal and public health.

The Department argues in particular that its "routine husbandry practices" exemption is consistent with the statutory mandate and is an appropriate means to permit the continuation of practices that should be permitted. It points out that in response to criticism that its original definition of "routine husbandry practices" was too broad, it introduced and adopted the amended definition, limiting such practices only to those that are "commonly taught" at veterinary schools, land grant colleges,[8] and universities or by agricultural extension agents. At the same time, the Department urges the Court to reject petitioners' assertion that it did not review the curricula of these institutions before relying on them as part of its safe harbor. The Department notes instead that it consulted with educators and experts, reviewed various curricula, texts, federal and state statutes, as well as state and national standards, and asserts that it therefore fully discharged its statutory obligations.

The Department also urges this Court to reject petitioners' other arguments that the regulations fail to establish enforceable standards, as well as the challenges to each of the specific practices that the agency elected to include within the subsections identifying techniques that are permissible. It asserts that it has faithfully carried out its mandate to ensure that the practices used in animal husbandry are humane, and has exercised its expertise in order to do so. In support of this argument, the Department explains that in those cases in which it identified practices

8. The National Association of State Universities and Land-Grant Colleges explains that "[a] land-grant college or university is an institution that has been designated by its state legislature or Congress to receive the benefits of the Morrill Acts of 1862[, 7 *U.S.C.A.* §§ 301 to 308] and 1890[, 7 U.S.C.A. §§ 321 to 329]." *The Land-Grant Tradition* (1995), *available at* http://www.wvu.edu/~exten/about/land.htm (last visited July 8, 2008).

that are not humane, it has acted to eradicate them, pointing to its decision to ban full feed-removal forced molting.

The Department argues that the regulations set forth a baseline of behavior that farmers are free to exceed if they so desire and explains that underlying the regulations it adopted is the belief that farmers genuinely care for their animals and are aware of the basics of animal biology and behavior. As such, the Department urges us to reject the arguments raised by petitioners and to agree with the Appellate Division that there is no ground on which to invalidate any aspect of the regulations.

In addition to the arguments made by petitioners and by the Department, we granted leave to a number of other interested individuals and entities to file briefs as amicus curiae.

* * *

III.

We begin with a recitation of the well-established principles that inform our review of the final decisions of administrative agencies like the Department. Because the challenge brought by petitioners proceeds on multiple levels, we set forth the standards that apply to each.

First, the general parameters of our review are not controversial. Appellate courts ordinarily accord deference to final agency actions, reversing those actions if they are "arbitrary, capricious or unreasonable or [if the action] is not supported by substantial credible evidence in the record as a whole." Similarly, an appellate court generally will not reverse an agency action, including its action in promulgating regulations, unless: (1) the regulations at issue "violate[ ] the enabling act's express or implied legislative policies;" or (2) "there is [not] substantial evidence in the record to support the findings on which the agency based its action;" or (3) "in applying the legislative policies to the facts the agency clearly erred by reaching a conclusion that could not reasonably have been made upon a showing of the relevant factors." *In re Rulemaking,* N.J.A.C. 10:82-1.2 & 10:85-4.1, 117 N.J. 311, 325 (1989).

Moreover, in our review of an agency's interpretation of statutes within its scope of authority and its adoption of rules implementing its enabling statutes, we afford the agency great deference. As we have explained: "[s]uch deference is appropriate because it recognizes that 'agencies have the specialized expertise necessary to enact regulations dealing with technical matters and are "particularly well equipped to read . . . and to evaluate the factual and technical issues that . . . rulemaking would invite."'" For this reason, we begin with a presumption that an agency's regulations are both valid and reasonable and we place on the challenging party the burden of proving that the regulation violates the statute.

Nevertheless, if a regulation is "inconsistent with the statute it purports to interpret," it will be invalidated. As we have held, an agency "may not under the guise of interpretation . . . give the statute any greater effect than its language allows." "Thus, if the regulation is plainly at odds with the statute, [the court will] set it aside." Even if a regulation falls within the scope of the agency's legislative authority, it will nonetheless be invalidated if the agency "significant[ly]" fails "to provide . . . regulatory standards that would inform the public and guide the agency in discharging its authorized function," because a failure of that magnitude raises due process concerns. As we have explained, the "deference [we afford to agencies] does not require abdication by the judiciary of its function to assure that agency rulemaking conforms with basic tenets of due process, and provides standards to guide both the regulator and the regulated." In keeping with these familiar standards, we turn to our review of the particular regulations in issue.

IV.

A.

The regulations themselves are divided into several subchapters, each of which addresses a different aspect of the statutory mandate in the context of the care and treatment of domestic livestock. The first part of the regulations, N.J.A.C. 2:8-1.1 to -1.2, sets forth the agency's statement of purpose, its presumption that acts in accordance with the regulations will "not constitute cruelty . . . or inhumane care and treatment" in violation of the statute, N.J.A.C. 2:8-1.1, and lists the definitions that shall apply to the terms used in the regulations, N.J.A.C. 2:8-1.2.

The next six subchapters of the regulations set forth standards that relate to particular types of domestic livestock[;] . . . the majority of each subchapter is devoted to individualized practices and management techniques for each animal or group of animals.

For example, each includes subsections setting forth general provisions, as well as standards relating to "feeding," "watering," "keeping," "marketing and sale," and "care and treatment" of the particular group of animals in question. Each subchapter, however, also includes a subsection entitled "exceptions," that creates a so-called "safe harbor" provision. As to each type of farm animal, this provision identifies a number of particular practices that are explicitly permitted if they are performed by "knowledgeable individuals in a sanitary manner in a way to minimize pain," and authorizes other techniques by reference to "routine husbandry practices" as defined in N.J.A.C. 2:8-1.2.

The final subchapter of the regulations, N.J.A.C. 2:8-8.1 to -8.7, provides standards governing "the investigation and enforcement of alleged violations of humane standards" applicable to domestic livestock.

B.

In order to fully appreciate the challenges to the regulations and, in particular, the effect of the subsections that either explicitly permit certain practices or establish a safe harbor, we turn briefly to an analysis of the more general provisions of the laws that are designed to prevent and to punish cruelty to animals. The statutory provisions relating to the prevention of cruelty to animals are found in Chapter 22 of Title 4, which is devoted to Agriculture. As it is currently codified, that Chapter continues the existence of the NJSPCA and its county societies. . . .

As an integral part of the enforcement scheme, Chapter 22 includes several sections that define the meaning and scope of animal cruelty and its prevention. It does so in part by defining both in general and in very specific terms the acts that will constitute cruelty and by identifying the penalties, both civil and criminal, that will be imposed for particular violations. *See, e.g.,* N.J.S.A. 4:17-26.

In addition, however, the statute specifies a large variety of acts and practices that shall not be "prohibit[ed] or interfere[d] with," that is, acts and practices that shall not, by definition, constitute cruelty. *See* N.J.S.A. 4:22-16. These acts and practices include, for example, certain rather broadly defined scientific experiments, training of dogs for various purposes, and hunting and fishing in accordance with relevant regulations as to time and manner. It is in this section of the statute that the Legislature added, as part of the 1996 statutory amendment, a general exception from the acts comprising cruelty for "raising, keeping, care, treatment, marketing, and sale of domestic livestock" if performed in accordance with the regulations that were to be adopted pursuant to N.J.S.A. 4:22-16.1. *See* N.J.S.A. 4:22-16 (codifying L. 1995, c. 311, § 2).

The statute therefore, although it generally prohibits acts and practices that constitute cruelty, also explicitly permits other acts that fall within one of its exceptions. For purposes of this appeal, the result is that any act that meets the standards embodied in the Department's regulations as a permitted act, practice or technique, is, by definition, not an act of cruelty. As a result, all of the acts included in the several "safe harbor" provisions of these regulations, as long as they are performed in accordance with the standards that those provisions impose, are permitted by the statute because, by definition, they are not acts of cruelty.

By extension, however, if the safe harbor provisions themselves cannot be sustained, or if one or more of the acts now included in the safe harbor provisions lacks sufficient support in the record for it to withstand our review, the effect would not be that any of these procedures is banned. Rather, the effect would be that any of them could still be performed if otherwise consistent with the statutory definition of what is cruel and what is not. That is to say, even if this Court were to strike the safe harbor subsections in their entirety or strike the inclusion of specific practices that are now there permitted, it would not constitute a ban on those practices. Instead, the ordinary statutory provisions regarding what acts constitute cruelty, as well as those that govern the detection, investigation, and prosecution of violations, would operate as the appropriate regulatory mechanism pending promulgation of new regulations by the Department.

We turn, then, to a consideration of the issues raised in this appeal, which we analyze in light of this statutory and regulatory framework.

C.

In its lengthy consideration of the questions about animal cruelty in the context of domestic livestock, the Department compiled an extensive record. That record includes a wide variety of materials, representing input from numerous organizations (*e.g.*, Animal Welfare Institution, National Pork Board, United Egg Producers), individuals and interest groups from New Jersey and nationally (*e.g.*, Temple Grandin, Bernard Rollin, People for the Ethical Treatment of Animals, Farm Sanctuary, Professional Rodeo Cowboys Association), as well as materials from other states (*e.g.*, Pennsylvania, New York, Maine, Texas, West Virginia, Montana, New Mexico), and even from other countries (*e.g.*, England, Australia, New Zealand).

The record before this Court is not only extensive, but it is broad in its scope. On its face, the record demonstrates that the Department took seriously its charge to consider all aspects of the questions about the welfare of domestic livestock. In doing so, the Department did not simply consider the views and the input of farmers, agriculture professionals and their trade organizations, but it also received and took into account the views of animal rights activists and animal welfare organizations.

At the same time, the Department received input into its decisions from a wide variety of professionals, scholars, veterinarians, and other experts in all phases of animal welfare, animal health, and farming practices. The record includes a large number of scientific studies and scholarly publications reflecting both existing practices and trends, in this country and abroad, and representing current thinking about humane practices in the fields of animal husbandry, veterinary sciences, and agriculture. In addition, during the rulemaking process, the Department received and responded to thousands of comments, including many objections to its proposed regulations, in its effort to adopt regulations that more accurately carried out the legislative goal of ensuring that farm animals are treated humanely.

* * *

V.

Petitioners first assert that the regulations, in their entirety, fail to carry out the fundamental goal of the Legislature to have the Department create regulations that embody standards that are humane. They assert that the regulations neither comply with the meaning of humane as it is contemplated by the statute, nor do they even accord with the definition of humane that the agency itself adopted.

Petitioners first point out that, in enacting the statute, the Legislature referred explicitly to "humane" practices relating to livestock rather than, as other states have done, referring to a lesser standard, such as "routine" or "commonly practiced" management techniques. In order to give full meaning and effect to the intent of the Legislature, therefore, petitioners argue that the agency was required to look beyond the practices currently utilized and to identify and permit only those practices that meet this higher standard, but that it failed in this mission.

More to the point, petitioners point out that the Department itself adopted a definition of humane that many of the practices that are explicitly permitted or that fall within the safe harbor cannot meet. Although they point to several particular practices that they argue are examples of the way in which the regulations fall short, petitioners insist that this defect is so pervasive that the regulations cannot be sustained at all.

The Department argues that its regulations do not violate the requirements of the statute. The Department rejects the suggestion that the statute required an elevated standard and asserts that nothing in the regulations in fact violates the definition of humane that it adopted.

Our review of this record compels us to reject both aspects of petitioners' broad attack on these regulations. The statute that directed the Department to enact regulations relating to animal cruelty and adoption of humane practices, N.J.S.A. 4:22-16.1, comes to this Court with virtually no legislative history. The scant evidence that surrounds its passage, the conditional veto message, and the references included in various pronouncements in the time since its enactment, do not include evidence from which we can conclude that it was enacted as a response to complaints about particular agricultural practices or to domestic livestock management techniques generally. To be sure, we regard it as remedial legislation and we interpret it in that light, but there is no clue in this record about any particular evil that the legislation was designed to eradicate or even to remedy.

Plainly, the Department recognized that part of its charge was to adopt regulations that would ensure that the treatment of farm animals was humane, as opposed to merely reciting those practices that were accepted, routine, common, or prevalent. Just as plainly, the Department understood that the effectuation of its legislative mandate required that it adopt a definition of humane, because this is the critical term in the statute. As a result, the Department included in its regulations, both as originally proposed and as finally adopted, the following definition: "'Humane' means marked by compassion, sympathy, and consideration for the welfare of animals." N.J.A.C. 2:8-1.2(a).

In addition, although not part of the definition of "humane," the Department also proposed and adopted definitions of two related terms. As such, it defined both "Animal welfare" and "Well-being." The former, which is included in the list of defined terms, "means a state or condition of physical and psychological harmony between the animal and its surroundings characterized by an absence of deprivation, aversive stimulation, over stimulation or any other imposed condition that adversely affects health and productivity of the animal." *Ibid.* The latter, found in the same part of the regulations, is defined as follows: "'Well-being' means good health and welfare." *Ibid.*

We do not read in this statute or in these definitions any standard that requires that the regulations be invalidated in their entirety. In order to do so we would need to conclude either that the agency failed to consider the requirement of the statute that "humane" treatment be the touchstone or that, in light of the statutory standard and the definition adopted by the Department itself, its regulations as a whole are arbitrary, capricious or unreasonable. Indeed, because these regulations are the expression of the agency's determinations in an area within its technical expertise, in order to invalidate them in their entirety, we would need to discern an inherent flaw in the very process by which they were drafted and adopted or in the record that supports them.

The extensive record and careful response of the Department to the overwhelming number of comments does not permit us to so conclude. Even though there may be particular practices that the regulations specifically embrace and that might fall short of this lofty language, we cannot say that this is true as to each and every aspect of the regulations, or as to all of the practices that they permit. [¶] ... [M]atters included in the subchapter concerning cattle, for example, set forth broadly applicable requirements relating to adequate provision of water, N.J.A.C. 2:8-2.3, that have not been attacked as failing to meet any of the definitions of "humane" or its related terms as adopted by the Department. [¶] Likewise, the regulations governing many similar matters relating to the other types of farm animals are not challenged and appear to be uncontroversial in terms of whether or not they represent techniques that are humane. Regardless of one's personal view of the overall regulatory scheme or of domestic livestock management in general, the regulations as a whole are consistent with the meaning of the term "humane."

In so concluding, we are guided by two considerations. First, petitioners suggest that they have merely pointed to specific examples of treatment that they have identified as falling short of the definition of "humane," in an effort to illustrate a larger defect in the regulations. They argue that these examples alone should suffice to prove the bankruptcy of the process used by the Department in adopting the regulations and should therefore support a decision to invalidate the regulations in their entirety.

We, however, do not agree. Rather, we interpret petitioners' failure to suggest that the great majority of the practices permitted in these apparently uncontroversial requirements are not humane, as significant. That failure is instead evidence that they are not so wide of that mark that they constitute an agency action with which we should interfere. Although one or another of the specifically challenged practices within the regulations may individually fall short of the standard of review that we employ, that is an insufficient ground on which to invalidate the whole.

Second, the record reflects that the Department has considered objections to some of the originally proposed and adopted regulations and then concluded, on further review, that the objections were meritorious. In particular, as it relates to the challenged practice of full feed-removal during induced molting, the Department has not only been responsive to the continued objections to that particular technique, but has concluded that it should be banned. See 38 N.J.R. 4991(a) (Dec. 4, 2006). Far from the picture of an agency held hostage by the interests of agribusiness that petitioners would paint, the Department has not been unresponsive to arguments about specific practices that do not meet its definition of those that are humane.

These two considerations, in addition to our review of the record on appeal itself, inform our decision. The specific challenges to the regulations, both as to particular practices and as to the safe harbor provisions, do not, in and of themselves, nor in the larger context of the regulatory process, suggest that the Department failed to propose and adopt regulations that are essentially grounded upon a determination about what practices are humane. In the absence of some evidence that the regulations include some pervasive defect in process or content, we decline to invalidate them in their entirety.

VI.

Petitioners next challenge the inclusion in the regulations of language creating a safe harbor for any act or technique that meets the definition of "routine husbandry practices." N.J.A.C. 2:8-1.2. This exception, included in one of the subsections of each subchapter, essentially authorizes the use of any and all techniques that meet this definition because it identifies this class of practices as not being prohibited.[12]

The phrase "routine husbandry practices" is among the terms that the Department included in its section on definitions as follows:

> "Routine husbandry practices" means those techniques commonly taught by veterinary schools, land grant colleges, and agricultural extension agents for the benefit of animals, the livestock industry, animal handlers and the public health and which are employed to raise, keep, care, treat, market and transport livestock, including, but not limited to, techniques involved with physical restraint; animal handling; animal identification; animal training; manure management; restricted feeding; restricted watering; restricted exercising; animal housing techniques; reproductive techniques; implantation; vaccination; and use of fencing materials, as long as all other State and Federal laws governing these practices are followed.

[N.J.A.C. 2:8-1.2.]

Petitioners assert that the definition of "routine husbandry practices" is so broad and all-encompassing that it amounts to an improper delegation of the agency's authority, contrary to its legislative mandate. Moreover, they argue that the record reveals that the Department, in adopting this definition and this standard for what constitutes "humane," failed to even review or evaluate the practices that it would permit. In particular, they assert that the definition includes a wide variety of institutions, each of which has become the arbiter of which practices are humane, but that the Department did not undertake any analysis of these institutions. In part, they point out that the record includes no evaluation of any of the texts used or the curricula that they follow, and no investigation of their course catalogs or instructional personnel. In short, petitioners argue that there is nothing in the record that

---

12. In actuality, the regulations also require that, in order to be included in the safe harbor, any such practice must also be "performed in a sanitary manner by a knowledgeable individual and in such a way as to minimize pain." *See, e.g.,* N.J.A.C. 2:8-2.6(f). That aspect of the safe harbor is separately challenged by petitioners and we consider this separate criterion in the context of the specific practices that petitioners have attacked. *See* Point VII.B., *infra.*

would suggest that any of these institutions teaches practices that would meet the Department's own definition of "humane."

Amicus Rollin concurs, arguing that merely because a practice is routinely employed or taught, even if taught at a veterinary school, does not mean that it is humane. Rather, he argues that many practices taught at these institutions are motivated by concerns about the economics of agriculture, focusing on productivity alone, and ignoring any concerns about the welfare of the animals involved. As such, he argues that these practices, even if commonly taught, simply cannot be equated with practices or techniques that are also humane.

The Department argues that there is nothing in its definition of "routine husbandry practices" that fails to meet its mandate. It argues that the record fully supports its decision to rely on a variety of educational institutions as a mechanism to define and to identify permissible practices, contending that this choice was in keeping with its charge to create regulations that are "humane." In particular, the Department asserts that it undertook to review a variety of texts and curricula from many educational institutions as part of its consideration of this part of the regulations.

In support of its decision, the Department also points out that the statute itself directed the agency to cooperate with the New Jersey Agricultural Experiment Station, suggesting that this is evidence that the Legislature intended that the agency would rely on similar institutions, even to the point of including them within the safe harbor exception. Finally, the Department asserts that its mandate was not to create a complex series of detailed regulations about particular practices, but to implement general standards that would permit individual farmers to utilize their judgment in the same way that regulations governing doctors or accountants operate. In light of these considerations, the Department urges us to reject the challenge to the "routine husbandry practices" exception.

As adopted, this exception is different from the one that was proposed. To be sure, the originally proposed regulations included an exception for "routine husbandry practices," but defined that term in broader language. In place of the opening phrase in the regulations as adopted that refers to "techniques commonly taught by veterinary schools, land grant colleges, and agricultural extension agents," the original proposal included a different measuring stick. It referred to "techniques commonly employed and accepted as necessary or beneficial to raise, keep, care, treat, market, and transport livestock, . . ." During the notice and comment period, this standard was strongly criticized, both because it was inherently vague and for its apparent inclusion of practices that are not humane. In response, the Department commented that its initial definition "did not clearly reflect its intent that only those techniques commonly taught by veterinary schools, land grant colleges, and agricultural extension agents are considered appropriate." For this reason, the Department immediately proposed amendments to the regulations that resulted in the definition as it now stands.

Notwithstanding its assertion that the revised definition more accurately reflected its intent, and notwithstanding its insistence that its review was careful prior to its decision to effectively place into the hands of this wide-ranging and ill-defined group of presumed experts the power to determine what is humane, there is no evidence in the record that the Department undertook any review, organized or passing, of what these institutions actually teach. On the contrary, there is clear evidence in the record that the Department only attempted to collect and review the curricula of any of these institutions during the pendency of the appeal to this Court. Although one might well debate whether review of curricula or course guides alone would be sufficient, failing to do so at all leaves the agency's decision to rely on these institutions without any basis in the record.

Nor is there any evidence that the Department considered whether the techniques taught in these institutions, whatever those techniques might be, rest in any way on a concern about what practices are humane or have any focus other than expedience or maximization of productivity. Contrary to the Department's assertion, there is no evidence that it considered the intersection between the interests of those who attend these institutions or are taught by them and those who are concerned with the welfare of the animals.

Our review of this aspect of the appeal leads us to conclude that this part of the safe harbor exemption demonstrates two separate flaws. First, it cannot be denied that in enacting this statute, the Legislature directed the Department to achieve a specific goal and that it chose to do so in language that differed from similar statutes in other states. It is significant that the Legislature sought to exempt only "humane" practices from prosecution under the cruelty code. Whereas other states have exempted routine, common, or accepted practices from their cruelty codes, our Legislature chose not to use that language, selecting a different course.

To suggest, as the Department's "routine husbandry practices" definition implies, that the Legislature meant "routine" when it said "humane" would "abuse the interpretive process and . . . frustrate the announced will of the people." The wholesale adoption, as the equivalent of "humane," of "routine husbandry practices," however, does precisely that.

Second, in light of the direct mandate to the Department to adopt regulations that establish practices that are humane, the decision by that agency to authorize an exemption, and therefore to embrace wholesale any technique as long as it is "commonly taught" at any of these institutions, under the circumstances, is an impermissible subdelegation. As our Appellate Division has recognized, the "power . . . delegated by statute to an administrative agency cannot be subdelegated in the absence of any indication the Legislature so intends." In fact, because of the nature of the entities included within the safe harbor exemption, the Department did not simply engage in a subdelegation, but did so in favor of some entities that also might be described as private interests.

We are not persuaded, in these circumstances, that the direction from the Legislature to the Department to work with the New Jersey Agricultural Experiment Station is an indication that the Legislature intended that the agency would thereafter subdelegate its authority in so thorough a fashion. Although it might suggest that a limited subdelegation to that specific entity would be permitted, the Department went far beyond that narrow reading of the statute.

As an example, the Department could have reviewed the curriculum and faculty at a number of land grant colleges, universities, and veterinary schools and identified some where animal welfare concerns resulted in teaching of practices that meet the Department's definition of humane. Had it done so and had it then used those institutions as its safe harbor yardstick, there would be no basis for a challenge. Indeed, had the Department reviewed and relied on practices taught at Rutgers School of Environmental and Biological Sciences, formerly known as Cook College, and, perhaps, a veterinary school in New York or Pennsylvania, there would likely be no warrant for our interference. Instead, it accepted, without analysis, the practices that are taught in every veterinary school, land grant college, and agricultural extension agent not only in this state, but in the rest of the country and, it would appear, wherever they might be found around the globe. Although some of those institutions might teach or require practices that are far more humane than do our own, nothing in the record suggests that all of them will meet the standard set by our Legislature.

Our analysis of petitioners' objections to the several subsections of the regulations that create a safe harbor by reliance on "routine husbandry practices" compels us to conclude that these objections have merit. By adopting a definition of exceptional breadth, by failing to create an adequate record in support of this decision, and by implicitly permitting techniques that cannot meet the statutory mandate to base its regulations on a determination about what is humane, the Department has adopted regulations that are arbitrary and capricious. We therefore strike as invalid the definition of "routine husbandry practices," *see* N.J.A.C. 2:8-1.2, and that part of each of the subsections of the regulations referring thereto, see N.J.A.C. 2:8-2.6(f), -3.6(f), -4.7(e), -5.7(e)(2), -6.6(d), -7.6(d).

VII.

Petitioners also challenged individually a number of practices that are specifically permitted by the regulations, asserting that they are demonstrably inhumane and that the Department's authorization thereof is unsupported by sound science. In particular, petitioners point to several procedures utilized by some farming operations that are physically painful and, they contend, are emotionally distressing to the animals. At the same time, they argue, these same practices cannot be justified because they are often of little or no value. In response, the Department counters that there is ample scientific evidence in the record that supports the continued use of each of these procedures. Moreover, the Department asserts that because the regulations include limits on the manner and circumstances in which any of these disputed practices is permitted, the practical result is that each of them is only performed in a humane manner.

* * *

This part of the challenge focuses on several practices that are identified[14] in the regulations, as part of the safe harbor provisions or as otherwise permissible, and that therefore are presumptively humane. The challenged practices are: tail docking of cattle; use of crates or tethering of swine, cattle, and veal calves; castration (without required anesthesia) of cattle, horses, and swine; de-beaking of poultry; toe-trimming of turkeys (without required anesthesia); and transporting sick and downed cattle to slaughter.

A.

The first specific practice that petitioners attack relates only to dairy cattle. This practice, known as "tail docking," *see* N.J.A.C. 2:8-2.6(f), is a procedure that involves "the amputation of the lower portion of a dairy cow's tail." Lawrence J. Hutchinson, *Tail Docking for Cattle* (1997). Petitioners contend that tail docking cannot meet the Department's definition of humane, and they point to evidence of a consensus among scientists that tail docking is without any "apparent animal health, welfare, or human health justification." *See* C.L. Stull et al., *Evaluation of the scientific justification for tail docking in dairy cattle*, 220 J. Veterinary Med. Assoc. 1298, 1302 (May 1, 2002).

They further assert that tail docking causes acute pain and interferes with the ability of the affected animals to perform natural behaviors, including flicking their tails to chase away flies in the summer. *See* S.D. Eicher & J.W. Dalley, *Indicators of Acute Pain and Fly Avoidance Behaviors in Holstein Calves Following Tail-docking*, 85 J. Dairy Sci. 2850 (2002). Moreover, petitioners note that both the American (AVMA) and Canadian (CVMA) Veterinary Medical Associations oppose tail docking of dairy cattle, and they point to the AVMA's position paper that states: "[c]urrent scientific literature indicates that routine tail docking provides no benefit to the animal, and that tail docking can lead to distress during fly seasons." *See* AVMA, *Animal Welfare Position Statements: Tail Docking of Cattle* (2005), *see also* CVMA, *Animal Welfare Position Statements: Tail Docking of Dairy Cattle* (2003). Petitioners argue that a practice from which the animal derives no benefit, and that will cause it to suffer distress, cannot be humane.

The Department contends that, despite the AVMA's position paper, its decision to permit tail docking to continue to be performed complied with its statutory mandate to create humane standards. The agency points out that it responded to comments objecting to the practice, and that it reasoned that the practice should be

---

14. Petitioners also included in their brief an assertion that force-feeding of geese for the purpose of creating foie gras is not humane. They suggest that because the regulations do not specifically prohibit this practice, the regulations can be interpreted to permit a practice that is inhumane and are, therefore, defective. We perceive of this as an application to this Court to impose a ban on this particular practice, a request that would be inconsistent with the organizational structure of the statute and the regulations and, in our view, a request that is more properly within the province of the legislative branch.

permitted because it may lead to better milk quality and udder health, and it may also reduce the spread of diseases.

Nonetheless, the agency also commented that because the science is inconclusive concerning whether these benefits will be achieved, the Department "discourages" routine tail docking, leaving it to each producer to decide whether to engage in the practice. In doing so, the agency points out that its position is consistent with that espoused by the American Association of Bovine Practitioners, and it assures this Court that it intends to monitor the effects of this procedure and that it will ban the practice in the future if it concludes that the procedure is cruel or inhumane.

Although we recognize the considerable expertise that the Department brought to bear in reaching its decision to include tail docking within its list of permitted practices, it is difficult to find in this record any support for this particular practice, and none that meets the requisite standard of our review. The record amply demonstrates that, far from being humane, this practice is specifically disparaged by both the AVMA and the CVMA as having no benefit and as leading to distress. The only scientific evidence that even suggests that the practice might have some possible benefit is inconclusive at best.

More to the point, the record in support of the practice is so weak that even the industry trade group, like the Department, "discourages" it, leaving it apparently to the individual conscience of each dairy farmer. In light of the regulatory scheme, however, the practice was listed among those that are permitted and presumptively humane. The result is, therefore, to generally permit a practice for no apparent reason, and to permit it to be performed in accordance with no particular safeguards or standards, save for the Department's promise that it will ban tail docking in the future if it concludes that the practice is inhumane.

Apart from failing to adhere to the Legislative mandate that the agency permit only those practices that it finds to be humane (as opposed to not inhumane), because this practice finds no support at all in the record, to the extent that the regulation permits it, that aspect of the regulation is both arbitrary and capricious. In the absence of evidence in the record to support the practice or to confine it to circumstances in which it has a benefit and is performed in a manner that meets an objective definition of humane, this aspect of the regulation cannot stand.

B.

For purposes of our analysis, we have identified several of the challenged practices that we find it appropriate to consider together. This group comprises three specific practices that are similar in terms of petitioners' focus and our evaluation of the record: (1) castration of swine, horses, and calves; (2) de-beaking of chickens and turkeys; and (3) toe-trimming of turkeys. Each is a procedure that petitioners assert is, by and large, unnecessary, because each seeks to prevent behaviors, or the effects thereof, in which animals would likely not engage were they not raised in close quarters. In addition, petitioners challenge these practices because each is performed without anesthetics, thus causing the animals significant, if not severe, pain.

As to each of these practices, the Department implicitly recognizes that there are sound animal husbandry and management reasons for raising livestock in relatively close quarters that it elects not to prohibit. In light of that largely philosophical viewpoint, the Department asserts that its review of the scientific and professional literature supports its conclusion that the specific practices provide benefits to the health and safety of livestock. Moreover, the Department points out that its regulations address the question of pain and do so by adding the limitation on use of each of these procedures, requiring that they be performed by "knowledgeable persons" who are required to "minimize pain." In this manner, the agency asserts that it has ensured that each procedure will be performed in a manner that is in fact humane.

It is apparent from the record that each of these specific practices is rather controversial. Part of that controversy, however, stems from the larger question of whether farm animals are to be raised in close quarters or in spacious and relatively unconfined surroundings. That philosophical debate about how farm animals are raised and kept in general cannot help but affect one's views about whether some of these procedures are, on the one hand, pointless and cruel, or on the other hand, necessary techniques for managing the livestock in one's care.

That debate about whether domestic livestock should be kept in close quarters or left relatively unconfined, however, is not addressed in the statute. Nothing in the statute suggests that the Legislature intended to embrace the latter and reject the former; the record instead reflects that the agency was charged with finding an appropriate balance between the interests of animal welfare advocates and the need to foster and encourage agriculture in this state. Notwithstanding the ardent views of some of the individuals who have voiced opinions throughout the regulatory process, we do not view our role as including the right or the obligation to weigh in on that debate; we consider instead that it remains within the scope of the agency's expertise to strike a balance between the competing positions of the parties, guided only by the standards of review to which we have adverted.

The record reflects that there is evidence that demonstrates these practices confer a benefit on the animals in light of their living conditions. For example, castration is generally employed to reduce aggression between male animals, including horses and cattle, when they are kept together in a herd. Similarly, beak trimming is used to reduce such behaviors as cannibalism and pecking within a flock. In a like manner, toe-trimming is performed to prevent turkeys from climbing on one another and causing injury and to prevent them from inflicting injury on their caregivers or handlers. Although there are other management techniques that might achieve the desired results without employing these particular methods, there is sufficient credible evidence in the record to support the agency's conclusion that these techniques can be performed in a humane manner and should be permitted.

Were the issue before this Court merely a matter of deciding whether the scientific evidence supports the use of the procedures at all, our task would be a simple one; were that our task, we would be constrained to conclude that there is sufficient evidence in the record to support the Department's decision that they be permitted.

That, however, is not the only question before this Court. Instead, the question is whether there is sufficient support in the record for the Department's decision to specifically permit these practices in the context of its mandate that it adopt regulations that will ensure that the treatment of animals is humane.

As to that more specific question, petitioners argue that the particular procedures cannot be humane if they are performed without the use of anesthetics or other pain management techniques. They point to literature suggesting that all of these procedures are painful, often greatly or severely so.

The Department responds by pointing out that there is scientific evidence that supports the conclusion that use of anesthesia in animals is often not recommended. Moreover, the agency notes that both de-beaking and toe-trimming are specifically limited by reference to the maximum age of the poultry on which these procedures may be performed, itself an effort to limit the consequential pain and distress that these procedures cause.

In addition, the Department asserts that the key to ensuring humane treatment of the animals rests on the requirement that all of these procedures be performed by an "appropriately trained person." For this reason, the agency notes that its regulations do not give broad permission for the use of any of these procedures, but instead limit the practices in a significant way. Each such practice is permitted only if it is "performed in a sanitary manner by a knowledgeable individual and in such a way as to minimize pain." . . . Because of this limitation, the Department asserts that in practice the procedures will only be performed in a humane manner.

Our review of the record certainly supports the conclusion that the agency's determination, in general, that these procedures should be permitted is neither arbitrary nor capricious. We are, as part of this analysis, mindful of the significant limitations imposed relating to the age of the particular livestock on which some of these procedures may be performed, which we see as evidence of the agency's care in the decision-making process. Notwithstanding the foregoing, however, the limitation that the agency asserts is the lynchpin of ensuring that these procedures are performed in a humane manner cannot pass muster. The regulations do not define the terms "sanitary manner," "knowledgeable individual," or "minimize pain," nor is there any objective criteria against which to determine whether any particular individual performing the procedure measures up to these standards. As a result, the regulations that the Department suggests will ensure that the procedures will be accomplished in a humane manner provide no standard against which to test that they are in fact so performed. Although one farm may conclude that a knowledgeable individual, for example, means someone with either veterinary training or some similar level of expertise, another might conclude that merely having performed the procedure in the past, humanely or not, or merely having observed it being performed by others, humanely or not, meets the standard set forth in the regulations.

The lack of specificity in the regulations is illustrated by the Department's argument as set forth in its brief. There, notwithstanding the actual language of the regulations, the agency describes the intent of the regulation to be that an "experienced handler with skill and knowledge" must perform the various procedures, rather than merely a knowledgeable one. Moreover, in the agency's brief, it asserts that because the person performing the procedure will be "experienced" and will have "skill and knowledge," he or she will be able to individually assess and evaluate each animal so as to perform the procedure humanely. In that context, the agency argues that the phrase "minimize pain" provides an objective standard that can be followed and enforced.

Our review compels a contrary conclusion. The agency's subtle rephrasing suggests that the language used in the regulation is insufficient and that only a different, and perhaps a significantly higher standard, would suffice. Perhaps that subtle rephrasing suggests the standard that the Department intended to include in the regulation. Had the Department, for example, defined "knowledgeable individual" in terms of having been taught at a course given by a particular institution, or having had the technique demonstrated by a veterinarian or an agricultural extension agent, or by use of similarly objective criteria, it would likely withstand our scrutiny. Indeed, in the context of the kinds of farming operations prevalent in this State, were the Department to conclude, based on an appropriate record, that there is sufficient support to include within the definition a set of objective criteria that would apply to individuals who have learned practices through others in their farming family, it might also be permissible. It is the failure to give meaning to the term that makes it fall short, rather than the sufficiency of a basis on which to choose to rely on such individuals.

Similarly, without any standard as to what the regulation means in terms of minimizing pain, there is no standard at all. One could, of course, conclude that each of these practices causes pain for a period of time, but that the benefits outweigh that adverse consequence. At the same time, one might conclude that, in light of the mandate of the Legislature that all of these practices be performed only consistent with being humane, they can only be performed if sufficient pain medication or anesthesia is utilized. Alternatively, one might conclude that a particular practice is only humane if it is performed on an animal of a particular age or if a particular instrument is utilized. As it is, the Department adopted none of these standards.

The record reflects that the Department chose not to define the terms that form the basis for the inclusion of these practices as permissible and chose as well not to include specific requirements about the methods to use in performing these procedures. As such, however, this aspect of petitioners' challenge illustrates a significant flaw in this aspect of the regulations. Rather than creating a series of regulations that permit or disallow practices in accordance with whether they are humane, and rather than permitting practices only if performed in a specified manner, the agency instead authorized the practices in general and defined them as being humane by implicitly redefining humane itself. That is, the agency authorized the practices if performed by a knowledgeable person so as to minimize pain and equated that otherwise undefined person's choices with humane. This, however, has resulted in a regulation that is entirely circular in its logic, for it bases the definition of humane solely on the identity of the person performing the task, while creating the definition of that identity by using an undefined category of individuals of no discernable skill or experience.

Although it might be difficult to create a list of permitted practices with sufficient definition to ensure that they are in fact being performed humanely, the Legislature did not direct the Department to only do as much as it believed was expedient. We do not fault the Department for its decision not to attempt to create an exhaustive list of what is permitted and the precise circumstances that pertain. Nor do we dispute the Department's conclusion, as it is one that the Department is well-qualified to make, that these practices are beneficial to the animals or to the farmers. We do not suggest that these procedures cannot be carried out in a manner that is, objectively, humane. In the absence of sufficient guidance in the regulations to ensure that the practices are being performed in a manner that is humane, however, they should not be included within the blanket permission granted in these subsections.

Moreover, by including these practices in the subsections of the regulations that authorize them to be performed, the Department has created an unworkable enforcement scheme. That is to say, there is no standard against which to judge whether a particular individual is "knowledgeable" or whether a method is "sanitary" in the context of an agricultural setting or whether the manner in which the procedure is being performed constitutes a "way as to minimize pain." That being the case, we are constrained to conclude that these aspects of the regulations fail to fix a standard that will ensure that the practices are in fact humane and, at the same time, are too vague to establish a standard that is enforceable.

C.

Petitioners next attack the regulations relating to the use of crates and tethering for swine (sow gestation techniques) and for veal calves (cattle intended to be raised as "Special-Fed veal"), each of which they assert fails to meet the statutory standard of humane. In short, petitioners contend that these techniques do not permit the animals to move freely and to turn around and that they therefore cause significant distress in the animals not consistent with humane treatment. They rely on a number of publications relating to the use of crates for swine gestation that so conclude. . . . Petitioners further point out that this practice is banned in Florida, see Fla. Const. Art. X, § 21 (2005), and is currently being phased out and scheduled to be banned in member states of the European Union by 2013, see European Union Council Directive 2000/88/EC of 23 October 2001.

Petitioners refer to similar literature in support of their objections to the use of crates and tethering techniques for raising veal calves. They argue that this scientific evidence demonstrates that close confinement creates stress and causes the animals to engage in behaviors that demonstrate that they are in distress. . . .

In response, the Department also points to an impressive array of scientific studies that, it asserts, support the regulations that permit the use of crating and tethering techniques, particularly as they relate to sows. . . .

Although there are no veal farms in the State of New Jersey, as a result of which the challenge to the aspect of the regulation that would permit tethering or crates for their management is, perhaps, only theoretical, the Department also defends its decision to include permission for this technique in the regulations as well. In part, it does so by pointing out that the Legislature has twice declined to act on bills that would specifically require that veal calves be maintained in quarters that permit them to turn around completely, thus suggesting that the Legislature itself has considered this issue and spoken in a voice in full accord with the regulations.

In part, the agency relies on guidelines prepared and distributed by the American Veal Association (AVA). Those guidelines set forth four potential alternatives for housing veal calves, including the individual stall system that the regulations permit. The Department points out that the AVA Guide describes a number of sound reasons that support its decision to permit housing calves in individual stalls, including the reduced likelihood of disease passing among calves, a lessened possibility of fecal contamination, and greater ease in performing health examinations on the calves that result in less stress for the animals.

Our review of the literature relied on by the Department as compared with that cited by petitioners compels us to conclude that the agency's decision to permit these crating and tethering techniques, although controversial, falls well within its area of expertise. Moreover, the record demonstrates that the agency considered a wide variety of scientific and other studies before reaching its decision to include these particular management techniques within the regulations as permitted practices.

Far from simply adopting techniques already in place or embracing practices that serve only the economic ends of the agricultural community as petitioners suggest, these regulations reflect that the Department took seriously its mandate to identify humane practices, but did so in recognition of the need to balance those concerns with the interests of the farmers whose livelihood depends on such techniques and whose existence would be threatened were they to be banned. More to the point, because those aspects of the regulations are supported by sufficient credible evidence in the record, and because they are neither arbitrary nor capricious, we find no basis on which to interfere with them.

D.

Finally, petitioners argue that the regulations permit the transport of sick and downed animals to slaughter, a practice that is not humane. They assert that because the regulations permit cattle with an extremely low BCS [body condition scoring] to be accepted for slaughter, by implication, their transport is also permitted. *See* N.J.A.C. 2:8-2.2(b)(4)(iv) (cattle with body condition score of 1.0 (emaciated) is permitted at slaughter). They contrast this with the prohibition on the transport of such animals to market, arguing that this makes the regulation arbitrary and capricious. Petitioners argue that because "downed" animals are unable to stand or walk on their own, the process of loading them onto transport trucks is inherently painful.

In response, the Department suggests that petitioners have misinterpreted the regulation and have failed to consider the implication of federal law that bears upon the slaughter of disabled cattle for use in the food chain. In light of those significant limitations, the Department argues that a downed animal simply will not be transported for slaughter and that the only instance of a sick or downed animal being transported at all would, in all likelihood, involve taking it to a veterinarian for treatment.

Our review of the record reveals that the Department's reliance on the federal authorities does not completely address petitioners' concerns. As we understand it, the federal authorities on which the Department has relied are only designed to prevent downed animals from entering the food supply but do not otherwise prohibit them from being transported. The question thus remains whether the regulations, adopted by the Department, that permit their transport for slaughter can be sustained. This aspect of the regulations must be understood in its appropriate context.

The relevant regulations begin with a general requirement that sick or injured cattle must be treated or euthanized. *N.J.A.C.* 2:8-2.6(a). In fact, the regulation requires that treatment be "prompt" and that euthanasia be "humane." *Ibid.* The regulations specifically limit acceptable methods of euthanasia, incorporating by reference standards adopted by the AVMA. . . . As a result, the options available to a farmer who needs to euthanize an animal are limited.

The regulations also include a subsection that governs downed cattle. These regulations, like their federal counterparts, prohibit transport to a livestock market, but do not prohibit transport for other purposes. However, the regulations specifically prohibit dragging such an animal while it is conscious, and require that it be treated humanely, even if it is going to be slaughtered or euthanized.

During the notice and comment period, one commenter urged the Department to extend the prohibition on transport of downed cattle to livestock markets so that transport for slaughter would also be banned. The Department declined to do so, explaining that "[w]hile owners of downed animals may have the animal euthanized on the farm, the Department believes it is appropriate to provide some flexibility to owners on where and when slaughter may take place." Although there is evidence in the record that a downed animal "may suffer greatly," in light of the strict limits on permitted euthanasia methods, we cannot conclude that the Department's decision to permit farmers the option of choosing transport for slaughter is arbitrary or capricious. We therefore perceive of no failure on the part of the agency in its decision to adopt this regulation that requires our intervention.

VIII.

Our consideration of the issues raised in this appeal and our review of the record have led us to conclude that certain aspects of these regulations cannot be sustained. We do not intend, however, to suggest that the defects in the regulations are pervasive or that all of the many practices that the Department specifically considered and permitted cannot be performed in a humane manner. To be sure, we have concluded that the "routine husbandry practices" and the "knowledgeable individual and in such a way as to minimize pain" safe harbors cannot be sustained as written, but neither of these determinations effects a ban on any of the particular practices. Rather, any practice, technique, or procedure not otherwise prohibited by the regulations may be utilized by any farmer, risking only that the practice, technique, or procedure will be challenged by an appropriate enforcement authority as inhumane.

In such a proceeding, the burden of proving the facts, including that the particular practice as performed is inhumane, falls on the enforcing authority. *See N.J.S.A.* 4:22-1 (establishing the NJSPCA "for the purpose of the enforcement of all laws enacted for the protection of dumb animals; . . ."). In that context, some individuals utilizing some of these practices may be adjudged to have engaged in a practice that violates the animal cruelty statute, but others will not. *See N.J.S.A.* 4:22-17 (defining which acts and omissions constitute disorderly persons offenses and which are classified as third and fourth degree crimes); *N.J.S.A.* 4:22-26 (identifying which acts and omissions constitute animal cruelty punishable by civil fines and penalties).

Our decision, therefore, should not be understood to be a ban on the continuation of any specific practice, but merely a recognition that some of the standards that purport to define them so as to ensure that they are actually performed in a manner that meets the statute's command that all such practices be humane have fallen short.

IX.

The facial challenge to the regulations in their entirety is rejected. The specific challenges to the reliance on "routine husbandry practices" as defined in the regulations, and to the reliance on "knowledgeable individual and in such a way as to minimize pain" are sustained. The specific challenges to the practices, with the exception of the practice of tail docking, are otherwise rejected.

The judgment of the Appellate Division is affirmed in part and reversed in part and the matter is remanded to the Department for further proceedings consistent with this opinion.

Notes

1. The preceding case (*NJSPCA*) highlights several standard industry practices, as well as the controversy over the benefits and disadvantages of the practices. When courts are asked to review agency regulations that are adopted pursuant to statutes that authorize those regulations, the judicial scope of review is quite limited and courts must give significant deference to agency decisions. As long as the agency can provide some support for its decisions, courts must defer to those determinations, absent a showing of "arbitrary and capricious" reasoning or a decision that is contrary to law. *See Chevron v. NRDC,* 467 U.S. 837 (1984) (setting forth the federal doctrine that many state courts have adopted) (the "*Chevron* doctrine" is discussed further in Chapter 5).

2. Challenging government agency regulations regarding existing laws, or lack of enforcement of those laws, is one way to obtain better protections and living

conditions for animals. In these cases, laws have been enacted that, if properly applied by the agency promulgating the regulations and if adequately enforced, could effect a significant improvement in the lives of animals. Consider, for example, the impact on the lives and welfare of the animals to whom the New Jersey statute applies if the definition of "humane" included only those acts that did not cause pain or suffering, regardless of whether they constituted "routine husbandry practices."

3. Legislation relating to farmed animals has been increasing on the state level, both through the legislative process and voter initiatives, while there has been limited progress on the federal level.

In 2001, animal advocates sought to amend the Florida Constitution by a ballot initiative petition, to prohibit the "cruel and inhumane confinement of pigs during pregnancy" by eliminating the use of "gestation crates," because "[i]nhumane treatment of animals is a concern of Florida citizens." The Secretary of State submitted the petition to the Attorney General who, in turn, petitioned the Florida Supreme Court for an advisory opinion regarding its validity. The court found it valid, clearing the way for a statewide vote on the issue. *Advisory Opinion to the Attorney Gen. Re: Limiting Cruel and Inhumane Confinement of Pigs During Pregnancy*, 815 So. 2d 597 (Fla. 2002). The Florida Supreme Court's opinion did not address the merits of the initiative, although a concurring justice voiced the belief this is "a subject more properly reserved for legislative enactment." Florida voters approved the initiative and, as the *NJSPCA* court noted, it is now part of the Florida state constitution. FLA. CONST. art. X, § 21 (adopted 2002, but not effective until 2008).

As a practical matter, why might the animal advocates have chosen this constitutional amendment approach rather than use the more traditional means of lobbying legislators to act?

4. Other states followed Florida in banning such practices. *See, e.g.*, ARIZ. REV. STAT. § 13-2910.07 (enacted in 2006, but not effective until 2013; prohibits tethering or confining "any pig during pregnancy or any calf raised for veal, on a farm, for all or the majority of any day, in a manner that prevents such animal from: (1) [l]ying down and fully extending his or her limbs; or (2) [t]urning around freely"); OR. REV. STAT. § 600.150 (enacted in 2007, it was the first gestation crate ban enacted by a state legislature rather than by voter initiative); COLO. REV. STAT. § 35-50.5-102 (enacted in 2008, similar to the Arizona statute but without the "all or majority of any day" limitation); CAL. HEALTH & SAFETY CODE § 25990 (enacted in 2008 by a voter initiative known as "Proposition 2;" requires that calves raised for veal, pregnant pigs and also egg-laying hens be confined only in ways that allow the animals to lie down, stand up, fully extend their limbs (and wings) and turn around freely) (effective Jan. 1, 2015).

In 2018, California voters passed another initiative, "Proposition 12—Farm Animal Confinement Initiative." Unlike Proposition 2, Proposition 12 bans the sale of meat from calves raised for veal and pigs raised for their meat, and eggs from egg-laying hens, if those animals were treated in a "cruel manner" as defined in the statute. (The treatment required is similar to that required by Proposition 2.) The ban applies to all covered meat and eggs, regardless of where the animals were raised. Voter information sources about Proposition 12 indicate that part of the impetus for the new initiative may have been to respond to claims by some industry opponents that Proposition 2's behavioral standards were too vague. See *https://ballopedia.org /California Proposition 12, Farm Animal Confinement Initiative (2018)*.

The "phase-in" period for almost all of these laws is part of the compromise when the practices of large industries are affected. They provide an adjustment period so that any changes in housing or mechanical apparatus can be accomplished without significant interruption in production. For example, where facilities are required to move from "battery cages" to larger enclosures or cage-free operations, the phase-in period gives egg producers time to convert their facilities to the new standard.

Those who use animals for profit, especially those who use them for food, have challenged some of these statutes. California laws intended to prohibit what Californians believe to be products of cruelty from entry into California have been subjected to multiple challenges, as discussed later in this section. And not surprisingly, some of the same industry-based organizations that sue to overturn animal protection legislation also use their resources to fund campaigns against such propositions before an election. In *Californians for Humane Farms v. Schafer*, 2008 U.S. Dist. LEXIS 74861 (N.D. Cal. Sept. 29, 2008), a state ballot committee sponsored by various animal protection groups, family farmers, veterinarians and public health professionals, initiated litigation to prevent the USDA and the American Egg Board (AEB) from unlawfully spending several million dollars in federal funds to support a campaign against Proposition 2. The court granted an injunction prohibiting use of AEB funds in California until after the election.

After its enactment, Proposition 2 was the subject of several lawsuits that were litigated for years until reaching final resolution. In one case, the plaintiff was an egg producer who alleged that Proposition 2's behavioral requirements for egg-laying hens were unconstitutionally vague. In a short unpublished opinion, the Ninth Circuit rejected plaintiff's argument, affirming the district court's dismissal of the egg producer's complaint. *Cramer v. Harris*, 2015 U.S. App. LEXIS 1757 (9th Cir. Unpub. Feb. 4, 2015).

Because Proposition 2 covered only in-state conduct, and because Californians did not want eggs that came from "battery cage" hens sold in California, a second law was enacted. As explained in the following case, that law, known as "AB 1437" and codified at California Health & Safety Code section 25996, prohibits the sale of any egg (regardless of the state of origin) not produced in compliance with the requirements of Proposition 2. In the following case, several states unsuccessfully sued the State of California over the alleged effect of AB 1437 on the egg producers in their states. The central issue is not the merits or the propriety of farming practices, but focuses instead on a specialized form of standing known as "*parens patriae*," which means "parent of the nation." The doctrine allows states to sue on behalf substantial sections of their citizenry, subject to requirements that the states did not meet in the case below.

Missouri ex rel. Koster v. Harris

United States Court of Appeals, Ninth Circuit, 2017
847 F.3d 646

GRABER, Circuit Judge:

California enacted laws and regulations prescribing standards for the conditions under which chickens must be kept in order for their eggs to be sold in the state. Plaintiffs are six states, which sued to block enforcement of those laws and regulations before they took effect. We agree with the district court that Plaintiffs lacked standing to bring this case as *parens patriae*. We also hold that the district court did not err in denying Plaintiffs leave to amend their complaint. But because the action should have been dismissed without prejudice, we affirm but remand with instructions to dismiss the action without prejudice.

In the 2008 general election, California voters adopted Proposition 2, which enacted new standards beginning on January 1, 2015, for housing farm animals within California including, as relevant here, egg-laying hens. Cal. Health & Safety Code §§ 25990-94.

In 2010, California's legislature adopted Assembly Bill 1437 ("AB1437"), which mandated, also beginning on January 1, 2015, that "a shelled egg shall not be sold or contracted for sale for human consumption in California if the seller knows or should have known that the egg is the product of an egg-laying hen that was confined on a farm or place that is not in compliance with animal care standards set forth in [Proposition 2]." Cal. Health & Safety Code § 25996. Therefore, all eggs sold in California must comply with Proposition 2. In 2013, the California Department of Food and Agriculture promulgated egg-related regulations, including salmonella prevention measures and minimum cage sizes for egg-laying hens, all of which also carried an effective date of January 1, 2015. Cal. Code Regs. tit. 3, § 1350(d)(1).

On February 3, 2014, the State of Missouri filed a complaint in the Eastern District of California, asking the court to declare AB1437 and California Code §1350(d)(1) (collectively the "Shell Egg Laws") invalid, as violating the Commerce Clause or as preempted by federal statute, and to enjoin California from enforcing the laws. Plaintiffs then filed their First Amended Complaint (the "complaint"), joining the States of Nebraska, Oklahoma, Alabama, and Kentucky and the Governor of Iowa as additional plaintiffs. The Humane Society of the United States and the Association of California Egg Farmers ("Intervenors") moved to intervene as defendants, which the court allowed. Defendants filed a motion to dismiss for lack of subject matter jurisdiction; Intervenors filed their own, similar motions. The district court granted the motions to dismiss, with prejudice. The court concluded that Plaintiffs lacked standing as *parens patriae*, held that their claim was not justiciable, and denied leave to amend as futile. Plaintiffs timely appeal.

A. *Parens Patriae Standing*

States asserting *parens patriae* standing must meet both the basic requirements of Article III standing and the unique requirements of that doctrine. "To establish Article III standing, an injury must be concrete, particularized, and actual or imminent; fairly traceable to the challenged action; and redressable by a favorable ruling." In a *parens patriae* case, there are two additional requirements. First, "the State must articulate an interest apart from the interests of particular private parties, *i.e.*, the State must be more than a nominal party." Alfred L. Snapp & Son, Inc. v. Puerto Rico ex rel. Barez ("Snapp"), 458 U.S. 592, 607 (1982). Second, "[t]he State must express a quasi-sovereign interest." Id. On de novo review, we conclude that Plaintiffs have not met the first requirement. We therefore need not, and do not, reach the second part of the test, nor do we reach the issue of ripeness.

There are no "definitive limits on the proportion of the population of the State that must be adversely affected." *Snapp*, 458 U.S. at 607. But "more must be alleged than injury to an identifiable group of individual residents." *Id.* "[T]he indirect effects of the injury must be considered as well in determining whether the State has alleged injury to a sufficiently substantial segment of its population." *Id.*

Concerning the parties, the complaint alleges: "Missouri farmers produced nearly two billion eggs in 2012 and generated approximately $171 million in revenue for the state"; "Nebraska is one of the top ten largest egg producers in the United States"; "Alabama is one of the top fifteen largest egg producers in the United States"; "Kentucky farmers produced approximately 1.037 billion eggs in 2012 and generated approximately $116 million in revenue for the state"; "Oklahoma farmers produced more than 700 million eggs in 2012 and generated approximately $90 million in revenue for the state"; and "Iowa is the number one state in egg production[,] Iowa farmers produce over 14.4 billion eggs per year," and "[t]he cost to Iowa farmers to retrofit existing housing or build new housing that complies with AB1437 would be substantial."

The laws "forc[e] Plaintiffs' farmers either to forgo California's markets altogether or accept significantly increased production costs just to comply." That is, "Plaintiffs' egg farmers must choose either to bring their entire operations into compliance . . . or else simply leave the California marketplace." "[T]he necessary capital improvements [would] cost Plaintiffs' farmers hundreds of millions of dollars," and, without access to the California market, "supply would outpace demand by half a billion eggs, causing the price of eggs—as well as egg farmers' margins— to fall throughout the Midwest and potentially forc[e] some Missouri producers out of business. The same goes for egg producers in Nebraska, Alabama, Oklahoma, Kentucky, and Iowa."

In short, the complaint alleges the importance of the California market *to egg farmers* in the Plaintiff States and the difficult choice that *egg farmers* face in deciding whether to comply with the Shell Egg Laws. The complaint contains no specific allegations about the statewide magnitude of these difficulties or the extent to which they affect more than just an "identifiable group of individual" egg farmers.

Plaintiffs advance several theories to demonstrate "an interest apart from the interests of particular private parties" and an effect on "a sufficiently substantial segment of [the] population." First, Plaintiffs allege harm to their egg farmers. Second, Plaintiffs argue that the Shell Egg Laws will cause harmful fluctuations in the price of eggs. Finally, Plaintiffs allege that they will suffer discrimination from the Shell Egg Laws. For the reasons that follow, none of these theories establishes standing.

1. Alleged Harm to Egg Farmers

Alleging harm to the egg farmers in Plaintiffs' States is insufficient to satisfy the first prong of *parens patriae* standing. Other courts have recognized that *parens patriae* standing is inappropriate where an aggrieved party could seek private relief. The Second Circuit, for example, held that "*[p]arens patriae* standing . . . requires a finding that individuals could not obtain complete relief through a private suit." Here, complete relief would be available to the egg farmers themselves, were they to file a complaint on their own behalf.

Supreme Court cases in which private relief was held to be unlikely or unrealistic illustrate why *parens patriae* standing does not lie here. In *Missouri v. Illinois*, 180 U.S. 208 (1901), though never explicitly calling it a *parens patriae* case, the Supreme Court heard a sewage dispute between two states. The Court observed that "the nature of the injury complained of is such that an adequate remedy can only be found in this court at the suit of the state of Missouri." *Id.* at 241. The Court emphasized that the "health and comfort of the large communities inhabiting those parts of the state situated on the Mississippi River are not alone concerned, but contagious and typhoidal diseases introduced in the river communities may spread themselves throughout the territory of the state." *Id.* In other words, Missouri alleged that a public health hazard affected its entire population. By contrast, the Shell Egg Laws are not alleged to threaten the health of the entire population (or, indeed of anyone), and those directly affected — egg farmers — are capable of pursuing their own interests.

* * *

2. Alleged Fluctuation in the Price of Eggs

Plaintiffs argue that fluctuations in the price of eggs will harm consumers, thereby affecting a substantial segment of their populations and establishing *parens patriae* standing. Plaintiffs filed their complaint before the Shell Egg Laws took effect. As a result, their allegations about the potential economic effects of those laws, after implementation, were necessarily speculative. Indeed, Plaintiffs' allegations are inconsistent; the complaint alleges that prices will go either up or down. On the one hand, Plaintiffs allege that farmers must bring all egg facilities into compliance with the Shell Egg Laws, regardless of the proportion of their product actually bound for California, because the demand across markets fluctuates. The cost of "compliant" eggs will thus increase across the board. On the other hand, Plaintiffs allege that, if farmers decline to comply and they exit the California market, "the price of eggs . . . [would] fall throughout the Midwest." Neither of these alleged results is sufficient to support *parens patriae* standing.

At the outset, the unavoidable uncertainty of the alleged future changes in price makes the alleged injury insufficient for Article III standing. . . .

* * *

3. *Alleged Discrimination*

Finally, Plaintiffs' reliance on cases granting *parens patriae* standing to challenge discrimination against a state's citizens is misplaced. The Shell Egg Laws do not distinguish among eggs based on their state of origin. A statute that treats "both intrastate and interstate products" alike "is not discriminatory." *Ass'n des Eleveurs de Canards et d'Oies du Quebec v. Harris*, 729 F.3d 937, 948 (9th Cir. 2013).

In *Snapp*, Puerto Rico, acting as *parens patriae*, sued on behalf of its workers who allegedly suffered discrimination under a federal hiring program. The Court rejected "too narrow a view of the interests at stake." Although only 787 jobs were at issue, the nature of the discrimination affected all Puerto Ricans, so Puerto Rico could pursue relief for all residents under a *parens patriae* theory. But *Snapp* does not assist Plaintiffs because there is no discrimination here, whether to the few or to the many. As noted, California egg farmers are subject to the same rules as egg farmers from all other states, including California itself.

. . . Plaintiffs allege no trade barriers erected against their broader economies and, again, the Shell Egg Laws are not discriminatory. Accordingly, Plaintiffs' allegations of discrimination do not establish *parens patriae* standing.

* * *

The judgment of the district court is AFFIRMED and the case is REMANDED with instructions to dismiss this action without prejudice.

Notes

1. The foregoing case demonstrates the political connection that often exists between government and the agribusiness industry. This is just one of the recurring themes you will see throughout this chapter, particularly in Section 1.C addressing Ag-Gag laws. The close connection is sometimes even codified, especially in connection with federal programs intended to support the industry, as illustrated in the following excerpt:

> The U.S. Department of Agriculture ("USDA") oversees multiple federal programs established by Congress to promote certain agricultural commodities. These programs are funded by "checkoffs"—mandatory assessments that producers and importers pay on the sale or import of the commodity. The assessments are used to pay for a range of activities, including research and marketing of the commodities, and they subsidize well-known advertising campaigns, such as "Got Milk?," "Beef: It's What's for Dinner," and "The

Incredible, Edible Egg." This case involves the pork checkoff program and the trademarks associated with the slogan "Pork The Other White Meat."

The National Pork Board ("Board" or "NPB") is a fifteen-member board appointed by the Secretary of Agriculture that is responsible for developing and administering the pork checkoff program.

* * *

Congress created the pork checkoff program when it passed the Pork Act in 1985. 7 U.S.C. §4801 et seq. The Act's purpose is to "financ[e], through adequate assessments, . . . an effective and coordinated program of promotion, research, and consumer information" to "strengthen the position of the pork industry in the marketplace; and . . . maintain, develop, and expand markets for pork and pork products." 7 U.S.C. §4801(b) (2012). Pursuant to the Act, the Secretary issued the Pork Promotion, Research, and Consumer Information Order, which sets forth regulations to implement the Act. 7 U.S.C. §4803.

Humane Society of the U.S. v. Perdue, 290 F. Supp. 3d 5, 7, 9 (D.D.C. 2018) (the defendant, Sonny Perdue, was Secretary of the USDA at the time of the decision).

In that case, animal protection organizations and an independent pork producer challenged the USDA's annual approval of payments made by the National Pork Board to the National Pork Producers Council (NPPC), a trade lobbying association, to pay for the trademark for the "Pork The Other White Meat" slogan—which was no longer being used. (In 2006, with the Secretary's approval, the Board entered into an agreement to purchase trademarks from NPPC for a total of $60 million, over the course of twenty years.) Plaintiffs alleged that the NPPC was using "checkoff funds" supposedly intended for promotional activities to instead combat humane laws, despite a prohibition on using checkoff funds to influence legislation and government policy. The court acknowledged that "at least some portion of the money the Board pays NPPC under the Purchase Agreement ultimately goes to influencing legislation," but nevertheless concluded that because contracts between the Board and NPPC were contemplated by the Pork Act, this did not violate the prohibition against using the assessments to influence legislation. Given evidence that "The Other White Meat" slogan played no role in then-current marketing, the court enjoined the USDA from approving any future payments for it.

2. In addition to litigation, industry efforts to quash the spread of humane farm animal legislation has triggered attempts at a legislative response. In 2012 and again in subsequent years, Rep. Steven King (R-Iowa) proposed federal legislation to prevent any state from having higher agricultural standards than any other state, in an attempt to dismantle state and local laws such as Proposition 2 and many others aimed at providing some limited protections and improved standards for farmed animals. King's proposed bills actually would have affected hundreds of laws across the nation, so that all fifty states would regularly have to monitor the least restrictive laws in the country, and adapt their laws to those, for virtually any

product involving animals, vegetables or forest products. King's efforts have been unsuccessful.

3. Other California laws aimed at increasing protection for animals used for commercial purposes have been the subject of extensive litigation. *See, e.g., National Meat Ass'n v. Harris*, 132 S. Ct. 965 (2012) (meat industry group sued California to invalidate law requiring immediate euthanasia or veterinary treatment for animals on their way to slaughter who are too sick or injured to stand or walk) (excerpted later in this Chapter); *Chinatown Neighborhood Ass'n v. Brown*, 794 F.3d 1136 (9th Cir. Aug. 27, 2015), *cert. denied* (restaurateurs and distributors of shark fins unsuccessfully challenged California law banning possession and sale of detached shark fins under Supremacy and Commerce Clauses; two state court cases were also filed over the same law); *VIVA! Int'l Voice for Animals v. Adidas Promotional Operations, Inc.*, 41 Cal. 4th 929 (2007) (producer of athletic shoes containing kangaroo products failed to invalidate California law prohibiting importation of kangaroo skins).

California's statutes prohibiting the production and sale of *foie gras* (literally, "fatty liver") when made from force-fed birds have been the subject of multiple lawsuits that began immediately after the statutes went into effect. With the enactment of California Health and Safety Code sections 25980 *et seq.* ("Force Fed Birds"), California banned the production, sale, possession and importation of *foie gras*. Out-of-state producers of *foie gras* and California restaurateurs sued the state, alleging the law violated the Due Process and Commerce Clauses of the federal Constitution. The federal district court denied plaintiffs' request for a preliminary injunction on their Commerce Clause claims and the Ninth Circuit affirmed. *Association des Eleveurs de Canards et D'oies du Quebec v. Harris*, 729 F.3d 937 (9th Cir. 2013), *cert. denied*. The case was back before the Ninth Circuit four years later, after the district court granted plaintiffs' motion for summary judgment on preemption grounds.

Association des Eleveurs de Canards et d'Oies du Quebec v. Becerra

United States Court of Appeals for the Ninth Circuit, 2017
870 F.3d 1140

NGUYEN, Circuit Judge:

In 2004, California passed legislation to prohibit the practice of force-feeding ducks or geese to produce foie gras, an expensive delicacy made from their liver. California determined that the force-feeding process, which typically involves inserting a 10-to 12-inch metal or plastic tube into the bird's esophagus to deliver large amounts of concentrated food, is cruel and inhumane. The state therefore prohibited force-feeding a bird "for the purpose of enlarging the bird's liver beyond normal size," Cal. Health & Safety Code § 25981, as well as the in-state sale of products made elsewhere from birds force-fed in such a manner, *id.* §25982. The legislation does not ban foie gras itself, but rather the practice of producing foie gras by force-feeding. California provided a grace period of over seven and a half years for producers to transition to alternative methods of producing foie gras. *Id.* §25984.

On July 2, 2012, the day after the state law took effect, Plaintiffs sued the state of California, challenging only Health and Safety Code section 25982, the provision that bans the sale of products made from force-fed birds. Plaintiffs initially argued that the sales ban violates the Due Process and Commerce Clauses of the U.S. Constitution. After these claims were dismissed, Plaintiffs amended their complaint to allege that the federal Poultry Products Inspection Act (the "PPIA"), which has been on the books for over fifty years, preempts the state provision. The district court concluded that section 25982 is expressly preempted by the PPIA and granted Plaintiffs summary judgment. We reverse and remand.

I. BACKGROUND

Plaintiffs Hudson Valley Foie Gras and the Association des Éleveurs de Canards et d'Oies du Québec raise birds for slaughter and produce foie gras at their facilities in New York and Quebec, respectively; Plaintiff Hot's Restaurant Group is a restaurant in California that sells foie gras.

The foie gras products that Plaintiffs make and sell are produced by force-feeding birds to enlarge their livers. From the day they hatch, the birds undergo a regimented feeding process that lasts for about eleven to thirteen weeks. *Ass'n des Éleveurs de Canards et d'Oies du Québec v. Harris (Canards I)*, 729 F.3d 937, 942 (9th Cir. 2013). For the first few months, the birds are fed various pellets that are made available to them twenty-four hours a day. *Id.* Then, for a two-week period, the feeding pellets are available only during certain times of the day. *Id.* In the final stage of the feeding process, which lasts up to thirteen days, the birds are force-fed in a process called *gavage*, during which feeders use "a tube to deliver the feed to the crop sac at the base of the duck's esophagus." *Id.*

A. California's Force-Feeding Ban

In 2004, the California state legislature enacted a statutory framework to end the practice of force-feeding birds to fatten their livers. Cal. Health & Safety Code §§ 25980-25984. Section 25981 makes it illegal to force-feed a bird "for the purpose of enlarging the bird's liver beyond normal size." Section 25982, the only provision challenged in this case, prohibits selling a product "in California if it is the result of force feeding a bird for the purpose of enlarging the bird's liver beyond normal size." A "bird" is defined to include a duck or a goose, *id.* §25980(a), and "force-feeding" is defined as a process by which a bird consumes more food than it would typically consume voluntarily, conducted through methods such as "delivering feed through a tube or other device inserted into the bird's esophagus," *id.* §25980(b).

California's law was designed to rectify what the state considered an inhumane feeding practice. According to the legislative analysis of the law, force-feeding commonly requires a worker to hold the bird between her knees, grasp the bird's head, insert a 10-to 12-inch metal or plastic tube into the bird's esophagus, and deliver large amounts of concentrated meal and compressed air into the bird. The bird is force-fed up to three times a day for several weeks and its liver grows to ten times the size of a normal liver. This process is apparently "so hard on the birds that they would die from the pathological damage it inflicts if they weren't slaughtered first."

In enacting the force-feeding ban, California also considered a study conducted by the European Union's Scientific Committee on Animal Health and an Israeli Supreme Court decision. The European Union study concluded that force-feeding is detrimental to the welfare of birds, and the Israeli Supreme Court similarly concluded that force-feeding causes birds pain and suffering. In light of these and other factors, California decided to enact the ban, joining a growing list of countries around the world.[1]

California's legislature intended to ban not foie gras itself, but rather the practice of producing foie gras by force-feeding. The law's author, Senator John Burton, made clear when he introduced the bill that it "has nothing to do . . . with banning foie gras" and that it prohibits only the "inhumane force feeding [of] ducks and geese." Then-Governor Arnold Schwarzenegger echoed this sentiment in his signing statement: "This bill's intent is to ban the current foie gras production practice of forcing a tube down a bird's throat to greatly increase the consumption of grain by the bird. It does not ban the food product, foie gras." Signing Message of Governor Arnold Schwarzenegger, Sen. Bill 1520, 2003–2004 Reg. Sess. (Sept. 29, 2004). The legislature provided more than seven and a half years between the passage of the law and its effective date to allow producers to transition to producing foie gras without force-feeding. *Id.*; *see* Cal. Health & Safety Code § 25984(a) (This law "shall become operative on July 1, 2012.").

B. The PPIA

Originally enacted in 1957, the PPIA was intended to ensure that the nation's poultry products "are wholesome, not adulterated, and properly marked, labeled, and packaged." 21 U.S.C. § 451. The PPIA accomplishes this goal by, *inter alia*, authorizing the inspection of slaughterhouses and poultry-processing plants, 21 U.S.C. § 455, setting proper sanitation requirements, *id.* § 456, authorizing the Secretary of the U.S. Department of Agriculture ("USDA") to establish labeling and container standards, *id.* § 457, prohibiting the sale of adulterated, misbranded, or uninspected poultry products, *id.* § 458, establishing record-keeping requirements, *id.* § 460, and instituting storage and handling regulations, *id.* § 463. *See also Levine v. Vilsack*, 587 F.3d 986, 989 (9th Cir. 2009).

---

1. The following countries have instituted some form of a ban on force-feeding or foie gras products: Italy, the Netherlands, the Czech Republic, India, Luxembourg, Denmark, Finland, Norway, Poland, Israel, Sweden, Switzerland, Germany, and the United Kingdom. *See, e.g.*, Cal. Assemb. Comm. on Bus. & Professions, Analysis of S.B. 1520, 2003-2004 Reg. Sess., at 6 (June 20, 2004); Atish Patel, India Bans Import of Controversial Foie Gras, Wall St. J.: India Real Time (July 7, 2014, 7:59 PM), *https://blogs.wsj.com/indiarealtime/2014/07/07/india-bans-import-of-controversial-foie-gras/*; Michaela DeSoucey, Contested Tastes: Foie Gras and the Politics of Food 61 (2016).

In 1968, Congress passed the Wholesome Poultry Products Act, which amended the PPIA "to provide for cooperation with appropriate State agencies with respect to State poultry products inspection programs, and for other purposes." The 1968 amendment also added an express preemption clause to the PPIA, which states that "[m]arking, labeling, packaging, or *ingredient requirements . . . in addition to, or different than*, those made under [the PPIA] may not be imposed by any State." 21 U.S.C. § 467e (emphasis added). At issue here is whether California's ban on products made by force-feeding birds constitutes an "ingredient requirement" under the PPIA's preemption clause.

C. Procedural History

* * *

[*The District Court granted plaintiffs' motion for summary judgment, finding*] that section 25982 imposes an "ingredient requirement" and is expressly preempted by the PPIA. *Ass'n des Éleveurs de Canards et d'Oies du Québec v. Harris (Canards II)*, 79 F. Supp. 3d 1136, 1144-48 (C.D. Cal. 2015). The district court permanently enjoined California from enforcing section 25982.

* * *

III. DISCUSSION

Plaintiffs invoke three separate preemption doctrines in support of their view that the state ban on the sale of foie gras produced by force-feeding methods cannot be enforced. First, they argue that the federal PPIA expressly preempts section 25982 because it imposes an "ingredient requirement" on the production of foie gras. Second, relying on the doctrine of implied preemption, Plaintiffs contend that Congress intended to comprehensively regulate the field of poultry products and thus left no room for state laws such as section 25982. Finally, Plaintiffs argue that implied preemption also applies because section 25982 stands as an obstacle to the purpose of PPIA. We address each of Plaintiffs' arguments in turn.

A. Express Preemption

Plaintiffs' main argument, and the ground upon which the district court granted summary judgment, is that California's sales ban is expressly preempted because the PPIA prohibits states from imposing "ingredient requirements" that are "in addition to, or different than," the federal law and its regulations. 21 U.S.C. § 467e.

In determining whether section 25982 is preempted by the PPIA, Congress's intent "is the ultimate touchstone." Where the federal statute contains an express preemption clause, we must determine the substance and scope of the clause. In so doing, we assume "that the historic police powers of the States were not to be superseded by the Federal Act unless that was the clear and manifest purpose of Congress." And finally, "when the text of a pre-emption clause is susceptible of more than one plausible reading, courts ordinarily 'accept the reading that disfavors pre-emption.'"

We begin by noting two points of agreement between the parties. First, Plaintiffs do not dispute that California's historic police powers extend to issues of animal cruelty. *See Canards I*, 729 F.3d at 952 (highlighting that protecting animals, like safeguarding the health and safety of citizens, is a legitimate state interest). Because animal cruelty is a field traditionally regulated by the states, compelling evidence of an intention to preempt is required. Second, the parties also agree that Congress intended to preempt state laws regulating the *ingredients* of poultry products. The only dispute is whether California's sales ban imposes an "ingredient requirement" that is "in addition to, or different than, those made under [the PPIA]." 21 U.S.C. § 467e.

Plaintiffs argue that section 25982 imposes an "ingredient requirement" because it requires that foie gras be made only from the livers of birds who were not force-fed. Plaintiffs do not claim that foie gras produced from non-force-fed birds is in any way inferior to foie gras made from the livers of force-fed birds, only that federal law is silent on the former. The State counters that section 25982 does not address ingredients at all, but rather regulates California's market by proscribing the sale of products produced by force-feeding birds to enlarge their livers. And to the extent that section 25982 can be construed as a ban on foie gras itself, the State argues that the PPIA does not prevent a state from banning poultry products. Based on the ordinary meaning of "ingredient" and the plain language and purpose of the PPIA, we hold that section 25982 is not expressly preempted by the PPIA.

1. *"Ingredient Requirements" Refers to the Physical Composition of Poultry Products*

We must first determine the scope and substance of the PPIA's "ingredient requirements." Because the PPIA does not define the term "ingredient," we look to the ordinary meaning of the term. "Ingredient" is defined as "one of the foods or liquids that you use in making a particular meal." Macmillan English Dictionary 776 (2nd ed. 2007); *see also* New Oxford American Dictionary 893 (3rd ed. 2010) ("any of the foods or substances that are combined to make a particular dish"); Webster's New World Dictionary 248 (mod. desk ed. 1979) ("any of the things that make up a mixture; component"). Accordingly, the term "ingredient" as used in the PPIA is most naturally read as a physical component of a poultry product.

This reading of "ingredient" also draws support from the statutory scheme as a whole. For example, the PPIA allows the import of foreign poultry products only if, *inter alia*, the products "contain no dye, chemical, preservative, or ingredient which renders them unhealthful, unwholesome, adulterated, or unfit for human food." 21 U.S.C. § 466. Similarly, the PPIA's "Definitions" section contains phrases such as: "ingredients only in a relatively small proportion"; "to assure that the poultry ingredients in such products are not adulterated"; "common names of optional ingredients (other than spices, flavoring, and coloring) present in such food"; and "fabricated from two or more ingredients." 21 U.S.C. § 453. Only a physical component can be added in "relatively small proportion," "adulterated," or "fabricated" in the manner described in the PPIA. In addition, regulations implementing the PPIA use the term "ingredient" in a manner consistent with its ordinary meaning. *See, e.g.*, 9 C.F.R. §424.21 (approving a chart of ingredients, including: acidifiers, anti-foaming agents, artificial sweeteners, food binders and extenders, coloring agents, and proteolytic enzymes). The consistent usage of "ingredient" in the PPIA and its implementing regulations further confirms that the term is used to mean a physical component of a product. We ordinarily assume "that identical words used in different parts of the same act are intended to have the same meaning."

Congress made clear that the PPIA's "ingredient requirements" address the physical components of poultry products, not the way the animals are raised. *See Wyeth*, 555 U.S. at 565 (emphasizing that "the purpose of Congress is the ultimate touchstone in every pre-emption case" (quoting *Lohr*, 518 U.S. at 485)). The PPIA regulates "ingredient requirements" for the purpose of ensuring that poultry products are "wholesome, not adulterated, and properly marked, labeled, and packaged." 21 U.S.C. §451; *see id.* §452 (declaring Congressional policy of preventing distribution of "poultry products which are adulterated or misbranded"); *see also Armour & Co. v. Ball*, 468 F.2d 76, 80-81 (6th Cir. 1972) (explaining the purpose of "ingredient requirements" within the Federal Meat Inspection Act's ("FMIA") identical preemption clause). The PPIA therefore authorizes the USDA, acting through its Food Safety and Inspection Service ("FSIS"), to prescribe standards of identity or composition for poultry products. These "ingredient requirements" cannot be read to reach animal husbandry practices because the federal law "*does not regulate in any manner the handling*, shipment, or sale *of live poultry*." H.R. Rep. No. 85-465 at 1 (1957) (emphasis added).[2] The USDA has even represented in legal filings that "[t]he PPIA is wholly silent on the treatment of farm animals, (including feeding procedures) or methods of slaughter for poultry." Motion for Summary Judgment, at 2, *Animal Legal Def. Fund v. USDA*, No. 12-cv-04028 (C.D. Cal. Apr. 22, 2016), ECF No. 67; *id* at 3 ("[The FSIS] has no authority to regulate the care or feeding of birds prior to their arrival at the slaughter facility.")[3] Accordingly, the PPIA's "ingredient requirements" are limited to the physical components of poultry products and do not reach the subjects of animal husbandry or feeding practices.

The ordinary meaning of "ingredient" (in line with the statutory context and the presumption of consistent usage) and the purpose and scope of the PPIA together make clear that "ingredient requirements" pertain to the physical components that comprise a poultry product, not animal husbandry or feeding practices. Having

---

2. Although 21 U.S.C. §453(g)(2)(A) makes a passing reference to "live poultry," it does so only in the context of explaining circumstances in which a final poultry product could be deemed adulterated.

3. We again reject Plaintiffs' assertion that the USDA's Policy Book *requires* foie gras to come from force-fed birds. *Canards I*, 729 F.3d at 950 ("It says nothing about the force feeding of geese and ducks."). Moreover, the background memos and letters on which Plaintiffs rely are "couched in tentative and non-committal terms." *Reid v. Johnson & Johnson*, 780 F.3d 952, 965 (9th Cir. 2015). The USDA has explicitly stated that the PPIA does not address the treatment of farm animals (including feeding procedures) and, based on the plain language and purpose of the law, we agree.

determined the parameters of the PPIA's "ingredient requirements," we now turn to whether section 25982 can be construed as imposing an "ingredient requirement."

2. *California Law Does Not Impose a Preempted Ingredient Requirement*

California's ban on the in-state sale of foie gras produced by force-feeding contrasts starkly with the PPIA's conception of "ingredient requirements." Section 25982 does not require that foie gras be made with different animals, organs, or physical components. Nor does it require that foie gras consist of a certain percentage of bird liver. *Cf. Armour & Co.*, 468 F.2d at 80-81 (holding that a state law requiring a 12% protein content in sausage meat was preempted because, *inter alia*, federal regulations required only an 11.2% protein content). It simply seeks to prohibit a feeding method that California deems cruel and inhumane. Section 25982 therefore addresses a subject entirely separate from any "ingredient requirement": how animals are treated long before they reach the slaughterhouse gates.

Plaintiffs argue that while section 25982 may not appear to be an "ingredient requirement," the law functions as one because it requires the production of foie gras using non-force-fed, rather than force-fed, livers.[4] As an initial matter, it is not the livers that are force-fed, it is the birds. Regardless, Plaintiffs' reading of the PPIA would require us to radically expand the ordinary meaning of "ingredient." The difference between foie gras produced with force-fed birds and foie gras produced with non-force-fed birds is not one of ingredient. Rather, the difference is in the treatment of the birds *while alive*. "Force-fed" is not a physical component that we find in our poultry; it is a feeding technique that farmers use. The same logic applies to the difference between regular chicken and cage-free chicken. "Cage-free" is no more an "ingredient" than "force-fed." Although Plaintiffs invite us to expand the definition of "ingredients" to include animal husbandry practices, that is within Congress's bailiwick, not ours. *See, e.g., Henson v. Santander Consumer USA Inc.*, 137 S. Ct. 1718, 1725 (2017) ("And while it is of course our job to apply faithfully the law Congress has written, it is never our job to rewrite a constitutionally valid statutory text under the banner of speculation about what Congress might have done had it faced a question that, on everyone's account, it never faced."). The PPIA, which is silent on the topic of animal husbandry and feeding practices, may not be read to supplant state law on an entirely different topic. *See Cipollone v. Liggett Grp., Inc.*, 505 U.S. 504, 517, 523 (1992) ("Congress' enactment of a provision defining the pre-emptive reach of a statute implies that matters beyond that reach are not pre-empted.").

Alternatively, Plaintiffs argue that section 25982 is functionally a ban on *all* foie gras. According to Plaintiffs, section 25982 bans the "ingredient" of foie gras because it bans the *process* by which it is made, i.e. force-feeding. This argument fails for two independent reasons. First, nothing in the record before us shows that force-feeding is *required* to produce foie gras. The district court assumed, without deciding, that

---

4. Nearly all of the cases that Plaintiffs cite in their brief are irrelevant to the issue of "ingredient requirements" because they deal with other portions of the PPIA's preemption clause.

alternative methods of producing foie gras are available.[5] *Canards II*, 79 F. Supp. 3d at 1145 n.8. And as noted above, California never intended to ban foie gras entirely—only foie gras produced by force-feeding. *See* Signing Message of Governor Arnold Schwarzenegger, Sen. Bill 1520, 2003–2004 Reg. Sess. (Sept. 29, 2004); *Canards I*, 729 F.3d at 945 n.4 ("Section 25982, however, does not prohibit foie gras. It bans the sale of foie gras produced through force feeding, but would not ban foie gras produced through alternative methods."); Cal. Health & Safety Code § 25984 (providing an effective date over seven and a half years after passage so that producers could transition to alternative methods of producing foie gras). Section 25982 therefore precludes only Plaintiffs' preferred method of producing foie gras.

Moreover, even if section 25982 results in the total ban of foie gras regardless of its production method, it would still not run afoul of the PPIA's preemption clause. The PPIA targets the slaughtering, processing, and distribution of poultry products, 21 U.S.C. §§ 451-452, but it does not mandate that particular types of poultry be produced for people to eat. Its preemption clause regarding "ingredient requirements" governs only the physical composition of poultry products. Nothing in the federal law or its implementing regulations limits a state's ability to regulate the *types* of poultry that may be sold for human consumption. If foie gras is made, producers must, of course, comply with the PPIA. But if a state bans a poultry product like foie gras, there is nothing for the PPIA to regulate. The fact that Congress established "ingredient requirements" for poultry products that *are* produced does not preclude a state from banning products—here, for example, on the basis of animal cruelty—well before the birds are slaughtered.

Our conclusion here is consistent with rulings in both the Fifth and Seventh Circuits. In *Empacadora de Carnes de Fresnillo, S.A. de C.V. v. Curry*, the Fifth Circuit examined whether the FMIA's identical preemption clause was triggered by a Texas law that banned horsemeat. 476 F.3d 326, 333-35 (5th Cir. 2007). The court explained that the FMIA's preemption clause governs matters such as "meat inspection and labeling requirements. It in no way limits states in their ability to regulate what types of meat may be sold for human consumption in the first place." *Id.* at 333. Because the FMIA does not limit a state's ability to define which meats are available for human consumption, the court found that the federal law could not preempt Texas's horsemeat ban. *Id.*

Several months later, the Seventh Circuit reached the same conclusion. In *Cavel International, Inc. v. Madigan*, the plaintiff argued that the FMIA's preemption

5. Plaintiffs do not appear to dispute that alternative methods of producing foie gras are available. In fact, it appears that high-quality foie gras can be made without force-feeding birds. *See, e.g.,* Dan Barber, *A foie gras parable*, TED, July 2008, *available at* http://www.ted.com/talks/dan_barber_s_surprising_foie_gras_parable/transcript?language=en#t-98000; Lauren Frayer, *This Spanish Farm Makes Foie Gras Without Force-Feeding*, NPR: The Salt (Aug. 1, 2016, 4:27 PM), http://www.npr.org/sections/thesalt/2016/08/01/487088946/this-spanish-farm-makes-foie-gras-without-force-feeding (noting that the farmer's natural foie gras "won the Coup de Coeur, a coveted French gastronomy award (it's like the Olympics for foodies)").

clause swept aside state laws that banned the slaughter of horses for human consumption. 500 F.3d 551, 553 (7th Cir. 2007). The Seventh Circuit determined that this "argument confuses a premise with a conclusion." *Id.* The court explained:

> When the [FMIA] was passed (and indeed to this day), it was lawful in some states to produce horse meat for human consumption, and since the federal government has a legitimate interest in regulating the production of human food whether intended for domestic consumption or for export . . . it was natural to make the Act applicable to horse meat. That was not a decision that states must allow horses to be slaughtered for human consumption. The government taxes income from gambling that violates state law; that doesn't mean the state must permit the gambling to continue. Given that horse meat is produced for human consumption, its production must comply with the Meat Inspection Act. But if it is not produced, there is nothing, so far as horse meat is concerned, for the Act to work upon.

Id. at 553–54. Like the Fifth Circuit, the Seventh Circuit found that the FMIA is concerned with inspecting facilities at which meat is produced for human consumption, not "preserving the production of particular types of meat for people to eat." *Id.* at 554 (quoting *Empacadora de Carnes de Fresnillo*, 476 F.3d at 333).

Like the state bans on horsemeat in *Empacadora de Carnes de Fresnillo* and *Cavel*, section 25982 is not preempted by the PPIA even if it functions as a total ban on foie gras.[6] Presumably, Congress could have authorized force-fed bird products, but "Congress did not write the statute that way."

Instead of addressing *Empacadora de Carnes de Fresnillo* and *Cavel*, Plaintiffs rely on the Supreme Court's decision in *National Meat Ass'n v. Harris*, 565 U.S. 452 (2012). This case, however, bears little resemblance to *National Meat*. The California statute at issue in *National Meat* governed the slaughter of nonambulatory pigs. In order to ensure that slaughterhouses handled nonambulatory pigs in a particular way, the state statute included a sales ban on selling meat or products from such pigs.

The Supreme Court in *National Meat* found that the state statute was preempted because it regulated matters that fall within the heart of the FMIA's regulatory scope: the activities of slaughterhouses. According to the Court, the state law interfered in

---

6. Section 25982 was inspired, in part, by California's own ban on horsemeat. See Cal. Assemb. Comm. on Bus. & Professions, Analysis of S.B. 1520, 2003-2004 Reg. Sess., at 7 (June 20, 2004) (noting that there is only a small step between a ban on horse, cat, and dog meat and a ban on force-feeding birds). As societal values change, so too do our notions of acceptable food products. Like foie gras, horsemeat was once a delicacy. *Cavel*, 500 F.3d at 552. Today, many states, including California, ban horsemeat because they consider the idea of eating horse repugnant. *See id.*; Cal. Penal Code §§ 598c-598d. California, like a growing number of countries around the world, has concluded that force-fed foie gras is similarly repugnant. The PPIA and its preemption clause do not stand in the way of society's evolving standards regarding animal treatment. *Cf. Stevens*, 559 U.S. at 469 ("[T]he prohibition of animal cruelty itself has a long history in American law, starting with the early settlement of the Colonies."); see generally Emily Stewart Leavitt, *Animals and Their Legal Rights: A Survey of American Laws from 1641 to 1990* 1-47 (4th ed. 1990).

the operations of slaughterhouses, imposing requirements regarding the treatment of nonambulatory pigs that did not exist under the federal law and its regulations. The Court explained that while "a slaughterhouse may take one course of action in handling a nonambulatory pig" under the FMIA and its implementing regulations, "under state law the slaughterhouse must take another [course of action].". In distinguishing the nonambulatory pig law from the horsemeat bans in *Empacadora de Carnes de Fresnillo* and *Cavel*, the Court underscored that the horsemeat bans "work[] at a remove from the sites and activities that the FMIA most directly governs." Unlike the horsemeat cases, the Court found that the nonambulatory pig statute "reaches into the slaughterhouse's facilities and affects its daily activities." The Court thus concluded that the FMIA preempted California's nonambulatory pig statute.

National Meat does not apply here because it addressed a different preemption argument in the context of a very different state law.[7] As an initial matter, *National Meat* and the present case deal with different portions of the FMIA's and PPIA's parallel preemption clauses; while *National Meat* focused exclusively on the "premises, facilities and operations" portion of the FMIA's preemption clause, Plaintiffs here invoke only the "ingredient requirements" portion of the PPIA's preemption clause. Moreover, section 25982, like the horsemeat bans in *Empacadora de Carnes de Fresnillo* and *Cavel*, "works at a remove from the sites and activities that the [PPIA] most directly governs." *Nat'l Meat Ass'n*, 565 U.S. at 467. Section 25982 also does not reach into a poultry "slaughterhouse's facilities and affect[] its daily activities." *Id.* We therefore hold that the PPIA does not expressly preempt California Health and Safety Code section 25982.

B. Implied Preemption

Alternatively, Plaintiffs argue that the PPIA impliedly preempts section 25982 under the doctrines of field and obstacle preemption. Neither doctrine, however, applies here.

Under the doctrine of field preemption, "States are precluded from regulating conduct in a field that Congress, acting within its proper authority, has determined must be regulated by its exclusive governance." *Arizona v. United States*, 567 U.S. 387, 399 (2012). Courts may infer field preemption from a framework of regulation so pervasive "that Congress left no room for the States to supplement it" or where the federal interest is "so dominant that the federal system will be assumed to preclude enforcement of state laws on the same subject." *Id.* Plaintiffs concede that the PPIA does not regulate the field of animal care and feeding, but view the PPIA as broadly occupying the field of all edible products that result from raising poultry for food.

---

7. We also note that, unlike the FMIA at issue in *National Meat*, the PPIA does not explicitly incorporate the Humane Methods of Slaughter Act. We have not had the occasion to decide whether poultry should be considered "other livestock" under the Humane Methods of Slaughter Act, *see* 7 U.S.C. § 1902(a), and we need not decide that issue here.

Plaintiffs' field preemption argument ignores the states' role in poultry regulation. The express preemption clause at the heart of Plaintiffs' case clearly provides that the PPIA "shall not preclude any State . . . from making requirement[s] or taking other action, consistent with [the PPIA], with respect to any other matters regulated under [it]." 21 U.S.C. § 467e. It also explains that state laws regarding storage and handling are preempted *only if* the Secretary of Agriculture finds those laws to "unduly interfere with the free flow of poultry products in commerce. . . ." *Id.* In addition, states may implement standards for the inspection of poultry sold in-state, even if those standards are more rigorous than the ones imposed by federal law. Because the PPIA itself contemplates extensive state involvement, Congress clearly did not intend to occupy the field of poultry products. *See Empacadora de Carnes de Fresnillo*, 476 F.3d at 334 ("Congress did not intend to preempt the entire field of meat commerce under the FMIA.").

Plaintiffs' theory of obstacle preemption fares no better. Obstacle preemption, which is a form of conflict preemption, occurs "where the challenged state law 'stands as an obstacle to the accomplishment and execution of the full purposes and objectives of Congress.'" As with express preemption, courts "assume that 'the historic police powers of the States' are not superseded 'unless that was the clear and manifest purpose of Congress.'" *Arizona*, 567 U.S. at 400.

Plaintiffs fail to explain how section 25982 stands as an obstacle to the PPIA's objectives of ensuring that poultry products are "wholesome, not adulterated, and properly marked, labeled, and packaged." 21 U.S.C. § 451; *see also* 21 U.S.C. § 452. The PPIA most directly regulates "official establishments," where the "inspection of the slaughter of poultry, or the processing of poultry products," occurs. Section 25982, in contrast, prohibits what California finds to be a cruel feeding practice that occurs far away from the official establishments that the PPIA regulates. Moreover, nothing in section 25982 interferes with the USDA's "authority to inspect poultry producers for compliance with health and sanitary requirements, require[] inspection of poultry after slaughter, establish[] labeling requirements for poultry products, [or] allow[] for withdrawal of inspections for noncompliance and the imposition of civil and criminal penalties for the sale of adulterated products." As the Supreme Court has cautioned, we should not "seek[] out conflicts between state and federal regulation where none clearly exists." Accordingly, we conclude that section 25982 does not stand as an obstacle to accomplishing the PPIA's purposes.

IV. Conclusion

Because Health and Safety Code section 25982 is not preempted by the PPIA, California is free to enforce it. We REVERSE the district court's grant of summary judgment, VACATE the district court's permanent injunction, and REMAND the case for further proceedings consistent with this opinion.

Notes

1. On March 9, 2018, the *Association des Eleveurs* plaintiffs filed a petition for writ of certiorari to the U.S. Supreme Court, limited to a challenge to the Ninth Circuit's preemption decision. On January 7, 2019, the Supreme Court denied the plaintiffs' petition for *certiorari*. As a result, the law was in effect again.

2. The complex doctrine of preemption is grounded in the Supremacy Clause of the U.S. Constitution, U.S. Const. art. VI, cl. 2, which as a general matter provides that federal laws are superior to state laws where there is a direct conflict between the two. Nevertheless, the preemption doctrine begins with the presumption that the states' traditional police powers—including laws protecting public health and safety, as well as animal cruelty and welfare—should not be superseded by a federal act unless Congress has clearly intended that effect, whether through express preemption, conflict preemption or field preemption. As you will see from your readings in this chapter and elsewhere in the text, for more than thirty years preemption has been a recurring issue in cases addressing statutes and regulations affecting animals used in agribusiness.

3. Within days of the Ninth Circuit's 2017 decision in *Association des Eleveurs*, a federal district court in New York addressed some of the same issues. *Evolution Fast Food Gen. Partnership v. HVFG, LLC,* 2017 U.S. Dist. LEXIS 161129 (S.D.N.Y. Sept. 27, 2017). In that case, a California restaurant sued New York *foie gras* producers to enjoin them from selling any product in California made by force-feeding birds to enlarge their livers in any jurisdiction that prohibits cruelty to "any animal," and sought judicial declarations that (i) such practices constitute animal cruelty under New York's anti-cruelty law, (ii) the California statute is not preempted by federal law, and (iii) selling any such product in California is an unfair business practice under California statutes. Although not bound by the Ninth Circuit ruling in *Association des Eleveurs*, the court agreed with the Ninth Circuit's analysis and reached the same conclusion—that the federal PPIA does not preempt the California statute. Thus, all of plaintiff's claims based on California Health & Safety Code section 25982 survived defendants' motion to dismiss. The court did conclude, however, that the alleged violation of New York's anti-cruelty statute could not serve as a predicate for violation of California's unfair competition law.

4. In *Organic Consumers Ass'n v. Sanderson Farms, Inc.,* 284 F. Supp. 3d 1005 (N.D. Cal. 2018), plaintiffs were advocacy groups that focused on education and research and worked "to safeguard the rights and promote the views and interests of socially responsible consumers and farmers." Plaintiffs sued poultry processor Sanderson Farms under California's unfair competition/consumer misrepresentation statutes, and Sanderson argued that the PPIA (discussed in *Association des Eleveurs*) preempted their claims. The court disagreed, finding that the unfair competition laws were "complementary" to the federal law's protection of the quality and proper labeling of poultry products—and therefore not preempted. The court in *Animal Legal Defense Fund Boston, Inc. v. Provimi Veal Corp.,* 626 F. Supp. 278 (D.

Mass. 1986), discussed later in the chapter, addressed a related issue but found that the plaintiffs' attempted use of the state consumer misrepresentation statute was preempted by federal labeling laws.

5. Not only opponents of Section 25982 have initiated litigation over the statute; proponents have sued for enforcement of it. In *Animal Legal Defense Fund (ALDF) v. LT Napa Partners LLC*, 234 Cal. App. 4th 1270 (2015), ALDF alleged that the defendants violated Section 25982 by selling *foie gras* in their Napa restaurant. The defendants filed a motion to dismiss the case on the grounds that it was a "SLAPP suit" (Strategic Lawsuit Against Public Participation), arguing that the distribution of *foie gras* was a protected form of expressive conduct (a protest against the *foie gras* ban) not subject to challenge. The trial court denied the motion and, on appeal, the appellate court affirmed. The facts were as follows:

> Defendant Frank [managing member of LT Napa Partners LLC], who is the head chef at Napa restaurant La Toque [which is owned by LT Napa Partners LLC], has been a vocal opponent of Section 25982. For example, he testified at state senate hearings preceding passage of the law, publicly debated the merits of the ban, and authored a newspaper opinion article against the ban.

> After the ban went into effect, plaintiff paid an investigator to dine at La Toque on three occasions in September 2012, October 2012, and March 2013. On each occasion he requested *foie gras* and was told that if he ordered an expensive tasting menu he would receive *foie gras*. On two of the occasions it was described as a "gift" from the chef. He ordered the tasting menus and was served *foie gras*. He was not told he was served *foie gras* in protest against the *foie gras* ban and was not provided information about defendant Frank's opposition to the *foie gras* ban. [Fn 4: "In a declaration, Frank averred that, '[s]hortly after' the investigator's March 2013 visit, La Toque started 'presenting a protest card' when serving *foie gras*. He averred the cards explained his 'criticism of and opposition to' Section 25982."]

> Plaintiff brought the results of its investigation to Napa law enforcement authorities. Over the course of three months, plaintiff attempted to persuade the Napa authorities to take action based on the alleged violation of Section 25982 at La Toque, but the city attorney declined. Subsequently, plaintiff initiated the present suit, alleging a cause of action under the Unfair Competition Law ("UCL") (Bus. & Prof. Code §§ 17200, *et seq.*) based on defendants' alleged violation of Section 25982. Plaintiff does not request damages but seeks an injunction prohibiting defendants from "furnishing, preparing, or serving *foie gras* in any form or manner whatsoever."

234 Cal. App. 4th at 1275–76.

The court found that ALDF had "*Havens* standing" (see Chapter 5) to bring the lawsuit (having suffered injury-in-fact and lost money from having to divert significant resources as a result of defendants' conduct). On the merits, defendants did not dispute that the *foie gras* served at their restaurant was produced through force-feeding. The sole question was whether defendants' practice of serving it as part of a tasting menu constituted "sales" prohibited under the statute. Along with its own extensive analysis, the court relied on a California case and a California Attorney General Opinion interpreting a statute regarding liability for the sale of alcohol to minors, to conclude that the answer was yes.

6. Even before Section 25982 was enacted, the practices used to create *foie gras* were the subject of litigation. In *Humane Society of the U.S. v. Brennan*, 881 N.Y.S.2d 533 (App. Div. 2009), plaintiffs asserted that *foie gras* is an "adulterated food" and, therefore, cannot be sold pursuant to food safety laws. Under New York's Agriculture & Markets Law sections 199-a and 200, products of diseased animals are deemed "adulterated food" and may not be sold in the state. As described by the trial court, the gist of plaintiffs' claim was that "[t]he extreme hypertrophy (overgrowth) of their livers—the very goal of the process—is characterized through veterinary diagnosis as a pathological condition in the subject birds." Index No. 7704-06, RJI No. 01-06-ST7184 (N.Y. Supr. Ct., Albany Cty. Mar. 20, 2008), Decision, Order and Judgment, at 5. The basis for the adulteration claim was that "[a]t the time of their slaughter they are diseased animals, and the *foie gras* made from their livers is therefore the product of diseased animals" and, as such, "it is by definition an 'adulterated food product.'" *Id.* The trial court dismissed the action on the ground that plaintiffs had not suffered injury-in-fact and, therefore, did not have standing to sue. The court further concluded that the interests protected by the statute relating to adulterated food products were those of consumers, not those of the animals raised for slaughter. On appeal, the Appellate Division agreed that plaintiffs lacked standing; the court therefore did not address their remaining contentions.

7. As noted in footnote 1 of the *Association des Eleveurs* opinion, other countries, including Israel, have instituted some form of a ban on force-feeding or *foie gras* products. In 2001, Israel's parliament determined that force-feeding geese for the *foie gras* industry was cruel, and directed the agriculture office to ban the practice by the end of 2002. In 2003, Israel's High Court ruled that force-feeding geese was cruel, but recommended allowing the practice to continue until March 2005, by which time the Agriculture Ministry was to present new regulations relating to foie gras manufacture. HCJ 9232/01 *NOAH (Israeli Federation of Animal Protection Organizations) v. Attorney General*, Piskei Din 57(6) 212 (Isr. S.C. 2003). As translated by an animal protection organization in Israel (CHAI), Justice Rivlin commented:

> As for myself, there is no doubt in my heart that wild creatures, like pets, have emotions. They were endowed with a soul that experiences the emotions of joy and sorrow, happiness and grief, affection and fear. Some of them nurture special feelings towards their friend-enemy: man. Not all think so; but no one denies that these creatures also feel the pain inflicted upon them through physical harm or a violent intrusion into their bodies. Indeed, whoever wishes to may find, in the circumstances of this appeal,

prima facie justification for the acts of artificial force-feeding, justification
whose essence is the need to retain the farmer's source of livelihood and
enhance the gastronomic delight of others. . . . But this has a price — and
the price is reducing the dignity of Man himself.

http://www.animallaw.info/nonus/cases/cas_pdf/Israel2003case.pdf, at 39.

In January of 2005, the Knesset (Israel's parliament) Education Committee (which
is responsible for laws relating to the treatment of animals) ended the practice of
force-feeding geese in Israel. As stated by the Committee's chairwoman, "The time
has come to put an end to the drawn-out period of many years during which the
geese have suffered." Stuart Winer, *What's Bad For The Goose . . . Must Stop, Committee Rules*, JERUSALEM POST, Jan. 4, 2005. For a thorough analysis of the *NOAH* case
and a comparison of the relevant American laws at that time, *see* Mariann Sullivan &
David J. Wolfson, *What's Good for the Goose . . . The Israeli Supreme Court, Foie Gras,
and the Future of Farmed Animals in the United States*, 70 LAW & CONTEMP. PROBS.
139 (2007).

8. At the federal level in the United States, in 2007 several animal advocacy organizations petitioned the USDA and the Food Safety and Inspection Service (FSIS) to
promulgate regulations condemning *foie gras* as an adulterated food product under
the Poultry Products Inspection Act (PPIA), 21 U.S.C. §§ 451–472. As discussed in
Association des Eleveurs, the PPIA sets standards for the USDA to regulate the production and sale of poultry to protect consumers from adulterated poultry products. The FSIS denied the petition, and petitioners sued over the denial. The district
court first granted defendants' motion for judgment on the pleadings and dismissed
the case, holding that even though the organizations titled their document "Petition for Rulemaking," that they were actually not making "a request to make new
rules or modify existing rules" (the basis for a rulemaking petition), but simply
were "challenging a scientific conclusion and not a legal one. The USDA's denial of
Plaintiffs' petition shows that it disagrees with Plaintiffs' viewpoint that force-fed
foie gras is adulterated or diseased. . . ." The court concluded the advocates were not
entitled to judicial review under the Administrative Procedures Act because there
were "no legal issues to be considered concerning the USDA's petition denial." *Animal Legal Defense Fund v. U.S. Dept. of Agriculture (ALDF v. USDA)*, 2013 U.S. Dist.
LEXIS 40547 (C.D. Cal. Mar. 22, 2013).

On appeal, the Ninth Circuit reversed, holding that the denial of a petition to
initiate rulemaking is indeed reviewable under the Administrative Procedure Act.
ALDF v. USDA, 632 Fed. App'x 905, 908 (9th Cir. 2015). On remand, the court
granted defendants' summary judgment motion and again dismissed the case. The
court's analysis on the merits is excerpted below.

Animal Legal Defense Fund v. U.S. Dept. of Agriculture

United States District Court for the Central District of California, 2016
223 F. Supp. 3d 1008

* * *

3. Analysis

Plaintiffs challenge FSIS's decision on three grounds: (1) its explanation for why hepatic lipidosis does not render the liver unfit for human consumption is "nonsensical and irrational"; (2) its conclusion that there was insufficient evidence of a connection between consumption of force-fed foie gras and the onset of secondary amyloidosis in humans "ran counter to the evidence before it"; and (3) FSIS entirely failed to consider other bases purportedly included in the petition that support a finding that foie gras is unfit for human consumption.

i. Hepatic Lipidosis

Plaintiffs argue that FSIS gives a "nonsensical and irrational" explanation for why fatty livers caused by disease are unfit for human consumption, but livers fattened through force-feeding are not. First, they contend that the logic behind FSIS's reasoning is scientifically unsound. Second, they contend that neither the PPIA nor the relevant regulations distinguish between the causes of particular physiologic states (such as hepatic lipidosis). The Court disagrees.

As noted above, the Court must defer to an agency's scientific judgments. FSIS reasoned that although force-fed livers contain excess fat and thus could be characterized as affected by hepatic lipidosis, it is not a diseased or otherwise dangerous product because liver fattening is the normal and expected physiologic response to force-feeding.[6] FSIS contrasted this with hepatic lipidosis resulting from a disease process, which often causes—in addition to fat build up—inflammation, hemorrhaging, and a buildup of fibrin in the liver tissue, and which FSIS concedes *would* be a basis for condemning the bird. This explanation appears eminently reasonable, not "nonsensical and irrational," and is supported by both the administrative record and the agency's own scientists. While Plaintiffs strenuously argue that this is not a scientifically valid distinction, the Court is required to credit the agency's scientific conclusions over Plaintiffs' where, like here, the agency's reasoning is not totally implausible.

Plaintiffs' argument that the distinction is without basis in the statutory and regulatory scheme fares no better, because this is a classic case in which the Court should give *Chevron* and *Auer* deference to the agency's interpretation of the relevant statutes and regulations, respectively. The PPIA explicitly requires that the condemnation of poultry be based on "scientific fact, information, or criteria," and that such condemnation be achieved "through uniform inspection standards and

---

6. The bird is typically slaughtered before the fat deposits overwhelm the liver's ability to function.

uniform applications thereof." 21 U.S.C. § 452. Despite this, the PPIA and its implementing regulations are filled with broad and ambiguous phrases describing the bases for condemning poultry or removing it from commerce. Indeed, §453(g)(3) alone contains seven such words: "filthy," "putrid," "decomposed," "unsound," "unhealthful," "unwholesome," and "unfit." The implementing regulations contain only slightly less broadly worded phrases, such as "abnormal physiologic state," 9 C.F.R. § 381.83, "affected by an inflammatory process," and "general systemic disturbance," *id.* §381.86. The courts are obviously ill-equipped to make the scientific judgments necessary to determine which physiologic conditions render a bird "unsound" or "unwholesome" and thus in need of condemnation....

Here, there is nothing in the PPIA or the implementing regulations that renders FSIS's distinction between causes of hepatic lipidosis unreasonable. Plaintiffs point, for example, to the requirement that FSIS condemn any poultry carcass that "show[s] evidence of an abnormal physiologic state," 9 C.F.R. § 381.83, and argue that the phrase "abnormal physiologic state" precludes any consideration of what causes that state. However, this is far from the only reasonable interpretation of this phrase; indeed, the cause of the physiologic state may be *exactly* what makes it "abnormal." Similarly, the Court sees nothing inherent in the word "diseased," 21 U.S.C. § 460(d), that requires FSIS to totally disregard the cause of a physiologic state as a basis for condemnation (or, in this case, non-condemnation).

* * *

For these reasons, the Court concludes that FSIS acted within its discretion in rejecting the petitioners' arguments concerning hepatic lipidosis.

ii. Secondary Amyloidosis

Plaintiffs again attack the scientific reasoning, and the underlying statutory and regulatory constructions, behind FSIS's conclusion that the study petitioners presented to FSIS ("Solomon Study") did not show a connection between human consumption of foie gras and the onset of secondary amyloidosis. And, once again, the Court concludes that FSIS's conclusions and interpretations are rational.

FSIS provided a reasonable scientific explanation for its position. FSIS found that the Solomon Study did not evidence any connection between human consumption of foie gras and the onset of secondary amyloidosis because: (1) the experiments in the study were performed on mice, not humans, and humans are less susceptible than mice to developing secondary amyloidosis; (2) the mice were genetically engineered to have a pre-existing inflammatory process, making them even more susceptible to developing secondary amyloidosis; (3) the mice that developed secondary amyloidosis were injected or fed with "purified and concentrated amyloid fibrils extracted from foie gras," and that the removal of the fat from foie gras "could have altered how a normal stomach ... would have handled the ingestion"; (4) the authors of the study themselves never concluded that the study evidences a definite connection in healthy humans between eating foie gras and developing secondary amyloidosis, only that "it would seem prudent" for those genetically susceptible to developing secondary amyloidosis to "avoid" eating foie gras; and (5) the study's theory that persons with diabetes and Alzheimers may also be at an increased risk of developing secondary amyloidosis after consuming foie gras was speculative and not even tested in the study. Plaintiffs make conclusory assertions that these reasons are irrational, but give no concrete reason why they are outside the realm of scientific possibility. Instead, Plaintiffs simply highlight the study's findings about the link between foie gras and secondary amyloidosis in mice, and then state that this should be enough for FSIS to conclude that foie gras is also "unhealthful" for humans to consume. This is insufficient under the deferential standard of review for denials of rulemaking petitions.

* * *

As previously noted, the statutory scheme taken as a whole clearly points to affording FSIS discretion in carrying out the PPIA's objectives, which must include reasonable discretion as to the quantum of evidence needed before taking agency action as drastic as banning a food product entirely from the market. In other words, FSIS must have the discretion to determine what type and amount of scientific evidence crosses the threshold from scientific possibility to "scientific *fact*." 21 U.S.C. § 452 (emphasis added). Indeed, if Plaintiffs' interpretation of the PPIA were the rule, it would force FSIS to initiate rulemakings to ban and unban a poultry product every time any study came out that even touched on the health implications of the product. Not only would this destabilize the entire poultry market, it would wreak havoc on FSIS's resources. That cannot possibly be what Congress envisioned.

* * *

Note

Although no federal laws directly address the treatment of animals in factory farms, conditions in such industrial operations were the subject of Congressional debate in 2001.

Our inhumane treatment of livestock is becoming widespread and more and more barbaric. Six-hundred-pound hogs—they were pigs at one time—raised in 2-foot-wide metal cages called gestation crates, in which the poor beasts are unable to turn around or lie down in natural positions, and this way they live for months at a time.

On profit-driven factory farms, veal calves are confined to dark wooden crates so small that they are prevented from lying down or scratching themselves. These creatures feel; they know pain. They suffer pain just as we humans suffer pain. Egg-laying hens are confined to battery cages. Unable to spread their wings, they are reduced to nothing more than an egg-laying machine.

* * *

. . . Life must be respected and dealt with humanely in a civilized society.

147 Cong. Rec. S7311–12 (2001) (statement of Sen. Byrd (D-WV)).

While the acknowledgment of such treatment and conditions and the rejection of them in the Congressional Record at that time may have seemed promising, nearly two decades later, not only had no progress been made in federal protections for farmed animals, but bills (such as H.R. 4879/H.R. 3599, the "Protect Interstate Commerce Act;" and H.R. 2887, the "No Regulation Without Representation Act of 2017") aimed at dismantling state and local laws enacted to provide some limited protections and improved standards for farmed animals continued to be proposed in Congress. As the following case reflects, however, more than thirty years ago, at least one court held that federally-mandated practices regarding farmed animals should include consideration of the animals' welfare.

Humane Society of Rochester and Monroe County for Prevention of Cruelty to Animals, Inc. v. Lyng

United States District Court, Western District of New York, 1986
633 F. Supp. 480

TELESCA, U.S. District Judge. Plaintiffs in this action seek to have me convert the temporary restraining order I issued on April 4, 1986 into a preliminary injunction. Defendants oppose plaintiffs' motion, and have cross-moved to dismiss the action. For the reasons set forth below, the temporary restraining order is converted to a preliminary injunction, and defendants' motion to dismiss is denied.

BACKGROUND

The plaintiffs challenge the administratively prescribed method for branding cattle under the Dairy Termination Program ("DTP") as amended by the Food Security Act of 1985, P.L. 99-198. Under the program, the Commodity Credit Corporation ("CCC") is authorized to enter into contracts with producers of milk in the 48 states of the continental United States who agree to sell for slaughter or export all dairy cattle in which they have an interest and who, for a period of five years, agree not to acquire any interest in dairy cattle or the production of milk. Despite earlier measures to discourage over-production of milk, including the earlier Dairy Diversion Program and the freezing or reduction of the support price, the problem of milk supply exceeding commercial demand persisted. Thus to ensure a permanent reduction in milk production, and reduce the imbalance between supply and demand in the milk market, Congress established the Dairy Termination Program.

* * *

In implementing the program, the Secretary is authorized by the Act to issue a regulation requiring some method of identifying cattle subject to such contracts. In furtherance thereof, the Deputy Administrator, State and County Operation, adopted U.S. Department of Agriculture Notice LD-249 which provides that all female dairy cattle in the DTP program shall be branded within 15 days after the dairy farmer is notified that he has been accepted in the program. That document provides "All female dairy cattle must be branded with a hot branding iron. Freeze, chemical, or other branding methods are not acceptable." The plaintiffs attack that aspect of the publication claiming that it is arbitrary and capricious because it is inherently inhumane and therefore an unreasonable method of marking or identifying those cows earmarked for removal from production. The plaintiffs claim that the Government's rigid adherence to a plan of marking cows which calls for facial branding by hot-iron method, is unreasonable, arbitrary and capricious when another method or other methods which would not involve as much pain to the animal and are equally effective are not permitted under the plan.

FACTS

At this stage of the proceeding, the facts appear as follows. Plaintiff, Humane Society of Rochester and Monroe County for the Prevention of Cruelty to Animals, Inc. is a special corporation with a statutory charge to prevent and prosecute cruelty against animals. Some members of its staff are empowered as peace officers. In addition, under New York Not For Profit Corporation Law § 1403, plaintiff as a corporation for the prevention of cruelty to animals is specifically authorized to "... prefer a complaint before any court, tribunal or magistrate having jurisdiction, for the violation of any law relating to or affecting the prevention of cruelty to animals, and may aid in presenting the law and facts to such court, tribunal or magistrate in any proceeding therein." Plaintiffs Douglas D. Burdick and Mary Jane Burdick are dairy farmers who have been accepted into the Dairy Termination Program at issue in this case.

Plaintiffs specifically challenge the hot-iron face branding regulation published by defendants as U.S. Department of Agriculture Notice LD-249. They argue primarily that the regulation is arbitrary and capricious in violation of the Administrative Procedure Act, 5 U.S.C. § 706(2)(A).

* * *

At a preliminary injunction hearing held April 14th and 15th, 1986, plaintiffs presented eight witnesses. The first, Dr. Charles E. Short, D.V.M., a professor at Cornell University, testified that hot-iron facial branding was painful, could damage underlying facial structure (muscles used in chewing, salivary glands, and eyes), and that, because of the extent of enervation of the facial area, hot-iron branding was an "inhumane approach." He clearly outlined the potential for significant harm to the cows particularly if the branding process was inappropriately conducted.

Plaintiffs' second witness, Dr. Theodore H. Friend, a professor of applied animal behavior (his specialty is animal stress physiology) at Texas A & M University, testified regarding "freeze-branding" as an alternative to hot-iron branding. In freeze-branding, a branding iron is submerged in liquid nitrogen until it reaches the temperature of that nitrogen (−320 degrees F). It then is applied to the cow for 40 seconds, and causes short-term hair loss in the branded area, and eventually the hair grows back in white. However, if the brand is applied for 60 seconds, it causes permanent hair loss like a hot-iron brand. Dr. Friend testified that a freeze brand is just as visible on a white cow as a fire brand is on a black cow, from a distance of 40 to 50 feet. He testified that in his experience, no infections had ever resulted from freeze-branding, and the brand healed in approximately four weeks with only some itching. He testified that it was easier to freeze-brand, because a farmer could tell when the brand was cold enough when the nitrogen stopped bubbling, whereas only much practice could enable one to tell when a hot-iron brand was hot enough.[1] He also testified that, although a cow might react to a freeze-brand for a few seconds, the cow would become quiet almost immediately thereafter as the surrounding skin became numb.

Dr. William D. Whittier, D.V.M., a professor at V.P.I. College of Veterinary Medicine, testified that he prefers a freeze-brand because it is more legible and causes less pain to animals. Although Dr. Friend had testified that a brand should not be applied to the face of a cow (but if it were, that a freeze-brand should be used), Dr. Whittier had "no difficulty" with a freeze-brand applied to the face. He agreed that it was easier to use than a hot-iron because of the ability to tell when the iron had reached the proper temperature. He also felt it was easier because a farmer need only immobilize the head of a cow with, for example, a rope halter or a head catch, whereas "squeeze chutes" were recommended for hot-iron branding. He felt that any problem with visibility of freeze-brands on white-faced cows could be overcome by applying the brand for a longer time to remove the hair permanently. He also had had no experience with infections resulting from freeze branding. Although Dr. Friend felt that dairy farmers were more likely to have used freeze-brands than hot-iron brands, Dr. Whittier felt they were about equally common. He used dry ice rather than liquid nitrogen to cool the brand, and in his experience it took 30 to 35 seconds to brand a black cow, 40 to 45 seconds to brand a red cow, and 1¼ to 1½ minutes to brand a white cow.

Robert W. Birkenhauer of the Hasco Company, a manufacturer of cattle tags, also testified for plaintiffs. He testified that his company made both metal and plastic I.D. tags and notchers which could mark a cow by taking a notch out of its ear. He also produced a tattooing tool which would produce a two inch green tattoo in a cow's ear by perforating the skin on the ear and filling the perforation with dye. He testified that this brand would be visible from approximately 30 feet.

Dr. Short was then recalled as a witness. He testified that, based on the testimony of the other witnesses, freeze-branding would be preferable to hot-iron branding because it was less painful. He testified that it would be better to brand on the body of a cow rather than her face, and that he would recommend anesthesia before any face branding. He felt that tattoos were an acceptable alternative to branding, because they were easy, healed rapidly, resulted in minimal infection, and, in his experience, remained visible for 10 to 12 years.

---

1. Of course, this wouldn't be the case if the branding iron was electric thermostatically controlled, but LD-249 makes no mention of such a device.

* * *

Ronald Storm, the Chief Cruelty Investigator of the Humane Society of Rochester, testified that he would consider hot-iron branding on any part of a cow a violation of § 353 of the New York Agriculture and Markets Law. He also testified that, as far as he knew, no one had ever been prosecuted in New York for hot-iron branding. Dr. John F. Kullberg, the President of the American Society for the Prevention of Cruelty to Animals, testified that . . . it was clear to him that hot-iron face branding constitutes absolute cruelty to an animal when less painful alternatives are available.

Finally, plaintiff Douglas Burdick, a dairy farmer, testified that he was unwilling to hot-iron brand his cows on the face, in part because he feared prosecution by anti-cruelty organizations, and in part because he had experienced difficulties with a similar method of de-horning cows.

Dr. Lee E. Miller, D.V.M., testified on the Government's behalf. Unlike any of plaintiffs' witnesses, Dr. Miller had considerable experience with hot-iron face branding. He testified that there was no need for a squeeze chute, but only that the head of the cow need be immobilized. He also testified that the hot-iron did not seem to bother the cow after one second, that it did not cause any cows to lose milk producing capability and it did not instill fear of humans in the cow. He testified that freeze-branding, by contrast, caused facial swelling not caused by hot brands. In his judgment, hot branding was preferable because freeze-branding took much longer, the liquid nitrogen could cause freeze burn to the farmer or the cow, and could not be controlled as easily as an electric, thermostatically controlled hot-iron. In his experience, tattoos caused a far greater reaction from the cow because ears are more sensitive, tattoos get faint and difficult to read over time, and infection (especially by contagious warts) is much easier. He noted that he had seen hot-iron brands applied in the West become infected and/or smudged if the branding iron were heated on a fire too long or held on the cow too long. He found either type of brand equally difficult to camouflage. He testified that an electric branding iron (which costs $73.00) was needed for proper hot-iron branding, and probably should be applied by persons familiar with its use. After two weeks of hot-iron branding considerable numbers of cows on the jaw, he had noted no infections in any of them.

Richard C. Call, a dairy farmer from Genesee County, New York, testified that he had branded approximately 700 cows in his herd with an electric iron. Although he had never branded cows before, he was able to brand his cows with little difficulty by closing the stall around the head of the cow, gripping the cow's nose with a nose lead (a device compared to a pair of pliers), and branding the cow. His cows would react for one to two seconds, but would be able to eat normally the same afternoon they were branded. None of his cows developed infections from the hot-iron, and Mr. Call preferred the hot-iron because it was quicker and there was no risk of spilled liquid nitrogen.

Jerry Newcomb, the Administrator of the Dairy Termination Program, testified for defendants that he was responsible for the development of LD-249. He developed the regulation with the help of a veterinarian, Dr. Billy Johnson of the Animal and Plant Health Inspection Service (APHIS), and other staff members. He testified that the Department of Agriculture needed an immediate program which would result in visible, recognizable, and permanent identification of dairy cows to be taken out of production, because there was a concern about these cows being diverted (as had occurred under the predecessor Milk Diversion Program). He testified that pain to the animal was taken into consideration by the Department when looking at alternatives, and that, in particular, the Department had rejected freeze-branding as an alternative in part because of the additional stress caused to the animal by the lengthy branding process. He specifically stated that hot-iron branding was the only available alternative which effectively served the Program's purposes of identifying cows by a recognizable, permanent, and visible mark. Dr. Billy Johnson's testimony was essentially in agreement but added that LD-249 was patterned after the hot iron branding practices from one of the western states.

DISCUSSION

At the outset, I hold that all plaintiffs have standing to bring this action. The Humane Society is specifically authorized under New York State law to prosecute violations of animal cruelty laws. This differentiates it from the plaintiffs in *Sierra Club v. Morton*, 405 U.S. 727 (1972), and *Valley Forge Christian College v. Americans United for Separation of Church and State, Inc.*, 454 U.S. 464 (1982). Other courts have specifically recognized standing for animal protective societies in similar cases. The Burdicks' interests are evident: under the challenged regulation, they are forced against their will to brand their cows on the face with a hot-iron, and thereby expose themselves to the risk of prosecution for animal cruelty.

* * *

It has long been the public policy of this country to avoid unnecessary cruelty to animals. . . . Even the government's attorney conceded that if the avoidance of unnecessary cruelty to animals is not already government policy, it should be.

In the face of this public policy, the testimony before me indicates that defendants have obviously entirely failed to consider an important aspect of the problem before them when they drafted LD-249. Defendants argue that they considered the aspect of cruelty to animals specifically when they rejected freeze-branding. I reject this as not credible. The testimony before me establishes that freeze-branding causes less stress to the cow than hot-iron branding. Moreover, the predominant concern of defendants with the length of time taken to freeze-brand appears to be based more on inconvenience to farmers than on inconvenience to cows.

Most importantly, if cruelty to animals were indeed a consideration, LD-249 would not be drafted the way it is. The only testimony before me that hot-iron face branding was not unnecessarily cruel came from defendants' witnesses who had employed electric, thermostatically controlled hot-iron brands. Yet LD-249 is written to require farmers to brand solely with a hot-iron, whether or not they have access to an electric branding iron. It advises farmers that they can brand their cows by heating any three inch strip of iron, whether over a fire or with a blow torch then applying it to the cow twice to get an "X". Farmers are advised that an overheated iron can cause hair to burn which is particularly dangerous because the brand is being applied just below the cow's eye. Yet farmers are advised to keep on trying until they get it right. LD-249 clearly does not reflect the views of an agency which gave serious consideration to the prevention of cruelty to animals.

Accordingly, I find that plaintiffs have established a likelihood of success on the merits of their claim that LD-249 is arbitrary and capricious.

* * *

I further find that irreparable harm would result to plaintiffs if an injunction were not granted. On the testimony before me, the hot-iron face branding of cows appears to constitute a violation of the state anti-cruelty laws which the Humane Society is sworn to prevent. In addition, by branding their cows, the Burdicks would expose themselves to prosecution for violation of New York Agriculture and Markets Law § 353. Even more important is the prospect of not qualifying for the program if they fail to brand their cows within 15 days of acceptance. Membership in the program is limited to those applicants accepted as of April 1, 1986.

CONCLUSION

It is evident to me, as it should have been to the Department of Agriculture, that the type of branding espoused in LD-249 constitutes cruelty to animals. If the ASCS had been as concerned with cruelty to animals as they now claim to be, LD-249 would never have been adopted. The testimony before me clearly establishes that freeze-branding is a viable alternative to hot-iron branding since it causes less pain to cows and accomplishes all of the objectives outlined by defendants. Had defendants truly been concerned with preventing unnecessary cruelty to animals, they would have at least allowed farmers the option of either method.

Notes

1. While the *NJSPCA* (excerpted earlier in this chapter) case and some of the Notes that follow it considered standards for practices that may be deemed by courts, legislatures, government agencies and industry to constitute humane treatment, the courts have rarely gone so far as to suggest criminal liability for cruelty to animals where customary practices do not meet those standards. In the abstract, if a practice is not humane, is it necessarily illegal animal cruelty? If practices such as confinement in gestation crates or veal crates, the intensive overcrowding of egg-laying hens in small cages or the force-feeding of geese for the production of *foie gras* violate the literal language of a state anti-cruelty statute but the statute exempts customary farming practices, there is an implicit, if not explicit, legislative acceptance of cruelty to farmed animals. What are the public policy rationales or other possible bases for this?

2. In *Lyng*, two of the plaintiffs were dairy farmers who refused to engage in a federally required practice in part because they alleged that they feared prosecution

under the state's anti-cruelty laws. The court suggested that if the farmers complied with the federal requirement, which testimony from plaintiffs' experts indicated was "unnecessarily cruel," they would indeed be guilty of a crime under New York's anti-cruelty law. This was based solely on the representations of the local humane society, which asserted that hot-iron face branding was illegal. The court granted the farmers standing in the action based on the threat of prosecution. If the government could prove the local prosecutor would not charge the Burdicks, would that change the analysis?

3. The *NJSPCA* court concluded that the practice of cutting off or "docking" the tails of cows without anesthesia was "far from [] humane." Compare the case of *Hammer v. American Kennel Club*, 803 N.E.2d 766 (N.Y. 2003), excerpted in Chapter 3, where the plaintiff wanted to show his purebred Brittany Spaniel at competitions sponsored by the American Kennel Club (AKC) but he refused to dock his dog's tail. The gravamen of the complaint was that the AKC's tail-docking requirement encouraged dog owner/guardians to violate New York's anti-cruelty law (AGRIC. & MKTS. § 353). Because the court concluded that Hammer had no valid civil cause of action under the anti-cruelty statute, the court dismissed the complaint without determining whether docking a dog's tail would be deemed an act of cruelty in violation of section 353.

4. The early English case of *Waters v. Braithwaite*, 30 T.L.R. 107 (K.B. Div. 1913) addressed the issue of whether an act that causes unnecessary suffering can be deemed a violation of law even when the act is consistent with usual and customary commercial practices. In *Waters*, the defendant had walked a cow and her calf five-and-a-half miles while the cow was in "full milk" condition. The lower court determined that even though the cow had suffered from a distended udder and sores, no violation of law had occurred because the practice of walking similarly "overstocked" cows for some distance was common. On appeal, the higher court reversed, stating:

> [I]t was found that this treatment of cows was customary, the object being that the udder should be very much distended, so that possible purchasers might see that the cows were heavy milkers. It was not denied that this caused great pain; no one alleged that it produced any benefit to the cow, but, on the contrary, it was stated to do her harm. The only benefit there was might be that of the owner. It was said that the respondent caused the animal unnecessary pain. The case proved that the pain was unnecessary as far as the cow was concerned, and the respondent did cause unnecessary suffering by omitting to have her milked, or from being milked by muzzling the calf. If the custom of doing this did exist, it was time that it ceased, and people must find some other means of judging whether a cow was good milker or not.

Id. at 108. Consider other anti-cruelty cases you have read. Is the question of whether the acts are necessary or justified "as far as the [animal] was concerned" or as far as the defendant or society was concerned? Which should it be?

5. Reported cases involving farmed animal cruelty are relatively rare, but such cases do occur. *See, e.g., State v. Schott*, 384 N.W.2d 620 (Neb. 1986) (criminal neglect of cows and hogs); *State of New Jersey v. ISE Farms, Inc.*, Appeal No. A-45-00 (N.J. Super. Ct., Law Div., Mar. 8, 2001). In *ISE Farms*, the defendant disposed of two live hens on a pile of supposedly dead chickens. (Piles of dead animals are a common sight at many factory farms.) Both hens died shortly after being removed from the pile and taken for treatment by a witness who was touring defendant's facility when he saw the hens moving. At trial, defendant's site manager testified that it was not defendant's policy to throw away live chickens, but he described the corporate policy for handling "spent chickens or chickens that are down" as being euthanasia by "vertebrae dislocation"—breaking the chickens' necks by manually twisting them. When a veterinarian had examined the hens after they were removed from the trash, however, she found no sign of vertebrae dislocation. The veterinarian later moved out of state and was unavailable to testify at trial.

The customary practice of vertebrae dislocation was not at issue, but the municipal court found the defendant guilty on two counts of cruelty, admonishing the defendant's representative: "You better train your people better, you better get somebody who knows the difference between a live chicken or a dead chicken. If you're going to do it, you better do it right." Trial Tr. at 59, *ISE Farms* (N.J. Muni. Ct., Warren County, Oct. 17, 2000). On appeal, the conviction was overturned. The court found unanswered questions of "whether there was an attempt at vertebrae dislocation which was unsuccessful or whether in fact perhaps vertebrae dislocation was negligently done or attempted in this case or whether the employee in this case believed the chickens were even already dead and neglected to do it at all." Appeal Tr. at 49, *ISE Farms*, No. A-45-00 (N.J. Super. Ct. Law Div. Mar. 8, 2001). The veterinarian's unavailability at trial factored into the court's conclusion and its refusal to find beyond a reasonable doubt that defendant or its employee violated the state's anti-cruelty laws. *See also State of Missouri v. MOARK*, Case No. 05NW-CR1568 (Mo. Cir. Ct., Newton County, filed July 29, 2005) (settlement reached and damages paid where animal cruelty charges were filed against egg producer for "purposely kill[ing] chickens in a manner not allowed by law").

6. In *ISE Farms*, two attorneys in private practice acted as "private prosecutors." Where allowed under state law, this process allows interested attorneys to prosecute cruelty cases on behalf of the public entity, where the district attorney's office may not have the financial means or the interest to adequately work up the case and carry it through to conclusion.

In *Animal Legal Defense Fund v. Mendes*, 160 Cal. App. 4th 136 (2008), ALDF and individual consumers sued "calf ranchers" and their company that raised dairy calves in small crates, where the calves were unable to turn around or exercise. ALDF claimed that the method of intense and solitary confinement used by defendants violated Penal Code section 597t, one of California's many specialized anti-cruelty statutes, which requires that "adequate exercise" be provided to all confined animals. The consumer plaintiffs alleged unfair business practices under California

Business and Professions Code section 17200, *et seq.* (The consumer claims are discussed in the Notes after *ALDF v. Provimi Veal*, which follows these Notes.) In explaining the defendants' business, the court explained:

> Cows must give birth in order to produce milk. To maintain productivity in a dairy setting, cows are bred to give birth every 12 to 15 months. Female calves, essentially a byproduct of this necessity, can be raised and added to the producing herd after they have calved. The complaint alleges respondents raise the calves for about six months before returning them to the owners.

160 Cal. App. 4th at 140 n.2.

The complaint alleged that the defendants had approximately 12,000 calves at any one time. As summarized by the court:

> The factual core of the complaint is an allegation that calves are confined to isolation crates for up to 60 days at a time. Each crate is barely bigger than the calf and is not large enough to permit the calf to turn around or lie in a natural position for periods of rest. Only the bottoms of the crates are regularly washed, and fecal matter and other materials are washed from the top and sides of the crates only upon a change of occupant.

Id. at 140.

The trial court sustained the defendants' demurrer without leave to amend (thereby dismissing the case at the pleadings stage). On appeal, ALDF contended that Penal Code section 597t impliedly established a private right of action "in entities with a long-standing commitment to carrying out the laws protecting animals and a history of 'direct work in the area of animal cruelty law enforcement and protection.'" *Id.* at 141. The appellate court looked to the legislative history and comprehensive legislative scheme and rejected this contention.

7. Since very few jurisdictions allow advocates to pursue criminal convictions by acting as private prosecutors, advocates have looked to other avenues for civil lawsuits. One approach can be a "taxpayer standing" lawsuit. In California, for example, Code of Civil Procedure section 526a authorizes taxpayers to sue to "restrain[] and prevent[] any illegal expenditure of, waste of, or injury to, the estate, funds, or other property" of state or local government. The California Supreme Court has ruled that the use of this statute to enjoin criminal activity is prohibited. *Leider v. Lewis*, 2 Cal. 5th 1121 (2017) (arising from claims of elephant abuse at the Los Angeles zoo). *See also, ALDF v. Mendes* (rejecting the claim that California was improperly using taxpayers' funds by supporting cruelty to animals committed by the defendant); *Humane Soc'y of the U.S. v. State Board of Equalization*, 152 Cal. App. 4th 349 (2007) (rejecting taxpayer "waste" claim that an exemption from sales and use tax should not apply to "battery cage" chicken coops that were alleged to violate anti-cruelty laws).

8. Utilizing another litigation approach, in *Physicians Committee for Responsible Medicine v. Glickman*, 117 F. Supp. 2d 1 (D.D.C. 2000), the plaintiffs ("a collection of

individuals and groups") sought declaratory and injunctive relief for claims arising out of the appointment and operation of the Dietary Guidelines Advisory Committee for Year 2000 by the U.S. Department of Agriculture and the U.S. Department of Health and Human Services. The Dietary Guidelines "set forth recommended nutritional and dietary information, and are relied upon by federal agencies in carrying out their responsibilities under federal food, nutrition, and health programs." *Id.* at 2. Plaintiffs asserted that their views on nutrition and health were not adequately represented on the Committee. They sought a judgment declaring that defendants violated public disclosure requirements of the Federal Advisory Committee Act by failing to disclose all records prepared by or for the Committee. The court concluded the plaintiffs were entitled to declaratory relief to provide them "ammunition for their attack on the Committee's findings," although the court expressed no opinion as to how effective that "ammunition" would be. *Id.* at 5. The court also ruled that the Committee must disclose its members' sources of income and *curricula vitae*, to address the public interest in "learning whether a Committee member was financially beholden to a person or entity who had an interest in how the Dietary Guidelines might be amended" and in learning the "qualifications and affiliations" of the Committee members. What do you think the plaintiffs' goals were here?

9. As previously noted, civil actions may be brought not only against government agencies, but also against the industry corporations themselves. Lawsuits asserting false advertising claims under consumer protection statutes and unfair competition claims can be filed by animal advocates to try to ensure that the public is not misled about the conditions under which animals used for food products are kept. This type of effort has been used for some time. Consider the following case.

Animal Legal Defense Fund Boston, Inc. v. Provimi Veal Corp.

United States District Court, District of Massachusetts, 1986
626 F. Supp. 278

MAZZONE, District Judge. Disputes about food grow naturally out of our conviction that we are what we eat. This case, which questions the treatment of calves, illustrates this abiding and deeply-felt concern. The Animal Legal Defense Fund-Boston, Inc. ("ALDF") is a nonprofit charitable Massachusetts corporation whose members "promote animal welfare in purchasing their food." Convinced that calves raised for veal are mistreated, and that antibiotic drugs added to their feed endanger human health, the ALDF filed this action in Massachusetts state court. Defendant Provimi Veal Corporation ("Provimi"), a Wisconsin veal producer, buys calves raised by others in Massachusetts, slaughters them and sells the veal to meat distributors; Provimi's 1984 sales of veal in Massachusetts exceeded $1 million. Provimi also manufactures and sells pre-mixed and finished animal feeds and milk replacers.

Based on the Massachusetts consumer protection statute, Mass. Gen. Laws Ann. ch. 93A, §§ 1–11 (West 1984), the ALDF complaint seeks an order obligating Provimi to tell retail consumers how the calves that Provimi buys are raised. Its members, the ALDF complaint alleges, do not want to buy veal from calves raised in this cruel and unhealthful manner. Yet, because this information is not available to retail consumers, ALDF members have unwittingly bought and eaten Provimi veal. Other ALDF members feel they are unable to buy or eat veal at all.

The calves that Provimi buys in Massachusetts, the ALDF says, are raised in dark, confined pens; they are fed iron-deprived diets, which make them anemic so that their meat will be white rather than red. Their food also contains antibiotic drugs, such as penicillin and the tetracyclines, at dose levels below those required to treat an actual disease. These subtherapeutic doses are used to promote growth and to ward off disease.[5] Although Provimi does not raise its own calves, the ALDF contends that Provimi tells farmers how it wants them to be raised.

Provimi acts unfairly and deceptively because it does not tell consumers of its veal how the calves it buys are raised. Provimi buys "factory-farmed" veal calves that are "confined, intensively-raised [and] special-fed." Amended Complaint, para. 4. Such treatment is "cruel" and "fails adequately to meet the physiological and ethological needs of calves." *Id.* Members of the ALDF refuse to eat veal from calves raised this way because it would offend their "moral and aesthetic beliefs." Not telling consumers about this cruelty is unfair and deceptive, because it denies to consumers information they might consider important in deciding whether to buy Provimi's veal.

More complicated is the ALDF claim that Provimi ought to tell consumers that its veal might be unhealthful because it comes from calves that are fed antibiotics subtherapeutically. Bacteria immune to antibiotics flourish in animals whose feeds contain antibiotics. Resistance to antibiotics can pass from harmless bacteria in the animal's gut to other bacteria, such as salmonella, that can cause disease in humans. Resistant organisms passed to humans in meat render normal antibiotics ineffective against a wide range of infections. Patients may suffer prolonged illness or death while being treated with ineffective medicines. Consumers should be told about this health risk, the ALDF says, because it might influence their decision to buy veal; not telling them is unfair and deceptive.

The ALDF filed its complaint in Massachusetts state court in June, 1985. An amended complaint was filed a month later in July. Asserting diversity of citizenship, Provimi removed the case to this Court in August, 1985. Also in August, Provimi filed its answer, admitting that it buys calves and sells veal in Massachusetts, and

---

5. Subtherapeutic, continuous application of antibiotics in feed animals is believed to promote faster growth, improve feeding efficiency, and limit disease outbreaks, particularly among animals kept in crowded, confined quarters. Therapeutic application of antibiotics is intended to treat disease, once detected, and is administered in larger doses than for subtherapeutic use.

Exactly why and how subtherapeutic doses of antibiotics promote growth is not fully understood. Several explanations have been advanced. Antibiotics might increase an animal's metabolism. They might increase the rate at which the animal can absorb nutrients in its food. Most commonly accepted, it appears, is the theory that antibiotics limit subclinical diseases, those which may not cause evident symptoms but are nonetheless taxing to the animal. O. Schell, *Modern Meat* 11 (1984).

that it does not disclose to consumers how those calves are raised. Provimi advanced numerous affirmative defenses which it now presses in its motion for judgment on the pleadings. That motion is now before the Court.

The parties briefed the legal questions raised by the ALDF's amended complaint with vigor and at great length. Provimi filed a 46-page memorandum of law. In opposition, the ALDF filed a 93-page memorandum of law. Finally, Provimi responded with a 54-page reply brief.

Provimi raised numerous affirmative defenses in its answer and motion for judgment on the pleadings, but only two of them, preemption of the state law claim by federal law, and failure to state a claim on which relief can be granted, need be treated here.[6] For reasons explained more fully below, Provimi's motion must be granted and the ALDF amended complaint dismissed.

I.

The ALDF alleges that calves, raised according to Provimi's instructions, are treated cruelly because they are kept in cramped pens and are ill-fed. Even if the ALDF is right, however, Chapter 93A is an inappropriate remedy. The cruel treatment of animals violates criminal statutes which are enforced by public officials, not private organizations, no matter how well-intentioned.

Cruelty to animals is a crime in Massachusetts. *See, e.g.*, Mass. Gen. Laws Ann. ch. 272, §§ 77, 78A, 81, 85A (West Supp. 1985). These statutes are "directed against acts which may be thought to have a tendency to dull humanitarian feelings and to corrupt the morals of those who observe or have knowledge of those acts." Like nearly all criminal laws, these anti-cruelty statutes are enforced by public law enforcement officials. Cruelty to animals is an offense "against public morals, which the commission of cruel and barbarous acts tends to corrupt." It is true that officers of the Massachusetts Society for the Prevention of Cruelty to Animals, a private charitable and benevolent organization, do enforce these anti-cruelty statutes, but only when they have been appointed special police officers by the Commissioner of Public Safety.

It is also true that the ALDF does not, in the strict sense, try to enforce Massachusetts' criminal anti-cruelty statutes. It concedes it has no authority, as a private charitable organization, to do so. Instead, the ALDF insists that the Massachusetts consumer protection law gives concerned consumers a private right of action when violations of the anti-cruelty statutes affect them as consumers. Consumers have a

---

6. Provimi also contends that the ALDF lacks standing to litigate its concerns, that it did not send Provimi a demand letter before filing suit as required by the Massachusetts consumer protection statute, and that it did not join indispensable parties—the farmers who actually raise the veal calves Provimi buys. A good deal of the briefs is devoted to the standing question.

Although today's ruling assumes standing, it does not decide that difficult question. Nothing in this decision is meant to suggest that the ALDF's concerns about eating veal from mistreated calves, or about the health risks of feeding antibiotics subtherapeutically to livestock, are sufficient, or insufficient, to satisfy the constitutional standing requirements. The same holds true, of course, for the other affirmative defenses raised by Provimi but not decided here.

right to know that veal sold to them comes from cruelly mistreated calves; Provimi's failure to give consumers that information, not the cruel treatment itself, is the unfair and deceptive trade practice in violation of Chapter 93A. As adroit and skillful as this argument is, it is misdirected.

What makes Provimi's nondisclosure an unfair and deceptive trade practice is that it keeps consumers from knowing about a criminal violation, namely a violation of section 77. Not disclosing how calves are raised is deceptive, says the ALDF, because would-be veal buyers, including those who belong to the ALDF, might consider the criminally cruel treatment of calves raised for veal "relevant information," 940 C.M.R. 3.05(1), or a fact "the disclosure of which may have influenced the buyer or prospective buyer not to enter into the transaction . . ." 940 C.M.R. 3.16(2). An ALDF victory in this action would have an unmistakable effect: to enforce by means of an injunction obtained in a private lawsuit, a criminal statute enforceable only by public prosecutors and, in legislatively-sanctioned circumstances, private groups, among which the ALDF is not numbered.

Relying on the decision in *Dodd v. Commercial Union Ins. Co.*, 365 N.E.2d 802 (1977), the ALDF argues that Chapter 93A creates a private remedy for violations of other statutes which themselves do not provide for private enforcement actions. This reliance is misplaced, however. *Dodd* held that private plaintiffs could base a Chapter 93A action against an insurance company on violations of a second statute regulating unfair and deceptive insurance practices. That statute, Mass. Gen. Laws Ann. ch. 176D, did not provide for private actions and contemplated enforcement by the Commissioner of Insurance. *Dodd*, however, turned on a saving clause in Chapter 176D providing that it did not "relieve or absolve any person . . . from any liability under any other laws of this commonwealth." *Dodd* also concerned two regulatory statutes, both intended to protect consumers. "The mere existence of one regulatory statute," the *Dodd* court reasoned, "does not affect the applicability of a broader, nonconflicting statute, particularly when both statutes provide for concurrent coverage of their common subject matter." Notably, Chapter 93A was amended, following *Dodd*, and now explicitly provides that violations of Chapter 176D can be enforced in a Chapter 93A private action.

However well-intentioned it is, the ALDF is pursuing its goals along an improper avenue in this litigation. If convinced it has uncovered gross and systematic mistreatment of animals, the ALDF should concentrate its estimable advocacy urging public officials and the designated private animal protection organizations to proper action.

II.

The ALDF is also disturbed about what calves are fed and not fed. Calves raised for veal, like many food animals, eat medicated animal feeds which contain subtherapeutic levels [of] antibiotic drugs believed to promote growth. Humans who consume meat from these animals, the ALDF fears, also ingest bacteria resistant to antibiotic drugs. Such bacteria can cause serious illness, difficult to treat because normally effective antibiotic drugs would be useless. According to the ALDF, iron is omitted from the diet of calves so the veal will be pale and white rather than red.

The ALDF claims that calves raised on this antibiotic-rich, iron-deprived diet yield veal that is adulterated and unwholesome in violation of federal and Massachusetts regulations. Selling such veal violates Chapter 93A because it is an unfair trade practice not to comply with a Massachusetts public health statute or regulation, 940 C.M.R. 3.16(3). Similarly, it is an unfair and deceptive trade practice to violate any federal consumer protection statute. 940 C.M.R. 3.16(4). And not disclosing to consumers of veal that calves are fed antibiotic drugs is unfair and deceptive because it is important information that should be available to a consumer choosing whether to purchase veal. 940 C.M.R. 3.05(1), 3.16(2).

It is unnecessary to reach the merits of the ALDF's claims, however, because they are pre-empted by the comprehensive federal scheme regulating the labeling, packaging and marketing of meat and the use of medicated animal feeds. The ALDF's concerns are well-founded and quite serious. But this action, brought under a state consumer protection law, is an inappropriate remedy, and the ALDF's complaint must, therefore, be dismissed.

Under the Supremacy Clause, U.S. Const., Art. VI, cl. 2, state law claims, whether they are based on statute, regulation or common law, may be pre-empted in several circumstances. "First, when Congress, in enacting a federal statute has expressed a clear intent to pre-empt state law; second, when it is clear, despite the absence of explicit pre-emptive language, that Congress has intended, by legislating comprehensively, to occupy an entire field of regulation and has thereby left no room for the States to supplement federal law; and, finally, when compliance with both state and federal law is impossible." *Capital Cities Cable, Inc. v. Crisp*, 467 U.S. 691 (1984). The ALDF wrongly suggests that federal regulations are to be given less pre-emptive weight than federal statutes. "Federal regulations have no less pre-emptive effect than federal statutes." *Fidelity Federal Savings & Loan Assn. v. De La Cuesta*, 458 U.S. 141, 153–54 (1982). The ALDF's claim is based on the Massachusetts consumer protection statute and not on conflicting state regulations but that does not avoid pre-emption. "Regulation can be as effectively exerted through an award of damages as through some form of preventive relief. The obligation to pay compensation can be, indeed is designed to be a potent method of governing conduct and controlling policy."

The federal statutory and regulatory scheme involved here entails two federal statutes and two federal agencies. Food labeling generally is governed on the federal level by the Federal Food, Drug, and Cosmetic Act ("FDCA"), 21 U.S.C. §§ 301–392 (West Supp. 1985), and its regulations, which come under the administrative aegis of the Food and Drug Administration ("FDA").

Medicated animal feeds and drugs used in treating animals which are raised for human consumption are also controlled by the FDCA as part of its comprehensive scheme to protect the public from drugs that may be unsafe or ineffective for their intended uses. "New animal drugs," must be approved by the Food and Drug

Administration before they can be lawfully marketed. 21 U.S.C. § 360b(a)(1)(A). The FDA can refuse to approve a New Animal Drug Application if the drug is proven not safe, 21 U.S.C. § 360b(d)(1)(A) & (B), or that "there is a lack of substantial evidence that the drug will have the effect it purports or is represented to have under the conditions of use prescribed, recommended, or suggested in the proposed labeling thereof." 21 U.S.C. § 360b(d)(1)(E).

A drug that is not a "new animal drug" can be marketed without FDA approval. For a drug not to be considered a new animal drug, it must be "generally recognized" by qualified experts as safe and effective for each of its intended uses. 21 U.S.C. § 321(w).

Animal feeds that contain antibiotics are treated in a separate category parallel to new animal drugs. 21 U.S.C § 321(x). Medicated animal feeds must also win FDA approval, apart from approval of the animal drug itself, before they can be marketed. 21 U.S.C. § 360b(m).

Meat and meat food products shipped in interstate commerce are regulated by the Federal Meat Inspection Act, as amended by the Wholesome Meat Act, 21 U.S.C. §§ 601–695 (West Supp. 1985) ("FMIA"), and its regulations. The FMIA is administered by the United States Department of Agriculture ("USDA"). Enacted in 1907, the FMIA ensures that the "health and welfare of consumers [is] protected by assuring that meat and meat food products distributed to them are wholesome, not adulterated, and properly marked, labeled, and packaged." 21 U.S.C. § 602.

Combined, the FDCA and the FMIA form a comprehensive regulatory scheme intended to "protect the health and welfare of consumers and to prevent and eliminate burdens on commerce by assuring that meat and poultry products are wholesome and properly labeled."

The ALDF insists that Congress did not intend to entirely exclude all state regulation of food labels and animal drugs; that Congress was not concerned about bacteria in meat; and, that requiring a notice or label or warning "concerning the potential harmful effects of the genetically-altered" bacteria possibly contained in veal, would not conflict with federal regulations. I cannot agree, and for the reasons explained below, must conclude instead that the ALDF's Chapter 93A claim is preempted by the federal regulatory scheme.

First, to the extent the ALDF's amended complaint is based on violations of the FDCA or the parallel Massachusetts statute, Mass. Gen. Laws Ann. ch. 94, § 186 — which deem adulterated, food containing "any poisonous or deleterious substance which may render it injurious to health" — it is pre-empted. The ALDF says that Provimi violates the FDCA because it sells adulterated veal. It is true that veal containing salmonella bacteria resistant to antibiotics is adulterated, within the meaning of the FDCA. Diseases caused by drug-resistant bacteria may be prolonged and serious. A recent Centers for Disease Control study traced an outbreak of human food poisoning caused by salmonella bacteria resistant to several common antibiotics, to calves fed subtherapeutic doses of antibiotics. Holmberg, Osterholm, Senger & Cohen, 311 New Eng. J. of Med. 617 (1984).

But there is no allegation in the ALDF's complaint that Provimi has sold veal in Massachusetts contaminated with antibiotic-resistant salmonella. More important, the ALDF complaint fails to state a claim on which relief can be granted because no private right of action can be implied under the FDCA. Even assuming, for the moment, that the ALDF can show that Provimi violates the FDCA because its veal is adulterated, the state law authority for the injunctive relief it seeks—the Massachusetts consumer protection statute—is pre-empted by the FDCA. "A private right of action is equally inconsistent with the federal regulatory scheme, whether the right is based in federal or state law." Massachusetts cannot confer on private persons the power to enforce a federal statute whose enforcement Congress left to federal administrative agencies. Nor can the ALDF enforce Chapter 94, the Massachusetts statute which parallels the FDCA, in a private action under the Massachusetts consumer protection statute.

The same reasoning applies to the ALDF's claim that Provimi's veal is adulterated because calves are not fed iron. Iron, the ALDF argues, is a "valuable constituent" of veal; its absence renders veal an adulterated food. 21 U.S.C. § 342(b)(1). Nothing in the ALDF's brief suggests why veal must contain iron—it is the value of iron to humans that is important here, and not whether healthy calves require iron. Even assuming the ALDF is correct, however, this violation of the FDCA cannot support a private action under the Massachusetts consumer protection statute.

Second, the subtherapeutic and therapeutic use of antibiotics is controlled by a complicated and comprehensive federal statutory and regulatory scheme. Chapter 93A does not apply to "transactions or actions otherwise permitted under laws as administered by any regulatory board or officer acting under statutory authority of the Commonwealth or of the United States." Mass. Gen. Laws Ann. ch. 93A, § 3. Antibiotic use in animals that complies with the federal scheme does not violate the Massachusetts consumer protection statute. Nowhere in its pleadings does the ALDF allege that either farmers or Provimi fail to comply with the federal statutory and regulatory scheme.

Even if the ALDF avoided this exemption, however, the comprehensive federal statutory and regulatory scheme pre-empts any injunctive relief under Chapter 93A. The FDCA and its regulations establish complicated procedures by which new drugs proposed to be used in treating animals both subtherapeutically as feed additives and therapeutically, are approved before they can be marketed. Human safety is specifically considered, because it is in animals raised for food that these drugs and feeds will be used. 21 U.S.C. § 360b(d)(2). "The edible products of food-producing animals treated with such drugs" can contain only certain trace amounts of the drugs. 21 C.F.R. § 556 (1975). Further, regulations promulgated by the Secretary of Agriculture under the FMIA provide that all livestock slaughtered for human consumption shall be inspected before and after slaughter, to assure that these antibiotic levels are not exceeded. 9 C.F.R. §§ 309.16, 310.21 (1984). Food that contains approved animal drugs "or any substance formed in or on the food because of [the approved drug's] use" cannot be found to be adulterated. 21 U.S.C. § 360b(k).

The risk of antibiotic-resistant bacteria, the ALDF's particular concern, is not ignored in these regulations. In the early 1970s, the FDA assembled an Antibiotic Task Force to study the widespread subtherapeutic use of antibiotics in food-producing animals. That group recommended extensive further studies to assess the risk of an increase in antibiotic-resistant, bacterially-induced disease in humans or animals due to use of antibiotics as feed additives. In 1973, acting on the task force's advice, the FDA published 21 C.F.R. § 135.109 (since renumbered 558.15). The regulation proposed to revoke FDA approval for subtherapeutic use of antibiotics in two years unless data were submitted "which resolve conclusively the issues concerning their safety to man and animals." Studies of resistant salmonella are specifically called for. Drugs and animal feeds which were already approved were allowed to remain on the market while this testing was performed.

Thus, the federal statutory and regulatory scheme fully controls the use of antibiotics in animals, including possible health risks to humans. While it is true that the FDCA does not contain explicit pre-emptive language, Congress' intent to occupy the field of antibiotic use in animals, and to direct the States to leave all regulatory activity in that area to the federal government is clear.

Finally, the ALDF cannot escape the pre-emptive reach of the federal statutory and regulatory scheme by asking for an injunction simply obligating Provimi to tell consumers that the calves it buys are fed antibiotics subtherapeutically.

The ALDF wants Provimi to display on its "label or packaging" a "warning concerning the potential harmful effects of the genetically-altered salmonellae, or information that concerns the manner in which the veal calves were raised or procured." Even assuming Chapter 93A provides a basis for such a warning, it is plainly pre-empted by the federal regulatory scheme.

First, antibiotic use is thoroughly regulated by the FDCA. When Congress has fully occupied a field of regulation, even non-conflicting state regulation is pre-empted. Second, the ALDF's proposed warning is pre-empted by the FMIA which controls the labeling and packaging of meat and meat food products. Unlike the FDCA, it contains explicit pre-emption language; it permits some concurrent state regulation, but prohibits state "marking, labeling, packaging, or ingredient requirements in addition to, or different than, those" mandated by federal law. 21 U.S.C. § 678. The Secretary of Agriculture is authorized to prescribe "definitions and standards of identity or composition" for meat and meat food products which must be consistent with those prescribed under the FDCA. 21 U.S.C. § 607(c)(2). Meat and meat food products cannot be labeled until they have been inspected; inspections before and after slaughter assure that antibiotic tolerances set by the FDCA are not exceeded. 9 C.F.R. §§ 309.16, 310.21.

Federal law does not require meat and meat food product labels to carry a warning or an explanation about the subtherapeutic use of antibiotics. The ALDF seeks to impose requirements "in addition to or different than the federal requirements." It is true, as the ALDF contends, that Massachusetts can enact meat laws aimed at protecting the health and well-being of its citizens. Preparation of foodstuffs for market has traditionally been a matter of local concern. Still, meat ingredient standards, labeling and packaging have been pre-empted by the FMIA . . . and states cannot impose different or additional affirmative requirements on meat and meat food products.

Notes

1. What do you think ALDF's goals were in bringing this action? Is it a proper use of legal process to file an action in order to advance what appears to be a political, ethical/moral agenda? Should an organization be able to use the courts to effectuate its political wishes?

2. Can you think of any other, more traditional causes of action ALDF might have pled to achieve the same ends? Consider both federal and state law causes of action.

3. This case was at the forefront of a series of campaigns attacking the treatment of veal calves raised to produce "white," or "milk-fed," veal. In order to provide this meat for which consumers pay the highest prices, farmers take newborn calves from their mothers and lock them in crates, in which the calves cannot turn around or move freely. The calves are fed a diet absent of any iron or nutrients that would turn their flesh its natural pink color. Because of a high susceptibility to disease—caused by this inadequate diet and the denial of vital nutrients from their mothers' milk—the calves are given steady doses of antibiotics. The specialized treatment of these calves was spotlighted by animal protection groups, as an especially unnatural and harmful practice. The campaigns arguably were successful, by reducing the amount of veal eaten in America: in the 1970s, the average veal consumption per person in the United States was reportedly 3.5 pounds per year; as of 2013, the average was one-third of a pound per year. Ben Paynter, *Veal Farmers Adopt More Humane Methods*, N.Y. Times, Aug. 12, 2014. The efforts with respect to veal also educated many people about the production of veal in particular and the treatment of farmed animals in general. *See generally* Mary Esch, *Group Aids Farmers in Raising Animals More Humanely*, Dallas Morning News, May 3, 1987, at 12A; Robin Mather, *GNS Food Package*, Gannett News Service, May 2, 1989; Caroline E. Mayer, *Conflict Over Veal; Calf-Raising Techniques Are the Target of Animal-Welfare Groups*, Washington Post, June 14, 1989, at E01; Broderick Perkins, *Farmers, Activists Square Off Over Veal-Raising Methods*, San Diego Union-Tribune, July 20, 1989, at Food-26; Isabell Spindler, *Calves Deserve Better Treatment—Don't Eat Veal*, St. Petersburg Times 2, May 13, 1992, at 2. *See also* David J. Wolfson, *Beyond the Law: Agribusiness and the Systemic Abuse of Animals Raised for Food or Food Production*, 2 Animal L. 123 (1996).

4. In footnote 6, the *Provimi* court expressly sidestepped the issue of whether the plaintiffs had standing. Based on your knowledge of standing doctrine, was ALDF a proper plaintiff in this action?

5. The Federal Food, Drug and Cosmetic Act (FFDCA) regulates the use of medicated feeds and drugs given to animals raised for human consumption. The Federal Meat Inspection Act (FMIA) covers labeling and packaging of meat shipped in interstate commerce (as well as inspections and treatment of animals in slaughterhouses). The *Provimi* court concluded that together these statutes constitute a comprehensive federal scheme, which led to its ruling that ALDF's claim was preempted.

More than a quarter of a century after *Provimi*, federal preemption under the FMIA, FFDCA and other federal regulations remains a frequent issue in animal law cases, as you will see from some of your readings in this chapter and elsewhere in the text. For example, similar issues arise in the context of "cruelty-free" labeling, treatment of animals going to slaughter and the use of certain animals for clothing. *See, e.g.*, Bruce Friedrich, *Meat Labeling Through the Looking Glass*, 20 ANIMAL L. 79 (2013) (discussing the FMIA and preemption issues).

6. *Physicians Committee for Responsible Medicine (PCRM) v. McDonald's Corporation*, 187 Cal. App. 4th 554 (2010), involved claims related to California's "Proposition 65," (Cal. Health & Safety Code § 25249 *et seq.*) which requires businesses to provide warnings about potential carcinogens present at the businesses. Plaintiff sued seven chain restaurant corporations seeking an injunction, civil penalties and declaratory relief to prevent the defendants "from continuing to sell grilled chicken products to consumers without clear and reasonable warnings about the carcinogenic effects of those products," because of the alleged presence of carcinogens in the smoke produced by the grilling of chicken. The defendants contended that such potential Proposition 65 warnings were preempted by the federal Poultry Products Inspection Act (PPIA) because (i) "they conflicted with the federal policies promoting the thorough cooking of chicken to 'prevent the spread of foodborne illness'" and (ii) the PPIA established a "comprehensive and uniform federal scheme regulating labeling, processing and inspection of poultry." *Id.* at 561. The court held that the PPIA did not preempt Proposition 65 and remanded the case to the trial court for further proceedings. On remand, the trial court dismissed the claim, finding that certain defendants had posted Proposition 65 warnings and, as to other defendants, based on procedural issues regarding the timeliness of plaintiff's investigation into the facts before filing the lawsuit. The Court of Appeal affirmed. *PCRM v. Applebees Int'l Inc.*, 244 Cal. App. 4th 166 (2014).

7. Before filing a lawsuit, one animal advocacy organization registered a complaint with the Better Business Bureau, and submitted a simultaneous parallel petition to the Federal Trade Commission (FTC), contending that the "Animal Care Certified" logo used by United Egg Producers, Inc. (UEP) was misleading to consumers. As described in the National Advertising Review Board (NARB) Report No. 122 (May 10, 2004):

[Compassion Over Killing, Inc. (COK)] contended that the certification program was misleading in that the "animal care certified" logo, accompanied by a check mark, communicated to consumers that egg producers displaying the certification symbol, or seal, raised their hens in a humane fashion, when, in fact, compliance with the UEP certification guidelines did not ensure conformity with that expectation. UEP argued that it was not a national advertiser and therefore the certification program was beyond [National Advertising Division (NAD) of the Council of Better Business Bureaus]'s purview, and in any event, that the certification seal did not state or imply a humane level of care. UEP's position was that the certification logo simply communicated compliance with the animal husbandry guidelines reflected in the UEP certification standards.

NAD found that it had jurisdiction over the challenge because the UEP licensed its seal to be used by producers in labeling and advertising throughout the U.S. On the merits, based on its own judgment and expertise, as well as certain survey evidence that NAD considered persuasive but not dispositive, NAD agreed with the challenger and found that the seal conveyed a message that hens raised in compliance with the certification program were treated more humanely than the level of care reflected by the guidelines. NAD recommended discontinuance of the program as presently constituted. UEP appealed.

Id. at 1. On appeal, NARB affirmed the NAD's conclusions "with a somewhat different recommendation." *Id.* The NARB Report described the issue and the evidence as follows:

The issues presented on the merits are important ones for the parties, consumers, and the self-regulation system. Certification programs are important tools for communicating to consumers that certain products or services meet defined standards as established by the certifying organization. Entities displaying a seal are able to assure consumers that an independent third party has determined conformity to the applicable standards, which may be relevant to a determination by many consumers to purchase the goods or services in question, or their willingness to pay a premium price for certified products.

The UEP guidelines were developed in consultation with scientific experts. The parties appear to agree that they represent some improvement over practices generally used in the industry, although the extent of that improvement is disputed. The guidelines deal with issues such as the environment—the space afforded for each hen, access to clean drinking water, fresh air access, maintenance of body temperature; beak trimming; and molting, the practice of depriving hens of food and water to manipulate the egg-laying cycle. Independent audits are required of producers who display the certification logo to assure compliance.

The UEP guidelines recommend increased space for hens in cages, in the range of 67–86 square inches, although producers need not reach the 67 inch minimum until 2008. (67 square inches, while an improvement, is not enough space for a hen to flaps its wings.) The guidelines permit beak trimming in order to reduce pecking and cannibalism among the birds, although it may be done without anesthesia and thus painful. Finally, the guidelines suggest that molting longer than 4–5 days may give superior results, but require daily body weight loss monitoring and mortality, and recommend that mortality during the molting period should not substantially exceed normal flock mortality.

COK submitted the only evidence of consumer perception in this case. A 2000 poll by Zogby, Inc. showed that 75.4% of respondents found it unacceptable to starve hens for over a week to induce molting, something that is possible under the UEP guidelines, for example; that 86.2% found it unacceptable to densely crowd hens in cages, also allowed by the guidelines (even the 67 square inch standard to become effective in 2008 is less than a typical 8? × 11 inch piece of paper); and that 60.4% found that partially removing hens' beaks (allowed by the guidelines) was not acceptable. In addition, 80.7% said they would pay more for hens raised in a "humane" manner. As COK persuasively argues, it is unimaginable that consumers would consider treatment they find "unacceptable" to be humane treatment, even if it is care improved from earlier conditions, or a practical reality of the economics of egg production in the US.

. . . Here, the COK evidence is corroborative of the NAD's sound judgment that many consumers will take away from the "animal care certified" logo a message that the level of care is more humane than allowed by the UEP guidelines.

Id. at 2–3. The Report concluded with the following recommendation:

The panel recommends that the certification program either be discontinued in its present form or modified to more clearly communicate, through the UEP certification materials or as communication requirements placed on certified producers by UEP, that certification signifies the specific standard of care as set forth in the UEP guidelines.

Id. at 4.

While the petition with the FTC was pending, UEP changed its logo to "United Egg Producers Certified" rather than "Animal Care Certified."

COK and four individual plaintiffs then sued two supermarkets and Lehman's Egg Service, Inc., alleging unfair and deceptive trade practices under the District of Columbia's consumer protection statute, fraudulent and negligent misrepresentation and unjust enrichment, in connection with the same logo. *Compassion Over Killing, Inc., et al. v. Giant of Maryland LLC, d/b/a Giant Food Store, et al.,* Case No. 05-0001077 (D.C. Super. Ct.) (complaint filed Feb. 15, 2005). The allegations were consistent with those set forth in COK's complaint to the Better Business Bureau, which was referenced in the complaint in the D.C. action. The complaint sought injunctive relief, statutory and compensatory damages, and restitution. UEP intervened in the case shortly after the complaint was filed. The defendants, including UEP, filed motions to dismiss, asserting that all of the claims were either expressly preempted by the Egg Production Inspection Act (EPIA), 21 U.S.C. § 1036, or impliedly preempted by other federal regulatory statutes, and asserting that plaintiffs lacked standing. (Mem. Order Oct. 12, 2005, at 3–4.) Giant settled before the motions were heard. *Id.* at 3 n.1.

The court denied the motions to dismiss, finding no express preemption and distinguishing *ALDF v. Provimi Veal* because, unlike the plaintiffs in *Provimi*, the egg labeling plaintiffs sought "no affirmative labeling requirements." *Id.* at 9. The court further recognized that the "power to regulate marketing has traditionally been left to the states." *Id.*

In the following case, COK sued various government agencies after they each denied COK's petitions for rulemaking over egg carton labeling.

Compassion Over Killing v. U.S. Food & Drug Administration

United States Court of Appeals, Ninth Circuit, 2017
849 F.3d 849

MURGUIA, Circuit Judge:

Plaintiffs Compassion Over Killing, the Animal Legal Defense Fund, and six individual egg consumers submitted rulemaking petitions to Defendants U.S. Food and Drug Administration ("FDA"), Federal Trade Commission ("FTC"), Agricultural Marketing Service ("AMS"), and Food Safety and Inspection Service ("FSIS"), requesting that each agency promulgate regulations that would require all egg cartons to identify the conditions in which the egg-laying hens were kept during production. Each agency denied Plaintiffs' rulemaking petition. Plaintiffs initiated the underlying lawsuit claiming that each agency had acted arbitrarily and capriciously in dismissing their rulemaking petitions. The district court concluded that Defendants had each acted reasonably in denying Plaintiffs' petitions and granted summary judgment in favor of Defendants. We have jurisdiction pursuant to 28 U.S.C. § 1291, and we affirm.

I.

Plaintiffs submitted similar rulemaking petitions to the FDA, FTC, AMS, and FSIS requesting that each agency "take regulatory action to revise the current labeling requirements for eggs at [21 C.F.R. §§ 101, 115, 160], and/or to promulgate new regulations" that would require all egg cartons to identify the conditions in which the egg-laying hens were kept during production. The petitions specifically proposed that each agency develop regulations that would require all egg cartons to bear the labels "Free–Range Eggs," "Cage–Free Eggs," or "Eggs from Caged Hens," consistent with the living conditions of the hens. In support of the proposed regulations,

Plaintiffs argued that there is a strong consumer interest in buying eggs that are produced in cage-free environments. Plaintiffs also argued that, without the proposed regulations, consumers are being misled by certain statements and images on egg cartons that imply that the hens are being raised in cage-free environments. Plaintiffs provided several examples of various egg labels that present images of uncaged hens and contain phrases such as "all natural" or "animal friendly," arguing that these images and phrases likely mislead a consumer to believe that the hens are not being raised in cages. Plaintiffs also maintained that their proposed regulations are necessary because eggs from caged hens are nutritionally inferior to and carry a greater risk of Salmonella contamination than eggs from free-range hens.

Each agency denied Plaintiffs' petition for rulemaking. The FSIS and AMS explained that they could not promulgate the proposed regulations because they lacked the authority to take the requested action. The FTC explained that, based on the information Plaintiffs provided in the petition, it could not conclude that current egg-labeling practices were either "unfair or deceptive." The FTC also concluded that the petition had not sufficiently demonstrated that any misleading practice was "prevalent," as statutorily required for rulemaking. Lastly, the FTC explained that the agency's resources would be better used by combating any potentially deceptive practices through individual enforcement actions, rather than by promulgating new regulations.

The FDA denied Plaintiffs' request for rulemaking because it determined that Plaintiffs had failed to show that current egg labels omitted a "material" fact by not indicating the living conditions of the egg-laying hens. The FDA specifically explained that it could not determine that this information was material because Plaintiffs had not provided persuasive evidence that eggs from caged hens are either less nutritious or more likely to be contaminated with Salmonella than eggs from uncaged hens. The FDA also explained that consumer interest in the hens' living conditions, alone, is insufficient to establish that egg-production methods are a material fact that would permit the FDA to issue the requested regulations. Lastly, the FDA stated that it declined to promulgate the proposed labeling regulations because it could bring individual enforcement actions against any misbranded eggs, and "it would choose to use its limited resources on rulemakings of higher priority, such as those that are of greatest public health significance or are statutorily-mandated."

Plaintiffs filed this lawsuit, alleging that the FSIS, AMS, FTC, and FDA had each acted arbitrarily and capriciously in dismissing their rulemaking petitions. Plaintiffs moved for summary judgment, and Defendants filed a cross-motion for summary judgment, arguing that each agency had acted reasonably in denying Plaintiffs' rulemaking requests. The district court granted summary judgment for Defendants. Plaintiffs timely appealed.

II.

This Court reviews challenges to final agency action decided on summary judgment de novo and pursuant to Section 706 of the Administrative Procedure Act

("APA"). The APA requires the Court to "hold unlawful and set aside agency action, findings, and conclusions found to be . . . arbitrary, capricious, an abuse of discretion, or otherwise not in accordance with law." 5 U.S.C. § 706(2). When an agency refuses to exercise its discretion to promulgate proposed regulations, the Court's review "is 'extremely limited' and 'highly deferential.'" *Massachusetts v. EPA*, 549 U.S. 497, 527–28 (2007).

A.

Plaintiffs argue that the FSIS acted arbitrarily and capriciously by denying their rulemaking petition based on the agency's conclusion that it lacks the authority to promulgate the proposed regulations. Plaintiffs specifically argue that the FSIS has the authority to regulate the labeling of shell eggs under the Egg Products Inspection Act ("EPIA"), 21 U.S.C. §§ 1031–56.

The FSIS correctly concluded that it lacks the authority to promulgate Plaintiffs' proposed labeling regulations for shell eggs. The EPIA expressly distinguishes between the terms "egg products" and "eggs," and grants broad authority to the FSIS to regulate the labeling only of "egg products." *See* 21 U.S.C. § 1036(a) (stating that the FSIS may promulgate regulations mandating the disclosure of information "to assure that [egg products] will not have false or misleading labeling"); *see also id.* § 1033(f) (defining "egg product" as "any dried, frozen, or liquid eggs, with or without added ingredients, excepting products which contain eggs only in a relatively small proportion"); *id.* § 1033(g) (defining "egg" as "the shell egg of the domesticated chicken, turkey, duck, goose, or guinea"). Because Plaintiffs' proposed labeling regulations concern only shell eggs, they fall outside of the FSIS's labeling jurisdiction under the EPIA. Accordingly, we conclude that the FSIS did not act arbitrarily or capriciously in denying Plaintiffs' rulemaking petition.

* * *

D.

Plaintiffs argue that the FDA acted arbitrarily and capriciously in denying their rulemaking petition because the agency failed to consider their claims that egg cartons are widely misbranded not only because their labels omit material information, but also because current labeling practices *affirmatively* misrepresent the nature of the hens' living conditions. Plaintiffs also argue that the FDA improperly rejected their scientific evidence that the egg-laying hens' living conditions increase the risk of Salmonella-contamination and negatively affect the nutritional value of the eggs. Lastly, Plaintiffs contend that because the FDA failed to appropriately review their petition, the agency should not be permitted to summarily exercise its discretion to prioritize other agency goals in order to avoid addressing Plaintiffs' request for rulemaking.

The Federal Food, Drug, and Cosmetic Act ("FDCA"), 21 U.S.C. §§ 301–399f, prohibits the sale of misbranded food items. *See* 21 U.S.C. §§ 331(a). The FDA possesses discretionary authority to "promulgate regulations for the efficient enforcement of [the FDCA]." *Id.* § 371(a). Under the FDCA a food item is "misbranded" if its label "is false or misleading in any particular." *Id.* § 343(a)(1). Food labeling may be misleading through affirmative representations or through an omission of a material fact. *See id.* § 321(n).

To the extent Plaintiffs' petition argued that egg production methods were an omitted material fact that required disclosure because the hens' living conditions affect the likelihood of Salmonella-contamination or the nutritional value of the eggs, the FDA explained that Plaintiffs had provided insufficient reliable scientific evidence to support these claims. While Plaintiffs dispute the FDA's decision to reject their scientific evidence, the Court will not second guess the FDA's conclusion that these studies were insufficiently reliable, largely because they failed to control for relevant variables.

To the extent Plaintiffs' petition argued that egg-production methods were an omitted material fact that required disclosure in light of misleading affirmative representations that appear on egg cartons, the FDA explained that it could bring individual enforcement actions against any such misbranded food, as it has done in the past. The FDA also detailed its competing priorities given its limited resources and explained it had determined that, even if certain egg-labeling practices are misleading, proposed rulemaking was not the best use of its limited resources.

The decision to take enforcement action against misbranded eggs on a case-by-case basis, as opposed to promulgating regulations that would apply to all egg producers, is left to the broad discretion of the FDA. Similarly, the agency's decision to prioritize other projects is entitled to great deference by a reviewing court.

We note, however, that such broad discretion should not be construed as providing a blanket exception to APA review in any matter involving the allocation of agency resources. In denying a petition for rulemaking, an agency must, at a minimum, clearly indicate that it has considered the potential problem identified in the petition and provide a "reasonable explanation as to why it cannot or will not exercise its discretion" to initiate rulemaking.

Here, the FDA's explanation for denying Plaintiffs' rulemaking petition barely meets this low burden. The FDA could have better addressed Plaintiffs' evidence of misleading representations that appear on egg cartons to demonstrate that the agency fully appreciated one of the primary bases for Plaintiffs' rulemaking petition—that information concerning egg-laying hens' living conditions is necessary in order to correct the affirmative representations that frequently appear on egg labels and convey misleading information. The FDA's denial letter, however, reflects that the agency did consider Plaintiffs' evidence of affirmative misrepresentations that appear on egg labels but ultimately decided that individual enforcement actions would be preferable to promulgating the proposed regulations. Because the FDA is generally free to choose its procedural mode of administration and prioritize agency goals, we see no reason to remand the matter to the FDA to reconsider Plaintiffs' petition in this case.

III.

For the reasons stated above, the FSIS, AMS, FTC, and FDA each acted reasonably in denying Plaintiffs' rulemaking petitions. Accordingly, we affirm the district court's grant of summary judgment to Defendants.

Notes

1. In *People for the Ethical Treatment of Animals (PETA) v. California Milk Producers Advisory Board (CMAB)*, 125 Cal. App. 4th 871 (2005), PETA sued an industry-run trade board that had been created by a marketing order issued by the California Department of Food and Agriculture. Such boards are "administrative instrumentalities of the California Secretary of Food and Agriculture (the Secretary) and have no independent ability to implement policy or other actions without the approval of the Secretary." *Id.* at 875. As described by the court:

> The complaint alleges that for approximately the last two years, the CMAB has been engaged in an advertising program known as the "Happy Cows" campaign, which PETA contends is explicitly and implicitly untrue, deceptive, and misleading. It will suffice for this appeal to refer to the complaint's "Introductory Statement" for a description of the nature of the alleged misrepresentations contained in CMAB's advertisements:
>
> > This is a complaint seeking a permanent injunction against the defendants to prevent ongoing deceptive advertising practices in the false representations of the California dairy industry made in its "Happy Cows" advertisements. The theme of these advertisements is to portray spacious, grassy pastures on beautiful, rolling hills with a few cows grazing and wandering about and "enjoying" the ease, luxury, and contentment of life as a dairy cow in California. The tag line for each of the ads is "Great Cheese comes from Happy Cows. Happy Cows come from California." In reality, however, the vast majority of California's dairy cows live anything but easy, comfortable lives. They routinely spend their lives in 'dry' lots of grassless dirt (which become[] and remain[] mud throughout some months of the year), in sharp contrast to the "fictional," idyllic setting of the ads. They are repeatedly impregnated and then milked throughout their pregnancies. Their calves are taken away shortly after birth, many of whom are then condemned to veal crates. They commonly suffer from painful maladies from their intensive rearing. And when their worn bodies can no longer meet the inordinately high production demands of the industry, they are slaughtered. While plaintiffs do not ask the Court to rule on whether California cows are truly "happy," the nature of this complaint is that the conditions under which most California dairy cows are kept are so materially different (in a way that matters to, and misleads, consumers) than those depicted in the ads as to render them unlawfully deceptive and, therefore, subject to injunctive relief under California law.

Id. at 875–76. The complaint asserted three causes of action: (1) violation of California's prohibition against false and deceptive business advertising (CAL. BUS. & PROF. CODE § 17500 *et seq.*); (2) violation of the general Unfair Competition Laws (UCL) (CAL. BUS. & PROF. CODE § 17200 *et seq.*); and (3) violation of a statute prohibiting a specific form of false advertisements, those associated with "environmental misrepresentations" (CAL. BUS. & PROF. CODE § 17580 *et seq.*). In its claim for injunctive relief under the statutes, PETA sought to force a change in the advertisements and to halt the alleged misrepresentations.

The appellate court upheld the trial court's dismissal of the action on the ground that CMAB was a public entity and not a "person" that could be sued under these statutes. The court went on to look to the legislative history and statutory scheme. As described by the court, "[t]he creation of the CMAB is directly traceable to The California Marketing Act of 1937 (1937 Act), a breathtakingly extensive program of governmental assistance to this state's agriculture, designed specifically to advance the interests of all of this state's citizens." *Id.* at 881–82. The court noted that the 1937 Act provides a discretionary administrative complaint procedure for violation of the Act, which PETA had chosen not to undertake. Given the court's conclusion that the state legislature had "directly linked the work of CMAB in promoting California's agricultural economy through promotional campaigns to important public interests of the state," the court had "no hesitancy in concluding there would indeed be an 'infringement of sovereign power' for the CMAB to be subject to suit under the UCL for the content of one of its promotional campaigns." *Id.* at 883. The practical effect of the court's ruling was immunity for the industry group whose primary purpose was to advertise dairy products.

The court implicitly criticized PETA for not attempting an administrative remedy before filing the action. Consider the potential benefits and disadvantages of pursuing administrative versus judicial remedies.

2. In *Farm Sanctuary, Inc. v. Corcpork, Inc.*, No. BC321606 (Cal. Super. Ct., L.A. Cty. filed Sept. 16, 2004), a farmed animal rescue and advocacy group sued Corcpork, which was "engaged in the business of breeding and raising pigs for slaughter." The complaint alleged that

> . . . as part of its regular business practice, Corcpork keeps its pregnant sows in cramped, individual metal enclosures (known in the industry as "gestation crates") for months at a time. Gestation crates, as typically used in the industry, are approximately two feet wide and six feet long—dimensions that make it largely impossible for the confined sows to turn around. Furthermore, the gestation crates are placed on concrete and the sows are not provided with any bedding, so they are routinely forced to spend months at a time standing or laying on a hard, uncomfortable surface. Many sows confined in gestation crates suffer from sores on their bodies as a result of continuously rubbing against the side of their crates.

Complaint at ¶ 7. The complaint alleged that before the sows give birth, Corcpork moved them to "farrowing crates," which are substantially similar to the gestation crates. *Id.* at ¶ 11. The complaint further alleged:

> The intensive confinement of sows and consequent failure to provide them with an adequate exercise area has been scientifically demonstrated to cause numerous problems for the confined sows including joint damage, reduction in total bone mass, locomotory problems, cardiovascular problems and an increase in urinary tract infections. Intensive confinement has also been demonstrated to cause depression in sows which may be expressed through behaviors such as bar biting, head waving, licking, and so-called "vacuum chewing" where the animals chew nothing.

Id. at ¶ 13.

The legal basis for the lawsuit was California Business & Professions Code section 17200, *et seq.*, which prohibits any unlawful, unfair or fraudulent business practice. The complaint alleged that Corcpork's practices, though customary in the industry, violated California Penal Code section 597t, which requires that "[e]very person who keeps an animal confined in an enclosed area shall provide it with an adequate exercise area." Farm Sanctuary alleged that the Penal Code violation also constituted a violation of section 17200, which protects consumers from purchasing products created through illegal means. Complaint at ¶¶ 15, 17. Farm Sanctuary sought an injunction to stop Corcpork from "confining sows in gestation crates without access to an adequate exercise area." *Id.* at ¶ 18.

When the lawsuit was filed, California's unfair competition statutes included a private right of action for any person. A complaint could be filed by any person or organization "acting for the interests of itself, its members or the general public." Cal. Bus. & Prof. Code § 17204 (prior to amendment). These statutes were used by various nonprofit organizations and public interest groups, particularly in connection with environmental and consumer health concerns, to effectuate change on behalf of the public; but they also were used by some plaintiffs' attorneys to create what many considered frivolous lawsuits that harmed California businesses and that were intended solely to benefit the attorneys filing them. In light of the perceived and actual abuse of the statutes, section 17204 was amended by voter initiative in November of 2004, limiting the potential plaintiffs to any person "who has suffered injury in fact and has lost money or property as a result of such unfair competition." Cal. Bus. & Prof. Code § 17204 (2009). Thus, lawsuits could no longer be undertaken in the public interest by plaintiffs who had not suffered their own injury (like individuals seeking to protect animals)—severely limiting the number of potential plaintiffs.

Based on the amendment to section 17204, Corcpork prevailed on summary judgment on the ground that Farm Sanctuary lacked standing to sue under the statute. The court, therefore, did not reach the issue of whether Corcpork was violating the referenced anti-cruelty statute by keeping the sows confined, as it admitted to doing in its summary judgment motion. Mem. Pts. & Auths., at 1 ("Corcpork does not dispute that it uses the stalls or that the sows are not permitted to take more than a step or two forward or backward or to turn around in the stalls.").

On appeal, Farm Sanctuary argued, in part, that even if the statutory amendment applied, Farm Sanctuary had standing because it had suffered "injury in fact" as a result of the unfair competition. The court concluded that the new standard under the amendment required both injury in fact *and* loss of money or property. The court found Farm Sanctuary's admission that it had not lost money or property fatal to its standing argument. It, therefore, affirmed summary judgment in favor of Corcpork. *Farm Sanctuary, Inc. v. Corcpork, Inc.*, 2007 Cal. App. Unpub. LEXIS 634 (Jan. 26, 2007).

3. Before the *Farm Sanctuary* ruling was final, ALDF and three consumers had also sued Corcpork, alleging violation of California Penal Code section 597t (as well as Business & Professions Code section 17200, based on the economic injury suffered by the individuals). *ALDF v. Corcpork*, Case No. SCV 240050 (Cal. Super. Ct., Sonoma Cty.) (complaint filed Jan. 18, 2007). The consumers were people who ate pork products but believed the meat they ate had been produced in compliance with California's anti-cruelty laws. They alleged that because of the violation of section 597t, they had been injured when they purchased meat they would not have bought if they had known about the illegal conduct. The case settled before any rulings were issued. As part of the settlement, Corcpork agreed that it would eliminate its California pig breeding operations entirely, thereby ending the use of confinement crates in California, in exchange for a dismissal of the lawsuit.

A similar claim was rejected in *Animal Legal Defense Fund v. Mendes*, 160 Cal. App. 4th 136 (2008). Although plaintiffs alleged they had been duped into buying dairy products from cows treated in violation of the California anti-cruelty laws, the court rejected their claims, finding that they had only a "moral injury" and not an economic one. *Id.* at 560–61.

4. For a thorough discussion of false advertising claims in this context, *see* Carter Dillard, *False Advertising, Animals, and Ethical Considerations*, 10 ANIMAL L. 25 (2004).

5. In other cases that may affect nonhuman animals indirectly, plaintiffs have brought false advertising and consumer fraud claims based on alleged concerns regarding physical health effects on humans. *See, e.g., Gorran v. Atkins Nutritionals, Inc.*, 464 F. Supp. 2d 315 (S.D.N.Y. 2006), *aff'd*, No. 07-0120-CV, 2008 U.S. App. LEXIS 11146 (2d Cir. Unpub. May 22, 2008) (plaintiff alleged that he developed heart disease as a result of following the Atkins high protein (particularly meats)/ low carbohydrate diet that was popular in the United States for several years; complaint dismissed on the ground that Atkins' advice and ideas are noncommercial speech, protected by the First Amendment); *Pelman v. McDonald's Corp.*, 452 F. Supp. 2d 320 (S.D.N.Y. 2006) (class of parents and their children sued fast food

giant McDonald's for allegedly misrepresenting the nutritional benefits of its food, in violation of New York's consumer protection statute, alleging that children who ate McDonald's food on a regular basis developed detrimental health effects such as obesity, heart disease and high blood pressure); *Mills v. Giant of Maryland, LLC*, 441 F. Supp. 2d 104 (D.D.C. 2006), *aff'd*, 508 F.3d 11 (D.C. Cir. 2007) (class action by lactose-intolerant individuals against nine sellers of milk, seeking warning labels on milk; dismissed for failure to state a claim under D.C. tort law).

In *Physicians Committee for Responsible Medicine (PCRM) v. Tyson Foods, Inc.*, 119 Cal. App. 4th 120 (2004), PCRM alleged that Tyson made false and deceptive representations about chicken products that it sold to consumers in California. At that time, Tyson was the world's largest poultry producer and sold more than 25 percent of the total chicken meat products consumed by Americans.

The complaint alleges that Tyson engaged in two advertising campaigns, which disseminated false and deceptive statements about its products in violation of [California] Business and Professions Code section 17500. The first and second causes of action concern advertisements carried on the *all-recipes.com* Web site, in which Tyson allegedly portrayed chicken meat as a "heart-healthy" food and advised consumers to serve chicken "as often as you like." The advertisement then lists Tyson's chicken products that have been certified by the American Heart Association as being low in saturated fats and cholesterol. PCRM alleges that the advertisement creates "the false and misleading impression" that chicken "is a health food that can protect against the risk of developing heart disease." It alleges further that "the majority of Tyson chicken products contain substantial levels of fat and cholesterol, the consumption of which will not only fail to reduce the risk of heart disease, but is actually likely to increase such risk."

A second advertising campaign, alleged in the third through sixth causes of action, appeared in high-circulation magazines in California and was broadcast on television programs. PCRM alleges that "[e]ach advertisement claims that Tyson chicken products are 'all natural.' In particular, the ads state, 'You give them [referring to the reader's children] quality chicken that's all natural because you can.' In smaller print, the ads state, 'Every Tyson chicken product begins with all natural chicken. That means there are no additives, and it's minimally processed. And that means a lot.'" PCRM alleges that, in fact, "Tyson raises its chickens in a 'factory farm' system in which the chickens are genetic mutations that do not exist in nature, the chickens are vaccinated, the chickens are medicated immediately after being hatched, the chickens are crowded together by the tens of thousands under one roof, and the chickens are routinely and regularly fed antibiotics at therapeutic and sub-therapeutic levels to combat and prevent diseases facilitated by the unnatural overcrowding and to stimulate an unnatural growth rate." PCRM claims that the representations in this campaign not only constitute false advertising within the terms of Business and

Professions Code section 17500 but also an "unfair and fraudulent" business practice proscribed by Business and Professions Code section 17200.

The complaint prays for injunctive relief enjoining Tyson from making the alleged false and deceptive representations regarding its chicken products; requiring Tyson to undertake a public information campaign "to correct and remedy its current and prior false and deceptive advertising"; and requiring Tyson "to place appropriate warnings on its chicken products and on any advertising for its chicken products indicating the possible health consequences of consuming those products."

Id. at 123–24. The appellate court reversed the trial court's grant of Tyson's motion to strike certain causes of action. After Tyson later filed an affidavit attesting that the company was no longer running the ads in question and that it did not intend to do so in the future, PCRM dismissed the lawsuit.

Although *PCRM v. Tyson* achieved the remedy sought in the lawsuit, many of the foregoing cases illustrate the difficulties often faced by plaintiffs at the preliminary stages of litigation. When defendants are successful in obtaining dismissals at the pleadings stage, the substantive issues raised by these lawsuits are never considered by the courts and have less of a chance of obtaining public attention.

Are these issues more appropriately decided by the courts or the state and federal government agencies or legislatures? What interplay, if any, is there between lawsuits or legislation based on human health concerns and those in which the goal is improved conditions for the animals? As a question of public policy, should it matter if these lawsuits are brought by individuals with no concern about animal issues or if animal advocacy groups are involved? Should the plaintiffs' goals factor into the outcome?

6. False advertising claims on these issues also may be brought by industry competitors. For example, in *Sanderson Farms, Inc. v. Tyson Foods, Inc.*, 549 F. Supp. 2d 708 (D. Md. 2008), the plaintiffs (including Perdue Farms, Inc., a large chicken processing company) alleged violations of the federal Lanham Act, 15 U.S.C. § 1125(a), which prohibits false or misleading advertising and unfair trade practices in interstate commerce. The action arose out of Tyson's dissemination of allegedly false and misleading advertisements making unqualified claims that its chickens were "raised without antibiotics" and qualified claims that its chickens were "raised without antibiotics that impact antibiotic resistance in humans." *Id.* at 710. The court denied Tyson's motion to dismiss, *id.* at 720, and issued a preliminary injunction enjoining Tyson's advertisements. *Sanderson Farms, Inc. v. Tyson Foods, Inc.*, 547 F. Supp. 2d 491, 508–09 (D. Md. 2008) (concluding the public was being misled). The case was later consolidated with eight other similar lawsuits throughout the country and centralized in the District of Maryland under the federal multidistrict litigation rules. *In re Tyson Foods, Inc., Chicken Raised Without Antibiotics Consumer Litigation*, 582 F. Supp. 2d 1378 (J.P.M.L. 2008).

What import, if any, does such a case have for the chickens themselves? In *Sanderson Farms*, both the plaintiffs and the defendant were industrial-sized producers of chicken products. If the plaintiffs had instead been small organic farms raising cage-free chickens, would your answer be different?

7. One of the goals behind the false advertising and consumer fraud cases often is to increase public awareness—whether as a means to force a change in production methods or to alert consumers about industry practices. If consumers become aware of the conditions under which farmed animals are kept, and they find those conditions unacceptable, the public may motivate change by modifying their purchasing practices accordingly and giving the industry an economic incentive to improve these conditions.

8. Cases like *Provimi* and *PCRM v. Tyson Foods* may lead to unintended negative publicity if industry interests seek to silence public criticism or discussion of industrial practices. Where an entity files a lawsuit to quash public discourse or complaints about commercial practices, this type of action is known as a Strategic Lawsuit Against Public Participation, or "SLAPP suit," referenced earlier in this chapter. Anti-SLAPP statutes exist in most jurisdictions. SLAPP plaintiffs usually allege defamation and other business injury torts and claim large money damages. The anti-SLAPP statutes exist because, as a matter of public policy and freedom of speech and expression, it is deemed important to prevent the threat of large money judgments and expensive legal battles from discouraging public discussion of controversial matters.

In *Engler v. Winfrey*, 201 F.3d 680 (5th Cir. 2000), Texas cattlemen sued Oprah Winfrey, her production company and Howard Lyman (a guest on Oprah's television talk show), based on a segment on Oprah's show about "dangerous food" that discussed Mad Cow Disease (Bovine Spongiform Encephalopathy or "BSE") and beef industry practices of "ruminant-to-ruminant feeding" (the practice of feeding animal products and byproducts to cows). BSE is a type of Transmissible Spongiform Encephalopathies (TSEs) that can be caused by the practice of feeding cows, herbivores by nature, the brains and other central nervous system tissues of other cows. BSE was first discovered in England and spread to at least 25 countries between 1986 and 2008. The TSEs "have a debilitating neurological impact on their victims. After an incubation period of months or years, the diseases create myriad tiny holes in the brain, slowly deteriorating their victims' mental and physical abilities until death eventually results." *Ranchers Cattlemen Action Legal Fund v. United States Dept. of Agriculture*, 415 F.3d 1078, 1085 (9th Cir. 2005) (upholding implementation of USDA regulation allowing resumed importation of Canadian cows into the U.S.). In the *Winfrey* case, Oprah's guests claimed that ruminant-to-ruminant feeding created a high risk of BSE in the United States. The district court ruled, in part, that defendants did not knowingly disseminate false information about beef or beef industry practices. *Texas Beef Group v. Winfrey*, 11 F. Supp. 2d 858 (N.D. Tex. 1998). The Fifth Circuit affirmed on this ground, reasoning:

> Lyman's statements comparing the United States' cattlemen's and government's reaction to BSE to that in Great Britain and bewailing the failure to take any "substantial steps" to prevent a BSE outbreak in this country were a sincerely held opinion supported by the factual premise that only a mandatory ban on ruminant-to-ruminant feeding would dispense with the danger. The FDA imposed such a ban, with the approval of the cattle industry, only months after the Oprah Winfrey Show.

Engler, 201 F.3d at 688.

The media attention generated by the lawsuit brought by the cattlemen against Oprah Winfrey probably spread the word about Mad Cow Disease much further than if plaintiffs had simply let the issue drop after the original broadcast of the show.[g]

9. Primarily in response to media attention in the early 1990s over the effects of a pesticide (Alar) sprayed on apples, individual states began enacting so-called "veggie libel laws," similar to a Texas statute that was also at issue in *Winfrey*. The driving force behind the enactment of such laws in North Dakota (N.D. CENT. CODE §§ 32-44-01–32-44-04, allowing agricultural organizations to bring a claim for the disparagement of both agricultural products and practices) was the North Dakota Equine Ranching Association, consisting of twenty-nine family ranches that collected pregnant mares' urine (PMU) to be used in the production of the pharmaceutical Premarin (short for PREgnant MARes' urINe). Jennifer J. Mattson, Note, *North Dakota Jumps on the Agricultural Disparagement Law Bandwagon by Enacting Legislation to Meet a Concern Already Actionable Under State Defamation Law and Failing to Heed Constitutionality Concerns*, 74 N. DAK. L. REV. 89 (1998). Premarin is an estrogen-replacement therapy drug used to help relieve symptoms of menopause and treat osteoporosis. Manufactured by Wyeth-Ayerst Pharmaceuticals for more than fifty years, in 2000 it was the single most prescribed drug in the United States, holding over 80% of the estrogen replacement market, with more than nine million users. Lafcadio H. Darling, *Legal Protection for Horses: Care and Stewardship or Hypocrisy and Neglect?*, 6 ANIMAL L. 105, 121 (2000). The urine collection methods, summarized below, have been the subject of much controversy and debate.

> The mares, in their third or fourth month of an eleven-month pregnancy, are brought into the barns in late September or October and remain there for approximately six months. The stalls are approximately eight feet long, three and a half feet wide, and five feet high. Ropes or chains tether the mare and her vulva is fitted with a rubber collection cup. Due to this arrangement, the horse is limited in her ability to turn around, move backward or forward, or lie down. The mares are "rarely, if ever, taken off line and out of the harnesses for even a few brief hours of exercise." Each mare produces

---

g. For a first-hand account of the experience of one defendant in *Engler v. Winfrey, see* Howard Lyman, *Introduction: Free Speech, Animal Law, and Food Activism*, 5 ANIMAL L. i (1999). Mr. Lyman (who was also one of the defense experts in the *McLibel* case discussed in Note 11 below), a former cattle rancher and feedlot operator, became an outspoken advocate of vegetarianism.

approximately 0.5 to 0.75 gallons of urine per day, totaling ninety-one-hundred gallons for the entire collection season. The mares are taken off the production line just before they come to term and are allowed to foal in outdoor paddocks. Generally, the mares are impregnated again within a few weeks of foaling and nurse for three to four months, instead of the normal six month nursing period, and are returned to the collection barn in the fall. Estimates indicate that somewhere between 50,000 and 75,000 mares are used in Premarin production. If born foals, breeding stallions, premature mares, and replacement mares are included, "the total is considerably greater than 100,000."

Id. at 122. There has also been concern that water deprivation is utilized to increase estrogen concentration in the urine. *Id.* at 123. Further, a major concern among animal protection groups has been the ranchers' practice of disposing of excess foals as "byproducts of Premarin production." *Id.* The Humane Society of the United States characterized the practice as follows:

> A few mares may be kept for future PMU production. Some farmers breed registered horses hoping to sell the foals as riding prospects. And though a few have succeeded, many thousands of foals still go to unsheltered feedlots until they reach desirable market weight. Then they are slaughtered and their carcasses shipped for human consumption in Europe and Asia.

Id.

During the legislative hearings before the North Dakota statute was enacted, the ranchers told of their experiences with animal rights groups and national media outlets that publicized the alleged mistreatment and abuse of horses in the practice of collecting PMU. Mattson, *supra*, at 106. The North Dakota legislature responded by enacting an extremely broad statute, apparently tailored to favor equine ranchers, which at least one pro-rancher commentator has warned "fails to heed constitutionality concerns." *Id.* While animal rights activists may sometimes question their strength and effectiveness, particularly when their opponents are the agribusiness and pharmaceutical industries, they have been described by their opposition as "quite powerful." *Id.* On the other hand, another commentator noted that, for Wyeth-Ayerst, the protests of these groups was a "bearable burden," considering that Premarin was at that time "the largest selling prescription drug in the United States, and the envy of the entire industry." Sheldon Segal, *Introduction*, 23 N.Y.U. Rev. L. & Soc. Change 329, 332 n.7 (1997).

10. At about the same time, North Dakota was among several states that enacted statutes — the early "Ag-Gag" laws — criminalizing undercover investigations and videography at factory farms, other agricultural facilities and slaughterhouses, as well as animal research facilities. N.D. Cent. Code § 12.1-21.1–02 (2017) (originally enacted in 1991) ("No person without the effective consent of the owner may ... [e]nter an animal facility and use or attempt to use a camera, video recorder, or any other video or audio recording equipment," among other prohibitions). *See also*

Mont. Code Ann. § 81-30-103 (2017) (originally enacted 1991) ("Farm Animal and Research Facility Protection Act"); Kan. Stat. Ann. § 47-1825 (2018) (originally enacted 1990).

A decade later, as highly publicized videos of animal abuses at some of these facilities hit the internet and spread rapidly by YouTube and other internet sources, more states began introducing similar legislation, a limited number of which were enacted into law and were promptly subject to constitutional challenges, as discussed in Section 1.C of this chapter.

11. Just as the publicity over the Texas cattlemen's litigation against Oprah Winfrey may have been detrimental to the industry in the long run, the same held true with respect to a SLAPP lawsuit filed in England by McDonald's Corporation against two Greenpeace activists, which turned out to be of historic proportions and was described as "the biggest public relations disaster in history." Clare Dyer, *Libel Law Review over McDonald's Ruling*, Guardian, Feb. 16, 2005 ("*Dyer*"). *See also* James A. Wells, Notes & Comments, *Exporting SLAPPs: International Use of the U.S. "SLAPP" to Suppress Dissent and Critical Speech*, 12 Temp. Int'l & Comp. L.J. 457, 466 (1998) (describing the case as "a classic corporate Goliath against activist David, as McDonald's desire to censor criticism became more transparent throughout the trial, and public support for the defendants grew").

This case, *McDonald's Corp. v. Steel*, (1997) EWHC (Q.B.) 366 (England's High Court of Justice, Queen's Bench Division) ("*McLibel*"), brought factory farming practices and conditions to the public eye during the longest trial in the history of the English court system. The case spanned seven years (including 313 days of trial over a two-and-a-half year period) from filing until the June 1997 final judgment. The defendants were two activists, Helen Steel and David Morris, who, throughout the trial, represented themselves against McDonald's significant legal team. McDonald's claimed that the leaflets the activists distributed (describing factory farming practices) contained libelous and defamatory statements about McDonald's and the treatment of the animals who end up as food at McDonald's restaurants.

In hindsight, McDonald's may have regretted ever pursuing the matter through the courts. The negative publicity from international media coverage and the information revealed through the trial ultimately may have been more detrimental to the economic bottom line for McDonald's than the leaflet distribution, which was done by a small group of activists solely in London. *McLibel* is a landmark case— not only because the trial was epic in length or because the 1997 judgment was 800 pages long—but also because it was the first court opinion to find that certain customary practices in the raising and slaughtering of animals to be used for food are cruel and inhumane. The court recognized that this industry is like others that utilize those methods most effective at maximizing profits. After consideration of extensive testimony and documentary evidence, the court concluded:

> The practices which I have found to be cruel appear to have prevailed throughout the 1987 to 1990 period of relevant publication of the leaflet

and my ultimate conclusions so far as justification of the defamatory message of this part of the leaflet complained of is concerned, are as follows.

Laying hens which are used to produce eggs for [McDonald's] spend their whole lives in battery cages without access to open air or sunlight and without freedom of movement. I do not find the lack of open air or sunshine to be cruel, but the severe restriction of movement is cruel and [McDonald's] are culpably responsible for that cruel practice.

Broiler chickens which are used to produce meat for the [McDonald's] food spend their whole lives in broiler houses without access to open air and sunshine, I do not find this in itself cruel. However, they spend the last few days of their lives with very little room to move. The severe restriction of movement over those last few days is cruel and [McDonald's] are culpably responsible for that cruel practice.

A small, but not insignificant proportion of the sows which produce pigs which contribute to the supply of pork for [McDonald's] food in the U.K. spend virtually the whole of their lives in dry sow stalls, with no access to open air and sunshine and without freedom of movement. I do not find the lack of open air or sunshine to be cruel, but the severe restriction of movement is cruel and the Second Plaintiff is culpably responsible for that cruel practice.

Some pigs which are used to make [McDonald's] food in the U.K. spend the whole of their lives indoors and all or virtually all of them spend a significant part of their lives indoors. The situation is probably the same for the pigs which are used to make [McDonald's] food in the U.S. On the evidence which I have heard about their living conditions, I do not find this to be cruel, however.

It was not shown that cattle which are used to produce the Plaintiffs' food spend any significant part of their lives without access to open air and sunshine and without freedom of movement.

Nevertheless in my judgment the restriction of movement of laying hens throughout their lives in the U.K. and the U.S., and of broiler chickens in their last days in the U.K. and the U.S., and of some sows for virtually the whole of their lives in the U.K. is quite enough to justify the first particular charge of culpable responsibility for cruel practices in the way some of the animals spent their lives.

* * *

There are other cruel practices affecting chickens which are used to provide the Plaintiffs' food; calcium deficit resulting in osteopaenia in battery hens, the restriction of broiler breeders' feed with the result that they go hungry although bred for appetite, leg problems in broilers bred for weight, rough handling of broilers taken for slaughter and pre-stun electric shocks

> suffered by broilers on the way to slaughter. Those matters, for which
> [McDonald's is] in my judgment culpably responsible, go to strengthen my
> view that the sting of this part of the leaflet to the effect that [McDonald's
> is] culpably responsible for cruel practices in the rearing and slaughter of
> some of the animals which are used to produce their food is justified, true
> in substance and in fact.

Id. ((1997) EWHC (QB) 366). *See also* David J. Wolfson, *McLibel*, 5 ANIMAL L. 21 (1999) (providing an in-depth analysis of this case, the contradictions it exposes, and its possible ramifications). For more commentary on the *McLibel* case, as well as a complete record of the trial transcripts and final judgment, *see* McSpotlight, The McLibel Trial, *http://www.mcspotlight.org/case/*.

Despite the generally favorable ruling, defendants appealed those portions of the judgment against them; McDonald's, on the other hand, did not appeal. The English Appeal Court reversed Justice Bell and held in favor of Steel and Morris on several issues unrelated to animal cruelty, and reduced the award against them to £40,000. Not satisfied with anything less than a complete victory, Steel and Morris subsequently appealed the relatively small portion of the *McLibel* case that was decided against them (*i.e.*, the £40,000 award) to the European Court of Human Rights. On February 15, 2005, the European court ruled that the British court's ruling against Steel and Morris was unfair, in part because they were not granted legal aid. (The two had stated they were not able to afford lawyers; McDonald's reportedly spent an estimated £10 million on the case—roughly $18.8 million at the exchange rate around that time.) Heather Timmons, *Britain Faulted Over McDonald's Libel Case,* N.Y. TIMES, Feb. 16, 2005, at C5.

The European court ordered the British court to pay Steel and Morris, respectively, 35,000 Euros (roughly $45,000 at the exchange rate at that time) and 47,000 Euros (roughly $60,000) in costs and to offer them a retrial. As a result of this decision, the British government was directed to re-examine its legal aid regulations, which previously excluded defamation from legal aid. Counsel for Steel and Morris hailed their victory in the European court as a "turning point" in the law of libel. *Dyer, supra.*

For a thorough analysis of SLAPP suits generally, *see* George Pring & Penelope Canan, SLAPPs: GETTING SUED FOR SPEAKING OUT (1996). As detailed by the book's authors, animal activists have frequently been targeted by SLAPP suits, but they have also filed actions of their own that have been alleged to be SLAPP suits.

12. In the wake of the British *McLibel* decision (even before the European court ruling) and after aggressive campaigning by—and negotiations with—animal activist groups, both McDonald's and Burger King reportedly agreed to certain animal welfare concessions. For example, they agreed to purchase chicken meat and eggs only from suppliers who do not cut off the beaks of chicks without anesthesia or engage in "forced molting" practices. As noted in the *NJSPCA* case at the beginning of this section, "debeaking" is a common practice in which the end of the beak of young (and unanesthetized) egg-laying hens is cut off to reduce injuries from

pecking; and forced molting is a practice in which chickens are deprived of all food and/or water for a period of up to approximately two weeks, which forces them to shed their feathers and start a new egg-laying cycle. Both McDonald's and Burger King also agreed to require their suppliers to comply with guidelines providing for a minimal amount of additional space for the caged birds. In addition, they indicated they would conduct unannounced inspections of the chicken, pig and cow slaughterhouses supplying them with meat and eggs. Burger King also petitioned the U.S. Department of Agriculture to enforce the federal Humane Methods of Slaughter Act. Even with these measures in place, however, activist groups continued to press for further progress from the fast food industry. In fall of 2001, People for the Ethical Treatment of Animals (PETA) announced that the Wendy's fast food chain had agreed to meet the improved animal welfare standards to which McDonald's and Burger King had previously agreed. Animal activist organizations continue to monitor, to the extent possible, the extent to which these companies adhere to their agreements in this regard. In 2009, PETA renewed its campaign against McDonald's, claiming that McDonald's had not upheld its agreements regarding improved animal welfare standards.

13. In Europe, there has been more progress on these issues. In France, for example, battery cages were banned in 2012, although so-called "enriched cages" less than 12x12x12 inches were still allowed. But by 2018 a number of French companies, including three of the country's largest catering companies, vowed to completely stop selling eggs and egg products from caged birds by the year 2025. According to reports, figures from 2015 indicate that, at that time, 56% of laying hens in the European Union were kept in cages; 26% were "in barns"; 14% were "free range" and 4% were "organic"; while in the United Kingdom 42% were in cages. *https://www.connexionfrance.com/index.php/French-news/Laying-hens-in-France-to-be-freed-from-cages*.

14. An alternative approach for disseminating information publicizing the treatment of animals in industrial settings and increasing public awareness is through participation in corporate governance activities. Animal activist organizations today use shareholder initiatives as a means of disseminating information about a company's treatment of animals in the manufacture of its products. *See, e.g.*, John Cook, *Rights Group Asks Amgen to Halt Tests on Animals*, Seattle Post-Intelligencer, May 12, 2005, at A1 (noting that PETA had introduced shareholder resolutions at thirteen corporations thus far that year). Even if the initiatives are not approved by a majority of the shareholders, this process is effective in reaching large numbers of people. Consider, for example, *Lovenheim v. Iroquois Brands, Ltd.*, 618 F. Supp. 554 (D.D.C. 1985), which was among several suits that brought to light the treatment of geese raised for the production of *foie gras*. The opinion stated:

> Pâté de foie gras is made from the liver of geese. According to [plaintiff's] affidavit, force-feeding is frequently used in order to expand the liver and thereby produce a larger quantity of pâté. [Plaintiff's] affidavit also contains a description of the force-feeding process:

> Force-feeding usually begins when the geese are four months old. On some farms where feeding is mechanized, the bird's body and wings are placed in a metal brace and its neck is stretched. Through a funnel inserted 10–12 inches down the throat of the goose, a machine pumps up to 400 grams of corn-based mash into its stomach. An elastic band around the goose's throat prevents regurgitation. When feeding is manual, a handler uses a funnel and stick to force the mash down.
>
> Plaintiff contends that such force-feeding is a form of cruelty to animals.

Id. at 556 n.2. In that case, the court granted a shareholder a preliminary injunction barring a *foie gras* importing company from excluding from proxy materials information concerning a proposed resolution the shareholder intended to offer at an upcoming meeting. The resolution called upon the company's directors to

> form a committee to study the methods by which its French supplier produces pâté de foie gras, and report to the shareholders its findings and opinions, based on expert consultation, on whether this production method causes undue distress, pain or suffering to the animals involved and, if so, whether further distribution of this product should be discontinued until a more humane production method is developed.

Id. at 556. The issue before the court was the application of section 14(a) of the Securities Exchange Act of 1934, 15 U.S.C. §78n(a) and the shareholder proposal rule promulgated by the Securities and Exchange Commission (Rule 14a-8). The court agreed with the shareholder that the rule prohibited omission of his proposal because the proposal had "ethical or social significance."

The shareholder in *Lovenheim* referred to animal protection laws in effect in all fifty states and the District of Columbia to support his position that his proposal was ethically and socially significant. The case did not, however, address the issue of whether the force-feeding of geese by the company's French supplier would constitute a violation of American anti-cruelty statutes. As discussed at length earlier in this section, however, in 2005 California enacted express statutory prohibitions against the force-feeding of ducks and geese, as well as the sale of products that came from force-fed ducks or geese, though the law (CAL. HEALTH & SAFETY CODE §§ 25980–25984) was still not in effect and tied up in litigation until early 2019, when the U.S. Supreme Court denied the plaintiffs' petition for *certiorari* review, which resulted in the law going into effect.

15. In Illinois, after famed Chicago chef Charlie Trotter announced that he would no longer serve *foie gras* in his restaurants, a Chicago city alderman proposed an ordinance that would ban *foie gras* in all Chicago restaurants. Fran Spielman & Lisa Donovan, *Alderman Wants Foie Gras Off Menus*, CHICAGO SUN-TIMES, Apr. 7, 2005, at 17. The ban was approved and went into effect in 2006, at which time the Illinois Restaurant Association and a few Chicago chefs who were proponents of *foie gras* initiated a campaign to repeal the ordinance. They also filed suit, claiming that the ordinance violated the Illinois and U.S. Constitutions. The federal district court

rejected their claims and granted the city's motion to dismiss. *Illinois Restaurant Ass'n v. City of Chicago*, 492 F. Supp. 2d 891 (N.D. Ill. 2007). In May of 2008, however, while the case was on appeal, the Chicago City Council voted 37–6 to repeal the ban.

Meanwhile, in 2007 renowned chef Wolfgang Puck announced that his restaurants would no longer serve *foie gras*. According to his press release at the time, he would be "raising the bar on treating farm animals." The press release went on to state:

> A key initiative of Wolfgang's all-natural and organic evolution is a comprehensive, first-of-its-kind humane farm animal treatment program created in partnership with the Humane Society of the United States (HSUS) and with advice from Farm Sanctuary. This historic nine-point program aims to stop the worst practices associated with factory farming. . . .

Puck claimed that within a few months of the release, along with eliminating *foie gras* from their menus, his restaurants would only "use and serve eggs from cage-free hens not confined to battery cages," only serve pork and veal using animals that had not been confined to crates, and "continue to offer and expand vegetarian selections on all menus," among other steps to incorporate practices promoting human health and animal welfare.

16. The conditions under which factory-farmed animals live (and die) were brought to a broader audience in a book by Matthew Scully, who, from 2001 through 2004, served as special assistant and deputy director of speechwriting for President George W. Bush. *See* Matthew Scully, DOMINION: THE POWER OF MAN, THE SUFFERING OF ANIMALS, AND THE CALL TO MERCY (2002). In addition to his public speaking engagements and other writings on this issue, Scully brought his insights to a politically conservative audience (that might not otherwise be exposed to such a message) in a 2005 cover story in The American Conservative magazine. Matthew Scully, *Fear Factories: The Case for Compassionate Conservatism—For Animals*, AMERICAN CONSERVATIVE, May 23, 2005, at 7–14. The magazine cover framed the subject of the article as, "Torture on the Farm: Why Conservatives Should Care About Animal Cruelty."

Even though concerns have been expressed in the past by some politicians over the conditions in which farmed animals are raised and slaughtered, farmers who seek to raise their animals in what they consider to be a natural "organic farming" setting may run afoul of the law. One such farmer is Joel Salatin, who has published several books on the subject of organic farming.

> Salatin himself makes no secret of his feelings about the agribusiness bureaucracy: he hates it. A favorite line is, "Everything I do is illegal," and he will readily regale a visitor with tales of his travails in keeping the right to process his own chickens in an immaculate, open-air backyard operation ([the state of] Virginia argued that it was "inherently unsanitary" because it didn't have walls). He bemoans the fact that federal meat-processing regulations force him to send his cattle and hogs to commercial locker-plants and thus surrender control over the final stage of a process throughout which he has

tended them with such care. (He thinks government should allow mobile abattoirs that could do on-farm slaughtering for small-scale operations.) At a time when homeland-security experts warn of the vulnerabilities of a food-supply system based on large-scale production, centralized processing and long-distance transportation, he complains that politicians of both parties call for only "more centralization."

Todd S. Purdum, *High Priest of the Pasture*, N.Y. Times Magazine, May 1, 2005, at 76.

17. Industrialized farm operations create enormous amounts of both liquid and solid waste, the disposal of which must comply with the Clean Water Act (33 U.S.C. §§ 1251–1387), which controls discharges of pollutants into U.S. waters. The Environmental Protection Agency (EPA), the agency charged with implementing this Act, has determined that "concentrated animal feeding operations" (known as CAFOs) are "point sources" of pollution and must comply with the Act's requirements. CAFOs also emit hazardous and non-hazardous materials into the air, and must meet the requirements of the Clean Air Act (CAA) (42 U.S.C. §§ 7401–7671q). Although a detailed primer of these significant environmental laws is beyond the scope of this book, it is important to note that these laws, as well as other federal and state environmental laws, may be useful tools for individuals and organizations concerned about the problems created by these large operations.

18. While animal-protective laws may be evolving gradually, the process is very slow and far from uniform, particularly as applied to different species. For example, if a cat or dog was force-fed in the same manner as geese raised for *foie gras*, there is little doubt that the practice would be deemed unacceptable and a violation of anti-cruelty statutes here and abroad. Moreover, the slaughter and consumption of dogs and cats (and horses to a lesser extent) for human consumption has been expressly prohibited by statute in many U.S. states.

B. Slaughter Laws and Related Issues

As discussed on the Senate floor by U.S. Senator Robert Byrd (D-WV) in 2001, concern about the treatment of animals used for food products does not stop when the animals leave the farm:

Last April, the Washington Post detailed the inhumane treatment of livestock in our Nation's slaughterhouses. A 23-year-old Federal law requires that cattle and hogs to be slaughtered must first be stunned, thereby rendered insensitive to pain, but mounting evidence indicates that this is not always being done, that these animals are sometimes cut, skinned, and scalded while still able to feel pain.

A Texas beef company, with 22 citations for cruelty to animals, was found chopping the hooves off live cattle. In another Texas plant with about two dozen violations, Federal officials found nine live cattle dangling from an overhead chain. Secret videos from an Iowa pork plant show hogs squealing and kicking as they are being lowered into the boiling water that will soften their hides, soften the bristles on the hogs and make them easier to skin.

I used to kill hogs. I used to help lower them into the barrels of scalding water, so that the bristles could be removed easily. But those hogs were dead when we lowered them into the barrels.

The law clearly requires that these poor creatures be stunned and rendered insensitive to pain before this process begins.[h] Federal law is being ignored. Animal cruelty abounds. It is sickening. It is infuriating. Barbaric treatment of helpless, defenseless creatures must not be tolerated even if these animals are being raised for food — and even more so, more so. Such insensitivity is insidious and can spread and is dangerous. Life must be respected and dealt with humanely in a civilized society.

So for this reason I have added language in the supplemental appropriations bill that directs the Secretary of Agriculture to report on cases of inhumane animal treatment in regard to livestock production, and to document the response of USDA regulatory agencies.

The U.S. Department of Agriculture agencies have the authority and the capability to take action to reduce the disgusting cruelty about which I have spoken.

Oh, these are animals, yes. But they, too, feel pain. These agencies can do a better job, and with this provision they will know that the U.S. Congress expects them to do better in their inspections, to do better in their enforcement of the law, and in their research for new, humane technologies. Additionally, those who perpetuate such barbaric practices will be put on notice that they are being watched.

I realize that this provision will not stop all the animal life in the United States from being mistreated. It will not even stop all beef, cattle, hogs and other livestock from being tortured. But it can serve as an important step toward alleviating cruelty and unnecessary suffering by these creatures.

147 Cong. Rec. S7311–12 (2001).

By the Fall of 2001, Congress had passed two resolutions (S. 45 and H.R. 175) expressing the "sense of Congress" that the Secretary of Agriculture should follow existing law by resuming violation tracking and reporting under the Humane Methods of Slaughter Act (HMSA) and by fully enforcing the Act to ensure humane livestock slaughter. In response, the USDA hired seventeen veterinarians to oversee

---

h. This statement, unfortunately, is not entirely true. In fact, the Humane Methods of Slaughter Act (7 U.S.C. § 1901 *et seq.*) requires *either* that the animals be "rendered insensible to pain," whether by "a single blow or gunshot or an electrical, chemical or other means," *or* that they be slaughtered under religious standards where they are *not* rendered insensible to pain. 7 U.S.C. § 1902.

the two thousand slaughterhouses throughout the United States. Philip Brasher, *USDA Hiring Vets to Enforce Humane Laws at Meat Plants, Creating Database to Track Violations*, Associated Press, Nov. 2, 2001 (LEXIS News).

In 2013, the USDA's Office of the Inspector General (OIG) issued a report entitled "Food Safety and Inspection Service — Inspection and Enforcement Activities at Swine Slaughter Plants." (Audit Report 24601–0101-41; *see http://www.usda.gov/oig /webdocs/24601–0001-41.pdf*.) The stated objectives of the OIG audit were "to identify areas of risk in FSIS' inspection of swine plants, evaluate FSIS controls over food safety and humane handling, and determine if appropriate enforcement actions were taken against plants that violated FMIA [Federal Meat Inspection Act] and HMSA." FSIS inspects more than 600 plants authorized to slaughter pigs. The OIG reviewed enforcement actions taken against these plants in fiscal years 2008 through 2011 and conducted thirty site visits. The OIG Report summed up its findings as follows:

> The [FSIS] enforcement policies do not deter swine slaughter plants from becoming repeat violators of the [FMIA]. As a result, plants have repeatedly violated the same regulations with little or no consequence. We found in 8 of the 30 plants we visited, inspectors did not always examine the internal organs of carcasses in accordance with FSIS inspection requirements, or did not take enforcement actions against plants that violated food safety. As a result there is reduced assurance of FSIS inspectors effectively identifying pork that should not enter the food supply.
>
> * * *
>
> Finally, we found that FSIS inspectors did not take appropriate enforcement actions in 8 of the 30 plants we visited for violations of the [HMSA]. We reviewed 158 humane handling noncompliance records (violations) issued to the 30 plants and found 10 instances of egregious violations where inspectors did not issue suspensions. As a result, the plants did not improve their slaughter practices, and FSIS could not ensure humane handling of swine. FSIS concurred with all of our recommendations [for improvement].

(OIG information page accompanying the Report.)

The Report noted that "[u]nlike post-mortem food safety inspections, humane handling inspections are only performed on a limited basis." OIG Report at 22. During the audit, the OIG observed the process of stunning pigs before slaughter for only thirty minutes at the relatively few plants visited (5% of the 600 total pig slaughterhouses), yet the Report provided multiple specific examples of observed HMSA violations. *Id.* at 23–25. The OIG recommended that FSIS submit a plan describing how it will minimize reliance on the inspectors' subjective judgment to ensure consistent application and enforcement of the HMSA and related regulations. *Id.* at 27. The FSIS's response stated that it implemented required supplemental training for its inspectors and that by August 31, 2013 it would hire a new "Humane Handling Enforcement Coordinator" to, among other things, increase the frequency of noncompliance review and develop a database to track the reviews and any suspensions. *Id.*

The meat industry has long been targeted because of human health concerns over the consumption of tainted meat, in addition to animal welfare issues. In a case involving adulterated meat products, the Seventh Circuit noted:

> According to a 2001 Gallup poll, only 6 percent of American adults are veg-etarians. We think that percentage would jump dramatically if the other 94 percent read the record in this case. This panel has read the record and will be recommending that more broccoli, rutabagas, asparagus, cauli-flower, kohlrabi, and tofu burgers be served at future court dinners.

United States v. Mantas, 274 F.3d 1127, 1128 (7th Cir. 2001) (defendants guilty of improperly storing adulterated products).

One author investigated cockfighting and then visited a Tyson Foods chicken factory in Arkansas — a factory that took in 1.3 million birds each week to be slaughtered and turned out "an endless stream of chicken parts and precooked wings." Burkhard Bilger, NOODLING FOR FLATHEADS 58 (2000). He noted that major chicken processor Perdue Farms' public relations department had not allowed him to enter or tour their factory. On the other hand, his guide at the Tyson factory he visited was a "rare believer in full disclosure," yet "nearly refused" Bilger's request to see the "killing floor." Upon viewing it, he described the killing floor as "the nightmarish finale, the tunnel of fear," where the "stench of spilled intestines was overwhelming." *Id.* at 59. After summarizing the slaughtering process, Bilger compared it to the cockfighting he had witnessed:

> These are things we don't want to know, that we zone away beyond city limits, and most meat producers are happy to oblige us. Every year we eat more chicken meat and see less and less of the living birds, and this strikes us as normal. Animal rights activists, of course, condemn poultry factories as well as cockfighting, but most of us aren't that consistent. We're appalled at blood sports, yet when activists picket slaughterhouses or send lurid photos to the media, we resent them, deem them unrealistic. Like cockfighters, they threaten a cherished illusion: that society, in growing up, has lost its taste for blood.

Id. at 59–60. *See also* Elizabeth L. DeCoux, *In the Valley of the Dry Bones: Reuniting the Word "Standing" With Its Meaning In Animal Cases*, 29 WM. & MARY ENVT'L. L. & POL'Y REV. 681, 684 (Spring 2005) ("The popular name[] of [the Humane Methods of Slaughter Act] . . . paint[s] a peaceful picture, far removed from the blood, stench, filth, and screams of the slaughterhouse. . . .").

Jones v. Butz

United States District Court, Southern District of New York, 1974
374 F. Supp. 1284

PALMIERI, District Judge. This action involves a challenge, under the Free Exercise and Establishment Clauses of the First Amendment, to the Humane Slaughter Act (the Act), 7 U.S.C. § 1901 *et seq.* (1970), and in particular to the provisions relating to ritual slaughter as defined in the Act and which plaintiffs suggest involve the Government in the dietary preferences of a particular religious group.

The plaintiffs consist of a group of six individuals and three organizations hereinafter described. They seek injunctive relief as well as a declaration that the questioned statutory provisions are violative of the Constitution.

* * *

The Statutory Provisions Involved

Section 1 of the Act (7 U.S.C. § 1901) declares it to be the policy of the United States "that the slaughtering of livestock and the handling of livestock in connection with slaughter shall be carried out only by humane methods." And section 3 provides:

> The public policy declared in this Chapter shall be taken into consideration by all agencies of the Federal Government in connection with all procurement and price support programs and operations and after June 30, 1960, no agency or instrumentality of the United States shall contract for or procure any livestock products produced or processed by any slaughterer or processor which in any of its plants or in any plants of any slaughterer or processor with which it is affiliated slaughters or handles in connection with slaughter livestock by any methods other than methods designated and approved by the Secretary of Agriculture. . . .

7 U.S.C. § 1903. The plaintiffs' challenge to the Act is directed to sections 2(b), 5, and 6 (7 U.S.C. §§ 1902(b), 1905, and 1906). Section 2 provides:

> § 1902. Humane methods
>
> No method of slaughtering or handling in connection with slaughtering shall be deemed to comply with the public policy of the United States unless it is humane. Either of the following two methods of slaughtering and handling are hereby found to be humane:
>
> (a) in the case of cattle, calves, horses, mules, sheep, swine, and other livestock, all animals are rendered insensible to pain by a single blow or gunshot or an electrical, chemical or other means that is rapid and effective, before being shackled, hoisted, thrown, cast, or cut; or
>
> (b) by slaughtering in accordance with the ritual requirements of the Jewish faith or any other religious faith that prescribes a method of slaughter whereby the animal suffers loss of consciousness by anemia of

the brain caused by the simultaneous and instantaneous severance of the carotid arteries with a sharp instrument.

Section 4(c) provides:

Handling in connection with such slaughtering which necessarily accompanies the method of slaughter described in subsection (b) of this section shall be deemed to comply with the public policy specified by this section.[3]

Section 5 of the Act provides for the establishment of an advisory committee to assist in implementing the Act's provisions, with one of the members of the advisory committee being a "person familiar with the requirements of religious faiths with respect to slaughter." 7 U.S.C. § 1905. Section 6 provides:

Nothing in this Chapter shall be construed to prohibit, abridge, or in any way hinder the religious freedom of any person or group. Notwithstanding any other provision of this Chapter, in order to protect freedom of religion, ritual slaughter and the handling or other preparation of livestock for ritual slaughter are exempted from the terms of this Chapter. For the purposes of this section the term 'ritual slaughter' means slaughter in accordance with 1902(b) of this title.

7 U.S.C. § 1906.

The Parties

The plaintiffs are six individuals and three organizations having in common a professed commitment to "the principle of the humane treatment of animals" and to "the principle of the separation of church and state." The complaint alleges that each of the individual plaintiffs is a taxpayer, that two of the individual plaintiffs abstain from eating any meat or meat products because of the alleged inhumane treatment of animals prior to slaughter, and that the other individual plaintiffs are consumers of meat who have at times unwittingly eaten meat that allegedly was slaughtered according to the "religious exception" contained in sections 2(b) and 6 of the Act. Two of the organization plaintiffs are unincorporated associations whose members reside in the Southern District of New York; and one is a not-for-profit corporation organized under the laws of New York with its principal offices in New York City.

Defendants are the Secretary of Agriculture, the Acting Administrator of Consumer and Market Services of the Department of Agriculture, and "John Doe," who has since been identified as Rabbi Joseph Soloveitchik, the member of the advisory committee authorized under section 5 who is familiar with the requirements of religious faiths with respect to slaughter.

Intervention has been permitted pursuant to Rule 24, Fed. R. Civ. P., to seven individuals and five organizations speaking for a large number of the estimated

---

3. Although this sentence appears in § 1904(c) it is manifest that it was placed there by mistake since it makes reference to the method set out in § 1902(b).

6 million Jews in the United States and representative of the "entire spectrum of Jewish organizational life." The intervenors contend that if the Act is held unconstitutional, they and their members will be deprived of their right to eat ritually slaughtered meat.

The intervenors have an undoubted interest in the legislation under consideration here inasmuch as it affects the production of kosher[4] meat, which is slaughtered according to the ritual method described in section 2(b). This interest is different and distinct from the interest of the federal officials who have been named as defendants in this action and whose responsibility it is to administer the provisions of the Act. In addition, we are persuaded that intervention here will not delay the disposition of the action and will not cause any perceptible prejudice to any existing party. Moreover, the intervenors appeared before Congressional committees at the time the Act was under consideration by Congress and were therefore in a unique position to inform the Court regarding factual matters raised by this action.

Standing to Sue

The question of standing, vigorously contested in the briefs and upon the argument, presents no serious obstacle to a consideration of the merits. Defendants argue that plaintiffs cannot show that they have suffered any injury in fact by reason of the so-called religious exception of the Act and that therefore they lack standing to maintain this action. Plaintiffs, on the other hand, contend that they, or that at least one of them, have sustained the requisite injury either as taxpayers, in that the Act governs procurement of meat and meat products by the federal government; as consumers of meat who, as a practical matter, are unable to distinguish between meat produced according to subsection (a) and that produced according to subsection (b) of section 2 of the Act, and who therefore are "forced to eat ritually prepared meat"; or as citizens whose moral, religious, and aesthetic beliefs are offended because they are unable to refrain from eating ritually prepared meat. Plaintiffs contend that these alleged injuries are sufficient to confer standing to challenge the constitutionality of the Act.

The Supreme Court has recently made it clear that the plaintiffs' asserted injury may reflect "'aesthetic, conservational, and recreational' as well as economic values." *Sierra Club* [*v. Morton*, 405 U.S. 727 (1972)]. The fact that the interests claimed to have been injured are shared by many rather than few does not make them less deserving of legal protection through the judicial process. To have standing it is only necessary that the plaintiffs be among the class of persons injured.

---

4. Although the plaintiffs have apparently avoided use of the term "Kosher" and have used the expression "ritually prepared meat" in describing their alleged grievances, the defendants and the intervenors have occasionally used the term "Kosher." It has not been made clear that the two are not interchangeable. Kosher is the Jewish term for any food or vessels for food made ritually fit for use. Ritually slaughtered meat is not necessarily Kosher meat. Not all animals slaughtered in accordance with the ritual requirements of the Jewish faith are Kosher. *See* 13 Encyclopedia Britannica, Verbo "Kosher," at 493 (1959 ed.).

* * *

That the plaintiffs' commitment to the principles of humane treatment of animals and to the separation of church and state is deeply held and sincere is not doubted. The intervenors profess to be no less committed to the same principles, and indeed their religious beliefs have a long historical association with the humane treatment of animals. The sole question here is whether the plaintiffs have suffered the requisite injury or have a personal stake in the outcome of this controversy so that the Court can be assured that the issues will be framed with the necessary specificity, that the issues will be contested with the necessary adverseness, and that the litigation will be pursued with the necessary vigor as to make it capable of judicial resolution. *See Flast v. Cohen*, 392 U.S. 83, 106 (1968).

This is not a generalized dispute in which plaintiffs seek to air "generalized grievances about the conduct of government," *id.*; plaintiffs have raised a specific attack on a particularized legislative enactment, alleging that it is in violation of specific constitutional provisions in the First Amendment. The Act in question establishes as the policy of the United States that animals are to be treated humanely prior to and during the slaughtering process, and in addition provides that the Act's provisions with respect to what methods of slaughter are humane shall govern the procurement of all meat and meat products by the federal government through the expenditure of federal moneys. In addition to the moneys spent by the federal government for procurement,[6] there are some moneys spent to pay the travel and subsistence expenses of the members of the advisory committee authorized under section 5 of the Act and to administer the other provisions of the Act. Plaintiffs' allegations of injury in their role as federal taxpayers are therefore sufficient to meet the criteria of *Flast v. Cohen, supra.*

But apart from their status as taxpayers, plaintiffs' allegations of injury as consumers and citizens are sufficient to confer standing here. Plaintiffs allege that the Act contains a religious exception making it impossible as a practical matter to be certain of purchasing meat from animals slaughtered by a process that they consider humane and consistent with the policy of the United States as declared in section 1 of the Act. Plaintiffs contend that this uncertainty causes injury to their moral principles and aesthetic sensibilities. These allegations are substantially comparable to the allegations of environmental injury in *United States v. S.C.R.A.P., supra*, where the Court sustained the standing of plaintiffs. Although the Act in its operative provisions regulates directly only government procurement, we are willing to accept that governmental refusal to purchase the meat of animals slaughtered by the ritual method would so influence production in the great packing houses as to save plaintiffs from the uncertainty of which they complain; indeed, the general

---

6. The United States Department of Agriculture, for example, procures meat under the National School Lunch Act, 42 U.S.C. § 1751 *et seq.*, the Child Nutrition Act of 1966, 42 U.S.C. §§ 1771–1786, and under 7 U.S.C. § 612c as implemented by 15 U.S.C. § 713c.

structure of the Act rather suggests that Congress believed government procurement policy could have that kind of impact on methods of slaughter and handling in general.

The Meaning of the Statutory Provisions

Two aspects of the legislative history deserve special mention; first, that in passing these provisions Congress was fully informed with respect to the method of slaughter according to the Jewish ritual method, as well as the handling of livestock prior to such slaughter; and secondly, that the legislative history indicates that opinion among Jewish organizations regarding the inclusion of sections 2(b), 4(c) and 6 of the Act was divided.[7]

The declaration of humaneness becomes a focal point of inquiry in the case. The plaintiffs do not challenge the right of any slaughterer or religious group to slaughter livestock by means of a throat cut administered skillfully with a sharp knife—the Jewish ritual slaughtering method known as shehitah. Nor do the plaintiffs challenge the Congressional finding that the throat cut method is a humane method of slaughter. The crux of their complaint rests upon the proposition that in failing to require that the animal be rendered insensible to pain before the handling process, and thus before it is shackled and hoisted, the provisions permitting ritual slaughter are offensive to and inconsistent with the humane purposes of the Act and have a special religious purpose in contravention of the First Amendment. In effect, therefore, the plaintiffs contend that the provisions of the Act (sections 2(b) and 6) constitute an exemption from the application of subdivision (a), an act of cruelty to the animal so slaughtered, and a violation of the Religion Clauses of the First Amendment.

Congress characterizes as humane, in section 2 of the Act, either of two methods of "slaughtering and handling." The two methods are set forth in disjunctive paragraphs. The first subdivision (a), relates to the method by which the animal is "rendered insensible to pain" by some form of stunning—mechanical, electrical or chemical—before being shackled and hoisted. The second, subdivision (b), provides for an alternative method—slaughter "in accordance with the ritual requirements of the Jewish faith or any other religious faith" without making any express reference to the shackling or hoisting or any pre-slaughter handling procedure. It was conceded, however, upon the argument by counsel for the intervenors, that in practice, because of Department of Agriculture regulations, the Jewish slaughter method often involves the animal's being shackled and hoisted before the animal suffers loss of consciousness. [8] It is precisely this to which the plaintiffs object. They

---

7. Certain members of the orthodox Jewish community were alarmed with respect to the implications of the proposed legislation both with regard to the possible restriction of pre-slaughter handling and to the possibility of anti-Semitic propaganda which had accompanied similar legislation in other countries.

8. Upon the argument counsel for the intervenors made the following uncontradicted statement:
    "In Israel, and indeed, in the old traditional Jewish method, the animal would be laying down on its side, and the throat would be cut on the floor.

contend that such prior hoisting and shackling is inhumane. The plaintiffs' argument can be paraphrased in substantially the following manner: section 2(a) specifically provides that the animal must be rendered insensible before being shackled and hoisted. The general declaration of policy by Congress contained in section 1 is that only humane methods of slaughter should be carried out. Yet section 2(b) appears to be opposed to the declaration of policy and to be inconsistent with 2(a) because the animal suffers no loss of consciousness during the preliminary shackling and hoisting procedure under the ritual method. Yet this method as well as the method described in 2(a) are both "found to be humane" by the express provisions of the introductory paragraph of section 2; and perhaps by the misplaced provision in section 4(c) as well. Plaintiffs assert that such legislative inconsistency can be explained only as so clear a piece of deference to the tenets of one religious group as to violate the First Amendment.

The intervenors have made a persuasive showing that Congress was fully and competently advised with respect to Jewish ritual practices. It developed at the argument that the shackling and hoisting were not part of the Jewish ritual; but that under Jewish ritual practice it was essential that the animal be conscious at the time of the administration of the throat cut. This appears to be the reason why ritually slaughtered animals are sometimes shackled and hoisted before being killed—a practice prohibited in the Act with respect to other animals. Accepting, arguendo, that this constitutes an inconsistency in the statute, the question remains as to whether that inconsistency in any way violates the plaintiffs' rights under the Establishment Clause or the Free Exercise Clause of the First Amendment. Since Congress has determined that the Jewish ritual method is humane under the Act, the plaintiffs' arguments reduce themselves to whether they are really alleging an injury to themselves or an injury to the livestock to be slaughtered in the future, not by way of the throat cut which they concede is humane but because of the pre-slaughter handling which they suggest is not. In this connection section 4(c), the misplaced provision of the statute, expressly referred to section 2(b), setting forth the ritual method of slaughter, and stated that handling necessarily connected with such method "shall be deemed to comply with the public policy specified" by the statute. The draftsmen apparently attempted, perhaps inartistically, to avoid the appearance of inconsistency. But if there is inconsistency in the statute the plaintiffs have not persuaded us that they have suffered a deprivation of rights under the First Amendment.

"That is not permitted under Department of Agriculture regulations for sanitary reasons. You can't put an animal down in a Department of Agriculture inspected plant on the ground.

"The consequence is that the way the animal is positioned for slaughter in many slaughter houses that use the Jewish ritual method is that it is what is called shackled and hoisted. It is picked up by its legs, and it is turned upside down so that the throat cut can be administered."

We note at the outset of the analysis that we do not read subdivision (b) to be an exception to subdivision (a) of section 2. Phrased as it is in the disjunctive, the statute makes neither (a) nor (b) an exception to the other. The described methods are alternative methods; neither is dependent upon the other for the ascertainment of its meaning, and each one is supported by legislative history as a justifiable legislative determination that the stated method of slaughter is indeed humane.

The Establishment Clause

Despite this, plaintiffs assert that subsection (b), in permitting slaughterers to slaughter in accordance with the ritual method and, by implication, to handle livestock by whatever means is appropriate prior to such slaughter, had a religious purpose—the protection of a religious belief—and therefore violated the Establishment Clause.

Congress considered ample and persuasive evidence to the effect that the Jewish ritual method of slaughter, and the handling preparatory to such slaughter, was a humane method. It formulated a general policy after evaluating the abundant evidence before it.[10] Congress did not create a religious preference, nor did it create an exception to any general rule. The intervenors have made a persuasive showing that Jewish ritual slaughter, as a fundamental aspect of Jewish religious practice, was historically related to considerations of humaneness in times when such concerns were practically non-existent.

Since we regard the questioned statute as a Congressional declaration of policy, it necessarily follows that the proper forum for the plaintiffs is the Congress and not the courts. The Court cannot be asked to choose among methods of slaughter or pre-slaughter handling of livestock and to decide which is humane and which is not. We do not sit as a "super-legislature to weigh the wisdom of legislation."

The Constitutional clause against establishment of religion by law "does not ban federal or state regulation of conduct whose reason or effect merely happens to coincide or harmonize with the tenets of some or all religions." *McGowan v. Maryland*, 366 U.S. 420, 442 (1961). Thus the Congressional finding of humaneness in section 2 of the Act was an appropriate legislative function; and its coincidence with a ritual procedure under Jewish religious law does not undercut its validity or propriety.

Even assuming, *arguendo*, that Congress permitted the throat-cutting method of slaughter out of deference to the religious beliefs of many orthodox Jews, and chose out of similar deference not to restrain the prior handling of livestock attendant upon such ritual slaughter, Congress did not thereby violate the First Amendment. The accommodations of religious practices by granting exemptions from statutory

---

10. . . . Senator Hubert H. Humphrey, chairman of the Subcommittee and one of the principal proponents of the legislation, said on the floor of the Senate during debate that . . . ["n]ot only is [Kosher slaughter] a procedure accepted as a humane method of slaughter, but it is so established by scientific research."

obligations have been upheld in the Sunday closing cases and in the conscientious objector cases.

* * *

The lesson to be drawn from these Sunday closing and conscientious objector cases is this: that if Congress acted here out of deference to the religious tenets of many orthodox Jews it did so constitutionally and in substantially the same way as it accommodated the Sabbatarians and conscientious objectors by the exemptions in the applicable statutes.

The plaintiffs have placed much emphasis upon the holding of the Supreme Court in *Abington School District v. Schempp*, 374 U.S. 203 (1963), which held Bible reading in the public schools required by state action to be a violation of the Establishment Clause. We do not regard this holding as inconsistent with our views. The requirement in *Abington* that there be a secular legislative purpose[12] is met here by the manifest Congressional intent to establish humane standards for the slaughter of livestock. That one of the provisions of the Act defining humaneness coincided with the method for Jewish ritual slaughter, and even that a wholesale exemption was provided for ritual slaughter and accompanying preparation of livestock to accommodate a religious practice quite apart from the finding of humaneness, neither advanced nor inhibited religion within the intendment of the holding in *Abington*.

In its later decision in *Lemon v. Kurtzman*, 403 U.S. 602, 612–613 (1971), the Supreme Court set forth the three tests to be applied in determining whether a law violates the Establishment Clause: "First, the statute must have a secular legislative purpose; second, its principal or primary effect must be one that neither advances nor inhibits religion . . . finally, the statute must not foster 'an excessive government entanglement with religion.'" It is clear that the sections of the Act here under attack do not violate these tests. Read in the context of the entire statute, they have a secular purpose; their principal or primary effect is to provide for humane slaughter; and they do not foster excessive government entanglement with religion.

We do not find it necessary to discuss the holdings of the Supreme Court under the Establishment Clause which are concerned with an excessive entanglement of government with religion because there is no entanglement here. The governmental functions involved have no connection with any religious practices. The only government expenditure attributable to allegations in the complaint is the sum of $210.05 paid to Rabbi Joseph Soloveitchik for travel and subsistence expenses as a member of the advisory committee authorized under section 5. These expenses

---

12. The Supreme Court there stated:
   "The test may be stated as follows: what are the purpose and the primary effect of the enactment? If either is the advancement or inhibition of religion then the enactment exceeds the scope of legislative power as circumscribed by the Constitution. That is to say that to withstand the strictures of the Establishment Clause there must be a secular legislative purpose and a primary effect that neither advances nor inhibits religion." 374 U.S. at 222, 83 S. Ct. at 1571.

were paid for the period January 28, 1959 to July 15, 1963. We attribute no significance to this expenditure because it is both *de minimis* and stale.

The Free Exercise Clause

Insofar as plaintiffs' attack is based on the Free Exercise Clause rather than the Establishment Clause, the answer to it is that they have failed to demonstrate any coercive effect of the statute with respect to their religious practices. The plaintiffs suggest that they are being forced "knowingly or unknowingly" to eat ritually slaughtered meat, while in some cases they have been forced to cease eating meat. Apart from other failings in the claim, they do not allege any impingement upon the practice of any religion of their own. The plaintiffs' assertion of ethical principles against eating meat resulting from ritual slaughter is not sufficient. In the absence of a showing of coercive effect on religious practice, a meritorious claim under the Free Exercise Clause has not been made out. By making it possible for those who wish to eat ritually acceptable meat to slaughter the animal in accordance with the tenets of their faith, Congress neither established the tenets of that faith nor interfered with the exercise of any other.

Defendants' motion for summary judgment is granted, dismissing the complaint with prejudice.

Plaintiffs' motion for summary judgment is denied.

* * *

Notes

1. The case establishes the following conundrum: (a) "humane killing" requires that an animal be rendered insensible prior to being shackled and hung upside down before the severing of the carotid artery that results in death; (b) a killing is "inhumane" if a conscious animal is shackled and hung upside down before being killed; (c) kosher slaughter requires animals to be shackled and hung upside down while conscious; and (d) kosher slaughter is "humane killing."

2. Does it matter that more than a thousand years ago kosher slaughter may have been the most efficient and "healthy" (for people eating the animals) way to kill animals for meat? Should it matter if the practice was considered humane in Biblical times, if the practice is inhumane by today's standards?

3. When the *Jones v. Butz* opinion was issued, the HMSA applied only to slaughterhouses that contracted with and sold their final products to the federal government. A subsequent amendment expanded HMSA coverage to all slaughterhouses inspected by the Food Safety and Inspection Service, which covers virtually all meat produced commercially for human consumption in the United States.

4. In *Church of Lukumi Babalu Aye v. City of Hialeah*, 508 U.S. 520, 538 (1993), excerpted in Chapter 5, the Supreme Court effectively held that the legislative body of the City of Hialeah could not determine which practices involving animals would be allowed in the city. Here, the court almost does the reverse, deferring to the

determination of Congress that ritual kosher-type slaughter is humane. In each case the religious practice prevails over the animal welfare issues. The courts are indirectly balancing the compelling interest in religious freedom against the interest in preventing animal cruelty. Each case turns somewhat on its facts and the surrounding issues—in *Lukumi Babalu Aye*, the targeting of Santerians and their practices by the City of Hialeah, and in *Jones v. Butz*, the implications for the kosher/ritual meat industry and some consumers if ritual slaughter was ruled to be inhumane and, therefore, illegal.

If the Santerians (whose practices were challenged in *Lukumi Babalu Aye*) rather than Jews practiced kosher slaughter, do you think the practice of hanging conscious animals upside down by their back legs would still be considered humane?

5. The United States is not the only country in which "humane slaughter" and religious exemptions have been addressed. For example, Poland engaged in a series of affirmations and rejections of a ritual slaughter exemption to its Animal Protection Act of 1997's requirement that animals may be slaughtered only by methods that decrease pain to the lowest possible level. Over the course of nearly two decades, the same humane slaughter exception as discussed in *Jones* was in, and then out, several times. The discussion centered on whether the exemption unconstitutionally violated the right to religious freedom, whether it appropriately protected the public morals, and whether it was justified, given all the other accepted conduct that harms animals (such as hunting). In 2014 the Act was found to be unconstitutional because it did not include an exception for religious slaughter methods.

For a comprehensive look at the Polish discussion, see Aleksandra Lis and Tomasz Pietrzykowski, *Animals as Objects of Ritual Slaughter: Polish Law after the Battle over Exceptionless Mandatory Stunning*, GLOBAL J. OF ANIMAL LAW 1, 4 (Vol. 2, 2015). The authors argue for a balancing between religious freedoms and moral duties toward animals and propose "neutral limits of religious freedom" and application of "principles of proportionality" in an effort to achieve such a balance.

6. On January 1, 2013, the European Union's Regulation 1099/2009 (adopted in 2009) on the protection of animals came into effect, providing uniform rules throughout the European Union relating to the slaughter of animals—requiring stunning before slaughter, but providing a ritual slaughter exemption. The Regulation, however, allowed member states to preserve or establish their own laws providing higher standards of animal protection, as long as such departures from the Regulation were formally reported to the European Commission. Some European countries, including Sweden, Norway and Denmark, prohibit animal slaughter without prior stunning, with no exception. In 2017, voters in Belgium's largest territory (its Walloon region) voted to do the same (effective Sept. 1, 2019), and similar legislation has been proposed in Belgium's northern Flemish region as well.

For a summary of European laws on this issue as of early 2018, see "Legal Restrictions on Religious Slaughter in Europe" (Law Library of Congress, March 2018).

7. In 2018, the Israeli government moved toward enacting legislation to gradually phase out (within a three-year period) the transport of live sheep and cattle from Australia and Europe into Israel to be slaughtered there for food, in response to revelations of the extremely poor conditions and animal suffering, disease and death during transport. The legislative effort had bipartisan support. Regarding the legislation, Israel's Prime Minister reportedly stated on Facebook at that time: "It's our duty to act and correct this enormous suffering caused to animals."

8. Turning attention back to the United States, the HMSA applies to methods of slaughtering or "handling *in connection with* slaughtering...." 7 U.S.C. § 1902 (emphasis added). It has always been assumed that it applies only to the actual slaughter process in slaughterhouses, and no other period of an animal's life. In December 2001, People for the Ethical Treatment of Animals filed a rulemaking petition, asking the U.S. Department of Agriculture (USDA) to implement rules under the HMSA to protect animals raised for food and other commercial uses from birth until they are slaughtered. The petition was based on the proposition that if any animals have been brought into existence for no other purpose than to be slaughtered, then from the moment of their births they are being handled "in connection with" slaughter. The editors are not aware of any response from the USDA.

9. In *Levine v. Conner*, 540 F. Supp. 2d 1113 (N.D. Cal. 2008), *vacated and remanded by Levine v. Vilsack*, 587 F.3d 986 (9th Cir. 2009), plaintiffs sued the USDA, challenging the agency's determination that chickens, turkeys and other avian species slaughtered for food were not covered by the HMSA. The district court concluded that the undefined term "livestock" in the HMSA was not intended to include those winged species, which represent more than ninety percent of all animals killed for food each year. The court's ruling meant there was no requirement that these animals be treated humanely in connection with slaughter. On appeal, the Ninth Circuit found that plaintiffs did not meet the "redressability" prong of standing under Article III of the federal Constitution (see Chapter 5) and vacated the district court opinion with instructions to dismiss the lawsuit. 587 F.3d at 997. The Ninth Circuit's order left intact the federal government's decision that birds are not covered by the HMSA.

10. *Farm Sanctuary, Inc. v. Department of Food and Agriculture*, 63 Cal. App. 4th 495 (Cal. Ct. App. 1998), addressed slaughter exceptions in California's analog to the HMSA, which, like those challenged in *Jones v. Butz*, were tied to religious and "ritualistic" practices. California Food and Agricultural Code section 19501, part of the state Humane Slaughter Law (HSL), like the HMSA, requires animals to be slaughtered after being "rendered insensible to pain" or without being rendered insensible to pain if the slaughter is "in accordance with ritual requirements of the Jewish or any other religious faith that prescribes a method of slaughter whereby the animal suffers loss of consciousness by anemia of the brain caused by the simultaneous and instantaneous severance of the carotid arteries with a sharp instrument." The California law, in contrast to the HMSA, includes birds within its coverage, and Farm Sanctuary's lawsuit alleged that the ritualistic slaughter provisions permitted

inhumane slaughter of birds, and therefore conflicted with the humane intention of the law.

The court rejected Farm Sanctuary's challenge to the law but produced a notable decision with respect to the ripeness (one of the justiciability/gatekeeper doctrines discussed in Chapter 5) of the challenge. The holding also established Farm Sanctuary's standing for purposes of the lawsuit, and included some compelling statements about allowing those who seek to protect animals to have a place at the bar when animals' interests could be negatively impacted:

> In determining whether a controversy is ripe, we use a two-prong test: (1) whether the dispute is sufficiently concrete to make declaratory relief appropriate; and (2) whether the withholding of judicial consideration will result in a hardship to the parties.

> * * *

> In this case, the ripeness test is satisfied. As to the first prong, the question before us is not so abstract or hypothetical that we should await a better factual scenario. Farm Sanctuary contends that the ritualistic slaughter regulation is invalid on its face because it is inconsistent with the HSL....

> As to the second prong, a significant and imminent injury is inherent in further delay. If as Farm Sanctuary contends, the ritualistic slaughter regulation authorizes a wholesale exemption from the HSL, poultry may be slaughtered through *inhumane* methods. By delaying a decision on the merits, we run the risk of allowing the needless suffering of animals—the evil that the HSL was intended to prevent.

> We realize that Farm Sanctuary and its members might not face any hardship if we decline to reach the merits of the case. The HSL was enacted for the benefit of *animals*. If the ritualistic slaughter regulation is invalid, it will result in an unlawful injury to poultry, not humans. In essence, the affected animals in this case are the real parties in interest. In these unique circumstances, we should focus on the potential harm to the beneficiaries of the statute.

> Further, as a practical matter, Farm Sanctuary should be allowed to challenge the ritualistic slaughter regulation. Assuming that the regulation authorizes an exemption from the HSL's humane slaughter requirement, someone who is granted an exemption is not about to challenge the regulation. By the same token, someone who is denied an exemption might seek to overturn the denial but would not attack the regulation's creation of an exemption. Thus, unless an organization like Farm Sanctuary is permitted to challenge the department's rulemaking authority, the ritualistic slaughter regulation will be immune from judicial review.... As one court has observed: "Where [a statute] is expressly motivated by considerations of humaneness toward animals, who are uniquely incapable of defending their

own interests in court, it strikes us as eminently logical to allow groups specifically concerned with animal welfare to invoke the aid of the courts in enforcing the statute." (*Animal Welfare Institute v. Kreps* (D.C. Cir. 1977) 561 F.2d 1002, 1007 (dictum).)

Moreover, declaratory relief is appropriate where "questions of public interest . . . are involved." [¶] We think it clear that the slaughtering of animals through humane methods, as required by the HSL, is a matter of public importance. "It has long been the public policy of this country to avoid unnecessary cruelty to animals." (*Humane Soc. of Rochester & Monroe Cty. v. Lyng* (W.D.N.Y. 1980) 633 F. Supp. 480, 486.)

63 Cal. App. 4th at 502–04.

Remember that in state courts, Article III, section 2, of the U.S. Constitution does not apply to restrict a court's ability to obtain jurisdiction over disputes or a plaintiff's standing to sue, unless the particular state's courts have adopted the federal standards for their own.

11. The *Farm Sanctuary* court acknowledged that humane treatment of animals is a "matter of public importance." The farmed animal industry has publicly agreed with that statement. As with the language of the anti-cruelty statutes discussed in Chapter 3, definitions of "cruelty" and "humane" may be subjective. The lack of an objective legal standard for these terms that are central to the treatment of animals is partly responsible for the ongoing debate and the slow change in industry practices. The best way to regulate agribusiness may be to proscribe specific practices like the use of battery cages, gestation crates and veal crates, or the unanesthetized procedures performed on many species of animals used for food (such as castration and tail docking). These are objectively identifiable acts that do not suffer from the same interpretive ambiguity as words like "humane" and "cruel."

12. For more on these issues, see Bruce Friedrich, *Ritual Slaughter, Federal Preemption, and Protection for Poultry: What Legislative History Tells Us About USDA Enforcement of the Humane Slaughter Act*, 24 ANIMAL L. 137 (2018).

13. Shifting from general rules regarding slaughter to American sentiments about certain animals, the next case (which was discussed in the *Association des Eleveurs* case excerpted earlier in this chapter, for its preemption analysis) illustrates a state's ability to exercise its desires regarding identified species and the legal arguments that may be made by the industry to prevent the enforcement of those social mores. In issuing its opinion in favor of the state's right to regulate and to prevent the slaughter of horses, the Seventh Circuit also provided commentary on the culinary decisions made by people based on the species of the animals who may become food.

Cavel International, Inc. v. Madigan

United States Court of Appeals, Seventh Circuit, 2007
500 F.3d 551

POSNER, Circuit Judge.

Horse meat was until recently an accepted part of the American diet—the Harvard Faculty Club served horse-meat steaks until the 1970s. No longer is horse meat eaten by Americans, Christa Weil, "We Eat Horses, Don't We?," *New York Times,* Mar. 5, 2007, p. A19, though it is eaten by people in a number of other countries, including countries in Europe; in some countries it is a delicacy. Meat from American horses is especially prized because our ample grazing land enables them to eat natural grasses, which enhances the flavor of their meat. Mary Jacoby, "Why Belgians Shoot Horses in Texas For Dining in Europe," *Wall St. J.,* Sept. 21, 2005, p. 1.

Cavel International, the plaintiff in this case, owns and operates the only facility in the United States for slaughtering horses. Until recently it was one of three such facilities, but the other two, both in Texas, stopped slaughtering horses after the Fifth Circuit upheld a Texas law similar to the Illinois law challenged in this case. *Empacadora de Carnes de Fresnillo, S.A. de C.V. v. Curry,* 476 F.3d 326, 336–37 (5th Cir. 2007).

Cavel's slaughterhouse, located in DeKalb, Illinois, near Chicago, has some sixty employees and slaughters some 40,000 to 60,000 horses a year, out of a total of about 700,000 horses that either are killed or die of natural causes in the United States annually. Cavel buys its horses for about $300 apiece from brokers who obtain them at auctions. The company has been in operation for 20 years and has some $20 million in annual revenues.

Horses are the only animals that Cavel slaughters, and it represented to us without contradiction that if it loses this case it will have to shut down. The Texas slaughterhouses were more eclectic—they slaughtered, besides horses, such sources of "atypical meat products" as bison and ostrich. But they too represented to the courts that if forbidden to slaughter horses they would have to shut down, though it appears that after a brief shutdown they reopened, adding cattle to their menu, as it were.

In the United States, horses are killed in slaughterhouses only when the horses' flesh is destined for eating by human beings or (a detail to be considered later) zoo animals. The flesh of horses that is intended for pet food is obtained from the corpses hauled to rendering plants for disposal; the plants also produce glue and other products from the carcasses. (All these businesses are in terminal decline. Jeffrey McMurray, "Some Horses Left to Starve as Market for Meat Shrivels," *Chi. Tribune,* Mar. 15, 2007, p. 3.) Unlike Cavel's slaughterhouse, a rendering plant's methods of producing meat from dead horses do not have to comply with the requirements that the federal Meat Inspection Act, 21 U.S.C. §601, prescribes for the production of meat, expressly including horse meat, §§601(j), (w), intended for human consumption. The Act is fully applicable to Cavel, *see* 21 U.S.C. §617, even though Cavel's entire output is exported to such countries as Belgium, France, and Japan. Indeed, Cavel is the subsidiary of a Belgian company.

On May 24 of this year, the Illinois Horse Meat Act, 225 ILCS 635, was amended to make it unlawful for any person in the state either "to slaughter a horse if that person knows or should know that any of the horse meat will be used for human consumption," §635/1.5(a), or "to import into or export from this State, or to sell, buy, give away, hold, or accept any horse meat if that person knows or should know that the horse meat will be used for human consumption." §635/1.5(b). (Prior to the amendment, the statute merely required a license to slaughter horses and imposed various inspection, labeling, and other regulatory restrictions on licensees. The prohibition has made these provisions academic.) Cavel claims that the amendment violates both the federal Meat Inspection Act and the commerce clause—the provision in Article I, section 8, of the federal Constitution that in terms merely empowers Congress to regulate interstate and foreign commerce but that has been interpreted to limit the power of states to regulate interstate and foreign commerce even in the absence of federal legislation inconsistent with the state regulation.

Cavel moved for a preliminary injunction against the enforcement of the amendment. The district court declined to issue it, on the ground that Cavel had failed to make a strong showing that it was likely to prevail on the merits. Cavel appealed, and we enjoined the application of the amendment to Cavel pending our decision of its appeal.

The challenge based on the Meat Inspection Act need detain us only briefly. Cavel points to the Act's preemption clause—"requirements within the scope of this Act with respect to premises, facilities and operations of any establishment at which inspection is provided under title I of this Act [including facilities at which horses are slaughtered, 21 U.S.C. §§601(d), (j)] which are in addition to, or different than those made under this Act may not be imposed by any State or Territory or the District of Columbia," §678—and argues that it signifies Congress's decision to sweep aside any state law that would render the federal requirements inapplicable to Cavel's slaughterhouse by forbidding horses to be slaughtered. The argument confuses a premise with a conclusion. When the Meat Inspection Act was passed (and indeed to this day), it was lawful in some states to produce horse meat for human consumption, and since the federal government has a legitimate interest in regulating the production of human food whether intended for domestic consumption or for export—exporting meat unfit for human consumption would be highly damaging to the nation's foreign commerce—it was natural to make the Act applicable to horse meat. That was not a decision that states must allow horses to be slaughtered for human consumption. The government taxes income from gambling that violates state law; that doesn't mean the state must permit the gambling to continue. Given that horse meat is produced for human consumption, its production must comply with the Meat Inspection Act. But if it is not produced, there is nothing, so far as horse meat is concerned, for the Act to work upon.

Of course in a literal sense a state law that shuts down any "premises, facilities and operations of any establishment at which inspection is provided" is "different" from the federal requirements for such premises, but so literal a reading is untenable. If despite its title the Meat Inspection Act were intended to forbid states to shut down slaughterhouses, it would have to set forth standards and procedures for determining whether a particular slaughterhouse or class of slaughterhouses should be shut down; and it does not. The Act is concerned with inspecting premises at which meat is produced for human consumption, *see, e.g.*, 21 U.S.C. §606, rather than with preserving the production of particular types of meat for people to eat.

The more difficult question is whether the horse-meat amendment violates the commerce clause as interpreted to prohibit state regulations that unduly interfere with the foreign commerce of the United States. Cavel fastens on subsection (b) of the Illinois amendment, which forbids the importing and exporting of horse meat for human consumption. But that provision is not addressed to Cavel; it is addressed to a middleman who having procured horse meat from Cavel tries to export it, or that imports horse meat to Illinois hoping to induce Americans to eat it. (We assume that the terms "import" and "export" refer to bringing horse meat into Illinois from another state, or shipping it to another state, as well as to importing horse meat from and exporting it to a foreign country.) The provision directed at Cavel is subsection (a), which forbids the slaughtering of horses for human consumption. If that subsection is valid, Cavel loses its case.

The clearest case of a state law that violates the commerce clause is a law that discriminates in favor of local firms. Suppose a state passed a law that forbade the importation of wild baitfish. That would be a discrimination against interstate and foreign commerce. . . .

There is no discrimination in the present case insofar as the prohibition against slaughter is concerned. If a local firm (remember that Cavel is foreign-owned) wanted to slaughter horses, it could not do so. No local merchant or producer benefits from the ban on slaughter.

* * *

"Where the statute regulates evenhandedly to effectuate a legitimate local public interest, and its effects on interstate commerce are only incidental, it will be upheld unless the burden imposed on such commerce is *clearly* excessive in relation to the putative local benefits." *Pike v. Bruce Church, Inc.*, 397 U.S. 137, 142 (1970) (emphasis added).

* * *

Cavel argues . . . that Illinois's ban on slaughtering horses for human consumption serves no purpose at all. The horses will be killed anyway when they are too old to be useful and what difference does it make whether they are eaten by people or by cats and dogs? But the horse meat used in pet food is produced by rendering plants from carcasses rather than by the slaughter of horses, and the difference bears on the effect of the Illinois statute. Cavel pays for horses; rendering plants do not. If your horse dies, or if you have it euthanized, you must pay to have it hauled to the rendering plant, and you must also pay to have it euthanized if it didn't just die on you. So when your horse is no longer useful to you, you have a choice between selling it for slaughter and either keeping it until it dies or having it killed. The option of selling the animal for slaughter is thus financially more advantageous to the owner, and this makes it likely that many horses (remember that Cavel slaughters between 40,000 and 60,000 a year) die sooner than they otherwise would because they can be killed for their meat. States have a legitimate interest in prolonging the lives of animals that their population happens to like. They can ban bullfights and cockfights and the abuse and neglect of animals.

Of course Illinois could do much more for horses than it does—could establish old-age pastures for them, so that they would never be killed (except by a stray cougar), or provide them with free veterinary care. But it is permitted to balance its interest in horses' welfare against the other interests of its (human) population; and it is also permitted to take one step at a time on a road toward the humane treatment of our fellow animals.

There is a wrinkle in this analysis, however, though unremarked by the parties. Zoos feed a considerable amount of horse meat to their charges. Brad Haynes, "Zoos in a Pickle Over Horse Meat", *Seattle Times*, Aug. 14, 2007, *http://seattletimes .nwsource.com/html/ localnews/2003835227-horsemeat14m.html* (visited Sept. 18, 2007). For living proof, we reproduce a photograph from Haynes's article, with its caption: [*Ed. Note: At this point in the opinion the court inserted a picture with the following caption:*] "Kwanzaa, a young South African lion at Cameron Park Zoo in Waco, Texas, celebrates his birthday with a cake made from 10 pounds of horse meat, plus whipped cream and a carrot." As the article explains, American zoos, seeing the handwriting on the wall so far as the domestic slaughter of horses is concerned, are shifting to importing horse meat. So the slaughter of horses will continue. For all we know, Cavel may seek out a new market in America's zoos. We do not know why, with the cessation of horse slaughtering at the Texas slaughterhouses, Cavel has not done so already.

But even if no horses live longer as a result of the new law, a state is permitted, within reason, to express disgust at what people do with the dead, whether dead human beings or dead animals. There would be an uproar if restaurants in Chicago started serving cat and dog steaks, even though millions of stray cats and dogs are euthanized in animal shelters. A follower of John Stuart Mill would disapprove of a law that restricted the activities of other people (in this case not only Cavel's owners and employees but also its foreign consumers) on the basis merely of distaste, but American governments are not constrained by Mill's doctrine.

The careful reader will have noted that we have so far been discussing the legal principles governing state burdens on interstate commerce, though the Illinois statute burdens foreign commerce. Quite apart from economic consequences, an interference by a state with foreign commerce can complicate the nation's foreign relations, which are a monopoly of the federal government; states are not permitted to have their own foreign policy, their own embassies and consuls and ambassadors, and so forth. "Foreign commerce is pre-eminently a matter of national concern. 'In international relations and with respect to foreign intercourse and trade the people of the United States act through a single government with unified and adequate national power.' *Board of Trustees v. United States*, 289 U.S. 48, 59 (1933)." *Japan Line, Ltd. v. County of Los Angeles*, 441 U.S. 434, 448–51 (1979).

Suppose Cavel were the only source of horse meat for human consumption in Europe and the law provoked European governments into remonstrating with our State Department, which in response submitted to us an amicus curiae brief denouncing the law.... [¶] ... [Cavel] did not tell the district court and has not told us what percentage of the horse meat consumed by Europeans it supplies and thus whether its being closed down is likely to have a big effect on the price of horse meat in Europe. And while it is true that the foreign minister of Belgium wrote a letter to Governor Blagojevich inquiring about the status of the bill that became the horse-meat amendment, he did not say that his government was opposing the bill. So far as we know, there was no follow-up (we have not been told whether the letter was answered and if so what the answer said); and we have heard nothing from any other foreign government or from the State Department.

The curtailment of foreign commerce by the amendment is slight and we are naturally reluctant to condemn a state law, supported if somewhat tenuously by a legitimate state interest, on grounds as slight as presented by Cavel. Yet we are not entirely happy about having to uphold the Illinois statute. That the company is foreign-owned and its entire output exported means that the shareholders and consumers harmed by the amendment have no influence in Illinois politics, though there is no hint in the history of the amendment of local hostility to foreigners but only of indifference to them, in the remark of the state's agriculture director that "there is no *domestic* market for horsemeat and, *therefore*, no need for this practice to continue in Illinois." Governor's Office Press Release, "Gov. Blagojevich Signs Legislation Banning the Slaughter of Horses in Illinois for Human Consumption," May 24, 2007, *www.illinois.gov/PressReleases/ShowPressRelease.cfm?SubjectID =3&RecNum=5995* (visited Sept. 5, 2007) (emphasis added).

The fact that the governor's signing statement acknowledges the role of the Hollywood actress Bo Derek, author of the book *Riding Lessons: Everything That Matters in Life I Learned From Horses* (2002), in outlawing the slaughtering of horses could be thought to inject a frivolous note into a law that forces the closing of a business that has very little to do with the people of Illinois. But this is not a basis for invalidating a nondiscriminatory statute that interferes minimally with the nation's foreign commerce and cannot be said to have no rational basis.

Although the appeal is from the denial of a preliminary injunction, the merits of Cavel's challenge to the horse-meat law have been fully briefed and argued and there are no unresolved factual issues the resolution of which in a trial would alter the result. In such a case, courts treat the appeal as if it were from a final judgment. So the judgment is affirmed, the suit dismissed with prejudice, and the injunction that we granted pending appeal dissolved.

Notes

1. "The lone cowboy riding his horse on a Texas trail is a cinematic icon. Not once in memory did the cowboy eat his horse, but film is an imperfect mirror for reality." *Empacadora de Carnes de Fresnillo, S.A. de C.V. v. Curry*, 476 F.3d 326, 328 (5th Cir. 2007) (concluding that the Texas statute banning horse slaughter for human consumption was valid; holding that two Texas slaughterhouses could be prosecuted for violating the statute). As noted in *Cavel v. Madigan*, the two Texas facilities stopped slaughtering horses after the Fifth Circuit issued its decision in *Empacadora*.

2. In addition to Texas and Illinois, several other states have similar statutory bans on horse slaughter and the sale of horse meat for human consumption. *See, e.g.,* CAL. PENAL CODE § 598c ("Prohibition of Horse Slaughter and Sale of Horsemeat for Human Consumption Act of 1998") ("[I]t is unlawful for any person to possess, to import into or export from the state, or to sell, buy, give away, hold, or accept any horse with the intent of killing, or having another kill, that horse, if that person knows or should have known that any part of that horse will be used for human consumption."); CAL. PENAL CODE § 598d ("[H]orsemeat may not be offered for sale for human consumption. No restaurant, café, or other public eating place may offer horsemeat for human consumption.").

3. As the *Cavel* court pointed out, however, horsemeat may still be used in pet food (though this rarely happens any more) and for zoo animals; and horses continue to be slaughtered outside the United States for human food and inside America for other reasons. Do you think the cessation of the slaughter of American horses in America for human consumption was merely a pyrrhic victory for the horses or are there broader ramifications?

With the cessation of the domestic horse slaughter operations, more horses have been sent from the U.S. to Canada and Mexico to be slaughtered, enduring longer transports than might have been necessary if they were being shipped domestically. Horse slaughter supporters claim that conditions in slaughterhouses in foreign countries are worse than those in America; although those opposed to horse slaughter debate the issue and U.S. Department of Agriculture reports from the last American horse slaughterhouses demonstrated major violations of humane handling practices, presumably in part because of the difference in behavior of horses and other animals traditionally slaughtered for food. From an animal advocate's perspective, how would you balance these types of risks and/or realities in deciding whether to direct your efforts toward banning certain conduct within the United States? What factors would you consider? On what grounds could you argue that the legal prohibition in America of any practice considered to be cruel or inhumane to animals is a victory for animals? On what grounds could you make the contrary argument?

4. The *Cavel* case came about because in May of 2007 Illinois amended the Illinois Horse Meat Act, prohibiting the slaughter of horses for human consumption in Illinois and, therefore, directly impacting Cavel's business (which was the only horse slaughterhouse in America at the time).

Before then, HSUS and other plaintiffs were litigating against the federal government as a means of curtailing horse slaughter nationwide. *See, e.g., Humane Society of the U.S. v. Johanns*, 520 F. Supp. 2d 8 (D.D.C. 2007) (excerpted in Chapter 9). When the complaint was filed, "horses were slaughtered at three different foreign-owned facilities in the United States [two in Texas and the Cavel plant] to provide horse meat for human consumption abroad and for use in zoos and research facilities domestically." *Id.* at 12. The *Johanns* case related to "the web of legislation and regulations pertaining to the inspection of such horses prior to slaughter." *Id.* More specifically, in 2005, Congress amended the FY 2006 Agricultural Appropriations Act to prohibit the use of funds under the Act for the salaries or expenses of personnel to inspect horses under the Federal Meat Inspection Act. Since all slaughterhouses killing horses for human consumption are required to undergo inspections, the effect of the amendment was to prohibit the slaughter of horses for human consumption. In response, the three horse slaughter facilities then operating filed a petition for emergency rulemaking with the USDA to create a "fee-for-service" inspection program for the required inspections. As a result, an Interim Final Rule was issued, amending the federal meat inspection regulations to allow the horse slaughter facilities to pay for inspections under such a fee-for-service program. The plaintiffs in *HSUS v. Johanns* sued the USDA, alleging that by creating this program without first conducting any environmental review under the National Environmental Policy Act (NEPA), the USDA had violated NEPA and the Council on Environmental Quality's implementing regulations, abused its discretion, and acted arbitrarily and capriciously in violation of the Administrative Procedure Act. The slaughterhouses intervened in the case. Before the case was resolved, the Seventh Circuit issued its decision in *Cavel v. Madigan*, thereby closing the doors of the one then-existing slaughterhouse that was killing horses for human consumption. (The two Texas plants had been closed after the Fifth Circuit's ruling in *Empacadora de Carnes de Fresnillo, S.A. de C.V. v. Curry*, 476 F.3d 326, 336–37 (5th Cir. 2007).) *HSUS v. Johanns* also resulted in a positive ruling for the horse protection advocates, with the court ruling that the USDA's failure to even consider its NEPA obligations was arbitrary and capricious. The USDA chose not to appeal that decision and did not engage in any NEPA review with respect to the fee-for-service program; the fee-for-service program was thus eliminated as a viable option to continue horse slaughter.

5. The funding prohibition discussed in the preceding Note—colloquially known as a "defund"—was reinstated annually through 2011, accomplishing its intended effect of prohibiting nationwide the slaughter of horses for human consumption. *See* Remarks of Senator John Ensign (R-NV), 151 CONG. REC. S 10,218 (Sept. 20, 2005) ("The goal of our amendment is simple: to end the slaughter of America's

horses for human consumption overseas."). For the FY 2012 budget, however, Congress failed to renew its funding ban, thus opening the door for horse slaughter for human consumption to resume in this country. Due to the controversial nature of horse slaughter, however, bipartisan Congressional efforts were undertaken to prevent resumption of this industry. In 2013, both the House and Senate Appropriations Committees unanimously amended the FY 2014 Agriculture Appropriations bill to reinstate the defund and eliminate funding for the inspection of horse slaughter facilities. On January 17, 2014, President Obama signed the bill, withdrawing government funding for horse slaughter inspections, effectively preventing American horse slaughter from starting again. Because of the concerted opposition to horse slaughter, discussed in further detail in Note 8 below, as of the time of publication of this edition, no horse slaughter for human consumption has occurred in the U.S. since 2007.

6. Particular objections to horse slaughter have been raised based on concerns regarding (1) the cruelty inherent in horse slaughter, (2) the dangerous nature of horse meat to consumers because of the number of unregulated substances horses are given before slaughter, and (3) the potential environmental harm that could result from the reinstitution of commercial horse slaughter in America. For example, almost all American horses are given a wide variety of drugs and other substances that are banned from use in those animals raised for human consumption, which renders horses' blood and tissue contaminated and dangerous to consume. Moreover, discarding the byproducts of horse slaughter poses environmental and public health risks when wastewater and blood from slaughter operations seep into the ground and water supply, and offal and adulterated tissue are discarded in landfills.

In 2012, Front Range Equine Rescue (Front Range), along with HSUS, filed rulemaking petitions with the federal Food & Drug Administration and the USDA, asking the agencies to issue rules that would provide for the proper screening of horses and preclude any who had been given prohibited substances from being used for human food. (Front Range also petitioned the federal Bureau of Land Management to stop the sale of wild horses gathered from the range to individuals who then sell them to slaughter facilities.)

After Congress lifted the funding ban in 2012, the USDA's Food Safety and Inspection Service (FSIS) issued inspection grants to two commercial equine slaughter facilities, allowing them to begin slaughtering horses. Front Range, HSUS and other organizations and individuals immediately sued USDA officials seeking a declaration that the agency had violated NEPA by giving the inspection grants without proper environmental review, and asking the court to set aside the two grants that had been issued. The plaintiffs also moved to enjoin the federal defendants from authorizing slaughter while the lawsuit was pending. The two slaughterhouse companies (and a third that had applied for an inspection grant but had not received one) intervened. The district court noted that the USDA never refuted that "horse slaughter operations have 'significantly' impacted the environment within the meaning of NEPA as set forth in 40 C.F.R. § 1508.27," citing to the *Johanns* case discussed in Note 4. *Front Range Equine Rescue, et al. v. Vilsack*, Civ. No.1:13-cv-MCA-RHS (D.N.M. Nov. 1, 2013). The court granted the plaintiffs' motion for a temporary restraining order, but denied their request for permanent injunction and dismissed the case. On appeal, the Tenth Circuit dismissed the case as moot because (1) Congress had resumed the funding prohibition by that time, and (2) one slaughterhouse "decided to abandon all plans to slaughter equines and asked FSIS to withdraw its grant of inspection," another surrendered its inspection grant for horse slaughter, and the third was not slaughtering horses at that time, had not been given an FSIS inspection grant and also lacked the necessary state permits to switch to equine slaughter. *Front Range Equine Rescue v. Vilsack*, 782 F.3d 565 (10th Cir. 2015).

7. On December 26, 2013, the New Mexico Attorney General filed a lawsuit (in which Front Range Equine Rescue intervened) against Valley Meat Company and its operator in Roswell, New Mexico, asking for an injunction to stop the horse slaughterhouse from opening. A temporary restraining order was issued on December 30 and, after an extended hearing, the court found that horse meat was adulterated and horse slaughter environmentally hazardous, and granted an injunction on all four of the Attorney General's claims, which included allegations of potential violations of New Mexico's Water Quality Act, Food Act, nuisance and consumer misrepresentation laws. *State of New Mexico ex rel. Gary K. King, Attorney General v. Valley Meat Co. et. al.*, Case No. D-101-CV-2013-03197 (N.M. Dist. Ct., Santa Fe County, First Jud. Dist., Jan. 17, 2014). The case ultimately settled, with Valley Meat agreeing never to slaughter horses.

8. Federal bills explicitly banning the transport and/or slaughter of horses in the United States for human consumption have been introduced over the years, but as of the date of publication of this edition, none had passed into law. *See, e.g.,* H.R. 3781 (2002) ("American Horse Slaughter Prevention Act"); H.R. 503 (2005) (introduced by Representative John Sweeney (R-NY) to amend the Horse Protection Act, 15 U.S.C. § 1821, "to prohibit the shipping, transporting, moving, delivering, receiving, possessing, purchasing, selling, or donation of horses and other equines to be slaughtered for human consumption, and for other purposes"); and H.R. 2966/S.1176 (2011) (American Horse Slaughter Prevention Act of 2011). In 2005, Representative Sweeney stated: "This inhumane and disgusting practice, which serves only to promote animal cruelty, needs to be brought to an end. . . . Support for this legislation is stronger than ever, and I look forward to the day when the American horse no longer ends up on a dinner plate overseas." *Rep. Sweeney Reintroduces Horse Slaughter Legislation*, U.S. FED. NEWS, Feb. 1, 2005.

9. The notion of what is "inhumane and disgusting" varies between cultures and countries. In most of the Western world, societal sentiment is that eating dog, cat or wild-caught "bushmeat" (meat from wild animals including wild cats, chimpanzees and other primates) is taboo. In some Asian countries, however, dog meat is a staple and favored food of a segment of the population. And some African tribes

consider the consumption of bushmeat to be part of their social and spiritual heritage. *See United States v. Manneh*, 2008 U.S. Dist. LEXIS 105209 (E.D.N.Y. Dec. 31, 2008) (defendant claiming religious exemption convicted of illegally importing bushmeat; inspectors found and seized "65 individual pieces of bushmeat, including skulls, limbs and torsos").

With respect to dog and cat meat, its consumption is not only deemed unacceptable, it is explicitly banned by statute in some states. *See, e.g.*, GA. CODE ANN. § 26-2-160 (2017) (prohibits sale of dog meat for human consumption; all dog meat sold for other purposes must be in packages, with label showing contents and stating that contents are "NOT FOR HUMAN CONSUMPTION"); N.J. STAT. ANN. § 4:22-25.4 (2017) (prohibits selling or bartering for sale of dog or cat flesh for human consumption, provided that person "knew or reasonable should have known" that flesh was from domestic dog or cat); N.J. STAT. ANN. § 4:22-26(y) (2017) (animal cruelty to "knowingly sell or barter or offer for sale or barter, at wholesale or retail, for human consumption, the flesh of a domestic dog or cat or any product made in whole or in part from the flesh of a domestic dog or cat"); N.Y. AGRIC. & MKTS. LAW § 96-e (2018) ("It shall be unlawful for any slaughterhouse, abattoir or other place or establishment, or for any person, to slaughter or butcher domesticated dog (*canis familiaris*) or domesticated cat (*felis catus* or *domesticus*) to create food, meat or meat products for human or animal consumption.").

Note that the New York statute bans the slaughter of dogs and cats to create food products for human *or animal* consumption, whereas the other referenced statutes, like the horse slaughter prohibitions, ban sale or slaughter only for *human* consumption.

If the "inhumane and disgusting practice" of slaughtering horses (or dogs, cats or non-human primates) for human consumption "serves only to promote cruelty [and] needs to be brought to an end," how do we reconcile that notion with the suffering and slaughter of billions of other animals used for food and clothing each year? If Representative Sweeney was correct, what is the basis for the accepted social distinction? Should longstanding societal practices and norms be the primary justification for disparate treatment of different species of sentient beings? As a practical matter, can social norms and historical practices be taken out of the equation when laws are enacted or amended? If you were to attempt a wholly objective evaluation of which sentient animals, if any, the law should permit to be slaughtered for food, what factors would you take into account?

10. The Seventh Circuit in *Cavel* and the Fifth Circuit in *Empacadora* held that the Federal Meat Inspection Act (FMIA) did not preempt state laws prohibiting the slaughter of horses for human consumption. Five years later, without disturbing those rulings, the United States Supreme Court reached an arguably different result when addressing the question of whether the FMIA preempted a California law requiring the immediate euthanasia (and therefore prohibiting the slaughter for consumption) of certain nonambulatory or "downed" animals (those who are too sick or injured to stand or walk) found in slaughterhouses. While the statute

covered all animals going to slaughter, as well as a variety of places they might be found, the case before the Court addressed only downed pigs and only downed pigs that were found in slaughterhouses.

National Meat Association v. Harris

United States Supreme Court, 2012
565 U.S. 452, 132 S. Ct. 965, 181 L. Ed. 2d 950

Justice KAGAN delivered the opinion of the Court.

The Federal Meat Inspection Act (FMIA or Act), 21 U.S.C. § 601 *et seq.*, regulates the inspection, handling, and slaughter of livestock for human consumption. We consider here whether the FMIA expressly preempts a California law dictating what slaughterhouses must do with pigs that cannot walk, known in the trade as nonambulatory pigs. We hold that the FMIA forecloses the challenged applications of the state statute.

I

A

The FMIA regulates a broad range of activities at slaughterhouses to ensure both the safety of meat and the humane handling of animals. First enacted in 1906, after Upton Sinclair's muckraking novel *The Jungle* sparked an uproar over conditions in the meatpacking industry, the Act establishes "an elaborate system of inspecti[ng]" live animals and carcasses in order "to prevent the shipment of impure, unwholesome, and unfit meat and meat-food products." *Pittsburgh Melting Co. v. Totten*, 248 U.S. 1, 4–5 (1918). And since amended in 1978, see 92 Stat. 1069, the FMIA requires all slaughterhouses to comply with the standards for humane handling and slaughter of animals set out in the Humane Methods of Slaughter Act of 1958, (HMSA), 72 Stat. 862, 7 U.S.C. § 1901 *et seq.*, which originally applied only to slaughterhouses selling meat to the Federal Government.

The Department of Agriculture's Food Safety and Inspection Service (FSIS) has responsibility for administering the FMIA to promote its dual goals of safe meat and humane slaughter. Over the years, the FSIS has issued extensive regulations to govern the inspection of animals and meat, as well as other aspects of slaughterhouses' operations and facilities. See 9 CFR § 300.1 *et seq.* (2011). The FSIS employs about 9,000 inspectors, veterinarians, and investigators to implement its inspection regime and . . . [i]n fiscal year 2010, those personnel examined about 147 million head of livestock and carried out more than 126,000 "humane handling verification procedures."

The FSIS's inspection procedure begins with an "ante-mortem" examination of each animal brought to a slaughterhouse. See 9 CFR § 309.1. If the inspector finds no evidence of disease or injury, he approves the animal for slaughter. If, at the other end of the spectrum, the inspector sees that an animal is dead or dying, comatose, suffering from a high fever, or afflicted with a serious disease or condition, he designates the animal as "U.S. Condemned." . . . A condemned animal (if not already dead) must be killed apart from the slaughtering facilities where food is produced, and no part of its carcass may be sold for human consumption. See § 309.13(a); 21 U.S.C. § 610(c).

The inspector also has an intermediate option: If he determines that an animal has a less severe condition — or merely suspects the animal of having a disease meriting condemnation — he classifies the animal as "U.S. Suspect." See 9 CFR § 309.2. That category includes all nonambulatory animals not found to require condemnation.[2] See § 309.2(b). Suspect livestock must be "set apart," specially monitored, and (if not reclassified because of a change in condition) "slaughtered separately from other livestock." § 309.2(n). Following slaughter, an inspector decides at a "post-mortem" examination which parts, if any, of the suspect animal's carcass may be processed into food for humans. See 9 CFR pts. 310, 311.

The regulations implementing the FMIA additionally prescribe methods for handling animals humanely at all stages of the slaughtering process. Those rules apply from the moment a truck carrying livestock "enters, or is in line to enter," a slaughterhouse's premises. And they include specific provisions for the humane treatment of animals that cannot walk. See 9 CFR § 313.2(d). Under the regulations, slaughterhouse employees may not drag conscious, nonambulatory animals, see § 313.2(d)(2), and may move them only with "equipment suitable for such purposes," § 313.2(d)(3). Similarly, employees must place nonambulatory animals, as well as other sick and disabled livestock, in covered pens sufficient to protect the animals from "adverse climatic conditions." See § 313.2(d)(1); § 313.1(c).

The FMIA contains an express preemption provision, at issue here, addressing state laws on these and similar matters. That provision's first sentence reads: "Requirements within the scope of this [Act] with respect to premises, facilities and operations of any establishment at which inspection is provided under . . . this [Act] which are in addition to, or different than those made under this [Act] may not be imposed by any State." 21 U.S.C. § 678.[3]

B

In 2008, the Humane Society of the United States released an undercover video showing workers at a slaughterhouse in California dragging, kicking, and electro-shocking sick and disabled cows in an effort to move them. The video led the Federal Government to institute the largest beef recall in U.S. history in order to prevent consumption of meat from diseased animals. Of greater relevance here, the video also prompted the California legislature to strengthen a pre-existing statute

---

2. The FSIS's regulations define "non-ambulatory disabled livestock" as "livestock that cannot rise from a recumbent position or that cannot walk, including, but not limited to, those with broken appendages, severed tendons or ligaments, nerve paralysis, fractured vertebral column, or metabolic conditions." § 309.2(b).

3. The preemption provision also includes a saving clause, which states that the Act "shall not preclude any State . . . from making requirement[s] or taking other action, consistent with this [Act], with respect to any other matters regulated under this [Act]." 21 U.S.C. § 678; see n. 10, *infra*.

governing the treatment of nonambulatory animals and to apply that statute to slaughterhouses regulated under the FMIA.

As amended, the California law—§ 599f of the state penal code—provides in relevant part:

"(a) No slaughterhouse, stockyard, auction, market agency, or dealer shall buy, sell, or receive a nonambulatory animal.

"(b) No slaughterhouse shall process, butcher, or sell meat or products of nonambulatory animals for human consumption.

"(c) No slaughterhouse shall hold a nonambulatory animal without taking immediate action to humanely euthanize the animal." Cal. Penal Code Ann. § 599f (West 2010).

The maximum penalty for violating any of these prohibitions is one year in jail and a $20,000 fine. See § 599f(h).

Petitioner National Meat Association (NMA) is a trade association representing meatpackers and processors, including operators of swine slaughterhouses. It sued to enjoin the enforcement of § 599f against those slaughterhouses, principally on the ground that the FMIA preempts application of the state law. The District Court granted the NMA's motion for a preliminary injunction, reasoning that § 599f is expressly preempted because it requires swine "to be handled in a manner other than that prescribed by the FMIA" and its regulations. App. to Pet. for Cert. 36a. But the United States Court of Appeals for the Ninth Circuit vacated the injunction. According to that court, the FMIA does not expressly preempt § 599f because the state law regulates only "the kind of animal that may be slaughtered," and not the inspection or slaughtering process itself.

* * *

II

The FMIA's preemption clause sweeps widely—and in so doing, blocks the applications of § 599f challenged here. The clause prevents a State from imposing any additional or different—even if non-conflicting—requirements that fall within the scope of the Act and concern a slaughterhouse's facilities or operations. And at every turn § 599f imposes additional or different requirements on swine slaughterhouses: It compels them to deal with nonambulatory pigs on their premises in ways that the federal Act and regulations do not. In essence, California's statute substitutes a new regulatory scheme for the one the FSIS uses. Where under federal law a slaughterhouse may take one course of action in handling a nonambulatory pig, under state law the slaughterhouse must take another.

Consider first what the two statutes tell a slaughterhouse to do when (as not infrequently occurs) a pig becomes injured and thus nonambulatory sometime after delivery to the slaughterhouse.[5] Section 599f(c) prohibits the slaughterhouse

---

5. The percentage of pigs becoming nonambulatory after delivery varies by slaughterhouse

from "hold[ing]" such an animal "without taking immediate action to humanely euthanize" it. And § 599f(b) provides that no part of the animal's carcass may be "process[ed]" or "butcher[ed]" to make food. By contrast, under the FMIA and its regulations, a slaughterhouse may hold (without euthanizing) any nonambulatory pig that has not been condemned. And the slaughterhouse may process or butcher such an animal's meat for human consumption, subject to an FSIS official's approval at a post-mortem inspection. The State's proscriptions thus exceed the FMIA's. To be sure, nothing in the federal Act requires what the state law forbids (or forbids what the state law requires); California is right to note that "[t]he FMIA does not mandate that 'U.S. Suspect' [nonambulatory] animals . . . be placed into the human food production process." But that is irrelevant, because the FMIA's preemption clause covers not just conflicting, but also different or additional state requirements. It therefore precludes California's effort in § 599f(b) and (c) to impose new rules, beyond any the FSIS has chosen to adopt, on what a slaughterhouse must do with a pig that becomes nonambulatory during the production process.

Similarly, consider how the state and federal laws address what a slaughterhouse should do when a pig is non-ambulatory at the time of delivery, usually because of harsh transportation conditions.[6] Section 599f(a) of the California law bars a slaughterhouse from "receiv[ing]" or "buy[ing]" such a pig, thus obligating the slaughterhouse to refuse delivery of the animal. But that directive, too, deviates from any imposed by federal law. A regulation issued under the FMIA specifically authorizes slaughterhouses to buy disabled or diseased animals (including nonambulatory swine), by exempting them from a general prohibition on such purchases. See 9 CFR § 325.20(c). And other regulations contemplate that slaughterhouses will in fact take, rather than refuse, receipt of nonambulatory swine. Recall that the FMIA's regulations provide for the inspection of all pigs at delivery—in the case of nonambulatory pigs, often right on the truck. They further instruct slaughterhouses to kill and dispose of any nonambulatory pigs labeled "condemned," and to slaughter separately those marked "suspect." In short, federal law establishes rules for handling and slaughtering nonambulatory pigs brought to a slaughterhouse, rather than ordering them returned to sender. So § 599f(a) and the FMIA require different things of a slaughterhouse confronted with a delivery truck containing nonambulatory swine. The former says "do not receive or buy them"; the latter does not.

The Humane Society counters that at least § 599f(a)'s ban on buying nonambulatory animals escapes preemption because that provision applies no matter when or

---

from 0.1 percent to over 1 percent. See McGlone, Fatigued Pigs: The Final Link, Pork Magazine 14 (Mar.2006). About 100 million pigs are slaughtered each year in the United States, see Dept. of Agriculture, National Agricultural Statistics Service, Livestock Slaughter 13 (Jan.2011), so those percentages work out to between 100,000 and 1,000,000 pigs.

6. According to one estimate, almost half of one percent of the pigs slaughtered annually in the United States become nonambulatory during the trip from farm to slaughterhouse. See National Pork Board, Transport Quality Assurance Handbook 25 (Version 4, 2010). About half that many die during transport. See ibid.

where a purchase takes place. The argument proceeds in three steps: (1) §599f(a)'s ban covers purchases of non-ambulatory pigs made prior to delivery, away from the slaughterhouse itself (say, at a farm or auction); (2) the State may regulate such offsite purchases because they do not involve a slaughterhouse's "premises, facilities and operations," which is a condition of preemption under the FMIA; and (3) no different result should obtain just because a slaughterhouse structures its swine purchases to occur at delivery, on its own property.

But this argument fails on two grounds. First, its preliminary steps have no foundation in the record. Until a stray comment at oral argument, neither the State nor the Humane Society had disputed the NMA's assertion that slaughterhouses buy pigs at delivery (or still later, upon successful ante-mortem inspection). Nor had the parties presented evidence that a significant number of pigs become non-ambulatory before shipment, when any offsite purchases would occur. The record therefore does not disclose whether §599f(a)'s ban on purchase ever applies beyond the slaughterhouse gate, much less how an application of that kind would affect a slaughterhouse's operations. And because that is so, we have no basis for deciding whether the FMIA would preempt it. Second, even assuming that a State could regulate offsite purchases, the concluding step of the Humane Society's argument would not follow. The FMIA's preemption clause expressly focuses on "premises, facilities and operations"—at bottom, the slaughtering and processing of animals at a given location. So the distinction between a slaughterhouse's site-based activities and its more far-flung commercial dealings is not, as the Humane Society contends, an anomaly that courts should strain to avoid. It is instead a fundamental feature of the FMIA's preemption clause.

For that reason, the Humane Society's stronger argument concerns California's effort to regulate the *last* stage of a slaughterhouse's business—the ban in §599f(b) on "sell[ing] meat or products of nonambulatory animals for human consumption." The Government acknowledges that the FMIA's preemption clause does not usually foreclose "state regulation of the commercial sales activities of slaughterhouses." And the Humane Society asserts, in line with that general rule, that §599f(b)'s ban on sales does not regulate a slaughterhouse's "operations" because it kicks in only after they have ended: Once meat from a slaughtered pig has passed a post-mortem inspection, the Act "is not concerned with whether or how it is ever actually sold." At most, the Humane Society claims, §599f(b)'s ban on sales offers an "incentiv[e]" to a slaughterhouse to take nonambulatory pigs out of the meat production process. And California may so "motivate[ ]" an operational choice without running afoul of the FMIA's preemption provision.

But this argument mistakes how the prohibition on sales operates within §599f as a whole. The sales ban is a criminal proscription calculated to help implement and enforce each of the section's other regulations—its prohibition of receipt and purchase, its bar on butchering and processing, and its mandate of immediate euthanasia. The idea—and the inevitable effect—of the provision is to make sure that slaughterhouses remove nonambulatory pigs from the production process (or keep them out of the process from the beginning) by criminalizing the sale of their meat. That, we think, is something more than an "incentive" or "motivat[or]"; the sales ban instead functions as a command to slaughterhouses to structure their operations in the exact way the remainder of §599f mandates. And indeed, if the sales ban were to avoid the FMIA's preemption clause, then any State could impose any regulation on slaughterhouses just by framing it as a ban on the sale of meat produced in whatever way the State disapproved. That would make a mockery of the FMIA's preemption provision. Cf. *Engine Mfrs. Assn. v. South Coast Air Quality Management Dist.*, 541 U.S. 246, 255, 124 S.Ct. 1756, 158 L.Ed.2d 529 (2004) (stating that it "would make no sense" to allow state regulations to escape preemption because they addressed the purchase, rather than manufacture, of a federally regulated product). Like the rest of §599f, the sales ban regulates how slaughterhouses must deal with non-ambulatory pigs on their premises. The FMIA therefore preempts it for all the same reasons.

III

California's and the Humane Society's broadest argument against preemption maintains that all of §599f's challenged provisions fall outside the "scope" of the FMIA because they exclude a class of animals from the slaughtering process. See 21 U.S.C. §678 (preempting certain requirements "within the scope of this [Act]"). According to this view, the Act (and the FSIS's authority under it) extends only to "animals that are going to be turned into meat,"—or to use another phrase, animals that will "be slaughtered . . . for purposes of human food production." Section 599f avoids the scope of the Act, respondents claim, by altogether removing nonambulatory pigs from the slaughtering process.[8] The Ninth Circuit accepted this argument, analogizing §599f to state laws upheld in two other Circuits banning the slaughter of horses for human consumption. 599 F.3d, at 1098 (discussing *Cavel Int'l., Inc. v. Madigan*, 500 F.3d 551 (C.A.7 2007), and *Empacadora de Carnes de Fresnillo, S.A. de C.V. v. Curry*, 476 F.3d 326 (C.A.5 2007)). According to the Court of Appeals, "states are free to decide which animals may be turned into meat." 599 F.3d, at 1098, 1099.

We think not. The FMIA's scope includes not only "animals that are going to be turned into meat," but animals on a slaughterhouse's premises that will never suffer that fate. The Act's implementing regulations themselves exclude many classes of animals from the slaughtering process. Swine with hog cholera, for example, are disqualified, see 9 CFR §309.5(a); so too are swine and other livestock "affected with anthrax," §309.7(a). Indeed, the federal regulations prohibit the slaughter of any

---

8. California's brief sometimes casts its argument in terms of the "operations" language of the FMIA's preemption clause (although the State appeared to abandon this phrasing at oral argument). In this version of the claim, California contends that the "operations" of a slaughterhouse are only those "of federal concern," and that excluding a class of animals from the slaughtering process does not impinge on such operations. We see no real difference between saying that a categorical exclusion of animals does not implicate "operations of federal concern" and saying that it does not fall within the scope of the Act. Accordingly, our answer to both forms of the argument is the same.

nonambulatory *cattle* for human consumption. See § 309.3(e). As these examples demonstrate, one vital function of the Act and its regulations is to ensure that some kinds of livestock delivered to a slaughterhouse's gates will *not* be turned into meat. Under federal law, nonambulatory pigs are not among those excluded animals. But that is to say only that § 599f's requirements differ from those of the FMIA—not that § 599f's requirements fall outside the FMIA's scope.

Nor are respondents right to suggest that § 599f's exclusion avoids the FMIA's scope because it is designed to ensure the humane treatment of pigs, rather than the safety of meat. That view misunderstands the authority—and indeed responsibility—that the FMIA gives to federal officials. Since 1978, when Congress incorporated the HMSA's standards, the FMIA has required slaughterhouses to follow prescribed methods of humane handling, so as to minimize animals' pain and suffering. See 21 U.S.C. §§ 603(b), 610(b). A violation of those standards is a crime, see § 676, and the Secretary of Agriculture can suspend inspections at—and thus effectively shut down—a slaughterhouse that disobeys them, see §§ 603(b), 610(c). To implement the Act's humane-handling provisions, the FSIS has issued detailed regulations, see 9 CFR pt. 313, including some specifically addressing animals that cannot walk, see §§ 313.2(d), 313.1(c). Those rules, as earlier noted, apply throughout the time an animal is on a slaughterhouse's premises, from the moment a delivery truck pulls up to the gate. So the FMIA addresses not just food safety, but humane treatment as well. Even California conceded at oral argument that the FSIS could issue regulations under the FMIA, similar to § 599f, mandating the euthanasia of nonambulatory swine. If that is so—and it is, because of the FSIS's authority over humane-handling methods—then § 599f's requirements must fall within the FMIA's scope.

The Circuit decisions upholding state bans on slaughtering horses, on which the Ninth Circuit relied, do not demand any different conclusion. We express no view on those decisions, except to say that the laws sustained there differ from § 599f in a significant respect. A ban on butchering horses for human consumption works at a remove from the sites and activities that the FMIA most directly governs. When such a ban is in effect, no horses will be delivered to, inspected at, or handled by a slaughterhouse, because no horses will be ordered for purchase in the first instance. But § 599f does not and cannot work in that way. As earlier noted, many nonambulatory pigs become disabled either in transit to or after arrival at a slaughterhouse. So even with § 599f in effect, a swine slaughterhouse will encounter nonambulatory pigs. In that circumstance, § 599f tells the slaughterhouse what to do with those animals. Unlike a horse slaughtering ban, the statute thus reaches into the slaughterhouse's facilities and affects its daily activities. And in so doing, the California law runs smack into the FMIA's regulations. So whatever might be said of other bans on slaughter, § 599f imposes requirements within—and indeed at the very heart of—the FMIA's scope.[10]

---

10. We finally reject California's argument, that our reading of the FMIA's preemption provision renders its saving clause insignificant. That clause provides that States may regulate slaughterhouses

IV

The FMIA regulates slaughterhouses' handling and treatment of nonambulatory pigs from the moment of their delivery through the end of the meat production process. California's §599f endeavors to regulate the same thing, at the same time, in the same place—except by imposing different requirements. The FMIA expressly preempts such a state law. Accordingly, we reverse the judgment of the Ninth Circuit, and remand this case for further proceedings consistent with this opinion.

Notes

1. With the exception of its holding striking the statute's prohibition on selling meat from downed pigs, the Supreme Court was very careful to limit the preemptive scope of its opinion to activities within the geographical boundaries of the slaughterhouse. *NMA v. Harris* thus left the California law intact with respect to nonambulatory animals found in stockyards, at dealers and auction yards, and even on trucks on their way to the slaughterhouse. Accordingly, California Penal Code section 599f, if properly enforced, still has the potential to eliminate a significant amount of animal abuse and suffering.

In this regard, in *People v. Santorsola*, 225 Cal. App. 4th Supp. 12 (2014), the defendant was charged with selling nonambulatory animals at his auction, in violation of Section 599f. The trial court dismissed the charges, concluding that they were preempted by the FMIA, based on *NMA v. Harris*. On appeal, the court reversed.

> The People argue that section 599f is preempted only to the extent that it seeks to regulate premises, facilities and operations of establishments at which inspections are provided under the FMIA and so does not preempt the provisions that apply to livestock auctions like those conducted by respondent, which are contained in subdivisions (d) and (e) of section 599f. Respondent argues that there is no language in *Harris* that specifically singles out auction houses as exempt from the FMIA contending that the Supreme Court specifically referenced slaughterhouses only because the petitioner there, National Meat Association, was "a trade association representing meatpackers and processors, including operators of swine slaughterhouses" and "sued to enjoin the enforcement of §599f against those slaughterhouses. . . ."

---

as to "other matters," not addressed in the express preemption clause, as long as those laws are "consistent with" the FMIA. 21 U.S.C. §678. So, for example, the Government acknowledges that state laws of general application (workplace safety regulations, building codes, etc.) will usually apply to slaughterhouses. Moreover, because the FMIA's express preemption provision prevents States from imposing only "addition[al]" or "different" requirements, §678, States may exact civil or criminal penalties for animal cruelty or other conduct that also violates the FMIA. See §678; cf. *Bates v. Dow Agrosciences, LLC*, 544 U.S. 431, 447 (2005) (holding that a preemption clause barring state laws "in addition to or different" from a federal Act does not interfere with an "equivalent" state provision). Although the FMIA preempts much state law involving slaughterhouses, it thus leaves some room for the States to regulate.

* * *

... Respondent does not identify any part of the FMIA that would require inspection of an auction where cattle are bought and sold, but are not killed, canned, salted, packed, or rendered and this court has not found any such provision.

Nor do the federal regulations governing the inspections under the FMIA show an intent to extend the scope of inspections beyond those at the places where animals are killed and their carcasses processed.

* * *

... "When the holding pens of an official establishment are located in a public stockyard and are reserved for the exclusive use of the establishment, such pens shall be regarded as part of the premises of that establishment and the operator of the establishment shall be responsible for compliance with all requirements of the regulations in this subchapter with respect to such pens." (9 C.F.R § 309.1(b) (2014).) There is nothing in the record that would show that respondent's auction is a holding pen located in a public stockyard and reserved for the use of an official establishment, and so respondent's auction is not brought within the preemptive scope of the FMIA by the regulations governing its enforcement.

Because respondent's auction is not an establishment subject to inspection under the FMIA, the charges alleged against respondent based on the violation of Penal Code section 599f, subdivisions (d) and (e) are not preempted and the judgment of the trial court dismissing those charges is reversed.

225 Cal App. 4th Supp. at 16–18.

2. The Supreme Court in *NMA v. Harris* also made it clear that federal law does not preempt state laws that are "equivalent" to the FMIA. Therefore, state anti-cruelty laws can be enforced in slaughterhouses, and their penalties invoked, to the extent the requirements they impose are not "in addition to or different from" those under the FMIA and its incorporation of the HMSA.

3. The Supreme Court in *NMA v. Harris* reversed the Ninth Circuit's opinion, which held, *inter alia*, that the states' traditional power to regulate the treatment of animals within their borders logically extended to the determinations made by the California legislature in enacting section 599f:

The district court sought to distinguish *Cavel* and *Empacadora*: "A non-ambulatory pig is not a 'type of meat.' A pig is a pig. A pig that is laying down is a pig. A pig with three legs is a pig. A fatigued or diseased pig is a pig. Calling it something else does not change the type of meat produced." In effect, the district court reasoned that states may ban the slaughter of certain species, but once a state allows a species to be slaughtered, it cannot impose further restrictions. Hogwash.

States aren't limited to excluding animals from slaughter on a species-wide basis. What if a state wanted to ban the slaughter of a specific breed of pig but not the entire species? Or to allow wild dogs and horses to be slaughtered, but not domesticated companions? And what if, in response to a population problem, a state only banned the slaughter of female cattle? Or, perhaps due to ethical concerns, prohibited the slaughter of pregnant or newborn animals, or the slaughter of non-free-range animals? Regulating what kinds of animals may be slaughtered calls for a host of practical, moral and public health judgments that go far beyond those made in the FMIA. These are the kinds of judgments reserved to the states, and nothing in the FMIA requires states to make them on a species-wide basis or not at all. Federal law regulates the meat inspection process; states are free to decide which animals may be turned into meat.

It is possible that a state may go too far in regulating what "kind of animal" may be slaughtered. For example, a state may feel that federal inspection standards for diamond-skin disease (9 C.F.R. § 311.6), arthritis (*id.* § 311.7) or sexual odor of swine (*id.* § 311.20) are too lenient. The state may try to establish stricter inspection standards, and style the new standards as a regulation of the "kind of animal" that may be slaughtered: "The kind of pig that tests positive under procedure X for sexual odor may not be slaughtered." Or enforcement of a state regulation of what "kind of animal" may be slaughtered might require certain inspections: "Pigs with arthritis may not be slaughtered. Slaughterhouses shall perform Y and Z procedures to screen for the condition." Such regulations could effectively establish a parallel state meat-inspection system.

We need not decide what limits the express preemption provision places on such regulations. California's prohibition of the slaughter of nonambulatory animals does not duplicate federal procedures; it withdraws from slaughter animals that are unable to walk to their death. This prohibition doesn't require *any* additional or different inspections than does the FMIA, and is thus not a regulation of the "premises, facilities and operations" of slaughterhouses. There is no express preemption here.

National Meat Ass'n v. Brown, 599 F.3d 1093, 1098–99 (9th Cir. 2010), *rev'd sub nom. National Meat Ass'n v. Harris*, 132 S. Ct. 965 (2012), and *vacated sub nom. National Meat Ass'n v. Harris*, 680 F.3d 1193 (9th Cir. 2012).

4. There is an easily traceable connection between the number of nonambulatory animals in the slaughter pipeline and modern practices that lead to animals who grow to extreme muscle and body size in a historically short period of time. Does California Penal Code section 599f have any influence on these practices of intensive confinement and fast-growth high-yield animal production?

5. The California law was based on the legislature's recognition that animals who were too sick or injured to stand or walk (1) were possibly suffering significantly

and should thus be immediately euthanized and (2) had a much higher chance of having diseases that could be passed on to consumers. The law was based in both animal welfare concerns and in the commercial interest in keeping California pork products healthy for consumers. Plaintiff National Meat Association seemed to be arguing that it did not consider these to be important enough concerns to justify the loss of a small percentage of profit for the pork industry. These issues were not considered when the Supreme Court found the California law was preempted in slaughterhouses, demonstrating the power of the Supremacy Clause even in cases involving a clash between areas long within the purview of the states and federal policy/agency alignment with commercial interests.

6. Several states in addition to California have enacted legislation to address the concerns over "downed" animals being slaughtered for meat. *See, e.g.,* WASH. REV. CODE ANN. § 16.52.225 (enacted in 2004, prohibiting anyone from transporting or accepting delivery of downed animals (not limited to cows) at slaughterhouses, feedlots or livestock markets; also requiring that non-ambulatory animals be "humanely euthanized"); 510 ILL. COMP. STAT. ANN. § 70/7.5 (2017); OR. REV. STAT. § 167.351 (2017); MICH. COMP. LAWS § 287.127a (2018). The editors are not aware of any challenges to these laws.

7. In *Baur v. Veneman*, 352 F.3d 625 (2d Cir. 2003), plaintiffs (Michael Baur and Farm Sanctuary, Inc.) sued the Secretary of Agriculture and the USDA under the FMIA and the Federal Food, Drug, and Cosmetic Act, 21 U.S.C. §§ 301–399a (FFDCA), seeking to have the USDA ban the use of downed livestock as food for human consumption. The complaint alleged that such animals, who collapse for unknown reasons and are too ill to walk or stand prior to slaughter, are particularly likely to be infected with Transmissible Spongiform Encephalopathies, such as Mad Cow Disease (BSE) (discussed in the Notes earlier in this chapter). When the case was filed, USDA regulations allowed downed livestock to be used for human consumption after passing a mandatory post-mortem inspection by a veterinary officer. Plaintiffs claimed this policy violated the FMIA and the FFDCA and further alleged that the consumption of downed animals creates a serious risk of disease transmission—most specifically the risk that humans will contract a variant of Creutzfeldt-Jakob Disease, a fatal disease caused by eating beef products contaminated with BSE. The lower court granted defendants' motion to dismiss for lack of standing, based on plaintiffs' failure to establish a cognizable injury under Article III, section 2 of the U.S. Constitution. The Second Circuit Court of Appeals reversed, holding that "exposure to an enhanced risk of disease transmission may qualify as injury-in-fact in consumer food and safety suits" and that plaintiffs had alleged a "sufficiently credible risk of harm" to survive a motion to dismiss.

In 2004, the USDA adopted an interim rule preventing the slaughter of downed cows for human food. 69 Fed. Reg. 1862 (Jan. 12, 2004) (codified July 13, 2007, at 9 C.F.R. pts. 309, 310, 318). That rule provided a loophole, however, allowing downed cows to be processed for human food if they did not become nonambulatory until after they reached the slaughterhouse. Those animals had to be inspected but could still be slaughtered as long as they could stand. The loophole led to abusive practices by slaughterhouse workers attempting to coerce the downed cows to stand, such as those discussed in Note 8 and in the *National Meat Association* case with respect to the Hallmark slaughter facility. In 2009, the USDA adopted a new rule permanently banning the slaughter of *all* downed adult cows for food. 9 C.F.R. § 309.3.

8. After HSUS obtained evidence of cruelty being committed at the Hallmark plant, it filed a complaint (as "Relator," providing evidence to the U.S. Attorney General, based on which the government later intervened as plaintiff) under the federal False Claims Act (FCA) (31 U.S.C. §§ 3729, *et seq.*), alleging that defendants Hallmark Meat Packing Company and others falsely certified to the USDA that cows slaughtered at Hallmark's Chino, California facility were handled humanely and in accordance with the law. Additional claims included fraudulent concealment, negligent misrepresentation, payment by mistake and breach of contract. Hallmark had entered into an agreement with Westland Meat Company (another defendant) pursuant to which Hallmark slaughtered the cows and Westland processed the meat for human consumption. In 2003, Westland bid for and was awarded 140 contracts for the USDA's National School Lunch Program, whereby Hallmark/Westland meat would be consumed by thousands of schoolchildren around the country. An important element of the bidding process is the bidder's certification that it has complied with all relevant federal laws and regulations. During the term of the School Lunch contracts, however, an HSUS employee worked at the Hallmark slaughter facility and videotaped extensive footage showing the cruel handling of non-ambulatory cows, allegedly violating 31 U.S.C. § 3729(a)(1) of the FCA (among other provisions), for "False Certification of Compliance with Humane Handling/Downer/Non-Ambulatory Disabled Cattle Provisions." Additional testimony provided by a former Hallmark employee who had worked there for 25 years further confirmed that downed cows were routinely mishandled and treated inhumanely during his employment at Hallmark. Based on this and other evidence, in cross-motions for summary judgment brought by both sides, the court found triable issues of fact and denied most of the motions. *United States of America, ex rel The Humane Society of the United States v. Hallmark Meat Packing Co., et al.,* 2013 U.S. Dist. LEXIS 126945 (C.D. Cal. Apr. 30, 2013).

Note that if the HSUS employee's videotaping at the facility had taken place in a state with a so-called "Ag-Gag" law in effect (discussed in Section 1.C of this chapter), this conduct, disclosing illegal and inhumane activities at the facility, itself may have been a criminal offense. As noted in *NMA v. Harris*, after the results of the investigation were disclosed, 143 million pounds of beef were recalled, reportedly the largest recall in U.S. history. Associated Press, *California Beef Plant Worker Sentenced in Abuse Case*, USA TODAY (Sept. 24, 2008).

After the cross-motions for summary judgment did not resolve the case, a settlement was reached, with the defendants paying over $3 million, and a final judgment was entered against Westland for more than $155 million, the largest monetary judgment ever based on animal abuse. As noted in Chapter 3, before the civil case settlement, in a separate criminal proceeding, two Hallmark employees who were caught on video abusing the animals were charged with and pled guilty to violations of California Penal Code sections 597 (animal cruelty) and 599f (regarding mistreatment of non-ambulatory animals).

9. The USDA's ban on the slaughter of downed adult cows did not extend to other downed animals such as pigs, sheep and other species; nor did it cover calves. Two rulemaking petitions subsequently were filed to address these issues. Farm Sanctuary filed a petition seeking a rule that would permanently ban the slaughter of all downed animals and HSUS filed a narrower petition trying to close the loophole excluding calves from the downed cow rule. In July of 2016, the USDA issued a final rule, closing the regulatory loophole allowing the slaughter of calves who are too sick or injured to walk, instead requiring that they be promptly and humanely euthanized. 9 C.F.R. 309 (2016).

10. While not generally farmed in the traditional sense, more fish (and some marine mammals) are killed and eaten for food than all land animals combined — and their protections have been at the center of legislation and litigation for years. The Marine Mammal Protection Act, discussed in Chapter 9, provides special protections for the animals identified in the title of the law, but does not directly address commercial fisheries. There are a few federal laws governing commercial fisheries, most notably the Magnuson-Stevens Fishery Conservation and Management Act, 16 U.S.C. § 1801 *et seq.*, and each state has licensing and harvesting requirements and restrictions based on species and other criteria. One of the most controversial fishing practices is that of "shark finning."

Shark fin soup is common fare internationally and in some areas of the United States. It has been estimated that each year the fins from between twenty-six and seventy-three million sharks are used to supply the global demand for shark fins, which fuels shark finning activity. Shelley C. Clark, *et al., Global estimates of shark catches using trade records from commercial markets,* ECOLOGY LETTERS, 9: 1115–126 (2006). The commercial "finners" pull live sharks from the sea and slice off their fins, and sometimes their tails, saving only those parts. The sharks, still alive and profusely bleeding, are then tossed back into the ocean where they die. In the past century, shark finning has contributed to an estimated 90 percent decline in some shark populations across the globe. E. Griffin *et al.,* PREDATORS AS PREY: WHY HEALTHY OCEANS NEED SHARKS 3 (Oceana 2008). As shark populations plummet, conservationists and scientists are becoming increasingly concerned about the protection of sharks and the well-being of the oceans, and legislatures and international bodies have taken action to combat the practices threatening shark populations. Paula Walker, *Oceans in the Balance: As the Sharks Go, So Do We,* 17 ANIMAL L. 97, 114 (2010).

For its part, the United States enacted the Shark Finning Prohibition Act of 2000 (SFPA) as an amendment to the Magnuson-Stevens Act, making shark finning within the jurisdiction of the United States a federal crime. 16 U.S.C. § 1857(1)(P) (2000). Additionally, the SFPA calls for the Secretary of Commerce to enter into treaties to protect shark species and establish an international ban on finning. 16 U.S.C. § 1822 (2000). In 2011, the Shark Conservation Act of 2010 (SCA), Pub. L. No. 111-348, increased shark protection and strengthened the SFPA by making it illegal to remove shark fins at sea and requiring all landed sharks (sharks brought to mainland ports) to have fins and tails attached.

This issue has also been addressed at the state level, because the federal law does not govern state sales, possession or treatment of fish, nor does it control international fishing operations. For example, in 2012 California enacted a law making it illegal to possess, sell, offer for sale, trade or distribute a detached shark fin without a permit. CAL. FISH & GAME CODE §§ 2021, 2021.5 ("Shark Fin Law"). In enacting the law, the California legislature made the following official findings:

(a) Sharks, or elasmobranchs, are critical to the health of the ocean ecosystem.

(b) Sharks are particularly susceptible to decline due to overfishing because they are slow to reach reproductive maturity and birth small litters, and cannot rebuild their populations quickly once they are overfished.

(c) Sharks occupy the top of the marine food chain. Their decline is an urgent problem that upsets the balance of species in ocean ecosystems and negatively affects other fisheries. It constitutes a serious threat to the ocean ecosystem and biodiversity.

(d) The practice of shark finning, where a shark is caught, its fins cut off, and the carcass dumped back into the water, causes tens of millions of sharks to die each year. Sharks starve to death, may be slowly eaten by other fish, or drown because most sharks need to keep moving to force water through their gills for oxygen.

(e) Data from federal and international agencies show a decline in shark populations worldwide.

(f) California is a market for shark fin and this demand helps drive the practice of shark finning. The market also drives shark declines. By impacting the demand for shark fins, California can help ensure that sharks do not become extinct as a result of shark finning.

(g) Shark fin often contains high amounts of mercury, which has been proven dangerous to consumers' health.

CAL. STATS. 2011, Ch. 524 (A.B. 376) § 1(a)-(g).

Two lawsuits were filed in 2012 challenging California's Shark Fin Law. The Humane Society of the United States, the Asian Pacific American Ocean Harmony Alliance and the Monterey Bay Aquarium Foundation intervened in both actions. In state court, plaintiff alleged violation of the Takings and Commerce Clauses of the federal constitution. Plaintiffs in federal court claimed the Shark Fin Law violated the Due Process, Commerce, Equal Protection and Supremacy Clauses. The federal case included a claim that the law had been motivated by racial animus, notwithstanding that the law's main sponsor was a Chinese-American, that many prominent Chinese-Americans supported the Shark Fin Law and that seven state legislators of Asian and Pacific Islands descent voted in favor of the law. *See* Michael Conathan and Rebecca Friendly, *Landmark Shark Fin Bill Awaits Signature of California Governor Jerry Brown*, THINK PROGRESS (Oct. 7, 2011), at *http://thinkprogress.org /climate/2011/ 10/07/338880/landmark-shark-fin-bill-awaits-signature-of-california-governor-jerry-brown/*. In addition, a February 2011 poll found that 70% of California's Chinese-American voters supported legislation to ban shark finning. *Id.*

The state case was dismissed after the court sustained defendants' demurrer with respect to the Takings Clause. *Asian American Rights Committee of California v. Edmund Brown et al.*, Case No. CGC-12-517723 (Cal. Super. Ct., San Francisco County, complaint filed Jan. 27, 2012). In the federal case, the court denied plaintiffs' motion for a preliminary injunction and the Ninth Circuit affirmed that ruling. *Chinatown Neighborhood Ass'n v. Brown*, 2013 WL 4517073 (9th Cir. Aug. 27, 2013) (unpublished). The district court then granted defendants' motion to dismiss, without leave to amend, the Ninth Circuit affirmed, and the Supreme Court denied *certiorari* review. *Chinatown Neighborhood Ass'n v. Harris*, 794 F.3d 1136 (9th Cir. 2015), *cert. denied*, 136 S. Ct. 2448 (2016).

C. "Ag-Gag" Laws

As noted earlier in this chapter, in the early 1990's several states enacted statutes criminalizing undercover investigations and unconsented photography or videography at factory farms, other agricultural facilities and slaughterhouses, and animal research facilities. N.D. CENT. CODE § 12.1-21.1–02 (2017) (originally enacted in 1991) ("No person without the effective consent of the owner may . . . [e]nter an animal facility and use or attempt to use a camera, video recorder, or any other video or audio recording equipment," among other prohibitions); MONT. CODE ANN. § 81-30-103 (2017) (originally enacted 1991) ("Farm Animal and Research Facility Protection Act"); KAN. STAT. ANN. § 47-1825 (2018) (originally enacted 1990). Such laws are known colloquially as "Ag-Gag" laws because they seek to "gag" disclosure of and discussions relating to the treatment of the animals at such facilities.

A decade later, as highly publicized videos of animal abuses at some of these facilities hit the internet and spread rapidly by YouTube and other internet sources, more states began introducing similar legislation, a limited number of which were enacted into law. Promptly upon enactment, lawsuits were filed asserting constitutional challenges to the Ag-Gag laws.

> The story of Upton Sinclair provides a clear illustration of how the First Amendment is implicated by [Ag-Gag laws]. Sinclair, in order to gather material for his novel, *The Jungle*, misrepresented his identity so he could get a job at a meat-packing plant in Chicago. Sinclair's novel, a devastating exposé of the meat-packing industry that revealed the intolerable labor conditions and unsanitary working conditions in the Chicago stockyards in the early 20th century, "sparked an uproar" and led to the passage of the

Federal Meat Inspection Act, as well as the Pure Food and Drug Act. Today, however, Upton Sinclair's conduct would expose him to criminal prosecution under [Idaho's Ag-Gag law].

Animal Legal Defense Fund v. Otter, 118 F. Supp. 3d 1195, 1201-02 (D. Idaho 2015) (finding Idaho's Ag-Gag laws constitutional), *reversed in part by Animal Legal Defense Fund v. Wasden*, 878 F.3d 1184 (9th Cir. 2018).

The following case and Notes that follow present different approaches by various courts addressing constitutionality questions relative to different states' Ag-Gag laws.

Animal Legal Defense Fund v. Herbert

United States District Court, District of Utah, 2017
263 F. Supp. 3d 1193

Utah recently joined the growing number of states to enact so-called "ag-gag" laws—laws that target undercover investigations at agricultural operations. Utah's version operates, in relevant part, by criminalizing both lying to get into an agricultural operation and filming once inside. Plaintiffs contend the law violates their First Amendment rights. For the reasons below, the court agrees.

BACKGROUND

For as long as farmers have put food on American tables, the government has endeavored to support and protect the agricultural industry. In an address to Congress shortly after the Revolutionary War, George Washington, an ardent tobacco farmer, declared that "agriculture is of primary importance," and argued that the rapid growth of the young nation rendered "the cultivation of the soil more and more an object of public patronage." Congress heeded the call, and federal legislation in the ensuing decades led to the development of millions of acres of farmland across the country.

As agriculture expanded, so too did governmental investment in it. Toward the end of the nineteenth century, President Lincoln established the Department of Agriculture—known then as "The People's Department"—and Congress began providing cash to states to conduct agricultural research. In the mid-twentieth century, following the Great Depression, President Roosevelt's administration went so far as to pay farmers to stop growing crops and to destroy existing crops and livestock in order to stabilize prices by artificially limiting supply. To this day, the federal government has continued to support the agricultural industry through measures like nonrecourse loans, subsidies, and price guarantees, as have the states, all of which have enacted right-to-farm laws.[5] In short, governmental protection of

---

5. Rita-Marie Cain Reid & Amber L. Kingery, *Putting A Gag on Farm Whistleblowers: The Right to Lie and the Right to Remain Silent Confront State Agricultural Protectionism*, 11 J. Food L. & Pol'y 31, 34 (2015); Charlene C. Kwan, *Fixing the Farm Bill: Using the "Permanent Provisions" in Agricultural Law to Achieve WTO Compliance*, 36 B.C. Envtl. Aff. L. Rev. 571, 575–85 (2009).

the American agricultural industry is not new, and has taken a variety of forms over the last two hundred years.

What is new, however, is the recent spate of state laws that have assumed an altogether novel approach: restricting speech related to agricultural operations. These so-called "ag-gag" laws have their genesis in the 1990s. Around that time, animal rights advocates had begun conducting undercover investigations to expose animal abuse at various facilities.[6] After these initial investigations became public, Kansas, Montana, and North Dakota all enacted ag-gag laws. The laws criminalized entering an animal facility and filming without consent.[8]

Nobody was ever charged under these laws, and for nearly two decades no new ag-gag legislation was introduced. That changed, however, after a series of high profile undercover investigations were made public in the mid to late 2000s. To name just a few, in 2007, an undercover investigator at the Westland/Hallmark Meat Company in California filmed workers forcing sick cows, many unable to walk, into the "kill box" by repeatedly shocking them with electric prods, jabbing them in the eye, prodding them with a forklift, and spraying water up their noses.[9] A 2009 investigation at Hy-Line Hatchery in Iowa revealed hundreds of thousands of unwanted day-old male chicks being funneled by conveyor belt into a macerator to be ground up live.[10] That same year, undercover investigators at a Vermont slaughterhouse operated by Bushway Packing obtained similarly gruesome footage of days-old calves being kicked, dragged, and skinned alive.[11] A few years later, an undercover investigator at E6 Cattle Company in Texas filmed workers beating cows on the head with hammers and pickaxes and leaving them to die.[12] And later that year, at Sparboe Farms in Iowa, undercover investigators documented hens with gaping, untreated wounds laying eggs in cramped conditions among decaying corpses.[13]

The publication of these and other undercover videos had devastating consequences for the agricultural facilities involved. The videos led to boycotts of facilities

---

6. *See* Lewis Bollard, *Ag-Gag: The Unconstitutionality of Laws Restricting Undercover Investigations on Farms*, 42 Envtl. L. Rep. News & Analysis 10960, 10962 (2012).

8. Kan. Stat. Ann. §47-1827(c) (2012); Mont. Code Ann. §81-30-103 (2011); N.D. Cent. Code Ann. §§12.1-21.1-01 (2011).

9. Matthew L. Wald, *Meat Packer Admits Slaughter of Sick Cows*, N.Y. Times (Mar. 13, 2008), *http://www.nytimes.com/2008/03/13/business/13meat.html*.

10. *Agriculture Industry Defends Itself Over Grisly Iowa Chick Video*, L.A. Times (Sept. 5, 2009, 11:50 AM), *http://latimesblogs.latimes.com/unleashed/2009/09/agriculture-industry-defends-itself-over-grisly-iowa-chick-video.html*.

11. *Vermont Slaughterhouse Closed Amid Animal Cruelty Allegations*, L.A. Times (Nov. 3, 2009, 4:12 PM), *http://latimesblogs.latimes.com/unleashed/2009/11/vermont-slaughterhouse-closed-amid-animal-cruelty-allegations.html*.

12. Kevin Lewis, *Charges Filed in E6 Cattle Case*, Plainview Daily Herald (May 26, 2011, 11:30 AM), *http://www.myplainview.com/news/article/Charges-filed-in-E6-Cattle-case-8414335.php*.

13. *McDonald's Cuts Egg Supplier After Undercover Animal Cruelty Video*, L.A. Times (Nov. 18, 2011, 2:24 PM), *http://latimesblogs.latimes.com/money_co/2011/11/mcdonalds-cuts-egg-supplier-after-undercover-animal-cruelty-video.html*.

by McDonald's, Target, Sam's Club, and others.[14] They led to bankruptcy and closure of facilities and criminal charges against employees and owners.[15] They led to state-wide ballot initiatives banning certain farming practices.[16] And they led to the largest meat recall in United States history, a facility's entire two years' worth of production.[17]

Over the next three years, sixteen states introduced ag-gag legislation.[18] Iowa's was the first to go into effect. It was introduced in the wake of the Iowa Sparboe Farms video, in addition to the publication of several other undercover investigations in Iowa.[19] According to its sponsors, the bill's purpose was "to crack down on activists who deliberately cast agricultural operations in a negative light and let cameras roll rather than reporting abuse immediately," and to stop "subversive acts" that could "bring down the industry," including acts committed by "extremist vegans."[20] The Iowa law prohibits obtaining access to an agricultural production facility under false pretenses and lying on a job application with the intent to commit an unauthorized act.[21]

Utah's bill came less than a month later. Representative John Mathis, the sponsor of the House bill, declared the bill was motivated by "a trend nationally of some propaganda groups . . . with a stated objective of undoing animal agriculture in the United States." Another representative (a farmer by trade) stated that the bill was targeted at "a group of people that want to put us out of business," and noted that farmers "don't want some jack wagon coming in taking a picture of them." Senator David Hinkins, the sponsor of the Senate bill, declared the bill was meant to address the "vegetarian people that [are] trying to kill the animal industry" by "hiding cameras and trying to . . . modify the films and stuff like that," explaining "[t]hat's what we're trying to prevent here."

The bill ultimately enacted in Utah consists of four provisions: a lying provision, and three recording provisions. The lying provision criminalizes "obtain[ing] access to an agricultural operation under false pretenses." The three recording provisions criminalize: (1) bugging an agricultural operation; (2) filming an agricultural operation after applying for a position with the intent to film; and (3) filming

14. Bollard, *supra* note 6, at 10960.

15. *Id.* at 10963; Matthew Shea, *Punishing Animal Rights Activists for Animal Abuse: Rapid Reporting and the New Wave of Ag-Gag Laws*, 48 Colum. J.L. & Soc. Probs. 337, 338 (2015); *Vermont Slaughterhouse Closes Amid Animal Cruelty Allegations*, L.A. Times (Nov. 3, 2009), http://latimesblogs.latimes.com/unleashed/2009/11/vermont-slaughterhouse-closed-amid-animal-cruelty-allegations.html.

16. Bollard, *supra* note 6, at 10963.

17. David Brown, *UDSA Orders Largest Meat Recall in U.S. History*, Wash. Post (Feb. 18, 2008), http://www.washingtonpost.com/wp-dyn/content/article/2008/02/17/AR2008021701530.html.

18. Jessalee Landfried, Note, *Bound & Gagged: Potential First Amendment Challenges to "Ag-Gag" Laws*, 23 Duke Envtl. L. & Pol'y F. 377, 378–79 (2013).

19. *See Undercover Investigations*, Mercy for Animals, http://www.mercyforanimals.org/investigations (listing various undercover operations).

20. Bollard, *supra* note 6, at 10965.

21. Iowa Code Ann. §717A (2012).

an agricultural operation while trespassing.[27] Governor Herbert signed the bill into law on March 20, 2012.

On February 8, 2013, Plaintiff Amy Meyer became the first person to be charged under the new law, and seemingly the only person in the country to ever be charged under an ag-gag law.[29] Meyer was arrested while filming what appeared to be a bulldozer moving a sick cow at a slaughterhouse in Draper City, Utah. Meyer was on public property at the time—meaning her actions did not fall within the statute—but the State nonetheless brought charges. It later dismissed the case against Meyer without prejudice.

Meyer, along with Animal Legal Defense Fund (ALDF) and People for the Ethical Treatment of Animals (PETA), subsequently filed this lawsuit against Gary Herbert in his capacity as Governor of Utah and Sean Reyes in his capacity as Attorney General of Utah (collectively, "the State"). Plaintiffs challenge the Act as an unconstitutional restriction on speech in violation of the First Amendment and as a violation of the Equal Protection Clause of the Fourteenth Amendment. Both sides have moved for summary judgment.[32]

ANALYSIS

Plaintiffs argue the Act is unconstitutional because it violates their First and Fourteenth Amendment rights. The State contends some or all Plaintiffs lack standing to sue, and even if some have standing, the Act is constitutional. The court first addresses the State's standing arguments, and then turns to the merits.

---

27. [*Utah Code §76-6-112 (2012)*.] The full text is below:
   (1) As used in this section, "agricultural operation" means private property used for the production of livestock, poultry, livestock products, or poultry products.
   (2) A person is guilty of agricultural operation interference if the person:
      (a) without consent from the owner of the agricultural operation, or the owner's agent, knowingly or intentionally records an image of, or sound from, the agricultural operation by leaving a recording device on the agricultural operation;
      (b) obtains access to an agricultural operation under false pretenses;
      (c) (i) applies for employment at an agricultural operation with the intent to record an image of, or sound from, the agricultural operation;
         (ii) knows, at the time that the person accepts employment at the agricultural operation, that the owner of the agricultural operation prohibits the employee from recording an image of, or sound from, the agricultural operation; and
         (iii) while employed at, and while present on, the agricultural operation, records an image of, or sound from, the agricultural operation; or
      (d) without consent from the owner of the operation or the owner's agent, knowingly or intentionally records an image of, or sound from, an agricultural operation while the person is committing criminal trespass, as described in *Section 76-6-206*, on the agricultural operation.
29. Leighton Akio Woodhouse, *Charged with the Crime of Filming a Slaughterhouse*, The Nation (July 31, 2013), *http://www.thenation.com/article/charged-crime-filming-slaughterhouse/*.
32. The court grants summary judgment if the movant shows there is "no genuine dispute as to any material fact" and the movant is "entitled to judgment as a matter of law." Fed. R. Civ. P. 56(a).

Standing

This is not the court's first time addressing Plaintiffs' standing to sue. The State initially moved to dismiss the case on this basis, and the court determined Plaintiffs had properly alleged standing. Notwithstanding the State's present objections, the court concludes that Plaintiffs have now sufficiently substantiated those allegations through declarations and deposition testimony.

The Constitution limits this court to deciding justiciable cases or controversies, a restriction courts have distilled into a three-part inquiry. To show standing to sue, a plaintiff must demonstrate (1) an injury, (2) caused by the conduct complained of, (3) that is redressible. This inquiry becomes somewhat complicated when the alleged injury, as here, is a chilling effect on speech based on a threat of future prosecution. On the one hand, "allegations of a subjective chill" or "of possible future injury do not satisfy the injury in fact requirement." On the other, "a plaintiff need not expose himself to actual arrest or prosecution to be entitled to challenge a statute."

To balance these competing interests—the constitutional requirement that an alleged injury be sufficiently concrete and the notion that a plaintiff need not take the final step of breaking the law before suing—the Tenth Circuit has developed a three-part test for a plaintiff alleging injury based on a chilling effect on speech. Such a plaintiff must demonstrate: (1) that in the past, the plaintiff engaged in the kind of speech implicated by the statute; (2) that the plaintiff has a desire, but no specific plans, to engage in the speech; and (3) that the plaintiff presently has no intention of engaging in the speech because of a credible threat the statute will be enforced.

All three Plaintiffs meet this standard. Meyer has previously engaged in speech implicated by the statute. As discussed, on one occasion she was actually arrested and charged with violating the statute. She wishes to continue engaging in speech related to animal activism, but currently has no plans to do so for fear she will be arrested again. Similarly, members of ALDF and PETA have also engaged in undercover operations in which they lied to get into agricultural facilities and filmed once inside. They now wish to conduct operations at agricultural facilities in Utah. But they presently have no intention to do so because they fear Utah may prosecute them—and rightfully so, as the State already prosecuted Meyer for conduct even less clearly covered by the Act.

The State does not meaningfully object to any of these contentions. Rather, it argues only that "Plaintiffs have not shown they have any concrete plans to actually violate the law." But that is not what the law requires. The Tenth Circuit has explicitly disclaimed any requirement that a plaintiff have actual plans to violate the challenged statute. As discussed, to establish standing to sue based on a chilling effect on speech, a plaintiff must demonstrate only "a present desire, *though no specific plans*, to engage in such speech." Plaintiffs here have met that burden.

The First Amendment

Turning to the merits, Plaintiffs argue the Act impermissibly restricts their free speech rights under the First Amendment. The First Amendment limits the State's ability to enact laws that restrict speech. Not all speech is protected by the First Amendment, but if a law restricts speech that is protectable, the State must justify the law by articulating the problem it is meant to address and demonstrating that the law is properly tailored to address that problem.

Thus, the First Amendment analysis proceeds in three parts. The court first determines whether the Act's lying and recording provisions implicate protectable speech—that is, whether the First Amendment even applies. If so, the court next decides what level of scrutiny to apply to each provision, which in turn dictates what showing the State must make to justify them. Last, the court assesses whether the State has made that showing.

A. Whether the First Amendment Applies

The first question is whether the lying[45] and recording criminalized by the Act are protectable speech under the First Amendment. The State contends the lying and recording criminalized by the Act can never be protected by the First Amendment, so the court need not engage in a First Amendment analysis. As to lying, it concedes that lies are "speech" for First Amendment purposes, but it argues that the lies implicated by the Act fall within a category the Supreme Court has deemed unprotectable. And recording, the State argues, is not speech to begin with, so it is similarly not protected by the First Amendment. Plaintiffs have the burden of demonstrating otherwise.

1. The Lying Provision

Generally, when a law restricts speech, it is subject to some level of scrutiny. Since the early days of the Republic, however, there have been certain categories of speech that do not enjoy First Amendment protection. These categories consist of speech that has such little value, and is so likely to cause harm, that the court need not conduct a case-by-case First Amendment analysis because any regulation of the speech will clearly be upheld. They include obscenity, defamation, child pornography, fraud, and true threats, among others.

Recently, in *United States v. Alvarez*, the Supreme Court addressed whether false statements belong on this list of unprotectable speech. The Court ultimately concluded that lies are not categorically unprotectable by the First Amendment, but lies that cause "legally cognizable harm" do fall outside of First Amendment protection.[50] Thus, the threshold question here is whether all of the lies prohibited by the Act cause legally cognizable harm. If so, the lying provision is immune from

---

45. As discussed, the statute actually criminalizes gaining access under "false pretenses"; the parties use "lying" as shorthand, and the court follows that lead.

50. [*U.S. v. Alvarez*, 567 U.S. 709 (2012)] at 719. No majority opinion emerged from *Alvarez*, but the plurality, concurrence, and dissent all agreed that lies are not categorically outside of First Amendment protection. . . . . Indeed, the plurality and concurrence are largely in agreement as to which lies are subject to First Amendment protection; where they depart, as discussed below, is on what level of scrutiny to apply.

First Amendment scrutiny. But if any of the lies prohibited by the Act do not cause legally cognizable harm, those lies are protectable under the First Amendment and the lying provision of the Act criminalizing them is subject to scrutiny.

The parties do not dispute this is the applicable standard, but they vigorously dispute whether the lies prohibited by the Act—"obtain[ing] access to an agricultural operation under false pretenses"—cause legally cognizable harm. The State contends they do, and points to two types of harm it believes necessarily result from such lies: (1) danger to animals and employees, and (2) trespass over property persons otherwise could not access. Plaintiffs disagree, arguing that people who lie to gain access to an agricultural facility will cause neither of these harms.

a. Danger to Animals and Employees

The State's first alleged harm—danger to animals and employees—likely qualifies as "legally cognizable harm" under *Alvarez*. But there is no evidence in the record that lying to gain access to an agricultural facility will necessarily harm animals or employees. It is certainly conceivable that some lies used to gain access to a facility might result in such harm—the job applicant, for example, who lies about being trained to use heavy equipment, or who represents that he has a safety certification he does not actually possess. But plenty of lies that fall within the purview of the Act would cause no harm at all to animals or workers—the applicant who says he has always dreamed of working at a slaughterhouse, that he doesn't mind commuting, that the hiring manager has a nice tie. Because the Act as written criminalizes lies that would cause no harm to animals or workers—i.e., lies that enjoy First Amendment protection—this rationale fails to place the lying provision outside of First Amendment scrutiny.

b. Trespass Harm

The State's other argument is that access to private property in and of itself, when procured through misrepresentation, constitutes trespassing, and trespassing is a legally cognizable harm (meaning these misrepresentations would enjoy no First Amendment protection under *Alvarez*). Plaintiffs, for their part, contend that lying to gain access is not trespassing. Consent, they argue, is a defense to trespassing, and by definition anybody charged under the Act's lying provision would have obtained consent to enter (albeit through misrepresentation). Thus, the initial question is whether misrepresentation negates consent—that is, whether a person who lies to obtain permission to access private property is a trespasser.

The answer, it seems, is not always. Neither the Utah appellate courts nor the Tenth Circuit have not spoken on the issue, but the Fourth and Seventh Circuits have. Both concluded that it depends on the type of harm (if any) the liar causes. [51] Specifically, if the person causes harm of the type the tort of trespass seeks to

---

51. *See Desnick v. Am. Broad. Cos., Inc.*, 44 F.3d 1345, 1352 (7th Cir. 1995) (Lying to gain access constitutes trespass only when the access results in an "invasion . . . of any of the specific interests that the tort of trespass seeks to protect."); *see also Food Lion, Inc. v. Capital Cities/ABC, Inc.*,

protect—interference with ownership or possession of the land—then her consent to enter becomes invalid, and from that point on she is not merely a liar, but a trespasser as well. But if the liar does not interfere with ownership or possession of the land, her consent to access the property remains valid, notwithstanding that it was obtained nefariously through misrepresentation. Thus, a competitor who enters a business to steal secrets while posing as a customer is a trespasser, as is the man who is invited into a home while posing as a repairman, but is in fact just a busybody looking to snoop around (because both have interfered with ownership or possession of the property). But the liar who causes no trespass-type harm—the restaurant critic who conceals his identity, the dinner guest who falsely claims to admire his host, or the job applicant whose resume falsely represents an interest in volunteering, [57] to name a few—is not guilty of trespassing (because no interference has occurred). In other words, under this reasoning, lying to gain entry, without more, does not itself constitute trespass.

Thus, merging the Fourth and Seventh Circuit's trespass conclusions (that a liar is not a trespasser unless and until she causes trespass-type harm) with *Alvarez*'s First Amendment conclusion (that a law criminalizing lies is immune from First Amendment scrutiny only if the lies cause legally cognizable harm), the following standard emerges: the Act here is immune from First Amendment scrutiny under the State's trespass theory only if those who gain access to an agricultural operation under false pretenses subsequently cause trespass-type harm, meaning interference with ownership or possession of the property. In those instances, they have negated their consent to enter, they are trespassers (and have therefore caused legally cognizable harm), and their lies, under *Alvarez*, receive no First Amendment protection. But if those who lie to gain access do not necessarily cause trespass-type harm (and thus, in turn, do not necessarily cause legally cognizable harm), their lies retain First Amendment protection under *Alvarez*, and the Act remains subject to scrutiny.

It is certainly possible that a lie used to gain access to an agricultural facility could cause trespass-type harm; a protestor, for example, might pose as a prospective customer, and then, after being let in the door, begin causing a scene or damaging property. But the Act also sweeps in many more trivial, harmless lies that have no discernable effect on whether a person is granted access, and, consequently, on whether a person causes any trespass-type harm. Indeed, given its broad language ("obtain[ing] access to an agricultural operation under false pretenses"), the Act on its face criminalizes, for example, an applicant's false statement during a job interview that he is a born-again Christian, that he is married with kids, that he is a fan of the local sports team. It criminalizes putting a local address on a resume when the applicant is actually applying from out of town. In short, the Act criminalizes a broad swath of lies that result in no harm at all, much less interference with ownership or

---

194 F.3d 505, 517 (4th Cir. 1999) (agreeing with "*Desnick*'s thoughtful analysis about when a consent to enter that is based on misrepresentation may be given effect").

57. *See Food Lion*, 194 F.3d at 518 (declining to "turn[] successful resume fraud into trespass").

possession of the facility—lies that are therefore entitled to First Amendment protection under *Alvarez*.

… [T]he State argued … that the court should read a causation requirement into "false pretenses" to narrow its scope solely to lies that are material to a person's access. In other words, under the State's proposed interpretation, a lie falls within the Act only if a person gains access *because of* the lie—the applicant, for example, who lies about supporting the local sports team has not violated the Act unless the agricultural facility owner would not have given consent to enter had he known the applicant in fact preferred the crosstown rival.

Setting aside the potential vagueness doctrine implications for reading this type of subjective requirement into a criminal statute, the State's proposed solution likely does not save the Act from First Amendment review. At least under the approach adopted by the Fourth and Seventh Circuits, the fact that a lie was the reason the landowner granted consent to enter (and not merely an unrelated white lie) does not alter the harm calculation. According to these courts, a liar does not become a trespasser merely because a property owner would have withheld consent to enter the property had he known the truth. In *Desnick*, the Seventh Circuit concluded that undercover ABC investigators who represented themselves to an ophthalmic clinic as potential patients and then covertly filmed their visit did not commit trespass because they had consent to enter and caused no trespass-type harm; there was no sneaking into areas to which they were not granted access, no publication of intimate details of anyone's life, no theft of trade secrets, no disruption of office activities, etc. And it did not matter, according to the court, that the clinic "would not have agreed to the entry of the test patients into its offices had it known they wanted eye examinations only in order to gather material for a television expose of the Center and that they were going to make secret videotapes of the examinations." What mattered was they obtained consent to enter, and they subsequently caused no trespass-related harm to vitiate that consent.

Nor did the Fourth Circuit in *Food Lion* find it relevant that "consent [was] given *because of* the misrepresentations."[64] There, ABC reporters falsified their resumes and obtained jobs at a Food Lion grocery store where they surreptitiously recorded various health violations. The Fourth Circuit noted it could find no authority for the proposition "that consent based on a resume misrepresentation turns a successful job applicant into a trespasser the moment she enters the employer's premises." The court concluded that the reporters' resume fraud did not amount to trespass because it did not interfere with "the ownership and peaceable possession of land," regardless of the fact that the store owner would not have allowed the reporters on the property but for the fact that they concealed their identities.[67] Thus, like the

---

64. *Food Lion, Inc.*, 194 F.3d at 518 (emphasis added).
67. *Id.* The *Food Lion* court ultimately upheld the reporters' trespass convictions, concluding that although their consent to enter was not vitiated by the lies on their resumes, they subsequently exceeded the scope of that consent by recording non-public areas of the store. *Id.* at 519. This part

Seventh Circuit, the Fourth Circuit ultimately concluded that lying to gain entry, without more, does not render someone a trespasser.

At what point, then, does an invited guest become a trespasser as a result of making misrepresentations to a private property owner? At least in this court's view, the issue is both complicated and mired in competing policy considerations. Consider, for example, the owner of a landscaping company who bids on a project to provide landscaping services to an architectural firm, but misrepresents in his bid the experience of his company. The owner falsely claims the company has completed fifty similar projects, when in fact it would be his first project as a landscaper, and provides fifty sample images of "previous projects," when in fact those images were merely lifted from the Internet. The architectural firm hires the landscaper solely on the strength of his false experience and the quality of work in the fake images. The landscaper nevertheless completes the project on time, for the price bid, and in a manner exceeding the expectations of the architectural firm.

What legally cognizable trespass harm has the firm suffered? The Fourth and Seventh Circuits would conclude, none. There is ample room for disagreement with that conclusion, and the Utah appellate courts or Tenth Circuit might well adopt a different analysis. But absent guidance from these courts, the approach taken by the Fourth and Seven Circuits is persuasive to this court. That is, something more than access by misrepresentation seems necessary to cause trespass-related harm. The mere knowledge (or lack of knowledge, as the case may be) that an invited guest was less than truthful, without more, may cause some harm, but it is difficult to see how that harm alone becomes legally cognizable.[68]

For these reasons, the court opts to follow the reasoning of the Fourth and Seventh Circuits that gaining access to a business by concealing an organizational affiliation, even if that concealment was the reason access was granted, does not alone cause a legally cognizable trespass harm. Applying that reasoning here, at least some lies criminalized by the Act enjoy First Amendment protection. As discussed above, the plain language of the Act criminalizes a host of trivial, harmless misrepresentations, and for that reason alone it is subject to First Amendment scrutiny. And under the reasoning of the Fourth and Seventh Circuits, the answer does not change even if the court were persuaded it could faithfully construe "false pretenses" in the Act to more narrowly criminalize only those lies that actually induce a property owner to grant access to an agricultural facility, as urged by the State. In other

---

of the holding is not relevant to this case both because it was based on North Carolina state law, and, more importantly, because here the plain language of the Act punishes not only those who exceed their consent, but also those who lie to get in the door but then act entirely within the scope of their consent and are otherwise indistinguishable from any other employee.

68. To be clear, this analysis is focused only on trespass-related harm with regard to access itself. The invited guest is obviously not immune from liability for other tortious conduct she may commit after being invited onto the property. For example, the property owner may still obtain relief through tort remedies (including trespass) if the guest later steals trade secrets, invades private spaces, destroys property, assaults employees, or the like.

words, absent an additional showing of harm, under either interpretation, at least some of the lies criminalized by the Act retain First Amendment protection.

c. Harm Related to Offers of Employment

The State's final argument is that even if access alone does not cause "legally cognizable harm" under *Alvarez*, obtaining a job under false pretenses does, so the Act's lying provision (which presumably covers lying to get a job, among other types of access) is not subject to First Amendment scrutiny. For this proposition the State relies on the following line from *Alvarez*:

> Where false claims are made to effect a fraud or secure moneys or other valuable considerations, say offers of employment, it is well established that the Government may restrict speech without affronting the First Amendment.[69]

If the Act solely criminalized obtaining an offer of employment under false pretenses, this argument might carry some weight. Instead, however, the Act criminalizes "obtain[ing] access . . . under false pretenses," which sweeps in a host of lies unrelated to lying to gain employment, including, for example, lying about wanting to take a tour, lying about an interest in acquiring the facility, or lying about wanting to write an article about the facility for Modern Farmer. Because the Act criminalizes more than just lies to gain employment, *Alvarez*'s reference to "offers of employment" is not a basis to exempt the Act from First Amendment scrutiny. Indeed, this proposition is borne out by *Alvarez* itself. In that case, the statute at issue criminalized lying about receiving the Medal of Honor, which presumably includes lying about receiving the Medal of Honor in order to get a job open only to Medal recipients. But the fact that a subset of the lies criminalized were lies to gain employment did not bring the statute outside First Amendment protection. Rather, because it swept in First Amendment-protected lies (even if it also swept in unprotected lies), it was subject to scrutiny.

For the same reason, the false pretenses provision in the Act is subject to First Amendment scrutiny. It may be that some of the misrepresentations criminalized by the Act cause legally cognizable harm, but not all do. Thus, if the State wishes to criminalize these misrepresentations, the Act must survive First Amendment scrutiny.

2. The Recording Provisions

The court next addresses whether the First Amendment applies to the Act's recording provisions. Unlike lying, which the State concedes is speech but argues is nonetheless unprotected in this case, the State argues the act of recording is not speech to begin with. According to the State, it may place any restriction on recording— including, presumably, banning it entirely—without having to justify the restriction under the First Amendment. Plaintiffs, by contrast, contend that recording is First

---

69. *United States v. Alvarez*, 567 U.S. 709, 723 (2012).

Amendment speech, so the government must justify the Act's recording restrictions and demonstrate they are narrowly tailored.

There has been no definitive word from the Supreme Court or the Tenth Circuit on whether recording is speech for First Amendment purposes. But based on the Supreme Court's treatment of similar issues, it appears the answer likely is yes. Over a half-century ago, the Court declared that movies themselves are protected by the First Amendment, concluding that New York had to justify its decision to ban any movie the state deemed "sacrilegious." More recently, the Court affirmed that laws restricting "visual [and] auditory depiction[s], such as photographs, videos, or sound recordings," are subject to First Amendment scrutiny, so the government was required to justify a statute that banned "crush videos" depicting the torture and killing of small animals.[71]

Thus, the Court has made clear that restrictions on recordings themselves are subject to scrutiny, and while it has not yet addressed whether such scrutiny extends to restrictions on the *making* of those recordings, it has recognized that "[l]aws enacted to control or suppress speech may operate at different points in the speech process"—for example, taxing ink and paper purchased to print newspapers. Taking these principles together—that recordings are speech and that pre-speech restrictions are treated similarly to restrictions on speech itself—it appears the Court likely would conclude that making a recording is an act that can enjoy First Amendment protection.

Several circuits have more directly confronted the question, and have reached the same conclusion. The Seventh Circuit, for example, determined that "[t]he act of *making* an audio or audiovisual recording is necessarily included within the First Amendment's guarantee of speech and press rights as a corollary of the right to disseminate the resulting recording." Indeed, the undisputed right to *broadcast* a video recording would mean very little, the court explained, if the government could circumvent that right by regulating with impunity the *making* of the recording instead. Other circuits are in accord.

* * *

In sum, it appears the consensus among courts is that the act of recording is protectable First Amendment speech. And this court agrees. Were the law otherwise, as the State contends, the State could criminalize, for example, creating music videos, or videos critical of the government, or any video at all, for that matter, with impunity. In other words, the State could do indirectly what the Supreme Court has made clear it cannot do directly. Because recordings themselves are protected by the First Amendment, so too must the making of those recordings be protected. This is not to say the State cannot regulate the act of recording; it is merely to say that if it wishes to do so, the State must justify and narrowly tailor the restriction, as with any other constraint on protected speech.

---

71. *United States v. Stevens*, 559 U.S. 460, 468, 482 (2010).

3. The Private Property Distinction

The State's final argument is that even if the lying and recording criminalized by the Act are otherwise protectable speech, the First Amendment plays no role in this case because the Act applies only to speech on private property, and the First Amendment does not apply on private property. According to the State, "private property rights extinguish . . . First Amendment rights." And by that logic, speech on agricultural facilities enjoys no First Amendment protection.

This argument finds no support in the case law. In its papers, and again at oral argument, the State relied on four Supreme Court cases: *Lloyd Corp v. Tanner* (the First Amendment does not compel the owner of a shopping center to allow people to protest on the property), *Hudgens v. NLRB* (the First Amendment does not compel a store owner to allow employees to protest on the property), *Branzburg v. Hayes* (the First Amendment does not shield a reporter from revealing a confidential source to a grand jury), and *Pell v. Procunier* (the First Amendment does not compel a prison to allow journalists access to prisoners). But these cases are not on point. Indeed, the State's reliance on these cases (and its argument in general) confuses two related but distinct concepts: a landowner's ability to exclude from her property someone who wishes to speak, and the government's ability to jail the person for that speech. The cases cited by the State deal with the first concept. They stand for the proposition that the First Amendment is typically not a defense to generally-applicable tort laws. Specifically, as relevant here, they hold that the First Amendment does not provide a license to trespass on private property, and, as a corollary, nor does it provide a defense in a trespass suit. In short, the cases cited by the State answer the question of whether a landowner can remove someone from her property or sue for trespass even when the person wishes to exercise First Amendment rights. And generally, as the cases make clear, the answer is yes.

But that is not the question before the court. The question here is whether the State (not a private landowner) can prosecute (not sue for damages) a person based on her speech on private property. And at this point in the analysis, the question is the threshold one of whether it can do so without even justifying or tailoring the law. The State cites no authority for this proposition. Nor has the court found any, and seemingly for good reason: it is contrary to basic First Amendment principles.

If a person's First Amendment rights were extinguished the moment she stepped foot on private property, the State could, for example, criminalize any criticism of the Governor, or any discussion about the opposition party, or any talk of politics whatsoever, if done on private property. This runs directly afoul of the First Amendment, which "was fashioned to assure unfettered interchange of ideas for the bringing about of political and social changes desired by the people," whether in the public square or in private coffee shops and cafes.

In sum, the fact that speech occurs on a private agricultural facility does not render it outside First Amendment protection. Nobody disputes that owners of an agricultural facility can immediately remove from the property any person speaking in ways the owners find objectionable. But if the State wants to criminalize the same speech, it must justify the law under the First Amendment.

B. What Level of Scrutiny Applies

Having concluded that both the lying and recording provisions of the Act are subject to First Amendment scrutiny, the court turns to the question of what level of scrutiny is warranted. Restrictions on speech are subject either to strict or intermediate scrutiny. Which level applies depends on whether the government criminalized the speech "because of disagreement with the message it conveys" — what is known as a "content-based" law. A law is content based — and therefore subject to strict scrutiny — if determining whether someone violated the law requires looking at what was said. But if assessing a violation does not require reviewing the message itself, the law is content neutral, and is subject to intermediate scrutiny. With this framework in mind, the court will address the scrutiny that applies to the lying and recording provisions.

1. The Lying Provision

* * *

As discussed, the question is whether the law is content based, which requires determining whether "enforcement authorities [must] examine the content of the message that is conveyed to determine whether a violation has occurred." The provision at issue here criminalizes "obtain[ing] access to an agricultural operation under false pretenses." Thus, whether someone violates the Act depends on what they say. If, for example, enforcement authorities know only that an applicant represented to an agricultural facility that she attended a particular school, that alone is not sufficient to determine whether the Act was violated. Rather, the authorities must take the next step of examining the content of the message: what school did she say she attended, and is that the school she actually attended? The falsity of the speech cannot be determined without looking to the content of the message. This means the provision is content based, and subject to strict scrutiny.

The State argues the lying provision is content neutral because it "prohibits all persons, regardless of the message they intend to disseminate, from lying to gain access to agricultural operations." But the test is not whether the Act prohibits some or all persons from lying. And what message (if any) a person wishes to disseminate *after* accessing a facility is irrelevant. The speech in question is the lie itself, and the only way to know whether a lie is a lie is to review what was said. This is perhaps the quintessential example of a content-based restriction.

2. The Recording Provisions

The next question is whether the recording provisions of the Act are content based. Each provision criminalizes "record[ing] an image of, or sound from, [an] agricultural operation." And "agricultural operation" is defined as "private property used for the production of livestock, poultry, livestock products, or poultry products." So the question is whether criminalizing the recording of a particular location is a content-based restriction.

The State contends it is not. According to the State, the Act does not restrict *what* is said, but rather *where* it is said. In other words, the State's position is that the Act is not a content-based restriction but rather a permissible location-based restriction.

That might be so if the Act criminalized recording an image "*at* an agricultural operation." But the Act criminalizes recording an image "*of* an agricultural operation." The distinction is not trivial. Indeed, the use of "of" rather than "at" means the Act does not bar all filming at an agricultural operation, so it is not location based. For example, a person standing on agricultural operation property who films a passing flock of geese is certainly at an agricultural operation, but nobody watching the film would contend it was a recording "of an agricultural operation." An employee who takes a photo of a sunset through the window of an agricultural operation is at the facility, but he has not snapped a shot "of an agricultural operation." In short, if a person walks off an agricultural facility with a recording, the only way to know whether she is criminally liable under the Act is to view the recording. That makes the provision content based, and subject to strict scrutiny.

C. Whether the Act Withstands Strict Scrutiny

Having concluded the Act is subject to strict scrutiny, the court must decide whether it withstands this review. The presumption is that it does not. The State may rebut this presumption by demonstrating that "the restriction furthers a compelling interest" and that the restriction "is narrowly tailored to achieve that interest."[97]

On first blush, this inquiry appears to pit the First Amendment broadly against the privacy and property interests of landowners. Indeed, it might seem to involve a weighing of the value of undercover investigations against the wisdom and reasoning behind laws suppressing them. Ultimately, however, because of both the breadth of the Act and the narrow grounds on which the State defended it, these complex policy questions never really materialize in this case.

Instead, in its briefing, the State confined the court's analysis to four discrete government interests it contends support the Act, arguing: (1) the Act protects animals from diseases brought into the facility by workers; (2) it protects animals from injury resulting from unqualified or inattentive workers; (3) it protects workers from exposure to zoonotic diseases; and (4) it protects workers from injury resulting from unqualified or inattentive workers. . . . .

As an initial matter, it is not clear that these were the actual reasons motivating the Act. Indeed, the legislative history surrounding the Act appears entirely devoid of any reference to an intention by the State to protect the safety of animals or workers. Rather, as discussed, it is rife with discussion of the need to address harm caused by "national propaganda groups," and by "the vegetarian people" who are "trying to

---

97. *Id.* at 2231. Because Plaintiffs have mounted a facial challenge, if the court concludes the "statute fails the relevant constitutional test" — in this case, strict scrutiny — then "it can no longer be constitutionally applied to anyone." *Doe v. City of Albuquerque*, 667 F.3d 1111, 1127 (10th Cir. 2012).

kill the animal industry," "a group of people that want to put [agricultural facilities] out of business."

But even assuming animal and employee safety were the State's actual reasons for enacting the Act, there is no indication that those interests are actually threatened by people who lie to get in the door or record once inside. At oral argument, the State conceded that the "record does not show that Plaintiffs' undercover operatives have created any of the diseases [employers] risk, or that Plaintiffs' undercover operatives have caused an injury to another worker."[101] In other words, the harm targeted by the Act is entirely speculative. And harm that is "mere[ly] speculat[ive] . . . does not constitute a compelling state interest."

Further, even if the State had demonstrated that protecting animals and employees from undercover investigators is a compelling interest, the State has not shown the Act is narrowly tailored to address this problem. To survive strict scrutiny, a law must be "actually necessary" to achieve the State's interests, and may not be over or underinclusive. It is not at all clear from the record that the Act is actually necessary to address perceived threats to animals and employees from undercover investigators, especially given the slew of content-neutral alternatives discussed by the State's own expert.[104] Not only is the Act seemingly not necessary to remedy the State's alleged harms, it is an entirely overinclusive means to address them. It targets, for example, the employee who lies on her job application but otherwise performs her job admirably, and it criminalizes the most diligent well-trained undercover employees. And it is simultaneously underinclusive because it does nothing to address the exact same allegedly harmful conduct when undertaken by anyone other than an undercover investigator.

What the Act appears perfectly tailored toward is preventing undercover investigators from exposing abuses at agricultural facilities. The State has not argued

---

101. Dkt. 199 at 114. The only basis the State provided to connect undercover investigators with harm to animals or employees is "some evidence in the record of Plaintiffs' undercover operatives perhaps prolonging suffering of animals by not reporting abuse in a timely manner." *Id.* The State has not argued that one of the compelling interests furthered by the Act is quickly addressing animal abuse by agricultural operations. But even if it had, the Act is not even remotely tailored to that end. Several states have addressed this exact concern by passing mandatory disclosure laws, requiring employees who record abuse to turn over the recording to authorities within a certain time period. *See, e.g.,* Mo. Rev. Stat. § 578.013 (2012). The court makes no determination about the constitutionality of such a provision, but notes only that it is seemingly both more narrowly tailored to and more effective at addressing delays in reporting animal abuse than are the provisions at issue here.

104. *See, e.g.,* Dkt. 88-1 at 5-6, 12 (discussing various measures to protect against biosecurity threats, including "personal protective equipment or procedures required for anyone entering/exiting the premises," "lines of separation, protective outwear, donning and doffing practices," "information addressing employee movement practices," "limiting traffic (people and equipment) onto farms," "on-farm movement control of pigs, material, and people," "disinfection of vehicles, equipment, and appropriate disposal of dead pigs and slurry," and "training programs for the safety of . . . workers").

this as a government interest motivating the Act. And had it done so, it is not clear whether that interest could be sufficiently compelling to withstand strict scrutiny. But that question is for another day. The court's analysis today addresses only the interests the State now relies on: health and safety of animals and employees. To that end, the State has provided no evidence that animal and employee safety were the actual reasons for enacting the Act, nor that animal and employee safety are endangered by those targeted by the Act, nor that the Act would actually do anything to remedy those dangers to the extent they exist. For these reasons, the Act fails strict scrutiny.

CONCLUSION

There can be no doubt that today, over 200 years after Washington implored Congress to safeguard the agricultural industry, the industry remains crucially important to the continued viability of the nation. Similarly important to the nation's continued viability, however, is the safeguarding of the fundamental rights Washington helped enshrine into the Constitution. Utah undoubtedly has an interest in addressing perceived threats to the state agricultural industry, and as history shows, it has a variety of constitutionally permissible tools at its disposal to do so. Suppressing broad swaths of protected speech without justification, however, is not one of them.

The court concludes that Utah Code § 76-6-112 is unconstitutional. Plaintiffs' Motion for Summary Judgment is granted. The State's Motion for Summary Judgment is denied. The clerk is directed to close the case.

Notes

1. The State of Utah did not appeal the district court's ruling in *ALDF v. Herbert*.

2. As noted by the court, the strong interconnection between government and the agribusiness industry dates back to the founding of this country and "remains crucially important to the continued viability of the nation." The tension between a desire for more humane alternatives to food production and the drive to maximize profit and meet market demand fuels the ongoing debate over farmed animal treatment. The Ag-Gag laws are an outgrowth of that longstanding debate and governmental desire to protect the agribusiness industry.

3. The *ALDF v. Herbert* court recognized that "[w]hat the Act appears perfectly tailored toward is preventing undercover investigators from exposing abuses at agricultural facilities"—although Utah claimed the bill was supported by health and safety concerns for animal and employees. In *Animal Legal Defense Fund v. Wasden*, 878 F.3d 1184 (9th Cir. 2018), the Ninth Circuit reviewed the legislative history of Idaho's Ag-Gag law and concluded that it demonstrated two purposes behind the law. According to the court, one purpose was to prevent physical harm to agricultural facilities from unwanted intruders with criminal motives, and the second purpose was to stop the dissemination of videotapes of undercover investigation, because farmers were being "persecuted in the court of public opinion."

4. The factual background in *Wasden* involved an undercover "activist" getting a job, filming instances of animal cruelty, and releasing the results on the internet to broad viewership. Relying in significant part on *U.S. v. Alvarez*, 567 U.S. 709 (2012), (discussed and relied upon in *Herbert*), the court summarized the tensions in the case, explaining that it was "sensitive to journalists' constitutional right to investigate and publish exposés on the agricultural industry. . . . However, the First Amendment right to gather news within legal bounds does not exempt journalists from laws of general applicability." Walking that fine line, the court delivered a ruling that severed only limited aspects of the statute it believed violated the First Amendment.

The court found that Idaho's law violated the First Amendment to the extent it prohibited misrepresentations made by individuals in order to enter an agricultural facility, and to the extent it banned "audio and video recordings of a production facility's operations." Relying on *Alvarez*, the court held that because activists seeking to expose animal cruelty, or journalists interested in a story, were not acting "for the purpose of material gain" or "material advantage," and because the misrepresentation itself did not "inflict a legally cognizable harm," it was protected by the First Amendment, and the state could not criminalize those misrepresentations. In essence, because speech was involved and the speaker was only lying to gain entry—not to secure a job (even though the activists did that also)—the speech could not be prohibited.

> . . . [T]he misrepresentation provision of subsection (a) regulates protected speech while "target[ing] falsity and nothing more." Such regulation is subject to the "most exacting scrutiny." Idaho's chosen restriction on speech must be "actually necessary" to achieve a compelling government interest, and there must be a "direct causal link between the restriction imposed and the injury to be prevented." Subsection (a) cannot survive this high bar.

> Even assuming Idaho has a compelling interest in regulating property rights and protecting its farm industry, criminalizing access to property by misrepresentation is not "actually necessary" to protect those rights. If, as Idaho argues, its real concern is trespass, then Idaho already has a prohibition against trespass that does not implicate speech in any way. If instead, as a number of the legislators made clear and the dairy lobby underscored, the statute was intended to quash investigative reporting on agricultural production facilities, then the speech aspect of the statute prohibiting misrepresentations is even more problematic. The focus of the statute to avoid the "court of public opinion" and treatment of investigative videos as "blackmail" cannot be squared with a content-neutral trespass law.

Wasden, 878 F.3d at 1196–97.

The court noted, however, that in its view in order to "fix the First Amendment problem," Idaho needed only to excise the word "misrepresentation" from the statute, so that the law would still prohibit entry on agricultural production facilities property "by force, threat, or trespass."

With respect to the prohibition on filming or recording "conduct of an agricultural production facility's operations," the court found this was "a classic example of a content-based restriction that cannot survive strict scrutiny."

5. But the *Wasden* court's ruling was a mixed one for undercover investigators, upholding the part of the statute that prohibited "misrepresentations to obtain records" of an agricultural production facility, or to obtain employment for material gain. The court's rationale for the different holdings is that obtaining records under false pretenses—as opposed to just a false statement—causes a "legally cognizable harm" that a state is empowered to prohibit without constitutional concerns. The court explained: "Acquiring records by misrepresentation results in something definitively more than does entry onto land—it wreaks actual and potential harm on a facility and bestows material gain on the fibber . . . and does not run afoul of the First Amendment." 878 F.3d at 1200.

With respect to the employment aspect of the ruling, the statutory language is key to the holding. Idaho's law criminalizes "knowingly '[o]btain[ing] employment with an agricultural production facility by . . . misrepresentation with the intent to cause economic or other injury' to the facility's operations, property, or personnel." Because this would amount to a "lie made for material gain," the court followed the Supreme Court's holding in *Alvarez* and upheld this part of the statute. This part of the holding means that the law still could put a significant chill on activists seeking to expose animal cruelty in agricultural production facilities.

6. One of the problems the *Wasden* court identified with the statute was the broad definition of "agricultural production facility" and "agricultural production," which meant that the statute prohibited conduct "not only in the context of a large-scale dairy facility or cattle feedlot, but also grocery stores, garden nurseries, restaurants that have an herb garden or grow their own produce, llama farms that produce wool for weaving, beekeepers, a chicken coop in the backyard, a field producing crops for ethanol, and hardware stores, to name a few." The court's comment identifies a recurring difficulty for legislators trying to restrict activities involving food products.

7. The plaintiffs in *Wasden* also challenged the law under the Equal Protection Clause. Because of the acknowledged animus towards animal welfare groups and reporters with a particular message, the court invoked "searching scrutiny" but ultimately decided the statute did not violate equal protection, given that the statute had a legitimate purpose—prohibiting interference by wrongful conduct—in addition to its impermissible purpose—quashing protected First Amendment conduct. In so ruling, the court reversed the district court in *ALDF v. Otter*, 118 F. Supp. 3d 1195, 1209–12 (D. Idaho 2015), *reversed in part, affirmed in part* [by *Wasden*], where the court undertook a thorough analysis, found no legitimate purpose supported by the legislative record and therefore held that the law violated the Equal Protection Clause.

8. One judge in *Wasden* dissented in part. He would have taken the majority's ruling one step further in favor of the State, upholding the entire statute, focusing

on trespass and the "ancient right" of "an owner of real property to exclude all others from his property."

9. Notably absent from both *Wasden* and *Herbert* opinions is anything more than a passing mention of the public policy against cruelty to animals (at least outside the context of the agribusiness industry) — both historically (as discussed in Chapter 3) and in modern society — and the efforts of animal activists and journalists to promote that policy by opening the proverbial doors and windows of the industry to the public.

10. For articles on Ag-Gag laws, *see, e.g.,* Nicole E. Negowetti, *Seattle University Law Review Symposium: Re-Tooling Food Law: How Traditional Legal Models Can Be Re-Tooled for Food System Reform: Article & Essay: Opening the Barnyard Door: Transparency and the Resurgence of Ag-Gag & Veggie Libel Laws,* 38 Seattle U.L. Rev. 1345 (Summer, 2015); Matthew Shea, *Punishing Animal Rights Activists for Animal Abuse: Rapid Reporting and the New Wave of Ag-Gag Laws,* 48 Colum. J.L. & Soc. Probs. 337 (Spring, 2015); Gabriela Wolfe, *Note: Anything But Ag-Gag: Ending the Industry-Advocate Cycle,* 66 Syracuse L. Rev. 367 (2016).

Section 2. Animals in Research and the Animal Welfare Act

Tens of millions of animals are used each year in American research facilities for a variety of purposes. For example, animals are commonly used to develop or test the danger or toxicity of new and existing cleaning and cosmetic products, medical procedures and medications; they are also used to extract specific biological substances, such as insulin, for research and therapy. Exact figures for the numbers of animals used and the types of research performed are impossible to obtain because no accurate reporting system exists. This is particularly the case for birds, rats and mice bred for use in research. It has been estimated that they represent roughly 95% to 99% of the sentient beings used in research facilities, but there are no reliable data for how many are used or what is done to them because they are not covered by the Animal Welfare Act (AWA) (7 U.S.C. §§ 2132–2158). According to an "Annual Report: Animal Usage by Fiscal Year" prepared by the Animal and Plant Health Inspection Service of the United States Department of Agriculture (USDA), more than 820,000 animals *other than birds, rats and mice* were used in research in the United States in 2016. The report further breaks down animal usage by type: 60,979 dogs; 18,898 cats; 71,188 nonhuman primates; 183,237 guinea pigs; 102,633 hamsters; 139,391 rabbits; 12,196 sheep; 20,597 other farm animals; and 161,467 other animals.

A. Scientific, Legal and Public Debate

Two controversial issues in this area are (1) the use of nonhuman animals in invasive biomedical research and testing, and (2) the efficacy of the AWA as protective legislation, given its limited control of the treatment of research animals and the fact that it does not address specific research protocols or the manner and method by which the animals can be used.

This topic is controversial because of a significant philosophical split between those who support the use of animals in invasive biomedical research and non-invasive psychological and behavioral research, and those who believe the use of animals in this way is unethical because it is inhumane, immoral and violates the animals' interests in not being harmed.[a] A secondary, but important, scientific dispute revolves around the actual benefit of research on animals, *i.e.*, whether animal-based research protocols produce supportable scientific results that can lead to improved health or care for humans (or animals). Research advocates argue in favor of animal testing by relying heavily on the premise that the research is essential to developing new medicines and medical procedures to save lives. They dismiss arguments that animal testing does not adequately demonstrate the effect that a particular drug or procedure will have in other settings, or on humans. They usually do not address the ethical issues or whether the perceived benefit to humans is worth the cost to animals. *See* Jack H. Botting & Adrian R. Morrison, *Animal Research is Vital to Medicine*, Scientific American, Feb. 1997, at 83–85.

Opponents of research explain that because each species has significant physiologic, psychological and metabolic differences, animal experiments can render misleading results or even contribute to illnesses or death by failing to predict the toxic (or beneficial) effects of drugs in humans, and that numerous alternative methods to research on animals are available and will yield better, safer results. These alternatives include computer modeling as well as "epidemiological studies, clinical intervention trials, astute clinical observation aided by laboratory testing, human tissue and cell cultures, autopsy studies, endoscopic examination and biopsy, as well as new imaging methods." Neal D. Barnard & Stephen R. Kaufman, *Animal Research is Wasteful and Misleading*, Scientific American, Feb. 1997, at 81.

Commentators point out that the "growing body of scientific literature critically assessing the validity of animal experimentation generally (and animal modeling specifically) raises important concerns about its reliability and predictive value for human outcomes and for understanding human physiology;" and that "animal experimentation often significantly harms humans through misleading safety studies, potential abandonment of effective therapeutics, and direction of resources away from more effective testing methods." Aysha Akhtar, *The Flaws and Human Harms of Animal Experimentation*, 24 Cambridge Quarterly of Healthcare Ethics 407, 407 (2015). In addition, ethics scholars and political scientists worldwide have argued that "the ongoing paradigm shift in society's view of animals prompts a

---

a. A third type of scientific investigation involves solely observational work, where the animals involved are not required to engage in any harmful or manipulated behaviors. This research, done both in the field and in sanctuary settings, usually carried out only when it will benefit the species being observed/investigated, does not raise the same concerns.

serious re-evaluation of the values underpinning the routine use of sentient nonhuman animals in research." Pers-Anders Svärd (Dept. of Political Science, Stockholm Univ.), *Normative Dilemmas in Sweden's Ethical Review Policy for Animal Experiments*, 5 GLOBAL J. OF ANIMAL LAW 1, Issue No. 2 (2017).

Another area of discussion is the conflict between animal anti-cruelty laws (and the public policy that supports them) and the scientific community's claim of constitutional protection (as a matter of protected "speech" under the First Amendment) for medical research. *See, e.g.*, Thomas Kelch, *Animal Experimentation and the First Amendment*, 22 W. NEW ENG. L. REV. 467 (2001). Kelch discusses what he believes to be the fallacy of according protection to research and experimentation as speech, finding no constitutional support for the "mythical transformation" of otherwise clear cruelty violations into constitutionally-protected science/speech. *Id.* at 468. The message in Kelch's article is that legislators and judges alike should recognize this fiction, despite its long-term acceptance, and begin to examine research in the context of anti-cruelty and other animal-protection laws. One issue to be resolved is whether there is a speech component to research that merits any protection. In other words, where on the traditional legal speech-conduct continuum used in First Amendment jurisprudence does medical research fall?

A major barrier to opponents of animal research is the majority opinion that research on animals is justified by its outcome, in an "ends justifies the means" approach to the issue. This societal perception has been effectively codified so that most states have specific exemptions from the anti-cruelty laws for research activities, thus eliminating any successful challenge along the lines that Kelch suggests. *See* William A. Reppy, Jr., *Broad Exemptions in Animal-Cruelty Statutes Unconstitutionally Deny Equal Protection of the Law*, 70 LAW & CONTEMP. PROBS. 255 (Winter 2007).

Animal protection advocates often use public records act requests, undercover investigations and other methods to obtain information about research activities. Protests against research have taken the form of direct action and violence. *See generally* Dane E. Johnson, *Cages, Clinics, and Consequences: The Chilling Problems of Controlling Special-Interest Extremism*, 86 OR. L. REV. 249 (2007). Such undercover investigations and other actions have prompted some states to enact the so-called "Ag-Gag" laws addressed in Section 1 of this chapter, criminalizing undercover investigations and videography at research facilities as well as at slaughterhouses and other agribusiness facilities.

Lawsuits have challenged the efficacy of animal testing as well. For example, in 2005, a products liability complaint was filed by an individual against the manufacturer of the drug Vioxx. *Tufford v. Merck & Co., Inc.*, No. ATL-L-4211-05 MT (N.J. Super. Ct. Law Div., Atlantic Cty.) (1st Am. Cmplt. filed Aug. 5, 2005). The complaint contained considerable discussion about the manufacturer's alleged "improper reliance on animal testing," including detailed analysis of the testing that was conducted. *Id.*, 1st. Am. Cmplt. at ¶¶ 5–71. It also focused the issue by quoting from exemplar cases where courts rejected animal testing evidence. *Id.* at ¶¶ 72–73. *See, e.g., In re "Agent Orange" Product Liability Litigation*, 611 F. Supp. 1223, 1241 (E.D.N.Y. 1985)

("The animal studies are not helpful in the instant case because they involve different biological species. They are of so little probative force and are so potentially misleading as to be inadmissible."); *Richardson by Richardson v. Richardson-Merrell, Inc.*, 857 F.2d 823, 830 (D.C. Cir. 1988).

In *Lockheed Litigation Cases*, 23 Cal. Rptr. 3d 762 (2005) (*depublished, superseded by grant of review*), plaintiffs sought damages for injuries allegedly caused by exposure to toxic chemicals and relied heavily on testimony by their expert, Dr. Daniel Teitelbaum, on the issue of causation. Dr. Teitelbaum, in turn, based his testimony on animal toxicology studies, but the trial court concluded that these studies (along with other studies he relied on) did not provide a reasonable basis on which to conclude that any of the toxic chemicals could cause disease. As a result, his testimony was excluded by the lower court before trial and the defendant's motion to dismiss the complaint was granted. On appeal, plaintiffs argued that excluding Dr. Teitelbaum's testimony was in error, and that the dismissal was procedurally improper. The appellate court affirmed the lower court's decision, and concluded that reliance on animal studies was misplaced:

> The court in its tentative ruling noted several shortcomings in Dr. Teitelbaum's reliance on animal studies, including his failure to explain the significance of differences between human beings and the animals studied (species extrapolation) and his failure to explain how to extrapolate from the high doses given to animals to the lower doses to which human beings may be subjected (dosage extrapolation). The court stated in its tentative ruling that absent further explanation Dr. Teitelbaum's reliance on animal studies was unreasonable. The court offered the parties the opportunity to present additional evidence on the extrapolation issues. Plaintiffs declined the opportunity. The court therefore concluded in its final order excluding expert testimony that Dr. Teitelbaum could not reasonably rely on the animal studies.

> On appeal, Plaintiffs do not attempt to explain why the animal studies that Dr. Teitelbaum relied on are probative of causation in human beings. Instead, they argue categorically that animal studies generally are reliable for this purpose, particularly when combined with other evidence.

> An animal study may or may not provide reasonably reliable support for an opinion on causation in human beings. Differences between human beings and other species, including differences in absorption, distribution, and metabolism of substances, may affect toxicity. (Goldstein & Henifin, *Reference Guide on Toxicology in Reference Manual on Scientific Evidence, supra,* at 419.) The high doses typically used in animal experiments compared with the much lower levels to which human beings typically may be exposed make it necessary to consider the relationship between dose and response, the shape of the dose-response curve at lower levels of exposure, and the possibility that exposure may not cause a disease when the

exposure is below a threshold level. (*Id.* at 409, 410; Green et al., *Reference Guide on Epidemiology in Reference Manual on Scientific Evidence*, *supra*, at 377 & n.119; Searcy-Alford, *A Guide to Toxic Torts* § 10.02[6][b], at 10–47 (2004).) In light of these concerns, reliance on a particular animal study may be unwarranted. To justify reliance on a particular animal study, an expert should explain why reliance is warranted.

Plaintiffs have not shown that Dr. Teitelbaum adequately explained why his reliance on the animal studies was warranted and do not explain why his reliance on the animal studies on which he relied was warranted. Plaintiffs therefore have not shown error in the court's conclusion that the animal studies provide no reasonable basis to support Dr. Teitelbaum's opinion.

Id. at 779–80. In an interesting turn of events, the California Supreme Court granted review, and the case was fully briefed, at which point the court dismissed the petition for review because "circumstances, arising since review was granted, . . . require[d] a majority of the permanent members of the court to recuse themselves." The court declined a request for publication of the appellate court opinion, so the case has no precedential value. 83 Cal. Rptr. 3d 478 (Cal. 2007) (dismissing petition for review).

The debate over animal experimentation shows no sign of abating in the near future. How this may impact the future development of laws affecting animal research is an open question. It is clear that the research community itself is exploring new alternatives to testing protocols that do not involve animals. At the request of the Environmental Protection Agency, the National Research Council ("NRC"), in conjunction with the National Academy of Sciences, conducted a comprehensive review of then-current toxicity-testing methods and strategies and proposed a long-term vision and strategy for testing going forward. In 2007, the Committee on Toxicity Testing and Assessment of Environmental Agents published its report of nearly 200 pages, entitled *Toxicity Testing in the 21st Century: A Vision and a Strategy*. The Committee was comprised of more than twenty scholars, academics, industry representatives and scientists. Only one member was a representative of an animal protection organization (Dr. Martin Stephens of the Humane Society of the United States). In the report, the Committee recommended phasing out all animal-based toxicity testing over the subsequent twenty years. Its recommendation was based on the conclusion that the most efficient, productive and accurate testing is performed using non-animal testing alternatives. Animal advocates have expressed support for the NRC recommendation because if implemented, it would keep millions of animals from being used in research.

The use of live animals in educational institutions is also the focus of controversy. Students' desires to opt out of such practices have been the subject of litigation and legislation. As a result, virtually all veterinary schools now offer, upon student request, alternative options to the invasive or lethal use of animals. Medical schools followed the same trend. According to a 2016 survey by Physician's Committee for

Responsible Medicine, all United States medical schools stopped using live animals to teach basic concepts in human physiology, pharmacology and/or surgery.

B. AWA History and Overview

In response to public outcry after the publication of popular media articles reporting pets being stolen and sold for research, in 1966 Congress enacted Public Law (P.L.) 89-544, known as the Laboratory Animal Welfare Act, which set minimum standards for the care, housing, sale and transport of dogs, cats, primates, rabbits, hamsters, guinea pigs and other animals held on the premises of animal dealers or laboratories. The Act also required the licensing of cat and dog dealers and research facilities and the identification of dogs and cats to prevent their theft. The first amendment to the Laboratory Animal Welfare Act was passed in 1970 (P.L. 91-579), at which point the name of the law was changed to the Animal Welfare Act, based on an expansion of its coverage. This amendment extended coverage to regulate other warm-blooded animals designated by the Secretary of Agriculture, when used in research, exhibition or the wholesale pet trade. The amendment required the licensing of all animal dealers. It also added the requirement for the "appropriate use of anesthetic, analgesic, or tranquilizing drugs in prescribed circumstances." *Id.*

In 1972, the Secretary of Agriculture enacted a rule that specifically excluded birds, mice, rats, horses and farmed animals from the definition of "animal" under the AWA. *See* Henry Cohen, *The Legality of the Agriculture Department's Exclusion of Rats and Mice From Coverage Under the Animal Welfare Act*, 31 Sᴛ. Lᴏᴜɪs U. L.J. 543 (1987). Although this regulation was challenged successfully on the merits in *Animal Legal Defense Fund v. Madigan*, 781 F. Supp. 797 (D.D.C. 1992), the judgment subsequently was vacated on the ground that plaintiffs lacked standing. *See Animal Legal Defense Fund v. Espy*, 23 F.3d 496 (D.C. Cir. 1994), discussed in Chapter 5. As further explained below, this was not the end of this issue.

In 1976, the AWA was amended to prohibit most animal fighting ventures and regulate the commercial transportation of animals. 90 Stat. 417 (1976). Animals sold as pets (except in pet stores) and those used in exhibition were added to the list of protected animals; and research institutions were placed in the same category as exhibitors and dealers with respect to the imposition of fines for violations. (Previously, research facilities were subject to a cease and desist order, which they would have to violate before a fine could be imposed.) These amendments also made government research facilities subject to the same standards set forth in the AWA for private institutions.

In 1985, another amendment, titled the Improved Standards for Laboratory Animals Act strengthened AWA standards for laboratory animal care, increased enforcement of the AWA, mandated training for those who handle animals, and created Institutional Animal Care and Use Committees (IACUCs) at each institution using regulated animals. 99 Stat. 1650 (1985). These committees ostensibly oversee animal care at the institution and are meant to ensure that alternatives are considered in experiments that cause pain or suffering to animals. 7 U.S.C. §§ 2143(b)(1) *et seq.* In addition, the 1985 amendment required some exercise for dogs and a physical environment that "promotes the psychological well-being of primates."

In 1990, provisions in the Food, Agriculture, Conservation and Trade Act of 1990 were added to the AWA. 7 U.S.C. §§ 2137, 2138, 2158, 2159 (1990). This amendment established more stringent recordkeeping requirements for dealers who obtain animals from "random sources." In this context, "random source" means "dogs and cats obtained from animal pounds or shelters, auction sales, or from any person who did not breed and raise them on his or her premises." 9 C.F.R. §§ 2.132 *et seq.*; 9 C.F.R. § 1.1. Another provision authorized the Secretary to seek an injunction to stop certain licensed entities from continuing to violate the AWA while charges are pending in cases of stolen animals or where an animal's health is in serious danger or may become endangered. 7 U.S.C. § 2159 (1990).

In 1998, the issue of which beings were "animals" protected under the AWA was again brought to the courts. The Alternative Research and Development Foundation ("ARDF") sued the USDA, arguing that the exclusion of rats, mice and birds was arbitrary and capricious and improperly based on economic concerns rather than on scientific or ethical considerations. ARDF sought an amendment to the AWA's definition of "animals" to include birds, rats and mice, thereby granting them protection under the AWA. *See Alternatives [sic] Research & Development Foundation v. Glickman*, 101 F. Supp. 2d 7 (D.D.C. 2000) (noted in Chapter 5). In 2000, ARDF and the USDA announced a settlement stipulating that the USDA would initiate and complete, within a reasonable time, a rulemaking procedure on the regulation of rats, mice and birds under the AWA. Weeks later, this agreement was superseded by the 2001 Agricultural Appropriations Act, which included a provision that prevented the USDA from using appropriated funds to begin rulemaking on this issue until, at the earliest, a year later.

In 2002 (while the USDA was still prohibited from engaging in rulemaking on the exclusion of birds, rats and mice from the AWA), the federal "Farm Bill" contained an amendment by Senator Jesse Helms (R-NC) to exclude "birds, mice of the genus *Mus* and rats of the genus *Rattus*, bred for use in research" from the AWA definition of the term "animal." The amendment was signed into law that year, despite ongoing investigations at several well-known research institutions regarding inadequate care and negligent deaths of numerous animals used in laboratories. In 2004, the USDA published a Final Rule in the Federal Register amending the AWA regulations to reflect the 2002 Farm Bill amendment to the AWA's definition of the term "animal." 9 C.F.R. § 1.1 (2004); 69 Fed. Reg. 31513, 31513–14 (June 4, 2004). This ended the fight over the exclusion of birds, rats and mice bred for use from AWA coverage.

Because of the compromise language, which covered only members of those species "bred for use in research," an undefined (but probably in the thousands if not the tens or hundreds of thousands) number of birds, rats and mice are still covered by the AWA. For example, all birds used in any commercial venture—sales, display, public exhibition—are still covered by the AWA. However, despite technical coverage under the AWA since 2002, no regulations have been published by the relevant agency (the Animal Plant and Health Inspection Service).

In 2007, the AWA was amended to strengthen anti-dog fighting provisions, with the enactment of the Animal Fighting Prohibition Enforcement Act. 18 U.S.C. §49. In 2008, a provision in the Farm Bill increased fines for violation of the AWA from $2,500 to $10,000 per violation, per day (7 U.S.C. §2156), and contained language addressing the use of cats and dogs in federal research. Under that section, the National Institutes of Health (NIH) was to seek an independent review of the use of "Class B" dogs and cats and the USDA was required to review the NIH report. "Class B" dogs and cats refers to those animals purchased or otherwise acquired by licensed dealers who resell them to research institutions.

In 2009, the NIH released its report as required under the Farm Bill. The report, titled "Scientific and Humane Issues in the Use of Random Source Dogs and Cats in Research," raised ongoing concerns with random source animals, stating: "[T]estimony provided to the Committee by USDA officials made it clear that despite new enforcement guidelines and intensified inspection efforts, not all origins of animals are or can be traced. The USDA simply cannot assure that stolen or lost pets will not enter research laboratories via the Class B dealer system." Despite these findings, a small number of Class B dealers still operated as of December 2013. At the end of 2015, Congress passed the Consolidated Appropriations Act of 2016, which included language that defunds some Class B dealer licensing:

> None of the funds made available by this Act may be used to carry out any activities or incur any expense related to the issuance of licenses under section 3 of the Animal Welfare Act (7 U.S.C. 2133), or the renewal of such licenses, to class B dealers who sell dogs and cats for use in research, experiments, teaching, or testing.

CONSOLIDATED APPROPRIATIONS ACT OF 2016, PUB. L. No. 114-113, § 753, 129 STAT. 2284 (2015). This language was renewed in the Consolidated Appropriations Act of 2017. However, as of 2018, Class B dealers were still legally allowed to sell warm-blooded animals other than dogs or cats for use in research.

In 2013, the USDA adopted a rule closing a loophole that allowed Internet sales of pets to avoid federal oversight of their operations. 9 C.F.R. Parts 1 and 2; 78 F.R. 57227-01, 2013 WL 5206012. The AWA generally requires that cat, dog and other pet breeders obtain a license, comply with minimum standards of animal care and submit to occasional inspections to verify compliance with the law. However, the AWA exempts retail pet stores based on the USDA's assumption that purchasers can see the animals' living conditions first-hand so that inspections are unnecessary. Breeders who sell online had been taking advantage of this exemption by claiming their websites qualified as retail pet stores. This led to the creation of subpar breeding facilities with no oversight to ensure minimum standards of care. The USDA ruled closed that loophole by requiring the purchasers' physical presence at the property for a breeder to qualify for the retail pet store exemption. For more on this issue, *see* Section 2.D of this chapter.

Unlike some other federal environmental protection laws, such as the Endangered Species Act, 16 U.S.C. §§ 1531–1543, the AWA does not include a "citizen suit provision" or otherwise provide a private right of action that would allow interested parties to sue for its enforcement. Thus, lawsuits based on AWA violations typically are brought under the Administrative Procedure Act, 5 U.S.C. § 701, *et seq.*

C. Nonhuman Primates

In the following case (an earlier opinion of which, containing the factual background of the case, is excerpted in Chapter 5), the AWA was used in an effort to ensure proper care was given to primates in a roadside zoo. Although it does not deal with animals in research facilities, it does demonstrate a court's analysis of some of the same regulations applicable to research facilities and, therefore, is pertinent to the present discussion.

Animal Legal Defense Fund, Inc. v. Glickman
United States Court of Appeals, District of Columbia Circuit, 2000
204 F.3d 229

WILLIAMS, Circuit Judge. In *Animal Legal Defense Fund, Inc. v. Glickman*, 154 F.3d 426 (D.C. Cir. 1998) (en banc), we held that plaintiff Marc Jurnove has standing to challenge regulations promulgated by the Secretary of Agriculture in 1991 that purport to set "minimum requirements . . . for a physical environment adequate to promote the psychological well-being of primates." 7 U.S.C. § 2143(a) (1)-(2). The en banc court left untouched the panel's decision that Animal Legal Defense Fund lacked standing. The court referred the merits—the question whether the Secretary's regulations satisfy that statutory mandate and the Administrative Procedure Act—to a future panel. Finding that the regulations do meet the statutory and APA tests, we reverse the district court's decision to the contrary.

* * *

In 1985 Congress passed the Improved Standards for Laboratory Animals Act, Pub. L. No. 99-198, 99 Stat. 1645, amending the Animal Welfare Act of 1966. *See* 7 U.S.C. § 2131 *et seq.* The 1985 amendments directed the Secretary of Agriculture to promulgate "standards to govern the humane handling, care, treatment, and transportation of animals by dealers, research facilities, and exhibitors." *Id.* § 2143(a) (1). The Act specified that among these must be "minimum requirements . . . for a physical environment adequate to promote the psychological well-being of primates." *Id.* § 2143(a)(1)-(2).

There are over 240 species of non-human primates, ranging from marmosets of South America that are a foot tall and weigh less than half a pound to gorillas of western Africa standing six feet tall and weighing up to 500 pounds. It proved no simple task to design regulations to promote the psychological well-being of such varied species as they are kept and handled for exhibition and research. Notice of intent to issue regulations was first published in the *Federal Register* in 1986, 51 Fed. Reg. 7950 (1986), but the Secretary did not publish proposed regulations until 1989. 54 Fed. Reg. 10897 (1989). After receiving a flood of comments (10,686 timely ones, to be precise), the Secretary reconsidered the regulations and published new proposed regulations in 1990. 55 Fed. Reg. 33448 (1990). After receiving another 11,392 comments, he adopted final regulations in 1991. 56 Fed. Reg. 6426 (1991); 9 C.F.R. § 3.81.

The final regulations consist of two separate modes of regulation, typically known as engineering standards and performance standards. The former dictate the required means to achieve a result; the latter state the desired outcomes, leaving to the facility the choice of means. *See* 56 Fed. Reg. at 6427 (discussing engineering and performance standards generally). The Secretary identifies five guidelines that he considers engineering standards, which in substance require as follows: (1) restraints are generally prohibited subject to certain exceptions as determined by the attending veterinarian or the research proposal, 9 C.F.R. § 3.81(d); (2) primary enclosures must be "enriched" so that primates may exhibit their typical behavior, such as swinging or foraging, *id.* § 3.81(b); (3) certain types of primates must be given special attention, including infants, young juveniles, individually housed primates, and great apes over 110 pounds, again in accord with "the instructions of the attending veterinarian," *id.* § 3.81(c); (4) facilities must "address the social needs of nonhuman primates . . . in accordance with currently accepted professional standards . . . and as directed by the attending veterinarian," but they may individually house primates under conditions further specified in the regulations, *id.* § 3.81(a); and (5) minimum cage sizes are set according to the typical weight of different species, *id.* § 3.80(b)(2)(i).

To implement these guidelines and to promote the psychological well-being of the primates, facilities must develop performance plans:

> Dealers, exhibitors, and research facilities must develop, document, and follow an appropriate plan for environment enhancement adequate to promote the psychological well-being of nonhuman primates. The plan must be in accordance with the currently accepted professional standards as cited in appropriate professional journals or reference guides, and as directed by the attending veterinarian. This plan must be made available to APHIS [Animal and Plant Health Inspection Service] upon request, and, in the case of research facilities, to officials of any pertinent funding agency.

Id. § 3.81.

Jurnove primarily maintains that nothing about these regulations establishes "minimum requirements . . . for a physical environment adequate to promote the psychological well-being of primates," and that the Secretary's use of performance plans and his apparent deference to on-site veterinarians amount to an impermissible delegation of his legal responsibility.

The district court agreed. *Animal Legal Defense Fund v. Glickman* ("*ALDF*"), 943 F. Supp. 44 (D.D.C. 1996). It held that the regulation "fails to set standards," by which the district court meant engineering standards, and that "the regulation completely delegates the establishment of such standards to the regulated entities" because "[a]t best, the regulation refers these entities to the direction of their attending veterinarians—who are not under the control of the agency." The district court also concluded that the Secretary had a duty to require social housing of primates given a finding by the Secretary that "[i]n general, housing in groups promotes psychological well-being more assuredly than does individual housing." As the court read the regulation "the agency delineates only when social grouping might not be provided," and therefore "the regulation does not contain any minimum requirement on a point recognized by the agency itself as critical to the psychological well-being of primates."

* * *

Jurnove argues that the plain language of the statute—the Secretary shall establish "minimum requirements . . . for a physical environment adequate to promote the psychological well-being of primates"—requires that the Secretary spell out exactly how primates may and may not be housed and handled (*i.e.*, engineering standards), or at least spell out the "minimum requirements" in this manner. The Secretary's emphatic first response is: we did.

Jurnove consistently reads the regulations, as did the district court, as if the only "requirement" of the facilities is the production of a performance plan and that, basically, anything goes—provided the facilities honor what he views as the empty formality of finding some sort of support from "currently accepted professional standards as cited in appropriate professional journals or reference guides" and from "the attending veterinarian." 9 CFR §3.81. This reading yields an obvious parade of horribles. Facilities will find unscrupulous veterinarians to rubber-stamp outrageous practices, and fringe periodicals will be the coin of the animal realm. This, argues Jurnove, is not the setting of "standards" or "minimum requirements" that the statute plainly commands.

We need not decide when performance standards alone could satisfy a congressional mandate for minimum requirements, or whether the sort of agency deference depicted by Jurnove could ever do so. The regulations here include specific engineering standards. The most obvious example is the regulation of cage sizes, *id.* §3.80, which even Jurnove grants is an engineering standard. Jurnove attempts to discount the "primary enclosure" requirements because they appear in a different section of the regulations, and the Animal Welfare Act had previously mandated standards for "housing." But the Secretary stated that the cage requirements were set as part of the standards for promoting psychological well-being, 56 Fed. Reg. at 6468, and it is perfectly permissible to implement congressional commands through complementary regulations, some of which serve multiple goals.

The Secretary's requirement bases cage size on the weight of the primate, with special provisions for great apes, whereas the previous regulations merely required "sufficient space to allow each nonhuman primate to make normal postural adjustments with adequate freedom of movement." 56 Fed. Reg. at 6469. By hiking the requirements, the Secretary addressed an issue that Congress considered one of the central elements of a primate's psychological well-being. The statutory language speaks of minimum requirements for the "physical environment" of the primate, 7 U.S.C. § 2143(a)(2)(B), and the Conference Committee noted that "[t]he intent of standards with regard to promoting the psychological well-being of primates is *to provide adequate space* equipped with devices for exercise consistent with the primate's natural instincts and habits." H.R. Conf. Rep. No. 99-447, at 594 (1985) (emphasis added).

Similarly, the regulations on environmental enrichment, special consideration of certain primates (infants, juveniles, etc.), and restraint devices all plainly provide engineering standards. 9 C.F.R. § 3.81(b)–(d). The facilities "must" provide environmental enrichment and special consideration for certain primates, *id.* § 3.81(b), (c), and they "must not" maintain primates in restraint devices "unless required for health reasons as determined by the attending veterinarian or by a research proposal approved by the Committee at research facilities," *id.* § 3.81(d). The regulation on restraints then makes clear that even where a veterinarian approves of restraints, there are still limits: Maintenance under such restraint must be for the shortest period possible. In instances where long-term (more than 12 hours) restraint is required, the nonhuman primate must be provided the opportunity daily for unrestrained activity for at least one continuous hour during the period of restraint, unless continuous restraint is required by the research proposal approved by the Committee at research facilities. *Id.*

Although research facilities may be allowed to restrain primates continuously, this limited exception is not offered to non-research handlers and is in keeping with the statute's bar on the Secretary from interfering with research. *See* 7 U.S.C. § 2143(a)(6)(A)(i)-(iii).

These "requirements" may be minimal but they are clearly mandatory. Jurnove argued, and the district court agreed, that this case begins and ends with the fact that the Secretary provided *no* engineering standards. But in fact he did.

It of course remains possible that the engineering and performance standards chosen by the Secretary are not enough to meet the mandate of "minimum requirements." We assess this issue under the familiar doctrine that if Congress has spoken to the precise question at issue, we must "give effect to the unambiguously expressed intent of Congress," but if Congress has not, we defer to a permissible agency construction of the statute. *Chevron U.S.A., Inc. v. NRDC*, 467 U.S. 837, 842–43 (1984).

Here Jurnove's Exhibit A (and indeed his only serious example) is the Secretary's handling of primates' "social grouping." In 1989 the Secretary proposed to include a requirement of group housing for primates, saying that he intended to emphasize that nonhuman primates must be grouped in a primary enclosure with compatible members of their species or with other nonhuman primate species, either in pairs, family groups, or other compatible social groupings, whenever possible and consistent with providing for the nonhuman primates' health, safety, and well-being, unless social grouping is prohibited by an animal care and use procedure and approved by the facility's Committee. This proposal was based on evidence that "nonhuman primates are social beings in nature and require contact with other nonhuman primates for their psychological well-being," and that "[s]ocial deprivation is regarded by the scientific community as psychologically debilitating to social animals."

The final rule, of course, refrained from imposing such a general group housing requirement. Jurnove (stating his case in the best light) would tie the agency to its 1989 proposal on two theories: He argues first under *Chevron* that because of this finding any interpretation of the statute not recognizing social grouping as one of the "minimum requirements" could not be a reasonable interpretation of the statute. And second he claims that the Secretary's decision was arbitrary and capricious because he failed to explain it adequately, in violation of the Administrative Procedure Act. . . .

The Secretary's 1989 proposal was at odds with comments already in the record. For example, comments of the American Psychological Association had noted the wide disparities in social behavior among primates, with some forming large troops of 50 to 100 or more, others living in small groups of 10 to 20, and still others spending their lives in almost solitary isolation or as pairs in the wild. The 1989 proposal itself then generated new opposing comments, most notably from the University of Chicago, which pointed out that group housing "can significantly increase the incidence of trauma, the spread of upper respiratory and gastrointestinal diseases and more recently has been responsible for the outbreak of Simian Acquired Immune Deficiency Syndrome." Moreover, according to these comments, an image of nonhuman primates blissfully coexisting in groups is a substantially incomplete depiction of species-typical behavior. Again, as the University of Chicago informed the Secretary: "Even in compatible groups in no specific distress, species typical activities include threatening, chasing, fighting, wounding, hair-pulling, food competition, dominance challenges and reversals, and displacement of subordinate animals from food, water and shelter. Such activity can threaten the animals' health and well-being."

The Secretary took account of such comments, just as the designers of "notice and comment" rulemaking intended. He pointed to expressions of concern that "social grouping would endanger the animal's [sic] welfare by increasing noise and fighting," 55 Fed. Reg. at 33491, and to contentions that differences among species (there are, recall, over 240) required "discretion be used in deciding whether to employ group housing," *id*. Although it is true (as the district court noted and Jurnove here argues) that even in the final rulemaking the Secretary observed that "[i]n general, housing in groups promotes psychological well-being more assuredly than does individual housing," 943 F. Supp. at 60 (quoting 56 Fed. Reg. at 6472–73), that generality was obviously qualified by the remarks just quoted.

Thus the Secretary proposed a new regulation on social grouping: The environment enhancement plan must include specific provisions to address the social needs of nonhuman primates of species known to exist in social groups in nature. Such specific provisions must be in accordance with currently accepted professional standards, as cited in appropriate professional journals or reference guides, and as directed by the attending veterinarian. 55 Fed. Reg. at 33525; 9 C.F.R. § 3.81(a) (final rule same). The regulation then offers "exceptions" to the social needs provision if the primate is vicious or debilitated, if it carries contagious diseases, or if its potential companions are not compatible. *Id.* § 3.81(a)(1)–(3). Even though social grouping is no longer formally mandated (facilities must only produce a "specific" plan for action that addresses "social needs"), the Secretary rightly argues that the enumeration of the "exceptions" makes social grouping the "norm."

Contrary to the view of the district court, the statute did not force the Secretary to require social grouping and then specify exceptions. To the contrary, we accord agencies broad deference in choosing the level of generality at which to articulate rules. Nothing in the statutory mandate required greater specificity. . . . [B]ecause the Secretary was reasonably concerned that more precise specification might cause harm, it was entirely reasonable under the statute for him to choose a relatively flexible standard.

The explanation that renders the Secretary's interpretation of the statute reasonable also serves to establish that the final rule was not arbitrary and capricious. Where "Congress delegates power to an agency to regulate on the borders of the unknown, courts cannot interfere with reasonable interpretations of equivocal evidence"; courts are most deferential of agency readings of scientific evidence. There is little question that the Secretary was forced to regulate "on the borders of the unknown" in setting the baseline of rights to "psychological well-being" for nonhuman primates, or at least how to "promote" their psychological well-being. In changing the design of the regulations, the Secretary pointed to substantial conflicting evidence on whether a stringent social grouping requirement was a good idea, and thus his final policy judgment on social grouping was reasonable.

Jurnove may well be correct that some of the Secretary's regulations may prove difficult to enforce, or even difficult to augment through subsequent "interpretation." But the requirements such as the ones on cage size and restraints are eminently enforceable, and the Secretary has begun to offer interpretations likely to assist both regulatees and enforcers. *See Draft Policy on Environment Enhancement for Nonhuman Primates,* 64 Fed. Reg. 38145 (1999).

* * *

The decision of the district court is *Reversed.*

Notes

1. Agencies have broad authority to establish rules pursuant to Congressional mandate. ALDF argued the standards ultimately promulgated by the Secretary were wholly insufficient and therefore did not comply with the agency's requirement. Consider the different perspectives the court and ALDF have with regard to what constitutes the agency's discretion to adopt "minimum standards." Are there other potential bases on which to impact the conditions under which some zoo or research animals are kept?

2. With respect to conditions of confinement, special attention has been paid to the more than 80,000 primates registered with the USDA (which does not include the estimated 11,000 to 15,000 undocumented "pet" primates). As discussed in *Glickman*, because of the complex psychological needs of these highly evolved animals, in 1985 Congress directed the USDA to "promulgate . . . minimum requirements" necessary for these facilities to provide "a physical environment adequate to promote the psychological well-being of primates." 7 U.S.C. § 2143(a)(2)(B). In response to this directive, in 1991 the USDA issued regulations requiring regulated facilities to formulate "psychological enhancement plans" for primates, but left to those entities the determination of the content and substance of those plans. 9 C.F.R. § 3.81.

3. Although the Endangered Species Act (ESA), 16 U.S.C. §§ 1531, *et seq.*, is addressed in Chapter 9, the history of its special listing of chimpanzees is worth noting. From 1989 until 2015, chimpanzees were subject to a "split listing," so that chimpanzees in the wild were given the greatest protection as an "endangered" species, while chimpanzees in captivity (including research, entertainment, public display and exhibition) were treated as a "threatened" species, subject to a special rule that allowed them to be used for almost any purpose. *See former rule at* 50 C.F.R. § 17.40; 55 Fed. Reg. 9129 (1990).

In June 2013 Fish & Wildlife Service (FWS) published a proposed final rule to eliminate the split listing, finding that

> the Act does not allow for captive-held animals to be assigned separate legal status from their wild counterparts on the basis of their captive state, including through designation as a separate distinct population segment (DPS). It is also not possible to separate out captive-held specimens for different legal status under the Act by other approaches. Therefore, we are proposing to eliminate the separate classification of chimpanzees held in captivity and list the entire species, wherever found, as endangered under the Act.

78 Fed Reg. 35202 (2013). In 2015, the rule became final, effectively ending all use of chimpanzees in America, whether for entertainment (not including zoos), public use, or research. While applications for a permit to engage in research can still be submitted and reviewed by FWS, the authors are unaware of FWS receiving any such applications.

4. The Chimpanzee Health Improvement Maintenance and Protection Act enacted in 2000, commonly referred to as the "CHIMP Act," created a federal mechanism to "retire" chimpanzees owned by the federal government. It amended the Public Health Service Act to provide a system of sanctuaries for chimpanzees that have been designated as "no longer needed" in research. It includes requirements for sanctuaries, criteria for "acceptance of chimpanzees into the system" and standards for chimpanzee "retirement." 42 U.S.C.A. § 283m. As originally written, the CHIMP Act allowed chimpanzees to be brought out of retirement and placed back in research facilities. This loophole was never used and in 2007 was changed so that, once retired, the chimpanzees can never be removed from the sanctuary or subjected to any invasive research. As of 2018, Chimp Haven, a nonprofit sanctuary in Louisiana, held the sole contract to provide retirement to federally owned chimpanzees. Finding sanctuary space for retired federal research chimpanzees and funding to support them remains, and likely will always be, a significant challenge.

While government funding limitations may impede retirements, private funding may play a role. A coalition of chimpanzee sanctuaries known as the North American Primate Sanctuary Alliance (NAPSA), which includes Chimp Haven, was formed in 2010, in part to address collectively important issues in the chimpanzee community. Members of NAPSA are "committed to providing space for any chimps the NIH wants to retire." James Gorman, *U.S. to Begin Retiring Most Research Chimps*, N.Y. TIMES, June 26, 2013 (science section).

D. Breeders, Dealers and Puppy Mills

As noted earlier in the AWA overview, regulation of breeders, dealers and the retail sales of animals falls within the purview of the AWA. Many researchers purchase the animals they use from commercial dealers who are regulated under the AWA, but the definition of what constitutes a "dealer" is not always clear.

Associated Dog Clubs of New York State, Inc. v. Vilsack

United States District Court, District of Columbia, 2014
75 F. Supp. 3d 83

CHRISTOPHER R. COOPER, United States District Judge.

With few exceptions, there is nothing one can buy in a traditional store that cannot be bought online as well. It should come as no surprise, then, that the Internet unleashed a growing online market for pet sales. Prompted by this expansion of sight-unseen sales over the Internet, the Department of Agriculture, through the Animal and Plant Health Inspection Service ("APHIS"), issued a new rule that redefined "retail pet store"—a statutory category of pet sellers exempt from regulation by the agency. Whereas APHIS previously exempted from regulation all outlets that sold certain animals directly to the public, its revised retail pet store definition exempted only face-to-face sellers. Many online sellers thus became subject to regulation for the first time. The new rule brought howls from small breeders anxious over the potential costs of regulatory oversight. A collection of those breeders—through some 42 separate dog and cat clubs—seek to bring APHIS to heel, arguing that the agency exceeded its statutory authority in issuing the new rule. But the clubs are barking up the wrong tree: Their complaints are more policy disagreements with APHIS's regulatory approach than they are valid legal objections to APHIS's authority and the process it followed in adopting the rule. Because APHIS acted within its authority in promulgating the rule and otherwise complied with the requirements of the Administrative Procedures Act, the Court will grant summary judgment for the agency.

I. Background

Congress passed the Animal Welfare Act ("AWA"), 7 U.S.C. §2131 *et seq.*, in 1966 "to insure that animals intended . . . for use as pets are provided humane care and treatment," *id.* §2131(1). The Act gives the Secretary of Agriculture authority, which has been delegated to APHIS, to promulgate regulations that require "animal dealers" to be licensed, keep records, and maintain humane facilities. *Id.* §§2133, 2143. The AWA exempts "retail pet stores" from the definition of "animal dealers"—making them free from all regulation by APHIS—but the statute does not define that term. *Id.* §2132(f). Congress left that task to the Secretary. Accordingly, APHIS issued a regulation in 1971 defining "retail pet store" to mean "any retail outlet where animals are sold only as pets at retail." It later created a *de minimis* exception from regulation for any person who maintains three or fewer breeding females and who sells only the offspring of those females for pets or exhibition. Although both APHIS and Congress considered several alternative definitions over the years, these regulations remained relatively unchanged over the next several decades.

In 2010, however, the Department of Agriculture Office of the Inspector General ("OIG") published an audit report critical of APHIS's inspection program. OIG, APHIS Animal Care Program Inspections of Problematic Dealers, Audit Report 33002–4–SF ("OIG Report") (May, 2010), Administrative Record ("AR") 146–214. Among other issues, the report documented a pack of complaints by owners of sick or injured animals purchased from unregulated online sellers. The report observed, however, that '[l]arge breeders that sell AWA-covered animals over the Internet . . . [we]re exempt from [APHIS's] inspection and licensing requirements" because online sellers fell within the definition of retail pet stores. It therefore urged APHIS to seek legislation to cover these unregulated entities. APHIS responded favorably to the recommendation, assuring the OIG that it was promoting a bill that "would place dogs sold directly to the public via the Internet . . . within the jurisdiction of the AWA."

Instead of continuing to pursue legislative change, however, APHIS determined that "the AWA's definition of a regulated 'dealer' is sufficiently broad to allow us to clarify—without legislation—the regulatory definition of a 'retail pet store' so that Internet retail sales of regulated animals are covered[.]"APHIS thus published a notice of proposed rulemaking to limit the retail pet store exemption to only those outlets where "each buyer physically enters [the store] in order to personally observe the animals[.]"

* * *

After receiving over 75,000 comments, which both supported and opposed the new rule, APHIS promulgated the new definition of "retail pet store" in September 2013. Along with the new definition, the rule change also expanded the *de minimis* exception from three to four breeding females. The pertinent sections of the final rule provide:

> Retail pet store means a place of business or residence at which the seller, buyer, and the animal available for sale are physically present so that every buyer may personally observe the animal prior to purchasing and/or taking custody of that animal after purchase[.]

9 C.F.R. § 1.1.

> The following persons are exempt from the licensing requirements. . . . Any person who maintains a total of four or fewer breeding female dogs, cats, and/or small exotic or wild mammals . . . and who sells, at wholesale, only the offspring of these [breeding females], which were born and raised on his or her premises, for pets or exhibition, and is not otherwise required to obtain a license.

Id. § 2.1(a)(3)(iii).

Plaintiffs, a collection of 42 dog and cat clubs and registries,[1] then brought this suit, alleging that the agency's rulemaking violated the Administrative Procedure Act ("APA"), 5 U.S.C. § 706. Approximately three months later, Congress passed the Agricultural Act of 2014, Pub.L. No. 113–79, which amended the AWA to, among other things, exempt from licensing "a dealer or exhibitor under this Act if the size of the business is determined by the secretary to be *de minimis*." *Id.* § 12308 (italics added). The Conference Report for the bill explains that the amendment was meant to codify APHIS's prior *de minimis* exception, so that APHIS could focus "its limited budget and inspection and enforcement staff on entities that pose the greatest risks to animal welfare and public safety." 160 Cong. Rec. H1269–01. The Conference Report also recommended that APHIS engage in rulemaking to further define the *de minimis* exception given "confusion among the regulated industry" over the term "breeding female." *Id.* The Agricultural Act did not affect APHIS's new definition of retail pet store. After the clubs brought suit, the Humane Society of the United States filed a motion to intervene to defend the rule, which the Court granted. The dog clubs, the Secretary, and the Humane Society have now cross-moved for summary judgment.

---

1. With no offense to our feline friends, the Court will refer to the Plaintiffs as "dog clubs" or simply "clubs."

II. Standard of Review

Summary judgment in an APA case supported by an administrative record generally does not apply the standard set forth in Federal Rule of Civil Procedure 56(a). Instead, the district court's role "'is to determine whether or not as a matter of law the evidence in the administrative record permitted the agency to make the decision it did.'" "Summary judgment thus serves as a mechanism for deciding, as a matter of law, whether the agency action is supported by the administrative record and is otherwise consistent with the APA standard of review."

III. Analysis

The dog clubs have two main bones of contention with the new rule. First, they argue that APHIS exceeded its regulatory authority under the AWA by changing the agency's long-established definition of "retail pet store," which they view as inconsistent with the new definition. Second, the clubs contend that the agency's rulemaking process was arbitrary and capricious because APHIS underestimated the number of breeders that would be affected by the new rule, minimized the fiscal impact of the rule on those breeders, and arbitrarily covered smaller breeders despite the fact that the OIG only identified problems with large Internet sellers.

A. Authority Under the AWA

Chevron, U.S.A. v. Natural Resources Defense Council, 467 U.S. 837 (1984), establishes a two-part inquiry to determine whether an agency charged with implementing a statute has arrived at a permissible interpretation of the law. First, if a law directly addresses the precise question at issue, Congress's directive is, of course, controlling. Second, if the statute is silent or ambiguous regarding the matter at hand, "'the question for the court is whether the agency's interpretation is based on a permissible construction of the statute in light of its language, structure, and purpose.'" The court must defer to any reasonable agency interpretation; the interpretation need not be the one "deemed *most* reasonable by the courts[,]"

As the Secretary and the clubs both agree, the D.C. Circuit in *Doris Day Animal League v. Veneman*, 315 F.3d 297 (D.C.Cir.2003), found the meaning of "retail pet store" in the AWA to be ambiguous. *Id*. at 300 ("there is enough play in the language of the Act to preclude us from saying that Congress has spoken to the issue with clarity"). Thus, the only question before the Court is whether, under *Chevron* step-two, the agency's new rule is a reasonable construction of the term. The Court concludes that it is.

The new rule limits the retail pet store exemption to outlets where the seller, buyer, and animal are physically present at each sale, while the old rule considered any retail outlet, including mail-order or online sellers, to be exempt from AWA regulation. APHIS justified the limitation by explaining that face-to-face buyers are able to inspect the seller's premises and the animals. Online buyers, by contrast, generally cannot determine the animal's condition before receiving the pet and may never see the seller's facilities. Particularly in light of the recent growth in online sales, the Secretary posited that this lack of oversight by online buyers justified bringing sight-unseen sales within the scope of APHIS regulation.

The Secretary's justification for the rule is reasonable on its face. The dog clubs nevertheless maintain that APHIS exceeded its authority because the new definition of retail pet store is inconsistent with the agency's prior definition, which had allowed unregulated sight-unseen sales for 47 years and which APHIS defended against an APA challenge as recently as 2003. But that dog won't hunt. An agency may change, or even reverse, longstanding positions while enjoying *Chevron* deference so long as it provides a reasoned explanation for doing so. APHIS has provided such an explanation here. The clubs overstate the regulatory change in any event: The prior rule did not expressly exempt sight-unseen sales; it merely failed to address them. Thus, APHIS's new approach is more accurately described as closing a loophole than reversing a settled position. As APHIS explained, it updated the definition to address the "dramatic rise in sight unseen sales" brought on by the Internet. Closing a loophole because it has grown into a significant regulatory gap is a sufficiently reasoned explanation for adopting a new agency position.

Despite the clubs' assertions to the contrary, the Secretary's current position is not inconsistent with the government's litigation position in *Doris Day*, where a previous Secretary defended the prior retail pet store definition. The government's position in *Doris Day* was that the definition of retail pet store was not clearly established, and APHIS's interpretation of the term was reasonable in light of that ambiguity. The government still maintains that the term is open for interpretation; it simply argues that both the prior and current definitions are reasonable. Moreover, the primary defense of the regulation advanced by the Secretary in *Doris Day* was that "'retail dealers . . . are already subject to a degree of self-regulation and oversight by persons who purchase animals from the retailers' homes.'" As discussed above, that justification does not apply to online sales. See OIG Report, AR 185 ("for Internet breeders, there is no degree of self-regulation and oversight because consumers do not have access to their facilities"). Accordingly, the prior Secretary's position in *Doris Day* does not undercut APHIS's authority to promulgate the rule at issue here.

The dog clubs also contend that APHIS's revision of the retail pet store definition through rulemaking is inconsistent with its prior commitment to address its concerns about online sellers via legislation. They rely on *American Mining Congress v. United States Army Corps of Engineers*, 951 F. Supp. 267 (D.D.C. 1997), where the district court rejected the agency's revised definition of "discharge" under the Clean Water Act. In a footnote, the court observed in passing that the agency had intended to clarify the term through legislation before issuing the challenged regulation. But the court did not rely on this fact in holding that the text and legislative history of the Clean Water Act did not support the agency's interpretation. *American Mining Congress* therefore does not help the clubs, and they have not offered any other authority for the proposition that an agency's stated intention to pursue legislative change forever bars it from seeking the same result through regulation.

The clubs also argue that APHIS exceeded its authority because Congress acquiesced in the prior definition of "retail pet store" by reenacting the AWA several times without modifying the definition. When Congress reenacts a statute but does not modify an Agency's interpretation of a regulatory provision, it can be evidence that Congress has endorsed the interpretation. APHIS emphasizes, however, that Congress reenacted the AWA *after* the rule change as well. Indeed, although the Court is somewhat leery of congressional acquiescence arguments generally, the subsequent passage of the Agricultural Act of 2014 creates a particularly sturdy footing for the argument that Congress acquiesced to the new definition. That is so because the Agricultural Act codified one aspect of the AWA exemption—the historic *de minimis* exception—but did not affect the brand-new "retail pet store" definition. Similarly, the Conference Report on the bill urges APHIS to clarify the meaning of "breeding female" but does not mention the new definition of "retail pet store." Both the Act and its legislative history thus suggest that members of Congress specifically considered the retail pet store exemption immediately after APHIS changed the definition but left the change untouched. Short of explicit endorsement, it is difficult to imagine a better example of congressional acquiescence to a regulatory change.

* * *

IV. Conclusion

For reasons stated above, the Court will grant the Defendants' and Intervenor–Defendant's motions for summary judgment and deny the Plaintiffs' motion. The Court will issue an order consistent with this opinion.

Notes

1. The court in *Associated Dog Clubs* frequently refers to *Doris Day Animal League v. Veneman*, 315 F. 3d 297 (D. C. Cir. 2003). In *Doris Day*, an animal welfare group challenged the validity of a regulation exempting breeders who sell dogs from their residences from AWA licensing requirements. The *Doris Day* court ruled against the animal welfare group and held that the regulation was a reasonable interpretation of Congressional intent. While the court did not interpret the term "retail pet store" as broadly as plaintiffs, legislative efforts to protect animals who are subjects of commercial breeding and sales operations were ongoing at that time and have continued since. For example, in 2001, the "Puppy Protection Act" was introduced in Congress to amend the AWA "to address the widespread suffering that occurs from unsanitary and inhumane conditions in 'puppy mills.'" Laurie Fulkerson, *2001 Legislative Review*, 8 ANIMAL L. 259, 281 (2002) ("*Fulkerson*"). Puppy mills are "dog breeding operation[s] in which the health of the dogs is disregarded in order to maintain a low overhead and maximize profits." *Avenson v. Zegart*, 577 F. Supp. 958, 960 (D. Minn. 1984).

> The Act recognized that puppies and adults in puppy mills suffer from, among other things, lack of protection from the elements, infestation from

rodents and insects, over-breeding, lack of proper veterinary care, and lack of socialization with humans. Females are bred too young, often at the time of their first estrus. Puppies and adults tend to suffer from disease due to overcrowding and inbreeding, and often do not live long or healthy lives. In addition, unwanted animals are often killed.

Fulkerson, at 281–82, citing to S.R. 1478 (107th Cong. 2001).

The Puppy Protection Act sought to rectify these problems by (i) mandating that female dogs be at least one year old before they are bred, and (ii) designating that females would not be bred more than three times in a twenty-four month period. S.R. 1478. The Act also sought to develop standards for socializing the dogs, based on recommendations from animal welfare and behavior experts. *Id*. In addition, it would have provided civil and criminal penalties for violators. *Id*.

The Act created a great deal of controversy, in large part due to its definition of "breeders."

Groups such as the American Kennel Club and the National Animal Interest Alliance, interpret the amendment as regulating even one-time breeders, and fear that government intrusion into all dog breeding will result in a lowering, rather than a raising, of standards. The opposition feels that engineered standards for socialization could be too rigid and too reflective of true working socialization techniques, and that any deviation would result in a violation. In addition, the opposition believes that this amendment would take USDA inspectors away from their jobs in investigating "puppy mills" and put them into roles of ensuring that the 300,000 licensed breeders in the United States are complying with the amendment. Those in support of the amendment, such as the HSUS and the Doris Day Animal League, believe that the term "breeders," as defined in the amendment, covers all manner of breeders. Supporters of the amendment feel that closing down puppy mills and providing humane breeding are such important issues that they trump any small governmental intrusion potentially faced by "responsible" breeders.

Fulkerson, at 282–83.

The Puppy Protection Act passed in the Senate but did not pass in the House of Representatives. In 2013, federal lawmakers introduced legislation to close a loophole in the AWA regulations that then allowed dogs to be sold over the Internet without any oversight or standards of care, thereby allowing large, commercial breeders who sell puppies online or directly to the public to escape the licensing and inspection requirements that apply to breeders selling dogs to pet stores. S. 395 and H.R. 847 — known as the PUPS Act, or "Puppy Uniform Protection and Safety Act" — ultimately did not pass. Since that time, similar bills have been introduced, but as of this publication none have passed.

2. In addition to promoting animal welfare, strictly regulating online breeder sales helps protect consumers. A recent phenomenon is internet sales fraud involving

online pet sales. A licensed breeder will post a photo of an animal for sale. Another person, engaging in fraud, will then use that photo in an advertisement for an animal that does not exist, thereby defrauding a buyer out of several hundreds, if not thousands, of dollars. The problem is not isolated and is in fact quite prevalent. In 2015, an internal report with the Federal Trade Commission indicated receipt of 37,000 complaints related to fraudulent online pet-sales. Karin Brulliard, *How much is that doggy on the website? It might not even exist.* WASH. POST, Sept. 28, 2017.

3. The ASPCA has estimated that approximately 500,000 puppies are sold annually by pet stores; in 1997 the Humane Society of the United States estimated that 90% of those puppies came from puppy mills. Adam J. Fumarola, *With Best Friends Like Us Who Needs Enemies? The Phenomenon of the Puppy Mill, the Failure of Legal Regimes to Manage It, and the Positive Prospects of Animal Rights*, 6 BUFF. ENVT'L. L.J. 253, 262, 263 (1999). Fumarola's article discusses "the atrocities and horrors that make up this recent American phenomenon" of puppy mills, which developed after World War II when the USDA "began promoting the raising of dogs as a crop" as an alternative means for farmers to make money. *Id.* at 261–62. There is little case law on these issues, but the cited article discusses the legal means of addressing them— by regulating the source (through the AWA, private nuisance claims, local zoning laws and anti-cruelty statutes) and by regulating the distributors (through products liability and breach of contract claims, and state animal dealer legislation). *Id.* at 267–82. As the author recognizes, however, these avenues have been ineffective at improving industry standards and conditions. At best, local prosecutors or other government agencies, animal protection organizations or concerned individuals may succeed in limiting or closing down a single operation in the locality, but the wholesale practices continue, in practical effect unregulated.

Additionally, like other large-scale industry efforts using animals in commercial ventures, all of the larger operations occur behind closed doors, unviewed by the public and unknown to the agencies established to monitor such situations. Complex levels of operations similar to those in organized crime may often insulate the producers of the animals from the oversight and authority of those who have the power to enforce the laws being broken.

In the end, public awareness and consumer action—by adopting rather than purchasing companion animals and by refusing to make any purchases from retailers (over the Internet or in stores)—may be the most effective means of ending the puppy mill industry. At the same time, states are starting to consider, and in several cases pass, legislation to address the problem of puppy mills. For example, in 2009 Tennessee enacted the Tennessee Commercial Breeder Act, which requires operations with more than twenty unsterilized female dogs kept for breeding to be licensed, inspected and follow humane care standards; requires commercial breeding operations to comply with state sales tax requirements and be subject to licensure and inspection; and holds mass dog producers accountable to consumers by ensuring they are subject to the consumer protection act. TENN. CODE ANN. §§ 44-17-701–715.

Pennsylvania is another state that has passed legislation intended to combat the problems inherent with puppy mills. 3 Pa. Stat. Ann. § 459-101-1205 (Dog Law). The Pennsylvania Department of Agriculture enacted regulations to enforce Pennsylvania's Dog Law, which included a provision allowing nursing female dogs to be kept in enclosures with 50% metal flooring. The regulation was challenged as directly contradicting the Dog Law's express prohibition against metal flooring in primary enclosures of dogs who are more than twelve weeks old. The court agreed, struck down the regulation and granted summary judgment in favor of the plaintiffs (ALDF and Pennsylvania dog owners who were members of ALDF). *Keith v. Commonwealth ex rel. Pa. Dep't of Agric.*, 151 A.3d 687 (Pa. Commw. Ct. 2016). Thus, it is not enough that such laws are enacted, but animal advocates need to remain apprised of regulations later enacted to enforce such laws, to assure that they are not contrary to the express language or intent of the laws, as this one was determined to be.

In 2017, California became the first state to enact a bill prohibiting the sale of commercially bred dogs, cats and rabbits in pet stores. Assembly Bill No. 485, enacted as Cal. Health & Safety Code § 122354.5 (effective Jan. 1, 2018; operative Jan. 1, 2019) and as amendments to other Code sections. The statute allows retail pet stores to sell only animals obtained from rescue groups, animal shelters, humane societies, or animal control agencies; and the stores must maintain records indicating the source of each animal they sell. Though California was the first state to fully ban the sale of commercially bred companion animals, at least one more state (Maryland) enacted a similar bill in 2018, and more than 250 localities in twenty-two states and several provinces in Canada ban the sales of commercially bred animals. Some of the laws cover only dogs and cats, and some also cover rabbits, and they vary in the restrictions imposed and the sources of the animals who can be sold. For more information, see *https://bestfriends.org/resources/puppy-mills/jurisdictions-retail-pet-sale-bans*.

There is wide-ranging public support for these laws. But like the agribusiness industry and restaurant challenges to laws aimed at improving the conditions under which animals are raised and slaughtered to be food products (often immediately after the laws take effect), so too have breeders and pet stores promptly sued to overturn these ordinances. The grounds here too are often arguments under the Supremacy (claiming preemption by the AWA and/or state laws), Dormant Commerce, Takings, Equal Protection and Contract Clauses of the U.S. Constitution. These ordinances have withstood almost every challenge, which at the time of publication have been reviewed in several federal circuit courts of appeals as seen in the next case and the Notes that follow it.

New York Pet Welfare Association v. City of New York

United States Court of Appeal, Second Circuit, 2017
850 F.3d 79

Edward R. Korman, District Judge:

Home to more than a million dogs and cats, New York City (collectively with two individual defendants, "the City") has long worked to address a tangle of problems surrounding the companion animal business—including irresponsible breeding of animals destined for the City market, their subsequent sale to unwitting consumers, and an overpopulation of unwanted animals. Armed with a new grant of authority from the Legislature, the City enacted a package of laws in 2015 that aimed to mitigate these issues by regulating the sale of dogs and cats in pet shops.

On the day they were to take effect, the New York Pet Welfare Association ("NYPWA") brought this suit to block two of these mandates. The first—the "Sourcing Law"—requires that pet shops sell only animals acquired from breeders holding a Class A license issued under the federal Animal Welfare Act ("AWA"), and the second—the "Spay/Neuter Law"—requires that pet shops sterilize each animal before releasing it to a consumer. NYPWA claims that the Sourcing Law violates the "dormant" *Commerce Clause* and is preempted by the AWA, and that the Spay/Neuter Law is preempted by New York law. The district judge dismissed NYPWA's entire complaint. NYPWA appeals, and we affirm.

BACKGROUND

I. Federal, State, and City Regulation of Commerce in Animals

The commercial breeding and sale of companion animals is subject to a web of overlapping federal, state, and local regulation. The Animal Welfare Act, 7 U.S.C. § 2131 et seq., is the only federal law addressed to the trade and treatment of dogs and cats intended for use as pets. The AWA applies broadly, covering any "dealer"— a "person who, in commerce, for compensation or profit, delivers for transportation, or transports, except as a carrier, buys, or sells, or negotiates the purchase or sale of . . . any dog or other animal . . . [for] use as a pet," *id.* § 2132(f)—but the statute itself does not deal in details. Rather, it sets up a general structure and tells the Secretary of Agriculture to fill in the blanks. The AWA requires most dealers to be federally licensed, but leaves it to the Secretary to design the licensing scheme and define specific standards of care that dealers must abide by.

The Secretary has created three licensing categories of dealers: Class A breeders, Class B distributors, and exempt breeders. Class A breeders include all dealers subject to licensure "whose business involving animals consists only of animals that are bred and raised on the premises." 9 C.F.R. § 1.1. Class B distributors include all dealers subject to licensure "whose business includes the purchase and/or resale of any animal," including brokers who "negotiate or arrange for" the purchase or sale of animals, but do not take possession or ownership of them. *Id.* Exempt breeders do not need licenses so long as they have four or fewer breeding females, and sell only their offspring. 9 C.F.R. § 2.1(a)(3)(iii), (vii).

Despite its breadth, the AWA has always explicitly contemplated continuing state and local regulation of commerce in animals. The Act authorizes the Secretary "to cooperate with the officials of the various States or political subdivisions thereof in effectuating the purposes of this Act and of any State . . . or municipal legislation or ordinance on the same subject." (codified as amended at 7 U.S.C. § 2145(b)). Moreover, in 1985, Congress directed that the federal standards applicable to dealers under the AWA "shall not prohibit any State . . . from promulgating standards in addition to those . . . promulgated by the Secretary." (codified at 7 U.S.C. § 2143 (a)(8)).

Indeed, many states have specifically regulated the sale of dogs and cats. Many of these laws are motivated by concern that large-scale commercial breeders — often maligned (whether fairly or not) as "puppy mills" — prioritize profit over humane treatment and responsible breeding, and target them for special scrutiny. *See, e.g.,* N.Y. Agric. & Mkts. Law § 405 (requiring yearly inspections of dealers who sell more than 25 animals per year); *see also* American Society For The Prevention Of Cruelty To Animals, State Puppy Mill Chart (last updated June 16, 2015), *archived at https:// perma.cc/HTK3-ZNQ4.*

In addition to regulating large breeders directly, some jurisdictions have also opted to regulate the pet shops through which poorly bred or ill-treated animals are often sold. Some of these laws simply provide consumers additional protection by strengthening warranties and mandating disclosures about the animal. Over the last several years, however, many jurisdictions have enacted laws that sharply limit — or simply eliminate — pet shops' ability to acquire dogs and cats from commercial sources. Three states limit pet shops' sale of commercially bred dogs to animals obtained from federal licensees with clean records.[4] And numerous local governments have gone farther, banning pet shops from selling *any* animal not acquired from a shelter or humane society.[5]

Until recently, New York law blocked any efforts by the City to regulate its own pet shops. The Pet Dealer Act (codified at N.Y. Agric. & Mkts. Law § 400-a (repealed 2014); N.Y. Gen. Bus. Law § 753-e (repealed 2014)), expressly preempted "any local

---

4. Connecticut requires pet shops to source only from USDA licensees without recent citations for violating the AWA, *see* Act of June 3, 2014 (codified at Conn. Gen. Stat. § 22-354(b)); New Jersey accepts sourcing from either USDA licensees without recent citations for violating the AWA, or from animal control facilities, rescue organizations, or shelters, *see* Act of Feb. 5, 2015 (codified at N.J. Rev. Stat. § 56:8-95.1); and Virginia mandates sourcing either from persons without recent citations for AWA violations, or from a humane society or animal shelter, *see* Act of Mar. 27, 2015 (codified at Va. Code Ann. § 3.2-6511.1).

5. So far as we are aware, Los Angeles enacted the first local ordinance regulating the sourcing practices of pet shops in 2012, barring all sales of dogs or cats in pet shops except those obtained from animal shelters or humane societies. *See* L.A., Cal., Ordinance 182309 (Sept. 10, 2012) (codified as amended at L.A., Cal., Municipal Code § 53.73). Among major cities and counties, Chicago, *see* Chi., Ill., Municipal Code § 4-384-015(b), San Diego, *see* San Diego, Cal., Municipal Code § 42.0706, and Las Vegas, *see* Las Vegas, Nev., Municipal Code § 7.40.315(A), have enacted similar laws. Cook County, Illinois, *see* Cook Cty., Ill., Code Of Ordinances § 10-13(a), allows pet shops to source from Class A breeders in addition to shelters. For a listing of local ordinances banning or limiting the sale of dogs and cats in pet shops, see Best Friends Animal Society, Jurisdictions With Retail Pet Sale Bans (last visited Jan. 4, 2017), *archived at https://perma.cc /8DFA-PLWS.*

law . . . regulating or licensing pet dealers." In 2014 the Legislature changed course, explicitly providing that nothing in the Pet Dealer Act should be construed to "limit or restrict any municipality from enacting or enforcing a local law . . . governing pet dealers . . . including a law . . . governing the source of animals sold or offered for sale by pet dealers, and the spay or neuter of such animals." N.Y. Agric. & Mkts. Law § 407; N.Y. Gen. Bus. Law § 753-d).

II. The Challenged Laws

Shortly thereafter, the New York City Council began considering several new laws regulating pet shops. After multiple hearings and extensive testimony on the proposed regulations, the City enacted, *inter alia*, the Sourcing Law (N.Y.C. Admin. Code § 17-1702), and the Spay/Neuter Law (N.Y.C. Admin. Code § 17-804(b)).

The Sourcing Law provides that City pet shops may obtain dogs or cats *only* directly from federally-licensed Class A breeders (who sell only animals bred and raised on their own premises). Moreover, pet shops may buy only from breeders whose federal license has not been suspended within the last five years, have not been recently cited for violating the AWA by the U.S. Department of Agriculture, and provide a sworn affidavit that they have never been convicted of violating certain animal protection laws. Pet shops are also expressly forbidden from selling animals knowingly obtained from Class B distributors (who purchase and resell animals), and forbidden by implication from selling animals obtained from exempt breeders (who cannot obtain a Class A license because they have fewer than five breeding females). Notably, the same sourcing rules do not apply to animal shelters or animal rescue organizations.

The Spay/Neuter Law prohibits pet shops from releasing any dog or cat to a consumer unless it has been sterilized by a veterinarian. The Law specifically defines "sterilization" as such an operation performed on a "dog or cat that is at least eight weeks of age and that weighs at least two pounds." Animal shelters are also generally required to sterilize dogs and cats before releasing them, but their obligation to do so is subject to a number of exceptions not applicable to pet shops.

DISCUSSION

Review of a dismissal under Fed. R. Civ. P. 12(b)(6) is de novo. We consider the facts alleged in the complaint, documents attached to it or incorporated by reference, and matters subject to judicial notice. We accept well-pleaded allegations and draw all reasonable inferences in the plaintiff's favor.

I. Federal Preemption

A. Obstacle Preemption

NYPWA argues that the district judge erred in holding that the Sourcing Law is not preempted by the AWA. There are several well-established categories of preemption, but NYPWA alleges only that one—obstacle preemption—applies here. Federal law preempts conflicting state laws, and the Supreme Court has long recognized that a conflict exists when a state law "stands as an obstacle to the accomplishment . . . of the full purposes and objectives of" federal law. NYPWA argues that the Sourcing Law obstructs the Animal Welfare Act by interfering with its system of licensing for animal dealers. We disagree.

Preemption analysis rests on two fundamental principles. First, every preemption case starts with the presumption that Congress did not intend to displace state law. Because this presumption rests on our "respect for the States as independent sovereigns in our federal system," it is especially strong in areas where states traditionally wield police powers. The heavy burden of overcoming this presumption falls on the party alleging preemption, who must show that the conflict between the federal and state laws "is so direct and positive that the two . . . cannot be reconciled or consistently stand together."

Second, since preemption is ultimately a question of statutory construction, it is always a matter of intent, "even where that intent must be inferred." We look to the intent of Congress to determine the preemptive force of a statute, but in evaluating preemption by a regulation, we focus on the agency's intent. Divining Congress's intent is always "a matter of judgment, to be informed by examining the federal [scheme] as a whole and identifying its purpose and intended effects." We apply the same "ordinary pre-emption principles" whether the relevant federal law is a statute or a regulation. We turn to that inquiry now.

B. The Animal Welfare Act Does Not Preempt the Sourcing Law

Because obstacle analysis hinges on the purposes of the federal scheme, "we must first ascertain those objectives as they relate to the federal law[s] at issue." NYPWA's federal preemption claim is very specific, arguing only that the Sourcing Law obstructs the system of dealer licenses authorized by the AWA and implemented by the Secretary of Agriculture. The threshold task, then, is to determine the purpose of *that licensure scheme* as it relates to the broader objectives of the AWA and its implementing regulations.

Nevertheless, despite NYPWA's narrow focus, neither party squarely addresses the issue. The City argues wrongly that the AWA does not preempt the Sourcing Law because they share the goal of promoting the humane treatment of animals. Broad harmony of purpose will not save a state law from preemption if it "interferes with the methods by which the federal statute was designed to reach [its] goal." NYPWA misses the point as well when it focuses too narrowly on the fact that the Sourcing Law blocks particular pet dealers from acting in ways that federal law standing alone would allow. It explains how those strictures interfere with the business models of *individual licensees*, but not how they interfere with the role of the licensing *system* in advancing the statute's overall goals. The question is whether the Sourcing Law blocks the licensure system from fulfilling the specific role that Congress and the Secretary of Agriculture intend it to play in advancing the goals of the AWA.

Neither Congress nor the Secretary has explained the purpose of licensure in the overall AWA scheme. Nevertheless, a careful analysis of the AWA's provisions suggests that licensure is best understood as a system of compulsory registration designed to require dealers to provide information that would facilitate the Act's objective of creating a nationwide system of animal welfare inspections.

Inspections are central to the AWA: the statute directs the Secretary to carry out inspections to determine whether dealers are violating the Act, 7 U.S.C. § 2146(a), and requires that federal inspectors have access to dealers' premises, animals, and records, *id.* The regulations implementing that provision give federal officials broad latitude to inspect and document all aspects of a dealer's business without giving prior notice. *See* 9 C.F.R. § 2.126. Indeed, the portion of the statute captioned "Administration and enforcement" deals exclusively with empowering the Secretary to inspect and otherwise investigate regulated parties. *See* 7 U.S.C. § 2146. Put simply, the Secretary's nationwide authority to proactively inspect for violations is the AWA's primary enforcement mechanism. *See* U.S. Department Of Agriculture, Animal Welfare Act Enforcement (last modified Oct. 3, 2016), *archived at* *https://perma.cc/YRK4-7ENE*.

Of course, to make a nationwide inspection program effective, the Secretary has to know what to inspect. At a minimum, he has to know who the dealers are and where to find them. But that presents a problem—how is the Secretary supposed to get that information? To be sure, Congress could have directed him to simply start looking for dealers on his own. But even in 1966 the AWA swept broadly, covering "live dogs, cats, monkeys . . . , guinea pigs, hamsters, and rabbits," and the job of finding every dog and cat dealer in the United States (to say nothing of its hamsters) would have been enough to make the Secretary, in his few, fleeting, hopeful moments, wish longingly to trade places with Sisyphus. The AWA aims to solve this problem through a system of compulsory licensure. In requiring dealers to obtain federal licenses, the Act and the Secretary's regulations require regulated parties to make themselves known to regulators, and to turn over the information that is pertinent to enforcing the Act.

We also note that this view of licensure as facilitating inspection finds some measure of support in the Department of Agriculture's approach to the AWA. Its regulations, for example, generally do not prescribe the information required to obtain a license, *except* to expressly require that applicants provide a mailing address and "a valid premises address where animals, animal facilities, equipment, and records may be inspected for compliance." 9 C.F.R. § 2.1(a)(1). The Secretary's decision to require a satisfactory inspection as a precondition to the issuance of a license also suggests that the agency intends licensure to further the AWA's enforcement mechanisms. *See* 9 C.F.R. § 2.3(b). Moreover, in a recent statement of basis and purpose, the Secretary justified his decision to exempt certain small breeders from licensing on the grounds that, as "low-risk" facilities, they did not need "Federal oversight." 78 Fed. Reg. 57227, 57240 (2013). Since inspection constitutes the bulk of oversight, the agency's decision to forego licensing where oversight is unnecessary is consistent with our view that licensure is an administrative mechanism meant to facilitate the inspection regime that gives the AWA teeth.

The second step in our analysis is ascertaining whether the Sourcing Law stands as an obstacle to that purpose. It clearly does not. Breeders and distributors' ability to sell to City pet shops has no bearing on the licensing scheme's ability to facilitate federal enforcement activities. Distributors will still have to get licenses, will still have to provide information to federal officials, and will still have to open their facilities to federal inspection. And of course, exempt breeders will still be excluded from the licensing system as a matter of federal law.

C. NYPWA's Preemption Arguments Are Meritless

NYPWA's arguments appear to rest on a very different view of licensure's role that is never clearly articulated, but that we nevertheless consider and reject. NYPWA argues that the AWA's regulations grant animal dealers a federal right to engage in any line of business they wish without state interference. NYPWA finds these rights in both federal action—licensing certain animal dealers—and federal inaction—determining that other animal dealers do not need licenses. The unspoken but inescapable implication of NYPWA's position is that the Secretary's intent was simply to preempt the field of trade in animals.

Where Congress legislates in an area that is within the states' traditional police powers, intent to preempt the field will ordinarily not be inferred unless such intent is "clear and manifest." This is just such a field, *see, e.g., Reid v. Colorado*, 187 U.S. 137, 148 (1902) (upholding a state statute regulating trade in cattle and horses sourced from certain areas as a valid exercise of police powers), and we do not detect the requisite intent in the licensure system. The mere creation of a federal licensing scheme does not indicate that Congress wanted to displace state law.

Significantly, the text of the AWA unambiguously envisions continuing state animal welfare regulation. Congress has expressly authorized the Secretary, in implementing the Act, to "cooperate with" local officials "in carrying out the purposes of . . . [the AWA] and of any State, local, or municipal legislation or ordinance on the same subject." 7 U.S.C. § 2145(b). The Secretary may preempt only to the extent that Congress has delegated him the power to do so. Section 2145(b)'s explicit grant of authority to the Secretary to cooperate with state officials carrying out state law makes it clear that Congress did not intend that the statute displace all state regulation of the field.

II. Commerce Clause

A. Overview

The Commerce Clause empowers Congress "to regulate Commerce . . . among the several States," U.S. Const. Art. I, § 8, cl. 3, but also has a corresponding "negative" or "dormant" aspect that "limits the power of local governments to enact laws affecting interstate commerce." Analysis of state and local laws under the dormant Commerce Clause treads a well-worn path. First, we determine whether the challenged law "discriminates against interstate commerce," or "regulates evenhandedly with only incidental effects on interstate commerce."

In this context, discrimination "means differential treatment of in-state and out-of-state economic interests that benefits the former and burdens the latter." Discriminatory laws are permissible only if the state shows they are "demonstrably justified by a valid factor unrelated to economic protectionism." This justification must show "a legitimate local purpose that cannot be adequately served by reasonable nondiscriminatory alternatives."

Laws that impose only incidental burdens on interstate commerce, however, are subject to a much more forgiving standard. Under the balancing test of *Pike v. Bruce Church, Inc.*, 397 U.S. 137, 142 (1970), we will uphold a nondiscriminatory law unless the challenger shows that "the burden imposed on [interstate] commerce is clearly excessive in relation to the putative local benefits."

B. The Sourcing Law Does Not Discriminate Against Interstate Commerce

The Supreme Court has recognized three modes of discrimination against interstate commerce: a law may discriminate on its face, harbor a discriminatory purpose, or discriminate in its effect. On appeal, NYPWA raises three different theories of discriminatory effect.

First, NYPWA contends that the Sourcing Law discriminates against out-of- state breeders, because "many" (not all) of them cannot afford the expense of reaching the New York City marketplace except by selling to Class B distributors, who resell animals to pet shops but are now prohibited from engaging in such commerce within the City. The Commerce Clause, however, "protects the interstate market, not particular interstate firms." The Sourcing Law may make it difficult or impossible for some out-of-state breeders to sell to City pet shops, but so long as others are able to, "interstate commerce is not subjected to an impermissible burden simply because a[] . . . regulation causes some business to shift from one interstate supplier to another."

Based on NYPWA's complaint, we have every reason to believe that some out-of-state breeders will sell directly to City pet shops. After all, NYPWA alleges that pet shops depend on puppy sales for a significant portion of their revenues and that the vast majority of Class A breeders are located outside New York. With or without the Sourcing Law, City pet shops will need to import puppies into New York, and the interstate market will have every incentive to meet demand. The Sourcing Law is not invalid merely because it favors out-of-state breeders who are able to make direct sales over those who are not.

NYPWA's second theory of discriminatory effect is that by shifting the City pet market away from pet shops—which buy most of their animals from dealers outside New York—and towards animal shelters and rescues ("rescue entities"), the Sourcing Law disadvantages out-of-state pet dealers in favor of local rescue entities for access to the City pet market. The City, in turn, contends that commercial dealers and rescue entities are so dissimilarly situated as to be incomparable. We need not resolve the City's argument, because even assuming that the two are similarly situated, NYPWA still fails to show discrimination against interstate commerce. The complaint alleges that rescue entities are vigorous participants in the *interstate* market for companion animals. Rescue entities "obtain dogs and cats from across the country," which they sell "throughout the City." To the extent the Sourcing Law makes it easier for rescue entities, and harder for breeders, to compete in the City, it merely shifts business from one interstate actor to another.

Finally, NYPWA argues that the Sourcing Law discriminates against interstate commerce because the vast majority of Class B distributors (who buy from breeders for resale to pet shops, and are barred by the Sourcing Law from selling to City pet shops) are located outside New York. The Supreme Court has considered and rejected the argument that a "statute is discriminatory because it will apply most often to out-of-state entities" in a market that has more out-of-state than in-state participants, and there is no need to say any more here.

C. The Sourcing Law Survives Pike Balancing

Because the Sourcing Law does not discriminate against interstate commerce, under the *Pike* balancing test, we will uphold it unless NYPWA can show that the incidental burden it imposes on such commerce is clearly excessive in relation to the local benefits. An incidental burden is one that weighs more heavily on interstate commerce than intrastate commerce. We have recognized three types of 'incidental' burdens: regulations that have a disparate impact on in- versus out-of-state entities, laws that regulate beyond the state's borders, and laws that create regulatory inconsistencies between states. *Id.*

First, NYPWA fails sufficiently to allege that the burden of selling directly to City pet shops, rather than through distributors, will fall disproportionately on out-of-state breeders. Even drawing the extremely favorable inference that the burden of direct sales will correlate directly with the seller's distance from the City, NYPWA still has not pled a disparate impact. The cost of doing business in many markets is higher for faraway sellers than for nearby ones, and the Sourcing Law does not violate the Commerce Clause merely because of that fact. Where the cost of compliance with the Sourcing Law would be the same in Pittsburgh as in Buffalo, the Law cannot be said to impose a special burden on interstate commerce.

Second, NYPWA does not demonstrate that the Sourcing Law 'directly controls commerce occurring wholly outside' of New York. It argues that the Sourcing Law will have such an effect when out-of-state exempt breeders increase the scale of their operations in order to qualify for Class A licenses, which are only available to breeders with more than four breeding females. The Commerce Clause, however, does not void every law that causes behavior to change in other states. Rather, the measure of extraterritoriality is whether the Sourcing Law "inescapably require[s]" breeders to operate on the City's terms even when doing business elsewhere. That standard is not met here, where the Sourcing Law attaches no significance to breeders' conduct with respect to animals sold outside the City.

Finally, NYPWA has pled no facts indicating that the Sourcing Law is 'in substantial conflict with a common regulatory scheme in place in other states.' The complaint contains no allegations at all that the Sourcing Law will create an interstate regulatory conflict. Even if we were to consider allegations raised for the first time on appeal, NYPWA's opening brief simply concludes, without support, that the Sourcing Law conflicts with the laws of other states. NYPWA does cite some examples in its reply brief, but they do not conflict either with the Sourcing Law or with each other — a breeder may simultaneously hold a Class A license and possess only five breeding females, each of which produces only one litter per year. We need not explore hypothetical conflicts of our own design, since '[i]t is not enough to point to a risk of conflict[ ] . . . ; there must be an actual conflict between the challenged regulation and those [already] in place.'

Moreover, the City has identified a number of local benefits that are clearly unrelated to economic protectionism. Requiring pet shops to purchase directly from Class A breeders protects consumers by making it impossible to obscure the source of an animal by using a middleman, enhances animal welfare by reducing the incidence of disease and behavioral problems associated with irresponsible breeding, and alleviates the burden of providing care in public shelters for animals abandoned because of such problems.

Nevertheless, because we hold the Sourcing Law to be nondiscriminatory, there is no reason to reach the question of whether these non-protectionist justifications would be sufficient to overcome a presumption of per se invalidity and because NYPWA has not demonstrated any incidental burden on interstate commerce, there is no need to consider the weight these local benefits should carry in the Pike balancing test. Because the Sourcing Law imposes no incidental burdens on interstate commerce, it cannot impose any that are clearly excessive in relation to its local benefits, and therefore survives scrutiny under the dormant Commerce Clause.

III. State Preemption

* * *

The Spay/Neuter Law is not preempted by New York's laws governing veterinary medicine, or by its animal cruelty laws.

* * *

CONCLUSION

The Sourcing and Spay/Neuter Laws address problems of significant importance to the City and its residents. It appears that the City has enforced them for more than a year, with no apparent ill effects. Because the challenged laws are not preempted by either state or federal law, and do not offend the Commerce Clause, we affirm the district court's order dismissing NYPWA's complaint.

Notes

1. NYPWA appealed the dismissal to the United States Supreme Court, which denied the petition for writ of *certiorari*.

2. As the Second Circuit noted, in 2014 New York State enacted laws explicitly allowing municipalities within the State to enact laws more stringent than the

State's Pet Dealer Act, which New York City, among other New York State cities, did. Arizona, however, took the opposite approach. In *Puppies 'n Love v. City of Phoenix*, a pet store and individuals sued the City of Phoenix challenging an ordinance prohibiting pet stores from selling dogs and cats supplied by commercial breeders. The court allowed the Humane Society of the United States (HSUS) to intervene as a defendant to challenge to the ordinance. The court granted summary judgment in favor of the City and HSUS, ruling that the ordinance did not violate the U.S. or Arizona Constitutions and was not preempted by state law. 116 F. Supp. 3d 971 (D. Ariz. 2015), *vacated*, 283 F. Supp. 3d 815 (D. Ariz. 2017). While an appeal of that 2015 ruling was pending, however, the state legislature enacted a law that, contrary to the ordinance, specifically allowed pet stores to sell dogs and cats obtained from commercial breeders that meet certain requirements. Ariz. Rev. Stat. § 44-1799.10. The statute contains an express preemption provision, stating that any local ordinance imposing stricter requirements on pet dealers is preempted. Ariz. Rev. Stat. § 44-1799.11.

In light of the new statute, the plaintiffs filed a motion to dismiss in the Ninth Circuit, arguing that the statute mooted the case; the City and HSUS opposed the motion. The Ninth Circuit remanded the case to the district court "for consideration of the effect, if any," of the new legislation. Addressing the preemption issue, the court explained:

> The Arizona Constitution has a home-rule charter provision. Under this provision, "eligible cities may adopt a charter—effectively, a local constitution—for their own government without action by the state legislature." "The purpose of the home rule charter provision of the Constitution was to render the cities adopting such charter provisions as nearly independent of state legislation as was possible. Under it a city may provide for the exercise of every power connected with the proper and efficient government of the municipality where the legislature has not entered the field." ...

> As a charter city, Defendant "may exercise all powers granted by its charter, provided that such exercise is not inconsistent with either the constitution or general laws of the state." Defendant "is granted autonomy over matters of local interest." ...

> ... The relevant inquiry "hinges on whether the subject matter is characterized as of statewide or purely local interest." A court does not balance the evidence to determine whether the state or the city has a more pressing interest; the question is limited to the nature of the legislation's subject matter.

283 F. Supp. 3d at 819–20. After analysis of the issue, the court held that the subject matter clearly implicated both state and local concerns and, therefore, the ordinance was preempted. *Id.* at 822 ("Although the Court does not doubt that the City has real interests in the regulation of pet stores and the sources of the animals they sell, state interests are involved as well.").

The City and HSUS also argued that the judgment in their favor should not be vacated because plaintiffs persuaded the State to pass the statute. The court rejected the argument, however, because other courts had held "broadly that lobbying efforts do not cause federal or state legislative enactments," a holding which was "based on separation of powers principles and eschews any judicial inquiry into the causes of legislative action."

3. In *Park Pet Shop, Inc. v. City of Chicago*, 872 F.3d 495 (7th Cir. 2017), the court addressed many of the same legal issues as addressed by the Second Circuit in *NYPWA* and by *Puppies 'n Love*, upholding the ordinance, in the absence of an express state law preemption and with the following context:

> This case challenges Chicago's "puppy mill" ordinance, which limits the sources from which pet stores may obtain dogs, cats, and rabbits for resale. The ordinance provides that pet retailers in the city "may offer for sale only those dogs, cats, or rabbits" obtained from an animal control or care center, pound, or kennel operated by local, state, or federal government or "a humane society or rescue organization." Chicago, Ill., Code § 4-384-015(b) (2016).

The Seventh Circuit affirmed. In so doing, it explained the background and legislative intent behind the law:

> In 2014 the Chicago City Council acted to address concerns that pet stores in the city sourced their animals from large mill-style breeders, which are notorious for deplorable conditions and abusive breeding practices, including over-breeding, inbreeding, crowded and filthy living conditions, lack of appropriate socialization, and inadequate food, water, and veterinary care. The Council determined that mill-bred pets develop health and behavioral problems, creating economic and emotional burdens for pet owners and imposing financial costs on the City as owners abandon their physically or emotionally challenged pets or surrender them to the shelter operated by the City's Commission on Animal Care and Control. Nearly a third of all animals that come into the City's care are owner surrenders — the second largest source of dogs and cats taken in by the Commission (strays are the largest). Chicago budgets about $300,000 each year for its shelter service and spends more than $500,000 every year to euthanize animals.

> The Council determined that extinguishing the supply of puppy-mill pets to local pet stores would serve several important policy goals. Among other things, it would (1) limit financial support to mill operators; (2) reduce the financial and emotional toll on Chicago consumers who purchase mill-bred pets with latent physical and behavioral problems; (3) boost placement of shelter pets; and (4) reduce the City's animal-care and euthanization costs. The Council also determined that banning the retail sale of mill-bred pets may also promote pet adoption from the City's shelter, which would benefit Chicago residents because the $65 pet adoption fee both offsets the cost

to taxpayers of operating the shelter and gives Chicagoans ready access to cheaper pets.

The Council accordingly adopted the . . . ordinance restricting the sources from which pet stores in the city may obtain dogs, cats, or rabbits for resale. . . .

872 F.3d at 497–98.

As the foregoing illustrates, there are multiple public health and safety, as well as animal welfare, reasons for these laws.

4. Also in Illinois, the Missouri Pet Breeders Association, along with three Cook County, Illinois, pet shops and their owners sued to invalidate a county ordinance that limited pet store sales of dogs, cats and rabbits from a breeder that (among other requirements) holds a USDA Class "A" license and "owns or possesses no more than five (5) female dogs, cats or rabbits capable of reproduction in any twelve (12) month period." *Missouri Pet Breeders v. County of Cook,* 119 F. Supp. 3d 865 (N.D. Ill. 2015). The court summarized the plaintiffs' claims as follows:

The pet stores claim that they will go out of business if the ordinance takes effect, because there are not enough breeders that meet the ordinance's requirements to supply Cook County pet stores with the desired number of specialty pets. Plaintiffs also claim that the ordinance will impact out-of-state breeders, including the Missouri breeders who MPBA represents. Even though breeders are not directly regulated, the ordinance would effectively ban local pet shops from selling pets imported from many out-of-state breeders. Plaintiffs also contend that breeders outside of Illinois will lose business in the following way: the ordinance does not regulate breeders' direct sales to consumers, so breeders without licenses can sell to Cook County residents without restriction. Thus, Cook County residents who want specialty breeds and cannot find them at Cook County pet stores (because their supply will be essentially wiped out) will instead purchase dogs directly from breeders. According to plaintiffs, Cook County consumers will be more likely to buy from in-state breeders, as few will be willing to travel to another state to purchase an animal. Thus, out-of-state breeders will lose business to Illinois breeders.

Id. at 869. As in the other cases discussed above, the court rejected plaintiffs' arguments and dismissed the complaint. Plaintiffs appealed, and then voluntarily dismissed their appeal.

5. In *Maryeli's Lovely Pets, Inc. v. City of Sunrise,* 2015 U.S. Dist. LEXIS 98451 (S.D. Fla. June 24, 2015), plaintiffs challenged a similar ordinance "to combat the ills of excessive breeding." *Id.* at *1.

"Puppy mills" and "kitten factories," the Ordinance [No. 577] states, are more likely to breed animals with genetic disorders and to subject animals to inhumane housing conditions and indiscriminate disposal when they reach the end of their profitable breeding cycle. The ready availability of mill and factory animals leads to impulse purchasing by consumers and, after the animals outgrow their "initial puppy or kitten appeal," can result in their abandonment or mistreatment. (*See id.*) But the Ordinance is discriminatory, Lovely Pets argues, because it requires Lovely Pets "to purchase its puppies only from Sunrise-based Hobby Breeders." The Court disagrees and grants the City's Motion for Summary Judgment as it relates to Lovely Pets's Commerce Clause and Equal Protection claims.

* * *

The Ordinance seeks to curb the practice of purchasing animals from "puppy mills" and the resulting problems of mistreatment and abandonment. The City enacted the Ordinance, believing, among other things, that:

> the restriction of the retail sale of dogs and cats in pet stores in the City will reduce impulse purchases of pets, which can lead to abandonment or mistreatment of the animals once they have outgrown their initial puppy or kitten appeal and will also encourage pet consumers to adopt dogs and cats from shelters where proposed owners are screened for their suitability with respect to the animal, thus reducing the likelihood that the animal will be mistreated or abandoned and thereby saving animals' lives and reducing the cost to the public of sheltering animals[.]

Protecting the health and welfare of domestic animals is a legitimate governmental interest; indeed, courts around the country have so held. *See e.g., Kerr v. Kimmell*, 740 F. Supp. 1525, 1529 (D. Kan. 1990) ("The court finds that a legitimate local public interest is served by the stated purposes of the Act, i.e., quality control and humane treatment of animals."); *Perfect Puppy, Inc.*, [98 F. Supp. at 417] ("There can be little dispute that promoting the humane treatment of animals is a legitimate local interest."); *Mo. Pet Breeders Ass'n v. Cnty. of Cook*, [106 F. Supp. 3d 908, 919 (N.D. Ill. 2015)] ("The ordinance's breeder-size limitations are plausibly designed to reduce the number of animals sold in Cook County that are obtained from mass-breeding facilities. This restriction is rationally related to a legitimate government interest, even if it does not include all animals from mass-breeding facilities.")

Id. at *1-*2, *12-*13. As part of the plaintiff's Equal Protection argument, the pet store compared itself to animal shelters and animal rescue organizations—a comparison which the court soundly rejected:

> Lovely Pets argues that it is treated differently than similarly situated entities under the Ordinance. The Ordinance "is under-inclusive because [it] specifically exempts both animal shelters and animal rescue organizations from the requirement that any purchases of puppies come solely

from locally-licensed Hobby Breeders[,]" claims Lovely Pets. These entities, Lovely Pets writes, "'stand on equal footing' with [it] and have 'the potential [to purchase dogs from puppy mills.'" But to compare Lovely Pets with animal shelters and rescues is to compare apples to oranges.

To consider two entities similarly situated, they "must be 'prima facie identical in all relevant respects." In a similar case, another district court confronted the same comparison of for-profit pet stores and non-profit animal rescues. *See Perfect Puppy, Inc. v. City of E. Providence*, 98 F. Supp. 3d 408 (D.R.I. 2015) [*aff'd in part and appeal dismissed by* 2015 U.S. App. LEXIS 21243 (1st Cir. Dec. 8, 2015)]. The *Perfect Puppy* court concluded, and this Court agrees, that "on the most basic level, the entities are dissimilar: Plaintiff is a for-profit business that sells dogs, while the entities to which Plaintiff compares itself are not-for-profits that rescue and shelter them. The only similarity would seem to be that both involve dogs. But that is like saying a homeless shelter is similarly situated to a luxury hotel because both provide rooms to sleep in." *Id.* at 419. The law of equal protection requires more than superficial similarity and where entities are not similarly situated, there is no equal protection violation.

2015 U.S. Dist. LEXIS 98451 at *9-*10.

6. As noted in some of the excerpts above, part of reason these ordinances have been and continue to be enacted is to combat the problems caused by "puppy mills." The horrifying conditions of these factory breeding operations has come to the public's attention partly as a result of undercover investigations that are now the target of Ag-Gag laws addressed in Section 1.C of this chapter. While most of the cases challenging these laws are in the context of animals raised and slaughtered as food, puppy mills are very much a part of the same agribusiness industry, prompting at least one lawsuit challenging an Ag-Gag law in this context. *Animal Legal Defense Fund v. Reynolds,* 297 F. Supp. 3d 901 (S.D. Iowa 2018) (suit challenging Iowa's Ag-Gag law, Iowa Code section 717A.3A).

In *ALDF v. Reynolds,* the court explained the background of Ag-Gag laws and the connection with puppy mills as follows:

Undercover investigations have long been an important tool used by journalists and advocacy groups to gather information about the inner workings of slaughterhouses and other agricultural facilities. Because Iowa is the nation's largest producer of pork and eggs, as well as a major source of other animal products, agricultural facilities in Iowa have been subject to numerous such investigations in recent years. For example, a 2008 undercover investigation at an Iowa pig farm revealed instances of workers beating pigs with rods and sticking clothespins into pigs' eyes and faces, leading to criminal charges being filed against multiple employees. Undercover investigations in the 2000s at a kosher slaughterhouse in Iowa revealed instances of cows being slaughtered not in accordance with kosher practices, such as by having their tracheas removed with meat hooks while fully conscious, and cows remaining conscious for minutes after their throats had been slit. Similar undercover investigations in other states have resulted in felony convictions for cruelty to animals or have spurred formal investigations by federal and state regulators. Undercover investigations at agricultural production facilities document other issues besides animal cruelty, such as unsafe working conditions, improper food safety practices, violations of labor law, or violations of environmental law.

Most agricultural facilities, such as slaughterhouses, are not open to the public. Investigators have thus typically gained access to facilities by securing employment at the facilities through standard hiring channels. Investigators serve as regular employees performing the tasks demanded of them but also document activities in the facilities—such as animal cruelty, unsanitary conditions, pollution, sexual misconduct, and violations of labor law—using hidden recording equipment. Most undercover investigations use employees new to a facility rather than existing employees, who are often reluctant to become whistleblowers due to fear of retaliation, the risk of termination, and immigration concerns. Employers, meanwhile, seek to prevent undercover investigations by inquiring during the application process about whether a candidate has any connections to certain animal protection organizations. At other agricultural facilities, such as large-scale commercial dog breeding facilities, undercover investigators instead pose as breeders or brokers to gain access.

Id. at 908-09. The plaintiffs were "a collection of national and local non-profit organizations that engage in advocacy they allege is impaired by § 717A.3A," including ALDF, PETA and the following organization:

Bailing Out Benji is an Iowa non-profit organization that promotes the welfare of dogs and companion animals and raises awareness about puppy mills in the state. Prior to the enactment of §717A.3A, Bailing Out Benji conducted undercover investigations into puppy mills by sending its volunteers to puppy mills, stating or implying that they were breeders or brokers, and collecting video or photographic evidence of animal abuse. Bailing Out Benji also previously used material gained from another organization's undercover investigations in its advocacy materials and public education activities. Bailing Out Benji alleges that it now no longer conducts undercover investigations or is able to use material gained from other organizations' undercover investigations in Iowa.

Id. at 910.

At the pleadings stage, on a motion to dismiss, the court concluded that the plaintiffs met standing requirements (i) because they "plausibly alleged that they reasonably decided to refrain from conducting undercover investigations and that they face a credible threat of prosecution," thereby alleging an injury in fact sufficient to confer standing, and (ii) based on diversion of organizational resources to combat the statute. The court undertook a lengthy analysis of First Amendment issues and, based on the following allegations, concluded that "Plaintiffs have plausibly alleged an intent to disfavor a subset of messages based on their viewpoint."

> The Complaint alleges that the Iowa Legislature, in enacting §717A.3A, did so to stifle viewpoints critical of modern large-scale agricultural animal production methods. The Complaint contains examples of statements from legislators disparaging animal activists in connection with the proposed legislation. Section 717A.3A, consistent with this alleged intent, only applies to false statements made at agricultural facilities, and not to other private property in any other industry that might be targeted by undercover investigators who are *not* animal activists, such as food service establishments or childcare facilities.

Id. at 926.

On the Equal Protection claim, the court noted that "the text of §717A.3A contains no classification targeting animal welfare activists" and agreed with defendants' argument that "individual statements from legislators do not suffice to allege animus on the part of the state legislature as a whole." The court also noted that two of the plaintiffs were advocacy organizations that were not primarily engaged in "animal-rights" advocacy, and therefore found it "clear" that the statute applied to all activists and that it merely singled out agribusiness facilities for special protection. Accordingly, the court followed the Ninth Circuit's decision in *Wasden* (excerpted in Section 1.C of this chapter) and granted the motion to dismiss the Equal Protection claims, concluding that plaintiffs had not plausibly alleged that the statute was "inexplicable by anything but animus toward the class it affects."

7. In *NYPWA*, it was an association of breeders, dealers and pet stores that filed suit, in part, based on spay/neuter requirements. On the other side of the spay/neuter issue, however, in *Take Me Home Rescue v. Luri*, 208 Cal. App. 4th 1342 (2012), an animal rescue organization sued a foster caregiver for failing to spay a dog, Lily, put in her care, alleging breach of contract and conversion. Under California statutory law (Cal. Food & Agric. Code § 30503(a)), rescue organizations must spay or neuter dogs in their care. The plaintiff rescue group claimed to have explained this to the defendant when it released Lily to her to care for the dog until her health improved sufficiently for her to be spayed. The trial court issued a preliminary injunction to force the foster caregiver to have the dog spayed or return her to the rescue group. She appealed, arguing that Lily was exempt from the spay requirement because Lily was in agility training. The appellate court affirmed the judgment, upholding the injunction. In doing so, the court concluded that Take Me Home would likely have succeeded on the merits and that Take Me Home was much more likely to be irreparably harmed by Lily not being spayed than the foster caregiver was by having her spayed. "Luri is but one pet owner, and can either spay Lilly or adopt another dog; on the other hand, Take Me Home's entire existence

depends on its ability to place pets that it obtains from shelters in adoptive homes."
Id. at 1352.

8. Some cases have focused more on procedural violations of the AWA than actual harm to the animals. One such case is *Toney v. Glickman*, 101 F.3d 1236 (8th Cir. 1996), in which a husband and wife who sold animals to research facilities were found to have committed hundreds of violations of the AWA:

> [T]he Toneys kept records that falsely identified the source of many of the dogs they obtained and contained incorrect information about the sources; (2) they used forged certificates when selling at least 44 dogs to research facilities; (3) they failed to hold at least 190 animals for the five days required by the Act and then altered their records in some instances to conceal their violations; (4) they willfully failed to identify properly 60 dogs on the premises; (5) they failed to record other necessary information on 13 of those 60 dogs; (6) they willfully kept records that contained false information on an "undeterminable" number of the 60; and (7) they provided unsafe and unsanitary housing and contaminated food to the dogs.

Id. at 1239. The Administrative Law Judge (ALJ) in the underlying case fined the Toneys $200,000, permanently revoked their license to sell animals to research facilities and ordered them to cease and desist from the prohibited practices. The appellate court upheld the ALJ decision, except as to specific charges that they had "falsely received" dogs from an individual and from one of several "pounds." The case was remanded for the ALJ to recalculate the fine without considering those specific violations. In its opinion, the court made the following statements regarding the purpose and intent of the AWA:

> The Toneys repeatedly point out that there is no evidence that they have dealt in stolen dogs, and no one has argued to the contrary. The Animal Welfare Act does not penalize only those who steal dogs or who purchase stolen dogs. It also penalizes those who violate the regulations that are designed to make dog stealing more difficult. It may seem unfair to the Toneys that they are being punished when they have not helped to steal any dogs, but that does not change the fact that they repeatedly, and, in some cases, flagrantly violated the law. The law may or may not be overly harsh, but is our job to uphold it.

Id. at 1243.

9. The use of stolen dogs in research facilities is an ongoing problem, with a long history. For example, in *U.S. v. Linville*, 10 F.3d 630 (9th Cir. 1993), the court summarized the activities of Brenda Linville, David Stephens and Tracy Lynne Stephens as follows:

> [Defendants] developed a scheme to make money by taking advantage of trusting pet owners. Linville would fraudulently obtain pets from

owners who placed "Free to Good Home" ads in local newspapers. She would tell the owners that she wanted the animals as pets and would provide good homes for them. In fact she planned to sell and did sell the animals to David and Tracy Stephens (doing business as D & T Kennels), whom Linville knew would in turn sell the pets to institutions for medical research purposes. On one occasion, Linville specifically told a pet owner that she would not sell her dogs for medical research, signed a statement to that effect and promised to notify the owner if she ever did consider selling the dogs for medical research. Linville nonetheless sold those dogs to the Stephenses for resale to medical research facilities, and, as a result, the dogs died.

To perpetrate the fraud and conceal the animals' whereabouts from their owners, Linville obtained the names of individuals who had recently renewed their driver licenses and gave that information to the Stephenses to record in their United States Department of Agriculture (USDA) acquisition records as the names of people who had supposedly sold animals to the kennel.

Id. at 631.

10. In response to pressure by the public and various organizations, Congress has considered several bills that make the theft of any animal for the purpose of reselling to a research facility a federal crime. For example, The Pet Safety and Protection Act of 2004, Senate Bill 2346 (which did not pass) would have eliminated authorization in the AWA for Class B dealers who sell animals to research facilities from "random sources." ("Random source" animals, as discussed earlier in this section, are usually strays, seized shelter animals, animals purchased from flea markets or obtained through "free to good home" advertisements and, occasionally, stolen pets.) This bill was reintroduced in 2006 and again in 2008, neither of which passed. In 2015, however, the NIH prohibited the use of dogs from Class B dealers, thereby negating the need for Congressional action on this particular issue as long as the prohibition remains in effect.

E. Animal Cruelty

Taub v. State

Court of Appeals of Maryland, 1983
296 Md. 439, 463 A.2d 819

COUCH, Judge. The issue in this case is whether the animal cruelty statute, Maryland Code (1957, 1976 Repl. Vol.), Article 27, § 59, is applicable to a research institute conducting medical and scientific research pursuant to a federal program. For reasons to be discussed herein we hold that it is not.

Dr. Edward Taub was the chief scientific investigator in charge of animal research at the Institute for Behavioral Research (IBR) which operated a laboratory in Silver

Spring, Maryland. This laboratory was funded by the National Institutes of Health (NIH) under a series of grants outlining the specific animal research to be done by the laboratory. The United States Department of Agriculture (USDA) was charged with making periodic announced and unannounced inspections of the laboratory pursuant to the Federal Animal Welfare Act, 7 U.S.C.A. §§ 2131–2156 (1973 and 1976 Supp.).

During the period May–September, 1981, Dr. Taub, under an NIH grant, was conducting research to gain information to help retrain human beings afflicted with a stroke. In an effort to learn to retrain limbs damaged by a stroke, Dr. Taub simulated the effects of a stroke by creating an animal model of the conditions in humans. This was accomplished by surgically abolishing all sensation in the limb of a monkey; thereafter, experiments could be performed to retrain that limb. The surgical procedure is known as somatosensory deafferentation.

Acting on information furnished by a former employee of the laboratory, Montgomery County police investigated conditions therein, seizing a colony of monkeys pursuant to an order of court. Thereafter, in January, 1982, the county State's Attorney filed a seventeen count information against Dr. Taub charging him with violation of Maryland Code (1957, 1976 Repl. Vol.), Article 27, § 59, with regard to seventeen different monkeys. Following a trial in the District Court, Dr. Taub was found guilty of failing to provide necessary veterinary care for six of the monkeys and was acquitted of all other charges. Upon appeal to the circuit court, a jury found Dr. Taub guilty of one charge of failing to provide necessary veterinary care for one monkey known as Nero.

We granted *certiorari* to consider a question of public importance.

While Dr. Taub has raised several issues concerning the constitutionality of section 59, preemption of this section by the Federal Act, and certain alleged errors in the trial court's evidentiary rulings, we believe the matter may be disposed of by our conclusion that section 59 simply is inapplicable to Dr. Taub and the laboratory and thus the charges against him should be dismissed. We recognize that this issue was not raised previously although it was discussed at oral argument. Under Maryland Rule 813 our scope of review is "ordinarily" limited to questions raised and decided by the trial court. Nevertheless, as the rule employs the term "ordinarily," it permits exceptions and we have occasionally decided cases on issues not previously raised. *See, e.g., Squire v. State*, 368 A.2d 1019 (1977). Because our conclusion as to this issue is completely dispositive of the case, we shall consider it.

By Chapter 198 of the Laws of Maryland, 1890, the legislature, for the first time, made it a misdemeanor for "any person who wilfully sets on foot, instigates, engages in, or in any ways furthers any act of cruelty to any animal, or any act tending to produce such cruelty, or by any act, conduct, neglect, or omission wilfully causes, permits or suffers any animal to undergo any species of torture or cruelty. . . ." Torture and cruelty were thereafter defined "to include everything whereby *unjustifiable* physical pain, suffering, or death [w]as caused or permitted. . . ." (Emphasis added.)

In 1904, this chapter became sections 57 and 58 of Article 27 without change. The next legislative action of significance, pertinent to the issue before us, occurred in 1955, when a specific penalty for violation of the section was provided. In 1957, the legislature removed from the penalty provision the language "in the discretion of the Court." By Chapter 718 of the Laws of 1963, the penalty provision was changed to provide for up to ninety days imprisonment. The legislature increased the fine provision to $1,000.00, in 1966. In 1972, the legislature repealed the pertinent sections and enacted a new section 59 to read as follows:

> Any person who (1) overdrives, overloads, deprives of necessary sustenance, tortures, torments, cruelly beats, mutilates or cruelly kills; or (2) causes, procures or authorizes these acts; or (3) having the charge or custody of an animal, either as owner or otherwise, inflicts unnecessary suffering or pain upon the animal, or unnecessarily fails to provide the animal with proper food, drink, air, space, shelter or protection from the weather, is guilty. . . .

Section 62 was amended to define "torment", otherwise it remained essentially unchanged. In 1975, section 59 was repealed and reenacted with the language as it was at the time of the inception of this case, as set forth below:

> Any person who (1) overdrives, overloads, deprives of necessary sustenance, tortures, torments, cruelly beats, mutilates or cruelly kills; or (2) causes, procures or authorizes these acts; or (3) having the charge or custody of an animal, either as owner or otherwise, inflicts unnecessary suffering or pain upon the animal, or unnecessarily fails to provide the animal with nutritious food in sufficient quantity, necessary veterinary care, proper drink, air, space, shelter or protection from the weather, is guilty of a misdemeanor and shall be punishable by a fine not exceeding $1,000 or by imprisonment not to exceed 90 days, or both. Customary and normal veterinary and agricultural husbandry practices including but not limited to dehorning, castration, docking tails, and limit feeding, are not covered by the provisions of this section. In the case of activities in which physical pain may unavoidably be caused to animals, such as food processing, pest elimination, animal training, and hunting, cruelty shall mean a failure to employ the most humane method reasonably available. It is the intention of the General Assembly that all animals shall be protected from intentional cruelty, but that no person shall be liable for criminal prosecution for normal human activities to which the infliction of pain to an animal is purely incidental and unavoidable.

It can be readily seen that the legislature has consistently been concerned with the punishment of acts causing "unnecessary" or "unjustifiable" pain or suffering. Furthermore, clearly the legislature recognized that there are certain normal human activities to which the infliction of pain to an animal is purely incidental and unavoidable. . . .

In addition, we are confident that the legislature was aware of the Federal Animal Welfare Act which was, in part, to insure that animals intended for use in research facilities would be provided humane care and treatment. Under the terms of that Act, a research facility is required to register with the Secretary of Agriculture (7 U.S.C.A. § 2136 (1973, 1976 Supp.)), to comply with standards promulgated by the Secretary to govern the humane handling, care, and treatment of animals (§ 2143 (1976 Supp.)), is subject to inspection of their animals and records (§ 2147 (1973)), and is subject to civil and criminal penalties, as well as a cease and desist order for any violation of the Act (§ 2149(b) and (c) (1976 Supp.)). Thus the Act provides a comprehensive plan for the protection of animals used in research facilities, while at the same time recognizing and preserving the validity of use of animals in research (§ 2146 (1973 and 1976 Supp.)).

Moreover, the involved laboratory was subject to detailed regulations of the Secretary of Agriculture (9 C.F.R. §§ 3.75–3.91 (1978)) which set forth specifications for humane handling, care, treatment, transportation of nonhuman primates, and for veterinary care. With respect to the latter, again provision is made for a recognition and preservation of the validity of research purposes.

Lastly, being a recipient of an NIH grant, the laboratory became subject to pertinent regulations thereof governing the care and treatment of animals used in the research which was the subject of the grant (U. S. Dept. of Health, Education, and Welfare, Public Health Service, NIH Publication No. 80-23, Guide for the Care and Use of Laboratory Animals (rev. 1978, reprinted 1980)).

Accordingly, we do not believe the legislature intended section 59 of Article 27 to apply to this type of research activity under a federal program. We shall, therefore, reverse Dr. Taub's conviction and remand this matter to the Circuit Court for Montgomery County with instructions to dismiss the criminal information.

* * *

Notes

1. The Maryland Court of Appeals held that the AWA provides a comprehensive plan for protecting animals used in research facilities and that the Maryland legislature must have contemplated the AWA in enacting the anti-cruelty laws. The court reached this opinion despite the fact that the Maryland legislature had enacted its anti-cruelty laws more than a century before the AWA was ever contemplated.

2. If the court is correct, there is a blanket exemption for the practices of researchers with federal grants. The prohibition on animal cruelty is traditionally a state power, yet the court here effectively holds that federal laws addressing research have preemptive power—without ever ruling explicitly on the federal preemption doctrine (which would likely not support this ruling). Is there a comprehensive federal policy supporting any and all animal research that overrides the traditional state power to legislate with respect to animal cruelty? The issue of federal preemption

has been addressed in other cases regarding the treatment of animals (including the *National Meat Association v. Harris* excerpted in Section 1 of this chapter), but never in connection with such a broad edict that effectively writes a research exemption into all state anti-cruelty laws.

3. *Taub* is a landmark and unique case in that an animal researcher was convicted at the trial court level of violating state anti-cruelty laws for activity related to his laboratory work. Analyze the different standards applied under the AWA and the Maryland anti-cruelty laws that result in the difference in liability.

4. In *DeHart v. Town of Austin*, 39 F.3d 718 (7th Cir. 1994), the owner and operator of an exotic animal buying, breeding, raising and selling operation challenged the constitutionality of an ordinance prohibiting the possession of "wild animals" within the boundaries of the township of Austin, Indiana. He based his suit in part on the ground that the AWA preempted the ordinance, in an argument similar to the rule adopted by the Maryland Court of Appeals in *Taub*. The *DeHart* court rejected the argument, because federal permission or regulation of activity does not constitute a prohibition on state or local regulation of the same activity. The court held the ordinance was not preempted:

> [I]t is clear that the Animal Welfare Act does not evince an intent to preempt state or local regulation of animal or public welfare. Indeed, the [AWA] expressly contemplates state and local regulation of animals. . . . In summary, the purpose of the [AWA] is to foster humane treatment and care of animals and to protect the owners of animals from the theft of their animals.

Id. at 722. Compare the holding in *Taub* with that in *DeHart*. In *Taub*, the court concluded that state anti-cruelty laws simply do not apply to animals in research facilities, a *de facto* declaration without any legal support. The *DeHart* court concluded that state laws regulating (or prohibiting) possession of animals can apply to animals who would otherwise be covered under the AWA, if possession was legal. Can these two opinions be reconciled? Under the *Taub* rationale, could an animal be afforded greater protection if his genus or species is not encompassed by the AWA — in other words, could a laboratory mouse be better protected under state anti-cruelty laws than a dog (or monkey, as in *Taub*) whose protection falls under the AWA?

5. In *ALDF v. Provimi Veal*, 626 F. Supp. 278 (D. Mass. 1986) (excerpted earlier in this chapter), the court found state claims were in part preempted by a pervasive scheme of federal statutes and regulations under the Federal Food, Drug and Cosmetic Act and the Federal Meat Inspection Act and that, in combination, this extensive regulatory scheme fully occupied the area at issue (labeling of meat), thus prohibiting even non-conflicting state regulation. If the AWA did not contain language that expressly contemplated state and local regulation of animals, might DeHart have successfully argued that the regulations enacted under the authority of the AWA also qualify as a pervasive scheme, making it reasonable to conclude that Congress intended exclusive federal regulation of this area?

F. Disclosure of Information

The *Taub* case is commonly known as "The Silver Springs Monkey Case," and it catapulted a nascent animal rights organization into national prominence. The former employee who initially brought the case to the attention of state authorities was Alex Pacheco, one of the co-founders of People for the Ethical Treatment of Animals (PETA). What is not clear in the excerpted decision is the fact that much of the evidence presented by Mr. Pacheco was collected secretly. In more recent years, research laboratories have become more sophisticated about the danger posed to their reputations if they hire employees who are likely to, or intend to, record laboratory activities and make that information public. Thus, separate and apart from the "Ag-Gag" laws addressed at length earlier, hiring processes have become more elaborate and new employees are commonly required to sign confidentiality agreements. When employees breach those agreements, laboratories are more likely to file suit.

In 2005, one company that described itself as a "laboratory that conducts biological safety evaluations for the pharmaceutical and biotechnology industries" sued a former employee (Lisa Leitten) for allegedly fraudulently gaining employment for the purpose of obtaining confidential and proprietary information regarding the treatment of animals used in research by the laboratory. *Covance Laboratories, Inc. v. People for the Ethical Treatment of Animals, et al.*, Chancery No. 2005–2590 (Va. Cir. Ct., Fairfax Cty., June 3, 2005) (1st Am. Bill of Cmplt. at ¶ 4). The laboratory also sued PETA for allegedly conspiring to injure its business by publicly disseminating such information. The case settled, with PETA paying nothing to Covance and being allowed to continue to show its excerpt of the videotaped footage of activities inside Covance labs and to cooperate with federal investigations into Covance.

The settlement followed a ruling several months earlier in favor of PETA's European arm (PETA Europe Ltd.) in a parallel action filed by Covance in England. *Covance Laboratories Ltd., et al. v. Covance Campaign, et al.*, Claim No. 5C-00295 (High Ct. of Justice, Chancery Div., Leeds Dist. Registry, June 16, 2005) (judgment denying injunction to prevent PETA Europe from publication of investigator's videotaped footage). Covance filed the British lawsuit based on press releases by PETA Europe (a British organization) and Covance Campaign ("a loose affiliation of individuals who operate a website called *www.covancecampaign.com*") of videotaped footage obtained by a secret observer. In the judgment, the court commented on the content of the footage as follows:

> In the course of his submissions, Mr Browne [counsel for PETA Europe] described the video as "horrendous," a word which [counsel for Covance] in his reply characterised as "emotive" and "subjective." Mr Browne's rhetoric may owe something to forensic license, but having watched the video, I am unable to say that his language is far short of the mark. I would myself regard the description "highly disturbing" as fitting the video precisely. I take just two aspects of what can be seen, the rough manner in which

animals [are] handled and the bleakness of the surroundings in which they are kept. These are matters which, even to a viewer with no particular interest in animal welfare, at least cry out for explanation.

Id. at ¶ 32.

Later in the opinion, the court considered the defendants' "public interest" defense:

It has long been established that the fact that disclosure would be in the public interest is an answer to a claim for an injunction to restrain the publication of confidential information. The public interest in publication is a matter which the court is now directed to take into account by section 12(4)(a)(ii) of the Human Rights Act 1998. In my judgment, this is a case in which the public interest defence has an unusually strong chance of success at trial. Accordingly, at this stage of the proceedings, it must tell heavily against CL USA [Covance] in its efforts to show likelihood of success, as it is required to do by section 12(3) of the Human Rights Act 19998.

The point is almost so obvious as not to require much by way of spelling it out. CL USA is part of a global group of companies which develops and markets pharmaceutical products. As is well known the testing of products on animals in laboratories is a common (and, it may well be, necessary) part of the work done by pharmaceutical manufacturers. In my judgment, concern that laboratory animals should be treated with basic decency and with the minimum pain consistent with the procedures to which they are subjected is a matter of legitimate interest to substantial sections of the public. I refer to persons who are particularly concerned with the welfare of animals; and (this is probably by far the larger group) to those who, given a choice of drugs, would prefer to use drugs produced by a manufacturer who treated laboratory animals in the way which I have just mentioned rather than a manufacturer whose treatment of animals was abusive. Put in terms which are more specific to this case, there is a legitimate public interest in seeing material which may enable people to reach a view as to where, on the spectrum of treatment, CL USA is to be found.

The fact that serious allegations of breaches of federal and state law has [*sic*] been made against CL USA also supports the public interest defence. It is not, in my judgment, an answer to say that everything can be left to the regulatory authorities.

Id. at ¶¶ 54–56.

The court went on to address defendants' claim that they were correcting a "misleading impression," explaining as follows:

In Woodward v. Hutchins[1] Lord Denning MR said:

---

1. [1977] 1 WLR 760 at pp. 673, 764.

"If a group of this kind [pop stars] seek publicity which is to their advantage, it seems to me that they cannot complain if a servant or employee of theirs afterwards discloses the truth about them. If the image which they fostered was not a true image, it is in the public interest that it should be corrected. In these cases of confidential information it is a matter of balancing the public interest in maintaining the confidence against the public interest in knowing the truth.... In this case the balance comes down in favour of the truth being told, even if it should involve some breach of confidential information. As there should be 'truth in advertising', so there should be truth in publicity. The public should not be misled. So it seems to me that the breach of confidential information is not a ground for granting an injunction."

Covance Incorporated's website contains a statement which reads, in part, as follows:

"Animal Welfare Statement

Covance Code of Respect for Animals in Research and Development

... As one of the world's leading providers of preclinical drug development services and other services to advance safety, we accept both the legal and the moral obligation to be a leader in assuring that animals in our care are treated in accordance with all applicable rules and with high standards of respect and compassion. In addition to law and ethics, this obligation is scientifically important because failure to meet these rules and standards can undermine the validity of scientific research. Toward that end, all of us at Covance will follow these principles:

1. We will treat animals in our care with respect. We honor the contribution that animals in our care make to lifesaving advances and will treat these animals with the respect that they deserve.

2. We will strictly follow all applicable laws and regulations for animal treatment.

* * *

4. We will minimize animal discomfort....

5. We will take steps to ensure that our employees and processes meet these standards...."

Whether CL USA has been in breach of federal or state legislation is a matter which has still to be determined in the United States. I leave that question to one side. Nonetheless, a comparison of what is said in the statement from which I have quoted and what may be seen in the video (and read, at length, in Ms Leitten's written record of her time at the Primate Toxicology Department) is a comparison between two different worlds. The case is caught squarely by what was said by Lord Denning in *Woodward v. Hutchins*. If, as seems highly likely on the evidence so far available, the group of which CL USA forms part has fostered a misleading impression, PETA Europe is entitled to correct it publicly.

Id. at ¶¶ 58–60. As noted above, the court dismissed the application for injunctive relief.

The following case is an example of litigation that can result when employees step forward to disclose mistreatment of animals. This case involved the treatment of circus animals. Due to their temporary presence in any jurisdiction, long-term treatment of traveling circus animals can be tracked only by reports from circus employees, who often have obvious motivations not to speak about any problems they observe.

Hagan v. Feld Entertainment, Inc. d/b/a Ringling Bros. and Barnum & Bailey Circus

United States District Court, Eastern District of Virginia, 2005
365 F. Supp. 2d 700

SMITH, Judge. This matter is before the court on plaintiff's motion to remand [to state court] and defendant's motion to dismiss. For the reasons outlined below, plaintiff's motion to remand is GRANTED in part and MOOTED in part. Defendant's motion to dismiss is GRANTED in part and DENIED in part.

I. Factual and Procedural History

[*On a motion to dismiss, all facts alleged in the complaint are taken as true. The court cited to the complaint as it set forth the following facts.*] Plaintiff, Frank Hagan ("Hagan"), is a resident and citizen of Virginia. Defendant, Feld Entertainment, Incorporated ("Feld"), is a Virginia corporation with its principal place of business in Virginia. Beginning in March 1993, Hagan was hired by Feld to work for Ringling Bros. and Barnum & Bailey Circus ("Ringling Bros."). Hagan worked intermittently for Feld from March 1993 until 2000. Beginning on or about March 7, 2000, Hagan worked continuously for Feld without interruption until he was terminated on July 21, 2004.

In December 2003 Feld assigned Hagan to work as a lion handler for Ringling Bros. As part of his job, he fed and watered the lions, cleaned their cages, cared for their transport on the train, and cared for them at the performance site. He spent between twelve and fourteen hours every day with the lions.

On or about 11:00 a.m. on July 12, 2004, the Ringling Bros. train left Phoenix, Arizona, headed for Fresno, California. At the three train stops during the day, Hagan checked on the lions, during which time the lions seemed healthy. The next day, July 13, 2004, Hagan watered down the lions at approximately 8:30 a.m. That day the train traveled through the Mojave desert where temperatures reached upwards of one hundred degrees. At approximately 9:30 a.m. Hagan called Ringling Bros.' Train Master Gene Petis ("Petis") to inform him that the train needed to be stopped so that Hagan could again water down the lions. Petis advised Hagan that the train could not stop because it was behind schedule. Thereafter Jarak, another lion handler, attempted without success to contact Jeff Steele, General Manager of Ringling Bros., to request a train stop to water down the lions. Finally, at 2:45 p.m., the train stopped in Arizona. Between 8:30 a.m. and 2:45 p.m. the lions had no drinking water and they were not watered down.

When the train stopped, Hagan immediately went to the lion car where he discovered that a two-year-old lion named Clyde was unresponsive and was lying in the fetal position with his tongue hanging out, eyes rolled back in his head, and barely breathing. When Hagan placed his hands on Clyde in an attempt to help him, he realized that Clyde's body was extremely hot. As Hagan attempted to help Clyde, the lion died. After sitting and crying with Clyde's body for a period of time, Hagan once again tried to contact Steele, but was unsuccessful. He was, however, able to reach Ringling Bros.' Operations Manager, John Griggs ("Griggs"), who told him to move Clyde's body to the meat truck and to not say a word about it to anyone.

The train arrived in Fresno, California, shortly before midnight on July 13, 2004. On or about July 14, 2004, Hagan was ordered to move Clyde's body from the meat car to a Ryder rental truck. He was also ordered to pressure wash the meat car to remove Clyde's hair and blood before the United States Department of Agriculture ("U.S.D.A.") inspectors arrived. When the U.S.D.A. inspectors arrived, Hagan was taken to another location where he was questioned by Feld's legal counsel. Hagan was told not to talk to anyone about Clyde's death, which Hagan understood to mean no conversations with the U.S.D.A. inspectors. Hagan continued to talk about Clyde's death and was threatened and intimidated by Steele not to talk about it with anyone. On July 21, 2004, while still in California, Hagan was terminated and he and his daughter were left in California with no way to get home. The reason given for the termination was that Hagan caused a power outage.

* * *

[II] B. Underlying State Claims

1. Wrongful Discharge

California recognizes the tort of wrongful discharge. A claim for wrongful discharge exists when an "employer's discharge of an employee violates fundamental principles of public policy." Generally, California courts have found that an employee was discharged in violation of public policy where the employee was discharged after the employee: "(1) refused to violate a statute; (2) performed a statutory obligation; (3) exercised a constitutional or statutory right or privilege; or (4) reported a statutory violation for the public's benefit." *Green v. Ralee Engineering Co.*, 960 P.2d 1046, 1051 (Cal. 1998). A claim for wrongful discharge also exists if the employee is discharged after reporting a statutory violation to management and other employees, but not to a government official or other enforcement entity. The statutory violation may exist at either the state or federal level. *See id*. at 1059. Additionally, an employee's allegation that a federal regulation, rather than a statute or constitution, was violated is sufficient to show that the employee was discharged in contravention of public policy. As a final limiting factor, the statute (or regulation) in question must be "designed to protect the public or advance some substantial public policy goal." *Id.* [at 1061].

Plaintiff alleges a prima facie case of wrongful discharge. He alleges that he was discharged for reporting to management and other employees a statutory violation of the Animal Welfare Act, 7 U.S.C. § 2131 *et seq.*, and the California Penal Code § 597 *et seq.* (prohibiting cruelty to animals).[2] The Animal Welfare Act ("the Act") authorizes the Secretary of Agriculture to promulgate standards and rules governing the humane handling, care, treatment and transportation of animals by exhibitors. 7 U.S.C. § 2143(a). Pursuant to this grant of rulemaking authority, the Secretary of Agriculture promulgated rules requiring that animals in transit be observed at least once every four hours to ensure that ambient temperature is within a specified range and that animals are not in physical distress. 9 C.F.R. § 3.140. If animals are in obvious physical distress, the carrier is required to provide veterinary care as soon as possible. 9 C.F.R. § 3.140. Live animals are not to be subjected to surrounding air temperatures in excess of 85 degrees Fahrenheit and care must be taken to ensure that animals do not suffer physical trauma. 9 C.F.R. § 3.142. The facts as alleged by plaintiff indicate that these regulations were violated when no one observed the lions for over six hours, the ambient air temperature was greater than it should have been, and care was not taken to insure that animals suffered no physical distress. Allegedly, as a result of these violations, a lion died and plaintiff was fired because he complained to management and other employees about violations of the Animal Welfare Act.

While it may be difficult to determine what constitutes a public policy source, at the core it must have a legislative root and be of fundamental concern to the general public, rather than to an individual. *See Gantt v. Sentry Ins.*, 824 P.2d 680, 684, 687–88 (Cal. 1992). In order to meet the first prong, that the public policy has a legislative root, a plaintiff's public policy source in a wrongful discharge claim must be tethered to a statutory or constitutional provision. *See Green*, 960 P.2d at 1051. A regulation that accomplishes the purpose of a statute is properly tethered to a public policy source. California courts recognize that "if a statute that seeks to further a public policy objective delegates the authority to adopt administrative regulations to an administrative agency in order to fulfill that objective, and that agency adopts regulations that are within the scope of its statutory policy, then those regulations may be manifestations of important public policy." *Id.* at 1056.

The regulations accompanying the Animal Welfare Act are closely related to the statutory language and advance the stated purpose of the Animal Welfare Act.

---

2. While some of Feld's actions may have been criminal under the California penal statute had they occurred in California, the actions occurred in Arizona, not California. Thus, it is unclear whether the California penal statute could serve as a public policy source in this case. However, as the Animal Welfare Act and regulations clearly qualify as a public policy source, it is unnecessary for the court to make this determination.

The stated purpose of the Act is "to insure that animals intended for use . . . for exhibition purposes . . . are provided humane care and treatment." 7 U.S.C. § 2131. The Act grants the Secretary of Agriculture the authority to promulgate rules and standards to govern the humane handling of animals. The Secretary is directed to set minimum standards for "handling, housing, feeding, watering, sanitation, ventilation, shelter from extremes of weather and temperatures, adequate veterinary care . . . necessary for humane handling, care or treatment of animals." 7 U.S.C. § 2143. The rules and standards promulgated under this grant of power are found in 9 C.F.R. 3 *et seq.* The rules that defendant allegedly violated about which plaintiff complained, namely failure to observe animals at regular intervals, failure to water animals properly, failure to maintain proper handling temperatures, and failure to prevent physical distress, directly flow from the legislative grant of power to the Secretary in 7 U.S.C. § 2143. Furthermore, these regulations carry out the stated purpose of the Act in insuring that animals in interstate commerce are treated humanely. *See* 7 U.S.C. § 2143. In sum, while the alleged violations by the defendant are regulatory in nature, they are sufficiently tethered to a statute to constitute public policy.

The Animal Welfare Act and accompanying regulations further an important public policy concern, the welfare of animals in commerce, thereby meeting the final limiting factor of California law for a wrongful discharge claim. There are two primary factors California courts look to in determining whether a statute furthers public policy. First, the matter must affect "society at large rather than a purely personal or proprietary interest of the plaintiff." *Gantt*, 824 P.2d at 684. The Act clearly benefits society at large rather than the personal interests of the plaintiff. The Act is designed to insure that the nation's animals in interstate commerce are treated in a safe and humane manner. Society as a whole, rather than an individual such as the plaintiff, benefits from the humane handling of animals. In examining whether the Act was meant to protect the public, the District of Columbia Circuit found that "the legislative history of both the 1985 amendments to the Animal Welfare Act and the 1970 act that first included animal exhibitions within the AWA confirms that Congress acted with the public's interest in mind." *Animal Legal Defense Fund, Inc. v. Glickman*, 154 F.3d 426, 444 (D.C. Cir. 1998). The Act was designed to benefit the public at large rather than specific individuals.

Second, the matter must be fundamental, substantial, and well-established at the time of the wrongful discharge. The Act and its accompanying regulations are fundamental. The statement of policy accompanying the Act states that it is "essential" to regulate how animals are treated in interstate commerce. 7 U.S.C. § 2131. The statute is substantial in that it sets out a broad-based statutory and regulatory framework for the treatment of animals used in research facilities, for exhibition purposes, and for pets. It is the "core federal statute regulating animal use and abuse." *United States v. Thompson*, 118 F. Supp. 2d 723, 724 (W.D. Tex. 1998). The public policy embodied in the statute of treating animals humanely is well-established; the statute was originally passed in 1966. Its requirements were made applicable to exhibitors, such as circuses showcasing animals, in 1970. Pub. L. 91-579 (1970), as codified in 7 U.S.C. § 2131. Defendant has been on notice since that time of the policy purpose of the Act.

In sum, plaintiff has presented a prima facie case of wrongful discharge under California law. As alleged, he was fired after complaining to management about violations of a federal statute. A colorable state law claim has been made, and the court DENIES defendant's motion to dismiss the wrongful discharge claim. . . .

Notes

1. The *Hagan* court also considered plaintiff's claim for intentional infliction of emotional distress. Under California's Labor Code, if the employee's physical or emotional injury, or both, occurred during the "normal course of the employment relationship," the state's workers' compensation system generally provides the sole remedy and the plaintiff would not be entitled to damages for emotional distress. *Hagan*, 365 F. Supp. 2d at 710. The court noted that "[t]he defendant's conduct itself may have been abnormal and inhumane, making the circumstances surrounding Clyde's death distasteful or outrageous," but the "acts constituting defendant's misconduct all occurred during the normal course of the employment relationship." *Id.* at 711. On that basis, the court dismissed plaintiff's emotional distress claim.

2. In addition to employment practices, employee guidelines and the restrictions encompassed by Ag-Gag laws, laboratories also have become increasingly more resistant to making public any information about their research activities. This leads to more requests for information by concerned individuals and organizations under state and federal public records acts. (See further discussion of the open records acts earlier in this Chapter.) Many lawsuits have arisen out of such requests and laboratory refusals to comply. For example, in *State ex rel. Physicians Committee for Responsible Medicine v. Board of Trustees of Ohio State University*, 843 N.E.2d 174 (Ohio 2006), Physicians Committee for Responsible Medicine (PCRM) alleged the University failed to comply with the Ohio Public Records Act in response to PCRM's request for information relating to the University's Spinal Cord Injury Training Program, which trains researchers on a method of inducing spinal cord injuries in laboratory animals. The Ohio Supreme Court concluded that the intellectual property exception to the Public Records Act supported the University's refusal to release the records and denied PCRM's writ.

In *Mississippi State University v. PETA*, 992 So. 2d 595 (Miss. 2008), the court summarized the facts and its conclusion as follows:

> Following Mississippi State University's ("MSU") denial of its records request, People for the Ethical Treatment of Animals, Inc. ("PETA") filed a complaint in the Chancery Court of Oktibbeha County seeking disclosure. In its initial request, PETA sought records relating to any and all research projects, tests, and/or experiments that initially received funding and/or sponsorship and any and all installments thereof, in whole or in part, from

The Iams Company ("Iams") or an affiliate and for which *in vivo* animal research was conducted at MSU from 1999 to date.

For the period requested, MSU and Iams entered into a series of "Agreement[s]," "Research Agreement[s]," "Non-Disclosure Agreement[s]," and "Agreement[s] to Provide Animal Care Facilities and Technical Services." These agreements provided for "secrecy of information," "no disclosure of confidential information," and "intellectual property rights," and mandated that "[b]oth parties agree to comply with all relevant federal, state, county, and municipal executive orders, rules, regulations, ordinances and laws." For example, MSU warranted that its animal care facilities "conform to the animal care and use guidelines set forth by the United States Animal Welfare Act[,] . . . regulations set forth in 9 CFR parts 1, 2, and 3[,] . . . and other applicable laws and policies regarding the care and use of vertebrate animals for research and training purposes."

PETA's request subsequently was modified to seek only Institutional Animal Care and Use Committee ("IACUC") records for projects, tests, and experiments funded by Iams, the creation of which were a requisite condition under MSU's agreements with Iams. Thus, PETA sought a compilation of data and information recorded on animal care protocol review forms prepared by MSU in conjunction with Iams, with whom it contracted to perform studies and research. The protocol review forms included, *inter alia*, the name of the principal investigator(s); title of the project; project period; project summary; proposed species of animals; numbers of animals; experimental design; rationale for involving animals in the study and justification for using the species selected; care and use of the animals; names and qualifications of personnel involved in the project; protocol updates and amendments; and history of protocols. The purpose of the studies and research, as well as the type and number of animals, was controlled by contractual agreements between the sponsor (Iams) and institution (MSU). Federal law mandates the use of protocols when live vertebrate animals are involved in research. After Iams was granted leave to intervene, it filed a "Motion for an Order Prohibiting the Disclosure of Exempt Information," unopposed by MSU, asserting that the documents PETA requested were exempt from disclosure pursuant to *Mississippi Code Annotated Sections 25-61-9(3)* and *79-23-1(3)*. Following an *in camera* review of the subject records, the chancellor entered her order which, *inter alia*, stated that "IACUC is governed by rules adopted by it and MSU, as well as by rules imposed by applicable federal and state law[,]" but then concluded that the exemptions were largely inapplicable and ordered disclosure to PETA, subject to limited conditions. From that order, MSU and Iams filed their "Joint Notice of Appeal."

Id. at 595–97. On appeal, the court concluded that PETA had "failed to rebut the evidence presented by MSU and Iams that the data and information requested in the subject records constituted trade secrets and or confidential commercial and financial information of a proprietary nature developed by MSU under contract with Iams." Therefore, the court found that the data and information requested by PETA was "exempted from the provisions of the Mississippi Public Records Act, in harmony with applicable federal law."

In *Citizens for Alternatives to Animal Labs, Inc. v. Board of Trustees of State University of New York*, 703 N.E.2d 1218 (N.Y. 1998), petitioners sought access to certificates provided to a research facility from random source dealers. ("Random source" animals are discussed earlier in this section.) The certificates "contain[ed] various data, including the name and address of the person, pound, or shelter from which the dog or cat was purchased or otherwise acquired by the dealer, and an assurance that such person or entity was notified that the acquired animal may be used for research or educational purposes." The lower court found that the defendant, State University of New York (SUNY) was not an "agency" under the Freedom of Information Law (FOIL) because it was not "performing a governmental or proprietary function for the state." New York's highest court reversed, holding:

> Under FOIL, an "agency" is "any . . . governmental entity performing a governmental or proprietary function for the state." Public Officers Law § 86(3). A "record" is "any information kept, held, filed, produced or reproduced by, with or for an agency . . . in any physical form whatsoever." *Id.* at § 86(4). SUNY is an "agency" under FOIL, and respondents concede that SUNY HSC-B [the Health Science Center at Brooklyn, where SUNY conducts biomedical research using animals] is an integral part of SUNY. Furthermore, SUNY HSC-B is fulfilling SUNY's mission to provide educational services to the people of the State by "facilitat[ing] basic and applied research for the purpose of the creation and dissemination of knowledge vital for continued human [and] scientific . . . advancement." Education Law § 351(c).

Id. at 1220.

In *Medlock v. Board of Trustees of University of Massachusetts*, 580 N.E.2d 387 (Mass. 1991), the issue was whether the Massachusetts open meeting law, G.L.c. 30A, §§ 11A and 11AH, applied to the IACUCs created by the University of Massachusetts in compliance with the AWA. The defendant argued that the open meeting law did not apply to IACUC meetings because the Legislature had limited the requirement of open meetings to the University Board of Trustees itself. The trial court held that because the Board of Trustees was not expressly excluded from the definition of "governmental body," the meetings of the Board and any committee created by it must have open meetings. The appellate court, however, reversed and concluded that even if the IACUC is a governmental body, it does not conduct "meetings" within the meaning of the Open Meeting Law, and therefore, need not meet in public:

> We do not suggest that the law does not recognize that there is public concern about the manner in which animals are cared for and used. The Animal

Welfare Act and G. L. c. 140, § 174D, are results of that concern. The place for public expression and vigilance, however, is not at the research facility but at the public hearings where care and use standards are formulated and violations punished, as well as at the facility inspection report repository.

Although the defendant committees determine whether the care and use of animals for research purposes at the University and its medical school are consistent with Federal and State standards, they do not consider or discuss public policy matters in order to arrive at a decision on any public business.

580 N.E.2d at 391–92. For a critical look at the role of IACUCs, *see* Katharine M. Swanson, *Carte Blanche for Cruelty: The Non-Enforcement of the Animal Welfare Act*, 35 U. MICH. J.L. REFORM 937 (2002).

Both *Citizens for Alternatives to Animal Labs* and *Medlock* explore issues relating to public access to information generated as a result of AWA requirements. These cases, however, seem to come to contrary conclusions. Can the holdings be reconciled?

In *Physicians Committee for Responsible Medicine v. National Institutes of Health*, 326 F. Supp. 2d 19 (D.D.C. 2004), plaintiff sought to obtain an unredacted copy of a grant application submitted by a doctor/university professor to the NIH, relating to the development of a feline model of a neurological disease and drug abuse. NIH argued that the application was exempt from the federal FOIA, 5 U.S.C. § 552, as a trade secret, commercial information or inter-agency or intra-agency memorandum. Although the doctor believed potential commercial harm could come from "trade secrets" contained in the application being made public and argued that early disclosure could affect his ability to have his findings published, the court was not persuaded. It found that the doctor was a "noncommercial" scientist, affiliated with an educational institution, whose research was fully funded by U.S. taxpayers. As such, he was unable to show that the redacted information consisted of commercially viable information likely to be used in the production of trade commodities. The court also found that the data was not confidential and that the doctor was not acting as a consultant to the government when he submitted his application. Thus, no trade secret or commercial information was at risk and the application was not a document that qualified as an inter-agency or intra-agency memoranda.

3. In *In Defense of Animals v. U.S. Dept. of Agriculture*, 656 F. Supp. 2d 68 (D.D.C. 2009), the plaintiff sued to obtain records relating to a USDA investigation of Huntingdon Life Sciences, Inc. (HLS), a company involved in extensive invasive animal research. HLS' parent company intervened. The USDA had refused to produce over 1000 pages of records, asserting disclosure would cause HLS to suffer "competitive harm." Defendants based the refusal on "FOIA Exemption 4," which allows an agency to withhold "trade secrets and commercial or financial information obtained from a person and privileged or confidential." 5 U.S.C. § 552(b)(4). The case was litigated for four years and went to trial, which is rare in FOIA cases.

Extensive expert testimony was presented at trial and the court issued a 31-page opinion, finding that defendants had not met their burden of proving a substantial likelihood of competitive harm. The court also found defendants had not proven that all "reasonably segregable" documents that were not exempt from disclosure had been produced.

The "competitive harm" claim has come up in a number of cases. Some courts have viewed the exemption narrowly and compelled disclosure. *See, e.g., Boeing Co. v. U.S. Dep't of the Air Force*, 616 F. Supp. 2d 40 (D.D.C. 2009); *In Defense of Animals v. U.S. Dep't of Agric.*, 587 F. Supp. 2d 178 (D.D.C. 2008). Where defendants have presented sufficient evidence of the anticipated competitive harms, however, courts have upheld the nondisclosure. *See, e.g., Customs & Int'l Trade Newsletter v. U.S. Customs & Border Prot.*, 588 F. Supp. 2d 51 (D.D.C. 2008); *NYC Apparel FZE v. U.S. Customs & Border Prot.*, 484 F. Supp. 2d 77 (D.D.C. 2007).

4. In February 2017, the USDA removed its animal welfare records from its website, including records of all Animal Welfare Act (AWA) violations. In the months that followed, organizations filed Freedom of Information Act (FOIA) requests in order to view the data. In return, some of these organizations received nearly 2,000 pages of completely blacked-out data. Natasha Daily and Rachael Bale, *We Asked the Government Why Animal Welfare Records Disappeared. They Sent 1,700 Blacked-Out Pages,* Nat'l Geographic (May 1, 2017). The reasoning the USDA provided for the removal of the records was similarly opaque. It stated: "Based on our commitment to being transparent, remaining responsive to our stakeholders' informational needs, and maintaining the privacy rights of individuals, APHIS [the agency responsible for AWA inspections and oversight] is implementing actions to remove documents." In August 2017, the USDA rolled out its new Public Search Tool. However, the information contained in the available records was still heavily redacted and eliminated most of the names of AWA violators. Animal advocacy groups have sued in order to gain access to the full records, although as of this publication none had been successful, with courts ruling that they cannot order an agency to release its records. *See,* Delcianna Winders, *Fulfilling the Promise of eFOIA's Affirmative Disclosure Mandate,* 95 Denv. L. Rev. 910 (2018).

As of this publication, one of the more recent lawsuits in this area was *Humane Soc'y of the U.S. v. Animal & Plant Health Inspection Service, et al.*, Civil Action No. 18-646 (D.D.C., complaint filed March 21, 2018). The litigation was in its early stages when this edition went to press.

5. Researchers in all fields have a vested interest in maintaining a high level of security around their work and underlying research until they are able to sell or publish their findings. However, in the case of researchers who use nonhumans as their subjects, should a more liberal rule be instituted allowing for closer scrutiny throughout the research project? If so, how could such a rule be crafted to allow for appropriate oversight and yet protect the researchers' proprietary interest in the research?

G. Animal Exhibition under the AWA

Other businesses that impact a significant number of captive animals—usually exotic ones—are circuses and zoos. These enterprises are, when not exempted, subject to local and state laws governing cruelty to animals (as discussed in Chapter 3), as well as the keeping, exhibition and housing of exotic animals under the AWA and state and local law. Some animals may also be covered by specific laws protecting identified species, such as the Endangered Species Act (discussed briefly earlier in this chapter and in Chapter 9).

Animals used for "exhibition purposes" are covered by the AWA, 7 U.S.C. § 2132(g), and exhibitors of covered animals (including zoos, circuses, traveling exhibitors, carnivals) are regulated as well. 7 U.S.C. § 2132(h). The AWA also oversees "intermediate handlers" who transport animals, as well as the carriers involved in transport of animals. 7 U.S.C. § 2132(l), (j). The AWA prescribes minimum standards for "handling, housing, feeding, watering, sanitation, shelter from extremes of weather and temperatures, and adequate veterinary care." 7 U.S.C. § 2143(a)(2)(A). The requirement "for a physical environment adequate to promote the psychological well-being of primates" was discussed earlier in this chapter. 7 U.S.C. § 2143(a)(2)(B).

State and local laws aid in protecting animals used for "exhibition purposes," particularly those in circuses. Statutes exist in at least twenty-three states to regulate exhibited animals at both the local and state-wide level. Some bans are very narrow in scope, banning a specific instrument or a type of animal from use in exhibits. *See, e.g.,* PITTSBURGH MUNI. CODE Title 6, Art. III, § 637.02 (banning the use of bull hooks, whips, bats, and other objects on exotic animals); R.I. GEN. LAWS § 4-1-43 (statewide ban on the use of bullhooks on elephants). Others are broader in scope, banning the use of wild animals generally or specific wild animals in traveling exhibits or exhibits of any kind. *See, e.g..* SAN FRAN. HEALTH CODE Art. 1B § 3 (banning wild or exotic animals in performances); 520 ILL. COMP. STAT 10/3.5 (amending the state Endangered Species Act by banning the use of elephants in traveling animal acts).

The American Zoo and Aquarium Association (AZA) is a voluntary membership organization that provides internal accreditation for zoos and aquariums, and certification for member zoos, refuges, sanctuaries and other facilities. (There are also sanctuary groups that are self-policing and, like the AZA, carry no legal authority.) The AZA sets standards for accreditation and certification, but as a private, self-governing organization, it does not have legal authority to enforce laws or even to enforce its own standards, other than by removal from its membership. Many zoos are not certified by the AZA, but this does not bar them from operating. AZA membership and accreditation does establish a certain set of minimum standards, but it also carries with it strongly recommended or compulsory participation in breeding programs and loan protocols to other accredited zoos. To varying degrees, the federal government also provides oversight by the USDA, in compliance with AWA requirements.

Shifting regulatory standards for zoos and aquaria are not limited to the United States. In 2017, France imposed significantly stricter regulations on aquaria operating in the country and banned the breeding of captive dolphins and killer whales. These regulations included a ban on direct contact between animals and the public and required enlarging dolphin and whale enclosures by 2020. In January of 2018, however, France's highest administrative court overturned the ban, citing procedural irregularities in the legislation. *Top French court reverses ban on breeding whales, dolphins*, Reuters (Jan. 29. 2018). Vancouver, British Columbia attempted to ban the keeping of cetaceans in its city parks; however, the British Columbia Supreme Court struck down the bylaw, claiming the park board lacked standing to change the charter. Derrick Penner, *Vancouver park board to appeal court decision that overturned cetacean-ban bylaw*, Vancouver Sun (Mar. 2, 2018). India has succeeded in avoiding this issue altogether. In 2013, the Ministry of Environment and Forests in India banned the establishment of a dolphinarium in the country, citing the intelligence and sensitivity of cetaceans along with the compromise of their survival in captivity.

Chapter 7

Contracts

As animals are considered property under the law, they cannot be parties to contracts. There are many circumstances, however, in which they are the subjects of contracts or contractual disputes. Billions of animals are sold every year. In addition, companion animals may be the focus of landlord/tenant disputes, homeowners' association regulations and custody disputes upon dissolution of relationships. And a growing topic in society today is the issue of exemptions to pet restrictions in leases, community development regulations or local ordinances under state and federal housing regulations and, more broadly, under state and federal laws preventing discrimination against the disabled and elderly.

Every time an animal companion is turned over to a caregiver, groomer or veterinarian, a contract is created. This type of contract generally is viewed as a bailment. Because they raise both tort and contract issues, bailments were discussed in Chapter 4 in connection with veterinary malpractice cases. Bailment cases may involve companion animals as well as animals kept for profit. Product liability issues, such as warranties and the Uniform Commercial Code, also arise in cases involving animals. Insurance policies represent another type of contract where animals may be an issue.

This chapter focuses on some of the more common circumstances in which courts have considered the unique issues that arise when animals are the subject of contractual agreements, and in which the law is continuing to evolve.

Section 1. Housing Issues

A. Pet Restrictions in Leases and Community Developments

Young v. Savinon

Superior Court of New Jersey, Appellate Division, 1985
201 N.J. Super. 1, 492 A.2d 385

DREIER, J. Defendants appeal from a decision of the Special Civil Part enforcing a "no pets" provision in defendants' renewal leases. Defendants had been tenants in plaintiff's apartments prior to his acquiring title. Their earlier leases did not prohibit pets, but upon renewal after plaintiff's purchase, the leases contained a new "no pets" provision.

At issue before us is whether under the facts of this case the "no pets" provision should be sustained. The trial judge found herself bound by *Terhune Courts v. Sgambati*, 394 A.2d 416 (Cty. D. Ct. 1978), *aff'd o.b.* 406 A.2d 1330 (App. Div. 1979), *certif. den.* 420 A.2d 331 (1980), and upheld plaintiff's right to dispossess defendants unless they removed their dogs.

At the time of the trial in 1982 defendant Possumato had been residing in the premises with her daughter, now a teenager, for six years and had brought her dog with her when she moved in. She had owned the dog four years at that time, and thus the dog must now be 12 to 13 years old. The wife of defendant Savinon had lived in their apartment for only a year at the time of trial, but had owned the dog for some time prior to moving into the apartment. The dog is now between 12 and 13 years old. The dog is her constant companion and her attachment to the animal is also partially due to the fact that it had belonged to her sister until her sister's death. The third defendant, Mrs. Brosonski, first lived in the apartment in 1973, and as of the time of trial had lived there for 8 of the past 9 years. Her dog also is between 13 and 14 years old. The dogs are respectively a German shepherd, a Scottish terrier and a Chihuahua.

Testimony established that the premises are located near warehouses, which are unoccupied at night, and that there are bars in the area. People are known to "hang out" around the building at night; drunks often throw beer bottles or fight at night in the alleyway near the premises, waking up the tenants; the tenants have also experienced attempted break-ins. The entrance door to the building has been forced open, and one year prior to the trial a man had been stabbed to death in the building. Both the defendants and other tenants testified that the presence of the dogs make all of the tenants feel safer, since they give warning when strangers approach.

Prior to plaintiff's purchase of the building, the landlord imposed no condition prohibiting pets, and defendants all moved in with their pets with knowledge of former landlord's policy. In December 1981 when plaintiff purchased the premises he was aware that five animals were maintained in the twelve unit apartment house.[1] Plaintiff, who is afraid of dogs, admits purchasing the premises with the intention of forcing the tenants either to get rid of their pets or move.

None of the dogs belonging to the defendants has been the subject of any but the most minor complaint by another tenant or by the prior or present landlord. None of the dogs is permitted out of its apartment unattended.

At the trial defendants presented testimony by Dr. Aaron Katcher, an Associate Professor of Psychology at the University of Pennsylvania and a specialist concerning the influence of companion animals on the mental and physical health of

---

1. In addition to the three dogs belonging to defendants, a cat was owned by another tenant, and the superintendent of the premises owned a dog which he still possessed at the time of trial. Actually, there was a sixth animal. One of the defendants owned a fish, which plaintiff also demanded be removed in his initial notices.

their owners. His testimony established that the loss of their pets to people such as defendants would cause significant health problems, especially if the loss is due to a defendant being forced to give up his or her pet as opposed to the pet's dying a natural death. Defendants could be expected to suffer grief and depression as great as that suffered at the loss of a family member and, in addition, suffer from a sense of guilt and loss of self-esteem. On a positive note, the witness testified to studies showing that the presence of a pet lowers blood pressure, decreases anxiety, combats depression and generally increases the owner's health. In fact, the presence of pets generally lowers the rate of mortality. As to Mrs. Savinon, and defendants Possumato and Brosonski, Dr. Katcher testified that one would be increasingly unwilling to leave her home, another would suffer a worsening in her cardiovascular system and increased hypertension and the third would experience severe grief, especially since this woman would not only grieve for the loss of her dog but suffer a reawakened grief for the loss of her sister, the dog's former owner. He expected that if these women were forced to choose between giving up their pets or moving, they would feel forced to move.

This case was tried twice. After the first trial the complaints were dismissed on procedural grounds. In the second trial it was stipulated that the testimony initially taken could be considered by the judge who, on April 20, 1983, granted judgments for possession against the three defendants. A stay was entered pending this appeal.

Prior to the enaction of the Anti-Eviction Act, N.J.S.A. 2A:18-61.1 *et seq.*, a landlord had the right to refuse to renew a lease for practically any reason, other than a basis that would be in violation of the Law Against Discrimination, N.J.S.A. 10:5-1 *et seq.* The Anti-Eviction Act, however, limited the causes for eviction and required that landlords be "reasonable" in their relations with their tenants insofar as placing restrictions upon a tenant's activities. These restrictions could be placed in the rules and regulations promulgated by the landlord, in the lease covenants themselves, or in changes in the terms and conditions contained in a renewal lease. These sections all require, however, that the provisions be "reasonable."

The court in *Terhune Courts v. Sgambati, supra*, assumed that an outright ban on pets was reasonable, citing *Housing Auth., Atlantic City v. Coppock*, 136 N.J. Super. 432, 435 (App. Div. 1975). As has been recently explained by us in *Royal Associates v. Concannon*, 200 N.J. Super. 84, 90–91 (App. Div. 1985), the discussion in the *Atlantic City* case was *dictum* and was also stated as an assumption without an analysis of the impact of the statement in the particular case. Likewise, in *Terhune Courts*, the court assumed that it was bound by a prior appellate determination that a "no pets" provision was reasonable, irrespective of the facts. The court there also reasoned that it was limited to assessing the agreements of landlord and tenant during only the current term of the lease, without reference to any agreement concerning their continuing relationship. The fallacy in that argument can be demonstrated by assuming that a landlord made a promise at the commencement of the first lease that a tenant would be charged 80% of the rental charged to the other tenants for the same size apartment for so long as the tenant remained at the premises. If after a few renewals of the lease at such rate the landlord determined to charge the tenant the full rental, contending that any agreement to the contrary had been made during the term of a prior lease and, therefore, terminated with the end of that lease, would a court permit such repudiations? We think not. A landlord may make an abiding agreement outside of the lease that is intended to transcend the provisions of individual leases, and which may be enforced. The tenant, of course, must carry the burden of proof and demonstrate that the separate agreement was made. In *Royal Associates v. Concannon, supra,* we found an express contract, not denied by the landlord, that the tenants could keep their dog so long as they controlled it. The tenants had satisfied their commitment, and the landlord was estopped from enforcing the "no pets" provision of the lease during the lifetime of the animal so long as the tenants continued to comply with their agreement to control it.

In the case before us, the prior landlord rented the apartment to tenants knowing they possessed dogs. Given the ages and family situations of the tenants it was reasonable to expect that the tenants would be attached to their animals. Agreements between the landlord and tenant need not be in writing nor even be expressed in words. Enforceable agreements also may be implied in fact from the conduct of the parties. If the prior landlord by his actions bound himself to permit the continued possession of these animals by their owners and this implied contract also transcended the term of the then-current lease, the former landlord could have conveyed to his transferee no greater rights than he possessed. . . . In this case the purchaser was aware that the Anti-Eviction Act permitted only reasonable changes in the lease terms or a landlord's rules or regulations, and that the premises were subject to that Act. Plaintiff also was familiar with the then-current tenants, that these defendants possessed dogs and that their possession of the animals was not in violation of any term of their leases.

This is not to say that a landlord may not validly prohibit pets in rental premises owned by him. The only blanket exception to this right is contained in N.J.S.A. 10:5-29.2 governing guide dogs for a handicapped, blind or deaf person. The issue here, however, is whether the prohibition shall operate retroactively to force the removal of pets already owned by tenants in a situation where there was no lease violation when the pets were acquired. In *Terhune Courts* and in the trial court's opinion here, the trial judges determined that the test of reasonableness was to be applied solely to the landlord's interest. In the context of the Anti-Eviction Act the term applies to the lease provision, not the landlord's or tenant's sole interest. Since the "no pets" provision may be enforced in a summary dispossess or declaratory judgment proceeding, if a tenant claims special circumstances, the reasonableness of the prohibition relating to both the landlord and the tenant in his or her particular circumstances should be inquired into by the court.

The tenant may be able to show a waiver or estoppel. *See Royal Associates v. Concannon, supra. See also Jasontown Apts. v. Lynch,* 382 A.2d 688 (App. Div. 1978), where the reasonableness of the "no pets" provision was stipulated, but the tenant was entitled to a hearing to determine in the circumstances of that case if the provision had been waived. *Accord Shannon & Luchs v. Tindal*, 415 A.2d 805 (Ct. App. D.C. 1980); *Doerr v. Maher*, 85 N.E.2d 363 (1949); *see also Ocean Gate Associates Starrett Systems, Inc. v. Dopico*, 441 N.Y.S.2d 34, 35 (Civ. Ct. 1981) (where the dog was needed to afford protection to a handicapped owner and thus the "no pets" provision was unenforceable) and *Majors v. Housing Auth. DeKalb Cty.*, 652 F.2d 454, 458 (5th Cir. 1981) (where it was alleged that the mental deficiency of the tenant required the companionship of a dog and the case was remanded for a factual determination to see whether the "no pets" provision would be enforced).

In the case before us there was extensive psychological testimony concerning both the bonding between the defendants and their dogs and the adverse effect to the tenants if the provision were to be enforced against them. This testimony stood unimpeached. The trial judge determined that she could not consider the reasonableness of the "no pets" provision from the standpoint of the tenants under *Terhune Courts*. She correctly found that she was bound by prior appellate authority. We now find, however, that such statement of the law in *Terhune Courts* was in error.

Rather than remand this matter for reconsideration by the trial judge, we will exercise our original jurisdiction under *R.* 2:10-5 and render a complete determination of this matter. Based upon the factual testimony and the psychological expert's opinion, and considering the conduct of the prior landlord known to the plaintiff, we find that it would be unreasonable to enforce the "no pets" provision with respect to the defendants and their present pets. Through attrition, defendants' apartments will be brought into compliance.

By this determination, we should not be misunderstood as avoiding all "no pets" provisions in leases. Such provisions have been found reasonable from a landlord's point of view and should be enforced unless the landlord has expressly or impliedly permitted particular pets to be maintained, is otherwise estopped from enforcing the provision, or if a tenant who had previously been allowed to maintain a pet upon the premises can show that it is unreasonable to enforce the provision under the particular circumstances of the case before the court.

The judgments of possession appealed from are reversed and the complaints are hereby dismissed.

Notes

1. There is no question that landlords can and often do ban companion animals from leased premises. Disputes should be avoidable where the ban is enforced consistently and potential tenants are aware at the outset of the relationship. The real world issue arises most frequently, however, where tenants have been living with a companion animal and suddenly are given notice that they are in violation of the lease and must vacate the premises or get rid of the animal. Often this is due to a change in circumstances, as in *Young*, where there was a new property owner; or where a new neighbor or building manager doesn't like animals. With respect to dogs in particular, disputes may arise because of frequent barking or concern

about perceived problems unique to particular breeds or larger dogs. As noted in *Young*, where there is no applicable state law or local ordinance and the federal Fair Housing Act does not cover the situation, general principles of waiver and estoppel may apply.

2. In *Young*, the court agreed that the tenants should prevail, but only allowed them to keep their current companion animals until the animals died, and thereafter they could not have any more. Is there a legal basis for the court's decision?

3. The import of *Young* arguably is limited because it is based on the "reasonableness" standard of the New Jersey Anti-Eviction Act. The case has a more substantial significance because of the court's acceptance of extensive unimpeached testimony regarding the bond between defendants and their dogs. The opinion signals a departure from the traditional property-based judicial consideration of animals. As you have seen in your readings thus far, cases throughout the text reflect courts' increasing recognition of the emotional and psychological bond that often exists between humans and their companion animals. This bond is becoming more and more widely acknowledged by the judiciary, legislators, scientists and society as a whole.

4. Some of the litigation that arises from landlord/tenant disputes regarding companion animals can be avoided by the enactment of general tenant protection laws, such as New Jersey's Anti-Eviction Act, or more specific local ordinances. For example, New York City Administrative Code, ch. 2, section 27-2009.1 ("Rights and responsibilities of owners and tenants in relation to pets") provides, in relevant part:

> a. Legislative declaration. The council hereby finds that the enforcement of covenants contained in multiple dwelling leases which prohibit the harboring of household pets has led to widespread abuses by building owners or their agents, who knowing that a tenant has a pet for an extended period of time, seek to evict the tenant and/or his or her pet often for reasons unrelated to the creation of a nuisance. Because household pets are kept for reasons of safety and companionship and under the existence of a continuing housing emergency it is necessary to protect pet owners from retaliatory eviction and to safeguard the health, safety and welfare of tenants who harbor pets under the circumstances provided herein, it is hereby found that the enactment of the provisions of this section is necessary to prevent potential hardship and dislocation of tenants within this city.

> b. Where a tenant in a multiple dwelling openly and notoriously for a period of three months or more following taking possession of a unit, harbors or has harbored a household pet or pets, the harboring of which is not prohibited by the multiple dwelling law, the housing maintenance or the health codes of the city of New York or any other applicable law, and the owner or his or her agent has knowledge of this fact, and such owner fails within this three month period to commence a summary proceeding or action to enforce a lease provision prohibiting the keeping of such household pets, such lease provision shall be deemed waived.

* * *

d. The waiver provision of this section shall not apply where the harboring of a household pet causes damage to the subject premises, creates a nuisance or interferes substantially with the health, safety or welfare of other tenants or occupants of the same or adjacent building or structure.

e. The New York city housing authority shall be exempt from the provisions of this section.

Such laws essentially codify the common law principles of waiver and estoppel, and remove the factual question regarding what constitutes sufficient notice to be deemed a waiver or estoppel.

5. In 1998, Title I of the United States Housing Act of 1937 was amended to add 42 U.S.C. section 1437z-3(a), "Pet Ownership in Public Housing," which provides, in pertinent part:

A resident of a dwelling unit in public housing . . . may own 1 or more common household pets or have 1 or more common household pets present in the dwelling unit of such resident, subject to the reasonable requirements of the public housing agency, if the resident maintains each pet responsibly and in accordance with applicable State and local public health, animal control, and animal anti-cruelty laws and regulations. . . .

Prior to the enactment of this section, federal law permitted companion animals only in housing dedicated strictly to senior citizens and disabled persons. The amendment permits all residents of most federally-assisted housing to have a companion animal or animals, provided they do so responsibly and in compliance with applicable laws and requirements.

6. Individuals who choose to reside in community developments are subject to homeowners' association rules, regulations and bylaws, which will govern many aspects of living in the community, especially those affecting the use of "common areas" that all in the community have the option of utilizing. In addition, most homeowners' association regulations dictate, in some respects, certain conditions of habitation within the dwelling units. Through covenants, conditions and restrictions ("CC&Rs") or similar provisions of mutual agreement and governance, homeowners enter into a form of contract whereby purchasers and residents agree to be bound by generally applicable rules in exchange for owning property and/or residing in the community development.

In the abstract, it may seem unreasonable to expect that such rules and regulations would dictate the type of personal property that homeowners may keep within their dwelling unit. At the same time, it must be understood that community living requires some degree of agreed-upon rules and that individuals have the right to enter into contracts that legally limit conduct of private community members. So while a limit on red lamps might be too unreasonable to be supported, companion animals fall into a *sui generis* category of property. Restrictions on the type, number or size of companion animals thus may be found in homeowners' association rules, regulations and/or bylaws, and usually are upheld against challenges. Animal guardians may try to override the rules and to find exceptions or limits to the extent of permissible restrictions with respect to animals, as the cases discussed in the following Notes demonstrate.

In *Nahrstedt v. Lakeside Village Condominium Association*, 8 Cal. 4th 361 (1994), a homeowner in a condominium complex sued to prevent the homeowners' association from enforcing a pet restriction, asserting that the restriction was "unreasonable" as applied to her because she kept her three cats indoors and because her cats were "noiseless" and "created no nuisance." The intermediate appellate court agreed with her, but the California Supreme Court majority did not.

> Under the holding we adopt today, the reasonableness or unreasonableness of a condominium use restriction that the Legislature has made subject to [Cal. Civil Code] section 1354 is to be determined *not* by reference to facts that are specific to the objecting homeowner, but by reference to the common interest development as a whole. As we have explained, when, as here, a restriction is contained in the declaration of the common interest development and is recorded with the county recorder, the restriction is presumed to be reasonable and will be enforced uniformly against all residents of the common interest development *unless* the restriction is arbitrary, imposes burdens on the use of lands it affects that substantially outweigh the restriction's benefits to the development's residents, or violates a fundamental public policy.

* * *

> We conclude, as a matter of law, that the recorded pet restriction of the Lakeside Village condominium development prohibiting cats or dogs but allowing some other pets is not arbitrary, but is rationally related to health, sanitation and noise concerns legitimately held by residents of a high-density condominium project such as Lakeside Village, which includes 530 units in 12 separate 3-story buildings.

8 Cal. 4th at 386.

Should the special relationship between guardians and their animals be a factor in deciding the validity of pet restrictions as opposed to other types of homeowner restrictions? Is there a way in which to craft a restriction that would recognize a unique status for animals, while still protecting the interests of other property owners in the community?

Consider how animals are different from other inanimate property, and whether those differences are sufficient to automatically trigger a more rigorous consideration of community interests. For example, should the presence of a barbecue grill (with attendant smells and fire risks) and the presence of a dog or cat, be analyzed the same way for purposes of determining nuisance values? What about other human activities such as smoking? How do the potential health and safety dangers of smoking in one's private residence compare to the potential threat to human health and safety of having a cat or dog? How would you balance all of the stakeholders' interests in these examples?

The *Nahrstedt* majority discussed the history of the law of covenants and equitable servitudes, generally, but did not focus on any special considerations with respect to the issue of companion animals and their relationship with humans. The dissent, however, relied on that connection significantly, as excerpted below.

"There are two means of refuge from the misery of life: music and cats."[1]

I respectfully dissent. While technical merit may commend the majority's analysis, its application to the facts presented reflects a narrow, indeed chary, view of the law that eschews the human spirit in favor of arbitrary efficiency. In my view, the resolution of this case well illustrates the conventional wisdom, and fundamental truth, of the Spanish proverb, "It is better to be a mouse in a cat's mouth than a man in a lawyer's hands."

As explained below, I find the provision known as the "pet restriction" contained in the covenants, conditions, and restrictions (CC&R's) governing the Lakeside Village project patently arbitrary and unreasonable within the meaning of Civil Code section 1354. Beyond dispute, human beings have long enjoyed an abiding and cherished association with their household animals. Given the substantial benefits derived from pet ownership, the undue burden on the use of property imposed on condominium owners who can maintain pets within the confines of their units without creating a nuisance or disturbing the quiet enjoyment of others substantially outweighs whatever meager utility the restriction may serve in the abstract. It certainly does not promote "health, happiness [or] peace of mind" commensurate with its tariff on the quality of life for those who value the companionship of animals. Worse, it contributes to the fraying of our social fabric.

* * *

2. *The burden*.

* * *

Both recorded and unrecorded history bear witness to the domestication of animals as household pets. Throughout the ages, dogs and cats have provided human beings with a variety of services in addition to their companionship—shepherding flocks, guarding life and property, hunting game, ridding the house and barn of vermin. Of course, the modern classic example is the assist dog, which facilitates a sense of independence and security for disabled persons by enabling them to navigate their environment, alerting them to important sounds, and bringing the world within

---

1. Albert Schweitzer.

their reach. Emotionally, they allow a connection full of sensation and delicacy of feeling.

Throughout the ages, art and literature, as well as mythology, depict humans in all walks of life and social strata with cats and dogs, illustrating their widespread acceptance in everyday life. Some religions have even incorporated them into their worship. Dogs and cats are also admired for the purity of their character traits. Closer to home, our own culture is populated with examples of the well-established place pets have found in our hearts and homes.

In addition to these historical and cultural references, the value of pets in daily life is a matter of common knowledge and understanding as well as extensive documentation. People of all ages, but particularly the elderly and the young, enjoy their companionship. Those who suffer from serious disease or injury and are confined to their home or bed experience a therapeutic, even spiritual, benefit from their presence. Animals provide comfort at the death of a family member or dear friend, and for the lonely can offer a reason for living when life seems to have lost its meaning. In recognition of these benefits, both Congress and the state Legislature have expressly guaranteed that elderly and handicapped persons living in public-assistance housing cannot be deprived of their pets. (12 U.S.C. § 1701r-1; Health & Saf. Code, § 19901.) Not only have children and animals always been natural companions, children learn responsibility and discipline from pet ownership while developing an important sense of kindness and protection for animals. Single adults may find certain pets can afford a feeling of security. Families benefit from the experience of sharing that having a pet encourages. While pet ownership may not be a fundamental right as such, unquestionably it is an integral aspect of our daily existence, which cannot be lightly dismissed and should not suffer unwarranted intrusion into its circle of privacy.

3. *The benefit.*

What is gained from an uncompromising prohibition against pets that are confined to an owner's unit and create no noise, odor, or nuisance?

To the extent such animals are not seen, heard, or smelled any more than if they were not kept in the first place, there is no corresponding or concomitant benefit. Pets that remain within the four corners of their owners' condominium space can have no deleterious or offensive effect on the project's common areas or any neighboring unit. Certainly, if other owners and residents are totally *unaware* of their presence, prohibiting pets does not in any respect foster the "health, happiness [or] peace of mind" of anyone except the homeowners association's board of directors, who are thereby able to promote a form of sophisticated bigotry. In light of the substantial and disproportionate burden imposed for those who must forego virtually any and all association with pets, this lack of benefit renders a categorical ban unreasonable under Civil Code section 1354.

The proffered justification is all the more spurious when measured against the terms of the pet restriction itself, which contains an exception for domestic fish and birds. A squawking bird can readily create the very kind of disturbance supposedly prevented by banning other types of pets. At the same time, many animals prohibited by the restriction, such as hamsters and the like, turtles, and small reptiles, make no sound whatsoever. Disposal of bird droppings in common trash areas poses as much of a health concern as cat litter or rabbit pellets, which likewise can be handled in a manner that avoids potential problems. Birds are also known to carry disease and provoke allergies. Neither is maintaining fish without possible risk of interfering with the quiet enjoyment of condominium neighbors. Aquarium water must be changed and disposed of in the common drainage system. Leakage from a fish tank could cause serious water damage to the owner's unit, those below, and common areas. Defendants and the majority purport such solicitude for the "health, sanitation and noise concerns" of other unit owners, but fail to explain how the possession of pets, such as plaintiff's cats, under the circumstances alleged in her complaint, jeopardizes that goal any more than the fish and birds expressly allowed by the pet restriction. This inconsistency underscores its unreasonableness and discriminatory impact.

* * *

5. Conclusion.

Our true task in this turmoil is to strike a balance between the governing rights accorded a condominium association and the individual freedom of its members. To fulfill that function, a reviewing court must view with a skeptic's eye restrictions driven by fear, anxiety, or intolerance. In any community, we do not exist *in vacuo*. There are many annoyances which we tolerate because not to do so would be repressive and place the freedom of others at risk.

In contravention, the majority's failure to consider the real burden imposed by the pet restriction unfortunately belittles and trivializes the interest at stake here. Pet ownership substantially enhances the quality of life for those who desire it. When others are not only undisturbed by, but *completely unaware of*, the presence of pets being enjoyed by their neighbors, the balance of benefit and burden is rendered disproportionate and unreasonable, rebutting any presumption of validity. Their view, shorn of grace and guiding philosophy, is devoid of the humanity that must temper the interpretation and application of all laws, for in a civilized society that is the source of their authority. As judicial architects of the rules of life, we better serve when we construct halls of harmony rather than walls of wrath.

8 Cal. 4th at 370–97 (Arabian, J., dissenting).

7. After *Nahrstedt*, the California legislature enacted California Civil Code section 1360.5 ("Pets within common interest developments"), which became operative in 2001, and was later replaced by Civil Code section 4715 ("Pets"), which provides (as the predecessor statute did), in pertinent part:

> (a) No governing documents shall prohibit the owner of a separate interest within a common interest development from keeping at least one pet within the common interest development, subject to reasonable rules and regulations of the association. . . .

> (b) For purposes of this section, "pet" means any domesticated bird, cat, dog, aquatic animal kept within an aquarium, or other animal as agreed to between the association and the homeowner.

While the legislature defined "pet" to include any "animal as agreed to between the association and the homeowner," as a practical matter there are likely to be relatively few instances where a homeowners' association would agree that other types of animals (aside from those specifically listed) should be encompassed by the statute.

In *Villas de las Palmas Homeowners Association v. Terifaj*, 33 Cal. 4th 73 (2004), a condominium owner asserted that the enactment of section 1360.5 called into question *Nahrstedt*'s ultimate conclusion that the "no pet restriction" in that case was not unreasonable. In *Terifaj*, the governing document at issue was amended before 2001. The court concluded that to "allow section 1360.5 to undermine *Nahrstedt*'s holding in this case would essentially render section 1360.5's operative date meaningless." *Id.* at 93. The court went on to conclude that by enacting section 1360.5 "the Legislature did not declare that prohibiting pets is unreasonable, but merely demonstrated a legislative preference for allowing homeowners in common interest developments to keep at least one pet." *Id.* The court went on to quote its observation in *Nahrstedt* that "prohibiting pets is 'rationally related to health, sanitation and noise concerns legitimately held by residents' of common interest developments." *Id.* The court noted that *Nahrstedt* involved a "high-density" project, but concluded that the "concerns expressed in that case apply equally" to the Palm Springs condominiums at issue in *Terifaj*, which many of the owners, including the defendant, did not use as a primary residence but merely visited periodically or seasonally. *Id.* at 79, 93.

The reasoning of *Terifaj* was adopted by the North Dakota Supreme Court in *Riverside Park Condominium Unit Owners Association v. Lucas*, 691 N.W.2d 862 (N. Dak. 2005) (concurring with "rational relationship" discussion in *Terifaj* and *Nahrstedt*). In *Lucas*, the amended declaration of covenants and restrictions provided that no animal "shall be raised, bred, or kept by any unit owner. . . ." The homeowner asserted that his ex-wife's fifteen-pound West Highland White Terrier visited him at "irregular, infrequent times, probably approximately 24 days a year, with no scheduled times per month." *Id.* at 867. He argued that the word "kept" in the declaration is ambiguous and that a visiting dog is not "kept" for purposes of the restriction. The court concluded that "when the dog is there alone or is staying overnight no reasonable mind can dispute that the dog is being kept" by the homeowner. *Id.* at 872 (citing to the "periodic or seasonal" visits by the homeowner in *Terifaj*). Do you agree with the court's conclusion? The court provided no guidance as to when an animal is being "kept" in violation of the restrictions as opposed to permissibly visiting. At what point would you draw that line?

8. Where there is no statute addressing the issue, total bans on companion animals in common interest developments generally have been upheld by courts across the country. *See, e.g., Noble v. Murphy*, 612 N.E.2d 266 (Mass. App. Ct. 1993). Short of a total ban, many other limitation parameters could exist. Restrictions could be applied by species, breed, number of animals or size of the animals within a species. Would the restriction in *Nahrstedt* have met the California Supreme Court's test of "reasonableness" if it merely limited the number of cats and dogs in a dwelling unit, as opposed to effectuating a total ban? What if it excluded cats, but not dogs? Or vice versa? What if it permitted cats and dogs, but limited the weight of any given dog to twenty pounds? What about fifty or 100 pounds?

9. Even if a restriction otherwise would be enforceable, it may not be upheld if it has been selectively enforced. *See, e.g., Prisco v. Forest Villas Condo. Apts., Inc.*, 847 So. 2d 1012 (Fla. Dist. Ct. App. 2003) (reversing summary judgment in favor of the association based on questions of fact as to whether the restriction had been selectively enforced). In that case, there was a ban on any "pets whatsoever," except fish and birds. The homeowner plaintiff wanted to have a dog living with her. The trial court had concluded that the fact that other homeowners had been allowed to keep cats was not a selective enforcement because "cats are not the same as dogs." *Id.* at 1015. The appellate court found the difference to be irrelevant given the scope of the restriction — "What does matter is that neither a cat nor a dog is a fish or a bird, so both should be prohibited." *Id.*

If you were retained by a developer to draft a homeowners' association's bylaws and regulations, would you recommend including a "pet restriction"? If so, what limitations would you recommend imposing? What problems could arise in trying to enforce the restriction?

B. Exceptions to Pet Restrictions in Housing: "Service" and "Support" Animals

Under federal law and many parallel state laws, "support" or "service" animals are allowed to live with their human companions, despite "no pet" restrictions, where a health care provider certifies that the animal provides valuable support or assistance to a disabled person's mental or physical health. Under federal law, the Americans with Disabilities Act (ADA) (42 U.S.C. § 12101 *et seq.*) was enacted to prevent disparate treatment of disabled individuals and public settings with respect to the receipt of government services and public accommodations, as well as in employment; whereas the Fair Housing Act (FHA) (42 U.S.C. § 3601 *et seq.*) provides similar protections for housing choices. The standards under the two statutes and their state law analogs, while similar, are not identical.

Although the analysis may vary slightly depending on whether courts are focusing on federal law or state law, and the language of any state statute at issue, the key issues in companion animal/disability cases generally are (i) whether the individual seeking the accommodation is "disabled" within the meaning of the statute, (ii) whether the animal is a "reasonable accommodation" for the disability, and (under the ADA) (iii) whether the animal must be a "properly trained service animal" to qualify as a reasonable accommodation. Litigation in this area has been extensive.

Outside the housing arena, the ADA allows for "service animals" to be reasonable accommodations for disabled persons under appropriate circumstances, where those individuals are seeking to obtain the benefit of services available to the public. The regulations implementing the ADA define "service animal" to mean: ". . . any dog that is individually trained to do work or perform tasks for the benefit of an individual with a disability. . . . [T]he provision of emotional support, well-being, comfort, or companionship do not constitute work or tasks for the purposes of this definition." 28 C.F.R. § 36.104.

As noted, one issue addressed by courts has been whether an animal is required to be a trained "service" animal as required under the ADA in order to be a reasonable accommodation under the FHA. The implementing regulations revised by the Department of Housing and Urban Development (HUD) in 2008 made clear that the answer is no, at least under the federal FHA.

> [The ADA] generally provides that a public accommodation "shall modify policies, practices, or procedures to permit the use of a service animal by an individual with a disability." The FHA, in contrast with the ADA, does not regulate disability discrimination by public accommodations and in places of public accommodation. Rather, the FHA, *inter alia*, makes it illegal to discriminate against handicapped individuals in providing housing. 42 U.S.C. § 3604(f)(1). Simply stated, there is a difference between not requiring the owner of a movie theater to allow a customer to bring her emotional support dog, which is not a service animal, into the theater to watch a two-hour movie, an ADA-type issue, on one hand, and permitting the provider of housing to refuse to allow a renter to keep such an animal in her apartment in order to provide emotional support to her and to assist her to cope with her depression, an FHA-type issue, on the other.

> Based upon the foregoing alone, this Court would conclude that accommodations under the FHA regarding animals are not limited to service animals. However, additional indicia demonstrate that the two federal agencies charged with enforcing that statute, HUD and the DOJ, take the opposite position from that advocated herein by [the mutual housing corporation]. For instance, HUD recently revised its regulations concerning pet ownership by the elderly and persons with disabilities residing in HUD-assisted, public housing. *See Pet Ownership for the Elderly and Persons with Disabilities*, 73 F.R. 63834-38 (October 27, 2008). The revised regulation excludes from HUD's regulations prohibiting pet ownership in public

housing "animals that are used to assist, support, or provide service to persons with disabilities." 24 CFR § 5.303. HUD has explained that the revised rule applies not just to service animals, as defined by the regulations implementing the ADA, but also to support and therapy animals. 73 F.R. 63834. Such animals are defined to include those "providing emotional support to persons who have a disability related need for such support." *Id.* As can be seen, HUD has declined to limit its regulation on keeping animals to those that have been individually trained, unlike the regulations implementing the ADA. HUD explained its reasons for doing so:

> Finally, the Department believes that removing the animal training requirement ensures equal treatment of persons with disabilities who need animals in housing as a reasonable accommodation, for a wide variety of purposes. While many animals are trained to perform certain tasks for persons with disabilities, others do not need training to provide the needed assistance. For example, there are animals that have an innate ability to detect that a person with a seizure disorder is about to have a seizure and can let the individual know ahead of time so that the person can prepare. This ability is not the result of training, and a person with a seizure disorder might need such an animal as a reasonable accommodation to his/her disability. Moreover, emotional support animals do not need training to ameliorate the effects of a person's mental and emotional disabilities. Emotional support animals by their very nature, and without training, may relieve depression and anxiety, and/or help reduce stress-induced pain in persons with certain medical conditions affected by stress.

Overlook Mut. Homes, Inc. v. Spencer, 666 F. Supp. 2d 850, 858-59 (S.D. Ohio 2009). In response to public comment against the revision before it was finalized, HUD further explained:

> The Department does not agree that the definition of the term "service animal" contained in the Department of Justice regulations implementing the ADA should be applied to the Fair Housing Act and Section 504. The ADA governs the use of animals by persons with disabilities primarily in the public arena. There are many areas where the ADA and the Fair Housing Act and Section 504 contain different requirements. For example, accessibility is defined differently under the ADA than under the Fair Housing Act and Section 504.
>
> The Fair Housing Act and HUD's Section 504 regulations govern the use of animals needed as a reasonable accommodation in housing. HUD's regulations and policies pertaining to reasonable accommodation were constructed specifically to address housing and, furthermore, were enacted prior to the development and implementation of the ADA regulations. Thus, the requirements for assistance/service animals must be evaluated in the appropriate context of housing, and are independent

of the ADA regulations that were formulated to meet the needs of persons with disabilities in a different context and were adopted subsequent to HUD's regulations.

There is a valid distinction between the functions animals provide to persons with disabilities in the public arena, i.e., performing tasks enabling individuals to use public services and public accommodations, as compared to how an assistance animal might be used in the home. For example, emotional support animals provide very private functions for persons with mental and emotional disabilities. Specifically, emotional support animals by their very nature, and without training, may relieve depression and anxiety, and help reduce stress-induced pain in persons with certain medical conditions affected by stress. Conversely, persons with disabilities who use emotional support animals may not need to take them into public spaces covered by the ADA.

Id. at 63836. Although the revised rule applies only to HUD-assisted public housing, as opposed applying to housing generally, as does the FHA, the rationale in support thereof is equally applicable to all types of housing regulated by the FHA.

Overlook Mut. Homes, 666 F. Supp. 2d at 860.

In *Association of Apartment Owners of Liliuokalani Gardens at Waikiki v. Taylor,* 892 F. Supp. 2d 1268 (D. Haw. 2012), where the defendant sought to keep his dog, Nell, as an accommodation for his mental disability, the court addressed the same issue, also noting the then-recent development in the law.

As a preliminary matter, the Court considers the development of the FHA and state law to include not only "service animals," but "assistance animals" as reasonable accommodations. Taylor and [*amicus*] have presented persuasive arguments that the FHA state law, while not explicitly embracing "emotional support animals" as unequivocal "reasonable accommodations," does not preclude them as such. HUD and the DOJ have shown an increasing acceptance of emotional support animals, and *Haw. Rev. Stat.* §515-3, while not explicitly mentioning emotional support animals, invites the possibility of their acceptance with the broad limitation of "use of an animal." Accordingly, this Court acknowledges that the law has changed since [*Prindable v. Ass'n of Apt. Owners of 2987 Kalakaua,* 304 F. Supp. 2d 1245 (D. Haw. 2003), *aff'd, Dubois v. Ass'n of Apt. Owners of 2987 Kalakaua,* 453 F.3d 1175] was decided in 2003 by increasing acceptance of "assistance animals" as possible "reasonable accommodations."

Upon a close reading of the *Prindable* decision, the Court notes that Judge Kay did not confront the exact issue presently before this Court. . . . Plainly, the analysis in *Prindable* was focused solely on whether Einstein was a "service animal," which requires some indicia of specialized training.

Conversely, the present case requires the Court to consider whether Nell is an "assistance animal" that, by her very presence, provides emotional support to ameliorate Taylor's disability. As extensively briefed by Taylor and [*amicus*], the concept of an "assistance animal," distinguishable from a "service animal," is a relatively recent occurrence and has become more prominent in the law in the nine years since the district court decided *Prindable*. Because this Court is not confronting the same issue as the *Prindable* court, it need not adopt the ADA definition of "service animal" or otherwise conclude that an untrained animal is not a reasonable accommodation per se.

Taylor, 892 F. Supp. 2d at 1285-86 (distinguishing and noting the developments in the law since *Prindable* without reaching the issue of whether the dog was an "individually trained service animal"). *See also Fair Housing of the Dakotas, Inc. v. Goldmark Property Mngmt, Inc.*, 778 F. Supp. 2d 1028, 1036 (D.N.D. 2011) (concluding that the ADA "service animal" definition did not apply to the FHA reasonable accommodations standard; "the FHA encompasses all types of assistance animals regardless of training, including those that ameliorate a physical disability and those that ameliorate a mental disability").

The *Taylor* court went on to conclude that it "cannot say, as a matter of law, that an untrained emotional support animal unequivocally is or is not a reasonable accommodation under the FHA," finding instead that a fact-specific inquiry must be undertaken and a case-by-case determination made. 892 F. Supp. 2d at 1287.

Notes

1. While it is clear that the FHA does not require an animal to be a specially trained "service" animal, state analogs with different wording may not be construed in the same manner. For example, in *Timberlane Mobile Home Park v. Washington State Human Rights Commission*, 95 P.3d 1288 (Wash. Ct. App. 2004), the Washington State Human Rights Commission filed a complaint on behalf of two tenants against their landlord mobile home park, under Washington's analog to the FHA. The Washington law stated that only animals trained to assist or accommodate disabled persons can qualify as "service animals." The tenant (Candida) suffered from severe migraine headaches several times a week. Candida acquired Spicey, a Pomeranian dog, when Spicey was five weeks old. When Spicey was about eight months old, she began responding to Candida's migraines by alerting others that Candida needed assistance. The landlord contended that Spicey was not a "service animal" under the statute because she was not trained to assist Candida. The unchallenged findings by the administrative law judge (ALJ) were that "(1) although Spicey did not receive training to do so, she will 'freak out' and get [Candida's brother] when Candida has a severe migraine incident, and (2) it is possible Spicey would not have been trainable as a service animal, but by March 1998, Spicey assisted Candida in alleviating her migraine condition by bringing her

assistance when she was unable to help herself." *Id.* at 1291. Based on these findings, the ALJ concluded that "'[n]ot much [training] is required' of an alert dog, that Spicey had a 'propensity' to alert others to Candida's needs, and that Spicey 'achieves what she wants — attention to [Candida] — [which] is in itself positive reinforcement of desired behavior and thus a form of training.'" *Id.* The appellate court reversed, holding that the ALJ's finding and its ruling in favor of the tenant (which had been affirmed by the trial court) were "at odds" with the conclusion that Spicey was a "service animal" under the Washington statute, which "plainly requires that the animal's training be for the purpose of assisting or accommodating a disabled person." *Id.* According to the appellate court, "the ALJ's reasoning that Spicey's training consisted of getting what she wanted . . . would make any family pet a service animal." *Id.*

Consider the potential alternative interpretations of the "training" required to qualify for coverage under these statutes. What parameters can be used to judge training? Where a statute requires the animal to be "trained for the purpose of assisting or accommodating a disabled person's sensory, mental, or physical disability" (as the Washington statute did), what facts short of formal training might support a finding in favor of the tenant?

2. In *Presidential Village, LLC v. Phillips,* 158 A.3d 772 (Conn. 2017), the Connecticut Supreme Court held that the trial court had erred in relying on the "spirit" of certain HUD regulations to rule in favor of a tenant who kept an emotional support dog in her federally subsidized rental apartment in violation of a pet restriction in her lease. In that case, however, the issue was whether the tenant was "disabled" under the statutory language, *i.e.,* whether she demonstrated "a physical or mental impairment that substantially limits one or more of [her] major life activities." The court concluded: "Although one may be sympathetic to the emotional benefits that Mellow [the dog] provides to the defendant and her family given their traumatic family history, we nevertheless disagree with the trial court's conclusion that allowing them to keep Mellow in the apartment is consistent with 'the spirit of the [department's] regulations' absent evidence that any one of them had a 'physical or mental disability affecting a major life activity.'" *Id.* at 783.

3. A result favoring the tenant was reached in *Green v. Housing Authority of Clackamas County, Oregon,* 994 F. Supp. 1253 (D. Or. 1998). In that case, plaintiffs sued under the FHA and the ADA when faced with eviction after buying a hearing assistance dog.

> There is no dispute that Jeremy is a qualified individual with a disability, or that [Defendant] HACC is a public entity as defined by the ADA. The dispute, specifically, is whether plaintiffs' hearing assistance dog was really, in fact, a hearing assistance dog — or simply a household pet. HACC argues that the dog was not an appropriate accommodation for Jeremy's disability because the plaintiffs were unable to produce any "verification" that the dog was a "certified" hearing assistance trained animal. HACC admits that a disabled person has an absolute right to an assistance animal, and that it

was capable of accommodating plaintiffs' request for a hearing dog without incurring significant financial or administrative burdens. HACC relies on its own internal policy to make the determination of whether an animal is an assistance animal. Plaintiffs contend that there exists no federal or state statutes which allow the defendant to decide whether the dog is an assistance animal.

* * *

[T]here is no federal or Oregon certification process or requirement for hearing dogs, guide dogs, companion animals, or any type of service animal. There is no federal or Oregon certification of hearing dog trainers or any other type of service animal. The only requirements to be classified as a service animal under federal regulations are that the animal be (1) individually trained, and (2) work for the benefit of a disabled individual. There is no requirement as to the amount or type of training a service animal must undergo. Further, there is no requirement as to the amount or type of work a service animal must provide for the benefit of the disabled person. 28 C.F.R. § 36.104. The regulations establish minimum requirements for service animals.

Plaintiffs claim that the dog underwent individual training at home and was also trained by a professional trainer. Plaintiffs state that the dog alerted Jeremy to several sounds, including knocks at the door, the sounding of the smoke detector, the telephone ringing, and cars coming into the driveway. HACC's requirement that an assistance animal be trained by a certified trainer of assistance animals, or at least by a highly skilled individual, has no basis in law or fact. There is no requirement in any statute that an assistance animal be trained by a certified trainer.

Id. at 1255–56. The court granted summary judgment in favor of plaintiffs, concluding that they "should have been allowed to keep the dog as an assistance animal chosen by plaintiffs to help Jeremy enjoy equal access to the programs and services provided by HACC to all tenants." *Id.* at 1257.

In *Auburn Woods I Homeowners Ass'n v. Fair Employment and Housing Commission*, 121 Cal. App. 4th 1578 (2004), Ed and Jayne Elebiari both suffered "from severe depression and found that taking care of a dog alleviated their symptoms and enabled them to function more productively." Specifically, with their companion Pooky to care for,

Jayne's agitation lessened, her concentration improved, her interpersonal relationships improved, she slept better, and the acts of self-mutilation became less severe. The dog also had a positive effect on Ed by keeping Ed occupied. Ed took the dog for walks and played with her. The dog alleviated depression for both Jayne and Ed, and enabled them to enjoy each other's company more. Dr. Schnitzler believed that the Elebiaris' moods and affects improved after getting the dog. . . .

Id. at 1584–85. Under California's Fair Employment and Housing Act (FEHA), which includes a prohibition on disability discrimination in housing, the Elebiaris sought permission to have Pooky live with them at their condominium development (which prohibited pets), but the homeowners' association refused. Pooky was removed because of the association's refusal to allow her to stay. A central issue in the Elebiaris' lawsuit was whether Pooky could qualify as a reasonable accommodation under the FEHA. The court found that "it is clear that, under the right circumstances, allowing a pet despite a no-pets policy may constitute reasonable accommodation." *Id.* at 1593. "[B]ecause a [statutorily-defined] service animal was not at issue here, there was no requirement that the Elebiaris present evidence that their dog was specially trained to alleviate their disabilities. Pooky did not need special skills to help ameliorate the effects of the Elebiaris' disabilities. Rather, it was the innate qualities of a dog, in particular a dog's friendliness and ability to interact with humans, that made [her] therapeutic here." *Id.* at 1596.

Do the facts in *Green* and *Auburn Woods* warrant a different result than in *Timberlane Mobile Home Park*?

4. As discussed above, disabled individuals seeking to have an animal live with them where such animals are prohibited must show (1) they have a covered disability and (2) the requested accommodation is reasonable and necessary. One of the factors required to satisfy the second element is to establish a nexus between the disability and the need for the animal. While in many cases this is obvious and easily established (*e.g.*, dogs who assist those who are hearing or vision impaired), in some cases it is not so clear. *Kennedy House, Inc. v. Philadelphia Commission on Human Relations*, 143 A.3d 476 (Pa. Commw. Ct. 2016), addressed this issue. The case involved Jan Rubin's "request for a housing accommodation in the form of a waiver of [the] no-dog policy" of a residential cooperative building (Kennedy House), in which she wished to purchase an apartment. Kennedy House denied her application, and Rubin sued.

Ms. Rubin suffered from severe physical ailments that caused constant pain, as well as other conditions, all of which made it difficult for her to stand or sit for more than a short period. The facts established that "[t]o assist her in everyday life, Ms. Rubin employs two part-time caregivers and is assisted by her 10- or 11- year-old Plott Hound named Mira." In support of her need for Mira, Ms. Rubin's primary care physician stated that she "benefit[ted] from the support of a service dog," and that her dog's companionship was "consistent with her needs associated with her disability." Ms. Rubin testified that Mira did not help her with mobility issues but that "'[Mira] has a timing thing that goes off in her and she reminds me what I am supposed to be doing.'" She further testified that Mira was not specially trained, but assisted her at home.

> "When I am not able to leave the house for long periods of time, my companion dog gives me emotional support. . . . My companion dog reminds me to wake up, eat meals, and go to sleep when required." Ms. Rubin further alleges that her request for accommodation was reasonable because "my

companion dog would always be on a leash[,] ... would avoid elevator cars with other residents[,] ... would exit through the rear entrance instead of the lobby[, and p]ublic and private areas would be kept clean and odor free."

143 A.3d at 480.

Kennedy House took the position that Ms. Rubin had not established that there was "a sufficient nexus between her disability and the assistance provided by her dog" and that "a reasonable accommodation in the form of an assistance animal would only be required under the law when a dog is specially trained to assist a disabled person."

The court noted that "[t]he difficulty presented is distinguishing between a disability-related need for an assistance animal and a beloved, and intuitive, pet." The court cited federal guidance that advised that "[a]n assistance animal is not a pet. It is an animal that works, provides assistance or performs tasks ... or provides emotional support that alleviates one or more identified symptoms or effects of a person's disability." Given that Ms. Rubin alleged no mental disability, but only a physical one, the court found that she had not met her burden on the required nexus:

> We agree with Kennedy House that the nexus that must be demon-
> strated is between the disability described in the medical information
> and the assistance provided by the animal. Here, the medical information
> provided by her physician documented Ms. Rubin's issues with mobility;
> however, there is no question that Mira does not provide assistance to Ms.
> Rubin directly related to her mobility, the only disability documented by
> Dr. Wynne. Ms. Rubin explicitly stated that Mira *does not* assist her with
> her mobility; instead, Mira assists her by *reminding* her to take medications
> and *reminding* her to get out of bed. (emphasis added). It is Ms. Rubin, as
> the complaining party, that bears the burden of proving that an accommo-
> dation is necessary. Because Ms. Rubin did not demonstrate a need for her
> assistance animal directly related to the disability described by her physi-
> cian, we cannot conclude that Ms. Rubin satisfied her burden.

Id. at 490 (emphasis in original) (followed by citation to multiple cases regarding assistance animals and the nexus element).

5. In *Bhogaita v. Altamonte Heights Condo. Ass'n, Inc.*, 765 F.3d 1277, 1289 (11th Cir. 2014), the trial court allowed plaintiff's dog to remain in the courtroom at his side while he testified. On appeal, the condominium association argued that the dog's presence was unfairly prejudicial, as it suggested that the plaintiff needed the dog by his side at all times. The Eleventh Circuit deferred to the trial court's broad discretion to allow the dog to "remain present as a demonstrative exhibit."

6. In one of the first cases on the issue, *Majors v. Housing Authority of County of DeKalb, Georgia*, 652 F.2d 454 (5th Cir. 1981) (cited in the *Young v. Savinon* opin-ion), the plaintiff challenged an eviction from government-subsidized housing for violation of a "no pets" provision in her lease. The parties stipulated that Ms. Majors' "mental disability requires that she be permitted to keep the dog in her

apartment." Suing under the predecessor statute to the ADA, plaintiff claimed she was excused from the no-pets lease provision in light of the federal law. The district court granted summary judgment in favor of the landlord, and the Fifth Circuit Court of Appeals reversed—finding triable issues of fact on whether plaintiff was an "otherwise qualified handicapped individual" under the statute, whether the handicap required the companionship of a dog, and what, if any, reasonable accommodations could be made by the Housing Authority. In so doing, the court noted:

> By enforcing the no pet rule, the Housing Authority has effectively deprived Ms. Majors of the benefit of the housing program. . . . In the summary judgment posture of this case, we must recognize as reasonable the inference that the Housing Authority could readily accommodate Ms. Majors. Even if the "no pet" rule is itself imminently [sic] reasonable, nothing in the record rebuts the reasonable inference that the Authority could easily make a limited exception for that narrow group of persons who are handicapped and whose handicap requires (as has been stipulated) the companionship of a dog. Such accommodation falls well within the kind of reasonable accommodation required by the regulation. . . .

Id. at 457–58.

7. Another "nexus" case like *Kennedy Homes* is *In re Kenna Homes Co-op. Corp.*, 557 S.E. 2d 787 (W. Va. 2001), in which the plaintiff housing project filed a declaratory relief action to determine the propriety of its rules prohibiting pets. The tenants intervened as defendants, asserting that the rules were invalid under the federal Fair Housing Act (FHA) and the West Virginia analog to that law—both facially (because the rules allegedly were more restrictive than the statutes) and as applied to them. The court rejected both arguments. One of the plaintiffs suffered from juvenile rheumatoid arthritis, high blood pressure and depression, and the other plaintiff suffered from peptic ulcer disease, heart palpitations and an abnormally fast heart rate. A physician submitted a statement that plaintiffs' two dogs were a "medical necessity" to address "both the physical and mental need for companionship as well as the confinement due to the various illnesses." *Id.* at 792. The trial court concluded that none of plaintiffs' physicians' statements "correlate dogs generally, or the [plaintiffs'] two dogs, specifically, to the claimed disabilities." *Id.* The West Virginia Supreme Court agreed, concluding that "[p]alliative care and the ordinary comfort of a pet are not sufficient to justify a request for service animal under FHA or the West Virginia FHA." However, the court went on to note:

> We recognize that some chronic and severe psychoses, such as schizophrenia, can substantially restrict a person's ability to form and sustain human relationships of friendship, companionship, and affection. Research has shown that a companion pet can in some cases materially improve the quality of life of such persons. Nothing in this opinion would bar the balanced consideration of a well-documented request for approval of a companion pet in such a case.

Id. at 800 n.15 (citation omitted).

Subsequent to the *Kenna Homes* decision above, the federal housing agency (HUD) sued Kenna Homes,

> alleging that it had violated the FHA by implementing a rule which limited the types of dogs residents could keep to dogs that were trained and certified for a particular disability, a rule which had the effect of denying a mentally impaired resident the ability to keep a dog which provided emotional support. *United States v. Kenna Homes Cooperative Corp.*, Case No. 2:04-783 (S.D.W.Va.) at Doc. # 1. Kenna Homes and the Government subsequently entered into a consent decree, under which the former agreed to adopt an exception to any rule preventing residents from keeping pets, by permitting disabled residents to have service animals or emotional support animals. An emotional support animal was defined as an animal, "the presence of which ameliorates the effects of a mental or emotional disability."

Overlook Mut. Homes, Inc. v. Spencer, 666 F. Supp. 2d 850, 860-61 (S.D. Ohio 2009).

8. The issue of whether an exemption to a "no pet" restriction is warranted in a particular case involves a "fact-sensitive examination" and a "cost-benefit balancing" that takes into account the needs of both the landlord and the tenant. *Oras v. Housing Authority of the City of Bayonne*, 861 A.2d 194, 202, 204 (N.J. Super. Ct., App. Div. 2004) (reversing summary judgment in favor of landlord and remanding for factual determination under New Jersey state statutes); *North Dakota Fair Housing Council, Inc. v. Allen*, 319 F. Supp. 2d 972 (D.N.D. 2004) (where the tenant allegedly suffered from major depressive disorder, panic disorder and attention deficit disorder and claimed her dog was therapeutic and helped her cope with her disabilities, the court denied the landlord's summary judgment motion, finding questions of fact as to whether the tenant was disabled and whether the dog was a reasonable or necessary accommodation under the FHA).

9. While dogs are most frequently the species at issue in these cases, they are not the only ones. *See, e.g., Crossroads Apts. Assocs. v. LeBoo*, 578 N.Y.S. 2d 1004 (1991) (triable issues of fact existed as to whether a mentally ill tenant required a cat in order to use and enjoy his apartment); *HUD v. Dutra*, 1996 WL 657690 (HUDALJ Nov. 12, 1996) (a disabled tenant's enjoyment of his apartment and quality of life greatly increased by having a cat and therefore demonstrated the need for exemption from the no-pet rule); *Janush v. Charities Housing Dev. Corp.*, 169 F. Supp. 2d 1133 (N.D. Cal. 2000) (where the tenant/plaintiff suffered from "severe mental health disability" and her treating psychiatrist testified that plaintiff's two birds and two cats were necessary to plaintiff's mental health and lessened the effects of the disability by providing her with companionship, the court denied defendant's summary judgment motion to allow for a "fact-intensive, case-specific determination" as to the reasonableness of the request to keep the animal companions).

Section 2. "Service" and "Support" Animals in Contexts Other Than Housing

The ADA and animal law have aligned outside of the housing area as well. In fact, the ADA applies across a very broad range of activities, and includes businesses and services open to the public such as hotels and other lodging places, restaurants and bars, public gathering places, entertainment venues, service and social service establishments, schools from preschool through the graduate level, and even hospitals and locked psychiatric wards. *See, e.g.,* 42 U.S.C. § 12181(7)(a)-(l). In January of 2017, at the Annual Meeting of The Association of American Law Schools (AALS), the AALS Sections on Animal Law, on Disability Law and on Law and Mental Disability co-sponsored a symposium addressing the use of animals as living accommodations in various contexts, including many of the aforementioned, as well as in the housing context. A series of articles from that symposium were subsequently published. *See* 24 Animal L. 1-97 (2018).

In recent years, service animals and emotional support animals on planes have become an increasingly contentious topic—both in terms of incidents and species. For instance, in June of 2017, a passenger was mauled by an emotional support dog while putting on his seat belt on a Delta flight. The incident led Delta to release statistics showing an increased prevalence of animals on flights. Delta claimed that the number of service and emotional support animals on flights increased 150% from 2015 to 2017. Incidents, including bites, also increased, doubling from 2016 to 2017. Karlin Brulliard, *Fur and Fury at 40,000 Feet as More People Bring Animals on Planes*, Wash. Post, Jan. 22, 2018.

Under the ADA, dogs are the only service animals seen on flights (given the impracticality of flying with miniature horses—the only other animal that may be designated as a service animal under the ADA, as addressed in Note 5 below). However, the Air Carrier Access Act (ACAA) (14 C.F.R. § 382.117), rather than the ADA, applies to emotional support animals, which are subject to different rules and restrictions than service animals. Unlike the ADA, the ACAA requires accommodation of almost any species of animal (excluding only snakes, other reptiles, rodents, spiders and ferrets) as an emotional support animal, unless the air carrier can show the animal would be a direct threat to the health or safety of others, or is too large or heavy to safely accommodate on the plane. With the increased prevalence of emotional support animals, media attention has focused on the more exotic species of emotional support animals accompanying passengers on flights. In 2014, a woman was escorted off a U.S. Airways flight at Connecticut's Bradley Airport when her emotional support pig defecated on the floor. In 2015, a woman flew home to Seattle for Christmas with her emotional support turkey, without incident. In January 2018, a woman and her emotional support peacock were denied access to a United Airlines flight at Newark Airport in New Jersey. The peacock reportedly did not fit the airline's size guidelines, such that the ACAA may have provided authority for the airline to deny access. David Schaper, *New Barking Orders for Documenting Support Animals Before Boarding Planes*, NPR (Feb. 1, 2018).

Unlike the ADA, which restricts the inquiries that can be made, the ACAA does permit the airlines to require documentation from a treating mental health professional that the passenger has a recognized "mental or emotional disability" and requires the presence of the emotional support animal. Aside from the restrictions noted above and the documentation requirements, airlines have no discretion regarding accommodation of emotional support animals under the AACA and must comply with the ADA relative to service animals.

Notes

1. In *Crowder v. Kitagawa*, 81 F.3d 1480 (9th Cir. 1996), plaintiffs were a class of visually-impaired persons who relied on guide dogs to carry out their daily activities. At the time of the lawsuit, Hawaii had a mandatory 120-day quarantine for carnivorous animals (including dogs and cats) entering the state. Plaintiffs argued that the quarantine, designed to prevent the importation of rabies (Hawaii is rabies-free), violated the ADA, as well as the plaintiffs' constitutional rights of travel, equal protection and substantive due process. The district court rejected their claims. The Ninth Circuit, ruling only on the ADA issue, remanded for the lower court to reconsider whether there was a reasonable accommodation that would allow plaintiffs to use their guide dogs and still protect against rabies transmission. The Ninth Circuit concluded that, without such an accommodation, the quarantine "effectively prevents [plaintiffs] from enjoying the benefits of state services and activities in violation of the ADA" and therefore might constitute impermissible discrimination:

> Although Hawaii's quarantine requirement applies equally to all persons entering the state with a dog, its enforcement burdens visually-impaired persons in a manner different and greater than it burdens others. Because of the unique dependence upon guide dogs among many of the visually-impaired, Hawaii's quarantine effectively denies these persons — the plaintiffs in this case — meaningful access to state services, programs, and activities while such services, programs, and activities remain open and easily accessible by others. The quarantine, therefore, discriminates against the plaintiffs by reasons of their disability.

Id. at 1484.

In 2003, Hawaii's quarantine program changed to provide owner/guardians with the option of avoiding the quarantine completely, or having a five-day quarantine, as opposed to the 30-day to 120-day quarantine for non-guide dogs and non-service dogs. The rules are relaxed if guardians comply with certain requirements including two rabies vaccinations, special testing and microchip placement. *See* Haw. Admin. Rules § 4-29-2, *et seq.* The revised rules also provide a complete exemption from quarantine for guide dogs and service dogs meeting specified criteria.

Could Hawaii quarantine humans known to have or be susceptible to certain diseases that are not present on the Hawaiian islands?

2. The ADA has broad applications with respect to service animals. In *Johnson v. Gambrinus Co./Spoetzl Brewery*, 116 F.3d 1052 (5th Cir. 1997), the court required a brewery to allow a guide dog on a public tour of the brewery, notwithstanding the brewery's blanket "no animals" policy based on its interpretation of federal food safety regulations, and notwithstanding the fact that the brewery offered a personal human guide instead of the animal guide. *See also Lentini v. California Center for the Arts, Escondido*, 370 F.3d 837, 839 (9th Cir. 2004) (concluding that a small dog was a service animal that "provided minimal protection and retrieved small dropped items" for a quadriplegic, who used a wheelchair for mobility; holding that modification of a concert hall's policies to allow a patron to attend performances with her service animal who may have made disruptive noises at past performances, if such behavior would have been acceptable if engaged in by humans, was a necessary and reasonable accommodation under the ADA).

3. Consider the case of *In the Matter of Lillian Kline*, No. A-1788-95T5 (N.J. Super. Ct. App. Div. July 12, 1996) referenced in Chapter 4, in which the connection between a disabled person and her service dogs was applied in a different context. In that case, appellant, Ms. Kline, was a qualified disabled person under the ADA, who was assisted by two service dogs. When a neighbor's son was walking one of the dogs, the boy and the dog were attacked by a group of teenagers who threatened the boy and threw stones at the dog. Although the dog was not physically harmed, the trauma affected her temperament and her ability to continue to function as a service dog, so that she would have to be retrained or replaced. Ms. Kline sought compensation from the New Jersey Violent Crimes Compensation Board (the "Board") as a "victim," defined under the relevant state statute as "a person who is injured or killed" by the commission of a violent crime. The Board denied the claim, concluding that the victim of the crime was a dog rather than a person, and it was the dog who sustained the injury. The appellate court disagreed:

> In the unique circumstances of this case, we are satisfied that the Board read the relevant statutory provisions too narrowly by unduly limiting the concept of "person." In our view, the status of the dog permits the finding that the injury was done not only to the dog but also to appellant. That is to say, in view of the function of the dog as a veritable extension of appellant's own body, an injury to the dog is tantamount to an injury to appellant's person. We have little doubt that damage, for example, to an artificial limb would constitute injury to the person. We see no reason for distinguishing between that situation and the physical extension afforded the person by a seeing-eye dog or, as here, a trained service dog.

The appellate court went on to note that the appellant had witnessed the attack on the dog from her window and that she had apparently sustained mental distress by witnessing the attack and as a result of its aftermath. On these two separate bases, the court concluded that the appellant should have the opportunity to support her claim. The court reversed the Board's denial of the claim and remanded for reconsideration.

4. Miniature horses have come to be an increasingly common assistance animal—enough that, as noted above, they have been designated as the only species other than dogs to qualify as "service animals" under the Americans with Disabilities Act (regulations relating to public accommodations), as long as they satisfy certain "assessment factors":

(i) The type, size, and weight of the miniature horse and whether the facility can accommodate these features;

(ii) Whether the handler has sufficient control of the miniature horse;

(iii) Whether the miniature horse is housebroken; and

(iv) Whether the miniature horse's presence in a specific facility compromises legitimate safety requirements that are necessary for safe operation.

28 C.F.R. § 35.136(i)(2).

In *Anderson v. City of Blue Ash*, 798 F.3d 338 (6th Cir. 2015), the plaintiff's daughter suffered "from a number of disabilities that affect[ed] her ability to walk and balance independently" and a miniature horse enabled her "to play and exercise in her back yard without the assistance of an adult." There was a history of disputes between the City and the mother (including a criminal conviction for violation of a municipal ordinance banning horses from residential properties) over the keeping of various animals, including at one point two miniature horses to assist her daughter and, at the time of this lawsuit, a single miniature horse, named Ellie. On appeal after the trial court granted summary judgment in favor of the City, Anderson (the mother) contended that Ellie met the ADA requirements because Ellie was individually trained to steady Anderson's daughter as she walked in the backyard and help her stand after she would fall. The City countered that the requirements were not met because Ellie did not help the girl with her daily activities, such as going to school; the girl could walk without Ellie; Ellie did not assist the girl inside the house; and the horse's primary instructor held no certification in service-animal training. The Sixth Circuit rejected the City's arguments, noting that the ADA regulations have no certification requirements, and further stating:

We are not persuaded by, nor do we find any authority to support, the proposition that an animal must be needed in all aspects of daily life or outside the house to qualify for a reasonable modification under the ADA. Many service animals are trained to provide specialized assistance that may be necessary only at certain times or places. *See* 28 C.F.R. § 35 app. A (discussing tasks commonly performed by service animals).

798 F.3d at 354. The Sixth Circuit found disputed issues of fact that precluded summary judgment in favor of the City on Anderson's ADA claim for a reasonable modification of the ordinance to keep Ellie at her house and, accordingly reversed the trial court ruling on that claim.

Note that although *Anderson v. City of Blue Ash* involves the question of whether the miniature horse could be kept in the back yard of a home, it addresses both Fair Housing Act questions (on which the appellate court largely affirmed summary judgment) and also the ADA regulation of public accommodation of otherwise prohibited animals, because the law at issue was a municipal ordinance restricting ownership of "farm animals" at private residences. So it was a law that governed housing, but the court focused in large part on the ability of disabled residents to obtain access to government programs, services and activities available to nondisabled individuals.

5. Consider whether a dangerous, illegal, captive wild animal can, or should, legally qualify as a reasonable accommodation for a disabled person. In *Pruett v. State of Arizona*, 606 F. Supp. 2d 1065 (D. Ariz. 2009), the plaintiff suffered juvenile onset diabetes, which caused her to be unaware of life-threatening sudden onsets of hypoglycemia (low blood sugar). During these periods she became dizzy and unable to take measures to remedy the situation, and could become unconscious if glucose was not administered. Pruett obtained a chimpanzee who was trained to retrieve sugar and press a medical alert button when Pruett was in distress. Chimpanzees are classified as "restricted wildlife" in Arizona (such that it is prohibited, without exception, to keep them as companion animals or service animals), because they are deemed to be "inherently dangerous animals capable of transmitting serious diseases and causing serious injury or death to human beings." (For a discussion of chimpanzee attacks on humans where chimpanzees were not properly confined, see Chapter 1.) The plaintiff claimed the ADA preempted Arizona state wildlife laws that prohibited ownership and possession of chimpanzees. The *Pruett* court considered alternative options available to the plaintiff (all of which she had rejected, but which the court felt were adequate) and dismissed the case, concluding that allowing her to possess the chimpanzee would not be a reasonable accommodation, in light of the reasons for the Arizona prohibition against doing so.

Section 3. Dissolution of Marriage and Other Relationships: Custody Disputes

Many individuals consider their companion animals to be members of their family, despite the animals' legal status as property. Upon divorce or dissolution of marriage or other cohabitation relationships, when judicial intervention is sought to determine the fate of companion animals (who are technically considered property, like other items to be distributed), courts are left to grapple with their unique position — property that may be considered a family member by either or both parties in the relationship.

The first four short cases in this section provide a historical glimpse at the animal custody issue and demonstrate courts struggling, sometimes subtly, with the issues the courts faced directly in the more recent cases excerpted later in this section, and which some state legislatures are now starting to address as well.

Akers v. Sellers

Appellate Court of Indiana, En Banc, 1944
114 Ind. App. 660, 54 N.E.2d 779

CRUMPACKER, Chief Judge. This is a controversy over the ownership and possession of a Boston bull terrier dog upon which the appellant, while declining to measure its true value to him in mere money, has placed an arbitrary value of $25. Were we to judge the importance of these proceedings by such a fictitious standard of value we would be inclined to resent this appeal as a trespass on the court's time and an imposition on our patience, of which quality we trust we are possessed to a reasonable degree. But we have in mind Senator Vest's immortal eulogy on the noble instincts of a dog so we approach the question involved without any feeling of injured dignity but with a full realization that no man can be censured for the prosecution of his rights to the full limit of the law when such rights involve the comfort derived from the companionship of man's best friend.

The parties to this litigation were at one time husband and wife. We conclude from the record that their union was not blessed with children, but some seven years ago there came into their lives the Boston terrier which is the subject of this controversy. He was the gift of a doctor of veterinary medicine with whom he had been left to board by a former owner who had never sought his return. What his age may have been at the time is not disclosed, but, assuming that he was then a pup, it is apparent that he is now about to enter the mellow years when those qualities most to be desired in a dog are at their peak, and the natural springtime inclination to roam, common to all males of whatever specie, is on the wane. Despite the tie and cementing influence of this little Boston terrier, the marriage of the parties proved not to have been made in heaven and the appellee sought and obtained a divorce. The court wherein such divorce was decreed, feeling perhaps that the care and custody of the dog of the parties was not an inescapable appendage to their domestic controversy, failed to make any order in reference to the same and the wife, being left in the possession of the domicile on separation from her husband, just naturally came into the custody of the dog. Whether the learned judge who heard the appellant's petition for divorce would have made such disposition of the dog had the matter been called to his attention, we are, of course, unable to say. Whether the interests and desires of the dog, in such a situation, should be the polar star pointing the way to a just and wise decision, or whether the matter should be determined on the brutal and unfeeling basis of legal title, is a problem concerning which we express no opinion.

We recognize, however, the tragedy of his consignment to the appellee if, in fact, his love, affection and loyalty are for the appellant. However that may be, the appellant, insisting that legal title and the dog's best interests are in accord and both rest in him, brought this suit in replevin and upon the trial thereof was unsuccessful. The record presents no question for our consideration except that the evidence is insufficient to sustain the decision of the court and that the same is contrary to law. We find evidence tending to prove that the dog in controversy was first given to the appellant and by him, in turn, given to the appellee. This is sufficient to support the decision, and as there is no reason shown why possession should not accompany ownership such decision is not contrary to law. We feel that had the trial court seen fit to apply Solomon's test and offered to cut the dog in halves, awarding one part to each claimant, the decision might have been for the appellant, as the appellee has failed to show sufficient interest in the controversy, or its subject, to file an answer below or favor us with a brief on appeal. The fact, however, that we may possibly have more confidence in the wisdom of Solomon than we do in that of the trial court hardly justifies us in disturbing its judgment.

Affirmed.

Bennett v. Bennett

District Court of Appeal of Florida, First District, 1995
655 So. 2d 109

WOLF, Judge. Husband, Ronald Greg Bennett, appeals from a final judgment of dissolution of marriage which, among other things, awarded custody of the parties' dog, "Roddy." The husband asserts that (1) the trial court erred in awarding the former wife visitation with the parties' dog, and (2) the trial court erred in modifying the final judgment to increase the former wife's visitation rights with the dog. We find that the trial court lacked authority to order visitation with personal property; the dog would properly be dealt with through the equitable distribution process.

A brief recitation of the procedural history will demonstrate the morass a trial court may find itself in by extending the right of visitation to personal property. The parties stipulated to all issues in the final judgment of dissolution of marriage except which party would receive possession of the parties' dog, "Roddy." After a hearing, the trial court found that the husband should have possession of the dog and that the wife should be able to take the dog for visitation every other weekend and every other Christmas.

The former husband contested this decision and filed a motion for rehearing alleging that the dog was a premarital asset. He also filed a motion for relief from final judgment and an amended motion for rehearing. The wife replied and filed a motion to strike former husband's amended motion for rehearing and a motion for contempt. The former wife requested that the trial court transfer custody of the dog because the former husband was refusing to comply with the trial court's order concerning visitation with the dog.

A hearing on these motions was held on September 27, 1993. The wife's counsel filed [a] motion requesting the trial court to change custody, or in the alternative, change visitation. The trial court denied the former husband's motion for rehearing and granted the former wife's . . . motion to change visitation. Thus, the trial court's ruling on visitation now reads:

> 7. Dog, Roddy: The former Husband, Ronald Gregory Bennett, shall have custody of the parties' dog "Roddy" and the former Wife, Kathryn R. Bennett n/k/a Kathryn R. Rogers shall have visitation every other month beginning October 1, 1993. The visitation shall begin on the first day of the month and end on the last day of the month.

Based on the history of this case, there is every reason to believe that there will be continued squabbling between the parties concerning the dog.

While a dog may be considered by many to be a member of the family, under Florida law, animals are considered to be personal property. *County of Pasco v. Riehl*, 620 So. 2d 229 (Fla. 2d DCA 1993), and *Levine v. Knowles*, 197 So. 2d 329 (Fla. 3d DCA 1967). There is no authority which provides for a trial court to grant custody or visitation pertaining to personal property. § 61.075, Fla. Stat. (1993).

While several states have given family pets special status within dissolution proceedings (for example, *see Arrington v. Arrington*, 613 S.W.2d 565 (Tex. App. 1981)), we think such a course is unwise. Determinations as to custody and visitation lead to continuing enforcement and supervision problems (as evidenced by the proceedings in the instant case). Our courts are overwhelmed with the supervision of custody, visitation, and support matters related to the protection of our children. We cannot undertake the same responsibility as to animals.

While the trial judge was endeavoring to reach a fair solution under difficult circumstances, we must reverse the order relating to the custody of "Roddy," and remand for the trial court to award the animal pursuant to the dictates of the equitable distribution statute.

Arrington v. Arrington

Court of Civil Appeals of Texas, Fort Worth, 1981
613 S.W.2d 565

HUGHES, Justice. Albert C. Arrington has appealed the judgment which divorced him from his wife, Ruby D. Arrington, divided their property and made Mrs. Arrington managing conservator of Bonnie Lou, their dog.

* * *

Bonnie Lou is a very fortunate little dog with two humans to shower upon her attentions and genuine love frequently not received by human children from their divorced parents. All too often children of broken homes are used by their parents to vent spite on each other or they use them as human ropes in a post divorce tug-of-war. In trying to hurt each other they often wreak immeasurable damage on the innocent pawns they profess to love. Dogs involved in divorce cases are luckier than children in divorce cases—they do not have to be treated as humans. The office of "managing conservator" was created for the benefit of human children, not canine.

A dog, for all its admirable and unique qualities, is not a human being and is not treated in the law as such. A dog is personal property, ownership of which is recognized under the law. 3 Tex. Jur.3d 513 §§ 4 & 5, "Animals as Property" (1980). There was testimony that Bonnie Lou was given to Mrs. Arrington over ten years ago.

Mr. Arrington agreed to Mrs. Arrington's custody of the dog if he could have reasonable visitation. He does not complain of lack of visitation; only that he was not appointed managing conservator. We overrule point of error no. 7 with the hope that both Arringtons will continue to enjoy the companionship of Bonnie Lou for years to come within the guidelines set by the trial court. We are sure there is enough love in that little canine heart to "go around". Love is not a commodity that can be bought and sold—or decreed. It should be shared and not argued about.

* * *

We affirm.

In re The Marriage of Stewart
Court of Appeals of Iowa, 1984
356 N.W.2d 611

PRIOR HISTORY: Appeal from the Iowa District Court for Marshall County—Roger F. Peterson, Judge. Respondent, Joan Wilson, appeals from the decree entered in this dissolution action. She contends that the property division is inequitable and that she should have been awarded alimony. She also contends that she should have been awarded the family dog.

DISPOSITION: AFFIRMED.

SACKETT, Judge. Jay and Joan were married in 1977. At the time of marriage Joan had a college degree; Jay was within a year and one-half of obtaining a degree in veterinary medicine. Joan has been employed throughout the marriage in the sale of agricultural and animal products. Jay's parents paid him his school expenses and gave him $100 per month while he was in school. Joan's income supplied the balance of the family expenses.

A home was purchased with a $5,500 loan or gift from Joan's parents. The home was in Joan's name. Jay, with the help of a noninterest bearing loan from his parents purchased a half interest in a veterinary practice in Grundy Center.

* * *

III. CUSTODY OF PERSONAL PROPERTY

Joan contends the trial court erred in not awarding the dog, Georgetta, to her.

Jay gave Joan the dog in question for Christmas. When the parties separated the dog remained with Jay. The dog accompanies Jay to the office and spends a substantial portion of the day with Jay.

The trial court found that custody of the dog should be with Jay.

A dog is personal property and while courts should not put a family pet in a position of being abused or uncared for, we do not have to determine the best interests of a pet.

We have considered the property division as a whole. We find no reason to disturb the trial court's decision on the award of the dog to Jay. We affirm the decision of the trial court.

AFFIRMED.

Note

Compare and contrast the historical cases you just read with the more recent cases excerpted below and discussed in the Notes that follow.

Houseman v. Dare

Superior Court of New Jersey, Appellate Division, 2009
405 N.J. Super. 538, 966 A.2d 24

GRALL, J.A.D. Plaintiff Doreen Houseman appeals from a judgment of the Family Part awarding her $1500 for a dog she and defendant Eric Dare jointly owned when they separated and ended their engagement to be married. Alleging that she and Dare had an oral agreement giving her possession of the dog that Dare breached by wrongfully retaining the dog after a post-separation visit, Houseman sought specific performance of the agreement and a judgment declaring her ownership of the animal.[1] Prior to trial, the court determined that pets are personal property that lack the unique value essential to an award of specific performance. On appeal Houseman claims that the pretrial ruling was erroneous as a matter of law. We agree and remand for further proceedings.[2]

* * *

The following facts are not in dispute. Houseman and Dare had a relationship for thirteen years. In 1999 they purchased a residence, which they owned as joint

---

1. Houseman also alleged that Dare converted the dog and claimed that money damages were inadequate to redress the harm she sustained as a consequence of that tort. See *Restatement (Second) of Torts* § 946 (1979). Because the rights of ownership and possession Houseman seeks to vindicate are based solely on the alleged oral agreement, there is no need to discuss this claim, which, if viable, would be fully addressed by an award of specific performance of the oral agreement.

2. By leave granted, the Animal Legal Defense Fund and Lawyers in Defense of Animals both filed a brief as amicus curiae. They urge us to adopt a rule that requires consideration of the best interests of the dog.

tenants and made their home. In 2000 they engaged to marry, and in 2003 they purchased a pedigree dog for $1500, which they registered with the American Kennel Club reporting that they both owned the dog. In May 2006 Dare decided to end his relationship with Houseman. At that time, Dare wanted to stay in the house and purchase Houseman's interest in the property. In June 2006, Houseman signed a deed transferring her interest in the house to Dare. When she vacated the residence on July 4, 2006, Houseman took the dog and its paraphernalia with her. She left one of the dog's jerseys and some photographs behind as mementos for Dare.

The trial court limited presentation of evidence about the parties' dog in accordance with its pretrial ruling foreclosing Houseman's claim for specific performance and the parties' stipulation that $1500 was the intrinsic value of the dog. Nonetheless, the record includes the following information relevant to Houseman's claim that she and Dare had an oral agreement about the dog that Dare breached after they separated.

According to Houseman, "from the minute [Dare] told [her they] were breaking up, he told [her she] could have" the dog. She and Dare agreed that she would get the dog . . . [¶] Dare acknowledged that Houseman raised the question of who would get the dog after he broke their engagement. . . . [H]e did not expressly deny that he agreed to give Houseman the dog. . . .

Dare and Houseman did not have a written agreement about the dog, but after Houseman left the residence she allowed him to take the dog for visits after which he returned the pet to her. According to Houseman, when she asked Dare to memorialize their agreement about the dog in a writing, he told her she could trust him and he would not keep the dog from her. Although Dare admitted to making that promise in his answer to Houseman's complaint, he offered no testimony on that point at trial.

In late February 2007, Houseman left the dog with Dare when she went on vacation. On March 4, 2007, she asked Dare for the dog, but the pet was not returned. Houseman filed the complaint that initiated this litigation on March 16, 2007, and when trial commenced in December 2007 Dare still had the dog.

* * *

At the conclusion of trial, the court found Houseman's testimony to be "extremely" and "particularly credible." The court noted that Houseman testified "without guile," "was truthful" and answered even the "hard questions . . . in a way that would not have been advantageous to her." On those grounds, the court accepted her testimony.

The court made the following findings relevant to the dog:

> I'm more than satisfied, hearing Ms. Houseman testify, that the dog was in no way related to the sale of the house. They may have an understanding about the dog. She thought she was getting the dog. He picked the dog up later. He has the dog. We know what the value of the dog is. The dog is worth

$1500. I believe it's now in Mr. Dare's possession. He'll pay Ms. Houseman
$1500 [the full value stipulated by the parties] for the dog.

The foregoing passage suggests, although not with unmistakable clarity, that the
court found that Houseman established an oral agreement under which she was to
obtain possession and ownership of the dog. Despite that finding and solely on the
ground that Dare had possession of the dog at that time, the court awarded Dare
possession and Houseman the dog's stipulated value.

The court's conclusion that specific performance is not, as a matter of law, available to remedy a breach of an oral agreement about possession of a dog reached
by its joint owners is not sustainable. The remedy of specific performance can be
invoked to address a breach of an enforceable agreement when money damages are
not adequate to protect the expectation interest of the injured party and an order
requiring performance of the contract will not result in inequity to the offending
party, reward the recipient for unfair dealing or conflict with public policy.

Specific performance is generally recognized as the appropriate remedy when
an agreement concerns possession of property such as "heirlooms, family treasures
and works of art that induce a strong sentimental attachment." [*Restatement (Second) of Contracts*] at § 360 comment b. That is so because money damages cannot
compensate the injured party for the special subjective benefits he or she derives
from possession.

On the same reasoning, when personal property has such special subjective value
courts have determined that an award of possession of personalty is the only adequate remedy for tortious acquisition and wrongful detention of property. *See Burr
v. Bloomsburg*, 101 *N.J. Eq.* 615, 621, 138 *A.* 876 (Ch.1927); *see also Restatement (Second) of Torts* § 946 (1979). And, consideration of special subjective value is equally
appropriate when a court is called upon to exercise its equitable jurisdiction to
resolve a dispute between joint owners of property that cannot be partitioned or
sold without hardship or violation of public policy. *See Woodruff v. Woodruff*, 44
N.J. Eq. 349, 358, 16 *A.* 4 (Ch.1888) (considering sentiments asserted in resolving
a dispute about a farm that favored leaving undivided possession with the party
who had remembrances and associations with the property owned by her father and
grandfather).

The special subjective value of personal property worthy of recognition by a
court of equity is sentiment explained by facts and circumstances—such as the
party's relationship with the donor or prior associations with the property—that
give rise to the special affection. *See Burr, supra*, 101 *N.J. Eq.* at 621–25, 138 *A.* 876;
Pomeroy, *Specific Performance of Contracts* §§ 12, 34 (3d ed. 1926). In a different
context, this court has recognized that pets have special "subjective value" to their
owners. *Hyland v. Borras*, 316 *N.J. Super.* 22, 25 (App. Div.1998) (concluding that
the owner of an injured dog was entitled to recover costs of treatment that exceeded
replacement cost); *see also Pitney v. Bugbee*, 98 *N.J.L.* 116, 120, 118 *A.* 780 (Sup.
Ct.1922) (noting the importance of the "companionship" of animals to humans in

concluding that a bequest to the Society for Prevention of Cruelty to Animals was exempt from tax as a transfer to a benevolent and charitable organization). Courts of other jurisdictions have considered the special subjective value of pets in resolving questions about possession. *See, e.g., Morgan v. Kroupa*, 702 A.2d 630, 633 (1997) (affirming a decision awarding possession of a dog to a person who found the lost pet, "diligently attempted to locate the dog's owner and responsibly sheltered and cared for the animal for over a year").

There is no reason for a court of equity to be more wary in resolving competing claims for possession of a pet based on one party's sincere affection for and attachment to it than in resolving competing claims based on one party's sincere sentiment for an inanimate object based upon a relationship with the donor. *See Burr, supra*, 101 *N.J. Eq.* at 626, 138 *A.* 876. In both types of cases, a court of equity must consider the interests of the parties pressing competing claims for possession and public policies that may be implicated by an award of possession. *Cf. Juelfs v. Gough*, 41 P.3d 593, 597 (Alaska 2002) (approving modification of a property settlement agreement providing for shared possession of a dog because the arrangement assumed cooperation between the parties that did not exist); *Akers v. Sellers*, 54 N.E.2d 779, 779–80 (Ind. Ct. App. 1944) (speculating that the interests of the pet might be different but finding the evidence adequate to support an award of possession to the wife, rather than husband, on the ground that the husband had given her the dog).

In those fortunately rare cases when a separating couple is unable to agree about who will keep jointly held property with special subjective value (either because an agreement is in dispute or there is none) and the trial court deems division by forced sale an inappropriate or inadequate remedy given the nature of the property, our courts are equipped to determine whether the assertion of a special interest in possession is sincere and grounded in "facts and circumstances which endow the chattel with a special . . . value" or based upon a sentiment assumed for the purpose of litigation out of greed, ill-will or other sentiment or motive similarly unworthy of protection in a court of equity. *Burr, supra*, 101 *N.J. Eq.* at 626, 138 *A.* 876. We are less confident that there are judicially discoverable and manageable standards for resolving questions of possession from the perspective of a pet, at least apart from cases involving abuse or neglect contrary to public policies expressed in laws designed to protect animals, *e.g.*, N.J.S.A. 4:22-17 to -26; *see Morgan, supra*, 702 A.2d at 633 (noting that "[h]owever strong the emotional attachments between pets and humans, courts simply cannot evaluate the 'best interests' of an animal" and resolving a dispute about possession in light of the interests asserted by the parties).

We conclude that the trial court erred by declining to consider the relevance of the oral agreement alleged on the ground that a pet is property. Agreements about property jointly held by cohabitants are material in actions concerning its division. They may be specifically enforced when that remedy is appropriate.

Houseman's evidence was adequate to require the trial court to consider the oral agreement and the remedy of specific performance. The special subjective value of the dog to Houseman can be inferred from her testimony about its importance to her and her prompt effort to enforce her right of possession when Dare took action adverse to her enjoyment of that right. Her stipulation to the dog's intrinsic monetary value cannot be viewed as a concession that the stipulated value was adequate to compensate her for loss of the special value given her efforts to pursue her claim for specific performance at trial. *See Burr, supra,* 101 *N.J. Eq.* at 629, 138 A. 876 (concluding that a payment made on demand to avoid loss of an heirloom did not bar a claim for possession based on an assertion that money damages were inadequate). And, Dare did not establish that an order awarding specific performance would be harsh or oppressive to him, reward Houseman for unfair conduct or violate public policy. To the contrary, assuming an oral agreement that Dare breached by keeping the dog after a visit, an order awarding him possession because he had the dog at the time of trial would reward him for his breach.

Recognizing that the trial court is in the best position to evaluate the equities implicated by Houseman's request for possession of the dog, and that Dare had no reason to present relevant evidence because he had possession of the dog when the trial court made its improvident pretrial ruling on specific performance, we . . . [¶] reverse and remand to the trial court that part of the judgment awarding Dare possession of the dog and Houseman $1500 for her interest in the pet for further proceedings in conformity with this opinion.

Notes

1. The appellate court remanded the case to the trial court for further proceedings in accord with the published opinion. According to news reports later that year, the trial court ruled that "neither party had an exclusive right to Dexter." Mary Pat Gallagher, *Splitting Couple Awarded Joint Possession of Pet Pug,* Law.com, Sept. 24, 2009, *available at* http://www.law.com/jsp/article.jsp?id=1202434029986. Instead, the court found Dexter was joint property and therefore awarded joint ownership of the dog, instituting rotating, five-week visitation rights between Houseman and Dare. According to news reports, the court did not refer to "custody"—which would be appropriate for a child, for example; instead, he addressed only "possession," indicating Dexter's property status. The trial court's decision was affirmed without written opinion. *Houseman v. Dare,* 2010 N.J. Super. Unpub. LEXIS 2498 (App. Div. Oct. 15, 2010) ("the judge concluded that the parties did not have an oral agreement and entered an order requiring the joint owners to each have sole possession of the property at specified times during the calendar year;" the appellate division found the arguments raised by Dare on appeal were "without sufficient merit to warrant discussion in a written opinion").

2. Nearly thirty years after *Stewart,* the Iowa Court of Appeals addressed animal custody issues in *In re Marriage of Berger,* 834 N.W.2d 82 (Iowa Ct. App. 2013) to determine disposition of the family's ten-year-old golden retriever, Max.

The district court opined the "biggest issue" regarding the dog was which party would be more available to care for him. In awarding Max to Cira, the district court noted she has been responsible for taking him to the veterinarian and, because she stays at home, would have more time than Joe to provide attention for the dog.

On appeal, the court cited to *Stewart* for the proposition that dogs are property and "courts do not have to determine a pet's best interests when making a property division." But the court also noted the recognition in *Houseman v. Dare* that "pets have a 'special subjective value' to their owners" and a law review article's recognition that "while current legal framework does not coincide with modern public sentiment about pets, the law is changing," citing to Eric Kotloff, Note, *All Dogs Go to Heaven . . . Or Divorce Court: New Jersey Un "leashes" a Subjective Value Consideration to Resolve Pet Custody Litigation in Houseman v. Dare*, 55 VILL. L. REV. 447, 447–49 (2010). After a short recitation of factors weighing in favor of the trial court's decision, the appellate court affirmed the award, finding "the property distribution to be equitable."

Travis v. Murray

Supreme Court of New York, New York County, 2013
42 Misc. 3d 447, 977 N.Y.S.2d 621

OPINION

Matthew F. Cooper, J.

People who love their dogs almost always love them forever. But with divorce rates at record highs, the same cannot always be said for those who marry. All too often, one time happy spouses end up as decidedly unhappy litigants in divorce proceedings. And when those litigants own a dog, matrimonial judges are called upon more and more to decide what happens to the pet that each of the parties still loves and each of them still wants. This case concerns one such dog, a two and a half year-old miniature dachshund named Joey.

Joey finds himself in a tug-of-war between two spouses in the midst of a divorce proceeding to end their extremely short and childless marriage. In fact, the only issue in this case is what will become of the parties' beloved pet. Plaintiff, Shannon Louise Travis (plaintiff), alleges that the defendant, Trisha Bridget Murray (defendant), wrongfully took Joey at the time the couple separated. Consequently, by way of this motion, she seeks not only an order requiring defendant to return Joey to her, but an order awarding her what she terms "sole residential custody" of the dog.

Background

* * *

Coincidentally, with a new canine case before me, [one] of New York City's major publications ran an opinion piece examining the unique relationship between dogs and people. The piece, "Dogs Are People, Too," which appeared in the Sunday Review section of the *New York Times*, urges that dogs be granted what the author calls "personhood." In taking this position, the author, a neuroscientist, relies on M.R.I. scans that he contends show dogs to have a range of emotions similar to those of human beings (Gregory Berns, *Dogs Are People, Too*, New York Times, Oct. 6, 2013, §SR at 5, col 1).

* * *

What is even more surprising [*than the dearth of media regarding animal custody*], considering New Yorkers' dedication to their dogs and their propensity for litigation, is that there are so few reported cases from the courts of this state dealing with pet custody in general and no cases at all making a final award of a pet to either side in the context of a divorce. As a result, courts are left with little direction with respect to questions surrounding dog custody: Can there be such a thing as "custody" of a canine? If so, how is a determination to be made? And if not, how does the court decide what happens when a couple divorces and each of them wants the beloved dog as her own?

Facts and Parties' Contentions

Plaintiff and defendant were married on October 12, 2012. . . . On February 6, 2011, while the parties were living together but before they married, plaintiff bought Joey from a pet store. At the time of his purchase, Joey was a ten week-old puppy.

On June 11, 2013, defendant moved out of the marital apartment while plaintiff was away from New York on a business trip. Defendant took some furniture and personal possessions with her. She also took Joey. According to plaintiff, defendant first refused to tell her where Joey was but then later claimed that she had lost him while walking in Central Park.

Plaintiff filed for divorce on July 11, 2013. Two months after the commencement of the divorce, plaintiff brought this motion. . . . [¶] Plaintiff argues that Joey is her property because she bought him with her own funds prior to the marriage. She alleges that defendant, in effect, stole the dog when she removed him from the marital apartment and subsequently relocated him to Maine. Moreover, asserting that she "was the one who cared for and financially supported Joey on a primary basis," plaintiff contends that it is in Joey's "best interests" that he be returned to her "sole care and custody."

Defendant opposes the motion in all respects. In so doing, she states that Joey was a gift to her from plaintiff as a consolation for her having to give away her cat at plaintiff's insistence. Defendant further contends that she shared financial responsibility for the dog, that she "attended to all of Joey's emotional, practical, and logistical needs," and that "Joey's bed was next to [her] side of the marital bed." Finally, defendant submits that it is in Joey's "best interests" not to be with plaintiff, but instead to be with her mother in Maine, where defendant can see him regularly and where he is "healthy, safe and happy."

Thus, both sides invoke two different approaches in determining which one should be awarded Joey. The first approach is the traditional property analysis, with plaintiff maintaining that Joey is her property by virtue of having bought him and defendant maintaining that the dog is hers as a result of plaintiff having gifted him to her. The second approach is the custody analysis, with each side calling into play such concepts as nurturing, emotional needs, happiness and, above all, best interests—concepts that are firmly rooted in child custody analyses.

Discussion

Whatever one may think of treating our dogs like people—whether it is called "humanification," "personhood," or some other means of endowing dogs with humanlike qualities—it is impossible to deny the place they have in our hearts, minds and imaginations. From Odysseus's ever-faithful dog Argo in Homer's *The Odyssey*, to the All-American collie Lassie, to the Jetsons' futuristic canine Astro, to Dorothy's little dog Toto too, they are beloved figures in literature, movies and television. . . .

It is also obvious that dogs, and household pets in general, receive an ever increasing amount of our time, attention and money.[2] Where once a dog was considered a nice accompaniment to a family unit, it is now seen as an actual member of that family, vying for importance alongside children. The depth of this familial attachment is evidenced by statistics cited in "Bones of Contention: Custody of Family Pets," which appeared in the 2006 *Journal of the American Academy of Matrimonial Lawyers* (Ann Hartwell Britton, *Bones of Contention: Custody of Family Pets, 20 J. Am. Acad. Matrim. Law 1* [2006]). These statistics show that 76% of pet owners feel guilty about leaving their pets at home, 73% have signed a greeting card "from the dog," 67% take their pets to the veterinarian more often than they go to their own doctors, 41% take their dogs on vacation with them, and 38% telephone their pets so the animals can hear their voices when they are away. Perhaps even more striking is the article's report that "a Gallup Poll showed most pet owners would not trade their pets for even $1 million in cash."

While the dog owners of New York might uniformly regard their pets as being far more than mere property, the law of the State of New York is in many ways still largely at odds with that view. The prevailing law, which has been slow to evolve, is that, irrespective of how strongly people may feel, a dog is in fact personal property—sometimes referred to as "chattel"—just like a car or a table. . . .

Replevin is the means by which non-matrimonial actions regarding ownership and possession of dogs have generally come before New York courts (*see e.g. LeConte v Lee, 35 Misc 3d 286, 935 N.Y.S.2d 842 [Civ Ct, NY County 2011]* [Bubkus, a maltese]; *see also Cent. W. Humane Socy., Inc. v Hilleboe, 202 Misc 881, 884, 116 N.Y.S.2d 403 [Sup Ct, Westchester County 1952]* [discussing the value of dogs in general and an owner's property rights in them]; *Mongelli v Cabral, 166 Misc 2d 240, 632 N.Y.S.2d 927 [Yonkers City Ct 1995]* [small claims action over Peaches,

---

2. According to *The Atlantic*, Americans spent $52 billion on their pets in 2012 (Derek Thompson, TheAtlantic.com, *These 4 Charts Explain Exactly How Americans Spend $52 Billion on Our Pets in a Year,* http://www.theatlantic.com/business/archive/2013/02/these-4-charts-explain-exactly-how-americans-spend-52-billion-on-our-pets-in-a-year/273446/ [Feb. 23, 2013]). This sum, which is greater than the gross national product of Bulgaria, is twice the annual amount we spent on our pets 20 years ago.

a Molluccan Cockatoo]). With the standard for replevin being "superior possessory right in the chattel," it is the property rights of the litigants, rather than their respective abilities to care for the dog or their emotional ties to it, that are ultimately determinative.

Even in the one reported case where a New York court awarded temporary possession of a pet in the context of a divorce proceeding, *C.R.S. v T.K.S. (192 Misc. 2d 547, 746 N.Y.S.2d 568 [Sup Ct, NY County 2002])*, the award to the wife of the couple's "five year-old chocolate labrador retriever" was based solely on the fact that the dog was an "interspousal gift" to her. Any doubt that the court in C.R.S. was utilizing a strict property analysis in its granting of temporary possession is confirmed by the direction in the decision that "[t]he determination of the final distributive award of the dog will be made at trial. A credit for any proven value of the dog could be made at that time" *(Id. at 550)*. The clear implication is that the Labrador retriever was to be "distributed" just like any other item of marital property subject to equitable distribution, be it a television or a set of dishes.

Nevertheless, at the same time that the traditional property view has continued to hold sway, there has been a slow but steady move in New York case law away from looking at dogs and other household pets in what may be seen as an overly reductionist and utilitarian manner. One of the first of these cases, *Corso v Crawford Dog and Cat Hospital, Inc., (97 Misc. 2d 530, 415 N.Y.S.2d 182 [Civ Ct, Queens County 1979]) [excerpted in Chapter 4 of the text]*, involved a veterinarian who wrongfully disposed of the remains of the plaintiff's poodle and then attempted to conceal the fact by putting the body of a dead cat in the dog's casket. Finding that the distressed and anguished plaintiff was entitled to recover damages beyond the market value of the dog, the court held that "a pet is not just a thing but occupies a special place somewhere in between a person and a personal piece of property" *(Id. at 531)*.

In this same vein, the Appellate Division, Second Department, in a 2008 case brought by a cat owner against an animal shelter, cited the extensive array of laws that exist in New York for the protection of pets *(Feger v Warwick Animal Shelter, 59 A.D.3d 68, 870 N.Y.S.2d 124 [2d Dept 2008])*. The court, after observing that "[t]he reach of our laws has been extended to animals in areas which were once reserved only for people," went on to underscore that "[t]hese laws indicate that companion animals are treated differently from other forms of property. Recognizing companion animals as a special category of property is consistent with the laws of the State . . ." *(Id. at 72)*.

Courts in other states have also had occasion to deviate from the strict pets-equal-property viewpoint to find that household pets have a special status surpassing ordinary personalty or chattel. In a widely-cited decision involving a "mixed-breed dog, Boy," the Vermont Supreme Court, drawing on Corso's statement that a pet is "somewhere in between a person and a personal piece of property," noted that "modern courts have recognized that pets do not fit neatly within traditional property law principles" *(Morgan v Kroupa, 167 Vt. 99 [1997])*.

Likewise, the Wisconsin Supreme Court in *Rabideau v City of Racine (243 Wis2d 486, 491, 627 NW2d, 795, 798 [2001]*[internal footnotes omitted]), stated the following:

> [W]e are uncomfortable with the law's cold characterization of a dog . . . as mere "property." Labeling a dog "property" fails to describe the value human beings place upon the companionship that they enjoy with a dog. A companion dog is not a fungible item, equivalent to other items of personal property.

See also Juelfs v. Gough, 41 P.3d 593 [Alaska 2002][in a "custody" battle over Coho, a chocolate Labrador retriever, giving some credence to the ex-wife's claim that "a pet is not just a thing"]; *Bueckner v Hamel, 886 S.W.2d 368, 377–78 [Tex App Ct–Hous 1994]*[Freckles, a one-year-old Dalmatian and Muffin, a two-year-old Australian shepherd]["Society has long since moved beyond the untenable Cartesian view that animals are unfeeling automatons and, hence, *mere* property"], *writ denied* [1995]; *Goodby v Vetpharm, Inc., 182 Vt. 648 [2007]*["Pets may be distinguished from other chattel by the mutual relationship: Pet owners love their pets and their pets love them back"]).

It is from this state though, and from the First Department in particular, that we have one of the most important statements from a "modern court" as to the "de-chattelization" of household pets. The case *Raymond v Lachmann (264 A.D.2d 340, 695 N.Y.S.2d 308 [1st Dept 1999])* is certainly the most relevant to the inquiry as to how a court should best proceed when dealing with a dispute like the one over Joey. In *Raymond*, the court was called upon to resolve the issue of who was entitled to "ownership and possession of the subject cat, Lovey, nee Merlin."[4] In a short, poignant opinion, the court wrote:

> Cognizant of the cherished status accorded to pets in our society, the strong emotions engendered by disputes of this nature, and the limited ability of the courts to resolve them satisfactorily, on the record presented, we think it best for all concerned that, given his limited life expectancy, Lovey, who is now almost ten years old, remain where he has lived, prospered, loved and been loved for the past four years.

(Id. at 341).

Raymond is significant for both what it does and does not do. The decision is a clear statement that the concept of a household pet like Lovey being mere property is outmoded. Consequently, it employs a new perspective for determining possession

---

4. Because the case before me is about a dog, this decision, with the exception of one cited case concerning a bird, has largely focused on dogs. Yet, it must be acknowledged that cats, for reasons that might be hard to fathom by dog-owners, also play an important role in our lives as companion pets. And even though cats are far less visible in this city, as they neither walk on leashes — usually — nor play in dog runs, they are clearly experiencing a wave of popularity not equaled since ancient Egypt, when their hieroglyphic images adorned obelisks and tombs.

and ownership of a pet, one that differs radically from the traditional property analysis. This new view takes into consideration, and gives paramount importance to, the intangible, highly subjective factors that are called into play when a cherished pet is the property at issue. The factors touched upon in the decision include the concern for Lovey's well-being as an elderly cat and the special relationship that existed between him and the person with whom he was living, a relationship that is described, rather nicely, as one where Lovey has "loved and been loved." In making its determination to keep Lovey in his present home, the First Department apparently concluded that the intangibles transcended the ordinary indicia of actual ownership or right to possession such as title, purchase, gift, and the like.

After reviewing the progression of the law in both New York and other states, it can be concluded that in a case such as this, where two spouses are battling over a dog they once possessed and raised together, a strict property analysis is neither desirable nor appropriate. Although Joey the miniature dachshund is not a human being and cannot be treated as such, he is decidedly more than a piece of property, marital or otherwise. As a result, whether plaintiff bought Joey from the pet store with her own funds or whether defendant received him from plaintiff as a gift is only one factor to consider when determining what becomes of him.

But if not a strict property analysis, what should be the process by which Joey's fate is decided and what standard should be applied in making that determination? Should the court adopt a custody analysis similar to that used for child custody? And if so, is the well-established standard of "best interests of the child" to be replaced by that of "best interests of the canine?"

Because of the paucity of New York case law addressing these matters, it is useful to turn once again to decisions from the courts of other states. There are a small number of cases that actually use the term "custody" in making an award of a dog to a spouse or ex-spouse (*see e.g. Juelfs, 41 P.3d 593* [granting "sole custody" of Coho the chocolate Labrador retriever to ex-husband]; *Van Arsdale v Van Arsdale, 2013 WL 1365358, *4 [2013]* ["The parties shall have joint legal custody of the labrador retrievers but the labrador retrievers' principal place of residence shall be with plaintiff"]). One decision, *Placey v Placey (51 So. 3d 374 [Ala. Ct. Civ. App. 2010]),* in which the court relied on an Alabama animal protection statute in awarding "a dog named Preston" to one family member over another, goes so far as to expressly refer to the "best interests" of the dog.

The majority of cases from other jurisdictions, however, have declined to extend child custody precepts to dog disputes. Some have been plainly dismissive. . . . [¶] Still, there is a good body of case law from other states that, while not embracing the application of child custody principles to cases of dog ownership and possession, takes a nuanced position that considers at least some of the factors traditionally associated with child custody (*see e.g. Baggett v Baggett, 2013 WL 4606383, *12 [Tenn Ct App 2013]* ["As to ownership of the parties' dogs, it is evident that the trial court considered their needs and the ability of the parties to care for them"]; *Aho v Aho,*

2012 WL 5235982, *5 [Mich Ct App 2012] ["[T]he trial court found that awarding Finn [the dog] to plaintiff was proper in order to keep all of the animals together"]; *see also Wolf v Taylor, 224 Or App 245, 250 [2008]* [while not directly addressing issue of whether agreement regarding visitation of a dog is enforceable, positing that it "certainly is an interesting question"]).

With the exception of *Placey*, the Alabama case, even the decisions employing custody or custody-like considerations to dog disputes have uniformly rejected the application of a "best interests" standard. As the Vermont Supreme Court stated in *Morgan*, a case pitting the former owner of a lost dog against its finder: "[T]he trial court was correct that family law provides an imperfect analogue. However strong the emotional attachments between pets and humans, courts simply cannot evaluate the best interests' of an animal" (*167 Vt at 103*). [*The court went on to discuss the New Jersey Houseman v. Dare case excerpted in the text after this case.*]

Although the opinion by the First Department in *Raymond* can be read as a firm declaration that household pets enjoy a status greater than mere chattel, the decision, irrespective of its use of language that is in some ways suggestive of a child custody, does not direct that the resolution of a pet dispute be undertaken by engaging in a process comparable to a child custody proceeding. Nor does it state that a court should utilize a best interests standard in determining to whom the pet should be awarded. In fact, the term "best interests" appears nowhere in the decision. Instead, the term that is used is "best for all concerned" (*Id. at 341*). Thus, when the parties here cite Raymond for the proposition that Joey's "best interests" must be considered in determining their competing claims for him, the citation is inapposite.

Child custody battles are difficult, painful and emotionally wrenching experiences for all concerned: the parties, the children, the attorneys and the court. The New York State Court of Appeals, in writing about one facet of child custody, relocation, could have been describing custody cases in general when it stated that such cases "present some of the knottiest and most disturbing problems that our courts are called upon to resolve." A determination in a custody proceeding must be guided by the overriding and well established standard of the child's best interests. A court needs a tremendous amount of information upon which to make a best interests finding. This almost always necessitates the appointment of an attorney for the children; the appointment of a forensic psychiatrist or psychologist to evaluate the children and the parties as well as to conduct collateral interviews with teachers, child care providers, pediatricians and the like; the taking of extended testimony, both from lay and expert witnesses; and the court hearing from the children themselves in an *in camera* proceeding.

Obviously, the wholesale application of the practices and principles associated with child custody cases to dog custody cases is unworkable and unwarranted. As has been noted in decisions previously cited, it is impossible to truly determine what is in a dog's best interests. Short of the type of experimental canine M.R.I.s discussed in the *New York Times* piece "Dogs are People, Too," there is no proven or practical means of gauging a dog's happiness or its feelings about a person or a place other than, perhaps, resorting to the entirely unscientific method of watching its tail wag. The subjective factors that are key to a best interests analysis in child custody—particularly those concerning a child's feelings or perceptions as evidenced by statements, conduct and forensic evaluations—are, for the most part, unascertainable when the subject is an animal rather than a human.

Even if there were a method to readily ascertain in some meaningful manner how a dog feels, and even if a finding could be made with regard to a dog's best interests, it is highly questionable whether significant resources should be expended and substantial time spent on such endeavors. It is no secret that our courts are overwhelmed with child custody cases, cases in which the happiness and welfare of our most precious commodity, children, are at stake. To allow full-blown dog custody cases, complete with canine forensics and attorneys representing not only the parties but the dog itself, would further burden the courts to the detriment of children. Such a drain of judicial resources is unthinkable. This does not mean, however, that cases like this one, in which it appears that each spouse views the dog as a family member and sincerely believes that he would be better off in her care, should be given short shrift. After all, matrimonial judges spend countless hours on other disputes that do not rise to a level of importance anywhere near that of children. If judicial resources can be devoted to such matters as which party gets to use the Escalade as opposed to the Ferrari, or who gets to stay in the Hamptons house instead of the Aspen chalet, there is certainly room to give real consideration to a case involving a treasured pet.

With this in mind, it is appropriate that the parties here be given a full hearing. Full does not mean extended; the hearing shall not exceed one day. The standard to be applied will be what is "best for all concerned," the standard utilized in *Raymond*. In accordance with that standard, each side will have the opportunity to prove not only why she will benefit from having Joey in her life but why Joey has a better chance of living, prospering, loving and being loved in the care of one spouse as opposed to the other. To this end, the parties may need to address questions like: Who bore the major responsibility for meeting Joey's needs (i.e., feeding, walking, grooming and taking him to the veterinarian) when the parties lived together? Who spent more time with Joey on a regular basis? Why did plaintiff leave Joey with defendant, as defendant alleges, at the time the couple separated? And perhaps most importantly, why has defendant chosen to have Joey live with her mother in Maine, rather than with her, or with plaintiff for that matter, in New York?

At this juncture, it should be made clear that, absent an appeal, the one-day hearing to determine who gets Joey will be the final proceeding on this issue. The award of possession will be unqualified. This means that whichever spouse is awarded Joey will have sole possession of him to the complete exclusion of the other. Although regrettably a harsh and seemingly unfeeling outcome, it is the only one that makes sense. As has been stated, our judicial system cannot extend to dog owners the same time and resources that parents are entitled to in child custody proceedings. The extension of an award of possession of a dog to include visitation or joint custody—components of child custody designed to keep both parents firmly involved in the child's life—would only serve as an invitation for endless post-divorce litigation, keeping the parties needlessly tied to one another and to the court (*see Juelfs, 41 P3d at 597* ["[T]he parties were unable to share custody of Coho without severe contention"]).[6] While children are important enough to merit endless litigation, as unfortunate as that litigation may be, dogs, as wonderful as they are, simply do not rise to the same level of importance.

Conclusion

The changes in the way society regards dogs and other household pets all but insures that cases involving the type of dispute seen here will only increase in frequency. In Raymond, the First Department referred to "the limited ability of the courts to resolve" such cases (*Id. at 341*). It is my hope that the analysis engaged in here, including the survey of cases from both New York and other states, will help other courts more successfully deal with the conflict that ensues when a couple separates, a marriage ends, and a Joey, . . . a Bubkus, or a Lovey is left in the wake.

In accordance with the foregoing, plaintiff's motion is granted to the extent of setting the case down for a hearing to determine who shall have final possession of the dog, Joey. . . .

* * *

Notes

1. The court in *Travis v. Murray* noted that *Raymond v. Lachmann* considered the "best interests of all concerned" but did not apply a "best interests" *of the animal* standard (which would more directly parallel the "best interests of the child" standard). Do you think this legal distinction can make a difference in practical effect? Should animal advocates press the courts to apply the child custody "best interests" standard or is "best interests of all concerned" equally or more advantageous strategically to reach the optimal outcome for animals in custody disputes?

2. A large number of companion animal custody disputes are between individuals who were never married, whether prior romantic partner, roommates or family members. With the rise in cases of this sort, the field expands exponentially. Less than a year after *Travis v. Murray* was decided, in the following case another New York state trial court took "the next step in recognizing that pets are more than just 'personal property' when it comes to resolving a dispute between owners."

---

6. Although courts should not entertain applications for "joint custody or visitation" with regard to a pet, the parties are, of course, always free, and in fact are encouraged, to informally make their own arrangements. . . .

Hennett v. Allan

Supreme Court of New York, Albany County, 2014
43 Misc. 3d 542, 981 N.Y.S.2d 293

Michael C. Lynch, J.

Plaintiff commenced this action seeking to recover possession of a black Labrador retriever named "Earthsea, the Duke of Dunnsville" or "Duke" for short. The parties were involved in a non-marital relationship for over 15 years and lived together [with "Duke" for 4 years], when defendant moved out. . . . While there is a dispute as to which party purchased the dog, Duke's title and registration was placed in their joint names.

On July 23, 2013, the defendant signed an acknowledged statement that reads as follows:

> "I, William Allan, Jr., waive any and all claims I might have against Alisha Hennet.

> "I, William Allan, Jr., waive any and all rights and titles to the property located at 290 Settles Hill Rd. Altamont, NY 12009 along with any and all materials and possessions located therein.

> "As of today, July 23, 2013, I William Allan, Jr., have removed all personal property from above said property and forever relinquish rights and claims [to] anything left behind. All personal property remaining at above said residence is therefore sole and exclusive property of Alisha Hennet.

> "I certify that the above statements are true and complete."

The statement was signed in conjunction with a refinancing of the mortgage on the Settles Hill property, with defendant quitclaiming his title interest in the property to plaintiff. Plaintiff continues to own and reside in the Settles Hill property while defendant has acquired a separate residence. In his answer, defendant admits that Duke resided at the Settles Hill residence on July 23, 2013. On August 1, 2013, defendant took possession of Duke and has maintained possession ever since, notwithstanding plaintiff's demands that he return Duke to her. This replevin action ensued.

By notice of motion . . . , plaintiff seeks an award of summary judgment and an order . . . directing the sheriff to seize and return Duke to her. Defendant has opposed the request, insists that Duke is his dog, and seeks an accounting as to the personal property distributed between the parties.

To begin, the court agrees with plaintiff that the only issue before the court is a determination of the parties' respective claims to Duke. . . .

Essentially, plaintiff maintains that since defendant has admitted Duke resided at the Settles Hill residence on July 23, 2013, he released any claim to Duke under the terms of the release agreement. In opposition, defendant maintains he only signed the release as part of the refinancing closing. . . .

Defendant maintains he never intended to release any interest in Duke and that his signing the release was a mistake. For her part, plaintiff denies making any misrepresentations as to the terms of the release and asserts that she observed defendant read and sign the release at closing.

* * *

. . . Since defendant acknowledges reading the release, these express terms negate any claim of a plausible reliance on plaintiff's purported misrepresentation. As such, the release stands.

The further question is whether the reference to personal property in the release extends to Duke.

Traditionally, dogs have been defined as "personal property" under New York law. Correspondingly, replevin has been utilized to recover possession of dogs in non-matrimonial actions.

There has been a more recent trend, however, to treat companion dogs as more than just property. In a thoughtful and careful analysis of the prevailing case law, Judge Cooper in Travis v Murray (977 N.Y.S.2d 621 [2013]) concluded that a strict property analysis should not be used to resolve a dispute between divorcing spouses over possession of their dachshund (id.). Instead, relying upon the First Department's recognition of "the cherished status accorded to pets in our society" in Raymond v Lachmann (264 A.D.2d 340, 341, 695 N.Y.S.2d 308 [1999]), Judge Cooper opted to apply a "best for all concerned" standard, rejecting the application of a "best interests" custody standard as unworkable.

* * *

Courts are essentially at a crossroads in determining whether a strict property analysis should still govern disputes between dog owners. This dilemma is not unlike that facing the Court of Appeals more than a century ago in *Mullaly v People* (86 N.Y. 365 [1881], *supra*). The defendant in *Mullaly* argued that he could not be convicted for stealing a dog. Remarkably, "[a]t common law the crime of larceny could not be committed by feloniously taking and carrying away a dog" (*Id.* at 366). The rationale "for this rule as to stealing dogs [was] the baseness of their nature and the fact that they were kept for the mere whim and pleasure of their owners" (*id.* at 366-367). The Court of Appeals readily rejected the common-law standard giving due recognition to the often heroic attributes of dogs and their close connection to people. In so holding, the Court observed that "[t]he artificial reasoning upon which these rules were based are wholly inapplicable to modern society" (*Id.* at 367). In this manner, the law in New York first recognized that dogs were "personal property."

Today, we should take the next step in recognizing that pets are more than just "personal property" when it comes to resolving a dispute between owners. In such disputes, to adopt the characterization of the Second Department in [*Feger v Warwick Animal Shelter*, 59 A.D.3d 68, 71, 870 N.Y.S.2d 124 [2008]], pets should be recognized as a "special category of property." It follows that the reference to "personal property" in the subject release does not extend to Duke. Certainly, the attachment each party professes to have with Duke would only be consistent with recognizing that Duke falls within a "special category of property" that is simply not covered by the release.

We are thus left with a dispute between two people as to which party should retain possession of Duke. . . .

Given this factual dispute, as in *Travis*, the court finds that a hearing should be held to determine which party should be awarded sole possession of Duke. . . . Since both parties profess a strong relationship with Duke and extensive involvement in his care, in essence the court is left with endeavoring to render a fair determination as to which party through his or her conduct has the most genuine right of possession. This inquiry necessitates a review of the circumstances as to how Duke was acquired and cared for, and the actual arrangement between the parties for spending time with Duke after defendant left the Settles Hill Road residence.

Accordingly, the parties' respective motions for summary judgment are denied. . . .

Notes

1. Other parties and courts in New York subsequent to *Travis v. Murray* have relied on it to apply a "best interests" standard. In *Mitchell v. Snider*, 2016 Misc. LEXIS 2078 (N.Y.C. Civ. Ct. Unpub. Mar. 18, 2016), before trial the parties stipulated that the applicable standard for determining who would get custody of a couple's five-year-old Labrador Retriever named Django would be "the best interests of all concerned," as set forth in *Travis v. Murray*. The court first looked to past New York cases, including *Raymond v. Lachmann* and cases after *Travis v. Murray*, including *Hennet v. Allan*. It then explained the factors to be considered in making its determination.

> Although important, ownership is just one factor to consider when determining who should possess the dog based on the best for all concerned analysis. The court must also consider intangible factors such as why each party would benefit from having the dog in his or her life and why the dog has a better chance of prospering, loving and being loved in the care of one party or the other (*Raymond*, 264 A.D.2d at 341; *Travis*, 42 Misc. 3d at 460). Additionally, the court considers who is in the best position to meet the dog's daily physical and emotional needs based on a healthy, active lifestyle, time constraints, type of home and yard, emotional bond, safety concerns, financial ability, opportunities to socialize with other dogs, access to dog-friendly parks and outdoor activities and access to veterinary care and pet stores. The court will also consider each party's ability to care for the dog, including, but not necessarily limited to, feeding, watering, walking, grooming, bathing petting, playing, training, taking the dog to the veterinarian and engaging in other recreational and dog-friendly activities.

2016 Misc. LEXIS at *5-*6. After reviewing in detail the extensive testimony by both plaintiff and defendant, the court awarded sole custody to the defendant, concluding:

> Based on the totality of the evidence, the court finds that it is best for all concerned for Defendant to retain sole possession of Django. Django has lived at the same location with Defendant without incident for 4 1/2 years, except during the year when the parties alternated caring for him. Django has thrived and prospered without Plaintiff in his life for almost two years. To suddenly uproot Django and send him across the country to live with Plaintiff would disrupt the dog's daily routine, healthy and energetic life-style and loving and happy home. The current environment appears to enhance the chances of both Django and Defendant living a long and prosperous life together.

Id. at *15.

2. As noted in Chapter 2 (Section 3), state legislatures have now begun to step in on this issue as well, directing courts in those jurisdictions to apply a similar standard. In Alaska, in issuing a judgment in a marital dissolution case where the parties have a companion animal, the court has discretion to make a determination with respect to "the ownership or joint ownership of the animal, taking into consideration the well-being of the animal." ALASKA STAT. § 25.24.160(a)(5) (enacted 2016; effective Jan. 17, 2017). An Illinois statute removes that discretion and *requires* courts to consider the animals' interests:

> If the court finds that a companion animal of the parties is a marital asset, it shall allocate the sole or joint ownership of and responsibility for a companion animal of the parties. In issuing an order under this subsection, the court shall take into consideration the well-being of the companion animal. . . .

750 ILL. COMP. STAT. 5/503(n) (enacted 2017; effective Jan. 1, 2018).

3. Although the court in *Travis v. Murray* was willing to consider the "best interests of all concerned," the court confined presentation of argument and evidence to a one-day hearing. In one protracted divorce case more than a decade earlier, the custody battle between an anesthesiologist and his wife over their dog, Gigi, lasted approximately two years. It culminated in a three-day trial, roughly half of which reportedly related to custody of Gigi, who the couple had adopted from a shelter two years before filing for divorce, and after the husband's dog died. *Perkins v. Perkins*, Case Nos. D442128 and D442154 (Cal. Super. Ct., San Diego Cty. 1998–2000). The trial included a "day in the [dog's] life" video (taken by Mrs. Perkins); a report from a "canine bonding" expert (retained at the court's suggestion), who observed Gigi in each household (during an interim shared-custody period); and testimony from family members. Documentary evidence reportedly included a birthday card to a "special Mom" signed "Love, Gigi." The retained expert's report concluded that both spouses were loving caretakers, but recommended that Mrs. Perkins get primary custody of Gigi because she worked at home and her neighborhood was

safer for Gigi than her husband's neighborhood. The court awarded custody to Mrs. Perkins.

4. The *Travis v. Murray* court also declined to risk embroiling the court in extended battles over a court-ordered shared custody, though it encouraged parties to informally make their own arrangements in that regard. Some of the problems that can arise with shared visitation are exemplified in the *Juelfs v. Gough* case cited by both the *Travis* court and the *Houseman* court. In *Juelfs v. Gough*, 41 P.3d 593 (Alaska 2002), a 1993 marriage dissolution decree between Julie and Stephen Gough provided for shared ownership of their dog, Coho.

> On March 28, 2000, Julie filed a motion requesting the dissolution agreement be reviewed due to Stephen's alleged failure to allow Julie her allotted time with Coho. Stephen opposed the motion, alleging that two other dogs at Julie's residence threatened Coho's life. Furthermore, he alleged that, during one incident when the dogs were fighting, Julie's boyfriend separated the dogs by pulling Coho's leg, thus dislocating it at the elbow requiring Coho to be under "constant care and medication." . . .
>
> [The judge] issued his decision in the matter on April 20, 2000. In it, he awarded "legal and physical custody of Coho" to Stephen and allowed Julie "reasonable visitation rights as determined by" Stephen. . . .
>
> * * *
>
> In September 2000, the parties sought reciprocal restraining orders against each other as the result of an altercation between them that occurred when Stephen sought to regain custody of Coho after Julie had taken the dog for a visit without Stephen's permission. Julie then filed a request for a hearing to review the custody settlement. On September 19, 2000, [the judge] ruled that although the court had remained hopeful that "some type of visitation could still occur between Ms. Gough and Coho" it has not worked. Therefore, the court found that Julie and Stephen should no longer have any contact whatsoever. The court also reaffirmed its previous ruling granting custody of Coho to Stephen stating, "Ms. Gough has no rights whatsoever to Coho and may not demand visitation or take the dog from Mr. Gough." The court then imposed a six-month restraining order prohibiting the parties from contacting each other except through counsel.
>
> In October 2000, Julie moved for a change in custody of Coho, requesting physical custody of Coho on weekends from Saturday at eight o'clock a.m. until Sunday at eight o'clock p.m. . . .

41 P.3d at 594–95.

In his opposition to Julie's motion, Stephen asserted that it was "in the best interests of Coho" that he be awarded sole custody. The court revoked the shared custody and awarded sole physical and legal custody of Coho to Stephen. The Alaska Supreme Court affirmed.

5. In *Brooks Brann v. Patti Dalby*, Civil No. 99HL04290 (Cal. Super. Ct., Orange Cty. 2001), it was the parties themselves who initially rejected shared custody and visitation arrangements. In that case, an unmarried couple disputed custody of Guinness, their four-year-old dog. Brann sought custody of Guinness, plus $10,000 in emotional distress damages and $15,000 in punitive damages because Dalby allegedly kept Guinness from him. Although Brann described Guinness as his "best friend and loyal companion," his attorney litigated the case from a different perspective, stating: "This is just a property dispute; the property happens to be a dog." Richard Marosi, *Dog Fight; Couple Who Separated Now In Custody Battle—Over A Rottweiler*, L.A. Times, April 4, 2000, at B1. Dalby's counsel, however, recognized the broader ramifications of the case and argued that companion animals in general, and Guinness in particular, are and should be recognized by the law as being much more than mere objects of property. (Telephone interview with Dalby's counsel, Robert Newman (May 4, 2000).) Dalby urged the court to consider the interests of all concerned, including Guinness and his canine companion at her home. After a week-long trial, the judge concluded that the parties jointly owned Guinness and, in Solomonic fashion, he was prepared to order that the property (*i.e.*, Guinness) be sold to a third party, with the proceeds to be split between Brann and Dalby. To avoid that result, Dalby agreed to what she believed would be the lesser of two evils for Guinness. Under a stipulated judgment, Brann obtained custody of Guinness subject to certain conditions (including visitation rights, access to veterinary records and the right to regain custody of Guinness if Brann was no longer willing or able to care for him). Although the judge commended Dalby for putting Guinness's interests before her own, her action did not cause him to change his decision and award custody of Guinness to her.

6. One means used by some couples to avoid or minimize the risk of future custody battles if the marriage does not last is to include a provision in a prenuptial or postnuptial (during the marriage) agreement to address custody issues. While it may be difficult to prospectively anticipate emotional attachments and practical considerations that might arise with future companion animals, these agreements at least may provide guidance to the courts even if the agreements do not entirely eliminate or resolve a subsequent custody dispute.

Section 4. The Sale of "Goods" and "Products"

As the cases discussed below illustrate, just as animals are treated as property under the law, they may also be deemed to be "products," or "goods" subject to the Uniform Commercial Code (UCC) and similar state statutes. *See, e.g., Embryo Progeny Assocs. v. Lovana Farms, Inc.*, 416 S.E.2d 833 (Ga. Ct. App. 1992) (sales of cows and other animals are transactions in goods under the UCC); *Key v. Bagen*, 221 S.E.2d 234 (Ga. Ct. App. 1975) (sale of a horse); *Young & Cooper, Inc. v. Vestring*, 521 P.2d 281 (Kan. 1994) (sale of cows).

There is mixed authority, however, as to whether or not a live animal is a "product" for purposes of strict products liability. *See Sease v. Taylor's Pets, Inc.*, 700 P.2d 1054 (Or. Ct. App. 1985) (skunk purchased from a pet store was a product); *Beyer v. Aquarium Supply Co.*, 94 Misc. 2d 336 (N.Y. Supr. Ct. 1977) (diseased hamsters were products). *But see, e.g., Anderson v. Farmers Hybrid Co.*, 408 N.E.2d 1194, 1199 (Ill. App. Ct. 1980). In *Anderson,* where the defendants sold diseased pigs, which subsequently infected and caused the death of several other pigs in the buyer's lot, the court stated:

> [T]he changeable nature and health of living creatures, and the potential effect of events and conditions outside the control of the seller on such creatures, lead us to conclude that the trial court was correct in finding that the gilts [*unbred female pigs used for breeding purposes*] at issue in this case are not products for purposes of imposing strict liability in tort under section 402A. While a "product" may be unchanged from its natural state, viable, and not the result of manufacturing processes, it must also be of a fixed nature at the time it leaves the seller's control. Thus, while blood or mushrooms, both sold in their natural state, may be products, their nature, as products, is fixed, or is intended to be fixed, prior to the time they enter the stream of commerce. If properly packaged, they are not easily affected by internal or external processes in the same way a living creature is so affected. Living creatures, such as the swine in the instant case, are by their nature in a constant process of internal development and growth and they are also participants in a constant interaction with the environment around them as part of their development. Thus, living creatures have no fixed nature in the same sense as the blood or the mushrooms can be said to have a fixed nature at the time they enter the stream of commerce.

See also Kaplan v. C Lazy U Ranch, 615 F. Supp. 234, 238 (D. Colo. 1985) (rejecting the plaintiffs' "novel" contention that a horse and saddle at a riding facility constituted a "product," the court cited to *Anderson* and noted that due to their changing nature "[g]enerally, living things do not constitute 'products' within the scope of the strict tort liability doctrine"); *Latham v. Wal-Mart Stores, Inc.*, 818 S.W.2d 673, 676 (Mo. Ct. App. 1991) (where the plaintiff bought a bird infected with psittacosis, contracted the disease from the bird and sued the seller, the court rejected the claim: "We tend to agree with the Illinois view [in *Anderson* and a prior case] that due to their mutability and their tendency to be affected by the purchaser, animals should not be products under 402A as a matter of law."). For further discussion of this issue, *see* Daniel A. Harvey, *The Applicability of Strict Products Liability to Sales of Live Animals*, 67 Iowa L. Rev. 803 (1982).

The sale of goods and products inevitably leads to disputes over express and implied warranties. Breach of warranty cases involve all types of property. Such cases, often involving "warranties of soundness," arose in the 1800s in conjunction with the sale of human slaves, who were legally classified as property at that time, as discussed in Chapter 2. *See, e.g., Hodgkins v. Fletcher,* 10 Cal. App. 690, 708 (1909), and cases cited therein. The sale of animals is no exception in this regard.

In *Alpert v. Thomas,* 643 F. Supp. 1406 (D. Vt. 1986), for example, plaintiffs trained, bred and sold Arabian horses for profit. Defendant was a full-time farm operator and breeder who, at that time, owned several Crabbet mares. Prior to purchasing Raxx, a 20-year-old Russian Arabian stallion owned by plaintiffs, defendant requested a breeding soundness test to evaluate and guarantee his ability to breed. A breeding soundness guarantee was customary in the industry when a horse was being purchased for commercial breeding. No such test was performed on Raxx before the purchase and no breeding soundness guarantee was included in the written contract of sale, but plaintiffs' representative verbally guaranteed the horse to be sound for breeding. After paying a portion of the purchase price and unsuccessfully attempting to use Raxx to impregnate a mare, breeding evaluation examinations performed at defendant's request revealed that Raxx was an "unsatisfactory prospective breeder" due to a deficiency of normal sperm. Plaintiffs sued to recover the remaining purchase price, plus interest and costs; and defendant counterclaimed for rescission of the sale or, in the alternative, for damages arising from plaintiffs' breach of express and implied warranties, fraud and misrepresentation.

The court concluded that Raxx did not conform to the contract in two ways. First, based on the verbal assurances of breeding soundness, his infertility was a breach of express warranties under Vermont's product liability statutes. Second, Raxx failed to conform to the statutory implied warranty of merchantability. The attempted sale of Raxx was rescinded and declared null and void. The court ordered that plaintiffs return the portion of the purchase price already paid, plus interest, and that defendant also recover the expenses reasonably incurred in the transportation, care, custody and insurance of Raxx from the date of his delivery to the time of judgment.

While physical defects may form the basis for a breach of warranty claim, "psychological idiosyncrasies" generally do not. *See, e.g., O'Connor v. Judith B. and Roger C. Young, Inc.,* 1995 U.S. Dist. LEXIS 21111 (N.D. Cal. June 30, 1995) (no recovery where horse's erratic behavior affected his suitability for competition). For more on this subject, *see* John Alan Cohan, *The Uniform Commercial Code as Applied to Implied Warranties of "Merchantability" and "Fitness" in the Sale of Horses,* 73 Ky. L.J. 665 (1985).

A different result than in *Alpert v. Thomas* was reached under slightly different facts in *Connor v. Bogrett,* 596 P.2d 683 (Wyo. 1979), which involved the sale of a registered Black Labrador Retriever. In this case, plaintiff purchased the dog for field trial competitions. He was knowledgeable about Labrador Retrievers, had competed with his dogs in field trial competitions, had owned one national champion, and had also judged field trial competitions. In fact, he had judged this particular dog in field trials. Before the purchase, plaintiff's own veterinarian examined the dog. The veterinarian testified that his examination revealed hip dysplasia, which can result in excessive motion of the hip joint, giving rise to changes that may result in arthritis. The veterinarian recommended against purchasing the dog. In subsequent discussions with the seller, the dog was compared to another Labrador Retriever who had hip dysplasia but had still performed successfully in field trials and had become a national champion. Plaintiff ultimately purchased the dog, gave him additional training, and entered him in field trials. On one occasion, he provided the dog for breeding purposes. It appeared that at least once plaintiff had shot the dog with a shotgun which, according to the court, was apparently a "recognized technique" for training Retrievers for field trial competition. Later in the year, the dog became less willing to perform in competitions. Upon re-examination, x-rays revealed definite evidence of osteoarthritis, which had not been present on previous x-rays. Plaintiff's veterinarian recommended that he return the dog to the seller. When plaintiff returned with the dog, the seller refused to agree to the rescission of the contract and return of the dog. After an angry exchange between the parties, plaintiff released the dog in the seller's yard and left. Plaintiff then sued to rescind the contract; defendant counterclaimed to recover the balance of the purchase price and the reasonable value of services furnished to care for, maintain and train the dog after he was abandoned by plaintiff in the seller's yard. The parties later raised theories under the Uniform Commercial Code (UCC) (applicable to contracts for sales of products). The trial court granted the seller's summary judgment motion on the claim for the balance of the purchase price; denied plaintiff's motion for return of the purchase price already paid; and left for trial the question of damages claimed by the seller in connection with the maintenance, care and training of the dog after abandonment.

On appeal, plaintiff claimed the dog's continued physical ability to compete in field trial competition was a condition of the agreement, resulting in an express warranty under Wyoming's version of the UCC. The seller relied on other sections of the Wyoming statutes, contending there was no express warranty and that the statutory language relating to an affirmation of the value of goods or a statement purporting to be the seller's opinion or commendation does not create a warranty. The appellate court affirmed, holding that plaintiff had accepted the dog, *i.e.*, the "goods," by acting in ways consistent with ownership; and that the seller's expressions relative to the potential of this dog were merely nonbinding expressions of opinion or commendation. The court further concluded from the record that plaintiff did not rely on the seller's comments and, therefore, such comments would not serve as a basis of the bargain. In reaching this result, the court reasoned:

> Since animals are "fragile creatures, susceptible to myriad maladies, detectable and undetectable," for a seller to warrant the future physical condition of a dog such as this, particularly when the buyer has examined it and been apprised of the potential of a disease which developed, requires a very precise contract. Here, since neither the buyer nor the seller could assume to have the power to actually control those events, the possibility of such a condition appropriately is described as a gamble, with the risk of such eventualities being assigned to the buyer.

Id. at 688. The majority also held that the cost of caring for the dog after plaintiff left him in the seller's yard should be considered as incidental damages, since plaintiff's return of the dog manifested his anticipatory breach of the contract. Two justices concurred in the result, but on different grounds. The concurring justices concluded that the costs of caring for the dog were beyond the scope of the contract and were not the type of damages contemplated by Wyoming law.

Most of the cases noted in this section involve animals maintained for sale and/ or profit, who are treated as goods and products, even though the courts must necessarily recognize the changeable and idiosyncratic nature of these living beings. Once again, the question arises: Should a legal distinction be made between animals raised for profit and companion animals? If so, how might companion animals sold by breeders and pet stores fit into the scheme? What about, for example, mice factory-farmed for use in research or even as food for reptile pets versus mice who are companion animals?

If a higher legal status is attributed to companion animals, might that place greater restrictions on operations like "puppy mills" (*see* Chapter 6)? Is that a goal that should be pursued as a matter of public policy? Considering that raising and selling farm animals for food is deemed to be an acceptable practice in our society, should there be a different legal standard for those species deemed by society to be companion animals?

Section 5. Insurance

Several types of insurance contracts should be considered when discussing contractual issues involving animals. Some of the issues that arise are significant—such as breed-specific policy exclusions—while others only tangentially present animal law issues, but are worth noting nonetheless.

Statistics in 2003 indicated that dog bites accounted for 25% of homeowners' insurance liability claims, amounting to $321.6 million in payouts from insurance companies. Rodd Zolkos, *Homeowners insurers should throw these dogs a bone*, Industry Focus (Bus. Ins. Supp.) 2 (Mar. 2005) ("*Zolkos*"). Dog bite claims are so common that some insurance companies offer, or have offered, extensive tips on how to be a responsible dog owner in their policyholder newsletters and/or on their websites. *See, e.g., id.* (referring to State Farm's tips "on its Web site and through brochures, advocating training, neutering and proper socialization of the animal"); SAFECO Customer News, Spring/Summer 2000.

Statistics from the Insurance Information Institute in 2017 indicated dog bites accounted for more than one-third of homeowners' insurance liability claims, amounting to more than $600 million in payouts in 2016 alone. According to the report, the average claim costs insurers $33,230. Katherine Chiglinsky, *Dog-Bite Claims Surge 18% as Children Bear Brunt of Attacks*, Bloomberg News, Apr. 10, 2017.

In 2000, the Insurance Information Network of California (an insurance industry group) indicated that approximately 70% of insurance companies then planned to refuse renewal to any policyholders whose dogs have cost the insurers money. *Moneynotes*, Newsweek, p. 78 (Mar. 6, 2000). However, not every such instance warrants an insurer's cancellation of an existing policy. *See, e.g., Aegis Security Ins. Co. v. Pennsylvania Ins. Dept.*, 798 A.2d 330, 332 (Pa. Commw. Ct. 2002) ("The mere presence of or the introduction into a home of a dog, even of a breed known to be aggressive, is not a basis for finding a substantial increase of hazard absent some showing that the particular dog creates that risk.").

Some insurance companies have taken the issue a step further — refusing to issue or renew policies based on the dog's breed, rather than whether that specific dog has ever demonstrated a propensity to bite. *See, e.g.,* Larry Cunningham, *The Case Against Dog Breed Discrimination By Homeowners' Insurance Companies*, 11 Conn. L.J. 1 (Fall 2004) ("*Cunningham*") (the author, a law professor, was denied insurance coverage by various insurance companies because one of his dogs was a Rottweiler and the other, Saffy, was part Chow); *Zolkos, supra* ("Many insurers keep breed blacklists, and homeowner applicants with dogs on those rosters find themselves facing higher premiums or possibly being denied coverage by certain insurers."). The relatively recent phenomenon of breed discrimination in insurance was preceded by the enactment of breed-specific legislation at the state and local level. (These statutes are addressed in Chapter 5.) These laws are generally a response to highly publicized attacks by certain breeds, particularly "pit bulls." *Cunningham*, at 6. As Cunningham explains, however, these practices are not supported by statistical or scientific evidence that the perceived "dangerous" breeds are more likely to bite than any other type of dog. *Id.* at 17–37.

Given that breed-specific statutes generally have been upheld, is there any reason why this practice by insurance companies wouldn't be legally justified? In the instance above, Mr. Cunningham disclosed to the insurance companies that his dog Saffy was part Chow. The article indicates he knew Saffy's parents were a Chow and a Labrador Retriever. As a practical matter, if a potential policyholder has an elderly mixed-breed dog who has always been gentle and friendly towards human and nonhuman animals, is it reasonable for an insurer to deny coverage if the applicant discloses that the dog may be a Rottweiler or "pit bull" mix? What if the dog was a purebred Rottweiler or "pit bull"?

If a guardian lives with a mixed-breed dog who could conceivably be part "pit bull" but also physically resembles another breed that is not on the list of "uninsurable" breeds, what obligation does he have to respond to an insurance company questionnaire about the dog's breed? If the guardian does not disclose on an insurance application seeking the identity of the breed that the dog appeared to be part "pit bull," and if the dog later bites someone, should the guardian expect the insurance company to pay the claim? How strong an argument do you think the insurer would have that the guardian misrepresented a material fact in the application?

In *Quincy Mutual Fire Insurance Co. v. Gramegna*, 2008 U.S. Dist. LEXIS 17244 (D. Conn. Mar. 6, 2008), the insured (Gramegna) had a policy with an insurance company that did not insure owners of certain breeds of dogs, including Rottweilers. When Gramegna filled out his insurance application his Rottweiler dog was staying at his father's house. The record in the case did not reflect how long the dog stayed there; only that he was there the day Gramegna filled out the application. Gramegna responded "no" to the application question "is a dog or any other pet owned or kept on the premises?" The court found the question to be ambiguous and ruled that Gramegna's answer did not constitute a material misrepresentation warranting rescission of the policy.

Homeowners' insurance policies generally contain an exclusion which precludes from coverage loss for certain business property or arising out of "business pursuits." In *Wiley v. Travelers Ins. Co.*, 534 P.2d 1293 (Okla. 1974), the court determined an insured homeowner who bred, raised and sold St. Bernard puppies for profit was engaged in a "business pursuit" within the meaning of his homeowners' policy. *See also Weiss v. Allstate Ins. Co.*, 49 A.D.3d 1251 (N.Y. App. Div. 2008) (where insureds' barn was used for a horse breeding and boarding business, business pursuits exclusion applied). Such policies also generally exclude coverage for damage caused by "domestic animals." *See, e.g., Smith v. State Farm Fire & Cas.*, 381 So. 2d 913 (La. Ct. App. 1980) (holding that a cow was a "domestic animal" under the policy's exclusionary provision, so that when the policyholder's cow fell into his swimming pool and damaged the pool, the resultant damage was not covered under the policy).

Homeowners' policies contain both property and liability coverage components. Under the property coverage, such policies generally cover damage caused by "vandalism and malicious mischief." One issue that has arisen is whether damage to property caused by a "wild" animal can constitute "vandalism and malicious mischief" within the meaning of such policies. In *Montgomery v. United Services Auto. Ass'n*, 886 P.2d 981 (N.M. Ct. App. 1994), the insurance policy defined vandalism and malicious mischief as "intentional and malicious damage." The court held that damage to the policyholder's personal property caused by a bobcat was not covered under the policy because a bobcat cannot develop the requisite intent or malice. In addition to his formal judgment, the trial judge poetically announced the ruling orally, stating, in part, as follows:

> Alas, it is written in the law
>
> that the animal with the paw
>
> does not have the mind
>
> to do the damage of this kind.
>
> And so, I'm sorry, the Plaintiff won't get paid.
>
> That's how the contract was made.
>
> This policy does not apply

when the bobcat runs awry.

In this case the bobcat needs "intent."

Or did he just rely on his scent?

Id. at 981 n.1. *See also Roselli v. Royal Ins. Co.*, 538 N.Y.S.2d 898 (App. Div. 1989) (apartment damaged by a deer); *Ditloff v. State Farm Fire & Cas. Co.*, 406 N.W.2d 101, 104 (Neb. 1987) (stating, in *dicta*, that cows could not form the necessary intent to have caused willful or malicious damage to property). The same conclusion was reached by an Alabama court, where a deer crashed through a window and damaged a home.

> There is no question but that the popular meaning of vandalism is the intentional and malicious destruction of property. Such act requires a human mind capable of forming the requisite intent of committing a wrongful act, resulting in senseless destruction or damage to property either public or private.
>
> An animal, such as a deer, to the human mind, and in law, is incapable of forming an intent to commit a wrongful act or to act maliciously. An animal, nonhuman, acts or reacts instinctively without knowledge of right or wrong as defined by man.

Stack v. Hanover Ins. Co., 329 So. 2d 561, 562 (Ala. Civ. App. 1976). The court therefore held that the destruction of the policyholder's property by the deer's independent action was not covered under the insurance policy.

Unlike property policies, liability insurance policies (including the liability portion of homeowners' policies that may be relevant in dog bite cases) require insurers not only to pay for damage, but also to defend potentially covered lawsuits against the policyholder. As a practical point, insurance companies often are involved in the background defending policyholders in cases alleging tortious harm to animals, including but not limited to veterinary malpractice cases (as discussed in Chapter 4).

With respect to insurance coverage for harm *to* animals, property insurance policies, such as homeowners' policies, may provide coverage on a limited basis. The following are a few examples: Example No. 1: "We'll only cover live animals if the animals die during transit, and the death is caused directly by fire, lightning, wind storm, collision or the overturn of the vehicle the animals are being transmitted in." Example No. 2: "Live animals, birds and fish, meaning live animals, birds and fish you're holding for sale or that you have sold but not yet delivered, are covered only if they die or have to be destroyed because of direct physical loss caused by [a covered cause of loss such as fire, lightning, vandalism, *etc.*]." Example No. 3: "We'll cover [animals and pets] only if you're actually holding them for sale, or if they're sold but not yet delivered and if they're described in the coverage summary."

While standard form insurance policies generally do not provide coverage for injuries to companion animals, health insurance policies can be purchased for companion animals. Note that these policies do not cover pre-existing conditions.

Routine care and treatment also is likely to be excluded. These policies generally are designed to cover injuries resulting from accidents and diseases that are not preventable by vaccine, and that are not congenital or hereditary in nature. Life insurance covering animals (generally animals maintained for profit), such as equine or livestock mortality insurance, can also be purchased. *See, e.g., Lasma Corp. v. Monarch Ins. Co. of Ohio*, 764 P.2d 1118 (Ariz. 1988).

The Animal Law Committee of the Tort Trial & Insurance Practice Section (TIPS) of the American Bar Association issues a newsletter that often includes articles on insurance issues relating to animals. Relevant articles may also be found in the TIPS law journal. *See, e.g.,* Adam P. Karp & Margrit Lent Parker, *Recent Developments in Animal Tort and Insurance Law*, 51 Tort Trial & Ins. Prac. L.J. 245 (Winter 2016); Adam P. Karp & Margrit Lent Parker, *Recent Developments in Animal Tort and Insurance Law*, 50 Tort Trial & Ins. Prac. L.J. 179 (Winter 2015).

Chapter 8

Wills and Trusts

No study of animals and the law would be complete without considering the disposition of animals upon the death of their owners/guardians. Providing for the care of an animal after the testator's death is far more complicated than the disposition of other personal property, and it can require a more complex legal analysis than even providing for minor children. As you will see in this chapter, some people believe their companion animals would not be properly cared for by anyone else and thus seek to have their animals killed upon their death. Others attempt to provide for their animals, only to be stopped by the laws of testacy, or by potential beneficiaries seeking to obtain funds set aside for the animals' care and/or for the animals' designated new caregivers. As with all cases involving wills and trusts, the court's role is to determine and effectuate the testator's intent, unless certain exceptions apply, including whether the directives in the will are contrary to law or public policy.

As discussed later in this chapter, all fifty states have codified specifications for valid companion animal trusts, which alleviates some of the problems animal guardians have had in the past when trying to ensure that their animals would receive the intended care and protections after their guardians have died.

Section 1. Validity of Will Provisions: Historical Perspective

A. Will Provisions Providing for the Destruction of Companion Animals upon the Testator's Death

In re Capers' Estate

Common Pleas Court of Allegheny County, Pennsylvania, 1964
34 Pa. D. & C.2d 121

RAHAUSER, J., November 12, 1964—Ida M. Capers, the owner of two Irish setters named "Brickland" and "Sunny Birch", died January 27, 1963. Her will provided, among other things:

> "FIFTH: I direct that any dog which I may own at the time of my death be destroyed in a humane manner and I give and grant unto my Executors hereinafter named full and complete power and discretion necessary to carry out the same."

The executors of the estate filed a petition for declaratory judgment, February 28, 1963. At that time, the court directed that the hearing on the declaratory judgment would be held at the time of the audit. At the audit of the estate a date was set for the disposition of the prayer of petitioners.

The petition prays that the court determine the rights and duties of the executors by reason of the aforementioned clause in the will of the above decedent.

* * *

The tradition of this court is to consider with care all matters that come before it, whether they concern the disposition of animals of small value or estates of vast resources.

One of the pertinent matters that came to the court's attention was an address of the late Senator George G. Vest, of Missouri, when he was a young lawyer. He became involved in a lawsuit where his client was suing a neighbor for killing a pet dog. Many of the things that Senator Vest said in his address to the jury are applicable here and, because they are so well stated, they will be made a part of this opinion, having some bearing on the matter before the court. His memorable words are as follows:

> "The best friend a man has in the world may turn against him and become his enemy. His son or daughter that he has reared with loving care may prove ungrateful. Those who are nearest and dearest to us, those whom we trust with our happiness and good name, may become traitors to their faith.

> "The money that a man has he may lose. It flies away from him, perhaps when he needs it most. A man's reputation may be sacrificed in a moment of ill-considered action.

> "The people who are prone to fall on their knees to do us honor when success is with us may be the first to throw the stone of malice when failure settles its cloud upon our heads.

> "The one absolutely unselfish friend that a man can have in this selfish world, the one that never deserts him, the one that never proves ungrateful or treacherous, is his dog.

> "Gentlemen of the jury, a man's dog stands by him, in prosperity and poverty, in health and sickness. He will sleep on the cold ground, where the wintry wind blows and the snow drives fiercely if only he may be near his master's side. He will kiss the hand that has no food to offer; he will lick the wounds and sores that come in encounter with the roughness of the world. He guards the sleep of his pauper master as if he were a prince.

> "When all other friends desert, he remains. When riches take wing and reputation falls to pieces, he is as constant in his love as the sun in its journey through the heavens.

"If fortune drives his master forth an outcast in the world, friendless and homeless, the faithful dog asks no higher privilege than that of accompanying him to guard against danger, to fight his enemies, and when the last scene of all comes and death takes the master in its embrace and his body is laid away, there by his graveside will the noble dog be found, his head between his paws, his eyes said but open in alert watchfulness, faithful and true even unto death."

The will of decedent provided that the executors of her estate should follow a prescribed course of action in dealing with her Irish setters. There was uncertainty on the part of the executors, if they should take such drastic action without the authority of the court. The governor of the State ordered the Attorney General of Pennsylvania to intervene to prohibit the executors from carrying out the illegal purposes of the will.

* * *

The executors properly filed this petition for declaratory judgment. Had they carried out the provisions of decedent's will, they would have followed an inhumane course of action from which there is no appeal and would have established a precedent that this court believes is not in accord with the law.

The court has studied the petition and the testimony given at the hearing and concludes that the questions involved are:

1. Was the petition for declaratory judgment proper?
2. What was the purpose and intent of testatrix?
3. Is it against public policy to hold valid a clause in a will directing the summary destruction of decedent's property after death?
4. Does the Wills Act authorize a decedent to direct the summary destruction of her property?
5. What is the present status of the two Irish setters mentioned in decedent's will?
6. What should the executors do under the present circumstances with the two Irish setters mentioned in the will of the decedent?
7. Does the prayer of the petition require the court to pass on the propriety of the executors' duties as to an appeal from the ruling of the court?

The petition is properly before the court and must be disposed of.

In the analysis of the petition, after first determining that the court has jurisdiction, the court must then determine what is the intent of testatrix as evidenced from the four corners of the will.

Let us consider the second question, which deals with the intent of testatrix.

It is apparent that testatrix was deeply interested in the humane care and treatment of animals. She left the greater part of her fortune for these purposes.

The testimony at the hearing indicated that the chief objects of decedent's affection were the two Irish setters mentioned in her will.

She was interested that they would be given the same care after her death that she gave them while she lived. She evidently feared that either they would grieve for her or that no one would afford them the same affection and kindness that they received during her life.

She, accordingly, made the above provision in her will for their destruction.

Testimony indicates that she was mistaken on both above points.

The record is clear on this fact.

Dr. John P. Childress, a veterinarian who was known to Miss Capers and whom she employed during her life testified to the degree of care Miss Capers gave the two Irish setters and to the affection that she exhibited in her attention to them.

He testified as follows:

* * *

"Q. A moment ago you said you took care of the dogs while Miss Capers was living, as well as subsequent to the time of her death. Can you describe the care that Miss Capers gave them?

"A. Well, all I can say is that Miss Capers lived on Fifth Avenue and I live in Wexford, and she would hire a taxicab to bring the dogs all the way over to my office; or she would have me come all the way over to her home, if the dogs required any medical attention. This was because she felt that for some reason, I would give the dogs better services, than perhaps someone else might. But there were many qualified veterinarians who had been closer to her than I, to provide services, but this did not matter: Her home was for her dogs. She had Kennel facilities. The car was for the dogs, when she had a car. She had a separate area in the basement of her home, for grooming, bathing and taking care of these two dogs. They were her entire reason for existence, I would think. I spent many hours reassuring her, whenever she was upset over something that had gone wrong with either Sunnybur or Brickland.

"Q. Did she ever discuss with you, or express her concern, of what would happen to the dogs following her death?

"A. No. I don't think she was contemplating passing away; and I daresay the only way she cared for the dogs—her biggest concern would be, if she passed away, that they would not be cared for; and I am familiar with the provisions in Miss Capers' Will; and I feel, knowing her and the care that she had given the dogs and how dear they were to her, would be the concern that they would not receive the same type of care; and I am sure,—this is of course conjectural on my part—but I am sure this was the main reason for the item in her Will.

* * *

"Q. Have you had occasion to attend to dogs under the care of Mr. and Mrs. Miller?

"A. Yes, I have.

"Q. Would you tell us of the maintenance facilities of Mr. and Mrs. Miller?

"A. Yes. One time when Mr. and Mrs. Miller were out of town, they left word with other relatives who were staying at the Home caring for their own dogs, that if anything should happened to either of the dogs, I should be called; and one of the dogs developed an ear infection, and I called. When I got to the place, the two Irish Setters were in the Home, as I would be if I were a member of the family. There were rugs for the dogs to lie on. There were other dogs besides Sunnybur (sic) and Brickland, and they were all together, quite content and very, very happy.

* * *

"Q. Has there been adequate space where Mr. and Mrs. Miller is, for dogs to run?

"A. Absolutely. They have a farm type house out in the country, with adequate facilities for exercise. . . . I would say the dogs are even happier in the present situation than they were with Miss Capers. Miss Capers lived inside, and everything was done for them. However, she lived on Fifth Avenue, and the dogs had to be walked with a leash, and Miss Capers could not do this at all times and she would have to hire someone to walk the dogs for her.["]

* * *

The testimony clearly shows the basis for the provision of the will has been eliminated. There is no lack of care. There is no reason for carrying out the literal provision of the will. That decedent would rather see her pets happy and healthy and alive than destroyed, there can be no doubt.

Other testimony confirms what this witness suggests and what the court concludes. We, therefore, believe that the intent of testatrix would be carried out if her two favored Irish setters were placed where they are given the same care and attention that she bestowed on them; where they are doubtlessly as happy and contented as they were during the life of the owner.

This brings us to the third question. Is it against public policy to hold valid a clause in a will directing the summary destruction of certain of decedent's property after her death?

There is no question of the strength of the public sentiment in favor of preserving the lives of these animals. This is in accord with the upward development of the humane instinct in mankind for the preservation of life of all kinds, not only of human life but of the life of the lesser species. Man has come to realize that he has an ethical duty to preserve all life, human or not, unless the destruction of such other life is an absolute necessity.

If affirmation of life and ethics are inseparably combined, it indeed would be unethical to carry out the literal provisions of paragraph five of decedent's will. Paragraph 5 of decedent's will would confiscate the life of the two setters for no purpose. It would be an act of cruelty that is not sanctioned by the traditions and purposes of this court, and would conflict with its established public policy.

* * *

The general hue and cry against the destruction of these two animals was felt so strongly that the Attorney General of the State of Pennsylvania intervened for the purpose of preserving their lives.

The Attorney General ... states that the testamentary direction to destroy the dogs is against public policy. ...

Here, there is a unanimity of opinion that to destroy these two Irish setters that have displayed nothing but fidelity and affection would be an act of gross inhumanity.

The facts in this case are within that group of cases that are labeled "the clearest cases" of violation of public policy and it is, therefore, the basis for legal decision.

* * *

This brings us to the fourth question involved: Did decedent, Ida M. Capers, have a right under the Wills Act to order her executors to destroy the two Irish setters that were the property of her estate?

Whatever right exists to have the provisions of decedent's will carried out must be found in the Wills Act in force at the time of the death of decedent.

It is well known that in England, until recent period, the practice of allowing the owner of property to dispose of it after death, was exercised under considerable restraint.

The purpose of the [English] statutes ... was to authorize the owner of property to pass on that property to other owners. The right to make a will was never intended to bestow on an owner of property the right to order it destroyed after his death.

* * *

... [T]he court is of the opinion that testatrix had no right under the Wills Act to order her executors to destroy the two Irish setters after her death.

This brings us to the fifth consideration as to what is the present status of the Irish setters, Brickland and Sunny Birch. At the audit and at the date of the hearing, of which all parties were notified, the only party to appear and make an offer for the dogs, was the kennel keeper, Thomas L. Miller. There had been substantial offers for the two Irish setters at previous times, but at the date of the audit when the parties should have known that they had to be in court and make their bid for this property of decedent, they failed to do so.

The court, at the time of the audit, allowed $24 per week to the kennel keeper of the two setters. The dogs have been with Thomas L. Miller since January 1963, a period of approximately 98 weeks. Mr. Miller, therefore, would be entitled to approximately $2,500 for keeping these animals. The testimony indicates that Mr. Miller testified that he would waive the cost of keeping Brickland and Sunny Birch, for the privilege of obtaining their ownership.

* * *

The court will withhold a decree of distribution for a period of 20 days, to enable the Western Pennsylvania Humane Society and Mr. Thomas Miller to come to an arrangement with reference to these dogs which will be satisfactory to the said parties and in accordance with the foregoing opinion.

Notes

1. Why did Ida Capers include a provision for her dogs to be humanely killed upon her death? Do you think her reasons were valid? If so, can you articulate a public policy that is consistent with humane principles and yet still allow such a provision to be enforceable?

2. The following case illustrates a variation on the court's holding in *Capers Estate*. In the *Howard Brand* case, the court invokes the common law doctrine known as *cy pres*, by which the court tries to carry out the intention of the creator of the trust (or the testator) as closely as possible even when to do so literally would be impossible or even illegal. *Cy pres* is a common doctrine in cases such as these. As you read *In re Estate of Howard H. Brand*, consider whether the definition of "public policy" in this context is likely to shift with time, and if so, how the doctrine of *cy pres* may be impacted, if at all.

In re Estate of Howard H. Brand

Probate Court, Chittenden County, Vermont, March 17, 1999
No. 28473 (Unpublished)

FOWLER, Probate Judge. [*Editors' Note: Testator's third codicil to his will provided for the destruction of his motor vehicle and all animals owned by him at the time of his death. The Coalition to Save Brand's Horses filed a motion to intervene in the probate proceedings and a motion for preliminary injunction.*]

The Coalition to Save Brand's Horses (hereinafter referred to as the Coalition) is an unincorporated association which includes: Mary Ingham, a Williston resident who has spent significant time with the animals in question and is a prior owner of one of the animals; The Vermont Humane Federation, Inc., a membership organization whose members include Vermont's Humane Societies; The Vermont Volunteer Services for Animals Humane Society, an organization authorized by Vermont Law to interfere with acts of cruelty to animals; the Humane Organization for Retired Standardbred Equines, Vermont Chapter (hereinafter Vermont H.O.R.S.E.), an organization that screens applicants for and provides post-placement monitoring of rescued horses in Vermont; and the Student Animal Defense fund, a Vermont-based affiliate of the national organization located at Vermont Law School. The

Coalition to Save Brand's Horses was granted leave to intervene in the proceeding pursuant to V.R.C.P. 24(b) and V.R.P.P. 17.

CONCLUSIONS OF LAW

The issue before the court is one of first impression in the State of Vermont: can a decedent legally request destruction of healthy livestock as part of his Last Will and Testament? The question arises from the following language, as set forth in the Third Codicil of Howard H. Brand:

"TENTH C"

"If at the time of my death I am still the owner of any animals, including any horses and/or a mule, I direct my Executor to have such animals destroyed."

During the hearing on allowance of the Will, Attorney Fitzpatrick testified that Howard Brand was fully aware that his death was imminent, and clearly understood the nature of the directive concerning his livestock. In fact, Attorney Sheehey had previously prepared wills for Mr. Brand which had included similar language. It is Attorney Fitzpatrick's belief that Howard Brand wished to have his animals destroyed so as to avoid the possibility that they would fall victim to inhumane treatment in the years following Mr. Brand's death. (It is interesting to note that Mr. Brand also directed that his Cadillac be crushed, and that demolition take place in the presence of the Executor, who was further directed to certify to the court that the vehicle had been completely destroyed).

The Coalition contends that the provision of Howard Brand's Will calling for destruction of his animals should be stricken and prohibited from being carried out by the Executor as a violation of public policy in Vermont. In the alternative, the Coalition urges the court to exercise its inherent authority to amend the Will under the doctrine of *cy pres* in order to assure that the actual intent of the testator is realized.

The court does not set aside a provision in a person's Last Will and Testament lightly. It is the right of a citizen of this state to execute a Last Will and Testament, and a fundamental responsibility of the probate court to ensure that the decedent's last wishes are carried out. Indeed, many procedural safeguards are in place for that purpose.

"It is a cardinal principle that, in construing a will, the first and chief object is to ascertain the intention of the testator, from the language used, since, so far as it may be legally carried out, that governs. Such intention is to be ascertained from a consideration of the context of the will and the circumstances attending the making of it. And force and effect are to be given to every clause of the will."

There is no doubt as to the clear directive set forth in Howard Brand's Third Codicil, and the Executor has thus been entrusted with the task of carrying out the Decedent's directives, to the extent permissible by law. And, as crisply stated by the Estate, it is quite true that Humane Societies are legally authorized to euthanize injured, sick, homeless or unwanted pets and animals. 13 V.S.A. section 371(a). In addition, animals are raised for human consumption, and those who own animals may put them to death personally without fear of legal reprisal. Why then, queries the Estate, should questions arise when a person directs by Will that his animals be destroyed?

In part, the answer lies in distinctions historically drawn between "companion" animals and animals that are raised, owned, or merely controlled (*i.e.*, the deer herd) for other purposes. In addition, there is a distinction between what a person may do himself and what he may cause another to do on his behalf. This distinction between the rights of a testator and those of an executor has roots in early common law.

"Although the arbitrary rules and canons of testamentary construction are subordinate to the intention of the testator, it is universally recognized that the testatorial intention, even where clearly ascertainable, must yield to an established rule of law or public policy if it is in conflict therewith. Common examples of situations in which the testator's intention is overcome upon this theory are afforded by wills whose terms disregard the rule in Shelly's case, or the rule against perpetuities. In such cases the will must fail of effect, not because the intent of the testator does not control the construction, but because the law will not permit his intent to be accomplished." *In re Kuttler's Estate*, 325 P.2d 624, 626 (1958).

The phrase "against public policy" has been characterized as that which conflicts with the morals of the time and contravenes any established interest of society. Acts are said to be against public policy "when the law refuses to enforce or recognize them, on the ground that they have a mischievous tendency, so as to be injurious to the interests of the state, apart from illegality or immorality." *Dille v. St. Luke's Hosp.*, 196 S.W.2d 615, 620 (Mo. 1946).

Public policy may be found in the constitution, statutes, and judicial decisions of this state or the nation. But in a case of first impression, where there are no guiding statutes, judicial decisions, or constitutional provisions, "a judicial determination of the question becomes an expression of public policy provided it is so plainly right as to be supported by the general will." *In re Mohler's Estate*, 22 A.2d 680, 683 (PA 1941). In the absence of guidance from authorities in its own jurisdiction, courts may look to the judicial decisions of sister states for assistance in discovering expressions of public policy.

Other states that have considered the issue of animal destruction in wills have found such clauses to violate public policy, including but not limited to: *Smith v. Avalino* [sic], No. 225698 (Super. Ct., San Francisco County, June 1980), in which a California court found invalid on public policy grounds a will provision directing the destruction of a dog; *In re Capers Estate*, 34 D & C 2d 121 (PA 1964), in which a Pennsylvania court invalidated on public policy grounds a will provision directing the destruction of two dogs; *In re Estate of Hack*, No. 97-P-274 (3d Jud. Cir., Madison County, Ill. 1998), where in the court found a will provision ordering the testator's dog to be killed to be against public policy; and *In re Estate of Clive Wishart* (28 September 1992) (Newcastle, New Brunswick N/M/74/92), wherein a Canadian court drew heavily upon United States precedent to hold that a will provision directing the destruction of four horses was void and should not be carried out because to do so would be contrary to public policy.

Although the discussion regarding the future of Mr. Brand's animals occurs within the realm of property law, the unique type of "property" involved merits special attention. "Property" in domestic pets is of a highly qualified nature, possession of which may be subject to limitation and control. *Morgan v. Kroupa*, 702 A.D. 630, 634 (Vt. 1997). Courts in other jurisdictions have also recognized the distinction between companion animals and other forms of personal property in landlord tenant cases,[1] tort actions, and even divorce decrees. The mere fact that this court has received more than fifty letters from citizens across the nation concerned about the outcome of this case, and not a single communication addressing Mr. Brand's desired destruction of his perfectly good Cadillac, underscores the point.

An *Amicus Curiae* brief was submitted in connection with this case by Attorney Derek St. Pierre of San Francisco, California, on behalf of the national, non-profit organization entitled "In Defense of Animals." He states, in part, the following:

> "The study of property is the study of social relations. Property rights are significant in their ability to create expectations of specific treatment in social dealings with others. The Anglo-American concept of property creates an artificial legal dualism with two types of entities: persons and property. This division between the concepts of 'people' and 'property' is not as logical as it appears. Inanimate objects sometimes fall into the category of people,[3] and living beings can find themselves in the category of property. Nonhuman animals are currently categorized as personal property.[4] Despite this categorization, observation and logic illustrate the unique quality of this living, breathing property in comparison to most other forms of inanimate property.
>
> Property law must be understood and viewed within its historical context. Not long ago, the concept of property included various classes of humans. In the Seventeenth century, Africans brought into the United States were bought and sold as chattel.[5] During the same period, women, once married, became the property of their husbands.[6] Possibly the biggest barrier to the exertion of rights by either group was their status as property.

---

1. *New York Life Ins. Co. v. Dick*, 335 N.Y.S.2d 802, 811 (1972).

3. Corporations and ships are considered people for the purposes of the law and can sue and be sued.

4. Gary Francione, Animals, Property and the Law, 34–35 (1995).

5. William M. Wiecek, *The Origins of the Law of Slavery in British North America*, 17 Cardozo L. Rev. 1711, 1779 (1996).

6. Winston E. Landley & Vivian C. Fox, Women's Rights in the United States 7 (1994).

By definition, this categorization relegated both slaves and married women to a position with few legally cognizable rights.

The current position of nonhuman animals in our society is rooted in this long history of subjugation and domination by humans over humans.[7] Science, theology, and social myths have all played a part in establishing modern relationships between humans and nonhuman animals. In this country, the transition of slaves and married women from property to people came through a change in perspective away from a focus on the differences that separated the dominant from the subservient groups.[8] As the rationale to support subjugation lost its significance, the groups at issue gained ever widening protection by the law.

The situation of nonhuman animals, although clearly not identical, is analogous to that formerly occupied by slaves and married women. Humans do not possess any characteristics which are not shared by at least one other species. Nonhuman animals use tools, communicate with language, display emotions, have social relations, establish culture, display rational thought and even exhibit altruism. The converse is also true. There are no shortcomings displayed by nonhuman animals that are not also reflected in human behavior."

While it is argued by the Estate that Howard Brand intended to prevent future cruelty to his horses by ordering their death, it would seem to this court that a death sentence imposed upon healthy, if aging, animals might be considered cruel in its own right. Surely any person who has observed an animal threatened with harm can attest to its preference for survival over death.

* * *

The content of nearly all letters received by the court in connection with this case may be summed up in this quote from a letter written by Alfredo and Nicola Kuba of California:

"... The word animal comes from the Latin 'anima,' meaning soul. These poor souls are in your hands, please, do not allow people to grant death wishes in their will, especially when those being killed are helpless creatures without a voice ..." The letter goes on to quote St. Francis of Assisi, Alice Walker, and, finally, George Bernard Shaw, as follows: "The worst sin toward our fellow creatures is not to hate them, but to be indifferent to them. That is the essence of inhumanity."

States presently regulate human use and interaction with animals through anti-cruelty statutes. Increasingly, states are viewing cruelty toward animals as a serious

---

7. Steven Wise, *How Nonhuman Animals Were Trapped in an* [sic] *Nonexistent Universe*, 1 ANIMAL L. 15 (1995).

8. *See* Derek St. Pierre, *The Transition From Property to People: The Road to the Recognition of Rights for Non-Human Animals*, 9 HASTINGS WOMEN'S L.J. 255 (Summer 1998).

offense against society. Our social history and cultural development illustrate an increasing understanding of this concept and of the rights of nonhuman animals. Consequently, public policy and Vermont law should operate to allow these animals the opportunity to continue living.

Having stated all of the foregoing, the court turns to consider the best means by which to carry out Howard Brand's stated desire for his animals. If the court does not permit destruction of the horses, the next best option would assure the animals' continued existence in a manner which closely resembles the life they enjoyed while Howard Brand was living. This may be accomplished through use of the doctrine of *cy pres*, by which the intention of the party is carried out *as near as may be,* when it would be impossible or illegal to give it literal effect. *Burr's Executors v. Smith*, 7 Vt. 241 (1835).

The court is mindful of the fact that animals may be sold or given away by an owner at will, and thus their lives may be subject to change for the worse as time goes by, potentially culminating in just the sort of neglect or cruelty Howard Brand sought to avoid through the terms of his will. To ensure that such an ending does not befall the animals at issue here, the court will oversee the placement of Mr. Brand's horses and will prohibit any future transfer of ownership without prior approval of the court.

The court is without sufficient information at this time to make a ruling as to the appropriate disposition of Howard Brand's horses. Further hearing will be held for that purpose.

ORDER

Wherefore, it is found that the terms of the Third Codicil of Howard Brand, as set forth in Paragraph Tenth C, mandating the destruction of any animals owned by Mr. Brand at his death, are hereby deemed void as against public policy. The terms of the Codicil will be amended pursuant to the doctrine of *cy pres* to allow for the continued existence of the horses under humane conditions. Further hearing will be scheduled for the purpose of taking evidence on the issue of an appropriate placement for them.

Notes

1. As noted in *Estate of Brand*, other courts addressing the same issue have agreed it would violate public policy to enforce a will provision directing the destruction of an animal. In *Smith v. Avanzino*, No. 225698 (Cal. Super. Ct., San Francisco County, June 17, 1980) (also known as the *Sido* case), referenced by the *Brand* court, the testatrix's will provided for the immediate destruction of her small, mixed-breed dog upon her death. The San Francisco Society for the Prevention of Cruelty to Animals (SPCA) obtained custody of the dog, Sido, after the testatrix's death and refused to release Sido, thereby preventing implementation of the terms of the will. The executor sued the SPCA, seeking custody of Sido for the purpose of carrying out the will provision. After extensive publicity and public outcry, the California legislature

passed a special statute, specifically to save Sido. California Senate Bill 2509 passed unanimously and was signed into law on June 16, 1980, one day before the court hearing to determine Sido's disposition. The bill provided, in part:

> The legislature hereby finds that under the facts meeting the description set forth in Section 1 of this act, the testator, having the best interests of her pet dog in mind, would not wish her instructions for the destruction of the pet dog carried out were she cognizant of the present circumstances assuring the well-being and happy future for the dog, occurring as the result of unexpected developments following her death.
>
> In order to prevent the unnecessary and undesirable killing of animals, pursuant to the requirements of decedents' wills, it is necessary that this act go into immediate effect.

* * *

Although a telephone call from the governor to the court during the June 17 hearing confirmed that the issue was moot, the court nonetheless resolved the matter on the record:

> First of all, we have to proceed somewhat in a legal fashion because that is our function here, and that can't be governed by sentiment and by the correspondence and communications that we have received from the public, although they definitely bear in the issue, as I will share in just a moment.
>
> The right to make a will is a privilege which all of us have. It is given to us by law. The purpose of a will, each layman will concur, is to permit an individual upon his death to see that his assets pass to individuals of his choice. Section 20 of our Probate Code provides that a person who is over the age of 18 years may dispose of his property by will.
>
> Now, the word "dispose" in this sense means to pass along to someone else, that someone else succeed as the owner thereof. The word "dispose" cannot be interpreted to mean that of destroying, damaging. There is a good deal of case law that could be cited in support of that.
>
> As a result, the Court finds that the provision of the will before us is invalid in that it seeks to do under the will that which the law does not permit. Further, that the actions in this regard violate public policy.
>
> But there remains one further matter of public policy and breach of the law that I think should be shared herein; that the will seeks to have carried out an act which I find to be illegal.
>
> The Municipal Code of the City and County of San Francisco as well as the Penal Code makes specific provisions as to what is to be done with animals insofar as their death is concerned. In this City and County of San Francisco it is the Animal Control Officer who has the jurisdiction, and the statute spells out the conditions under which the death of an animal may be decreed and carried out by him.

Now, stray dogs, abandoned dogs, have rights under our statute which must be carefully followed. Our dog Sido cannot be deemed an abandoned dog or a stray dog. Her plight resulted due to the death of her mistress. Her Sido is entitled to nothing less than which we afford to stray dogs.

To permit the direction of the decedent here to be carried out would, again, violate existing statute and be contrary to public policy.

* * *

With respect to the actual disposition of Sido, the court stated: "Let's rise to the exception in this instance and do what I think would be to the best interest of the dog."

2. In light of the public policy considerations and persuasive case authority, the outcome in *Sido* may have been the same even without the national media coverage and public outcry. The function of the courts, however, is merely to interpret and apply existing law. Codification of laws by state legislatures, with careful drafting, can serve to limit judicial discretion. In *Sido*, the media and the public undoubtedly influenced state legislators to remove any risk that the court would enforce the will as drafted and order Sido put to death, by expeditiously and unanimously passing California Senate Bill 2509. As you have seen throughout your study of animal law, the *Sido* case illustrates once again how changes in the law can be effectuated through the legislative process and the courts — but motivation may also come from groups and individuals who increase public awareness and recognition of the need for change.

3. Other courts addressing the issue of destruction of a companion animal upon a testator's death may find that such a practice does not violate public policy. In November of 2014, Connie Ley of Dearborn County, Indiana died, leaving a will authorizing her friend Barbara Gilbert to decide the fate of any animals Ley owned at the time of her death. Ley gave two options: send the animal to Best Friends Animal Society in Kanab, Utah (Best Friends) or have the animal euthanized, cremated, and buried with Ley.

Before Ms. Gilbert decided on Ley's dog Bela's fate, the Animal Legal Defense Fund (ALDF) intervened. Driven partially by public outcry, ALDF sought to enjoin as a public nuisance Ley's estate from euthanizing Bela and to appoint a guardian *ad litem* to consider Bela's best interests moving forward. However, Ms. Gilbert ultimately decided to send Bela to Best Friends before ALDF's petition was heard, and Bela was transferred there at the end of December 2014. In an amended complaint filed in January of 2015, ALDF requested a declaratory judgment pursuant to Indiana's nuisance laws, declaring that "to euthanize Bela, a healthy animal, solely because of the provision in the will . . . would constitute a public nuisance" and, further, that the provision in Ley's will concerning the disposition of Bela was void as it is against public policy. The court did not agree that euthanizing a healthy animal was against public policy or a public nuisance, citing Bela's documented aggression as legitimate grounds for the provision in Ley's will. Further, the court stated:

A pet owner's right to euthanize an animal during the owner's lifetime does not constitute a nuisance under Indiana law and it therefore would not constitute a nuisance to have a pet or animal euthanized upon the owner's death ... No public policy exists in Indiana prohibiting the euthanasia of animals during the owner's lifetime or following the owner's death.

Creating such a public policy ... would necessarily create an irreconcilable conflict causing potential problems for animal owners, farmers, veterinarians, animal shelters, animal control agencies, and humane societies.

ALDF v. Estate of Connie Ley and Doug Denmure, Cause No. 15C01-1412-MI-090 (Ind. Cir. Ct., Dearborn Cty. Jul. 6, 2015).

Do you agree with the court? Regardless of your answer, what conflicts can you foresee being created by a public policy prohibiting the euthanasia of animals pursuant to will directives?

4. With respect to pet destruction provisions, regardless of public policy, if a will is uncontested or if any conflicts are resolved among the parties, courts may not be given the opportunity to step in to protect the animal or, even if they are, some courts may determine that the testator's intent overrides competing interests of public policy. It is impossible to know how many such provisions have been enforced without intervention (or with approval) by the courts. Indeed, if there is no interested party willing to fight for the animal's life, these provisions will likely get carried out by executors without question.

B. Will Provisions Providing for the Care of Companion Animals upon Testator's Death: The Rule Against Perpetuities

In re Howells' Estate

Surrogate's Court of New York, Kings County, 1932
145 Misc. 557, 260 N.Y.S. 598

WINGATE, S. The statement has frequently been made that judicial tribunals struggle to preserve the validity of a testamentary instruction and do not yield to a construction producing intestacy unless such a course is absolutely inevitable. It is believed that the natural connotation of such a statement is far too broad. The office of the court in any proceeding for testamentary construction is twofold. ... It must first interpret the meaning of the will, ascertaining what the testator intended by the language employed when read in the light of the circumstances surrounding him at the time of its execution, and when this has been determined, it must adjudicate the legal effect and consequences of the directions as thus interpreted.

It is only in the process of interpretation that the principle of presumed, or rather of desired, validity obtains. If the will is ambiguous and capable of two or more meanings, one of which is lawful and another contrary to law, the alternative which results in effectiveness rather than that which spells invalidity, should be adopted. This, the noted statement means and nothing more. "Only where there is fair room for two constructions may the court take the one to preserve rather than to overturn the instrument." The testator, not the court, must make the disposition of his property. All the latter can do is, so far as legal rules permit, to effectuate the disposition which the testator has directed. It cannot make a new and valid will for him if he has failed in this respect.

Approaching the task of interpretation of the will at bar, and taking seat in testatrix's arm chair, . . . it is found that testatrix was a married woman, apparently a school teacher by occupation, living apart from her husband. Her sole next of kin was a sister with whom she was apparently out of sympathy, since her name was coupled in the will with that of testatrix's estranged husband, as intentionally disinherited. The place in her affections usually occupied by family or relatives seems to have been taken by pets, of which two cats and three dogs survived her. She appears also to have been interested in one Charles E. Rattray, who was a retired policeman, living with his sister on a pension. Rattray was no blood relation to testatrix.

With this meager background of pertinent facts, the provisions of the will must next be examined. It is apparently a homemade affair, and, after directing payment of debts, giving a specific bequest of a piano already in the possession of the beneficiary, and a general legacy of $500 to a woman living in the same house, proceeded as follows:

> "*Fifth.* All the rest, residue and remainder of my estate, both real, personal and mixed, and wheresoever the same may be situate [sic], and any unused balance of moneys derived under Option No. 1 from the Teachers' Retirement System I give in trust unto my Executor hereinafter named to and for the following uses and purposes:

> * * *

> "I further authorize and empower and hereby direct my said Executor or the successor Trustee of my estate to apply the balance of the income from my estate to the care, comfort and maintenance of Charles E. Rattray and should conditions arise during the lifetime of Charles E. Rattray which would bring about the need of more income for his necessary care, comfort and maintenance, in addition to the amount of income herein directed to be applied to or paid for his support, that then and in such case my Executor or his successor Trustee of my estate is authorized and directed to use such portion of the principal of said trust estate as is required to amply provide for his care, comfort and maintenance.

> "*Sixth.* Upon the death of said Charles E. Rattray or should he predecease me, then upon my death I authorize and direct my Executor or the successor Trustee of my estate to expend an amount not to exceed $400 to provide a suitable stone to mark my last resting place and such additional sum as is necessary to provide for the perpetual care of my burial plot.

* * *

"*Eighth*. I authorize and empower my Executor or the successor Trustee of my estate to retain any part or portion of my estate as long as he or she shall consider it to be for the benefit of my estate to do so and to provide for the care of my pet animals while they live.

"*Ninth*. I designate the Teachers' Welfare Loan Fund as residuary devisee, legatee and beneficiary to receive the remainder of my estate held in trust by my executor or his successor Trustee of whatsoever kind and wherever located. I do this in recognition of the worthy purposes for which the Fund has been created and because it has been truly helpful to me. It is my desire and wish to help perpetuate its usefulness to others who like myself may require assistance in their hour of need.["]

* * *

From the disclosed situation of the testatrix, coupled with the directions of the will, the conclusion is inescapable that her dominant testamentary desire was to provide for the care and welfare of her pet animals who constituted her sole immediate family. The first charge upon the income of the residue of the estate was dedicated to their comfort and maintenance. Only after this was attended to, was any portion thereof devoted to any other use. Her paramount interest in her pets was further demonstrated by the fact that whereas she gave a power of invasion of principal in favor of Rattray, should conditions arise in his life which made such a course necessary, the power of the court to make direction in this regard was expressly limited by the grant of authority to the trustee in Item eighth to retain so much of the fund in his hands as might be necessary to care for her pet animals.

The validity of a testamentary trust in this State must be determined, *inter alia*, by the provisions of sections 11 of the Personal Property Law and 42 of the Real Property Law which provide in substance that absolute ownership of property shall not be suspended for a period longer than during the continuance, and until the termination, of not more than two lives in being at the death of the testator.

In the will at bar no express time for termination of the trust is given. The directions are merely to pay so much of the income as shall be directed by testatrix's named friends for the care and maintenance of her pet animals, and the balance to Charles E. Rattray.

The learned referee in this proceeding has read the sixth item of the will as amounting to a direction that the trust shall end at Rattray's death. The court is unable to agree with his conclusion in this regard. The terms of that direction are merely that upon his death, or upon testatrix's death should he predecease her, the executor shall pay from the principal fund the sum of $400 for a monument upon her grave and a reasonable sum for its perpetual care. This provision does not by express terms or necessary implication affect any portion of the principal other than such $400 and additional reasonable sum, and merely deducts this amount from the total principal dedicated for the prescribed purposes.

Had Rattray predeceased the testatrix, far from the trust never having come into existence, as the referee concludes, the primary purpose of the testatrix to provide for the welfare of her pet animals would have remained. An interpretation, therefore, that Rattray's predecease of testatrix would have prevented any portion of the trust from coming into existence, could be attained only by the complete deletion from the will of the entire direction for use of the trust income for the support of the animals. Such a conclusion would be in direct conflict with the basic principle that in the interpretation of a written document all of its words shall be given effect if at all possible.

The contention of the executor differs somewhat from the conclusion of the referee, and is to the effect that the limited power of invasion of principal granted to the trustee constitutes an implication that the trust was primarily for the benefit of Rattray in spite of the express words of the testator dedicating the first income of the trust to use for the benefit of the animals. The conclusive reply to this position is that the authorization for invasion amounted merely to a limited condition subsequent on the continuance of the trust, which condition subsequent being uncertain of performance, will not avail to bring the trust as an entirety within the provisions of the statute, since it is primary that, ". . . to render such future estates valid, they must be so limited that in every possible contingency, they will absolutely terminate at such period, or such estates will be held void."

Since, under the terms of the will, the use of any portion of the principal for Rattray was expressly conditioned on the happening of future events making possible a demonstration that circumstances had transpired which "would bring about the need for more income" for his necessary care, which events, being in the future, could not be foretold, it follows that viewing the matter from the time of death of the testatrix, this authority for invasion was not a limitation which "in every possible contingency" would absolutely terminate the trust within his lifetime. Obviously he had no claims upon the trust fund until testatrix's death. Even if, at the moment of her death, his situation had been such as to require more than the balance of the income dedicated to him after the satisfaction of the prior wants of the pets, there would be no assurance that he would live for a period long enough to exhaust the principal, or, indeed, even for a day. It follows, therefore, that the authority for invasion of principal cannot be deemed a limitation which "will absolutely terminate" the trust within his lifetime.

Since there is no express or necessarily implied condition absolutely terminating the trust until the death of all of the pet animals who survive the testatrix and of Rattray, the sole question remaining for solution on this branch of the case is as to whether a trust for the application of income for the lives of one human being and five domestic animals comes within the inhibitions of the statute.

It is primary that a portion of a human life is to be considered as a life in computing "lives in being" within the terminology of the statute, wherefore, the argument which has been advanced that the lives of cats and dogs are commonly known to be of shorter duration than those of human beings, possesses no relevancy to the determination. It is a matter of common knowledge that such domestic animals frequently live to ages of ten or beyond, and it would be absurd to assert that any measuring life which might extend for a period of ten years beyond the death of the testator, or even for an appreciable fraction thereof, was an inconsequential limitation. Had the trust been limited upon the lives of five relatives of the testatrix who were all of the ages of sixty-seven or above, plus the life of Rattray, no one would have the temerity to assert that the suspension was valid, yet the expectancy of life of an individual of sixty-seven years, according to the American Experience Table of Mortalities, is precisely ten years.

Counsel have cited no authority in which the question of the validity of a testamentary benefit for domestic animals has been adjudicated, and the independent research of the court has disclosed only two. The first in point of time is *Matter of Dean — Cooper-Dean v. Stevens* (41 Ch. Div. 552), decided in England in 1889. By the terms of the will, testator gave to his trustees his horses and dogs and charged his estate, devised in earlier items of his will, "with the payment to my trustees for the term of fifty-years commencing from my death, if any of the said horses and hounds shall so long live, of an annual sum of £750. And I declare that my trustees shall apply the said annual sum payable to them under this clause in the maintenance of the said horses and hounds for the time being living." This provision was attacked on several grounds, the most seriously asserted being that the beneficiaries were unable to enforce performance. In sustaining the direction, the court says (at p. 557):

> "Is there then anything illegal or obnoxious to the law in the nature of the provision, that is, in the fact that it is not for human beings, but for horses and dogs? It is clearly settled by authority that a charity may be established for the benefit of horses and dogs, and, therefore, the making of a provision for horses and dogs, which is not a charity, cannot of itself be obnoxious to the law, provided, of course, that it is not to last for too long a period."

A very recent and far more apposite decision is found in the advance sheets for April, 1932, of the Irish Reports in the case of *Matter of Kelly — Cleary v. Dillon* (1932 Irish Rep. 255) which was a decision of the High Court of Justice, Saorstate Eirann, rendered on April fourteenth of this year. The pertinent bequest in the will there under construction read: "I leave one hundred pounds sterling to my executors and trustees for the purpose of expending four pounds sterling on the support of each of my dogs per year." In the course of an elaborate opinion which upheld the validity of the trust for twenty-one years, but no longer, the court says (beginning at p. 260):

> "If the lives of the dogs or other animals could be taken into account in reckoning the maximum period of 'lives in being and twenty-one years afterwards,' any contingent or executory interest might be properly limited, so as only to vest within the lives of specified carp, or tortoises, or other animals that might live for over a hundred years, and for twenty-one years afterwards, which, of course, is absurd. 'Lives' means human lives. It was suggested that the last of the dogs could in fact not outlive the testator by

778 8 · WILLS AND TRUSTS

more than twenty-one years. I know nothing of that. The court does not enter into the question of a dog's expectation of life. In point of fact neighbor's dogs and cats are unpleasantly long-lived; but I have no knowledge of their precise expectation of life. Anyway the maximum period is exceeded by the lives even of specified butterflies and twenty-one years afterwards. And even, according to my decision—and, I confess, it displays this weakness on being pressed to a logical conclusion—the expiration of the life of a single butterfly, even without the twenty-one years, would be too remote, despite all the world of poetry that may be thereby destroyed. In *Robinson v. Hardcastle* (2 Bro. C.C. 22, at p. 30) Lord Thurlow defined a perpetuity in these words: 'What is a perpetuity, but the extending the estate beyond a life in being, and twenty-one years after?' Of course by 'a life' he means lives; and there can be no doubt that 'lives' means lives of human beings, not of animals or trees in California."

It is, of course, apparent from this language of the court that were it construing a statute similar to our own, which limits the duration of a trust to two lives in being, without the addition of the twenty-one-year period, it must have declared any trust not limited upon human lives wholly bad. In the case at bar it is unnecessary for the court to go to the extent of holding that a trust cannot be limited other than on human lives, since here there is no question of whether a limitation on the lives of *two* domestic animals would infringe upon the terms of the statute, since on the facts of the case there were *five* of them. It is probable, however, in view of the phraseology of subdivision 3 of section 96 of the Real Property Law, referring to the "use of any *person*," that such result would be unavoidable even were two only in existence at testatrix's death. In any event, it may be said with assurance that the present trust, limited on the lives of five animals and one human being, is bad.

* * *

The final result is that all the dispositive provisions of the will above quoted are ineffectual and void, and that the testatrix must be determined to have died intestate with respect to the property covered thereby.

* * *

Notes

1. This case highlights the difficulty posed by the common law Rule Against Perpetuities (which prohibits "a grant of an estate unless the interest must vest, if at all, no later than twenty-one years . . . after the death of some person alive when the interest was created") when companion animal lives are at stake. The Rule Against Perpetuities Act has now been enacted in many states and provides that the writer of a trust can, in lieu of lives in being and twenty-one years as a measuring period, opt for a ninety-year period in gross—long enough for almost any turtle or parrot, the longest-lived companion animals. *See, e.g.,* Fla. Stat. § 689.225 (2008).

2. For more on the historical perspective, *see* James T. Brennan, *Bequests for the Care of Specific Animals*, 6 Duq. L. Rev. 15 (1967–68). For a discussion of the enforceability of animal trusts under the laws of countries other than the United States, *see* Kenneth McK. Norrie, *Trusts for Animals*, 22 J.L. Soc'y Scotland 386 (1977) (Scottish law); Philip Jamieson, *Trusts for the Maintenance of Particular Animals*, 14 Univ. Queensland L.J. 175 (1987) (Australian law). Bequests to animal charities, as opposed to bequests for the care of specific animals, are discussed in Philip Jamieson, *On Charity's Edge — The Animal Welfare Trust*, 13 Monash U.L. Rev. 1 (1987).

3. Twenty years after the *Howells* case, another New York court cited to *Howells* and reached a similar result. In *In re Filkins' Will*, 120 N.Y.S. 2d 124 (N.Y. Surrogate's Ct., Monroe County 1952), the will provision at issue read as follows:

> I give, devise and bequeath to Lottie E. Filkins, widow of my deceased brother Clarence G. Filkins, whatever automobile I may own at the time of my decease and my residence where I now reside, including all of the land and outbuildings as well as all furniture, household furnishings and housekeeping appliances in the house, and I direct that she shall have the right to use and occupy said premises immediately upon my death. This bequest and devise, however, are made expressly contingent upon the said Lottie E. Filkins furnishing proper care for any and all pets which I may own at the time of my decease for as long as they shall live.

The court concluded that the provision for the care of the testatrix's companion animals was a condition subsequent, which could not operate to disturb the vested interests of the beneficiary. Moreover, citing to *Howells*, the court concluded that "[s]ince the condition is based on the lives of several animals, it clearly is void under the statute against unlawful suspension of the power of alienation." *Id.* at 126.

As the following case demonstrates, where animals' lives are not at stake, courts have upheld will provisions that clearly evidenced the testators' concerns about their companion animals, but which, in the strictest sense, may or may not have met all the traditional requirements for such bequests.

In re Estate of Searight: Department of Taxation of Ohio

Court of Appeals of Ohio, Ninth Appellate District, Wayne County, 1950
87 Ohio Ct. App. 417, 95 N.E.2d 779

HUNSICKER, Judge. George P. Searight, a resident of Wayne County, Ohio, died testate on November 27, 1948. Item "third" of his will provided:

> "I give and bequeath my dog, Trixie, to Florence Hand of Wooster, Ohio, and I direct my executor to deposit in the Peoples Federal Savings and Loan Association, Wooster, Ohio, the sum of $1000.00 to be used by him to pay Florence Hand at the rate of 75 cents per day for the keep and care of my dog as long as it shall live. If my dog shall die before the said $1000.00 and the

interest accruing therefrom shall have been used up, I give and bequeath whatever remains of said $1000.00 to be divided equally among those of the following persons who are living at that time, to wit: Bessie Immler, Florence Hand, Reed Searight, Fern Olson and Willis Horn."

At the time of his death, all of the persons, and his dog, Trixie, named in such item third, were living. Florence Hand accepted the bequest of Trixie, and the executor paid to her from the $1000 fund, 75 cents a day for the keep and care of the dog. The value of Trixie was agreed to be $5.

The Probate Court made a determination of inheritance tax due from the estate of George P. Searight, deceased, the pertinent part of this judgment reading as follows:

"The court further finds that the value of the dog Trixie is taxable as a succession to Florence Hand: that the said dog inherits the sum of $1000.00 with power to consume both the interest and principal at a limited rate; that the state of Ohio (Sec. 5332) levying a tax on successions to property does not levy a tax upon the succession to any property passing to an animal; that the $1000.00 bequest to said dog is therefore not taxable; that the remainder of the $1000.00, if any, remaining after the death of said dog is taxable in the hands of the remaindermen; that there is no certain life expectancy of said dog, and that a tax should therefore be assessed upon the entire bequest to the contingent beneficiaries, . . .

"Wherefore, it is ordered by the court that Florence Hand, as successor to the title of the said dog Trixie, be taxed at the rate prescribed by law on the value of said dog, to wit, $5.00; that Bessie Immler, Florence Hand, Reed Searight, Fern Olson and Willis Horn, as contingent beneficiaries and remaindermen of the said $1000.00, each be taxed on $200.00 at the rate prescribed by law, subject to refund or assessment of any excess as indicated in the findings herein. . . ."

The Department of Taxation of Ohio appeals to this court from such judgment, claiming the Probate Court erred: In holding that the bequest in item third to the extent it was paid to Florence Hand for the care of Trixie, is not a succession to property passing in trust or otherwise, to or for the use of a person; in not holding that the bequest of $1000 to the extent it was to be paid to Florence Hand for the care of Trixie was a bequest or succession to the said Florence Hand, subject to Ohio inheritance taxes; in holding that the bequest of $1000 was a bequest to a dog to the extent it is paid to Florence Hand for the care of Trixie; in holding that a bequest of $1000 to the extent it is paid to Florence Hand for the care of Trixie is not subject to Ohio inheritance taxes; in holding that a bequest for the care of Trixie is a valid bequest; in not holding that the sum of $1000 was a succession of property passing to the remaindermen named in item third; in not making a final order holding that the entire bequest of $1000 was subject to Ohio inheritance taxes on the amount of $200 due to each remainderman.

The questions presented by this appeal on questions of law are:

1. Is the testamentary bequest for the care of Trixie (a dog) valid in Ohio—

   (a) as a proper subject of a so-called "honorary trust"?

   (b) as not being in violation of the rule against perpetuities?

2. Is the bequest set forth in item third of testator's will subject to the inheritance tax laws of Ohio?

1(a). The creation of a trust for the benefit of specific animals has not been the subject of much litigation in the courts, and our research, and that of able counsel in this case, have failed to disclose any reported case on the subject in Ohio. The few reported cases in this country, in England and in Ireland have been the subject of considerable comment by the writers of text books and by the law reviews of leading law schools. *See*: *Mitford v. Reynolds*, 60 Eng. Rep., 812, 16 Simons 105 (trust for horses); *Pettingall v. Pettingall*, 11 L.J. Ch., 176, 8 English and Empire Digest, 264 (trust for horses and hounds); *In re Dean, Cooper-Dean v. Stevens*, 41 L.R. Ch. D. 552 (trust for horses and hounds); *Willett v. Willett*, 247 S.W. 739, (trust for dog allowed on the basis of a statute exempting both trusts for humane purposes and those for charitable purposes from the definite beneficiary requirement); [also citing to *In re Kelly, supra*; and *In re Howells, supra*].

We do not have, in the instant case, the question of a trust established for the care of dogs in general or of an indefinite number of dogs, but we are here considering the validity of a testamentary bequest for the benefit of a specific dog. This is not a charitable trust, nor is it a gift of money to the Ohio Humane Society or a county humane society, which societies are vested with broad statutory authority for the care of animals.

Text writers on the subject of trusts and many law professors designate a bequest for the care of a specific animal as an "honorary trust"; that is, one binding the conscience of the trustee, since there is no beneficiary capable of enforcing the trust.

The rule in Ohio, that the absence of a beneficiary having a legal standing in court and capable of demanding an accounting of the trustee is fatal and the trust fails, was first announced in *Mannix, Assignee, v. Purcell*, 19 N.E. 572.

The text writer for Ohio Jurisprudence on the subject of trusts (40 Ohio Jurisprudence, page 85 *et seq.*), Professor Harry W. Vanneman of Ohio State University Law School, says, in section 68:

> "Where property is conveyed or devised to a trustee for certain purposes, such as maintenance of graves, saying of masses, erection of monuments, care of certain animals, and the like, although the object of the bounty cannot enforce the trust, and, the trust not being a charity, the attorney general has no duty with respect to it, nevertheless, contrary to the doctrine of the preceding section, the trust does not fail if the trustee is willing to carry it out and erect the monument, care for the animals, *etc.*, provided the trust will not continue for a period longer than the rule against perpetuities.

The trustee cannot hold beneficially, and, if he is unwilling to carry out the power entrusted to him, he will hold as resulting trustee for the proper person. Such a trust has been designated as an 'honorary trust' because there is no beneficiary capable of enforcing it. . . ."

* * *

The object and purpose sought to be accomplished by the testator in the instant case is not capricious or illegal. He sought to effect a worthy purpose—the care of his pet dog.

Whether we designate the gift in this case as an "honorary trust" or a gift with a power which is valid when exercised is not important, for we do know that the one to whom the dog was given accepted the gift and indicated her willingness to care for such dog, and the executor proceeded to carry out the wishes of the testator.

"Where the owner of property transfers it upon an intended trust for a specific non-charitable purpose, and there is no definite or definitely ascertainable beneficiary designated, no trust is created; but the transferee has power to apply the property to the designated purpose, unless he is authorized by the terms of the intended trust so to apply the property beyond the period of the rule against perpetuities, or the purpose is capricious." I Restatement of the Law of Trusts, section 124.

To call this bequest for the care of the dog, Trixie, a trust in the accepted sense in which that term is defined is, we know, an unjustified conclusion. The modern authorities, as shown by the cases cited earlier in this discussion, however, uphold the validity of a gift for the purpose designated in the instant case, where the person to whom the power is given is willing to carry out the testator's wishes. Whether called an "honorary trust" or whatever terminology is used, we conclude that the bequest for the care of the dog, Trixie, is not in and of itself unlawful.

In Ohio, by statute, the rule against perpetuities is specifically defined, and such statute further says: "It is the intention by the adoption of this section to make effective in Ohio what is generally known as the common law rule against perpetuities."

It is to be noted, in every situation where the so called "honorary trust" is established for specific animals, that, unless the instrument creating such trust limits the duration of the trust—that is, the time during which the power is to be exercised—to human lives, we will have "honorary trusts" established for animals of great longevity, such as crocodiles, elephants and sea turtles.

See: Gray, The Rule Against Perpetuities (Fourth Ed.), section 896.3.

Restatement of the Law of Property, section 374, states the maximum period allowed by the rule against perpetuities as:

"(a) lives of persons who are

"(i) in being at the commencement of such period, and

"(ii) neither so numerous nor so situated that evidence of their deaths is likely to be unreasonably difficult to obtain; and "(b) twenty-one years; and

"(c) any period or periods of gestation involved in the situation to which the limitation applies."

This same text, with reference to the application of such rule to "honorary trusts," says, at section 379:

"A limitation of property on an intended trust is invalid when, under the language and circumstances of such limitation,

"(a) the conveyee is to administer the property for the accomplishment of a specific noncharitable purpose and there is no definite or definitely ascertainable beneficiary designated; and

"(b) such administration can continue for longer than the maximum period described in Section 374; and

"(c) destructibility of the trust, of the sort described in Section 373, is absent."

The lives, in being, which are the measure of the period set out in the rule against perpetuities, must be determined from the creating instrument.

If we then examine item third of testator's will, we discover that, although the bequest for his dog is for "as long as it shall live," the money given for this purpose is $1000 payable at the rate of 75¢ a day. By simple mathematical computation, this sum of money, expended at the rate determined by the testator, will be fully exhausted in three years and 238 1/3 days. If we assume that this $1000 is deposited in a bank so that interest at the high rate of 6% per annum were earned thereon, the time needed to consume both principal and interest thereon (based on semi-annual computation of such interest on the average unused balance during such six month period) would be four years, 57 1/2 days.

It is thus very apparent that the testator provided a time limit for the exercise of the power given his executor, and that such time limit is much less than the maximum period allowed under the rule against perpetuities.

We must indulge the presumption that the testator was cognizant of the rule against perpetuities and the construction placed upon it by the courts, and that he prepared his will possessed of such knowledge.

We therefore conclude that the bequest in the instant case for the care of the dog, Trixie, does not, by the terms of the creating instrument, violate the rule against perpetuities.

2. We next consider the problem of the inheritance tax, if any, to be levied on the bequest contained in item third of testator's will.

Section 5332, General Code ... determines that a tax shall be levied upon succession to all property passing to a person, institution or corporation. Certainly, a dog is neither an institution nor a corporation. Can it be successfully contended that a dog is a person? A "person" is defined as "3. A human being." Webster's New International Dictionary, Second Edition.

We have herein above indicated that the bequest for the dog, Trixie, comes within the designation of an "honorary trust," and, as such, is proper in the instant case. A tax based on the amount expended for the care of the dog cannot lawfully be levied against the monies so expended, since it is not property passing for the use of a "person, institution or corporation."

The executor herein had a power granted to him to use the funds for the support of the dog, which he proceeded to fulfill. Is it possible that such a power could be considered as a power of appointment within the terms of subsection 4 of section 5332, General Code, and, hence, subject to taxation thereunder?

On this point, we need look for no other authority than that contained in 3 Restatement of the Law of Property (Future Interests), section 318 (2), which states the rule as follows:

> "(2) The term power of appointment does not include a power of sale, a power of attorney, a power of revocation, a power to cause a gift of income to be augmented out of principal, a power to designate charities, a charitable trust, a discretionary trust, or an honorary trust."

Thus, an intended trust (honorary trust) for the support of a specific animal does not create a power of appointment, as such term is used in the inheritance tax statute.

We therefore conclude that no succession tax may be levied against such funds as are expended by the executor in carrying out the power granted to him by item third of testator's will. The judgment of the Probate Court is affirmed.

Notes

1. As discussed in the next section, modern statutes enacted in most states have helped alleviate the difficulties previously encountered when testators have tried to ensure proper care for their companion animals. But these statutes do not remove all hurdles faced by an estate trying to effectuate companion animal provisions, especially when large sums of money are at stake.

For example, take the case of *In re Estate of Sidney Altman*, Case No. BP039093 (Cal. Super. Ct., Los Angeles County, 2000). According to reports, Altman, a bathroom fixture magnate who died in 1996, left his Beverly Hills home and $350,000 to his dog Samantha. The will nominated Marie Dana, Altman's female companion of six years, to be Samantha's legal guardian and to care for her until Samantha's death. Dana was to receive an annual tax-free stipend of $60,000, provided that she care for Samantha. The will also provided for a one-time payment of $50,000 to Dana for a shopping spree and for redecorating the house. The lump sum of $350,000 was provided for Samantha's living expenses and care. A separate $150,000 was left to the executor who was to assure the quality of Samantha's life by investigating the situation on a quarterly basis. The will provided that upon Samantha's death, "the arrangement" with Dana was to be canceled, the house was to be sold and the money was to be distributed to specified animal welfare groups which were the charities designated in the will.

Dana, who was nearly thirty years younger than Altman, asserted that she and Altman had a contractual agreement — he had promised to always support her and provide a home, in exchange for which she would be his lifetime companion and confidant. Her attorney, who asserted that the will did not reflect the depth of his relationship with Dana, was quoted as saying that "she feels she shouldn't be treated worse than a dog." Christopher Reed, *Woman Goes to Court Over Will that Favors Dead Boyfriend's Dog*, SAN DIEGO UNION TRIB., Sept. 27, 1998, at A30. Early in the case, Dana sought $2.7 million. The judge urged the parties to reach a compromise settlement and sent the case to mediation. Confidential negotiations ensued to resolve the dispute.

Should public policy preclude individuals from leaving more of their assets to nonhuman loved ones than to human family, friends or significant others?

2. In another case, a Maryland court enforced a holographic (handwritten) will provision leaving all assets to the testatrix's white Spitz dog, Master Teddy. *In re Estate of Crawford*, [No. Unkn.] (Md. Cir. Ct., Montgomery County, 1986).[1] The one-paragraph will did not designate a caretaker, provide for disposition of the remainder after the dog's death, or provide specific guidelines for Teddy's care or the assets to be used for his care. Judge L. Leonard Ruben nonetheless painstakingly assured that the testatrix's intent was effectuated. As background, the testatrix, Celeste Crawford, had been ill for some time before her death at the age of 77 in 1984. She had undergone multiple operations over a five-year period, ultimately having her leg amputated. According to Karl Feissner, the attorney who described his role as counsel for both Master Teddy and Crawford's former tenant (George Schnabble), after each operation (and until her death) Teddy spent his days on the ottoman by Crawford's chair at all times, leaving her side only when her Schnabble came to take Teddy out for a walk. Upon learning of her death and the will provision, Crawford's six siblings contested the will, arguing that they should not be forced to wait for the dog's death to inherit the proceeds from the sale of the house. In his petition filed in January 1986, counsel for Teddy and Schnabble asserted, "Teddy shall live where he is and stand as many monuments [do] to 'man's best friend.' Loyalty and love are what this will stands for — it is what we should all stand for." *Dog, Family Square Off Over House*, SUNDAY STAR-NEWS (Wilmington, N.C.), Jan. 26, 1986, at 1.

Agreeing that Teddy was "loyalty personified" (as later described by Judge Ruben), the court concluded Crawford was more than justified in leaving all her assets for Teddy's benefit. After the heirs rejected a settlement offer suggested by the

---

1. Details regarding this case and the surrounding facts were obtained from telephone interviews with Hon. L. Leonard Ruben (Ret.) and attorney Karl G. Feissner (counsel representing Master Teddy and George Schnabble in this case), on March 29, 1999 and March 25, 1999, respectively. The editors thank them for sharing their recollections.

court, the court denied their request for distribution before Teddy's death. Schnabble agreed to remain in the house to care for Teddy. In order to fully effectuate Crawford's intent, the court designated Schnabble as Teddy's caretaker, ordered him to remain living in the house with Teddy, and set a nominal rent for Schnabble to pay. The court specified that Master Teddy was to be treated as the testatrix would have treated him. The court received biannual status reports regarding Teddy's care. Further demonstrating his flexibility, when attorney Feissner one day brought Teddy to the court (as a client who could not speak for himself and had a right to be present), the judge suggested that Master Teddy might be amenable to waiting in the witness room with the option of turning on the courtroom speaker. Teddy remained there with the Sheriff during the proceedings.

Several years after that ruling, the heirs expressed concern that another white Spitz might be substituted for Master Teddy upon his death. They then sought an order that Teddy's hind leg be tattooed for identification. Schnabble and the veterinarian asserted the tattooing process would inflict needless trauma on the dog, since he could be identified by photographs and x-rays. An agreement was ultimately reached with the heirs, allowing for a thorough examination of Master Teddy (who was 13 years old at the time of the agreement) to satisfy all parties that another dog had not been substituted. In addition, according to his attorney, Teddy was "finger-printed" at the Canadian Embassy, by a noseprinting technique routinely utilized by the Royal Canadian Mounted Police.

Teddy lived a long life and Schnabble died less than one year after Teddy's death. The remainder of the estate was depleted to the extent that after Teddy's death the heirs received less than half of the original settlement offer suggested by the court and rejected by the heirs early in proceedings.

Section 2. Companion Animal Trusts

"Pet trusts," created through either common law or statutory provisions, have become frequently used vehicles for owners to ensure the continuing care of their companion animals after death or incapacitation. *See, e.g.,* Breahn Vokolek, Comment, *America Gets What it Wants: Pet Trusts and a Future for its Companion Animals,* 76 UMKC L. Rev. 1109 (2008). By 2016, all fifty states had enacted some form of pet trust statute, as discussed later in this section. This has been motivated by an increased desire to ensure the health and safety of companion animals after their owners die and because prior attempts to use the traditional law met many challenges, some of which are illustrated by the following case.

In re Estate of Russell

Supreme Court of California, 1968
70 Cal. Rptr. 561, 444 P.2d 353

SULLIVAN, Associate Justice. Georgia Nan Russell Hembree appeals from a judgment (Prob. Code, §1240) entered in proceedings for the determination of heirship (§§1080–1082) decreeing *inter alia* that under the terms of the will of Thelma L. Russell, deceased, all of the residue of her estate should be distributed to Chester H. Quinn.

Thelma L. Russell died testate on September 8, 1965, leaving a validly executed holographic will written on a small card. The front of the card reads:

"Turn the card   March 18-1957

                                I leave everything

                                I own Real &

                                Personal to Chester

                                H. Quinn & Roxy Russell

                                Thelma L. Russell"

The reverse side reads:

                                "My ($10.) Ten dollar gold

                                Piece & diamonds I leave

                                To Georgia Nan Russell.

                                Alverata, Geogia [sic]."

Chester H. Quinn was a close friend and companion of testatrix, who for over 25 years prior to her death had resided in one of the living units on her property and had stood in a relation of personal trust and confidence toward here. Roxy Russell was testatrix' pet dog which was alive on the date of the execution of testatrix' will but predeceased her. Plaintiff is testatrix' niece and her only heir-at-law.

In her petition for determination of heirship plaintiff alleges, *inter alia*, that 'Roxy Russell is an Airedale dog'; that section 27 enumerates those entitled to take by will; that 'Dogs are not included among those listed in . . . Section 27. Not even Airedale dogs'; that the gift of one-half of the residue of testatrix' estate to Roxy Russell is invalid and void; and that plaintiff was entitled to such one-half as testatrix' sole heir-at-law.

* * *

The trial court found, so far as is here material, that it was the intention of testatrix 'that Chester H. Quinn was to receive her entire estate, excepting the gold coin and diamonds bequeathed to' plaintiff and that Quinn 'was to care for the dog, Roxy Russell, in the event of Testatrix's death.' The language contained in the Will concerning the dog, Roxy Russell, was precatory in nature only, and merely indicative of the wish, desire and concern of Testatrix that Chester H. Quinn was to care for the dog, Roxy Russell, subsequent to Testatrix's death. The court concluded that testatrix intended to and did make an absolute and outright gift to Mr. Quinn of all the residue of her estate, adding: 'There occurred no lapse as to any portion of the residuary gift to Chester H. Quinn by reason of the language contained in the Will concerning the dog, Roxy Russell, such language not having the effect of being an attempted outright gift or gift in trust to the dog. The effect of such language is merely to indicate the intention of Testatrix that Chester H. Quinn was to take the entire residuary estate and to use whatever portion thereof as might be necessary to care for and maintain the dog, Roxy Russell.' Judgment was entered accordingly. This appeal followed.

Plaintiff's position before us may be summarized thusly: That the gift of one-half of the residue of the estate to testatrix' dog was clear and unambiguous; that such gift was void and the property subject thereof passed to plaintiff under the laws of intestate succession; and that the court erred in admitting the extrinsic evidence offered by Quinn but that in any event the uncontradicted evidence in the record did not cure the invalidity of the gift.

We proceed to set forth the rules here applicable which govern the interpretation of wills.

First, as we have said many times: "The paramount rule in the construction of wills, to which all other rules must yield, is that a will is to be construed according to the intention of the testator as expressed therein, and this intention must be given effect as far as possible." (*Estate of Wilson* (1920) 184 Cal. 63, 66–67.) The rule is imbedded in the Probate Code. (§ 101.) Its objective is to ascertain what the testator meant by the language he used.

When the language of a will is ambiguous or uncertain resort may be had to extrinsic evidence in order to ascertain the intention of the testator. We have said that extrinsic evidence is admissible "to explain any ambiguity arising on the face of a will, or to resolve a latent ambiguity which does not so appear." (*Estate of Torregano* (1960) 54 Cal. 2d 234, 246, citing § 105.) A latent ambiguity is one which is not apparent on the face of the will but is disclosed by some fact collateral to it.

* * *

In order to determine initially whether the terms of any written instrument are clear, definite and free from ambiguity the court must examine the instrument in the light of the circumstances surrounding its execution so as to ascertain what the parties meant by the words used. Only then can it be determined whether the seemingly clear language of the instrument is in fact ambiguous. "Words are used in an endless variety of contexts. Their meaning is not subsequently attached to them by the reader but is formulated by the writer and can only be found by interpretation in the light of all the circumstances that reveal the sense in which the writer used the words. The exclusion of parol evidence regarding such circumstances merely because the words do not appear ambiguous to the reader can easily lead to the attribution to a written instrument of a meaning that was never intended." (*Universal Sales Corp. v. California etc. Mfg. Co.* (1942) 20 Cal. 2d 751, 776 (Traynor, J., concurring).) "The court must determine the true meaning of the instrument in the light of the evidence available. It can neither exclude extrinsic evidence relevant to that determination nor invoke such evidence to write a new or different instrument." (*Laux v. Freed* (1960) 53 Cal. 2d 512, 527 (Traynor, J., concurring).)

* * *

Accordingly, we think it is self-evident that in the interpretation of a will, a court cannot determine whether the terms of the will are clear and definite in the first place until it considers the circumstances under which the will was made so that the judge may be placed in the position of the testator whose language he is interpreting. (*Cf.* Code Civ. Proc., § 1860.) Failure to enter upon such an inquiry is failure to recognize that the "ordinary standard or 'plain meaning,' is simply the meaning of the people who did not write the document." (9 Wigmore, *op.cit. supra*, § 2462, p. 191.)

* * *

As we have explained, what is here involved is a general principle of interpretation of written instruments, applicable to wills as well as to deeds and contracts. Even when the answer to the problem of interpretation is different for different kinds of written instruments, "it appears in all cases as a variation from some general doctrine." (9 Wigmore, *op.cit. supra*, § 2401, p. 7.) Under the application of this general principle in the field of wills, extrinsic evidence of the circumstances under which a will is made (except evidence expressly excluded by statute) may be considered by the court in ascertaining what the testator meant by the words used in the will. If in the light of such extrinsic evidence, the provisions of the will are reasonably susceptible of two or more meanings claimed to have been intended by the testator, "an uncertainty arises upon the face of a will" (§ 105) and extrinsic evidence relevant to prove any of such meanings is admissible (*see* § 106), subject to the restrictions imposed by statute (§ 105). If, on the other hand, in the light of such extrinsic evidence, the provisions of the will are not reasonably susceptible of two or more meanings, there is no uncertainty arising upon the face of the will (§ 105; *see Estate of Beldon* (1938) 11 Cal. 2d 108, 117; *Estate of Pierce* (1948) 32 Cal. 2d 265, 272; *Estate of Carter, supra*, 47 Cal. 2d 200, 207) and any proffered evidence attempting to show an intention different from that expressed by the words therein, giving them the only meaning to which they are reasonably susceptible, is inadmissible. In the latter case the provisions of the will are to be interpreted according to such meaning. In short, we hold that while section 105 delineates the manner of ascertaining the testator's intention "when an uncertainty arises upon the face of a will," it cannot always be determined whether the will is ambiguous or not until the surrounding circumstances are first considered.

* * *

We said in *Estate of Beldon, supra*, 11 Cal. 2d 108, 111–112, "'The making of a will raises a presumption that the testator intended to dispose of all his property.

Residuary clauses are generally inserted for the purpose of making that disposition complete, and these clauses are always to receive a broad and liberal interpretation, with a view of preventing intestacy as to any portion of the estate of the testator, and this general rule is in harmony with the declaration of our code that the provisions of a will must be construed, if possible, so as to effect that purpose.' (*O'Connor v. Murphy*, 147 Cal. 148, 153.) But there is no room for application of the rule if the testator's language, taken in the light of surrounding circumstances, will not reasonably admit of more than one construction. . . . If [testator] used language which results in intestacy, and there can be no doubt about the meaning of the language which was used, the court must hold that intestacy was intended." Therefore, if having ascertained in the instant case that the provisions of the will are not reasonably susceptible of two or more meanings, we conclude that the only meaning to which the words expressed by testatrix are reasonably susceptible results in intestacy, we must give effect to her will accordingly.

Examining testatrix will in the light of the foregoing rules, we arrive at the following conclusions: Extrinsic evidence offered by plaintiff was admitted without objection and indeed would have been properly admitted over objection to raise and resolve the latent ambiguity as to Roxy Russell and ultimately to establish that Roxy Russell was a dog. Extrinsic evidence of the surrounding circumstances was properly considered in order to ascertain what testatrix meant by the words of the will, including the words: 'I leave everything I own Real & Personal to Chester H. Quinn & Roxy Russell' or as those words can now be read 'to Chester H. Quinn and my dog Roxy Russell.'

However, viewing the will in the light of the surrounding circumstances as are disclosed by the record, we conclude that the will cannot reasonably be construed as urged by Quinn and determined by the trial court as providing that testatrix intended to make an absolute and outright gift of the entire residue of her estate to Quinn who was 'to use whatever portion thereof as might be necessary to care for and maintain the dog.' No words of the will give the entire residuum to Quinn, much less indicate that the provisions for the dog is merely precatory in nature. Such an interpretation is not consistent with a disposition which by its language leaves the residuum in equal shares to Quinn and the dog. A disposition in equal shares to two beneficiaries cannot be equated with a disposition of the whole to one of them who may use 'whatever portion thereof as might be necessary' on behalf of the other. (*See* § 104; *cf. Estate of Kearns* (1950) 36 Cal. 2d 531, 534–536.) Neither can the bare language of a gift of one-half of the residue to the dog be so expanded as to mean a gift to Quinn in trust for the care of the dog, there being no words indicating an enforceable duty upon Quinn to do so or indicating to whom the trust property is to go upon termination of the trust. 'While no particular form of expression is necessary for the creation of a trust, nevertheless some expression of intent to that end is requisite.' (*Estate of Doane, supra*, 190 Cal. 412, 415; *see* § 104; *Estate of Marti* (1901) 132 Cal. 666, 669, 61 P. 964; *Estate of McCray* (1928) 204 Cal. 399, 402; *Estate of Sargavak, supra*, 41 Cal. 2d 314, 319, citing cases.)

Accordingly, since in the light of the extrinsic evidence introduced below, the terms of the will are not reasonably susceptible of the meaning claimed by Quinn to have been intended by testatrix, the extrinsic evidence offered to show such an intention should have been excluded by the trial court. Upon an independent examination of the will we conclude that the trial court's interpretation of the terms thereof was erroneous. Interpreting the provisions relating to testatrix' residuary estate in accordance with the only meaning to which they are reasonably susceptible, we conclude that testatrix intended to make a disposition of all of the residue of the estate to Quinn and the dog in equal shares; therefore, as tenants in common. As a dog cannot be the beneficiary under a will (s 27; see 1 Page on Wills, op. cit. supra, s 17.21, p. 851) the attempted gift to Roxy Russell is void.

* * *

The judgment is reversed and the cause is remanded with directions to the trial court to set aside the findings of fact and conclusions of law; to make and file findings of fact and conclusions of law in conformity with the views herein expressed; and to enter judgment accordingly. Such findings of fact, conclusions of law and judgment shall be prepared, signed, filed and entered in the manner provided by law. Plaintiff shall recover costs on appeal.

Notes

1. For more information on the Roxy Russell case, *see* Emily Gardner, *An Ode to Roxy Russell: A Look at Hawaii's New Pet Trust Law*, 11 Haw. Bar J. 30 (2007).

2. As noted earlier, under the common law, pet trusts could be invalidated for violating the Rule Against Perpetuities and because pet trusts historically failed to meet some of the basic requirements needed to establish a trust. Over the past several decades, but before pet trust statutes were enacted, some courts responded to this barrier by finding ways to allow for "honorary pet trusts." As the next cases illustrate, however, not all such "honorary" trusts were enforceable.

In re Stewart's Estate

Common Pleas Court of Montgomery County, Pennsylvania,
Orphans Court Division, 1979
13 Pa. D. & C.3d 488

TAXIS, J. At the time of audit, the court was asked to approve a reserve of $5,000 for decedent's three cats and the consequent prepayment of several residuary bequests and to make a finding as to whether a specific residuary devise was a deemed.

Decedent died on September 27, 1978, leaving a will dated July 12, 1975 and survived by her three cats. After specifically disposing of her books, decedent left the residue of her estate in trust to her executrix for the maintenance, care and feeding of her three cats: "Preserved," the 14-year-old mother, and her two 13-year-old offspring, "Marmalade" and "Relish." Following the death of the last surviving cat, decedent devised to Georgette M. Most her real property in Tucson, Arizona; $1,000 to the Women's S.P.C.A. of Philadelphia, Pennsylvania; $1,000 to Grace Gonzales; $4,200 to Alice L. Podolyn; and the residue of the estate to Wellesley College.

The residuary estate, which is to be placed in trust, amounts approximately to $76,000, an excessive sum for the care of Preserved, Marmalade and Relish. Such a trust constitutes an honorary trust, which cannot be given effect because decedent has not named a person, corporation or association with a beneficial interest capable of enforcing the duties of the trustee. However, this does not mean that Preserved, Marmalade, and Relish should live the rest of their natural lives without adequate funds. Such would be contrary to the intent of decedent. But it is also clear that decedent intended that, after the deaths of her four-footed friends and the payment of some minor bequests, the remainder goes to Wellesley College. By requesting that contributions be made to listed funds at the College should the residuary estate exceed $15,000, decedent indicated a recognition that the better part of the estate might remain after the death of her pets. Furthermore, were the accountant to hold all of these funds in trust for the pets, greater inheritance tax would be incurred, which would be contrary to decedent's intent to benefit Wellesley College, a charity not subject to the tax.

Although such a trust cannot be given effect, there is precedent for creating a reserve of sufficient funds for the benefit of the pets, in order to accomplish the intent of the decedent and where the executrix has agreed to undertake the responsibility: *Lyon Est.*, 67 Pa. D. & C.2d 474 (1974); *Renner Est.*, 358 Pa. 409 (1948); 20 Pa. C.S.A. § 6104.

The accountant has made an arrangement with Grace Gonzales, who is a legatee under the will and who did housework for decedent for many years, to take care of Preserved, Marmalade and Relish in her home for $75 per month. In addition, to conserve the fund, the accountant has agreed to pay inheritance tax annually as the principal is consumed.

Due to inflation and the rising cost of cat food, the accountant requests that the court award to her the sum of $5,000 to be deposited by her in a savings account, subject to the condition that upon the death of the last cat, the balance shall be paid to Wellesley College. Wellesley College has agreed to the arrangement provided that they now receive the balance of the residue. The reserve fund is herewith approved.

As evidenced by satisfactions of award, the accountant has distributed $1,000 each to Grace Gonzales and the Women's S.P.C.A. of Philadelphia and $4,200 to Alice L. Rosenthal, formerly Alice L. Podolyn, which distributions, under the provisions of the will, were to have been made after the death of the last surviving cat. However, in light of the views expressed in this adjudication, the distributions are herewith approved.

* * *

Notes

1. In an effort to combat the type of common law challenges seen in the cases in this chapter, especially those regarding the enforceability of "honorary pet trusts," every state has enacted some form of statute that authorizes trusts for the care of companion animals and guides the courts in effectuating testamentary intent. The following text provides a brief summary of the various forms of statutory language relied upon or adopted by different jurisdictions.

States with pet trust statutes generally have either (i) followed the Uniform Trust Code (UTC), (ii) followed the Uniform Probate Code (UPC), or (iii) drafted laws, sometimes incorporating aspects of the UTC and UPC, and taken individualized approaches to one or more provisions of the statute.

Section 408 of the UTC provides, in relevant part:

Uniform Trust Code § 408. Trust for Care of Animal.

(a) A trust may be created to provide for the care of an animal alive during the settlor's lifetime. The trust terminates upon the death of the animal or, if the trust was created to provide for the care of more than one animal alive during the settlor's lifetime, upon the death of the last surviving animal.

(b) A trust authorized by this section may be enforced by a person appointed in the terms of the trust or, if no person is so appointed, by a person appointed by the court. A person having an interest in the welfare of the animal may request the court to appoint a person to enforce the trust or to remove a person appointed.

(c) Property of a trust authorized by this section may be applied only to its intended use, except to the extent the court determines that the value of the trust property exceeds the amount required for the intended use. Except as otherwise provided in the terms of the trust, property not required for the intended use must be distributed to the settlor, if then living, otherwise to the settlor's successors in interest.

The following states have either adopted section 408 of the Uniform Trust Code or modeled their pet trust statutes after that section: Alabama (ALA. CODE § 19-3B-408), Arkansas (ARK. CODE ANN. § 28-73-408), the District of Columbia (D.C. CODE § 19-1304.08), Florida (FLA. STAT. § 736.0408), Georgia (GA. CODE. ANN. § 53-12-28) Kansas (KAN. STAT. ANN. § 58a-408), Kentucky (KY. STAT. ANN. § 386B.4-080), Maine (ME. REV. STAT. ANN. title 18-B, § 408), Maryland (MD. EST & TRUSTS § 14-112), Massachusetts (MASS. GEN. LAWS ANN. ch. 203E, § 408), Minnesota (MINN. STAT. ANN. § 501C.0408), Mississippi (MISS. CODE ANN. § 91-8-408), Missouri (MO. ANN. STAT. § 456.4-408), Nebraska (NEB. REV. STAT. § 30-3834), New Hampshire (N.H. REV. STAT. ANN. § 564-B:4-408), New Mexico (N.M. STAT. ANN. § 46A-4-408), North Dakota (N.D. CENT. CODE § 59-12-08), Ohio (OHIO REV. CODE

Ann. §5804.08), Oregon (Or. Rev. Stat. §130.185), Pennsylvania (20 Pa. Cons. Stat. Ann. §7738), South Carolina (S.C. Code §62-7-408), Tennessee (Tenn. Code Ann. §35-15-408), Vermont (Vt. Stat. Ann. title 14A, §408), Virginia (Va. Code Ann. §55-544.08), West Virginia (W. Va. Code §44D-4-408), Wisconsin (Wis. Stat. Ann §701.0408) and Wyoming (Wyo. Stat. Ann. §4-10-409).

Section 2-907 of the UPC provides, in relevant part:

Uniform Probate Code § 2-907. Honorary Trusts; Trusts for Pets.

(a) [Honorary Trust.] Subject to subsection (c), if (i) a trust is for a specific lawful noncharitable purpose or for lawful noncharitable purposes to be selected by the trustee and (ii) there is no definite or definitely ascertainable beneficiary designated, the trust may be performed by the trustee for [21] years but no longer, whether or not the terms of the trust contemplate a longer duration.

(b) [Trust for Pets.] Subject to this subsection and subsection (c), a trust for the care of a designated domestic or pet animal is valid. The trust terminates when no living animal is covered by the trust. A governing instrument must be liberally construed to bring the transfer within this subsection, to presume against the merely precatory or honorary nature of the disposition, and to carry out the general intent of the transferor. Extrinsic evidence is admissible in determining the transferor's intent.

(c) [Additional Provisions Applicable to Honorary Trusts and Trusts for Pets.]

In addition to the provisions of subsection (a) or (b), a trust covered by either of those subsections is subject to the following provisions:

(1) Except as expressly provided otherwise in the trust instrument, no portion of the principal or income may be converted to the use of the trustee or to any use other than for the trust's purposes or for the benefit of a covered animal.

(2) Upon termination, the trustee shall transfer the unexpended trust property in the following order:

(A) as directed in the trust instrument;

(B) if the trust was created in a nonresiduary clause in the transferor's will or in a codicil to the transferor's will, under the residuary clause in the transferor's will; and

(C) if no taker is produced by the application of subparagraph (A) or (B), to the transferor's heirs under Section 2-711.

(3) For the purposes of Section 2-707, the residuary clause is treated as creating a future interest under the terms of a trust.

(4) The intended use of the principal or income can be enforced by an individual designated for that purpose in the trust instrument or, if

none, by an individual appointed by a court upon application to it by an individual.

(5) Except as ordered by the court or required by the trust instrument, no filing, report, registration, periodic accounting, separate maintenance of funds, appointment, or fee is required by reason of the existence of the fiduciary relationship of the trustee.

(6) A court may reduce the amount of the property transferred, if it determines that that amount substantially exceeds the amount required for the intended use. The amount of the reduction, if any, passes as unexpended trust property under subsection (c)(2).

(7) If no trustee is designated or no designated trustee is willing or able to serve, a court shall name a trustee. A court may order the transfer of the property to another trustee, if required to assure that the intended use is carried out and if no successor trustee is designated in the trust instrument or if no designated successor trustee agrees to serve or is able to serve. A court may also make such other orders and determinations as shall be advisable to carry out the intent of the transferor and the purpose of this section.

The following states have either adopted section 2-907 of the Uniform Probate Code or modeled their pet trust statutes after that section: Alaska (ALASKA STAT.§ 13.12.907), Arizona (ARIZ. REV. STAT.§ 14-2907), Colorado (COLO. REV. STAT. § 15-11-901), Hawaii (HAW. REV. STAT. § 560:7-501), Illinois (760 ILL. COMP. STAT. 5/15.2), Michigan (MICH. COMP. LAWS § 700.2722), Montana (MONT. CODE ANN. § 72-2-1017), North Carolina (N.C. GEN. STAT. § 36C-4-408), Rhode Island (R.I. GEN. LAWS § 4-23-1), South Dakota (S.D. CODIFIED LAWS §§ 55-1-21-55-1-22), Texas (TEX. PROP. CODE ANN. § 112.037) and Utah (UTAH CODE ANN. § 75-2-1001).

The UTC and the UPC largely mirror each other, as illustrated by the following table comparing some of their respective provisions:

Uniform Trust Code	Uniform Probate Code
A trust may be created for the care of an animal alive during the trustor's lifetime. § 408(a).	A trust for the care of a designated domestic or pet animal is valid. § 2-907(b).
The trust terminates upon the death of any covered animals. § 408(a).	The trust terminates when no living animal is covered by the trust. § 2-907(b).
The trust may be enforced by one appointed in the trust instrument or by the court. § 408(b).	The intended use can be enforced by an individual designated for that purpose in the instrument or by the court. § 2-907(c)(4).
A person having an interest in the welfare of the animal may request the court to appoint a person to enforce the trust or remove one so appointed. § 408(b).	An individual may apply to the court to have an individual designated to enforce the trust where the instrument has not designated such an individual. § 2-907(c)(4). A court may make other orders and determinations as shall be advisable to carry out the intent of the transferor. § 2-907(c)(7).

Uniform Trust Code	Uniform Probate Code
If the value of the trust exceeds the amount required for its intended use, the court may adjust it. § 408(c).	A court may reduce the amount of the property transferred if it substantially exceeds the amount required for the intended use. § 2-907(c)(6).
Unless otherwise specified in the trust instrument, excess property must be distributed to the settlor or the trustor's successors in interest. § 408(c).	Unexpended trust property must be transferred as directed in the trust instrument, or according to the trustor's will, or to the trustor's heirs, in that order. § 2-907(c)(2).

Despite the similarities between the UTC and the UPC, there are several notable differences. First, the UPC provides greater specificity as to the distribution of excess funds. When a trust fails to provide instructions for the distribution of excess funds, unexpended property under the UPC is transferred "as directed in the trust instrument, or according to the trustor's will, or to the trustor's heirs, in that order." UPC § 2-907(c)(2). The UTC, however, provides only that the court distribute excess property "to the settlor or the trustor's successors in interest." UTC § 408(c).

Second, only the UPC provides for honorary animal trusts in addition to companion animal (or pet) trusts. In general, honorary trusts are not enforceable except by statute. Where a statutory provision does exist (typically for the care of a person's pets or the maintenance of cemetery plots), it cannot extend beyond the period of the applicable state's version of the Rule Against Perpetuities, and implementation of the purposes of the trust is left to the honor of the transferee (hence the name). If he chooses not to effectuate the trust, the funds become property of the transferee. Because of these drawbacks, the UPC encourages courts to interpret pet trusts as companion animal trusts rather than honorary trusts. It does this by focusing on the trustor's intent, which generally would show a desire for the stronger provisions of the companion animal trust, and by allowing extrinsic evidence to elucidate such intent. § 2-907(b).

Third, only the UTC expressly allows a person with an interest in the welfare of the animal to petition the court to either appoint a person to enforce the trust or to remove a person already appointed. § 408(b). Under the UPC, interested individuals may only petition the court to appoint a person to enforce the trust if the trust instrument has not already designated such a person. § 2-907(c)(4). There is no provision in the UPC for an individual to petition for removal of a person designated to enforce the trust.

2. The following states have enacted pet trust statutes that are unique in at least some respects (as discussed further in the Notes that follow): California (CAL. PROB. CODE § 15212), Connecticut (CONN. GEN. STAT. ANN. § 45a-489a), Delaware (DEL. CODE ANN. title 12 § 3555), Idaho (IDAHO CODE ANN. § 15-7-601), Indiana (IND. CODE § 30-4-2-18), Iowa (IOWA CODE § 633A.2105), Louisiana (LA. REV. STAT. ANN. 9:2263), Nevada (NEV. REV. STAT. § 163.0075), New Jersey (N.J. STAT. ANN. § 3B:11-38), New York (N.Y. EST. POWERS & TRUSTS § 7-8.1),

Oklahoma (Okla. Stat. Ann. title 60, § 199), and Washington (Wash. Rev. Code §§ 11.118.005–110).

These states' statutes generally contain the following provisions in common with the UTC and the UPC: (1) the trust instrument must designate a specific purpose, animal or animals covered by the trust; (2) the trust instrument may specify an individual to enforce the terms of the trust, but failure to do so does not invalidate the trust; and (3) the court may appoint an individual to enforce the terms of the trust if the instrument fails to do so.

Several of these statutes are set forth below for purposes of comparison with the UTC and the UPC. The New York statute provides:

§ 7-8.1 Honorary trusts for pets

(a) A trust for the care of a designated domestic or pet animal is valid. The intended use of the principal or income may be enforced by an individual designated for that purpose in the trust instrument or, if none, by an individual appointed by a court upon application to it by an individual, or by a trustee. Such trust shall terminate when no living animal is covered by the trust, or at the end of twenty-one years, whichever occurs earlier.

(b) Except as expressly provided otherwise in the trust instrument, no portion of the principal or income may be converted to the use of the trustee or to any use other than for the benefit of a covered animal.

(c) Upon termination, the trustee shall transfer the unexpended trust property as directed in the trust instrument or, if there are no such directions in the trust instrument, the property shall pass to the estate of the grantor.

(d) A court may reduce the amount of the property transferred if it determines that amount substantially exceeds the amount required for the intended use. The amount of the reduction, if any, passes as unexpended trust property pursuant to paragraph (c) of this section.

(e) If no trustee is designated or no designated trustee is willing or able to serve, a court shall appoint a trustee and may make such other orders and determinations as are advisable to carry out the intent of the transferor and the purpose of this section.

N.Y. Est. Powers & Trusts Law§ 7-8.1.

The Idaho statute is not specific to animals, but provides for any kind of trust that serves a purpose the testator desires and that otherwise might not be valid under common law principles:

§ 15-7-601. Purpose Trusts.

(1) A trust may be created for any purpose, charitable or noncharitable, under the terms of a trust agreement or will. A noncharitable trust so created is a purpose trust and shall exist to serve a purpose.

(2) A purpose trust does not need a beneficiary.

(3) A purpose trust shall be enforceable on the terms set forth in the trust agreement by the person named to enforce the trust; provided however, that the failure to name a person to enforce the trust shall not void the trust or otherwise cause it to be unenforceable.

(4) A person named to enforce a purpose trust may resign or be removed or replaced in accordance with the trust.

(5) If the person named to enforce the trust resigns, or is removed, or is unwilling or unable to act, and if no successor is named in accordance with the trust, the trustee shall forthwith apply to the court having jurisdiction of the purpose trust for directions or for a person to be appointed by the court to enforce the trust. The court having jurisdiction of the purpose trust shall be empowered to make an order appointing a person to enforce the trust on such terms as it sees fit and to designate how successors will be named.

(6) During any period of time when no person is named or acting to enforce a purpose trust, the court having jurisdiction of the purpose trust shall have the right to exercise all powers necessary to enforce the trust in order to serve the purpose for which it was created.

(7) Any interested person, as defined in section 15-1-201(2[5]), Idaho Code, may bring an action under law or equity to enforce a purpose trust.

(8) Charitable trusts are not governed by this section.

(9) A purpose trust created prior to July 1, 2005, shall be valid and enforceable from the date of the trust's creation.

IDAHO CODE ANN. § 15-7-601.

In 2009, California repealed its old pet trust statute in favor of stronger provisions. Originally enacted in 1991, California's pet trust statute was much less explicit than the New York and Idaho statutes discussed above and many believed it would not have been enforceable if challenged. The former law, California Probate Code section 15212 ("Duration of Trust for Care of Animal"), merely provided:

A trust for the care of a designated domestic or pet animal may be performed by the trustee for the life of the animal, whether or not there is a beneficiary who can seek enforcement or termination of the trust and whether or not the terms of the trust contemplate a longer duration.

California's current statute (as of 2018) provides:

(a) Subject to the requirements of this section, a trust for the care of an animal is a trust for a lawful noncharitable purpose. Unless expressly provided in the trust, the trust terminates when no animal living on the date of the settlor's death remains alive. The governing instrument of the animal trust shall be liberally construed to bring the trust within this section, to presume against the merely precatory or honorary nature of the disposition, and to carry out the general intent of the settlor. Extrinsic evidence is admissible in determining the settlor's intent.

(b) A trust for the care of an animal is subject to the following requirements:

(1) Except as expressly provided otherwise in the trust instrument, the principal or income shall not be converted to the use of the trustee or to any use other than for the benefit of the animal.

(2) Upon termination of the trust, the trustee shall distribute the unexpended trust property in the following order:

(A) As directed in the trust instrument.

(B) If the trust was created in a nonresiduary clause in the settlor's will or in a codicil to the settlor's will, under the residuary clause in the settlor's will.

(C) If the application of subparagraph (A) or (B) does not result in distribution of unexpended trust property, to the settlor's heirs under Section 21114.

(3) For the purposes of Section 21110, the residuary clause described in subparagraph (B) of paragraph (2) shall be treated as creating a future interest under the terms of a trust.

(c) The intended use of the principal or income may be enforced by a person designated for that purpose in the trust instrument or, if none is designated, by a person appointed by a court. In addition to a person identified in subdivision (a) of Section 17200, any person interested in the welfare of the animal or any nonprofit charitable organization that has as its principal activity the care of animals may petition the court regarding the trust as provided in Chapter 3 (commencing with Section 17200) of Part 5.

(d) If a trustee is not designated or no designated or successor trustee is willing or able to serve, a court shall name a trustee. A court may order the transfer of the trust property to a court-appointed trustee, if it is required to ensure that the intended use is carried out and if a successor trustee is not designated in the trust instrument or if no designated successor trustee agrees to serve or is able to serve. A court may also make all other orders and determinations as it shall deem advisable to carry out the intent of the settlor and the purpose of this section.

(e) The accountings required by Section 16062 shall be provided to the beneficiaries who would be entitled to distribution if the animal were then deceased and to any nonprofit charitable corporation that has as its principal activity the care of animals and that has requested these accountings in writing. However, if the value of the assets in the trust does not exceed forty thousand dollars ($40,000), no filing, report, registration, periodic accounting, separate maintenance of funds, appointment, or fee is required by reason of the existence of the fiduciary relationship of the trustee, unless ordered by the court or required by the trust instrument.

(f) Any beneficiary, any person designated by the trust instrument or the court to enforce the trust, or any nonprofit charitable corporation that has as its principal activity the care of animals may, upon reasonable request, inspect the animal, the premises where the animal is maintained, or the books and records of the trust.

(g) A trust governed by this section is not subject to termination pursuant to subdivision (b) of Section 15408.

(h) Section 15211 does not apply to a trust governed by this section.

(i) For purposes of this section, "animal" means a domestic or pet animal for the benefit of which a trust has been established.

CAL. PROB. CODE § 15212.

The author and sponsor of the bill, Senator Leland Yee, explained the reason for upgrading the old pet trust law. "Pets are an important part of the American family . . . [The new bill] will make pet trusts enforceable and assure that the wishes of pet owners are respected." Patrick McGreevy, *New Law to Enforce Bequests for Pets*, L.A. TIMES, July 23, 2008, at 1.

3. New York, Idaho, California and all of the other states that have declined to adopt the UTC or the UPC may provide more, the same or fewer safeguards to protect a beneficiary animal's welfare by ensuring the trustor's intent is carried out. These select state provisions vary from the UTC, the UPC and each other on the following points: (1) the species or status of animals eligible for inclusion in a trust; (2) the powers of the court in overseeing and enforcing the trust; (3) who is entitled to enforce the trust; (4) who is entitled to use the trust property associated with the animals' care and protection (usually money, but sometimes real property or dwellings); (5) duration of the trust; (6) the degree of permissible involvement of interested persons or organizations; (7) construction of trust terms; and (8) admissibility of extrinsic evidence.

Animals eligible under the trust: State provisions all require the trust to designate an animal or animals to be cared for under the trust, but some contain additional eligibility requirements. Modeling its eligibility requirements after the honorary trust provision in UPC section 2-907(a), Idaho is perhaps the most inclusive in that it allows the trustor to designate any purpose for the funds. IDAHO CODE ANN. § 15-7-601(1). Mirroring UPC section 2-907(b), New York and California require beneficiary animals to be domestic or pet animals. While "domestic" may be statutorily defined in the state, possibly excluding traditionally "wild" animals, the word "pet" may allow a more subjective interpretation, which may encompass exotic animals and other non-domestic animals. Rather than limiting the type of animals who may be covered by the statutes, states like Delaware define animal as "any nonhuman member of the animal kingdom but shall exclude plants and inanimate objects" and borrow language from UTC section 408(a) requiring the animal named in the trust to be alive at the trustor's death. DEL. CODE ANN. title 12, § 3555(a); IND. CODE § 30-4-2-18(a); IOWA CODE § 633A.2105(2); NEV. REV. STAT. § 163.0075(1). Washington has declined to use language from either the UTC or the UPC, instead allowing trustors to designate any nonhuman vertebrate animal in a trust instrument. WASH. REV. CODE § 11.118.010.

Powers of the court: Courts in non-UTC or UPC states have powers similar to those conferred by the UTC and UPC. For instance, courts generally can appoint an individual to enforce the trust or to adjust the amount in trust if it substantially exceeds what is needed for the trust's stated purpose. *See, e.g.,* N.Y. EST. POWERS & TRUSTS LAW § 7-8.1(a), (d). In a revised version of UPC section 2-907(c)(7), providing blanket authorization to the court to make additional orders and determinations as necessary to carry out the intent of the trustor, some states also have directed courts to consider legislative intent in drafting the state's companion animal trust statute. CAL. PROB. CODE § 15212(d); N.J. STAT. ANN. § 3B:11-38(e); WASH. REV. CODE § 11.118.070.

Enforcement of the trust: Whether or not a state has adopted the UTC or the UPC, a trustor can designate an individual in the trust instrument to enforce the trust. If the instrument does not designate such an individual, the court may appoint one. Regarding court-appointed individuals, Nevada has adopted the UTC's approach (in section 408(b)) by allowing an individual with an interest in the animal's welfare to petition the court to appoint him or herself as trustee. NEV. REV. STAT. § 163.0075(3). Nevada provides an additional safeguard over the UTC, however, by expressly requiring a court to give preference to an individual with a demonstrated interest in the animal's welfare. *Id.* Washington's companion animal trust provision also provides an additional safeguard, allowing an individual with custody of the beneficiary animal to enforce the trust. WASH. REV. CODE § 11.118.050. By doing so, Washington expands the scope of individuals capable of enforcing the terms of the companion animal trust beyond those individuals designated in the trust or appointed by the court.

Do you think that Washington's approach goes as far as Nevada's in protecting animal welfare? Does an individual "with custody" necessarily have a demonstrated interest in the animal's welfare?

Use of property in trust: In addressing the appropriate uses of any type of property placed in trust, states have not strayed far from the language of the UTC or the UPC. Only two states have some variation on the requirement that property be applied in accordance with the terms of the trust: (1) Delaware has added the stipulation that care provided to the designated animal must be reasonable under the circumstances; and (2) Washington expressly allows the property in trust to be used to pay "reasonable compensation" to the trustee and reimburse the trustee for "reasonable costs incurred on behalf of the trust," even if the trust provides otherwise. Del. Code Ann. title 12, § 3555(f); Wash. Rev. Code § 11.118.030.

Duration of the trust: A slight majority of states that have declined to adopt the UTC or UPC have nevertheless adopted language from the model codes governing the duration of companion animal trusts. These provisions allow companion animal trusts to span the life or lives of the designated animal or animals. *See, e.g.,* Cal. Prob. Code § 15212(a). Several states have elected to retain their Rule Against Perpetuities by setting the termination date at the earlier of either the animal's death or 21 years. N.Y. Est. Powers & Trusts Law § 7-8.1(a); Iowa Code § 633A.2105(1); N.J. Stat. Ann. § 3B:11-38(a). Washington similarly has incorporated its Rule Against Perpetuities, but the statutory deadline is 150 years as opposed to 21 years. Wash. Rev. Code § 11.98.130.

Involvement of interested persons or organizations: States vary widely in the degree to which they allow interested persons or organizations to be involved in the administration or enforcement of companion animal trusts. Some states have declined to provide any such ability to petition the court. Iowa Code § 633A.2105; N.J. Stat. Ann. § 3B:11-38Similar to the UPC in this respect, New York allows an individual to apply to the court to appoint a trustee, but only where the trust instrument has failed to do so; and there is no requirement that the petitioning individual have an interest in the animal beneficiary's welfare. N.Y. Est. Powers & Trusts Law § 7-8.1(a). Unlike the UPC, however, New York's statute does not give the court power to make other orders and determinations necessary to carry out the trust. UPC § 2-907(c)(7). Thus, although stronger than the state statutes that do not provide for any such petitioning, the New York provision does little to safeguard against inadequate enforcement of the trust.

Idaho provides interested persons with greater latitude in that they may bring an action at law or equity to enforce the trust. Idaho Code Ann. § 15-7-601(7). However, "interested persons" is a defined term, limited to individuals with a property right in the trust, such as heirs would have. Idaho Code Ann. § 15-1-201(25). Such individuals may not share a concern for the beneficiary animal's welfare. The remaining non-UTC or UPC states provide greater protection for the beneficiaries—California, Delaware, Indiana, Nevada and Washington all allow persons with an interest in the welfare of the trust's designated animal or animals to petition the court regarding enforcement of the trust. Cal. Prob. Code § 15212(b)(3)(C); Del. Code Ann. title 12, § 3555(c); Ind. Code § 30-4-2-18(d); Nev. Rev. Stat. § 163.0075(3); Wash. Rev. Code § 11.118.050. Generally, states have modeled these provisions after the UTC, only allowing petitions requesting the appointment or removal of one appointed to enforce the trust. UTC § 408(b). California has elected to provide additional safeguards for the welfare of animals cared for by trusts; it grants persons or nonprofit, charitable organizations the ability to inspect animals, facilities or trust records. Cal. Prob. Code § 15212(f).

Construction of terms in the trust instrument: Some state provisions mirror the UPC's stipulation that terms in a trust instrument be construed in favor of finding a valid companion animal trust. CAL. PROB. CODE § 15212(a); NEV. REV. STAT. § 163.0075(1); WASH. REV. CODE § 11.118.080. Most non-UTC or UPC state provisions, however, are silent on the matter.

Extrinsic Evidence: Only three of the states opting out of the UTC or UPC models have expressly indicated that extrinsic evidence is allowed to determine the trustor's intent. CAL. PROB. CODE § 15212(a); WASH. REV. CODE § 11.118.080; OKLA. STAT. ANN. title 60, § 199.

4. Consider how you would assist a client in preparing a companion animal trust that would be upheld under any of the statutes discussed above. What information would you need? What contingencies would have to be anticipated? What would you recommend your client do to best ensure the client's testamentary intent will be effectuated?

5. In 2007, wealthy hotelier Leona Helmsley died, leaving $12 million to her 9-year-old dog named Trouble. A Manhattan judge later reduced Trouble's trust fund to $2 million, relying on an affidavit from the dog's caretaker that read: "Two million dollars . . . would be enough money to pay for Trouble's maintenance and welfare at the highest standards of care for more than 10 years, which is more tha[n] twice her reasonably anticipated life expectancy." Dareh Gregorian, *Screw the Pooch: Leona's Pup Loses $10M of Trust Fund*, N.Y. POST, June 16, 2008, at 3. As discussed above, the model codes and some state statutes may mandate that the courts measure the funds in a trust against the needs of designated animals. If there is no such requirement, do courts have the discretion to determine whether the amount of funds left in trust for the care of a companion animal are financially excessive? If so, what factors should be included in the determination?

Trouble died in 2011. Her caretaker had spent roughly $100,000 for her care and received $60,000 a year as payment for fulfilling his caretaker duties. The remainder of the $2 million reverted back to the Helmsley family trust.

Ms. Helmsley left most of the remainder of her estate (valued by some at $5 billion to $8 billion) to charity, providing discretion to her trustees to determine which charities should benefit. However, she also left a "mission statement" that instructed the trustees to use their discretion first for "purposes related to the provision of care of dogs" and then for "such other charitable activities as the Trustees shall determine." The story took a dramatic turn when the trustees of the estate indicated they did not intend to utilize any significant portion of the estate for animal protection. They obtained a court order granting them that authority, despite Helmsley's clear desire to have her money help dogs. *In the Matter of Helmsley*, 930 N.Y.S.2d 177 (N.Y. Surrogate's Ct., N.Y. Cty. 2009). In 2010, three animal protection groups moved to intervene in the ongoing estate case in New York, claiming an interest in ensuring Helmsley's wishes were met and a desire to have some part of her estate directed towards the welfare of dogs throughout the country. The court denied their motion, finding that they lacked standing to influence distribution of funds and reiterating that the trustees had sole discretion in that regard; the appellate court affirmed the ruling. *In the Matter of Rosenthal (as Trustees of the Leona M. and Harry B. Helmsley Charitable Trust)*, 99 A.D.3d 573 (N.Y. App. Div. 2012).

6. Hawaii safeguarded against individuals providing "unreasonable pet trust gifts to their pets" by including the following clause in its pet trust statute:

> The court may reduce the amount of the property transferred if it determines that the amount substantially exceeds the amount required for the intended use and the court finds that there will be no substantial adverse impact in the care, maintenance, health, or appearance of the designated domestic or pet animal. The amount of the reduction, if any, shall pass as unexpended trust property. . . .

HAW REV. STAT. § 560:7-501(b)(5).

7. Another method of providing for a companion animal is by creating a durable power of attorney, such as the following example:

> *Short Form of Durable Power of Attorney for Property Management [Pets] Under California Law*

> With respect to any animal that I own when this Power is executed or that is acquired thereafter, I give my attorney in fact the power to take any actions [he/she/they] believe[s] necessary or desirable in order to effectively maintain the animal, including the power to house, or to arrange for the housing, support, and maintenance of the animal, and to pay reasonable boarding, kenneling, and veterinary fees.

3 CAL. WILLS & TRUSTS § 1.13 (1997).

Chapter 9

Selected Wildlife Statutes

This chapter discusses some of the federal statutory and case law relating to the animals—unlike those covered in the rest of this casebook—who remain in a "wild" and noncaptive state.[a] The focus here is on law dealing with the attempt to protect and conserve wildlife in America and, to some extent, internationally. This is just a dip in the ocean of case law, statutes, and complex issues that arise where law and wildlife conservation meet. And this area could—and sometime does—constitute sufficient subject matter for an entire semester-long course. *See, e.g.*, Dale D. Goble & Eric T. Freyfogle, *et al.*, Wildlife Law: Cases and Materials (3d ed. 2017). This chapter provides a very brief discussion of a small sample of those laws, in order to provide a limited but hopefully meaningful glimpse into the world of wildlife law. Some of these statutes have already been touched upon in the constitutional law cases in Chapter 5, as litigation over them often involves constitutional issues.

Without question, the most significant and well-known federal animal protection law is the Endangered Species Act of 1973 (ESA), 16 U.S.C. §§ 1531–1544, discussed in the first section of the chapter, which can be a powerful and species-saving tool when properly applied. A valuable parallel is found in the Marine Mammal Protection Act of 1972, 16 U.S.C. §§ 1361–1407, which provides protections for marine mammals, and utilizes some language similar to the ESA.

The oldest wildlife protection law in America is the Lacey Act, 18 U.S.C. §§ 42-43, 16 U.S.C. §§ 3371-3378, which is discussed in the notes after the ESA section.

This chapter also discusses the Wild Free-Roaming Horses and Burros Act, 16 U.S.C. §§ 1331–1340. This law is included because, of all American wildlife, horses are among those that create the most controversy, carry the greatest emotional connection, and are most tied to America's history and formation.

A short section is also included on the National Environmental Policy Act of 1969, 42 U.S.C. §§ 4321–4347. While it is not an animal-related statute, it is a powerful tool for addressing government inaction or misfeasance and has been the basis for discussion earlier in the text. Along with the Administrative Procedure Act (which was the basis for cases discussed in Chapter 5 and is discussed in more detail

---

a. Compare the Animal Welfare Act, discussed in Chapter 6, which deals to some degree with captive "wild" animals (in commercial use, research, and display situations like zoos and aquariums), who are no longer living in the wild.

in the Notes after *Sierra Club v. Morton*), it is one of the most commonly used statutes in environmental and animal law cases. As you saw with several of the constitutional law cases in Chapter 5, some of the lawsuits brought to protect wildlife include claims under more than one of the foregoing statutes (and others not discussed here), depending on the species at risk and the factual setting of the case.

Some other statutes of note (not addressed here) are: African Elephant Conservation Act, 16 U.S.C. §§4201–424; Chimpanzee Health Improvement, Maintenance and Protection Act, 42 U.S.C. §287a-3a (discussed in Chapter 6); Magnuson-Stevens Fishery Conservation and Management Act, 16 U.S.C. 1801 § *et seq.*; Fish and Wildlife Conservation Act, 16 U.S.C. §§2901–2912 (2013); Migratory Bird Conservation Act, 16 U.S.C. §§715–715s; and Wild Bird Conservation Act, 16 U.S.C. §§4901–4916.

Section 1. Endangered Species Act

The Endangered Species Act of 1973 (ESA), 16 U.S.C. §§1531–1544, was signed by President Richard Nixon on December 28, 1973, and passed both houses of Congress by wide margins (390–12 in the House and 92–0 in the Senate). Although there had been prior laws protecting species in danger of extinction, the law Nixon signed was the strongest and broadest species protection bill to date; it covered not only all potentially endangered species (as opposed to prior laws which protected only vertebrates, mollusks and crustaceans) but also subspecies and even discrete populations within a species. It is designed to protect wildlife and their habitats (including resident flora) for the sake of biodiversity. The ESA's protections only extend to those species which are formally listed as "threatened" or "endangered," *id.* §1531(b) — distinct classifications for which the Act often accords essentially the same degree of protection. *Id.* §1533(d); *see also* Michael J. Bean & Melanie J. Rowland, THE EVOLUTION OF NATIONAL WILDLIFE LAW 201–202 (3d ed. 1997).

The ESA defines a "threatened species" as "any species which is likely to become an endangered species within the foreseeable future throughout all or a significant portion of its range." *Id.* §1532(20). Section 3(6) defines an "endangered species" as "any species which is in danger of extinction throughout all or a significant portion of its range . . ." *Id.* §1532(6). The term "significant portion of its range" has been a subject of much debate and judicial evaluation. *See, e.g., Humane Society of the United States v. Zinke*, 865 F.3d 585 (D.C. Cir. 2017), excerpted in this section.

The ESA also notably protects "any habitat of such species which is . . . considered to be critical habitat" and is designated as such under the Act. 16 U.S.C. §§1531(b)-(c), 1533(a)(3). "Critical habitat" is defined as:

> (i) the specific areas within the geographical area occupied by the species, at the time it is listed in accordance with the provisions of section 1533 of this title, on which are found those physical or biological features (I) essential to the conservation of the species and (II) which may require special management considerations or protection; and

(ii) specific areas outside the geographical area occupied by the species at the time it is listed in accordance with the provisions of section 1533 of this title, upon a determination . . . that such areas are essential for the conservation of the species.

Id. § 1532(5)(A).

The Supreme Court has declared that the ESA is "the most comprehensive legislation for the preservation of endangered species ever enacted by any nation." *Tennessee Valley Auth. v. Hill,* 437 U.S. 153, 180 (1978). It is intended "to provide a means whereby the ecosystems upon which endangered species and threatened species depend may be conserved, [and] to provide a program for the conservation of such endangered species and threatened species." 16 U.S.C. § 1531(b). The "plain intent of Congress in enacting this statute was to halt and reverse the trend toward species extinction, whatever the cost." *Defenders of Wildlife v. Babbitt,* 130 F. Supp. 2d 121, 124 (D.D.C. 2001) (internal quotes omitted). The U.S. Fish and Wildlife Service (FWS) must use "'all methods and procedures which are necessary to bring any [listed] species to the point at which the measures provided pursuant to this Act are no longer necessary.'" *Defenders of Wildlife v. Salazar,* 729 F. Supp. 2d 1207, 1210 (D. Mont. 2010) (quoting 16 U.S.C. § 1532(3)). The battleground for ESA litigants often focuses on a species' qualification for classification as a protected species, on the measures taken by the federal government to engage in appropriate conservation measures, and on efforts by FWS to limit the reach of the ESA.

Under the ESA, the responsibility for listing species and designating their critical habitat is split between the Secretary of the Interior—whose authority to list species is delegated to the FWS—and the Secretary of Commerce—who delegates to the National Marine Fisheries Service (NMFS). *See id.* § 1533(a).[b] For listing decisions, the Secretary of the Interior has jurisdiction over all threatened and endangered species, except those species over which the Secretary of Commerce was granted jurisdiction by an executive reorganization in 1970. NMFS oversees most marine species, including anadromous fish (fish that migrate from freshwater to saltwater), but excepting marine birds and sea otters.

The discretion of the Secretary of Commerce, *i.e.,* NMFS, to make determinations regarding listings is somewhat limited. NMFS decisions to *remove* a species from the threatened or endangered lists or to demote a species' listing classification from "endangered" to "threatened" must be approved by the Secretary of the Interior, although NMFS decisions to list a species or to upgrade its classification from "threatened" to "endangered" are not subject to such review. *Id.* § 1533(a)(2); *see also* 50 C.F.R. §§ 17.1-.3, 17.11-.12.

Listings, revisions to listing status and delistings may be instigated by either the proper Secretary/Service or any "interested person" who petitions the appropriate

---

b. Despite the Secretaries' delegation of their power to list species to the Services, all references in the ESA to listing matters are to the "Secretary," meaning the appropriate Secretary. *Id.* § 1532(15).

Secretary. 16 U.S.C. § 1533(a)-(b). In the case of a petition from outside the agency, the concerned Secretary must, within ninety days of receiving the petition, "[t]o the maximum extent practicable, . . . make a finding as to whether the petition presents substantial scientific or commercial information indicating that the petitioned action may be warranted" and must "promptly publish . . . in the Federal Register" each finding made pursuant to this process. *Id.* § 1533(b)(3)(A). If the petition contains such "substantial" information, then the Secretary must "promptly commence a review of the status of the species concerned." *Id.* Within twelve months of receipt of a petition requesting a change in listing status (either adding a species to the list, "uplisting," "downlisting," or "delisting"), the Secretary must assign one of the three following designations to the petitioned action: (i) not warranted, (ii) warranted, or (iii) "warranted, but . . . precluded" by inadequate resources to proceed with the proposal because of other "pending proposals [on which] expeditious progress is being made." *Id.* § 1533(b)(3)(B). The findings must be published in the Federal Register and, in the case of a petitioned action found to be "warranted," accompanied by "the complete text of a proposed regulation to implement such action." *Id.*

If the Secretary decides that a petitioned action is "warranted but precluded," that decision must be reviewed annually in order to reassess whether the proposal can yet be implemented. If a petitioned action is determined to be "warranted," then the Secretary must, within another twelve months, render and publish in the Federal Register either (1) a final regulation to implement the warranted action, or (2) "notice that the proposed regulation is being withdrawn" under section 1533(b)(6)(B)(ii), together with the finding on which such withdrawal is based.[c] *Id.* § 1533(b)(6)(A).

Section 4 of the ESA requires the Secretaries to base their final decisions about whether to list a species as threatened or endangered exclusively on the "best scientific and commercial data available." *Id.* § 1533(b)(1)(A). For an analysis of the application of this standard and a proposal for improved scientific peer review process under ESA section 4, see Joanna Wymyslo, *Legitimizing Peer Review in ESA Listing Decisions,* 33 ENVIRONS ENVTL. L. & POL'Y J. 135 (Fall 2009). Similarly, the Secretaries must base decisions about whether, under section 4(a)(3), a habitat should be designated "critical" (*i.e.,* essential to the conservation of threatened or endangered species) on the "best scientific data available . . . taking into consideration the economic impact, and any other relevant impact, of specifying any particular area as critical habitat." 16 U.S.C. § 1533(b)(2).

Once a species is listed as threatened or endangered, the ESA offers several different forms of protection. Section 4 mandates that the Secretary of the Interior develop and execute "recovery plans" for listed species. *Id.* § 1533(f)(1). These plans,

---

c. Under section 4(b)(6)(B), the Secretary has the option to extend this period for an additional six months in order to gather more data to try to resolve a "substantial disagreement regarding the sufficiency or accuracy of the available data relevant to the [proposed action] concerned." *Id.* § 1533(b)(6)(B).

which are designed to improve the health and viability of the species in order to (ide-ally) get the species at issue removed from the threatened or endangered list, call for government agencies and private parties to coordinate their efforts "for the conser-vation and survival of [listed] species." *Id.* In theory, such plans are to be instituted for each listed species, with the Secretary "giv[ing] priority to those endangered species or threatened species, without regard to taxonomic classification, that are most likely to benefit from such plans, particularly those species that are, or may be, in conflict with construction or other development projects or other forms of eco-nomic activity." *Id.* § 1533(f)(1)(A). In practice, however, these plans have become a generally impotent legal option—plans have actually been implemented for very few species, which may be attributable to Congress' failure to appropriate sufficient capital to adequately fund all of the plans. *See* J.B. Ruhl, *Section 7(a)(1) of the "New" Endangered Species Act: Rediscovering and Redefining the Untapped Power of Federal Agencies' Duty to Conserve Species*, 25 ENVTL. L. 1107, 1111, 1115 & nn.13, 35 (1995).

Section 7(a)(1) requires all federal agencies to implement programs to conserve listed species, 16 U.S.C. § 1536(a)(1), but like its section 4 counterpart, section 7(a)(1) has not had wide-ranging effect. *See* Bean & Rowland, *supra*, at 236; Ruhl, *supra*, at 1125–28. As a parallel, under section 7(a)(2), all federal agencies undertaking actions that may impact endangered species are required to consult with the Secre-tary to ensure that their activities are "not likely to jeopardize the continued exis-tence of any endangered species or threatened species or result in the destruction or adverse modification of [critical] habitat of such species. . . ." 16 U.S.C. § 1536(a)(2). Section 7(a)(1) broadly requires federal agencies to affirmatively carry out general (*i.e.*, non-event-specific) conservation programs. *Id.* § 1536(a)(1). Section 7(a)(2) is more limited in scope than section 7(a)(1), as section 7(a)(2) applies only to individual actions by federal agencies and thus cannot extend its prohibitions (on "jeopardy") beyond such particular agency actions. *Id.* § 1536(a)(2). Although sec-tion 7(a)(2) theoretically offers a much narrower reach than section 7(a)(1), the for-mer has proven to be infinitely more effective than the latter in that litigation under section 7 has been dominated by cases brought under subsection (a)(2), almost to the exclusion of claims under subsection (a)(1), as discussed below. *See generally* Bean & Rowland, *supra*, at 235–51.

Section 7(a)(1) has garnered a reputation as "the monumental underachiever of the ESA family," Ruhl, *supra*, at 1128, and the sparseness of meaningful case law wholly supports this critical characterization. *See* Bean & Rowland, *supra*, at 236. There are surprisingly few cases in which section 7(a)(1) has been invoked as the basis for a claim and, of these cases, almost none have addressed the section in a way that gives it any meaning, if not force. *Id.* at 236–39. However, a few cases have accorded section 7(a)(1) some substantive interpretation, albeit of limited favor to environmental advocates. Representative of this class of exceptions to the trend of neglecting—through either downplaying or excluding—section 7(a)(1) is *Pyramid Lake Paiute Tribe of Indians v. U.S. Dept. of the Navy*, 898 F.2d 1410 (9th Cir. 1990). In that case, the court concluded that in leasing acreage and adjoining water rights to local farmers "the Navy's reliance on the FWS biological 'no jeopardy' opinions was not arbitrary and capricious under section 7(a)(2) of the Act. Therefore, its refusal to adopt [an] alternative proposal for operation of the outlease program did not violate its affirmative obligation to conserve [the concerned] endangered species under section 7(a)(1) of the Act." *Id.* at 1421. The Ninth Circuit granted substantial deference to agency discretion "in deciding how to fulfill its duty to conserve" pursuant to section 7(a)(1) because the agency had taken at least *some* action. *Id.* at 1418.

Compare *Pyramid Lake* with *Florida Key Deer v. Stickney*, 864 F. Supp. 1222 (S.D. Fla. 1994), in which the federal district court concluded that the Federal Emergency Management Agency (FEMA) violated both section 7(a)(1), by failing to consider or undertake any action to fulfill its mandatory obligations under the ESA to conserve endangered species of deer allegedly harmed by the National Flood Insurance Program (NFIP) and section 7(a)(2), by failing to consult with the FWS as required by ESA, even after the FWS made a formal request for consultation on impact of the NFIP. The court held the agency had not discharged its responsibility under section 7(a)(1) since it had "failed to consider or undertake *any* action to fulfill its mandatory obligations under [the section]." *Id.* at 1238. (Emphasis in original.) *See also Florida Key Deer v. Paulison*, 522 F.3d 1133 (11th Cir. 2008) (later iteration of same case, affirming injunction of FEMA's issuance of new flood insurance without compliance with ESA). As *Pyramid Lake* suggests, where section 7(a)(1) has been examined by the courts, the results tend to parallel the presumed conclusions that would be reached under a section 7(a)(2) challenge. *See* Bean & Rowland, *supra*, at 237–38; *see generally* Ruhl, *supra*, at 1125–35.

Section 7(a)(1) retains substantial potential as a tool for compelling comprehensive restoration of listed species. *See* Oliver A. Houck, *The Endangered Species Act and Its Implementation by the U.S. Departments of Interior & Commerce*, 64 U. COLO. L. REV. 277, 327–28 & n.333 (1993). *Pyramid Lake* may have reduced the ESA's potential effect when it held "some discretion should be allowed" to federal agencies in fulfilling their obligations in this respect. 898 F.2d at 1418. However, "in the absence of firm guidance by the biological agencies, there is [still] considerable leeway as to what [section 7(a)(1)'s exact effect on conservation activities] will be." Houck, *supra*, at 327–28. *Pyramid Lake* may explain why section 7(a)(1) continues to be regarded as the "sleeping giant" of the ESA, Ruhl, *supra*, at 1109, and why its obligations "remain[] unclear and relatively unexplored." Bean & Rowland, *supra*, at 239. Section 7(a)(2), on the other hand, may be regarded as "the single most significant provision of the [ESA]." *Id.* at 240. The large body of case law examining section 7(a)(2) supports this description.

Similarly, section 9 of the ESA is considered by some as "[t]he most powerful regulatory consequence to flow from species listing," and "perhaps the most powerful regulatory provision in all of environmental law." Ruhl, *supra*, at 1115. Section 9 extends the ESA's coverage to private and public actors, and asserts no "person"— defined as all private and public entities, whether individuals or organizations— can "import[,] ... export[,] ... take[,] ... possess, sell, deliver, carry, transport, or ship" any endangered species of wildlife. 16 U.S.C. § 1538(a)(1). "Take" is defined expansively to mean "to harass, harm, pursue, hunt, shoot, wound, kill, trap, capture, or collect, or to attempt to engage in any such conduct." *Id.* § 1532(19).

Section 11 is the Act's enforcement mechanism. It authorizes citizen suits to be filed against any person who allegedly violated the Act, including the Secretaries of Interior and Commerce, when they perform in a nondiscretionary capacity. *Id.* § 1540(g). Examples of applicable acts are: (1) decisions to deny petitioned action regarding the listing of a species—*i.e.*, findings per section 4 that the proposed action is either not warranted or "warranted but precluded," *id.* § 1533(b)(3)(c)(ii); and (2) section 9's prohibition on takings. *Id.* § 1538(a)(1). Section 11 provides both civil and criminal penalties for violations. *Id.* § 1540. Civil penalties include damages of up to $25,000 per violation, *id.* § 1540(a), as well as a discretionary award of attorneys' fees to the prevailing party. *Id.* § 1540(g)(4). Criminal penalties are fines of up to $50,000 and/or up to one year in prison per violation. *Id.* § 1540(b).

Entire texts, treatises and casebooks have been written on the ESA, and the body of relevant law and scholarly commentary is extensive and complex. The presentation here is intended to provide only a brief overview/introduction to a few of the general concepts and overriding considerations.

The following case established the power of the ESA. The Secretary of the Interior, in response to petitions by scientists and environmentalists, found that completion of a major federal project, the construction of the Tellico Dam in the Tennessee Valley, would gravely imperil the survival of a three-inch long fish in the perch family known as the snail darter. The dam was nearly completed when the fish was discovered living in the river that would be impacted by the project, and the ESA had just recently been enacted. The Secretary listed the snail darter as an endangered species and declared the Little Tennessee River was a critical habitat of the fish. Plaintiffs in the case excerpted below sued to enjoin completion of the dam. The district court denied relief and dismissed the complaint on the ground that it was inequitable to halt the work so near to completion. The Court of Appeals reversed, holding that the record revealed a *prima facie* violation of ESA section 7 and that the equities could not override the Congressional mandate to protect endangered species and habitat. The U.S. Supreme Court then issued its opinion, as excerpted below.

Tennessee Valley Authority v. Hill

Supreme Court of the United States, 1978
437 U.S. 153, 98 S. Ct. 2279

MR. CHIEF JUSTICE BURGER delivered the opinion of the Court.

The questions presented in this case are (a) whether the Endangered Species Act of 1973 requires a court to enjoin the operation of a virtually completed federal dam—which had been authorized prior to 1973—when, pursuant to authority vested in him by Congress, the Secretary of the Interior has determined that operation of the dam would eradicate an endangered species; and (b) whether continued congressional appropriations for the dam after 1973 constituted an implied repeal of the Endangered Species Act, at least as to the particular dam.

* * *

I

Until recently the finding of a new species of animal life would hardly generate a cause célèbre. This is particularly so in the case of darters, of which there are approximately 130 known species, 8 to 10 of these having been identified only in the last five years. The moving force behind the snail darter's sudden fame came some four months after its discovery, when the Congress passed the Endangered Species Act of 1973 (Act), 87 Stat. 884, 16 U.S.C. § 1531 *et seq.* (1976 ed.). This legislation, among other things, authorizes the Secretary of the Interior to declare species of animal life "endangered" and to identify the "critical habitat" of these creatures. When a species or its habitat is so listed, the following portion of the Act—relevant here—becomes effective:

> "The Secretary [of the Interior] shall review other programs administered by him and utilize such programs in furtherance of the purposes of this chapter. All other Federal departments and agencies shall, in consultation with and with the assistance of the Secretary, utilize their authorities in furtherance of the purposes of this chapter by carrying out programs for the conservation of endangered species and threatened species listed pursuant to section 1533 of this title and *by taking such action necessary to insure that actions authorized, funded, or carried out by them do not jeopardize the continued existence of such endangered species and threatened species or result in the destruction or modification of habitat of such species* which is determined by the Secretary, after consultation as appropriate with the affected States, to be critical."

16 U.S.C. § 1536 (1976 ed.) (emphasis added).

* * *

II

We begin with the premise that operation of the Tellico Dam will either eradicate the known population of snail darters or destroy their critical habitat. Petitioner does not now seriously dispute this fact ... As we have seen, the Secretary promulgated regulations which declared the snail darter an endangered species whose critical habitat would be destroyed by creation of the Tellico Reservoir. Doubtless petitioner would prefer not to have these regulations on the books, but there is no suggestion that the Secretary exceeded his authority or abused his discretion in issuing the regulations. Indeed, no judicial review of the Secretary's determinations has ever been sought and hence the validity of his actions are not open to review in this Court.

Starting from the above premise, two questions are presented: (a) would TVA be in violation of the Act if it completed and operated the Tellico Dam as planned?

(b) if TVA's actions would offend the Act, is an injunction the appropriate remedy for the violation? For the reasons stated hereinafter, we hold that both questions must be answered in the affirmative.

(A)

It may seem curious to some that the survival of a relatively small number of three-inch fish among all the countless millions of species extant would require the permanent halting of a virtually completed dam for which Congress has expended more than $100 million. The paradox is not minimized by the fact that Congress continued to appropriate large sums of public money for the project, even after congressional Appropriations Committees were apprised of its apparent impact upon the survival of the snail darter. We conclude, however, that the explicit provisions of the Endangered Species Act require precisely that result.

One would be hard pressed to find a statutory provision whose terms were any plainer than those in § 7 of the Endangered Species Act. Its very words affirmatively command all federal agencies *"to insure* that actions *authorized, funded, or carried out* by them do not *jeopardize* the continued existence" of an endangered species or *"result* in the destruction or modification of habitat of such species...." 16 U.S.C. § 1536 (1976 ed.). (Emphasis added.) This language admits of no exception. Nonetheless, petitioner urges, as do the dissenters, that the Act cannot reasonably be interpreted as applying to a federal project which was well under way when Congress passed the Endangered Species Act of 1973. To sustain that position, however, we would be forced to ignore the ordinary meaning of plain language. It has not been shown, for example, how TVA can close the gates of the Tellico Dam without "carrying out" an action that has been "authorized" and "funded" by a federal agency. Nor can we understand how such action will *"insure"* that the snail darter's habitat is not disrupted.[18] Accepting the Secretary's determinations, as we must, it is clear that TVA's proposed operation of the dam will have precisely the opposite effect, namely the *eradication* of an endangered species.

Concededly, this view of the Act will produce results requiring the sacrifice of the anticipated benefits of the project and of many millions of dollars in public funds.[19]

---

18. In dissent, Mr. JUSTICE POWELL argues that the meaning of "actions" in § 7 is "far from 'plain,'" and that "it seems evident that the 'actions' referred to are not all actions that an agency can ever take, but rather actions that the agency is deciding whether to authorize, to fund, or to carry out."... Aside from this bare assertion, however, no explanation is given to support the proffered interpretation. This recalls Lewis Carroll's classic advice on the construction of language: "'When I use a word,' Humpty Dumpty said, in rather a scornful tone, 'it means just what I choose it to mean—neither more nor less.'" Through the Looking Glass, in The Complete Works of Lewis Carroll 196 (1939).

19. The District Court determined that failure to complete the Tellico Dam would result in the loss of some $53 million in nonrecoverable obligations. Respondents dispute this figure, and point to a recent study by the General Accounting Office, which suggests that the figure could be considerably less. The GAO study also concludes that TVA and Congress should explore alternatives to impoundment of the reservoir, such as the creation of a regional development program based on

But examination of the language, history and structure of the legislation under review here indicates beyond doubt that Congress intended endangered species to be afforded the highest of priorities.

When Congress passed the Act in 1973, it was not legislating on a clean slate. The first major congressional concern for the preservation of the endangered species had come with passage of the Endangered Species Act of 1966, 80 Stat. 926, repealed, 87 Stat. 903.[20] In that legislation Congress gave the Secretary power to identify "the names of the species of native fish and wildlife found to be threatened with extinction," §1(c), 80 Stat. 926, as well as authorization to purchase land for the conservation, protection, restoration, and propagation of "selected species" of "native fish and wildlife" threatened with extinction. §§2(a)–(c), 80 Stat. 926–927. Declaring the preservation of endangered species a national policy, the 1966 Act directed all federal agencies both to protect these species and "*insofar as is practicable and consistent with the[ir] primary purposes,* preserve the habitats of such threatened species on lands under their jurisdiction." *Id.* (Emphasis added.) The 1966 statute was not a sweeping prohibition on the taking of endangered species, however, except on federal lands, §4 (c), 80 Stat. 928, and even in those federal areas the Secretary was authorized to allow the hunting and fishing of endangered species. §4(d)(1), 80 Stat. 928.

* * *

In shaping legislation to deal with the problem thus presented, Congress started from the finding that "[t]he two major causes of extinction are hunting and destruction of natural habitat."

* * *

Witnesses recommended, among other things, that Congress require all landmanaging agencies "to avoid damaging critical habitat for endangered species and to take positive steps to improve such habitat." 1973 House Hearings 241 (Statement of Director of Mich. Dept. of Natural Resources).

* * *

As it was finally passed, the Endangered Species Act of 1973 represented the most comprehensive legislation for the preservation of endangered species ever enacted

---

a free-flowing river. None of these considerations are relevant to our decision, however; they are properly addressed to the Executive and Congress.

20. Prior federal involvement with endangered species had been quite limited. For example, the Lacey Act of 1900, 31 Stat. 187, partially codified in 16 U.S.C. §§667e and 701 (1976 ed.), and the Black Bass Act of 1926, 44 Stat. 576, as amended, 16 U.S.C. §851, *et seq.* (1976 ed.), prohibited the transportation in interstate commerce of fish or wildlife taken in violation of national, state, or foreign law. The effect of both of these statutes was constrained, however, by the fact that prior to passage of the Endangered Species Act of 1973, there were few laws regulating these creatures. The Migratory Bird Treaty Act, passed in 1918, 40 Stat. 755, as amended, 16 U.S.C. §703, *et seq.* (1976 ed.), was more extensive, giving the Secretary of the Interior power to adopt regulations for the protection of migratory birds. Other measures concentrated on establishing refuges for wildlife.

by any nation. Its stated purposes were "to provide a means whereby the ecosystems upon which endangered species and threatened species depend may be conserved," and "to provide a program for the conservation of such . . . species. . . ." In furtherance of these goals, Congress expressly stated in § 2(c) that "all Federal departments and agencies *shall* seek to *conserve endangered species* and threatened species. . . ." Lest there be any ambiguity as to the meaning of this statutory directive, the Act specifically defined "conserve" as meaning "to use and the use of *all methods and procedures which are necessary* to bring *any endangered species* or threatened species to the point at which the measures provided pursuant to this chapter are no longer necessary." Aside from § 7, other provisions indicated the seriousness with which Congress viewed this issue: Virtually all dealings with endangered species, including taking, possession, transportation, and sale, were prohibited, except in extremely narrow circumstances. The Secretary was also given extensive power to develop regulations and programs for the preservation of endangered and threatened species.[25] Citizen involvement was encouraged by the Act, with provisions allowing interested persons to petition the Secretary to list a species as endangered or threatened, and bring civil suits in United States district courts to force compliance with any provision of the Act . . .

* * *

The plain intent of Congress in enacting this statute was to halt and reverse the trend toward species extinction, whatever the cost. This is reflected not only in the stated policies of the Act, but in literally every section of the statute. All persons, including federal agencies, are specifically instructed not to "take" endangered species, meaning that no one is "to harass, harm,[30] pursue, hunt, shoot, wound, kill, trap, capture, or collect" such life forms. Agencies in particular are directed by §§ 2(c) and 3(2) of the Act to "use . . . all methods and procedures which are necessary" to preserve endangered species. In addition, the legislative history undergirding § 7 reveals an explicit congressional decision to require agencies to afford first priority to the declared national policy of saving endangered species. The pointed omission of the type of qualifying language previously included in endangered species legislation reveals a conscious decision by Congress to give endangered species priority over the "primary missions" of federal agencies.

---

25. A further indication of the comprehensive scope of the 1973 Act lies in Congress' inclusion of "threatened species" as a class deserving federal protection. Threatened species are defined as those which are "likely to become an endangered species within the foreseeable future throughout all or a significant portion of [their] range."

30. We do not understand how TVA intends to operate Tellico Dam without "harming" the snail darter. The Secretary of the Interior has defined the term "harm" to mean "an act or omission which actually injures or kills wildlife, including acts which annoy it to such an extent as to significantly disrupt essential behavioral patterns, which include, but are not limited to, breeding, feeding, or sheltering; *significant environmental modification or degradation which has such effects is included within the meaning of 'harm.'*" 50 C.F.R. § 17.3 (1976) (emphasis added).

It is not for us to speculate, much less act, on whether Congress would have altered its stance had the specific events of this case been anticipated. In any event, we discern no hint in the deliberations of Congress relating to the 1973 Act that would compel a different result than we reach here.

* * *

(B)

Having determined that there is an irreconcilable conflict between operation of the Tellico Dam and the explicit provisions of § 7 of the Endangered Species Act, we must now consider what remedy, if any, is appropriate. It is correct, of course, that a federal judge sitting as a chancellor is not mechanically obligated to grant an injunction for every violation of law. This Court made plain in *Hecht Co. v. Bowles*, 321 U.S. 321, 329 (1944), that "[a] grant of *jurisdiction* to issue compliance orders hardly suggests an absolute duty to do so under any and all circumstances." As a general matter it may be said that "[s]ince all or almost all equitable remedies are discretionary, the balancing of equities and hardships is appropriate in almost any case as a guide to the chancellor's discretion." Thus, in *Hecht Co.* the Court refused to grant an injunction when it appeared from the District Court findings that "the issuance of an injunction would have 'no effect by way of insuring better compliance in the future' and would [have been] 'unjust' to [the] petitioner and not 'in the public interest.'"

But these principles take a court only so far. Our system of government is, after all, a tripartite one, with each branch having certain defined functions delegated to it by the Constitution. While "[i]t is emphatically the province and duty of the judicial department to say what the law is," *Marbury v. Madison*, 1 Cranch 137, 177 (1803), it is equally—and emphatically—the exclusive province of the Congress not only to formulate legislative policies and mandate programs and projects, but also to establish their relative priority for the nation. Once Congress, exercising its delegated powers, has decided the order of priorities in a given area, it is for the Executive to administer the laws and for the courts to enforce them when enforcement is sought.

Here we are urged to view the Endangered Species Act "reasonably," and hence shape a remedy "that accords with some modicum of common sense and the public weal." . . . But is that our function? We have no expert knowledge on the subject of endangered species, much less do we have a mandate from the people to strike a balance of equities on the side of the Tellico Dam. Congress has spoken in the plainest of words, making it abundantly clear that the balance has been struck in favor of affording endangered species the highest of priorities, thereby adopting a policy which it described as "institutionalized caution."

Our individual appraisal of the wisdom or unwisdom of a particular course consciously selected by the Congress is to be put aside in the process of interpreting a statute. Once the meaning of an enactment is discerned and its constitutionality determined, the judicial process comes to an end. We do not sit as a committee of review, nor are we vested with the power of veto. The lines ascribed to Sir Thomas More by Robert Bolt are not without relevance here:

> The law, Roper, the law. I know what's legal, not what's right. And I'll stick to what's legal. . . . I'm *not* God. The currents and eddies of right and wrong, which you find such plain-sailing, I can't navigate, I'm no voyager. But in the thickets of the law, oh there I'm a forester. . . . What would you do? Cut a great road through the law to get after the Devil? . . . And when the last law was down, and the Devil turned round on you — where would you hide, Roper, the laws all being flat? . . . this country's planted thick with laws from coast to coast — Man's laws, not God's — and if you cut them down . . . d'you really think you could stand upright in the winds that would blow them? . . . yes, I'd give the Devil benefit of law, for my own safety's sake.

R. Bolt, *A Man for All Seasons*, Act I, p. 147 (Three Plays, Heinemann ed. 1967).

We agree with the Court of Appeals that in our constitutional system the commitment to the separation of powers is too fundamental for us to pre-empt congressional action by judicially decreeing what accords with "common sense and the public weal." Our Constitution vests such responsibilities in the political branches.

Notes

1. *TVA v. Hill* remains the leading case on the sanctity and force of the Endangered Species Act, despite forty years of efforts to force a judicial posture more in favor of a balancing of interests. And while many exceptions and limitations have been imposed on what seemed like the plain language of the Act, in some cases it continues to be the reason hundreds of species have a chance of survival.

2. In the real world of competing environmental and economic interests, the process of listing a species for ESA protection usually involves high-stakes political and legal battles. Theoretically, however, the decision hinges solely on scientific data. "The Act was amended in 1982 to ensure that the decision whether to list a species as endangered or threatened was based solely on an evaluation of the biological risks faced by the species, to the exclusion of all other factors." *Northern Spotted Owl v. Hodel*, 716 F. Supp. 479, 480 (W.D. Wash. 1988); 16 U.S.C. § 1533(b)(1)(A) (FWS must make listing determinations "solely on the basis of the best scientific and commercial data available . . ."); *Friends of Blackwater v. Salazar*, 691 F.3d 428, 432 (D.C. Cir. 2012) (the FWS is limited to consideration of the factors set up by the ESA and applicable regulations). In that case, involving the listing of the northern spotted owl, the court noted that "the ESA directs the Secretary of the Interior to determine whether any species have become endangered or threatened due to habitat destruction, overutilization, disease or predation, or other natural or manmade factors." *Id.* The court described the FWS's role in the listing process as follows: "The Service's role in deciding whether to list the northern spotted owl as endangered or

threatened is to assess the technical and scientific data in the administrative record against the relevant listing criteria in section 4(a)(1) and then to exercise its own expert discretion in reaching its decision." *Id.* at 481.

In *Northern Spotted Owl*, the FWS had assembled a panel of biologists to assess the viability of the owl population. The biologists concluded that continued harvesting of old growth trees in the Olympic Peninsula of Washington and Coast Range of Oregon would "likely lead to the extinction of the subspecies in the foreseeable future. . . ." *Id.* Despite this expert opinion, the FWS concluded that the owl population was viable, and decided not to list the species for ESA protection. The court held:

> The Service has failed to provide its own or other expert analysis supporting its conclusions. Such analysis is necessary to establish a rational connection between the evidence presented and the Service's decision. Accordingly, the United States Fish and Wildlife Service's decision not to list at this time the northern spotted owl as endangered or threatened under the Endangered Species Act was arbitrary and capricious and contrary to law. . . . The Court further finds that it is not possible from the record to determine that the Service considered the related issue of whether the northern spotted owl is a threatened species. This failure of the Service to review and make an express finding on the issue of threatened status is also arbitrary and capricious and contrary to law.

Id. at 483. The court then gave the FWS ninety days to provide an analysis of its decision that listing was not warranted.

3. For a thorough analysis of *TVA v. Hill* and other significant ESA cases up to 1997, *see* Michael J. Bean & Melanie J. Rowland, The Evolution of National Wildlife Law (3d ed. 1997). For additional perspective, *see* Donald C. Baur and Wm. Robert Irvin, Endangered Species Act: Law, Policy, and Perspectives (2d ed. 2010).

4. The ESA is a common tool for environmental and animal lawyers. Occasionally the ESA is used as a shield to support the desire to kill certain animals when they threaten the health of endangered populations. In a series of rulings in several related cases beginning in 2007 and continuing through 2013 involving the Bonneville Dam in Oregon, the fishing industry and the National Marine Fisheries Service (NMFS) sought authority to kill eighty-five sea lions who were eating endangered salmon; the Humane Society of the United States (HSUS) and others sued to prevent the killings. Plaintiffs brought claims under the National Environmental Policy Act (NEPA) and the Marine Mammal Protection Act (MMPA). Defendants asserted that under the ESA the injury to the endangered salmon population justified the sea lion killings despite the MMPA protections otherwise afforded the sea lions. A series of opinions ensued. *See, e.g., HSUS v. Guttierez*, 523 F.3d 990 (9th Cir. 2008) (granting stay of lethal actions with respect to sea lions); *HSUS v. Guttierez*, 527 F.3d 788 (9th Cir. 2008) (granting motion for stay of approval for 2008 season only); *HSUS v. Guttierez*, 558 F.3d 896 (9th Cir. 2009) (denying HSUS' request for stay of 2009 NMFS approval

to kill sea lions, pending appeal of summary judgment granted to NMFS); *HSUS v. Locke*, 626 F.3d 1040 (9th Cir. 2010) (affirming grant of partial summary judgment, but remanding to the district court for further proceedings on the MMPA claim); *HSUS v. Pritzker*, 2013 U.S. App. LEXIS 19861 (9th Cir. Sept. 27, 2013) (unpublished) (affirming judgment entered for defendants under both NEPA and MMPA).

Babbitt v. Sweet Home Chapter of Communities for a Great Oregon

Supreme Court of the United States, 1995
515 U.S. 687, 115 S. Ct. 2407

JUSTICE STEVENS delivered the opinion of the court. . . . Section 9 of the [ESA] makes it unlawful for any person to "take" any endangered or threatened species. The Secretary has promulgated a regulation that defines the statute's prohibition on takings to include "significant habitat modification or degradation where it actually kills or injures wildlife." This case presents the question whether the Secretary exceeded his authority under the Act by promulgating that regulation.

I

Section 9(a)(1) of the Act provides the following protection for endangered species:[1]

"Except as provided in sections 1535(g)(2) and 1539 of this title, with respect to any endangered species of fish or wildlife listed pursuant to section 1533 of this title it is unlawful for any person subject to the jurisdiction of the United States to—

"(B) take any such species within the United States or the territorial sea of the United States." 16 U.S.C. § 1538(a)(1).

Section 3(19) of the Act defines the statutory term "take":

"The term 'take' means to harass, harm, pursue, hunt, shoot, wound, kill, trap, capture, or collect, or to attempt to engage in any such conduct." 16 U.S.C. § 1532(19).

The Act does not further define the terms it uses to define "take." The Interior Department regulations that implement the statute, however, define the statutory term "harm":

"*Harm* in the definition of 'take' in the Act means an act which actually kills or injures wildlife. Such act may include significant habitat modification or degradation where it actually kills or injures wildlife by significantly impairing essential behavioral patterns, including breeding, feeding, or sheltering." 50 CFR § 17.3 (1994).

---

1. The Act defines the term "endangered species" to mean "any species which is in danger of extinction throughout all or a significant portion of its range other than a species of the Class Insecta determined by the Secretary to constitute a pest whose protection under the provisions of this chapter would present an overwhelming and overriding risk to man." 16 U.S.C. § 1532(6).

This regulation has been in place since 1975.[2]

A limitation on the §9 "take" prohibition appears in §10(a)(1)(B) of the Act, which Congress added by amendment in 1982. That section authorizes the Secretary to grant a permit for any taking otherwise prohibited by §9(a)(1)(B) "if such taking is incidental to, and not the purpose of, the carrying out of an otherwise lawful activity." 16 U.S.C. §1539(a)(1)(B).

* * *

Respondents in this action are small landowners, logging companies, and families dependent on the forest products industries in the Pacific Northwest and in the Southeast, and organizations that represent their interests. They . . . challenge the statutory validity of the Secretary's regulation defining "harm," particularly the inclusion of habitat modification and degradation in the definition. Respondents challenged the regulation on its face. Their complaint alleged that application of the "harm" regulation to the red-cockaded woodpecker, an endangered species, and the northern spotted owl, a threatened species, had injured them economically.

Respondents advanced three arguments to support their submission that Congress did not intend the word "take" in §9 to include habitat modification, as the Secretary's "harm" regulation provides. First, they correctly noted that language in the Senate's original version of the ESA would have defined "take" to include "destruction, modification, or curtailment of [the] habitat or range" of fish or wildlife, but the Senate deleted that language from the bill before enacting it. Second, respondents argued that Congress intended the Act's express authorization for the Federal Government to buy private land in order to prevent habitat degradation in §5 to be the exclusive check against habitat modification on private property. Third, because the Senate added the term "harm" to the definition of "take" in a floor amendment without debate, respondents argued that the court should not interpret the term so expansively as to include habitat modification.

The District Court considered and rejected each of respondents' arguments finding "that Congress intended an expansive interpretation of the word 'take,' an interpretation that encompasses habitat modification." 806 F. Supp. 279, 285 (1992). The court noted that in 1982, when Congress was aware of a judicial decision that had applied the Secretary's regulation, *see Palila v. Hawaii Dept. of Land and Natural Resources*, 639 F. 2d 495 (9th Cir. 1981) (*Palila I*), it amended the Act without using the opportunity to change the definition of "take." 806 F. Supp., at 284. The court stated that, even had it found the ESA "silent or ambiguous" as to the authority for the Secretary's definition of "harm," it would nevertheless have upheld the regulation as a reasonable interpretation of the statute. *Id*. at 285. The

---

2. The Secretary, through the Director of the Fish and Wildlife Service, originally promulgated the regulation in 1975 and amended it in 1981 to emphasize that actual death or injury of a protected animal is necessary for a violation. *See* 40 Fed. Reg. 44412, 44416 (1975); 46 Fed. Reg. 54748, 54750 (1981).

District Court therefore entered summary judgment for petitioners and dismissed respondents' complaint.

A divided panel of the Court of Appeals initially affirmed the judgment of the District Court. 1 F. 3d 1 (D.C. Cir. 1993). After granting a petition for rehearing, however, the panel reversed. 17 F. 3d 1463 (D.C. Cir. 1994). Although acknowledging that "[t]he potential breadth of the word 'harm' is indisputable," the majority concluded that the immediate statutory context in which "harm" appeared counseled against a broad reading; like the other words in the definition of "take," the word "harm" should be read as applying only to "the perpetrator's direct application of force against the animal taken. . . . The forbidden acts fit, in ordinary language, the basic model 'A hit B.'" *Id.* at 1465. The majority based its reasoning on a canon of statutory construction called *noscitur a sociis*, which holds that a word is known by the company it keeps.

The majority claimed support for its construction from a decision of the Ninth Circuit that narrowly construed the word "harass" in the Marine Mammal Protection Act of 1972, 16 U.S.C. § 1372(a)(2)(A), *see United States v. Hayashi*, 5 F. 3d 1278, 1282 (1993); from the legislative history of the ESA; from its view that Congress must not have intended the purportedly broad curtailment of private property rights that the Secretary's interpretation permitted; and from the ESA's land acquisition provision in § 5 and restriction on federal agencies' activities regarding habitat in § 7, both of which the court saw as evidence that Congress had not intended the § 9 "take" prohibition to reach habitat modification. Most prominently, the court performed a lengthy analysis of the 1982 amendment to § 10 that provided for "incidental take permits" and concluded that the amendment did not change the meaning of the term "take" as defined in the 1973 statute.

Chief Judge Mikva, who had announced the panel's original decision, dissented. In his view, a proper application of *Chevron* indicated that the Secretary had reasonably defined "harm" because respondents had failed to show that Congress unambiguously manifested its intent to exclude habitat modification from the ambit of "take." Chief Judge Mikva found the majority's reliance on *noscitur a sociis* inappropriate in light of the statutory language and unnecessary in light of the strong support in the legislative history for the Secretary's interpretation. He did not find the 1982 "incidental take permit" amendment alone sufficient to vindicate the Secretary's definition of "harm," but he believed the amendment provided additional support for that definition because it reflected Congress' view in 1982 that the definition was reasonable.

The Court of Appeals' decision created a square conflict with a 1988 decision of the Ninth Circuit that had upheld the Secretary's definition of "harm." *See Palila v. Hawaii Dept. of Land and Natural Resources*, 852 F. 2d 1106 (1988) (*Palila II*). The Court of Appeals neither cited nor distinguished *Palila II*, despite the stark contrast between the Ninth Circuit's holding and its own. We granted *certiorari* to resolve the conflict. Our consideration of the text and structure of the Act, its legislative history, and the significance of the 1982 amendment persuades us that the Court of Appeals' judgment should be reversed.

II

Because this case was decided on motions for summary judgment, we may appropriately make certain factual assumptions in order to frame the legal issue. First, we assume respondents have no desire to harm either the red-cockaded woodpecker or the spotted owl; they merely wish to continue logging activities that would be entirely proper if not prohibited by the ESA. On the other hand, we must assume, *arguendo*, that those activities will have the effect, even though unintended, of detrimentally changing the natural habitat of both listed species and that, as a consequence, members of those species will be killed or injured. Under respondents' view of the law, the Secretary's only means of forestalling that grave result — even when the actor knows it is certain to occur[9] — is to use his § 5 authority to purchase the lands on which the survival of the species depends. The Secretary, on the other hand, submits that the § 9 prohibition on takings, which Congress defined to include "harm," places on respondents a duty to avoid harm that habitat alteration will cause the birds unless respondents first obtain a permit pursuant to § 10.

The text of the Act provides three reasons for concluding that the Secretary's interpretation is reasonable. First, an ordinary understanding of the word "harm" supports it. The dictionary definition of the verb form of "harm" is "to cause hurt or damage to: injure." Webster's Third New International Dictionary 1034 (1966). In the context of the ESA, that definition naturally encompasses habitat modification that results in actual injury or death to members of an endangered or threatened species.

---

9. As discussed above, the Secretary's definition of "harm" is limited to "acts which actually kill or injure wildlife." 50 CFR § 17.3 (1994). In addition, in order to be subject to the Act's criminal penalties or the more severe of its civil penalties, one must "knowingly violate" the Act or its implementing regulations. 16 U.S.C. §§ 1540(a)(1), (b)(1). Congress added "knowingly" in place of "willfully" in 1978 to make "criminal violations of the act a general rather than a specific intent crime." H.R. Conf. Rep. No. 95-1804, p. 26 (1978). The Act does authorize up to a $500 civil fine for "[a]ny person who otherwise violates" the Act or its implementing regulations. 16 U.S.C. § 1540(a)(1). That provision is potentially sweeping, but it would be so with or without the Secretary's "harm" regulation, making it unhelpful in assessing the reasonableness of the regulation. We have imputed scienter requirements to criminal statutes that impose sanctions without expressly requiring scienter, but the proper case in which we might consider whether to do so in the § 9 provision for a $500 civil penalty would be a challenge to enforcement of that provision itself, not a challenge to a regulation that merely defines a statutory term. We do not agree with the dissent that the regulation covers results that are not "even foreseeable . . . no matter how long the chain of causality between modification and injury." . . . Respondents have suggested no reason why either the "knowingly violates" or the "otherwise violates" provision of the statute — or the "harm" regulation itself — should not be read to incorporate ordinary requirements of proximate causation and foreseeability. In any event, neither respondents nor their *amici* have suggested that the Secretary employs the "otherwise violates" provision with any frequency.

Respondents argue that the Secretary should have limited the purview of "harm" to direct applications of force against protected species, but the dictionary definition does not include the word "directly" or suggest in any way that only direct or willful action that leads to injury constitutes "harm." Moreover, unless the statutory term "harm" encompasses indirect as well as direct injuries, the word has no meaning that does not duplicate the meaning of other words that § 3 uses to define "take." A reluctance to treat statutory terms as surplusage supports the reasonableness of the Secretary's interpretation.[11]

Second, the broad purpose of the ESA supports the Secretary's decision to extend protection against activities that cause the precise harms Congress enacted the statute to avoid. . . . As stated in § 2 of the Act, among its central purposes is "to provide a means whereby the ecosystems upon which endangered species and threatened species depend may be conserved. . . ." 16 U.S.C. § 1531(b).

* * *

Respondents advance strong arguments that activities that cause minimal or unforeseeable harm will not violate the Act as construed in the "harm" regulation. Respondents, however, present a facial challenge to the regulation. Thus, they ask us to invalidate the Secretary's understanding of "harm" in every circumstance, even when an actor knows that an activity, such as draining a pond, would actually result in the extinction of a listed species by destroying its habitat. Given Congress' clear expression of the ESA's broad purpose to protect endangered and threatened wildlife, the Secretary's definition of "harm" is reasonable.[13]

Third, the fact that Congress in 1982 authorized the Secretary to issue permits for takings that § 9(a)(1)(B) would otherwise prohibit, "if such taking is incidental to,

---

11. In contrast, if the statutory term "harm" encompasses such indirect means of killing and injuring wildlife as habitat modification, the other terms listed in § 3 — "capture," "collect," "harass," "hunt," "kill," "pursue," "shoot," "trap," and "wound" — generally retain independent meanings. Most of those terms refer to deliberate actions more frequently than does "harm," and they therefore do not duplicate the sense of indirect causation that "harm" adds to the statute. In addition, most of the other words in the definition describe either actions from which habitat modification does not usually result (*e.g.*, "harass," "pursue") or effects to which activities that modify habitat do not usually lead (*e.g.*, "collect," "trap"). To the extent the Secretary's definition of "harm" may have applications that overlap with other words in the definition, that overlap reflects the broad purpose of the Act.

13. The dissent incorrectly asserts that the Secretary's regulation (1) "dispenses with the foreseeability of harm" and (2) "fail[s] to require injury to particular animals," . . . As to the first assertion, the regulation merely implements the statute, and it is therefore subject to the statute's "knowingly violates" language, *see* 16 U.S.C. §§ 1540(a)(1), (b)(1), and ordinary requirements of proximate causation and foreseeability. Nothing in the regulation purports to weaken those requirements. To the contrary, the word "actually" in the regulation should be construed to limit the liability about which the dissent appears most concerned, liability under the statute's "otherwise violates" provision. The Secretary did not need to include "actually" to connote "but for" causation, which the other words in the definition obviously require. As to the dissent's second assertion, every term in the regulation's definition of "harm" is subservient to the phrase "an act which actually kills or injures wildlife."

and not the purpose of, the carrying out of an otherwise lawful activity," 16 U.S.C. § 1539(a)(1)(B), strongly suggests that Congress understood § 9(a)(1)(B) to prohibit indirect as well as deliberate takings. The permit process requires the applicant to prepare a "conservation plan" that specifies how he intends to "minimize and mitigate" the "impact" of his activity on endangered and threatened species, 16 U.S.C. § 1539(a)(2)(A), making clear that Congress had in mind foreseeable rather than merely accidental effects on listed species. No one could seriously request an "incidental" take permit to avert § 9 liability for direct, deliberate action against a member of an endangered or threatened species, but respondents would read "harm" so narrowly that the permit procedure would have little more than that absurd purpose. "When Congress acts to amend a statute, we presume it intends its amendment to have real and substantial effect." *Stone v. INS*, 514 U.S. 386, 397 (1995). Congress' addition of the § 10 permit provision supports the Secretary's conclusion that activities not intended to harm an endangered species, such as habitat modification, may constitute unlawful takings under the ESA unless the Secretary permits them.

The Court of Appeals made three errors in asserting that "harm" must refer to a direct application of force because the words around it do.[15] First, the court's premise was flawed. Several of the words that accompany "harm" in the § 3 definition of "take," especially "harass," "pursue," "wound," and "kill," refer to actions or effects that do not require direct applications of force. Second, to the extent the court read a requirement of intent or purpose into the words used to define "take," it ignored § 11's express provision that a "knowin[g]" action is enough to violate the Act. Third, the court employed *noscitur a sociis* to give "harm" essentially the same function as other words in the definition, thereby denying it independent meaning. The canon, to the contrary, counsels that a word "gathers meaning from the words around it." *Jarecki v. G.C. Searle & Co.*, 367 U.S. 303, 307 (1961). The statutory context of "harm" suggests that Congress meant that term to serve a particular function in the ESA, consistent with, but distinct from, the functions of the other verbs used to define "take." The Secretary's interpretation of "harm" to include indirectly injuring endangered animals through habitat modification permissibly interprets "harm" to have "a character of its own not to be submerged by its association." *Russell Motor Car Co. v. United States*, 261 U.S. 514, 519 (1923).

---

15. The dissent makes no effort to defend the Court of Appeals' reading of the statutory definition as requiring a direct application of force. Instead, it tries to impose on § 9 a limitation of liability to "affirmative conduct intentionally directed against a particular animal or animals." . . . Under the dissent's interpretation of the Act, a developer could drain a pond, knowing that the act would extinguish an endangered species of turtles, without even proposing a conservation plan or applying for a permit under § 10(a)(1)(B); unless the developer was motivated by a desire "to get at a turtle," no statutory taking could occur. Because such conduct would not constitute a taking at common law, the dissent would shield it from § 9 liability, even though the words "kill" and "harm" in the statutory definition could apply to such deliberate conduct. We cannot accept that limitation. In any event, our reasons for rejecting the Court of Appeals' interpretation apply as well to the dissent's novel construction.

Nor does the Act's inclusion of the §5 land acquisition authority and the §7 directive to federal agencies to avoid destruction or adverse modification of critical habitat alter our conclusion. Respondents' argument that the Government lacks any incentive to purchase land under §5 when it can simply prohibit takings under §9 ignores the practical considerations that attend enforcement of the ESA. Purchasing habitat lands may well cost the Government less in many circumstances than pursuing civil or criminal penalties. In addition, the §5 procedure allows for protection of habitat before the seller's activity has harmed any endangered animal, whereas the Government cannot enforce the §9 prohibition until an animal has actually been killed or injured. The Secretary may also find the §5 authority useful for preventing modification of land that is not yet but may in the future become habitat for an endangered or threatened species. The §7 directive applies only to the Federal Government, whereas the §9 prohibition applies to "any person." Section 7 imposes a broad, affirmative duty to avoid adverse habitat modifications that §9 does not replicate, and §7 does not limit its admonition to habitat modification that "actually kills or injures wildlife." Conversely, §7 contains limitations that §9 does not, applying only to actions "likely to jeopardize the continued existence of any endangered species or threatened species," 16 U.S.C. §1536(a)(2), and to modification of habitat that has been designed "critical" pursuant to §4, 16 U.S.C. §1533(b)(2).[17] Any overlap that §5 or §7 may have with §9 in particular cases is unexceptional, and simply reflects the broad purpose of the Act set out in §2 and acknowledged in *TVA v. Hill*, 437 U.S. 153 (1978).

We need not decide whether the statutory definition of "take" compels the Secretary's interpretation of "harm," because our conclusions that Congress did not unambiguously manifest its intent to adopt respondents' view and that the Secretary's interpretation is reasonable suffice to decide this case. *See generally Chevron U.S.A. Inc. v. Natural Resources Defense Council, Inc.*, 467 U.S. 837 (1984). The latitude the ESA gives the Secretary in enforcing the statute, together with the degree of regulatory expertise necessary to its enforcement, establishes that we owe some degree of deference to the Secretary's reasonable interpretation. *See* Breyer, *Judicial Review of Questions of Law and Policy*, 38 Admin. L. Rev. 363, 373 (1986).

III

Our conclusion that the Secretary's definition of "harm" rests on a permissible construction of the ESA gains further support from the legislative history of the statute. The Committee Reports accompanying the bills that became the ESA do not specifically discuss the meaning of "harm," but they make clear that Congress intended "take" to apply broadly to cover indirect as well as purposeful actions. The Senate Report stressed that "'[t]ake' is defined . . . in the broadest possible manner

---

17. Congress recognized that §§7 and 9 are not coextensive as to federal agencies when, in the wake of our decision in *Hill* in 1978, it added §7(o), 16 U.S.C. §1536(o), to the Act. That section provides that any federal project subject to exemption from §7, 16 U.S.C. §1536(h), will also be exempt from §9.

to include every conceivable way in which a person can 'take' or attempt to 'take' any fish or wildlife." S. Rep. No. 93-307, p. 7 (1973). The House Report stated that "the broadest possible terms" were used to define restrictions on takings. H.R. Rep. No. 93-412, p. 15 (1973). The House Report underscored the breadth of the "take" definition by noting that it included "harassment, *whether intentional or not.*" *Id.* at 11 (emphasis added). The Report explained that the definition "would allow, for example, the Secretary to regulate or prohibit the activities of birdwatchers where the effect of those activities might disturb the birds and make it difficult for them to hatch or raise their young." *Id.* These comments, ignored in the dissent's welcome but selective foray into legislative history, support the Secretary's interpretation that the term "take" in §9 reached far more than the deliberate actions of hunters and trappers.

Two endangered species bills, S. 1592 and S. 1983, were introduced in the Senate and referred to the Commerce Committee. Neither bill included the word "harm" in its definition of "take," although the definitions otherwise closely resembled the one that appeared in the bill as ultimately enacted. Senator Tunney, the floor manager of the bill in the Senate, subsequently introduced a floor amendment that added "harm" to the definition, noting that this and accompanying amendments would "help to achieve the purposes of the bill." 119 Cong. Rec. 25683 (1973). Respondents argue that the lack of debate about the amendment that added "harm" counsels in favor of a narrow interpretation. We disagree. An obviously broad word that the Senate went out of its way to add to an important statutory definition is precisely the sort of provision that deserves a respectful reading.

The definition of "take" that originally appeared in S. 1983 differed from the definition as ultimately enacted in one other significant respect: it included "the destruction, modification, or curtailment of [the] habitat or range" of fish and wildlife. Hearings, at 27. Respondents make much of the fact that the Commerce Committee removed this phrase from the "take" definition before S. 1983 went to the floor. We do not find that fact especially significant. The legislative materials contain no indication why the habitat protection provision was deleted. That provision differed greatly from the regulation at issue today. Most notably, the habitat protection provision in S. 1983 would have applied far more broadly than the regulation does because it made adverse habitat modification a categorical violation of the "take" prohibition, unbounded by the regulation's limitation to habitat modifications that actually kill or injure wildlife. The S. 1983 language also failed to qualify "modification" with the regulation's limiting adjective "significant." We do not believe the Senate's unelaborated disavowal of the provision in S. 1983 undermines the reasonableness of the more moderate habitat protection in the Secretary's "harm" regulation.[19]

---

19. Respondents place heavy reliance for their argument that Congress intended the §5 land acquisition provision and not §9 to be the ESA's remedy for habitat modification on a floor statement by Senator Tunney:

The history of the 1982 amendment that gave the Secretary authority to grant permits for "incidental" takings provides further support for his reading of the Act. The House Report expressly states that "[b]y use of the word 'incidental' the Committee intends to cover situations in which it is known that a taking will occur if the other activity is engaged in but such taking is incidental to, and not the purpose of, the activity." H.R. Rep. No. 97–567, 31 (1982). This reference to the foreseeability of incidental takings undermines respondents' argument that the 1982 amendment covered only accidental killings of endangered and threatened animals that might occur in the course of hunting or trapping other animals. Indeed, Congress had habitat modification directly in mind: both the Senate Report and the House Conference Report identified as the model for the permit process a cooperative state-federal response to a case in California where a development project threatened incidental harm to a species of endangered butterfly by modification of its habitat. Thus, Congress in 1982 focused squarely on the aspect of the "harm" regulation at issue in this litigation. Congress' implementation of a permit program is consistent with the Secretary's interpretation of the term "harm."

* * *

"Many species have been inadvertently exterminated by a negligent destruction of their habitat. Their habitats have been cut in size, polluted, or otherwise altered so that they are unsuitable environments for natural populations of fish and wildlife. Under this bill, we can take steps to make amends for our negligent encroachment. The Secretary would be empowered to use the land acquisition authority granted to him in certain existing legislation to acquire land for the use of the endangered species program ... Through these land acquisition provisions, we will be able to conserve habitats necessary to protect fish and wildlife from further destruction.

"Although most endangered species are threatened primarily by the destruction of their natural habitats, a significant portion of these animals are subject to predation by man for commercial, sport, consumption, or other purposes. The provisions in S. 1983 would prohibit the commerce in or the importation, exportation, or taking of endangered species. ..." 119 Cong. Rec. 25669 (1973).

Similarly, respondents emphasize a floor statement by Representative Sullivan, the House floor manager for the ESA:

For the most part, the principal threat to animals stems from destruction of their habitat ... H.R. 37 will meet this problem by providing funds for acquisition of critical habitat ... It will also enable the Department of Agriculture to cooperate with willing landowners who desire to assist in the protection of endangered species, but who are understandably unwilling to do so at excessive cost to themselves.

Another hazard to endangered species arises from those who would capture or kill them for pleasure or profit. There is no way that Congress can make it less pleasurable for a person to take an animal, but we can certainly make it less profitable for them to do so.

Id., 30162.

Each of these statements merely explained features of the bills that Congress eventually enacted in § 5 of the ESA and went on to discuss elements enacted in § 9. Neither statement even suggested that § 5 would be the Act's exclusive remedy for habitat modification by private landowners or that habitat modification by private landowners stood outside the ambit of § 9. Respondents' suggestion that these statements identified § 5 as the ESA's only response to habitat modification contradicts their emphasis elsewhere on the habitat protections in § 7.

The judgment of the Court of Appeals is reversed.

Notes

1. If section 5 exists as an option for protecting threatened habitat via the federal government's purchasing power, is a broad definition of "harm" necessary? In fact, is it, as argued by the respondents, evidence the drafters intended a narrower definition?

2. As *Babbitt* makes clear, since the ESA's enactment, difficult questions have arisen regarding the definition of "take," particularly in determining the scope of the term "harm." *See, e.g.*, Alicia M. Griffin, *Beyond "Harm": Abandoning The Actual Injury Standard For Certain Prohibited Takings Under The Endangered Species Act By Giving Independent Meaning To Harassment*, 52 VAND. L. REV. 1831 (1999); Kelly A. Keenan, *They Paved Paradise And Put Up A Parking Lot: Babbitt v. Sweet Home Chapter Of Communities For A Great Oregon*, 60 ALB. L. REV. 1483 (1997); Diane S. L. Yuen, *Babbitt v. Sweet Home: Will The Endangered Species Act Survive?*, 18 U. HAW. L. REV. 909 (1996); Paul Boudreaux, *Understanding "Take" In The Endangered Species Act*, 34 ARIZ. ST. L.J. 733(Fall 2002). Prior to *Babbitt* a series of Ninth Circuit cases held that a claim under the ESA only required a showing that human conduct posed a significant *risk* of harm to a protected species: *Palila v. Haw. Dep't. of Land & Natural Res.*, 471 F. Supp. 985 (D. Haw. 1979) ("*Palila I*"), *aff'd*, 639 F. 2d 495 (9th Cir. 1981) ("*Palila II*"); *Palila v. Haw. Dep't. of Land & Natural Res.*, 649 F. Supp. 1070 (D. Haw. 1986) ("*Palila III*"), *aff'd*, 852 F.2d 1106 (9th Cir. 1988) ("*Palila IV*"); *Forest Conservation Council v. Rosboro Lumber Co.*, 50 F.3d 781 (9th Cir. 1995).

The FWS defines "harm" as "an act which actually kills or injures wildlife," although conduct that will cause future injury is subject to injunction under the ESA. After *Babbitt*, such acts may include significant habitat modification or degradation where it actually kills or injures wildlife by significantly impairing essential behavior patterns, including breeding, feeding or sheltering. 50 C.F.R. § 17.3 (2009).

Despite the FWS' efforts to delineate the scope of "harm" prohibited by the ESA, controversy raged for two decades over what kind of habitat modification would result in a statutory "harm."

In *Palila I*, national and local conservation groups alleged that the Hawaii Department of Land and Natural Resources' maintenance of feral sheep and goats in the endangered palila bird's habitat constituted a "taking" in violation of section 9. The palila lives exclusively in the mamane-naio forest on the slopes of Mauna Kea on the island of Hawaii and depends on the mamane trees for food, shelter and nest sites. By eating the seedlings and shoots of the mamane trees, the feral species allegedly prevented maturation of new mamane trees and regeneration of the forest upon which the palila depended for survival. Without requiring evidence of palila deaths, injuries or population decline, the district court found a section 9 taking based on the Secretary's definition of harm, even though the definition characterizes significant habitat modification or degradation as "harm" only when it actually kills or injures wildlife. The court reasoned implicitly that without continuous regeneration of the trees and forest, the birds eventually will lack food and shelter and thus were harmed. The court's analysis characterized processes that will cause harm to endangered species in the future as harm proscribed by the ESA. The Ninth Circuit affirmed in *Palila II*, finding a violation of the ESA because the maintenance of the feral sheep and goats in critical habitat posed a risk of harm to an endangered species. Seven years later, in response to a similar degradation of palila habitat by mouflon sheep, the court explained that a finding of "(actual) harm does not require death to individual members of the species; nor does it require a finding that habitat degradation is presently driving the species further toward extinction. Habitat destruction that prevents the recovery of the species by affecting essential behavioral patterns causes actual injury to the species and effects a taking under section 9 of the Act." *Palila III*, 649 F. Supp. at 1075. The district court found that the habitat degradation caused by the mouflon sheep was "actually presently injuring the palila by decreasing food and nesting sites" and therefore was harming the palila. *Id.* at 1080.

The Ninth Circuit in *Palila IV* agreed with the district court's treatment of the dichotomy between potential and actual harm, but declined to adopt the district court's interpretation of "harm" to include those activities that keep an endangered species at status quo, or prevents the population from recovering. *Id.* at 1110.

In *Forest Conservation Council v. Rosboro Lumber Co.*, 50 F.3d 781 (9th Cir. 1995), the court was called upon to resolve the scope of the term "harm" in a dispute between a group seeking to enjoin a lumber company from clear-cutting forty acres of timber on which one pair of northern spotted owls reportedly lived. The court ruled that an injury to an endangered species that allegedly will take place in the future constitutes ESA harm if the harm is reasonably certain to occur. Notably, *Babbitt* did not address *Rosboro*.

3. A large number of ESA takings claims have been litigated in the context of the definition of harm. The ESA's prohibition on "harassment" largely has been ignored by the courts and offers some clarity for the tangled "harm" webs. The regulatory definition of "harass," issued in 1975, characterizes the term as "an intentional or negligent act or omission which creates the likelihood of injuries to wildlife by annoying it to such an extent as to significantly disrupt normal behavior patterns which include, but are not limited to, breeding, feeding, or sheltering." 50 C.F.R. §17.3 (1998). The original definition of "harass" remains in effect, with a 1998 exemption for normal animal husbandry practices.

In promulgating the definitions for "harm" and "harass" the FWS noted that it intended to make "harass" applicable to those acts "with the potential for injury" and "harm" applicable to acts "which actually, (as opposed to potentially), cause injury." 40 Fed. Reg. 44,412, 44,413 (Sept. 26, 1975). The FWS later stated in the commentary accompanying the 1981 proposed redefinition of "harm" that, while a showing of a "likelihood of injury" meets the definition of "harass," "it will not result in criminal liability for habitat modification unless . . . the defendant also knew or reasonably should have known that his actions would be likely to injure" endangered or threatened species. 46 Fed. Reg. at 29,490 (June 2, 1981). However, because the words "habitat modification" appear in the definition of "harm" and not in the definition of "harass," arguably only a finding of "harm" provides redress for claims of habitat modification.

4. The Eleventh Circuit examined the meaning of "harm" under the ESA/MMPA in *People for the Ethical Treatment of Animals v. Miami Seaquarium*, 879 F.3d 1142 (11th Cir. 2018). Plaintiffs challenged the confinement of Lolita, an endangered killer whale:

> . . . Lolita was captured off the coast of Washington state when she was between three and six years old. Seaquarium purchased Lolita and she has lived at Seaquarium since September 24, 1970. Lolita is about twenty feet long and weighs around 8,000 pounds.
>
> Lolita lives in an oblong tank that, at its widest and deepest points, is eighty feet wide and twenty feet deep. A portion of the tank is occupied by a concrete platform on which Lolita's trainers stand. Stadium seating surrounds the tank. Lolita has not lived with another orca since 1980, when Hugo, her former companion, passed away . . .

Id. at 1144–45. Plaintiffs challenged the conditions of Lolita's confinement, claiming thirteen injuries that they alleged constituted actionable "harm" under the ESA. The injuries included:

> (1) Physical and psychological injury caused by Lolita's inability to engage in normal swimming and diving behaviors in her tank; (2) Psychological injury attributable to the absence of a socially compatible companion; . . . (6) "Surfer's eye," a condition caused by exposure to UV radiation for which Lolita requires twice-daily eye drops; (7) Blisters and wrinkles potentially caused by sun exposure; (8) Treatment with antibiotics, antifungals, pain medication, hormones, and antacids not used on wild orca; (9) General unhealthiness illustrated by: a mild kidney impairment, a high number of bacteria, past treatment for respiratory infections, and a potential recurring lung condition; (10) Abnormal behavior like listless floating, lying motionless near her tank's inflow valve, pattern swimming, etc.; (11) Significant wear in six teeth; (12) A tooth that has been drilled multiple times; and (13) Captivity conditions likely to reduce Lolita's lifespan

Id. at 1145 n.4. Plaintiffs also alleged stress and physical injuries caused by the dolphins with whom Lolita was housed.

The district court held that conduct must "gravely threaten" an endangered species in order to constitute take. The Eleventh Circuit rejected that holding, but upheld summary judgment for defendants, finding that plaintiffs had not alleged "serious harm," which it interpreted as the trigger for a finding of a taking under the ESA: "Under the ESA, 'harm' or 'harass[ment]' is only actionable if it poses a threat of serious harm." *Id.* at 1150.

5. One of the first species to be designated as endangered under the ESA was the gray wolf, *Canis lupus*, the largest wild member of the dog family, which had at one point lived in most regions of the country. Wolves are "highly adaptable habitat generalists," and if they are not persecuted by humans, can live anywhere that contains a sufficient population of ungulates. Wolves are highly mobile and may move "scores or even hundreds of miles until [they] locate[] suitable habitat."

The process of wolves moving away from their home packs is called "dispersal." The dispersal of wolves from their natal packs and territories is a normal and extremely important behavioral attribute of the species that facilitates the formation of new packs, the occupancy of vacant territories, and the expansion of occupied range by the "colonization" of vacant habitat. Wolf dispersal continues as wolves travel away from the more saturated habitats in their current range and into nearby areas where wolves are extremely sparse or absent. Dispersal is crucial to wolf population recovery, because dispersing wolves often reoccupy areas in which wolves were previously eradicated, a direct realization of the goals of the ESA. Additionally, dispersal helps maintain genetic diversity and expands the range of healthy populations. Dispersal occurs over large distances, with wide ranges of distances traveled.

Habitat destruction and government bounties in the Twentieth Century encouraged the widespread poisoning, trapping, and hunting of wolves, which eradicated the gray wolf from more than 95 percent of its range in the contiguous United States. Human-caused mortality continues to constitute the majority of documented wolf deaths. Despite these dire threats to their survival as a species, the FWS, along with individual states and special interest groups, have consistently sought to delist or remove federal protections from the gray wolf and return them to state management regimes.

At the time of the case below, the wolves at issue in that case represented the only sizable gray wolf population in the United States east of the Rocky Mountains, and they were found mainly in Minnesota, Wisconsin, and the Upper Peninsula of Michigan, with the majority of wolves in northern Minnesota. According to the FWS, this Great Lakes population included about 75 percent of the North American gray wolves south of Canada.

There are dozens of judicial opinions on the battles between animal welfare and wolf protection groups, on the one hand, and federal and state governments and private interest (hunting) groups on the other over the years. While they are too numerous and detailed to even summarize in this book, the following case touches on some of the issues raised in those cases.

Humane Society of the United States v. Zinke
United States Court of Appeals, District of Columbia Circuit, 2017
865 F.3d 585

Millett, Circuit Judge:

The gray wolf once roamed in large numbers across the contiguous forty-eight States. But by the 1960s, hunting, depredation, and habitat loss drove the gray wolf to the brink of extinction, and the federal government declared the gray wolf an endangered species. After a portion of the gray wolf population rebounded, the government promulgated the rule at issue here, which removes from federal protection a sub-population of gray wolves inhabiting all or portions of nine states in the Western Great Lakes region of the United States. The Humane Society of the United States challenges that rule as a violation of the Endangered Species Act of 1973 ("Act"), 16 U.S.C. § 1531 *et seq.*, and the Administrative Procedure Act ("APA"), 5 U.S.C. § 551 *et seq.* Because the government failed to reasonably analyze or consider two significant aspects of the rule—the impacts of partial delisting and of historical range loss on the already-listed species—we affirm the judgment of the district court vacating the 2011 Rule.

* * *

[I.]

[A.]

Congress enacted the Endangered Species Act "to halt and reverse the trend toward species extinction," and to do so "whatever the cost." As relevant here, a species is "endangered" if it "is in danger of extinction throughout all or a significant portion of its range [.]" 16 U.S.C. § 1532(6). A species is "threatened" if it "is likely to become an endangered species within the foreseeable future throughout all or a significant portion of its range." *Id.* § 1532(20).

The Endangered Species Act directs the Secretary of the Interior to apply five factors in determining whether a "species" is endangered or threatened: (i) "the present or threatened destruction, modification, or curtailment of [the species'] habitat or range"; (ii) "overutilization [of the species] for commercial, recreational, scientific, or educational purposes"; (iii) "disease or predation"; (iv) "the inadequacy of existing regulatory mechanisms"; and (v) "other natural or manmade factors affecting [the species'] continued existence." 16 U.S.C. § 1533(a)(1). In making that determination, the Secretary must rely on "the best scientific and commercial data available [.]" *Id.* § 1533(b)(1)(A). The Secretary of the Interior has delegated the authority to determine whether a species is "endangered" or "threatened" to the Fish and Wildlife Service ("Service").

The "species" that the Endangered Species Act protects are defined to include "any subspecies of fish or wildlife or plants, and," of most relevance here, "any distinct population segment of any species of vertebrate fish or wildlife which interbreeds when mature." 16 U.S.C. § 1532(16). The Act does not define "distinct population segment." Nor do agency regulations. The Service, however, has issued policy guidance stating that the existence of a "distinct population segment" turns upon the discreteness and significance of a sub-population as compared to the larger species population. [Federal] Policy emphasizes that the Service's authority to recognize distinct population segments should be "exercised sparingly."

* * *

Another key term in analyzing a species' need for protection — "range" — is also left undefined by the Act. In 2014, the Service adopted a policy statement defining "range" as a species' "'current range,' not [its] 'historical range.'" ("Range Policy".) The Range Policy further explains that a portion of a species' range will be considered "significant" if the species would be in danger of extinction or likely to become so in the foreseeable future without that portion of its range.

Once the Service determines that a species is endangered or threatened, it must add the species to a list of protected species in the Federal Register. 16 U.S.C. § 1533(c)(1). A listed species receives robust federal protections, including prohibitions on possessing, killing, selling, importing, or exporting its members. *Id.* § 1538(a). Any person that knowingly violates those prohibitions faces criminal sanctions, including fines of up to $50,000 or a year of imprisonment. *Id.* § 1540(b)(1).

* * *

[B.1.]

Regional subspecies of the taxonomic species "gray wolf" (*Canis lupis*) were declared endangered by the federal government between 1966 and 1976. . . .

With the wolves' numbers rebounding in certain areas, the federal government in 1978 reclassified the gray wolf from its regional listings into a single species listing divided into two groups: Minnesota gray wolves, which the Service determined had recovered to the point of only being threatened, and the gray wolf in the remaining forty-seven States, which remained endangered.

* * *

[C.1.]

This case is Round Three in the Service's effort to divide and delist gray wolves in the broader Western Great Lakes region. In 2011, the Service issued a final rule that . . . purported to "revise the boundaries of the Minnesota" gray wolf population to include the wolves in all or portions of eight other states. ("2011 Rule"). Specifically, the 2011 Rule designated the gray wolf population in Minnesota, Wisconsin, and Michigan, as well as portions of North Dakota, South Dakota, Iowa, Illinois, Indiana, and Ohio, as the Western Great Lakes Distinct Population Segment. In its next breath, the Service delisted that segment.

In doing so, the Service again expressly adopted the legal analysis in the Solicitor's Opinion regarding its authority to delist a . . . "distinct population segment."

The Service next considered whether the segment was endangered or threatened throughout all or a significant portion of its range. In making that determination, the Service explained that it would interpret "range" to mean "current range." The Service also clarified that it would consider a portion of a species' range to be "significant" if that portion is "important to the conservation of the species because it contributes meaningfully to the representation, resiliency, or redundancy of the species."

Finally, the Service concluded, after analyzing the five statutory endangerment factors, that the Western Great Lakes segment was neither endangered nor threatened throughout all or a significant portion of its range. The Service explained that existing rates of mortality from disease and human causes had been insufficient to prevent growth of the population, and that state plans provided adequate monitoring of and protection for the wolf segment.

[C.2.]

The Humane Society filed suit alleging that the 2011 Rule violated both the Endangered Species Act and the APA. The district court agreed with the Humane Society and vacated the 2011 Rule . . .

* * *

The district court further concluded that the rule was arbitrary and capricious because the Service failed to address how large losses in the gray wolf's historical range affected the determination that the Western Great Lakes segment was not endangered or threatened.

* * *

II

The Service's listing determinations are subject to review under Section 706 of the APA, 5 U.S.C. § 706. Under that standard, we must overturn an agency decision if it is "arbitrary, capricious, an abuse of discretion, or otherwise not in accordance with law." 5 U.S.C. § 706(2)(A).

We review the Service's interpretation of the Endangered Species Act under the familiar two-step *Chevron* framework. *See Chevron U.S.A., Inc. v. Natural Resources Def. Council, Inc.*, 467 U.S. 837 (1984). First, we apply the "traditional tools of statutory construction" to determine whether Congress has directly spoken to the question at issue. If the statute's meaning is clear, the inquiry ends and "we must give effect to the unambiguously expressed intent of Congress." If, however, "the statute is silent or ambiguous with respect to the specific issue," then we will defer to the agency's considered interpretation of the statute if it is "reasonable."

The central dispute in this case is whether the Endangered Species Act permits the Service to carve out of an already-listed species a "distinct population segment" for the purpose of delisting that segment and withdrawing it from the Act's aegis. We hold that the Act permits such a designation, but only when the Service first makes the proper findings.

A

* * *

The . . . text of the Endangered Species Act does not itself answer the question whether the Service can designate a distinct population segment from within an already-listed species.

B

Because the statute is "silent or ambiguous with respect to the specific issue" at hand, the question before this court becomes whether the Service's interpretation is "based on a permissible construction of the statute."

The Service's interpretation of Section 1533(c)(1) as allowing for the designation of a distinct population segment within a listed species is a reasonable reading of statutory text and—when properly undertaken, does not contravene the purposes of the Endangered Species Act.

* * *

The Service's position is . . . consonant with the purposes of the Endangered Species Act, which is to devote needed resources to the protection of endangered and threatened species, while abating the Act's comprehensive protections when a species—defined to include a distinct population segment—is recovered. The Service's interpretation ensures that the most resources can be brought to bear where a species continues to be threatened or endangered. In that regard, the Act's direction to the Service to evaluate the status of not just species, but subspecies and segments, 16 U.S.C. § 1532(16), signals Congress's intent to target the Act's provisions where needed, rather than to require the woodenly undifferentiated treatment of all members of a taxonomic species regardless of how their actual status and condition might change over time.

Another purpose of the Endangered Species Act is to foster state cooperation in the conservation of threatened or endangered species. Because the locations of distinct population segments not uncommonly correspond with geographical lines, empowering the Service to alter the listing status of segments rewards those States that most actively encourage and promote species recovery within their jurisdictions. On the other hand, continuing to rigidly enforce the Act's stringent protections in the face of such success just because recovery has lagged elsewhere would discourage robust cooperation. The Service's interpretation thus reasonably "encourage[s] the States *** through *** a system of incentives."

The Humane Society argues that Service action under the Act "must be, first and foremost, to provide protections to endangered or threatened species." True enough. But that premise does nothing to answer the specific question of whether the Service is permitted to tailor its protections to where they are most needed.

* * *

"When it enacted the [Endangered Species Act], Congress delegated broad administrative and interpretive power to the [Service]." And "[t]he task of defining and listing endangered and threatened species requires an expertise and attention to detail that exceeds the normal province of Congress." Given the ambiguity of the statutory text, the Humane Society's proffered interpretation of the Act as favoring the use of segments in a protective manner may very well be reasonable. But our task under *Chevron* is not to pick from amongst reasonable options. Our task is simply to determine whether the Service's interpretation of the ambiguous language is reasonable.

We hold that the Service permissibly concluded that the Endangered Species Act allows the identification of a distinct population segment within an already-listed species, and further allows the assignment of a different conservation status to that segment if the statutory criteria for uplisting, downlisting, or delisting are met.

C

Holding that the Service has the legal authority to identify a distinct population segment from within an already-listed species does not mean it did so properly here. In fact, it did not. The fundamental error in the Service's decision is that, in evaluating whether gray wolves in the Western Great Lakes region are a "distinct" population segment, the Service failed to address the impact that extraction of the segment would have on the legal status of the remaining wolves in the already-listed species. More specifically, the Service cannot find that a population segment is distinct—in the Service's words, that it is severable because it is "discrete" and "significant"—without determining whether the remnant itself remains a species so that its own status under the Act will continue as needed.

* * *

III

Under the Endangered Species Act, the determination of a species' endangered or threatened status turns on the threats that the species faces "throughout all or a significant portion of its range." The Service concluded that "range" refers to the species' current range at the time its status is evaluated or reevaluated for listing. The district court held that the Service's decision to delist the Western Great Lakes segment failed to adequately address the wolves' loss of historical range. Because the Service's interpretation of "range" as focusing on "current range" is reasonable, we uphold it. But because the Service categorically excluded the effects of loss of historical range from its analysis, we hold that the Service's conclusion about the ongoing threat to the Western Great Lakes segment within its current range was insufficiently reasoned, and therefore arbitrary and capricious.

A

Under *Chevron*, we ask first whether the Endangered Species Act speaks directly to the meaning of "range" and, if it does not, we must evaluate the reasonableness of the Service's interpretation. *See* 467 U.S. at 842–843.

The Endangered Species Act does not itself define "range." The definitions of "endangered" and "threatened" species, however, do use the present tense "is" to refer to the status of the species within its range. That seems to accord with the Service's position that "range" refers to "current range."

Still, focusing on verb tense does not get the Service very far. That is because the placement of "is" in the definitions seems most naturally to require that the species *currently* be endangered or threatened within its range, not to dictate the temporal scope of geographical evidence the Service is to consider. A species can be found to be endangered now—"*is* in danger of extinction,"—based just as easily on threats to the species throughout its historical range as on threats throughout its contemporary range. *Cf. Defenders of Wildlife v. Norton*, 258 F.3d 1136, 1145 (9th Cir. 2001) ("[A] species can be extinct 'throughout *** a significant portion of its range' if there are major geographical areas in which it is no longer viable but once was.") (second alteration in original).

* * *

... [T]raditional rules of statutory construction do not answer the question of whether "range" means current or historical range. Indeed, the Service and the Humane Society both acknowledge that the Act leaves open the possibility that "range" may refer to either current or historical range. The question then becomes whether the Service's interpretation of "range" as "current range" "is based on a permissible construction of the statute." It is.

Although the statute itself does not indicate the meaning of "range," the Service's interpretation is at least consistent with the Endangered Species Act's use of the present tense in provisions discussing the species' range. And it also accords with Section 1539(j)(2)(A)'s use of "current range" in reference to a species' listed range. In addition, focusing on the species' survival in the range it currently occupies is consonant with the purposes of the Endangered Species Act, because the threats that a species confronts where it currently lives often affect its continued survival the most and thus bear influentially on whether it should be listed.

For those reasons, we conclude that the Service's interpretation of "range" to focus on a species' current range is a reasonable interpretation of the Act.

B

As with the Service's designation of distinct population segments, the rub in this case is not with the Service's interpretation of the statute, but with its application of the statute to the record at hand ... The question ... remains whether the agency arbitrarily and capriciously "'failed to consider an important aspect of the problem' it faces."

We hold that the Service's analysis of the status of the Western Great Lakes segment within its current range wrongly omitted all consideration of lost historical range. Just because the Endangered Species Act does not compel the Service to interpret "range" to mean historical range, that does not mean that the Service can brush off a substantial loss of historical range as irrelevant to the species' endangered or threatened status. So says the Service itself: The Service's Range Policy is explicit that a species may be "endangered or threatened throughout all or a significant portion of its current range *because* [a] loss of historical range is so substantial that it undermines the viability of the species as it exists today."

That is an eminently sensible approach. Range loss can "result[ ] in a species for which distribution and abundance is restricted, gene flow is inhibited, or population redundancy is reduced to such a level that the entity is now vulnerable to extinction or likely to become so within the foreseeable future throughout all or a significant portion of its current range." In addition, "a species with a reduced range is at greater risk of all or most of its populations being affected by a catastrophic event such as a hurricane or fire."

In other words, an adequate evaluation of the threats confronting the survival of a species within its current range requires looking at more than just the current moment in time. The Service, consistent with its own Range Policy, also needs to consider the scope of the species' historical range, and the impact that material contraction or relocation might indicate for survival within a currently constricted or confined range.

There is, moreover, no question in this case that "gray wolves have been extirpated from most of the southern portions of their historical North American range." The Humane Society estimates that 95% of the gray wolf's historical range has disappeared. The Service does not dispute that figure.

Despite immense losses in the gray wolves' historical range—including the historical range of those wolves now occupying the Western Great Lakes area—the Service nowhere analyzed the impact of that loss on the survival of the gray wolves as a whole, the gray wolves remnant, or the Western Great Lakes segment. Such a failure to address "an important aspect of the problem" that is factually substantiated in the record is unreasoned, arbitrary, and capricious decisionmaking.

The Service does not deny the gap in its analysis. Instead, the Service points to its determination that the Western Great Lakes segment would remain viable in key portions of the Western Great Lakes area. That is a *non sequitur*. As the Range Policy explained, consideration of material changes in a species' historical range is critical to a reliable assessment of sustainability within the current range. So whatever the Service prognosticates about future viability in certain portions of the current range cannot be reliably reasoned if it was made in a historical vacuum. An important factor—the possible enduring consequences of significant loss of historical range—was left out of the analysis all together.

The Service also argues that the Act does not require the restoration of a species to its entire historical range. Okay. But giving adequate consideration to the effects of large losses of historical range on a species' survival going forward has nothing to do with where geographically a species must be restored. The only obligation at issue here is for the Service to contend with the implications of massive range loss for the species' endangered or threatened status within its current environment.

* * *

In sum, because the undisputedly vast loss of historical range is a salient factor in determining the endangered or threatened status of the Western Great Lakes segment and the remnant population within their current ranges, the Service's wholesale failure to address that factor renders the Service's decision unreasoned, arbitrary, and capricious.

* * *

Notes

1. Besides the ESA, there are other federal laws intended to protect some species of wildlife from reduction in population or unregulated exploitation. The federal Lacey Act is the oldest federal law regulating wildlife, and "[s]ince its enactment in 1900, a principal 'object and purpose' of the Lacey Act has been 'to regulate the introduction of American or foreign birds or animals in localities where they have not heretofore existed.' Lacey Act, ch. 553, § 1, 31 Stat. 187, 188 (1900) (codified as amended at 16 U.S.C. § 701)." *U.S. Ass'n of Reptile Keepers Inc. v. Zinke*, 852 F.3d 1131, 1133 (D.C. Cir. 2017).

The Act's "shipment clause" also authorizes the federal government "to designate certain species of animals as injurious to humans, wildlife, agriculture, horticulture, or forestry. When a species is designated as injurious, the Act prohibits any importation of the species into the United States or its possessions or territories. 18 U.S.C. § 42(a)(1). The Act additionally bars 'any shipment' of the species 'between the continental United States, the District of Columbia, Hawaii, the Commonwealth of Puerto Rico, or any possession of the United States.'" *Reptile Keepers*, 852 F.3d at 1132.

Until 2017, the government interpreted that latter "shipment clause" prohibition to include shipments of "injurious species" between states, as well as between the listed entities. In other words, the government took the position that the statute prohibited the transport of those species from one state to another within the continental United States.

2. The plaintiff in *Reptile Keepers* alleged that "ARK's members breed and sell reticulated pythons and green anacondas [which were designated as 'injurious species' by the Department of the Interior]. Its members have legally acquired each snake, but if the shipment clause prohibits all shipments of listed injurious species from one continental State to another, ARK's members would face criminal penalties (a fine or up to six months of imprisonment, *see* 18 U.S.C. § 42(b)) for shipping the two species across state lines." 852 F.3d at 1134.

Notably, the two species at issue "are no garden-variety snakes. Reticulated pythons can grow to a length of more than 28 feet and have been known to eat humans. Green anacondas are the world's heaviest snakes, attaining a weight in excess of 400 pounds and growing to about 22 feet in length. Both species can reproduce via parthenogenesis, a process by which numerous offspring can hatch from a female's unfertilized egg, enhancing the species' ability to establish themselves in the wild and to resist efforts to control their populations." *Id.*

Despite the obvious dangerous inherent in the identified species, and despite the government's arguments that its interpretation had been ratified by later Congressional action, the court was unmoved, and held that the shipment clause "prohibits the shipment of injurious species between the listed jurisdictions, including to and from the continental United States, but it does not speak to shipments between the 49 continental States." The practical result is that the transport of dangerous species like these snakes—and many others—could now commence unhindered by federal law. This would not, of course prevent any state from prohibiting the import of the reticulated python or any other species the state felt was dangerous and should be kept out of its borders. But while a federal prohibition would freeze transport nationwide, it is now up to each state to regulate this kind of activity.

Section 2. National Environmental Policy Act

The Humane Society of the United States v. Johanns

United States District Court, District of Columbia, 2007
520 F. Supp. 2d 8

KOLLAR-KOTELLY, District Judge. . . . [In Claim III,] Plaintiffs allege that, "by creating a fee-for-service ante-mortem horse slaughter inspection system without first conducting any environmental review under the National Environmental Policy Act [(NEPA)], 42 U.S.C. §4321, *et seq.*, [United States Department of Agriculture (USDA)] has violated NEPA and the [Council on Environmental Quality's (CEQ's)] implementing regulations, abused its discretion, and acted arbitrarily and capriciously in violation of the Administrative Procedure Act [(APA)], 5 U.S.C. §706(2)." Am. Compl. ¶ 98. The Parties, including Defendant-Intervenors, filed cross-dispositive motions as to Claim III. . . .

* * *

. . . Based on the Court's finding of a NEPA violation, the Court shall declare the Interim Final Rule to be in violation of the APA and NEPA, vacate the Interim Final Rule, and permanently enjoin the Food Safety and Inspection Service (FSIS) of the USDA from implementing the Interim Final Rule. . . .

I. BACKGROUND

A. *Factual History*

At the time Plaintiffs filed their Complaint, horses were slaughtered at three different foreign-owned facilities in the United States to provide horse meat for human consumption abroad and for use in zoos and research facilities domestically. The instant case pertains to the web of legislation and regulations pertaining to the inspection of such horses prior to slaughter.

On November 10, 2005, section 794 of the FY 2006 Agricultural Appropriations Act was signed into law. Introduced by members of Congress as an amendment to the FY 2006 Agricultural Appropriations Act, the Amendment provides:

> Effective 120 days after the date of enactment of this Act, none of the funds made available in this Act may be used to pay the salaries or expenses of personnel to inspect horses under section 3 of the Federal Meat Inspection

Act (21 U.S.C. Sec. 603) or under the guidelines issued under section 903 of the Federal Agriculture Improvement and Reform Act of 1996.

[*Because all horsemeat for human consumption must be inspected,*] Plaintiffs understand the FY 2006 Amendment to in effect prohibit the slaughter of horses for human consumption.

On November 23, 2005, Beltex Corporation, Dallas Crown, Inc., and Cavel International (collectively the "Slaughter Facility Operators") filed a petition for "emergency rulemaking" with the USDA to create a "fee-for-service" inspection program with respect to ante-mortem horse inspections and transportation-related horse inspections. On February 8, 2006, FSIS published in the *Federal Register* an amendment to 9 C.F.R. Pt. 352, "amending the Federal meat inspection regulations to provide for a voluntary fee-for-service program under which official establishments that slaughter horses will be able to apply for and pay for ante-mortem inspection." 71 Fed.Reg. 6337, 6337 (Feb. 8, 2006). The "interim final rule" was given an effective date of March 10, 2006. . . .

* * *

II. LEGAL STANDARDS

* * *

C. *National Environmental Policy Act*

NEPA, the "basic national charter for protection of the environment," 40 C.F.R. § 1500.1(a), requires that federal agencies take a "hard look" at the environmental consequences of their projects before taking action. 42 U.S.C. § 4332(C).

Pursuant to NEPA, an environmental impact statement ("EIS") must be prepared for "major Federal actions significantly affecting the quality of the human environment. . . ." 42 U.S.C. § 4332(C). The EIS must include "a detailed statement" regarding:

(i) the environmental impact of the proposed action,

(ii) any adverse environmental effects which cannot be avoided should the proposal be implemented,

(iii) alternatives to the proposed action,

(iv) the relationship between local short-term uses of man's environment and the maintenance and enhancement of long-term productivity, and

(v) any irreversible and irretrievable commitments of resources which would be involved in the proposed action should it be implemented.

42 U.S.C. § 4332(C)(i)-(v). In situations where an EIS is required, the agency is required to prepare "a concise public record of decision" that describes the factors it considered in making its decision, and must identify "all alternatives considered by the agency in reaching its decision, specifying the alternative or alternatives which were considered. . . ." 40 C.F.R. § 1505.2. The agency must "identify and discuss all

such factors including any essential considerations of national policy which were balanced by the agency in making its decision. . . ." *Id.*

However, an EIS may not be required under certain circumstances. First, "[a]n EIS is not required if the agency makes a determination based on a more limited document, an 'environmental assessment' ("EA") that the proposed action would not have a significant impact on the environment." *Sierra Club v. Mainella*, 459 F. Supp.2d 76, 81 (D.D.C.2006) (citing 40 C.F.R. §§ 1501.4, 1508.13). "The EA is to be a 'concise public document' that '[b]riefly provide[s] sufficient evidence and analysis for determining whether to prepare an [EIS].'" *Dep't of Transp. v. Pub. Citizen*, 541 U.S. 752, 757 (2004) (quoting 40 C.F.R. § 1508.9(a)). "If, pursuant to the EA, an agency determines that an EIS is not required under applicable CEQ regulations, it must issue a 'finding of no significant impact' (FONSI), which briefly presents the reasons why the proposed agency action will not have a significant impact on the human environment." *Id.* at 757–58 (citing 40 C.F.R. §§ 1501.4(e), 1508.13).

Second, a "categorical exclusion" may exempt certain agency actions from NEPA review. A "categorical exclusion" is defined by CEQ regulations as follows:

> a category of actions which do not individually or cumulatively have a significant effect on the human environment and which have been found to have no such effect in procedures adopted by a Federal agency in implementation of these regulations (§ 1507.3) and for which, therefore, neither an environmental assessment nor an environmental impact statement is required. . . . Any procedures under this section shall provide for extraordinary circumstances in which a normally excluded action may have a significant environmental effect.

40 C.F.R. § 1508.4. The USDA has issued NEPA regulations that "supplemen[t]," "incorporat[e]," and "adop[t]" the CEQ regulations described herein. 7 C.F.R. § 1b.1(a). Pursuant to 7 C.F.R. § 1b.4, certain USDA agencies and agency units, including FSIS, have been deemed to "conduct programs and activities that have been found to have no individual or cumulative effect on the human environment," and therefore "are excluded from the requirements of preparing procedures to implement NEPA. Actions of USDA agencies and agency units listed in paragraph (b) of this section are categorically excluded from the preparation of an EA or EIS unless the agency head determines that an action may have a significant environmental effect." 7 C.F.R. § 1b.4(a). However, "[n]otwithstanding the exclusions listed in . . . § 1b.4, or identified in agency procedures, agency heads may determine that circumstances dictate the need for preparation of an EA or EIS for a particular action. Agencies shall continue to scrutinize their activities to determine continued eligibility for categorical exclusion." 7 C.F.R. § 1b.3(c).

NEPA "requires that agencies assess the environmental consequences of federal projects by following certain procedures during the decision-making process." *City of Alexandria, Va. v. Slater*, 198 F.3d 862, 866 (D.C.Cir.1999). Ultimately, NEPA has twin aims. "First, it places upon an agency the obligation to consider every significant aspect of the environmental impact of a proposed action." *Baltimore Gas & Elec. Co.*, 462 U.S. at 97 (internal quotation omitted). "Second, it ensures that the agency will inform the public that it has indeed considered environmental concerns in its decisionmaking process." *Id.* Accordingly, NEPA's "mandate is essentially procedural." *City of Alexandria*, 198 F.3d at 866 (internal quotation omitted); *North Slope Borough v. Andrus*, 642 F.2d 589, 599 (D.C.Cir.1980) (NEPA requirements are essentially procedural and a court should not substitute its own policy judgment for that of the agency). "NEPA merely prohibits uninformed— rather than unwise—agency action." *Robertson v. Methow Valley Citizens Council*, 490 U.S. 332, 351 (1989). Compliance with the procedural requirements themselves, however, is not discretionary and a court may review the decision to forego production of an EIS.

Because NEPA provides no private right of action, Plaintiffs' claims have been brought under the APA. *See* 5 U.S.C. §706(2)(A). As such, "[t]he Court's role in reviewing a challenge to an agency's compliance with NEPA is limited to ensuring 'that the agency has adequately considered and disclosed the environmental impact of its actions and that its decision is not arbitrary and capricious.'" *Valley Ctmy. Pres. Comm'n v. Mineta*, 231 F.Supp.2d 23, 39 (D.D.C.2002) (quoting *Baltimore Gas & Elec. Co.*, 462 U.S. at 97–98). "While deferential, a court must thoroughly review an agency's decision and may not 'rubber stamp' decisions that are inconsistent with statutory mandate or congressional policy." *Gov't of the Province of Manitoba v. Norton*, 398 F.Supp.2d 41, 54 (D.D.C.2005).

III. DISCUSSION

While the Parties have appropriately filed Statements of Material Facts Not in Dispute, it is clear to the Court that at issue is whether Defendants were legally required to undertake some type of environmental review pursuant to NEPA prior to issuing the Interim Final Rule and that the underlying facts related thereto are not in dispute. . . .

* * *

As stated in the Court's March 14, 2006 Memorandum Opinion, Plaintiffs claim—and Defendants do not contest—that Defendants did not undertake any review pursuant to NEPA, nor did they prepare any NEPA document addressing the environmental impact associated with their issuance of the Interim Final Rule. Rather, Defendants (and Defendant-Intervenors) argue that Defendants were not required to subject the Interim Final Rule to review pursuant to NEPA because 1) the Interim Final rule did not constitute a "major Federal action" triggering NEPA requirements, and 2) the FSIS was "categorically exempt" from NEPA review requirements such that it was not required to subject the Interim Final Rule to such review. The Court shall address these arguments in turn, as well as Defendants' claim that even assuming *arguendo* that the Interim Final Rule was subject to review pursuant to NEPA, conflict between NEPA and another federal statute— specifically, the FMIA—precluded NEPA review.

A. *Issuance of the Interim Final Rule is a "Major Federal Action" that requires review pursuant to NEPA*

NEPA applies to "major Federal actions significantly affecting the quality of the human environment." 42 U.S.C. § 4332(C). Pursuant to 40 C.F.R. § 1508.18, a "major Federal action" includes "actions with effects that may be major and which are potentially subject to Federal control and responsibility. Major reinforces but does not have a meaning independent of significantly (§ 1508.27)." 40 C.F.R. § 1508.18. Accordingly, actions are deemed "major" if they "significantly" affect the environment as defined pursuant to 40 C.F.R. § 1508.27. Whether an action "significantly" affects the environment involves considerations of both "context" and "intensity." *Id.* A consideration of context "means that the significance of an action must be analyzed in several contexts such as society as a whole (human, national), the affected region, the affected interests, and the locality." *Id.* § 1508.27(a). An evaluation of "intensity," which refers to "the severity of the impact," includes an assessment of the following:

> (2) The degree to which the proposed action affects public health or safety. . . .
> (4) The degree to which the effects on the quality of the human environment are likely to be highly controversial. (5) The degree to which the possible effects on the human environment are highly uncertain or involve unique or unknown risks. . . . (9) The degree to which the action may adversely affect an endangered or threatened species or its habitat that has been determined to be critical under the Endangered Species Act of 1973.

Id. § 1508.27(b). "Effects," or impacts, include direct and indirect effects, and include

> ecological (such as the effects on natural resources and on the components, structures, and functioning of affected ecosystems), aesthetic, historic, cultural, economic, social, or health, whether direct, indirect, or cumulative. Effects may also include those resulting from actions which may have both beneficial and detrimental effects, even if on balance the agency believes that the effect will be beneficial.

40 C.F.R. § 1508.8.

> Pursuant to 40 C.F.R. § 1508.18, actions include:

> new and continuing activities, including projects and programs entirely or partly financed, assisted, conducted, regulated, or approved by federal agencies; new or revised agency rules, regulations, plans, policies, or procedures; and legislative proposals (§§ 1506.8, 1508.17). . . .

40 C.F.R. § 1508.18(a). Federal actions include the "[a]doption of official policy, such as rules, regulations, and interpretations adopted pursuant to the Administrative Procedure Act, 5 U.S.C. 551, *et seq.*; treaties and international conventions or agreements; formal documents establishing an agency's policies which will result in or substantially alter agency programs"; and "[a]doption of programs, such as a group of concerted actions to implement a specific policy or plan; systematic and

connected agency decisions allocating agency resources to implement a specific statutory program or executive directive." 40 C.F.R. § 1508.18(b)(1) & (3).

Neither Defendants nor Defendant-Intervenors refute Plaintiffs' argument that horse slaughter operations have "significantly" impacted the environment within the meaning of NEPA as set forth in 40 C.F.R. § 1508.27 . . . However, whether Plaintiffs' assessment of the "significance" of such impacts is correct is not presently subject to review, as it is clear that the related-NEPA analysis was never conducted by the agency in the first instance. Rather, both Defendants and Defendant-Intervenors claim that the Interim Final Rule does not constitute a major Federal action subject to review pursuant to NEPA because 1) Federal control is not implicated, and 2) the Interim Final Rule allegedly perpetuates the status quo. The Court will address these arguments in turn, as well as the key question of whether the impacts of the horse slaughter facilities themselves are sufficiently causally related to the Interim Final Rule such that they can be considered "effects" of the Rule itself.

1. *The Interim Final Rule is a Major Federal Action*

Defendants and Defendant-Intervenors argue that the Interim Final Rule is not a major Federal action subject to NEPA review because the Rule does not implicate Defendants' control over the horse slaughter operations themselves. Furthermore, Defendant-Intervenors claim that "Plaintiffs do not set forth any facts to suggest that the inspection-related activities conducted by the FSIS at the establishments — whether carried out pursuant to federal funding or the voluntary payment of fees — in and of themselves significantly affect the human environment, which clearly they do not. Instead, the crux of Plaintiffs' summary judgment argument is that the precursor slaughter operations conducted at Defendant-Intervenors' *privately owned and operated establishments* allegedly affect the human environment, and 'but for' the Interim Final Rule, those establishments would be forced to cease operating."

Defendants and Defendant-Intervenors mistakenly focus on "federal control" over non-federal actions in their filings. However, unlike the numerous cases cited by Defendants and Defendant-Intervenors, the federal "action" at issue in this case is not a non-federal program subject to federal funding and/or approval, but rather the agency's promulgation of the Interim Final Rule itself. Defendants and Defendant-Intervenors cannot (and do not) seriously argue that FSIS did not have control over the issuance of its own Rule. . . . In the instant case, the Interim Final Rule has already been issued such that this is the "federal action" undertaken.

* * *

While the promulgation of the Interim Final Rule itself unquestionably constitutes a major Federal action, some environmental effect must be caused by the Interim Final Rule for it to come within the rubric of NEPA. There is a major Federal action subject to NEPA review "whenever an agency makes a decision which permits action by other parties which will affect the quality of the environment."

Scientists' Inst. for Pub. Info. v. Atomic Energy Comm'n, 481 F.2d 1079, 1088–89 (D.C.Cir.1973).

Pursuant to CEQ regulations themselves, NEPA review is implicated by both foreseeable direct and indirect impacts:

* * *

Effects includes ecological (such as the effects on natural resources and on the components, structures, and functioning of affected ecosystems), aesthetic, historic, cultural, economic, social, or health, whether direct, indirect, or cumulative. Effects may also include those resulting from actions which may have both beneficial and detrimental effects, even if on balance the agency believes that the effect will be beneficial.

40 C.F.R. § 1508.8(b). "Indirect impacts need only to be 'reasonably foreseeable' to require an assessment of the environmental impact." *Friends of the Earth, Inc. v. U.S. Army Corps of Eng'rs*, 109 F.Supp.2d 30, 41 (D.D.C.2000). . . . [T]he Supreme Court, in a key 2004 case . . . held that the appropriate test in determining whether a particular effect was caused by a federal action was not a "but for" inquiry, but rather whether the federal action was the "legally relevant cause" of the effect. *Dep't of Transp. v. Public Citizen*, 541 U.S. 752, 769 (2004).

* * *

. . . Turning to the issues pending before this Court, both the legal framework surrounding ante-mortem inspections of horses to be slaughtered for consumption, and the intent of FSIS as expressed in the notice issued prior to the promulgation of the Interim Final Rule, reveal that the Rule is appropriately the "legally relevant cause" of the environmental effects of horse slaughter operations after the FY 2006 Amendment went into effect.

. . . [T]here is no intervening link between the Interim Final Rule and the horse slaughter operations and their environmental effects. . . . Pursuant to the FMIA, 21 U.S.C. § 603(a), "an [FSIS] examination and inspection of all amenable species" is required [before slaughter.]. . . . Defendants likewise admit that without the Interim Final Rule, the horse slaughter facilities would not continue to function as such.

* * *

. . . [T]he Interim Final Rule is the "legally relevant cause" of the environmental effects of the horse slaughter facilities after the FY 2006 Amendment went into effect. . . . [T]he horse slaughter operations and their environmental impacts are "functionally inseparable" from the fee-for-service inspections authorized by the Interim Final Rule because horse slaughtering for human consumption "may not take place" pursuant to the FMIA until the FSIS has conducted ante-mortem inspections. Accordingly, the environmental effects of horse slaughter operations themselves should have been assessed pursuant to NEPA prior to promulgating the Interim Final Rule, as they are "reasonably causally related" to be considered effects of the Rule itself.

* * *

B. *The Categorical Exclusion was arbitrarily and capriciously applied in this case*

* * *

Defendant-Intervenors broadly state, without providing any supporting case law, that "[t]he categorical exclusion of 7 C.F.R. § 1b.4(b)(6) does not require the agency head to make an affirmative determination that each particular activity of the FSIS shall be categorically excluded from NEPA's procedural requirements." Upon examining the case law and relevant statutes, the Court concludes that both NEPA and its implementing regulations preclude [this] interpretation that pursuant to 7 C.F.R. § 1b.4, a "categorically excluded" agency may ignore NEPA entirely.

* * *

Defendants' interpretation of 7 C.F.R. § 1b.4 as shielding the Interim Final Rule from any environmental consideration is arbitrary and capricious, as it is inconsistent with the terms of 7 C.F.R. § 1b.4 itself, as well as applicable CEQ regulations.

2. *Even under the "arbitrary and capricious standard," agencies subject to the exclusion provision delineated in 7 C.F.R. § 1b.4 must demonstrate consideration of NEPA in some fashion*

An agency cannot invoke a categorical exclusion for the first time in legal briefings when no such invocation exists in the record. . . . "Although the Court of Appeals has not addressed this particular issue, both judges of this Court that have considered the issue have found that a post hoc invocation of a categorical exclusion during litigation cannot justify a failure to prepare an EA or EIS. [citations omitted]" *Edmonds Inst. v. Babbitt,* 42 F.Supp.2d 1, 18 (D.D.C.1999). . . . Defendants' failure to give any consideration as to whether or not the Interim Final Rule invoked "extraordinary circumstances" such that it "may have a significant environmental effect," violated 7 C.F.R. § 1b.4 and NEPA's implementing regulations. Concretely, 7 C.F.R. § 1b.4 does not permit FSIS to avoid any consideration of whether extraordinary circumstances apply, and Defendants' interpretation to this effect is arbitrary and capricious.

Pursuant to USDA regulations, "[a]ctions of [the FSIS] are categorically excluded from the preparation of an EA or EIS unless the agency head determines that an action may have a significant environmental effect." 7 C.F.R. § 1b.4. However, this regulation does not exist in a vacuum. It is qualified by another USDA regulation — 7 C.F.R. § 1b.3(c) — as follows: "[n]otwithstanding the exclusions listed in paragraphs (a) of this section and § 1b.4, or identified in agency procedures, agency heads may determine that circumstances dictate the need for preparation of an EA or EIS for a particular action. Agencies *shall continue to scrutinize their activities* to determine continued eligibility for categorical exclusion." 7 C.F.R. § 1b.3(c) (emphasis added). Defendants' interpretation of 7 C.F.R. § 1b.4 would exempt the FSIS from any duty to scrutinize its activities in violation of 7 C.F.R. § 1b.3(c).

Furthermore, pursuant to 7 C.F.R. § 1b.2, "[e]ach USDA agency is responsible for compliance with this part, the regulations of CEQ, and NEPA." 7 C.F.R. § 1b.2(b). CEQ regulations require that "[a]ny procedures [invoked by an agency] under this [categorical exclusion] section *shall provide for extraordinary circumstances* in which a normally excluded action may have a significant environmental effect." 40 C.F.R. § 1508.4 (emphasis added). Defendants' interpretation of 7 C.F.R. § 1b.4 as having required only a determination over twenty years ago that all "FSIS activities have no significant environmental impact," see Defs.' Reply at 5, belies any compliance with FSIS's obligation to "provide for extraordinary circumstances in which a normally excluded action may have a significant environmental effect."

Ultimately, the Court agrees that "any notion that USDA may avoid NEPA review simply by *failing* even to consider whether a normally excluded action may have a significant environmental impact flies in the face of the CEQ regulations," Pls.' Mem. for Summ. J. at 36, as well as USDA's own NEPA regulations.

> *3. In the instant case, FSIS demonstrates that it did not give any consideration as to whether the Interim Final Rule should be exempt from the section 1b.4 exclusion provision*

The administrative record does not contradict Plaintiffs' assessment that "there is no evidence whatsoever that the 'agency head'—or any USDA official—even *contemplated* whether the rule 'may have a significant environmental effect' that should be considered in an EA or EIS, 7 C.F.R. § 1b.4, let alone made an affirmative contemporaneous determination that this exception to the general categorical exclusion for all FSIS programs should *not* apply here." Pls.' Mem. for Summ. J. at 32–33. *See also id.* at 36 ("[T]he Record contains no hint that USDA ever even considered whether the 'extraordinary circumstances' criteria applied to its decision.").

* * *

Plaintiffs state that the Administrative Record submitted by Defendants "contained no NEPA documentation in connection with the rule or petition, nor any indication that any USDA official had ever given any consideration to whether an EIS or EA should be prepared." Defendants do not refute this. Accordingly, . . . the Court concludes that Defendants have violated NEPA and its implementing regulations.

* * *

Accordingly, the Court shall vacate the Interim Final Rule, which was promulgated in violation of NEPA-mandated procedures and in violation of the law.

* * *

Notes

1. Unlike the other statutes discussed in this Chapter, NEPA is not focused on animals, but addresses procedural requirements placed on government agencies that intend to engage in activities that could have some impact on the environment, which can include the environment in which animals live. It does not address any

specific protection of animals or natural resources. Nevertheless, NEPA is one of the oldest and most often-used laws for environmental litigants. NEPA also serves as an important tool for defending the interests of animals. NEPA extends a critical procedural protection to animals and habitat anytime there is a "major federal action" which a federal agency has discretion to approve. NEPA requires that

> all agencies of the federal government shall . . . include in every recommendation or report on proposals for legislation and other major federal actions significantly affecting the quality of the human environment, a detailed statement by the responsible official on (i) the environmental impact of the proposed action; (ii) any adverse environmental effects which cannot be avoided should the proposal be implemented; (iii) alternatives to the proposed action; (iv) the relationship between local short-term uses of man's environment and the maintenance and enhancement of long-term productivity; and (v) any irreversible and irretrievable commitments of resources which would be involved in the proposed action should it be implemented.

42 U.S.C § 4332(2)(C) (2013).

2. NEPA governs the actions of federal agencies by requiring them to undertake specific tasks which involve the examination and weighing of the environmental effects and implications of certain actions. Thus, the statute's focus is on procedure. As the court in *Johanns* makes clear, NEPA is designed to ensure public participation and comment and an informed decision, but not to require particular results. *Vermont Yankee Nuclear Power Corp. v. Natural Res. Def. Counsel*, 435 U.S. 519, 558 (1978). Agency discretion to determine the particular course of action remains largely unchecked.

In general practice (subject to the exceptions and exclusions discussed in the preceding case), NEPA requires government officials intending to engage in "major federal actions" to prepare an Environmental Assessment (EA), 7 C.F.R. § 650.8, 40 C.F.R. § 1508.9, which evaluates the proposed action's likely effects on the environment. NEPA then directs officials to use this information to determine if the statute's provision requiring a more involved environmental impact statement (EIS) applies to the proposed action. 7 C.F.R. § 650.4; 40 C.F.R. § 1508.11. If the agency officials find that the proposed actions would have "no significant impact" on the environment, no EIS is required and the EA and "FONSI," or "finding of no significant impact," is the final act in this procedure. 22 C.F.R. § 161.7; 40 C.F.R. § 1508.13. If an EIS is required, an extensive set of research and reporting must be done by the government, with an opportunity for public comment as well.

As the opinion indicates, the definition of "major federal action" that significantly affects the environment—the trigger for an EIS—is a hotly contested issue, for a few reasons. First, Congress did not define "major" or "federal" or "major federal action" in the statute, and presumably intended these concepts to be interpreted independently by the agencies and the judiciary. The federal courts, functioning as the ultimate arbiters of NEPA, often consider the terms conjointly. *See* Daniel R. Mandelker,

NEPA LAW AND LITIGATION §§ 8:1, 8:6 (2d ed. revised 2002) ("Mandelker") (subsequently revised 2013). The term has been defined in the Council on Environmental Quality ("CEQ") regulations, as including "actions with effects that may be major and which are potentially subject to Federal control and responsibility," 40 C.F.R. § 1508.18, which still leaves the courts and litigants without significant guidance. These regulations are rules (and guidelines) for NEPA implementation binding on all federal agencies, are accorded substantial deference by courts and contain what the CEQ determined to be the majority court rule. *See* Mandelker, § 8:1.

3. While the CEQ regulations do not explicitly define federal actions, they do enumerate the following specific categories of activities which qualify as "federal action":

(1) the adoption of official policies, such as rules and regulations;

(2) the adoption of "formal plans . . . which guide or prescribe alternative uses of federal resources, upon which future agency actions will be based";

(3) the adoption of "programs, such as a group of concerted actions to implement a specific policy or plan" or "allocating agency resources to implement" a statutory program or executive directive; or

(4) the approval of specific projects such as "actions approved by permit or other regulatory decision as well as federal and federally assisted activities."

40 C.F.R. § 1508.18(b). *See also Sierra Club v. U.S. Dept. of Agric.*, 777 F. Supp. 2d 44, 58–64 (D.D.C. 2011) ("major federal action" under NEPA where federal agency had "long history of involvement" with electric power corporation, providing financial assistance and retaining "substantial control" over its coal-fired generating stations, particularly as related to the potential development of additional power plants at issue).

Once an action is found to be "federal," the next two steps require courts to determine whether it is "major" and whether it "significantly" affects the quality of the environment. The majority of the few cases that have considered these terms have focused on whether the action is "significant," with the issue of whether the action is "major" receiving far less attention. In these cases, some courts—and the CEQ (*see id.* § 1508.18)—have combined these considerations into a "unitary" test, under which an action is held to be major if it is significant. In the leading case of *Minnesota Public Interest Research Group v. Butz (I)*, 498 F.2d 1314 (8th Cir. 1974), the court adopted the unitary standard because the court felt it better promotes the policies behind NEPA. Other courts maintain the statute imposes a dual standard mandating that an action be *both* major and significant. *See, e.g., Nat'l Ass'n for the Advancement of Colored People v. Medical Ctr., Inc.*, 584 F.2d 619 (3d Cir. 1978) (adopting the dual standard because it adheres more strictly to the statutory language).

Under the unitary standard, the most common distinction between major and minor activities seems to be the relative size and magnitude of the activity (frequently assessed from an economic standpoint) and its corresponding potential impact on the environment. *See Nat'l Res. Defense Council, Inc. v. Hodel*, 435 F. Supp. 590, 598 (D. Or. 1977), *aff'd on other grounds sub nom, Nat'l Res. Defense Council, Inc. v. Munro*, 626 F.2d 134 (9th Cir. 1980) ("*Munro*") (joint private-federal hydro-electric power development program was a "major" action "in both the environmental and economic sense"); *see also* Mandelker, *supra*, § 8:6(3). Besides financial cost, courts performing this analysis have considered investment of time or other non-monetary resources, amount of planning, nature of construction and external-ized effects/costs, such as displacement of people or modification of the land. *See, e.g., Township of Ridley v. Blanchette*, 421 F. Supp. 435, 446 (E.D. Pa. 1976) ("major" projects are typically those which entail, *inter alia*, federal funding of at least one million dollars; "'major' is a term . . . [that] serves to differentiate between projects which do not involve sufficiently serious effects to justify the costs of completing an impact statement, and those projects with potential effects which appear to offset the costs in time and resources of preparing a statement"); *Natural Res. Defense Council, Inc. v. Grant*, 341 F. Supp. 356, 366 (E.D.N.C. 1972) (water channel project which extended 66 miles and cost $1.5 million — $706,000 of which was federal funding — was "major").

Other courts have employed the unitary causation standard, equating major sta-tus with the presence of significant effects. *See, e.g., Simmans v. Grant*, 370 F. Supp. 5 (S.D. Tex. 1974). These criteria provide only general direction to courts, ultimately forcing them to make subjective judgments about what qualifies as "major," by rely-ing on the following rule: larger, more involved activities with probably substantial effects tend to be classified as major; smaller, more limited activities with probably minimal effects tend to be classified as minor. Some examples of activities that were determined to be major are: the conversion of a large, partially federally-funded housing project, *Jones v. U.S. Dept. of Housing & Urban Dev.*, 390 F. Supp. 579 (E.D. La. 1974); and a bridge with 60% federal funding, *Monroe County Conservation Council, Inc. v. Volpe*, 472 F.2d 693 (2d Cir. 1972). Examples of "minor" activities are: partially federally-funded housing projects under agency directive that a mini-mum "threshold" project size exist to justify an EIS, *United Neighbors Civic Ass'n of Jamaica, Inc. v. Pierce*, 563 F. Supp. 200 (E.D.N.Y. 1983); minor traffic improve-ments, *Julis v. City of Cedar Rapids, Iowa*, 349 F. Supp. 88 (N.D. Iowa 1972); and a replacement bridge, *Sierra Club v. Hassell*, 636 F.2d 1095 (5th Cir. 1981). Mandelker, *supra*, § 8:6(3).

4. Determinations of "significan[ce]" under the dual standard are sometimes undertaken in an *ad hoc* manner, with different courts utilizing different tests. *See* Mandelker, *supra*, § 8:6(4)(a). Courts often turn to the CEQ regulations for the only true definition of "significant." *See* 40 C.F.R. § 1508.27. This is likely because NEPA does not offer an environmental "baseline" to use as a point of comparison for determinations of the significance of impacts, and because the courts and affected agencies have not established their own baselines. The "significan[ce]" of the activ-ity is an important consideration regardless of which standard — unitary or dual — is used. *See, e.g., Munro*, 626 F.2d 134.

The aforementioned CEQ regulations provide a framework that entails consideration of two factors: the action's "context" and its "intensity." The regulations require that proposed actions be "analyzed in several contexts, such as society as a whole . . . , the affected region, the affected interests, and the locality." *See* Mandelker, § 8:6(4)(b). Both the short-term and the long-term effects are also considered. The action's "intensity" "refer[s] to the severity of the impact." *Id.* Notably "[a] significant impact may exist even if the federal agency believes that on balance the effect will be beneficial." *Id.* The regulations identify the following factors which should be considered when assessing the severity/intensity of an impact:

1. the effects on public health and safety;

2. the unique characteristics of the relevant geographic area;

3. the degree to which the effects "are likely to be highly controversial;"

4. the degree to which the effects "are highly uncertain or involve unique or unknown risks;"

5. the cumulative effects of the action; and

6. whether the action threatens a violation of a federal, state, or local environmental law.

Id.

5. Ultimately, courts' determinations regarding significance are based on the facts of a given case. Some courts have expounded various criteria for making such determinations, although most of the criteria provide only generalized guidance. *See, e.g., Minnesota Pub. Interest Research Group v. Butz (I)*, 498 F.2d 1314, 1322 (8th Cir. 1974) ("significance" should be defined broadly: "NEPA is concerned with indirect effects as well as direct effects"); *Save Our Ten Acres v. Kreger*, 472 F.2d 463, 467 (5th Cir. 1973) ("significance" is attained when "the court finds that the project may cause a significant degradation of some human environmental factor (even though other environmental factors are affected beneficially or not at all)"); *Maryland-Nat'l Capital Park & Planning Comm'n v. U.S. Postal Serv.*, 487 F.2d 1029, 1040 (D.C. Cir. 1973) (enumerating four criteria to be used by courts in assessing "significance": (1) whether the agency has taken a "hard look" at the problem, rather than making "bald conclusions, unaided by preliminary investigation," (2) whether the agency has analyzed the pertinent areas of environmental concern, (3) whether the agency has made a "convincing case" that determinations of insignificant impact are justified, and (4) whether the agency has convincingly substantiated that determinations of *significant* impacts will be minimized by alterations in the project). *See also Humane Soc'y of the U.S. v. Hodel*, 840 F.2d 45 (D.C. Cir. 1988) (applying the four-part test after finding plaintiffs had standing to sue). One case, *Hanly v. Kleindienst (II)*, 471 F.2d 823 (2d Cir. 1972), applied an absolute, comparative test which would call for an EIS whenever a federal action results in "adverse environmental effects in excess of those created by existing uses in the area affected by it." *Id.* at 830–31; *see also* Mandelker, *supra*, § 8:6(4)(c). This standard equates NEPA's

provisions with a rule that mandates an EIS for any form of environmental degradation. This "nondegradation" principle coincides with NEPA's declaration of policy, which mandates "all practicable means" be employed to achieve "the widest range of beneficial uses of the environment without degradation." *See* 42 U.S.C. § 4331(b)(3). *Hanly*'s "absolute quantitative adverse environmental effects" standard might cover circumstances where the contemplated action would involve an environment that has already been degraded (an EIS may still be required under such circumstances) although it might not cover situations where the action's significance may be a function of its *qualitative* rather than *quantitative* impact. *See Hanly*, 471 F.2d at 830–31; Mandelker, *supra*, § 8:6(4)(c).

6. Courts have established that "major federal actions" include not only federal agency projects and private projects that the federal government has funded and/or approved, but also federal programs, rules and policies. *See* Mandelker, *supra*, §§ 8:1, 8:4(1). The CEQ regulations codify this case law by defining "major Federal action" as including "actions with effects that may be major and which are potentially subject to federal control and responsibility," as well as "projects and programs entirely or partly financed, assisted, conducted, regulated, or approved by federal agencies" and "new or revised agency rules, regulations, plans, policies, or procedures." 40 C.F.R. § 1508.18.

7. The actions of a non-federal entity can be considered "federal" if a federal agency has somehow "enabled" the non-federal party to act. For example, federal action occurs where permits, leases or other approvals are given under federal agency programs. *See Scientists' Inst. for Pub. Info., Inc. v. Atomic Energy Comm'n*, 481 F.2d 1079 (D.C. Cir. 1973). Courts make this determination on a case-by-case basis.

8. A multitude of cases have been brought in which plaintiffs asserted NEPA violations to force environmental review of actions that could negatively impact animals as well as humans. A few examples include *Front Range Equine Rescue v. Vilsack*, 782 F.3d 565 (10th Cir. 2015) (case challenged USDA failure to engage in NEPA review before granting federal inspection to horse slaughterhouses); *Anderson v. Evans*, 314 F.3d 1006 (9th Cir. 2003) (federal defendants did not satisfy NEPA when they issued a finding of "no significant impact" and permitted Makah Indian tribe to proceed with whale hunt) (discussed later in this chapter); *Center for Biological Diversity v. Salazar*, 695 F.3d 893 (9th Cir. 2012) (asserting claims under the MMPA, the ESA and NEPA, challenging FWS regulations under the MMPA that authorize incidental takes of polar bears and Pacific walruses resulting from oil and gas exploration activities in the Chukchi Sea and on the adjacent coast of Alaska, and challenging accompanying environmental review documents; summary judgment in favor of FWS affirmed); *Defenders of Wildlife v. U.S. Dept. of Navy*, 733 F.3d 1106 (11th Cir. 2013) (suit alleging violations under NEPA and the ESA challenged the Navy's decision to install an Undersea Warfare Training Range offshore of federally-designated critical habitat and adjacent to the only known calving grounds of the "highly endangered" North Atlantic right whale; summary judgment for defendants affirmed). The following is one such case that reached the U.S. Supreme

Court, and is especially instructive, because it analyzes NEPA and ESA claims, and also established the current federal standard for preliminary injunctive relief.

Winter v. Natural Resources Defense Council, Inc.

Supreme Court of the United States, 2008
555 U.S. 7, 129 S. Ct. 365, 172 L. Ed.2d 249

Chief Justice ROBERTS delivered the opinion of the Court.

"To be prepared for war is one of the most effectual means of preserving peace." So said George Washington in his first Annual Address to Congress, 218 years ago. One of the most important ways the Navy prepares for war is through integrated training exercises at sea. These exercises include training in the use of modern sonar to detect and track enemy submarines, something the Navy has done for the past 40 years. The plaintiffs complained that the Navy's sonar training program harmed marine mammals, and that the Navy should have prepared an environmental impact statement before commencing its latest round of training exercises. The Court of Appeals upheld a preliminary injunction imposing restrictions on the Navy's sonar training, even though that court acknowledged that "the record contains no evidence that marine mammals have been harmed" by the Navy's exercises.

The Court of Appeals was wrong, and its decision is reversed.

I

The Navy deploys its forces in "strike groups," which are groups of surface ships, submarines, and aircraft centered around either an aircraft carrier or an amphibious assault ship. Seamless coordination among strike-group assets is critical. Before deploying a strike group, the Navy requires extensive integrated training in analysis and prioritization of threats, execution of military missions, and maintenance of force protection.

Antisubmarine warfare is currently the Pacific Fleet's top war-fighting priority. Modern diesel-electric submarines pose a significant threat to Navy vessels because they can operate almost silently, making them extremely difficult to detect and track. Potential adversaries of the United States possess at least 300 of these submarines.

The most effective technology for identifying submerged diesel-electric submarines within their torpedo range is active sonar, which involves emitting pulses of sound underwater and then receiving the acoustic waves that echo off the target. Active sonar is a particularly useful tool because it provides both the bearing and the distance of target submarines; it is also sensitive enough to allow the Navy to track enemy submarines that are quieter than the surrounding marine environment. This case concerns the Navy's use of "mid-frequency active" (MFA) sonar, which transmits sound waves at frequencies between 1 kHz and 10 kHz.

Not surprisingly, MFA sonar is a complex technology, and sonar operators must undergo extensive training to become proficient in its use. . . . The Navy conducts regular training exercises under realistic conditions to ensure that sonar operators are thoroughly skilled in its use in a variety of situations.

The waters off the coast of southern California (SOCAL) are an ideal location for conducting integrated training exercises, as this is the only area on the west coast that is relatively close to land, air, and sea bases, as well as amphibious landing areas. [T]he SOCAL exercises include extensive training in detecting, tracking, and neutralizing enemy submarines.

Sharing the waters in the SOCAL operating area are at least 37 species of marine mammals, including dolphins, whales, and sea lions. The parties strongly dispute the extent to which the Navy's training activities will harm those animals or disrupt their behavioral patterns. The Navy emphasizes that it has used MFA sonar during training exercises in SOCAL for 40 years, without a single documented sonar-related injury to any marine mammal. The Navy asserts that, at most, MFA sonar may cause temporary hearing loss or brief disruptions of marine mammals' behavioral patterns.

The plaintiffs are the Natural Resources Defense Council, Jean-Michael Cousteau (an environmental enthusiast and filmmaker), and several other groups devoted to the protection of marine mammals and ocean habitats. They contend that MFA sonar can cause much more serious injuries to marine mammals than the Navy acknowledges, including permanent hearing loss, decompression sickness, and major behavioral disruptions. According to the plaintiffs, several mass strandings of marine mammals (outside of SOCAL) have been "associated" with the use of active sonar. They argue that certain species of marine mammals—such as beaked whales—are uniquely susceptible to injury from active sonar; these injuries would not necessarily be detected by the Navy, given that beaked whales are "very deep divers" that spend little time at the surface.

II

The procedural history of this case is rather complicated. The Marine Mammal Protection Act of 1972 (MMPA), 86 Stat. 1027, generally prohibits any individual from "taking" a marine mammal, defined as harassing, hunting, capturing, or killing it. 16 U.S.C. §§ 1362(13), 1372(a). The Secretary of Defense may "exempt any action or category of actions" from the MMPA if such actions are "necessary for national defense." § 1371(f)(1). In January 2007, the Deputy Secretary of Defense . . . granted the Navy a 2-year exemption from the MMPA for the training exercises . . . conditioned on the Navy adopting several mitigation procedures, including: (1) training lookouts and officers to watch for marine mammals; (2) requiring at least five lookouts with binoculars on each vessel to watch for anomalies on the water surface (including marine mammals); (3) requiring aircraft and sonar operators to report detected marine mammals in the vicinity of the training exercises; (4) requiring reduction of active sonar transmission levels by 6 dB if a marine mammal is detected within 1,000 yards of the bow of the vessel, or by 10 dB if detected within 500 yards; (5) requiring complete shutdown of active sonar transmission if a marine mammal is detected within 200 yards of the vessel; (6) requiring active sonar to be operated at the "lowest practicable level"; and (7) adopting coordination and reporting procedures.

The National Environmental Policy Act of 1969 (NEPA), 83 Stat. 852, requires federal agencies "to the fullest extent possible" to prepare an environmental impact statement (EIS) for "every . . . major Federal actio[n] significantly affecting the quality of the human environment." 42 U.S.C. §4332(2)(C) (2000 ed.). An agency is not required to prepare a full EIS if it determines—based on a shorter environmental assessment (EA)—that the proposed action will not have a significant impact on the environment. 40 CFR §§1508.9(a), 1508.13 (2007).

In February 2007, the Navy issued an EA concluding that the 14 SOCAL training exercises scheduled through January 2009 would not have a significant impact on the environment. App. 226–227. The EA divided potential injury to marine mammals into two categories: Level A harassment, defined as the potential destruction or loss of biological tissue (*i.e.*, physical injury), and Level B harassment, defined as temporary injury or disruption of behavioral patterns such as migration, feeding, surfacing, and breeding.

The Navy's computer models predicted that the SOCAL training exercises would cause only eight Level A harassments of common dolphins each year, and that even these injuries could be avoided through the Navy's voluntary mitigation measures, given that dolphins travel in large pods easily located by Navy lookouts. The EA also predicted 274 Level B harassments of beaked whales per year, none of which would result in permanent injury. Beaked whales spend little time at the surface, so the precise effect of active sonar on these mammals is unclear. Erring on the side of caution, the Navy classified all projected harassments of beaked whales as Level A. In light of its conclusion that the SOCAL training exercises would not have a significant impact on the environment, the Navy determined that it was unnecessary to prepare a full EIS.

Shortly after the Navy released its EA, the plaintiffs sued the Navy, seeking declaratory and injunctive relief on the grounds that the Navy's SOCAL training exercises violated NEPA, the Endangered Species Act of 1973 (ESA), and the Coastal Zone Management Act of 1972 (CZMA).[2] The District Court granted plaintiffs' motion for a preliminary injunction[, and after review by the Ninth Circuit, allowed]. . . . the Navy to use MFA sonar only as long as it implemented [additional] mitigation measures (in addition to the measures the Navy had adopted pursuant to its MMPA exemption)[, including] . . . shutting down MFA sonar when a marine mammal is spotted within 2,200 yards of a vessel; and powering down MFA sonar by 6 dB during significant surface ducting conditions, in which sound travels further than

---

2. The CZMA states that federal agencies taking actions "that affec[t] any land or water use or natural resources of the coastal zone" shall carry out these activities "in a manner which is consistent to the maximum extent practicable with the enforceable policies of approved State management programs." 16 U.S.C. §1456(c)(1)(A).

it otherwise would due to temperature differences in adjacent layers of water. The Navy filed a notice of appeal, challenging [those] two restrictions.

The Navy then sought relief from the Executive Branch. The President, pursuant to 16 U.S.C. § 1456(c)(1)(B), granted the Navy an exemption from the CZMA. . . . He concluded that compliance with the District Court's injunction would "undermine the Navy's ability to conduct realistic training exercises that are necessary to ensure the combat effectiveness of . . . strike groups."

* * *

III

A

A plaintiff seeking a preliminary injunction must establish that he is likely to succeed on the merits, that he is likely to suffer irreparable harm in the absence of preliminary relief, that the balance of equities tips in his favor, and that an injunction is in the public interest. . . .

* * *

"NEPA itself does not mandate particular results." *Robertson v. Methow Valley Citizens Council*, 490 U.S. 332, 350 (1989). . . . Instead, NEPA imposes only procedural requirements to "ensur[e] that the agency, in reaching its decision, will have available, and will carefully consider, detailed information concerning significant environmental impacts." *Id.* at 349. Part of the harm NEPA attempts to prevent in requiring an EIS is that, without one, there may be little if any information about prospective environmental harms and potential mitigating measures. Here, in contrast, the plaintiffs are seeking to enjoin—or substantially restrict—training exercises that have been taking place in SOCAL for the last 40 years. And the latest series of exercises were not approved until after the defendant took a "hard look at environmental consequences," id., as evidenced by the issuance of a detailed, 293-page EA.

As explained in the next section, even if plaintiffs have shown irreparable injury from the Navy's training exercises, any such injury is outweighed by the public interest and the Navy's interest in effective, realistic training of its sailors. A proper consideration of these factors alone requires denial of the requested injunctive relief. For the same reason, we do not address the lower courts' holding that plaintiffs have also established a likelihood of success on the merits.

B

A preliminary injunction is an extraordinary remedy never awarded as of right. . . . In this case, the District Court and the Ninth Circuit significantly understated the burden the preliminary injunction would impose on the Navy's ability to conduct realistic training exercises, and the injunction's consequent adverse impact on the public interest in national defense.

This case involves "complex, subtle, and professional decisions as to the composition, training, equipping, and control of a military force," which are "essentially professional military judgments." *Gilligan v. Morgan*, 413 U.S. 1, 10 (1973). We "give great deference to the professional judgment of military authorities concerning the relative importance of a particular military interest." *Goldman v. Weinberger*, 475 U.S. 503, 507 (1986). . . .

Here, the record contains declarations from some of the Navy's most senior officers, all of whom underscored the threat posed by enemy submarines and the need for extensive sonar training to counter this threat. . . . We accept these officers' assertions that the use of MFA sonar under realistic conditions during training exercises is of the utmost importance to the Navy and the Nation.

These interests must be weighed against the possible harm to the ecological, scientific, and recreational interests that are legitimately before this Court. Plaintiffs have submitted declarations asserting that they take whale watching trips, observe marine mammals underwater, conduct scientific research on marine mammals, and photograph these animals in their natural habitats. Plaintiffs contend that the Navy's use of MFA sonar will injure marine mammals or alter their behavioral patterns, impairing plaintiffs' ability to study and observe the animals.

While we do not question the seriousness of these interests, we conclude that the balance of equities and consideration of the overall public interest in this case tip strongly in favor of the Navy. For the plaintiffs, the most serious possible injury would be harm to an unknown number of the marine mammals that they study and observe. In contrast, forcing the Navy to deploy an inadequately trained antisubmarine force jeopardizes the safety of the fleet. Active sonar is the only reliable technology for detecting and tracking enemy diesel-electric submarines, and the President—the Commander in Chief—has determined that training with active sonar is "essential to national security."

The public interest in conducting training exercises with active sonar under realistic conditions plainly outweighs the interests advanced by the plaintiffs. Of course, military interests do not always trump other considerations, and we have not held that they do. In this case, however, the proper determination of where the public interest lies does not strike us as a close question.

C

Despite the importance of assessing the balance of equities and the public interest in determining whether to grant a preliminary injunction, the District Court addressed these considerations in only a cursory fashion.

* * *

The Court of Appeals held that the balance of equities and the public interest favored the plaintiffs, largely based on its view that the preliminary injunction would not in fact impose a significant burden on the Navy's ability to conduct its training exercises and certify its strike groups.

* * *

IV

As noted above, we do not address the underlying merits of plaintiffs' claims. . . .[5]

The factors examined above—the balance of equities and consideration of the public interest—are pertinent in assessing the propriety of any injunctive relief, preliminary or permanent. Given that the ultimate legal claim is that the Navy must prepare an EIS, not that it must cease sonar training, there is no basis for enjoining such training in a manner credibly alleged to pose a serious threat to national security. This is particularly true in light of the fact that the training has been going on for 40 years with no documented episode of harm to a marine mammal.

* * *

President Theodore Roosevelt explained that "the only way in which a navy can ever be made efficient is by practice at sea, under all the conditions which would have to be met if war existed." President's Annual Message, 42 Cong. Rec. 67, 81 (1907). We do not discount the importance of plaintiffs' ecological, scientific, and recreational interests in marine mammals. Those interests, however, are plainly outweighed by the Navy's need to conduct realistic training exercises to ensure that it is able to neutralize the threat posed by enemy submarines. The District Court abused its discretion by imposing a 2,200-yard shutdown zone and by requiring the Navy to power down its MFA sonar during significant surface ducting conditions. The judgment of the Court of Appeals is reversed, and the preliminary injunction is vacated to the extent it has been challenged by the Navy.

It is so ordered.

* * *

Justice GINSBURG, with whom Justice SOUTER joins, dissenting.

The central question in this action under the National Environmental Policy Act of 1969 (NEPA) was whether the Navy must prepare an environmental impact statement (EIS). The Navy does not challenge its obligation to do so, and it represents that the EIS will be complete in January 2009—one month after the instant exercises conclude. If the Navy had completed the EIS before taking action, as NEPA instructs, the parties and the public could have benefited from the environmental analysis—and the Navy's training could have proceeded without interruption. Instead, the Navy acted first, and thus thwarted the very purpose an EIS is intended to serve. To justify its course, the Navy sought dispensation not from Congress, but from an executive council that lacks authority to countermand or revise NEPA's requirements. I would hold that, in imposing manageable measures to mitigate

---

5. The bulk of Justice GINSBURG's dissent is devoted to the merits. For the reasons stated, we find the injunctive relief granted in this case an abuse of discretion, even if plaintiffs are correct on the underlying merits. As to the injunction, the dissent barely mentions the Navy's interests. We find that those interests, and the documented risks to national security, clearly outweigh the harm on the other side of the balance. . . .

harm until completion of the EIS, the District Court conscientiously balanced the equities and did not abuse its discretion.

* * *

II

NEPA "promotes its sweeping commitment" to environmental integrity "by focusing Government and public attention on the environmental effects of proposed agency action." "By so focusing agency attention, NEPA ensures that the agency will not act on incomplete information, only to regret its decision after it is too late to correct."

The EIS is NEPA's core requirement. In addition to discussing potential consequences, an EIS must describe potential mitigation measures and alternatives to the proposed course of action. The EIS requirement "ensures that important effects will not be overlooked or underestimated only to be discovered after resources have been committed or the die otherwise cast."

"Publication of an EIS . . . also serves a larger informational role." It demonstrates that an agency has indeed considered environmental concerns, and "perhaps more significantly, provides a springboard for public comment." . . .

In light of these objectives, the timing of an EIS is critical. CEQ regulations instruct agencies to "integrate the NEPA process with other planning at the earliest possible time to insure that planning and decisions reflect environmental values." 40 CFR § 1501.2 (1987). An EIS must be prepared "early enough so that it can serve practically as an important contribution to the decisionmaking process and will not be used to rationalize or justify decisions already made."

The Navy's publication of its EIS in this case, scheduled to occur after the 14 exercises are completed, defeats NEPA's informational and participatory purposes. The Navy's inverted timing, it bears emphasis, is the very reason why the District Court had to confront the question of mitigation measures at all. Had the Navy prepared a legally sufficient EIS before beginning the SOCAL exercises, NEPA would have functioned as its drafters intended: The EIS process and associated public input might have convinced the Navy voluntarily to adopt mitigation measures, but NEPA itself would not have impeded the Navy's exercises. . . .

* * *

[III.A.]

Equity's flexibility is important in the NEPA context. Because an EIS is the tool for uncovering environmental harm, environmental plaintiffs may often rely more heavily on their probability of success than the likelihood of harm. The Court is correct that relief is not warranted "simply to prevent the possibility of some remote future injury." "However, the injury need not have been inflicted when application is made or be certain to occur; a strong threat of irreparable injury before trial is an adequate basis." Wright & Miller, *supra*, § 2948.1, at 155–156 (footnote omitted). I agree with the District Court that NRDC made the required showing here.

B.

The Navy's own EA predicted substantial and irreparable harm to marine mammals. Sonar is linked to mass strandings of marine mammals, hemorrhaging around the brain and ears, acute spongiotic changes in the central nervous system, and lesions in vital organs. As the Ninth Circuit noted, the EA predicts that the Navy's "use of MFA sonar in the SOCAL exercises will result in 564 instances of physical injury including permanent hearing loss (Level A harassment) and nearly 170,000 behavioral disturbances (Level B harassment), more than 8,000 of which would also involve temporary hearing loss." 518 F.3d at 696. Within those totals, "the EA predicts 436 Level A harassments of Cuvier's beaked whales, of which, according to NOAA, as few as 1,121 may exist in California, Oregon and Washington combined. Likewise, the EA predicts 1,092 Level B harassments of bottlenose dolphins, of which only 5,271 may exist in the California Coastal and Offshore stocks." 518 F.3d, at 691–692.

* * *

In my view, this likely harm—170,000 behavioral disturbances, including 8,000 instances of temporary hearing loss; and 564 Level A harms, including 436 injuries to a beaked whale population numbering only 1,121—cannot be lightly dismissed, even in the face of an alleged risk to the effectiveness of the Navy's 14 training exercises. There is no doubt that the training exercises serve critical interests. But those interests do not authorize the Navy to violate a statutory command, especially when recourse to the Legislature remains open.

In light of the likely, substantial harm to the environment, NRDC's almost inevitable success on the merits of its claim that NEPA required the Navy to prepare an EIS, the history of this litigation, and the public interest, I cannot agree that the mitigation measures the District Court imposed signal an abuse of discretion. *Cf. Amoco Production Co. v. Gambell*, 480 U.S. 531, 545 (1987) ("Environmental injury, by its nature, can seldom be adequately remedied by money damages and is often permanent or at least of long duration, *i.e.*, irreparable. If such injury is sufficiently likely, therefore, the balance of harms will usually favor the issuance of an injunction to protect the environment.").

For the reasons stated, I would affirm the judgment of the Ninth Circuit.

Notes

1. The Supreme Court in *Winter* weighed animal interests against the need for a well-prepared military. Do you think there is some degree of animal injury that, if proven, would cause the Court to compromise the national defense? Or do you think it will always trump animal interests?

2. The Court also focuses on the purpose of NEPA, which is to provide information about potential harm to the environment and the possibility of reducing those harms. The Court seems to reason that because sonar has been occurring for decades, plaintiffs' claimed harms—based on current scientific evidence about

injuries to marine mammals—are not as important. Does the fact that a plaintiff has just discovered an adverse environmental impact change the government's duty to prevent that harm? Does NEPA allow ongoing challenges? If not, do any other federal laws provide an avenue for plaintiffs here?

3. While this ruling means the injuries to marine mammals may continue, the longer-lasting effect of *Winter* will surely be its change in the burden required for plaintiffs seeking preliminary injunctions in federal court. The Supreme Court increased that burden by making it clear that some governmental interests should be taken more seriously than animal interests and that the public interest (served by government conduct) must be given greater weight by courts determining whether to grant an injunction halting federal agency programs. *Winter* also dictates a more restrictive test than was previously available in cases involving temporary restraining orders and preliminary injunctions, eliminating the flexibility courts previously exercised when considering the factors of likelihood of success on the merits or irreparable injury.

4. For further analysis of the *Winter* case and events leading up to the decision, *see* Catherine Mongeon, *NRDC's Battle Against the Navy*, 35 ECOLOGY L.Q. 277 (2008).

Section 3. Marine Mammal Protection Act

The competing interest of humans and nonhuman animals has been a consistent theme throughout this course. As you will see from the cases and notes in this section, the Marine Mammal Protection Act (MMPA) represents another prime example of this pervasive conflict.

Like the Endangered Species Act, the MMPA prohibits anyone from "taking" ("harass, hunt, capture or kill") marine mammals, although there are a series of exceptions that allow takings—for research or display, as an incidental consequence of commercial fishing, or in line with conservation biology principles. Nevertheless, this aspect of the law is a potentially valuable tool where the covered species are at risk.

Committee for Humane Legislation v. Richardson

United States Court of Appeals, District of Columbia Circuit, 1976
540 F.2d 1141

I. INTRODUCTION

PER CURIAM. In this appeal we are asked to review a judgment of the District Court that the Secretary of Commerce, through the Director of the National Marine Fisheries Service (NMFS), has violated the provisions of the Marine Mammal Protection Act of 1972 by granting to the American Tunaboat Association a general permit for the practice of purse-seine fishing for yellowfin tuna "on porpoise." We concur with the conclusion of the District Court that the permit for fishing "on porpoise" was not issued in compliance with the requirements of the Act. Rather than order an immediate halt to operations of the tuna fleet, however, we have determined to stay the effect of the District Court order until January 1, 1977, for reasons stated hereinafter.

II. BACKGROUND

A. *Purse-Seine Fishing "on Porpoise"*

Prior to 1960 the most common method of fishing for yellowfin tuna was use of pole, line, and live bait. In the eastern tropical Pacific yellowfin tuna fishery, fishermen observed in the late 1950s that yellowfin habitually associate with certain species of dolphin (commonly called porpoise), and began setting their nets "on porpoise." When porpoise are spotted at the ocean surface, speedboats are deployed to herd them to where the net will be set. The tuna follow below the porpoise. The porpoise then are encircled with a cup-like purse-seine net, the open bottom of which is then drawn closed in the manner of a drawstring purse, trapping both the porpoise and the tuna beneath.

Although efforts are made to free the trapped porpoise,[4] purse-seine fishing has resulted in substantial incidental deaths of porpoise. Porpoise are air-breathing mammals, and may be suffocated if they become entangled in the net, or drowned as a result of shock or physical injury. The number of incidental porpoise deaths in recent years has been as follows:

1971   312,400

1972   304,600

1973   175,000

1974   97,800

1975   130,000 (est.)

The average number of porpoise killed each time purse-seine nets are "set" was 70 in 1971, 43 in 1972, 19 in 1973, 12 in 1974, and 17 in 1975.

The effectiveness of purse-seine fishing has led to dramatic increases in its use by the United States tuna fishing fleet. The catch of yellowfin tuna caught by United States purse-seiners on porpoise was 99,000 tons in 1974, or 60 percent of the total United States yellowfin catch (of 165,000 tons) and about 43 percent of the total United States tuna catch. For the period 1971–1974 purse-seiners fishing on porpoise accounted for 72 percent of the total catch of yellowfin.

---

4. Speedboats are used to stretch the net in an open position to permit the porpoise to swim out of the net without becoming entangled. As the net is brought aboard the seining vessel, the porpoise tend to congregate at the extreme end of the net, while tuna swim back and forth between the porpoise and the seiner. The seiner then follows a "backdown" procedure whereby it is backed rapidly to cause the corkline of the net to submerge at the end where the porpoise are located. When tuna swim toward this escape route, the vessel slows and the corkline bobs to the surface. The "backdown" procedure allows a substantial number of porpoise to escape unharmed.

B. *The Marine Mammal Protection Act of 1972*

The Marine Mammal Protection Act of 1972 was addressed in part to the growing problem of porpoise deaths incidental to commercial fishing. The Act was founded on a concern that certain species of marine mammals were in danger of extinction or depletion as a result of man's activities, and a concomitant belief that those species "should not be permitted to diminish below their optimum sustainable population."[7] A moratorium was imposed on taking and importation of all marine mammals, with a two-year exemption from the moratorium for taking of marine mammals incidental to the course of commercial fishing operations. [16 U.S.C. § 1371(a)(2).] Although the Secretary of Commerce was permitted to license incidental taking of marine mammals subsequent to the two-year exemption, the statute directs that "[i]n any event it shall be the immediate goal that the incidental kill or incidental serious injury of marine mammals permitted in the course of commercial fishing operations be reduced to insignificant levels approaching a zero mortality and serious injury rate."

The permits to be issued after the exemption period expired — on October 21, 1974 — were authorized under 16 U.S.C. § 1374, which in turn required compliance with regulations issued under section 1373. Section 1374 requires that the permit specify, *inter alia*, "the number and kind of animals which are authorized to be taken or imported," and the location, period, and method of the authorized taking. The applicant for a permit "must demonstrate to the Secretary that the taking or importation of any marine mammal under such permit *will be consistent with the purposes of this chapter and the applicable regulations established under section 1373 of this title*."[11] Section 1374(d)(3) (emphasis added).

---

7. 16 U.S.C. § 1361(2). "The term 'optimum sustainable population' means, with respect to any population stock, the number of animals which will result in the maximum productivity of the population of the species, keeping in mind the optimum carrying capacity of the habitat and the health of the ecosystem of which they form a constituent element." 16 U.S.C. § 1362(9). The House report on the proposed legislation emphasized that the benefit of the marine mammals was to be the paramount consideration:

[M]arine mammals are resources of great significance and . . . it is congressional policy that they should be protected and encouraged to develop consistent with sound policies of resource management. The primary objective of this management must be to maintain the health and stability of the marine ecosystem; this in turn indicates that the animals must be managed for their benefit and not for the benefit of commercial exploitation.

11. The House committee report found substantial safeguards in the requirement that a showing be made by the applicant for a permit:

In every case, the burden is placed upon those seeking permits to show that the taking should be allowed and will not work to the disadvantage of the species or stock of animals involved. *If that burden is not carried — and it is by no means a light burden — the permit may not be issued. The effect of this set of requirements is to insist that the management of the animal populations be carried out with the interests of the animals as the prime consideration.*

H.R. Rep. No. 92-707, at 18, U.S. Code Cong. & Admin. News 1972, p. 4151.

Section 1373, in turn, authorizes the Secretary to promulgate regulations "on the basis of the best scientific evidence available" for permits for taking marine mammals, "as he deems necessary and appropriate to insure that such taking will not be to the disadvantage of those species and population stocks and will be consistent with the purposes and policies set forth in section 1361 of this title." [12] The Act requires that prior to promulgating any such regulations the Secretary shall publish and make available to the public either before or concurrent with the publication of notice in the *Federal Register* of his intention to prescribe regulations under this section—

(1) a statement of the estimated existing levels of the species and population stocks of the marine mammal concerned;

(2) a statement of the expected impact of the proposed regulations on the optimum sustainable population of such species or population stock;

(3) a statement describing the evidence before the Secretary upon which he proposes to base such regulations; and

(4) any studies made by or for the Secretary or any recommendations made by or for the Secretary or the Marine Mammal Commission which relate to the establishment of such regulations.

C. *The Regulations*

On March 13, 1974 NMFS published notice of its intent to prescribe regulations for taking porpoise incidental to commercial fishing. It took this action despite its professed lack of knowledge as to the actual populations of porpoise, the optimum sustainable populations, or the effect of the takings on the optimum sustainable populations of porpoise.[13] Final regulations were promulgated on September 5, 1974, and the American Tunaboat Association was granted a general permit for the period October 21, 1974 to December 31, 1975 under which fishermen holding certificates of inclusion in the general permit were permitted to take an unlimited number of porpoise.

Despite subsequent warnings by the Marine Mammal Commission that the levels of incidental porpoise deaths would remain unacceptably high, NMFS did not impose a quota, although it later amended its regulations to require improved gear

---

12. 16 U.S.C. § 1373(a). The Secretary is directed to consider the following factors: (1) existing and future levels of marine mammal species and population stocks; (2) existing international treaty and agreement obligations of the United States; (3) the marine ecosystem and related environmental considerations; (4) the conservation, development, and utilization of fishery resources; and (5) the economic and technological feasibility of implementation. 16 U.S.C. § 1373(b).

13. "Estimates of porpoise kills by U.S. fishermen were 214,000 in 1970, 167,000 in 1971, and 228,000 in 1972. The importance of these kills in relation to optimum sustainable population is not known due to lack of knowledge of the sizes of porpoise populations and other population dynamics factors. Population modeling studies underway are scheduled to provide information on population sizes by October, 1974." 39 Fed. Reg. at 9685.

and techniques. The number of porpoise killed by commercial fishermen increased from 97,800 in 1974 to about 130,000 in 1975.

The American Tunaboat Association's application for renewal of its permit was granted on December 19, 1975. Although NMFS published population estimates for two species of porpoise, it again stated that it could not make any statement as to the optimum sustainable populations or the effect of the proposed taking, and determined to set no quota as to incidental deaths unless it appeared that the total number of deaths would exceed 70 percent of the final 1975 estimate. Although the Marine Mammal Commission again warned that there was no basis for assurance that porpoise stocks would not be harmed by the taking, NMFS expressed its belief in proposing regulations that existing porpoise populations would neither increase nor decrease as a result of the taking.

Appellees, various environmental protection organizations, filed suit in 1974 and 1975 to challenge the legality of the permits issued the American Tunaboat Association. The suits were consolidated, and on May 11, 1976 the District Court entered summary judgment for plaintiffs. The court found that the overriding purpose of the Marine Mammal Protection Act was protection of the animals' interests, and held that the Act required (1) that NMFS find that the effect of any proposed taking on the optimum sustainable populations of the species involved not be to the disadvantage of the animals, (2) that the permit specify the number and kind of animals which may be taken, and (3) that the applicant for a permit demonstrate that the taking will serve the purposes of the Act. The court declared the American Tunaboat Association's general permit void and ordered that no further permit be issued until the Act has been complied with. The effect of the decision has been stayed pending further order of this court.

III. ARGUMENT

The first major issue presented by this appeal is whether NMFS has discretion under the Marine Mammal Protection Act of 1972 to issue permits for incidental taking of marine mammals in the course of commercial fishing when estimates of the optimum sustainable population of the species involved and of the effect of that taking upon the optimum sustainable populations are not available.

As a preliminary matter, we may state our agreement with the District Court's conclusion that the Act was to be administered for the benefit of the protected species rather than for the benefit of commercial exploitation.[27] That general legislative intent, however, is not dispositive of the instant question. Congress was confronted

---

27. Appellants have sought to infer a different interpretation from 16 U.S.C. § 1361(6), which states the belief of Congress that marine mammals should be protected and encouraged "to the greatest extent feasible commensurate with sound policies of resource management. . . ." To the extent that that phrase may imply a qualification of the legislative purpose, we believe it is sufficient to note that the section goes on to provide that "the primary objective of this management should be to maintain the health and stability of the marine ecosystem." We also note that the explanation of this provision in H.R. Rep. No. 92-707, U.S. Code Cong. & Admin. News 1972,

directly with the conflict between protection of the porpoise and protection of the American tuna fishing industry; one result of that conflict was the express two-year exemption granted commercial fishermen from the moratorium on taking marine mammals. More significantly for this case, the committee reports contain strong language indicating that the Act was not intended to force tuna fishermen to cease operations. . . .

* * *

The Secretary, for example, in regulating the operations of the tuna industry with respect to the incidental catching of porpoises must consider the technical capability of these fishermen to avoid injury to porpoises. It is not the intention of the Committee to shut down or significantly to curtail the activities of the tuna fleet so long as the Secretary is satisfied that the tuna fishermen are using economically and technologically practicable measures to assure minimal hazards to marine mammal populations.

* * *

It is clear that Congress did not intend that the Marine Mammal Protection Act would force American tuna fishermen to cease operations; the Act does not prohibit purse-seine fishing on porpoise.[31] It is equally clear, however, that Congress intended that the requirements of the Act be complied with.

* * *

The specific requirements of the Act are indeed so clear as to require little discussion. 16 U.S.C. § 1373(d) requires that the Secretary [make available to the] public, *inter alia*, a statement of "the estimated existing levels of the species and population stocks" of the marine mammals to be taken, and a statement of the expected impact of the takings on the optimum sustainable populations of the species. As the House committee report explained, the Act was deliberately designed to permit takings of marine mammals only when it was *known* that taking would not be to the disadvantage of the species:

> In the teeth of this lack of knowledge of specific causes, and of the certain knowledge that these animals are almost all threatened in some way, it seems elementary common sense to the Committee that legislation should be adopted to require that we act conservatively—that no steps should be taken regarding these animals that might prove to be adverse or even irreversible in their effects until more is known. As far as could be done, we

---

p. 4154, stated that it "indicates that the animals must be managed for their benefit and not for the benefit of commercial exploitation."

31. The major concern at the time of enactment was that the Marine Mammal Protection Act not be read to prohibit many forms of commercial fishing solely because those methods result in incidental deaths of marine mammals. . . . We do not reach the question whether present levels of porpoise deaths incidental to commercial fishing constitute compliance with the requirement that deaths be ["]reduced to insignificant levels.["]

have endeavored to build such a conservative bias into the legislation here presented.

In promulgating the instant regulations in both 1974 and 1975, NMFS did not fulfill the requirement that it determine the impact of the takings on the optimum sustainable populations of the species of porpoise involved. The [American Tuna Boat Association's] statement that "[t]here is no evidence that the porpoise populations would substantially increase or decrease as a result of the regulations and reissuance of the general permit" is not at all responsive; the fact that actual stocks may be stable may supply little or nothing to the determination of effect on optimum sustainable populations. We therefore affirm the judgment of the District Court on this issue.

The second line of argument in this appeal concerns the requirement of 16 U.S.C. § 1374(b)(2)(A) that a permit "specify . . . the number and kind of animals which are authorized to be taken. . . ." The District Court held that NMFS had failed to satisfy this requirement inasmuch as no specified limit was placed on incidental takings. The Government has conceded on appeal that the Act requires that a permit contain a fixed number, and NMFS has amended 50 C.F.R. § 216.24(d)(2)(i)(A) to impose a limit of 78,000 on the total number of marine mammals which may be taken by those operating under the general permit.

Appellees contend, however, that the statute is not satisfied by aggregation of all marine mammals into one figure, relying on the express language of the Act that the permit specify both "number and kind." The determination whether the single quota established by NMFS is, in this case, in compliance with the Marine Mammal Protection Act may require development of evidence as to the suitability of aggregation in the context of purse-seine fishing on porpoise; it is a dispute which properly cannot be decided in the first instance by this court. We therefore remand the case to the District Court for prompt consideration and decision of this question.

The remaining statutory requirement relevant to this appeal is contained in 16 U.S.C. § 1374(d)(3): an applicant for a permit for taking marine mammals must demonstrate that the taking "will be consistent with the purposes of this chapter and the applicable regulations established under section 1373 of this title." Again, the purpose of the requirement was stated clearly in the legislative history:

> If that burden is not carried—and it is by no means a light burden—the permit may not be issued. The effect of this set of requirements is to insist that the management of the animal populations be carried out with the interests of the animals as the prime consideration.

The court has carefully examined the American Tunaboat Association's 1974 permit application and its 1975 renewal application. Neither contains any discussion of the predicted impact of the proposed takings on the optimum sustainable population of the porpoise species involved, or otherwise displays consistency with the purposes of the Marine Mammal Protection Act. We concur in the judgment of the District Court that the applications were deficient under the terms of the Act and should not have been granted. We therefore affirm the judgment of the District Court.

IV. REMEDIES

When this appeal was presented to the court on motions for stay pending review, it was represented by counsel for the Government that "[i]t is estimated that reasonably supportable scientific guesses at optimum sustainable populations of porpoise will not be available for 90 days." The request for stay was founded in part on the assertion that if ongoing research being conducted with the tuna fleet were permitted to continue figures could be obtained by autumn of this year. The court is now informed that "[i]t will take three to seven years for a scientifically valid figure."

The court granted a stay pending appeal in the belief that compliance with the Act could be effected within a short time and invalidation of the American Tunaboat Association's general permit thereby averted. We cannot, however, approve the suggestion of NMFS that it might not be in compliance with the Act as much as a decade after enactment. Our obligation is to enforce the law as it is written; the court may not be turned from its course by a proffer of statements that Congress really did not mean what it said.[39]

The court is aware, however, that the immediate impact of this decision would be disastrous to the commercial fishermen operating under the general permit. In further consideration of the efforts by the Government to achieve good faith compliance with the requirements of the Act, and of the need to conduct ongoing gear studies throughout the entire fishing season, we find it appropriate to continue our stay of the District Court order until January 1, 1977.

Notes

1. Did the court effectuate congressional intent by allowing the tuna fishermen to continue purse-seine fishing (at least temporarily), despite the court's agreement with the lower court that the permit for fishing "on porpoise" was not issued in compliance with the MMPA?

2. The MMPA was created because of the depletion of certain species of marine mammals and the need to maintain an "optimal sustainable population." The most sweeping provision of the MMPA, as it was first enacted, was the moratorium on "taking and importing" marine mammals and marine mammal products. 16 U.S.C. § 1371. The question of what constitutes a "taking" was litigated in *United States v. Hayashi*, 22 F.3d 859 (9th Cir. 1994). The Ninth Circuit held a fisherman who shot at (but did not intend to kill) porpoises to deter them from his catch did not commit a "taking" under the MMPA. According to the majority, such conduct

---

39. A major subject of controversy in the instant appeals has been the extent to which the American tuna fishing industry would be harmed by withdrawal of the general permit for purse-seine fishing on porpoise pending completion of the actions necessary to bring the parties into compliance with the Act. We accept as sufficiently demonstrated that the tuna fleet would be seriously harmed by such a ban. The arguments, however, properly should be addressed to Congress rather than to the courts. Balancing of interests between the commercial fishing fleet and the porpoise is entirely a legislative decision, dictated at present by the terms of the Act.

was "not the kind of direct, serious disruption of a porpoise's customary pursuits required to find a criminal 'taking.'" *Id.* at 865. After an in-depth analysis, the dissent concluded that "the majority's view is bad policy as well as bad law." *Id.* at 871. *See also* April Fisher & Amber Bell, Note, *Did United States v. Hayashi Fail To Provide A Safe Harbor For Marine Mammals Under The Marine Mammal Protection Act?*, 27 Golden Gate U.L. Rev. 67 (1997).

3. The MMPA is administered by two separate government agencies: the Department of Commerce, through the National Oceanic and Atmospheric Administration and the National Marine Fisheries Service (NMFS) (responsible for most marine mammals); and the Department of the Interior, through the Fish and Wildlife Service (responsible for walruses, polar bears, sea otters, and other marine mammals). 16 U.S.C. § 1362(11). One commentator has proposed a practical alternative to remedy the problem created by the conflicting duties of the agencies empowered to enforce the Act, by creation of an independent third group to deal with the countervailing interests of marine mammals and the fishing industry. Elise Miller, *The Fox Guarding the Henhouse: Conflicting Duties under the MMPA*, 31 Santa Clara L. Rev. 1063, 1073 (1991).

4. The MMPA authorizes the Secretary of Commerce to prescribe regulations with respect to the taking and importing of marine mammals. 16 U.S.C. § 1373. One controversial regulation adopted by the Secretary is the "observer" program, whereby vessels are required to "allow an observer duly authorized by the Secretary to accompany the vessel on any or all regular fishing trips for the purpose of conducting research and observing operations, including collecting information which may be used in civil or criminal penalty proceedings, forfeiture actions, or permit or certification sanctions." 50 C.F.R. § 216.24(e) (2013); *see also* 16 U.S.C. § 1413(a)(2)(B)(i) ("requiring observers on each vessel"). Tuna fishermen have complained bitterly about the observers placed aboard tuna ships to gather data on the number of porpoise or dolphin takes.[d] In the past, observers allegedly faced "seal bombs" set to explode near them to discourage them from reporting correct numbers, and were allegedly offered bribes to report lower takes. Nancy Kubasek, M. Neil Brown, Melissa Young & Wesley Hiers, *Protecting Marine Mammals: Time for a New Approach*, 13 UCLA J. Envtl. L. & Pol'y 1, 5–6 (1995). Moreover, captains on American ships had access to all of the observers' reports, placing the observers in a precarious position. *Id.* at 6.

The American Tunaboat Association sought an injunction against the NMFS, challenging the legislative and constitutional validity of the observer regulation requirement. The Ninth Circuit upheld the regulation on the grounds that it did not

---

d. Although dolphins and porpoises are scientifically classified as two taxonomically distinct species, they are so similar physiologically, behaviorally and morphologically that the terms are generally used interchangeably by courts, commentators and scientists. *See* David M. Levin, *Towards Effective Cetacean Protection*, 12 Nat. Resources Law. 549, 555 (1979).

contravene the MMPA and the observers' actions did not constitute an unreasonable search under the Fourth Amendment. *Balelo v. Baldridge*, 724 F.2d 753 (9th Cir. 1984).

5. The MMPA has been controversial in various respects, particularly trade relations with countries in the Eastern Tropical Pacific (ETP), a five-to-seven million square mile area of ocean spanning from the Southern California coast to Chile and extending west for nearly three thousand miles. *Earth Island Institute v. Mosbacher*, 746 F. Supp. 964, 966 (N.D. Cal. 1990) (enjoining importation of tuna from foreign countries unless per cent of dolphins taken is established and within statutory parameters). *See also* Deidre McGrath, Note, *Writing Different Lyrics to the Same Old Tune: The New (and Improved) 1997 Amendments to the Marine Mammal Protection Act*, 7 MINN. J. GLOBAL TRADE 431 (1998).

After two decades of debate behind closed doors as well as in the public forum, the MMPA was amended in 1992 by The International Dolphin Conservation Act (IDCA), also known as the "La Jolla Agreement." The IDCA established a global moratorium on purse-seining effective March 1, 1994. 16 U.S.C. §§ 1411–1418 (1992). It also authorized the Secretary of State to enter into international agreements to establish the moratorium. *Id.* § 1412(a). If a nation complied with the IDCA, the embargo imposed upon it under the MMPA would be lifted. *Id.* § 1412(b).

Additionally, due in part to media attention and resulting tuna boycotts by consumers concerned about the dolphin and porpoise deaths associated with the tuna industry, the Dolphin Protection Consumer Information Act, *id.* § 1385, was enacted. *See also Brower v. Daley*, 93 F. Supp. 2d 1071 (N.D. Cal. 2000) (federal agencies ordered to consider stress reports on dolphins before approving imports of tuna from ETP). The complaint in that case summarized plaintiff Samuel LaBudde's undercover investigation on a Panamanian vessel and resulting video footage which allegedly helped fuel the consumer boycott. The Act set forth the following Congressional findings:

> (1) dolphins and other marine mammals are frequently killed in the course of tuna fishing operations in the eastern tropical Pacific Ocean and high seas driftnet fishing in other parts of the world;

> (2) it is the policy of the United States to support a worldwide ban on high seas driftnet fishing, in part because of the harmful effects that such driftnets have on marine mammals, including dolphins; and

> (3) consumers would like to know if the tuna they purchase is falsely labeled as to the effect of the harvesting of the tuna on dolphins.

16 U.S.C. § 1385(b). *See also* Kristin L. Stewart, *Dolphin-Safe Tuna: The Tide is Changing*, 4 ANIMAL L. 111 (1998).

Several years later, following extensive lobbying by ETP countries, the United States negotiated an alternative to a complete tuna embargo. The negotiations led to the drafting of the Panama Declaration, which was signed October 4, 1995. In return for international recognition of obligations to protect dolphins in the ETP, the United States agreed to revise its definition of "dolphin-safe" in the MMPA. This became the impetus for the International Dolphin Conservation Program Act (IDCPA), 16 U.S.C. § 1411, *et seq.*

The 1997 IDCPA did not change the congressional finding that "[t]he yellow-fin tuna fishery of the Eastern Tropical Pacific Ocean has resulted in the deaths of millions of dolphins," 16 U.S.C. § 1411(a)(1), or the purported policy of the United States to "eliminate the marine mammal mortality resulting from the intentional encirclement of dolphins and other marine mammals in tuna purse-seine fisheries." *Id.* § 1411(b)(1). In fact, it added the congressional finding that "[r]ecognition of the International Dolphin Conservation Program will assure that the existing trend of reduced dolphin mortality continues; that individual stocks of dolphins are adequately protected; and that the goal of eliminating all dolphin mortality continues to be a priority." *Id.* § 1411(a)(4).

6. Although the MMPA, as originally written, recognized exceptions for commercial fishing operations, the stated "immediate goal" of the Act was that "the incidental kill or incidental serious injury of marine mammals permitted in the course of commercial fishing operations be reduced to insignificant levels approaching a zero mortality and serious injury rate." 16 U.S.C. § 1371(a)(2). As noted in *Fund for Animals v. Kreps*, 561 F.2d 1002 (D.C. Cir. 1977), new regulations adopted by the Secretary of Commerce in 1977 established a quota of 59,050 porpoise takes incidental to yellowfin tuna purse-seining for the calendar year of 1977. The 1980 amendments to the Act established an annual quota of 20,500 allowable takes—a quota which was extended indefinitely by the 1984 amendments and was still in effect ten years later due to the lobbying efforts of the tuna industry, despite the original zero mortality goal. Kubasek, *supra*, at 7. In any event, many American vessels avoided quotas completely by sailing under foreign flags, which caused dolphin kills by "foreign" fishing fleets to catapult from 20,000 to more than 100,000 per year from the time that the Act was enacted in 1972 until 1989. *Id. See also* McGrath, *supra*, at 435.

7. Not surprisingly, environmental watchdog groups and other concerned parties have looked to the courts to assure governmental compliance with the IDCPA. *See, e.g., Brower v. Daley*, 93 F. Supp. 2d 1071 (N.D. Cal. 2000) (environmental and animal protection groups claimed government agencies were ignoring evidence of serious impact on dolphins from purse seining); *Brower v. Evans*, 257 F.3d 1058, 1071 (9th Cir. 2001) ("*all* of the evidence indicated that dolphins were adversely impacted by the [purse-seine] fishery") (emphasis in original); *Earth Island Institute v. Hogarth*, 494 F.3d 757 (9th Cir. 2007) (further litigation on same issues of "dolphin-safe" labeling; holding arbitrary and capricious NMFS determinations of no significant impact with respect to effects of purse-seine tuna fishing on dolphins).

8. Beginning in 1990, a number of groups spearheaded by the International Marine Mammal Project (IMMP), started the Dolphin Safe Tuna Program. "Dolphin Safe" labels mean that the tuna in those cans is not caught in purse-seining operations. Through the active monitoring of 800 companies in 76 countries, compliance

resulted in a 99% reduction in dolphin deaths in tuna nets, as reported by the IMMP. Mexico refused to ban purse-seine fishing, meaning it was excluded from the Dolphin Safe program. It went to Congress, and sued the U.S. in the World Trade Organization (WTO) tribunal, alleging that imposition of the program violated international trade treaties. After initially ruling for Mexico, the WTO reversed its decision and ultimately ruled that the U.S. was in compliance with international free trade regulations.[e] On December 1, 2017, Mexico appealed the ruling. On December 14, 2018, the WTO issued its final decision, rejecting Mexico's appeal, upholding the use of the "Dolphin Safe" label for any tuna caught in nets in which dolphins are injured or killed.

9. As with many other animal protection statutes, the MMPA turned out to be less sweeping or effective than it may have first appeared to the public. For example, the Act originally allowed the government flexibility to exempt scientific research, public display and commercial fishing operations from the moratoria on takings and importation of marine mammals. 16 U.S.C. § 1371(a)(1). This section was expanded in 1994 to include exemptions for photography, education and commerce as well. *Id.* (*as amended by* Pub. L. No. 103-238, § 4(a)(1)). In addition, § 1371(b) provides that the MMPA does not apply to the taking of any marine mammal by any Indian, Aleut or Eskimo, under certain circumstances. Decades after its enactment, these exemptions remain controversial.

For example, in the late 1990s, the Makah Indian tribe of northwestern Washington announced plans to resurrect the tribal practice of whale hunting, which had been banned since the 1920s to protect the diminishing number of whales. Lawrence Watters & Connie Dugger, *The Hunt for Gray Whales: The Dilemma of Native American Treaty Rights and the International Moratorium on Whaling*, 22 COLUM. J. ENVTL. L. 319 (1997). In May 1999, the tribe successfully hunted a whale, amid vocal protests by marine mammal protectionists. *See, e.g.,* Rebekah Denn, *Sad Protesters Vow to Continue Their Fight*, SEATTLE POST-INTELLIGENCER, May 18, 1999, at A1.

The controversy over the Makah tribe whaling was addressed in *Anderson v. Evans*, 314 F.3d 1006 (9th Cir. 2003):

> [The] modern day struggle over whale hunting began when the United States granted support and approval to the Makah Tribe's ("the Tribe's") plan to resume whaling.

> The Tribe, a traditional Northwest Indian whale hunting tribe, had given up the hunt in the 1920s. In recent years, the Tribe leadership came to regret the cultural impact on the Tribe of the lapse of its whale hunting tradition. As part of a general effort at cultural revival, the Tribe developed plans to resume pursuing gray whales off the coast of Washington State and in the Strait of Juan de Fuca. The worldwide hunt for whales in the years the

---

e. *http://www.earthisland.org/journal/index.php/elist/eListRead/win_for_dolphins_wto_reverses_decision_us_dolphin_safe_tuna_label/*.

real-life Captain Ahabs roamed the high seas, however, seriously depleted the worldwide stock of the cetaceans. As a result of the near extinction of some species of whales, what had been a free realm for ancient and not-so-ancient mariners became an activity closely regulated under both federal and international law. This case is the second in which we have considered whether the federal government's approval of the Tribe's plans to pursue once again the Leviathan of the deep runs afoul of that regulation. *See Metcalf v. Daley,* 214 F.3d 1135 (9th Cir. 2000).

Id. at 1009. Plaintiffs sued under NEPA and the MMPA, with the court holding that the government, in authorizing the whaling plan, had violated both laws, and that the MMPA applied to the Tribe, and overrode any treaty rights the Tribe otherwise held. *Id.* at 1028–29.

10. The purse seining restrictions apply to all marine mammals. The question of what constitutes an excused "incidental take" under the MMPA (which avoids the prohibition on takes of marine mammals) arose in a case where the owners of a fishing vessel had known that whales were captured (and killed) in purse seine nets during extended tuna fishing operations. *Pacific Ranger, LLC v. Pritzker,* 211 F. Supp. 3d 196 (D.D.C. 2016). Plaintiffs owned a commercial fishing vessel and had been fined $127,000 for what they claimed were permissible "incidental" takes of whales in nets that had been set on marine mammals to catch tuna. The court first reaffirmed that while "protecting these mammals burdens the fishing industry to some degree, . . . there is no question that, under federal law, the interest in maintaining healthy populations of marine mammals comes first." *Id.* at 202–03.

The main issue the court decided in *Pacific Ranger* was what conduct constituted an "incidental" take — and therefore excused the killing of the whales. Plaintiffs argued that any take that was not lethal and intended specifically to catch and kill whales was excused. Given the policy behind the MMPA, the language of the regulations interpreting "incidental," and the deference given to an agency interpreting its own regulations, the court rejected plaintiffs' argument. *Id.* at 214-19. The court upheld the fines, confirming that "[o]nly accidental or non-intentional (*i.e.,* not deliberate) takes are excused; therefore, setting a purse seine net with knowledge that whales and other marine mammals are swimming among the targeted tuna is not." *Id.* at 219.

11. As discussed earlier in this section and as seen in the following case, the MMPA concerns not only domestic activities that adversely affect marine mammals but also certain foreign and extraterritorial activities.

Animal Welfare Institute v. Kreps

United States Court of Appeals, District of Columbia Circuit, 1977
561 F.2d 1002

J. SKELLY WRIGHT, Circuit Judge. These appeals arise from a complaint filed in the District Court challenging a decision by the Government appellees to waive the moratorium imposed by the Marine Mammal Protection Act (MMPA) so as to permit importation into the United States from South Africa of baby fur sealskins. Appellants are eight environmental groups. The District Court dismissed the suit on the ground that appellants lacked standing to sue. We reverse, holding that appellants do have standing and that the Government's decision to waive the ban on importing baby fur sealskins violates the Marine Mammal Protection Act.

I. HISTORY OF THE CASE

A brief sketch of the statutory scheme is necessary at this point. The MMPA imposes a moratorium on taking or importation of marine mammals or marine mammal products. The Director of the National Marine Fisheries Service (NMFS) can waive the moratorium to allow taking or importation according to the detailed procedural and substantive requirements of the Act. Waiving the moratorium is a two-stage process. In the first stage the agency must determine if there will be a waiver and promulgate regulations containing the terms of the waiver. In the second stage the agency may issue permits authorizing importation to particular applicants.

The annual harvest of baby seals takes place in South Africa in the fall of the year. In 1975 appellee Fouke Company, an importer, sought a waiver and a permit to allow it to import skins from the 1975 harvest. Throughout the administrative proceedings appellants vigorously opposed the waiver. In February 1976 the Director reached a decision that the Cape fur seal herd could sustain a taking of up to 70,000 seals per year. He therefore waived the moratorium on the condition that the total harvest in South Africa not exceed 70,000.

At this point appellants filed their complaint, alleging that the waiver was illegal because (1) seals less than eight months old would be imported, contrary to section 102(b)(2) of the Act; (2) nursing seals would be imported, contrary to the same section; (3) seals taken in an inhumane manner would be imported, contrary to section 102(b)(4); and (4) the program of taking marine mammals in South Africa is not consistent with the provisions and policies of the MMPA as required by section 101(a)(3)(A).

Soon after the complaint was filed and while Fouke's application for a permit was still pending, it became known that the 1975 harvest had exceeded 70,000 seals. Fouke therefore withdrew its application for a permit. Then, in June 1976, the District Court dismissed the suit on the ground that there was no longer a justiciable controversy since the waiver had been canceled by the failure of its condition. The error in this disposition, as the parties soon pointed out to the court, was that the waiver had continuing validity, subject to annual review, and the condition had failed only in regard to the 1975 harvest. The waiver remained and could become the basis for a permit to import in any future year in which the seal harvest did not exceed 70,000. Therefore, on July 22, 1976 the court vacated its order dismissing the suit and reinstated the complaint.

The Government then completed its 1976 annual review and decided that conditions continued to justify the waiver. In the fall of 1976 Fouke applied for a permit to import some 13,000 sealskins from the 1976 harvest. Notice of the application was published in the Federal Register and appellants promptly submitted their views, urging that the application be denied or at least held in abeyance pending resolution of their suit challenging the waiver. However, notice that the permit had been granted appeared on December 15, 1976. Appellants immediately moved in the District Court for a temporary restraining order and preliminary injunction aimed at preventing importation of the 13,000 sealskins covered by the permit. The District Court denied appellants' motion and dismissed the suit, holding that appellants lacked standing to sue.

Appellants appealed. On December 28, 1976 this court refused to enjoin the importation pending appeal, but agreed to expedite the appeal, and it was stipulated that the briefs on appeal would address the merits of the validity of the waiver as well as the issue of standing.

* * *

III. THE MERITS

A. *Age Limitation*

Appellants charge that the Government appellees' decision to waive the moratorium is illegal in four respects. The first is that it would permit importation of sealskins from animals that were less than eight months old at the time of taking, in contravention of section 102(b)(2) of the MMPA.[46]

In the waiver decision and the regulations implementing it the Government defined eight months old to mean "eight months old as determined by using a mean birthdate for the Cape fur seal of December 1 for any one pupping season." Thus the Government deems any seal killed on or after August 1 each year old enough to be imported. The Government defends this regulation on the ground that some such method for determining the age of animals in the wild is a practical necessity. We agree, but the method chosen by the Government blatantly violates the Act.

It is undisputed that the annual pupping season for Cape fur seals is from November to December. Five percent of the new seals are born by November 14, 50 percent by December 1, and 95 percent by December 18. The Government considered these data and deliberately chose a formula which permits fully *half* the seals imported to be less than eight months old when killed. This interpretation flatly contradicts the plain language of the statute: "It is unlawful to import into the United States any marine mammal if such mammal was . . . less than eight months old. . . ." The legislative history confirms that Congress meant to refer to individual animals, not groups or populations with a mean age of eight months. This is also the view of the Marine Mammal Commission, an expert body created by the MMPA to advise the Secretary of Commerce.

---

46. 16 U.S.C. § 1372(b)(2) (Supp. V 1975). The statute prohibits importation of marine mammals and marine mammal products if the animal was "nursing at the time of taking, or less than eight months old, whichever occurs later."

We agree with the Government "that it is impossible to avoid entirely the chance that a *single* sealskin might be imported from an underage seal." But, faced with this problem, the Government has decided to allow *half* the sealskins imported to be from underage seals. This formula is so far from meeting the statutory standard that it must be rejected.[52]

B. Nursing

The statute also prohibits importation of sealskins from animals who were "nursing at the time of taking. . . ." The Government determined that this provision, like the age limitation, would be impossible to administer unless the agency established some general standard for all seals. In the waiver and regulations the Government set such a standard: first, it ruled that "nursing" means "nursing which is obligatory for the physical health and survival of the nursing animal"; second, it ruled that each and every seal has ceased obligatory nursing by August 1. Appellants contend that there is nothing in the statute or the legislative history to justify the distinction between "obligatory" and "convenience" nursing and that, in any event, all seals have not ceased obligatory nursing by August 1.

In order to decide whether the Government's distinction is consistent with the statute, it is necessary to know what the purpose of the "nursing" prohibition was. Why was Congress concerned about the killing of nursing animals? The legislative history sheds little light on this question. But the parties agree the restriction does not relate to reproduction or maintenance of the seal population, because seals do not reproduce until a least a year after they have ceased all nursing. Rather, it appears that Congress was responding to an emotional conviction that killing babies who were still nursing was intolerably cruel. The legislative history speaks of "public indignation" and "public opinion." Nursing seems to have been used as a measure of infancy, of vulnerability and helplessness. While it is admittedly unusual to find a statutory purpose based entirely on emotional concerns, it is perfectly proper in the context of a statute which also prohibits killing in an "inhumane" manner, where humane is defined as involving "the least possible degree of pain and suffering practicable to the mammal involved." There is surely no "resource management" explanation for this provision; nor is there, as far as we know, for the nursing prohibition.

Assuming then that the statute responded to emotional concerns, there is clearly no justification for the technical distinction between obligatory and convenience nursing which the Government grafted onto the statute. The statute is plain; it bars importation of any animal which was "nursing at the time of taking." It is undisputed that seals cease all nursing by October each year, when the mother seals leave the rookeries. Therefore, as in the case of age, there was available to the Government a workable, standard method of applying the provision. Instead, the Government

---

52. While we do not decide what date the Government could lawfully establish, it appears on the basis of the data before us that December 18, when about 95% of the seals have been born, would be a logical choice; thus all seals could be deemed to be at least eight months old if they are killed on or after August 18 each year.

invented a distinction whose only purpose was to allow more importation of seals.[58] As the Marine Mammal Commission stated in opposing the Government's decision:

> As in the case of mean date of birth, the concept of obligate nursing is necessary in order to resolve a special problem faced by the applicant and is not necessary in order to remedy any fatal defect in the Act. . . .
>
> . . . Contrived arguments that the applicant can import an animal which was killed because it did not *need* to nurse in order to survive but was only doing so as a *convenience* [are] irrelevant and inadequate for purposes of satisfying the categorical, unqualified statutory mandate of section 102(b)(2). . . .

Because we reject the Government's use of the obligatory nursing concept to narrow the unambiguous command of the statute, we do not reach the question of when obligatory nursing ceases.

C. *Humane Manner*

Appellants' third contention is that the Government's decision to waive the moratorium is illegal in that it allows importation of seals taken in an inhumane manner, in violation of section 102(b)(4) of the Act. Humane is defined to mean "that method of taking which involves the least possible degree of pain and suffering practicable to the mammal involved."

The parties agree that the most humane method of killing is the so-called "stun and stick" method. The method involves three stages: (1) the roundup drive; (2) clubbing the animal so as to render it unconscious; and (3) severing the great arteries or heart with a knife to kill the animal quickly. The parties also agree that this is the method used in South Africa, but appellants claim that it is not properly put into practice there. Appellants contend that humaneness requires that each seal be rendered instantly and permanently unconscious by a single blow. They cite testimony that in South Africa as many as 40 percent of the seals required a second blow. They also allege that practices at harvests where no observers are present can be presumed to be worse than those observed by the witnesses.

Unlike appellants' claims regarding age and nursing, which involved questions of statutory interpretation, their humaneness contention involves only a finding of fact. The Director of the National Marine Fisheries Service made a determination on the administrative record that the South African harvest was conducted

---

58. The regulation followed a report by a National Marine Fisheries Service representative, who had visited South Africa, that nursing is the critical question regarding a waiver of the moratorium under the Marine Mammal Protection Act. During this trip, the stomachs of 20 seals were examined. The majority contained no food while one contained milk, indicating some seals were still nursing. The final resolution of the question would seem to depend upon either one of two actions:

    1. An amendment of the Act, or

    2. A legal determination that the Act refers to obligatory nursing only and a biological determination that obligatory nursing is completed by a predetermined date.

in a humane manner. Our role in reviewing this finding is limited; we can reject it only if it is not supported by substantial evidence. While we might agree that South Africa's record of stunning seals with a single blow could certainly be improved,[64] we cannot say that the Director's finding is not supported by substantial evidence on the record as a whole. There was expert testimony that multiple blows were not necessarily inhumane, provided they were delivered within a minimal period of time. Two out of three observers concluded that the harvest they observed was, overall, humane. And the record before us provides no solid support for appellants' speculation that other harvests were undoubtedly worse. Therefore, we affirm the Director's finding on this point.

D. *Consistency with the MMPA*

The MMPA provides that

> no marine mammal or marine mammal product may be imported into the United States unless the Secretary certifies that the program for taking marine mammals in the country of origin is consistent with the provisions and policies of this chapter. . . .

The Secretary did so certify in the decision to waive the moratorium, but appellants contend that the certification is invalid because the record does not support a finding that South Africa's sealing practices are consistent with the provisions and policies of the MMPA.

Our decision on this claim is dictated by our holdings on appellants' other claims. Even if we assume that South Africa killed no seals prior to August 1,[67] as dictated by the Government appellees' construction of the age and nursing provisions of the Act, the record shows that up to 50 percent of them were less than eight months old and many of them were still nursing. The Government used its mean birth date and obligatory nursing constructs to legitimate these killings, but we have held that the Government interpretations do not comply with the Act. It is therefore clear that South Africa's sealing program is not consistent with the provisions of the MMPA, in that South Africa kills many animals which are nursing or less than eight months old at the time of taking.

Appellants offer as an additional ground for invalidating the certification the fact that the MMPA is based on a policy of "optimum sustainable population" (OSP) while South Africa's sealing program is based on a policy of "maximum sustainable yield" (MSY). Both OSP and MSY are efforts to quantify how many animals can be taken each year without depleting the population. However, both are exceedingly difficult to apply with any precision. The MMPA sets as a goal "to obtain an optimum sustainable population keeping in mind the optimum carrying capacity of the habitat." But in our view the definitions of both OSP and optimum carrying

---

64. Appellants point out that at the American seal harvest in the Pribilof Islands a second blow is required to render the seal unconscious in less than 5% of the clubbings.

67. Appellants assert that the harvest began as early as June at some sites.

capacity are singularly unenlightening; each is defined in terms of the other.[69] The Government, conceding that it has had trouble with the terms, has decided that OSP is not a fixed population level at all but a population range.

We are reluctant to jump into this fray. The Director found that the South African seal population is healthy and growing and that what South Africa is trying to achieve via MSY—a healthy seal herd in a balanced ecosystem—is consistent with what the MMPA seeks to achieve via OSP. Appellants disagree, saying that MSY inherently means harvesting more animals than OSP. But appellants admit that they too do not really know what either term means, and they do not deny that the seal herds are growing under South African management. On the basis of this cloudy record, we cannot conclude that MSY is definitely inconsistent with OSP. We do not foreclose the question for the future, however, when experience and sharper definitions might require a different conclusion.

IV. CONCLUSION

... [T]he Government's decision to waive the moratorium on importation of baby fur sealskins contravenes the MMPA in that it permits importation of skins taken from animals who were less than eight months old or who were nursing at the time of taking. For the same reason the Secretary's certification that South Africa's sealing program is consistent with the provisions and policies of the MMPA is invalid. Accordingly, the waiver decision and the regulations implementing it are hereby set aside.

Notes

1. Consider the court's finding that it was legitimate to prohibit importation of baby seal skins based on emotional arguments against killing nursing babies. Are there other plausible reasons for this prohibition? The court agreed with NMFS that taking more than one blow to kill the seals was not necessarily inhumane. Is this finding consistent with the statutory intent?

2. International controversy over the annual Canadian seal hunt comes up each year as the hunt begins. The European Union, Russia, and other countries have banned the importation of seal skins, which would have significant impacts on the fur-producing countries. These bans also create the potential for sanctions with respect to the countries' involvement in international trade agreements that

---

69. 16 U.S.C. § 1362 reads in part:

(8) The term "optimum carrying capacity" means the ability of a given habitat to support the optimum sustainable population of a species or population stock in a healthy state without diminishing the ability of the habitat to continue that function.

(9) The term "optimum sustainable population" means, with respect to any population stock, the number of animals which will result in the maximum productivity of the population or the species, keeping in mind the optimum carrying capacity of the habitat and the health of the ecosystem of which they form a constituent element.

prohibit such restrictions where the products are still sold in the country. Dispute resolution processes in the international arena are ongoing on this issue.

3. Based on your readings, does the MMPA appear to be more or less effective than the Endangered Species Act in protecting the animals who are the purported beneficiaries of the law?

4. In *United States v. Mitchell*, 553 F.2d 996 (5th Cir. 1977), defendant was an American citizen convicted of violating the MMPA when he hunted dolphins in the Bahamas. Dolphin hunting was legal under Bahamian law. The sole issue before the court was whether the MMPA applied to Americans in foreign waters. The Fifth Circuit concluded it did not, and reversed the conviction. The Court based its decision on the language of the MMPA, the need (or lack of need) to apply it extraterritorially and the presumption against extraterritorial application of federal statutes.

5. The capture of marine mammals by or for exhibitors and marine parks, in which Mitchell was involved, has been the subject of criticism by animal advocates. *See, e.g., Animal Prot. Inst. of America v. Mosbacher*, 799 F. Supp. 173 (D.D.C. 1992) (*API*) (challenging permits for the importation of six false killer whales from Japan by Shedd Aquarium in Chicago; court concluded the Secretary did not abuse his discretion in issuing the permits). In *API*, the whales were the subject of an annual "nuisance drive," where whales are intentionally beached by Japanese fishermen who claim the whales interfere with their fishing operations by depleting the fish stocks. Lavonne R. Dye, Note, *The Marine Mammal Protection Act: Maintaining the Commitment to Marine Mammal Conservation*, 43 Case W. Res. 1411, 1413, 1420 (1993). Those who are not sold for display are slaughtered by the fishermen. *Id.* at 1423.

In challenging the permits, the *API* plaintiffs asserted the Secretary failed to comply with the MMPA provision that provides that the Secretary of Commerce may issue permits for the importation of marine mammals for public display only if doing so is "in accord with sound principles of resource protection and conservation," and only if the Secretary certifies the country from which the marine mammal is imported has a program for taking marine mammals that is consistent with the MMPA. 16 U.S.C. § 1371(a)(3)(A). Since Japan has no such program—and is in fact an outspoken advocate in favor of resuming worldwide commercial whaling—plaintiffs asked the court to reject the permits.

Not everyone agreed, however, that plaintiffs were acting in the whales' best interest. In her law review article, Lavonne Dye suggested section 1371(a)(3)(A) is antithetical to the conservationist intent of the MMPA. By prohibiting the importation of animals from Japan, she asserted, section 1371(a)(3)(A) prevents marine parks from saving marine mammals from the fatal fishery drives. *Id.* She argues it is preferable for marine mammals to be captured, displayed and studied at a marine park than to be slaughtered by the fishermen. *Id.* at 1444–48. Do you agree? What approaches might protect whales in foreign waters without this Hobson's choice?

The district court did not address these concerns in *API v. Mosbacher*. Finding no guidance in the legislative history, the court concluded the restrictions of section 1371(a)(3)(A) were inapplicable, in light of the broader language in section 1371(a)(1)—which specifically applies to importation for public display and does not expressly require a consistent takings program in the exporting country. *API*, 799 F. Supp. at 179.

6. Attempts to import rare Beluga whales were blocked by the National Marine Fisheries Service and the federal court in *Georgia Aquarium, Inc. v. Pritzker*, 135 F. Supp. 3d 1280 (N.D. Ga. 2015). The court upheld each of the agency's grounds for denying the aquarium's permit, including its inability to prove the importation would not increase other takings and that the imported whales were not nursing at the time of capture.

Section 4. Wild Free-Roaming Horses and Burros Act

In 1971, Congress passed the Wild Free-Roaming Horses and Burros Act (WFHBA), 16 U.S.C. §§ 1331–1340, finding and declaring that

> wild free-roaming horses and burros are living symbols of the historic and pioneer spirit of the West; that they contribute to the diversity of life forms within the Nation and enrich the lives of the American people; and that these horses and burros are fast disappearing from the American scene.

16 U.S.C. § 1331.

Wild horses and burros are the progeny of animals introduced to North America by early Spanish explorers. They once roamed the western rangelands in vast herds. But over time, desirable grazing land was fenced off for private use, while the animals were slaughtered. The herds began to dwindle, and the remaining animals were driven to marginal, inhospitable grazing areas.

Alarmed at the decline of these herds, Congress enacted the WFHBA to protect the wild horses and burros from "capture, branding, harassment, or death." 16 U.S.C. § 1331. According to congressional findings, they had been cruelly slain, used for target practice and harassed for sport. S. Rep. No. 242, 92d Cong., 1st Sess., *reprinted in* 1971 U.S. CODE CONG. & AD. NEWS 2149, 2149. Congress also found that the wild horses and burros had been exploited by commercial hunters who sold them to slaughterhouses for the production of pet food and fertilizer. *See also* Johnston, *The Fight to Save a Memory*, 50 TEXAS L. REV. 1055, 1056–57 (1972).

Despite their emotional connection to national origins, some argue that wild horses can cause serious damage to their habitat, especially when confined to a given area of land. Grazing and trampling of grass and dirt cause significant effects that become problems for commercial interests interested in using the same land for grazing of cows and other livestock (who also negatively impact open spaces by compacting and trampling grass and dirt). Balancing the commercial interests of ranchers and the energy industry on one hand and the wild horses on the other has been at the core of controversy over BLM's implementation of the Act. As of 2001, for every wild horse on BLM lands, one hundred cattle were grazing. Kristen H. Glover, *Managing Wild Horses on Public Lands: Congressional Action and Agency Response,* 79 N.C. L. REV. 1108, 1120 (2001). *See, e.g., Mountain States Legal Found. v. Hodel,* 799 F.2d 1423, 1425 (10th Cir. 1986) (damage to private lands caused by wild horses and burros protected by the Act did not constitute a "taking," even though the animals' grazing habits had diminished the property value, where owners were not deprived of all "economically viable use" of the land). *See also* Kenneth P. Pitt, *The Wild Free-Roaming Horses and Burros Act: A Western Melodrama,* 15 ENVTL. L. 503, 505 (1985).

The Bureau of Land Management (BLM) is charged with implementing the WFHBA. *Kleppe v. New Mexico,* 426 U.S. 529 (1976) (finding the Act constitutional). BLM manages a larger area of land than any other federal agency—264 million acres, which equates to roughly one-eighth of the United States. Glover, *supra,* at 1109. BLM's implementation of the WFHBA has led to the filing of numerous lawsuits, by ranchers as well as by animal advocates. The sampling of cases in this section explores the meaning and intent of the WFHBA, and the place of wild horses and burros in the scheme of natural resources management.

Colorado Wild Horse and Burro Coalition, Inc. v. Salazar

United States District Court, District of Columbia, 2009
639 F. Supp. 2d 87

MEMORANDUM OPINION

ROSEMARY M. COLLYER, District Judge.

Plaintiffs challenge the decision of the Bureau of Land Management ("BLM"), an agency of the U.S. Department of the Interior, to remove all wild horses from the West Douglas Herd Area in Colorado. They argue, *inter alia,* that the decision violates the Wild Free-Roaming Horses and Burros Act ("Wild Horse Act" or "Act"), 16 U.S.C. § 1331, *et seq.* Defendants counter that BLM's decision to remove the West Douglas Herd is a reasonable exercise of BLM's discretion and is entitled to *Chevron* deference. Before the Court are cross motions for summary judgment. For the reasons explained herein, the Court finds that BLM's decision to remove the West Douglas Herd exceeds the scope of authority that Congress delegated to it in the Wild Horse Act. The Court will grant in part Plaintiffs' motion for summary judgment, deny Defendants' cross motion for summary judgment, and set aside BLM's decision.

I. FACTS

The West Douglas Herd Area encompasses 123,387 acres of federal land managed by BLM and 4,754 acres of private land in Northwestern Colorado, southwest of the town of Rangely and approximately 50 miles north of Grand Junction. It is located within the White River Resource Area. In the first census conducted by BLM in 1974, it counted 9 wild horses in the West Douglas Herd Area. BLM estimates that there are now 147 wild horses in the herd area.

In 1975, BLM drafted a White River Resource Area Management Framework Plan that provided a framework for managing multiple uses in the area, including the management of the wild horses. In 1980, BLM issued an updated Management Framework Plan which recommended that all horses west of Douglas Creek (later designated as the West Douglas Herd Area) be removed because other resource activities in this area (namely, energy exploration) were causing the horses to disperse into areas where they did not roam in 1971, when the Wild Horse Act was enacted. In 1985, for reasons not fully explained, BLM unsuccessfully attempted to completely remove wild horses from the West Douglas Herd Area.

On July 1, 1997, the Colorado State Director of BLM signed a Record of Decision for the White River Resource Area Management Plan that called for the total removal of wild horses in the West Douglas Herd Area by 2007. However, BLM decided to reconsider its decision and to conduct further analysis before commencing the removal of the West Douglas Herd.

On April 28, 2005, BLM published an environmental assessment that considered two alternatives: Alternative A, removing all wild horses from the West Douglas Herd Area by 2007; and Alternative B, managing a small herd of 29–60 wild horses in this area. On August 29, 2005, Kent E. Walter, Field Manager for BLM's White River Field Office, issued a proposed Decision Record and a Finding of No Significant Impact with respect to his decision to implement Alternative A, removing all wild horses from the West Douglas Herd Area. Mr. Walter's proposed decision was protested by five parties, including counsel for Plaintiffs in this case.

* * *

On July 14, 2008, BLM released its 2008 West Douglas Herd Area Wild Horse Removal Final Decision Record and Environmental Assessment ("2008 Gather Plan"), authored by Mr. Walter, which provided that "[a]ll wild horses will be removed from within and outside the [West Douglas Herd Area] beginning no sooner than October 1, 2008" and that "[t]he gather methods used will include helicopter drive trapping, helicopter assisted roping, water trapping, or bait trapping." [The gather never occurred.] BLM currently plans to remove 100 horses from the West Douglas Herd Area pursuant to the 2008 Gather Plan beginning on September 27, 2009. . . .

Plaintiffs are four associations organized to protect wild horses and one equine veterinarian, a former contract veterinarian for BLM, who frequently visits the West Douglas Herd Area to see and enjoy the wild horses. Plaintiffs filed their Third Amended Complaint on March 24, 2009, seeking, *inter alia,* a declaration that the 2008 Gather Plan exceeds BLM's discretion in the Wild Horse Act and an order setting aside the 2008 Gather Plan as *ultra vires.* Pending before the Court are cross motions for summary judgment.

II. LEGAL STANDARDS

A. Standard of Review

Under the Administrative Procedure Act ("APA"), 5 U.S.C. § 551, *et seq.,* "[a]gency action made reviewable by statute and final agency action for which there is no other adequate remedy in a court are subject to judicial review." [footnote] *Id.* § 704. The APA provides that the reviewing court *shall* "hold unlawful and set aside agency action . . . found to be . . . in excess of statutory jurisdiction, authority, or limitations, or short of statutory right." *Id.* § 706(2)(C). "To determine if the Secretary has exceeded his statutory authority under 5 U.S.C. § 706(2)(C), the Court must engage in the two-step inquiry required by *Chevron.*" *Anna Jacques Hosp. v. Leavitt,* 537 F. Supp. 2d 24, 29–30 (D.D.C. 2008). "If the intent of Congress is clear, that is the end of the matter; for the court, as well as the agency, must give effect to the unambiguously expressed intent of Congress." *Chevron,* 467 U.S. at 842–43. "[I]f the statute is silent or ambiguous with respect to the specific issue, the question for the court is whether the agency's answer is based on a permissible construction of the statute." *Id.* at 843.

* * *

III. ANALYSIS

* * *

B. The Wild Horse Act

The Wild Horse Act provides that "Congress finds and declares that wild free-roaming horses and burros are living symbols of the historic and pioneer spirit of the West; that they contribute to the diversity of life forms within the Nation and enrich the lives of the American people; and that these horses and burros are fast disappearing from the American scene." 16 U.S.C. § 1331. The Act further provides that "[i]t is the policy of Congress that wild free-roaming horses and burros shall be protected from capture, branding, harassment, or death; and to accomplish this they are to be considered in the area where presently found, as an integral part of the natural system of the public lands." [11] *Id.* It is a federal crime to remove a wild free-roaming horse or burro from public lands, convert a wild free-roaming horse or burro to private use, or kill or harass a wild free-roaming horse or burro. *See id.* § 1338(a)(1)-(3).

Congress delegated to the Secretary of Agriculture and the Secretary of the Interior jurisdiction over all wild free-roaming horses and burros "for the purpose of management and protection in accordance with the provisions of this chapter." *Id.* § 1333(a). Section 1333(a) provides that "[t]he Secretary is authorized and directed to protect and manage wild free-roaming horses and burros as components of the public lands, and he may designate and maintain specific ranges on public lands as sanctuaries for their protection and preservation. . . ." It further provides that "[t]he Secretary shall manage wild free-roaming horses and burros in a manner that is designed to achieve and maintain a thriving natural ecological balance on the public lands" and that "[a]ll management activities shall be at the minimal feasible level . . . in order to protect the natural ecological balance of all wildlife species which inhabit such lands, particularly endangered wildlife species."

---

11. BLM has interpreted the term "where presently found" to mean "the geographic area identified as having been used by a herd as its habitat in 1971." 43 C.F.R. § 4700.0-5(d) (definition of "herd area").

Section 1333(b)(1) requires BLM to maintain a current inventory of wild horses and burros so that it can "make determinations as to whether and where an over-population exists and whether action should be taken to remove excess animals; determine appropriate management levels of wild free-roaming horses and burros on these areas of public lands; and determine whether appropriate management levels should be achieved by the removal or destruction of excess animals, or other options (such as sterilization, or natural controls on population levels)." Section 1333(b)(2) provides that when BLM determines "that an overpopulation exists on a given area of the public lands and that action is necessary to remove excess animals, [the Secretary] shall immediately remove excess animals from the range so as to achieve appropriate management levels." The term "excess animals" is defined as "wild free-roaming horses or burros (1) which have been removed from an area by the Secretary pursuant to applicable law or, (2) which must be removed from an area in order to preserve and maintain a thriving natural ecological balance and multiple-use relationship in that area." *Id.* § 1332(f).

Section 1333(b)(2) specifically provides an "order and priority" for removal of excess animals "until all excess animals have been removed so as to restore a thriving natural ecological balance to the range, and protect the range from the deterioration associated with overpopulation."[13] Specifically, it first provides that BLM "shall order old, sick, or lame animals to be destroyed in the most humane manner possible." Second, BLM "shall cause such number of additional excess wild free-roaming horses and burros to be humanely captured and removed for private maintenance and care for which [the Secretary] determines an adoption demand exists by qualified individuals. . . ." Third, and as a last resort, BLM "shall cause additional excess wild free-roaming horses and burros for which an adoption demand by qualified individuals does not exist to be destroyed in the most humane and cost efficient manner possible." In § 1333(e), Congress also gave BLM authority to sell any excess animal that is more than 10 years old or that has been offered unsuccessfully for adoption at least three times.

Congress stipulated five conditions upon which the animals "shall lose their status as wild free-roaming horses or burros and shall no longer be considered as falling within the purview of this chapter." *Id.* § 1333(d). The first is if title to an excess animal has passed to a qualified individual for adoption or private maintenance. The second is if an excess animal has been transferred for private maintenance or adoption and "die[s] of natural causes before passage of tile." The third is if an excess animal is destroyed by BLM "pursuant to subsection (b) of this section." The fourth is if a wild free-roaming horse or burro dies of natural causes on public lands or private lands where the animal was maintained and BLM has authorized

---

13. The term "range" is defined as "the amount of land necessary to sustain an existing herd or herds of wild free-roaming horses and burros, which does not exceed their known territorial limits, and which is devoted principally but not necessarily exclusively to their welfare in keeping with the multiple-use management concept for the public lands." 16 U.S.C. § 1332(c).

disposal of the animal. And the fifth is if a wild free-roaming horse or burro is destroyed or dies "for purposes of or incident to the program authorized in this section." Any excess animal that is sold by BLM pursuant to § 1333(e) also is no longer "considered to be a wild free-roaming horse or burro for the purposes of this chapter." *Id.* § 1333(e)(4).

Finally, § 1339, entitled "Limitation of authority," provides that "[n]othing in this chapter shall be construed to authorize the Secretary to relocate wild free-roaming horses or burros to areas of the public lands where they do not presently exist."

[C.] BLM's Authority to "Manage" Wild Free-Roaming Horses and Burros

Against this backdrop, Defendants take the extreme position that it is within BLM's discretion to remove the entire West Douglas Herd, a herd comprised of wild free-roaming horses that Defendants conceded at oral argument BLM has not determined to be "excess animals." [¶] The Court declines to afford BLM's interpretation deference. *E.g., Am. Horse Prot. Ass'n, Inc. v. Watt,* 694 F.2d 1310, 1319 (D.C. Cir. 1982) (noting that under the Wild Horse Act "the Secretary's discretion remains bounded" and that "[h]is orders are subject to review and may be overturned if his action is arbitrary").

The initial inquiry under *Chevron* is "whether Congress has directly spoken to the precise question at issue." *Chevron,* 467 U.S. at 842. "If the intent of Congress is clear, that is the end of the matter; for the court, as well as the agency, must give effect to the unambiguously expressed intent of Congress." *Id.* at 842–43. However, "if the statute is silent or ambiguous with respect to the specific issue, the question for the court is whether the agency's answer is based on a permissible construction of the statute." *Id.* at 843. The "specific issue" here is not whether BLM may remove an entire herd of wild free-roaming horses and burros, as Defendants assert; the "specific issue" is whether BLM may remove an entire herd of wild free-roaming horses and burros that BLM concededly has not determined to be "excess animals" within the meaning of the Wild Horse Act.[16] For the following reasons, the Court finds that Congress clearly intended to protect non-excess wild free-roaming horses and burros from removal, and that BLM's removal authority is limited to those wild free-roaming horses and burros that it determines to be "excess animals" within the meaning of the Wild Horse Act.[17]

BLM's authority to "manage" wild free-roaming horses and burros is expressly made subject to "the provisions of this chapter[,]" 16 U.S.C. § 1333(a), including the provision that "[i]t is the policy of Congress that wild free-roaming horses and burros shall be protected from capture. . . ." *Id.* § 1331. It would be anomalous to

---

16. The Court expresses no opinion about whether BLM has the authority to remove an entire herd that it has determined, in accordance with the Wild Horse Act, to be "excess animals."

17. Alternatively, and for the same reasons, the Court finds that BLM's decision to remove an entire herd of concededly non-excess wild free-roaming horses and burros is an impermissible construction of the Wild Horse Act under step two of *Chevron*.

infer that by authorizing the custodian of the wild free-roaming horses and burros to "manage" them, Congress intended to permit the animals' custodian to subvert the primary policy of the statute by capturing and removing from the wild the very animals that Congress sought to protect *from* being captured and removed from the wild.

Defendants argue that the horses will not be "eradicated" or "eliminated" inasmuch as BLM intends to continue to manage the horses *not* in the wild but through private adoption or long-term care. But BLM's directive is "to protect and manage *wild free-roaming* horses and burros *as components of the public lands. . . .*" 16 U.S.C. § 1333(a) (emphasis added). Congress did not authorize BLM to "manage" the wild horses by corralling them for private maintenance or long-term care as *non*-wild free-roaming animals *off* of the public lands. Upon removal for private adoption and/or long-term care, the West Douglas Herd would forever cease to be "wild free-roaming" horses "as components of the public lands" contrary to Congress's intent to protect the horses from capture.

Moreover, the statute expressly provides that BLM's "management activities *shall* be at the *minimal* feasible level. . . ." *Id.* (emphasis added). It is difficult to think of a "management activity" that is farther from a "minimal feasible level" than removal. While Congress did not specifically define "manage," it did provide a list of the "management activities" it envisioned. The management activities that Congress had in mind were for BLM to "make determinations as to whether and where an overpopulation exists and whether action should be taken to *remove excess animals;* determine appropriate management levels of wild free-roaming horses and burros on these areas of public lands; and determine whether appropriate management levels should be achieved by the *removal or destruction of excess animals,* or other options (such as sterilization, or natural controls on population levels)." *Id.* § 1333(b)(1) (emphasis added). Conspicuously omitted from this list is any reference to a determination by BLM to remove non-excess animals.

Further, Congress prescribed a detailed statutory procedure for removing excess animals. *See id.* § 1333(b)(2)(A)-(C). Congress "specified both the circumstances under which BLM may determine that an overpopulation of wild horses exists and the means the Agency may use to control horse populations." *Am. Horse Protection Ass'n,* 694 F.2d at 1316. Yet there is no procedure in the statute for removing non-excess animals. While it is true, as Defendants argue, that nothing in the statute expressly precludes BLM from removing non-excess animals, it would make no sense for Congress to provide detailed procedures for removing excess animals but no procedure at all for removing non-excess animals. For this reason, the Court rejects Defendants' proposed construction that § 1333(b) *requires* the removal of excess animals whereas § 1333(a) *permits* the removal of non-excess animals. In light of the statute's purpose to protect wild free-roaming horses and burros, the Court finds that the only plausible inference to be drawn from the omission of any procedure for removing non-excess animals is that Congress did not intend for BLM's management authority to be so broad.

This inference is bolstered by the fact that Congress specifically excluded from the Act's coverage those excess animals that are adopted, sold, or destroyed following removal by BLM pursuant to § 1333(b), *see* 16 U.S.C. § 1333(d) & (e)(4), but the Act contains no exclusion for the adoption, sale, or destruction of non-excess animals removed by BLM pursuant to § 1333(a), the provision of the statute authorizing BLM to "manage" wild free-roaming horses and burros. In addition, Congress expressly limited BLM's authority "to relocate wild free-roaming horses or burros to areas of the public lands where they do not presently exist." *Id.* § 1339. Given the policy expressed in the statute, it would make no sense to prohibit BLM from relocating wild horses to public lands where they did not historically exist but permit BLM to take the more drastic measure of removing non-excess animals from the public lands altogether.

Finally, the Court notes that the original 1971 Act contained a provision that empowered the Secretary to destroy wild free-roaming horses or burros "when in his judgment such action is necessary to preserve and maintain the habitat in a suitable condition for continued use." Congress repealed that provision in 1978 and replaced it with the current provision which speaks only to BLM's authority to remove and destroy *excess* animals. *See* Pub. L. No. 95-514, § 14(a), 92 Stat. 1803, 1808 (Oct. 25, 1978); *see also* H.R. Rep. No. 95-1737, at 14 (1978) ("The conferees further agreed to retain the House bill's mandate to the Secretaries to remove *excess* wild horses and burros from the public lands.") (emphasis in original). The Court infers from that repeal that Congress intended to eliminate BLM's discretion to destroy non-excess animals. Insofar as BLM's decision to remove the West Douglas Herd makes the horses eligible for eventual destruction,[19] the decision is contrary to Congress's intent in the 1978 amendments to preclude BLM from destroying non-excess animals in order to maintain the habitat.

Defendants protest that because wild free-roaming horses will continue to inhabit the Piceance-East Douglas Herd Management Area, BLM's decision to remove the West Douglas Herd will not result in the removal of all of the horses historically found in the Douglas Creek wild horse herd unit. The argument misses the point. Defendants admit that "[t]he area of wild horse use at the passage of the Act was an area of 187,970 acres known as the 'Douglas Creek wild horse herd unit,'" and that the herd unit encompassed the area that the West Douglas Herd now inhabits. That "BLM will continue to manage horses in the Douglas Creek herd unit because wild horses will be maintained in the Piceance-East Douglas HMA," Defs.' Mem. at 15, does nothing to remedy BLM's lack of statutory authority to remove non-excess

---

19. As already noted, Defendants aver that "the horses will be removed from West Douglas but BLM will manage the horses elsewhere, through adoption or long-term care." Answer to 3d Am. Compl. ¶ 2. However, given Defendants' broad interpretation of BLM's management authority, Defendants' averment is of little comfort that BLM will not later decide to destroy the West Douglas Herd, should adoption prove unsuccessful and long-term care too expensive.

animals historically found in the Douglas Creek herd unit, including the West Douglas Herd Area.

IV. CONCLUSION

For the foregoing reasons, the Court finds that the 2008 Gather Plan was "in excess of statutory jurisdiction, authority, or limitations, or short of statutory right." 5 U.S.C. § 706(2)(C). A prerequisite to removal under the Wild Horse Act is that BLM first determine that an overpopulation exists and that the wild free-roaming horses and burros slated for removal are "excess animals." BLM concededly has not made such a determination with respect to the horses in the West Douglas Herd Area. Accordingly, Plaintiffs' motion for summary judgment will be granted in part, Defendants' cross motion for summary judgment will be denied, and the 2008 Gather Plan will be set aside. . . .

Notes

1. In 2010, after the above ruling, BLM proposed a new gather of wild horses in the West Douglas Herd Area and the Coalition and others again filed suit. *Colorado Wild Horse & Burro Coalition, Inc. v. Salazar*, 890 F. Supp. 2d 99 (D.D.C. 2012). In 2011, BLM withdrew its proposal. The parties then disputed whether the court should invalidate the 2005 Decision Record referenced in the above excerpt (which had been approved in 2007) and declare that BLM has no authority to eliminate the entire West Douglas Herd or any other herd of wild horses. The court concluded that without a specific gather plan at issue the case was not ripe for review.

2. In *Animal Protection Institute v. Hodel*, 860 F.2d 920 (9th Cir. 1988), the Ninth Circuit addressed a challenge to the BLM's practice of adopting wild horses to individuals who plaintiffs claimed BLM knew or should know would be selling the horses to slaughter. The court reviewed the legislative history, stating, "[t]his legislation was necessary to correct intolerable abuses of these animals by those seeking to exploit them for private use and profit." *Id.* at 926. The court noted that "[c]ommercial exploitation encompasses the use of animals as bucking horses in rodeos and the slaughter of animals for processing into pet food." *Id.* at 923 n.3. The court recognized that Congress created a one-year waiting period before title changed hands from the federal government to individuals, "to act as a safeguard to insure humane treatment by establishing a probationary period for adopters," and concluded, "[l]egislative history thus reveals that Congress intended the one-year wait for title transfer to act as a probationary period that would weed out unfit adopters." *Id.* at 927.

The BLM had been issuing title to adopters who openly professed an intention to sell adopted horses to slaughterhouses, which the court found antithetical to the expressed desire of the framers of the WFHBA:

> The Secretary's disregard for the announced future intentions of adopters undercuts Congress' desire to insure humane treatment for wild horses and burros. In fact, it renders the adoption process a farce, for the one-year

requirement of humane treatment and care serves no purpose if on the day the one-year period expires, the adopter can proceed to the slaughterhouse with his horses or burros.

Id.

3. Animal protection groups have sued not only over the BLM's "adopt-a-horse" program, but also when the BLM allowed ranchers to take action themselves to eliminate the horses. In *American Horse Prot. Ass'n v. United States*, 551 F.2d 432 (D.C. Cir. 1977), ranchers rounded up wild horses after notifying BLM officials. The horses were trapped and left unattended overnight. During the night, four horses died by falling over a cliff and three horses caught their hooves in rocks and could not be freed. As stated by the court, the record indicated that the ranchers then "disposed of the three by cutting their throats and pushing their bodies over the cliff." *Id.* at 435. The surviving horses were sent to Nebraska "to be slaughtered for dog food." *Id.* Some died en route, but the remaining horses were rescued and held by BLM pending a determination of ownership. *Id.*

The Act defines "wild free-roaming horses and burros" as "all unbranded and unclaimed horses and burros on public lands in the United States." 16 U.S.C. § 1332(b). Congress did leave the door open, however, for individual assertions of ownership of animals on public lands, subject to state law restrictions. 16 U.S.C. § 1335. The question presented on appeal in *American Horse Protection* was whether determination of ownership was to be made by federal or state officials. The court held that the final determination is reserved for the federal government, and remanded to the district court for findings consistent with that decision. The court noted, however, that even assuming the ranchers owned the horses, "the Act and implementing regulations would not permit the ranchers to round them up without first complying with prescribed procedures." 551 F.2d at 435 n.21.

4. Disputes over BLM's disposition of "excess" wild horses have continued. Many groups continue to monitor BLM's programs and have complained that many horses intended for safe-haven adoptions are actually sent to slaughterhouses. *Settlement Protects Wild Horses; Adopters Must Vow Not to Sell Animals for Slaughter,* Dallas MORNING NEWS, Oct. 19, 1997, at 41A. After an investigation in 1997, BLM was accused of selling wild horses to individuals who intended to send the horses to slaughter. *Id.* The Fund for Animals and API filed suit to stop the alleged practice. *Id.* The lawsuit settled. As part of the settlement, BLM agreed to submit to the Office of Management and Budget the following language to be inserted into the (1) Private Maintenance and Care Agreement and (2) Application for Title:

Under the penalty of prosecution for violating 18 U.S.C. 1001, which makes it a federal crime to make false statements to any agency of the United States, I hereby state that I have no intent to sell this wild horse or burro for slaughter or bucking stock, or for processing into commercial products, within the meaning of the Wild and Free-Roaming Horse and Burro Act, 16 U.S.C. 1331, *et seq.*, and regulations, 43 C.F.R. 4700.0-5(c).

Settlement Agreement, *Animal Prot. Inst. of Am., Inc. v. Babbitt*, No. CV-R 85-365-HDM (D. Nev. filed Oct. 15, 1997).

5. In 2004, Congress approved a rider ("the Burns Amendment") to the 3,300-page federal budget that reversed three decades of government policy protecting the horses from slaughter. The Burns Amendment, submitted by Senator Conrad Burns (R-Mont.), overrode the one-year requirement by providing that "excess" animals "shall be made available for sale without limitation." Fiscal Year 2005 Omnibus Appropriations Act, Pub. L. No. 108-447, Div. E, § 142 (replacing the former 16 U.S.C. § 1333(e)).

Since that time, multiple attempts have been made to restore the prohibition on the commercial sale and slaughter of wild free-roaming horses and burros. The bills have provided for the deletion of 16 U.S.C. § 1333(e) (as revised by the Burns Amendment) and the addition of language that eliminates the option of sale or transfer of wild free-roaming horses or burros or their body parts for consideration for processing into commercial products.

Also since the Burns Amendment, the BLM has acted somewhat inconsistently regarding the issue of wild horses going to slaughter. BLM's contracts with adopters and purchasers of wild horses included a provision that the horses would not be sold for slaughter and Congress has consistently prohibited the BLM from selling wild horses for commercial use, through the budget process. Concerns over the sale of wild horses to slaughter continued for years. In late 2012, an individual was identified who reportedly had sold as many as 1700 wild horses into the slaughter pipeline. *See, e.g.*, Mark Stricherz, *Man Under Federal Investigation For Selling Wild Horses To Slaughter Houses Worked On Salazar Family Farm*, The Colorado Observer, Nov. 16, 2012. In response, Secretary of Interior, Ken Salazar, claimed he would impose stricter regulations to prevent a recurrence. *See, e.g.*, Dave Philipps, *Salazar tightens rules to guard against wild horse slaughter*, Colorado Springs Gazette, Dec. 8, 2012.

6. A recurring problem for plaintiffs in cases challenging the BLM's decision-making with respect to wild horse gathers is that the horses may be gathered before the courts can rule. The BLM usually provides limited notice about these gathers, so plaintiffs may not be able to prepare the necessary documents to file a complaint and motion for temporary restraining order (TRO) and get a ruling before the horses are captured. If the district court denies plaintiffs' request for a TRO or preliminary injunction, it is even more unlikely that the appellate court will rule until after the gather has taken place. In either scenario, the government will likely argue that the case is moot and that, therefore, the courts have lost jurisdiction. *See, e.g.*, *In Defense of Animals v. United States Dept. of Interior*, 648 F.3d 1012, 1013 (9th Cir. 2011) ("interlocutory appeal from the denial of a preliminary injunction is moot because the roundup sought to be enjoined has taken place"); *Cloud Foundation v. U.S. Bureau of Land Management*, 2013 U.S. Dist. LEXIS 53371 (D. Nev. Mar. 26, 2013). In *Cloud Foundation*, the district court had denied plaintiffs' motion for

preliminary injunction. The Ninth Circuit initially issued a TRO but then lifted it and the gather went forward and was concluded while appeal of the district court's ruling was pending. After the *In Defense of Animals* decision was issued, plaintiffs voluntarily dismissed their appeal. Ruling on the merits of whether the round-up had been accomplished in violation of the WFHBA, the district court granted summary judgment in favor of the government, noting BLM's "significant discretion" in its interpretation of the WFHBA and its obligations thereunder. *Id.* at *19.

For a discussion of the mootness doctrine as applied to wild horse gathers, *see* Amy L. Gleghorn, *Unbridled Power And The Wild Horses And Burros Act*, 15 Mo. Envtl. L. & Pol'y. R. 151 (Fall 2007).

7. In *Habitat for Horses v. Salazar*, 745 F. Supp. 2d 438 (S.D.N.Y. 2010), the plaintiffs filed suit to stop a horse gather. The court first denied plaintiffs' application for a TRO that the BLM cease removal of wild horses and return those already removed. The following day, plaintiffs renewed their application, premised on the deaths of two horses during the gather operations. The court denied the renewed application and later denied plaintiffs' motion for preliminary injunction. Defendants then filed motions to dismiss the case. The court expressed sympathy for the horses and the issues plaintiffs raised but nonetheless construed the law against them and granted defendants' motions.

> At the outset, this Court recognizes the need to ensure the continued existence of viable wild horse populations in the West. While over two million horses roamed freely in the nineteenth century, only 37,000 remain wild today. And the North Piceance removal, if it is ever completed, will reduce the rangelands open to those remaining few. This Court also appreciates the harmful effects of the removal process, as evidenced by the death of several wild horses during the North Piceance removal in October 2010. Nevertheless, this Court is bound to follow the law, not its sympathies. Accordingly, for the following reasons [set forth in the opinion], Defendants' motions are granted.

Habitat for Horses v. Salazar, 2011 U.S. Dist. LEXIS 197267, *2 (S.D.N.Y. Sept. 7, 2011).

8. The "wild horse problem" has garnered increased attention from all sectors. According to BLM documentation, in 2017 the wild horse and burro population was at its highest point since the agency began managing horses in 1971. The agency's first population census, conducted in 1971, estimated that there were 25,345 wild horses and burros on public rangelands. As of 2016, the agency's population census estimated that there were 67,027 wild horses and burros.[f]

In its 2013 report, the National Academy of Sciences (NAS) found that "management practices are facilitating high horse population growth rates," and emphasized

---

f. *See* https://www.blm.gov/programs/wild-horse-and-burro/about-the-program/myths-and-facts.

that the BLM's ill-considered and unscientific "removals are likely to keep the population at a size that maximizes population growth rate."[g]

In fiscal year 2015, BLM spent $49 million maintaining captured wild horses in off-range facilities, which constituted 46% of the entire budget of the agency's wild horse and burro program. Such a large expenditure has limited the agency's ability to properly manage wild horses on the range and led to a bipartisan search for solutions. In September 2016, the BLM's Wild Horse and Burro Advisory Board — an independent body — recommended euthanizing all 45,000 formerly wild horses currently being kept in long-term holding, in order to eliminate the burden on the federal government of maintaining the horses for life. This proposal was quickly withdrawn (in a few days), likely owing to the overwhelming backlash from the public to the concept of slaughtering tens of thousands of these American icons.

As this edition went to press, the debate over how best to address American's wild horses continued.

9. Advocates recommend that the involved federal agencies cease managing horse and burro populations solely through conducting gather and removals. One possible alternative solution to the problem that has been suggested is the use of fertility control and contraceptives on the range, which, when used properly, can be effective tools to manage populations of free-roaming equines. However, according to BLM data, the BLM's use of such tools has been minimal.[h] But advocates assert that if the agency were to commit to actually using fertility control and treating a significant portion of the remaining horses in any given area with population fertility control tools, the population levels would likely be reduced and stabilized.

Fallini v. Hodel

United States Court of Appeals, Ninth Circuit, 1992
963 F.2d 275

GOODWIN, Circuit Judge. Joe, Susan, and Helen Fallini operate a cow and calf ranch on approximately 2,700 acres of deeded land in Nye County, Nevada, and hold grazing permits on 657,520 acres of public land in the Reveille Allotment of the Tonopah Resource Area. The competition between domestic cattle and free roaming wild horses for food and water on these public lands has produced folk lore, movies, legislation, and litigation.

The government appeals a judgment in favor of the Fallinis and adverse to the Bureau of Land Management, which is charged with the administration of public lands under the Taylor Grazing Act of 1934, 43 U.S.C. § 315, *et seq.* (1988) (as amended). We must consider whether the Fallinis violated their federal range

---

g. National Research Council of the National Academies of Sciences. 2013. "Using Science to Improve the BLM Wild Horse and Burro Program: A Way Forward." 5-6, 81-91 (2013 NAS Report).

h. *https://www.blm.gov/programs/wild-horse-and-burro/about-the-program/program-data*, Population Growth Suppression Treatments.

improvement permit when they installed highway guardrails around one of their water holes to discourage wild horses from grazing the surrounding land. Concluding that they did not, we affirm the district court.

I. BACKGROUND

The Fallini operation, known as the Twin Springs Ranch, depends on the public lands of the Reveille Allotment for grazing during that part of the year in which natural forage is produced on the desert. The Fallini permits include the right to develop deep wells at their own expense, but they also provide that the water thus produced be made available to wildlife.

The Fallinis rotate their cattle from one area to another by closing access to one water hole and opening access to another. Virtually all of the useable water within the Allotment is artificially produced including Deep Well, the site with which this case is concerned. The central Nevada mountains enjoy minimal rainfall and light accumulations of winter snow. The resulting moisture appears only briefly on the surface, and cattlemen since pioneer times have relied on wells in order to take advantage of the seasonal pasture within the Allotment. With the coming of rural electrification and advanced technology in the 1930s, the development of deep wells made it feasible to graze cattle in areas that had until then been the exclusive habitat of desert wildlife.

In September of 1967 the BLM, pursuant to section 4 of the Taylor Grazing Act, 43 U.S.C. § 315c, issued the Fallinis a range improvement permit, designated Deep Well, authorizing them to maintain and use a stock-watering facility on public lands inside the Allotment.[2] The permit at Deep Well—one of several issued to the Fallinis over the years authorizing improvements at the major water sources within the Allotment—allows the Fallinis to make improvements so that nearby grazing lands can be available for cattle grazing.

In 1971 Congress enacted the Wild Free-Roaming Horses and Burros Act, 16 U.S.C. §§ 1331–1340. At that time, according to stipulations by the parties, approximately 130 wild horses roamed within the Reveille Allotment but no wild horses or burros roamed within the vicinity of Deep Well. By 1984, however, approximately 1,800 wild horses inhabited the Allotment, and several hundred of these horses, attracted by the Fallinis' stock-watering facility, grazed the land surrounding Deep Well.

In late 1983, the Fallinis, without first obtaining BLM approval, installed highway guardrails across the entrances to nine of their water troughs within the Reveille Allotment, including Deep Well. The guardrails were erected at a height and in a manner that would prevent access to the water by wild horses; the guardrails do not bar access by cattle or indigenous wildlife.

---

2. This section of the Act provides that "[f]ences, wells, reservoirs, and other improvements necessary to the care and management of the permitted livestock may be constructed on the public land ... under permit issued by the authority of the Secretary." 43 U.S.C. § 315c.

On December 23, 1983, the BLM's manager for the Reveille Allotment issued a proposed decision stating that the installation of the guardrails constituted a modification of the watering facility and violated the Fallinis' improvement permit because BLM approval had not first been obtained as required by the applicable regulations. The proposed decision required removal of the guardrails within 15 days and stated that failure to do so would result in cancellation of the Fallinis' permit. The Fallinis removed the guardrails at every water source except Deep Well and protested the BLM's proposed decision as it applied to Deep Well. On May 3, 1984, the BLM cancelled the Deep Well permit.

The Fallinis appealed the BLM's decision to an administrative law judge who found that the Fallinis "have not violated the conditions of the . . . permit involved in this case nor any applicable federal regulations." The BLM appealed to the Interior Board of Land Appeals (IBLA) which reversed the administrative law judge.

The Fallinis then appealed to the district court. Judge Foley made four rulings: first, the installation of the guardrails did not require prior BLM approval; second, the BLM acted beyond its authority and jurisdiction; third, the BLM's decision was tainted by improper political influence; and fourth, the BLM's decision effected a regulatory taking of the Fallinis' water rights in violation of the Fifth Amendment.

II. STANDARDS OF REVIEW

This decision involving the application of law to facts over which the parties disagree, calls for review without deference to the trial court's application of law, but with proper respect to the trial court's determination of the facts.

Final decisions of the IBLA are reviewed under the Administrative Procedure Act, 5 U.S.C. § 706(2). Section 706 states that the reviewing court shall,

> hold unlawful and set aside agency action, findings and conclusions found to be . . . (A) arbitrary, capricious, an abuse of discretion, or otherwise not in accordance with the law; (B) contrary to constitutional right . . . ; or (C) in excess of statutory jurisdiction, authority, or limitations. . . .

Id. The scope of judicial review under this standard is narrow, and this court "cannot merely substitute [its] judgment for that of the IBLA."

An agency's interpretation of the governing statute or of its own regulations is entitled to deference, but courts are the final authorities on issues of statutory and regulatory construction. The applicable standard of review is whether the agency decision "was based upon a consideration of the relevant factors and whether there has been a clear error of judgment."

III. DISCUSSION

A. *Violation of the Range Improvement Permit*

The IBLA found that the Fallinis violated permit conditions and modified their range improvement at Deep Well without first obtaining BLM approval, in violation of 43 C.F.R. § 4140.1(b)(2). That regulation provides that persons may be subject to civil and criminal penalties for "[i]nstalling, using, maintaining, modifying, and/ or removing range improvements without authorization." Because the installation of guardrails was intended to and did deter wild horses from watering at Deep Well, the pivotal question was whether this alteration of the water hole gates to exclude unwanted horses was a "modification" that required prior BLM authorization. The trial court held that it was not. In reviewing the trial court's approach to the IBLA decision, two words become important: "gate" and "wildlife."

The permit for Deep Well allows the permittee to install "4 Steel gates" and requires wildlife access to water. The permit provides in relevant part that "[a]ny public lands or impounded waters will be available for wildlife use" and that the permit "is subject to cancellation for noncompliance with the rules and regulations now or hereafter approved by the Secretary of the Interior."

The Fallinis contend that their highway guardrails are gates, and both the IBLA and the trial court agreed. This may have been an unwarranted stretch of language, but it is not challenged on appeal. The permit requires the permittee to allow access to the impounded water by "wildlife." There seems to be no question but that water pumped from a deep well into a storage tank and then allowed to flow into watering troughs is "impounded." We turn then to the meaning of wildlife.

Ordinarily there would be little basis for quibbling about whether wild horses are wildlife. However, in a forensic range war, words can take on strange meanings. Here the trial court held that the term "wildlife" as used in the Fallinis' 1967 permit did not include feral horses. In this respect, we hold that the trial court's finding was not clearly erroneous.

Although the Fallinis' permit and its specifications were never subsequently changed, the record indicates that the Deep Well facility was changed numerous times over the years. The specified improvements were repaired, replaced, and substituted, and in some respects substantially altered. Until 1983, none of the different or additional installations was determined by the BLM to be a "modification" for which prior agency approval was required.

The IBLA concluded that the guardrails were gates and thus fell within the categories of improvements listed in the Deep Well permit. The IBLA chose to disregard definitional questions about what constituted a gate and instead focused on the purpose the gates were intended to serve. The IBLA then determined that the purpose underlying the installation of the guardrails—impeding wild horse access to the water while allowing cattle access—differed from the original purpose authorizing the installation of gates in the 1967 permit. Accordingly, the IBLA ruled that the installation of the guardrails constituted a modification requiring prior BLM approval.

Noting that an agency acts arbitrarily when it entirely fails "to consider an important aspect of the problem" before it, the district court concluded that the IBLA failed to consider the purposes of the Taylor Grazing Act in construing the intent of the parties in 1967 and the purpose for which the Deep Well range improvement permit was issued.

The intent of the parties in drafting the permit is a question of fact. In construing the permit language, the trial court accepted the Fallinis' view that the language should mean what it meant to the parties in 1967 when the permit was issued, and not what it might mean 20 years later after Congress had dramatically changed the legal environment in which range management would occur in the future.

The 1971 wild horse legislation shortly resulted in the proliferation of feral horses in numbers that far exceeded both the carrying capacity of the range and the imagination of the parties at the time the permits were granted. When the Fallinis' permit was issued, small scattered bands of wild horses roamed the intermountain deserts of central Nevada as well as other similar ranges in neighboring states. But wild horses were not considered "wildlife" for grazing permit purposes. It was customary for ranchers to round up redundant wild horses and ship them off for purposes that aroused the indignation and political energy of urban voters. For range permits in 1967 "wildlife" included the occasional mountain sheep, mule deer, antelope, coyote, kit fox and the birds and rodents that make up the fauna that have evolved in an almost waterless desert.

As the district court recognized, no sane rancher would spend thousands of dollars to drill a deep well and build associated water works in order to attract a population of wild horses that would eat and uproot all the grass for miles around the water hole. Before the Fallinis developed the Deep Well water facility, the few wild horses in that part of Nevada searched elsewhere for feed and water. After the laws were changed to protect the horse population, the water developed by the Fallinis attracted the recently protected and rapidly multiplying horses in numbers that made this confrontation between horses and cows on the same range inevitable.

The trial court reasoned that the BLM could not claim that a purpose of the range improvement permit was to provide water to wild horses because none had roamed the Deep Well area at the time the permit was issued. Thus, based on the permit's language and surrounding circumstances, the court concluded "that 'wildlife' does not include 'wild horses' . . ." The court went on to say that the guardrails did not violate the permit conditions. *Fallini*, 725 F. Supp. at 1117. We agree.

The trial court noted that the primary purpose of the Taylor Grazing Act is "to promote the highest use of the public lands pending its final disposal." 43 U.S.C. § 315. We have stated that "the purpose of the Taylor Grazing Act is to stabilize the livestock industry and protect the rights of sheep and cattle growers from interference." *Kidd v. United States Dep't of the Interior, Bureau of Land Management*, 756 F.2d 1410, 1411 (9th Cir. 1985).

With these principles in mind, the trial court correctly turned to the original purpose of the permit in deciding that the failure to obtain prior approval before erecting the guardrails did not constitute a violation of the permit terms.

B. *Other Issues*

The district court announced three alternative grounds for its decision. First, the court accepted the Fallinis' argument that the BLM acted beyond its authority and jurisdiction by appropriating the Deep Well water in a manner contrary to state water laws. The district court also concluded that "improper political considerations tainted the agency's exercise of its discretion." The court read the record as showing that the BLM's decision to cancel the Deep Well permit was improperly influenced by wild horse activists. The court cited no evidence, however, that the IBLA's decision was affected in any way by political pressure. As a final alternative ground for its decision, the district court held that the BLM's cancellation of the Deep Well permit constituted a regulatory taking of the Fallinis' water rights in violation of the Fifth Amendment.

Because we find adequate reasons to affirm the district court without reaching the state law, political influence, or takings issues, there is no need for us to rule on them.

* * *

Notes

1. Does the majority's decision square with the intent of the WFHBA?

2. For further background and history regarding the Taylor Grazing Act, *see Public Lands Council v. Babbitt*, 929 F. Supp. 1436 (D. Wyo. 1996). In that case, ranchers alleged 1995 regulations governing the administration of livestock grazing on public lands managed by BLM violated the Taylor Grazing Act, NEPA and the Administrative Procedure Act, among others. The federal district court ruled that portions of the new regulations opposed by the ranchers were unlawful and violated the Taylor Grazing Act. On appeal, the Tenth Circuit reversed the district court to the extent it had ruled in favor of the ranchers. *Public Lands Council v. Babbitt*, 167 F.3d 1287 (10th Cir. 1999).

The Tenth Circuit noted that while stabilizing the livestock industry is one of several purposes of the Taylor Grazing Act, as set forth in the Act's uncodified preamble, the actual text of the statute refers only to "safeguarding the rangeland and providing for its orderly use as primary objectives." *Id.* at 1298 n.5. The court found it "significant" that "BLM lands support only a small portion of the livestock industry." *Id.* at 1299.

"Only twenty-two percent of western beef cattle producers have federal grazing permits. Similarly, only nineteen percent of western sheep producers hold federal grazing permits.... The Secretary is free to consider this fact in balancing the need for industry stability against the need to protect federal lands from deterioration." *Id.*

The opinion noted that between 1934 and 1976, "grazing regulation was limited, and the early regulations were actually the creation of the ranchers themselves." *Id.* at 1299 n.7. Accordingly, the court concluded that "[p]erpetuating grazing decisions handed down in the 1940s may well be inconsistent with the ongoing statutory command that the Secretary protect the federal lands, especially where the grazing decisions were largely made by the ranchers themselves. *Id.* at 1299. The United States Supreme Court affirmed the Tenth Circuit ruling, holding that the Secretary is "free reasonably to determine just how, and the extent to which, 'grazing privileges' shall be safeguarded, in light of the grazing Act's basic purposes." *Public Lands Council v. Babbitt*, 529 U.S. 728, 742 (2000).

2. Articles discussing BLM's management of wild horses on public lands and related issues include: Elspeth Visser, *Note: The Continuing Saga of Wild Horse Management: Finding a Balance in the Case of One of America's Iconic Symbols*, 41 Wm. & Mary Envtl. L. & Pol'y Rev. 683 (Spring 2017); Nadia Aksentijevich, *Note: An American Icon in Limbo: How Clarifying the Standing Doctrine Could Free Wild Horses and Empower Advocates*, 41 B.C. Envtl. Aff. L. Rev. 399 (2014); Lafcadio H. Darling, *Legal Protection for Horses: Care and Stewardship or Hypocrisy and Neglect?*, 6 Animal L. 105 (2000); Elizabeth A. Thomasian, *Should The Wild Free-Roaming Horses And Burros Act Of 1971 Be Reigned In Or Turned Out To Pasture?*, 22 San Joaquin Agric. L.R. 189 (2012–2013); Kristen H. Glover, *Managing Wild Horses on Public Lands: Congressional Action and Agency Response*, 79 N.C.L. Rev. 1108 (2001).

Appendix A

Definitions of "Animal" in Selected State Statutes

State Statute	Definition
ALASKA STAT. § 11.61.145 (2017)	(Promoting an exhibition of fighting animals). "'[A]nimal' means a vertebrate living creature not a human being, but does not include fish."
ARIZ. REV. STAT. ANN. § 13-2910 (2017)	(Cruelty to animals; . . .). "'Animal' means a mammal, bird, reptile or amphibian."
CAL. PENAL CODE § 599B (2018)	(Malicious mischief). "'[A]nimal' includes every dumb creature."
DEL. CODE ANN. TITLE 11, § 1325 (2018)	(Cruelty to animals; . . .). "'Animal' shall not include fish, crustacea or molluska."
HAW. REV. STAT. ANN. § 711-1109(1) (B) (2017)	(Cruelty to animals in the second degree). Makes it an offense to "mutilate[ ], poison[ ], or kill[ ] without need any animal other than insects, vermin, or other pests."
IND. CODE ANN. § 35-46-3-3 (2018)	(Offenses relating to animals). "'[A]nimal' does not include a human being."
KY. REV. STAT. ANN. §525.130 (2018)	(Cruelty to animals . . .). Makes it a second degree offense to subject "any animal" to "cruel or injurious treatment" or to cause any animal "to fight for pleasure or profit (including, but not limited to being a spectator or vendor at an event where a four-legged animal is caused to fight for pleasure or profit."
LA. REV. STAT. ANN. § 14:102.1 (2017)	(Cruelty to animals; simple and aggravated). The statute makes it a crime to mistreat "living animals" without further defining "animal."
ME. REV. STAT. ANN. TITLE 7, § 3907 (2017)	(Animal Welfare Act). "'Animal' means every living, sentient creature not a human being."
MASS. GEN. LAWS ANN. CH. 272, § 77 (2018)	(Cruelty to animals). Makes it an offense to use "a live animal" as lure or bait, "except . . . as lure or bait in fishing."
MICH. COMP. LAWS ANN. § 750.50 (2018)	([C]rimes against animals, . . .). "'Animal' means any vertebrate other than a human being."
MISS. CODE ANN. § 97-41-1 (2018)	(Living creatures not to be cruelly treated). Text does not use the word "animal" but instead protects "any living creature."
N.H. REV. STAT. ANN. § 644:8 (2018)	(Cruelty to animals). "'Animal' means a domestic animal, a household pet or a wild animal in captivity."

State Statute	Definition
N.Y. Agric. & Mkts. Law § 350 (2017)	(Code sections including general and specific anti-cruelty laws). "'Animal', as used in this article, includes every living creature except a human being." (Statute further defines "companion animal" or "pet" as "any dog or cat, and . . . any other domesticated animal normally maintained in or near the household of the owner . . . [but] shall not include a 'farm animal'. . . .")
N.C. Gen. Stat. § 14-360 (2017)	(Cruelty to animals). "'[A]nimal' includes every living vertebrate in the classes Amphibia, Reptilia, Aves, and Mammalia except human beings."
S.C. Code Ann. § 47-1-40 (2018)	(Ill-treatment of animals generally). "Animals" is undefined, but the section expressly does not apply to "fowl."
S.D. Codified Laws § 40-1-1 (2018)	(Cruelty, abuse and injury to animals). "Animal" means "any mammal, bird, reptile, amphibian, or fish, except humans."
Tenn. Stat. Ann. § 39-14-201 (2018)	(Criminal offenses against property). "Animal" means "a domesticated living creature or a wild creature previously captured."
Tex. Penal Code Ann. § 42.09 (2017)	(Cruelty to livestock animals). "'Livestock animal' means: (A) cattle, sheep, swine, goats, ratites, or poultry commonly raised for human consumption; (B) a horse, pony, mule, donkey, or hinny; (C) native or nonnative hoofstock raised under agriculture practices; or (D) native or nonnative fowl commonly raised under agricultural practices."
Utah Code Ann. § 76-9-301 (2017)	(Cruelty to animals). "'Animal' means . . . a live, nonhuman vertebrate creature." (In defining "animal," the statute also makes a variety of exceptions for zoological animals, livestock, and wildlife.)
Va. Code Ann. §§ 3.2-6500, 3.2–6570 (2017)	(Cruelty to animals). "For purposes of § 3.2-6522, animal means any nonhuman vertebrate species except fish." "For the purposes of § 3.2-6570, animal means any nonhuman vertebrate species including fish except those fish captured and killed or disposed of in a reasonable and customary manner."

Appendix B

Tennessee Code Annotated

"General Patton Act of 2003" (formerly T-Bo Act)[1]
Tenn. Code Ann. § 44-17-403 (2018)

Death of pet caused by negligent act of another — Damages

(a) (1) If a person's pet is killed or sustains injuries which result in death caused by the unlawful and intentional, or negligent, act of another or the animal of another, the trier of fact may find the individual causing the death or the owner of the animal causing the death liable for up to *five thousand dollars ($5,000)* in noneconomic damages; provided, that if such death is caused by the negligent act of another, the death or fatal injury must occur on the property of the deceased pet's owner or caretaker, or while under the control and supervision of the deceased pet's owner or caretaker.

(2) *If an unlawful act resulted in the death or permanent disability of a person's guide dog, then the value of the guide dog shall include, but shall not necessarily be limited to, both the cost of the guide dog as well as the cost of any specialized training the guide dog received.*

(b) As used in this section, "pet" means any domesticated dog or cat normally maintained in or near the household of its owner.

(c) Limits for noneconomic damages set out in subsection (a) shall not apply to causes of action for intentional infliction of emotional distress or any other civil action other than the direct and sole loss of a pet.

(d) Noneconomic damages awarded pursuant to this section shall be limited to compensation for the loss of the reasonably expected society, companionship, love and affection of the pet.

(e) This section shall not apply to any not-for-profit entity or governmental agency, or its employees, negligently causing the death of a pet while acting on the

---

1. Italicized text reflects the following changes (effective June 15, 2004) from the original "T-Bo Act": (i) the amount in section (a)(1) was increased from the original four thousand dollars; (ii) section (a)(2) was added; and (iii) the former section (f) was deleted. Former section (f) provided: "The provisions of this section shall apply only in incorporated areas of any county having a population in excess of seventy-five thousand (75,000) according to the 1990 federal census or any subsequent census."

behalf of public health or animal welfare; to any killing of a dog that has been or was killing or worrying livestock as in § 44-17-203; nor shall this section be construed to authorize any award of noneconomic damages in an action for professional negligence against a licensed veterinarian.

(f) [*Deleted by 2004 amendment.*]

Illinois Compiled Statutes Annotated

Humane Care for Animals Act
510 Ill. Comp. Stat. 70/16.3 (2018)

Civil actions.

Any person who has a right of ownership in an animal that is subjected to an act of aggravated cruelty under Section 3.02 or torture under Section 3.03 in violation of this Act [510 ILCS 70/3.02 or 510 ILCS 70/3.03] or in an animal that is injured or killed as a result of actions taken by a person who acts in bad faith under subsection (b) of Section 3.06 or under Section 12 of this Act [510 ILCS 70/3.06 or 510 ILCS70/12] may bring a civil action to recover the damages sustained by that owner. Damages may include, but are not limited to, the monetary value of the animal, veterinary expenses incurred on behalf of the animal, any other expenses incurred by the owner in rectifying the effects of the cruelty, pain, and suffering of the animal, and emotional distress suffered by the owner. In addition to damages that may be proven, the owner is also entitled to punitive or exemplary damages of not less than $500 but not more than $25,000 for each act of abuse or neglect to which the animal was subjected. In addition, the court must award reasonable attorney's fees and costs actually incurred by the owner in the prosecution of any action under this Section or exemplary damages of not less than $500 but not more than $25,000 for each act of abuse or neglect to which the animal was subjected. In addition, the court must award reasonable attorney's fees and costs actually incurred by the owner in the prosecution of any action under this Section.

The remedies provided in this Section are in addition to any other remedies allowed by law.

In an action under this Section, the court may enter any injunctive orders reasonably necessary to protect animals from any further acts of abuse, neglect, or harassment by a defendant.

The statute of limitations for a violation of this Act is 2 years.

Index